Collins EUROPE
ESSENTIAL ROAD ATLAS

Published by Collins
An imprint of HarperCollins Publishers
Westerhill Road
Bishopbriggs
Glasgow G64 2QT
www.harpercollins.co.uk

First published 2004

New edition 2017

© HarperCollins Publishers Ltd 2017
Maps © Collins Bartholomew Ltd 2017

Collins® is a registered trademark of HarperCollins Publishers Ltd

A catalogue record for this book is available from the British Library

ISBN 978-0-00-826251-8

10 9 8 7 6 5 4 3 2 1

Printed by RR Donnelley APS Co Ltd, China

All mapping in this atlas is generated from Collins Bartholomew digital databases. Collins Bartholomew, the UK's leading independent geographical information supplier, can provide a digital, custom, and premium mapping service to a variety of markets.
For further information:
Tel: +44 (0)141 306 3752
e-mail: collinsbartholomew@harpercollins.co.uk
or visit our website at: www.collinsbartholomew.com

If you would like to comment on any aspect of this book, please contact us at the above address or online.
e-mail: collinsmaps@harpercollins.co.uk

 facebook.com/collinsref @collins_ref

Contents

Distance map and chart
ii – iii   Map symbols
iii   Map symbols and country identifiers
iv   International road signs and travel web links
v   Key to map pages
vi – xvii Route planning maps   1:4 654 000
2 – 181   Road maps   1:1 000 000
182 – 187 Road maps   1:750 000
188 – 191 Index to place names   1:750 000
192 – 207 City through-route maps
    192 Amsterdam, Athina, Barcelona, Belfast
    193 Beograd, Berlin, Bern, Birmingham
    194 Bonn, Bordeaux, Bratislava, Brussel/Bruxelles
    195 Bucureşti, Budapest, Cardiff, Chişinau
    196 Dublin, Edinburgh, Firenze, Frankfurt
    197 Glasgow, Göteborg, Den Haag, Hamburg
    198 Helsinki, İstanbul, København, Köln
    199 Leipzig, Lisboa, Ljubljana, London
    200 Lyon, Madrid, Manchester, Marseille
    201 Milano, München, Napoli, Oslo
    202 Palermo, Paris, Podgorica, Praha
    203 Rīga, Roma, Rotterdam, Sankt Peterburg
    204 Sarajevo, Sevilla, Skopje, Sofia
    205 Stockholm, Strasbourg, Tallinn, Torino
    206 Toulouse, Valencia, Venezia, Vilnius
    207 Warszawa, Wien, Zagreb, Zürich

208 – 211 City street plans
    208 Amsterdam, Athina, Berlin, Bern
    209 Brussel/Bruxelles, Dublin, Helsinki, København
    210 Lisboa, London, Madrid, Oslo
    211 Paris, Roma, Stockholm, Wien

212 – 272 Index to place names   1:1 000 000

           Driving information and web links

Map symbols

Road maps	Carte routière	Strassenkarten
E55 Euro route number	Route européenne	Europastrasse
A13 Motorway	Autoroute	Autobahn
Motorway – toll	Autoroute à péage	Gebührenpflichtige Autobahn
Motorway – toll (vignette)	Autoroute à péage (vignette)	Gebührenpflichtige Autobahn (Vignette)
37 Motorway junction – full access	Echangeur d'autoroute avec accès libre	Autobahnauffahrt mit vollem Zugang
12 Motorway junction – restricted access	Echangeur d'autoroute avec accès limité	Autobahnauffahrt mit beschränktem Zugang
Motorway services	Aire de service sur autoroute	Autobahnservicestelle
309 Main road – dual carriageway	Route principale à chaussées séparées	Hauptstrasse – Zweispurig
Main road – single carriageway	Route principale à une seule chaussée	Hauptstrasse – Einspurig
516 Secondary road – dual carriageway	Route secondaire à chaussées séparées	Zweispurige Nebenstrasse
Secondary road – single carriageway	Route secondaire à seule chaussée	Einspurige Nebenstrasse
Other road	Autre route	Andere Strasse
Motorway tunnel	Autoroute tunnel	Autobahntunnel
Main road tunnel	Route principale tunnel	Hauptstrassetunnel
Motorway/road under construction	Autoroute/route en construction	Autobahn/Strasse im Bau
Road toll	Route à péage	Gebührenpflichtige Strasse
Distance marker 16 Distances in kilometres 10 Distances in miles (UK only)	Marquage des distances Distances en kilomètres Distances en miles (GB)	Distanz-Markierung Distanzen in Kilometern Distanzen in Meilen (GB)
Steep hill	Colline abrupte	Steile Strasse
2587 Mountain pass (height in metres)	Col (Altitude en mètres)	Pass (Höhe in Metern)
Scenic route	Parcours pittoresque	Landschaftlich schöne Strecke
International airport	Aéroport international	Internationaler Flughafen
Car transport by rail	Transport des autos par voie ferrée	Autotransport per Bahn
Railway	Chemin de fer	Eisenbahn
Tunnel	Tunnel	Tunnel
Funicular railway	Funiculaire	Seilbahn
Rotterdam Car ferry	Bac pour autos	Autofähre
▲2587 Summit (height in metres)	Sommet (Altitude en mètres)	Berg (Höhe in Metern)
▲ Volcano	Volcan	Vulkan
Canal	Canal	Kanal
International boundary	Frontière d'Etat	Landesgrenze
Disputed International boundary	Frontière litigieuse	Umstrittene Staatsgrenze
Disputed Territory boundary	Frontière territoriale contestée	Umstrittene Gebietsgrenze
GB Country abbreviation	Abréviation du pays	Regionsgrenze
Urban area	Zone urbaine	Stadtgebiet
28 Adjoining page indicator	Indication de la page contigüe	Randhinweis auf Folgekarte
National Park	Parc national	Nationalpark

1:1 000 000

1 centimetre to 10 kilometres

0	10	20	30	40	50	60	70	80 km

1 inch to 16 miles

0	10	20	30	40	50 miles

City maps and plans	Plans de ville	Stadtpläne
★ Place of interest	Site d'interêt	Sehenswerter Ort
▬ Railway station	Gare	Bahnhof
Parkland	Espace vert	Parkland
Woodland	Espace boisé	Waldland
General place of interest	Site d'interêt général	Sehenswerter Ort
Academic/Municipal building	Établissement scolaire/installations municipales	Akademisches/Öffentliches Gebäude
Place of worship	Lieu de culte	Andachtsstätte
Transport location	Infrastructure de transport	Verkehrsanbindung

Places of interest

Symbol	English	Français	Deutsch
🏛	Museum and Art Gallery	Musée / Gallerie d'art	Museum / Kunstgalerie
	Castle	Château	Burg / Schloss
	Historic building	Monument historique	historisches Gebäude
	Historic site	Site historique	historische Stätte
	Monument	Monument	Denkmal
	Religious site	Site religieux	religiöse Stätte
	Aquarium / Sea life centre	Aquarium / Parc Marin	Aquarium
	Arboretum	Arboretum	Arboretum, Baumschule
	Botanic garden (National)	Jardin botanique national	botanischer Garten
	Natural place of interest (other site)	Réserve naturelle	landschaftlich interessanter Ort
	Zoo / Safari park / Wildlife park	Parc Safari / Réserve sauvage / Zoo	Safaripark / Wildreservat / Zoo
	Other site	Autres sites	Touristenattraktion
	Theme park	Parc à thème	Freizeitpark
	World Heritage site	Patrimoine Mondial	Weltkulturerbe
	Athletics stadium (International)	Stade international d'athlétisme	internationales Leichtathletik Stadion
	Football stadium (Major)	Stade de football	Fußballstadion
	Golf course (International)	Parcours de golf international	internationaler Golfplatz
	Grand Prix circuit (Formula 1) / Motor racing venue / MotoGP circuit	Circuit auto-moto	Autodrom
	Rugby ground (International - Six Nations)	Stade de rugby	internationales Rugbystadion
	International sports venue	Autre manifestation sportive	internationale Sportanlage
	Tennis venue	Court de tennis	Tennis
Valcotos	Winter sports resort	Sports d'hiver	Wintersport

Country identifiers

Code	English	Français	Deutsch
A	Austria	Autriche	Österreich
AL	Albania	Albanie	Albanien
AND	Andorra	Andorre	Andorra
B	Belgium	Belgique	Belgien
BG	Bulgaria	Bulgarie	Bulgarien
BIH	Bosnia and Herzegovina	Bosnie-et-Herzégovine	Bosnien und Herzegowina
BY	Belarus	Bélarus	Belarus
CH	Switzerland	Suisse	Schweiz
CY	Cyprus	Chypre	Zypern
CZ	Czechia (Czech Republic)	République tchèque	Tschechische Republik
D	Germany	Allemagne	Deutschland
DK	Denmark	Danemark	Dänemark
DZ	Algeria	Algérie	Algerien
E	Spain	Espagne	Spanien
EST	Estonia	Estonie	Estland
F	France	France	Frankreich
FIN	Finland	Finlande	Finnland
FL	Liechtenstein	Liechtenstein	Liechtenstein
FO	Faroe Islands	Iles Féroé	Färöer-Inseln
GB	United Kingdom GB & NI	Grande-Bretagne	Grossbritannien
GBA	Alderney	Alderney	Alderney
GBG	Guernsey	Guernsey	Guernsey
GBJ	Jersey	Jersey	Jersey
GBM	Isle of Man	Île de Man	Insel Man
GBZ	Gibraltar	Gibraltar	Gibraltar
GR	Greece	Grèce	Griechenland
H	Hungary	Hongrie	Ungarn
HR	Croatia	Croatie	Kroatien
I	Italy	Italie	Italien
IRL	Ireland	Irlande	Irland
IS	Iceland	Islande	Island
L	Luxembourg	Luxembourg	Luxemburg
LT	Lithuania	Lituanie	Litauen
LV	Latvia	Lettonie	Lettland
M	Malta	Malte	Malta
MA	Morocco	Maroc	Marokko
MC	Monaco	Monaco	Monaco
MD	Moldova	Moldavie	Moldawien
MK	Macedonia (F.Y.R.O.M.)	Ancienne République yougoslave de Macédoine	Ehemalige jugoslawische Republik Mazedonien
MNE	Montenegro	Monténégro	Montenegro
N	Norway	Norvège	Norwegen
NL	Netherlands	Pays-Bas	Niederlande
P	Portugal	Portugal	Portugal
PL	Poland	Pologne	Polen
RKS	Kosovo	Kosovo	Kosovo
RO	Romania	Roumanie	Rumänien
RSM	San Marino	Saint-Marin	San Marino
RUS	Russia	Russie	Russland
S	Sweden	Suède	Schweden
SK	Slovakia	République slovaque	Slowakei
SLO	Slovenia	Slovénie	Slowenien
SRB	Serbia	Sérbie	Serbien
TN	Tunisia	Tunisie	Tunisien
TR	Turkey	Turquie	Türkei
UA	Ukraine	Ukraine	Ukraine

International road signs and travel web links

Informative signs

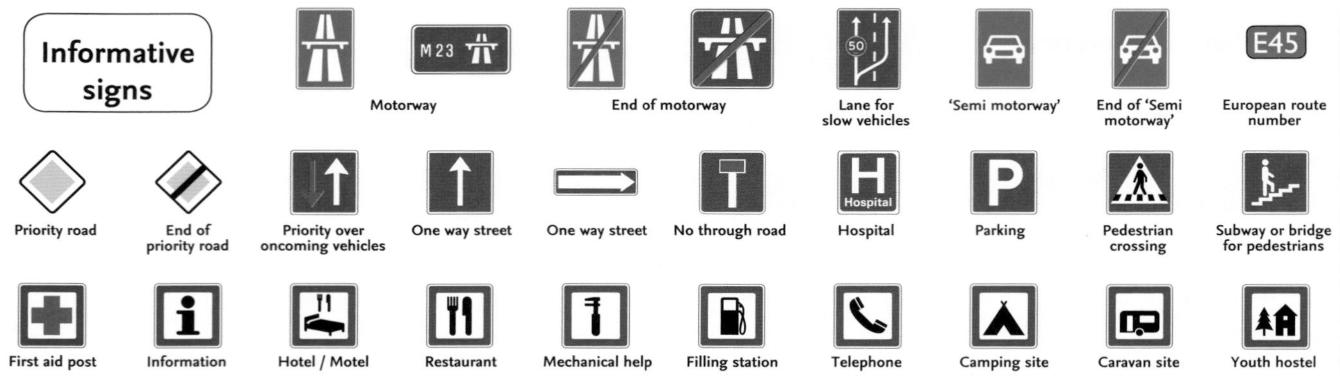
Motorway
End of motorway
Lane for slow vehicles
'Semi motorway'
End of 'Semi motorway'
European route number
Priority road
End of priority road
Priority over oncoming vehicles
One way street
One way street
No through road
Hospital
Parking
Pedestrian crossing
Subway or bridge for pedestrians
First aid post
Information
Hotel / Motel
Restaurant
Mechanical help
Filling station
Telephone
Camping site
Caravan site
Youth hostel

Warning signs

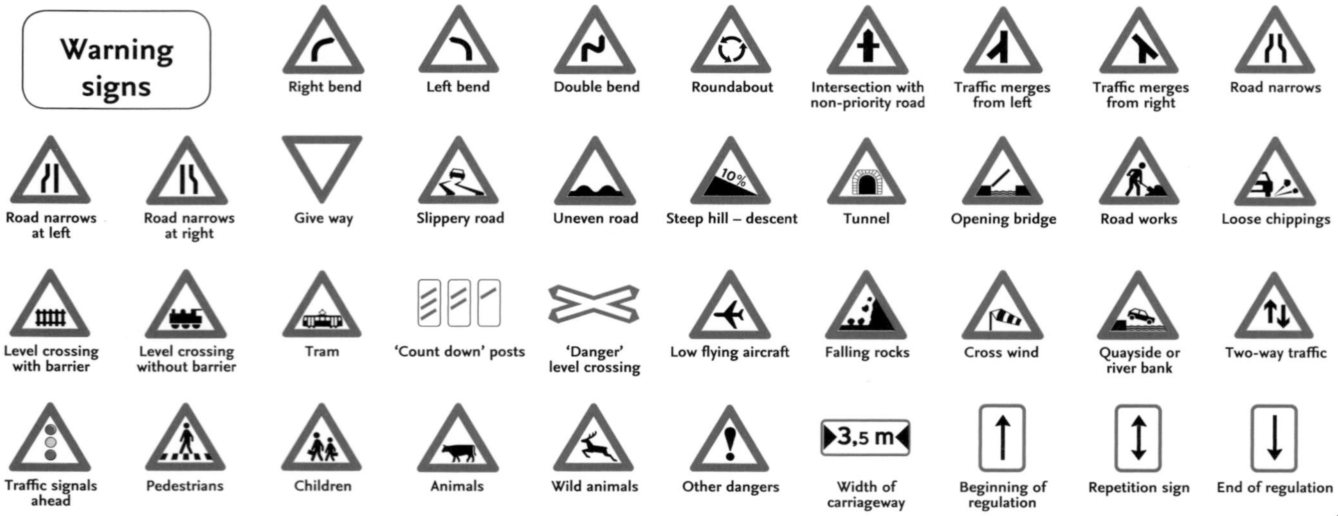
Right bend
Left bend
Double bend
Roundabout
Intersection with non-priority road
Traffic merges from left
Traffic merges from right
Road narrows
Road narrows at left
Road narrows at right
Give way
Slippery road
Uneven road
Steep hill – descent
Tunnel
Opening bridge
Road works
Loose chippings
Level crossing with barrier
Level crossing without barrier
Tram
'Count down' posts
'Danger' level crossing
Low flying aircraft
Falling rocks
Cross wind
Quayside or river bank
Two-way traffic
Traffic signals ahead
Pedestrians
Children
Animals
Wild animals
Other dangers
Width of carriageway
Beginning of regulation
Repetition sign
End of regulation

Regulative signs

End of all restrictions
Halt sign
Customs
No stopping ("clearway")
No parking/waiting
Priority to oncoming vehicles
Use of horns prohibited
Roundabout
Direction to be followed
Pass this side
Minimum speed limit
End of minimum speed limit
Cycle path
Footpath
Riders only
All vehicles prohibited
No entry for all vehicles
No right turn
No u-turns
No entry for motor cars
No entry for all motor vehicles
Lorries prohibited
Buses and coaches prohibited
No trailers
Motorcycles prohibited
Mopeds prohibited
Cycles prohibited
No entry for pedestrians
No overtaking
End of no overtaking
No overtaking for lorries
End of no overtaking for lorries
Laden weight limit
Axle weight limit
Width limit
Height limit
Maximum speed limit
End of speed limit

Travel & route planning

Driving information	www.drive-alive.co.uk
The AA	www.theaa.com
The RAC	www.rac.co.uk
ViaMichelin	www.viamichelin.com
Bing Maps	www.bing.com/mapspreview
Motorail information	www.seat61.com/Motorail
Ferry information	www.aferry.com
Eurotunnel information	www.eurotunnel.com/uk/home/

General information

UK Foreign & Commonwealth Office	www.gov.uk/government/organisations/foreign-commonwealth-office
Country profiles	www.cia.gov/library/publications/resources/the-world-factbook/index.html
World Heritage sites	whc.unesco.org/en/list
World time	wwp.greenwichmeantime.com
Weather information	www.metoffice.gov.uk

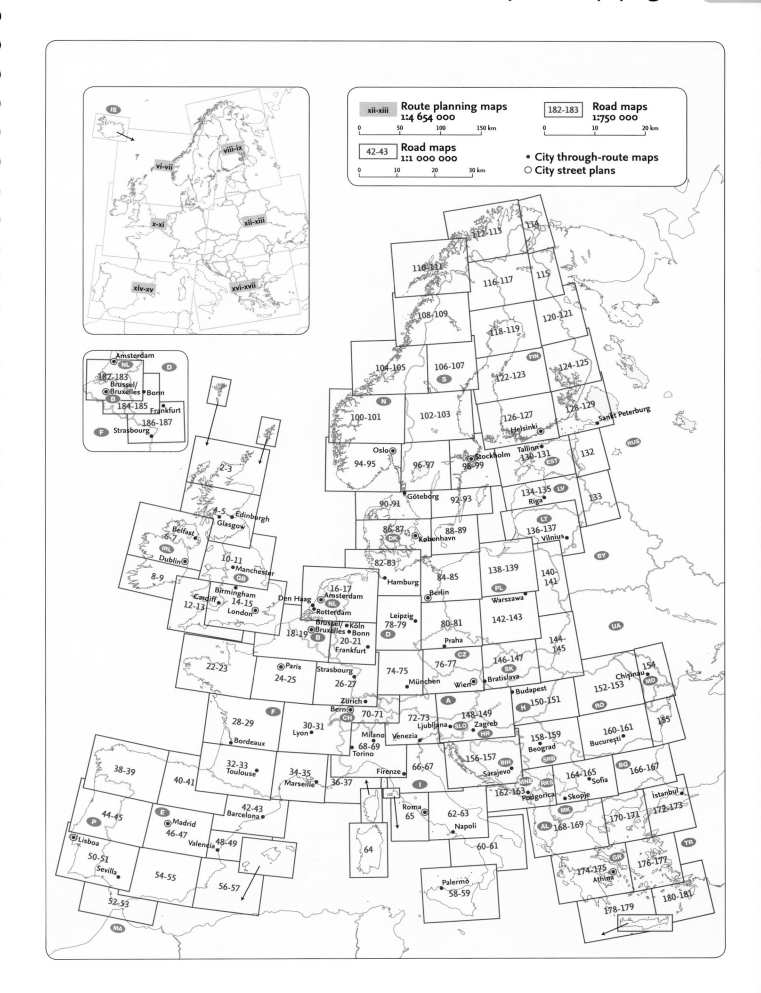

Route planning maps
xii-xiii
1:4 654 000
0   50   100   150 km

Road maps
182-183
1:750 000
0   10   20 km

Road maps
42-43
1:1 000 000
0   10   20   30 km

• City through-route maps
○ City street plans

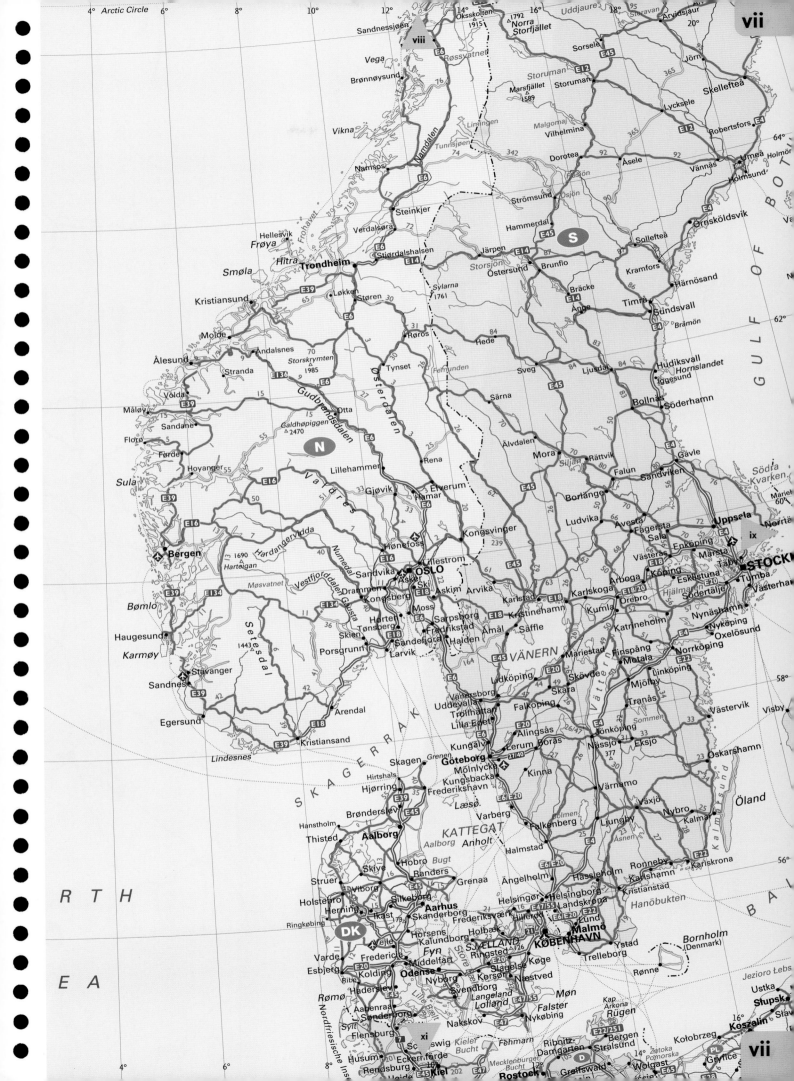

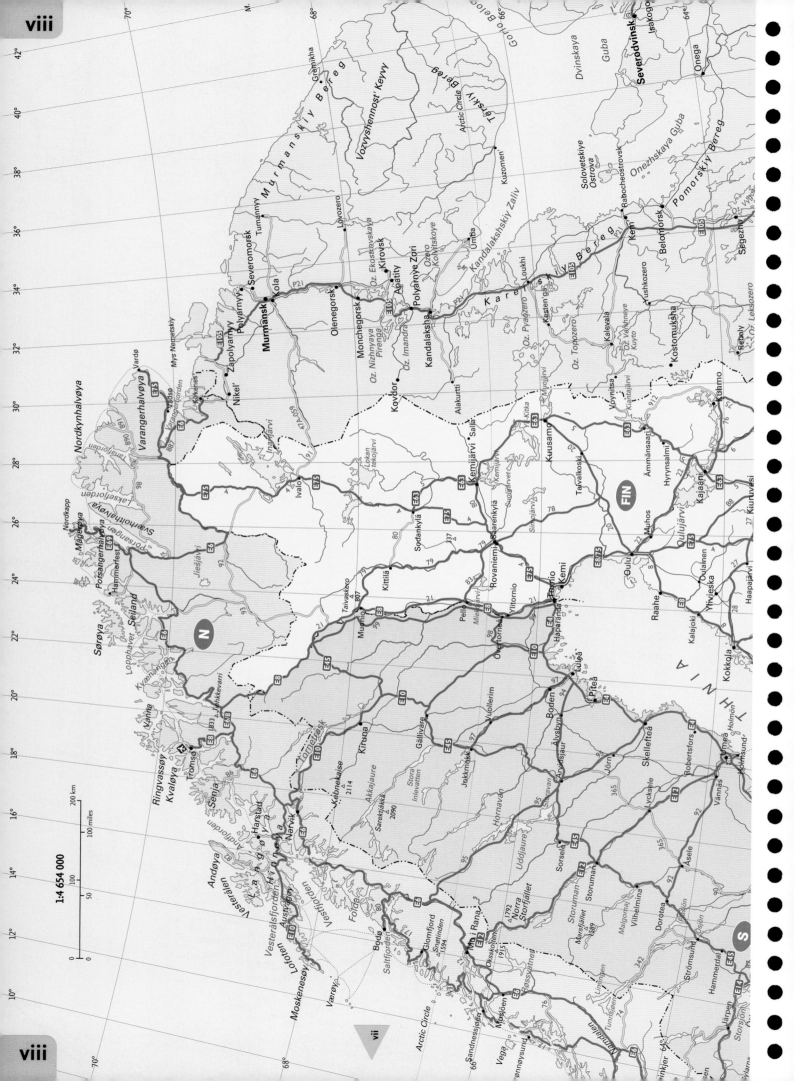

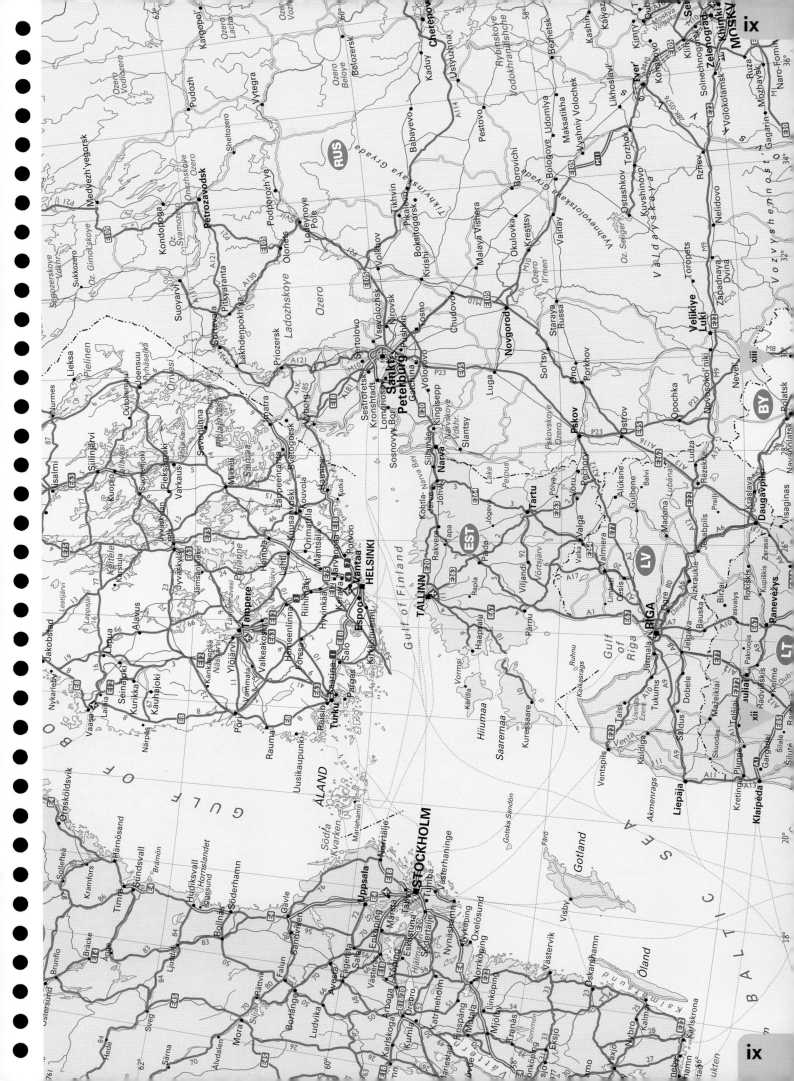

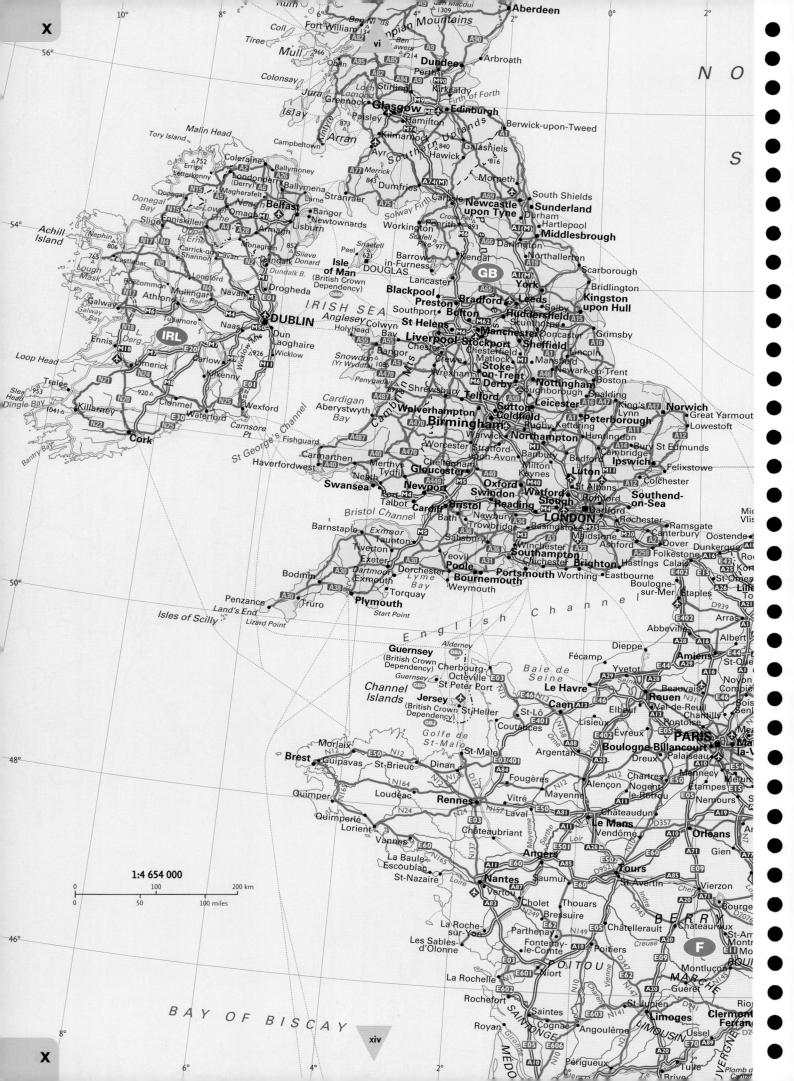

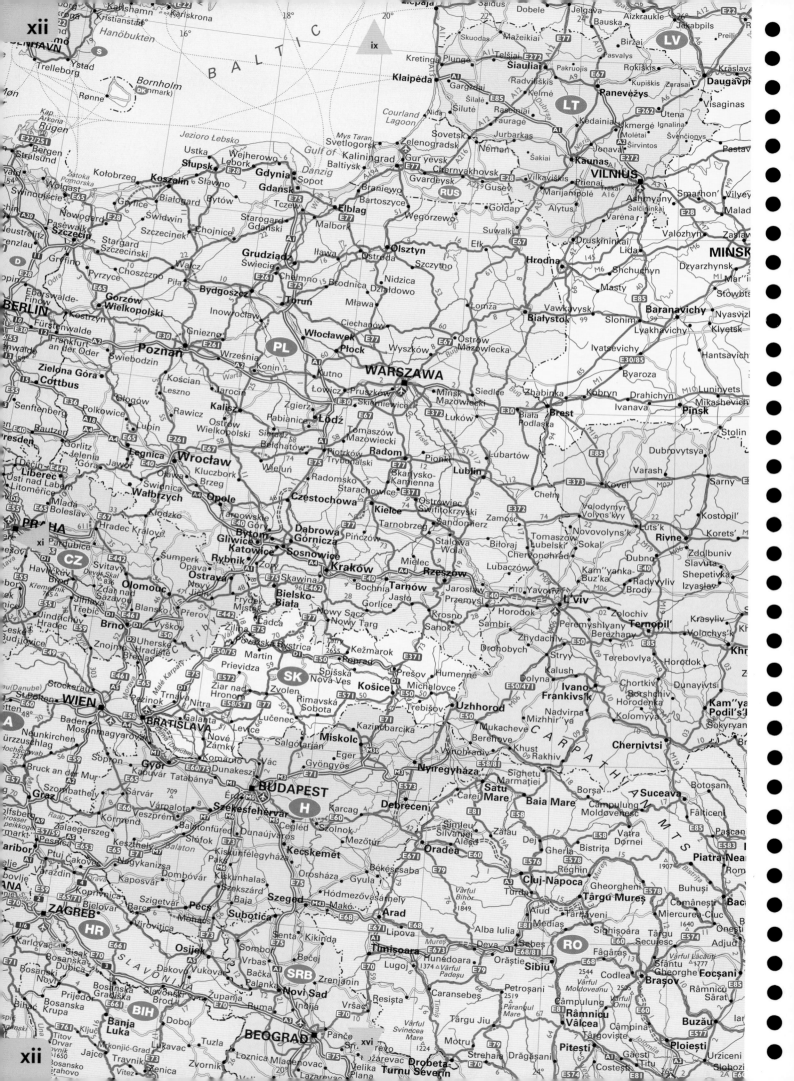

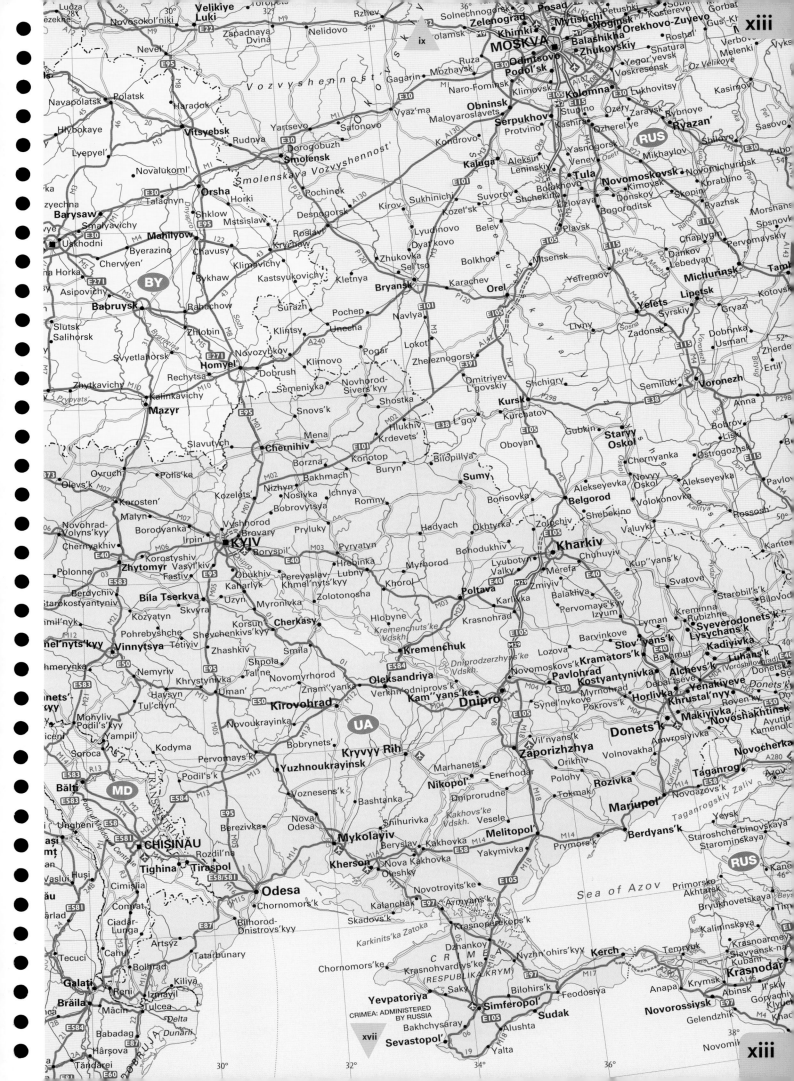

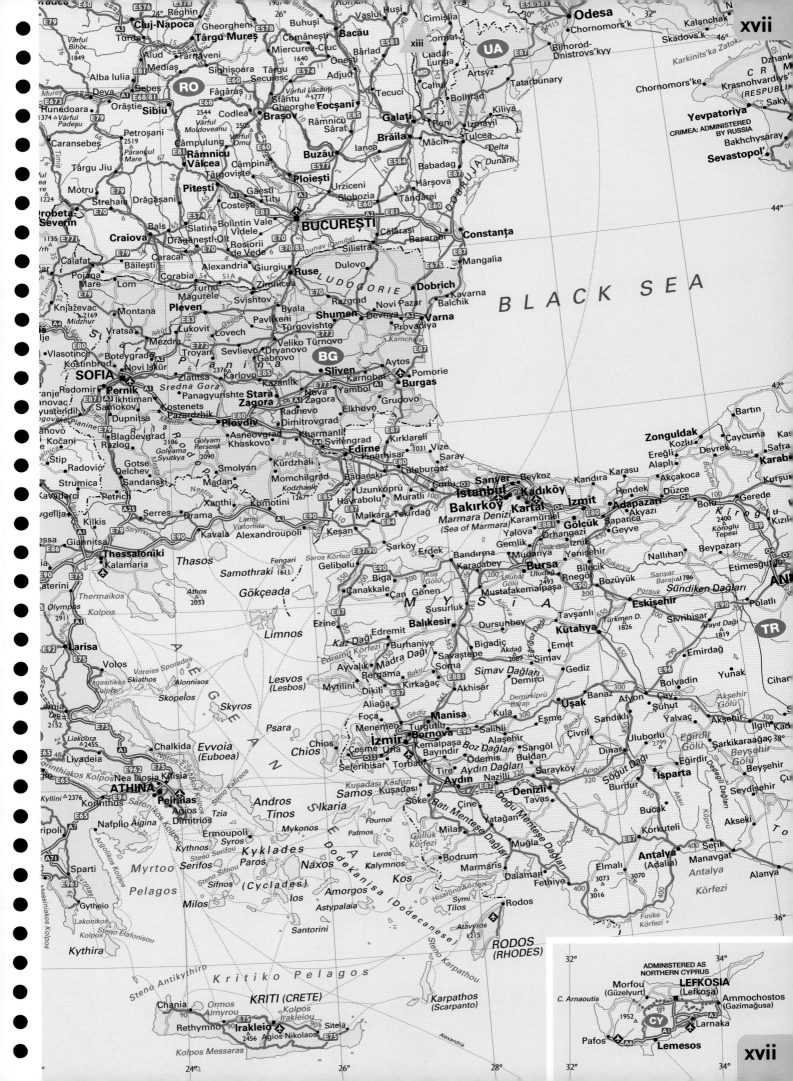

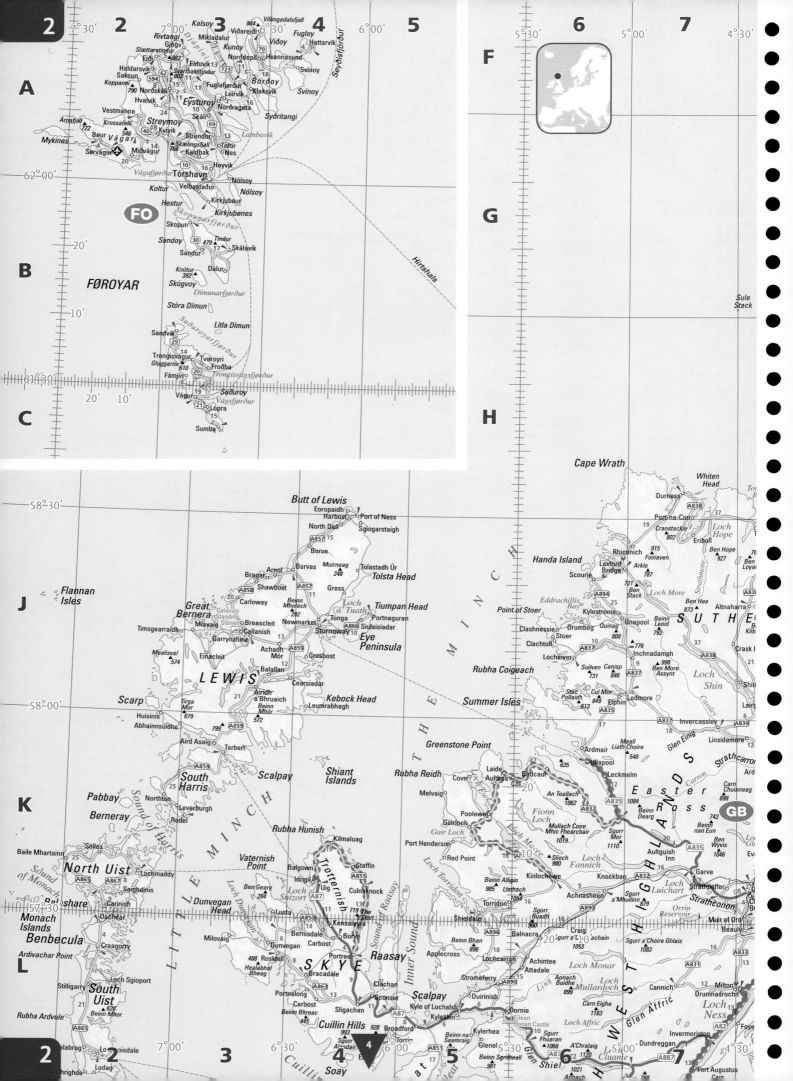

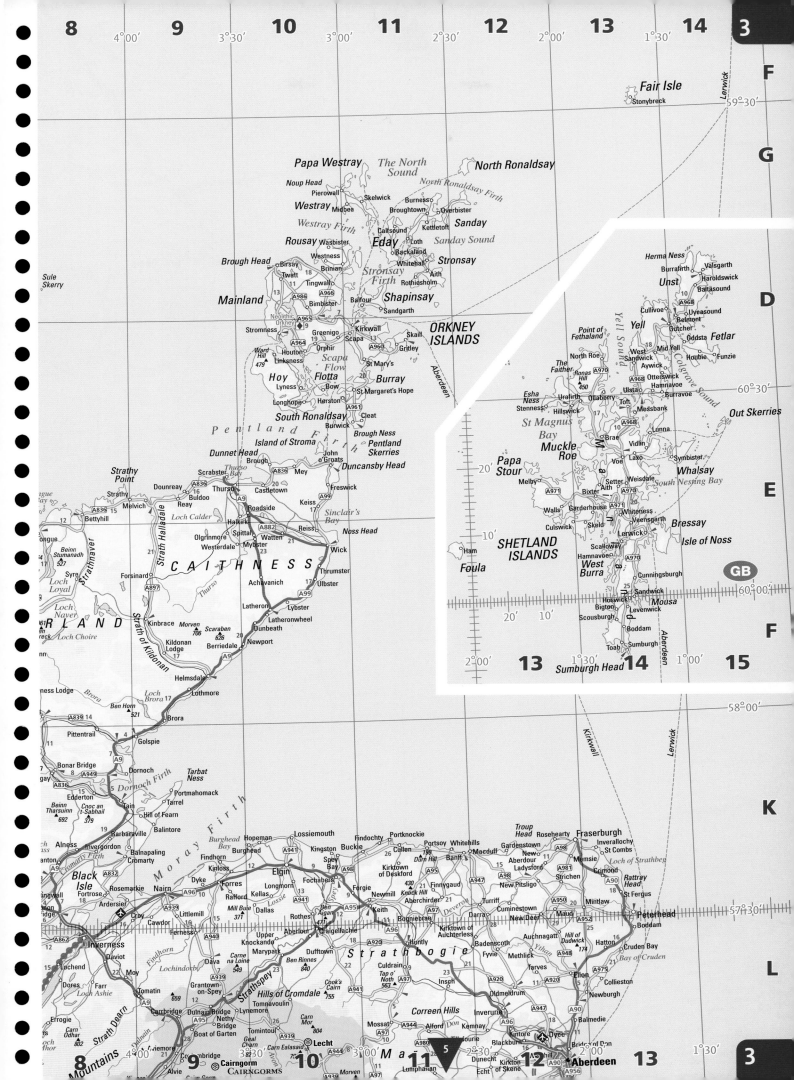

F

4°00'   3°30'   3°00'   2°30'   2°00'   1°30'

Fair Isle
Lerwick
Stonybreck   59°30'

G

Papa Westray   *The North*   North Ronaldsay
                     Sound
Noup Head   Pierowall   Skelwick   *North Ronaldsay Firth*
                    Burness
Westray   Midbea   Broughtown   Overbister   Sanday
Westray Firth   Caltsound   Kettletoft   Loth
                    Backaland
Rousay   Wasbister   Eday   Whitehall   Stronsay
                         Sanday Sound
Brough Head   Birsay   Westness   Backaland
            Twatt   Brinian   Aith   Rothiesholm
        18   Tingwall   *Stronsay*
Mainland   11   A986   Bimbister   Balfour   *Firth*   Shapinsay   D
        13   A966   Sandgarth
        Neolithic   A965   ORKNEY
        Orkney◆9   Kirkwall   ISLANDS
    Stromness   19   Greenigo   Skaill
            A964   Orphir   Scapa   A960   Gritley
        Ward   Houton   St Mary's
        Hill   Linksness   *Scapa*   Burray
        479   *Flow*
            Hoy   Flotta   St Margaret's Hope
                Lyness   Bow
                    Horston   A961   Cleat
            Longhope   South Ronaldsay   Burwick
                         Brough Ness
        Pentland   *Firth*   Island of Stroma   *Pentland*
                             Skerries
            Dunnet Head   Brough   John
Strathy   Scrabster   *Thurso*   Mey   o'Groats   Duncansby Head
Point   Dounreay   A836   *Bay*   Freswick
        16   Thurso   A9   Castletown   Aberdeen
    Strathy   Buldoo   20   Keiss
Melvich   Reay   Roadside   Sinclair's
A836   15   A9   Halkirk   *Bay*
Bettyhill   Loch Calder   Spittal   A882   Reiss   Noss Head
                    Olgrinmore   Watten   23   Wick
        21   Westerdale   Mybster   CAITHNESS   Thrumster
                Achavanich   A99   Ulbster
    Forsinard   Latheron   Lybster
        A897   *Thurso*   Latheronwheel
            Kinbrace   Morven   Scaraben   Dunbeath
                706   626   Newport
        Kildonan   Berriedale
        Lodge
            Helmsdale
        Brora
    Loch Brora 17   Lothmore

SHETLAND / ORKNEY inset (right panel):

Herma Ness
Burrafirth   Valsgarth
    Unst   Haroldswick
        10   Baltasound
Cullivoe   A968   Uyeasound
    Yell   Belmont
        18   Gutcher   Oddsta   Fetlar
Point of   West   Mid Yell   Houbie   Funzie
Fethaland   Sandwick   Aywick
North Roe   A968   Otterswick
The   Ronas   A970   Hamnavoe
Faither   Hill   Ulsta   Burravoe   60°30'
    450
Esha   Urafirth   Toft   Out Skerries
Ness   Stenness   Ollaberry   A968
    St Magnus   Hillswick   Mossbank
    Bay   A968   Lunna
    Muckle   17   Brae
    Roe   Vidlin
Papa   A970   Laxo   Symbister
Stour   Melby   Voe   Whalsay
            Setter   A970   *South Nesing Bay*
    Walls   Bixter   Aith   Weisdale
        A971   A971   Whiteness
            Garderhouse   Veensgarth   Bressay
    Culswick   Skeld   A971   Lerwick   Isle of Noss
            20   Scalloway
SHETLAND   Hamnavoe   A970
ISLANDS   West   25   Cunningsburgh   GB
    Foula   Burra   Sandwick
            Hoswick   Mousa
        Bigton   Levenwick   60°00'
            Scousburgh
        Boddam
    20'   10'   Toab   Sumburgh
                Boddam
        13   Sumburgh Head   **14**   **15**
2°00'   1°30'   1°00'

F

58°00'

Brora
A839 14
Ben Horn   Loch Brora
521   Brora
Pittentrail   Golspie
Bonar Bridge   A9
    A949   Dornoch   Tarbat
    A836   Ness
Edderton   Portmahomack
    Tain   Tarrel
Beinn   Cnoc an   Hill of Fearn
Tharsuinn   t-Sabhail
692   379   Balintore
        Barbaraville   Kirkwall   Lerwick   K
Alness   Invergordon   Balnapaling
        Cromarty
Black   A832   *Moray   Firth*
Isle   Fortrose   Rosemarkie   Nairn
    Ardersier
        A939   Croy   Cawdor
Inverness   Daviot   Littlemill   Forres   A96   10
        Moy   Ferness   Elgin   57°30'
    Dores   Farr   Carrbridge   Peterhead
    Loch Ashie   Tomatin
        659   Grantown-on-Spey
            Strathspey   Hills of Cromdale
                     Tomnavoulin
8   9   10   Carn   11   12   13   **3**
4°00'   3°00'   2°30'
    Cairngorm   Lecht   M
    CAIRNGORMS   5   Aberdeen

Moray / Aberdeenshire (lower right):

Troup   Rosehearty   Fraserburgh
Head   Inverallochy
        A98   St Combs
Burghead   Hopeman   Lossiemouth   Findochty   Portknockie   Portsoy   Whitehills   Macduff   New   Memsie
Bay   Kingston   Buckie   Cullen   Gardenstown   Aberdour
Burghead   Spey   A98   *Durn Hill*   Banff   Ladysford   A98   Strichen   Loch of Strathbeg
    A941   Bay   199   Kirktown   A95   A981   Crimond   A90
Findhorn   Fochabers   of Deskford   Finnygaud   New Pitsligo   Rattray
Kinloss   Elgin   9   430   Knock Hill   A947   Head
Dyke   Forres   Longmorn   Forgie   Newmill   Knock   Aberchirder   Turriff   Cuminestown   St Fergus
    Rafford   Kellas   A941   Keith   A97   *Deveron*   New Deer   Maud   Peterhead
Mill Buie   Dallas   Lossie   Rothes   A95   Bogniebrae   Darra   A952   Boddam
371   Ben   Craigellachie   Kirkton of   A948   Hill of
    Upper   Aigan   A96   Huntly   Auchterless   Badenscoth   Dudwick   Hatton
Cawdor   Knockando   Aberlour   12   *Strathbogie*   Fyvie   Methlick   174   Cruden Bay
    Marypark   Dufftown   A920   Insch   Auchnagatt   Tarves   Bay of Cruden
Findhorn   Carne   Ben Rinnes   Culdrain   A920   A920   Ellon   A975
    na Loine   840   Tap o'   23   *Ythan*   Colliesto
    549   Noth   Insch   Oldmeldrum   Newburgh
Lochindorb   563   A97   Inverurie   A947
A939   Mossat   Alford   A944   Kemnay   A96   Balmedie
Carrbridge   Nethy   Tomintoul   Correen Hills   A97   Kintore   Dyce
Dulnain Bridge   Bridge   Carn   Lumphanan   Blackburn   Bridge
    A95   Lynemore   Mor   Geal   Echt   of Don
Boat of Garten   804   Charn   Carn Ealasaid   Dunecht   Kirkton   A90
            Lecht   of Skene   A956
M   a   i   n
5   Lumphanan   Aberdeen
8   **9**   **10**   **11**   **12**   **13**
Cairngorm

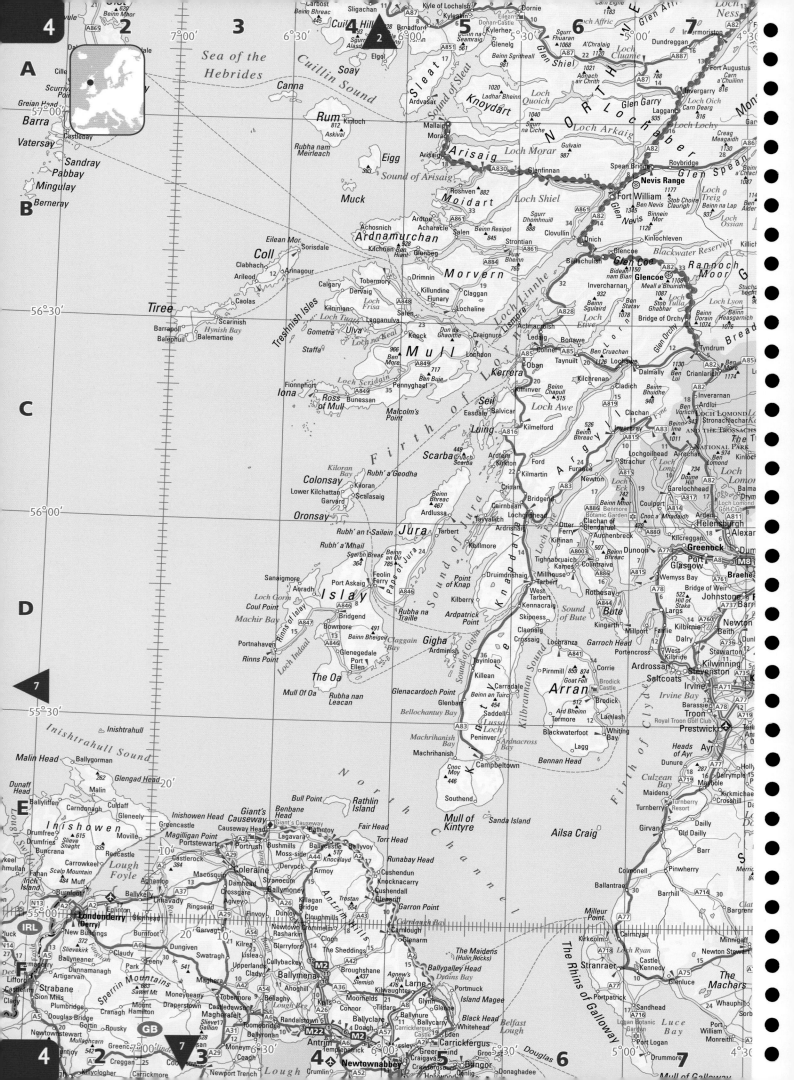

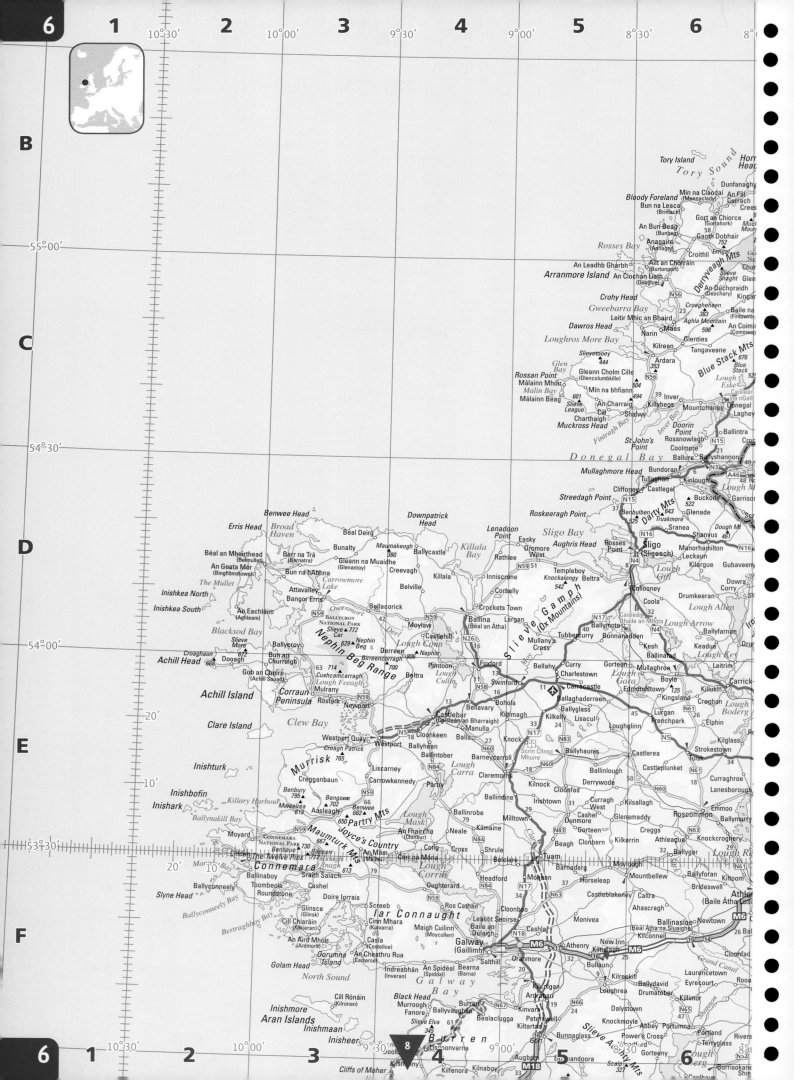

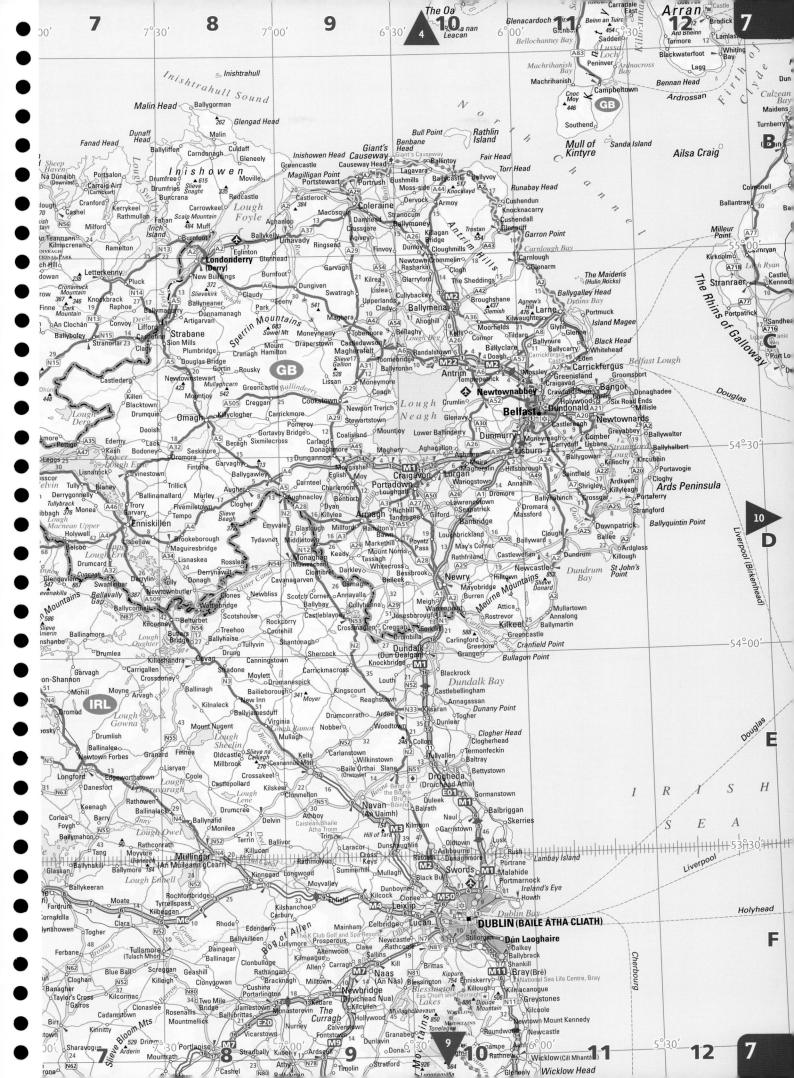

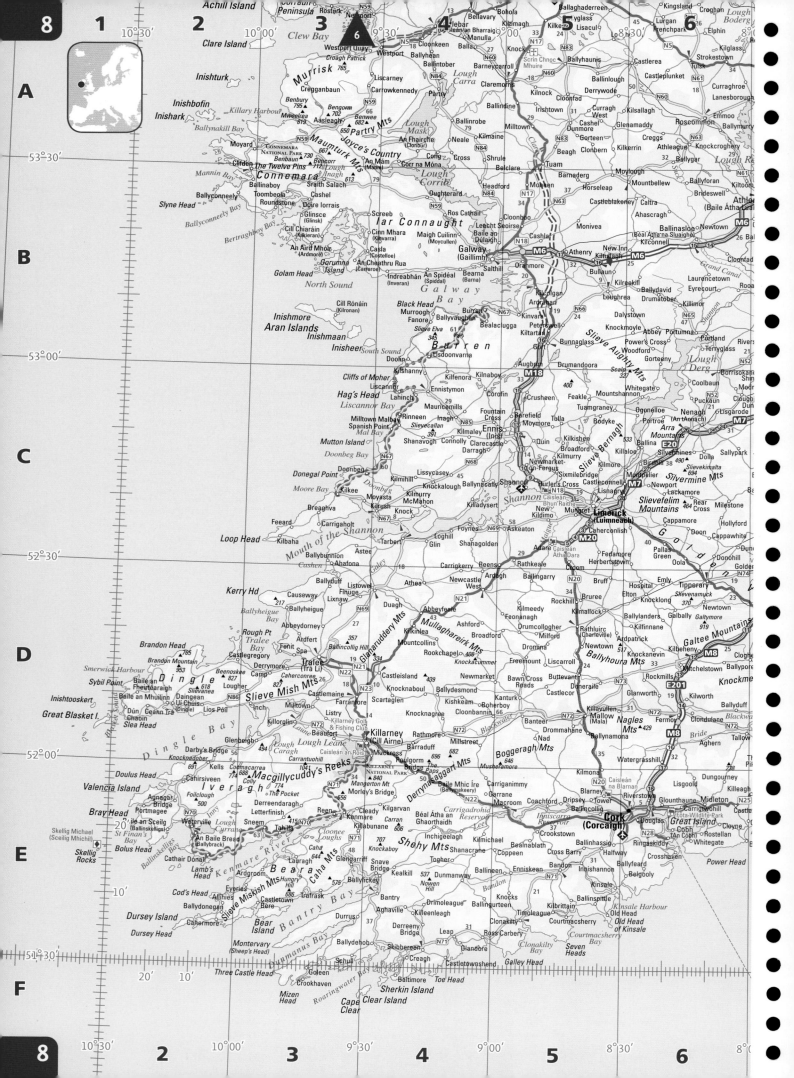

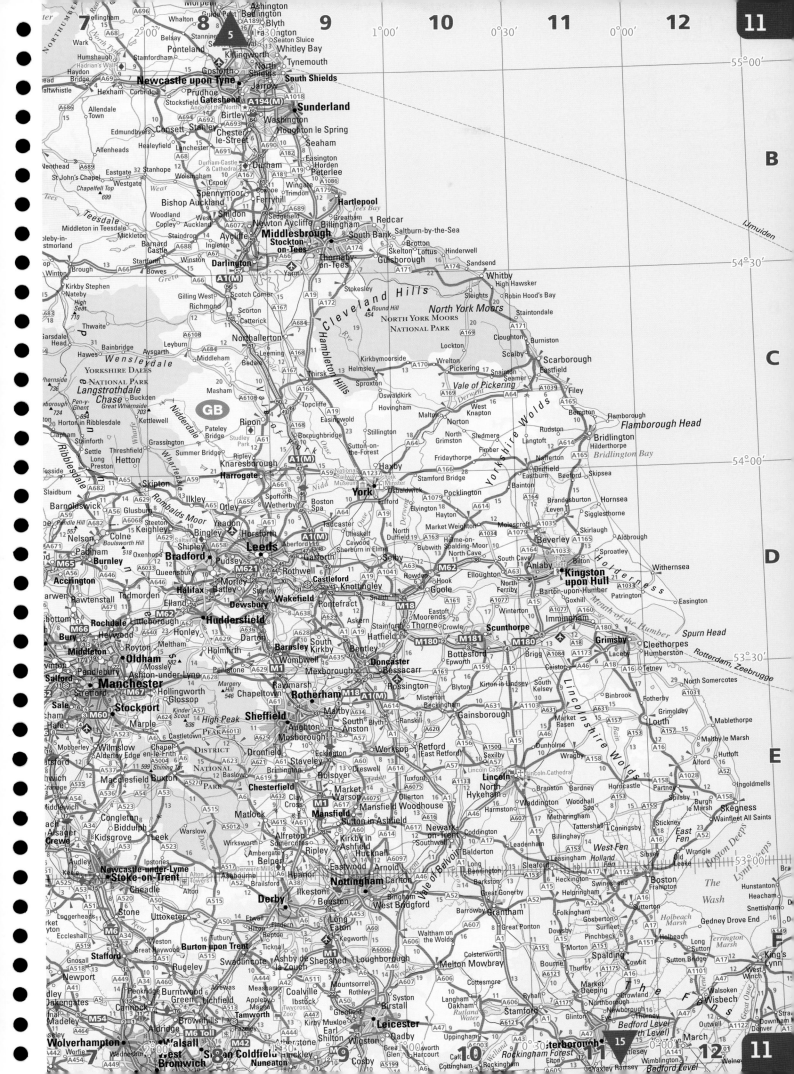

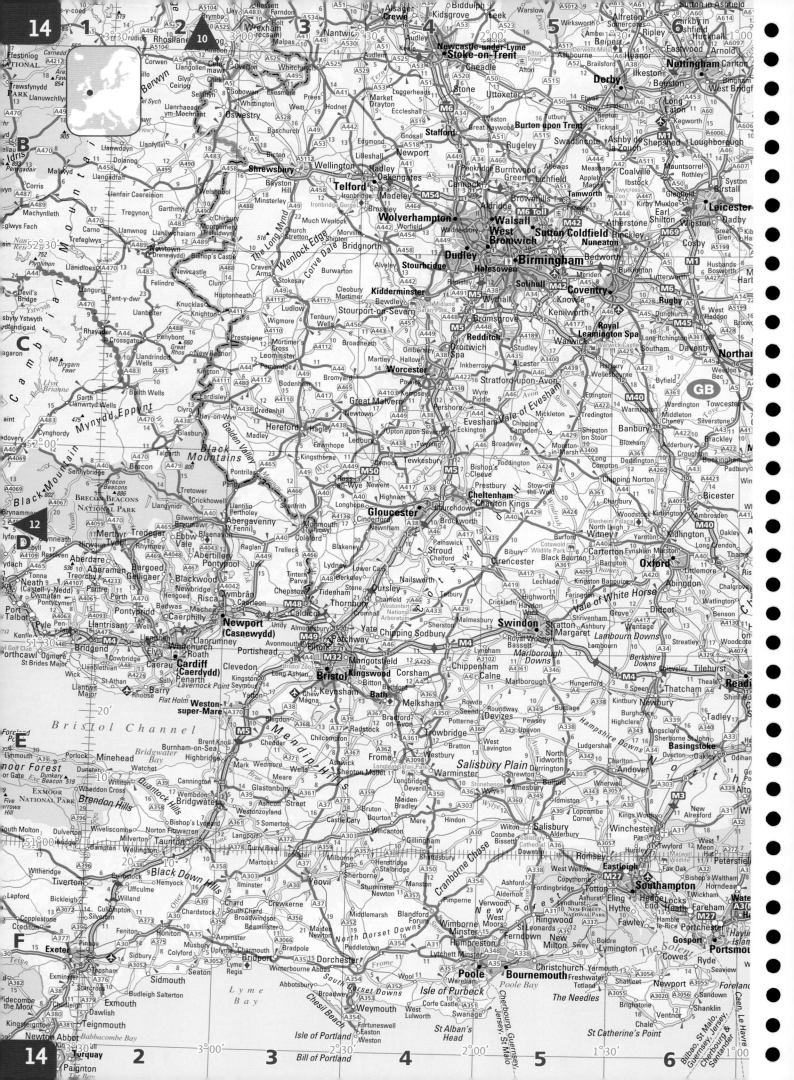

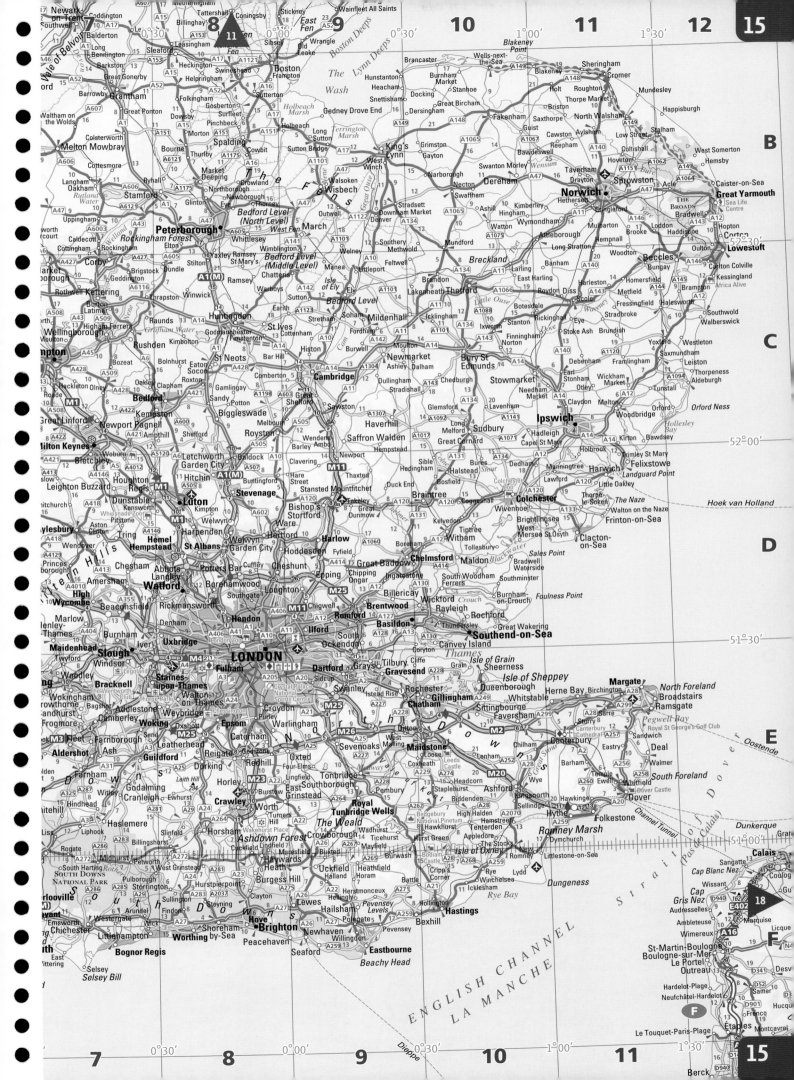

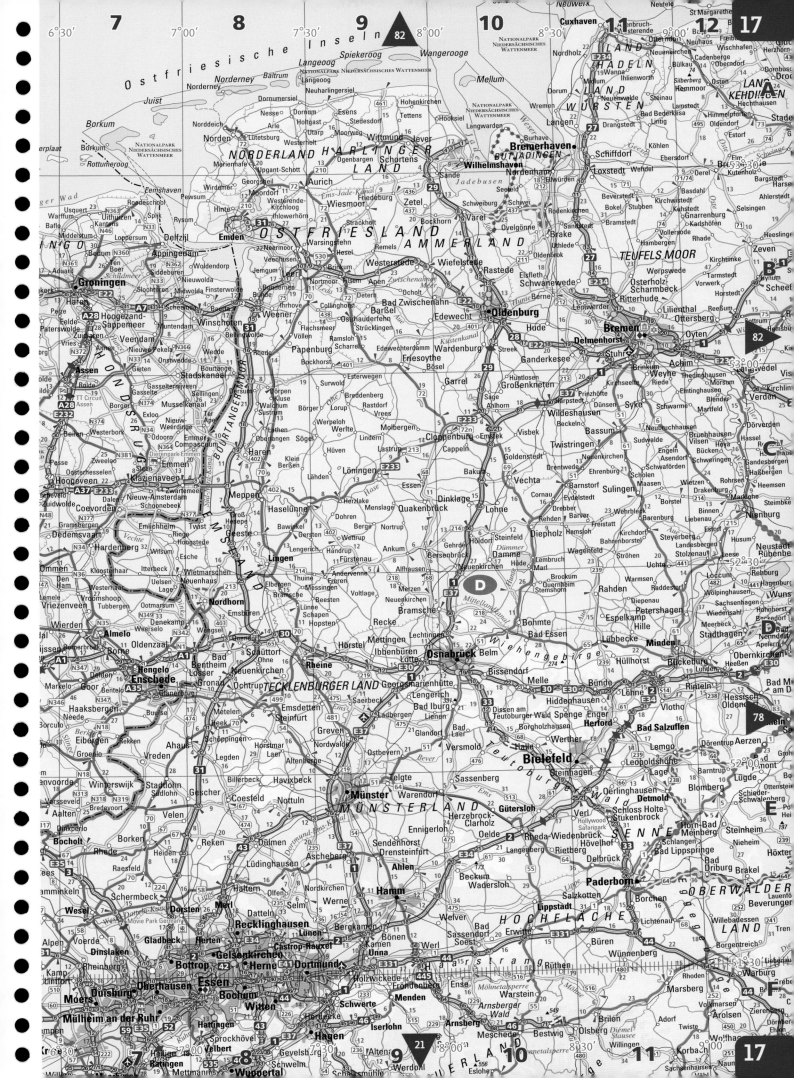

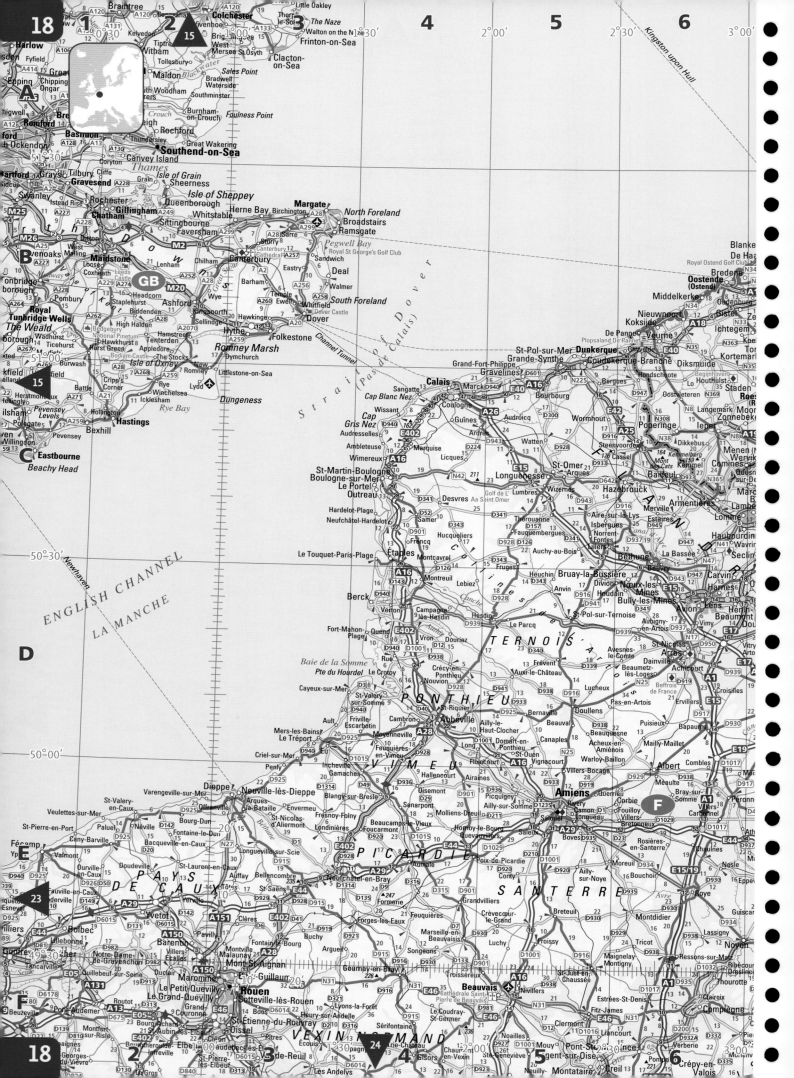

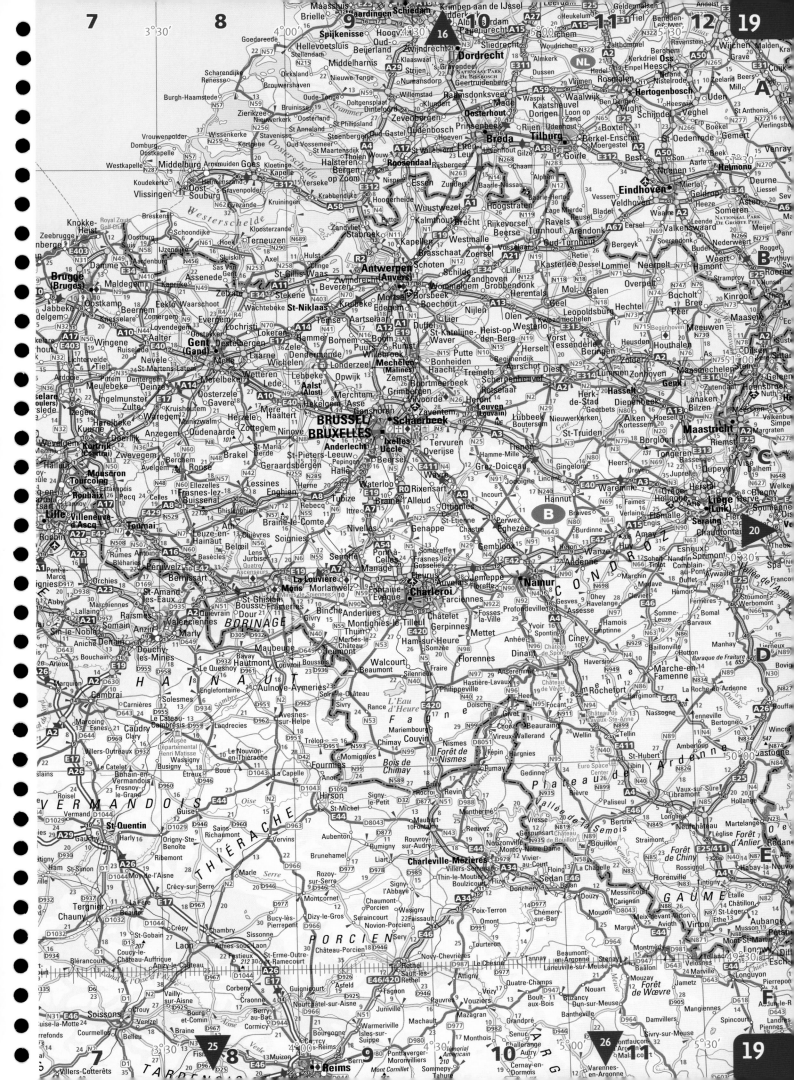

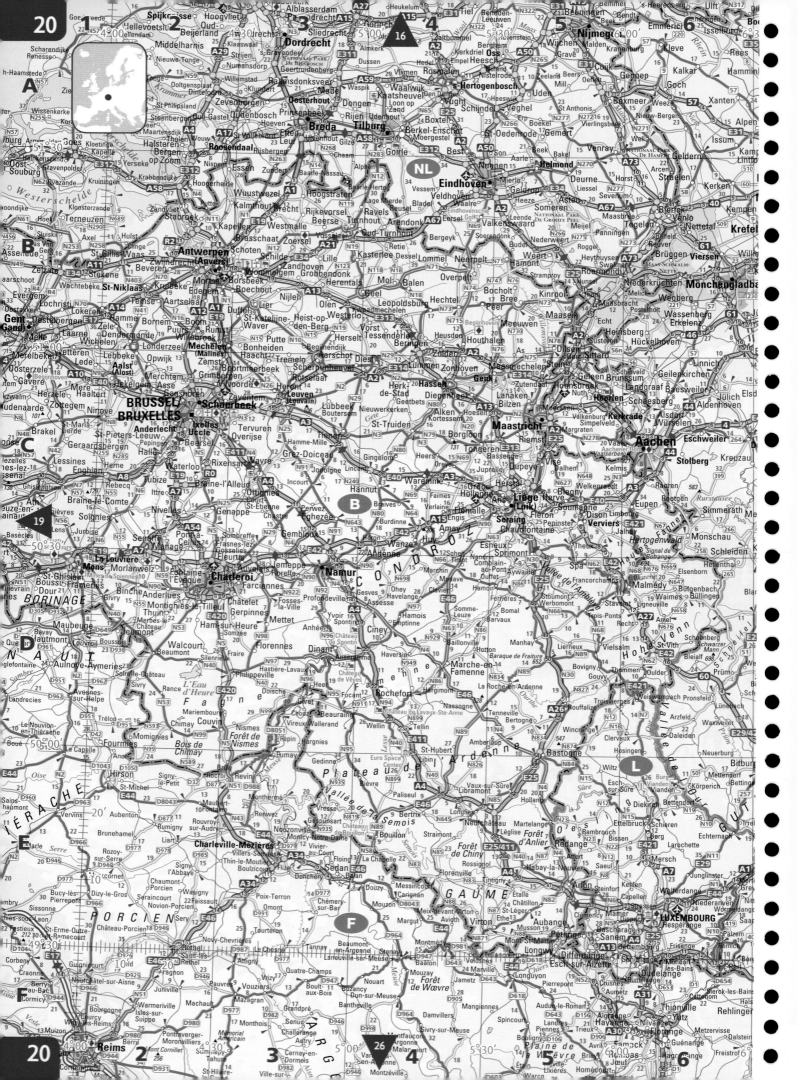

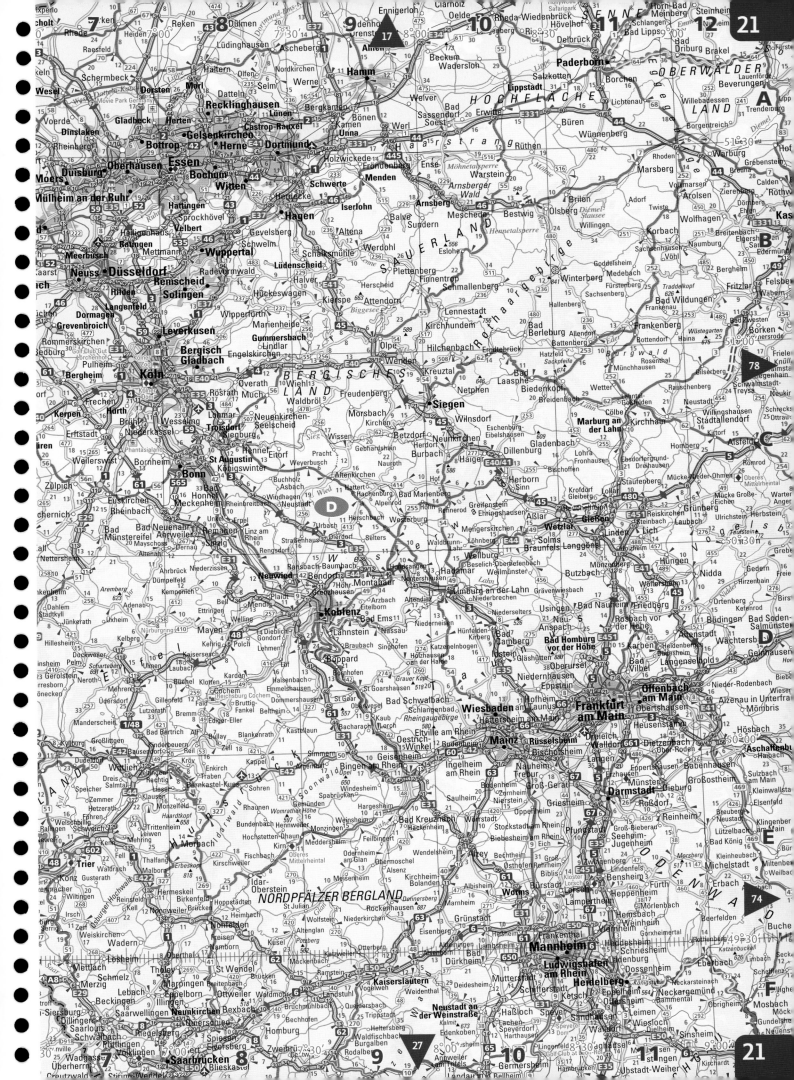

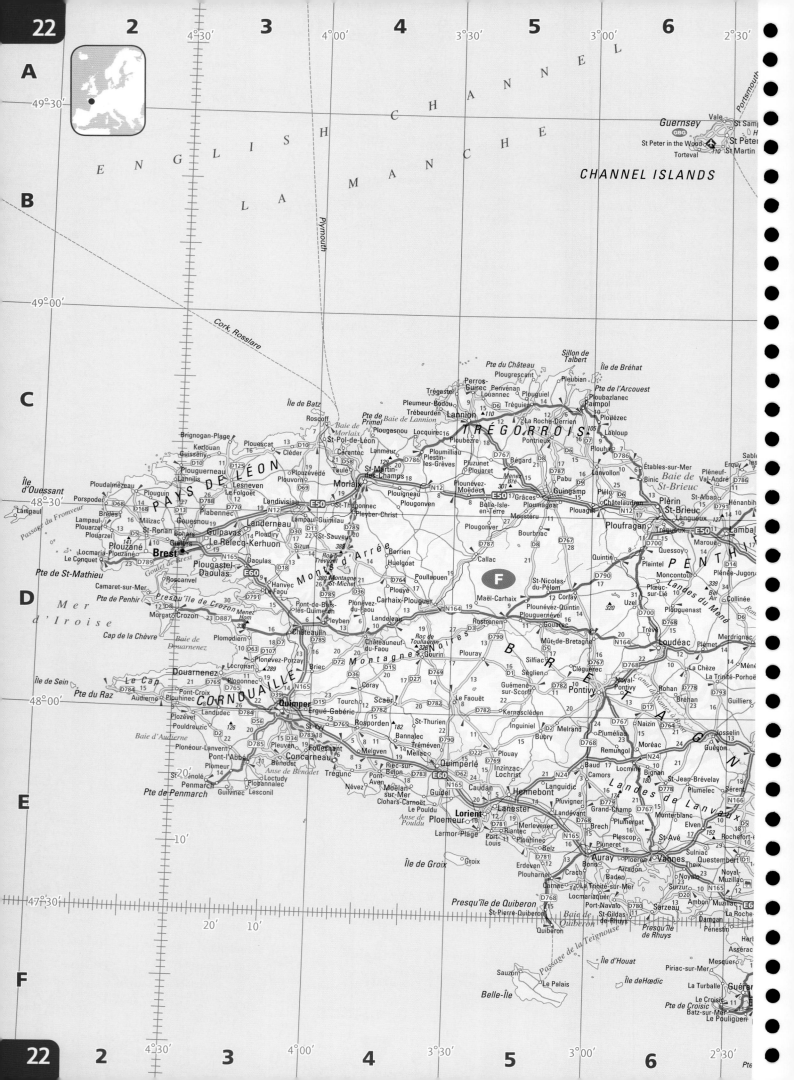

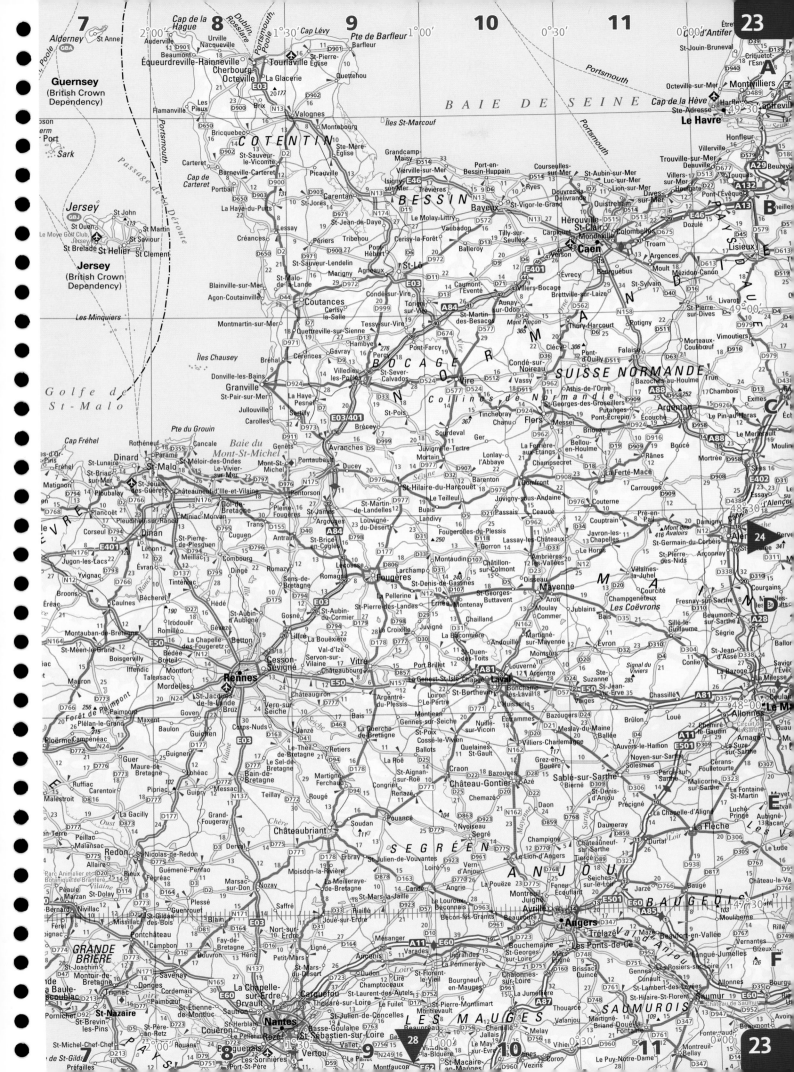

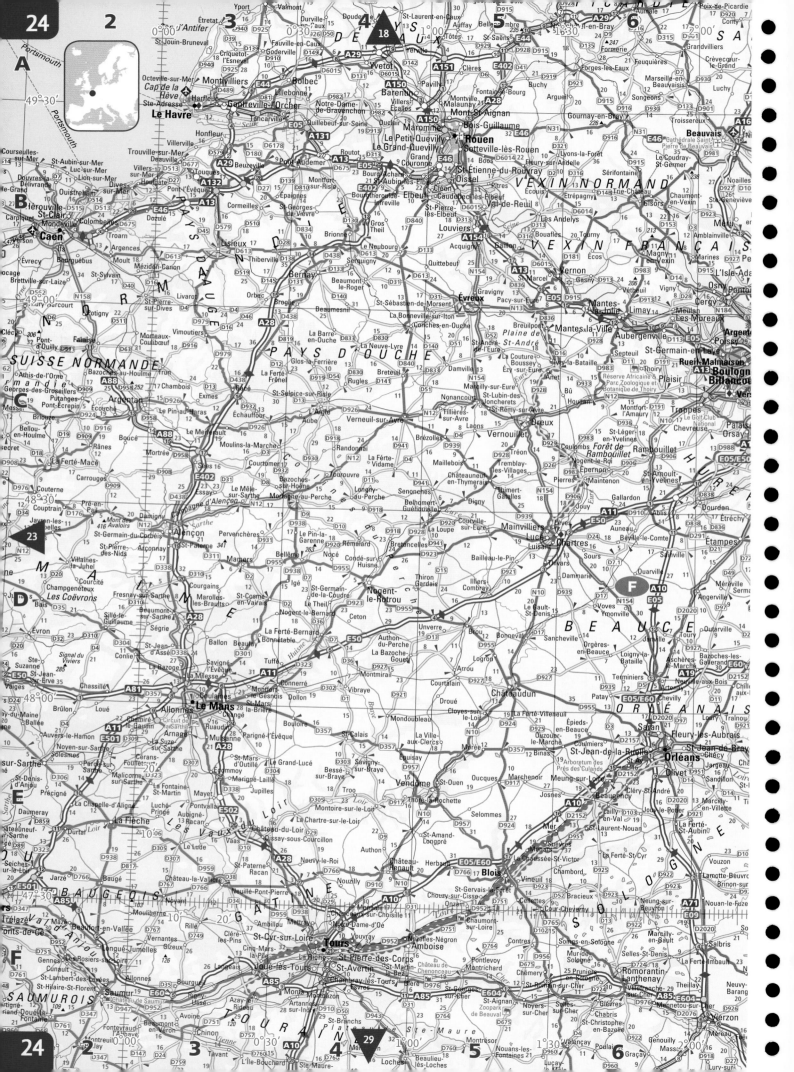

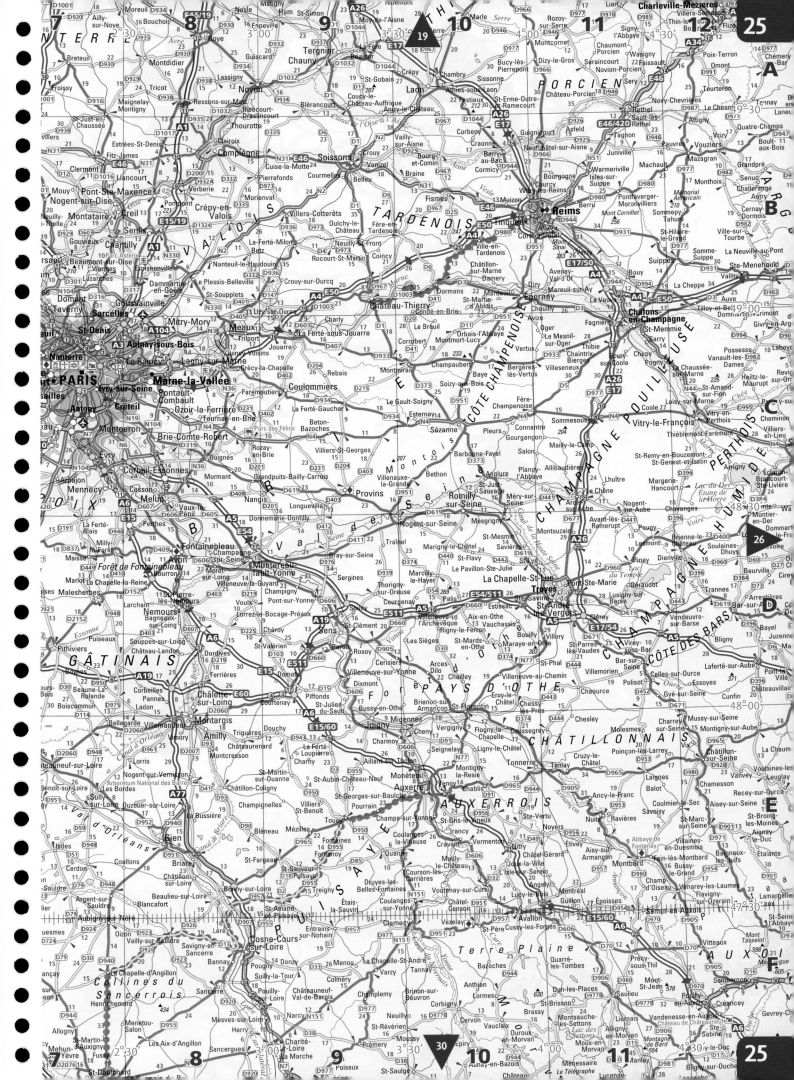

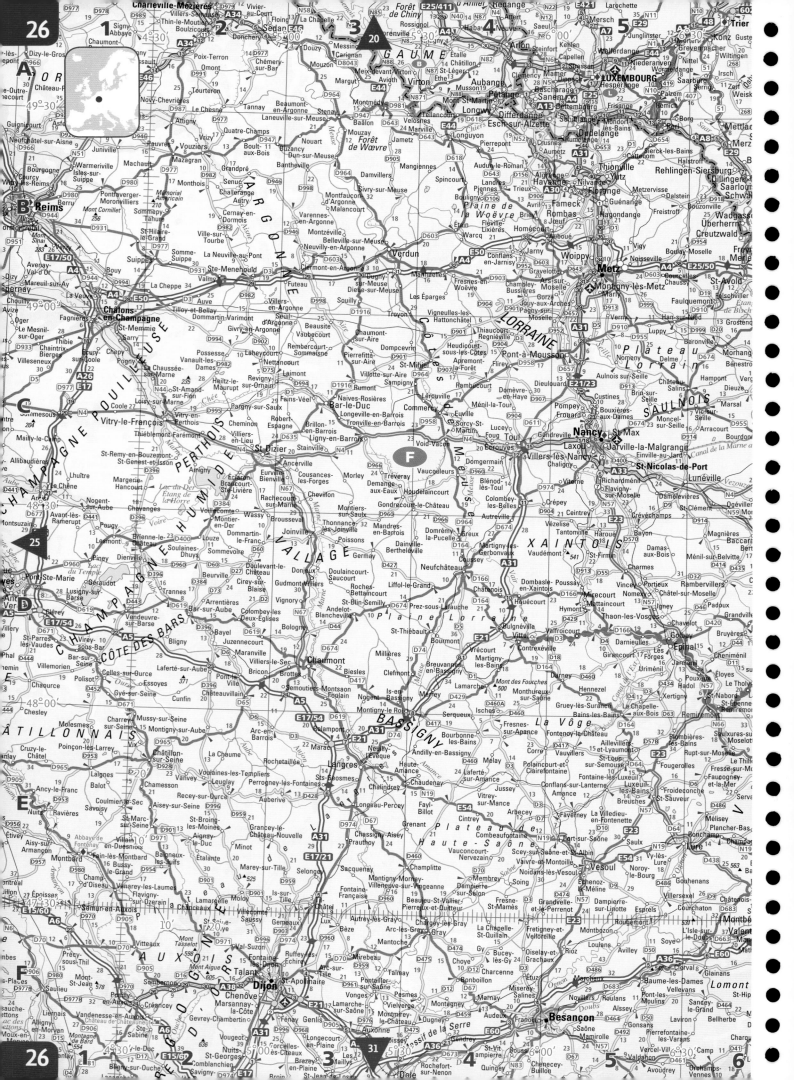

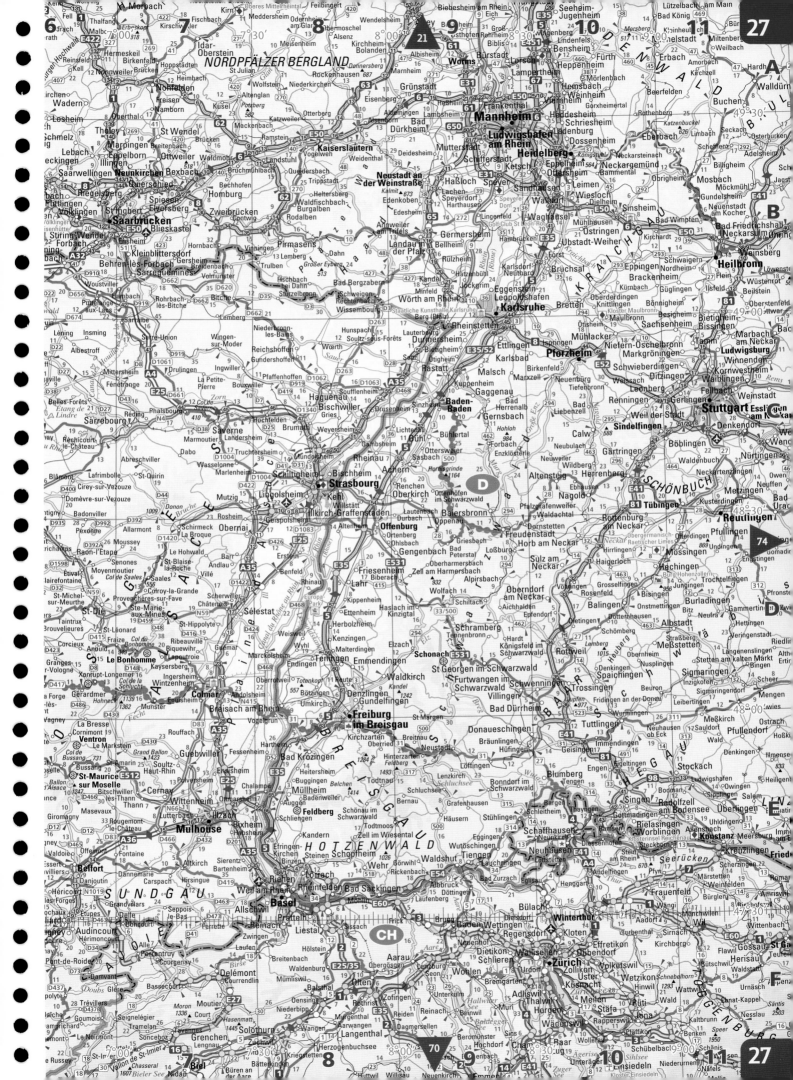

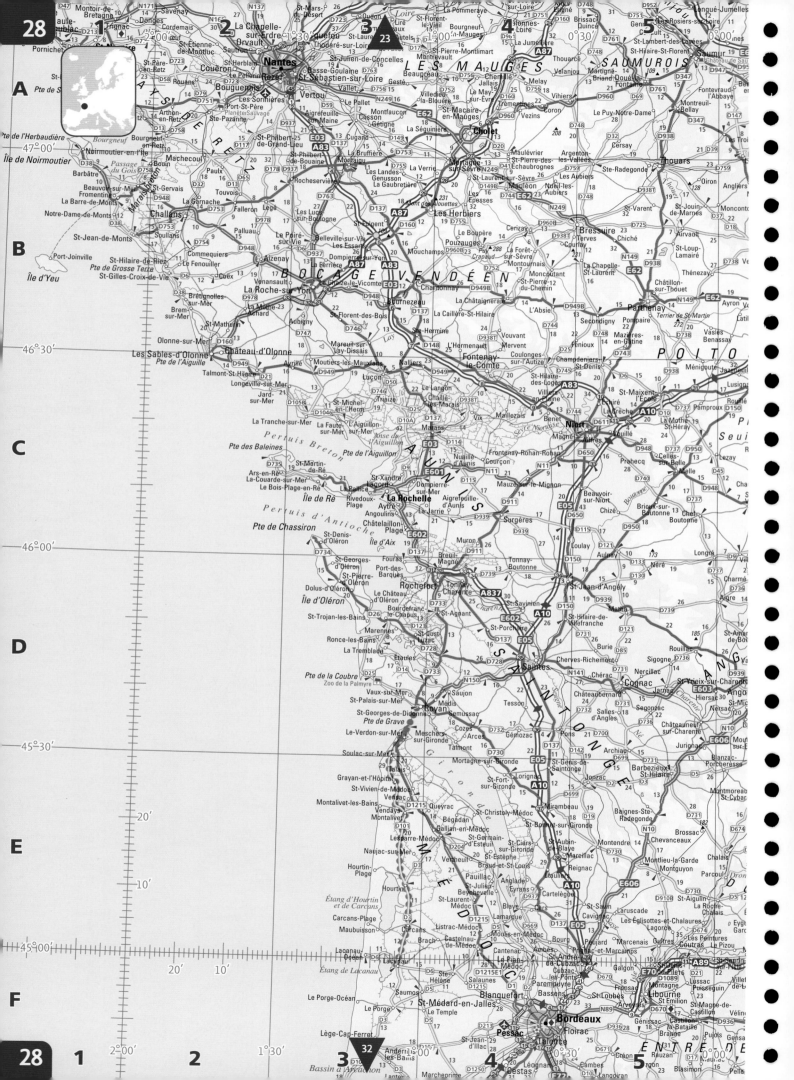

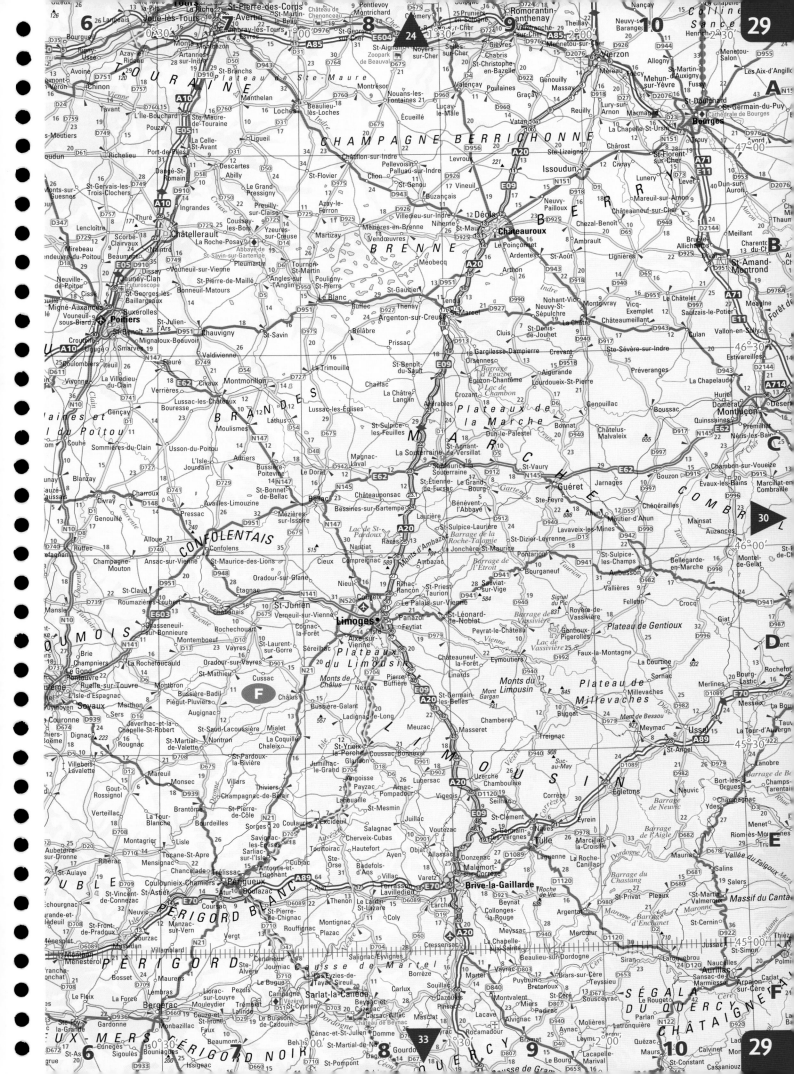

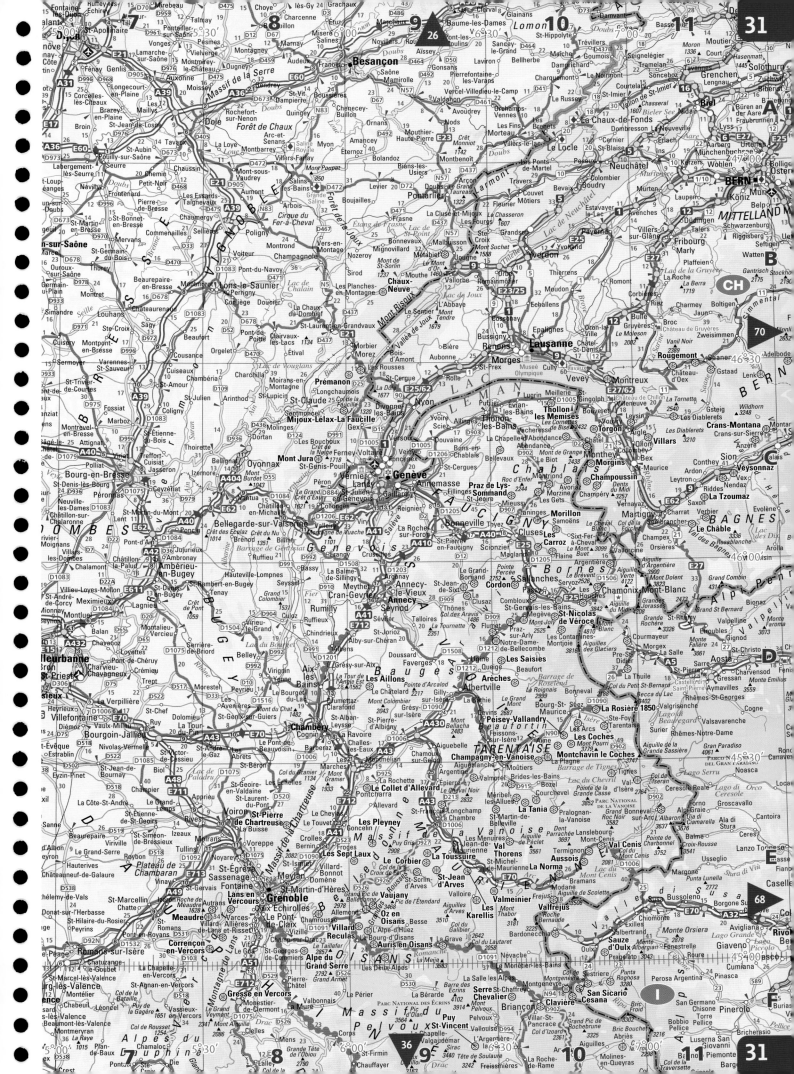

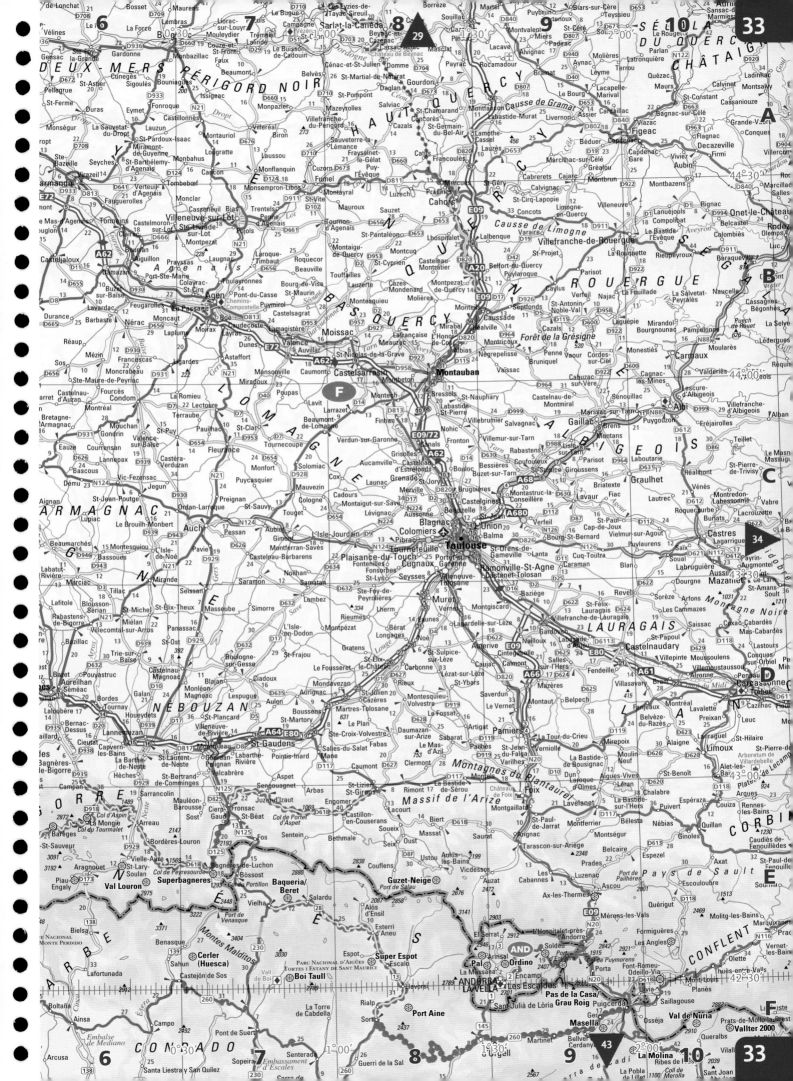

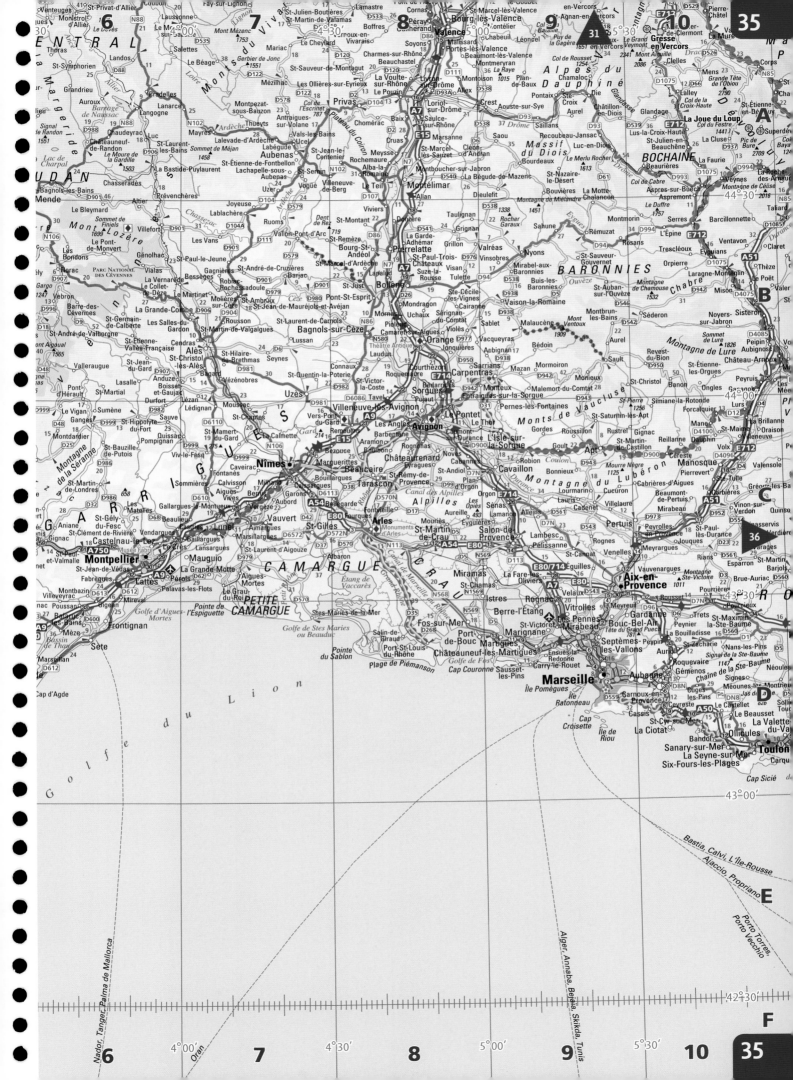

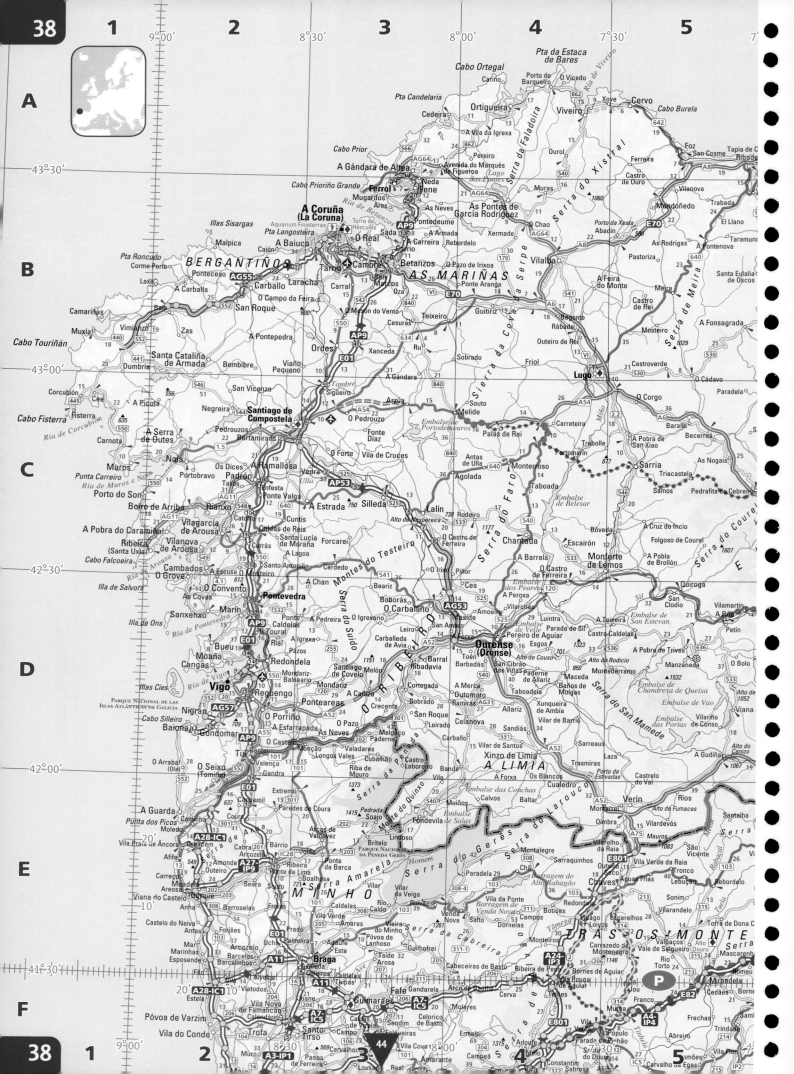

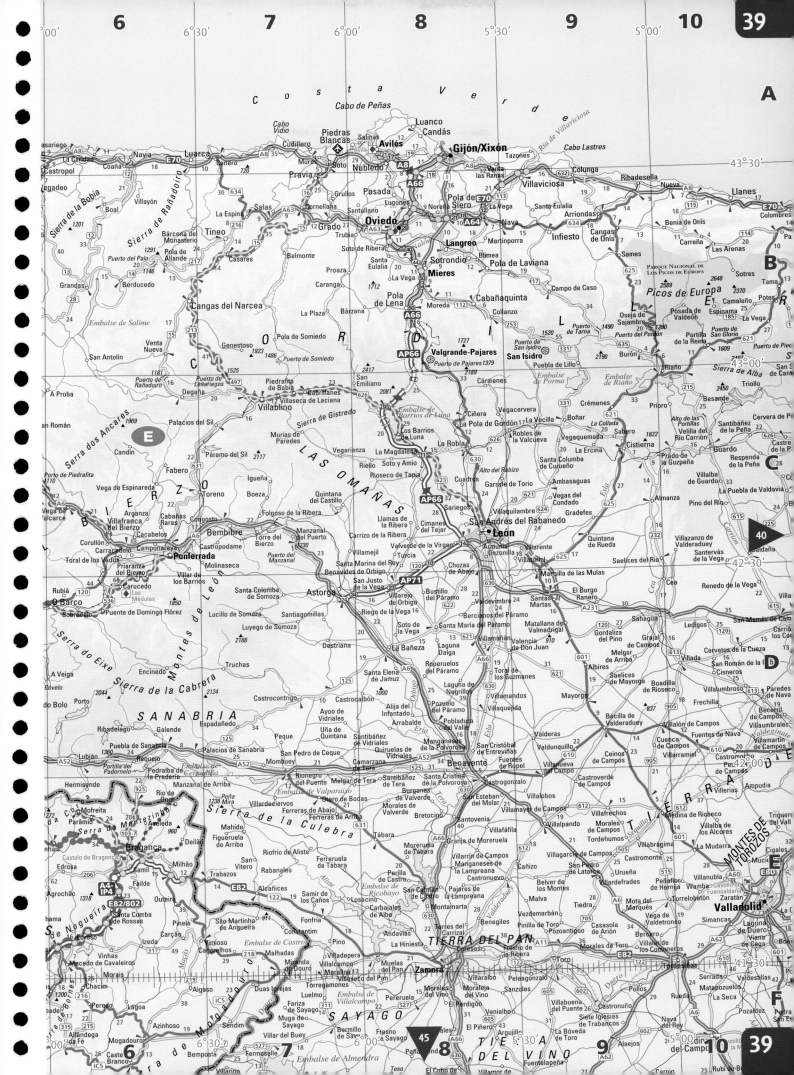

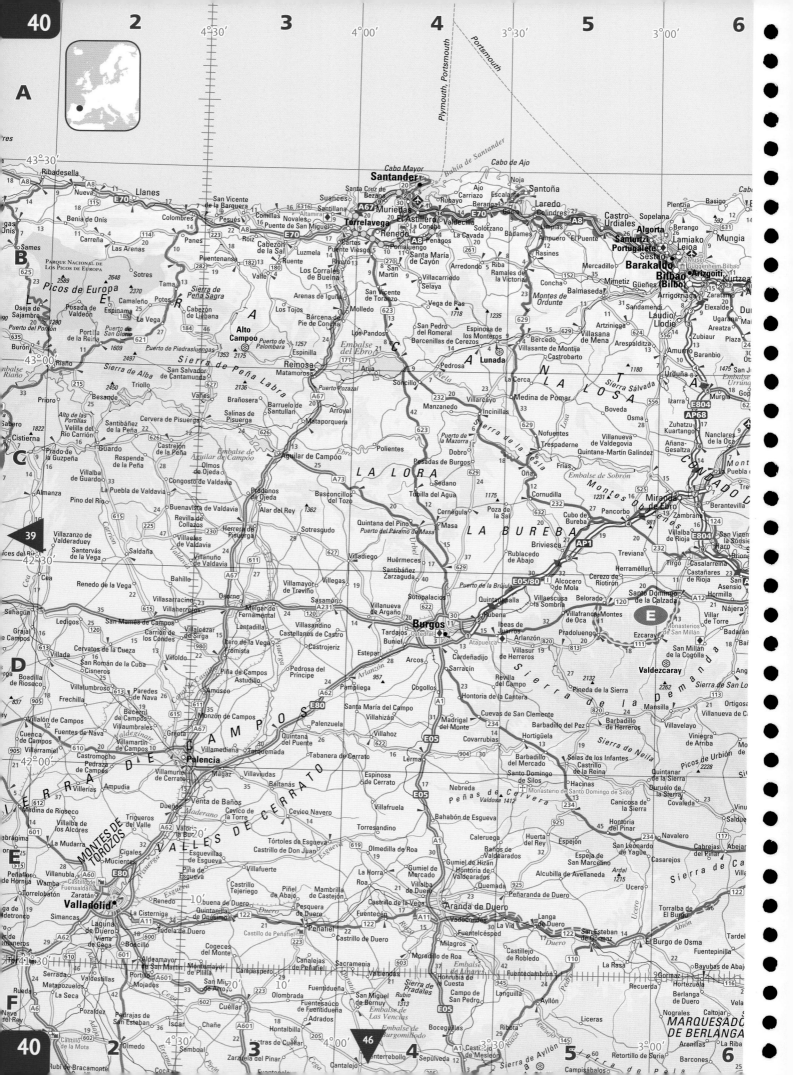

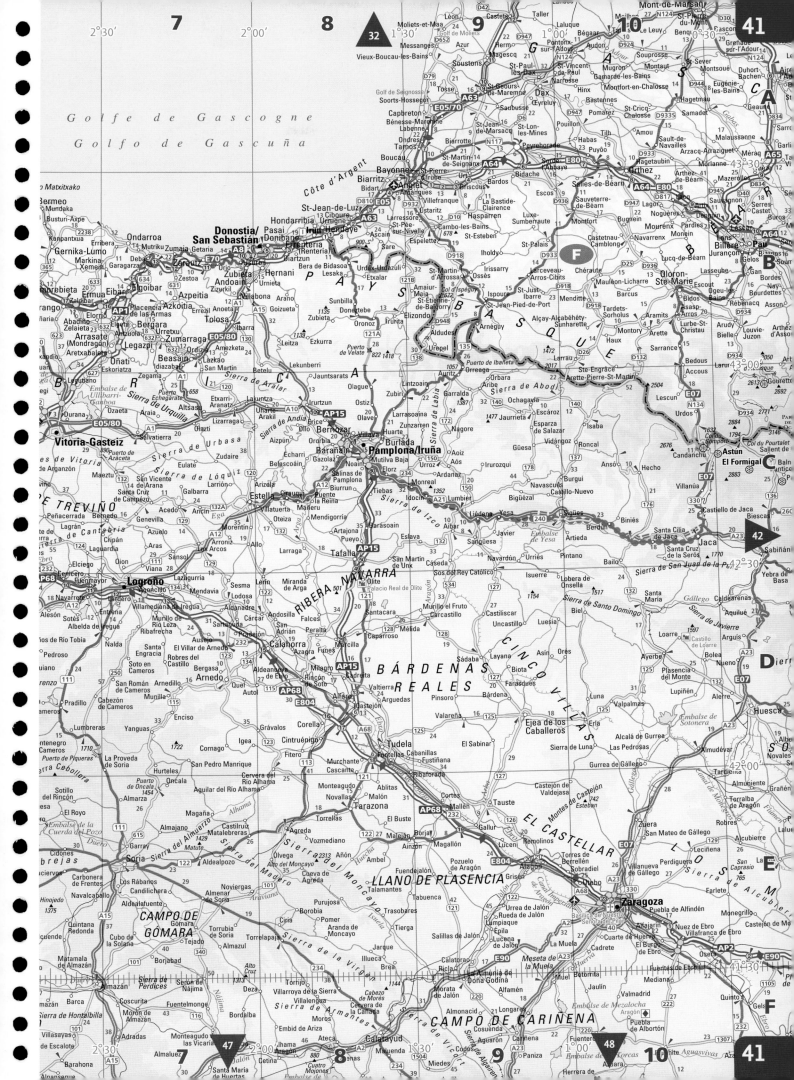

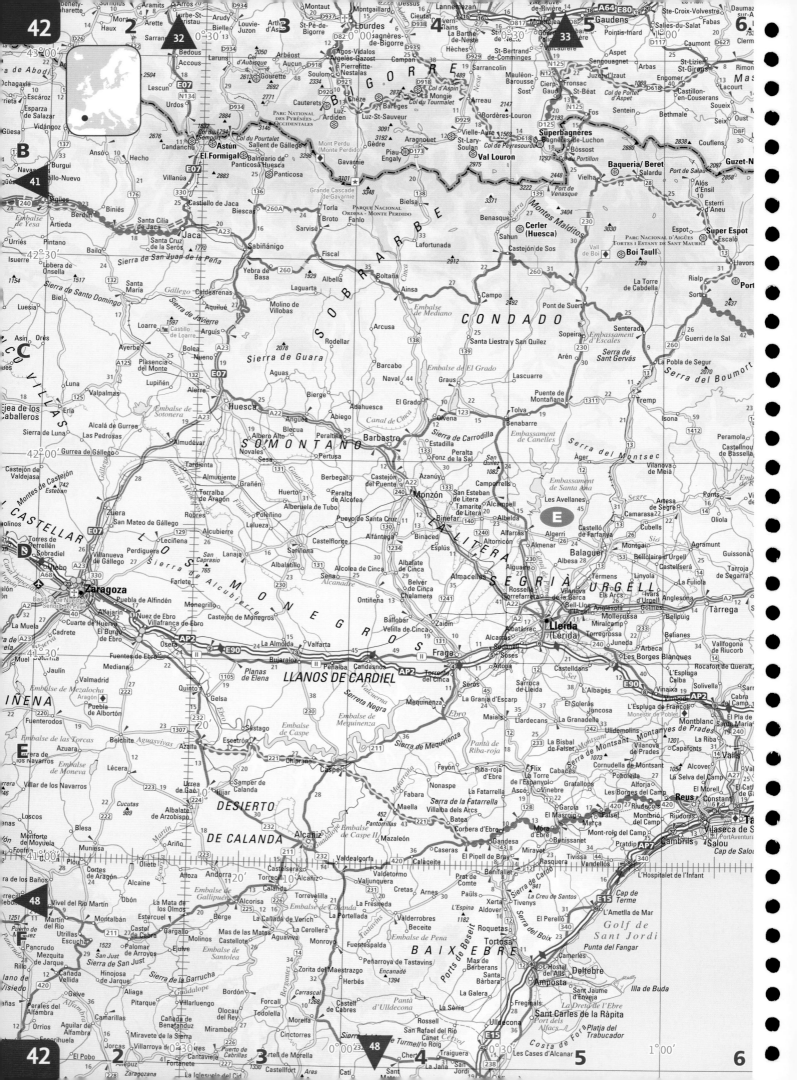

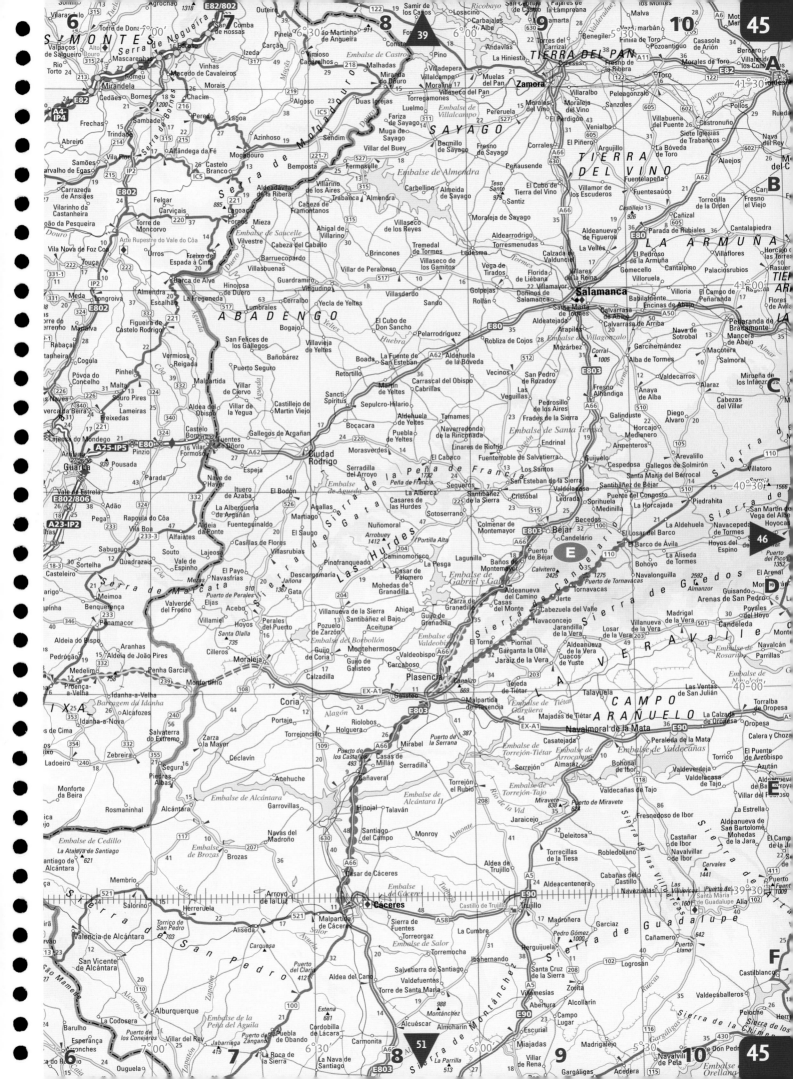

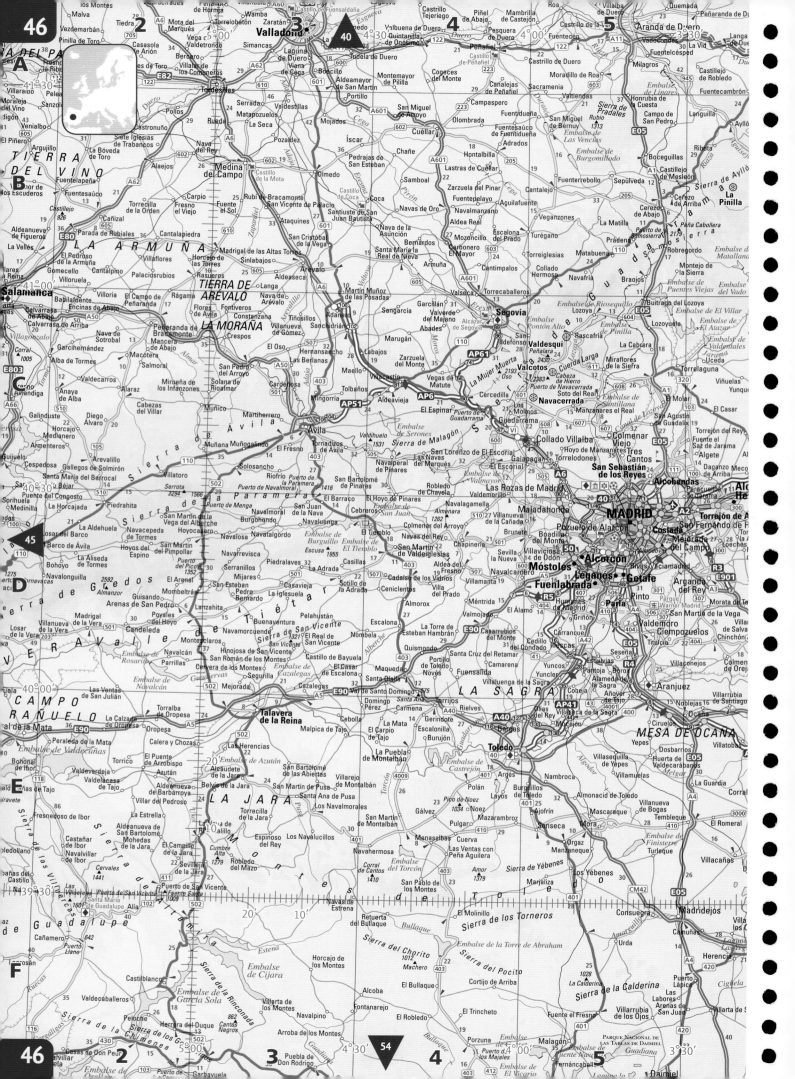

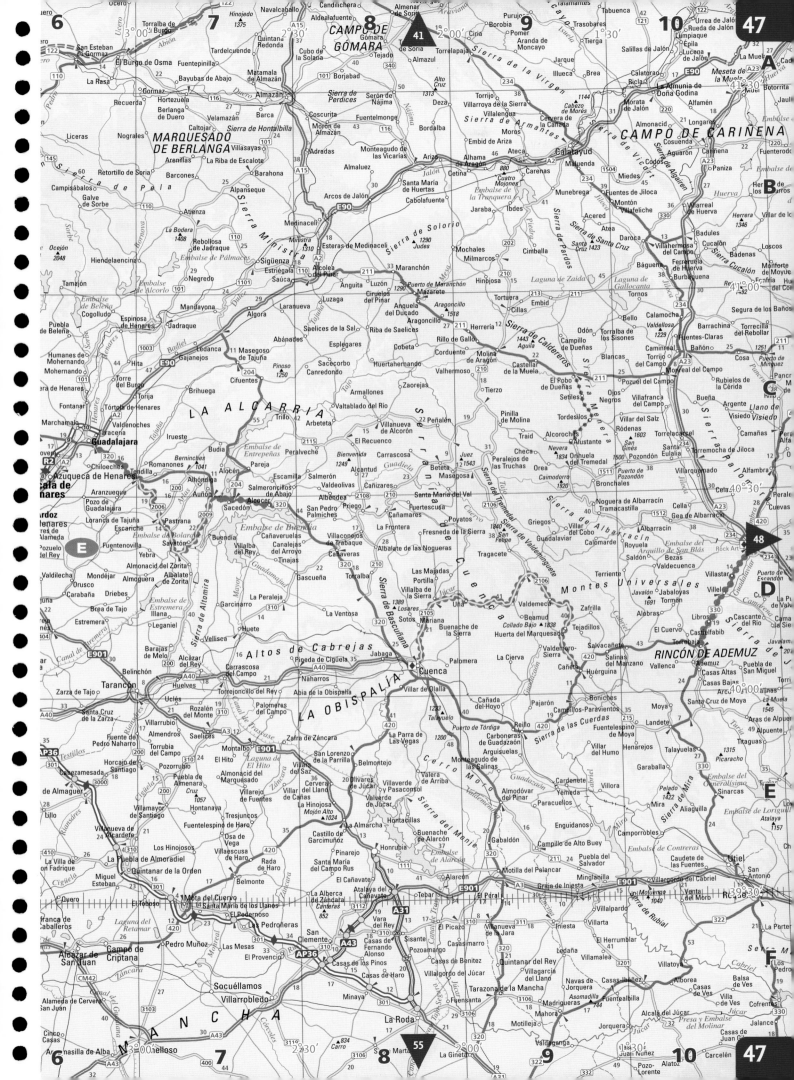

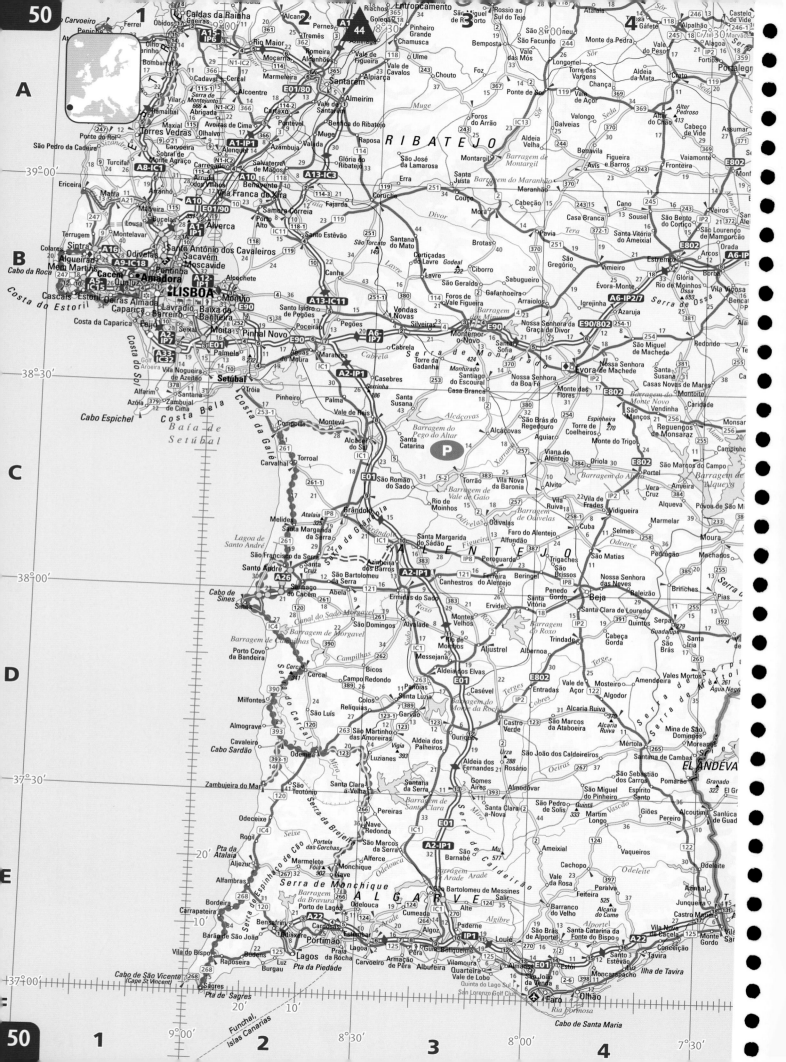

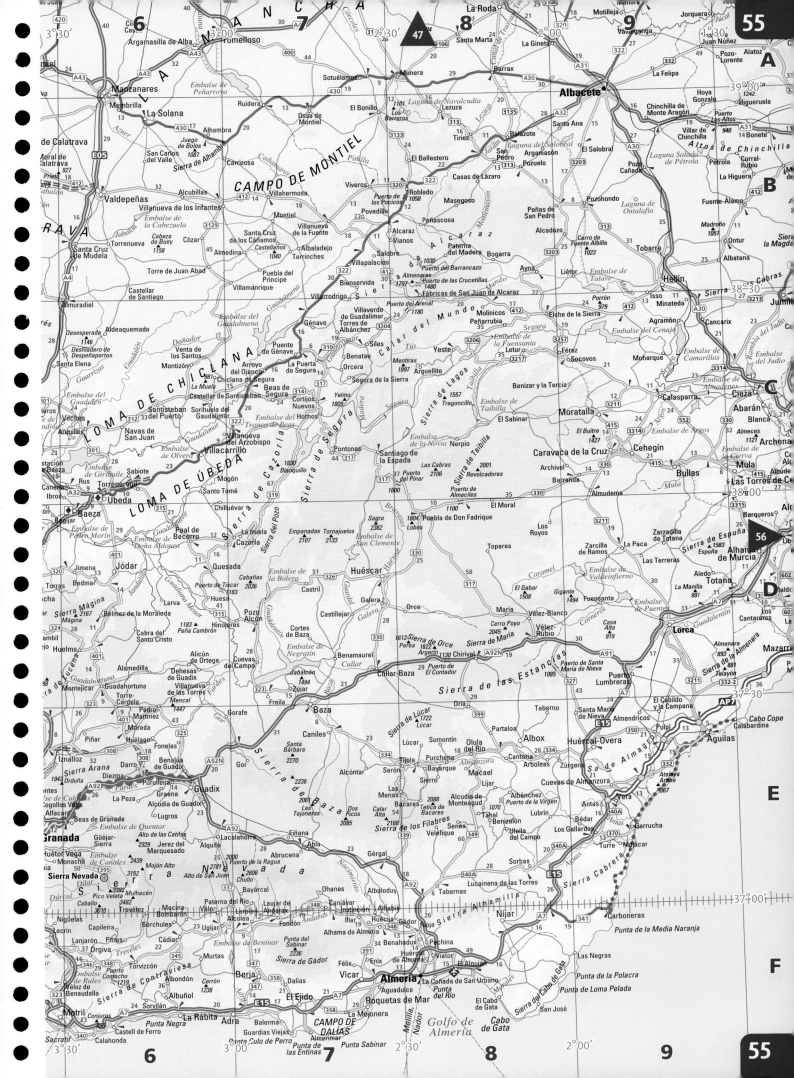

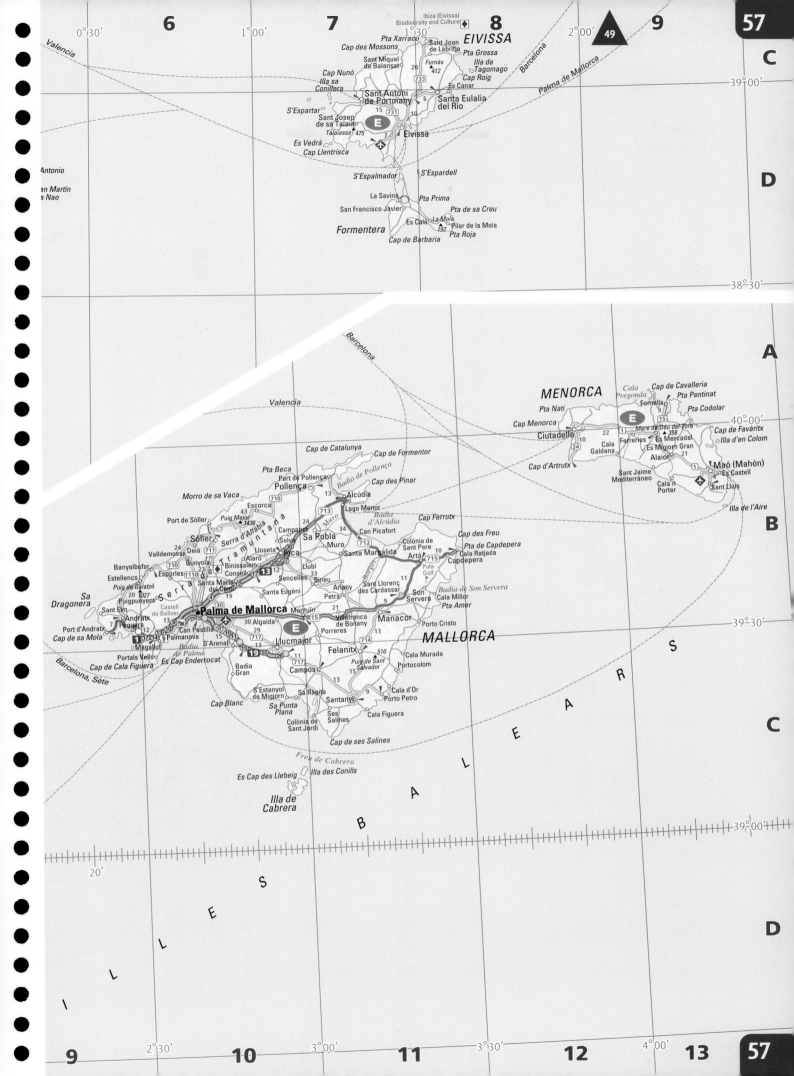

6 0°30′ **7** 1°00′ 1°30′ **8** 2°00′ **49** **9**

C

D

Valencia

an Martín
a Nao

Antonio

Ibiza (Eivissa)
Biodiversity and Culture ◆
EIVISSA

Pta Xarracó
Cap des Mossons
Sant Joan
de Labritja
Cap Nunó
Illa sa
Conillera
Sant Miquel
de Balansat
20
Furnás
412
Pta Grossa
Illa de
Tagomago
733
Cap Roig
Es Canar
Sant Antoni
de Portmany
6
Santa Eulalia
del Río
S'Espartar
15
731
Sant Josep
de sa Talaia
10
Talaiassa 475
E
Eivissa
Es Vedrà
Cap Llentrisca

Barcelona
Palma de Mallorca

39°00′

S'Espalmador
S'Espardell

La Savina
Pta Prima
San Francisco Javier
Pta de sa Creu
Es Caló
La Mola
192
Pilar de la Mola
Pta Roja
Formentera
Cap de Barbaria

38°30′

A

B

C

D

Valencia

Barcelona

MENORCA
Cala
Pregonda
Cap de Cavalleria
Pta Nati
Fornells
Pta Pentinat
Cap Menorca
Pta Codolar
Ciutadella
E
15
Mare de Déu del Toro
22
358
Cap de Favàritx
24
1
Illa d'en Colom
Cala
Galdana
Ferreries
Es Mercadal
Es Migjorn Gran
Alaior
21
Cap d'Artrutx
Sant Jaime
Mediterráneo
Cala'n
Porter
1
Maó (Mahón)
Es Castell
Sant Lluís
Illa de l'Aire

40°00′

Cap de Catalunya
Cap de Formentor
Pta Beca
Port de Pollença
Cap des Pinar
Morro de sa Vaca
Pollença
13
Badia de Pollença
Escorca
710
Alcúdia
43
Lago Menor
Puig Major
713
Badia
1436
Muro
d'Alcúdia
Cap Ferrutx
Port de Sóller
Campanet
24
34
Can Picafort
Cap des Freu
Sóller
Serra d'Alfàbia
Selva
Sa Pobla
Colònia de
Pta de Capdepera
711
Muro
712
Sant Pere
10
Cala Ratjada
Valldemossa
Deià
Lloseta
Santa Margalida
Artà
715
Capdepera
24
Alaró
30
Pula
Banyalbufar
Bunyola
Inca
Golf
710
Binissalem
Llubí
Estellencs
Esporles
13
Consell
Sencelles
Sineu
Son
Puig de Galatzó
1110
23
Llorenç
Son
Badia de Son Servera
1027
Santa Maria
Anany
des Cardassar
Servera
Sa
del Camí
19
Petra
Cala Millor
Dragonera
Puigpunyent
Santa Eugèni
Pta Amer
Sant Elm
Castell
de Bellver
Montuïri
21
Villafranca
Manacor
Port d'Andratx
Andratx
Palma de Mallorca
30 Algaida
de Bonany
Porto Cristo
Peguera
13
Can Pastilla
29
Porreres
13
Cap de sa Mola
12
10
717
MALLORCA
1
Palmanova
S'Arenal
Llucmajor
Felanitx
Cala Murada
Portals Vells
15
22
11
510
Portocolom
Barcelona, Sète
19
126
Campos
Puig de Sant
Salvador
Cap de Cala Figuera
Es Cap Enderrocat
Badia
13
Cala d'Or
Gran
717
9
Porto Petro
S'Estanyol
Sa Ràpita
Santanyí
de Migjorn
Santanyí
Ses
Sa Punta
Salines
Cala Figuera
Plana
Cap Blanc
Colònia de
Sant Jordi
Cap de ses Salines

Freu de Cabrera
Es Cap des Llebeig
Illa des Conills

Illa de
Cabrera

B
A
L
E
A
R
S

39°30′

C

39°00′

D

I
L
L
E
S
B
A
L
E
A
R
S

20′

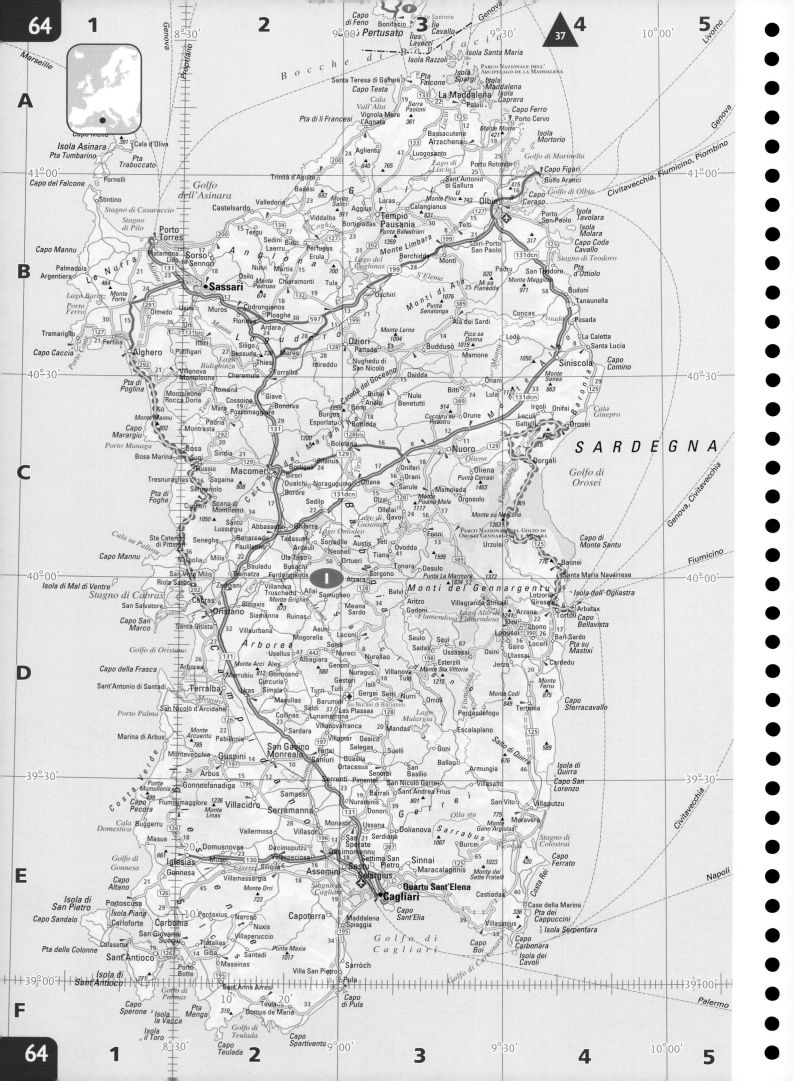

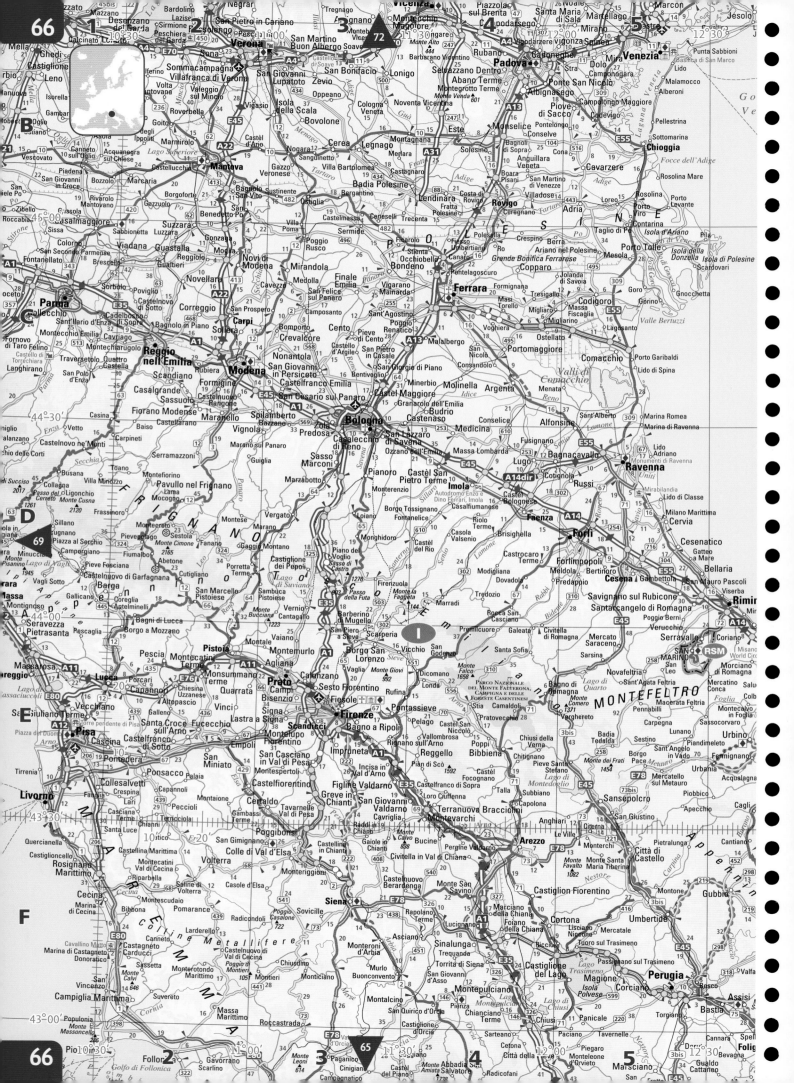

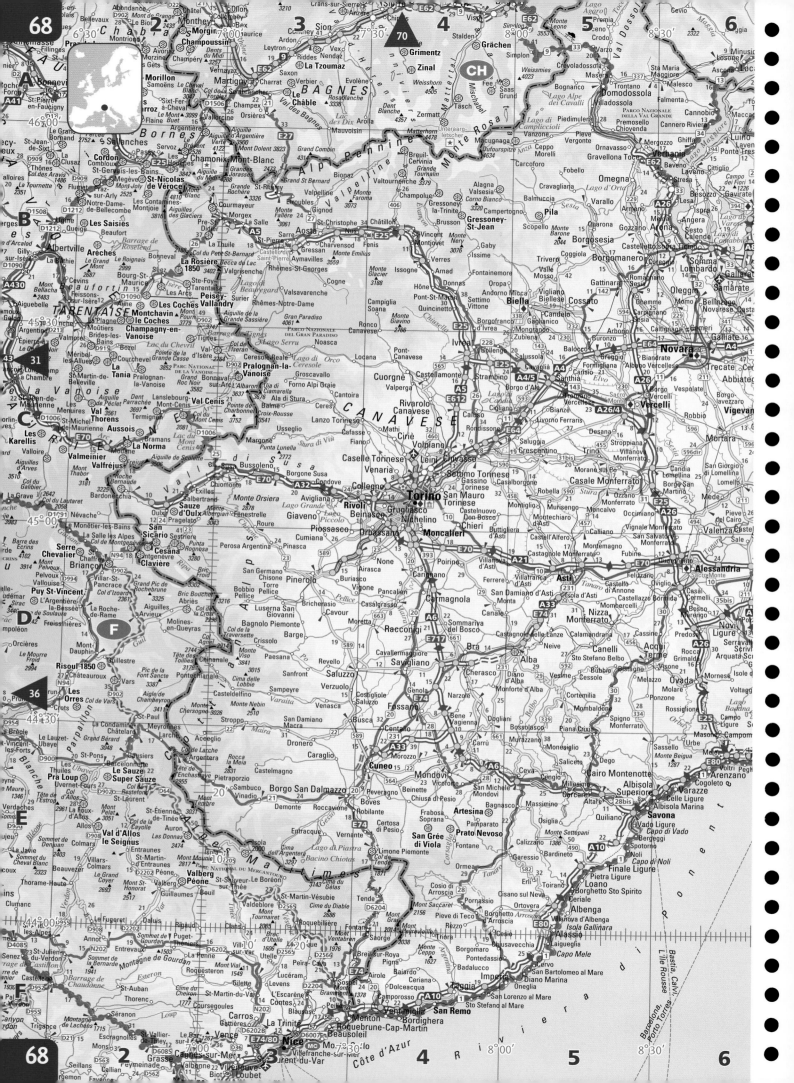

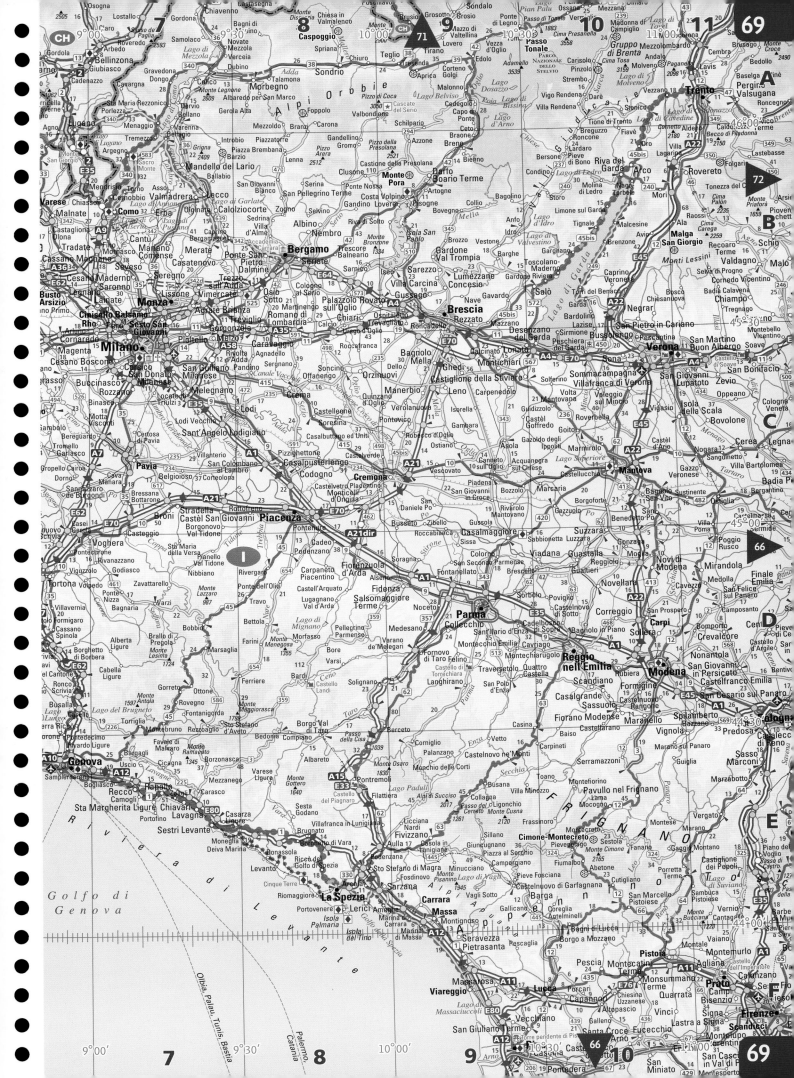

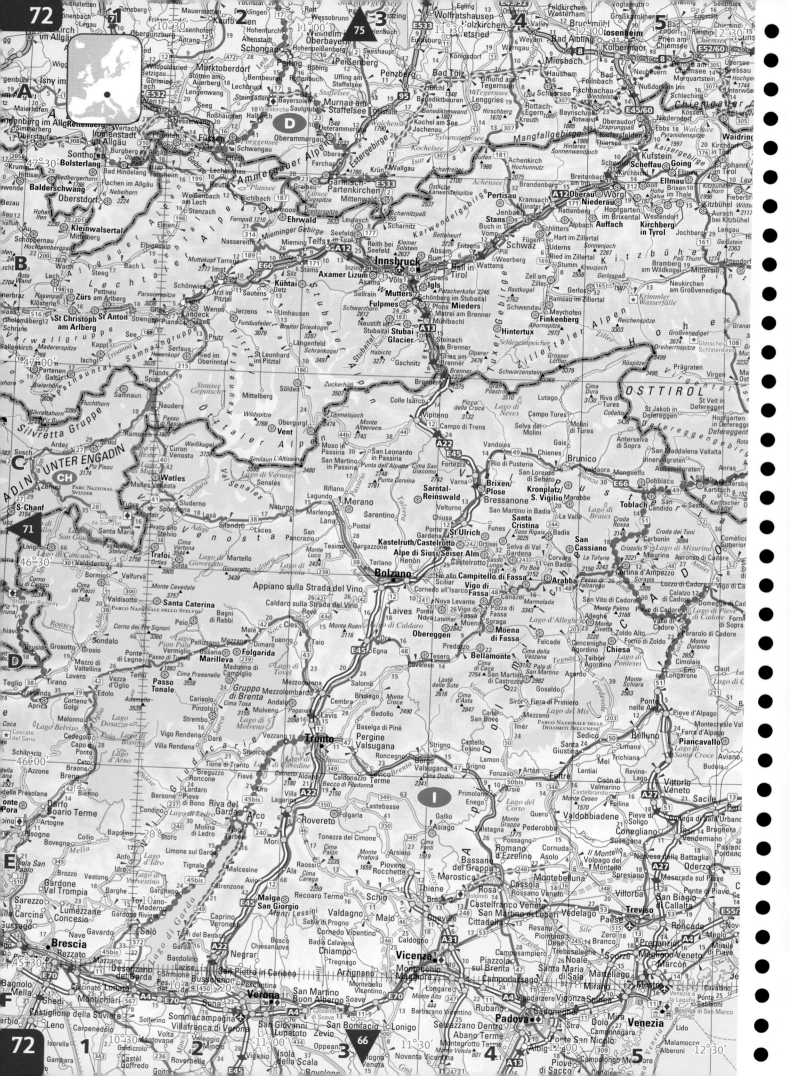

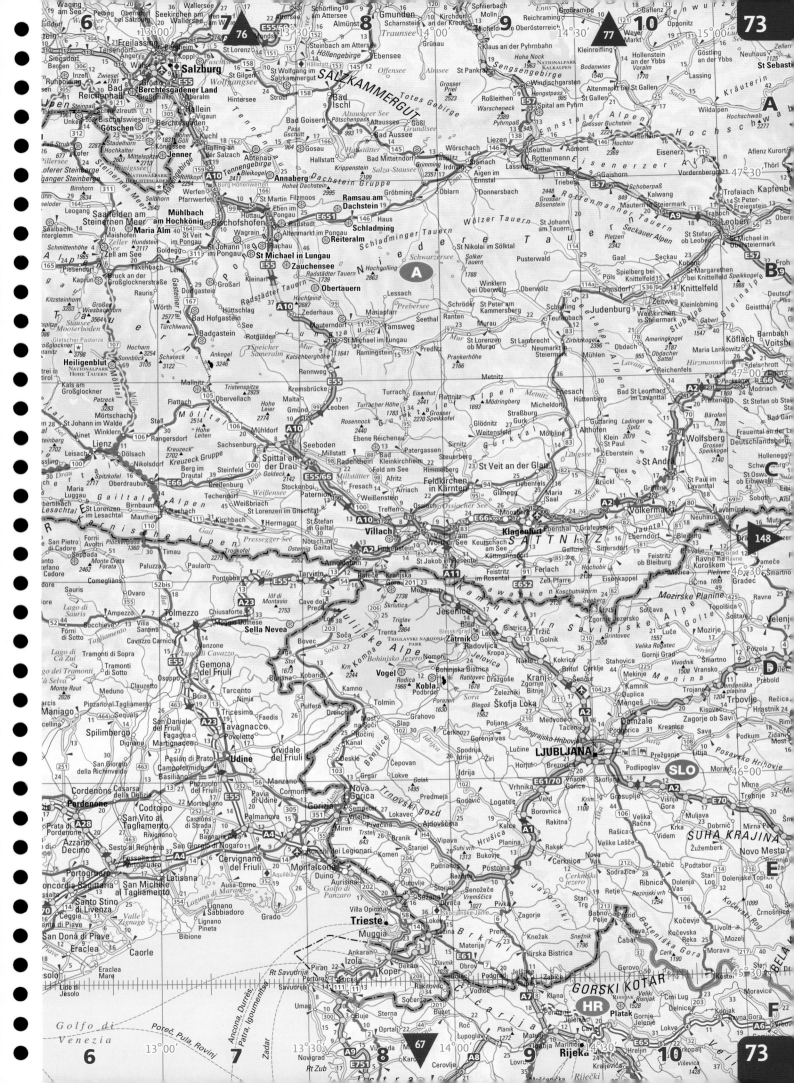

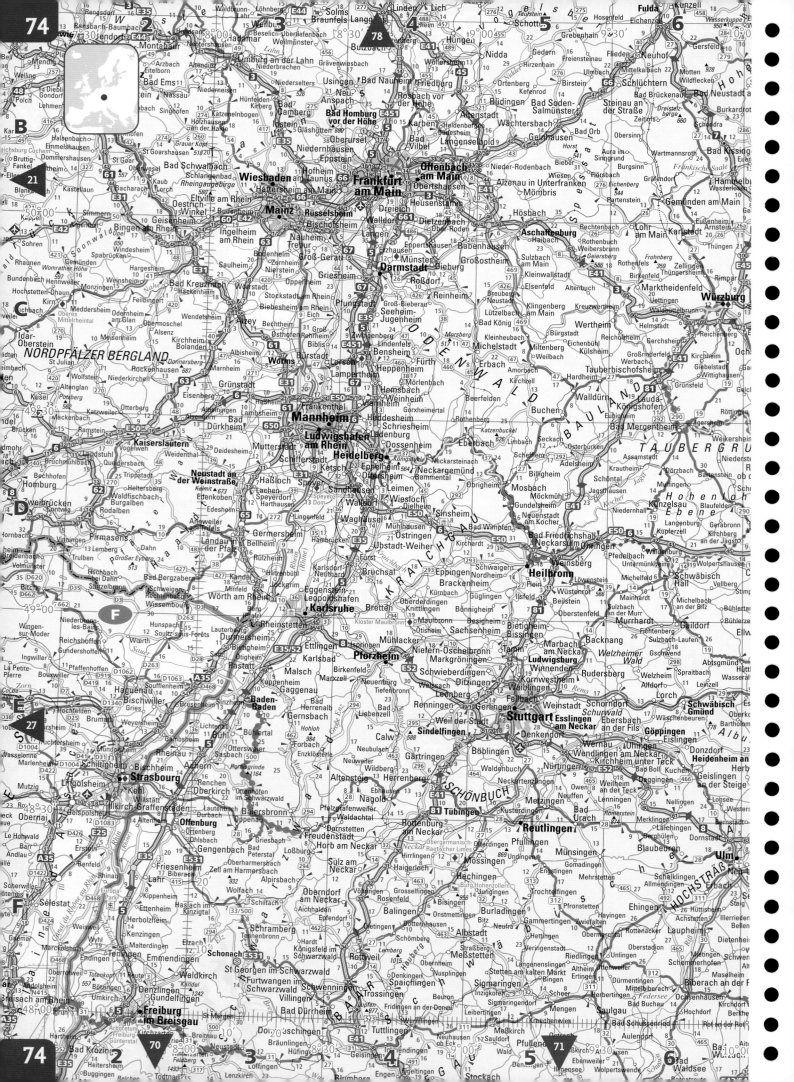

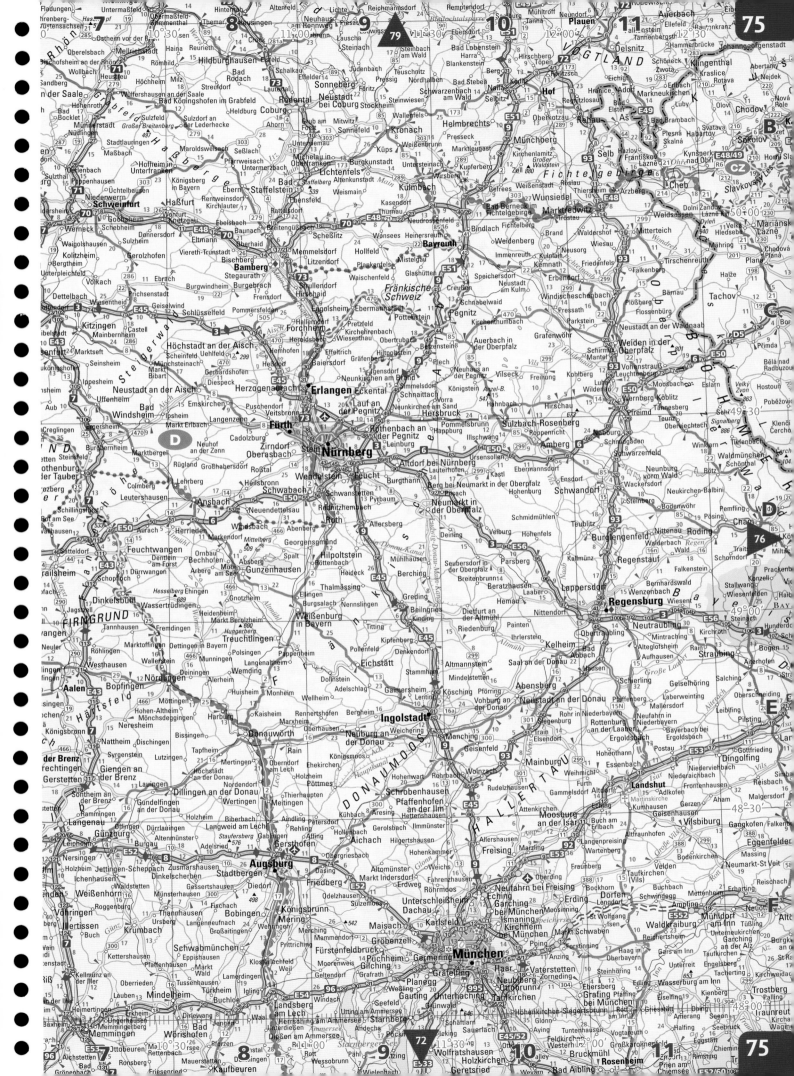

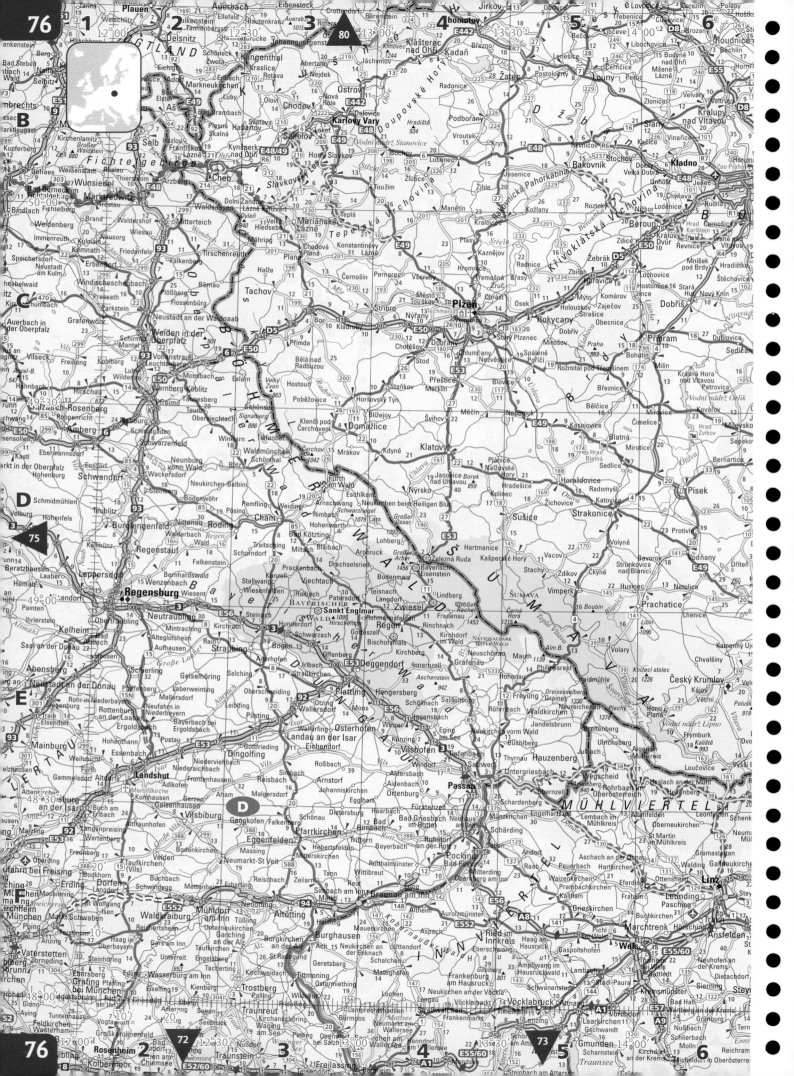

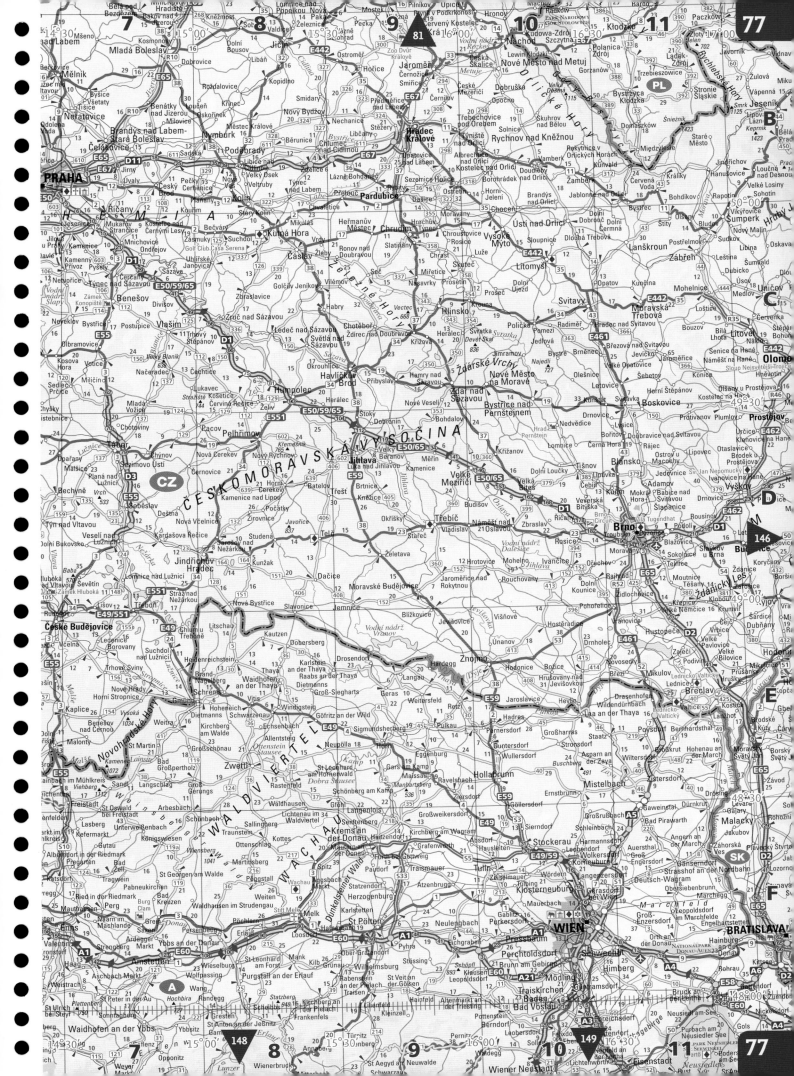

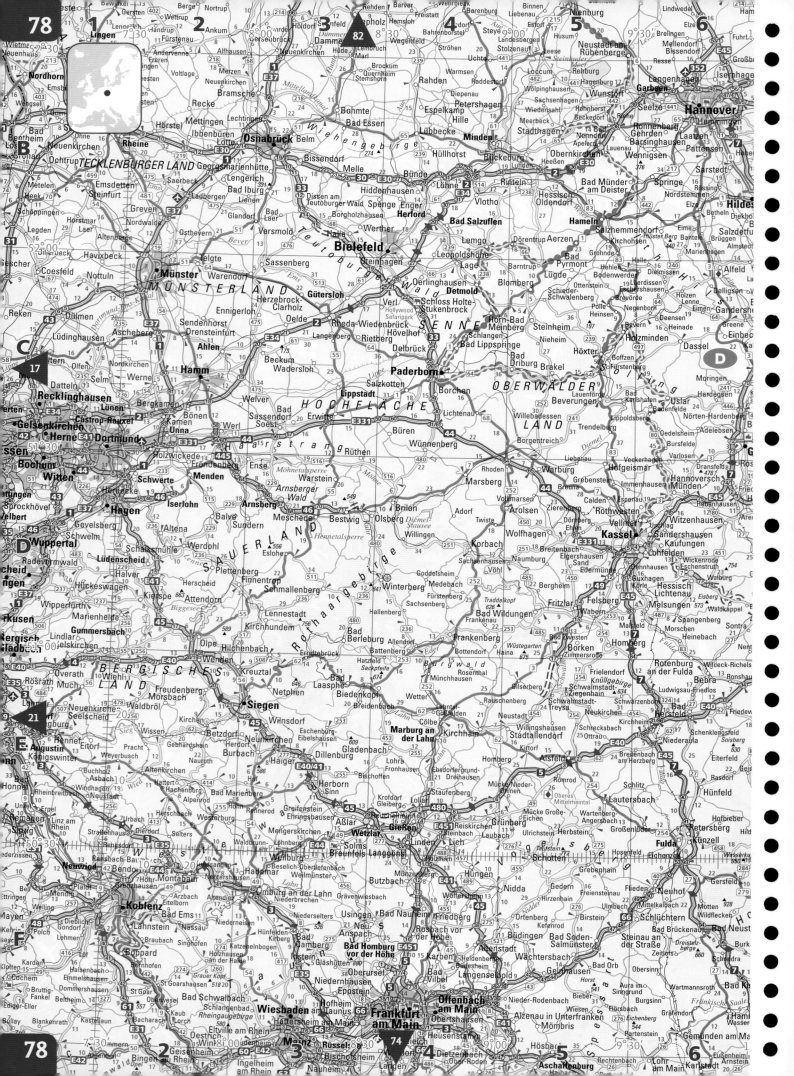

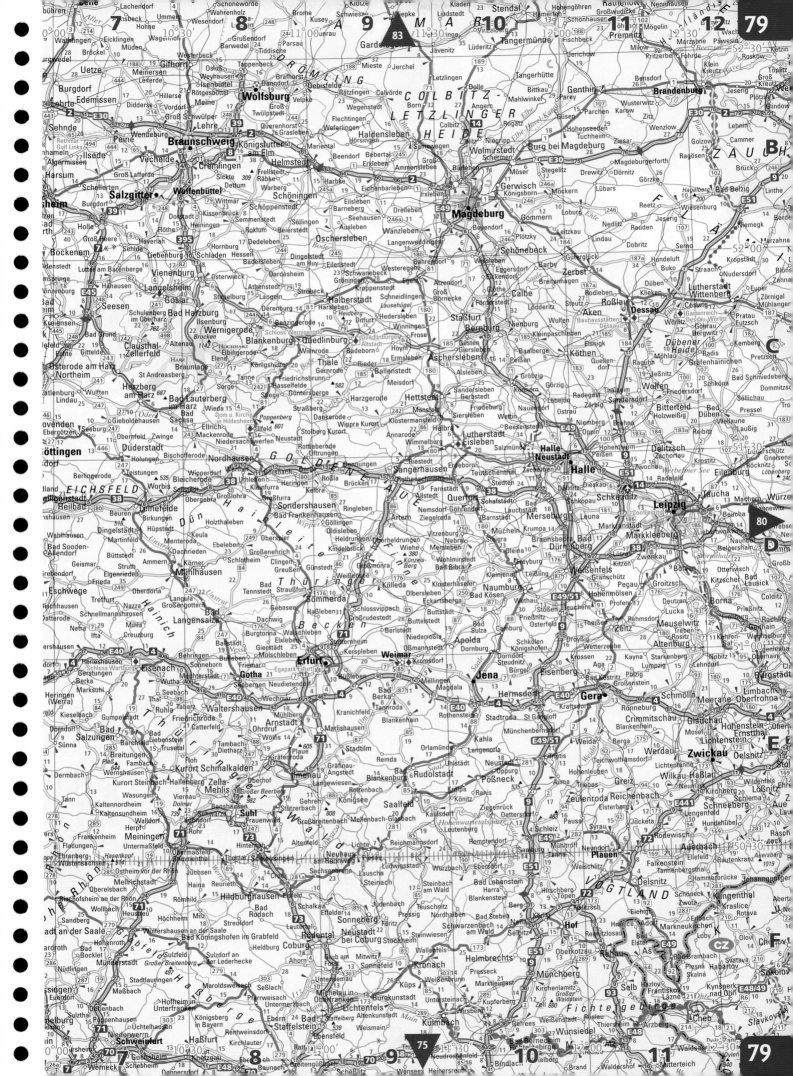

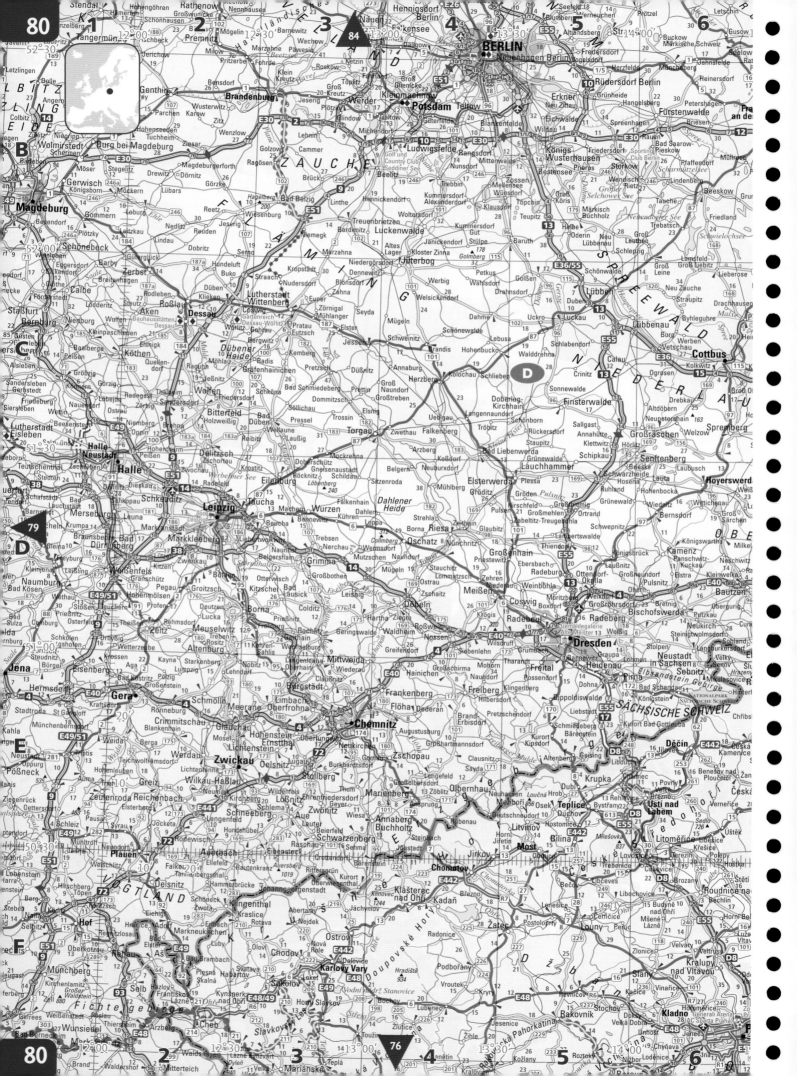

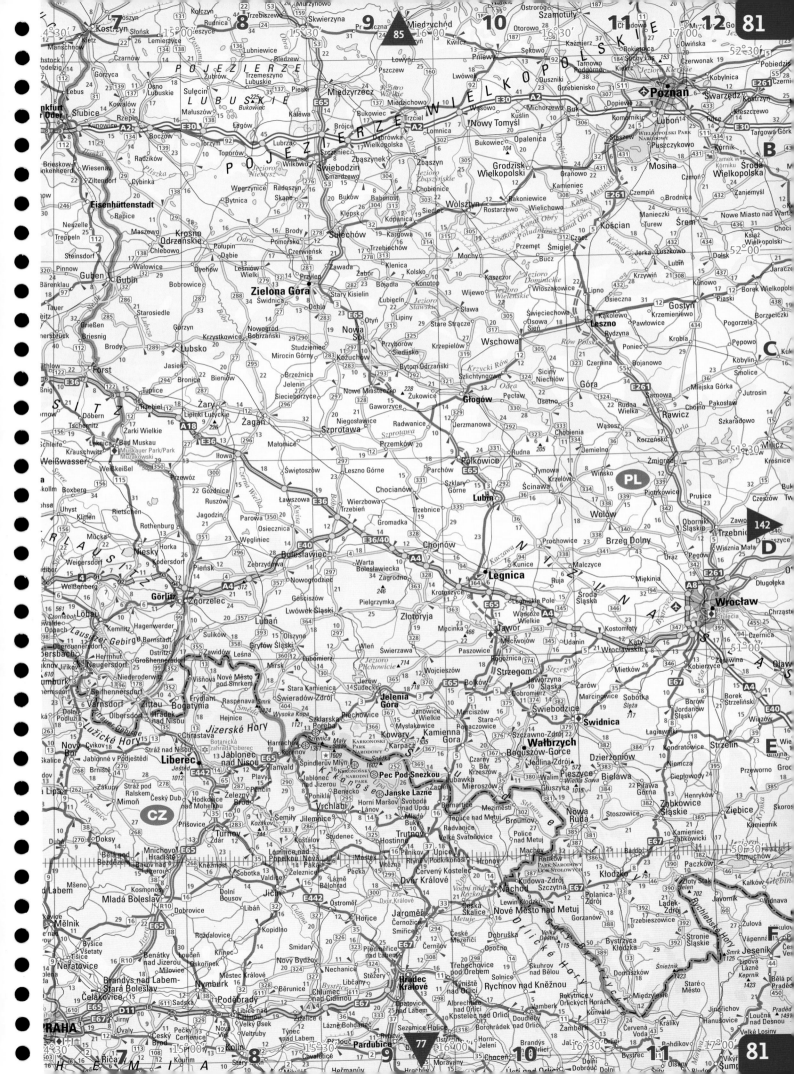

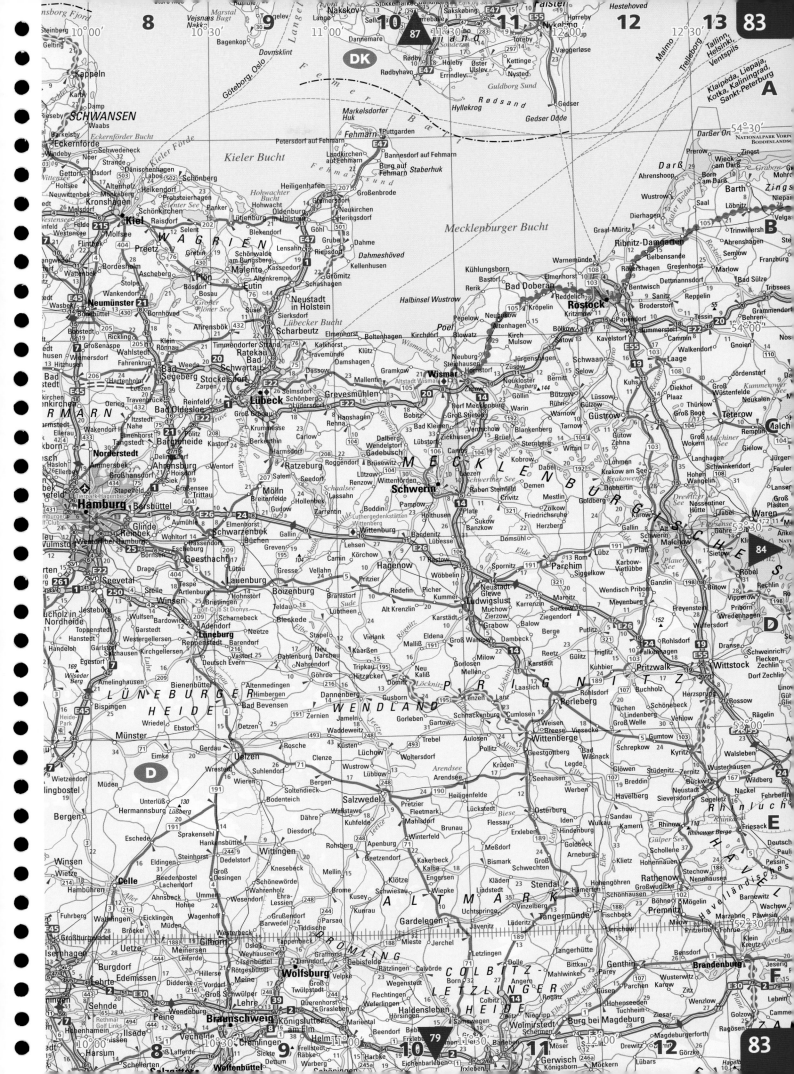

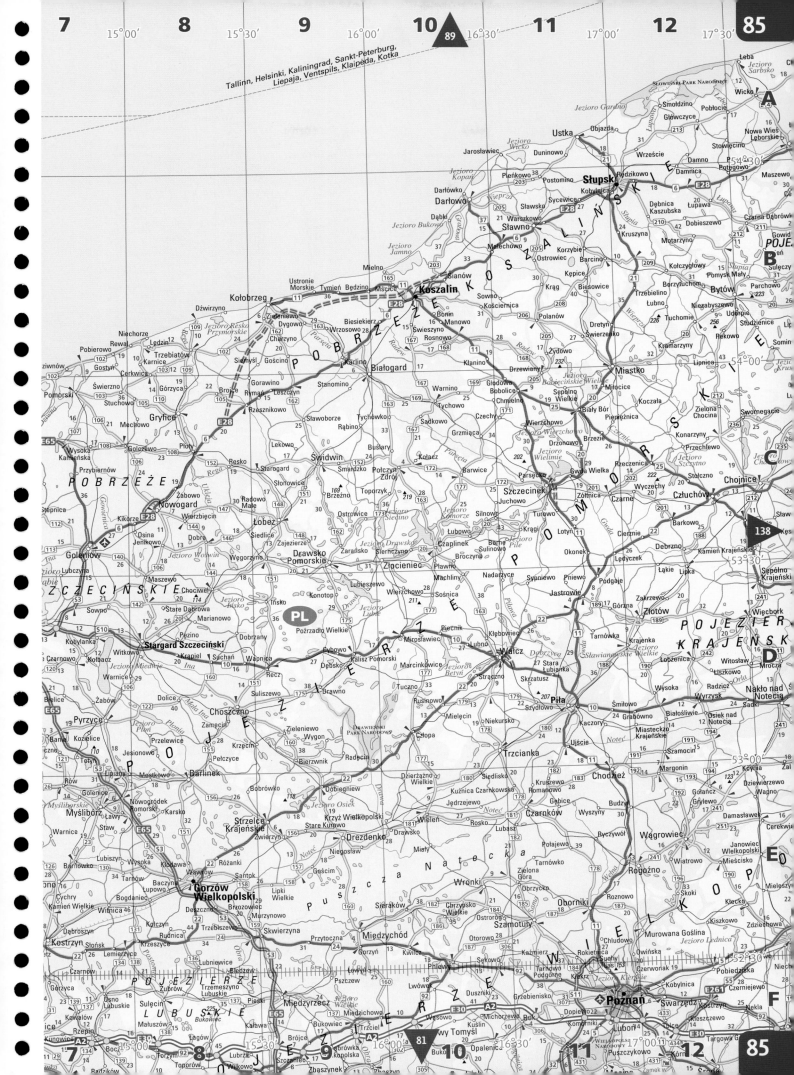

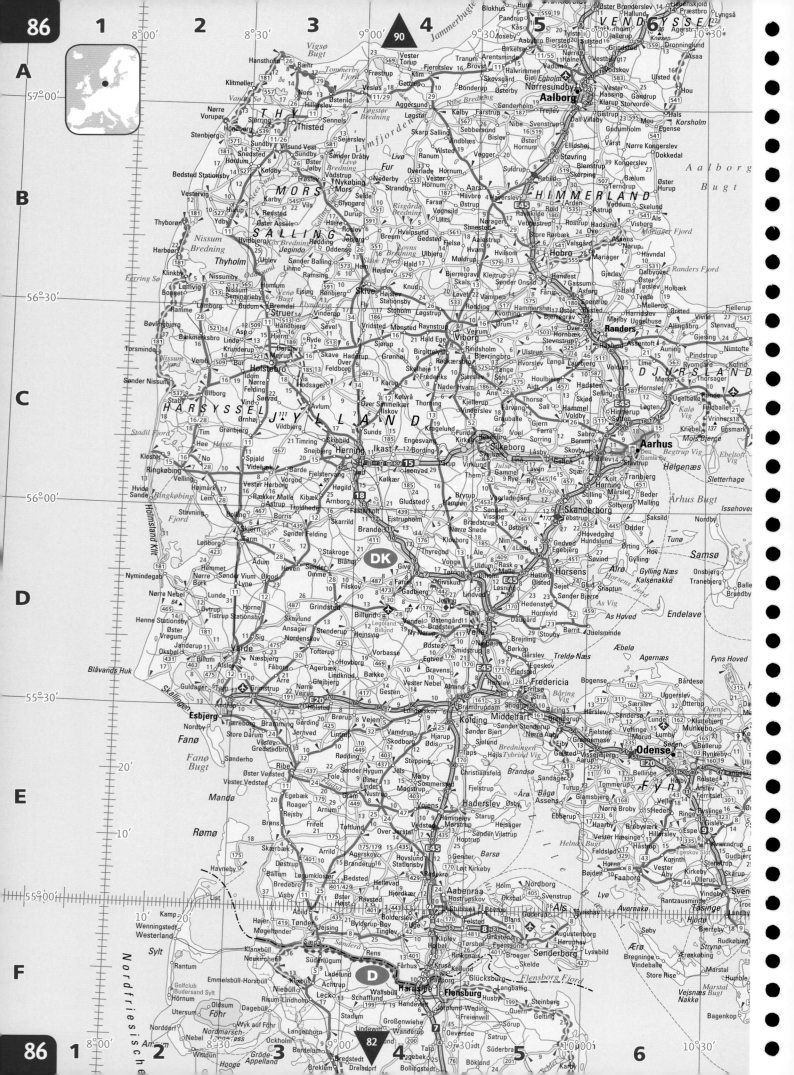

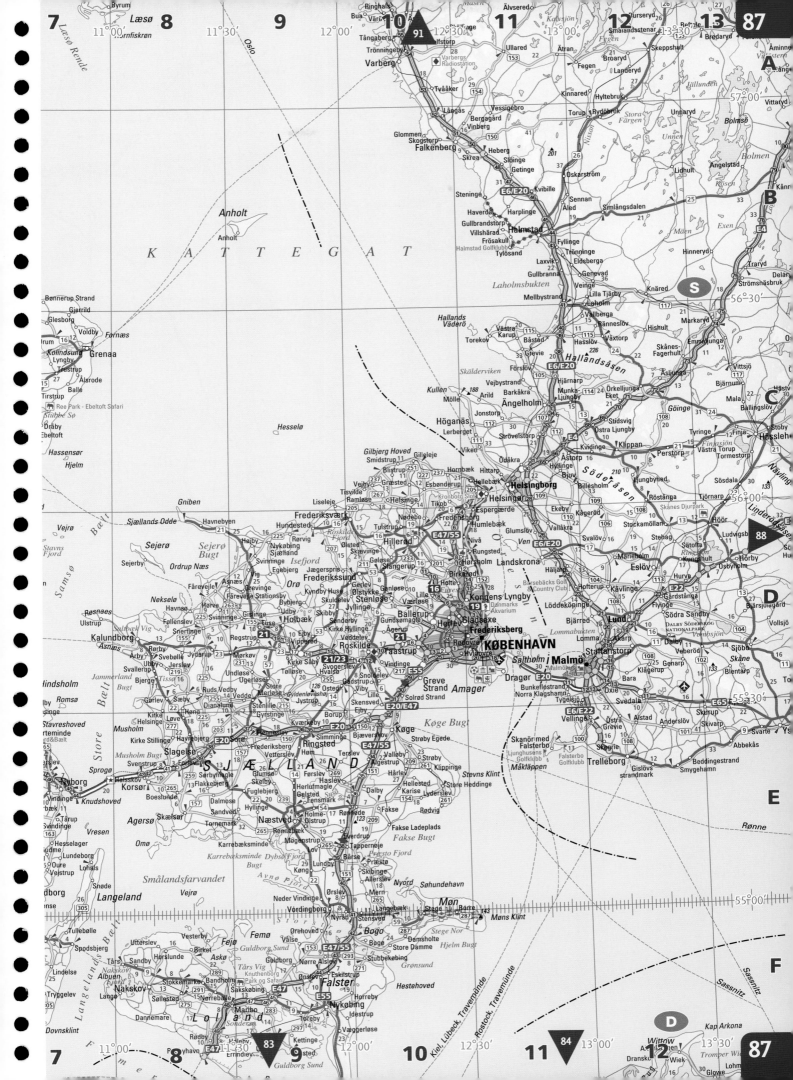

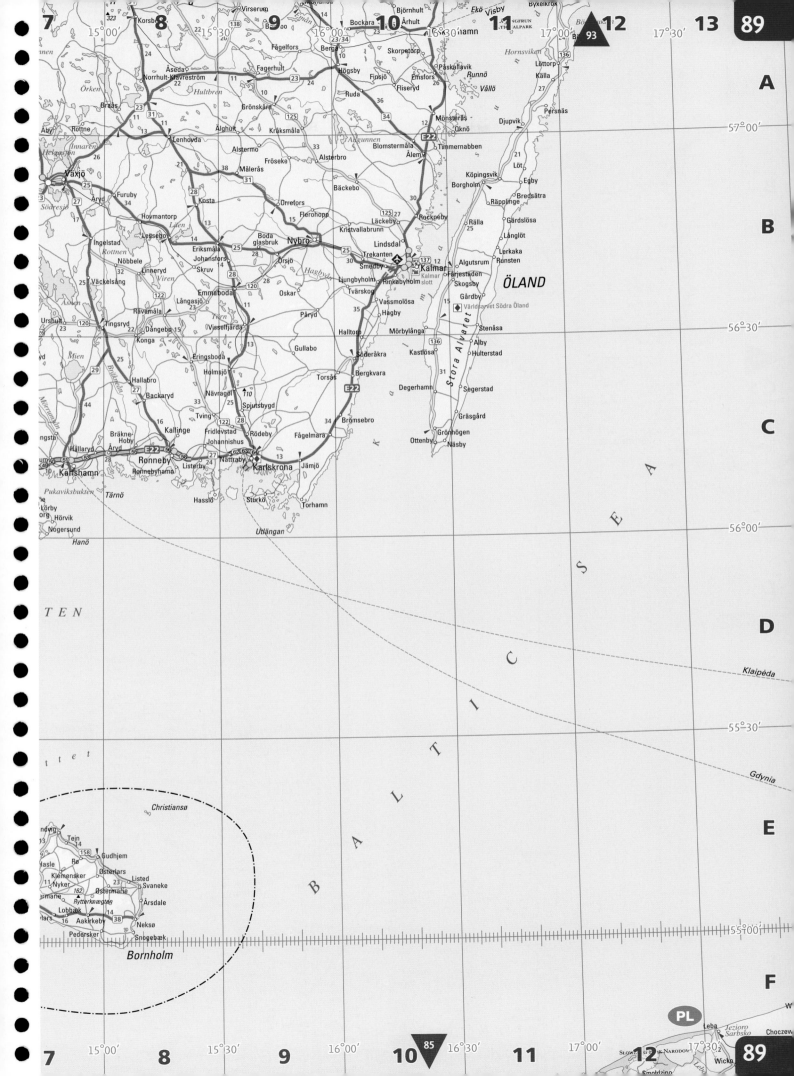

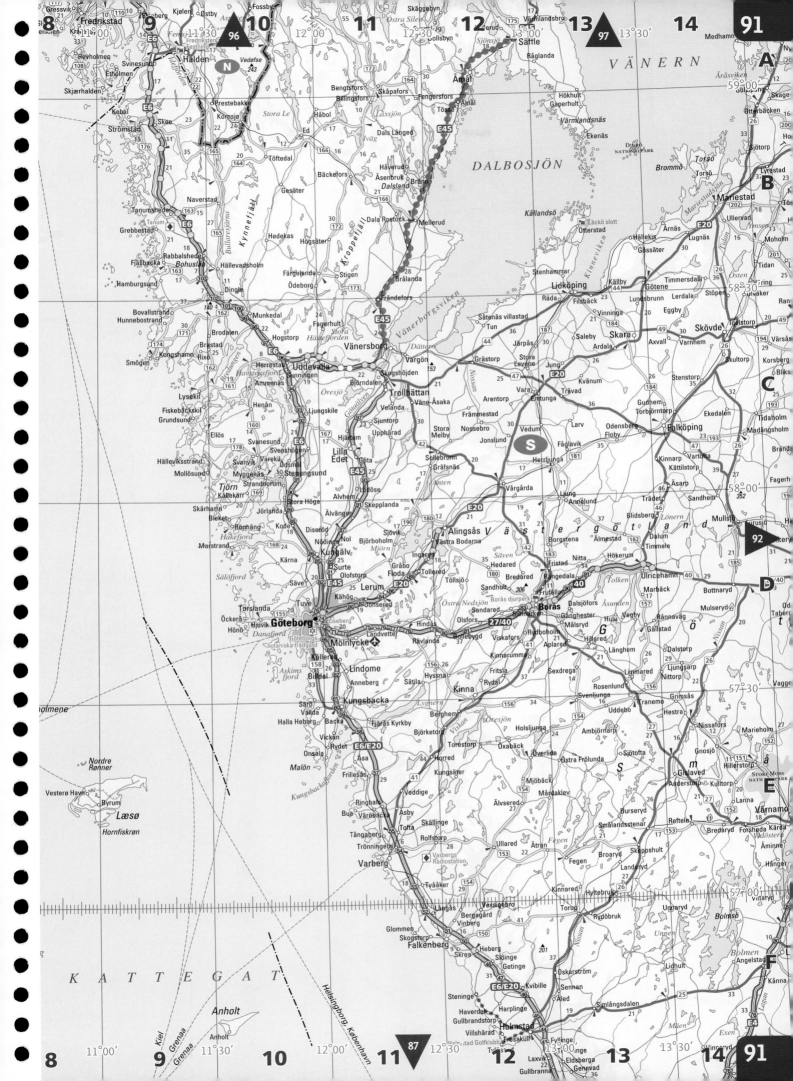

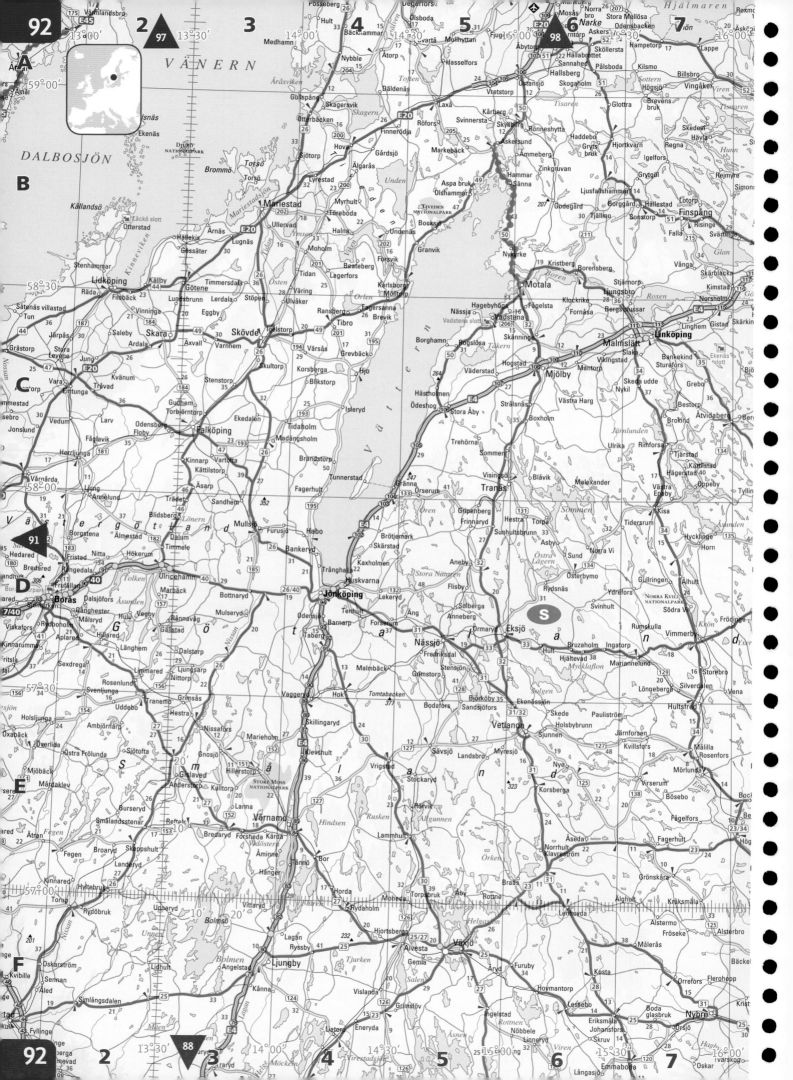

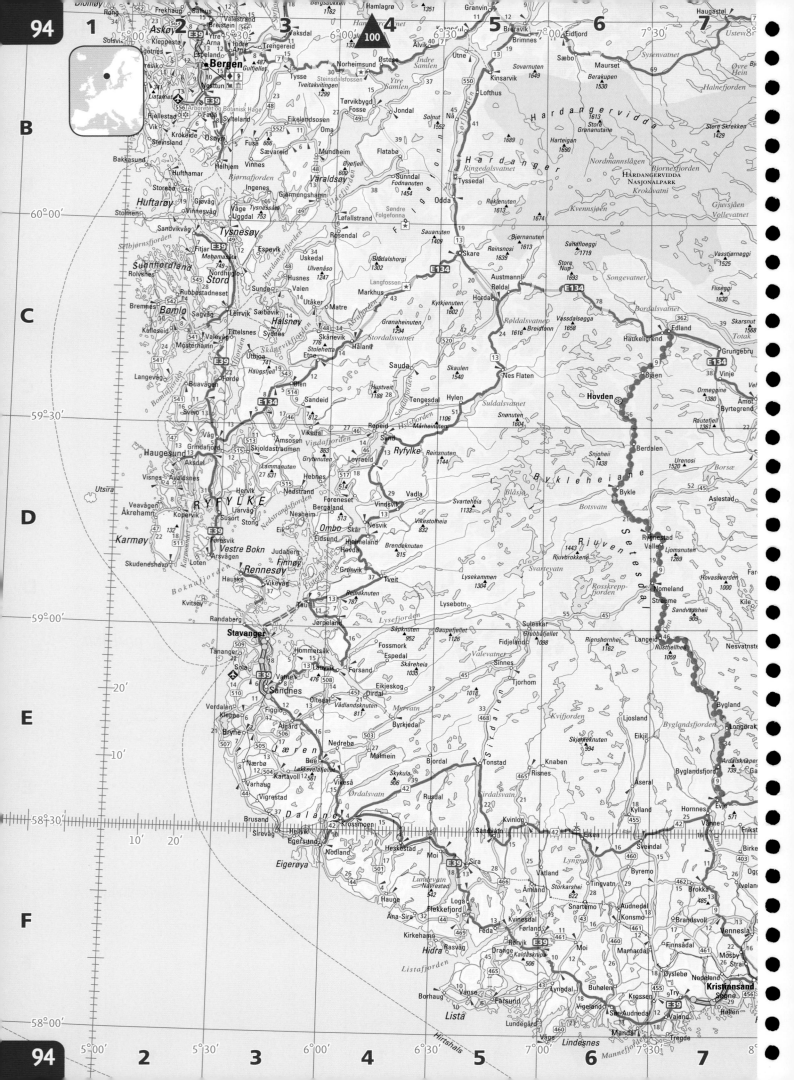

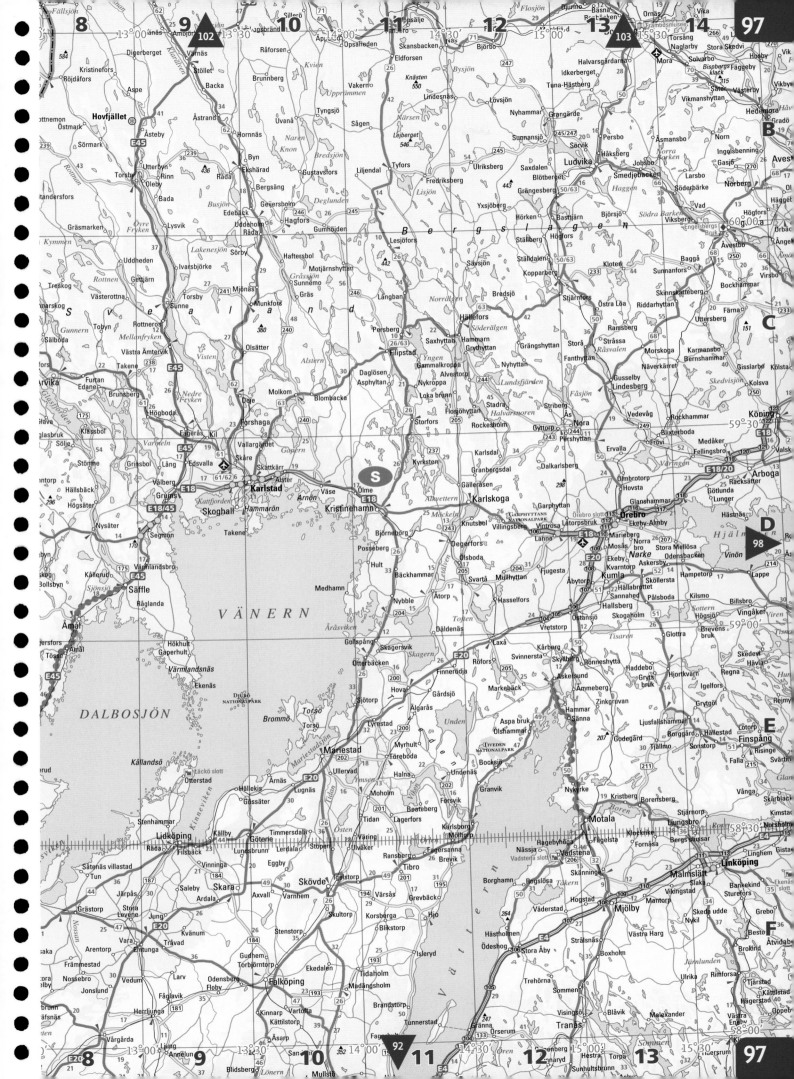

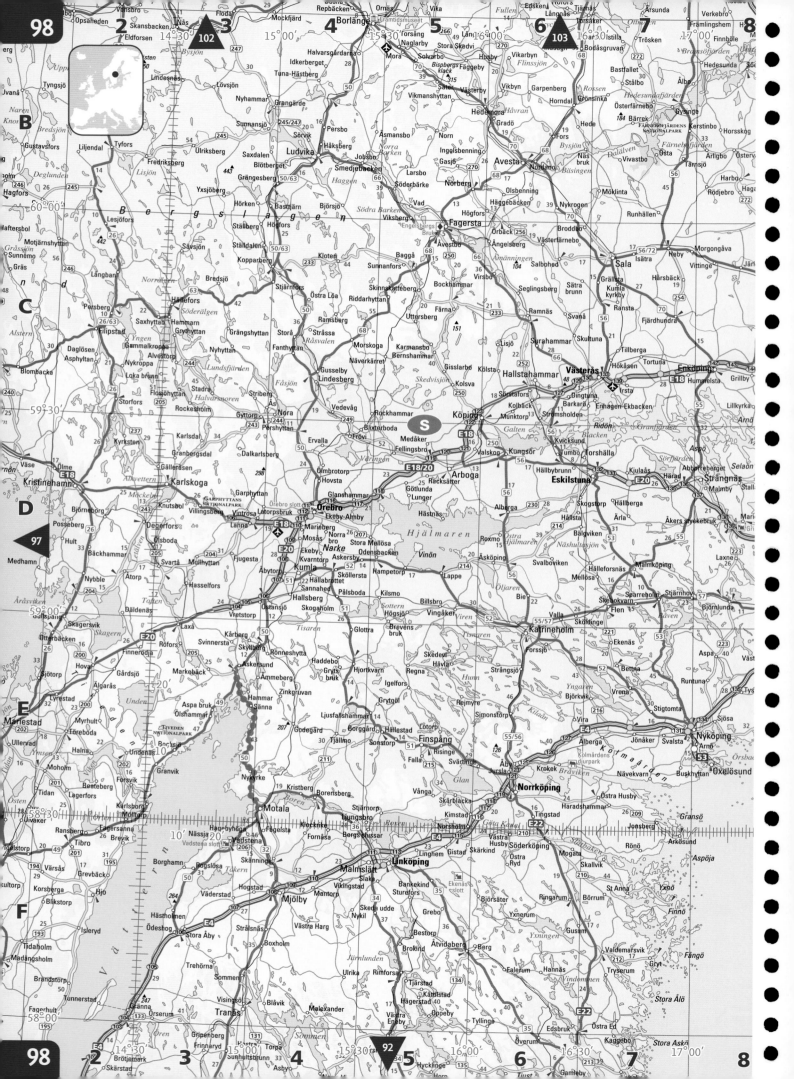

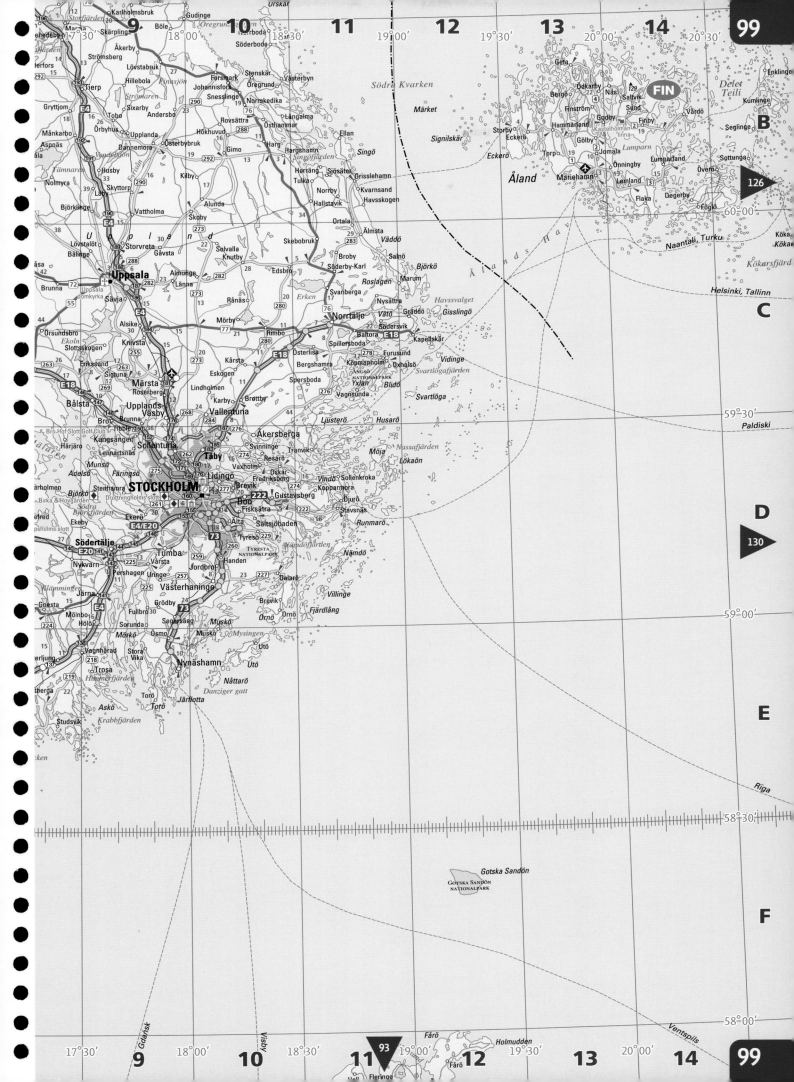

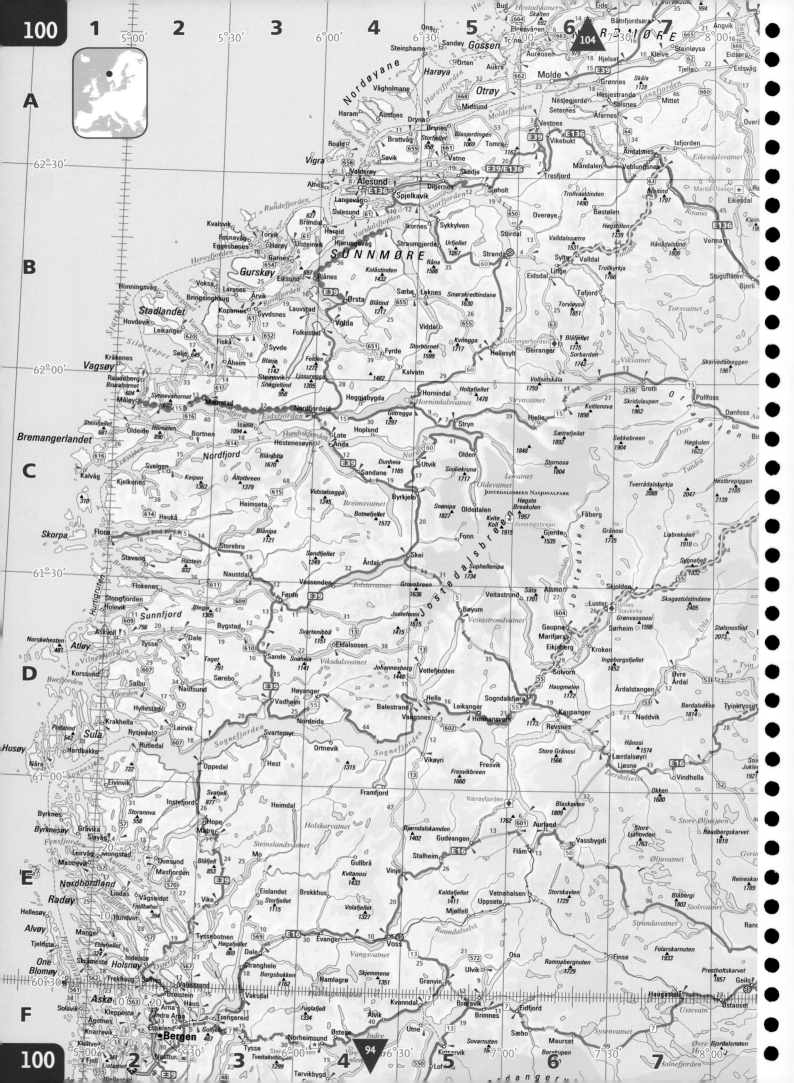

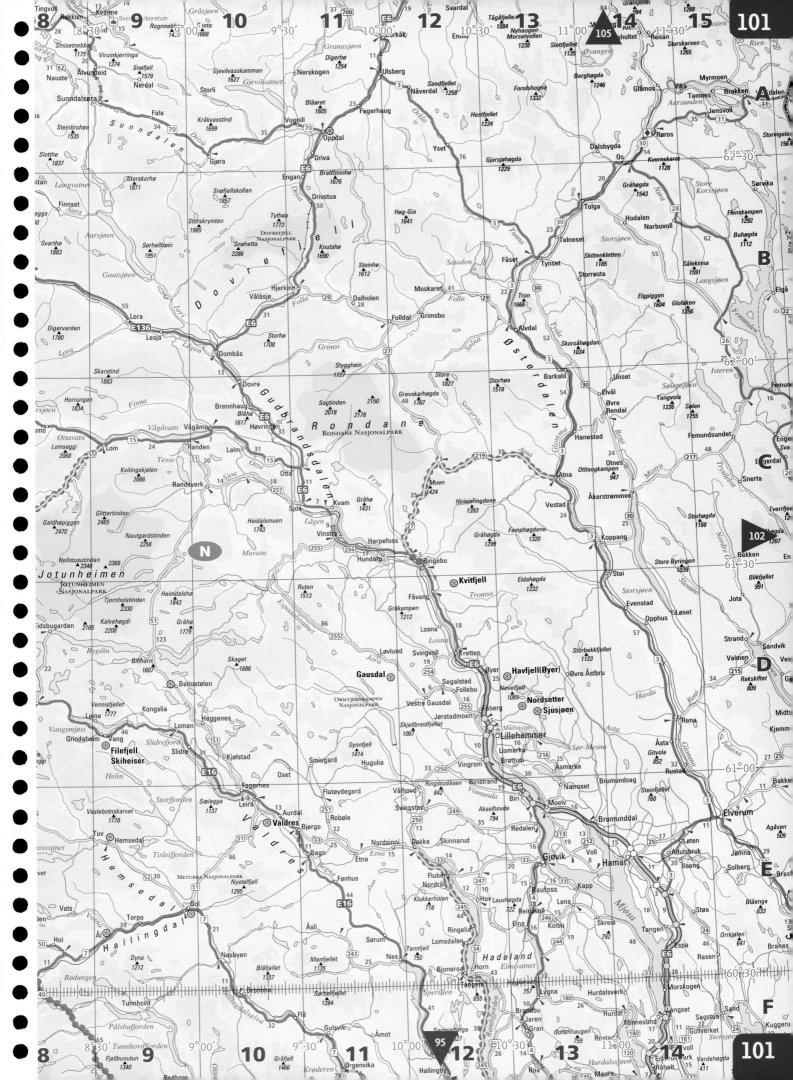

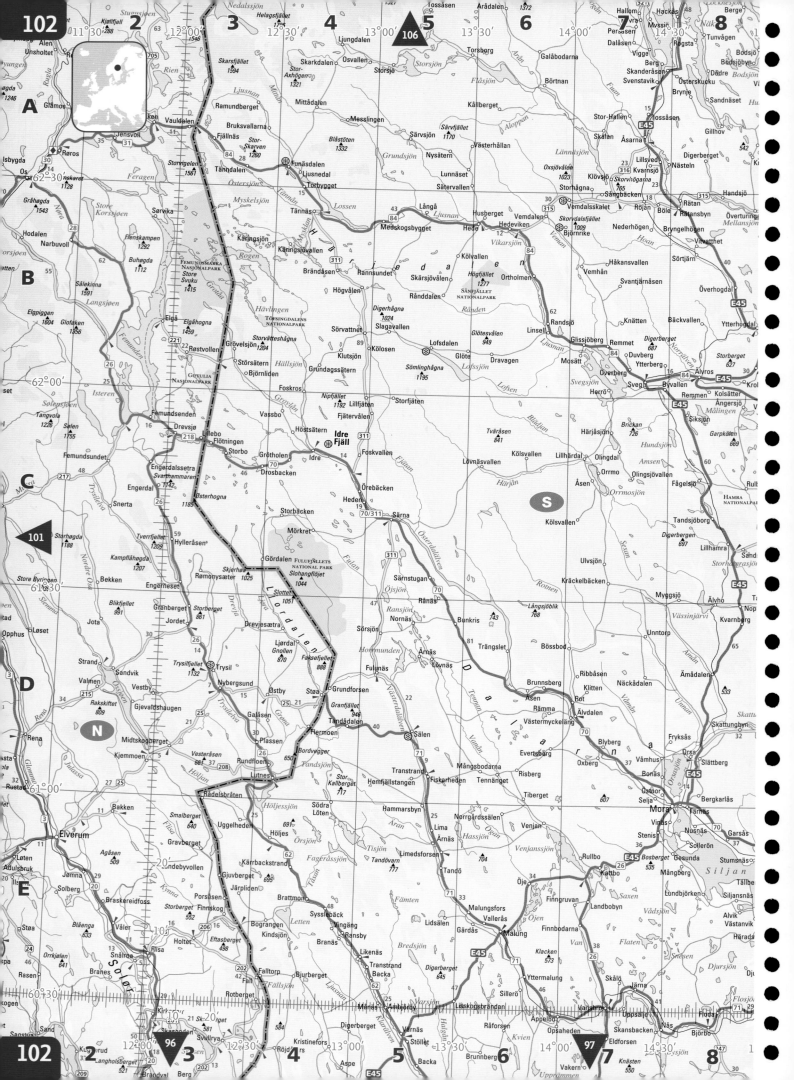

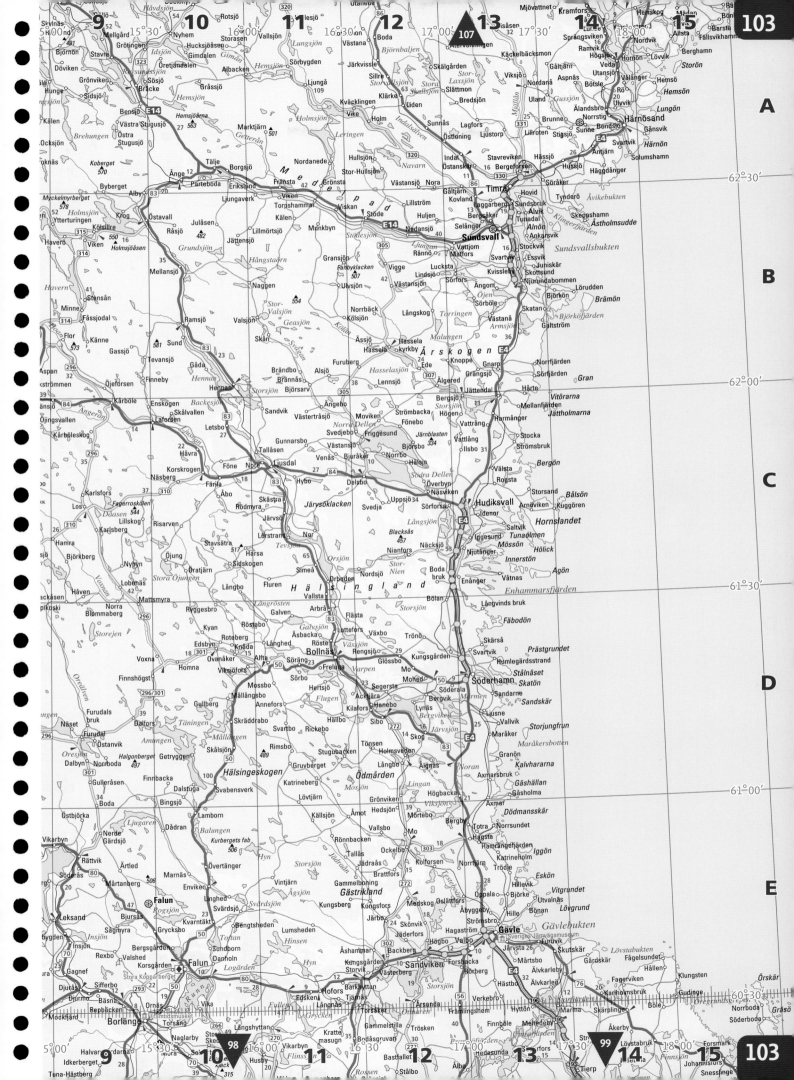

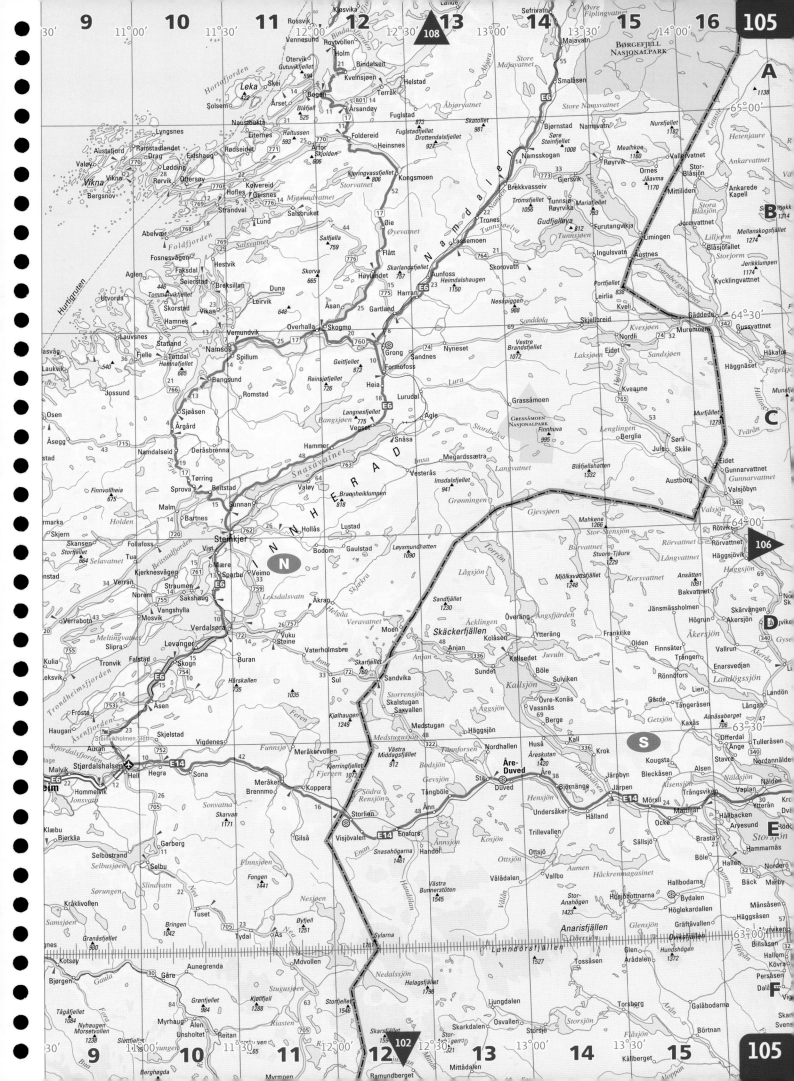

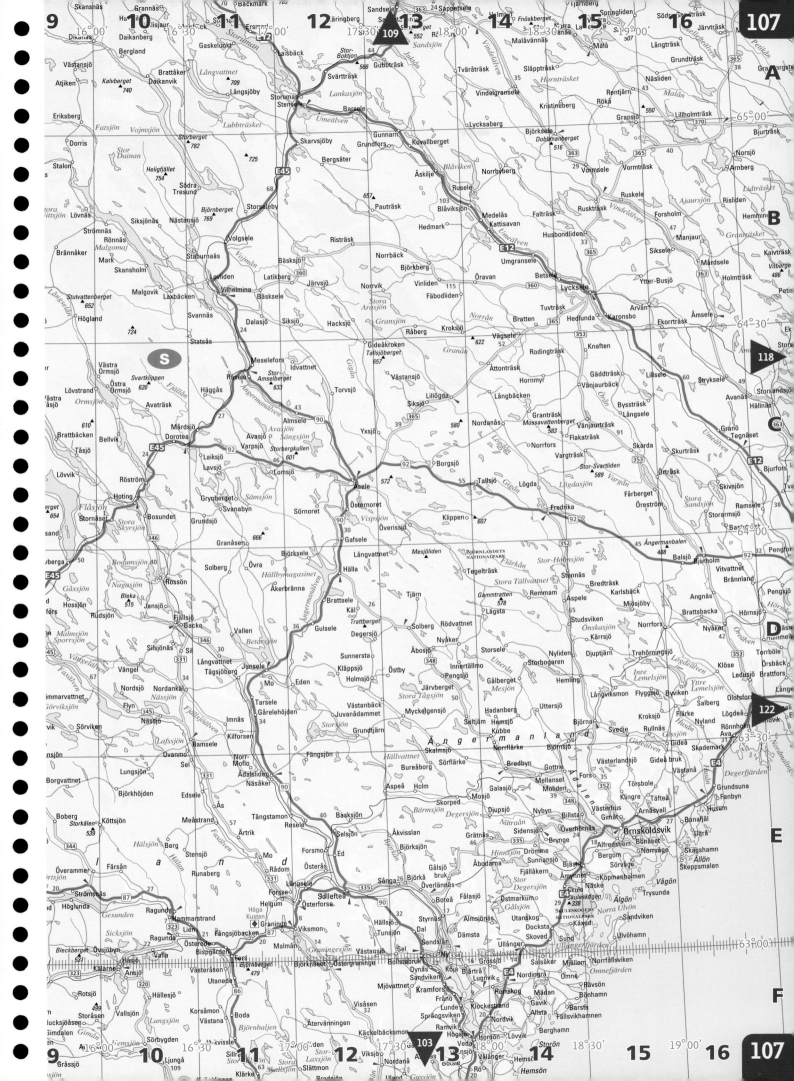

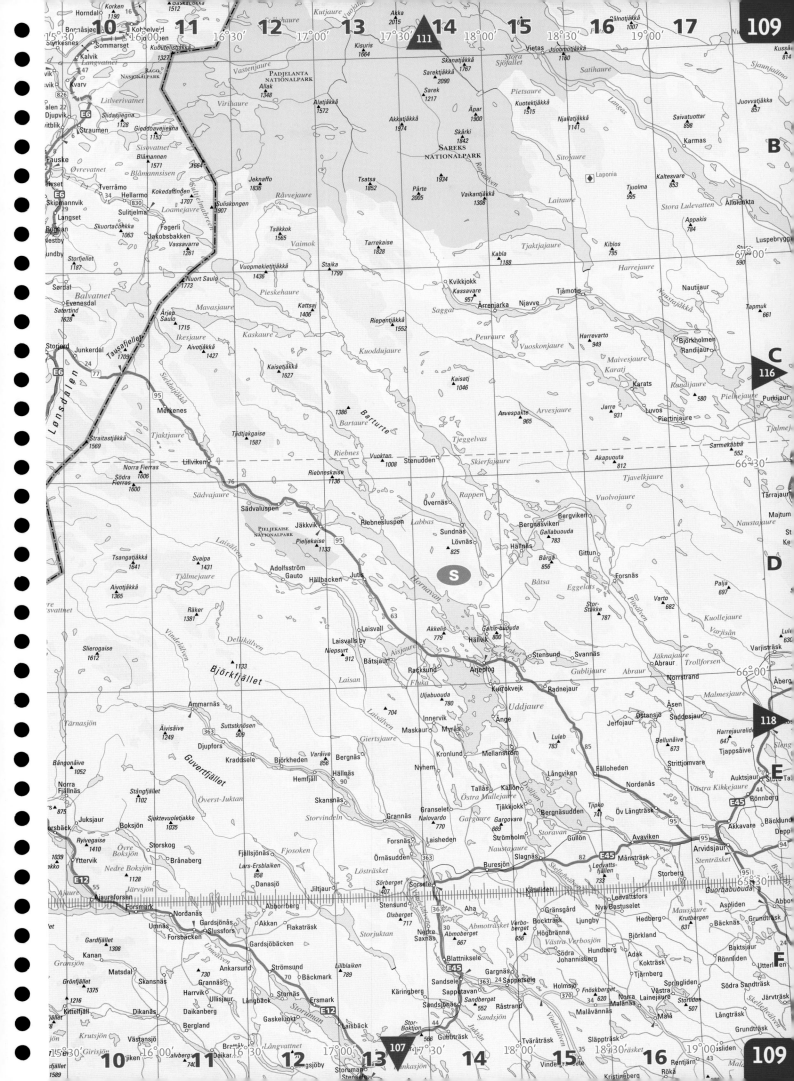

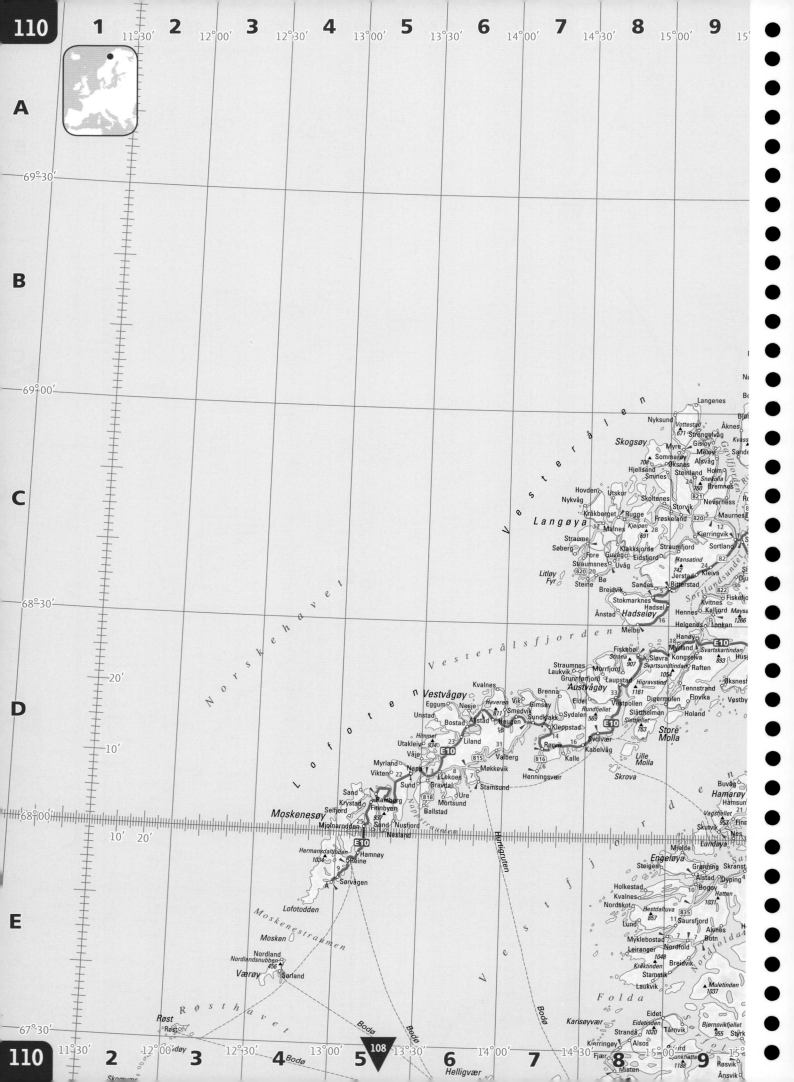

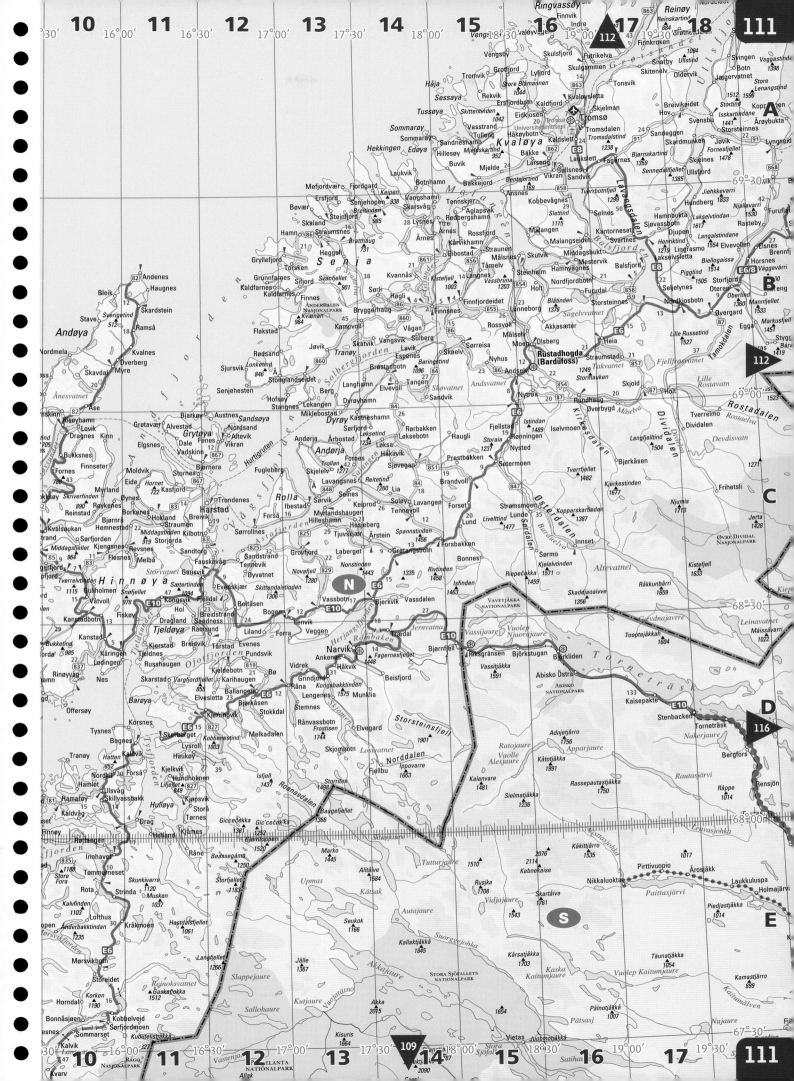

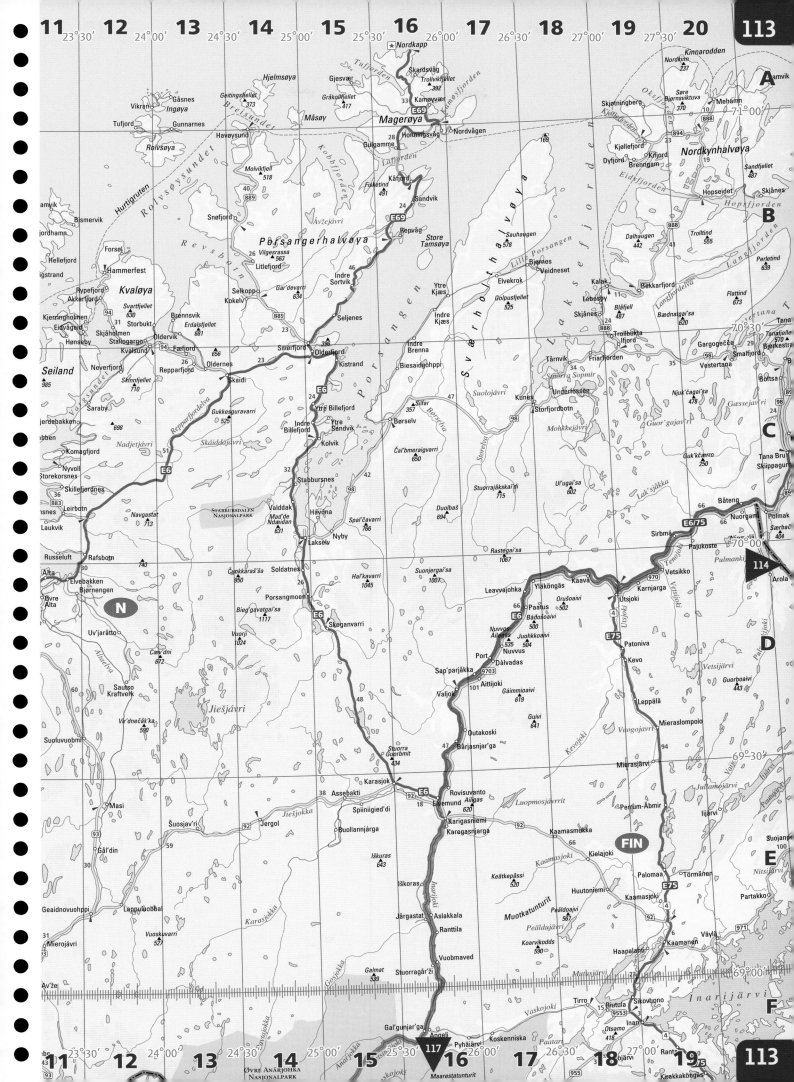

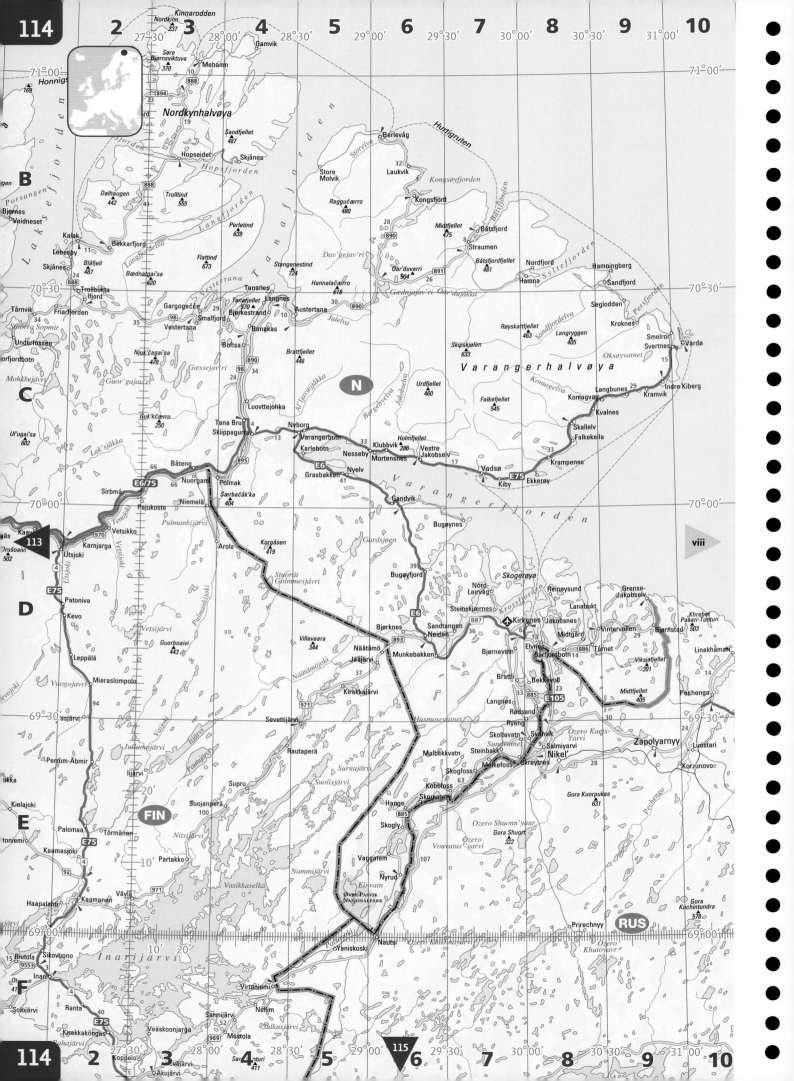

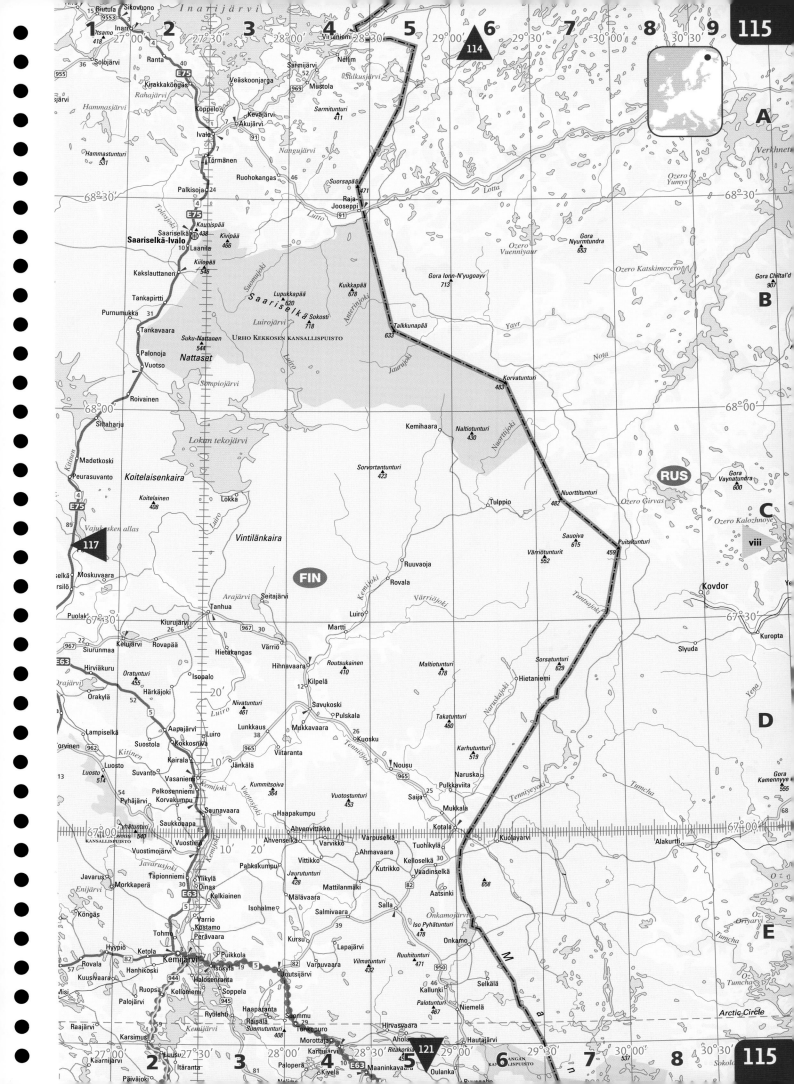

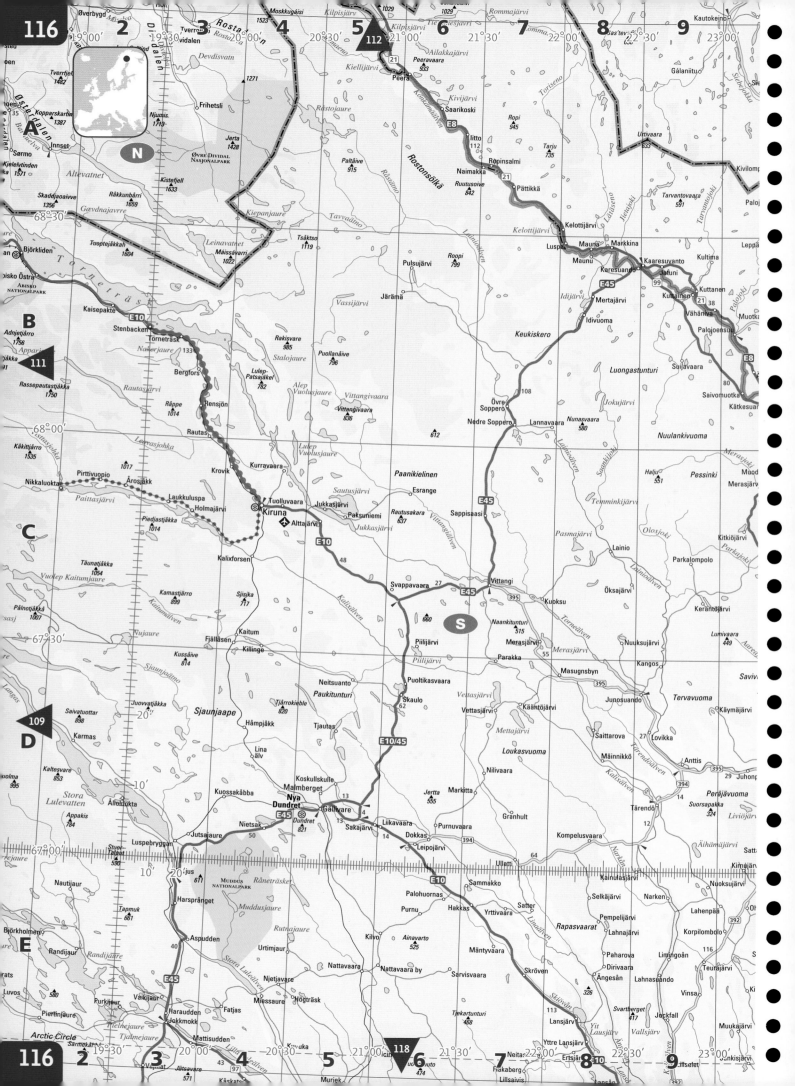

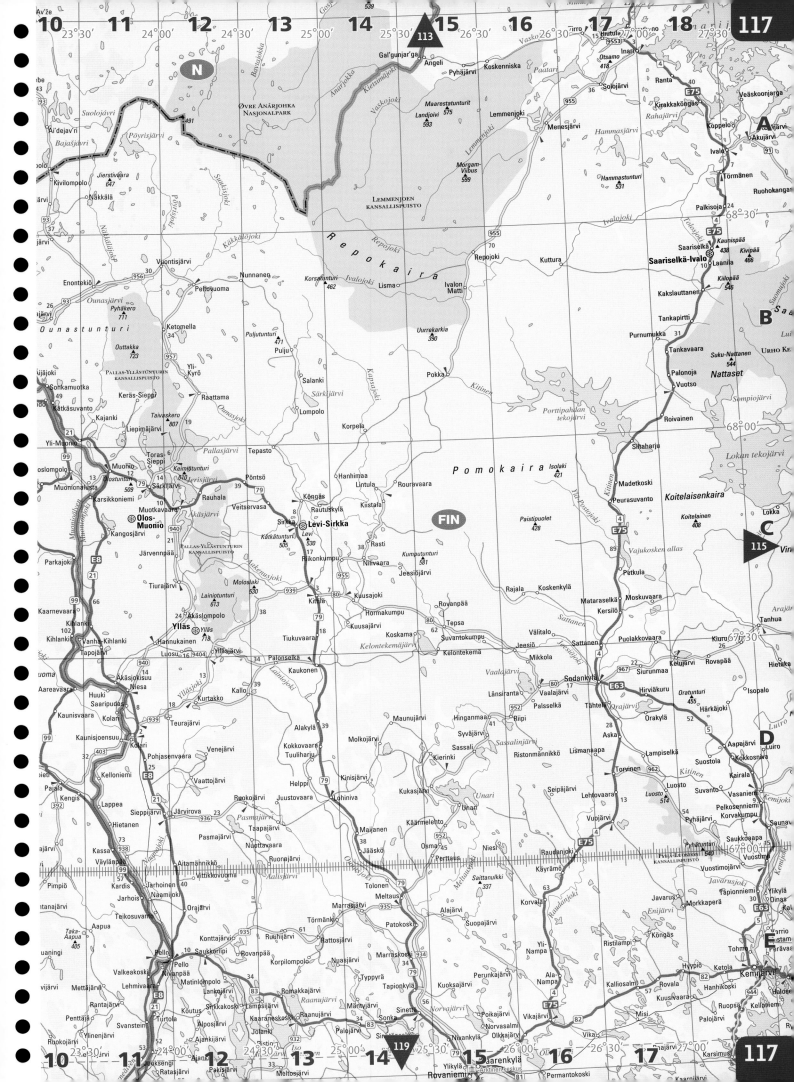

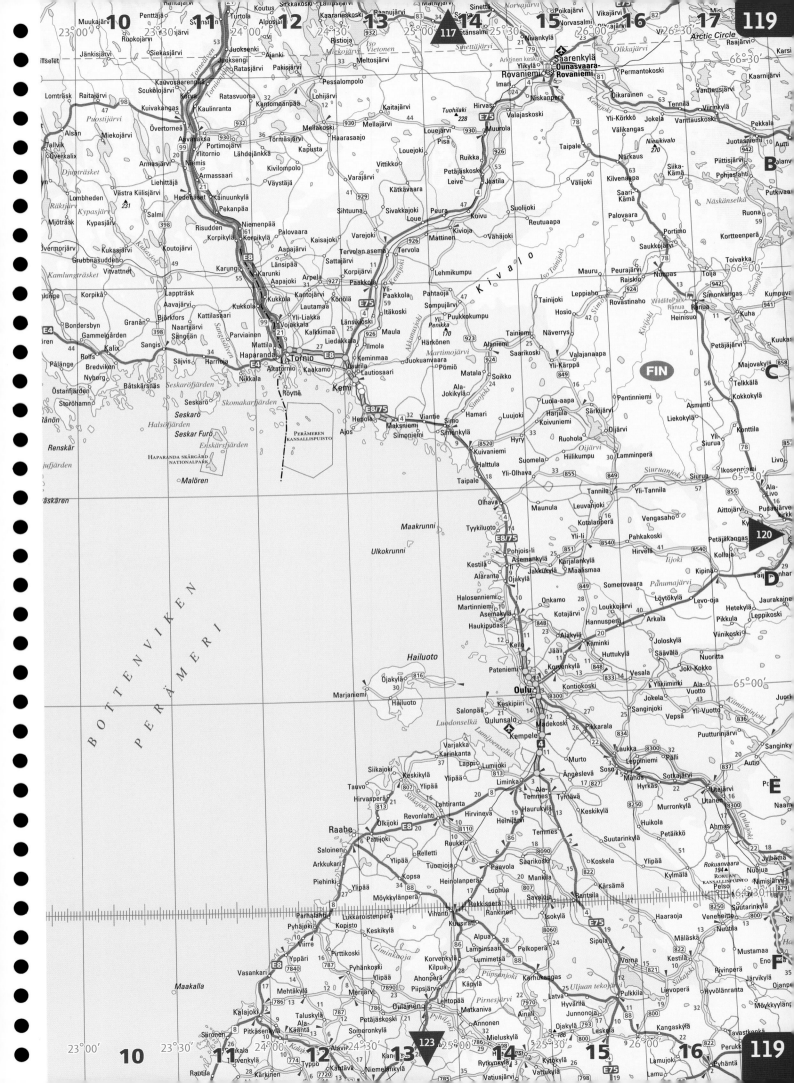

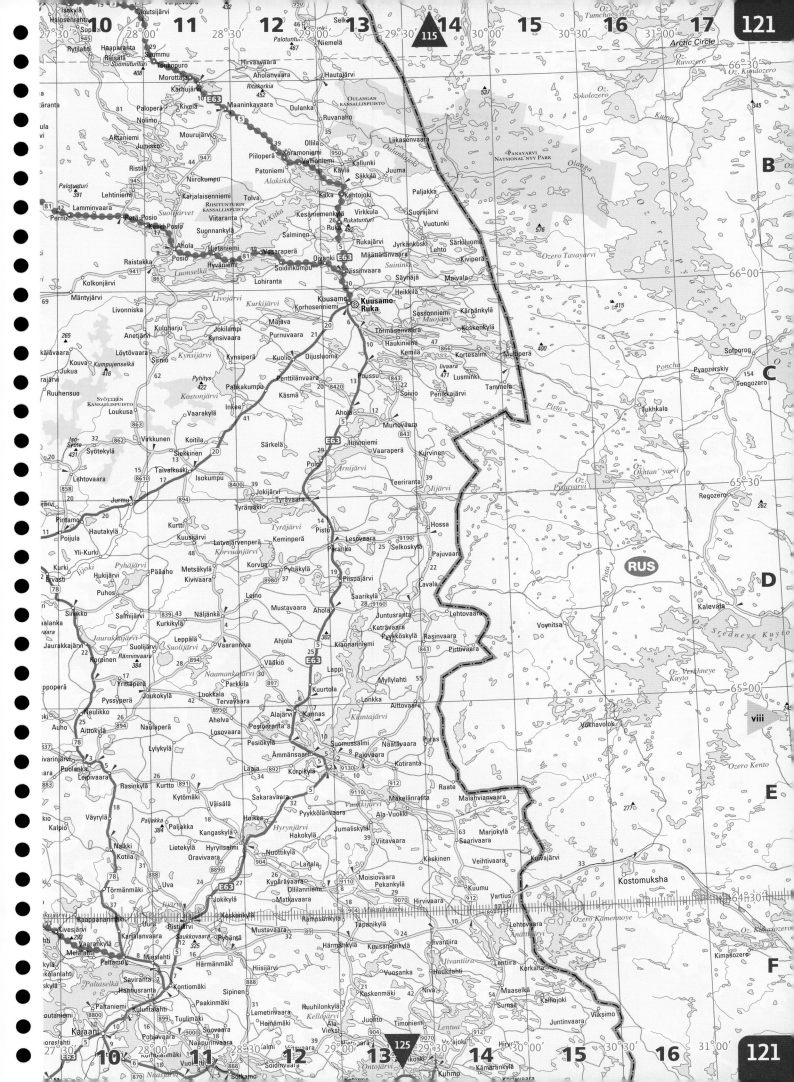

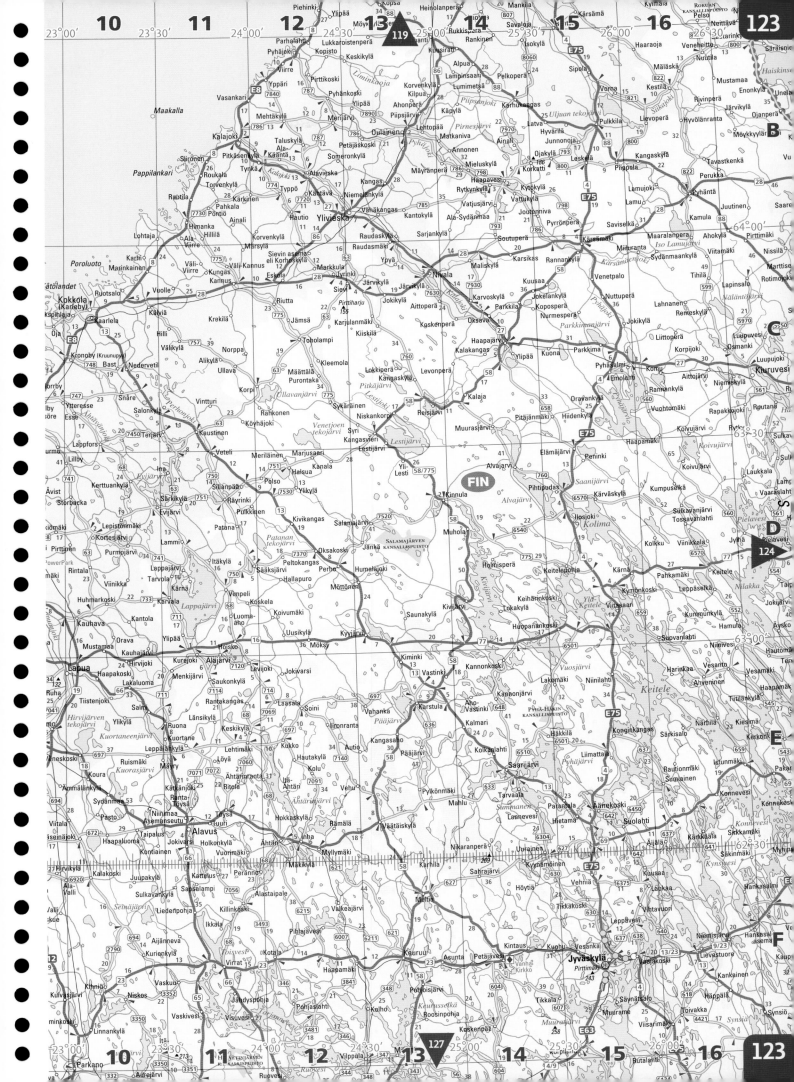

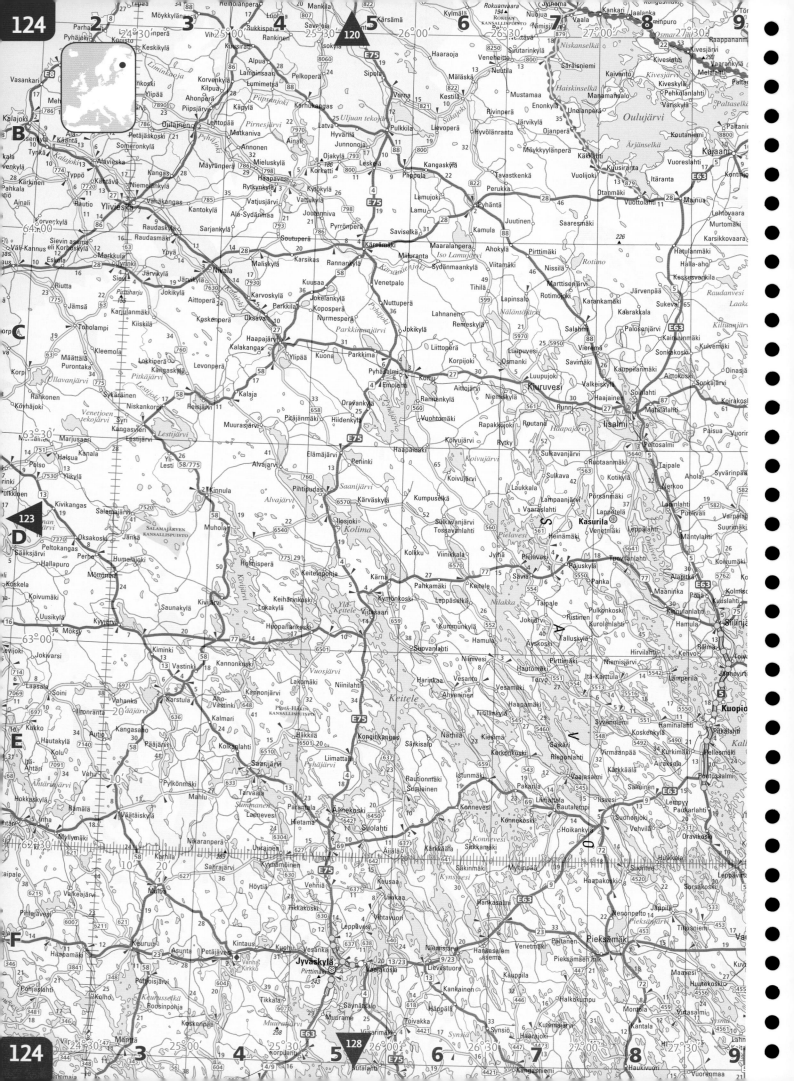

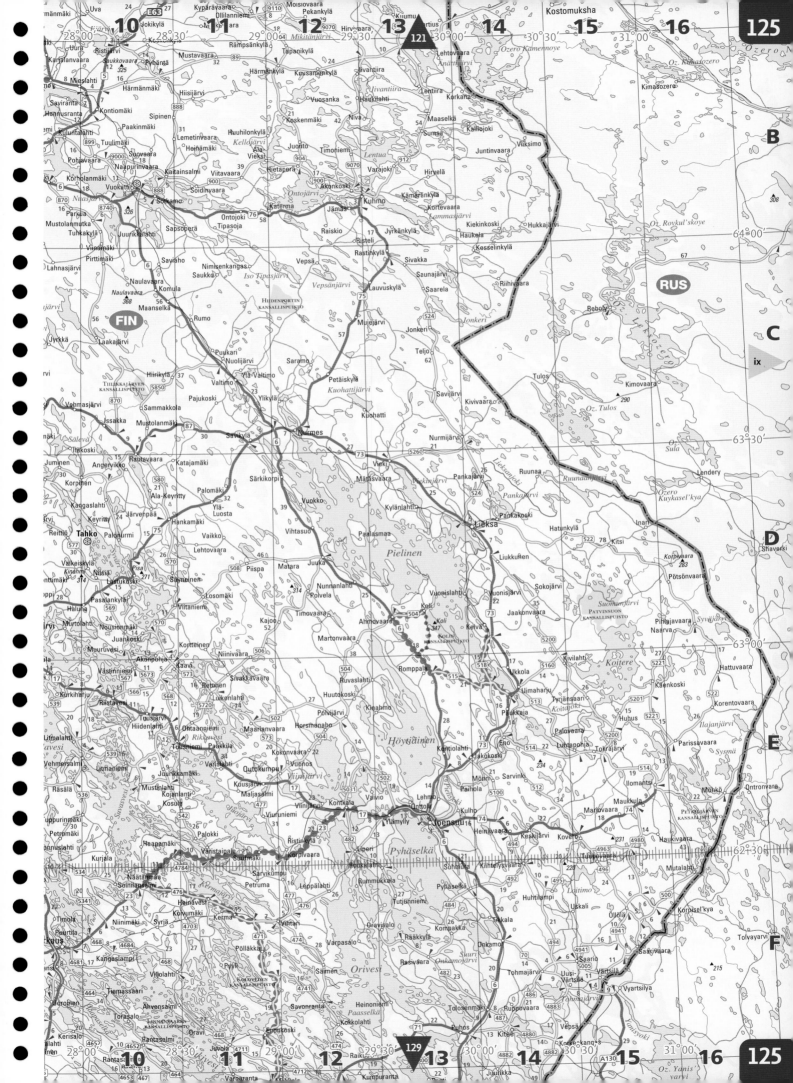

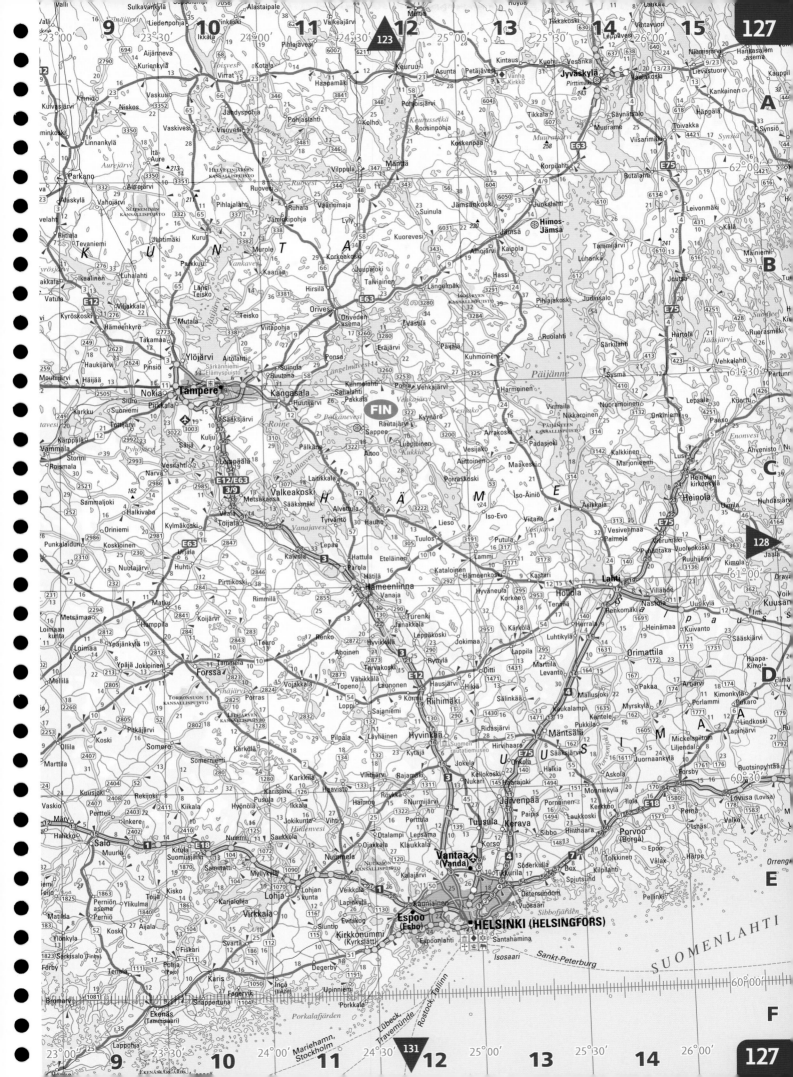

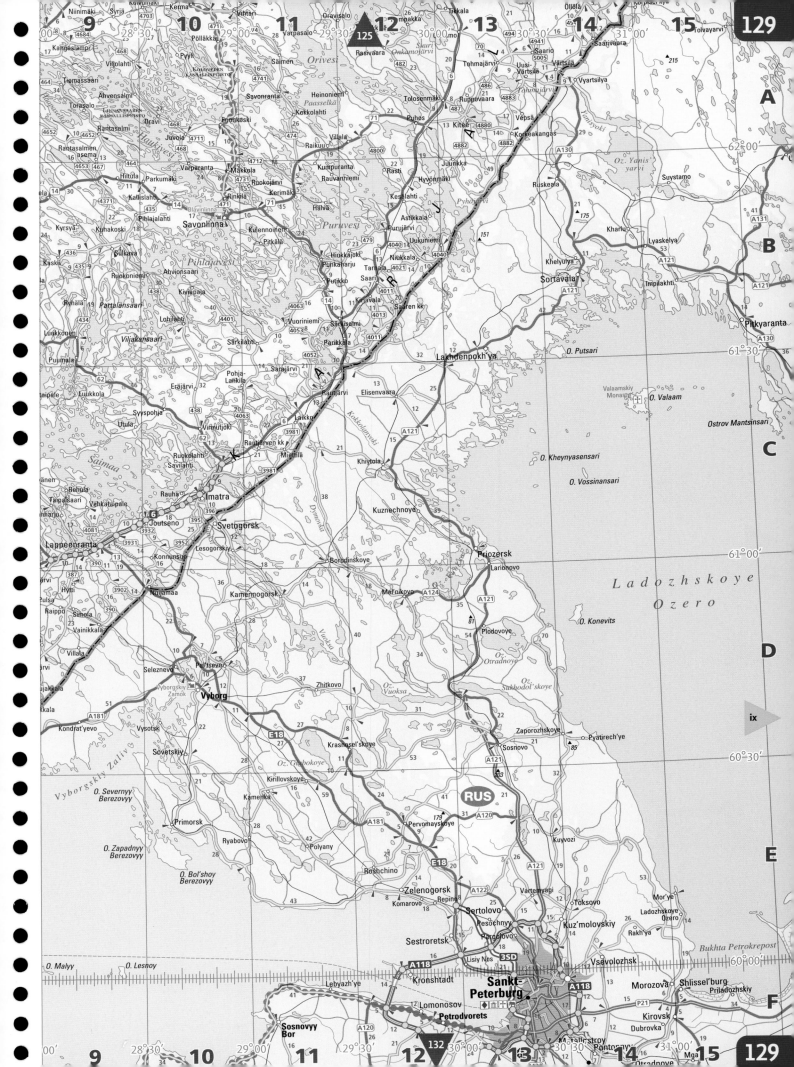

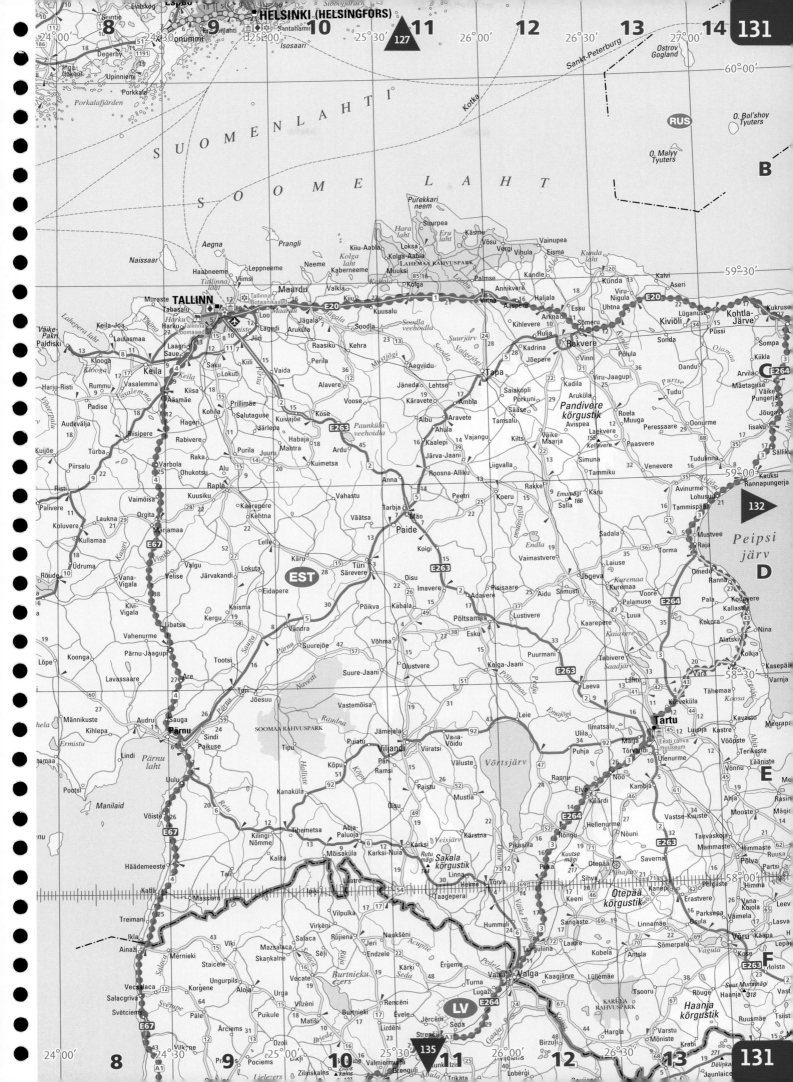

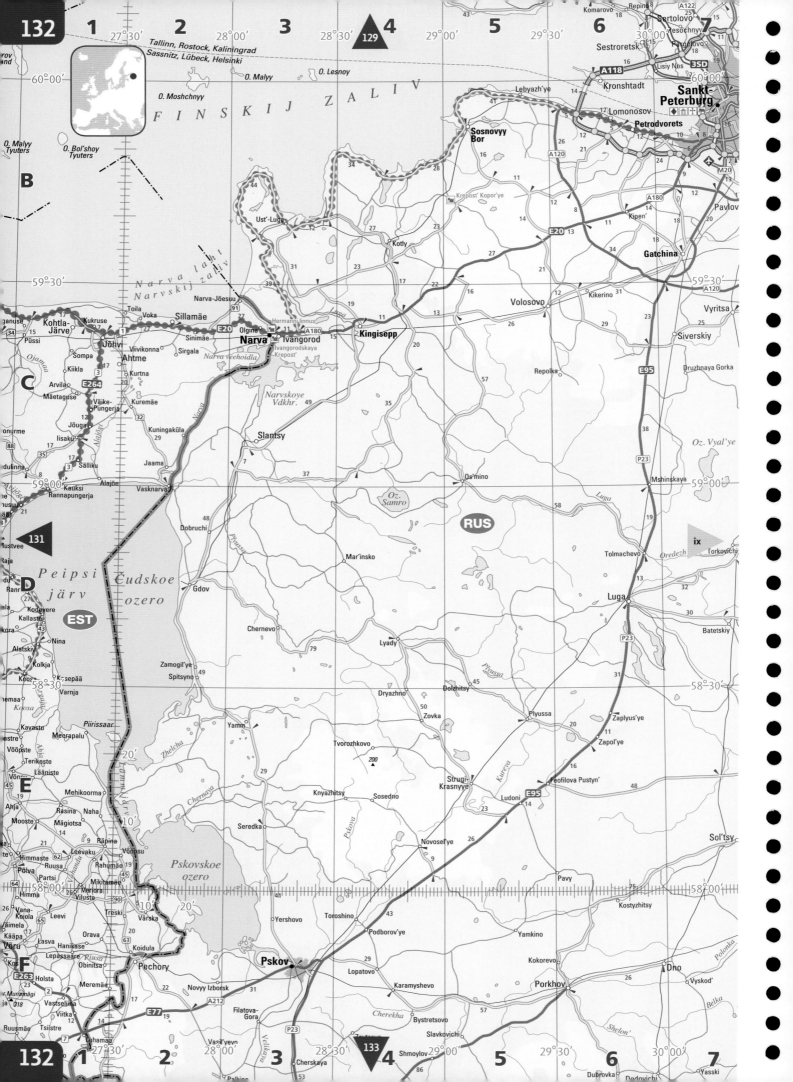

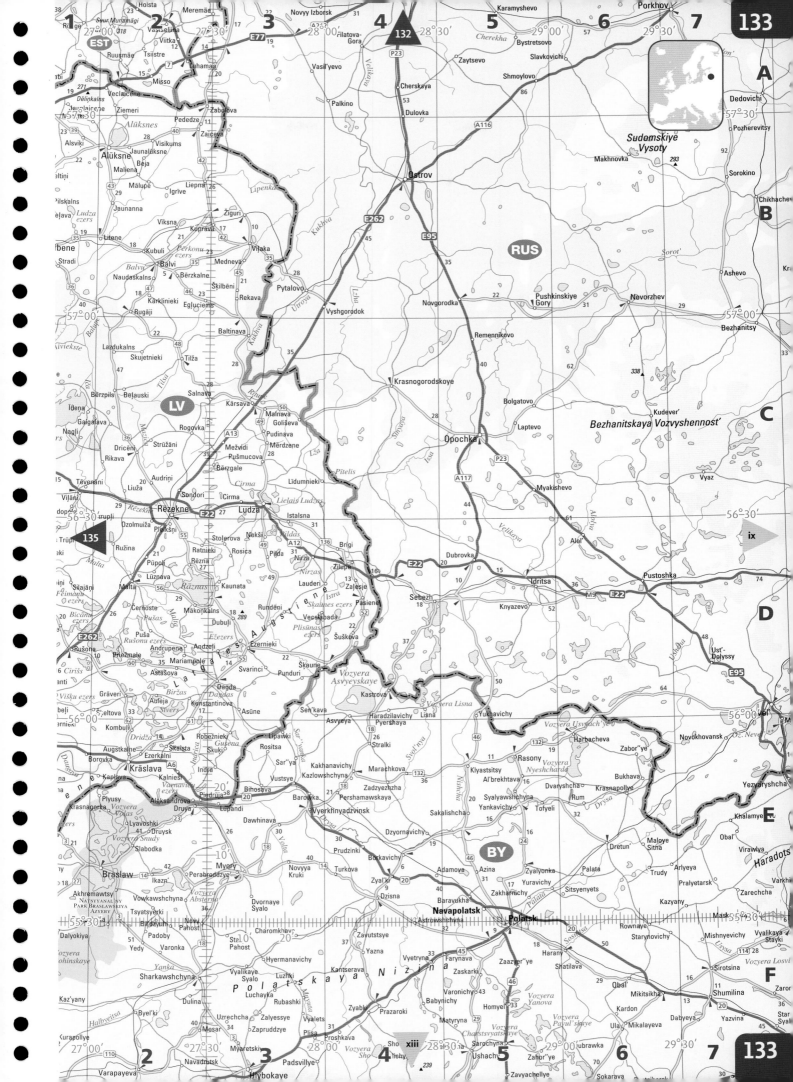

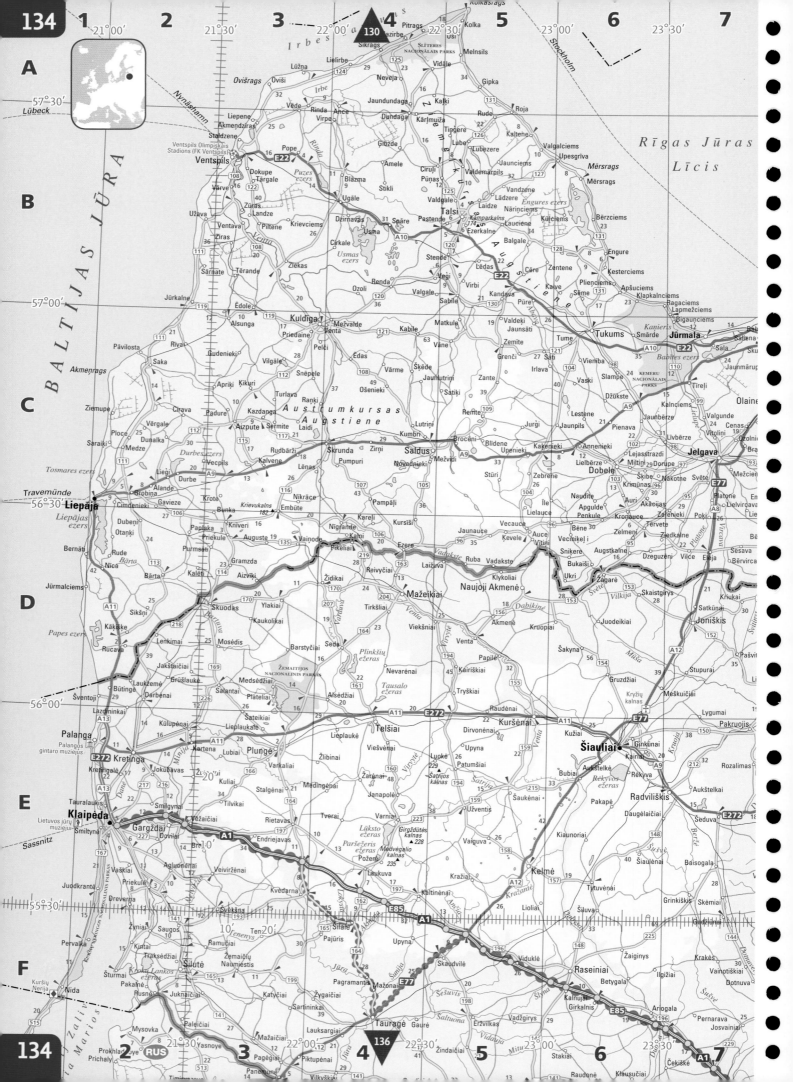

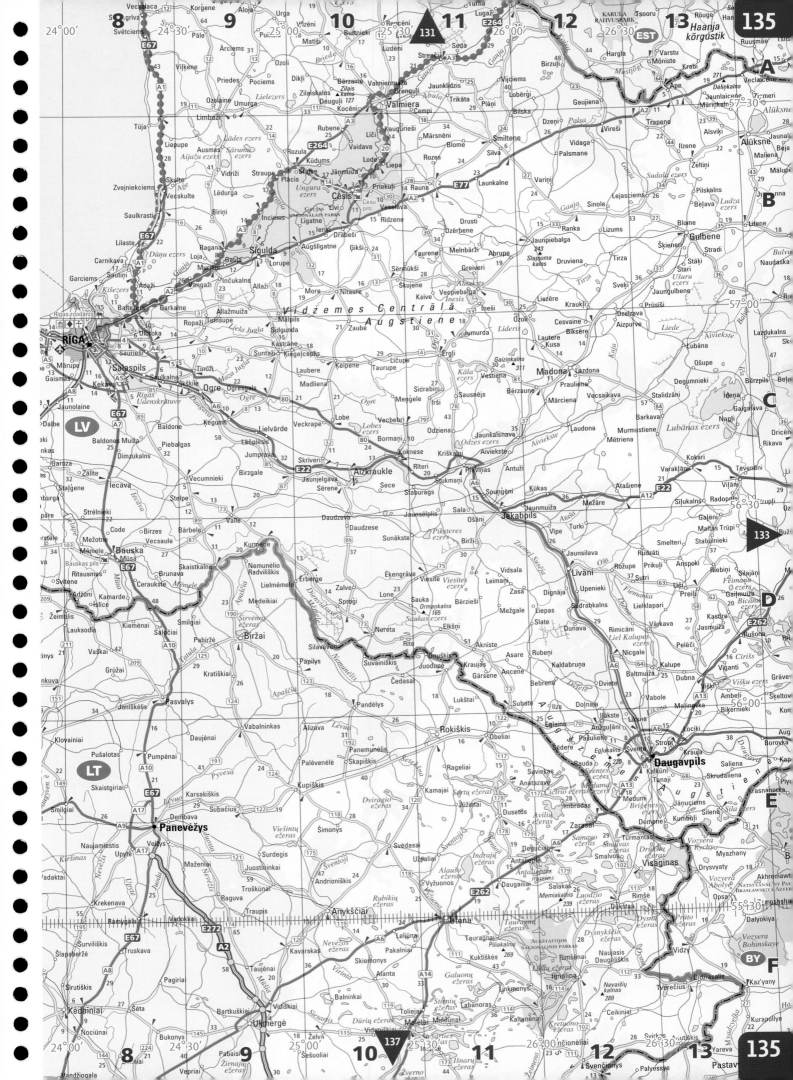

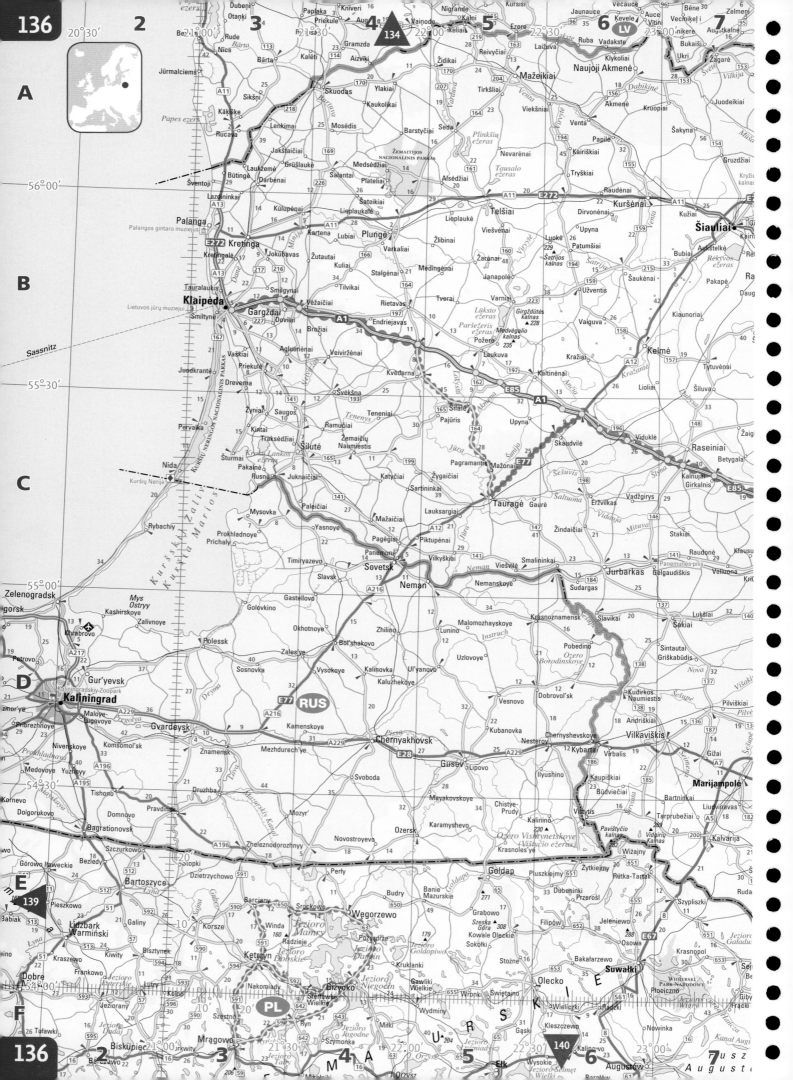

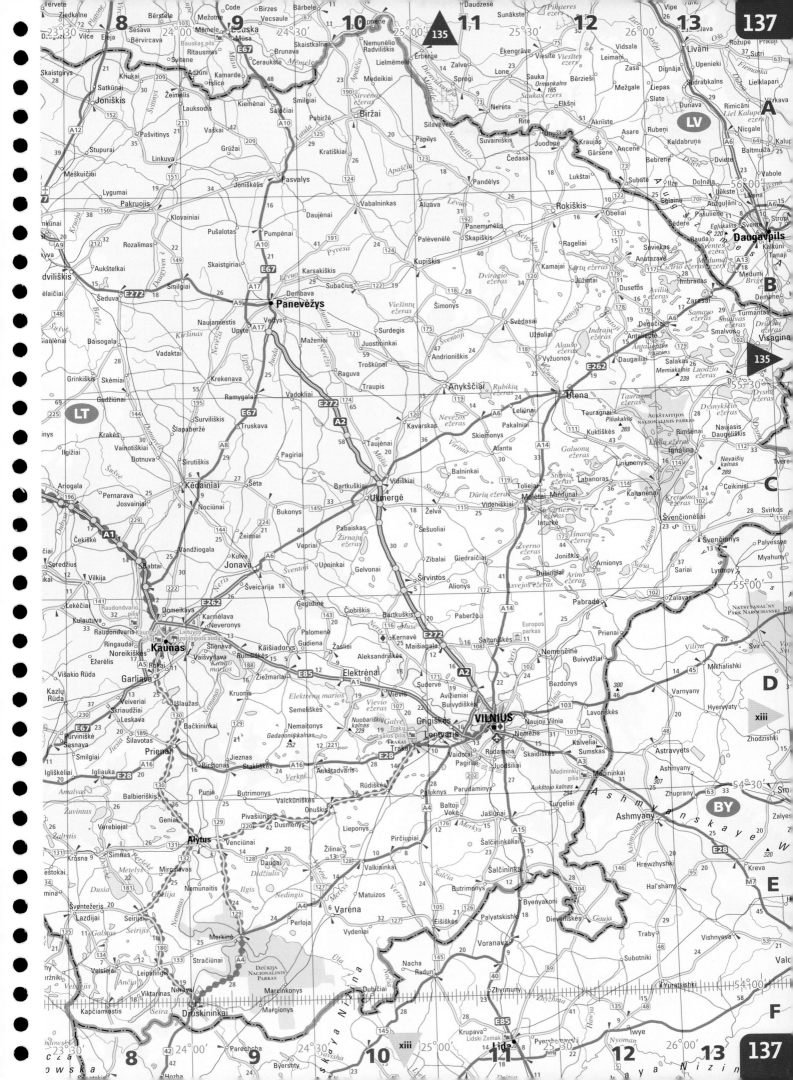

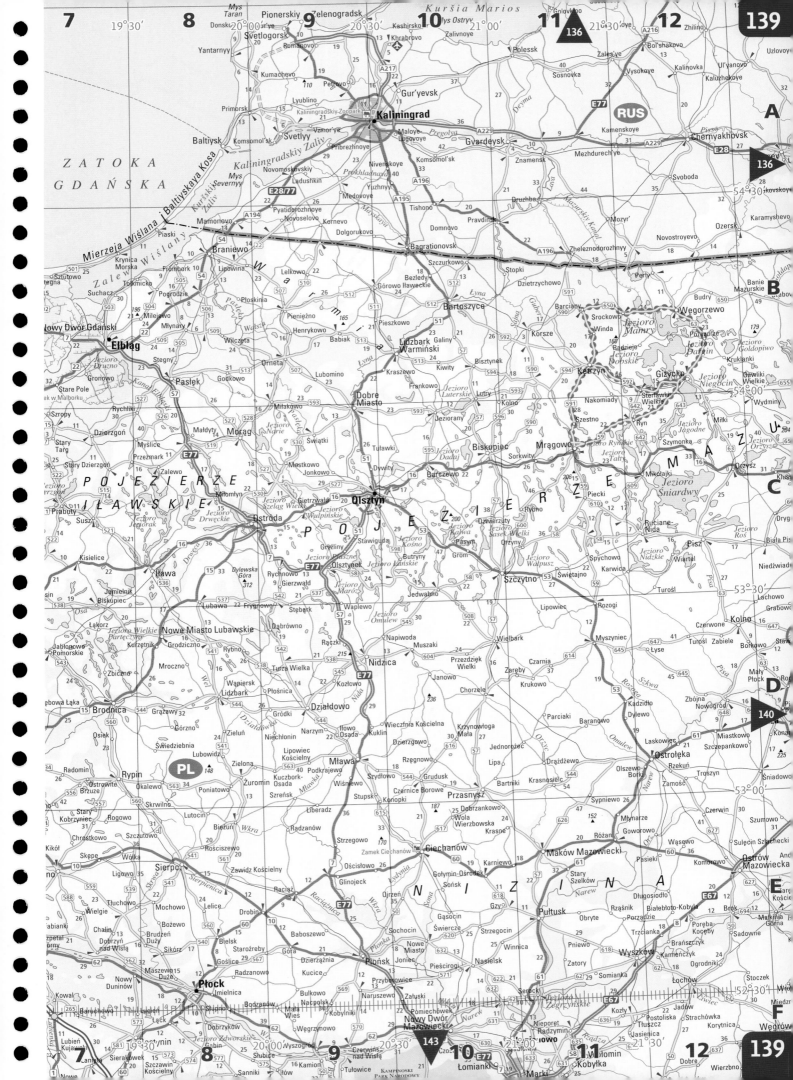

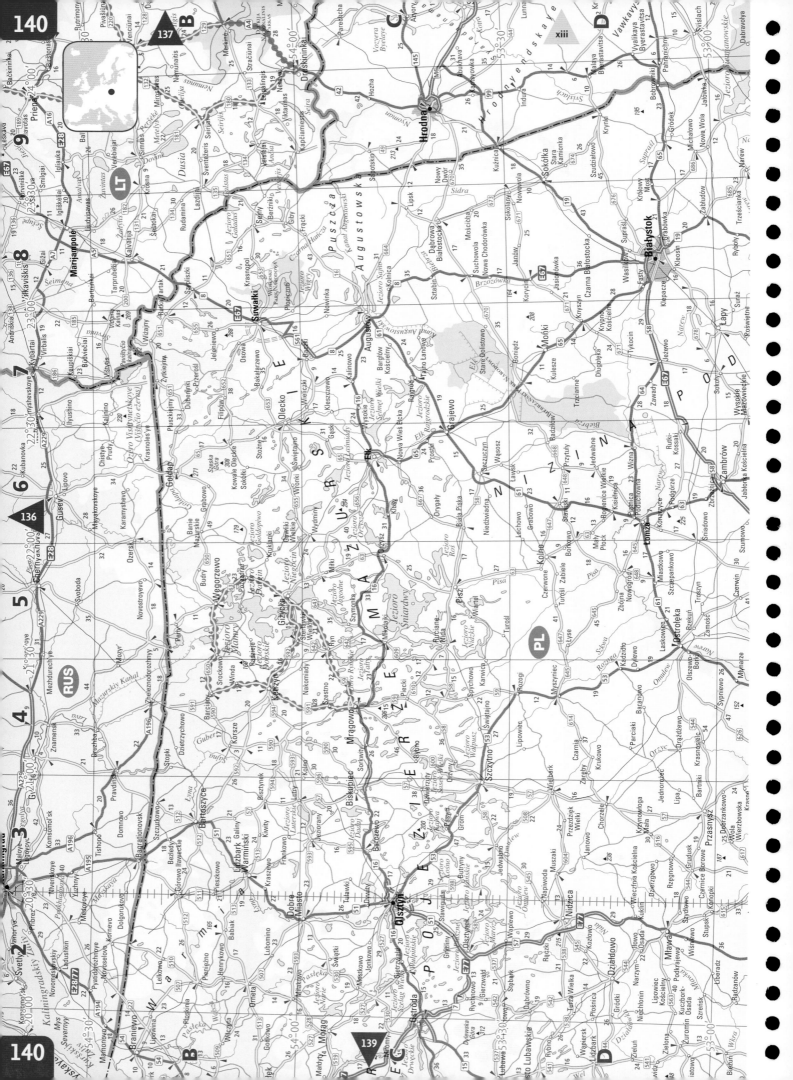

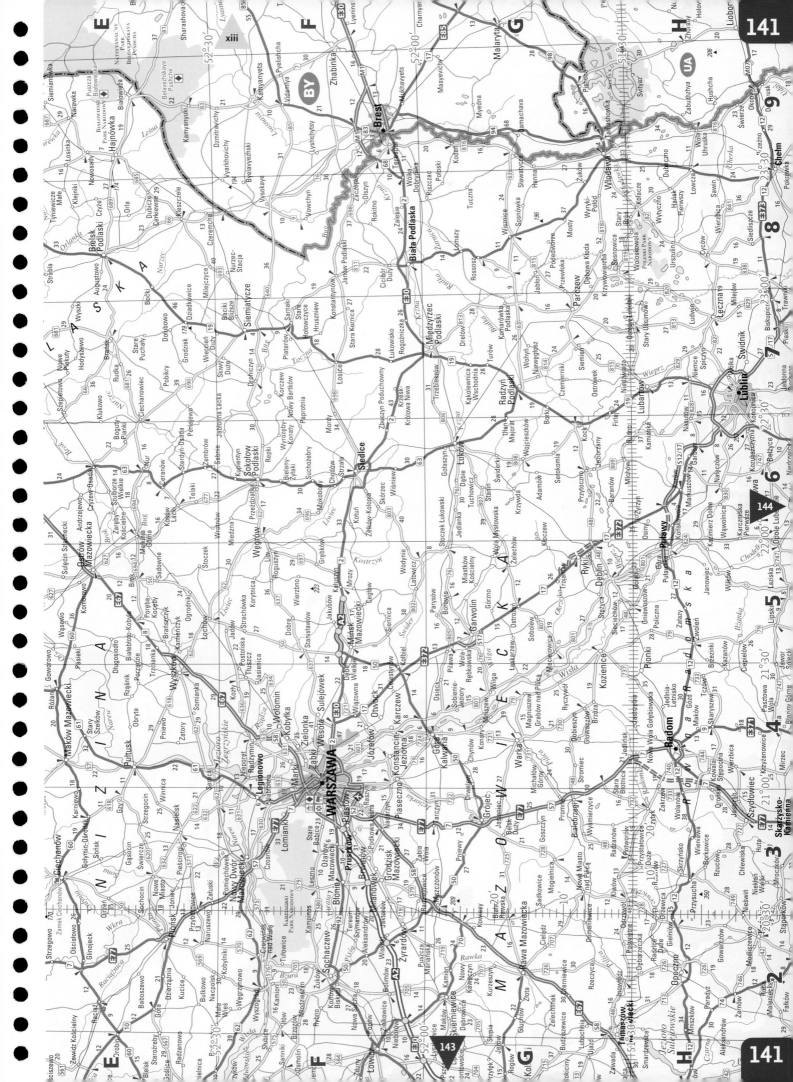

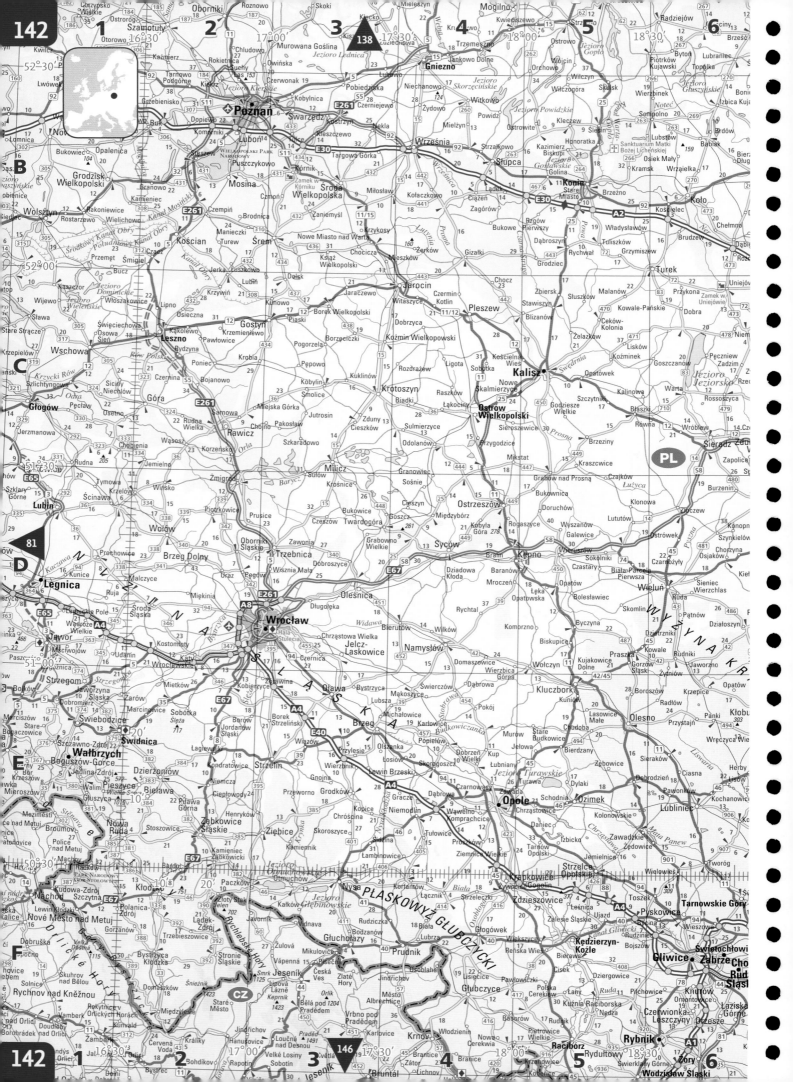

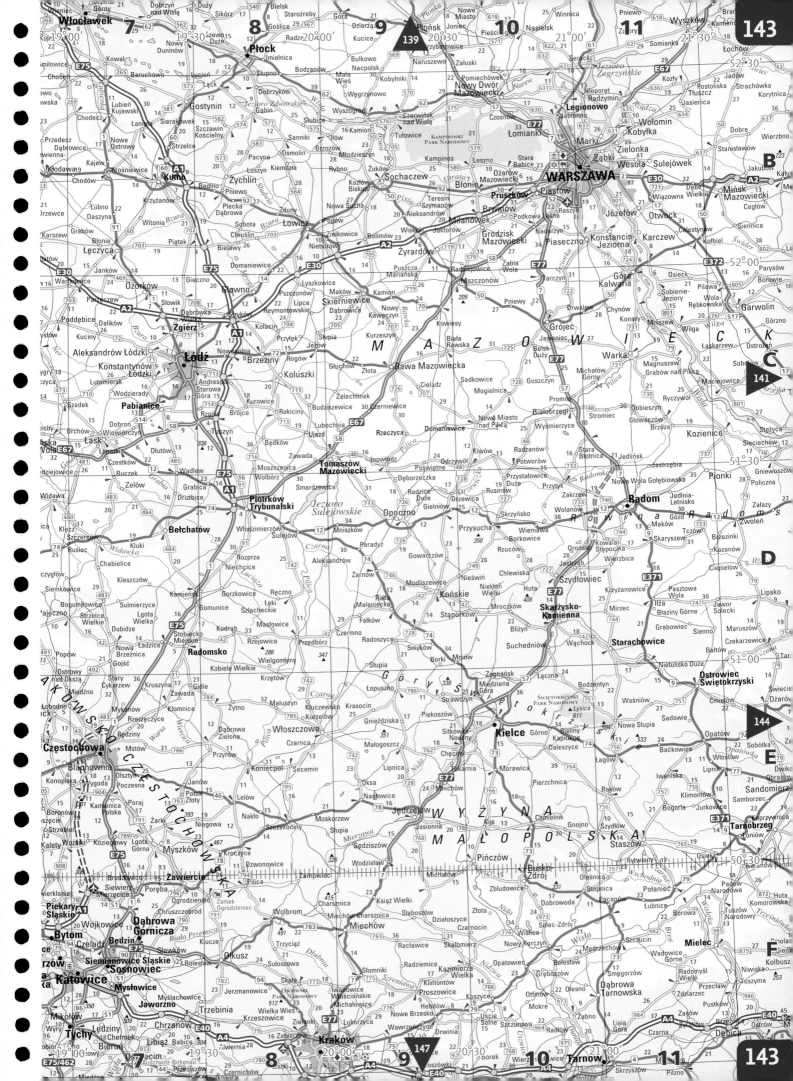

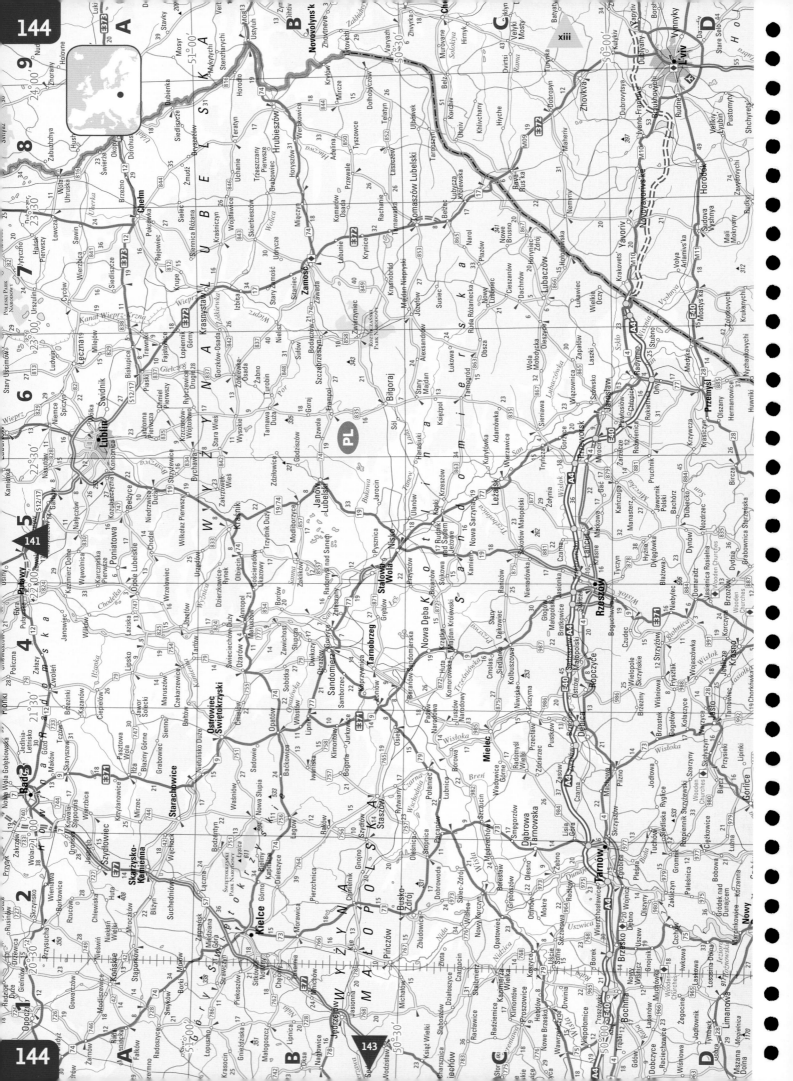

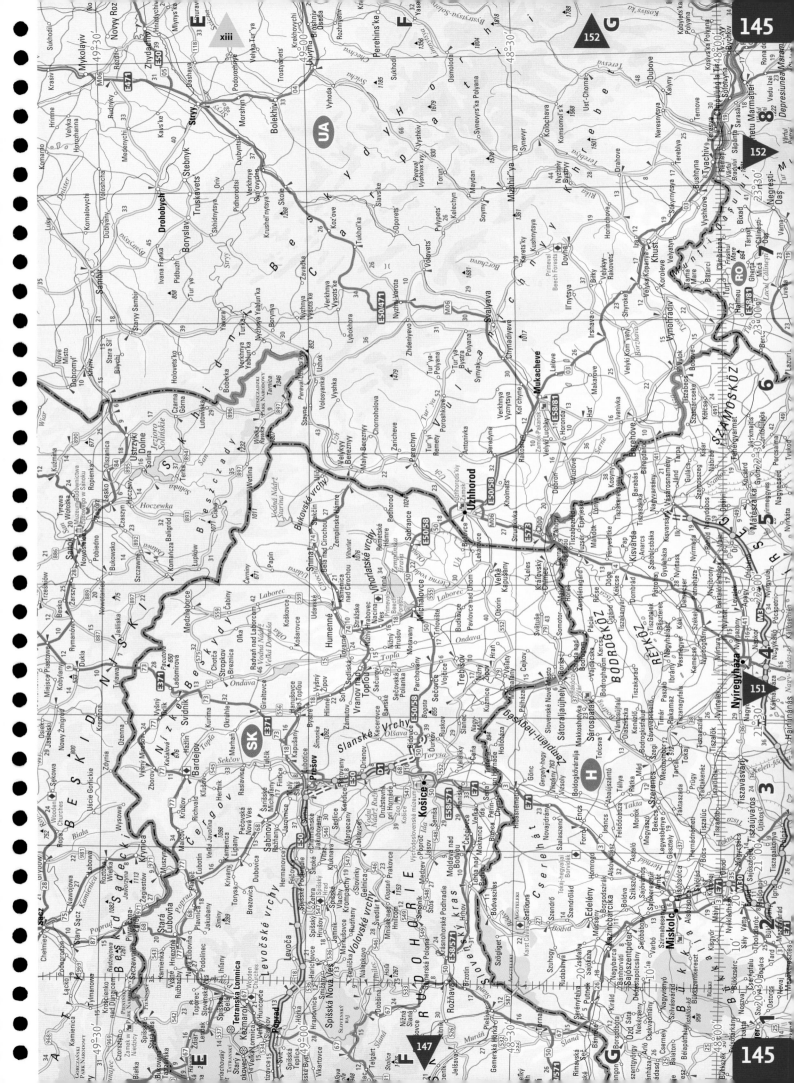

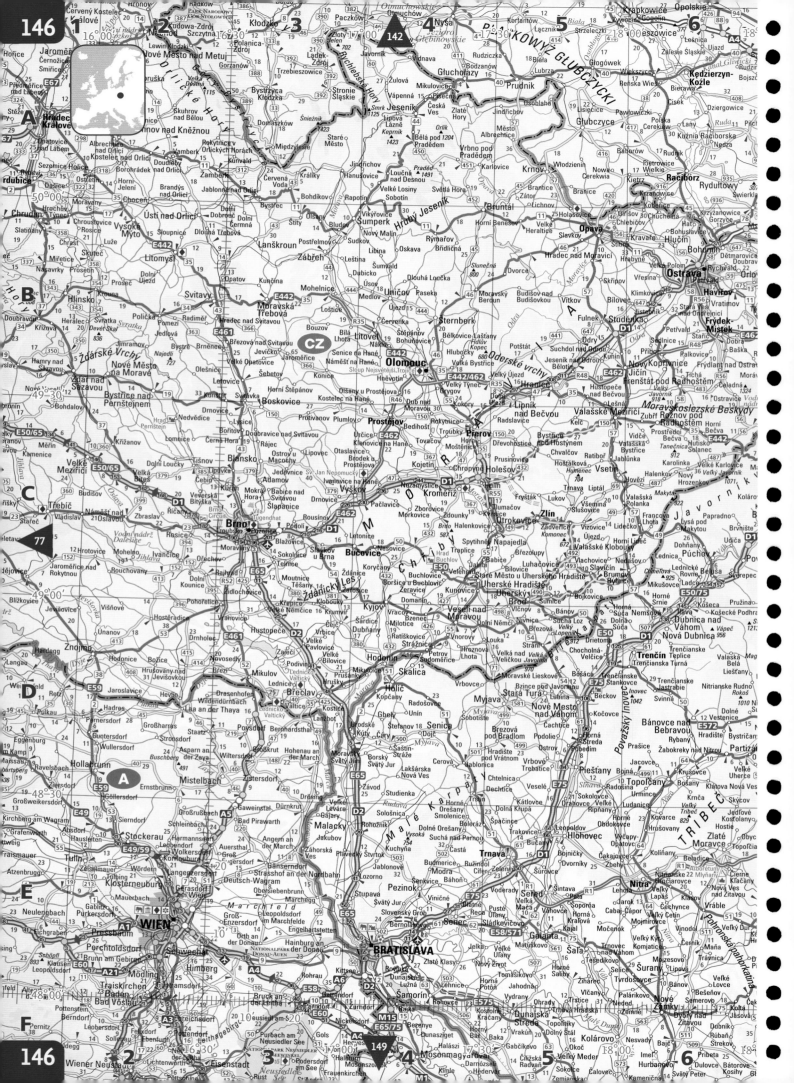

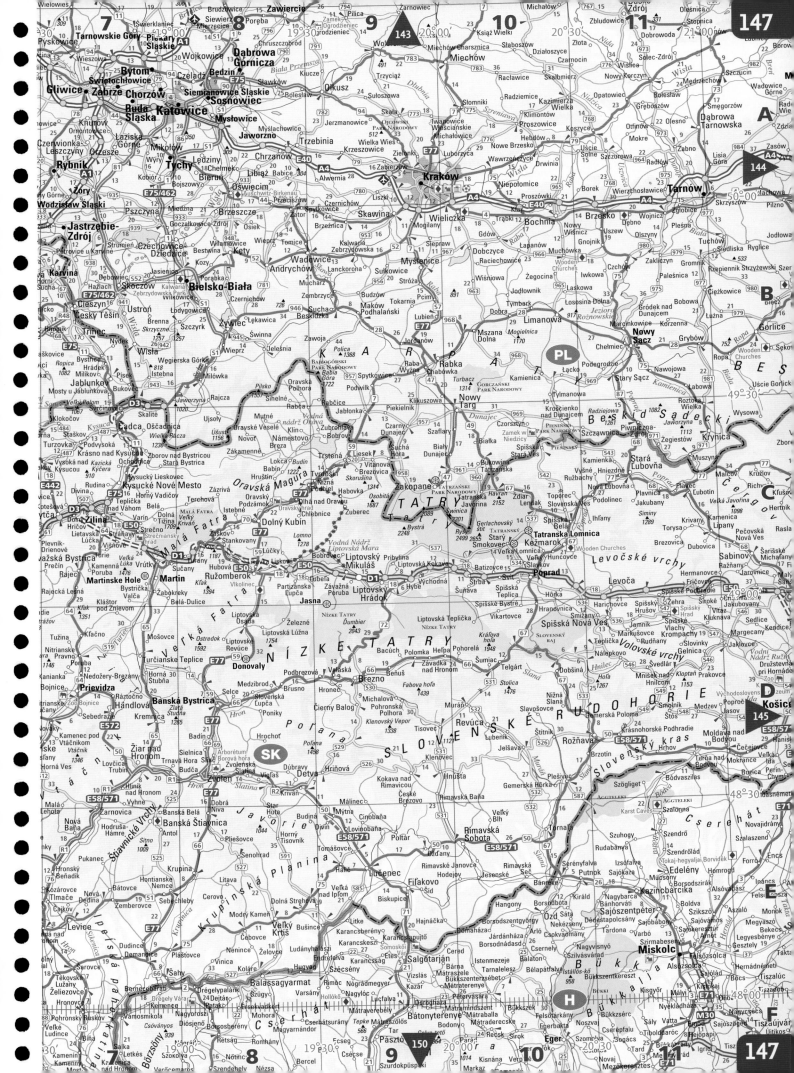

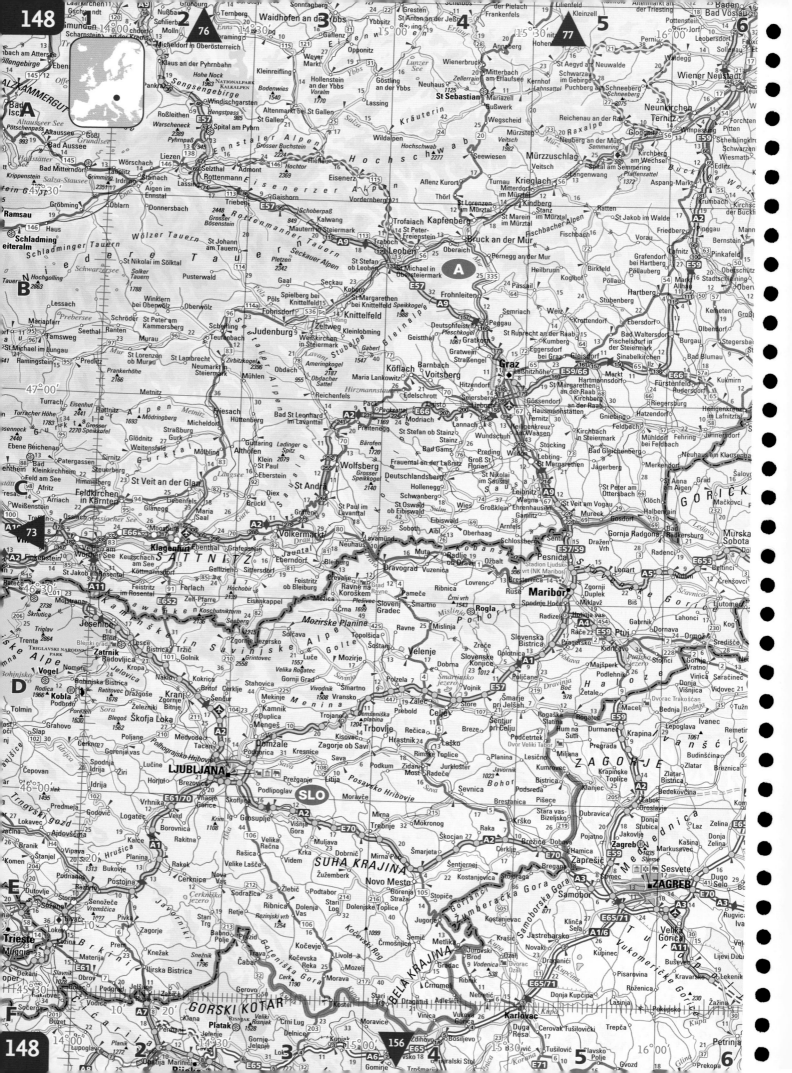

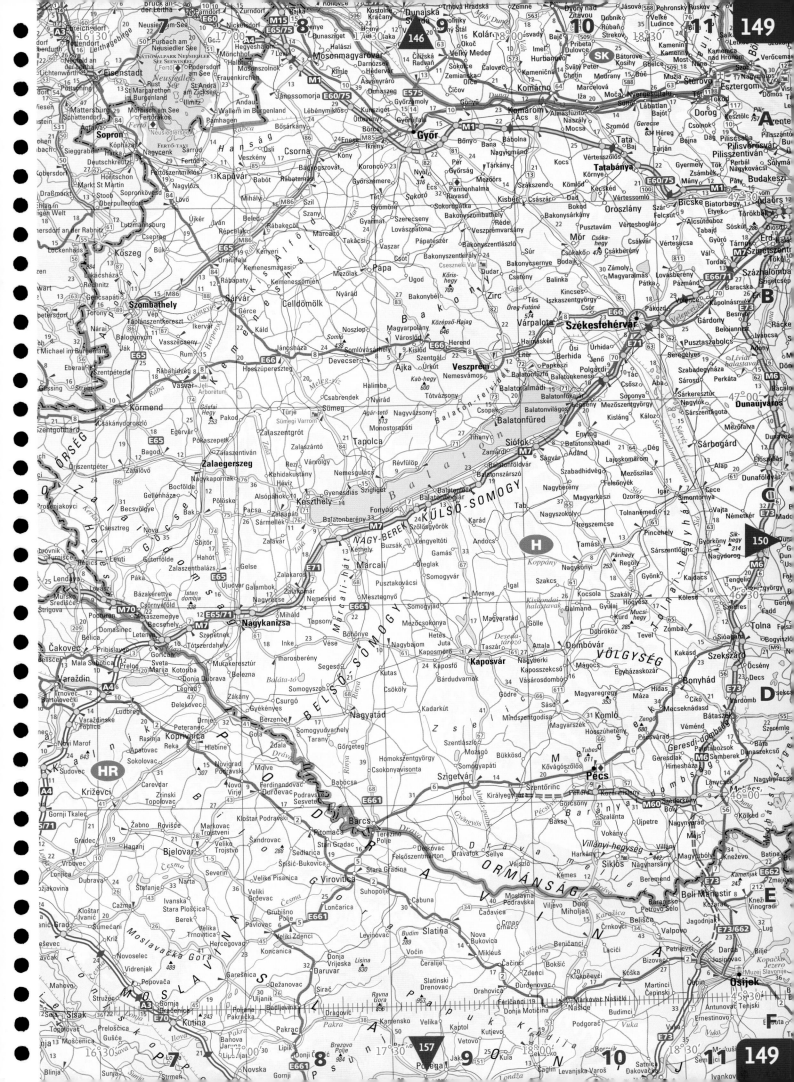

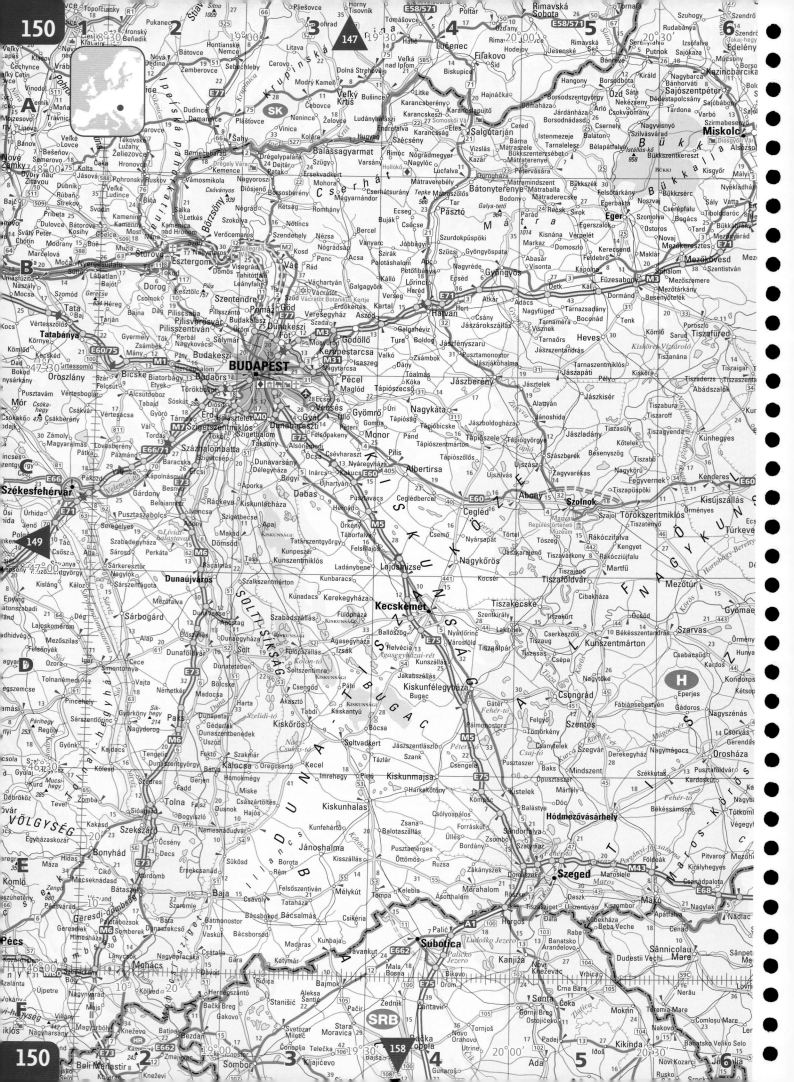

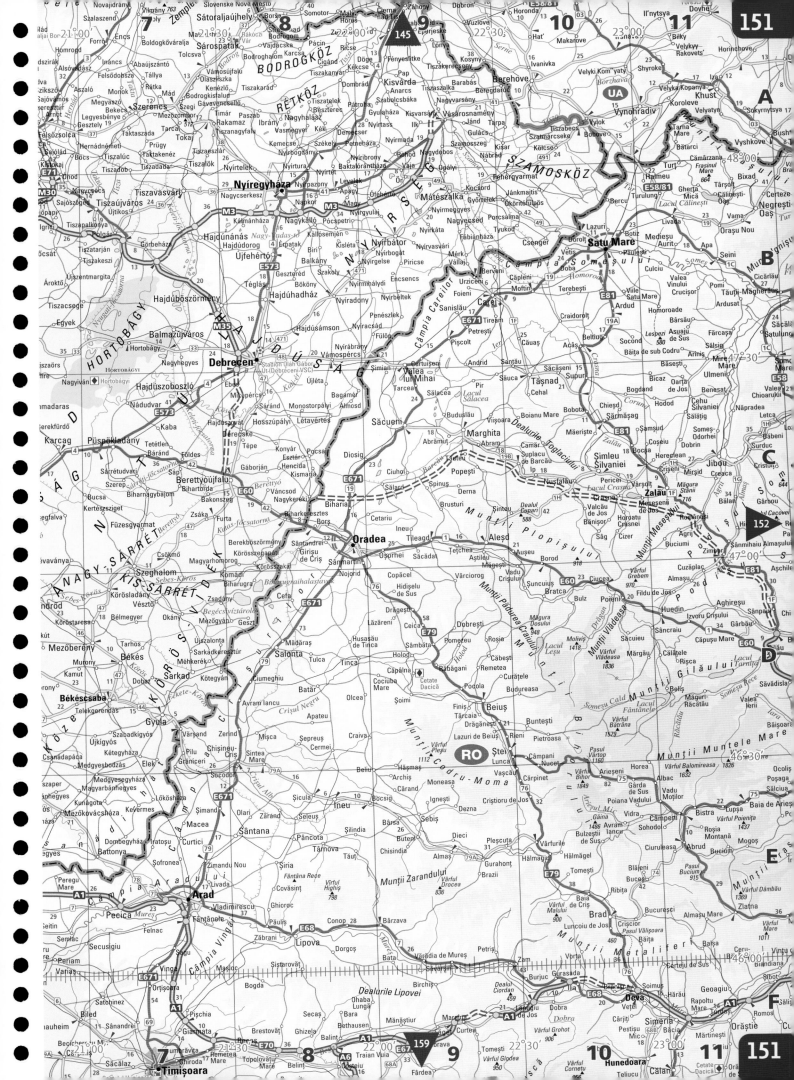

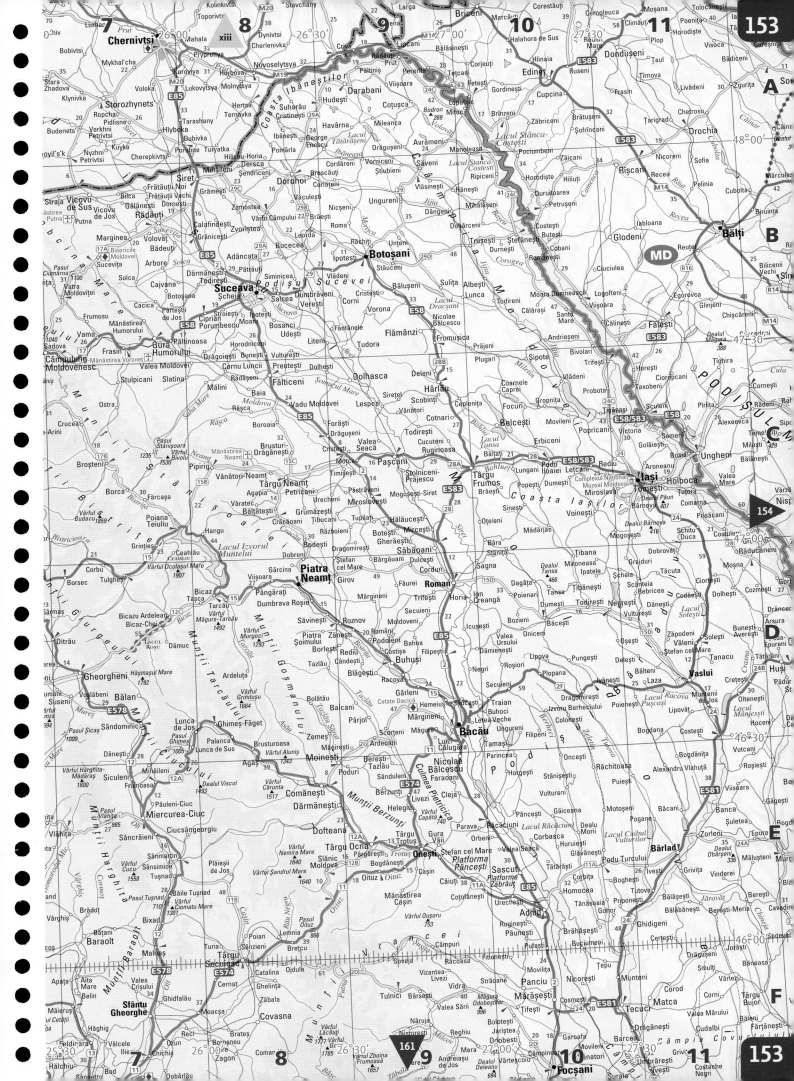

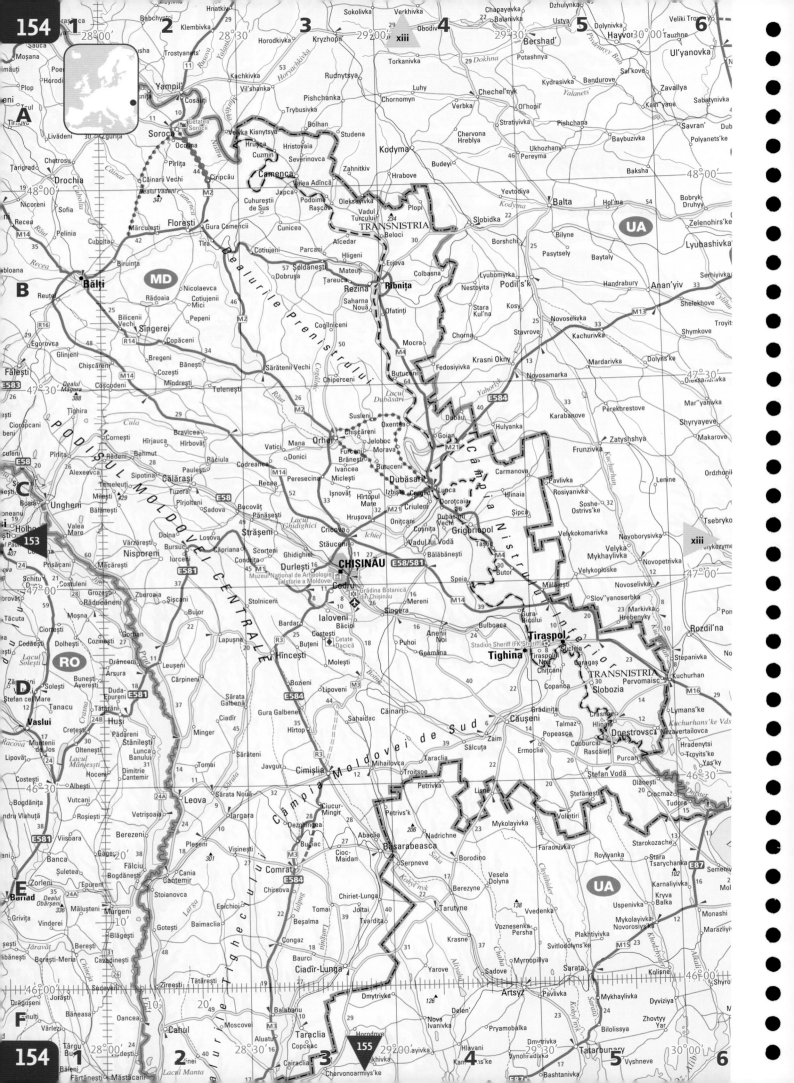

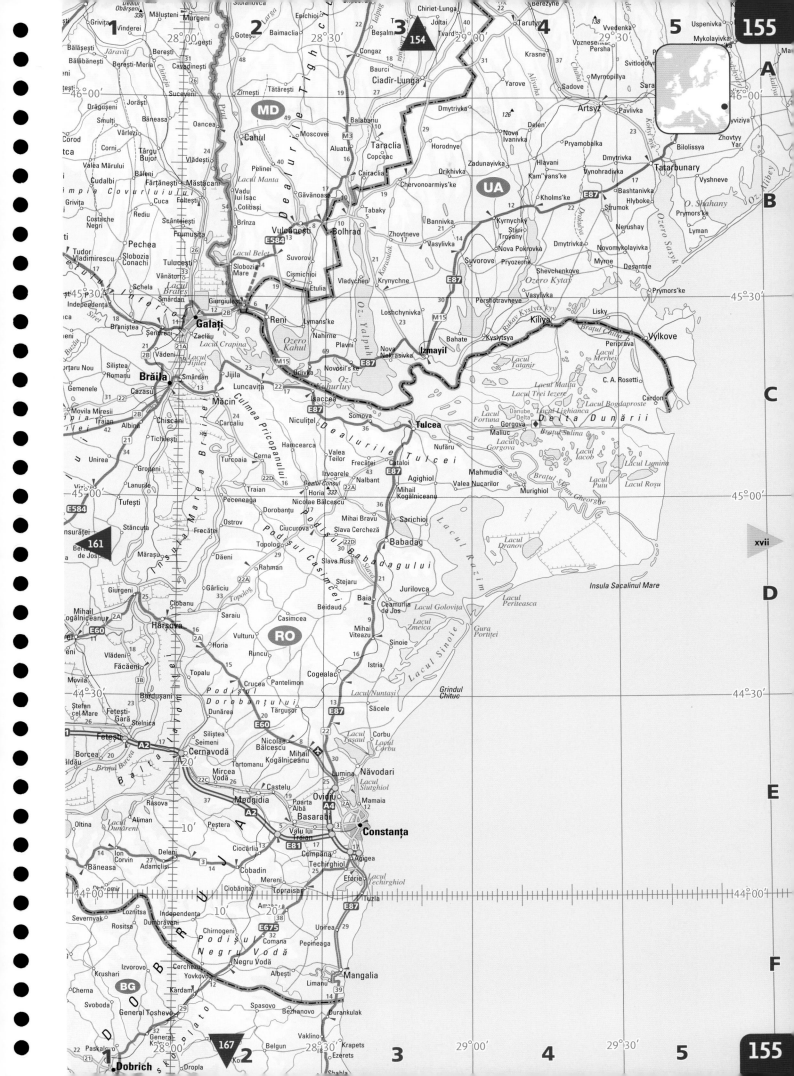

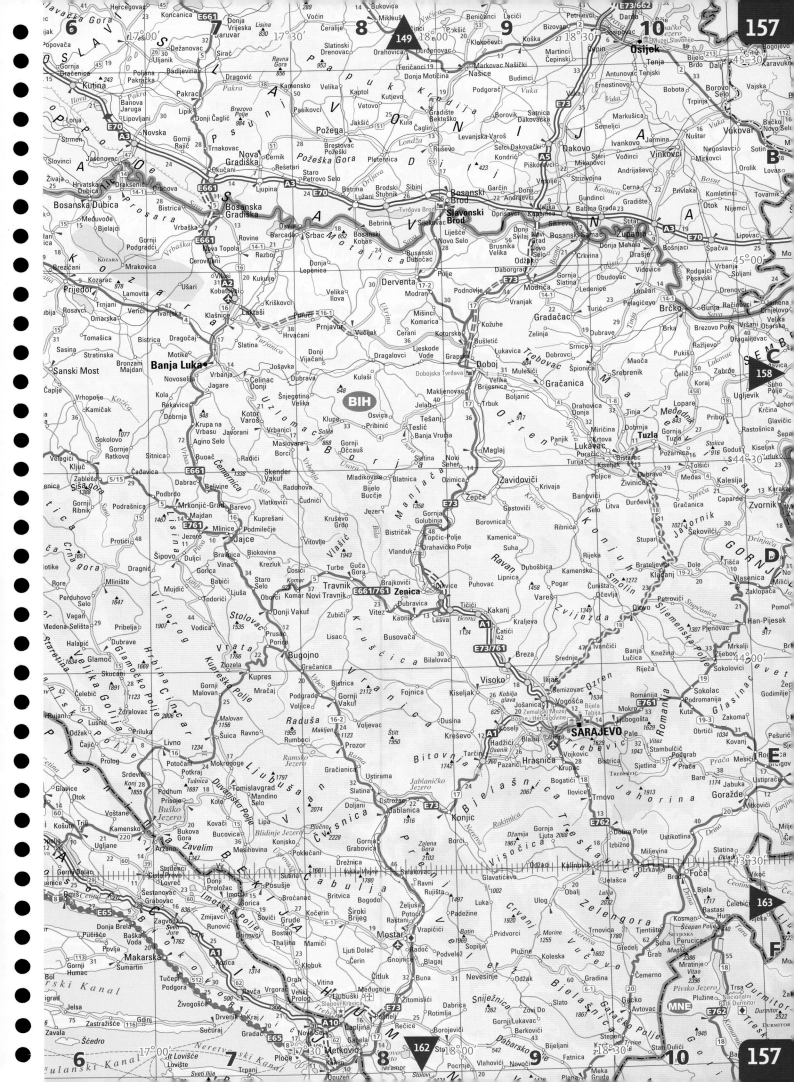

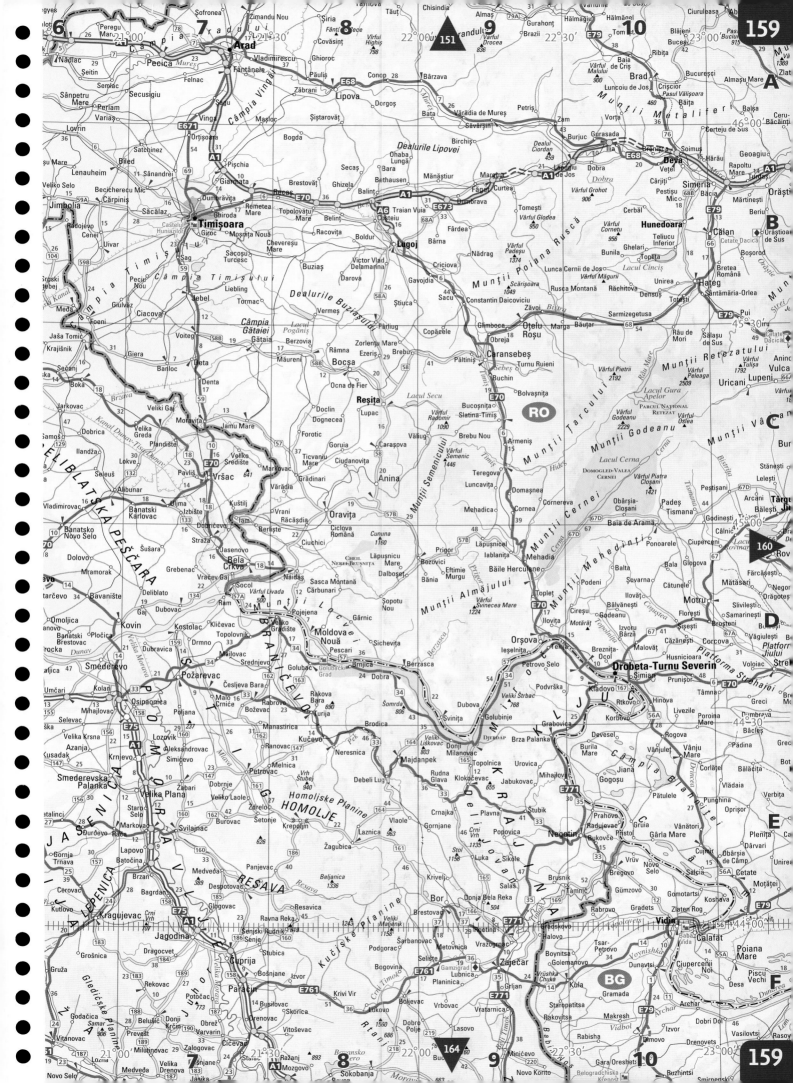

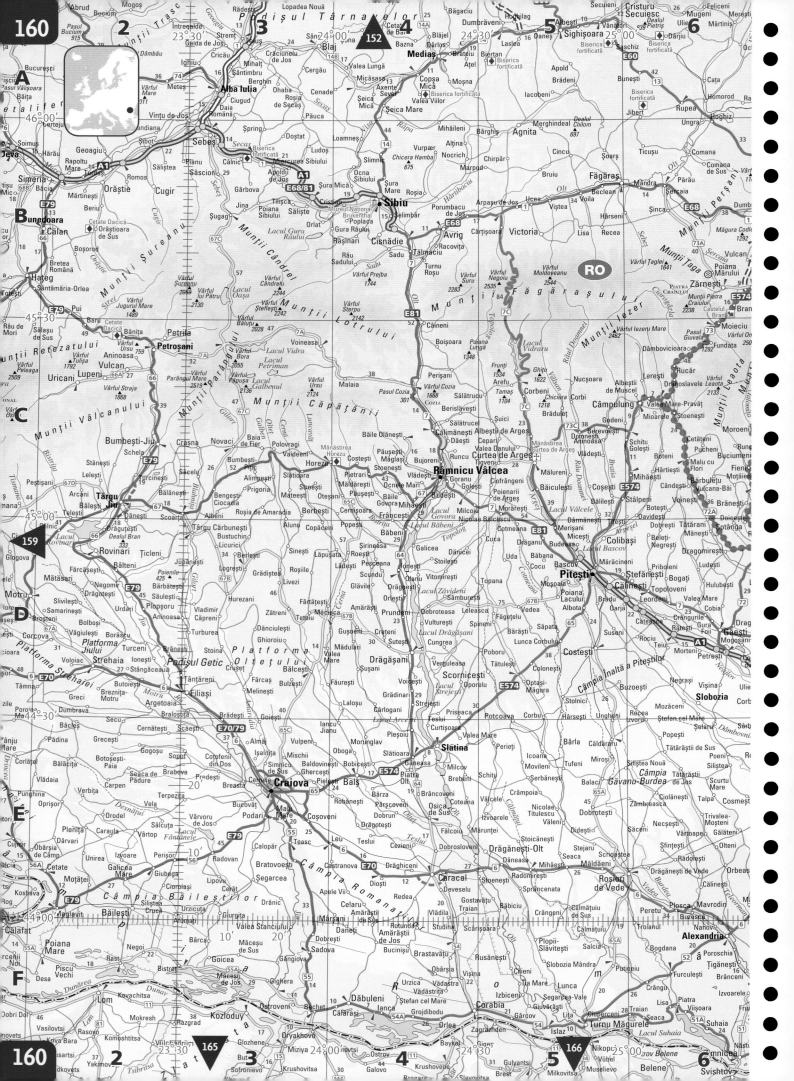

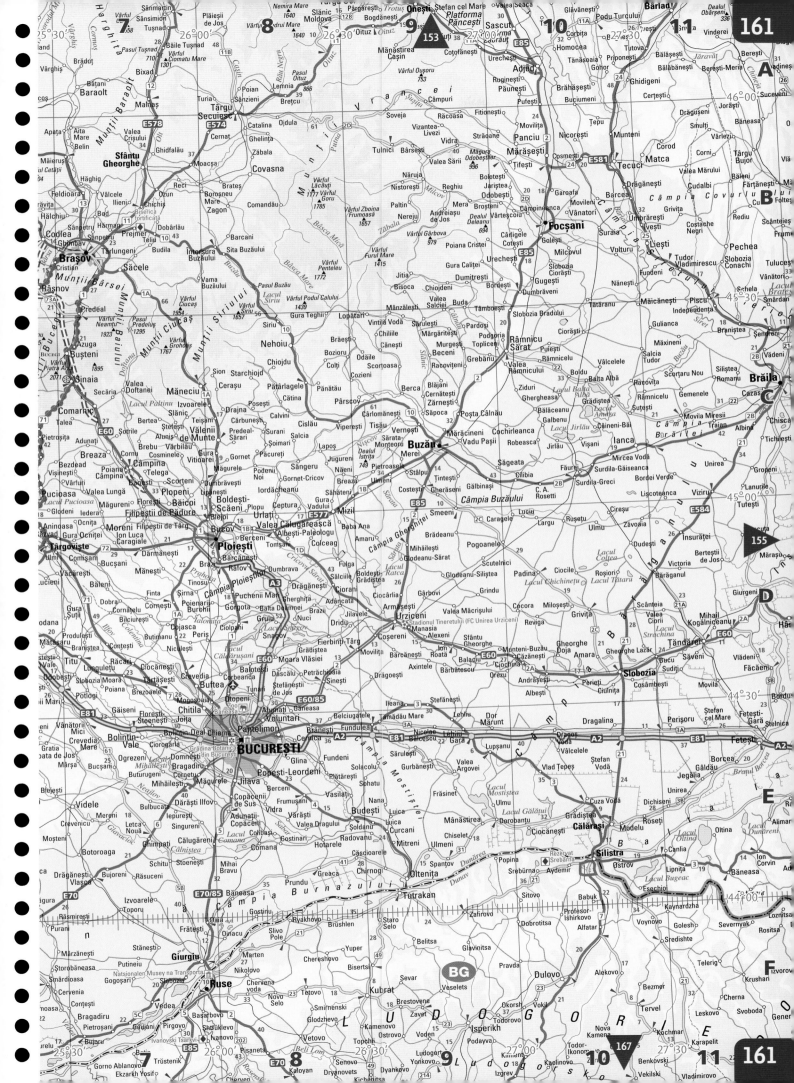

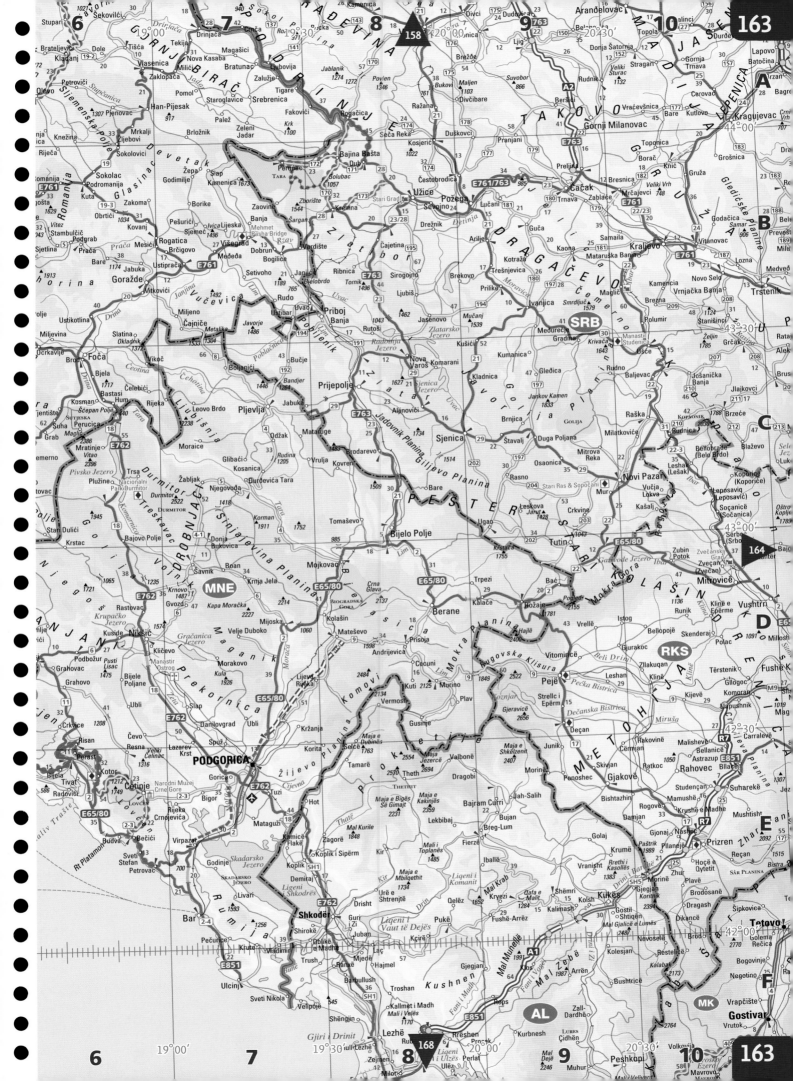

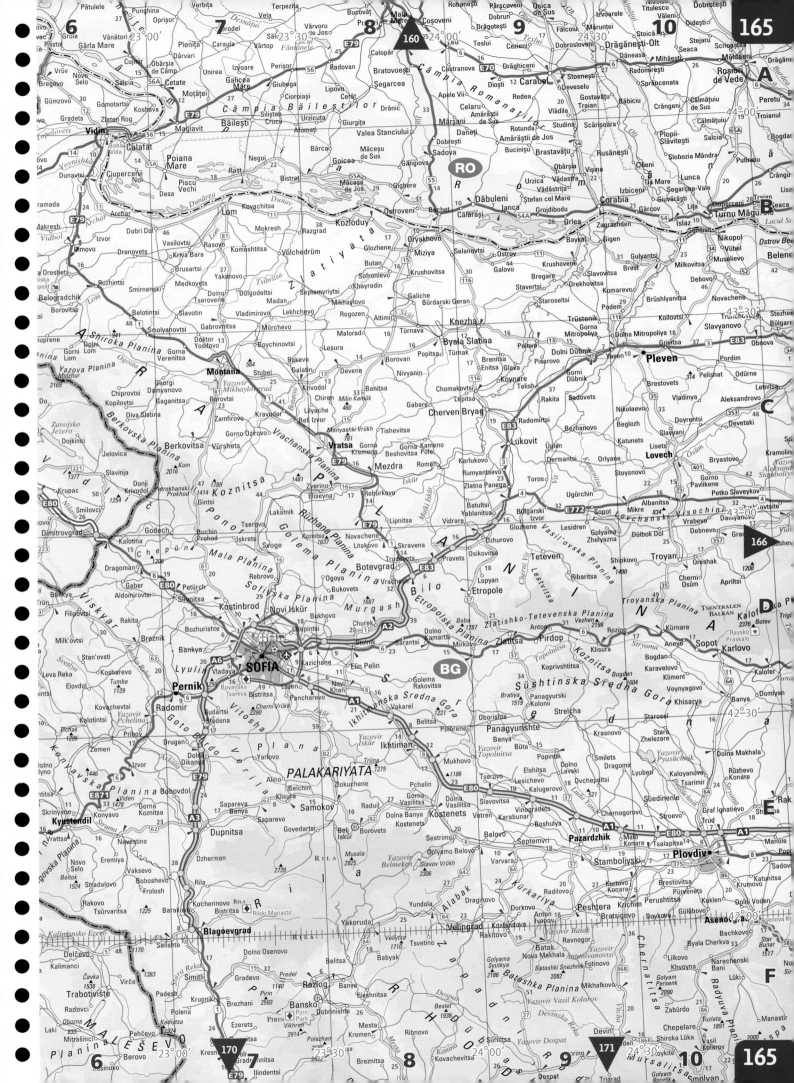

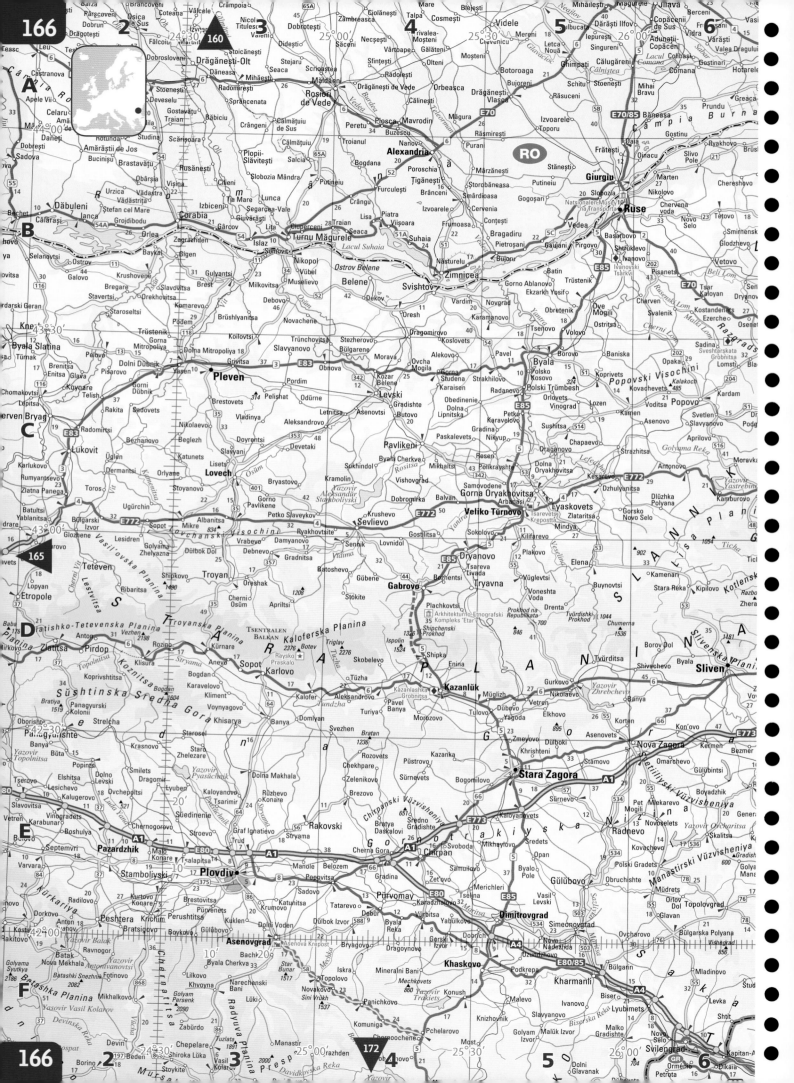

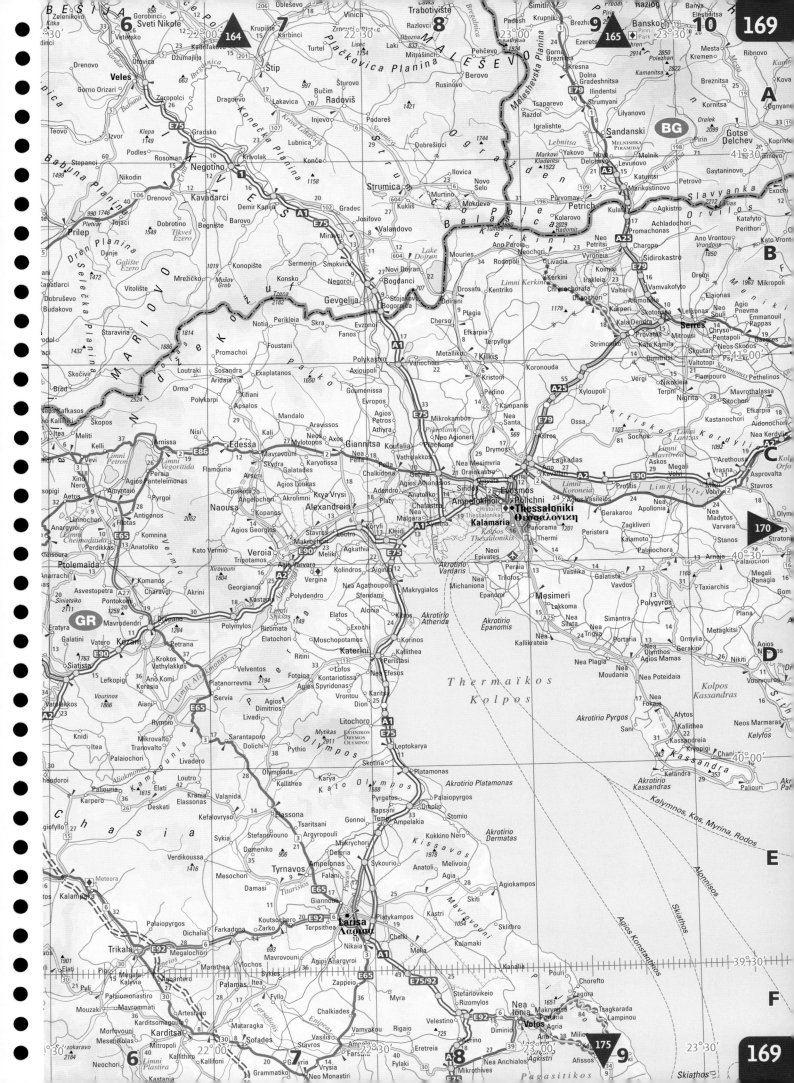

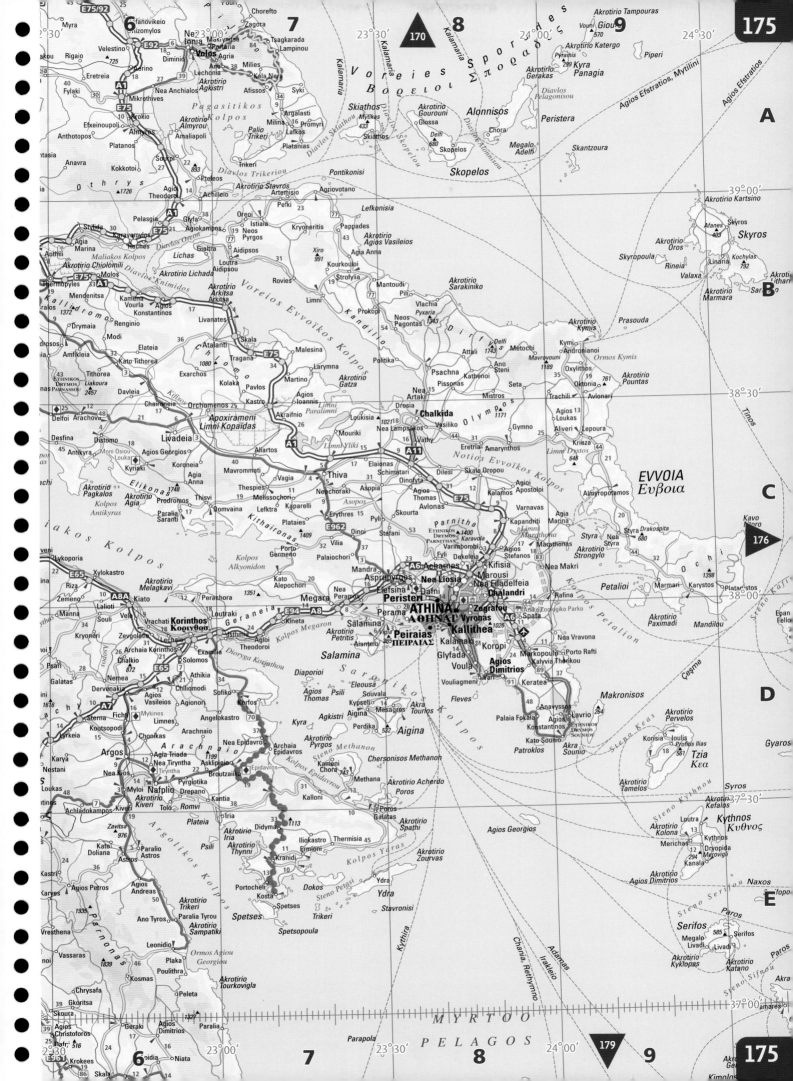

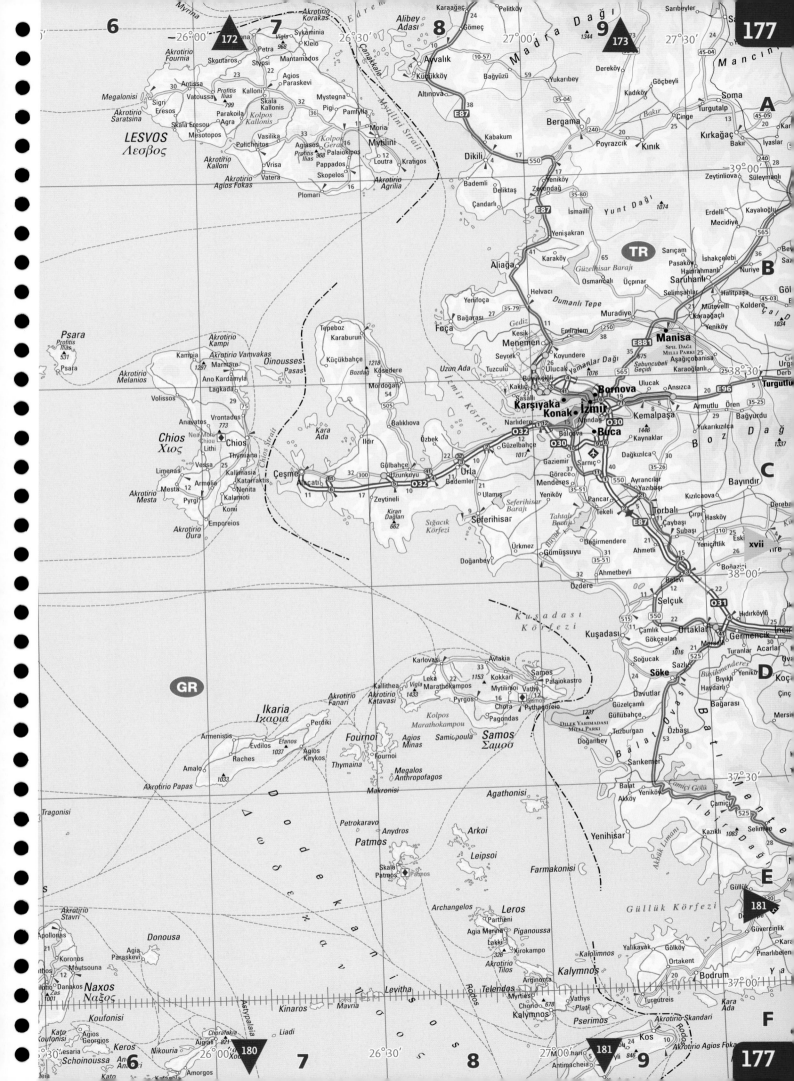

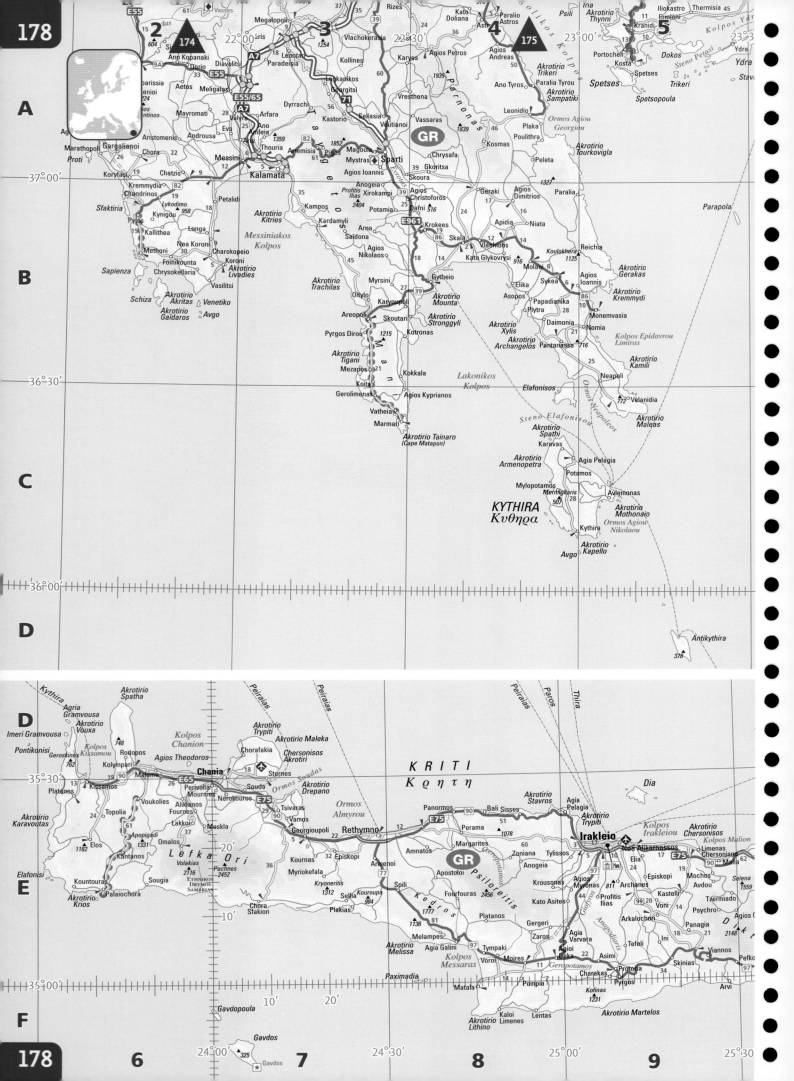

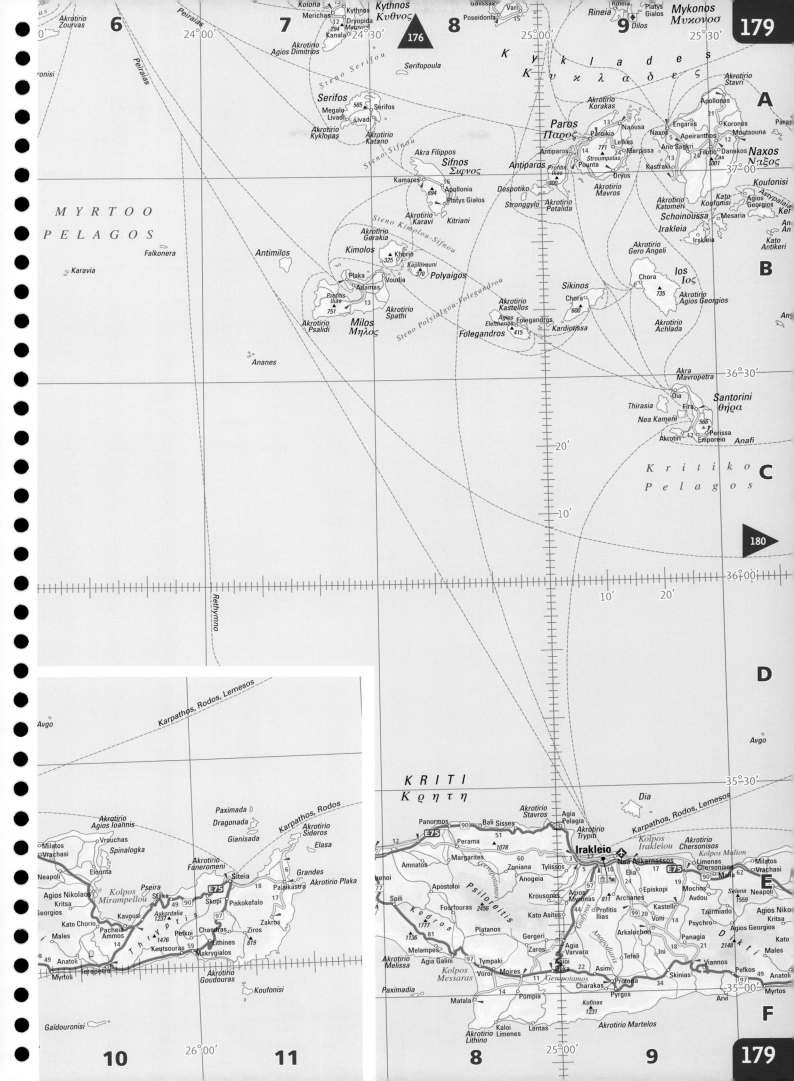

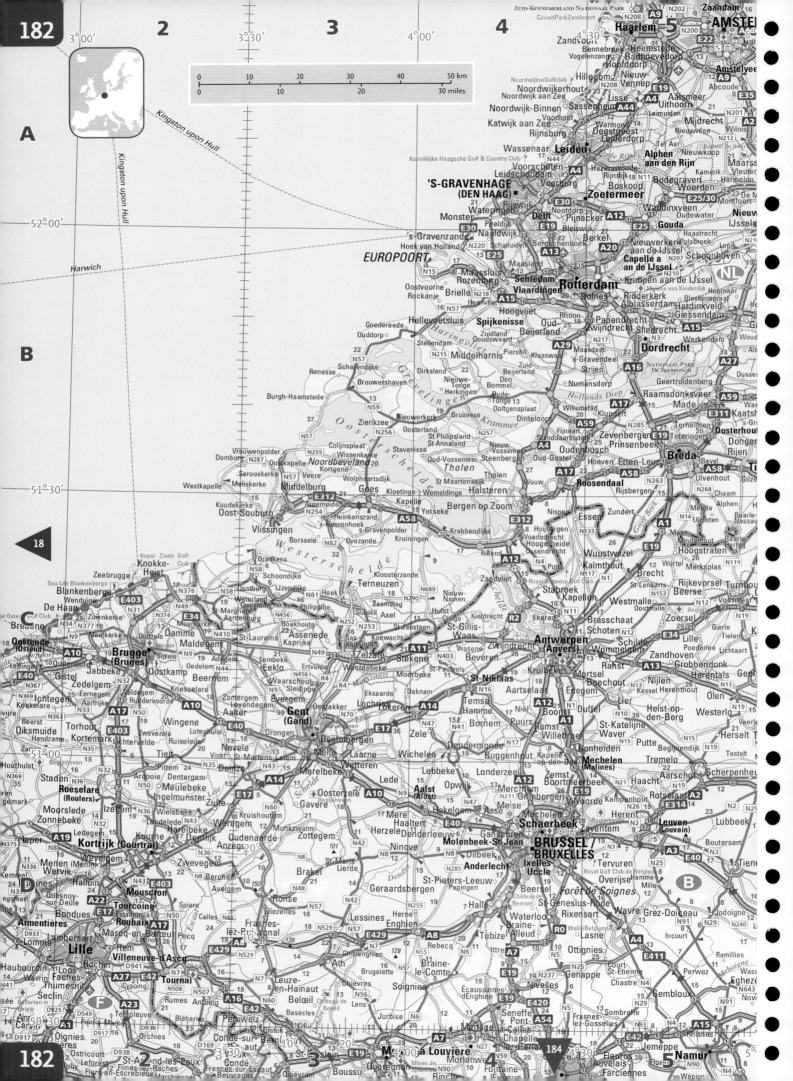

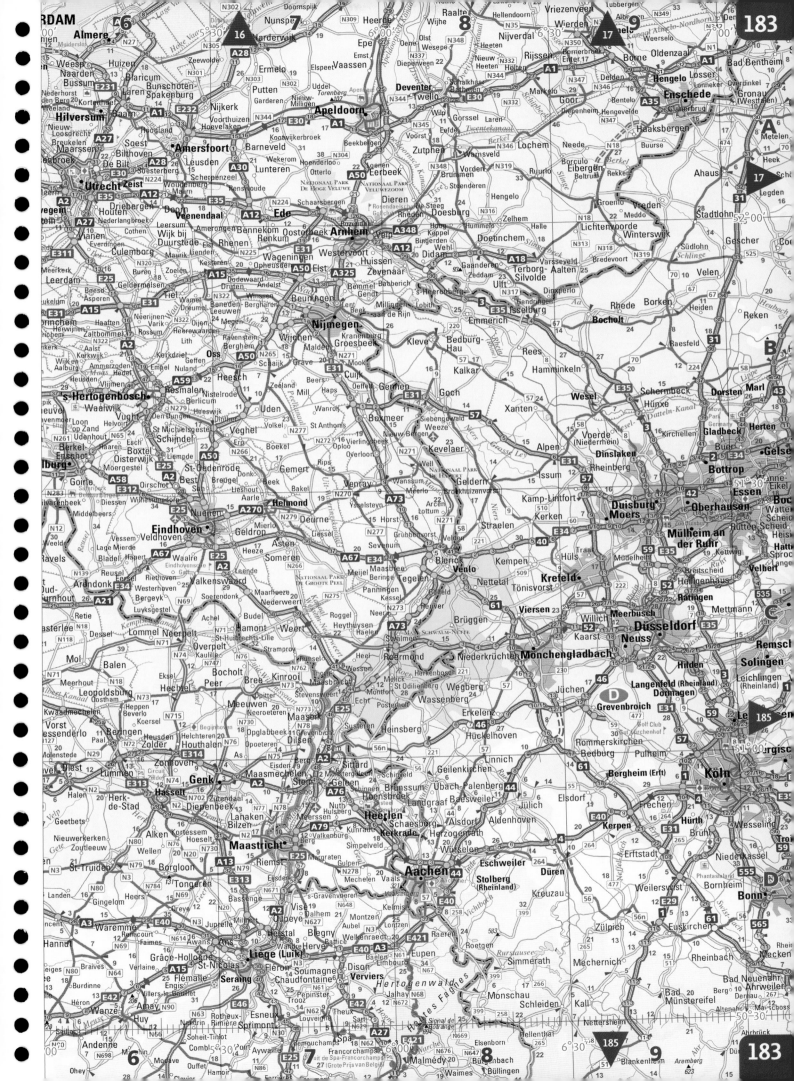

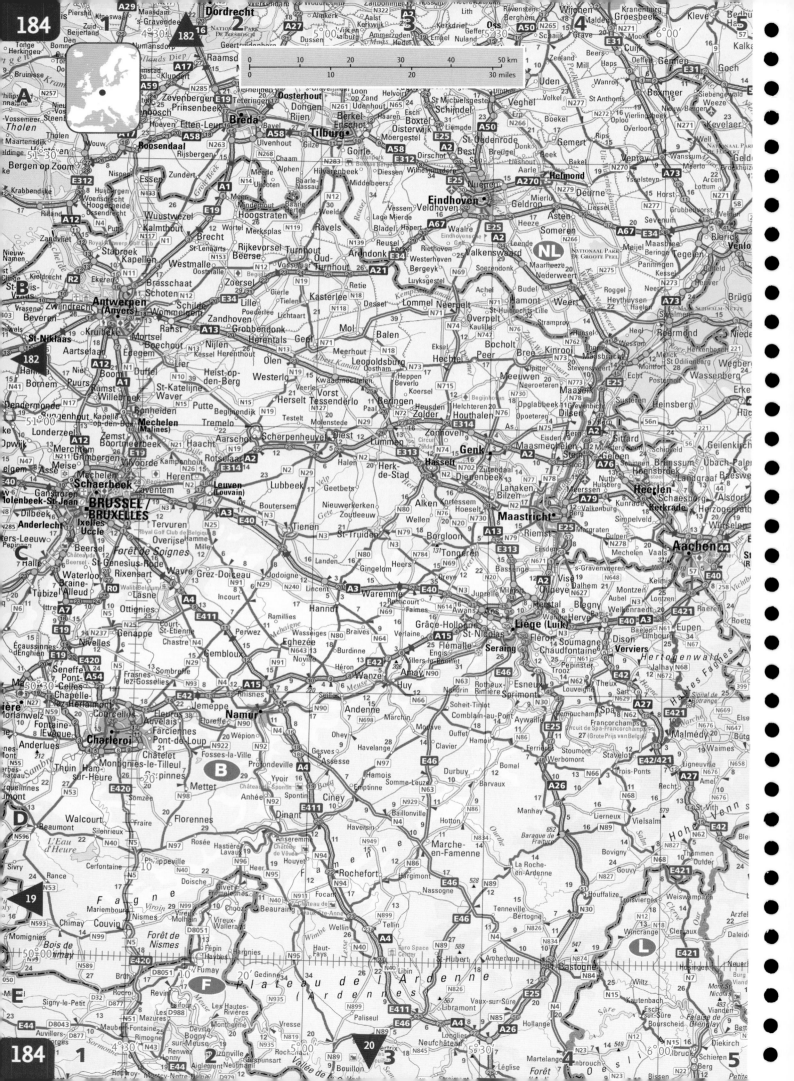

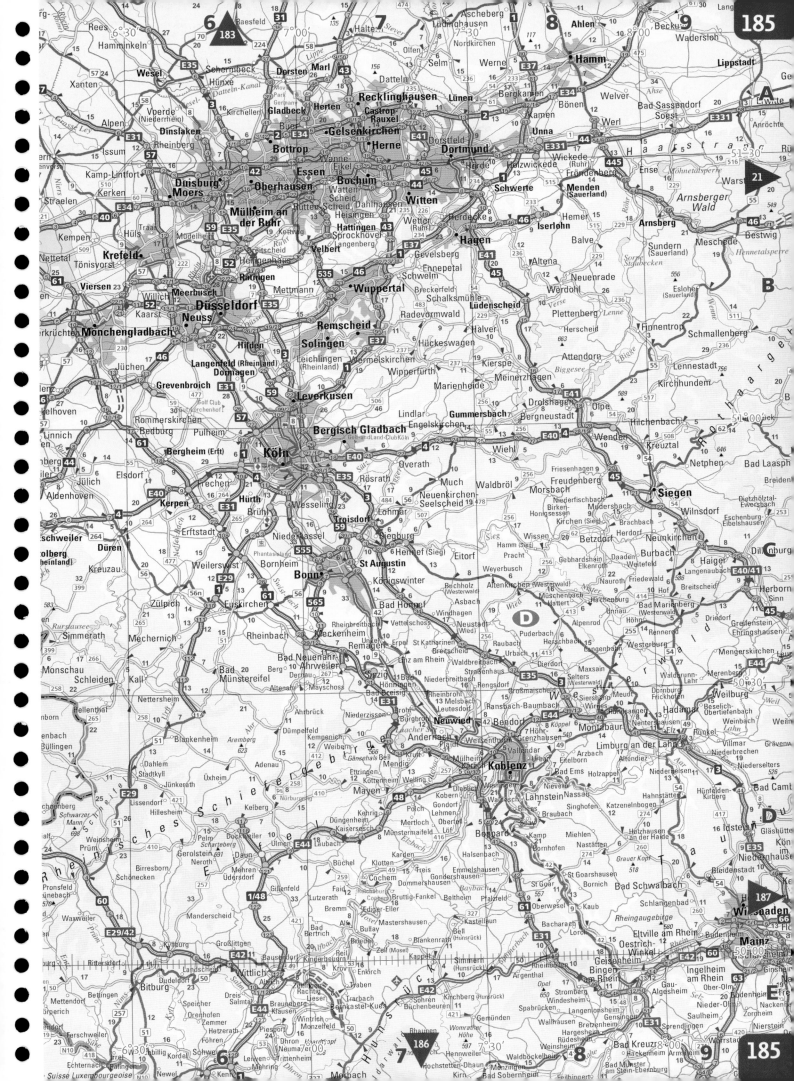

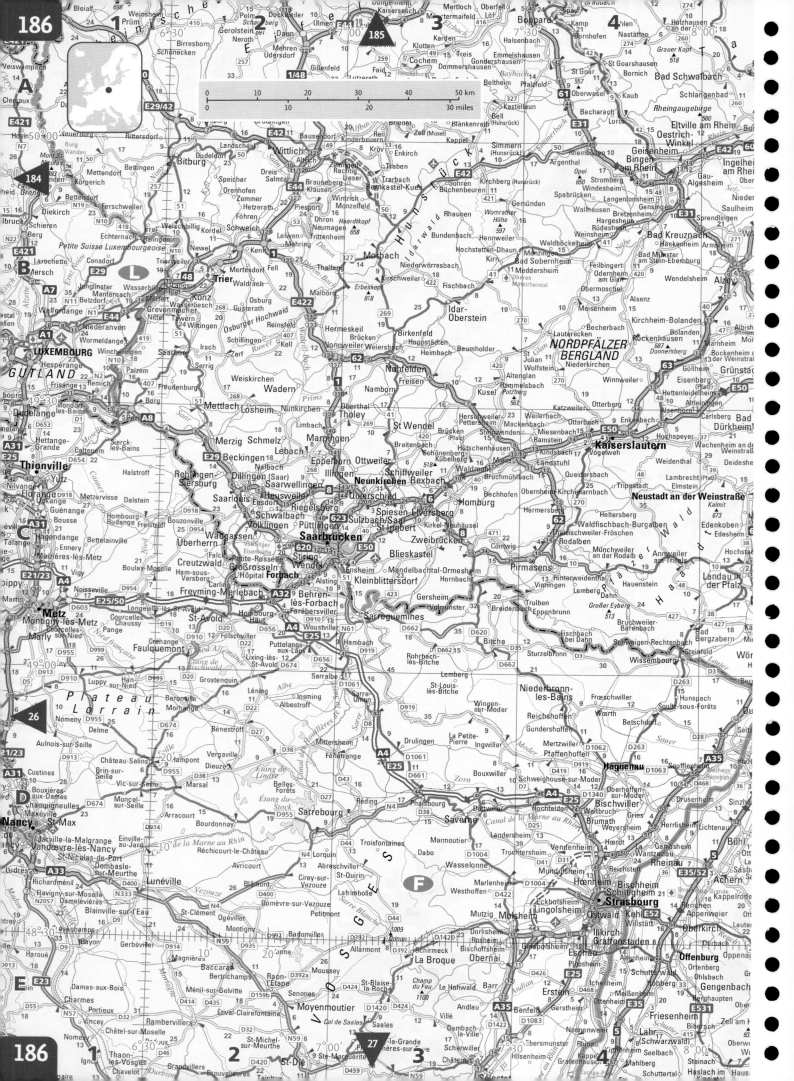

A

Aachen D 183 D8
Aalen D 187 D9
Aalsmeer NL 182 A5
Aalst B 182 D4
Aalst NL 183 B6
Aalten NL 183 B9
Aalter B 182 C2
Aardenburg NL 182 C2
Aarle NL 183 C7
Aarschot B 182 D5
Aartrijke B 182 C2
Aartselaar B 182 C4
Abcoude NL 182 A5
Abreschviller F 186 D3
Abtsgmünd D 187 D8
Achel B 183 C6
Achern D 186 D5
Achstetten D 187 E8
Adegem B 182 C2
Adelmannsfelden D 187 D8
Adelsheim D 187 C7
Adenau D 185 D6
Aglasterhausen D 187 C6
Ahaus D 183 A10
Ahlen D 185 A8
Ahrbrück D 183 E9
Aichhalden D 187 E6
Aiglemont F 184 E2
Albergen NL 183 A9
Albertshofen D 187 B9
Albestroff F 186 C2
Albisheim (Pfrimm) D 186 B5
Alblasserdam NL 182 B5
Aldenhoven D 183 D8
Alf D 185 D7
Alfdorf D 187 D8
Alken D 183 D7
Allarmont F 186 E3
Allmendingen D 187 E8
Almelo NL 183 A9
Almere NL 183 A6
Almkerk NL 182 B5
Alost B 182 D4
Alpen D 183 B9
Alpenrod D 185 C8
Alphen NL 182 C5
Alphen aan den Rijn NL 182 A5
Alpirsbach D 187 E5
Alsbach D 187 B6
Alsdorf D 183 D8
Alsenborn D 186 C4
Alsenz D 186 B4
Alsheim D 185 E9
Alsting F 186 C2
Altena D 185 B8
Altenahr D 183 D9
Altenbuch D 187 B7
Altendiez D 185 D8
Altenglan D 186 B3
Altenheim D 186 E4
Altenkirchen (Westerwald) D 185 C8
Altenstadt D 187 A6
Altensteig D 187 D6
Altheim (Alb) D 187 D7
Althengstett D 187 D6
Altleiningen D 186 B5
Altrich D 185 E6
Alzenau in Unterfranken D 187 A7
Alzey D 186 B4
Amay D 183 D6
Amberloup B 184 D4
Ameide NL 182 B5
Amel B 184 A5
Amerongen NL 183 B6
Amersfoort NL 183 A6
Ammerbuch D 187 D6
Ammerzoden NL 183 B6
Amnéville F 186 C1
Amorbach D 187 B7
Amstelveen NL 182 A5
Amsterdam NL 182 A5
Amstetten D 187 D8
Andelst NL 183 B7
Andenne B 183 E6
Anderlecht B 182 D4
Anderlues B 182 E4
Andernach D 185 D7
Andlau F 186 E3
Anhée B 184 D1
Annœullin F 182 C1
Annweiler am Trifels D 186 C4
Anröchte D 185 A9
Ans B 183 D7
Anseremme B 184 D2
Antoing B 182 D2
Antwerpen B 182 C4
Anvers B 182 C4
Anzegem B 182 D2
Apeldoorn NL 183 A7
Appenweier D 186 D4
Arcen NL 183 C8
Ardooie B 182 C2
Arendonk B 183 C6
Argenthal D 185 E8
Armentières F 182 D1
Armsheim D 185 E9
Arnemuiden NL 182 C3
Arnhem NL 183 B7
Arnsberg D 185 B9
Arnstein D 187 B8
Arracourt F 186 D2
Arry F 186 C1
Arzbach D 185 D8
Arzfeld D 185 D5
As B 183 C7
Asbach D 185 C7
Aschaffenburg D 187 B7
Ascheberg D 185 A8
Asperen NL 183 B6
Assamstadt D 187 C8
Asse B 182 D4
Assenede B 182 C3
Assesse B 184 D3
Asten NL 183 C7
Ath B 182 D3
Attendorn D 185 B8
Aub D 187 B9
Aubel B 183 D7
Aubenton F 184 E1
Auby F 182 E2
Aulnois-sur-Seille F 186 D1
Aura im Sinngrund D 187 A8
Auvelais B 182 E5
Auvillers-les-Forges F 184 E1
Avelgem B 182 C3
Avricourt F 186 D2

B

Awans B 183 D6
Axel NL 182 C3
Aywaille B 183 E7

Baarle-Hertog B 182 C5
Baarle-Nassau NL 182 C5
Baarn NL 183 A6
Babberich NL 183 B8
Babenhausen D 187 B6
Baccarat F 186 E2
Bacharach D 185 D8
Backnang D 187 D7
Bad Bentheim D 183 A10
Bad Bergzabern D 186 C4
Bad Berleburg D 185 B9
Bad Bertrich D 185 D7
Bad Boll D 187 D8
Bad Breisig D 185 C7
Bad Camberg D 185 D9
Bad Dürkheim D 186 B5
Bad Ems D 185 D8
Baden-Baden D 187 D5
Bad Friedrichshall D 187 C7
Bad Herrenalb D 187 D5
Badhoevedorp NL 182 A5
Bad Homburg vor der Höhe D 187 A6
Bad Honnef D 185 C7
Bad Hönningen D 185 C7
Bad Kissingen D 187 A9
Bad König D 187 B7
Bad Kreuznach D 185 E8
Bad Laasphe D 185 C9
Bad Liebenzell D 187 D6
Bad Marienberg (Westerwald) D 185 C8
Bad Mergentheim D 187 C8
Bad Münstereifel D 183 D9
Bad Neuenahr-Ahrweiler D 183 D10
Badonviller F 186 D2
Bad Orb D 187 A7
Bad Peterstal D 187 E5
Bad Rappenau D 187 C7
Bad Sassendorf D 185 A9
Bad Schönborn D 187 C6
Bad Schwalbach D 185 D9
Bad Sobernheim D 185 E8
Bad Überkingen D 187 D8
Bad Urach D 187 E7
Bad Vilbel D 187 A6
Bad Wildbad im Schwarzwald D 187 D6
Bad Wimpfen D 187 C7
Baelen B 183 D7
Baesweiler D 183 D8
Baiersbronn D 187 D5
Baillonville B 184 D3
Bakel NL 183 C7
Balingen D 187 E6
Balve D 185 B8
Bammental D 187 C6
Barneveld NL 183 A7
Baronville F 186 D2
Barr F 186 E3
Bartenstein D 187 C8
Bartholomä D 187 D8
Barvaux B 184 D3
Basècles B 182 D3
Bassenge B 183 D6
Bastogne B 184 D4
Bathmen NL 183 A8
Battice B 183 D7
Baumholder D 186 B3
Bausendorf D 185 D6
Bavel NL 182 B5
Bayon F 186 E1
Beaumont B 184 D1
Beauraing B 184 D2
Becherbach D 186 B4
Bechhofen D 186 C3
Bechtheim D 187 B5
Beckingen D 186 C2
Beckum D 185 A9
Bedburg D 183 D9
Bedburg-Hau D 183 B8
Beek NL 183 B7
Beek NL 183 B7
Beekbergen NL 183 A7
Beerfelden D 187 B6
Beernem B 182 C2
Beers NL 183 B7
Beerse B 182 C5
Beersel B 182 D4
Beerst B 182 C1
Beesd NL 183 B6
Begijnendijk B 182 C5
Behren-lès-Forbach F 186 C2
Beilstein D 187 C8
Beimerstetten D 187 E8
Belfeld NL 183 C8
Bell D 185 D7
Bell (Hunsrück) D 185 D7
Bellenberg D 187 E9
Belles-Forêts F 186 D2
Bellheim D 187 C5
Belœil B 182 D3
Beltheim D 185 D7
Beltrum NL 183 A9
Bemmel NL 183 B7
Bendorf D 185 D8
Beneden-Leeuwen NL 183 B6
Bénestroff F 186 D2
Benfeld F 186 E4
Bennebroek NL 182 A5
Bennekom NL 183 A7
Bensheim D 187 B6
Bentelo NL 183 A9
Berchem B 182 D3
Berg D 183 D9
Berg L 184 E5
Berg NL 183 D7
Berg NL 183 D7
Berg (Pfalz) D 187 D5
Bergen op Zoom NL 182 C4
Bergeyk NL 183 C6
Bergharen NL 183 B7
Berghaupten D 186 E4
Bergheim (Erft) D 183 D9
Berghem NL 183 B7
Berghülen D 187 D8
Bergisch Gladbach D 183 D10
Bergkamen D 185 A8
Bergneustadt D 185 B8
Bergschenhoek NL 182 B5
Bergtheim D 187 B9
Beringe NL 183 C7
Beringen B 183 C6

Berkel NL 182 B4
Berkel-Enschot NL 183 B6
Berlicum NL 183 B6
Bernissart B 182 E3
Bernkastel-Kues D 185 E7
Bernstadt D 187 D9
Bertrange L 184 B1
Bertrichamps F 186 E2
Bertrix B 184 E3
Beselich-Obertiefenbach D 185 D9
Besigheim D 187 D7
Bessenbach D 187 B7
Best NL 183 B6
Bestwig D 185 B9
Betschdorf F 186 D4
Bettelainville F 186 C1
Bettembourg L 186 B1
Bettendorf L 184 E5
Betzdorf D 185 C8
Betzdorf L 186 B1
Beuningen NL 183 B7
Beuvrages F 182 E2
Beveren B 182 C4
Beverlo B 183 C6
Bexbach D 186 C3
Biberach D 186 E5
Biblis D 187 B5
Bieber D 187 A7
Biebesheim am Rhein D 187 B5
Bietigheim D 187 D5
Bietigheim-Bissingen D 187 D7
Bièvre B 184 E3
Billigheim D 187 C7
Bilthoven NL 183 A6
Bilzen B 183 D7
Bingen am Rhein D 185 E8
Bingerden NL 183 B8
Birkenau D 187 B6
Birkenfeld D 186 B3
Birkenfeld D 187 B8
Birkenfeld D 187 D6
Birken-Honigsessen D 185 C8
Birresborn D 185 D6
Bischbrunn D 187 B7
Bischheim F 186 D4
Bischoffsheim F 186 E3
Bischofsheim D 185 E9
Bischwiller F 186 D4
Bisingen D 187 E6
Bissen L 184 E5
Bitburg D 185 E6
Bitche F 186 C3
Bladel NL 183 C6
Blainville-sur-l'Eau F 186 D1
Blâmont F 186 D2
Blankenberge B 182 C2
Blankenheim D 183 E9
Blankenrath D 185 D7
Blaricum NL 183 A6
Blaton B 182 D3
Blaubeuren D 187 E8
Blaufelden D 187 C8
Blaustein D 187 E8
Blegny B 183 D7
Bléharies B 182 D2
Bleialf D 185 D5
Bleidenstadt D 185 D9
Bleiswijk NL 182 A5
Blerick NL 183 C8
Bleskensgraaf NL 182 B5
Blieskastel D 186 C3
Blokzijl NL 183 A7
Bobenheim-Roxheim D 187 B5
Bocholt B 183 C7
Bocholt D 183 B9
Bochum D 185 B8
Bockenheim an der Weinstraße D 187 B5
Bodegraven NL 182 A5
Bodelshausen D 187 E6
Bodenheim D 185 E9
Boechout B 182 C4
Boekel NL 183 B7
Boekhoute B 182 C3
Bogny-sur-Meuse F 184 E2
Böhl D 187 C5
Bolanden D 186 B5
Bolnes NL 182 B5
Bomal B 184 D4
Bondorf D 187 D6
Bondues F 182 C1
Bönen D 185 A8
Bonheiden B 182 C5
Bonn D 183 D10
Bönnigheim D 187 C7
Boom B 182 C4
Boortmeerbeek B 182 D5
Boppard D 185 D7
Borculo NL 183 A9
Borg D 186 B1
Borgloon B 183 D6
Borken D 183 B9
Born NL 183 C7
Borne NL 183 A9
Bornem B 182 C4
Bornerbroek NL 183 A9
Bornheim D 183 D9
Bornhofen D 185 D8
Bornich D 185 D8
Borssele NL 182 C3
Boskoop NL 182 A5
Bottrop D 183 B9
Bouillon B 184 E3
Boulay-Moselle F 186 C1
Bourdonnay F 186 D2
Bourscheid L 184 E5
Bousse F 186 C1
Boussu B 182 E3
Boutersem B 182 D5
Bouxières-aux-Dames F 186 D1
Bouxwiller F 186 D3
Bouzonville F 186 C2
Bovigny B 184 D4
Boxberg D 187 C8
Boxmeer NL 183 B7
Boxtel NL 183 B6
Brachbach D 185 C8
Brackenheim D 187 C7
Braine-l'Alleud B 182 D4
Braine-le-Comte B 182 D4
Braives B 183 D6
Brasschaat B 182 C4
Braubach D 185 D8
Brauneberg D 185 E6
Braunfels D 185 C9
Braunsbach D 187 C8
Brecht B 182 C5
Breckerfeld D 185 B7

Breda NL 182 B5
Bredene B 182 C1
Bredevoort NL 183 B9
Bree B 183 C7
Breidenbach F 186 C3
Breitenbach D 186 C3
Breitscheid D 183 C9
Breitscheid D 185 C7
Breitscheid D 185 C7
Bremm D 185 D7
Brensbach D 187 B6
Breskens NL 182 C3
Bretten D 187 C6
Bretzenheim D 185 E8
Bretzfeld D 187 C7
Breuberg-Neustadt D 187 B7
Breugel NL 183 B7
Breukelen NL 183 A6
Briedel D 185 D7
Brielle NL 182 B4
Brin-sur-Seille F 186 D1
Broekhuizenvorst NL 183 C8
Brohl D 185 D7
Brouvelieures F 186 E2
Brouwershaven NL 182 B3
Bruchköbel D 187 A6
Bruchmühlbach D 186 C3
Bruchsal D 187 C6
Bruchweiler-Bärenbach D 186 C4
Brücken D 186 B3
Brücken (Pfalz) D 186 C3
Brugelette B 182 D3
Bruges B 182 C2
Brugge B 182 C2
Brüggen D 183 C8
Brühl D 183 D9
Brühl D 187 C6
Bruinisse NL 182 B4
Brûly B 184 E2
Brumath F 186 D4
Brummen NL 183 A8
Brunehamel F 184 E1
Brunssum NL 183 D7
Brussel B 182 D4
Brücken D 186 B3
Bruttig-Fankel D 185 D7
Bruxelles B 182 D4
Büchel D 185 D7
Buchen (Odenwald) D 187 B7
Büchenbeuren D 185 E7
Buchholz (Westerwald) D 185 C7
Budel NL 183 C7
Büdenheim D 185 D9
Büdesheim D 185 E5
Buer D 183 B10
Buggenhout B 182 C4
Bühl D 186 D5
Bühlertal D 187 D5
Bühlertann D 187 C8
Bühlerzell D 187 C8
Bullay D 185 D7
Büllingen B 183 E8
Bundenbach D 185 E7
Bunschoten-Spakenburg NL 183 A6
Burbach D 185 C9
Burdinne B 183 D6
Buren NL 183 B6
Burgbrohl D 185 D7
Burgh-Haamstede NL 182 B3
Burgsinn D 187 A8
Burladingen D 187 E7
Bürstadt D 187 B5
Bütgenbach B 183 E8
Büttelborn D 187 B6
Bütthard D 187 B8
Buurse NL 183 A9

C

Calw D 187 D6
Capelle aan de IJssel NL 182 B5
Carling F 186 C2
Carlsberg D 186 C5
Carvin F 182 E1
Castrop-Rauxel D 185 A7
Cattenom F 186 C1
Ceintrey F 186 D1
Celles B 184 D2
Cerfontaine B 184 D1
Chaam NL 182 C5
Chaligny F 186 D1
Champigneulles F 186 D1
Chapelle-lez-Herlaimont B 182 E4
Charleroi B 182 E4
Charmes F 186 E1
Chastre B 182 D5
Château-Salins F 186 D2
Châtelet B 182 E4
Châtel-sur-Moselle F 186 E1
Châtenois F 186 E3
Chaudfontaine B 183 D7
Chavelot F 186 E1
Chièvres B 182 D3
Chimay B 184 D1
Chooz F 184 D2
Ciney B 184 D3
Cirey-sur-Vezouze F 186 D2
Clavier B 183 E6
Clervaux L 184 D5
Clinge NL 182 C4
Cochem D 185 D7
Coesfeld D 183 B10
Colijnsplaat NL 182 B3
Colroy-la-Grande F 186 E3
Comblain-au-Pont B 183 E7
Comines B 182 D1
Condé-sur-l'Escaut F 182 E3
Consdorf L 186 B1
Contwig D 186 C3
Cothen NL 183 A6
Courcelles B 182 E4
Courcelles-Chaussy F 186 C1
Courcelles-sur-Nied F 186 C1
Courrières F 182 E1
Courtrai B 182 D2
Court-St-Etienne B 182 D5
Couvin B 184 D2
Crailsheim D 187 C9
Créhange F 186 C2
Creutzwald F 186 C2
Crévéchamps F 186 D1
Cuijk NL 183 B7
Culemborg NL 183 B6
Custines F 186 D1
Cysoing F 182 D2

D

Daaden D 185 C8
Dabo F 186 D3
Dahlem D 185 D6
Dahlhausen D 183 C10
Dahn D 186 C4
Daknam B 182 C3
Daleiden D 184 D5
Dalhem B 183 D7
Dalstein F 186 C1
Damas-aux-Bois F 186 E1
Dambach-la-Ville F 186 E3
Damelevières F 186 D1
Damme D 182 C2
Darmstadt D 187 B6
Datteln D 185 A7
Daun D 185 D6
De Bilt NL 183 A6
Deerlijk B 182 D2
Degginden D 187 E8
De Haan B 182 C2
Deidesheim D 187 C5
Deinze B 182 D3
Delden NL 183 A9
Delft NL 182 A4
Delme F 186 D1
Den Bommel NL 182 B4
Denderleeuw B 182 D4
Dendermonde B 182 D4
Den Dungen NL 183 B6
Denekamp NL 183 A10
Den Haag NL 182 A4
Denkendorf D 187 D7
Dentergem B 182 D2
Dernau D 183 D10
Dessel B 183 C6
De Steeg NL 183 A8
Destelbergen B 182 C3
Dettelbach D 187 B9
Dettenhausen D 187 D7
Dettingen an der Erms D 187 D7
Dettwiller F 186 D3
Deurne NL 183 C7
Deventer NL 183 A8
Deville F 184 E2
Dhron D 185 E6
Didam NL 183 B8
Dieblich D 185 D7
Dieburg D 187 B6
Diekirch L 184 E5
Dielheim D 187 C6
Diemen NL 182 A5
Dienheim D 185 E9
Diepenbeek B 183 D6
Diepenheim NL 183 A9
Diepenveen NL 183 A8
Dierdorf D 185 C8
Dieren NL 183 A8
Diessen NL 183 C6
Diest B 183 D6
Dietzenbach D 187 B6
Dietzhölztal-Ewersbach D 185 C9
Dieuze F 186 D2
Dikkebus B 182 C1
Diksmuide B 182 C1
Dilbeek B 182 D4
Dillenburg D 185 C9
Dillingen (Saar) D 186 C2
Dilsen B 183 C7
Dinant B 184 D2
Dinklage D 182 A5
Dinslaken D 183 B9
Dinteloord NL 182 B4
Dinther NL 183 B6
Dinxperlo NL 183 B8
Dirksland NL 182 B4
Dirmstein D 187 B5
Dison B 183 D7
Ditzingen D 187 D7
Dockweiler D 185 D6
Dodewaard NL 183 B7
Doesburg NL 183 A8
Doetinchem NL 183 B8
Doische B 184 D2
Domburg NL 182 B3
Domèvre-sur-Vezouze F 186 D2
Dommershausen D 185 D7
Dongen NL 182 B5
Donk NL 183 C7
Donzdorf D 187 D8
Doorn NL 183 A6
Doornspijk NL 183 A7
Dordrecht NL 182 B5
Dorlisheim F 186 D3
Dormagen D 183 C9
Dornburg-Frickhofen D 185 C9
Dornhan D 187 E6
Dornstadt D 187 E8
Dornstetten D 187 E5
Dorsten D 183 B9
Dorstfeld D 185 A7
Dörzbach D 187 C8
Dossenheim D 187 C6
Dreieich D 187 B6
Dreis B 184 D3
Drensteinfurt D 185 A8
Dreumel NL 183 B6
Driebergen NL 183 A6
Driedorf D 185 C9
Drolshagen D 185 B8
Drongen B 182 C3
Drulingen F 186 D3
Drusenheim F 186 D4
Druten NL 183 B7
Dudelange L 186 C1
Dudeldorf D 185 E6
Duffel B 182 C5
Duisburg D 183 C9
Dümpelfeld D 185 D7
Düngenheim D 185 D7
Durbach D 186 D4
Durbuy B 184 D3
Düren D 183 D8
Durmersheim D 187 D5
Düsseldorf D 183 C9
Dussen NL 182 B5

E

Eberbach D 187 C6
Ebersbach an der Fils D 187 D8
Ebersmunster F 186 E4
Ebhausen D 187 D6
Écaussinnes-d'Enghien B 182 D4

Echt NL 183 C7
Echternach L 185 E5
Eckbolsheim F 186 D4
Ede NL 183 A7
Edegem B 182 C4
Edenkoben D 186 C5
Edesheim D 186 C5
Eefde NL 183 A8
Eeklo B 182 C3
Eerbeek NL 183 A8
Eernegem B 182 C2
Eersel NL 183 C6
Eggenstein-Leopoldshafen D 187 C5
Eghezée B 182 D5
Ehingen (Donau) D 187 E8
Ehningen D 187 D6
Ehringshausen D 185 C9
Eibelstadt D 187 B9
Eibergen NL 183 A9
Eich D 187 B5
Eichenbühl D 187 B7
Eijsden NL 183 D7
Eindhoven NL 183 C6
Einville-au-Jard F 186 D1
Eisden B 183 D7
Eisenberg (Pfalz) D 186 B5
Eislingen (Fils) D 187 D8
Eitelborn D 185 D8
Eitorf D 185 C7
Ekeren B 182 C4
Eksaarde B 182 C3
Eksel B 183 C6
Elchingen D 187 E9
Elfershausen D 187 A8
Elkenroth D 185 C8
Ellenberg D 187 C9
Ellezelles B 182 D3
Ellwangen (Jagst) D 187 D9
Elsdorf D 183 D9
Elsenborn B 183 E8
Elsenfeld D 187 B7
Elsloo NL 183 D7
Elspeet NL 183 A7
Elst NL 183 B6
Elst NL 183 B7
Eltville am Rhein D 185 D9
Elz D 185 D9
Emmelshausen D 185 D8
Emmerich D 183 B8
Empel NL 183 B6
Empfingen D 187 E6
Emptinne B 184 D3
Emst NL 183 A7
Engden D 183 A10
Engelskirchen D 185 C7
Enghien B 182 D4
Engis B 183 D6
Engstingen D 187 E7
Eningen unter Achalm D 187 E7
Enkenbach D 186 C4
Enkhout NL 183 E7
Ennepetal D 185 B7
Ennery F 186 C1
Enschede NL 183 A9
Ensdorf D 185 B9
Ense D 185 B9
Ensheim D 186 C3
Enter NL 183 A9
Enzklösterle D 187 D5
Epe NL 183 A7
Epfendorf D 187 E6
Eppelborn D 186 C2
Eppelheim D 187 C6
Eppenbrunn D 186 C4
Eppertshausen D 187 B6
Eppingen D 187 C6
Eppstein D 187 A5
Erbach D 187 B7
Erbach D 187 E8
Erftstadt D 183 D9
Erkelenz D 183 C8
Erlenbach am Main D 187 B7
Ermelo NL 183 A7
Erndtebrück D 185 C9
Erp NL 183 B7
Erpel D 185 C7
Erquelinnes B 184 D1
Erstein F 186 E4
Ertvelde B 182 C3
Erwitte D 185 A9
Erzhausen D 187 B6
Esch NL 183 B6
Eschau F 186 E4
Eschau D 187 B7
Eschborn D 187 A6
Eschenburg-Eibelshausen D 185 C9
Esch-sur-Sûre L 184 E4
Eschweiler D 183 D8
Eslohe (Sauerland) D 185 B9
Esneux B 183 E7
Essen B 182 C4
Essen D 183 C10
Essingen D 187 D9
Esslingen am Neckar D 187 D7
Estaimpuis B 182 D2
Estenfeld D 187 B9
Étival-Clairefontaine F 186 E2
Ettelbruck L 184 E5
Ettenheim D 186 E4
Etten-Leur NL 182 B5
Ettlingen D 187 D5
Ettringen D 185 D7
Eubigheim D 187 B8
Euerdorf D 187 A8
Eupen B 183 D8
Euskirchen D 183 D9
Eußenheim D 187 A8
Eutingen im Gäu D 187 E6
Everdingen NL 183 B6
Evergem B 182 C3

F

Faches-Thumesnil F 182 D2
Faid D 185 D7
Faimes B 183 D6
Falck F 186 C2
Fameck F 186 C1
Farcienes B 182 E5
Farébersviller F 186 C2
Faulbach D 187 B7
Faulquemont F 186 C2
Feilbingert D 185 E8
Fell D 186 B2
Fellbach D 187 D7
Fénétrange F 186 D3
Fépin F 184 D2
Ferrières B 183 E7

Ferschweiler D 185 E5
Fichtenberg D 187 D8
Fijnaart NL 182 B4
Finnentrop D 185 B8
Fischbach D 185 B3
Fischbach bei Dahn D 186 C4
Flavigny-sur-Moselle F 186 D1
Flein D 187 C7
Flémalle D 183 D6
Fléron B 183 D7
Flers-en-Escrebieux F 182 E2
Fleurus B 182 E5
Flines-lez-Raches F 182 E2
Florange F 186 C1
Floreffe B 182 E5
Florennes B 184 D2
Flörsbach D 187 A7
Flörsheim am Main D 187 A5
Flörsheim-Dalsheim D 187 B5
Focant B 184 D2
Föhren D 185 E6
Folschviller F 186 C2
Fontaine-l'Évêque B 182 E4
Forbach D 187 D5
Forbach F 186 C2
Forchtenberg D 187 C8
Forst D 187 C6
Fosses-la-Ville B 184 D2
Fraire B 184 D2
Frameries B 182 E3
Frammersbach D 187 A7
Francorchamps B 183 E7
Frankenthal (Pfalz) D 187 B5
Frankfurt am Main D 187 A6
Frasnes-lez-Buissenal B 182 D3
Frasnes-lez-Gosselies B 182 D4
Frechen D 183 D9
Freinsheim D 187 B5
Freisen D 186 B3
Freistroff F 186 C1
Fresnes-sur-Escaut F 182 E3
Freudenberg D 185 C8
Freudenberg D 187 B7
Freudenburg D 186 B2
Freudenstadt D 187 E5
Freyming-Merlebach F 186 C2
Friedewald D 185 C8
Friedrichsdorf D 187 A6
Friesenhagen D 185 C8
Friesenheim D 186 E4
Frisange L 186 B1
Fræschwiller F 186 D4
Fromelennes F 184 D2
Fröndenberg D 185 B8
Frouard F 186 D1
Fumay F 184 D2
Fürth D 187 B6

G

Gaanderen NL 183 B8
Gaggenau D 187 D5
Gaildorf D 187 D8
Gambsheim F 186 D4
Gammertingen D 187 E7
Gand B 182 C3
Ganshoren B 182 D4
Garderen NL 183 A7
Gärtringen D 187 D6
Gau-Algesheim D 185 E9
Gaukönigshofen D 187 B8
Gau-Odernheim D 185 E9
Gavere B 182 D3
Gebhardshain D 185 C8
Gechingen D 187 D6
Gedinne B 184 E2
Geel B 183 C6
Geertruidenberg NL 182 B5
Geesteren NL 183 A9
Geetbets B 183 D6
Geffen NL 183 B6
Geilenkirchen D 183 D8
Geiselbach D 187 A7
Geisenheim D 185 E8
Geislingen D 187 E6
Geislingen an der Steige D 187 D8
Geispolsheim F 186 D4
Gelchsheim D 187 B9
Geldermalsen NL 183 B6
Geldern D 183 B8
Geldersheim D 187 A9
Geldrop NL 183 C7
Geleen NL 183 D7
Gelnhausen D 187 A7
Gelsenkirchen D 183 B10
Gembloux B 182 D5
Gemert NL 183 B7
Gemmingen D 187 C6
Gemünd D 185 D5
Gemünden am Main D 187 A8
Genappe B 182 D4
Gendringen NL 183 B8
Gendt NL 183 B7
Gengenbach D 186 E5
Genk B 183 D7
Gennep NL 183 B7
Gensingen D 185 E8
Gent B 182 C3
Geraardsbergen B 182 D3
Gerabronn D 187 C8
Gerbéviller F 186 E2
Gerbrunn D 187 B8
Gerchsheim D 187 B8
Gerlingen D 187 D7
Germersheim D 187 C5
Gernsbach D 187 D5
Gernsheim D 187 B5
Gerolstein D 185 D6
Gerpinnes B 184 D2
Gerstetten D 187 D9
Gerstheim F 186 E4
Gescher D 183 B10
Gespunsart F 184 E2
Gesves B 184 D3
Gevelsberg D 185 B7
Ghislenghien B 182 D3
Giebelstadt D 187 B8
Gierle B 182 C5
Gillenfeld D 185 D6
Gilze NL 182 B5
Gingelom B 183 D6
Gingen an der Fils D 187 D8
Ginsheim D 185 E9
Gistel B 182 C1
Givet F 184 D2
Gladbeck D 183 B9
Glanerbrug NL 183 A9
Gläshütten D 187 A5
Goch D 183 B8

Goddelau D 187 B6
Goedereede NL 182 B3
Goes NL 182 B3
Göggingen D 187 D8
Goirle NL 183 B6
Göllheim D 186 B5
Gomadingen D 187 E7
Gomaringen D 187 E7
Gondelsheim D 187 C6
Gondershausen D 185 D7
Gondorf D 185 D7
Goor NL 183 A9
Göppingen D 187 D8
Gorinchem NL 182 B5
Gorssel NL 183 A8
Gorxheimertal D 187 B6
Gouda NL 182 A5
Goudswaard NL 182 B4
Gouvy B 184 D4
Graben-Neudorf D 187 C5
Grâce-Hollogne B 183 D6
Gräfendorf D 187 A8
Grafenrheinfeld D 187 B9
Grandvillers F 186 E2
Grave NL 183 B7
Greifenstein D 185 C9
Grevenbicht NL 183 C7
Grevenbroich D 183 C9
Grevenmacher L 186 B1
Grez-Doiceau B 182 D5
Gries F 186 D4
Griesbach D 187 E5
Griesheim D 187 B6
Grimbergen B 182 D4
Grobbendonk B 182 C5
Groenlo NL 183 A9
Groesbeek NL 183 B7
Gronau (Westfalen) D 183 A10
Groß-Bieberau D 187 B6
Großbottwar D 187 D7
Grosselfingen D 187 E6
Groß-Gerau D 187 B5
Großheubach D 187 B7
Großlangheim D 187 B9
Großlittgen D 185 D6
Großmaischeid D 185 C8
Großostheim D 187 B7
Großrinderfeld D 187 B8
Groß-Rohrheim D 187 B5
Großrosseln D 186 C2
Groß-Umstadt D 187 B6
Großwallstadt D 187 B7
Groß-Zimmern D 187 B6
Grostenquin F 186 D2
Grubbenvorst NL 183 C8
Grünsfeld D 187 B8
Grünstadt D 187 B5
Gschwend D 187 D8
Guénange F 186 C1
Güglingen D 187 C6
Gulpen NL 183 D7
Gummersbach D 185 B8
Gundelsheim D 187 C7
Gundershoffen F 186 D4
Guntersblum D 185 E9
Güntersleben D 187 B8
Gusterath D 186 B2
Gutach (Schwarzwaldbahn) D 187 E5

H

Haacht B 182 D5
Haaften NL 183 B6
Haaksbergen NL 183 A9
Haaltert B 182 D4
Haaren NL 183 B6
Haarlem NL 182 A5
Haastrecht NL 182 B5
Hachenburg D 185 C8
Hackenheim D 185 E8
Hadamar D 185 D9
Haelen NL 183 C7
Hagen D 185 B7
Hagenbach D 187 C5
Hagondange F 186 C1
Haguenau F 186 D4
Hahnstätten D 185 D9
Haibach D 187 B7
Haiger D 185 C9
Haigerloch D 187 E6
Haiterbach D 187 D6
Halen B 183 D6
Halfweg NL 182 A5
Halle B 182 D4
Halle NL 183 B8
Halluin B 182 D2
Halsenbach D 185 D8
Halsteren NL 182 B4
Halstroff F 186 C1
Haltern D 183 B10
Halver D 185 B7
Hambach F 186 C3
Hambrücken D 187 C6
Hamm D 185 A8
Hamm (Sieg) D 185 C8
Hamme B 182 C4
Hammelburg D 187 A8
Hamme-Mille B 182 D5
Hamminkeln D 183 B9
Hamoir B 183 E7
Hamois B 184 D3
Hamont B 183 C7
Hampont F 186 D2
Ham-sous-Varsberg F 186 C2
Ham-sur-Heure B 184 D1
Hanau D 187 A6
Handzame B 182 C2
Hannut B 183 D6
Han-sur-Nied F 186 D1
Hapert NL 183 C6
Haps NL 183 B7
Harderwijk NL 183 A7
Hardheim D 187 B7
Hardinxveld-Giessendam NL 182 B5
Harelbeke B 182 D2
Hargesheim D 185 E8
Hargimont B 184 D3
Hargnies F 184 D2
Harmelen NL 182 A5
Harnes F 182 E1
Haroué F 186 E1
Harthausen D 187 C5
Haslach im Kinzigtal D 186 E5
Hasselt B 183 D6
Haßloch D 187 C5
Haßmersheim D 187 C7
Hastière-Lavaux B 184 D2
Hattersheim am Main D 187 A5
Hattert D 185 C8
Hattingen D 183 C10
Hatzenbühl D 187 C5
Haubourdin F 182 D1
Hauenstein D 186 C4
Hausach D 187 E5
Hausen bei Würzburg D 187 B9
Haut-Fays B 184 D3
Havelange B 184 D3
Haversin B 184 D3
Hayange F 186 C1
Haybes F 184 D2
Hayingen D 187 E7
Hazerswoude-Rijndijk NL 182 A5
Hechingen D 187 E6
Hechtel B 183 C6
Heddesheim D 187 C6
Hedel NL 183 B6
Heek D 183 A10
Heel NL 183 C7
Heemstede NL 182 A5
Heenvliet NL 182 B4
Heer B 184 D2
Heerde NL 183 A8
Heerewaarden NL 183 B6
Heerlen NL 183 D7
Heers B 183 D6
Heesch NL 183 B7
Heeswijk NL 183 B6
Heeten NL 183 A8
Heeze NL 183 C7
Heidelberg D 187 C6
Heiden D 183 B9
Heidenheim an der Brenz D 187 D9
Heigenbrücken D 187 A7
Heilbronn D 187 C7
Heiligenhaus D 183 C9
Heimbach D 186 B3
Heimbuchenthal D 187 B7
Heimsheim D 187 D6
Heinkenszand NL 182 C3
Heino NL 183 A8
Heinsberg D 183 C8
Heisingen D 183 C10
Heist-op-den-Berg B 182 C5
Hekelgem B 182 D4
Helchteren B 183 C6
Heldenbergen D 187 A6
Hellendoorn NL 183 A8
Hellenthal D 183 E8
Hellevoetsluis NL 182 B4
Helmond NL 183 C7
Helmstadt D 187 B8
Heltersberg D 186 C4
Helvoirt NL 183 B6
Hem F 182 D2
Hemer D 185 B8
Hemsbach D 187 B6
Hengelo NL 183 A8
Hengelo NL 183 A9
Hengevelde NL 183 A9
Hénin-Beaumont F 182 E1
Hennef (Sieg) D 185 C7
Hennweiler D 185 E7
Heppen B 183 C6
Heppenheim (Bergstraße) D 187 B6
Herbeumont B 184 E3
Herborn D 185 C9
Herbrechtingen D 187 D9
Herdecke D 185 B7
Herdorf D 185 C8
Herent B 182 D5
Herentals B 182 C5
Herenthout B 182 C5
Herk-de-Stad B 183 D6
Herkenbosch NL 183 C8
Herkingen NL 182 B4
Hermersberg D 186 C4
Hermeskeil D 186 B2
Herne B 182 D4
Herne D 185 A7
Héron B 183 D6
Herrenberg D 187 D6
Herrlisheim F 186 D4
Herschbach D 185 C8
Herscheid D 185 B8
Herschweiler-Pettersheim D 186 C3
Herselt B 182 C5
Herstal B 183 D7
Herten D 183 B10
Herve B 183 D7
Herwijnen NL 183 B6
Herzele B 182 D3
Herzogenrath D 183 D8
Hespérange L 186 B1
Heßheim D 187 B5
Hettange-Grande F 186 C1
Hettenleidelheim D 186 B5
Hetzerath D 185 E6
Heubach D 187 D8
Heukelum NL 183 B6
Heusden B 183 C6
Heusden NL 183 B6
Heusenstamm D 187 A6
Heusweiler D 186 C2
Heythuysen NL 183 C7
Hilchenbach D 185 C9
Hilden D 183 C9
Hillegom NL 182 A5
Hillesheim D 185 D6
Hilsenheim F 186 E4
Hilvarenbeek NL 183 C6
Hilversum NL 183 A6
Hinterweidenthal D 186 C4
Hirrlingen D 187 E6
Hirschhorn (Neckar) D 187 C6
Hochfelden F 186 D4
Hochspeyer D 186 C4
Hochstadt (Pfalz) D 187 C5
Hochstetten-Dhaun D 185 E7
Höchst im Odenwald D 187 B6
Hockenheim D 187 C6
Hoek NL 182 C3
Hoek van Holland NL 182 B4
Hoenderloo NL 183 A7
Hœnheim F 186 D4
Hoensbroek NL 183 D7
Hœrdt F 186 D4
Hoeselt B 183 D6
Hoevelaken NL 183 A6
Hoeven NL 182 B5
Hof D 185 C9
Hofheim am Taunus D 187 A5
Hohberg D 186 E4
Höhn D 185 C8
Höhr-Grenzhausen D 185 D8
Hollange B 184 E4
Holten NL 183 A8
Holzappel D 185 D8
Holzgerlingen D 187 D7
Holzhausen an der Haide D 185 D8
Holzheim D 187 E9
Holzwickede D 185 A8
Hombourg-Budange F 186 C1
Hombourg-Haut F 186 C2
Homburg D 186 C3
Hoofddorp NL 182 A5
Hoogerheide NL 182 C4
Hoog-Keppel NL 183 B8
Hoogland NL 183 A6
Hoogstraten B 182 C5
Hoogvliet NL 182 B4
Hoornaar NL 182 B5
Hoppstädten D 186 B3
Horb am Neckar D 187 E6
Hörde D 185 B7
Hornbach D 186 C3
Horst NL 183 C8
Hösbach D 187 A7
Hosingen L 184 D5
Hotton B 184 D3
Houffalize B 184 D4
Houten NL 183 A6
Houthalen B 183 C6
Houthulst B 182 D1
Houyet B 184 D3
Hückelhoven D 183 C8
Hückeswagen D 185 B7
Huijbergen NL 182 C4
Huissen NL 183 B7
Huizen NL 183 A6
Hüls D 183 C8
Hulsberg NL 183 D7
Hulst NL 182 C4
Hummelo NL 183 A8
Hundsangen D 185 D8
Hünfelden-Kirberg D 185 D9
Hunsel NL 183 C7
Hunspach F 186 D4
Hünxe D 183 B9
Hürth D 183 D9
Hütschenhausen D 186 C3
Hüttisheim D 187 E8
Hüttlingen D 187 D9
Huy B 183 D6
Hymont F 186 E1

I

Ichenheim D 186 E4
Ichtegem B 182 C2
Idar-Oberstein D 186 B3
Idstein D 185 D9
Ieper B 182 D1
Iffezheim D 187 D5
Igel D 186 B2
Igersheim D 187 C8
Iggelheim D 187 C5
Igney F 186 E1
IJsselstein NL 183 A6
IJzendijke NL 182 C3
Illingen D 186 C3
illingen D 187 D6
Illkirch-Graffenstaden F 186 D4
Ilsfeld D 187 C7
Incourt B 182 D5
Ingelfingen D 187 C8
Ingelheim am Rhein D 185 E9
Ingelmunster B 182 D2
Ingwiller F 186 D3
Insming F 186 D2
Iphofen D 187 B9
Ippesheim D 187 B9
Irrel D 185 E5
Irsch D 186 B2
Iserlohn D 185 B8
Ispringen D 187 D6
Isselburg D 183 B8
Issum D 183 B8
Ittre B 182 D4
Ixelles B 182 D4
Izegem B 182 D2

J

Jabbeke B 182 C2
Jagsthausen D 187 C7
Jagstzell D 187 C9
Jalhay B 183 D7
Jarville-la-Malgrange F 186 D1
Jemeppe B 182 E5
Jockgrim D 187 C5
Jodoigne B 182 D5
Jouy-aux-Arches F 186 C1
Jüchen D 183 C8
Jülich D 183 D8
Jungingen D 187 E7
Junglinster L 186 B1
Jünkerath D 185 D6
Juprelle B 183 D7
Jurbise B 182 D3

K

Kaarst D 183 C9
Kaatsheuvel NL 183 B6
Kahl am Main D 187 A7
Kaisersesch D 185 D7
Kaiserslautern D 186 C4
Kalkar D 183 B8
Kall D 183 D9
Kalmthout B 182 C4
Kamen D 185 A8
Kamerik NL 182 A5
Kamp D 185 D8
Kampenhout B 182 D5
Kämpfelbach D 187 D6
Kamp-Lintfort D 183 C9
Kandel D 187 C5
Kapelle NL 182 C3
Kapellen B 182 C4
Kapelle-op-den-Bos B 182 C4
Kappel D 185 E7
Kappel-Grafenhausen D 186 E4
Kappelrodeck D 186 D5
Kaprijke B 182 C3
Karben D 187 A6
Karden D 185 D7
Karlsbad D 187 D6
Karlsdorf-Neuthard D 187 C6
Karlsruhe D 187 C5
Karlstadt D 187 B8
Kastellaun D 185 D7
Kasterlee B 182 C5
Katwijk aan Zee NL 182 A4
Katzenelnbogen D 185 D8
Katzweiler D 186 B4
Kaub D 185 D8
Kaulille B 183 C7
Kautenbach L 184 E5
Kehl D 186 D4
Kehlen L 186 B1
Kehrig D 185 D7
Kelberg D 185 D6
Kelkheim (Taunus) D 187 A5
Kell D 186 B2
Kelmis B 183 D8
Kempen D 183 C8
Kempenich D 183 E10
Kenn D 185 E6
Kerkdriel NL 183 B6
Kerken D 183 C8
Kerkrade NL 183 D8
Kerkwijk NL 183 B6
Kerpen D 183 D9
Kessel B 182 C5
Kessel NL 183 C8
Kesteren NL 183 B7
Ketsch D 187 C6
Kettwig D 183 C9
Kevelaer D 183 B8
Kieldrecht B 182 C4
Kierspe D 185 B8
Kinderbeuern D 185 D7
Kindsbach D 186 C4
Kinrooi B 183 C7
Kippenheim D 186 E4
Kirchardt D 187 C6
Kirchberg (Hunsrück) D 185 E7
Kirchberg an der Jagst D 187 C8
Kirchellen D 183 B9
Kirchen (Sieg) D 185 C8
Kirchheim D 187 B8
Kirchheim am Neckar D 187 C7
Kirchheim-Bolanden D 186 B5
Kirchheim unter Teck D 187 D7
Kirchhundem D 185 B9
Kirchzell D 187 B7
Kirkel-Neuhäusel D 186 C3
Kirn D 185 E7
Kirschweiler D 186 B3
Kist D 187 B8
Kitzingen D 187 B9
Klaaswaal NL 182 B4
Klausen D 185 E6
Kleinblittersdorf D 186 C3
Kleinheubach D 187 B7
Kleinrinderfeld D 187 B8
Kleinwallstadt D 187 B7
Kleve D 183 B8
Klingenberg am Main D 187 B7
Kloetinge NL 182 C3
Kloosterzande NL 182 C4
Klotten D 185 D7
Klundert NL 182 B5
Knesselare B 182 C2
Knittlingen D 187 C6
Knokke-Heist B 182 C2
Kobern D 185 D7
Koblenz D 185 D8
Koekelare B 182 C1
Koersel B 183 C6
Koewacht NL 182 C3
Kolitzheim D 187 B9
Köln D 183 D9
Königheim D 187 B8
Königsbronn D 187 D9
Königstein im Taunus D 187 A5
Königswinter D 185 C7
Konz D 186 B2
Kootwijkerbroek NL 183 A7
Kopstal L 186 B1
Kordel D 185 E6
Kornwestheim D 187 D7
Körperich D 185 E5
Kortemark B 182 C2
Kortenhoef NL 183 A6
Kortessem B 183 D6
Kortgene NL 182 B3
Kortrijk B 182 D2
Kottenheim D 185 D7
Koudekerke NL 182 C3
Krabbendijke NL 182 C4
Kranenburg D 183 B8
Krautheim D 187 C8
Krefeld D 183 C9
Kreuzau D 183 D8
Kreuztal D 185 C8
Kreuzwertheim D 187 B8
Krimpen aan de IJssel NL 182 B5
Kronau D 187 C6
Kronberg im Taunus D 187 A5
Kröv D 185 E7
Kruft D 185 D7
Kruibeke B 182 C4
Kruiningen NL 182 C4
Kruishoutem B 182 D3
Kuchen D 187 D8
Külsheim D 187 B8
Kunrade NL 183 D7
Künzelsau D 187 C8
Kupferzell D 187 C8
Kuppenheim D 187 D5
Kürnach D 187 B9
Kürnbach D 187 C6
Kusel D 186 B3
Kusterdingen D 187 D7
Kuurne B 182 D2
Kwaadmechelen B 183 C6
Kyllburg D 185 D6

L

Laarne B 182 C3
La Broque F 186 E3
Lachen-Speyerdorf D 187 C5
Ladenburg D 187 C6
Lafrimbolle F 186 D3
Lage Mierde NL 183 C6
Lahnstein D 185 D8
Lahr (Schwarzwald) D 186 E4
Laichingen D 187 E8
Laifour F 184 E2
Lallaing F 182 E2
La Louvière B 182 E4
Lambersart F 182 D2
Lambrecht (Pfalz) D 186 C5
Lambsheim D 187 B5
Lampertheim D 187 B5
Lanaken B 183 D7
Landau in der Pfalz D 186 C5
Landen B 183 D6
Landersheim F 186 D3
Landgraaf NL 183 D8
Landscheid D 185 E6
Landsmeer NL 182 A5
Landstuhl D 186 C4
Langemark B 182 D1
Langen D 187 B6
Langenau D 187 E9
Langenaubach D 185 C9
Langenberg D 183 C10
Langenberg D 185 A9
Langenburg D 187 C8
Langenfeld (Rheinland) D 183 C9
Langenhahn D 185 C8
Langenlonsheim D 185 E8
Langenselbold D 187 A7
Langsur D 186 B2
Lannoy F 182 D2
La Petite-Pierre F 186 D3
Laren NL 183 A6
Laren NL 183 A8
La Roche-en-Ardenne B 184 D4
Larochette L 186 B1
Lasne B 182 D4
Lattrop NL 183 A9
Laubach D 185 D7
Lauda-Königshofen D 187 B8
Lauf D 186 D5
Laufach D 187 A7
Lauffen am Neckar D 187 C7
Lautenbach D 186 D5
Lauterbourg F 187 D5
Lauterecken D 186 B4
Lauterstein D 187 D8
La Wantzenau F 186 D4
Laxou F 186 D1
Lebach D 186 C2
Le Ban-St-Martin F 186 C1
Lebbeke B 182 C4
Lede B 182 D3
Ledegem B 182 D2
Leende NL 183 C7
Leerdam NL 183 B6
Leersum NL 183 A6
Leffinge B 182 C1
Leforest F 182 E2
Legden D 183 A10
Léglise B 184 E4
Lehmen D 185 D7
Le Hohwald F 186 E3
Leichlingen (Rheinland) D 183 C10
Leiden NL 182 A5
Leiderdorp NL 182 A5
Leidschendam NL 182 A4
Leimen D 187 C6
Leimuiden NL 182 A5
Leinfelden-Echterdingen D 187 D7
Leinzell D 187 D8
Leiwen D 185 E6
Lembeke B 182 C3
Lemberg D 186 C4
Lemberg F 186 C3
Lendelede B 182 D2
Léning F 186 D2
Lennestadt D 185 B9
Lenningen D 187 D7
Lens B 182 D3
Lent NL 183 B7
Leonberg D 187 D7
Leopoldsburg B 183 C6
Les Hautes-Rivières F 184 E2
Les Mazures F 184 E2
Lessines B 182 D3
Leun D 185 C9
Leusden NL 183 A6
Leutesdorf D 185 D7
Leuven B 182 D5
Leuze-en-Hainaut B 182 D3
Leverkusen D 183 C9
L'Hôpital F 186 C2
Libin B 184 E3
Libramont B 184 E3
Lichtaart B 182 C5
Lichtenau D 186 D5
Lichtenvoorde NL 183 B9
Lichtervelde B 182 C2
Liège B 183 D7
Liempde NL 183 B6
Lienden NL 183 B7
Lier B 182 C5
Lierneux B 184 D4
Lieser D 185 E7
Lieshout NL 183 B7
Liessel NL 183 C7
Ligneuville B 184 D5
Lille B 182 C5
Lille F 182 D2
Limbach D 186 C2
Limbach D 187 C7
Limbourg B 183 D7
Limburg an der Lahn D 185 D9
Limburgerhof D 187 C5
Lincent B 183 D6
Lindenfels D 187 B6
Lindlar D 185 B7
Lingenfeld D 187 C5
Lingolsheim F 186 D4
Linnich D 183 D8
Linz am Rhein D 185 C7
Lippstadt D 185 A9
Lisse NL 182 A5
Lissendorf D 185 D6
Lith NL 183 B6
Lixing-lès-St-Avold F 186 C2
Lobith NL 183 B8
Lochem NL 183 A8
Lochristi B 182 C3
Loenen NL 183 A8
Löf D 185 D7
Lohmar D 185 C7
Löhnberg D 185 C9
Lohr am Main D 187 B8
Lokeren B 182 C4
Lomme F 182 D1
Lommel B 183 C6
Londerzeel B 182 D4
Longeville-lès-St-Avold F 186 C2
Longlier B 184 E3
Lonneker NL 183 A9
Lonny F 184 E2
Lonsee D 187 D8
Lontzen B 183 D8
Loon op Zand NL 183 B6
Loos F 182 D2
Lopik NL 182 B5
Lorch D 185 D8
Lorch D 187 D8
Lorquin F 186 D2
Lorsch D 187 B6
Losheim D 186 B2
Loßburg D 187 E5
Losser NL 183 A9
Lotenhulle B 182 C2
Lottum NL 183 C8
Louvain B 182 D5
Louveigné B 183 D7
Lovendegem B 182 C3
Löwenstein D 187 C7
Lubbeek B 182 D5
Lüdenscheid D 185 B8
Lüdinghausen D 185 A7
Ludres F 186 D1
Ludwigsburg D 187 D7
Ludwigshafen am Rhein D 187 C5
Luik B 183 D7
Lummen B 183 D6
Lünebach D 185 D5
Lünen D 185 A8
Lunéville F 186 D1
Lunteren NL 183 A7
Luppy F 186 D1
Lustadt D 187 C5
Luttenberg NL 183 A8
Lützelbach D 187 B7
Lutzerath D 185 D7
Luxembourg L 186 B1
Luyksgestel NL 183 C6

M

Maarheeze NL 183 C7
Maarn NL 183 A6
Maarssen NL 183 A6
Maarssenbroek NL 183 A6
Maasbracht NL 183 C7
Maasbree NL 183 C8
Maasdam NL 182 B5
Maaseik B 183 C7
Maasland NL 182 B4
Maasmechelen B 183 D7
Maassluis NL 182 B4
Maastricht NL 183 D7
Machelen B 182 D4
Mackenbach D 186 C4
Made NL 182 B5
Magnières F 186 E2
Mahlberg D 186 E4
Maikammer D 186 C5
Mainaschaff D 187 B7
Mainbernheim D 187 B9
Mainhardt D 187 C8
Mainz D 185 D9
Maizières-lès-Metz F 186 C1
Malborn D 186 B2
Maldegem B 182 C2
Malden NL 183 B7
Malines B 182 C4
Malmédy B 183 E8
Malsch D 187 D5
Manage B 182 E4
Mandelbachtal-Ormesheim D 186 C3
Manderscheid D 185 D6
Manhay B 184 D4
Mannheim D 187 C5
Manternach L 186 B1
Marange-Silvange F 186 C1
Marbach am Neckar D 187 D7
Marche-en-Famenne B 184 D3
Marchiennes F 182 E2
Marchin B 183 E6
Marcq-en-Barœul F 182 D2
Margraten NL 183 D7
Mariembourg B 184 D2
Marienheide D 185 B8
Markelo NL 183 A9
Markgröningen D 187 D7
Marktbreit D 187 B9
Marktheidenfeld D 187 B8
Marktseft D 187 B9
Marl D 183 B10
Marlenheim F 186 D4
Marly F 186 C1
Marmoutier F 186 D3
Marnheim D 186 B5
Marpingen D 186 C3
Marsal F 186 D2
Martelange B 184 E4
Marxzell D 187 D5
Maßbach D 187 A9
Mastershausen D 185 D7
Mattaincourt F 186 E1
Maubert-Fontaine F 184 E1
Maulbronn D 187 D6
Maurik NL 183 B6
Maxéville F 186 D1
Maxsain D 185 C8
Mayen D 185 D7
Mayschoss D 183 D10
Mechelen B 182 C4
Mechelen NL 183 D7
Mechernich D 183 D9
Meckenheim D 183 D10
Meckesheim D 187 C6
Meddersheim D 186 B4
Meddo NL 183 A9
Meer B 182 C5
Meerbusch D 183 C9
Meerhout B 183 C6
Meerkerk NL 182 B5
Meerle B 182 C5
Meerlo NL 183 B8
Meerssen NL 183 D7
Meetkerke B 182 C2
Meeuwen B 183 C7
Megen NL 183 B7
Mehren D 185 D6
Mehring D 185 E6
Mehrstetten D 187 E8
Meijel NL 183 C7
Meinerzhagen D 185 B8
Meise B 182 D4
Meisenheim D 186 B4
Meißenheim D 186 E4
Melick NL 183 C8
Meliskerke NL 182 B3
Melle B 182 C3
Menden (Sauerland) D 185 B8
Mendig D 185 D7
Menen B 182 D2
Mengerskirchen D 185 C9
Ménil-sur-Belvitte F 186 E2
Menin B 182 D2
Merbes-le-Château B 184 D1
Merchtem B 182 D4
Mere B 182 D3
Merelbeke B 182 D3
Merenberg D 185 C9
Merklingen D 187 D8
Merksplas B 182 C5
Mersch L 186 B1
Mertert L 186 B1
Mertesdorf D 186 B2
Mertloch D 185 D7
Mertzwiller F 186 D4
Merzig D 186 C2
Meschede D 185 B9
Mespelbrunn D 187 B7
Metelen D 183 A10
Mettendorf D 185 E5
Mettet B 184 D2
Mettlach D 186 C2
Mettmann D 183 C9
Metz F 186 C1
Metzervisse F 186 C1
Metzingen D 187 D7
Meudt D 185 D8
Meulebeke B 182 D2
Michelbach an der Bilz D 187 C8
Michelfeld D 187 C8
Michelstadt D 187 B7
Middelbeers NL 183 C6
Middelburg NL 182 B3
Middelharnis NL 182 B4
Middelkerke B 182 C1
Miehlen D 185 D8
Mierlo NL 183 C7
Miesau D 186 C3
Miesenbach D 186 C4
Mijdrecht NL 182 A5
Mill NL 183 B7
Millingen aan de Rijn NL 183 B8
Milmort B 183 D7
Miltenberg D 187 B7
Minderhout B 182 C5
Minfeld D 186 C5
Mirecourt F 186 E1
Mittelsinn D 187 A8
Mittersheim F 186 D2
Möckmühl D 187 C7
Modave B 183 E6
Moerbeke B 182 C3
Moergestel NL 183 B6
Moerkerke B 182 C2
Moers D 183 C9
Mögglingen D 187 D8
Möglingen D 187 D7
Mol B 183 C6
Molenbeek-St-Jean B 182 D4
Molenstede B 183 C6
Molsheim F 186 D3
Mömbris D 187 A7
Momignies B 184 D1
Moncel-sur-Seille F 186 D1
Mönchengladbach D 183 C8
Mondorf-les-Bains L 186 B1
Mons B 182 E3
Monschau D 183 D8
Monsheim D 187 B5
Mönsheim D 187 D6
Monster NL 182 A4
Montabaur D 185 D8
Montcy-Notre-Dame F 184 E2
Montfoort NL 182 A5
Montfort NL 183 C7
Monthermé F 184 E2
Montignies-le-Tilleul B 184 D1
Montigny F 186 D2
Montigny-lès-Metz F 186 C1
Montzen B 183 D7
Monzelfeld D 185 E7
Monzingen D 185 E8
Mook NL 183 B7
Moorslede B 182 D2
Morbach D 185 E7
Mörfelden D 187 B6
Morhange F 186 D2
Morlanwelz B 182 E4
Mörlenbach D 187 B6
Morsbach D 185 C8
Mortsel B 182 C4
Mosbach D 187 C7
Mössingen D 187 E7
Mouscron B 182 D2
Moussey F 186 E3
Moyenmoutier F 186 E2
Much D 185 C7
Mudau D 187 B7
Müdelheim D 183 C9
Mudersbach D 185 C8
Muggensturm D 187 D5
Mühlacker D 187 D6
Mühlhausen D 187 C6
Mulfingen D 187 C8
Mülheim an der Ruhr D 183 C9
Mülheim-Kärlich D 185 D7
Münchweiler an der Rodalb D 186 C4
Munderkingen D 187 E8
Mundolsheim F 186 D4
Munkzwalm B 182 D3
Münnerstadt D 187 A9
Münsingen D 187 E7
Münster D 187 B6
Munstergeleen NL 183 D7
Münstermaifeld D 185 D7
Murrhardt D 187 D8
Müschenbach D 185 C8
Mutterstadt D 187 C5
Mutzig F 186 D3

N

Naaldwijk NL 182 B4
Naarden NL 183 A6
Nackenheim D 185 E9
Nagold D 187 D6
Nalbach D 186 C2
Namborn D 186 B3
Namur B 182 E5
Nancy F 186 D1
Nandrin B 183 D6
Nassau D 185 D8
Nassogne B 184 D3
Nastätten D 185 D8
Nauheim D 187 B5
Nauroth D 185 C8
Neckarbischofsheim D 187 C6
Neckargemünd D 187 C6
Neckarsteinach D 187 C6
Neckarsulm D 187 C7
Neckartenzlingen D 187 D7
Nederhorst den Berg NL 183 A6
Nederlangbroek NL 183 A6
Nederweert NL 183 C7
Neede NL 183 A9
Neer NL 183 C8
Neerijnen NL 183 B6
Neeroeteren B 183 C7
Neerpelt B 183 C6
Nellingen D 187 D8
Nentershausen D 185 D8
Neroth D 185 D6
Nersingen D 187 E9
Netphen D 185 C9
Nettersheim D 183 E9

Nettetal D 183 C8
Neubrunn D 187 B8
Neubulach D 187 D6
Neuenbürg D 187 D6
Neuenkirchen-Seelscheid D 185 C7
Neuenrade D 185 B8
Neuenstadt am Kocher D 187 C7
Neuenstein D 187 C8
Neuerburg D 185 D5
Neufchâteau B 184 E3
Neuffen D 187 D7
Neufmanil F 184 E2
Neufra D 187 E7
Neuhausen D 187 D6
Neuhofen D 187 C5
Neu-Isenburg D 187 A6
Neuler D 187 D9
Neumagen D 185 E6
Neunkirchen D 185 C9
Neunkirchen D 186 C3
Neuss D 183 C9
Neustadt (Wied) D 185 C7
Neustadt an der Weinstraße D 186 C5
Neu-Ulm D 187 E9
Neuves-Maisons F 186 D1
Neuweiler D 187 D6
Neuwied D 185 D7
Nevele B 182 C3
Newel D 185 E6
Niederanven L 186 B1
Niederbrechen D 185 D9
Niederbreitbach D 185 C7
Niederbronn-les-Bains F 186 D4
Niederfischbach D 185 C8
Niederkassel D 183 D10
Niederkirchen D 186 B4
Niederkrüchten D 183 C8
Niederneisen D 185 D9
Niedernhall D 187 C8
Niedernhausen D 185 D9
Nieder-Olm D 185 E9
Nieder-Rodenbach D 187 A7
Niederselters D 185 D9
Niederstetten D 187 C8
Niederwerrn D 187 A9
Niederwörresbach D 186 B3
Niederzissen D 185 D7
Niefern-Öschelbronn D 187 D6
Niel B 182 C4
Nierstein D 185 E9
Nieuw-Bergen NL 183 B8
Nieuwegein NL 183 A6
Nieuwerkerk NL 182 B4
Nieuwerkerk aan de IJssel NL 182 B5
Nieuwerkerken B 183 D6
Nieuwe-Tonge NL 182 B4
Nieuw-Heeten NL 183 A8
Nieuwkoop NL 182 A5
Nieuw-Loosdrecht NL 183 A6
Nieuw-Milligen NL 183 A7
Nieuw-Namen NL 182 C4
Nieuwveen NL 182 A5
Nieuw-Vennep NL 182 A5
Nieuw-Vossemeer NL 182 B4
Nievern D 185 D8
Nijkerk NL 183 A6
Nijlen B 182 C5
Nijmegen NL 183 B7
Nijverdal NL 183 A8
Nilvange F 186 C1
Ninove B 182 D4
Nismes B 184 D2
Nispen NL 182 C4
Nistelrode NL 183 B7
Nittel D 186 B1
Nivelles B 182 D4
Nohfelden D 186 B3
Noisseville F 186 C1
Nomeny F 186 D1
Nomexy F 186 E1
Nonnenweier D 186 E4
Nonnweiler D 186 B2
Noordwijk aan Zee NL 182 A4
Noordwijk-Binnen NL 182 A4
Noordwijkerhout NL 182 A5
Nootdorp NL 182 A4
Nordheim D 187 C7
Nordkirchen D 185 A8
Nouzonville F 184 E2
Noville B 182 D5
Nüdlingen D 187 A9
Nuenen NL 183 C7
Nuland NL 183 B6
Numansdorp NL 182 B4
Nunkirchen D 186 C2
Nunspeet NL 183 A7
Nürtingen D 187 D7
Nuth NL 183 D7

O

Oberderdingen D 187 C6
Oberfell D 185 D7
Oberharmersbach D 186 E5
Oberhausen D 183 C9
Oberhausen-Rheinhausen D 187 C5
Oberhoffen-sur-Moder F 186 D4
Oberkirch D 186 D5
Oberkochen D 187 D9
Obermoschel D 186 B4
Obernai F 186 E3
Obernburg am Main D 187 B7
Oberndorf am Neckar D 187 E6
Obernheim-Kirchenarnbach D 186 C4
Ober-Olm D 185 E9
Ober-Roden D 187 B6
Oberrot D 187 C8
Obersinn D 187 A8
Obersontheim D 187 C8
Oberstenfeld D 187 C7
Oberthal D 186 B3
Oberthulba D 187 A8
Obertshausen D 187 A6
Oberursel (Taunus) D 187 A6
Oberwesel D 185 D8
Oberwolfach D 187 E5
Obrigheim D 187 C7
Obrigheim (Pfalz) D 187 B5
Ochsenfurt D 187 B9
Ochtrup D 183 A10
Odernheim am Glan D 186 B4
Oedelem B 182 C2
Oeffelt NL 183 B7
Oegstgeest NL 182 A5
Oene NL 183 A8
Oerlenbach D 187 A9
Oestrich-Winkel D 185 D8
Offenbach am Main D 187 A6
Offenbach an der Queich D 187 C5
Offenburg D 186 E4
Ofterdingen D 187 E7
Oftersheim D 187 C6
Ogéviller F 186 D2
Ohey B 183 E6
Ohlsbach D 186 E4
Öhringen D 187 C7
Oignies F 182 E1
Oijen NL 183 B6
Oirschot NL 183 B6
Oisterwijk NL 183 B6
Oldenzaal NL 183 A9
Olen B 182 C5
Olfen D 185 A7
Olpe D 185 B8
Olst NL 183 A8
Onstmettingen D 187 E6
Ooltgensplaat NL 182 B4
Oostakker B 182 C3
Oostburg NL 182 C2
Oostende B 182 C1
Oosterbeek NL 183 B7
Oosterhout NL 182 B5
Oosterland NL 182 B4
Oosterzele B 182 D3
Oostham B 183 C6
Oostkamp B 182 C2
Oostkapelle NL 182 B3
Oostmalle B 182 C5
Oost-Souburg NL 182 C3
Oostvoorne NL 182 B4
Ootmarsum NL 183 A9
Opglabbeek B 183 C7
Opheusden NL 183 B7
Opitter B 183 C7
Oploo NL 183 B7
Opoeteren B 183 C7
Oppenau D 187 E5
Oppenheim D 185 E9
Oppenweiler D 187 D7
Opwijk B 182 D4
Orchies F 182 E2
Orenhofen D 185 E6
Oreye B 183 D6
Ortenberg D 186 E4
Osburg D 186 B2
Oss NL 183 B7
Ossendrecht NL 182 C4
Ostend B 182 C1
Osterburken D 187 C7
Ostfildern D 187 D7
Osthofen D 187 B5
Ostricourt F 182 E2
Östringen D 187 C6
Ostwald F 186 D4
Ötigheim D 187 D5
Ötisheim D 187 D6
Ottenheim D 186 E4
Ottenhöfen im Schwarzwald D 187 D5
Otterbach D 186 C4
Otterberg D 186 B4
Otterlo NL 183 A7
Ottersweier D 186 D5
Ottignies B 182 D5
Ottweiler D 186 C3
Oud-Beijerland NL 182 B4
Ouddorp NL 182 B3
Oudenaarde B 182 D3
Oudenbosch NL 182 B5
Oudenburg B 182 C2
Oude-Tonge NL 182 B4
Oudewater NL 182 A5
Oud-Gastel NL 182 B4
Oud-Turnhout B 182 C5
Oud-Vossemeer NL 182 B4
Oudzele B 182 C2
Ouffet B 183 E6
Oulder B 184 D5
Oupeye B 183 D7
Overath D 185 C7
Overdinkel NL 183 A10
Overijse B 182 D5
Overloon NL 183 B7
Overpelt B 183 C6
Ovezande NL 182 C3
Owen D 187 D7

P

Paal B 183 C6
Padoux F 186 E2
Paliseul B 184 E3
Palzem D 186 B1
Pange F 186 C1
Panningen NL 183 C7
Papendrecht NL 182 B5
Partenstein D 187 A8
Pâturages B 182 E3
Pecq B 182 D2
Peer B 183 C6
Pelm D 185 D6
Pepingen B 182 D4
Pepinster B 183 D7
Perl D 186 C1
Péruwelz B 182 D3
Perwez B 182 D5
Petite-Rosselle F 186 C2
Petitmont F 186 D2
Pexonne F 186 E2
Pfaffenhofen an der Roth D 187 E9
Pfaffenhoffen F 186 D4
Pfalzfeld D 185 D8
Pfalzgrafenweiler D 187 D6
Pfedelbach D 187 C7
Pforzheim D 187 D6
Pfronstetten D 187 E7
Pfullingen D 187 E7
Pfungstadt D 187 B6
Phalsbourg F 186 D3
Philippeville B 184 D2
Philippine NL 182 C3
Philippsburg D 187 C5
Piershil NL 182 B4
Piesport D 185 E6
Pijnacker NL 182 A4
Pirmasens D 186 C4
Pittem B 182 D2
Plaidt D 185 D7
Plettenberg D 185 B8
Pliezhausen D 187 D7
Plobsheim F 186 E4
Plochingen D 187 D7
Ploegsteert B 182 D1
Plüderhausen D 187 D8
Poederlee B 182 C5
Polch D 185 D7
Polsbroek NL 182 B5
Pompey F 186 D1
Pont-à-Celles B 182 D4
Pont-à-Marcq F 182 D2
Pont-de-Loup B 182 E5
Poppenhausen D 187 A9
Portieux F 186 E1
Posterholt NL 183 C8
Poussay F 186 E1
Pracht D 185 C8
Prinsenbeek NL 182 B5
Profondeville B 184 D2
Pronsfeld D 185 D5
Provenchères-sur-Fave F 186 E3
Prüm D 185 D5
Puderbach D 185 C8
Pulheim D 183 C9
Putte B 182 C5
Putte NL 182 C4
Puttelange-aux-Lacs F 186 C2
Putten NL 183 A7
Püttlingen D 186 C2
Puurs B 182 C4

Q

Quaregnon B 182 E3
Queidersbach D 186 C4
Quendorf D 183 A10
Quesnoy-sur-Deûle F 182 D2
Quierschied D 186 C3
Quiévrain B 182 E3
Quiévrechain F 182 E3

R

Raalte NL 183 A8
Raamsdonksveer NL 182 B5
Radevormwald D 185 B7
Raeren B 183 D8
Raesfeld D 183 B9
Ralingen D 185 E6
Rambervillers F 186 E2
Rambrouch L 184 E4
Ramillies B 182 D5
Rammelsbach D 186 B3
Rammingen D 187 D9
Ramstein D 186 C4
Rance B 184 D1
Randersacker D 187 B8
Rangendingen D 187 E6
Ransbach-Baumbach D 185 D8
Ranst B 182 C5
Raon-l'Étape F 186 E2
Rastatt D 187 D5
Ratingen D 183 C9
Raubach D 185 C8
Ravels B 182 C5
Ravenstein NL 183 B7
Rebecq B 182 D4
Réchicourt-le-Château F 186 D2
Recht B 184 D5
Rechtenbach D 187 B8
Recklinghausen D 183 B10
Réding F 186 D3
Rees D 183 B8
Rehlingen-Siersburg D 186 C2
Reichelsheim (Odenwald) D 187 B6
Reichenbach D 187 B6
Reichenberg D 187 B8
Reicholzheim D 187 B8
Reichshoffen F 186 D4
Reichstett F 186 D4
Reil D 185 D7
Reilingen D 187 C6
Reinheim D 187 B6
Reinsfeld D 186 B2
Reken D 183 B10
Rekken NL 183 A9
Remagen D 185 C7
Remich L 186 B1
Remicourt B 183 D6
Remouchamps B 183 E7
Remscheid D 183 C10
Renchen D 186 D5
Renesse NL 182 B3
Rengsdorf D 185 C7
Renkum NL 183 B7
Rennerod D 185 C9
Renningen D 187 D6
Renswoude NL 183 A7
Renwez F 184 E2
Retie B 183 C6
Reusel NL 183 C6
Reutlingen D 187 E7
Reuver NL 183 C8
Revin F 184 E2
Rhaunen D 185 E7
Rhede D 183 B9
Rheden NL 183 A8
Rheinau D 186 D4
Rheinbach D 183 D9
Rheinberg D 183 B9
Rheinböllen D 185 E8
Rheinbreitbach D 185 C7
Rheinbrohl D 185 D7
Rheinstetten D 187 D5
Rheinzabern D 187 C5
Rhenen NL 183 B7
Rhens D 185 D8
Rhinau F 186 E4
Rhisnes B 182 D5
Rhoon NL 182 B4
Richardménil F 186 D1
Ridderkerk NL 182 B5
Riegelsberg D 186 C2
Riemst B 183 D7
Rieneck D 187 A8
Riethoven NL 183 C6
Rijen NL 182 B5
Rijkevorsel B 182 C5
Rijnsburg NL 182 A4
Rijsbergen NL 182 B5
Rijsel F 182 D2
Rijssen NL 183 A9
Rijswijk NL 182 A4
Rilland NL 182 C4
Rimbach D 187 B6
Rimogne F 184 E2
Rips NL 183 B7
Rittersdorf D 185 D5
Rixensart B 182 D5
Rochefort B 184 D3
Rochehaut B 184 E3
Rochin F 182 D2
Rockanje NL 182 B4
Rockenhausen D 186 B4
Rocroi F 184 E2
Rodalben D 186 C4
Roermond NL 183 C7
Roeselare B 182 D2
Roetgen D 183 D8
Roggel NL 183 C7
Röhlingen D 187 D9
Rohrbach-lès-Bitche F 186 C3
Rombas F 186 C1
Rommerskirchen D 183 C9
Ronse B 182 D3
Roosendaal NL 182 B4
Rosée B 184 D2
Rosenfeld D 187 E6
Rosheim F 186 D3
Rosmalen NL 183 B6
Rösrath D 185 C7
Roßdorf D 187 B6
Rossum NL 183 B6
Rot am See D 187 C9
Rothenberg D 187 B6
Rothenbuch D 187 B7
Rothenburg ob der Tauber D 187 C9
Rothenfels D 187 B8
Rotheux-Rimière B 183 D6
Rotselaar B 182 D5
Rottenacker D 187 E8
Rottenburg am Neckar D 187 E6
Rottendorf D 187 B9
Rotterdam NL 182 B5
Röttingen D 187 B8
Roubaix F 182 D2
Roulers B 182 D2
Rouvroy F 182 E1
Rouvroy-sur-Audry F 184 E2
Rozenburg NL 182 B4
Rozendaal NL 183 A7
Ruddervoorde B 182 C2
Rudersberg D 187 D8
Rüdesheim D 185 E8
Ruiselede B 182 C2
Rülzheim D 187 C5
Rumes B 182 D2
Rumigny F 184 E1
Rumst B 182 C4
Runkel D 185 D9
Rüsselsheim D 187 A5
Rutesheim D 187 D6
Rüthen D 185 B9
Rütten-Scheid D 183 C9
Ruurlo NL 183 A8

S

Saales F 186 E3
Saarbrücken D 186 C2
Saarburg D 186 B2
Saarlouis D 186 C2
Saarwellingen D 186 C2
Sachsenheim D 187 D7
St-Amand-les-Eaux F 182 E2
St-Avold F 186 C2
St-Blaise-la-Roche F 186 E3
St-Clément F 186 D2
St-Dié F 186 E2
Ste-Marguerite F 186 E2
Ste-Marie-aux-Mines F 186 E3
St-Firmin F 186 E1
St-Ghislain B 182 E3
St-Hubert B 184 D3
St-Louis-lès-Bitche F 186 D3
St-Max F 186 D1
St-Michel F 184 E1
St-Michel-sur-Meurthe F 186 E2
St-Nicolas B 183 D7
St-Nicolas-de-Port F 186 D1
St-Oedenrode NL 183 B6
St-Quirin F 186 D3
St-Vith B 184 D5
Salmtal D 185 E6
Sandhausen D 187 C6
Sankt Augustin D 185 C7
Sankt Goar D 185 D8
Sankt Goarshausen D 185 D8
Sankt Ingbert D 186 C3
Sankt Julian D 186 B4
Sankt Katharinen D 185 C7
Sankt Wendel D 186 C3
Santpoort NL 182 A5
Sarralbe F 186 D3
Sarrebourg F 186 D3
Sarreguemines F 186 C3
Sarre-Union F 186 D3
Sart B 183 D7
Sasbach D 186 D5
Sasbachwalden D 186 D5
Sassenheim NL 182 A5
Sas Van Gent NL 182 C3
Satteldorf D 187 C9
Saulheim D 185 E9
Saverne F 186 D3
Schaafheim D 187 B7
Schaarsbergen NL 183 A7
Schaerbeek B 182 D4
Schaesberg NL 183 D8
Schaijk NL 183 B7
Schalkhaar NL 183 A8
Schalksmühle D 185 B8
Scharendijke NL 182 B3
Schebheim D 187 B9
Schefflenz D 187 C7
Schelklingen D 187 E8
Schenkenzell D 187 E5
Schermbeck D 183 B9
Scherpenheuvel B 182 D5
Scherpenzeel NL 183 A6
Scherwiller F 186 E3
Schiedam NL 182 B4
Schieren L 184 E5
Schifferstadt D 187 C5
Schiffweiler D 186 C3
Schijndel NL 183 B6
Schilde B 182 C5
Schillingen D 186 B2
Schiltach D 187 E5
Schiltigheim F 186 D4
Schinnen NL 183 D7
Schinveld NL 183 D7
Schipluiden NL 182 B4
Schirmeck F 186 E3
Schlangenbad D 185 D9
Schleiden D 183 D8
Schmallenberg D 185 B9
Schmelz D 186 C2
Schnelldorf D 187 C9
Schnürpflingen D 187 E8
Schoenberg B 185 D5
Schöllkrippen D 187 A7
Schömberg D 187 D6
Schönaich D 187 D7
Schondra D 187 A8
Schönecken D 185 D5
Schönenberg-Kübelberg D 186 C3
Schöntal D 187 C8
Schoondijke NL 182 C3
Schoonhoven NL 182 B5
Schorndorf D 187 D8
Schoten B 182 C4
Schriesheim D 187 C6
Schrozberg D 187 C8
Schuttertal D 186 E4
Schutterwald D 186 E4
Schüttorf D 183 A10
Schwäbisch Gmünd D 187 D8
Schwäbisch Hall D 187 C8
Schwaigern D 187 C7
Schwalbach D 186 C2
Schwegenheim D 187 C5
Schweich D 185 E6
Schweigen-Rechtenbach D 186 C4
Schweighouse-sur-Moder F 186 D4
Schweinfurt D 187 A9
Schwelm D 185 B7
Schwerte D 185 B8
Schwieberdingen D 187 D7
Seckach D 187 C7
Seclin F 182 D2
Seebach D 187 D5
Seeheim-Jugenheim D 187 B6
Seilles B 183 E6
Seinsheim D 187 B9
Sélestat F 186 E3
Seligenstadt D 187 A6
Selm D 185 A7
Selters (Westerwald) D 185 C8
Seltz F 186 D5
Senden D 187 E9
Seneffe B 182 D4
Senones F 186 E2
Seraing B 183 D7
Serooskerke NL 182 B3
Serrig D 186 B2
Sevenum NL 183 C8
's-Gravendeel NL 182 B5
's-Gravenhage NL 182 A4
's-Gravenmoer NL 182 B5
's-Gravenpolder NL 182 C3
's-Gravenvoeren B 183 D7
's-Gravenzande NL 182 B4
's-Heerenberg NL 183 B8
's-Heerenhoek NL 182 C3
's-Hertogenbosch NL 183 B6
Siebengewald NL 183 B8
Siegburg D 185 C7
Siegen D 185 C9
Sierck-les-Bains F 186 C1
Siershahn D 185 D8
Signy-le-Petit F 184 E1
Sijsele B 182 C2
Silenrieux B 184 D1
Simmerath D 183 D8
Simmern (Hunsrück) D 185 E8
Simpelveld NL 183 D7
Sindelfingen D 187 D6
Singhofen D 185 D8
Sinn D 185 C9
Sinsheim D 187 C6
Sint Annaland NL 182 B4
Sint Anthonis NL 183 B7
Sint-Genesius-Rode B 182 D4
Sint-Gillis-Waas B 182 C4
Sint-Huibrechts-Lille B 183 C6
Sint Jansteen NL 182 C4
Sint-Katelijne-Waver B 182 C5
Sint-Laureins B 182 C3
Sint-Lenaarts B 182 C5
Sint Maartensdijk NL 182 B4
Sint-Margriete B 182 C3
Sint-Maria-Lierde B 182 D3
Sint-Martens-Latem B 182 C3
Sint Michielsgestel NL 183 B6
Sint-Niklaas B 182 C4
Sint Odilienberg NL 183 C8
Sint-Pauwels B 182 C4
Sint Philipsland NL 182 B4
Sint-Pieters-Leeuw B 182 D4
Sint-Truiden B 183 D6
Sinzheim D 187 D5
Sinzig D 185 C7
Sittard NL 183 D7
Sivry B 184 D1
Sleidinge B 182 C3
Sliedrecht NL 182 B5
Sluis NL 182 C2
Sluiskil NL 182 C3
Soerendonk NL 183 C7
Soest D 185 A9
Soest NL 183 A6
Soesterberg NL 183 A6
Soheit-Tinlot B 183 E6
Sohren D 185 E7
Soignies B 182 D4
Solingen D 183 C10
Sombreffe B 182 D5
Someren NL 183 C7
Somme-Leuze B 184 D3
Somzée B 184 D1
Son NL 183 B6
Soufflenheim F 186 D4
Soultz-sous-Forêts F 186 D4
Soumagne B 183 D7
Spa B 183 E7
Spabrücken D 185 E8
Spay D 185 D8
Speicher D 185 E6
Speyer D 187 C5
Spiere B 182 D2
Spiesen-Elversberg D 186 C3
Spijkenisse NL 182 B4
Spontin B 184 D3
Spraitbach D 187 D8
Sprendlingen D 185 E8
Sprimont B 183 D7
Sprockhövel D 185 B7
Stabroek B 182 C4
Staden B 182 D2
Stadtkyll D 185 D6
Stadtlohn D 183 B9
Staig D 187 E8
Standdaarbuiten NL 182 B5
Stavelot B 184 D4
Stavenisse NL 182 B4
Steenbergen NL 182 B4
Steenderen NL 183 A8
Stein NL 183 D7
Steinach D 186 E5
Steinfeld D 186 C5
Steinfeld D 187 B8
Steinheim am Albuch D 187 D9
Steinheim an der Murr D 187 D7
Steinsfeld D 187 C9
Steinwenden D 186 C4
Stekene B 182 C4
Stellendam NL 182 B4
Stevensweert NL 183 C7
Stimpfach D 187 C9
Stiring-Wendel F 186 C2
Stockstadt am Rhein D 187 B5
Stolberg (Rheinland) D 183 D8
Stoumont B 183 E7
Straelen D 183 C8
Straimont B 184 E3
Stramproy NL 183 C7
Strasbourg F 186 D4
Strassen L 186 B1
Straßenhaus D 185 C8
Strijen NL 182 B5
Stromberg D 185 E8
Sturzelbronn F 186 C4
Stuttgart D 187 D7
Suddendorf D 183 A10
Südlohn D 183 B9
Sulz am Neckar D 187 E6
Sulzbach am Main D 187 B7
Sulzbach an der Murr D 187 C7
Sulzbach-Laufen D 187 D8
Sulzbach/Saar D 186 C3
Sulzfeld D 187 C6
Sulzthal D 187 A9
Sundern (Sauerland) D 185 B9
Susteren NL 183 C7
Swalmen NL 183 C8

T

Taintrux F 186 E2
Talange F 186 C1
Tamm D 187 D7
Tantonville F 186 E1
Tauberbischofsheim D 187 B8
Tawern D 186 B2
Tegelen NL 183 C8
Tellin B 184 D3
Templeuve F 182 D2
Temse B 182 C4
Tenneville B 184 D4
Ter Aar NL 182 A5
Terborg-Silvolde NL 183 B8
Terheijden NL 182 B5
Terneuzen NL 182 C3
Tervuren B 182 D5
Tessenderlo B 183 C6
Testelt B 182 C5
Teteringen NL 182 B5
Thaleischweiler-Fröschen D 186 C4
Thalfang D 186 B2
Thaon-les-Vosges F 186 E1
't Harde NL 183 A7
Theux B 183 D7
Thionville F 186 C1
Tholen NL 182 B4
Tholey D 186 C3
Thommen B 184 D5
Thorn NL 183 C7
Thuin B 184 D1
Thüngen D 187 B8
Thüngersheim D 187 B8
Tiefenbronn D 187 D6
Tiel NL 183 B6
Tielen B 182 C5
Tielt B 182 D2
Tienen B 182 D5
Tilburg NL 183 B6
Tongeren B 183 D6
Tönisvorst D 183 C8
Torhout B 182 C2
Tourcoing F 182 D2
Tournai B 182 D2
Traar D 183 C9
Traben D 185 E7
Trarbach D 185 E7
Trebur D 187 B5
Treis D 185 D7
Tremelo B 182 D5
Trier D 186 B2
Trierweiler D 186 B2
Trippstadt D 186 C4
Trittenheim D 185 E6
Trochtelfingen D 187 E7
Troisdorf D 183 D10
Troisfontaines F 186 D3
Trois-Ponts B 184 D4
Troisvierges L 184 D5
Trooz B 183 D7
Truchtersheim F 186 D4
Trulben D 186 C4
Tubbergen NL 183 A9
Tübingen D 187 D7
Tubize B 182 D4
Turnhout B 182 C5
Twello NL 183 A8

U

Übach-Palenberg D 183 D8
Überherrn D 186 C2
Ubstadt-Weiher D 187 C6
Uccle B 182 D4
Üchtelhausen D 187 A9
Uckange F 186 C1
Uddel NL 183 A7
Uden NL 183 B7
Udenhout NL 183 B6
Üdersdorf D 185 D6
Uettingen D 187 B8
Uffenheim D 187 B9
Uhingen D 187 D8
Uithoorn NL 182 A5
Ulft NL 183 B8
Ulicoten NL 182 C5
Ulm D 187 E8
Ulmen D 185 D6
Ulvenhout NL 182 B5
Undingen D 187 E7
Unkel D 185 C7
Unna D 185 A8
Unnau D 185 C8
Untermünkheim D 187 C8
Unterpleichfeld D 187 B9
Urbach D 185 C8
Urbar D 185 D8
Urberach D 187 B6
Utrecht NL 183 A6
Üxheim D 185 D6

V

Vaals NL 183 D8
Vaassen NL 183 A7
Valkenburg NL 183 D7
Valkenswaard NL 183 C6
Vallendar D 185 D8
Vandœvre-lès-Nancy F 186 D1
Varik NL 183 B6
Varsseveld NL 183 B8
Vaux-sur-Sûre B 184 E4
Veenendaal NL 183 A7
Veere NL 182 B3
Veerle B 182 C5
Veghel NL 183 B7
Velbert D 183 C10
Veldegem B 182 C2
Velden NL 183 C8
Veldhoven NL 183 C6
Velen D 183 B9
Vellberg D 187 C8
Velp NL 183 B7
Vendenheim F 186 D4
Venlo NL 183 C8
Venray NL 183 B7
Vergaville F 186 D2
Verlaine B 183 D6
Verny F 186 C1
Verviers B 183 D7
Vessem NL 183 C6
Vettelschoss D 185 C7
Vianden L 184 E5
Vianen NL 183 B6
Vic-sur-Seille F 186 D2
Vielsalm B 184 D4
Vierlingsbeek NL 183 B7
Viernheim D 187 B6
Viersen D 183 C8
Vieux-Condé F 182 E3
Vigy F 186 C1
Villé F 186 E3
Villeneuve-d'Ascq F 182 D2
Villers-le-Bouillet B 183 D6
Villers-lès-Nancy F 186 D1
Villmar D 185 D9
Vilvoorde B 182 D4
Vincey F 186 E1
Vinkt B 182 C2
Vinningen D 186 C4
Vireux-Molhain F 184 D2
Vireux-Wallerand F 184 D2
Visé B 183 D7
Vlaardingen NL 182 B4
Vleuten NL 183 A6
Vlijmen NL 183 B6
Vlissingen NL 182 C3
Voerde (Niederrhein) D 183 B9
Vogelenzang NL 182 A5
Vogelweh D 186 C4
Vöhringen D 187 E6
Vöhringen D 187 E9
Volkach D 187 B9
Volkel NL 183 B7
Völklingen D 186 C2
Volmunster F 186 C3
Voorburg NL 182 A4
Voorhout NL 182 A4
Voorschoten NL 182 A4
Voorst NL 183 A8
Voorthuizen NL 183 A7
Vorden NL 183 A8
Vorst B 183 C6
Vosselaar B 182 C5
Vrasene B 182 C4
Vreden D 183 A9
Vreeland NL 183 A6
Vresse B 184 E2
Vriezenveen NL 183 A9
Vrouwenpolder NL 182 B3
Vught NL 183 B6

W

Waalre NL 183 C6
Waalwijk NL 183 B6
Waarschoot B 182 C3
Wachenheim an der Weinstraße D 187 C5
Wachtebeke B 182 C3
Wächtersbach D 187 A7
Waddinxveen NL 182 A5
Wadern D 186 B2
Wadersloh D 185 A9
Wadgassen D 186 C2
Wageningen NL 183 B7
Waghäusel D 187 C6
Waiblingen D 187 D7
Waibstadt D 187 C6
Waigolshausen D 187 B9
Waimes B 183 E8
Walcourt B 184 D1
Waldachtal D 187 E6
Waldböckelheim D 185 E8
Waldbreitbach D 185 C7
Waldbröl D 185 C8
Waldbrunn-Lahr D 185 C9
Waldbüttelbrunn D 187 B8
Waldenbuch D 187 D7
Waldenburg D 187 C8
Waldesch D 185 D8
Waldfischbach-Burgalben D 186 C4
Wald-Michelbach D 187 B6
Waldmohr D 186 C3
Waldrach D 186 B2
Waldsee D 187 C5
Waldstetten D 187 D8
Walferdange L 186 B1
Walldorf D 187 A6
Walldorf D 187 C6
Walldürn D 187 B7
Wallhausen D 185 E8
Wallhausen D 187 C9
Wamel NL 183 B6
Wandre B 183 D7
Wanne-Eikel D 183 B10
Wanroij NL 183 B7
Wanssum NL 183 B8
Wanze B 183 D6
Wapenveld NL 183 A8
Waregem B 182 D2
Waremme B 183 D6
Warmond NL 182 A5
Warnsveld NL 183 A8
Warstein D 185 B9
Wartmannsroth D 187 A8
Wäschenbeuren D 187 D8
Waspik NL 182 B5
Wasseiges B 183 D6
Wasselonne F 186 D3

Wassenaar NL 182 A4
Wassenberg D 183 C8
Wasseralfingen D 187 D9
Wasserbillig D 186 B2
Wasserliesch D 186 B2
Wasserlosen D 187 A9
Wateringen NL 182 A4
Waterland-Oudeman B 182 C3
Waterloo B 182 D4
Watten-Scheid D 183 C10
Wavre B 182 D5
Wavrin F 182 D1
Waxweiler D 185 D5
Waziers F 182 E2
Weelde B 182 C5
Weerselo NL 183 A9
Weert NL 183 C7
Weesp NL 183 A6
Weeze D 183 B8
Wegberg D 183 C8
Wehl NL 183 B8
Weibern D 183 E10
Weibersbrunn D 187 B7
Weidenstetten D 187 D8
Weidenthal D 186 C4
Weiersbach D 186 B3
Weikersheim D 187 C8
Weilbach D 187 B7
Weilburg D 185 D9
Weil der Stadt D 187 D6
Weilerbach D 186 C4
Weilerswist D 183 D9
Weilheim an der Teck D 187 D8
Weilmünster D 185 D9
Weinbach D 185 D9

Weingarten (Baden) D 187 C6
Weinheim D 187 B6
Weinsberg D 187 C7
Weinsheim D 185 D5
Weinsheim D 185 E8
Weinstadt D 187 D7
Weiskirchen D 186 B2
Weissach D 187 D6
Weißenhorn D 187 E9
Weißenthurm D 185 D7
Weiswampach L 184 D5
Weitbruch F 186 D4
Weitefeld D 185 C8
Weiterstadt D 187 B6
Wekerom NL 183 A7
Welkenraedt B 183 D7
Well NL 183 B8
Wellen B 183 D6
Wellin B 184 D3
Welling D 185 D7
Welschbillig D 185 E6
Welver D 185 A8
Welzheim D 187 D8
Wemeldinge NL 182 B4
Wendelsheim D 186 B5
Wenden D 185 C8
Wendlingen am Neckar D 187 D7
Wenduine B 182 C2
Wengsel (Isterberg) D 183 A10
Wépion B 182 E5
Werbach D 187 B8
Werbomont B 184 D4
Werdohl D 185 B8
Werkendam NL 182 B5

Werl D 185 A8
Wermelskirchen D 185 B7
Wernau D 187 D7
Werne D 185 A8
Werneck D 187 B9
Wertheim D 187 B8
Wervik B 182 D2
Wesel D 183 B9
Wesepe NL 183 A8
Wesseling D 183 D9
Wessem NL 183 C7
Westerburg D 185 C8
Westerheim D 187 D8
Westerhoven NL 183 C6
Westerlo B 182 C5
Westerstetten D 187 D8
Westervoort NL 183 B7
Westhausen D 187 D9
Westhofen D 187 B5
Westhoffen F 186 D3
Westkapelle NL 182 B2
Westmalle B 182 C5
Wetter (Ruhr) D 185 B7
Wetteren B 182 C3
Wevelgem B 182 D2
Weyerbusch D 185 C8
Weyersheim F 186 D4
Wichelen B 182 C3
Wickede (Ruhr) D 185 B8
Wiehl D 185 C8
Wielsbeke B 182 D2
Wierden NL 183 A9
Wiernsheim D 187 D6
Wiesbaden D 185 D9
Wiesen D 187 A7

Wiesensteig D 187 D8
Wiesloch D 187 C6
Wijchen NL 183 B7
Wijhe NL 183 A8
Wijk bij Duurstede NL 183 B6
Wijk en Aalburg NL 183 B6
Wildberg D 187 D6
Wilhelminadorp NL 183 C6
Willebroek B 182 C4
Willemstad NL 182 B4
Willich D 183 C9
Willstätt D 186 D4
Wilnis NL 182 A5
Wilnsdorf D 185 C9
Wilp NL 183 A8
Wiltingen D 186 B2
Wiltz L 184 E4
Wincheringen D 186 B1
Wincrange L 184 D4
Windesheim D 185 E8
Windhagen D 185 C7
Wingene B 182 C2
Wingen-sur-Moder F 186 D3
Winnenden D 187 D7
Winningen D 185 D8
Winnweiler D 186 B4
Winssen NL 183 B7
Winterswijk NL 183 B9
Wintrich D 185 E6
Wipperfürth D 185 B7
Wirges D 185 D8
Wissembourg F 186 C4
Wissen D 185 C8
Wissenkerke NL 182 B3
Witten D 185 B7

Wittighausen D 187 B8
Wittlich D 185 E6
Woensdrecht NL 182 C4
Woerden NL 182 A5
Woerth F 186 D4
Woippy F 186 C1
Wolfach D 187 E5
Wolfstein D 186 B4
Wolpertshausen D 187 C8
Wolphaartsdijk NL 182 B3
Wommelgem B 182 C5
Wormeldange L 186 B1
Worms D 187 B5
Wörrstadt D 185 E9
Wortel B 182 C5
Wörth am Main D 187 B7
Wörth am Rhein D 187 C5
Woudenberg NL 183 A6
Woudrichem NL 182 B5
Woustviller F 186 C3
Wouw NL 182 B4
Wuppertal D 183 C10
Würselen D 183 D8
Würzburg D 187 B8
Wüstenrot D 187 C7
Wuustwezel B 182 C5

X

Xanten D 183 B8

Y

Yerseke NL 182 C4
Ysselsteyn NL 183 C7
Yutz F 186 C1
Yvoir B 184 D2

Z

Zaamslag NL 182 C3
Zaandam NL 182 A5
Zaltbommel NL 183 B6
Zandhoven B 182 C5
Zandvliet B 182 C4
Zandvoort NL 182 A5
Zarren B 182 C1
Zaventem B 182 D4
Zeddam NL 183 B8
Zedelgem B 182 C2
Zeebrugge B 182 C2
Zeeland NL 183 B7
Zeewolde NL 183 A7
Zeiskam D 187 C5
Zeist NL 183 A6
Zeitlofs D 187 A8
Zele B 182 C4
Zelhem NL 183 A8
Zell (Mosel) D 185 D7
Zell am Harmersbach D 186 E5
Zell am Main D 187 B8
Zellingen D 187 B8
Zeltingen-Rachtig D 185 E7

Zelzate B 182 C3
Zemmer D 185 E6
Zemst B 182 D4
Zerf D 186 B2
Zevenaar NL 183 B8
Zevenbergen NL 182 B5
Zierikzee NL 182 B3
Zoelen NL 183 B6
Zoersel B 182 C5
Zoetermeer NL 182 A4
Zolder B 183 C6
Zomergem B 182 C3
Zonhoven B 183 D6
Zonnebeke B 182 D1
Zornheim D 185 E9
Zottegem B 182 D3
Zoutleeuw B 183 D6
Zuid-Beijerland NL 182 B4
Zuidland NL 182 B4
Zuienkerke B 182 C2
Zülpich D 183 D9
Zulte B 182 D2
Zundert NL 182 C5
Zutendaal B 183 D7
Zutphen NL 183 A8
Zweibrücken D 186 C3
Zwevegem B 182 D2
Zwevezele B 182 C2
Zwiefalten D 187 E7
Zwijndrecht B 182 C4
Zwijndrecht NL 182 B5
Zwingenberg D 187 B6

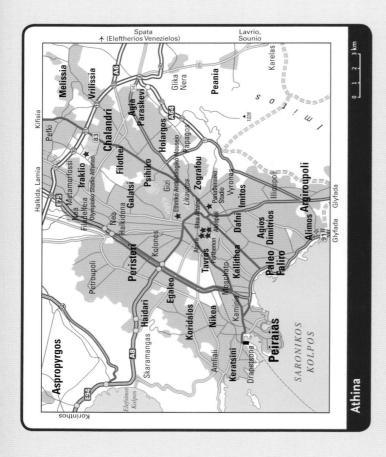

Athina

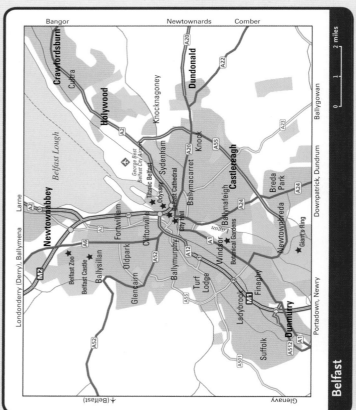

Belfast

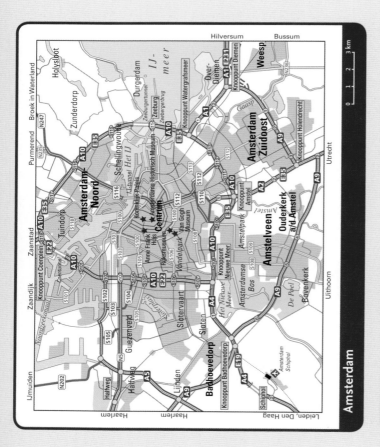

Amsterdam

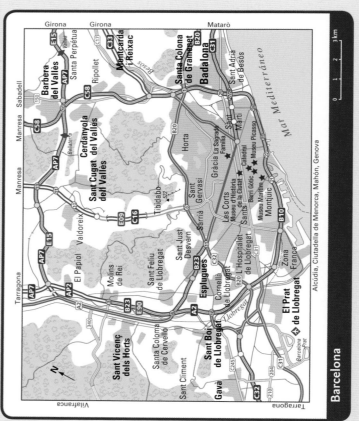

Barcelona

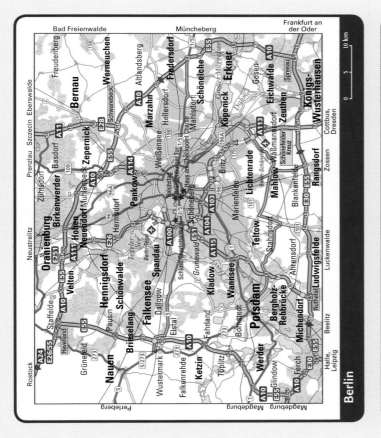

Berlin

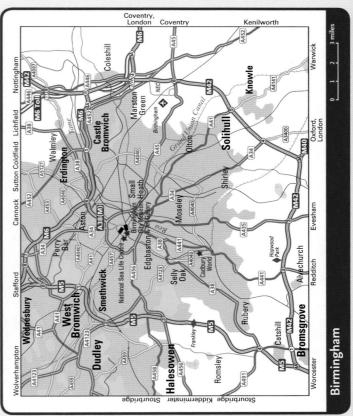

Birmingham

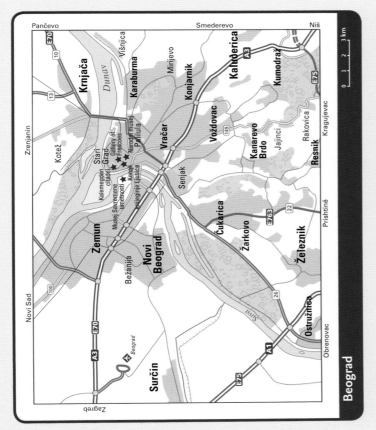

Beograd

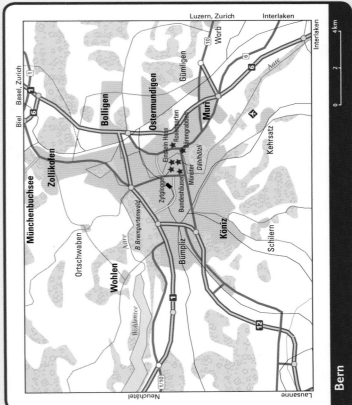

Bern

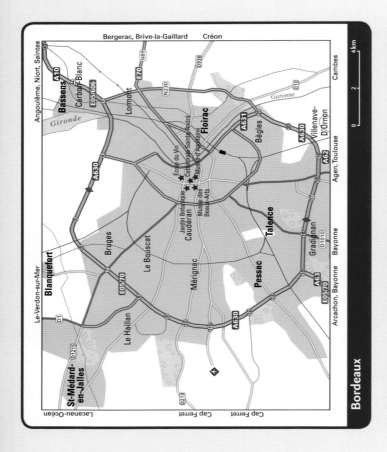

Bordeaux

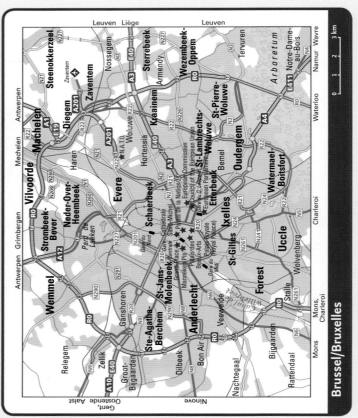

Brussel/Bruxelles

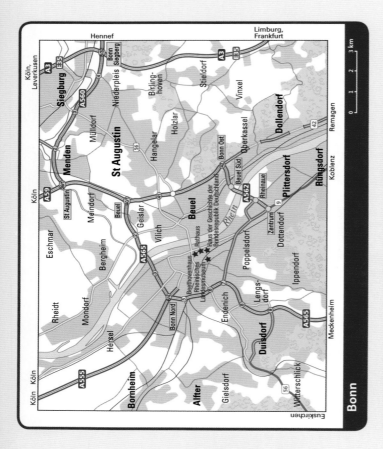

Bonn

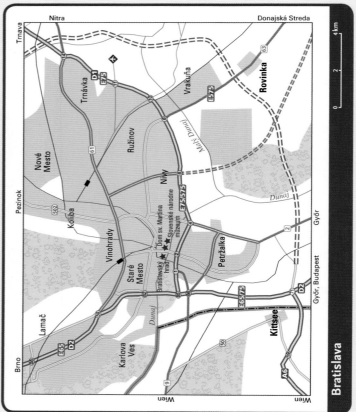

Bratislava

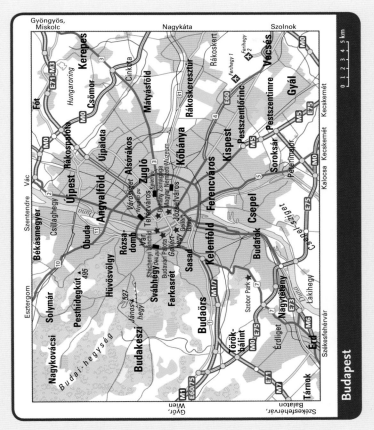

Budapest

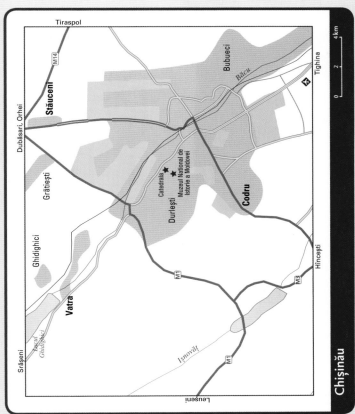

Chişinău

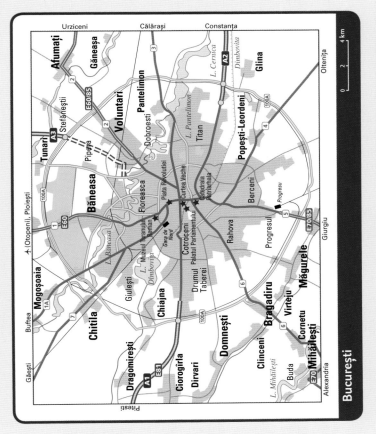

Bucureşti

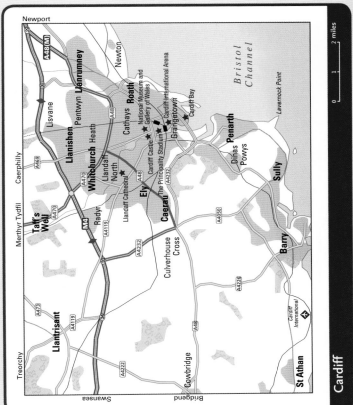

Cardiff

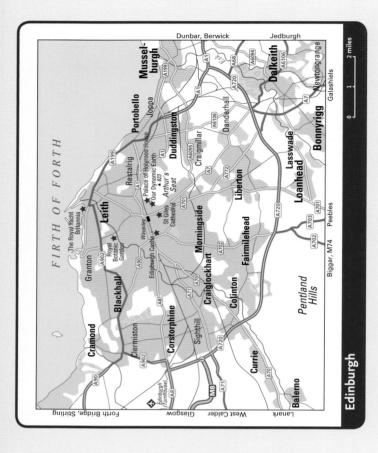

Edinburgh

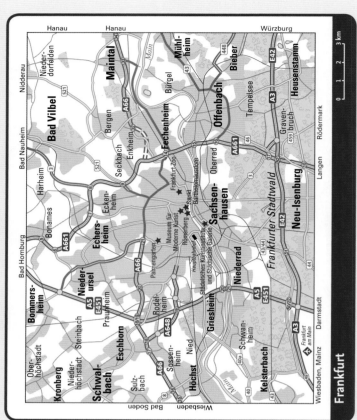

Frankfurt

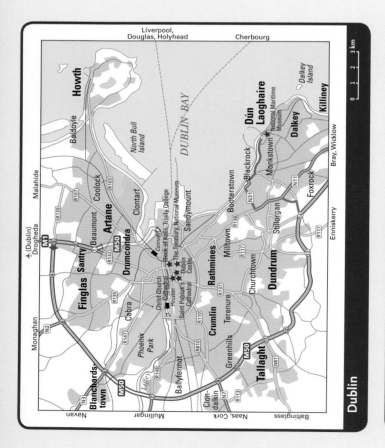

Dublin

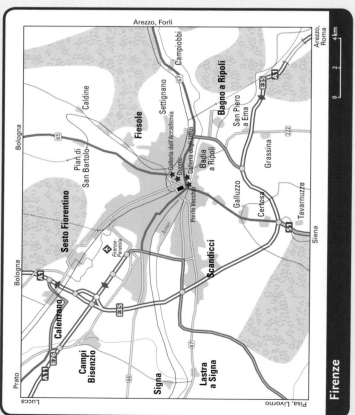

Firenze

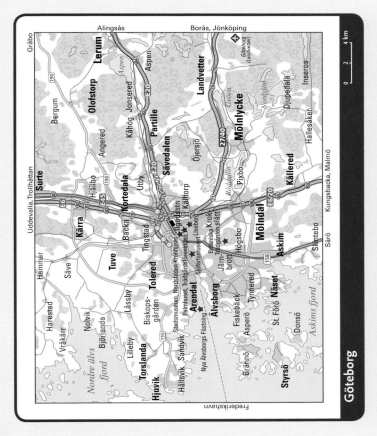

Göteborg

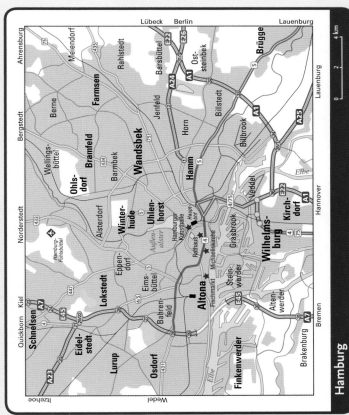

Hamburg

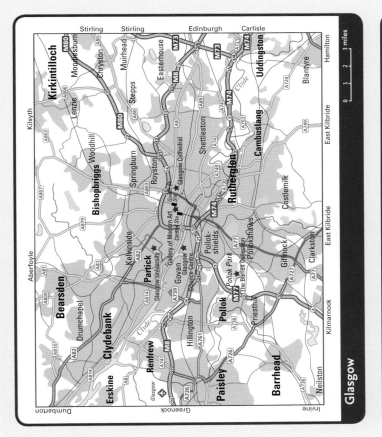

Glasgow

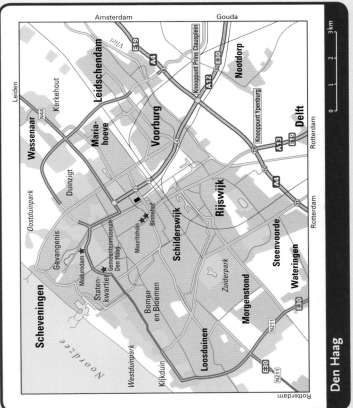

Den Haag

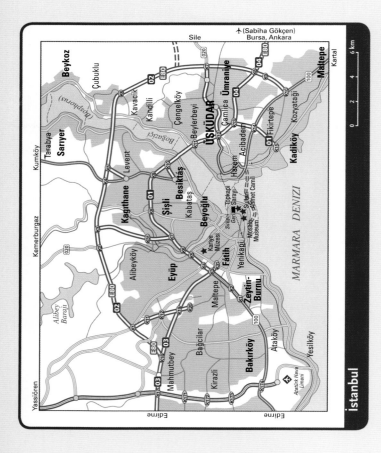

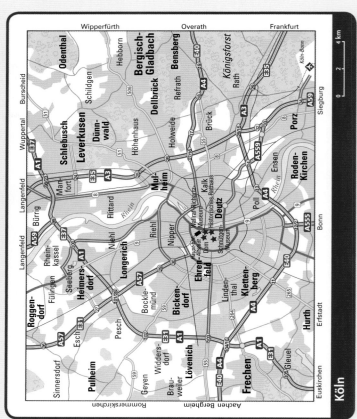

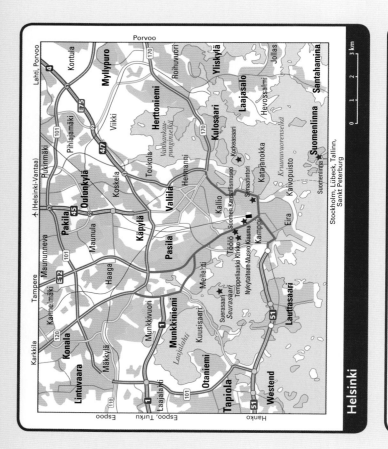

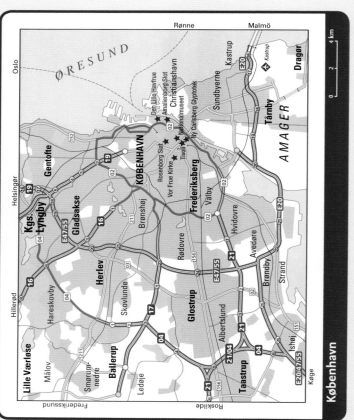

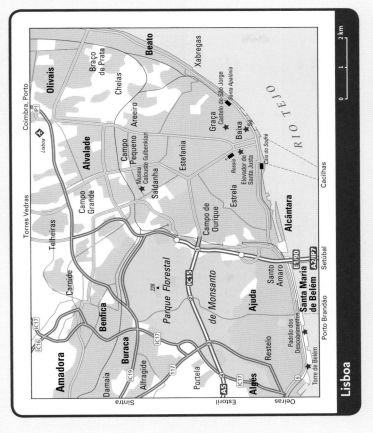

Lisboa

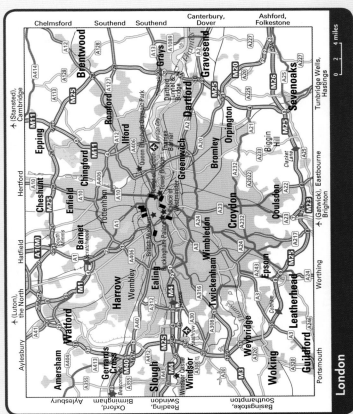

London

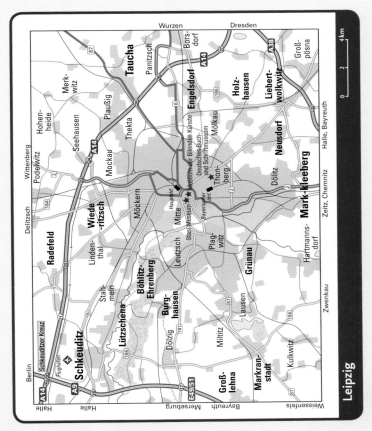

Leipzig

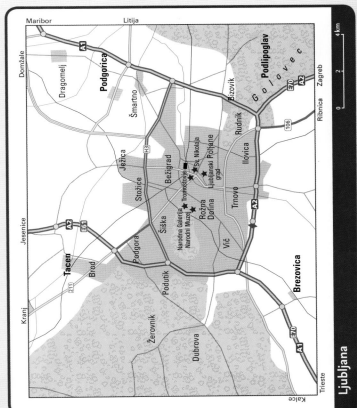

Ljubljana

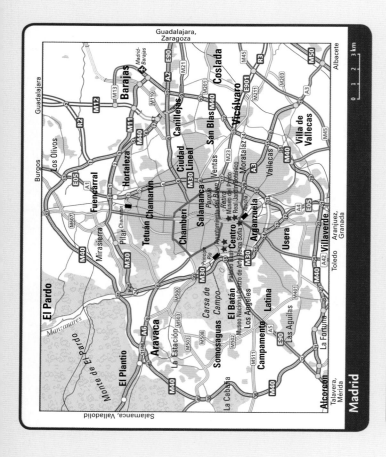

Madrid

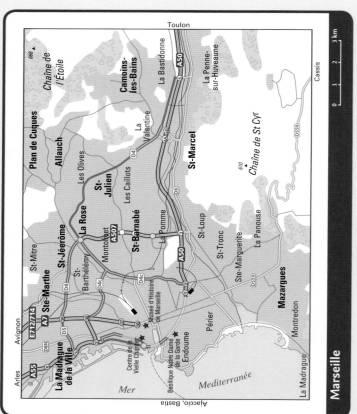

Marseille

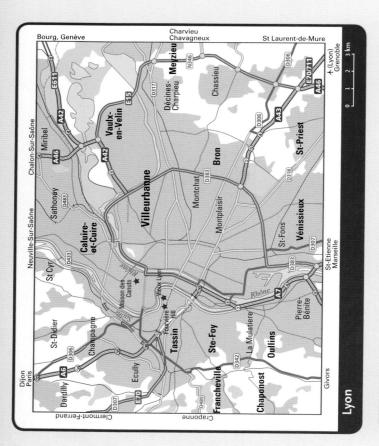

Lyon

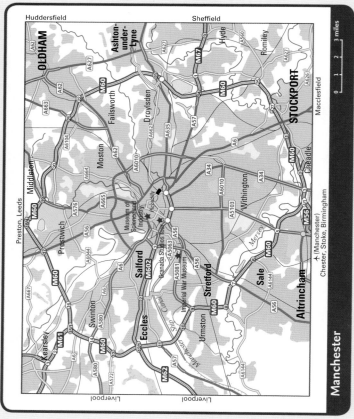

Manchester

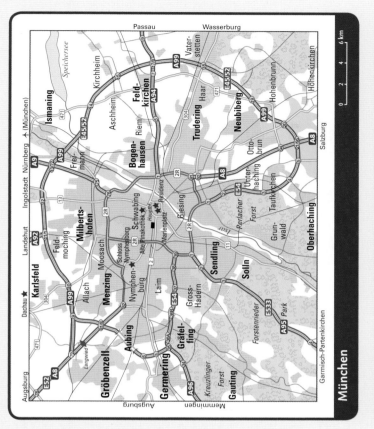

München

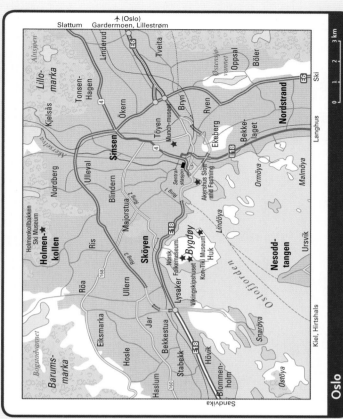

Oslo

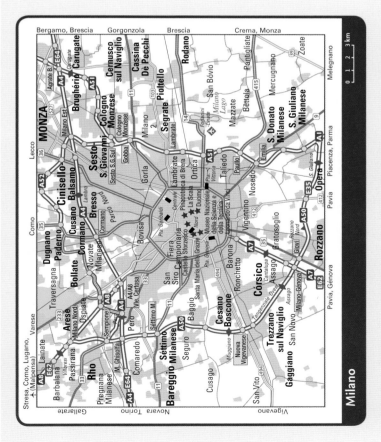

Milano

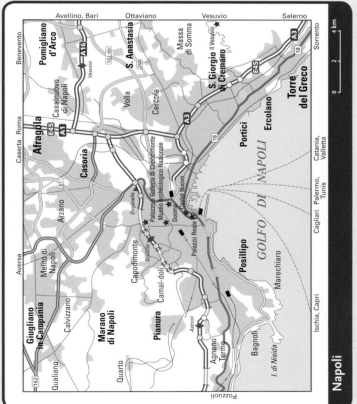

Napoli

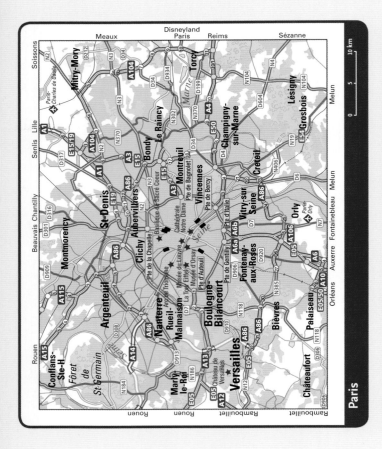

Paris

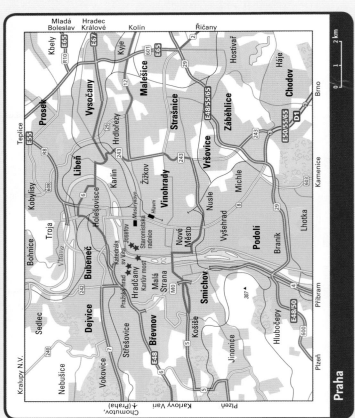

Praha

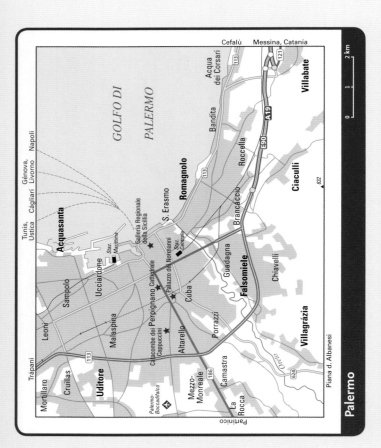

Palermo

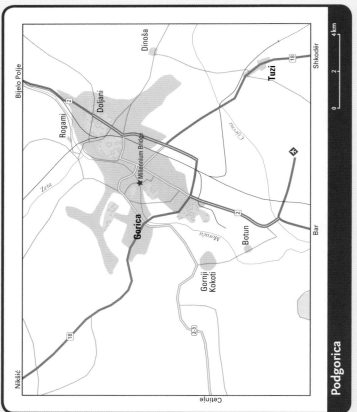

Podgorica

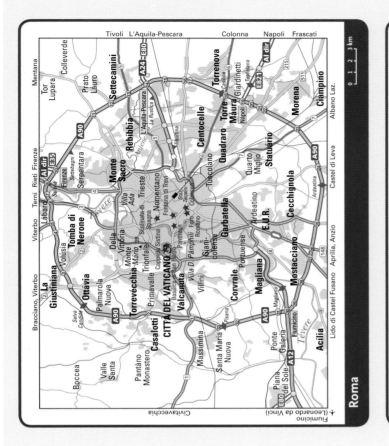

Roma

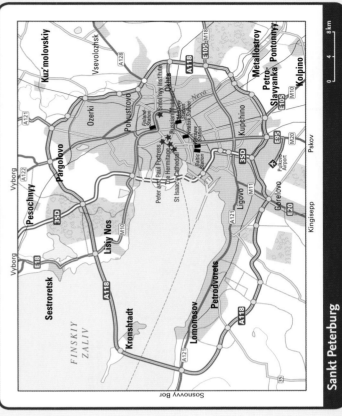

Sankt Peterburg

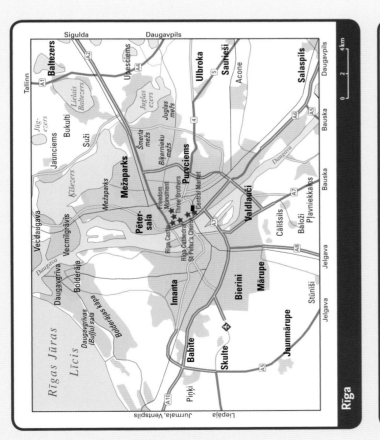

Rīga

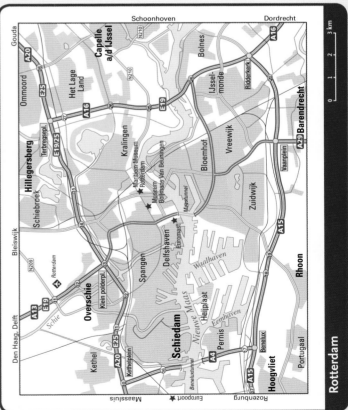

Rotterdam

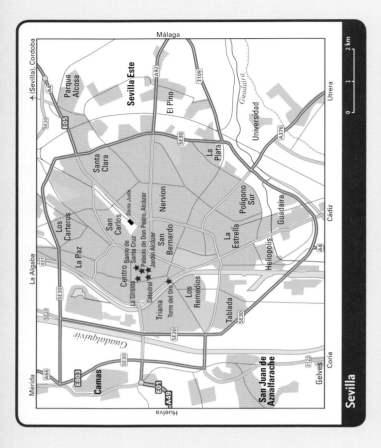

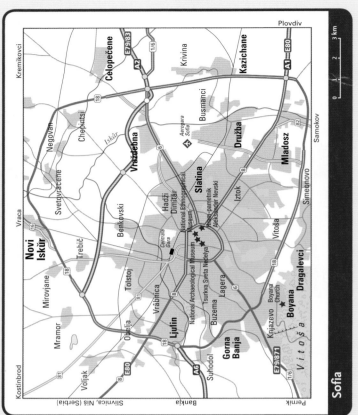

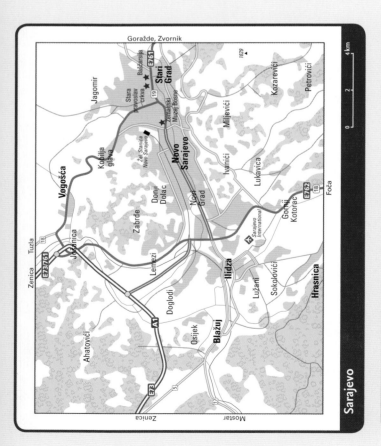

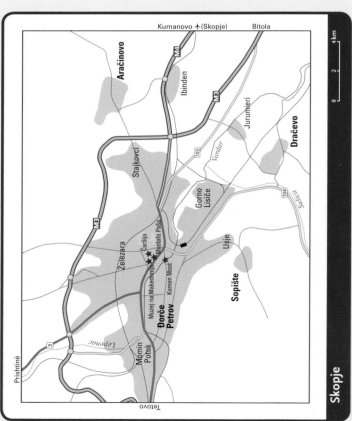

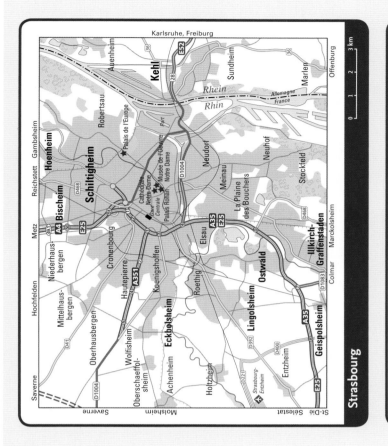

Strasbourg

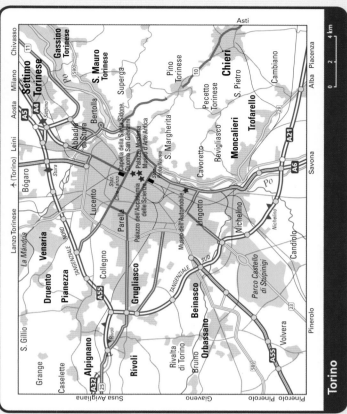

Torino

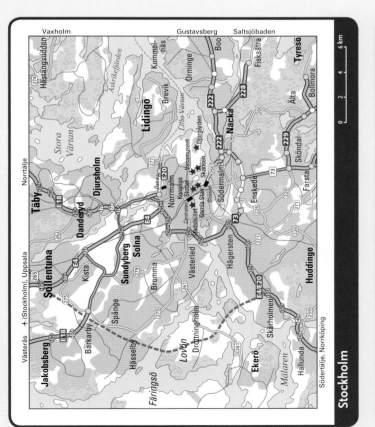

Stockholm

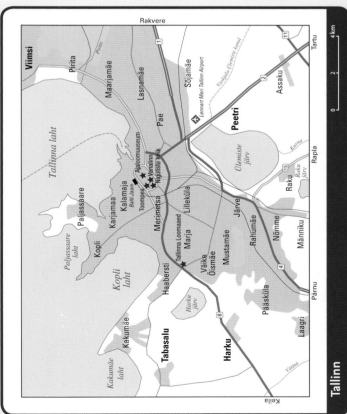

Tallinn

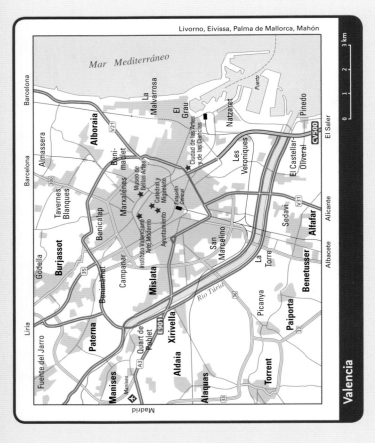

Valencia

Livorno, Eivissa, Palma de Mallorca, Mahón

Mar Mediterráneo

Barcelona · Almàssera · Alboraia · Beni-maclet · La Malvarrosa · El Grau · Natzaret · Pinedo · CV500 · El Saler

Godella · Tavernes Blanques · Benicalap · Campanar · Marxalenes · Ciudad de las Artes y de las Ciencias · Les Veroniques · El Castellar-Oliveral

Burjassot · Borbotnanet · Benimàmet · Museo de Bellas Artes · Catedral y Miguelete · Sedaví · Alfafar

Paterna · Mislata · Institut Valencià d'Art Modern · Ayuntamiento · San Marcelino · La Torre · Benetússer · Alicante · Albacete

Liria · Fuente del Jarro · Quart de Poblet · Xirivella · Aldaia · Picanya · Paiporta · Madrid

Manises · Alaquas · Torrent

Rio Túria

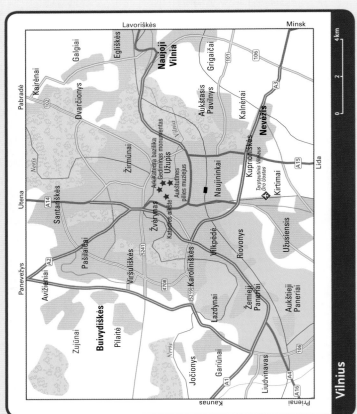

Vilnius

Lavoriškės · Minsk

Galgiai · Egliškės · Naujoji Vilnia · Grigaičiai

Kairėnai · Dvarčionys · Aukštasis Pavilnys · Kalnėnai · Nevėžis

Pabradė · Žirmūnai · Arkikatedra bazilika · Gedimino monumentas · Užupis · Kuprioniškės

Utena · Santariškės · Žvėrynas · Aukštutinės pilies muziejus · Naujininkai · Kirtimai

Paneveżys · Pašilaičiai · Karoliniškės · Vilkpėdė · Riovonys · Užusiensis

Avižieniai · Viršuliškės · Lazdynai · Žemieji Paneriai

Buivydiškės · Pilaitė · Jočionys · Gariūnai · Aukštieji Paneriai

Zujūnai · Liudvinavas · Prienai · Kaunas

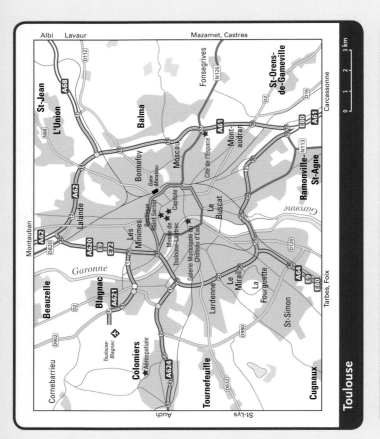

Toulouse

Albi · Lavaur · Mazamet, Castres

St-Jean · L'Union · Balma · St-Orens-de-Gameville

Fonsegrives · Carcassonne

Bonnefoy · Moscou · Mont-audran · Ramonville-St-Agne

Beauzelle · Lalande · Les Minimes · Basilique Saint Sernin · Capitole · Le Busca

Montauban · Blagnac · Galerie Municipale du Château d'Eau · Le Mirail · La Fourguette

Colomiers · Lardenne · St-Simon · Cugnaux

Cornebarrieu · Tournefeuille · Auch · St-Lys · Tarbes, Foix

Garonne · Aérospatiale · Toulouse-Blagnac

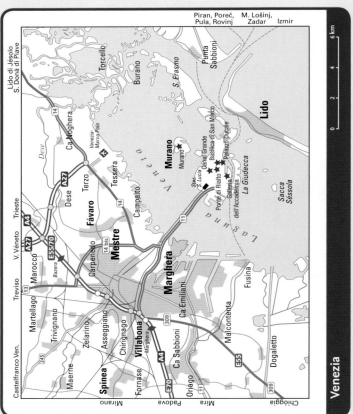

Venezia

Piran, Poreč, M. Lošinj, Pula, Rovinj · Zadar · Izmir

Lido di Jésolo S. Donà di Piave · Torcello · Burano · S. Erasmo · Punta Sabbioni

Ca'Noghera · Murano · Canal Grande · Basilica di San Marco · Lido

Tessera · Campalto · Galleria dell'Accademia · La Giudecca

Favaro · Mestre · Marghera · Fusina · Sacca Séssola

Treviso · Marocco · Carpenedo · Malcontenta · Dogaletto

Martellago · Trivignano · Villabona · Ca'Sabbioni · Chióggia

Spinea · Zelarino · Asseggiano · Chirignago · Ca'Emiliani

Maerne · Fornase · Oriàgo · Mira · Padova · Mirano

Castelfranco Ven. · V. Véneto · Trieste

Venezia

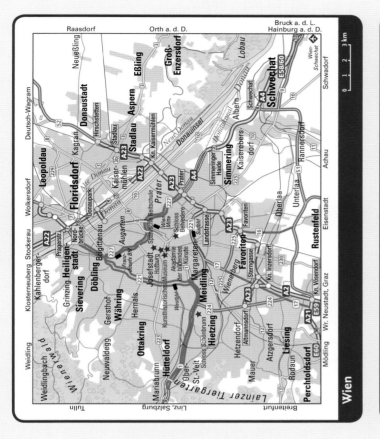

Wien

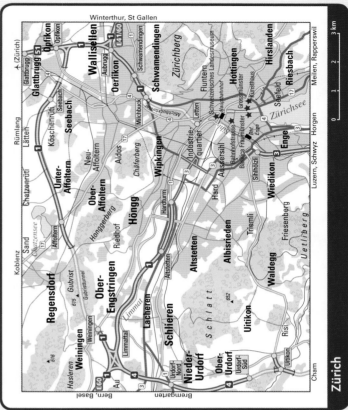

Zürich

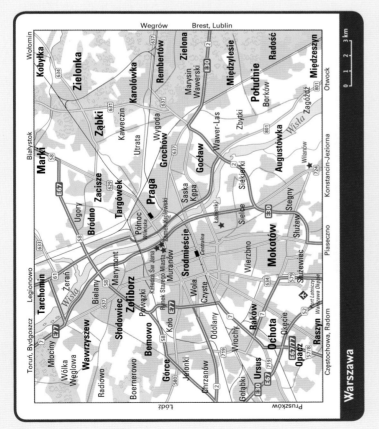

Warszawa

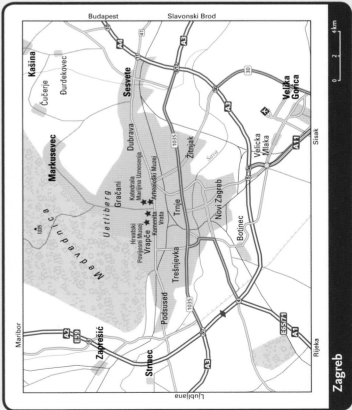

Zagreb

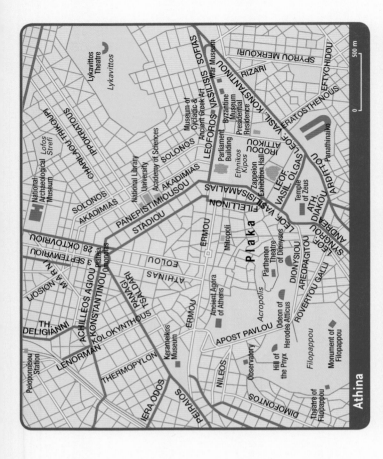

Athina

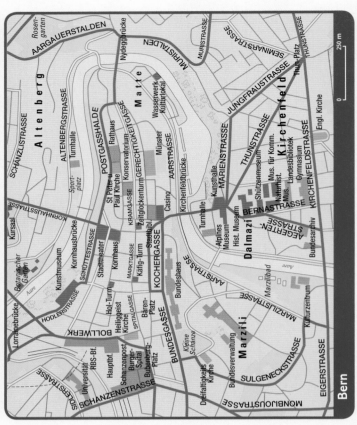

Bern

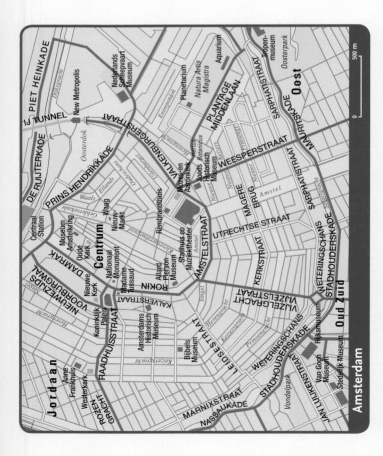

Amsterdam

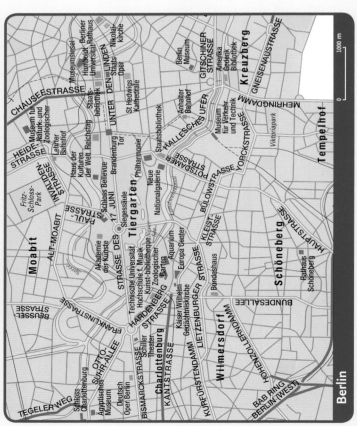

Berlin

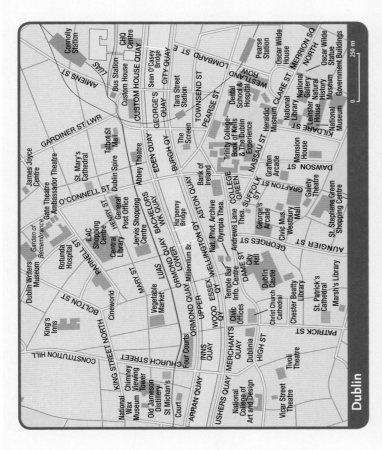

Dublin

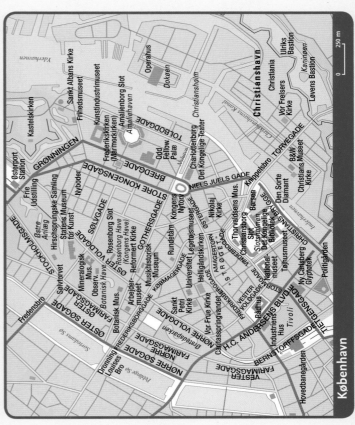

København

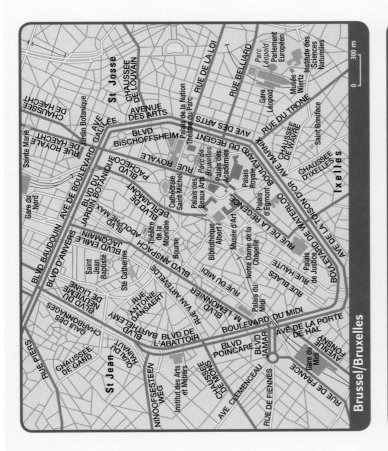

Brussel/Bruxelles

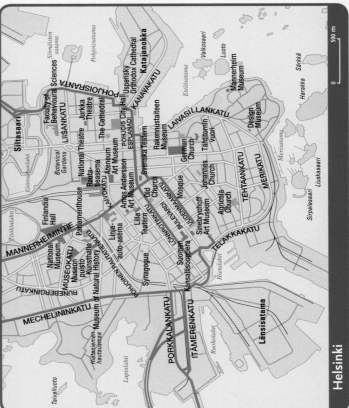

Helsinki

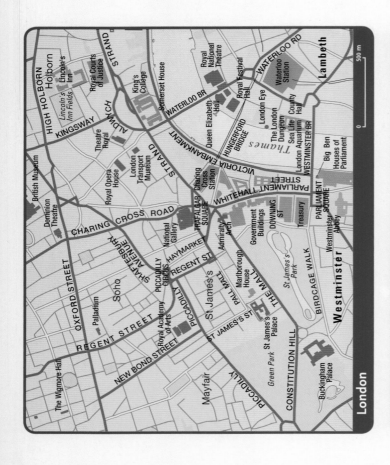

London

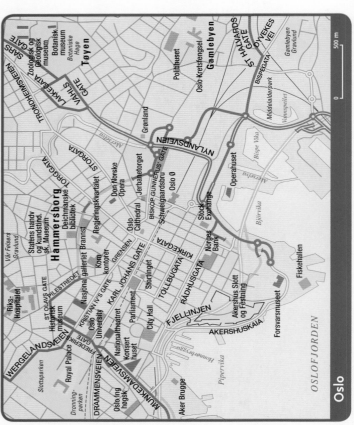

Oslo

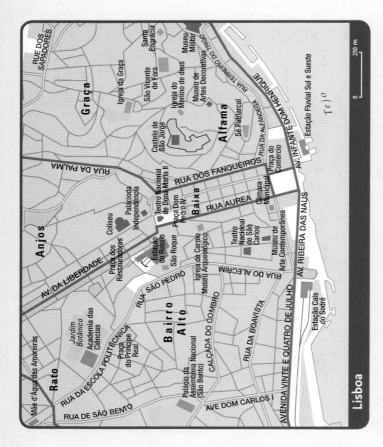

Lisboa

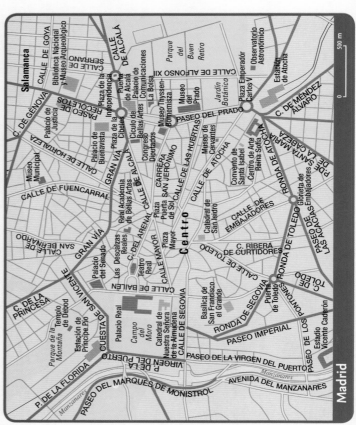

Madrid

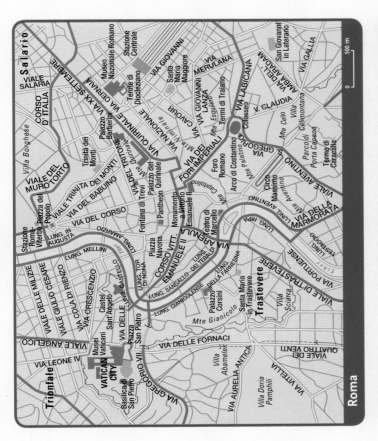

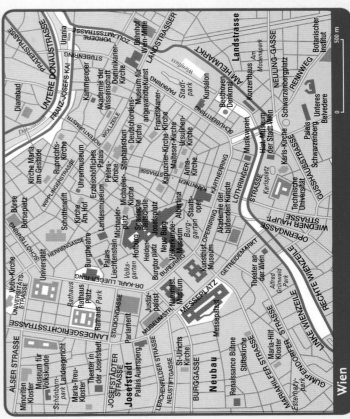

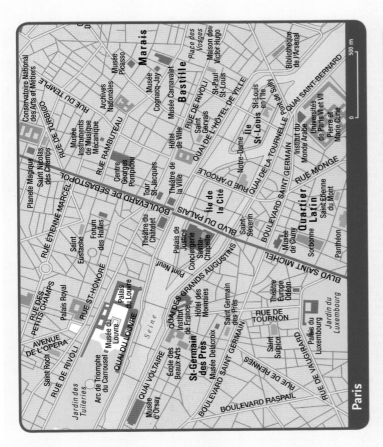

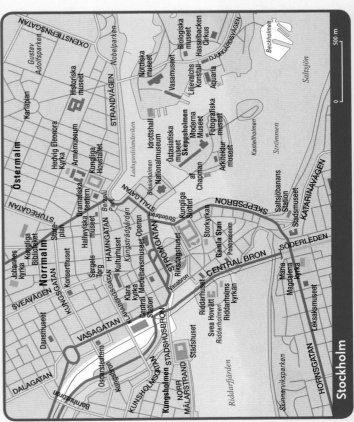

A

Å N 104 F7
Å N 110 E4
Å N 111 B12
Å N 111 C13
Aabenraa DK 86 E4
Aabybro DK 86 A5
Aachen D 20 C6
Aadorf CH 27 F10
Aakirkeby DK 89 E7
Aalborg DK 86 A5
Aalen D 75 E7
Aalestrup DK 86 B4
Aalsmeer NL 16 D3
Aalst B 19 C9
Aalst NL 183 B6
Aalten NL 17 E7
Aalter B 19 B7
Äänekoski FIN 123 E15
Aapajärvi FIN 115 D2
Aapajärvi FIN 119 B12
Aapajoki FIN 119 B12
Aapua S 117 E11
Aarau CH 27 F9
Aarberg CH 31 A11
Aardenburg NL 19 B7
Aareavaara S 117 D10
Aarhus DK 86 C6
Aarle NL 16 F5
A Armada E 38 B3
Aars DK 86 B5
Aarschot B 19 C10
Aartrijke B 182 C2
Aartselaar B 19 B9
Aarup DK 86 E6
Aarwangen CH 27 F8
Aasleagh IRL 6 E3
Ääsmäe EST 131 C9
Aaspere EST 131 C12
Aatsinki FIN 115 E5
Aavajärvi S 119 C11
Aavasaksa FIN 119 B11
Aba H 149 B11
Abaclia MD 154 E3
Abades E 46 C4
Abadín E 38 B5
Abadiño-Zelaieta E 41 B6
Abádszalók H 150 C6
A Baiuca E 38 B3
Abak TR 181 A7
Abalar TR 172 A6
Abánades E 47 C8
Abanilla E 56 E2
Abano Terme I 66 B4
Abarán E 55 C10
A Barrela E 38 C4
Abasár H 150 B5
Abaújszántó H 145 G3
Abbadia San Salvatore I 62 B1
Abbasanta I 64 C2
Abbekås S 87 E13
Abbeville F 18 D4
Abbey IRL 6 F6
Abbeydorney IRL 8 D3
Abbeyfeale IRL 8 D4
Abbeyleix IRL 9 C8
Abbey Town GB 5 F10
Abbiategrasso I 69 C6
Abborrberg S 109 F12
Abborreberget S 98 D8
Abborrträsk S 109 F17
Abbotsbury GB 13 D9
Abbots Langley GB 15 D8
Abcoude NL 16 D3
Abejar E 40 E6
Abejuela E 48 E3
Abela P 50 C2
Abelvær N 105 B10
Abenberg D 75 D8
Abenójar E 54 B4
Abensberg D 75 E10
Aberaeron GB 12 A6
Aberaman GB 13 B8
Aberchirder GB 3 K11
Aberdare GB 13 B8
Aberdaron GB 10 F2
Aberdeen GB 3 L12
Aberdovey GB 10 F3
Aberfeldy GB 5 B9
Aberffraw GB 10 E3
Aberford GB 11 D9
Aberfoyle GB 5 C8
Abergavenny GB 13 B8
Abergele GB 10 E4
Åberget S 109 E18
Abergwaun GB 12 B5
Abergynolwyn GB 10 F4
Aberlady GB 5 C11
Aberlour GB 3 L10
Abernethy GB 5 C10
Aberporth GB 12 A5
Abersoch GB 10 F2
Abertamy CZ 75 B12
Abertawe GB 13 B7
Abertillery GB 13 B8
Abertura E 45 F9
Aberuthven GB 5 C9
Aberystwyth GB 12 A6
Abetone I 66 D2
Abfaltersbach A 72 C6
Abhainnsuidhe GB 2 K2
Abia de la Obispalía E 47 D8
Abiego E 42 C3
Abild DK 86 F3
Abilly F 29 B7
Abingdon GB 13 B12
Abington GB 5 E9
Abisko Östra S 111 D16
Abja-Paluoja EST 131 E10
Abla E 55 E7
Ablis F 24 C6
Ablitas E 41 E8
Abmelaseter N 112 E6
Abo FIN 126 E7
Åbo S 103 C10
Åbodarna S 107 E14
Åbogen N 96 B7
Abondance F 31 C10
Abony H 150 C5
Åbosjö S 107 D13
Aboyne GB 5 A11
Abragão P 44 B4
Abram RO 151 C9
Abrămuț RO 151 C9
Abrantes P 44 F4
Abraur S 109 D16
Abreiro P 38 F5
Abreschviller F 27 C7
Abrest F 30 C3
Abriès F 31 F10
Abrigada P 44 F2
Abriola I 60 B5
Abrucena E 55 E7
Abrud RO 151 E11
Abrupe LV 135 B11
Absam A 72 B4
Absberg D 75 D8
Absdorf A 77 F9
Abtenau A 73 A7
Abtsgmünd D 74 E6
Abukhava BY 140 C10
Åby S 89 A7
Åby S 93 B8
Åbyen DK 90 D7
Åbyggeby S 103 E13
Åbyn S 118 D6
Åbytorp S 92 A6
Acaill IRL 6 E3
A Cañiza E 38 D3
A Carballa E 38 B2
Acarlar TR 177 D10
A Carreira E 38 B3
Acâș RO 151 B10
Acate I 58 E5
Accadia I 60 A4
Acceglio I 36 C5
Accettura I 60 C6
Acciano I 62 C5
Acciaroli I 60 C4
Accous F 32 E4
Accrington GB 11 D7
Accumoli I 62 B4
Acebo E 45 D7
Acedera E 45 F9
Acedo E 32 E1
Acehuche E 45 E7
Aceituna E 45 D8
Acered E 47 B9
Acerenza I 60 B5
Acerno I 60 B4
Acerra I 60 B2
Aceuchal E 51 B7
Ach A 76 F3
Achadh Mòr GB 2 J3
A Chan E 38 D3
Acharacle GB 4 B5
Acharnes GR 175 C8
Achavanich GB 3 J10
Achel B 183 C6
Achenkirch A 72 A4
Achern D 27 C9
Acheux-en-Amiénois F 18 D6
Achicourt F 18 D6
Achill IRL 6 E3
Achilleio GR 175 A6
Achim D 17 B12
Achintee GB 2 L6
Achladochori GR 169 B10
Achladokampos GR 175 D6
Achnacroish GB 4 B6
Achnasheen GB 2 K6
Achosnich GB 4 B4
Achstetten D 71 A9
Achtrup D 82 A6
Aci Castello I 59 D7
Aci Catena I 59 D7
Acireale I 59 D7
Aci Sant'Antonio I 59 D7
Aci Trezza I 59 D7
Acktjära S 103 D11
Acle GB 15 B12
A Coruña E 38 B3
Acquacalda I 59 B6
Acqualagna I 67 E6
Acquanegra sul Chiese I 66 B1
Acquapendente I 62 B1
Acquappesa I 60 E5
Acquaro I 59 B9
Acquarossa CH 71 E7
Acquasanta Terme I 62 B4
Acquasparta I 62 B3
Acquaviva Picena I 62 B5
Acquedolci I 59 C6
Acquigny F 24 B5
Acqui Terme I 37 B8
Acri I 61 E6
A Cruz do Incio E 38 C5
Ács H 149 A10
Acsa H 150 B3
Acuto I 62 D4
Ada SRB 150 F5
Adács H 150 B4
Adahuesca E 42 C3
Adak S 109 F16
Ådalsliden S 107 E11
Adamas GR 179 B7
Adamclisi RO 155 E1
Adamov CZ 77 D11
Adamova BY 133 E4
Adamów PL 141 G6
Adamówka PL 144 C6
Adamstown IRL 9 D9
Adămuș RO 152 E4
Adamuz E 53 A7
Adâncata RO 153 B8
Adâncata RO 161 D8
Ádánd H 149 C10
Adanero E 46 C3
Adão P 45 D6
Adare IRL 8 C5
Adatepe TR 173 D6
Adaúfe P 38 E3
Adavere EST 131 D11
Ādaži LV 135 B8
Adderbury GB 13 A12
Addlestone GB 15 E8
Adegem B 182 C2
Adelboden CH 31 C12
Adelebsen D 78 C6
Adelfia I 61 A7
Adelina PL 144 B8
Adelmannsfelden D 187 D8
Adelschlag D 75 E9
Adelsheim D 27 B11
Adelsried D 75 F8
Ademuz E 47 D10
Adenau D 21 D7
Adendorf D 83 D8
Adendro GR 169 C8
Adenstedt D 78 C6
Adjud RO 153 E10
Adlešiči SLO 148 E4
Adliswil CH 27 F10
Adlkofen D 75 E11
Admont A 73 A9
Adolfsström S 109 D12
Adony H 149 B11
Adorf D 75 B11
Adorf (Diemelsee) D 17 F11
Adoufe P 38 F4
Adra E 55 F6
Adradas E 41 F7
Adrados E 40 F3
Adrano I 59 D6
Adria I 66 B5
Adriani GR 171 B6
Adriers F 29 C7
Aduard NL 17 B6
Adulsbruk N 101 E14
Ådum DK 86 D3
Adunați RO 161 C7
Adunații-Copăceni RO 161 E8
Adutiškis LT 135 F13
Adzaneta de Albaida E 56 D4
Adžūni LV 135 D8
Aegviidu EST 131 C11
Aerino GR 169 F8
Ærøskøbing DK 86 F6
Aerzen D 17 D12
A Escusa E 38 C2
A Esfarrapada E 38 D2
A Estrada E 38 C3
Aetos GR 169 C6
Aetos GR 174 B3
Aetos GR 174 E4
Äetsä FIN 126 C8
Afantou GR 181 D8
Åfarnes N 100 A7
A Feira do Monte E 38 B4
Affing D 75 F8
Afife P 38 E2
Afissos GR 169 F9
Åfjord N 104 D8
Aflenz Kurort A 73 A11
A Fonsagrada E 38 B5
A Forxa E 38 D4
A Forxa E 38 D4
Åfoss N 90 A6
Afragola I 60 B2
Afritz A 73 C8
Afumați RO 160 E2
Afumați RO 161 D8
Afytos GR 169 D9
Aga D 79 E11
Ağaçli TR 173 B10
Ağaköy TR 173 D7
Agalas GR 174 D2
Agallas E 45 D8
A Gándara E 38 B3
A Gándara de Altea E 38 A3
Agapia RO 153 C8
Agăș RO 153 D8
Ágasegyháza H 150 D3
Agde F 34 D5
Agen F 33 B7
Àger E 42 C5
Agerbæk DK 86 D3
Agerskov DK 86 E4
Agersted DK 86 A6
Ågerup DK 87 D10
Ágfalva H 149 A7
Aggersund DK 86 A4
Aggius I 64 B3
Aggsbach Markt A 77 F8
Aghaboe IRL 9 C7
Aghagallon GB 7 C10
Aghalee GB 7 C10
Aghanloo GB 4 E3
Aghaville IRL 8 E4
Aghern IRL 8 D6
Aghione F 37 G10
Aghireșu RO 151 D11
Aghleam IRL 6 D2
Aghnagar Bridge IRL 8 E2
Agia GR 169 E8
Agia Anna GR 175 B7
Agia Anna GR 175 C6
Agia Effimia GR 174 C2
Agia Efthymia GR 174 C5
Agia Galini GR 178 E8
Agia Kyriaki GR 174 E4
Agia Marina GR 175 B6
Agia Marina GR 175 C9
Agia Marina GR 177 E8
Agia Paraskevi GR 168 D4
Agia Paraskevi GR 174 A3
Agia Paraskevi GR 177 E6
Agia Pelagia GR 178 C4
Agia Pelagia GR 178 E9
Agiasma GR 171 C7
Agiasos GR 177 A7
Agia Triada GR 174 D4
Agia Triada GR 175 D6
Agia Varvara GR 169 D7
Agia Varvara GR 178 E9
Agigea RO 155 E3
Agighiol RO 155 C3
Agino Selo BIH 157 C7
Agiofyllo GR 169 E6
Agioi Anargyroi GR 169 E7
Agioi Apostoloi GR 175 C8
Agioi Deka GR 178 E8
Agioi Theodoroi GR 169 E5
Agioi Theodoroi GR 175 A6
Agioi Theodoroi GR 175 D7
Agiokampos GR 169 E8
Agiokampos GR 175 B7
Agionori GR 175 D6
Agios Andreas GR 175 E6
Agios Athanasios GR 169 C8
Agios Athanasios GR 171 B6
Agios Charalampos GR 171 C9
Agios Christoforos GR 175 F5
Agios Dimitrios GR 169 D7
Agios Dimitrios GR 175 D8
Agios Dimitrios GR 175 F6
Agios Efstratios GR 171 E7
Agios Georgios GR 169 C7
Agios Georgios GR 174 B4
Agios Georgios GR 175 C6
Agios Georgios GR 177 F6
Agios Georgios GR 178 E9
Agios Germanos GR 168 C5
Agios Ioannis GR 174 E5
Agios Ioannis GR 175 C7
Agios Ioannis GR 178 B4
Agios Kirykos GR 177 D7
Agios Konstantinos GR 174 B3
Agios Konstantinos GR 174 D5
Agios Konstantinos GR 175 B6
Agios Konstantinos GR 175 D9
Agios Kyprianos GR 178 C3
Agios Leon GR 174 D2
Agios Loukas GR 169 C7
Agios Loukas GR 175 C9
Agios Mamas GR 169 D9
Agios Matthaios GR 168 F2
Agios Myronas GR 178 E9
Agios Nikolaos GR 168 E3
Agios Nikolaos GR 168 E5
Agios Nikolaos GR 169 D10
Agios Nikolaos GR 174 B2
Agios Nikolaos GR 174 B4
Agios Nikolaos GR 174 B4
Agios Nikolaos GR 178 B3
Agios Nikolaos GR 179 E10
Agios Panteleïmonas GR 169 C6
Agios Paraskevi GR 171 F10
Agios Petros GR 169 C8
Agios Petros GR 174 B2
Agios Petros GR 175 E6
Agios Spyridonas GR 169 D7
Agios Spyridonas GR 174 A2
Agios Stefanos GR 175 C8
Agios Stefanos GR 176 E5
Agios Thomas GR 175 C8
Agios Vasileios GR 169 C9
Agios Vasileios GR 175 D6
Agira I 59 D6
Agivey GB 4 E3
Agkathia GR 169 C7
Agkistro GR 169 B9
Aglapsvik N 111 B15
Aglasterhausen D 187 C6
Agle N 105 C13
Aglen N 105 B10
Agliana I 66 E3
Aglientu I 64 A3
Aglish IRL 9 D7
Agluonėnai LT 134 E2
Agnadello I 69 C8
Agnagar Bridge IRL 8 E2
Agnanta GR 168 F5
Agnantero GR 169 F6
Agneaux F 23 B9
Agnita RO 152 F5
Agno CH 69 A6
Agnone I 63 D6
Agolada E 38 C3
Agoncillo E 32 F1
Agon-Coutainville F 23 B8
Agordo I 72 D5
Agost E 56 E3
Agos-Vidalos F 32 D5
Ågotnes N 94 B2
Agra GR 177 A7
Agramón E 55 C9
Agramunt E 42 D6
Agrate Brianza I 69 B7
Agreda E 41 E8
Agrés E 56 D4
Agria GR 169 F9
Agridi GR 174 D4
Agrigento I 58 E4
Agrij RO 151 C11
Agrili GR 174 E4
Agrinio GR 174 B3
Agriovotano GR 175 A7
Agrochão P 39 E5
Agropoli I 60 C3
Ågskaret N 108 C5
Aguadulce E 53 B7
Aguadulce E 55 F7
A Guarda E 38 E2
Aguarón E 41 F9
Aguas E 42 C3
Águas Belas P 44 E4
Aguas de Busot E 56 D4
Águas de Moura P 50 B2
Águas Frias P 38 E5
Aguaviva E 42 F3
A Gudiña E 38 D5
Agudo E 54 B3
Águeda P 44 C4
Aguessac F 34 B5
Agugliano I 67 E7
Aguiar P 50 C4
Aguiar da Beira P 44 C5
Aguilafuente E 46 B4
Aguilar de Alfambra E 42 F2
Aguilar de Campóo E 40 C3
Aguilar de la Frontera E 53 A7
Aguilar del Río Alhama E 41 E8
Águilas E 55 E9
Agullana E 34 F4
Agullent E 56 D3
Aha S 109 F14
Ahafona IRL 8 C3
Aham D 75 E11
Ahascragh IRL 6 F6
Ahaus D 17 D8
Åheim N 100 B3
Ahelva FIN 121 E11
Ahigal E 45 D8
Ahigal de Villarino E 45 B8
Ahillones E 51 C8
Ahja EST 131 E14
Ahjola FIN 121 D12
Ahlainen FIN 126 B6
Ahlatli TR 167 E8
Ahlbeck D 84 C6
Ahlbeck D 84 C6
Ahlden (Aller) D 82 E7
Ahlen D 17 E9
Ahlerstedt D 17 B12
Ahlhorn D 17 C10
Ahmas FIN 119 E17
Ahmavaara FIN 115 E4
Ahmetbey TR 173 B8
Ahmetbeyli TR 177 C9
Ahmetçeeli TR 172 E6
Ahmetli TR 177 C9
Ahmovaara FIN 125 D13
Ahnsbeck D 79 A7
Ahoghill GB 4 F4
Ahoinen FIN 127 D11
Ahokylä FIN 123 C17
Ahola FIN 121 B11
Ahola FIN 121 C13
Ahola FIN 121 D13
Ahola FIN 124 D9
Aholanvaara FIN 115 E5
Ahonperä FIN 119 F13
Ahorn D 75 B8
Aho-Vastinki FIN 123 E14
Ahrbrück D 21 D7
Ahrensbök D 83 B9
Ahrensburg D 83 C8
Ahrenshagen D 83 B13
Ahrenshoop D 83 B12
Ähtäri FIN 123 E12
Ähtärinranta FIN 123 E12
Ahtme EST 132 C1
Ahula EST 131 C11
Ahun F 29 C10
Åhus S 88 D6
Ahveninen FIN 123 E16
Ahvenisto FIN 127 C16
Ahvensalmi FIN 125 F10
Ahvenselkä FIN 115 E4
Ahvenvittikko FIN 115 D4
Ahvionsaari FIN 129 B10
Aiani GR 169 D6
Aianteio GR 175 D7
Aibar E 32 E3
Aibl A 73 C11
Aichach D 75 F9
Aichhalden D 27 D9
Aichstetten D 71 B10
Ai'dejav'ri N 117 A10
Aidenbach D 76 E4
Aidipsos GR 175 B7
Aidone I 58 E5
Aidonochori GR 169 C10
Aidt DK 86 C5
Aidu EST 131 D12
Aiello Calabro I 59 A9
Aielo de Malferit E 56 D3
Aieta I 60 D5
Aiffres F 28 C5
Aigeira GR 174 C5
Aigen im Ennstal A 73 A9
Aigen im Mühlkreis A 76 E5
Aigiali GR 177 F6
Aigina GR 175 D7
Aiginio GR 169 D8
Aigio GR 174 C5
Aigle CH 31 C10
Aiglemont F 184 E2
Aignan F 33 C6
Aignay-le-Duc F 25 E12
Aigre F 28 D6
Aigrefeuille-d'Aunis F 28 C4
Aigrefeuille-sur-Maine F 28 A3
A Igrexa E 38 D3
Aiguafreda E 43 D8
Aiguebelle F 31 D9
Aigueblanche F 31 D10
Aigueperse F 30 C3
Aigues-Mortes F 35 C7
Aigues-Vives F 33 E9
Aigues-Vives F 34 D4
Aigues-Vives F 35 C7
Aiguilhe F 30 E4
Aiguilles F 31 F10
Aiguillon F 33 B6
Aigurande F 29 C9
Äijäjoki FIN 116 B10
Äijälä FIN 123 E16
Aijala FIN 127 E9
Aijänneva FIN 123 F11
Aillant-sur-Tholon F 25 E9
Aillas F 32 B5
Aillevillers-et-Lyaumont F 26 E5
Ailly-le-Haut-Clocher F 18 D4
Ailly-sur-Noye F 18 E5
Ailly-sur-Somme F 18 E5
Ailt an Chorráin IRL 6 C6
Aimargues F 35 C7
Aime F 31 D10
Ainali FIN 119 F14
Ainali FIN 123 B11
Ainay-le-Château F 29 B11
Ainaži LV 131 F8
Aindling D 75 E8
Ainet A 73 C6
Ainsa E 33 F6
Ainzón E 41 E9
Airaines F 18 E4
Airaksela FIN 124 E8
Airasca I 31 F11
Aird Asaig GB 2 K3
Airdrie GB 5 D9
Aire-sur-l'Adour F 32 C5
Aire-sur-la-Lys F 18 C5
Airidh a'Bhruaich GB 2 J3
Airola I 60 A3
Airole I 37 D7
Airolo CH 71 D7
Airvault F 28 B5
Aisey-sur-Seine F 25 E12
Aïssey F 26 F5
Aisymi GR 171 B9
Aisy-sur-Armançon F 25 E11
Aitamännikkö FIN 117 D12
Aita Mare RO 153 F7
Aiterhofen D 75 E12
Aith GB 3 E14
Aith GB 3 G11
Aitolahti FIN 127 B10
Aitoliko GR 174 C3
Aiton RO 152 D3
Aitona E 42 E4
Aitoo FIN 127 C11
Aitrach D 71 B10
Aitrang D 71 B11
Aittaniemi FIN 121 B10
Aittijoki FIN 113 D17
Aittojärvi FIN 119 D17
Aittojärvi FIN 123 C16
Aittokoski FIN 124 C8
Aittokylä FIN 121 E10
Aittoperä FIN 123 C13
Aittovaara FIN 121 D13
Aiud RO 152 E3
Aiviekste LV 135 C11
Aix-en-Othe F 25 D10
Aix-en-Provence F 35 C9
Aixe-sur-Vienne F 29 D8
Aix-les-Bains F 31 D8
Aizenay F 28 B2
Aizkraukle LV 135 C10
Aizpún E 32 E2
Aizpurve LV 135 C12
Aizpute LV 134 C3
Aizvīķi LV 134 D3
Ajaccio F 37 H9
Ajanki FIN 117 E12
Ajankijärvi FIN 117 E12
Ajat F 29 E8
Ajaureforsen S 109 E10
Ajdovščina SLO 73 E8
Ajka H 149 B9
Ajo E 40 B4
Ajofrín E 46 E5
Ajos FIN 119 C13
Akācijas LV 134 C6
Åkarp S 87 D12
Äkäsjokisuu FIN 117 D11
Äkäslompolo FIN 117 C12
Akasztó H 150 D3
Akçaova TR 181 B7
Akçasusurluk TR 173 D9
Akeld GB 5 D12
Aken D 79 C11
Åkerbränna S 107 D11
Åkerby S 99 B9
Åkerholmen S 118 C6
Åkersberga S 99 D10
Akersjön S 105 D16
Åkers styckebruk S 98 D8
Åkerstrømmen N 101 C14
Akheloy BG 167 D9
Akhremawtsy BY 133 E2
Akhtopol BG 167 E9
Akkan S 109 F12
Akkarfjord N 113 B12
Akkarvik N 112 C5
Akkasæter N 111 B16
Akkavare S 109 E17
Akkerhaugen N 95 D10
Akköy TR 171 E10
Akköy TR 177 E9
Akkrum NL 16 B5
Akmeņdziras LV 134 B3
Akmenė LT 134 D5
Åknes N 110 C9
Aknīste LV 135 D11
Akonkoski FIN 121 F13
Akonpohja FIN 125 D10
Akpinar TR 173 B10
Akraifnio GR 175 C7
Åkran N 105 D12
Akrata GR 174 C5
Åkrehamn N 94 D2
Akrini GR 169 D6
Akrolimni GR 169 C7
Akropotamos GR 170 C6
Akrotiri GR 179 C9
Aksakal TR 173 D9
Aksaz TR 173 D7
Aksdal N 94 D2
Aksnes N 104 F4
Akujärvi FIN 114 F3
Åkullsjön S 118 F5
Åkvisslan S 107 E13
Ål N 101 E9
Ala I 69 B11
Ala S 93 E13
Alacaat TR 173 E10
Alacant E 56 E4
Alacaoğlu TR 173 B7
Alaçati TR 177 C7
Alà dei Sardi I 64 B3
Ala di Stura I 31 E11
Alaejos E 39 F9
Alagna Valsesia I 68 B4
A Lagoa E 38 C2
Alagoa P 44 F5
Alagón E 41 E9
Alahärmä FIN 122 D9
Ala-Honkajoki FIN 126 B7
Alaigne F 33 D10
Alaior E 57 B13
Alájar E 51 D6
Alajärvi FIN 117 E15
Alajärvi FIN 121 E12
Alajärvi FIN 123 D11
Alajõe EST 132 C1
Ala-Jokikylä FIN 119 C14
Ala-Kääntä FIN 119 F12
Ala-Keyritty FIN 125 D10
Alakurtti RUS 115 E8
Alakylä FIN 117 D13
Alakylä FIN 119 D15
Alakylä FIN 126 B6
Ala-Livo FIN 119 D17
Alameda E 53 B7
Alameda de Cervera E 47 F6
Alameda de la Sagra E 46 D5
Alamedilla E 55 D6
Alamillo E 54 B3
Alan HR 67 B10
Ala-Nampa FIN 117 E16
Alanäs S 106 C9
Ālande LV 134 C2
Alandroal P 50 B5
Älandsbro S 103 A14
Alange E 51 B7
Alaniemi FIN 119 C14
Alanís E 51 C8
Alanta LT 135 F10
Alap H 149 C11
Alapitkä FIN 124 D9
Alaquàs E 48 F4
Alaranta FIN 119 D14
Alaraz E 45 C10
Alarcón E 47 E8
Alar del Rey E 40 C3
Alaró E 49 E10
Alarup AL 168 C4
Ålåsen S 106 D7
Alaskylä FIN 127 B8
Alassio I 37 C8
Alastaipale FIN 123 F11
Alastaro FIN 126 D8
Ala-Sydänmaa FIN 123 B14
Alata F 37 H9
Ala-Temmes FIN 119 E15
Alatoz E 47 F10
Alatri I 62 D4
Alatskivi EST 131 D14
Alattyán H 150 C5
Ala-Valli FIN 123 F9
Alavattnet S 106 C9
Alavere EST 131 C10
Ala-Vieksi FIN 121 F12
Alavieska FIN 119 F12
Ala-Viirre FIN 123 B11
Ala-Vuokki FIN 121 E13
Ala-Vuotto FIN 119 D16
Alavus FIN 123 E11
Alba I 37 B8
Alba Adriatica I 62 B5
Albac RO 151 E10
Albacete E 55 A9
Albacken S 103 A11
Alba de Tormes E 45 C9
Ålbæk DK 90 D7
Albagiara I 64 D2
Albaida E 56 D4
Alba Iulia RO 152 E3
Albaladejo E 55 B7
Alba-la-Romaine F 35 A8
Albalate de Arzobispo E 42 E3
Albalate de Cinca E 42 D4
Albalate de las Nogueras E 47 D8
Albalate de Zorita E 47 D7
Albalatillo E 42 D3
Alban F 33 C10
Albánchez E 55 E8
Albanella I 60 C4
Albanitsa BG 165 C10
Albano di Lucania I 60 B6
Albano Laziale I 62 D3
Albano Vercellese I 68 C5
Albanyà E 43 C9
Albaredo per San Marco I 69 A8
Albaret-le-Comtal F 30 F3
Albareto I 69 E8
Albaret-Ste-Marie F 30 F3
Albaron F 35 C7
Albarracín E 47 D10
Albatana E 55 B9
Albatàrrec E 42 D5
Albatera E 56 E3
Albbruck D 27 E9
Albelda E 42 D4
Albelda de Iregua E 41 D7
Albella E 32 F5
Albendea E 47 C8
Albendín E 53 A8
Albenga I 37 C8
Albeni RO 160 C3
Albens F 31 D8
Albentosa E 48 D3
Ålberga S 93 B9
Alberga S 98 D6
Albergaria-a-Velha P 44 C4
Albergaria dos Doze P 44 E3
Albergen NL 183 A9
Alberic E 48 F4
Alberndorf in der Riedmark A 77 F6
Albernoa P 50 D4
Albero Alto E 41 D11
Alberobello I 61 B8
Alberona I 60 A4
Alberoni I 66 B5
Alberschwende A 71 C9
Albersdorf D 82 B6
Albert F 18 E6
Albertacce F 37 G9
Alberta Ligure I 37 B10
Albertirsa H 150 C4
Albertshofen D 187 B9
Albertville F 31 D9
Alberuela de Tubo E 42 D3
Albesa E 42 D5
Albești RO 152 E5
Albești RO 153 B10
Albești RO 153 D11
Albești RO 155 F2
Albești RO 161 D10
Albeștii de Argeș RO 160 C5
Albeștii de Muscel RO 160 C6
Albești-Paleologu RO 161 D8
Albestroff F 27 C6
Albi F 33 C10
Albias F 33 B8
Albidona I 61 D6
Albignasego I 66 B4
Albina RO 155 C1
Albino I 69 B8
Albires E 39 D9
Albisheim (Pfrimm) D 21 E10
Albisola Marina I 37 C9
Albisola Superiore I 37 C9
Alblasserdam NL 16 E3
Ålbo S 98 B7
Albocàsser E 48 D5
Alboloduy E 55 E7
Albolote E 53 B9
Albon F 30 E6
Albondón E 55 F6
Alboraya E 48 E4
Alborea E 47 F10
Albota RO 160 D5
Albox E 55 E8
Albrechtice nad Orlicí CZ 77 B10
Al'brekhtava BY 133 E5
Albstadt D 27 D11
Albu EST 131 C11
Albudeite E 55 C10
Albufeira P 50 E3
Albujón E 56 F2
Albuñol E 55 F6
Albuñuelas E 53 C9
Alburquerque E 45 F7
Alby S 89 C11
Alby S 103 A9
Alby-sur-Chéran F 31 D9
Alcácer E 48 F4
Alcácer do Sal P 50 C2
Alcáçovas P 50 C3
Alcadozo E 55 B9
Alcafozes P 45 E6
Alcaine E 42 F2
Alcains P 44 E6
Alcalá de Guadaira E 51 E8
Alcalá de Gurrea E 41 D10
Alcalá de Henares E 46 D6
Alcalá del Júcar E 47 F10
Alcalá de los Gazules E 52 D5
Alcalá del Río E 51 D8
Alcalá del Valle E 51 F9
Alcalà de Xivert E 48 D5
Alcalá la Real E 53 B9
Alcalalí E 56 D4
Alcamo I 58 D2
Alcampell E 42 D4
Alcanadre E 32 F1
Alcanede P 44 F3
Alcanena P 44 F3
Alcanhões P 44 F3
Alcañices E 39 E7
Alcañiz E 42 E3
Alcántara E 45 E7
Alcantarilla E 56 F2
Alcantud E 47 C8
Alcaracejos E 54 C3
Alcara li Fusi I 59 C6
Alcaraz E 55 B8
Alcaria Ruiva P 50 D4
Alcarràs E 42 D5
Alcaucín E 53 C8
Alcaudete E 53 A8
Alcaudete de la Jara E 46 E3
Alçay-Alçabéhéty-Sunharette F 32 D4
Alcázar del Rey E 47 D7
Alcázar de San Juan E 47 F6
Alcedar MD 154 B3
Alcester GB 13 A11
Alçitepe TR 171 D10
Alcoba E 46 F4
Alcobaça P 44 E3
Alcobendas E 46 C5
Alcocer E 47 D7
Alcocero de Mola E 40 D5
Alcochete P 50 B2
Alcoentre P 44 F3
Alcoi E 56 D4
Alcolea E 53 A7
Alcolea E 55 F7
Alcolea de Calatrava E 54 B4
Alcolea de Cinca E 42 D4
Alcolea del Pinar E 47 B8
Alcolea del Río E 51 D8
Alcollarín E 45 F9
Alconchel E 51 B5
Alcóntar E 55 E7
Alcorcón E 46 D5
Alcorisa E 42 F3
Alcoroches E 47 C9
Alcossebre E 48 D5
Alcoutim P 50 E5
Alcover E 42 E6
Alcoy E 56 D4
Alcsútdoboz H 149 B11
Alcubierre E 41 E11
Alcubilla de Avellaneda E 40 E5
Alcubillas E 55 B6
Alcublas E 48 E3
Alcúdia E 57 B11
Alcudia de Guadix E 55 E6
Alcudia de Monteagud E 55 E8
Alcuéscar E 45 F8
Aldbrough GB 11 D11
Aldeacentenera E 45 E9

Aldeadávila de la Ribera *E* 45 B7
Aldea del Cano *E* 45 F8
Aldea del Fresno *E* 46 D4
Aldea del Obispo *E* 45 C7
Aldea del Rey *E* 54 B5
Aldea de Trujillo *E* 45 E9
Aldealafuente *E* 41 E7
Aldealpozo *E* 41 E7
Aldeamayor de San Martín *E* 39 E10
Aldeanueva de Barbarroya *E* 45 E10
Aldeanueva de Ebro *E* 41 D8
Aldeanueva de Figueroa *E* 45 B9
Aldeanueva de la Vera *E* 45 D9
Aldeanueva del Camino *E* 45 D9
Aldeanueva de San Bartolomé *E* 45 E10
Aldeaquemada *E* 55 C6
Aldea Real *E* 46 B4
Aldearrodrigo *E* 45 B9
Aldeaseca *E* 46 B3
Aldeatejada *E* 45 C9
Aldeavieja *E* 46 C4
Aldeburgh *GB* 15 C12
Aldehuela de la Bóveda *E* 45 C8
Aldehuela de Yeltes *E* 45 C8
Aldeia da Mata *P* 44 F5
Aldeia da Ponte *P* 45 D7
Aldeia de João Pires *P* 45 D6
Aldeia do Bispo *P* 45 D6
Aldeia dos Elvas *P* 50 D3
Aldeia dos Fernandes *P* 50 D3
Aldeia dos Palheiros *P* 50 D3
Aldeia Velha *P* 44 F4
Aldenhoven *D* 20 C6
Aldeno *I* 69 B11
Alderbury *GB* 13 C11
Alderholt *GB* 13 D11
Alderley Edge *GB* 11 E7
Aldersbach *D* 76 E4
Aldershot *GB* 15 E7
Aldinac *SRB* 164 B5
Aldinci *MK* 164 F3
Aldingham *GB* 10 C5
Aldomirovtsi *BG* 165 D6
Aldover *E* 42 F5
Aldridge *GB* 11 F8
Aldudes *F* 32 D3
Åle *DK* 86 D5
Åled *S* 87 B11
Aledo *E* 55 D9
Alekovo *BG* 161 F10
Alekovo *BG* 166 C4
Aleksandriškės *LT* 137 D10
Aleksandrova *LV* 133 E2
Aleksandrovac *SRB* 159 E7
Aleksandrovac *SRB* 163 C11
Aleksandrovo *BG* 165 C10
Aleksandrovo *BG* 166 D4
Aleksandrovo *BG* 167 E7
Aleksandrów *PL* 141 F2
Aleksandrów *PL* 141 H1
Aleksandrów Kujawski *PL* 138 E6
Aleksandrów Łódzki *PL* 143 C7
Aleksa Šantić *SRB* 150 F3
Aleksinac *SRB* 164 B4
Ålem *S* 89 B10
Ålen *N* 101 A14
Alençon *F* 23 D12
Alenquer *P* 44 F3
Alénya *F* 34 E4
Alerheim *D* 75 E8
Aléria *F* 37 G11
Alerre *E* 41 D11
Alès *F* 35 B7
Ales *I* 64 D2
Aleşd *RO* 151 C9
Alesón *E* 41 D6
Alessandria *I* 37 B9
Alessandria del Carretto *I* 61 D6
Alessandria della Rocca *I* 58 D3
Alessano *I* 61 D10
Ålesund *N* 100 B4
Alet-les-Bains *F* 33 D10
Alexandreia *GR* 169 C7
Alexandria *GB* 4 D7
Alexandria *RO* 160 F6
Alexandroupoli *GR* 171 C9
Alexandru Vlahuţă *RO* 153 E11
Alexeevca *MD* 153 C11
Alexeni *RO* 161 D9
Alexsandrów *PL* 144 C6
Alezio *I* 61 C10
Alf *D* 21 D8
Alfacar *E* 53 B9
Alfafar *E* 48 F4
Alfaiates *P* 45 D7
Alfajarín *E* 41 E10
Alfambra *E* 42 F1
Alfambras *P* 50 E2
Alfamén *E* 41 F9
Alfândega da Fé *P* 39 F6
Alfántega *E* 42 D4
Alfarim *P* 50 C1
Alfaro *E* 41 D8
Alfarràs *E* 42 D5
Alfatar *BG* 161 F10
Alfdorf *D* 74 E6
Alfedena *I* 62 D6
Alfeizerão *P* 44 E2
Alfeld (Leine) *D* 78 C6
Alfena *P* 44 B3
Alferce *P* 50 E3
Alfhausen *D* 17 C9
Alfonsine *I* 66 D5
Alford *GB* 3 L11
Alford *GB* 11 E12
Alforja *E* 42 E5
Alfredshem *S* 107 E15
Alfreton *GB* 11 E9
Alfta *S* 103 D11
Alfundão *P* 50 C3
Algaida *E* 57 B10
Algajola *F* 37 F9
Algámitas *E* 53 B6
Algar *E* 52 C5
Älgarås *S* 92 B4
Ålgård *N* 94 E3
Algarinejo *E* 53 B8
Algarrobo *E* 53 C8
Algatocín *E* 53 C6
Algeciras *E* 53 D6
Algemesí *E* 48 F4
Algered *S* 103 B12
Algermissen *D* 79 B6
Algerri *E* 42 D5
Algestrup *DK* 87 E10
Algete *E* 46 C6
Alghero *I* 64 B1
Älghult *S* 89 A9
Alginet *E* 48 F4
Älgnäs *S* 103 D12
Algodonales *E* 51 F9
Algodor *P* 50 D4
Algora *E* 47 C7
Algorta *E* 40 B6
Algoso *P* 39 F6
Algoz *P* 50 E3
Algrange *F* 20 F6
Alguaire *E* 42 D5
Alguazas *E* 56 E2
Algueirão-Mem Martins *P* 50 B1
Algueña *E* 56 E3
Algutsrum *S* 89 B11
Alhabia *E* 55 F7
Alhama de Almería *E* 55 F7
Alhama de Aragón *E* 41 F8
Alhama de Granada *E* 53 B9
Alhama de Murcia *E* 55 D10
Alhambra *E* 55 B6
Alhamn *S* 118 D7
Alhaurín de la Torre *E* 53 C7
Alhaurín el Grande *E* 53 C7
Alhendín *E* 53 B9
Alhojärvi *FIN* 127 B13
Alhóndiga *E* 47 C7
Ålhult *S* 92 D7
Alía *E* 45 F10
Alia *I* 58 D4
Aliaga *E* 42 F2
Aliağa *TR* 177 B8
Aliaguilla *E* 47 E10
Aliano *I* 60 C6
Aliartos *GR* 175 C7
Alibunar *SRB* 159 C6
Alicante *E* 56 E4
Alicún de Ortega *E* 55 D6
Alife *I* 60 A2
Alija del Infantado *E* 39 D8
Alijó *P* 38 F5
Alikianos *GR* 178 E6
Alikylä *FIN* 123 C11
Aliman *RO* 155 E1
Alimena *I* 58 D5
Aliminusa *I* 58 D4
Alimpeşti *RO* 160 C3
Alingsås *S* 91 D12
Alino *BG* 165 E7
Alionys 1 *LT* 137 C11
Aliseda *E* 45 F7
Alistrati *GR* 170 B5
Ali Terme *I* 59 C7
Aliveri *GR* 175 C9
Alizava *LT* 135 E10
Aljaraque *E* 51 E5
Aljezur *P* 50 E2
Aljinovići *SRB* 163 C8
Aljubarrota *P* 44 E3
Aljucén *E* 51 A7
Aljustrel *P* 50 D3
Alken *B* 19 C11
Alkkia *FIN* 122 F9
Alkmaar *NL* 16 C3
Allai *I* 64 D2
Allaire *F* 23 E7
Allambres *AL* 168 C2
Allan *F* 35 A8
Allanche *F* 30 E2
Allariz *E* 38 D4
Allarmont *F* 27 D7
Allassac *F* 29 E8
Allaži *LV* 135 B9
Allažmuiža *LV* 135 B9
Alle *CH* 27 F7
Alleghe *I* 72 D5
Allègre *F* 30 E4
Alleins *F* 35 C9
Allemond *F* 31 E9
Allen *IRL* 7 F9
Allendale Town *GB* 5 F12
Allendorf (Eder) *D* 21 B11
Allenheads *GB* 5 F12
Allensbach *D* 27 E11
Allentsteig *A* 77 E8
Allenwood *IRL* 7 F9
Allepuz *E* 42 G2
Allerona *I* 62 B1
Allersberg *D* 75 D9
Allershausen *D* 75 F10
Allerslev *DK* 87 E10
Allevard *F* 31 E9
Allex *F* 30 F6
Allibaudières *F* 25 C11
Alligny-en-Morvan *F* 25 F11
Allihies *IRL* 8 E2
Allingåbro *DK* 86 C6
Allinges *F* 31 C9
Allinge-Sandvig *DK* 89 E7
Alliste *I* 61 D10
Allmendingen *D* 74 F6
Allo *E* 32 E1
Alloa *GB* 5 C9
Allogny *F* 25 F7
Ålloluokta *S* 109 B17
Allonby *GB* 5 F10
Allonnes *F* 23 E12
Allonnes *F* 23 F12
Allons *F* 32 B5
Allos *F* 36 C5
Allouе *F* 29 C7
Alloza *E* 42 F2
Allschwil *CH* 27 E8
Allsta *S* 103 A15
Allstad *N* 110 D6
Allstedt *D* 79 D9
Allumiere *I* 62 C1
Alluy *F* 30 A4
Almacelles *E* 42 D4
Almáchar *E* 53 C8
Almada *P* 50 B1
Almadén *E* 54 B3
Almadén de la Plata *E* 51 D7
Almadenejos *E* 54 B3
Almagro *E* 54 B5
Almăj *RO* 160 E3
Almajano *E* 41 E7
Almalaguês *P* 44 D4
Almaluez *E* 41 F7
Almansa *E* 56 D2
Almansil *P* 50 E3
Almanza *E* 39 C9
Almaraz *E* 45 E9
Almargen *E* 53 B6
Almarza *E* 41 E7
Almaş *RO* 151 E9
Almásfüzitő *H* 149 A10
Almaşu *RO* 151 D11
Almaşu Mare *RO* 151 E11
Almazán *E* 41 F6
Almazora *E* 48 E4
Almazul *E* 41 E7
Almedina *E* 55 B7
Almedinilla *E* 53 B8
Almeida de Sayago *E* 39 F7
Almeirim *P* 44 F3
Almelo *NL* 17 D7
Almenar *E* 42 D5
Almenara *E* 48 E4
Almenar de Soria *E* 41 E7
Almendra *E* 45 B8
Almendra *P* 45 B6
Almendral *E* 51 B6
Almendralejo *E* 51 B7
Almendricos *E* 55 E9
Almendros *E* 47 E7
Almere *NL* 16 D4
Almería *E* 55 F8
Almerimar *E* 55 F7
Älmestad *S* 91 D13
Älmhult *S* 88 B6
Almind *DK* 86 D4
Almkerk *NL* 16 E3
Ålmo *N* 104 E4
Almodôvar *P* 50 D3
Almodóvar del Campo *E* 54 B4
Almodóvar del Pinar *E* 47 E9
Almodóvar del Río *E* 53 A6
Almofala *P* 44 C5
Almogía *E* 53 C7
Almograve *P* 50 D2
Almoguera *E* 47 D7
Almoharín *E* 45 F8
Almonacid de la Sierra *E* 41 F9
Almonacid del Marquesado *E* 47 E7
Almonacid del Zorita *E* 47 D7
Almonacid de Toledo *E* 46 E5
Almonaster la Real *E* 51 D6
Almondsbury *GB* 13 B9
Almonte *E* 51 E6
Almoradí *E* 56 E3
Almorchón *E* 51 B9
Almorox *E* 46 D4
Almosd *H* 151 C8
Almoster *P* 44 E4
Almsele *S* 107 C12
Almsjönäs *S* 107 E14
Älmsta *S* 99 C11
Almstedt *D* 79 B6
Almudema *E* 55 C9
Almudévar *E* 41 D10
Almuñécar *E* 53 C9
Almunge *S* 99 C10
Almuniente *E* 41 E11
Almünster *A* 73 A8
Almuradiel *E* 55 B6
Almussafes *E* 48 F4
Almvik *S* 93 D9
Almyropotamos *GR* 175 C9
Almyros *GR* 175 A6
Alnes *N* 100 B4
Alness *GB* 3 K8
Alnwick *GB* 5 E13
Alobras *E* 47 D10
Alocén *E* 47 C7
Aloja *LV* 131 F9
Alol' *RUS* 133 D6
Alonia *GR* 169 D8
Ålora *E* 53 C7
Alós d'Ensil *E* 33 E8
Alosno *E* 51 D5
Alost *B* 19 C9
Alost *B* 182 D4
Alovera *E* 47 C6
Alozaina *E* 53 C7
Alp *E* 33 F9
Alpalhão *P* 44 F5
Alpanseque *E* 41 F6
Alpbach *A* 72 B4
Alpedrinha *P* 44 D6
Alpedriz *P* 44 E3
Alpen *D* 17 E7
Alpenrod *D* 21 C9
Alpens *E* 43 C8
Alpera *E* 56 D2
Alphen *NL* 16 F3
Alphen aan den Rijn *NL* 16 D3
Alpiarça *P* 44 F3
Alpirsbach *D* 27 D9
Alpnach *CH* 70 D6
Alposjärvi *FIN* 117 E12
Alpua *FIN* 119 F14
Alpuente *E* 47 E11
Alpullu *TR* 173 B7
Alquería de la Condesa *E* 56 D4
Alquerías *E* 56 E2
Alqueva *P* 50 C4
Alquife *E* 55 E6
Alrance *F* 34 B4
Alrewas *GB* 11 F8
Als *DK* 86 B6
Alsager *GB* 11 E7
Alsån *S* 119 B9
Alsbach *D* 187 B6
Alsdorf *D* 20 C6
Alsėdžiai *LT* 134 D4
Alsen *S* 105 E15
Alsenborn *D* 21 F9
Alseno *I* 69 D8
Alsenz *D* 21 E9
Alsfeld *D* 21 C12
Alsheim *D* 185 E9
Alsike *S* 99 C9
Alsjö *S* 103 B11
Alsleben (Saale) *D* 79 C10
Alslev *DK* 86 D2
Alsmo *N* 100 D6
Alsónémedi *H* 150 C3
Alsópáhok *H* 149 C8
Alsos *N* 108 A8
Alsóvadász *H* 145 G2
Alsózsolca *H* 145 G2
Alsrode *DK* 87 C7
Ålstad *N* 110 E9
Alstad *S* 87 E12
Alstahaug *N* 108 E3
Alstakan *S* 97 C8
Alster *S* 97 D10
Alsterbro *S* 89 B9
Alstermo *S* 89 B9
Alsting *F* 186 C2
Alston *GB* 5 F12
Alsunga *LV* 134 C3
Alsvåg *N* 110 C9
Alsvik *N* 108 B7
Alsviķi *LV* 133 B1
Alta *N* 113 D11
Älta *S* 99 D10
Altafulla *E* 43 E6
Altamura *I* 61 B7
Altare *I* 37 C8
Altatornio *FIN* 119 C12
Altaussee *A* 73 A8
Altavilla Irpina *I* 60 B3
Altavilla Silentina *I* 60 B4
Altdöbern *D* 80 C6
Altdorf *CH* 71 D7
Altdorf *D* 75 E11
Altdorf bei Nürnberg *D* 75 D9
Alt Duvenstedt *D* 82 B7
Alte *P* 50 E3
Altea *E* 56 D4
Altefähr *D* 84 B4
Alteglofsheim *D* 75 E11
Alteidet *N* 112 C9
Altena *D* 17 F9
Altenahr *D* 21 C7
Altenau *D* 79 C7
Altenberg *D* 80 E5
Altenberge *D* 17 D8
Altenbruch-Westerende *D* 17 A11
Altenbuch *D* 74 C5
Altenburg *D* 79 E11
Altendiez *D* 21 D9
Altenfeld *D* 75 A8
Altenfelden *A* 76 F5
Altenglan *D* 21 E8
Altenhagen *D* 83 B11
Altenheim *D* 27 D8
Altenhof *D* 84 E5
Altenholz *D* 83 B8
Altenkirchen *D* 84 A4
Altenkirchen (Westerwald) *D* 21 C9
Altenkrempe *D* 83 B9
Altenkunstadt *D* 75 B9
Altenmarkt an der Triesting *A* 77 F9
Altenmarkt bei Sankt Gallen *A* 73 A10
Altenmarkt im Pongau *A* 73 B7
Altenmedingen *D* 83 D9
Altenmünster *D* 75 F8
Altenstadt *D* 21 D11
Altenstadt *D* 71 A10
Altenstadt *D* 71 B11
Altensteig *D* 27 C10
Altentreptow *D* 84 C4
Alter do Chão *P* 44 F5
Altes Lager *D* 80 B4
Altevik *N* 111 C12
Altfraunhofen *D* 75 F11
Altheim *A* 76 F4
Altheim *D* 27 D11
Altheim (Alb) *D* 187 D9
Althengstett *D* 187 D6
Althofen *A* 73 C9
Altier *F* 35 B6
Altimir *BG* 165 B8
Altîna *RO* 152 F4
Altındag *TR* 177 C9
Altinoluk *TR* 172 E6
Altinova *TR* 177 A8
Altıntaş *TR* 181 A8
Altkirch *F* 27 E7
Alt Krenzlin *D* 83 D10
Altlandsberg *D* 80 A5
Altleiningen *D* 21 E10
Altmannstein *D* 75 E10
Altnaharra *GB* 2 J8
Altofonte *I* 58 C3
Altomonte *I* 60 D6
Altomünster *D* 75 F9
Alton *GB* 11 F8
Alton *GB* 14 E7
Altopascio *I* 66 E2
Altorricón *E* 42 D4
Altötting *D* 75 F12
Altrich *D* 185 E6
Altrincham *GB* 11 E7
Alt Ruppin *D* 84 E3
Altsasu *E* 32 E1
Alt Schwerin *D* 83 C12
Altshausen *D* 71 B9
Altstätten *CH* 71 C9
Alttajärvi *S* 116 C5
Altura *E* 48 E4
Altusried *D* 71 B10
Alu *EST* 131 C9
Aluatu *MD* 154 F3
Alūksne *LV* 133 B2
Alund *S* 118 D6
Alunda *S* 99 B10
Aluniş *RO* 152 C3
Aluniş *RO* 152 D5
Aluniş *RO* 160 C5
Alunu *RO* 160 C3
Alustante *E* 47 C9
Alva *S* 93 E12
Alvaiázere *P* 44 E4
Alvajarvi *FIN* 123 D14
Alvalade *P* 50 D3
Alvaneu *CH* 71 D9
Älvängen *S* 91 D11
Alvarenga *P* 44 C4
Alvares *P* 44 D4
Álvaro *P* 44 E5
Alvdal *N* 101 B13
Älvdalen *S* 102 D7
Alvega *P* 44 F4
Alveley *GB* 13 A10
Alvelos *P* 38 E2
Alverca *P* 50 B1
Alverca da Beira *P* 45 C6
Alvesta *S* 88 B7
Alvestad *N* 111 C11
Alvestorp *S* 97 C12
Alvettula *FIN* 127 C11
Alvhem *S* 91 C11
Älvho *S* 102 D8
Alviano *I* 62 B2
Alvie *GB* 3 L9
Alvignac *F* 29 F9
Ålvik *N* 94 B4
Alvik *S* 102 E8
Alvik *S* 103 B13
Alvik *S* 118 C7
Alvito *I* 62 D5
Alvito *P* 50 C4
Älvkarleby *S* 103 E13
Älvkarleö *S* 99 A8
Alvnes *N* 108 B9
Alvnes *N* 110 E9
Alvoco da Serra *P* 44 D5
Älvros *S* 102 B8
Älvsbyn *S* 118 C6
Älvsered *S* 87 A11
Ålvund *N* 101 A9
Ålvundeid *N* 101 A9
Alwernia *PL* 143 F8
Alyki *GR* 174 A3
Alyth *GB* 5 B10
Alytus *LT* 137 E9
Alzenau in Unterfranken *D* 21 D12
Alzey *D* 21 E10
Alzira *E* 48 F4
Alzon *F* 34 C5
Alzonne *F* 33 D10
Åmådalen *S* 102 D8
Amadora *P* 50 B1
Amaiur-Maia *E* 32 D3
Åmål *S* 91 A12
Åmål *S* 91 B12
Amalfi *I* 60 B3
Amaliada *GR* 174 D3
Amaliapoli *GR* 175 A6
Amalo *GR* 177 D6
Amance *F* 26 E5
Amancey *F* 31 A9
Amandola *I* 62 B4
Amantea *I* 60 E6
Amara *RO* 161 D10
Amarante *P* 38 F3
Amarantos *GR* 168 E5
Amărăşti *RO* 160 D4
Amărăştii de Jos *RO* 160 F4
Amărăştii de Sus *RO* 160 F4
Amareleja *P* 51 C5
Amares *P* 38 E3
Amaroni *I* 59 B9
Amaru *RO* 161 D9
Amarynthos *GR* 175 C8
Amaseno *I* 62 E4
Amatrice *I* 62 B4
Amaxades *GR* 171 B8
Amay *B* 19 C11
Ambasaguas *E* 39 C9
Ambazac *F* 29 D8
Ambel *E* 41 E8
Ambeļi *LV* 135 D13
Amberg *D* 75 D10
Ambergate *GB* 11 E9
Ambérieu-en-Bugey *F* 31 D7
Amberloup *B* 19 D12
Ambert *F* 30 D4
Ambès *F* 28 E4
Ambierle *F* 30 C4
Ambillou *F* 24 F3
Ambjörby *S* 97 B9
Ambjörnarp *S* 91 E13
Ambla *EST* 131 C11
Amblainville *F* 24 B7
Amble *GB* 5 E13
Ambleside *GB* 10 C6
Ambleteuse *F* 15 F12
Amboise *F* 24 F4
Ambon *F* 22 E6
Ambrault *F* 29 B9
Ambrières-les-Vallées *F* 23 D10
Ambronay *F* 31 C7
Ambrosden *GB* 13 B12
Åmdals Verk *N* 95 D8
Ameglia *I* 69 E8
Ameide *NL* 182 B5
Ameixial *P* 50 E4
Amel *B* 20 D6
Amele *LV* 134 B4
Amelia *I* 62 B2
Amélie-les-Bains-Palalda *F* 34 F4
Amelinghausen *D* 83 D8
Amêndoa *P* 44 E4
Amendoeira *P* 50 D4
Amendolara *I* 61 D7
Amer *E* 43 C9
Amerang *D* 75 G11
A Merca *E* 38 D4
Amerongen *NL* 183 B6
Amersfoort *NL* 16 D4
Amersham *GB* 15 D7
Amesbury *GB* 13 C11
Amezketa *E* 32 D1
Amfikleia *GR* 175 B6
Amfilochia *GR* 174 B3
Amfipoli *GR* 169 C10
Amfissa *GR* 174 B5
Amieira *P* 50 C4
Amiens *F* 18 E5
Amilly *F* 25 E8
Äminne *FIN* 122 F7
Äminne *S* 87 A14
Åmland *N* 94 F5
Åmli *N* 90 A3
Åmli *N* 90 B3
Amlwch *GB* 10 E3
Ämmälänkylä *FIN* 123 E9
Ammanford *GB* 12 B7
Ämmänsaari *FIN* 121 E12
Ammarnäs *S* 109 E11
Åmmeberg *S* 92 B6
Ammenäs *S* 91 C10
Ammerbuch *D* 187 D6
Ammern *D* 79 D7
Ammersbek *D* 83 C8
Ammerzoden *NL* 183 B6
Ammochori *GR* 169 C5
Ammotopos *GR* 168 F4
Ammoudia *GR* 169 B9
Amnatos *GR* 178 E8
Amnéville *F* 186 C1
Amoeiro *E* 38 D4
Amonde *P* 38 E2
Amorbach *D* 21 E12
Amorebieta *E* 40 B6
Amorgos *GR* 177 F6
Amori *GR* 171 B10
Åmot *N* 94 C7
Åmot *N* 95 B11
Åmot *N* 95 C8
Åmot *N* 95 C11
Åmot *S* 103 E11
Åmotfors *S* 96 C7
Amou *F* 32 C4
Åmøyhamn *N* 108 C5
Ampelakia *GR* 169 E8
Ampeleia *GR* 169 F7
Ampelokipoi *GR* 169 C8
Ampelonas *GR* 169 E7
Ampezzo *I* 73 D6
Ampfing *D* 75 F11
Ampflwang im Hausruckwald *A* 76 F5
Amplepuis *F* 30 D5
Amposta *E* 42 F5
Ampthill *GB* 15 C8
Ampudia *E* 39 E10
Ampuero *E* 40 B5
Ampus *F* 36 D4
Amriswil *CH* 27 E11
Åmsele *S* 107 B16
Amsosen *N* 94 D3
Amstelveen *NL* 16 D3
Amsterdam *NL* 16 D3
Amstetten *A* 77 F7
Amstetten *D* 187 D8
Amulree *GB* 5 B9
Amurrio *E* 40 B6
Amusco *E* 40 D3
Amvrosia *GR* 171 B8
Amygdaleonas *GR* 171 C6
Amygdalia *GR* 174 C5
Åmynnet *S* 107 E15
Amyntaio *GR* 169 C6
Amzacea *RO* 155 F2
Anacapri *I* 60 B2
Anadia *P* 44 D4
Anafi *GR* 180 D3
Anafonitria *GR* 174 D2
Anagaire *IRL* 6 B6
Anagni *I* 62 D4
An Aird Mhóir *IRL* 6 F3
Añana-Gesaltza *E* 40 C6
Anan'yiv *UA* 154 B5
Anarcs *H* 145 G5
Anargyroi *GR* 169 C6
Anarrachi *GR* 169 D6
Anäset *S* 118 F6
Åna-Sira *N* 94 F4
Anatazavė *LT* 135 E11
Anatoli *GR* 168 E4
Anatoli *GR* 169 E8
Anatoli *GR* 179 E10
Anatoliki Fragkista *GR* 174 B4
Anatoliko *GR* 169 C6
Anatoliko *GR* 169 C8
Anavatos *GR* 177 C7
Anavra *GR* 174 A5
Anavra *GR* 175 A6
Anavyssos *GR* 175 D8
Anaya de Alba *E* 45 C10
An Baile Breac *IRL* 8 E2
An Baile Nua *IRL* 8 D5
An Bhlarna *IRL* 8 E5
An Bun Beag *IRL* 6 B6
An Cabhán *IRL* 7 E8
An Caiseal *IRL* 6 F3
An Caisleán Riabhach *IRL* 6 E6
An Caisléan Nua *IRL* 7 F10
An Caisléan Nua *IRL* 8 D4
An Cathair *IRL* 9 D7
Ance *LV* 134 A4
Ancelle *F* 36 B4
Ancene *LV* 135 D11
Ancenis *F* 23 F9
Ancerville *F* 26 C3
An Charraig *IRL* 6 C5
An Cheathru Rua *IRL* 6 F3
An Chill *IRL* 7 F9
Ancín *E* 32 E1
An Cionn Garbh *IRL* 6 C6
An Clochán *IRL* 7 C7
An Clochán Liath *IRL* 6 C6
An Cóbh *IRL* 8 E6
An Coimín *IRL* 7 C7
An Coireán *IRL* 8 E2
Ancona *I* 67 E8
Ancroft *GB* 5 D13
Ancrum *GB* 5 D11
Ancy-le-Franc *F* 25 E11
Anda *N* 100 C4
Andalo *I* 69 A11
Åndalsnes *N* 100 A7
Andau *A* 149 A8
Andavías *E* 39 E8
Anddalsvågen *N* 108 E3
Andebu *N* 95 D12
Andechs *D* 75 G9
Andeer *CH* 71 D8
Andelfingen *CH* 27 E10
Andelot-Blancheville *F* 26 D3
Andelst *NL* 16 E5
Andenes *N* 111 B11
Andenne *B* 19 D11
Anderlecht *B* 19 C9
Anderlues *B* 19 D9
Andermatt *CH* 71 D7
Andernach *D* 185 D7
Andernos-les-Bains *F* 28 F3
Andersbo *S* 99 B9
Anderslöv *S* 87 E12
Anderstorp *S* 88 A5
Andervenne *D* 17 C9
Andfiskå *N* 108 D7
Andijk *NL* 16 C4
Andilly-en-Bassigny *F* 26 E4
Andlau *F* 27 D7
Andoain *E* 32 D1
Andocs *H* 149 C9
Andolsheim *F* 27 D7
Andorf *A* 76 F5
Andørja *N* 111 C13
Andorno Micca *I* 68 B5
Andorra *E* 42 F3
Andorra la Vella *AND* 33 E9
Andosilla *E* 32 F2
Andouillé *F* 23 D10
Andover *GB* 13 C12
Andrano *I* 61 D10
Andrăşeşti *RO* 161 D10
Andratx *E* 49 E9
Andravida *GR* 174 D3
Andreas *GBM* 10 C3
Andreiaşu de Jos *RO* 153 F9
Andrespol *PL* 143 C8
Andrest *F* 33 D6
Andretta *I* 60 B4
Andria *I* 60 A6
Andrid *RO* 151 B9
Andrieşeni *RO* 153 B10
Andrijaševci *HR* 157 B10
Andrijevica *MNE* 163 D8
Andrioniškis *LT* 135 E10
Andriškiai *LT* 136 D6
Andritsaina *GR* 174 E4
Andronianoi *GR* 175 B9
Andros *GR* 176 D4
Androusa *GR* 174 E4
Andrup *DK* 86 D3
Andrupene *LV* 133 D2
Andrychów *PL* 147 B8
Andrzejewo *PL* 141 E6
Andselv *N* 111 B15
Andsnes *N* 112 C7
An Dúchoraidh *IRL* 6 C6
Andújar *E* 53 A8
Anduze *F* 35 B6
Andzeļi *LV* 133 D3
An Eachléim *IRL* 6 D2
Äneby *N* 95 B13
Aneby *S* 92 D5
Anela *I* 64 C3
Anenii Noi *MD* 154 D4
Ånes *N* 104 E4
Anet *F* 24 C5
Anetjärvi *FIN* 121 C10
Anevo *BG* 165 D10
Aneza *GR* 174 A2
An Fál Carrach *IRL* 6 B6
An Féar Bán *IRL* 7 F7
An Fhairche *IRL* 6 E4
Anfo *I* 69 B9
Ång *S* 92 D5
Anga *S* 93 E13
Ånge *S* 103 A10
Ånge *S* 105 E16
Ånge *S* 109 E14
An Geata Mór *IRL* 6 D2
Ängebo *S* 103 C11
Angeja *P* 44 C3
Ängelholm *S* 87 C11
Angeli *FIN* 113 F16
Angelniemi *FIN* 127 E8
Angelochori *GR* 169 C7
Angelokastro *GR* 174 B3
Angelokastro *GR* 175 D7
Ängelsberg *S* 97 C15
Angelstad *S* 87 B13
Angely *F* 25 E11
Anger *D* 73 A6
Angera *I* 68 B6
Angermünde *D* 84 D6
Angern *D* 79 B10
Angern an der March *A* 77 F11
Angers *F* 23 F10
Ångersjö *S* 102 C8
Ångersjö *S* 122 C3
Angersnes *N* 108 D4
Angervikko *FIN* 125 D10
Angerville *F* 24 D7
Ängesån *S* 116 E8
Ängesevä *FIN* 119 E15
Ängesträsk *S* 118 B8
Anghiari *I* 66 E5
Anglade *F* 28 E4
Angle *GB* 9 E12
Anglès *E* 43 D9
Anglès *F* 34 C4
Anglesola *E* 42 D5
Anglesona *E* 42 D6
Angles-sur-l'Anglin *F* 29 B7
Anglet *F* 32 D2
Angliers *F* 29 B6
Anglure *F* 25 C10
Angnäs *S* 107 D16
Angoisse *F* 29 E8
Ångom *S* 103 B13
An Gort *IRL* 6 F5
Angoulême *F* 29 D6
Angoulins *F* 28 C3
Angri *I* 60 B3
Angrie *F* 23 E10
Angüés *E* 42 C3
Anguiano *E* 40 D6
Anguillara Sabazia *I* 62 C2
Anguillara Veneta *I* 66 B4
Anguita *E* 47 B8
Angvik *N* 100 A8
Anha *P* 38 E2
Anhée *B* 19 D10
Anholt *DK* 87 B9
Aniane *F* 35 C6
Aniche *F* 19 D7
Anif *A* 73 A7
Anina *RO* 159 C8
Aninoasa *RO* 160 C2
Aninoasa *RO* 160 C5
Aninoasa *RO* 160 D2
Aninoasa *RO* 161 D6
Anizy-le-Château *F* 19 E7
Anjalankoski *FIN* 128 D6
Anjan *S* 105 D13
Anjum *NL* 16 B6
Ankaran *SLO* 73 E8
Ankarede Kapell *S* 105 B16
Ankarsrum *S* 93 D8
Ankarsund *S* 109 F12
Ankarsvik *S* 103 B13
Ankenes *N* 111 D13
Ankerlia *N* 112 E6
Ankershagen *D* 84 D3
Anklam *D* 84 C5
Ankum *D* 17 C9
Anlaby *GB* 11 D11
An Leadhb Gharbh *IRL* 6 C5
Anlezy *F* 30 B4
An Longfort *IRL* 7 E7
An Mám *IRL* 6 E3
An Mhala Raithní *IRL* 6 E3
An Móta *IRL* 7 F7
An Muileann gCearr *IRL* 7 E8
Ånn *S* 105 E13
Anna *E* 56 C3
Anna *EST* 131 C11
Annaberg *A* 77 G8
Annaberg-Buchholtz *D* 80 E4
Annaburg *D* 80 C4
Annagassan *IRL* 7 E10
Annagry *IRL* 6 B6
Annahilt *GB* 7 D10
Annahütte *D* 80 C5
Annalong *GB* 7 D11
Annamoe *IRL* 7 F10
Annan *GB* 5 F10
Anna Paulowna *NL* 16 C3
Annarode *D* 79 C9
An Nás *IRL* 7 F9
Annayalla *IRL* 7 D9
Annbank *GB* 4 E7
Anneberg *S* 91 D11
Anneberg *S* 92 D5
Annecy *F* 31 D9
Annecy-le-Vieux *F* 31 D9
Annefors *S* 103 D11
Annelund *S* 91 D13
Annemasse *F* 31 C9
Annen *NL* 17 B7
Annenieki *LV* 134 C6
Annestown *IRL* 9 D8
Anneyron *F* 30 E6
Annikvere *EST* 131 C12
Annœullin *F* 182 D1
Annonay *F* 30 E6
Annonen *FIN* 119 F14
Annopol *PL* 144 B4
Annot *F* 36 D5
Annweiler am Trifels *D* 21 F9
Ano Agios Vlasios *GR* 174 B4
Ano Amfeia *GR* 174 E5
Ano Chora *GR* 174 B4
Ano Diakofto *GR* 174 C5
Ano Drosini *GR* 171 B9
Anoeta *E* 32 D1
Anogeia *GR* 174 F5
Anogeia *GR* 178 E8
Ano Kalliniki *GR* 168 C5
Ano Kardamyla *GR* 177 B7
Ano Kavallari *GR* 169 C9
Ano Komi *GR* 169 D6
Ano Kopanaki *GR* 174 E4
Ano Lechonia *GR* 169 F9
Ano Lefkimmi *GR* 168 F3
Ano Mera *GR* 176 E5
Añón *E* 41 E8
Ano Poroia *GR* 169 B9
Anor *F* 19 E9
Añora *E* 54 C3
Ano Sagkri *GR* 176 E5
Ano Steni *GR* 175 B8

Ano Syros GR 176 E4
Ano Trikala GR 174 D5
Ano Tyros GR 175 E6
Anould F 27 D6
Añover de Tajo E 46 E5
Ano Vrontou GR 169 B10
Anquela del Ducado E 47 C8
Anras A 72 C6
An Rinn IRL 9 D7
Anröchte D 185 A9
An Ros IRL 7 E10
Ans B 19 C12
Ans DK 86 C5
Ansac-sur-Vienne F 29 D7
Ansager DK 86 D3
Ansbach D 75 D8
An Sciobairin IRL 8 E4
Anse F 30 D6
Ansedonia I 65 C4
Anseremme B 19 D10
Ansfelden A 76 F6
Ansião P 44 E4
Ansizca TR 177 C9
Ansjö S 103 A11
Ansnes N 181 B15
Ansó E 32 E4
An Spidéal IRL 6 F4
Anspoki LV 135 D13
Ansprung D 80 E4
Ånstad N 110 C8
Ånsvik N 109 B9
Antalieptė LT 135 E11
Antanhol P 44 D4
An tAonach IRL 8 C6
Antas E 55 E9
Antas P 38 E2
Antas P 44 C6
Antas de Ulla E 38 C4
An Teampall Mór IRL 9 C7
An Tearmann IRL 7 B7
Antequera E 53 B7
Anterselva di Sopra I 72 C5
Anthéor F 36 E5
Anthien F 25 F10
Anthili GR 175 B5
Anthotopos GR 175 A6
Anthrakitis GR 168 E4
Antibes F 36 D6
Antigonos GR 169 C6
Antikyra GR 175 C6
Antillo I 59 D7
Antimacheia GR 177 F9
An tInbhear Mór IRL 9 C10
Antiparos GR 176 E5
Antirrio GR 174 C4
Antisanti F 37 G10
Antissa GR 171 F9
Antjärn S 103 A14
Antnäs S 118 C7
Antoing B 19 C7
Antol SK 147 E7
Anton BG 165 D9
Anton Ivanov BG 165 E9
Antonivka UA 145 F6
Antonne-et-Trigonant F 29 E7
Antonovo BG 166 C6
Antony F 25 C7
Antraigues-sur-Volane F 30 F5
Antrain F 23 D9
Antrim GB 4 F4
Antrodoco I 62 C4
An tSeanga Mheáin IRL 6 C6
Antsla EST 131 F13
Anttis S 116 D9
Anttola FIN 128 B8
An Tulch IRL 9 C8
Antully F 30 B5
Antunovac Tenjski HR 149 F11
Antuži LV 135 C11
Antwerpen B 19 B9
Antzuola E 32 D1
An Uaimh IRL 7 E9
Anvers B 182 C4
Anvers B 19 B9
Anvin F 18 D5
Anykščiai LT 135 E10
Anzano di Puglia I 60 A4
Anzat-le-Luguet F 30 E3
Anzegem B 19 C7
Anzère CH 31 C11
Anzi I 60 B5
Anzin F 19 D7
Anzing D 75 F10
Anzio I 62 E3
Aoiz E 32 E3
Aoradh GB 4 D4
Aós E 32 E3
Aosta I 31 D11
Aouste-sur-Sye F 31 F7
Apa RO 151 B11
Apagy H 145 H4
Apahida RO 152 D3
Apaj H 150 C3
Apața RO 153 F7
Apateu RO 151 D8
Apátfalva H 150 E6
Apatin SRB 158 B2
Apatovac HR 149 D7
Apc H 150 B4
Ape LV 131 F13
Apecchio I 66 E5
A Pedreira E 38 D3
Apeiranthos GR 177 E6
Apeldoorn NL 16 D5
Apelern D 17 D12
Apele Vii RO 160 E4
Apen D 17 B9
Apenburg D 83 E10
Apensen D 82 D7
Aperi GR 181 E6
A Peroxa E 38 D4
Apgulde LV 134 C6
Apice I 60 A3
A Picota E 38 C2
Apidia GR 175 F6
Apiro I 67 F7
Aplared S 91 D13
A Pobla de Brollón E 38 C5
A Pobla de San Xiao E 38 C5
A Pobra de Trives E 38 D5
A Pobra do Caramiñal E 38 C2
Apoikia GR 176 D4
Apolakkia GR 181 D7
Apold RO 152 E5
Apolda D 79 D10
Apoldu de Jos RO 152 F3
Apollona GR 181 D7
Apollonas GR 177 E6
Apollonia GR 176 E5
A Pontenova E 38 B5
A Pontepedra E 38 B2
Åporka H 150 C3
Apostag H 149 C11
Apostoloi GR 178 E8
Äppelbo S 97 B11
Appenweier D 186 D4
Appenzell CH 27 F11
Appiano sulla Strada del Vino I 72 D3
Appietto F 37 G9
Appignano I 67 F7
Appingedam NL 17 B7
Appleby-in-Westmorland GB 10 B7
Appleby Magna GB 11 F8
Applecross GB 2 L5
Appledore GB 12 C6
Appledore GB 15 E10
Apprieu F 31 E7
Apremont-la-Forêt F 26 C4
Aprica I 69 A9
Apricale I 61 E6
Aprigliano I 61 E6
Apriki LV 134 C3
Aprilia I 62 D3
Aprilovo BG 166 C6
Apriltsi BG 165 D10
A Proba E 39 C6
Apsalos GR 169 C7
Apšuciems LV 134 B6
Apt F 35 C9
Aquaviva delle Fonti I 61 B7
Aquilonia I 60 B4
Aquilué E 32 F5
Aquino I 62 E5
Aracena E 51 D6
Arachnaio GR 175 D6
Arachova GR 175 C6
Aračinovo MK 164 E4
Arad RO 151 E7
Aradac SRB 158 C5
Arãdalen S 102 A6
Aradeo I 61 C10
Aragnouet F 33 E6
Aragona I 58 E4
Aragoncillo E 47 C8
Araia E 32 E1
A Ramallosa E 38 C2
Aramits F 32 D4
Aramon F 35 C8
Aranda de Duero E 40 E4
Aranda de Moncayo E 41 E8
Arandelovac SRB 158 E6
Aranhas P 45 D6
Aranitas AL 168 C2
Aranjuez E 46 D5
Arano E 32 D2
Aranzueque E 47 D6
Araovacik TR 173 E7
Arapaj AL 168 B2
Arapiles E 45 C9
Aras E 32 E1
Aras de Alpuente E 47 E10
Araswika N 104 E4
Aratos GR 171 B9
Araules F 30 E5
Aravete EST 131 C11
Aravissos GR 169 C7
Arazede P 44 D3
Arbanasi BG 166 C5
Arbatax I 64 D4
Arbeca E 42 D5
Arbecey F 26 E4
Arbedo CH 69 A7
Arbéost F 32 E5
Arberg D 75 D8
Arbesbach A 77 E7
Arbeteta E 47 C8
Arboga S 97 D14
Arboleas E 55 E8
Arbon CH 27 E11
Arbore RO 153 B7
Arborea I 64 D2
Arborio I 68 C5
Årbostad N 111 C13
Arbrå S 103 D11
Arbroath GB 5 B11
Arbúcies E 43 D9
Arbus I 64 D2
Årby DK 87 D8
Årbyn S 118 C8
Arcachon F 32 A3
Arcangues F 32 D2
Arcani RO 159 C11
Arce I 62 D5
Arcen NL 16 F6
Arc-en-Barrois F 26 E3
Arces F 28 D4
Arces-Dilo F 25 D10
Arc-et-Senans F 31 A8
Arcevia I 67 E6
Archaia Epidavros GR 175 D7
Archaia Korinthos GR 175 D6
Archaia Olympia GR 174 D4
Archanes GR 178 E9
Archangelos GR 181 D8
Archar BG 159 F10
Archena E 55 C10
Archidona E 53 B8
Archiş RO 151 D9
Archivel E 55 C9
Arcidosso I 65 B5
Árciems LV 131 F9
Arcis-sur-Aube F 25 C11
Arc-lès-Gray F 26 F4
Arco I 69 B10
Arco de Baúlhe P 38 F4
Arcola I 69 E8
Arçon F 31 B9
Arçonnay F 23 D12
Arcos E 40 D4
Arcos P 50 B4
Arcos de Jalón E 47 B8
Arcos de la Frontera E 52 C5
Arcos de las Salinas E 47 E10
Arcos de Valdez E 38 E3
Arcozelo P 38 C5
Arcozelo P 38 E2
Arc-sur-Tille F 26 F3
Arcusa E 33 F6
Arda BG 171 B7
Ardagger Markt A 77 F7
Ardagh IRL 8 C5
Ardal N 100 C4
Ardales E 53 C7
Årdalstangen N 100 D7
Ardanairy IRL 9 C10
Ard an Rátha IRL 6 C6
Ardara I 64 B2
Ardara IRL 6 C6
Ardauli I 64 C2
Ardea I 62 D3
Ardee IRL 7 E9
Ardeluța RO 153 D8
Arden DK 86 B5
Arden GB 4 C7
Ardentes F 29 B9
Ardeoani RO 153 D9
Ardersier GB 3 K8
Ardes F 30 E3
Ardez CH 71 D10
Ardfern GB 4 C6
Ardfert IRL 8 D3
Ardfinnan IRL 9 D7
Ardgay GB 3 K8
Ardglass GB 7 D11
Ardgroom IRL 8 E3
Ardino BG 171 A8
Ardkeen GB 7 D11
Ardlui GB 4 C7
Ardlussa GB 3 A6
Ardmair GB 2 J6
Ardminish GB 4 D5
Ardmore IRL 6 F3
Ardmore IRL 9 E7
Ardon CH 31 C11
Ardooie B 19 C7
Ardore I 59 C9
Ardpatrick IRL 8 D5
Ardrahan IRL 6 F5
Ardre S 93 E13
Ardres F 18 C4
Ardrishaig GB 4 C6
Ardrossan GB 4 D7
Ardscull IRL 7 F9
Ardtoe GB 4 B5
Ardu EST 131 C10
Ardud RO 151 B10
Ardusat RO 151 B11
Ardvasar GB 4 A5
Åre S 105 E14
Areatza E 40 B6
Arefu RO 160 C5
Areias P 44 E4
Arén E 42 C5
Arenas de Iguña E 40 B3
Arenas del Rey E 53 C9
Arenas de San Juan E 46 F6
Arenas de San Pedro E 45 D10
Arendal N 90 C4
Arendonk B 16 F4
Arendsee (Altmark) D 83 E10
Arengosse F 32 B4
Arenilla E 40 E6
Arenys de Mar E 43 D9
Arenzano I 37 C9
Areopoli GR 178 B3
Areosa P 38 E2
Ares E 38 B3
Arès F 28 F3
Ares del Maestre E 48 D4
Aresing D 75 E9
Arespalditza E 40 B5
Arethousa GR 169 C10
Arette F 32 D4
Arette-Pierre-St-Martin F 32 E4
Aretxabaleta E 41 B7
Arevalillo E 45 C10
Arévalo E 46 B3
Arezzo I 66 F4
Arfara GR 174 E5
Arfons F 33 D10
Arför N 105 B11
Argalasti GR 169 F9
Argallón E 51 F7
Argamasilla de Alba E 47 F6
Argamasilla de Calatrava E 54 B4
Argamasón E 55 B8
Arganda del Rey E 46 D6
Arganil P 44 D4
Arganza E 39 C6
Argegno I 69 B7
Argelès-Gazost F 32 D5
Argelès-sur-Mer F 34 E5
Argeliers F 34 D4
Argelita E 48 D4
Argenbühl D 71 B9
Argences F 23 B11
Argenta I 66 C4
Argentan F 23 C11
Argentat F 29 E9
Argente F 47 C10
Argentera I 36 C5
Argenteuil F 25 C7
Argenthal D 21 E9
Argentiera I 64 B1
Argentière F 31 D10
Argentine F 31 E9
Argenton-les-Vallées F 28 B5
Argenton-sur-Creuse F 29 B9
Argentré F 23 D10
Argentré-du-Plessis F 23 D9
Argent-sur-Sauldre F 25 E7
Argés E 46 E4
Argetoaia RO 160 D2
Arginonta GR 177 E8
Argonay F 31 D9
Argos GR 175 D6
Argos Orestiko GR 168 D5
Argostoli GR 174 C1
Argouges F 23 D9
Arguedas E 41 D8
Argueil F 18 E4
Arguellite E 55 C8
Arguís E 32 F5
Arguisuelas E 47 E9
Argujillo E 39 F8
Argyrades GR 168 F2
Argyropouli GR 169 E7
Arhavi TR 173 B8
Århus DK 86 C6
Ariano Irpino I 60 A4
Ariano nel Polesine I 66 C5
Ariany E 57 B11
Aribe E 32 E3
Aricia I 62 D3
Aridaia GR 169 C7
Arieşeni RO 151 E10
Arignac F 33 E9
Arija E 40 C4
Arild S 87 C11
Arileod GB 4 B3
Arilje SRB 158 F5
Arinagour GB 4 B3
Arinis RO 151 C11
Ariño E 42 E2
Arinsal AND 33 E8
Arinthod F 31 C8
Ariogala LT 134 F6
Aris GR 174 E5
Arisaig GB 4 B5
Aristomenis GR 174 E4
Arisvi GR 171 B9
Ariz P 44 C5
Ariza E 41 F7
Arizgoiti E 40 B6
Arizola E 32 E2
Årjäng S 96 D7
Arjona E 53 A8
Arjonilla E 53 A8
Arkala FIN 119 D16
Arkalochori GR 178 E9
Arkasa GR 181 F6
Arkelsjön GR 180 C3
Arkitsa GR 175 B7
Arkkukari FIN 119 E12
Arklow IRL 9 C10
Arkna EST 131 C12
Arkösund S 93 C9
Ärla S 98 D7
Arlanc F 30 E4
Arlanzón E 40 D5
Arle (Großheide) D 17 A8
Arlempdes F 30 F4
Arlena di Castro I 62 C1
Arles F 35 C8
Arleuf F 30 A5
Arleux F 19 D7
Arligbo S 98 B8
Arló H 145 G1
Arlon B 19 E12
Arló S 98 B8
Arluno I 69 B6
Arlyeya BY 133 E6
Armação de Pêra P 50 E3
Armadale GB 5 D9
Armadale GB 2 J3
Armağan TR 167 F8
Armagh GB 7 D9
Armallones E 47 C8
Armamar P 44 B5
Armáşeşti RO 161 D9
Armasjärvi S 119 B11
Armassaari FIN 119 B11
Armen AL 168 C2
Armenioi GR 174 A2
Armeniş RO 159 C9
Armenistis GR 177 D7
Armeno I 68 B5
Armenochori GR 168 C5
Armenoi GR 178 E7
Armenteros E 45 C10
Armentières F 18 C6
Armento I 60 C6
Armilla E 53 B9
Armissan F 34 D5
Armolia GR 177 C7
Armoy GB 4 E4
Armuña E 46 B4
Armuña de Almanzora E 55 E8
Armunia I 64 D3
Armutalani TR 181 C8
Armutlu TR 177 C10
Armutlu TR 173 D9
Arna GR 174 F5
Arnac-Pompadour F 29 E8
Arnad I 68 B4
Arnage F 23 E12
Arnaia GR 169 D10
Årnäs S 91 B14
Årnäs S 102 C5
Arnäsvall S 107 E15
Arnavutköy TR 173 B10
Arnay-le-Duc F 25 F11
Arnberg S 107 B16
Arnborg DK 86 C3
Arnbruck D 76 D3
Arnedillo E 41 D7
Arnedo E 41 D7
Arnéguy F 32 D3
Arnemark S 118 D6
Arnemuiden NL 16 F1
Arnfels A 148 C4
Arnhem NL 16 E5
Arnionys 1 LT 137 C12
Arnissa GR 169 C6
Arnö S 93 B10
Arnol GB 2 J3
Arnold GB 11 E9
Arnoldstein A 73 C7
Arnón HR 157 F7
Arnót H 145 G2
Arnöviken S 103 C13
Arnoyhamn N 112 C6
Arnprior GB 5 C8
Arnschwang D 76 D3
Arnstadt D 79 E8
Arnstein D 74 C6
Arnstorf D 76 E3
Arnum DK 86 E3
Aroania GR 174 D5
Åroktő H 151 B6
Arola FIN 113 D20
Arolla CH 31 C11
Arolsen D 17 F12
Aron F 23 D10
Arona I 68 B6
Aroneanu RO 153 C11
Aronkylä FIN 122 F8
Åros N 95 C12
Arosa CH 71 D9
Arosa P 38 E3
Årosjåkk S 111 E17
Arouca P 44 C4
Årøybukta N 111 A19
Arpajon F 25 C7
Arpajon-sur-Cère F 29 F10
Arpaşu de Jos RO 152 F5
Arpela FIN 119 B12
Arpino I 62 D5
Arquata del Tronto I 62 B4
Arquata Scrivia I 37 B9
Arques F 18 C5
Arques F 33 E10
Arques-la-Bataille F 18 E3
Arquillos E 55 C6
Arrabalde E 39 D8
Arracourt F 26 C5
Arradon F 22 E6
Arraiolos P 50 B4
Arrakoski FIN 127 C13
Arranhó P 50 B1
Arras F 18 D6
Arrasate E 41 B7
Årre DK 86 D3
Arreau F 33 E6
Arrén NL 183 C7
Arredondo E 40 B4
Arremølinos de León E 51 C7
Arrigny F 25 C12
Arrigorriaga E 40 B6
Arrild DK 86 E3
Arriondas E 39 B9
Arroba de los Montes E 46 F3
Arrochar GB 4 C7
Arronches P 45 F6
Arrone I 62 B3
Arroniz E 32 E1
Arrou F 24 D5
Arroyal E 40 C3
Arroyo de la Luz E 45 E7
Arroyo del Ojanco E 55 C7
Arroyo de San Serván E 51 B7
Arroyomolinos de León E 51 C7
Arruda dos Vinhos P 50 B1
Arry F 186 C1
Årsandøy N 105 A12
Årsdale DK 89 E8
Arseni RO 169 C7
Årset N 105 A11
Arsié I 72 E4
Arsiero I 69 B11
Årslev DK 86 E6
Arsoli I 62 C4
Ars-sur-Formans F 30 D6
Ars-sur-Moselle F 26 B5
Årstein N 111 C14
Årsunda S 98 A7
Årsura RO 153 D12
Arsvågen N 94 D2
Artà E 57 B11
Artajona E 32 E2
Artana E 48 E4
Artannes-sur-Indre F 24 F4
Artemisia GR 174 E5
Artemisio GR 174 D5
Artemisio GR 175 A7
Artèn I 72 D4
Artena I 62 D3
Artenay F 24 D6
Artern (Unstrut) D 79 D9
Artés E 43 D7
Artesa de Segre E 42 D6
Artesiano GR 169 F6
Arth CH 71 C7
Arthez-d'Asson F 32 D5
Arthez-de-Béarn F 32 D4
Arthon F 29 B9
Arthon-en-Retz F 23 C11
Artieda E 32 E4
Artigarvan GB 4 F2
Artigat F 33 D8
Artix F 32 D4
Artjärvi FIN 127 D15
Årtled S 103 E9
Artogne I 69 B9
Artsyz UA 154 F4
A Rúa E 38 D5
Arudy F 32 D5
Arukula EST 131 C10
Arukula EST 131 B13
Arundel GB 15 F7
Årvågen N 104 E5
Arvagh IRL 7 E7
Arvàn S 107 B16
Arvesund S 105 E16
Arveyres F 28 F5
Arvi GR 178 F9
Arvidsjaur S 109 E17
Arvidsträsk S 118 C5
Arvieu F 34 B4
Arvieux F 31 F10
Arvika N 100 B3
Arvika S 97 C8
Årviksand N 112 C6
Åryd S 89 B7
Arzachena I 64 A3
Arzacq-Arraziguet F 32 C5
Arzana I 64 D4
Arzano HR 157 E7
Arzberg D 75 B11
Arzberg D 80 C4
Arzfeld D 20 D6
Årzignano I 72 E3
Arzl im Pitztal A 71 C11
Arzúa E 38 C3
As B 19 B12
Aš CZ 75 B11
As N 95 C13
Ås N 105 A11
Ås S 96 C7
Ås S 106 E7
Åsa N 95 B12
Åsa S 91 E11
Asaa DK 86 A6
As Pontes de García Rodríguez E 38 B4
Aşağiçobanisa TR 177 B10
Aşağisevindikli TR 173 B8
Åsan N 105 B12
Asare LV 135 D11
Åsarna S 102 A7
Åsarp S 91 C14
Asasp-Arros F 32 D4
Asbach D 21 C8
Åsby S 103 D11
Ascain F 32 D2
Ascó E 42 E5
Asco F 37 G10
Ascoli Piceno I 62 B5
Ascoli Satriano I 60 A5
Ascona CH 68 A6
Ascou F 33 E9
As Covas E 38 D2
Åse N 111 B10
Åseda S 89 A8
Åsegg N 105 C9
Åsele S 107 C12
Åselet S 118 C4
Asemakylä FIN 119 D14
Asemanperä FIN 119 D14
Asemanseutu FIN 123 E11
Åsen N 105 D10
Åsen S 102 C7
Åsen S 102 D6
Åsen S 106 E7
Åsen S 109 E16
Asendorf D 17 C12
Asenovets BG 166 D5
Asenovgrad BG 165 E10
Asenovo BG 166 C6
Asenovtsi BG 165 C11
Åseral N 90 B1
Aseri EST 131 C13
Asfaka GR 168 E4
Asfeld F 19 F9
Asfendiou GR 177 F9
Asferg DK 86 B5
Asgårdstrand N 95 D12
Ash GB 15 E7
Åshammar S 103 E12
Ashbourne GB 11 E8
Ashbourne IRL 7 E10
Ashburton GB 13 D7
Ashbury GB 13 B11
Ashby de la Zouch GB 11 F9
Ashcott GB 13 C9
Ashevo RUS 133 B7
Ashford GB 13 D11
Ashford GB 15 E10
Ashford GB 7 F10
Ashford IRL 8 C4
Ashill GB 15 B10
Ashington GB 5 E13
Ashkirk GB 5 E11
Ashley GB 15 C9
Ashmyany BY 137 D13
Ashmyany BY 137 E12
Ashton-under-Lyne GB 11 E7
Ashurst GB 13 D11
Ashwick GB 13 C9
Asiago I 72 E4
Asikkala FIN 127 C14
Asila MA 52 F4
Asimi GR 178 E9
Asin E 32 F3
Asiros GR 169 C9
Ask N 95 C14
Aska FIN 117 D17
Askainen FIN 126 D6
Askeaton IRL 8 C5
Asker N 95 C12
Askern GB 11 D9
Askersby S 92 A6
Askersund S 92 B5
Askilje S 107 B13
Askim N 95 C14
Asklipieio GR 175 D7
Asklipieio GR 181 D7
Åskogen S 118 C7
Askola FIN 127 D14
Askos GR 169 C9
Askvoll N 100 D2
Asljunga S 87 C12
Åsmansbo S 97 B13
Åsmarka N 101 D13
Asmunti FIN 119 C17
Asnæs DK 87 D8
Åsnes N 96 B15
As Neves E 38 D3
As Nogais E 38 C5
Asola I 66 B1
Asolo I 72 E4
Asopia GR 175 C8
Asopos GR 178 B4
Asos GR 174 C1
Åsögg N 105 C9
Ásotthalom H 150 E4
Asp DK 86 C3
Aspa S 93 B9
Aspa bruk S 92 B5
Aspach A 76 F4
Aspan S 102 B8
Asparn an der Zaya A 77 E10
Asparukhovo BG 167 D8
Aspås S 106 E7
Aspatria GB 5 F10
Aspe E 56 E3
Aspe S 97 B8
Aspeå S 107 E12
Aspele S 107 D14
Aspen NL 183 B6
Asperg D 27 C11
Asperen NL 183 B6
Aspet F 33 D7
Asphyltan S 97 C11
Aspliden S 109 F17
Aspliden S 118 B7
Aspnäs S 99 B8
Aspnäs S 103 A14
Aspö S 91 E11
Asquins F 25 E10
Asmali TR 173 C8
Assamstadt D 74 D6
Asse B 19 C9
Assebakti N 113 E15
Asseiceira P 44 F3
Assemini I 64 E3
Assen NL 17 B7
Assenede B 16 F1
Assendelft NL 16 D3
Assens DK 86 E5
Assens DK 86 B6
Assentoft DK 86 C6
Asséraç F 23 F7
Assergi I 62 C5
Assesse B 19 D11
Assier F 33 A9
Assisi I 62 A3
Asso I 69 B7
Asson F 32 D5
Assoro I 58 D5
Assumar P 44 F6
Åsta N 101 D14
Astaffort F 33 B7
Astakos GR 174 B3
Åstan N 104 E7
Astašova LV 133 D2
Aste EST 130 E4
Åsteby S 97 B9
Astee IRL 8 C3
Asten A 76 F6
Asten NL 16 F5
Asti I 37 B8
Astikkala FIN 129 B12
Aştileu RO 151 C9
Astomilitsa GR 168 D4
Aston Clinton GB 15 D7
Astorga E 39 C7
Åstorp S 87 C11
Astradamovo RUS 133 B7
Astraki GR 178 B7
Astros GR 175 E6
Astrowna BY 133 F4
Astrowshchyna BY 133 F4
Astrup DK 86 B5
Astrup DK 86 C3
Astrup DK 90 E7
Astudillo E 40 D3
Astypalaia GR 180 C4
Asuaju de Sus RO 151 B11
Asûne LV 133 D3
Asuni I 64 D2
Asunta FIN 123 F13
Ásványráró H 146 F5
Asvestopetra GR 169 D6
Asvyeya BY 133 D4
Aszaló H 145 G2
Aszód H 150 B3
Atalaia P 44 F5
Atalaia P 44 F5
Atalanti GR 175 B7
Atalaya del Cañavate E 47 E8
Ataquines E 46 B3
Atarfe E 53 B9
Atašiene LV 135 C12
Atea E 47 B9
Ateca E 41 F8
A Teixeira E 38 D5
Atel RO 152 E4
Ateleta I 63 D6
Atella I 60 B5
Atena Lucana I 60 C5
Återvänningen S 103 A13
Atessa I 63 C6
Ath B 19 C8
Athani GR 174 B2
Athboy IRL 7 E9
Athea IRL 8 C4
Athenry IRL 6 F5
Athenstedt D 79 C8
Atheras GR 174 C1
Atherington GB 12 C6
Atherstone GB 11 F8
Athies F 18 E6
Athies-sous-Laon F 19 E8
Athikia GR 175 D6
Athina GR 175 D8
Athleague IRL 6 E6
Athlone IRL 7 F7
Áth Trasna IRL 8 D4
Atid RO 152 E6
Atienza E 47 B7
Atina I 62 D5
Aţintiş RO 152 E4
Atjiken S 107 A9
Atkár F 150 B4
Atna N 101 C13
Åtorp S 92 A4
Atouguia da Baleia P 44 F2
Ätran S 87 A11
Åtrask S 118 B7
Åträsk S 118 D5
Atri I 62 B5
Atripalda I 60 B3
Atsiki GR 171 E8
Attadale GB 2 L6
Attala H 149 D10
Attali GR 175 B8
Attanagh IRL 9 C8
Attnang A 76 F5
Attonträsk S 107 C14
Attu FIN 126 E7
Atur F 29 E7
Åtvidaberg S 92 C7
Atzara I 64 D3
Atzenbrugg A 77 F9
Atzendorf D 79 C10
Atzeneta del Maestrat E 48 D4
Au A 71 C9
Au CH 71 C9
Aub D 75 C7
Aubagne F 35 D10
Aubange B 19 E12
Aube F 24 C4
Aubel B 183 D7
Aubenas F 35 A7
Aubenton F 19 E9
Aubergenville F 24 C6
Auberive F 26 E3
Aubeterre-sur-Dronne F 29 E6
Aubiet F 33 C7
Aubignan F 35 B9
Aubignosc F 35 B10
Aubigny F 28 B3
Aubigny-en-Artois F 18 D6
Aubigny-sur-Nère F 25 F7
Aubin F 33 A10
Aubin CH 31 B9
Auboné F 20 F5
Aubord F 35 C7
Aubonne CH 31 B9
Aubusson F 29 D10

Auby F 19 D7
Aucamville F 33 C8
Auce LV 134 D5
Auch F 33 C7
Auchallater GB 5 B10
Auchenbreck GB 4 D6
Auchencairn GB 5 F9
Auchencrow GB 5 D12
Auchnagatt GB 3 L12
Auchterarder GB 5 C9
Auchtermuchty GB 5 C10
Auchy-au-Bois F 18 C5
Aucun F 32 E5
Audenge F 32 A3
Auderville F 23 A8
Audeux F 26 F4
Audevälja EST 131 C8
Audierne F 22 D2
Audincourt F 27 F6
Audlem GB 10 F6
Audley GB 11 E7
Audnedal N 90 C1
Audon F 32 C4
Audresselles F 15 F12
Audriņi LV 133 C2
Audru EST 131 E8
Audruicq F 18 C5
Audun-le-Roman F 20 F5
Aue D 79 E12
Auerbach D 75 A11
Auerbach in der Oberpfalz D 75 C10
Auersthal A 77 F11
Auffay F 18 E3
Aufhausen D 75 E11
Augbrim IRL 6 F5
Auggen D 27 E8
Augher GB 7 D8
Aughnacloy GB 7 D9
Aughrim IRL 6 F5
Aughrim IRL 9 C10
Aughton GB 11 E9
Augignac F 29 D7
Augsburg D 75 F8
Augšlīgatne LV 135 B10
Augstkalne LV 133 E2
Augstkalne LV 134 D6
Augusta I 59 E7
Auguste LV 134 D3
Augustenborg DK 86 F5
Augustów PL 136 F6
Augustowo PL 141 E8
Augustusburg D 80 E4
Auho FIN 121 E10
Aukan N 104 E4
Aukra N 100 A5
Aukrug D 82 B7
Aukštadvaris LT 137 D10
Aukštelkai LT 134 E7
Aukštelkė LT 134 E6
Auktsjaur S 109 E17
Auleja LV 133 D2
Aulendorf D 71 B9
Auletta I 60 B4
Aulla I 69 E8
Aullène F 37 H10
Aulnat F 30 D3
Aulnay F 28 C5
Aulnay-sous-Bois F 25 C8
Aulnois sur-Seille F 26 C5
Aulnoye-Aymeries F 19 D8
Aulon F 33 D7
Aulosen D 83 E11
Ault F 18 D3
Aultbea GB 2 K5
Aultguish Inn GB 2 K7
Aulus-les-Bains F 33 E8
Auma D 79 E10
Aumale F 18 E4
Aumetz F 20 F5
Aumont F 31 B8
Aumont-Aubrac F 30 F3
Aumühle D 83 C8
Aunay-en-Bazois F 25 F10
Aunay-sur-Odon F 23 B10
Auneau F 24 D6
Aunegrenda N 105 F10
Aunfoss N 105 B13
Auning DK 86 C6
Auñón E 47 C7
Aups F 36 D4
Aura FIN 126 D8
Aurach D 75 D7
Aurach bei Kitzbühel A 72 B5
Aura im Sinngrund D 74 B6
Auran N 105 E9
Auray F 22 E6
Aurdal N 101 E10
Aure N 104 E5
Aurec-sur-Loire F 30 E5
Aureilhan F 33 D6
Aureille F 35 C8
Aurejärvi FIN 123 G10
Aurel F 35 A9
Aurel F 35 B9
Aurensan F 32 C5
Aureosen N 100 A6
Auri LV 134 C6
Aurich D 17 B8
Aurignac F 33 D7
Aurillac F 29 F10
Auriol F 35 D10
Aurisina I 73 E8
Auritz E 32 E3
Aurland N 100 E6
Aurolzmünster A 76 F4
Auron F 36 C5
Auronzo di Cadore I 72 C5
Auros F 32 A5
Auroux F 30 F4
Aurskog N 95 C14
Ausa-Corno I 73 E7
Ausejo E 32 F1
Auşeu RO 151 C10
Ausleben D 79 B9
Ausmas LV 135 B9
Ausonia I 62 E5
Außervillgraten A 72 C5
Aussillon F 33 C10
Aussonne F 33 C8
Austafjord N 105 B9
Austbø N 95 C8
Austborg N 105 C15
Austertana N 114 C5
Austis I 64 C3
Austmannli N 94 C5
Austnes N 100 A4
Austnes N 105 B15
Austnes N 111 C12
Austråt N 104 D7
Austsmøla N 104 E4
Auterive F 33 D8
Authon F 24 E4
Authon F 36 C4
Authon-du-Perche F 24 D4
Autio FIN 119 E17
Autio FIN 123 E13
Autol E 41 D7
Autrans F 31 E8
Autreville F 26 D4
Autrey-lès-Gray F 26 F3
Autry F 19 F10
Autti FIN 119 B18
Auttoinen FIN 127 C13
Autun F 30 B5
Auve F 25 B12
Auvelais B 19 D10
Auvers-le-Hamon F 23 E11
Auvillar F 33 B7
Auvillers-les-Forges F 184 E1
Auxerre F 25 E10
Auxi-le-Château F 18 D5
Auxonne F 26 F3
Auxy F 30 B5
Auzances F 29 C10
Auzat F 33 E8
Auzat-la-Combelle F 30 E3
Aužgulāni LV 135 E12
Auzon F 30 E3
Ava FIN 126 E5
Ava S 107 D16
Avafors S 118 B8
Availles-Limouzine F 29 C7
Avaldsnes N 94 D2
Avallon F 25 E10
Avan S 118 C7
Avanäs S 107 C17
Avanca P 44 C3
Avançon F 36 B4
Avantas GR 171 C9
Avant-lès-Ramerupt F 25 D11
Avasjö S 107 C11
Avato GR 171 C7
Avaträsk S 107 C10
Avaviken S 109 E16
Avdira GR 171 C7
Avdou GR 178 E9
A Veiga E 39 D6
Aveiras de Cima P 44 F3
Aveiro P 44 C3
Avelar P 44 E4
Avelãs de Caminho P 44 D4
Aveleda P 38 E3
Aveleda P 39 E6
Avelgem B 19 C7
Avella I 60 B3
Avellino I 60 B3
Avenay-Val-d'Or F 25 B11
Avenches CH 31 B11
Avenhorn NL 16 C3
Avenida do Marquês de Figueroa E 38 A3
Avermes F 30 B3
Avers CH 71 E9
Aversa I 60 B2
Avesnes-le-Comte F 18 D6
Avesnes-sur-Helpe F 19 D8
Avesta S 98 B6
Åvestbo S 97 C14
Avetrano I 61 C9
Avezzano I 62 C4
Avgerinos GR 168 D5
Avià E 43 C7
Aviano I 73 D6
Aviemore GB 3 L9
Avigliana I 31 E11
Avigliano I 60 B5
Avigliano Umbro I 62 B2
Avignon F 35 C8
Ávila E 46 C3
A Vila da Igrexa E 38 A4
Avilés E 39 A8
Avilley F 26 F5
Avintes P 44 B3
Avinurme EST 131 D13
Avinyó E 43 D7
Avio I 69 B10
Avion F 18 D6
Avioth F 19 E11
Avis P 44 F5
Avispea EST 131 C12
Åvist FIN 122 D9
Avize F 25 C11
Avižieniai LT 137 D11
Avlakia GR 177 D8
Avlemonas GR 178 C5
Avliotes GR 168 E2
Avlonari GR 175 B9
Avlonas GR 175 C8
Avlum DK 86 C3
Avoca IRL 9 C10
Avoine F 23 F12
Avola I 59 F7
Avon F 25 D8
Avonmouth GB 13 B9
Avord F 29 A11
Avoriaz F 31 C10
Avoudrey F 26 F5
Avrămeni RO 153 A9
Avrămești RO 152 E6
Avram Iancu RO 151 D8
Avram Iancu RO 151 E10
Avranches F 23 C9
Avren BG 171 B9
Avricourt F 186 D2
Avrig RO 152 F4
Avril F 20 F5
Avrillé F 23 E10
Avrillé F 28 C3
Avtovac BIH 157 F10
Av'že N 112 E10
Awans B 183 D6
Axams A 72 B3
Axat F 33 E10
Axel NL 16 F1
Axente Sever RO 152 E4
Axintele RO 161 D9
Axioupoli GR 169 C8
Ax-les-Thermes F 33 E9
Axmar S 103 D13
Axmarsbruk S 103 D13
Axminster GB 13 D9
Axos GR 169 C7
Axvall S 91 C14
Ayamonte E 50 E5
Aycliffe GB 5 F13
Aydat F 30 D2
Aydemir BG 161 E10
Ayen F 29 E8
Ayerbe E 32 F4
Aying D 72 A4
Aylesbury GB 15 D7
Ayllón E 40 F5
Aylsham GB 15 B11
Aymavilles I 31 D11
Ayna E 55 B8
Aynac F 29 F9
Ayoo de Vidriales E 39 D7
Ayora E 47 F10
Ayr GB 4 E7
Ayrancilar TR 177 C9
Ayron F 28 B6
Ayşebaci TR 173 E8
Aysgarth GB 11 C8
Äyskoski FIN 123 D17
Äystö FIN 122 F7
Aytos BG 167 D8
Aytré F 28 C3
Ayvacik TR 171 E10
Ayvalik TR 172 F6
Aywaille B 19 D12
Azagra E 32 F2
Azaila E 41 F11
Azambuja P 44 F3
Azanja SRB 159 E6
Azanúy E 42 D4
Azaruja P 50 B4
Azatli TR 172 B6
Azay-le-Ferron F 29 B8
Azay-le-Rideau F 24 F3
Azé F 23 E10
Azerables F 29 C8
Azina BY 133 E5
Azinhaga P 44 F3
Azinhal P 50 E5
Azinheira dos Barros P 50 C3
Azinhoso P 39 F6
Azkoitia E 32 D1
Aznalcázar E 51 E7
Aznalcóllar E 51 D7
Azóia P 50 C1
Azpeitia E 32 D1
Azuaga E 51 C8
Azuara E 41 F10
Azuel E 54 C4
Azuelo E 32 E1
Azuga RO 161 C7
Azuqueca de Henares E 47 C6
Azur F 32 C3
Azután E 45 E10
Azy-le-Vif F 30 B3
Azyory BY 140 C10
Azzano Decimo I 73 E6
Azzone I 69 B9

B

Baalberge D 79 C10
Baâlon F 19 F11
Baar CH 27 F10
Baarle-Hertog B 16 F3
Baarle-Nassau NL 16 F3
Baarn NL 16 D4
Baba Ana RO 161 D8
Babadag RO 155 D3
Babaeski TR 173 B7
Babaköy TR 173 E9
Baban AL 168 C4
Băbana RO 160 D5
Babberich NL 183 B8
Babchyntsi UA 154 A2
Babenhausen D 21 E11
Băbeni RO 151 C11
Băbeni RO 160 D4
Babiak PL 136 E1
Babiak PL 138 F6
Babice CZ 146 C4
Babice PL 143 F7
Babice nad Svitavou CZ 77 D11
Babići BIH 157 D7
Băbiciu RO 160 E5
Babilafuente E 45 C10
Babimost PL 81 B9
Babín SK 147 C8
Babina SRB 164 D5
Babina Greda HR 157 B10
Babino Polje HR 162 D4
Babīte LV 135 C7
Babno Polje SLO 73 E10
Babócsa H 149 D8
Bábolna H 149 A9
Baborów PL 142 F4
Baboszewo PL 139 E9
Bábót H 149 A8
Babrrujë AL 168 B2
Babtai LT 137 C8
Babuk BG 161 E10
Babušnica SRB 164 C5
Babyak BG 165 F8
Babynichy BY 133 F4
Bać MNE 163 D9
Bač SRB 158 C3
Băcani RO 153 E11
Bacares E 55 E8
Bacău RO 153 D9
Baccarat F 27 D6
Baceno I 68 A5
Băcești RO 153 D10
Bach A 71 C10
Bacharach D 21 D9
Bachkovo BG 165 F10
Bachórz PL 144 D5
Băcia RO 151 F11
Baciki Bliższe PL 141 F7
Băcioi MD 154 D3
Baciu RO 152 D3
Bäck S 105 E16
Backa S 91 E10
Backa S 97 A9
Backa S 97 B9
Backaland GB 3 G11
Bačka Palanka SRB 158 C3
Backaryd S 89 C8
Bačka Topola SRB 150 F4
Backberg S 103 E12
Backe S 107 D10
Bäckebo S 89 B10
Bäckefors S 91 B11
Bäckhammar S 91 A15
Bački Breg SRB 150 F2
Bački Brestovac SRB 158 B3
Bački Jarak SRB 158 C4
Bački Monoštor SRB 150 F2
Bäckinkinai LT 137 D8
Bački Petrovac SRB 158 C4
Bäcklund S 109 E17
Bäckmark S 107 A11
Backnang D 27 C11
Bäcknäs S 109 F17
Bačko Dobro Polje SRB 158 B4
Bačko Gradište SRB 158 B5
Bačko Novo Selo SRB 157 B11
Bačko Petrovo Selo SRB 158 B5
Bačkovice PL 143 E11
Backträsk S 118 C6
Bäckvallen S 102 B8
Băcleș RO 159 E11
Bacoli I 60 B2
Bacqueville-en-Caux F 18 E2
Bácsalmás H 150 E3
Bácsbokod H 150 E3
Bácsborsód H 150 E3
Bacúch SK 147 D9
Baczyna PL 85 E8
Bada S 97 B9
Bad Abbach D 75 E11
Bad Aibling D 72 A5
Badajoz E 51 B6
Badalona E 43 E8
Badalucco I 37 D7
Badames E 40 B5
Badarán E 40 D6
Bad Aussee A 73 A8
Bad Bayersoien D 71 B12
Bad Bederkesa D 17 A11
Bad Belzig D 79 B12
Bad Bentheim D 17 D8
Bad Bergzabern D 27 B8
Bad Berka D 79 E9
Bad Berleburg D 21 B10
Bad Berneck im Fichtelgebirge D 75 B10
Bad Bertrich D 21 D8
Bad Bevensen D 83 D9
Bad Bibra D 79 D10
Bad Birnbach D 76 F4
Bad Blankenburg D 79 E9
Bad Blumau A 148 B6
Bad Bocklet D 75 B7
Bad Boll D 74 E6
Bad Brambach D 75 B11
Bad Bramstedt D 83 C7
Bad Breisig D 185 D7
Bad Brückenau D 74 B6
Bad Buchau D 71 A9
Bad Camberg D 21 D10
Badcaul GB 2 K6
Badderen N 112 D9
Bad Doberan D 83 B11
Bad Driburg D 17 E12
Bad Düben D 79 C12
Bad Dürkheim D 21 F10
Bad Dürrenberg D 79 D11
Bad Dürrheim D 27 D10
Badeborn D 79 C9
Badefols-d'Ans F 29 E8
Bad Elster D 75 B11
Bademler TR 177 C8
Bademli TR 171 F10
Bademli TR 173 D10
Bademli TR 177 B8
Bad Ems D 21 D9
Baden A 77 F10
Baden CH 27 F9
Baden F 22 E6
Bádenas E 47 B10
Baden-Baden D 27 C9
Bad Endorf D 72 A5
Badenscoth GB 3 L12
Badenweiler D 27 E8
Baderna HR 67 B8
Badersleben D 79 C8
Badesi I 64 B2
Bad Essen D 17 D10
Bădeuți RO 153 B7
Bad Fallingbostel D 82 E7
Bad Feilnbach D 72 A5
Bad Frankenhausen (Kyffhäuser) D 79 D9
Bad Freienwalde D 84 E6
Bad Friedrichshall D 21 F12
Bad Füssing D 76 F4
Bad Gams A 73 C11
Bad Gandersheim D 79 C7
Badgastein A 73 B7
Bad Gleichenberg A 148 C5
Bad Goisern A 73 A8
Bad Griesbach im Rottal D 76 F4
Bad Grönenbach D 71 B10
Bad Großpertholz A 77 E7
Bad Grund (Harz) D 79 C7
Bad Hall A 76 F6
Bad Harzburg D 79 C8
Bad Herrenalb D 27 C9
Bad Hersfeld D 78 E6
Bad Hindelang D 71 B10
Badhoevedorp NL 182 A5
Bad Hofgastein A 73 B7
Bad Homburg vor der Höhe D 21 D11
Bad Honnef D 21 C8
Bad Hönningen D 185 C7
Badia I 72 C4
Badia Calavena I 69 B11
Badia Gran E 49 F10
Badia Polesine I 66 B3
Badia Tedalda I 66 E5
Bad Iburg D 17 D10
Bădiceni MD 153 A12
Badín SK 147 D8
Bad Ischl A 73 A8
Bad Karlshafen D 78 C5
Bad Kissingen D 75 B7
Bad Kleinen D 83 C10
Bad Kleinkirchheim A 73 C8
Bad König D 21 E12
Bad Königshofen im Grabfeld D 75 B7
Bad Kösen D 79 D10
Bad Köstritz D 79 E11
Bad Kötzting D 76 D3
Bądkowo PL 138 E6
Bad Kreuzen A 77 F7
Bad Kreuznach D 21 E9
Bad Krozingen D 27 E8
Bad Laasphe D 21 C10
Bad Laer D 17 D10
Bad Langensalza D 79 D8
Bad Lauchstädt D 79 D10
Bad Lausick D 79 D12
Bad Lauterberg im Harz D 79 C7
Bad Leonfelden A 76 E6
Bad Liebenstein D 79 E7
Bad Liebenwerda D 80 C4
Bad Liebenzell D 27 C10
Bad Lippspringe D 17 E11
Badljevina HR 149 E8
Bad Lobenstein D 75 B10
Bad Marienberg (Westerwald) D 21 C9
Bad Mergentheim D 74 D6
Bad Mitterndorf A 73 A8
Bad Münder am Deister D 78 B5
Bad Münster-Ebernburg D 21 E9
Bad Münstereifel D 21 C7
Bad Muskau D 81 C7
Bad Nauheim D 21 D11
Bad Nenndorf D 17 D12
Bad Neuenahr-Ahrweiler D 21 C8
Bad Neustadt an der Saale D 75 B7
Badolato I 59 B10
Badolatosa E 53 B7
Bad Oldesloe D 83 C8
Badonviller F 27 C6
Bad Orb D 21 D12
Badovinci SRB 158 D3
Bad Peterstal D 27 D9
Bad Pirawarth A 77 F11
Bad Pyrmont D 17 E12
Bad Radkersburg A 148 C5
Bad Ragaz CH 71 C9
Bad Rappenau D 187 C7
Bad Reichenhall D 73 A6
Bad Rodach D 75 B8
Bad Saarow-Pieskow D 80 B6
Bad Sachsa D 79 C8
Bad Säckingen D 27 E8
Bad Salzdetfurth D 79 B7
Bad Salzuflen D 17 D11
Bad Salzungen D 79 E7
Bad Sankt Leonhard im Lavanttal A 73 C10
Bad Sassendorf D 17 E10
Bad Schandau D 80 E6
Bad Schmiedeberg D 79 C12
Bad Schönborn D 187 C6
Bad Schussenried D 71 A9
Bad Schwalbach D 21 D10
Bad Schwartau D 83 C9
Bad Segeberg D 83 C8
Bad Sobernheim D 185 E8
Bad Soden-Salmünster D 74 B5
Bad Sooden-Allendorf D 79 D6
Bad Staffelstein D 75 B8
Bad Steben D 75 B10
Bad Sulza D 79 D10
Bad Sülze D 83 B13
Bad Tennstedt D 79 D8
Bad Tölz D 72 A4
Bad Überkingen D 187 D8
Badules E 47 B10
Bad Urach D 27 D11
Bad Vilbel D 21 D11
Bad Vöslau A 77 G10
Bad Waldsee D 71 B9
Bad Waltersdorf A 148 B6
Bad Wildbad im Schwarzwald D 187 D6
Bad Wildungen D 21 B12
Bad Wilsnack D 83 E11
Bad Wimpfen D 21 F12
Bad Windsheim D 75 C7
Bad Wörishofen D 71 B11
Bad Wurzach D 71 B9
Bad Zell A 77 F7
Bad Zurzach CH 27 E9
Bad Zwesten D 21 B12
Bad Zwischenahn D 17 B10
Bække DK 86 D4
Bækmarksbro DK 86 C2
Baelen B 183 D7
Bælum DK 86 B6
Baena E 53 A8
Bærums Verk N 95 C12
Baesweiler D 20 C6
Baeza E 53 A10
Baflo NL 17 B7
Bagà E 43 C7
Băgaciu RO 152 E4
Bagaladi I 59 C8
Bagamér H 151 C8
Bağarasi TR 177 B8
Bağarasi TR 177 D10
Bagard F 35 B7
Bağcılar TR 181 B8
Bâgé-le-Châtel F 30 C6
Bagenalstown IRL 9 C9
Bagenkop DK 83 A9
Bages F 34 E4
Baggå S 97 C14
Bagheria I 58 C4
Bagn N 101 E11
Bagnacavallo I 66 D4
Bagnac-sur-Célé F 33 A10
Bagnara Calabra I 59 C8
Bagnaria I 37 B10
Bagnaria Arsa I 73 E7
Bagnasco I 37 C8
Bagneaux-sur-Loing F 25 D8
Bagnères-de-Bigorre F 33 D6
Bagnères-de-Luchon F 33 E7
Bagni di Lucca I 66 D2
Bagni di Masino I 69 A8
Bagni di Rabbi I 71 E11
Bagno a Ripoli I 66 E3
Bagno di Romagna I 66 E4
Bagnoli del Trigno I 63 D6
Bagnoli di Sopra I 66 B4
Bagnoli Irpino I 60 B4
Bagnolo in Piano I 66 C2
Bagnolo Mella I 66 B1
Bagnolo Piemonte I 31 F11
Bagnolo San Vito I 66 B2
Bagnols-les-Bains F 35 A6
Bagnols-sur-Cèze F 35 B8
Bagnoregio I 62 B2
Bagod H 149 C7
Bagolino I 69 B9
Bagrationovsk RUS 136 E2
Bagrdan SRB 159 E7
Bagshot GB 15 E7
Báguena E 47 B10
Bágyogszovát H 149 A8
Bağyurdu TR 177 C10
Bağyüzü TR 173 F6
Bahabón de Esgueva E 40 E4
Bahate UA 155 C3
Bahçeburun TR 181 B7
Bahçeköy TR 173 B10
Bahçeli TR 171 E10
Bahíllo E 39 D10
Bahmut MD 153 C12
Bahna RO 153 D9
Bahnea RO 152 E4
Báhoň SK 146 E4
Bahrenborstel D 17 C11
Bahrendorf D 79 C10
Baia RO 153 C8
Baia RO 155 D3
Baia de Aramă RO 159 D10
Baia de Arieș RO 151 E11
Baia de Criș RO 151 E10
Baia de Fier RO 160 C3
Baia della Zagare I 63 D10
Baia Mare RO 152 B3
Baiano I 60 B3
Baiardo I 37 D7
Baia Sprie RO 152 B3
Băicoi RO 161 C7
Băiculești RO 160 C5
Baiersbronn D 27 C9
Baiersdorf D 75 C9
Baignes-Ste-Radegonde F 28 E5
Baigneux-les-Juifs F 25 E12
Baile an Bhiataigh IRL 7 E10
Baile an Bhuinneánaigh IRL 8 C3
Baile an Chinnéidigh IRL 7 F10
Baile an Dúlaigh IRL 6 F4
Baile an Fheirtéaraigh IRL 8 D2
Baile an Mhóta IRL 6 D5
Baile an Mhuilinn IRL 8 D2
Baile an Róba IRL 6 E4
Baile an Sceilg IRL 8 E2
Baile Átha an Rí IRL 6 F5
Baile Átha Buí IRL 7 E9
Baile Átha Cliath IRL 7 F10
Baile Átha Fhirdhia IRL 7 E9
Baile Átha Í IRL 7 G9
Baile Átha Luain IRL 7 F7
Baile Átha Troim IRL 7 E9
Baile Brigín IRL 7 E10
Baile Coimín IRL 7 F9
Băile Govora RO 160 C4
Băile Herculane RO 159 D9
Baile Loch Riach IRL 6 F5
Baile Mhartainn GB 2 K2
Baile Mhic Andáin IRL 9 C8
Baile Mhic Íre IRL 8 E4
Baile Mhistéala IRL 8 D6
Bailén E 54 C5
Baile na Finne IRL 6 C6
Baile na Lorgan IRL 7 D9
Băile Olănești RO 160 C4
Baile Órthaí IRL 7 E9
Băilești RO 160 E2
Băile Tușnad RO 153 E7
Baile Uilcín IRL 7 E9
Bailieborough IRL 7 E9
Baillargues F 35 C7
Bailleau-le-Pin F 24 D5
Bailleul F 18 C6
Baillonville B 19 D11
Bailo E 32 E4
Baimaclia MD 154 E2
Bainbridge GB 11 C7
Bain-de-Bretagne F 23 E8
Baindt D 71 B9
Bains F 30 E4
Bains-les-Bains F 26 D5
Bainton GB 11 D10
Baio E 38 B2
Baiona E 38 D2
Bais F 23 D9
Bais F 23 D11
Baiso I 66 D2
Băișoara RO 151 D11
Baisogala LT 134 E7
Băița RO 151 E10
Băița de sub Codru RO 151 B11
Baix F 35 A8
Baixa da Banheira P 50 B1
Baixas F 34 E4
Baj H 149 A10
Baja H 150 E2
Bajč SK 146 F6
Bajgorë RKS 164 D3
Bajina Bašta SRB 158 F4
Bajmok SRB 150 F3
Bajna H 149 A11
Bajót H 149 A11
Bajovo Polje MNE 157 F10
Bajram Curri AL 163 E9
Bajša SRB 150 F4
Bak H 149 C7
Baka SK 146 F5
Bakacak TR 173 D7
Bakałarzewo PL 136 E6
Bakar HR 67 B10
Bakel NL 16 F5
Bakir TR 177 A10
Bakırköy TR 173 C10
Bakkasund N 94 B2
Bakke N 111 A16
Bakkeby N 112 D6
Bakkejord N 111 A15
Bakken N 101 E15
Bakko N 95 C9
Bakonszeg H 151 C7
Bakonybél H 149 B9
Bakonycsernye H 149 B10
Bakonysárkány H 149 B10
Bakonyszentkirály H 149 B9
Bakonyszentlászló H 149 B9
Bakonyszombathely H 149 B9
Bakov nad Jizerou CZ 77 B7
Baks H 150 D5
Baksa H 149 E10
Baksha UA 154 A5
Baktalórántháza H 145 H5
Baktsjaur S 109 F17
Bakum D 17 C10
Bakvattnet S 105 D16
Bäl S 93 D13
Bala GB 10 F4
Bala RO 159 D10
Balabancik TR 173 C6
Bălăbănești MD 154 C4
Bălăbănești RO 153 E11
Balabanu MD 154 F3
Bălăceanu RO 161 C10
Balaci RO 160 E5
Bălăcița RO 159 E11
Balaciu RO 161 D9
Balaguer E 42 D5
Balallan GB 2 J3
Balan F 19 E10
Balan F 31 D7
Bălan RO 151 C11
Bălan RO 153 D7
Bălănești MD 153 C12
Bălănești RO 160 C2
Balanivka UA 154 A4
Balaruc-les-Bains F 35 D6
Bălășești RO 153 E11
Bălăsinești MD 153 A9
Balassagyarmat H 147 E8
Balástya H 150 E5
Balat TR 177 D9
Balaton H 145 G1
Balatonalmádi H 149 B10
Balatonberény H 149 C8
Balatonboglár H 149 C9
Balatonfőkajár H 149 B10
Balatonföldvár H 149 C9
Balatonfüred H 149 C9
Balatonfűzfő H 149 B10
Balatonkenese H 149 B10
Balatonlelle H 149 C9
Balatonszabadi H 149 C10
Balatonszárszó H 149 C9
Balatonvilágos H 149 C10
Bălăușeri RO 152 E5
Balazote E 55 B8
Balbeggie GB 5 C10
Balbieriškis LT 137 D8
Balbigny F 30 D5
Balbriggan IRL 7 E10
Balcani RO 153 D9
Bălcești RO 160 D3
Balchik BG 167 C10
Balcilar TR 173 D6
Balçova TR 177 C9
Balderton GB 11 E10
Baldock GB 15 D8
Baldone LV 135 C8
Baldones Muiža LV 135 C8
Baldovinești RO 160 E4
Bale HR 67 B8
Baleizão P 50 C4
Balemartine GB 4 C3
Balen B 19 B11
Băleni RO 153 F11
Băleni RO 161 D7
Balephuil GB 4 C3
Balerma E 55 F7
Bălești RO 159 C11
Balestrand N 100 D5
Balestrate I 58 C3
Balfour GB 3 G11
Balfron GB 5 C8
Balgale LV 134 B5
Balgown GB 2 K4
Bälgviken S 98 D6
Bali GR 178 E8
Baligród PL 145 E5
Balikesir TR 173 E8
Baliklıçeşme TR 173 D7
Balikliova TR 177 C8
Bălilești RO 160 C5
Bälinge S 99 C9
Bälinge S 118 C7
Balingen D 27 D10
Balinka H 149 B10
Balinț RO 151 F8
Balintore GB 3 K9
Balje D 17 A12
Baljevac BIH 156 C4
Baljevac SRB 163 C10
Baljvine BIH 157 D7
Balk NL 16 C5
Balkány H 151 B8
Balkbrug NL 16 C6
Balla IRL 6 E4
Ballaban AL 168 D3
Ballabio I 69 B7
Ballachulish GB 4 B6
Ballaghaderreen IRL 6 E5
Ballaghkeen IRL 9 D10
Ballangen N 111 D12
Ballantrae GB 4 E6
Ballao I 64 D3
Ballasalla GBM 10 C2
Ballater GB 5 A10
Ballaugh GBM 10 C2
Balle DK 87 C7
Ballée F 23 E11
Ballee GB 7 D11
Ballen DK 86 D7
Ballenstedt D 79 C9
Balleroy F 23 B10
Ballerup DK 87 D10
Ballesteros de Calatrava E 54 B5
Balli TR 173 C7
Ballina IRL 6 D4
Ballina IRL 8 C6
Ballinaboy IRL 6 F2
Ballinafad IRL 6 D6
Ballinagar IRL 7 F8
Ballinagh IRL 7 E8
Ballinakill IRL 9 C8
Ballinalack IRL 7 E8
Ballinalee IRL 7 E7
Ballinamallard GB 7 D7
Ballinamore IRL 7 D7
Ballinamult IRL 9 D7
Ballinasloe IRL 6 F6
Ballincollig IRL 8 E5
Ballindine IRL 6 E5
Ballindooly IRL 6 F4
Ballineen IRL 8 E5
Ballingarry IRL 8 D5
Ballingarry IRL 9 C7
Ballingeary IRL 8 E4
Ballingry GB 5 C10
Ballingslöv S 87 C13
Ballingurteen IRL 8 E4
Ballinhassig IRL 8 E5
Ballinlough IRL 6 E5
Ballinluig GB 5 B9
Ballinrobe IRL 6 E4
Ballinskelligs IRL 8 E2
Ballinspittle IRL 8 E5
Ballintober IRL 6 E4
Ballintoy GB 4 E4
Ballintra IRL 6 C6
Ballintubber IRL 6 E4
Ballinure IRL 9 C7
Ballivor IRL 7 E9
Ballobar E 42 D4
Ballon F 23 D12
Ballon IRL 9 C9
Ballószög H 150 D4
Ballots F 23 E9
Ballsh AL 168 C2
Ballsnes N 111 A16
Ballstad N 110 D6
Ballstädt D 79 D8
Ballum DK 86 E3
Ballum NL 16 B5
Ballure IRL 6 C6
Ballybay IRL 7 D9
Ballybofey IRL 7 C7
Ballybrack IRL 7 F10
Ballybrack IRL 8 E2
Ballybrittas IRL 7 F8
Ballybunion IRL 8 C3
Ballybunnion IRL 8 C3
Ballycahill IRL 9 C7
Ballycanew IRL 9 C10
Ballycarry GB 4 F5
Ballycastle GB 4 E4
Ballycastle IRL 6 D4
Ballyclare GB 4 F5
Ballycolla IRL 9 C8
Ballyconneely IRL 6 F2
Ballyconnell IRL 7 D7
Ballycotton IRL 8 E6
Ballycroy IRL 6 D3
Ballydavid IRL 6 F6
Ballydehob IRL 8 E4
Ballydesmond IRL 8 D4
Ballydonegan IRL 8 E2
Ballyduff IRL 8 D3
Ballyduff IRL 8 D6
Ballyfarnan IRL 6 D6
Ballyfarnon IRL 6 D6
Ballyfeard IRL 8 E6

Ballyferriter IRL 8 D2
Ballyforan IRL 6 F6
Ballygar IRL 6 E6
Ballygarrett IRL 9 C10
Ballygawley GB 7 D8
Ballygeary IRL 9 D10
Ballyglass IRL 6 E5
Ballygorman IRL 4 E2
Ballygowan GB 7 C11
Ballyhaise IRL 7 D8
Ballyhalbert GB 7 D12
Ballyhale IRL 9 D8
Ballyhaunis IRL 6 E5
Ballyhean IRL 6 E4
Ballyheigue IRL 8 D3
Ballyjamesduff IRL 7 E8
Ballykeeran IRL 7 F7
Ballykelly GB 4 E2
Ballykilleen IRL 7 F8
Ballylanders IRL 8 D6
Ballylaneen IRL 9 D8
Ballylickey IRL 8 E4
Ballyliffen IRL 4 E2
Ballyliffin IRL 4 E2
Ballylynan IRL 9 C8
Ballymacarberry IRL 9 D7
Ballymacmague IRL 9 D7
Ballymadog IRL 9 E7
Ballymagorry GB 4 F2
Ballymahon IRL 7 E7
Ballymakeery IRL 8 E4
Ballymartin GB 7 D11
Ballymena GB 4 F4
Ballymoney GB 4 E3
Ballymore IRL 7 F7
Ballymote IRL 6 D5
Ballymurphy IRL 9 C9
Ballymurry IRL 6 E6
Ballynacally IRL 8 C4
Ballynafid IRL 7 E8
Ballynahinch GB 7 D11
Ballynahowen IRL 7 F7
Ballynakill IRL 7 F7
Ballynamona IRL 8 D5
Ballyneaner GB 4 F2
Ballynunty IRL 9 C7
Ballynure GB 4 F5
Ballyporeen IRL 8 D6
Ballyragget IRL 9 C8
Ballyroan IRL 9 C8
Ballyronan GB 4 F3
Ballyshannon IRL 6 C6
Ballyvaldon IRL 9 D10
Ballyvaughan IRL 6 F4
Ballyvoy GB 4 E4
Ballyvoyle IRL 9 D7
Ballywalter GB 7 C12
Ballyward GB 7 D10
Balma F 33 C9
Balmaha GB 4 C7
Balmaseda E 40 B5
Balmazújváros H 151 B7
Balme I 31 E11
Balmedie GB 3 L12
Balmuccia I 68 B5
Balnacra GB 2 L6
Balnapaling GB 3 K8
Balneario de Panticosa Huesca E 32 E5
Balninkai LT 135 F10
Balocco I 68 C5
Balogunyom H 149 B7
Balot F 25 E11
Balotaszállás H 150 E4
Balotești RO 161 D8
Balow D 83 D11
Balrath IRL 7 E10
Balș RO 160 E4
Balșa RO 151 E11
Balsa de Ves E 47 F10
Balsa Pintada E 56 F2
Balsareny E 43 D7
Balsfjord N 111 B17
Balsicas E 56 F3
Balsjö S 107 D16
Balsorano I 62 D5
Bålsta S 99 C9
Balsthal CH 27 F8
Balta RO 159 D10
Balta UA 154 B5
Balta Albă RO 161 C10
Balta Berilovac SRB 164 C5
Balta Doamnei RO 161 D8
Baltanás E 40 E3
Baltar E 38 E4
Baltasound GB 3 D15
Băltătești RO 153 C8
Bălțați RO 153 C10
Bălteni RO 153 D11
Bălteni RO 159 D11
Baltezers LV 135 B8
Bălți MD 153 B11
Baltimore IRL 8 F4
Baltinava LV 133 C3
Baltinglass IRL 9 C9
Baltiysk RUS 139 A8
Baltmuiža LV 135 D13
Baltoji Vokė LT 137 E11
Baltora S 99 C11
Bałtów PL 143 D12
Baltray IRL 7 E10
Băluşeni RO 153 B9
Balvan BG 166 C4
Bălvănești RO 159 D10
Balvano I 60 B5
Balve D 17 F9
Balvi LV 133 B2
Balvicar GB 4 C5
Balya TR 173 E8
Balzers FL 71 C9
Bamberg D 75 C8
Bamburgh GB 5 D13
Bammental D 21 F11
Bampini GR 174 B3
Bampton GB 13 B11
Bampton GB 13 D8
Bana H 149 A9
Banafjäl S 107 E16
Banagher IRL 7 F7
Banarli TR 173 B7
Banassac F 34 B5
Banatski Brestovac SRB 159 D6
Banatski Dvor SRB 158 B6
Banatski Karlovac SRB 159 C7
Banatsko Aranđelovo SRB 150 E5
Banatsko Karađorđevo SRB 158 B6
Banatsko Novo Selo SRB 159 D6
Banatsko Veliko Selo SRB 150 F6
Banbridge GB 7 D10
Banbury GB 13 A12
Banca RO 153 E11
Banchory GB 5 A12
Band RO 152 D4
Bande E 38 D4
Bandenitz D 83 D10
Bandholm DK 83 A10
Bandirma TR 173 D8
Bandol F 35 D10
Bandon IRL 8 E5
Bandurove UA 154 A5
Băneasa RO 153 F11
Băneasa RO 155 E1
Băneasa RO 161 E8
Bănești MD 154 B2
Bănești RO 161 C7
Banevo BG 167 D8
Banff GB 3 K11
Bångnäs S 106 B9
Bangor GB 4 F5
Bangor GB 10 E3
Bangor IRL 6 D3
Bangor Erris IRL 6 D3
Bangsund N 105 C10
Banham GB 15 C11
Bánhorváti H 145 G2
Bănia RO 159 D9
Banie PL 85 D7
Banie Mazurskie PL 136 E5
Baniska BG 166 C5
Bănișor RO 151 C10
Bănița RO 159 C11
Banite BG 171 A8
Banitsa BG 165 C8
Banja BIH 158 F3
Banja SRB 163 B8
Banja Lučica BIH 157 D10
Banja Luka BIH 157 C7
Banjani SRB 158 D4
Banja Vrućia BIH 157 C8
Bankekind S 92 C7
Bankeryd S 92 D4
Bankfoot GB 5 B9
Bankya BG 165 D6
Bankya BG 165 D7
Banloc RO 159 C7
Bannalec F 22 E4
Bannay F 25 F8
Bannesdorf auf Fehmarn D 83 B10
Bannewitz D 80 E5
Bannivka UA 155 B3
Bannockburn GB 5 C9
Bañobárez E 45 C7
Bañón E 47 C10
Banon F 35 B10
Baños de la Encina E 54 C5
Baños de Molgas E 38 D4
Baños de Montemayor E 45 D9
Baños de Río Tobía E 40 D6
Baños de Valdearados E 40 E4
Bánov CZ 146 D5
Bánov SK 146 E6
Banova Jaruga HR 149 F7
Bánovce nad Bebravou SK 146 D6
Banovići BIH 157 D10
Bánréve H 145 G1
Bansin D 84 C6
Banská Belá SK 147 E7
Banská Bystrica SK 147 D8
Banská Štiavnica SK 147 E7
Banské SK 145 F4
Bansko BG 165 F7
Bant NL 16 C5
Banteer IRL 8 D5
Banteln D 78 B6
Bantheville F 19 F11
Bantry IRL 8 E4
Banya BG 165 D10
Banya BG 165 E9
Banya BG 165 F8
Banya BG 166 D5
Banya BG 167 D9
Banyalbufar E 49 E10
Banyeres de Mariola E 56 D3
Banyliv UA 152 A6
Banyliv-Pidhirnyy UA 152 A7
Banyoles E 43 C9
Banyuls-sur-Mer F 34 F5
Banzi I 60 B6
Banzkow D 83 C11
Bapaume F 18 D6
Bar MNE 163 E7
Bara RO 151 F8
Băra RO 153 C10
Bara S 87 D12
Barabás H 145 G5
Baracska H 149 B11
Bărăganul RO 161 D11
Baragiano I 60 B5
Barahona E 41 F6
Barajas de Melo E 47 D7
Barajevo SRB 158 D5
Barakaldo E 40 B6
Barakovo BG 165 E7
Baralla E 38 C5
Barañain E 32 E2
Baranbio E 40 B6
Baránd H 151 C7
Baranello I 63 D7
Baranjsko Petrovo Selo HR 149 E10
Barano d'Ischia I 62 F5
Baranów PL 141 G6
Baranów PL 142 D5
Baranowo PL 139 D11
Baranów Sandomierska PL 143 F12
Barão de São João P 50 E2
Baraolt RO 153 E7
Baraqueville F 33 B10
Barásoain E 32 E2
Barassie GB 4 D7
Bărăști RO 160 D5
Baravukha BY 133 E5
Barbacena P 51 B5
Barbadás E 38 D4
Barbadillo de Herreros E 40 D5
Barbadillo del Mercado E 40 D5
Barbadillo del Pez E 40 D5
Barban HR 67 B9
Barbarano Vicentino I 66 B4
Barbaraville GB 3 K8
Barbaros TR 173 C7
Barbaste F 33 B6
Barbastro E 42 C4
Barbat HR 67 C10
Barbate de Franco E 52 D5
Bărbătescu RO 161 D9
Bărbătești RO 160 D3
Barbatovac SRB 164 C3
Barbâtre F 28 B1
Bārbele LV 135 D9
Barbentane F 35 C8
Barberà del Vallès E 43 D8
Barberaz F 31 D8
Barberino di Mugello I 66 D3
Barbezieux-St-Hilaire F 28 E5
Barbonne-Fayel F 25 C10
Bărbulețu RO 160 C6
Barbullush AL 163 F8
Barby (Elbe) D 79 C10
Barç AL 168 C4
Barca E 41 F6
Bârca RO 160 F3
Barcabo E 42 C4
Barcada BIH 157 B8
Barca de Alva P 45 B7
Bărcănești RO 161 D8
Bărcănești RO 161 D9
Barcani RO 161 B8
Barcarrota E 51 B6
Barcea RO 153 F10
Barcelinhos P 38 E2
Barcellona Pozzo di Gotto I 59 C7
Barcelona E 43 E8
Barcelonne-du-Gers F 32 C5
Barcelonnette F 36 C5
Barcelos P 38 E2
Bárcena del Monasterio E 39 B6
Bárcena de Pie de Concha E 40 B3
Barcenillas de Cerezos E 40 B4
Barchfeld D 79 E7
Barciany PL 136 E3
Barcillonnette F 35 B10
Barcin PL 138 E4
Barcino PL 85 B11
Barcis I 72 D6
Barcones E 40 F6
Barcos P 44 B5
Barcs H 149 E8
Barcus F 32 D4
Barczewo PL 136 F2
Bardal N 108 D5
Bardar MD 154 D3
Barde DK 86 C3
Bardejov SK 145 E3
Bárdena E 41 D9
Bardenitz D 80 B3
Bårdesø DK 86 D6
Bardi I 69 D8
Bardineto I 37 C8
Bardney GB 11 E11
Bardo PL 77 B11
Bardolino I 66 A2
Bardonecchia I 31 E10
Bardos F 32 D3
Bardowick D 83 D8
Bardsea GB 10 C5
Bárdudvarnok H 149 D9
Bare BIH 157 E10
Bare SRB 158 E6
Bare SRB 163 C8
Barefield IRL 8 C5
Barèges F 33 E6
Barenburg D 17 C11
Barendorf D 83 D9
Bärenklau D 81 C7
Bärenstein D 76 B4
Bärenstein D 80 E5
Barentin F 18 E2
Barenton F 23 C10
Barevo BIH 157 D7
Barfleur F 23 A9
Barga I 66 D1
Bargagli I 37 C10
Bargas E 46 E4
Bărgăuani RO 153 D9
Barge I 31 F11
Bargemon F 36 D5
Bargen CH 27 E10
Bargenstedt D 82 B6
Barghe I 69 B9
Bărghiș RO 152 F5
Bargischow D 84 C5
Bargłów Kościelny PL 140 C7
Bargoed GB 13 B8
Bargrennan GB 4 E7
Bargstedt D 17 B12
Bargteheide D 83 C8
Bargullas AL 168 C3
Barham GB 15 E11
Bar Hill GB 15 C9
Bari I 61 A7
Barić Draga HR 156 D3
Barile I 60 B5
Barilović HR 148 F5
Barinas E 56 E2
Båring DK 86 E5
Barì Sardo I 64 D4
Barisciano I 62 C5
Barjac F 35 B7
Bårjasnjar'ga N 113 D15
Barjols F 35 C11
Barkåkar N 95 D12
Barkåkra S 87 C11
Barkald N 101 C13
Barkarö S 98 C7
Barkava LV 135 C13
Barkelsby D 83 A7
Barkhyttan S 103 E11
Barkowo PL 85 C12
Barkston GB 11 F10
Bârla RO 160 E5
Bârlad RO 153 E11
Barleben D 79 B10
Bar-le-Duc F 26 C3
Barles F 36 C4
Barletta I 60 A6
Barley GB 15 C9
Barlinek PL 85 E8
Barlingbo S 93 D12
Barmouth GB 10 F3
Barmstedt D 82 C7
Bârna H 147 E9
Barna IRL 6 F4
Bârna RO 159 B9
Barnaderg IRL 6 F5
Barnard Castle GB 11 B8
Barnarp S 92 D4
Barnatra IRL 6 D3
Bârnau D 75 C11
Barnbach A 73 B11
Barneberg D 79 B9
Barneveld NL 16 D5
Barneville-Carteret F 23 B8
Barnewitz D 79 A12
Barneycarroll IRL 6 E5
Barnoldswick GB 11 D7
Bârnova RO 153 C11
Barnowko PL 85 E7
Barnsley GB 11 D9
Barnstädt D 79 D10
Barnstaple GB 12 C6
Barnstorf D 17 C11
Barntrup D 17 E12
Baronissi I 60 B3
Baronville F 26 C6
Baroševac SRB 158 E5
Barovo MK 169 B7
Barowka BY 133 E3
Barqueros E 55 D10
Barr F 27 D7
Barr GB 4 E7
Barracas E 48 D3
Barrachina E 47 C10
Barraduff IRL 8 D4
Barrafranca I 58 E5
Barral E 38 D3
Barrali I 64 E3
Barranco do Velho P 50 E4
Barrancos P 51 C6
Barranda E 55 C9
Barrapoll GB 4 C3
Barrax E 55 A8
Barre-des-Cévennes F 35 B6
Barreiro P 50 B1
Bärrek S 98 B7
Barrême F 36 D4
Barrhead GB 5 D8
Barrhill GB 4 E7
Barriada Nueva E 43 D8
Bàrrio P 38 E2
Barrio del Peral E 56 F3
Barrio Mar E 48 E4
Barrit DK 86 D5
Barr na Trá IRL 6 D3
Barroca P 44 D5
Barroselas P 38 E2
Barrowby GB 11 F10
Barrow-in-Furness GB 10 C5
Barruecopardo E 45 B7
Barruelo de Santullan E 40 C3
Barry GB 13 C8
Barry IRL 7 E7
Bârsa RO 151 E9
Barsac F 32 A5
Bârsana RO 145 H9
Bârsău RO 151 B11
Barsbüttel D 83 C8
Bârse DK 87 E9
Barsele S 107 A12
Bârsești RO 153 F9
Barsinghausen D 78 B5
Barßel D 17 B9
Barsta S 103 A15
Barstyčiai LT 134 D3
Bar-sur-Aube F 25 D12
Bar-sur-Seine F 25 D11
Bārta LV 134 D2
Bartenheim F 27 E7
Bartenstein D 74 D6
Barth D 83 B13
Bartholomä D 74 E6
Bartholomäberg A 71 C9
Bartkuškiai LT 135 F9
Bartkuškis LT 137 D10
Bartnes N 105 C10
Bartniki PL 139 D10
Bartninkai LT 136 E7
Barton GB 10 D6
Barton-upon-Humber GB 11 D11
Bartoszyce PL 136 E2
Baru RO 159 C11
Baruchowo PL 139 F7
Barulho P 45 F6
Barumini I 64 D3
Baruth D 80 B5
Barvas GB 2 J3
Barvaux B 19 D11
Barver D 17 C11
Barwedel D 79 A8
Barwice PL 85 C10
Barxeta E 56 C4
Bârza RO 160 E4
Bárzana E 39 B8
Bârzava RO 151 E9
Barzio I 69 B7
Bašaid SRB 158 B5
Basarabeasca MD 154 E3
Basarabi RO 155 E2
Basarbovo BG 161 F7
Bàscara E 43 C9
Bascharage L 20 E5
Baschi I 62 B2
Baschurch GB 10 F6
Basciano I 62 B5
Basconcillos del Tozo E 40 C4
Bascons F 32 C5
Bascous F 33 C6
Bascov RO 160 D5
Basdahl D 17 B12
Basècles B 19 C8
Basel CH 27 E8
Baselga di Pinè I 69 A11
Baselice I 60 A3
Bas-en-Basset F 30 E5
Băsești RO 151 C11
Bäsheim N 95 B10
Bashtanivka UA 154 F4
Basigo E 40 B6
Basildon GB 15 D9
Basiliano I 73 D7
Basingstoke GB 13 C12
Baška CZ 146 B6
Baška HR 67 C10
Baška Voda HR 157 F6
Baskemölla S 88 D6
Bäsksele S 107 B11
Bäsksjö S 107 B12
Basksjön S 107 E12
Baslow GB 11 E8
Bâsna S 97 A13
Bassacutena I 64 A3
Bassano del Grappa I 72 E4
Bassano Romano I 62 C2
Bassecourt CH 27 F7
Basse-Goulaine F 23 F9
Bassenge B 19 C12
Bassens F 28 F4
Bassiano I 62 D4
Bassoues F 33 C6
Bassum D 17 C11
Bassy F 31 D8
Bast FIN 123 C10
Båstad S 87 C11
Bastardo I 62 B3
Bastasi BIH 156 D5
Bastasi BIH 157 F10
Bastelica F 37 G10
Bastelicaccia F 37 H9
Bastennes F 32 C4
Bastfallet S 98 B7
Bastia F 37 F10
Bastia I 62 A3
Bastogne B 19 D12
Bastorf D 83 B11
Basttjärn S 97 B12
Bastumarks by S 118 E3
Bastuträsk S 107 C16
Bastuträsk S 118 E4
Báta H 149 D11
Bata RO 151 E9
Batajnica SRB 158 D5
Batak BG 165 F9
Batalha P 44 E3
Bățani RO 153 E7
Bătăr RO 151 D8
Bătarci RO 145 G7
Båtas S 106 B8
Bátaszék H 149 D11
Batea E 42 E4
Batelov CZ 77 D8
Båteng N 113 C20
Baterno E 54 B3
Batetskiy RUS 132 D7
Bath GB 13 C10
Bathford GB 13 C10
Bathgate GB 5 D9
Bathmen NL 16 D6
Batin BG 161 F7
Batina HR 149 E11
Batizovce SK 145 E1
Batković BIH 158 D3
Batley GB 11 D8
Batllavë RKS 164 D3
Bátmonostor H 150 E2
Båtnfjordsøra N 100 A7
Batočina SRB 159 E7
Bátonyterenye H 147 F9
Bátorove Kosihy SK 146 F6
Batoș RO 152 D5
Batoshevo BG 166 D4
Batovce SK 147 E7
Batovo BG 167 C9
Batrina HR 157 B8
Båtsfjord N 114 B7
Batsi GR 176 D4
Båtsjaur S 109 D13
Båtskärsnäs S 119 C10
Battenberg (Eder) D 21 B11
Bätterkinden CH 27 F8
Battice B 183 D7
Battipaglia I 60 B3
Battle GB 15 F9
Battonya H 151 E7
Batultsi BG 165 C9
Bátya H 150 E2
Batyatychi UA 144 C9
Batz-sur-Mer F 22 F7
Baucina I 58 D4
Baud F 22 E5
Bauduen F 36 D4
Bauen CH 71 D7
Baugé F 23 E11
Baugy F 25 F8
Bauladu I 64 C2
Baulon F 23 E8
Baume-les-Dames F 26 F5
Baumholder D 186 B3
Baunach D 75 C8
Baunei I 64 C4
Baurci MD 154 E3
Bausendorf D 21 D7
Bauska LV 135 D8
Băuțar RO 159 B10
Bautzen D 80 D6
Bavanište SRB 159 D6
Bavay F 19 D8
Bavel NL 182 B5
Baveno I 68 B6
Bavilliers F 27 E6
Bavorov CZ 76 D6
Bawdeswell GB 15 B11
Bawdsey GB 15 C11
Bawinkel D 17 C8
Bawn Cross Roads IRL 8 D5
Bayárcal E 55 E7
Bayarque E 55 E8
Baybuzivka UA 154 A5
Baye F 25 C10
Bayel F 25 D12
Bayerbach D 76 F4
Bayerbach bei Ergoldsbach D 75 E11
Bayerisch Eisenstein D 76 D4
Bayeux F 23 B10
Bayındır TR 177 C10
Bayır TR 181 B8
Bayırköy TR 172 D6
Baykal BG 160 F4
Bayon F 26 D5
Bayonne F 32 D3
Bayramiç TR 172 E6
Bayramiç TR 173 C6
Bayramli TR 173 B6
Bayreuth D 75 C10
Bayrischzell D 72 A5
Bayston Hill GB 10 F6
Baytaly UA 154 B5
Bayubas de Abajo E 40 E6
Baza E 55 D7
Bázakerettye H 149 C7
Bazas F 32 B5
Bazet F 33 D6
Bazièges F 33 D9
Bazillac F 33 D6
Bazna RO 152 E4
Bazoches F 25 F10
Bazoches-au-Houlme F 23 C11
Bazoches-les-Gallerandes F 24 D7
Bazoches-sur-Hoëne F 24 C3
Bazougers F 23 D10
Bazouges F 23 E10
Bazzano I 66 D3
Beaconsfield GB 15 D7
Beadnell GB 5 D13
Beagh IRL 6 E5
Bealach A Doirín IRL 6 E5
Bealach Conglais IRL 9 C9
Bealach Feich IRL 7 C7
Bealaclugga IRL 6 F4
Béal an Átha IRL 6 D4
Béal an Mhuirthead IRL 6 D3
Béal Átha an Ghaorthaidh IRL 8 E4
Béal Átha Beithe IRL 7 D9
Béal Átha hAmhnais IRL 6 E5
Béal Átha Liag IRL 7 E7
Béal Átha na Muice IRL 6 E5
Béal Átha na Sluaighe IRL 6 F6
Béal Átha Seanaidh IRL 6 C6
Béal Deirg IRL 6 D3
Béal Easa IRL 6 E4
Bealnablath IRL 8 E5
Beaminster GB 13 D9
Beamud E 47 D9
Beannchar IRL 7 F7
Beantraí IRL 8 E4
Beariz E 38 D3
Bearna IRL 6 F4
Bearsden GB 5 D8
Beas E 51 E6
Beasain E 32 D1
Beas de Granada E 53 B10
Beas de Segura E 55 C7
Beateberg S 92 B4
Beattock GB 5 E10
Beaucaire F 35 C8
Beaucamps-le-Vieux F 18 E4
Beauchastel F 30 F6
Beaucouzé F 23 F10
Beaufay F 24 D3
Beaufort F 31 B7
Beaufort F 31 D10
Beaufort IRL 8 D3
Beaufort-en-Vallée F 23 F11
Beaugency F 24 E6
Beaujeu F 30 C6
Beaujeu F 36 C4
Beaujeu-St-Vallier-Pierrejux-et-Quitteur F 26 E4
Beaulieu F 35 C7
Beaulieu-lès-Loches F 24 F5
Beaulieu-sur-Dordogne F 29 F9
Beaulieu-sur-Loire F 25 E8
Beaulon F 30 B4
Beauly GB 2 L8
Beaumarchés F 33 C6
Beaumaris GB 10 E3
Beaumesnil F 24 B4
Beaumetz-lès-Loges F 18 D6
Beaumont B 19 D9
Beaumont F 23 A8
Beaumont F 29 B6
Beaumont F 29 F7
Beaumont-de-Lomagne F 33 C7
Beaumont-de-Pertuis F 35 C10
Beaumont-en-Argonne F 19 E11
Beaumont-en-Véron F 23 F12
Beaumont-le-Roger F 24 B4
Beaumont-lès-Valence F 30 F6
Beaumont-sur-Oise F 25 B7
Beaumont-sur-Sarthe F 23 D12
Beaune F 30 A6
Beaune-La Rolande F 25 D7
Beaupréau F 23 F10
Beauquesne F 18 D5
Beauraing B 19 D10
Beaurepaire F 31 E7
Beaurepaire-en-Bresse F 31 B7
Beaurières F 35 A10
Beausite F 26 C3
Beausoleil F 37 D6
Beautor F 19 E7
Beauvais F 18 F5
Beauval F 18 D5
Beauvezer F 36 C5
Beauville F 33 B7
Beauvoir-sur-Mer F 28 B1
Beauvoir-sur-Niort F 28 C5
Beauzac F 30 E5
Beauzelle F 33 C8
Beba Veche RO 150 E5
Bebertal D 79 B9
Bebington GB 10 E5
Bebra D 78 E6
Bebrene LV 135 D12
Bebrina HR 157 B8
Beccles GB 15 C12
Becedas E 45 D9
Beceite E 42 F4
Bečej SRB 158 B5
Beceni RO 161 C9
Becerreá E 38 C5
Becerril de Campos E 39 D10
Becherbach D 186 B4
Bécherel F 23 D8
Bechet RO 160 F3
Bechhofen D 21 F8
Bechhofen D 75 D8
Bechlín CZ 76 B6
Bechtheim D 21 E10
Bechyně CZ 77 D6
Becicherecu Mic RO 151 F7
Bečići MNE 163 E6
Becilla de Valderaduey E 39 D9
Beçin TR 181 B7
Beckdorf D 82 D7
Beckedorf D 17 D12
Beckeln D 17 C11
Beckingen D 21 F7
Beckingham GB 11 E10
Beckov SK 146 D5
Beckum D 17 E10
Beclean RO 152 C4
Beclean RO 152 F5
Bécon-les-Granits F 23 F10
Bečov CZ 76 B5
Becsehely H 149 D7
Becsvölgye H 149 C7
Bečváry CZ 77 C8
Bedale GB 11 C8
Bédar E 55 E9
Bédarieux F 34 C5
Bédarrides F 35 B8
Bedburg D 21 C7
Bedburg-Hau D 183 B8
Beddgelert GB 10 E3
Beddingestrand S 87 E12
Bédée F 23 D8
Bedekovčina HR 148 D5
Beden BG 165 F9
Beder DK 86 C6
Bedford GB 15 C8
Bedihošť CZ 77 D12
Bjdków PL 143 C8
Bedlington GB 5 E13
Bedlno PL 143 B8
Bedmar E 53 A10
Bednja HR 148 D5
Bédoin F 35 B9
Bedollo I 69 A11
Bedonia I 37 B11
Bedous F 32 D4
Bedsted DK 86 E4
Bedsted Stationsby DK 86 B2
Béduer F 33 A9
Bedum NL 17 B7
Bedwas GB 13 B8
Bedworth GB 13 A12
Bjdzin PL 143 F7
Bjdzino PL 85 B9
Beedenbostel D 79 A7
Beeford GB 11 D11
Beek NL 16 E5
Beek NL 16 F5
Beek NL 183 D7
Beekbergen NL 183 A7
Beelitz D 80 B3
Beendorf D 79 B9
Beenz D 84 D4
Beerfelden D 21 E11
Beernem B 19 B7
Beers NL 16 E5
Beerse B 16 F3
Beersel B 19 C9
Beerst B 182 C1
Beerta NL 17 B8
Beesd NL 183 B6
Beesenstedt D 79 C10
Beeskow D 80 B6
Beesten D 17 D9
Beeston GB 11 F9
Beetsterzwaag NL 16 B6
Beetzendorf D 83 E10
Bégaar F 32 C4
Bégadan F 28 E4
Begaljica SRB 158 D6
Bégard F 22 C5
Begejci SRB 158 B6
Beğendik TR 172 C6
Begíjar E 53 A9
Begijnendijk B 19 B10
Beglezh BG 165 C10
Begnište MK 169 B6
Begonte E 38 B4
Begur E 43 D10
Behramkale TR 171 F10
Behren-lès-Forbach F 27 B6
Behren-Lübchin D 83 B13
Behringen D 79 D8
Beica de Jos RO 152 D5
Beidaud RO 155 D3
Beierfeld D 79 E12
Beierstedt D 79 B8
Beilen NL 17 C7
Beilngries D 75 D9
Beilstein D 27 B11
Beimerstetten D 187 E8
Beinasco I 37 A7
Beinette I 37 C7
Beinwil CH 27 F9
Beirã P 44 F6
Beisfjord N 111 D14
Beisland N 90 C3
Beith GB 4 D7
Beitostølen N 101 D9
Beitstad N 105 C10
Beiuș RO 151 D9
Beja LV 133 B2
Beja P 50 C4
Bejar AL 168 D2
Béjar E 45 D9
Bejís E 48 E3
Bekecs H 145 G3
Békés H 151 D7
Békéscsaba H 151 D7
Békéssámson H 150 E6
Békésszentandrás H 150 D5
Bekkarfjord N 113 B19
Bekken N 101 C15
Bekkevoll N 114 D8
Belá SK 147 C7
Bélâbre F 29 B8
Bela Crkva SRB 159 D7
Beladice SK 146 E6
Belá-Dulice SK 147 C7
Belalcázar E 51 B9
Belá nad Cirochou SK 145 F5
Bělá nad Radbuzou CZ 75 C12
Belanovce MK 164 E4
Belanovica SRB 158 E5
Bela Palanka SRB 164 C5
Bélapátfalva H 145 G1
Bělá pod Bezdězem CZ 77 A7
Bělá pod Pradědem CZ 77 B12
Belascoáin E 32 E2
Belauski LV 133 C2
Belava LV 135 B13
Belazaima do Chão P 44 C4
Belcaire F 33 E9
Belcastel F 33 B10
Belcești RO 153 C10
Bełchatów PL 143 D7
Belchin BG 165 E7
Belchite E 41 F10
Bělčice CZ 76 C5
Belciugatele RO 161 E8
Belclare IRL 6 F5
Belcoo GB 7 D7
Belderg IRL 6 D3
Beldibi TR 181 C8
Beled H 149 B8
Belegiš SRB 158 C5
Belej HR 67 C9
Belene BG 160 F6
Bélesta F 33 E9
Beleți-Negrești RO 160 D6
Belevi TR 177 C9
Belezna H 149 D7
Belfast GB 7 C11
Belfeld NL 16 F6
Belford GB 5 D13
Belfort F 27 E6
Belfort-du-Quercy F 33 B9
Belforte del Chienti I 67 F7
Belgern D 80 D4
Belgershain D 79 D12
Belgioioso I 69 C7
Belgodère F 37 F10
Belgooly IRL 8 E6
Belgun BG 155 F2
Belhomert-Guéhouville F 24 C5
Beli HR 67 B9
Belianes E 42 D6
Belica HR 149 D7
Beli Iskŭr BG 165 E8
Beli Izvor BG 165 C7
Beli Manastir HR 149 E11
Belin RO 153 F7
Belin-Béliet F 32 B4
Belinchón E 47 D6
Belinț RO 151 F8
Beli Potok SRB 164 B5
Beliș RO 151 D11
Belišće HR 149 E10
Belitsa BG 161 F9
Belitsa BG 165 D8
Belitsa BG 165 F8
Beliu RO 151 E9
Bělkovice-Lašťany CZ 146 B4
Bell D 21 D8
Bell (Hunsrück) D 185 D7
Bella I 60 B5
Bellac F 29 C8
Bellacorick IRL 6 D3
Bellaghy GB 4 F3
Bellaghy IRL 6 E5
Bellagio I 69 B7
Bellahy IRL 6 E5
Bellanicë RKS 163 E10
Bellano I 69 A7

Bellante I 62 B5
Bellaria I 66 D5
Bellavary IRL 6 E4
Bellavista I 51 E8
Bellclaire d'Urgell E 42 D5
Belleek GB 7 D10
Bellegarde F 25 E7
Bellegarde F 35 C8
Bellegarde-en-Marche F 29 D10
Bellegarde-sur-Valserine F 31 C8
Belle-Isle-en-Terre F 22 C5
Bellême F 24 D4
Bellenaves F 30 C3
Bellenberg D 71 A10
Bellencombre F 18 E3
Bellerive-sur-Allier F 30 C3
Belles-Forêts F 27 C6
Belleu F 19 F7
Bellevaux F 31 C10
Belleville F 30 C6
Belleville-sur-Meuse F 26 B3
Belleville-sur-Vie F 28 B3
Bellevue-la-Montagne F 30 E4
Belley F 31 D8
Bellheim D 21 F10
Bellherbe F 26 F6
Bellignat F 31 C8
Bellinge DK 86 E6
Bellingham GB 5 E12
Bellingwolde NL 17 B8
Bellinzago Novarese I 68 B6
Bellinzona CH 69 A7
Bellizzi I 60 B3
Bell-Lloc d'Urgell E 42 D5
Bello E 47 C10
Bellobrade RKS 163 C10
Bellopoje RKS 163 D10
Bellou-en-Houlme F 23 C11
Bellpuig E 42 D6
Bellreguard E 56 D4
Bellshill GB 5 D8
Belluno I 72 D5
Bellver de Cerdanya E 33 F9
Bellvis S 107 C10
Belm D 17 D10
Bélmegyer H 151 D7
Bélmez E 51 C9
Bélmez de la Moraleda E 53 A10
Belmont GB 3 D15
Belmont-de-la-Loire F 30 C5
Belmonte E 39 B7
Belmonte E 47 E7
Belmonte P 45 D6
Belmonte Calabro I 60 E6
Belmonte del Sannio I 63 D6
Belmonte in Sabina I 62 C3
Belmontejo E 47 E8
Belmont-sur-Rance F 34 C4
Belmullet IRL 6 D3
Belo Brdo RKS 163 C10
Belœil B 19 C8
Belogradchik BG 159 F10
Beloiannisz H 149 B11
Belorado E 40 D5
Beloslav BG 167 C9
Bělotín CZ 146 B5
Belotintsi BG 165 B6
Belovo BG 165 E9
Belozem BG 166 E4
Belp CH 31 B11
Belpasso I 59 D6
Belpech F 33 D9
Belper GB 11 E9
Belsay GB 5 E13
Belsh AL 168 C2
Belsk Duży PL 141 G3
Beltheim D 21 D8
Beltinci SLO 148 C6
Beltiug RO 151 B10
Beltra IRL 6 D5
Beltra IRL 6 E4
Beltrum NL 183 A9
Belturbet IRL 7 D8
Beluša SK 146 C6
Belušić SRB 159 F11
Belvédère-Campomoro F 37 H9
Belvedere Marittimo I 60 D5
Belvedere Ostrense I 67 E7
Belver de Cinca E 42 D4
Belver de los Montes E 39 E9
Belvès F 29 F8
Belvèze-du-Razès F 33 D10
Belvì I 64 D3
Belville IRL 6 D4
Belvís de la Jara E 46 E3
Belz F 22 E5
Belz UA 144 C9
Bełżec PL 144 C7
Bełżyce PL 141 H6
Bembibre E 38 B2
Bembibre E 39 C7
Bemmel NL 16 E5
Bemposta P 39 F7
Bemposta P 44 F4
Bempton GB 11 C11
Benabarre E 42 C4
Benacazón E 51 E7
Benahadux E 55 F8
Benahavís E 53 C6
Benalmádena E 53 C7
Benalúa de Guadix E 55 E6
Benalúa de las Villas E 53 B9
Benalup de Sidonia E 52 D5
Benamargosa E 53 C8
Benameji E 53 B7
Benamaurel E 55 D7
Benaocaz E 53 C6
Benaoján E 53 C6
Benasal E 48 D4
Benasau E 56 D4
Benasque E 33 E7
Benassay F 28 B6
Benatae E 55 C7
Benátky nad Jizerou CZ 77 B7
Benavente E 39 D8
Benavente P 50 B2
Benavides de Orbigo E 39 D8
Benavila P 44 F5
Benburb GB 7 D9
Bencatel P 50 B5
Bendorf D 21 D9
Bêne LV 134 D6
Benecko CZ 81 E9
Beneden-Leeuwen NL 16 E5
Benediktbeuren D 72 A3
Benedita P 44 F3
Benegiles E 39 E8
Bénéjacq F 32 D5
Benejama E 56 D3

Benejúzar E 56 E3
Benesat RO 151 C11
Benešov CZ 77 C7
Benešov nad Černou CZ 77 E7
Benešov nad Ploučnicí CZ 80 E6
Bénesse-Maremne F 32 C3
Benestare I 59 C9
Bénestroff F 27 C6
Benet F 28 C4
Benetutti I 64 C3
Bene Vagienna I 37 B7
Bénévent-l'Abbaye F 29 C9
Benevento I 60 A3
Benfeld F 27 D8
Benfica do Ribatejo P 44 F3
Bengeşti-Ciocadia RO 160 C3
Bengtsfors S 91 A11
Bengtsheden S 103 D10
Benia de Onís E 39 B10
Beniarbeig E 56 D5
Beniarrés E 56 D4
Beničanci HR 149 E10
Benicarló E 48 D5
Benicasim E 48 D5
Benidorm E 56 D4
Beniel E 56 E3
Benifaió E 48 F4
Benifallet E 42 F5
Benifallim E 56 D4
Benigánim E 56 D4
Benissa E 56 D5
Benissanet E 42 E5
Benitachell E 56 D5
Benitses GR 168 E2
Benizalón E 55 E8
Benizar y la Tercia E 55 C9
Benken CH 27 F11
Benkovac HR 156 D4
Benkovski BG 161 F10
Benkovski BG 171 B8
Benllech GB 10 E3
Benlloch E 48 D5
Bennebroek NL 182 A5
Bennekom NL 183 A7
Bennewitz D 79 D12
Bennungen D 79 D9
Benodet F 22 E3
Benquet F 32 C4
Bensafrim P 50 E2
Bensbyn S 118 C6
Bensdorf D 79 B11
Benshausen D 79 E8
Bensheim D 21 E11
Bensjö S 103 A9
Benson GB 13 B12
Bentelo NL 17 D7
Bentivoglio I 66 C3
Bentley GB 11 D9
Bentwisch D 83 B12
Bentzin D 84 C4
Beňuš SK 147 D9
Benzingerode D 79 C8
Beočin SRB 158 C4
Beograd SRB 158 D5
Bera de Bidasoa E 32 D2
Beragh GB 7 C8
Berane MNE 163 D8
Beranga E 40 B4
Berango E 40 B6
Berantevilla E 40 C6
Berat AL 168 C2
Beratzhausen D 75 D10
Berbegal E 42 D3
Berbeşti RO 160 C3
Berca RO 161 C9
Bercedo E 40 B5
Bercel H 147 F8
Berceni RO 161 D8
Berceni RO 161 E8
Bercero E 39 E9
Berceto I 69 D8
Berchem B 19 C8
Berchidda I 64 B3
Berching D 75 D9
Berchtesgaden D 73 A7
Bérchules E 55 F6
Bercianos del Páramo E 39 D8
Berck F 15 G12
Bercu RO 145 H6
Berdal N 104 E4
Berdalen N 94 D6
Berdún E 32 E4
Bere Alston GB 12 E6
Beregdaróc H 145 G6
Bereguardo I 69 C7
Berehomet UA 152 A6
Berehove UA 145 G6
Berek HR 149 E7
Berekböszörmény H 151 D8
Berekfürdő H 150 C6
Beremend H 149 E10
Bereşti RO 153 E11
Bereşti-Meria RO 153 E11
Bereşti-Tazlău RO 153 E9
Berettyóújfalu H 151 C8
Berevoeşti RO 160 C5
Berezeni RO 154 E2
Berezyne UA 154 E4
Berg D 71 B9
Berg D 75 B10
Berg D 183 D9
Berg L 20 E6
Berg N 96 B7
Berg N 108 F3
Berg NL 19 C12
Berg NL 183 D7
Berg S 92 C8
Berg S 102 A7
Berg S 107 E10
Berg (Pfalz) D 27 C9
Berga D 79 D9
Berga E 43 C7
Berga S 89 A10
Bergagård S 87 B11
Bergaland N 94 D4
Bergama TR 177 A9
Bergamo I 69 B8
Bergantino I 66 B3
Bergara E 32 D1
Bergasa E 32 F1
Bergatreute D 71 B9
Berg bei Neumarkt in der Oberpfalz D 75 D9
Bergby S 103 E13

Berge D 17 C9
Berge D 83 E11
Berge E 42 F3
Bergeforsen S 103 A13
Bergen D 73 A6
Bergen D 83 E7
Bergen D 84 B4
Bergen N 94 B2
Bergen NL 16 C3
Bergen (Dumme) D 83 E9
Bergen op Zoom NL 16 E2
Berger N 95 C12
Bergerac F 29 F6
Bergères-lès-Vertus F 25 C11
Bergesserin F 30 C6
Berget N 108 D6
Bergeyk NL 16 F4
Bergfors S 111 D18
Bergharen NL 183 B7
Bergheim D 73 A7
Bergheim D 186 E4
Bergheim D 75 B11
Bergheim (Edertal) D 21 B12
Bergheim (Erft) D 21 C7
Berghem NL 16 E5
Berghem S 91 E12
Berghin RO 152 E3
Berghülen D 74 F6
Berg im Drautal A 73 C7
Bergisch Gladbach D 21 C8
Bergkamen D 17 E9
Bergkarlås S 102 D8
Bergkvara S 89 C10
Bergland S 107 A10
Berglia N 105 C15
Bergmo N 112 D7
Bergnäs S 109 E13
Bergnäset S 118 C6
Bergnäsudden S 109 E15
Bergnäsviken S 109 D15
Bergneustadt D 185 B8
Bergö FIN 99 B13
Bergö FIN 122 E6
Bergom S 107 E15
Bergsåker S 103 B13
Bergsång S 97 B10
Bergsäter S 107 B12
Bergsbyn S 118 E6
Bergschenhoek NL 182 B5
Bergsgården S 103 E10
Bergshamra S 99 C11
Bergsjö S 103 C13
Bergsnov N 95 D9
Bergsnäs N 96 D6
Bergsviken S 118 D6
Bergtheim D 75 C7
Bergues F 18 C5
Bergün CH 71 D9
Bergvik S 103 D12
Bergviken S 109 D16
Bergwitz D 79 C12
Berhida H 149 B10
Beringe NL 183 C7
Beringel P 50 C4
Beringen B 19 B11
Berislăveşti RO 160 C4
Beriu RO 151 F11
Berja E 55 F7
Berka D 79 E7
Berkåk N 101 A12
Berkel NL 16 E2
Berkel-Enschot NL 16 E4
Berkeley GB 13 B10
Berkenthin D 83 C9
Berkheim D 71 A10
Berkhout NL 16 C4
Berkovići BIH 157 F9
Berkovitsa BG 165 C7
Berlanga E 51 C8
Berlanga de Duero E 40 F6
Berlevåg N 114 B6
Berlicum NL 183 B6
Berlin D 80 A4
Berlingerode D 79 D7
Berlişte RO 159 D7
Berlstedt D 79 D8
Bermatingen D 27 E11
Bermeo E 40 B6
Bermillo de Sayago E 39 F7
Bern CH 31 B11
Bernac-Dessus F 33 D6
Bernalda I 61 C7
Bernardos E 46 B4
Bernartice CZ 76 D6
Bernartice CZ 81 E9
Bernáti LV 134 D1
Bernau D 27 E9
Bernau D 84 E5
Bernau am Chiemsee D 72 A5
Bernaville F 18 D5
Bernay F 24 B4
Bernbeuren D 71 B11
Bernburg (Saale) D 79 C10
Berndorf A 77 G10
Berne D 17 B10
Bernecebaráti H 147 E7
Bernedo E 41 C7
Bernhardsthal A 77 E11
Bernhardswald D 75 D11
Bernin F 31 E8
Bernis F 35 C7
Bernkastel-Kues D 21 E8
Bernolákovo SK 146 E4
Bernsdorf D 80 D6
Bernshammar S 97 C14
Bernstadt D 74 E7
Bernstadt D 81 D7
Bernstein A 148 B6
Beromünster CH 27 F9
Beronovo BG 167 D7
Beroun CZ 76 C6
Berovo MK 165 F6
Berra I 66 C4
Berre-l'Étang F 35 D9
Berriedale GB 3 J9
Berrien F 22 D3
Berriozar E 32 E2
Berru F 19 F9
Berşenbrück D 17 C9
Bershad' UA 154 A5
Beršići SRB 158 E5
Bergby S 103 E13

Bërstele LV 135 D7
Bertamirans E 38 C2
Bertea RO 161 C7
Berteştii de Jos RO 155 D1
Bertinoro I 66 D5
Bertnes N 108 B8
Bertogne B 19 D12
Bertrange B 19 D12
Bertrichamps F 27 D6
Bertrix B 19 E11
Berveni RO 151 B9
Bërvircava LV 134 D7
Berwick-upon-Tweed GB 5 D12
Berzasca RO 159 D8
Bërzaune LV 135 C12
Bërzciems LV 134 B6
Bërzgale LV 133 C2
Bërzieši LV 135 D11
Bërzkalne LV 133 B2
Berzovia RO 159 C8
Berzunţi RO 153 E9
Beşalma MD 154 E3
Besalú E 43 C9
Besande E 39 C10
Bescanó E 43 D9
Besednice CZ 77 E7
Beška SRB 158 C5
Besko PL 145 D4
Besni Fok SRB 158 D5
Besnyő H 149 B11
Besozzo I 68 B6
Bessacarr GB 11 D9
Bessaker N 104 C8
Bessan F 34 D5
Bessay-sur-Allier F 30 C3
Bessbrook GB 7 D10
Besse F 31 E9
Besse-et-Saint-Anastaise F 30 D2
Bessèges F 35 B7
Bessenbach D 187 B7
Bessé-sur-Braye F 24 E4
Besse-sur-Issole F 36 E4
Bessières F 33 C9
Bessines-sur-Gartempe F 29 C8
Bessude I 64 B2
Best NL 16 E4
Bestensee D 80 B5
Bestorp S 92 C7
Bestwig D 17 F10
Bestwina PL 147 B8
Beszterec H 145 G4
Betanzos E 38 B3
Betelu E 32 D2
Bétera E 48 E4
Beteta E 47 C8
Bethausen RO 151 F8
Betheln D 78 B6
Bethesda GB 10 E3
Bethmale F 33 E8
Bethon F 25 C10
Béthune F 18 C6
Betna N 104 E4
Betnava SLO 148 D6
Beton-Bazoches F 25 C9
Betschdorf F 186 D4
Betsele S 107 B15
Bettainville F 186 C1
Bettembourg L 20 E6
Bettendorf L 20 E6
Bettingen D 20 E6
Bettna S 93 B9
Bettola I 37 B11
Betton F 23 D8
Bettyhill GB 3 H8
Bettystown IRL 7 E10
Betws-y-coed GB 10 E4
Betxi E 48 E4
Betygala LT 134 F6
Betz F 25 B8
Betzdorf D 21 C9
Betzdorf L 186 B1
Betzenstein D 75 C9
Betzigau D 71 B10
Beucha D 79 D12
Beuil F 36 C5
Beuningen NL 16 E5
Beuron D 27 E10
Beurville F 25 D12
Beuvrages F 182 E2
Beuvry F 18 C6
Bevagna I 62 B3
Beveren B 19 B9
Beverley GB 11 D11
Beverlo B 183 C6
Bevern D 78 C5
Beverstedt D 17 B11
Beverungen D 21 A12
Beverwijk NL 16 D3
Bewdley GB 13 A10
Bex CH 31 C11
Bexbach D 21 F8
Bexhill GB 15 F9
Beyağaç TR 181 B9
Beyazköy TR 173 B8
Beyçayiri TR 173 D6
Beyel TR 173 E10
Beyendorf D 79 B10
Beykoz TR 173 B11
Beynat F 29 E9
Beynost F 31 D7
Beyoba TR 177 B10
Beyobasi TR 181 C9
Bezas E 47 D10
Bezau A 71 C9
Bezdan SRB 150 F2
Bezdead RO 161 C6
Bezdonys LT 137 D12
Bèze F 26 F3
Bezenye H 146 F4
Bezhanitsy RUS 133 C7
Bezhanovo BG 165 C9
Béziers F 34 D5
Bezledy PL 136 E2
Bezmer BG 161 F10
Bezmer BG 166 E6
Bezouce F 35 C8

Bežovce SK 145 F5
Biadki PL 142 C4
Biała PL 142 F4
Biała Piska PL 139 C13
Biała Podlaska PL 141 G6
Biała Rawska PL 141 G2
Białe Błota PL 138 D4
Białobłoto-Kobyla PL 139 E12
Białka PL 145 E1
Białobrzegi PL 141 G3
Białośliwie PL 85 D12
Białogard PL 85 C9
Białowieża PL 141 E9
Biały Bór PL 85 C11
Biały Dunajec PL 147 C10
Białystok PL 140 D8
Biancavilla I 59 D6
Bianco I 59 C9
Biandrate I 68 C5
Bians-les-Usiers F 31 B9
Bianzè I 68 C5
Biar E 56 D3
Biarritz F 32 D2
Biarrotte F 32 C3
Biars-sur-Cère F 29 F9
Bias F 32 B3
Bias F 33 B7
Biasca CH 71 E7
Biatorbágy H 149 B11
Bibbiena I 66 E4
Bibbona I 66 F2
Biberach D 27 D9
Biberach an der Riß D 71 A9
Biberbach D 75 E8
Biberist CH 27 F8
Bibione I 73 E7
Biblis D 21 E10
Bibury GB 13 B11
Bicaj AL 163 E9
Bicaz RO 151 C11
Bicaz RO 153 D8
Bicaz-Chei RO 153 D7
Bicazu Ardelean RO 153 D7
Biccari I 60 A4
Bicester GB 13 B12
Bichiş RO 152 E4
Bichl D 72 A3
Bichlbach A 71 C11
Bickleigh GB 13 D7
Bicorp E 48 F3
Bicos E 50 D3
Bicske H 149 A11
Bicton GB 10 F6
Bidache F 32 D3
Bidart F 32 D2
Biddenden GB 15 E10
Biddinghuizen NL 16 D5
Biddulph GB 11 E7
Bideford GB 12 C6
Bidjovagge N 112 E10
Bidos F 32 D4
Bidovce SK 145 F3
Bie S 93 A8
Bieber D 21 D12
Biebesheim am Rhein D 21 E10
Biecz PL 144 D3
Biedenkopf D 21 C11
Biel CH 27 F7
Biel E 32 F3
Bielany-Żyłaki PL 141 F6
Bielawa PL 81 E11
Bielawy PL 143 B8
Bielefeld D 17 D11
Bielice PL 85 D7
Bieliny Kapitulne PL 143 E10
Biella I 68 B5
Bielle F 32 D5
Bielsa E 33 E6
Bielsk PL 139 E8
Bielsko-Biała PL 147 B8
Bielsk Podlaski PL 141 E8
Bienenbüttel D 83 D8
Bieniów PL 81 C8
Bienno I 69 B9
Bienservida E 55 B7
Bienvenida E 51 C7
Bierawa PL 142 F5
Bierdzany PL 142 E5
Bière CH 31 B9
Bierge E 42 C3
Bierné F 23 E10
Biersted DK 86 A5
Biert F 33 E8
Biertan RO 152 E5
Bieruń PL 143 F7
Bierutów PL 142 D4
Bierzwienna-Długa PL 142 B6
Bierzwnik PL 85 D9
Biesaidgohppi N 113 C16
Biescas E 32 E5
Biesenthal D 84 E5
Biesiekierz PL 85 B10
Biesles F 26 D3
Biesowice PL 85 B11
Biessenhofen D 71 B11
Bietigheim D 27 C9
Bietigheim-Bissingen D 27 C11
Bietikow D 84 D5
Bièvre B 19 E11
Bieżuń PL 139 E8
Biga TR 173 D7
Bigadiç TR 173 E9
Biganos F 32 A4
Bigastro E 56 E3
Bigaunciems LV 134 C7
Bigbury-on-Sea GB 13 E7
Biggar GB 5 D9
Biggleswade GB 15 C8
Bignan F 22 E6
Bignasco CH 71 E7
Bigor MNE 163 E7
Bigüézal E 32 E3
Biguglia F 37 F10
Bigaunciems LV 134 C7
Bihać BIH 156 C4
Biharia RO 151 C8
Biharkeresztes H 151 C8
Biharnagybajom H 151 C7
Bihartorda H 151 C7
Bihosava BY 133 E3
Bijela MNE 163 E6
Bijele Poljane MNE 163 D6
Bijeljani BIH 157 F9
Bijeljina BIH 158 D3
Bijelo Brdo HR 149 E11
Bijelo Bučje BIH 157 D7
Bijelo Polje MNE 163 C8
Bikernieki LV 135 E13
Bikovo SRB 150 F4
Bikšēre LV 135 C12
Bilá Lhota CZ 77 C11

Bilalovac BIH 157 D9
Bilbao E 40 B6
Bilbo E 40 B6
Bilbor RO 153 C7
Bilca RO 153 B7
Bilciureşti RO 161 D7
Bildudalur IS 190 D2
Bileća BIH 162 D5
Biled RO 151 F6
Bilgoraj PL 144 B6
Bilicenii Vechi MD 153 B12
Bilina CZ 80 E5
Bilisht AL 168 C4
Biljača SRB 164 E4
Bilje HR 149 E11
Bilka UA 145 G7
Billdal S 91 D10
Billerbeck D 17 E8
Billère F 32 D5
Billericay GB 15 D9
Billesholm S 87 C11
Billiat F 31 C8
Billigheim D 21 F12
Billingham GB 11 B9
Billinghay GB 11 E11
Billingsfors S 91 B11
Billingshurst GB 15 E8
Billom F 30 D3
Billsåsen S 105 E16
Billsbro S 92 A7
Billsta S 107 E15
Billum DK 86 D2
Billund DK 86 D4
Bilovec CZ 146 B6
Bilovice CZ 146 C5
Bilska LV 135 B11
Bilthoven NL 16 D4
Bilto N 112 E7
Bilton GB 11 C11
Bilyayivka UA 154 E6
Bilychi UA 145 E6
Bilyn UA 145 F7
Bilyne UA 134 B5
Bilzen B 19 C12
Bimbister GB 3 G10
Bíňa SK 147 F7
Binaced E 42 D4
Binas F 24 E5
Binasco I 69 C7
Binbrook GB 11 E11
Binche B 19 D9
Binde D 83 E9
Bindalseit N 105 A12
Bindlach D 75 C10
Bindslev DK 90 D7
Binefar E 42 D4
Bingen D 27 D11
Bingen am Rhein D 21 E9
Bingerden NL 183 B8
Bingham GB 11 F10
Binghamstown IRL 6 D2
Bingley GB 11 D8
Binic F 22 C6
Biniés E 32 E4
Binissalem E 49 E10
Binnen D 17 C12
Binz D 84 B5
Binzen D 27 E8
Biograd na Moru HR 156 E3
Biokovina BIH 157 D7
Biol F 31 E7
Bionaz I 31 D11
Biorra IRL 7 F7
Biosca E 43 D6
Biot F 36 D6
Biota I 41 D9
Birchington GB 15 E11
Birchiş RO 151 F9
Bircza PL 144 D5
Birdhill IRL 8 C6
Birgittelyst DK 86 C4
Biri N 101 E13
Birkeland N 90 C3
Birkeland N 90 C2
Birkenau D 21 E11
Birkenfeld D 21 E8
Birkenfeld D 27 C10
Birkenfeld D 74 C6
Birkenhead GB 10 E5
Birken-Honigsessen D 185 C8
Birkenwerder Berlin D 84 E4
Birkerød DK 87 D10
Birket DK 87 F8
Birketveit N 90 C2
Birkfeld A 148 B5
Birkungen D 79 D7
Birmingham GB 13 A11
Birnbaum A 73 C6
Biron F 33 A7
Birori I 64 C2
Birr IRL 7 F7
Birresborn D 21 D7
Birsay G 3 G10
Birstall GB 11 F9
Birstein D 21 D12
Birtavarre N 112 E6
Birtley GB 5 F13
Biruința MD 153 B12
Bîrzava RO 151 E8
Birzes LV 138 C8
Birzgale LV 135 C9
Biržai LT 135 D8
Biržu LV 135 D11
Birzuļi LV 131 F12
Biš SLO 148 C5
Bisaccia I 60 A4
Bisacquino I 58 D3
Biscarrosse F 32 B3
Biscarrosse-Plage F 32 B3
Bisceglie I 61 A7
Bischberg D 75 C8
Bischbrunn D 187 B7
Bischhausen (Waldkappel) D 78 D6
Bischheim F 27 C8
Bischoffen D 21 C10
Bischofferode D 79 D7
Bischofsheim D 21 E10
Bischofsheim an der Rhön D 74 B7
Bischofshofen A 73 B7
Bischofsmais D 76 E4
Bischofswerda D 80 D6
Bischofswiesen D 73 A6
Bischofszell CH 27 E11
Bischwiller F 27 C8

Bisenti I 62 B5
Biser BG 166 F5
Bisertci BG 161 F9
Bishop Auckland GB 5 F13
Bishop's Castle GB 10 G6
Bishop's Cleeve GB 13 B10
Bishop's Lydeard GB 13 C8
Bishop's Stortford GB 15 D9
Bishop's Waltham GB 13 D12
Bishopton GB 5 F9
Bisignano I 60 E6
Bisingen D 27 D10
Biskupice PL 141 H7
Biskupice PL 142 C5
Biskupice SK 147 E9
Biskupiec PL 136 F2
Biskupiec PL 139 C7
Bislev DK 86 B5
Bismark (Altmark) D 83 E11
Bismervik N 113 B11
Bismo N 101 C8
Bisoca RO 161 B9
Bispgården S 107 E11
Bispingen D 83 D8
Bissen L 20 E6
Bissendorf D 17 D10
Bissendorf (Wedemark) D 78 A6
Bissingen D 75 E8
Bistagno I 37 B8
Bistarac BIH 157 C10
Bistra RO 151 E11
Bistra RO 152 B4
Bistreț RO 160 F3
Bistrets BG 167 E8
Bistrica BIH 157 D7
Bistrica BIH 157 C7
Bistrica BIH 157 E10
Bistrica SLO 73 D9
Bistrica SLO 148 D5
Bistričák BIH 157 D9
Bistrița RO 152 C5
Bistrița Bârgăului RO 152 C5
Bistritsa BG 165 E7
Bistritsa BG 165 E7
Bisztynek PL 136 E2
Bitburg D 21 E7
Bitche F 27 B7
Bitetto I 61 A7
Bitinckë AL 168 C4
Bitola MK 168 B5
Bitonto I 61 A7
Bitschwiller-lès-Thann F 27 E7
Bitterfeld D 79 C11
Bitterstad N 110 C9
Bitti I 64 C3
Bitttkau D 79 B10
Bitton GB 13 C10
Bitz D 27 D11
Biurrun E 32 E2
Bivio CH 71 E9
Bivolari RO 153 B10
Bivona I 58 D3
Bixad RO 145 H7
Bixad RO 153 E7
Bixter GB 3 E14
Bizanet F 34 D4
Bizanos F 32 D5
Bjåen N 94 C6
Bjærangen N 108 C6
Bjæverskov DK 87 E10
Bjännberg S 122 C3
Bjärkøy N 111 C12
Bjärnum S 87 C13
Bjärred S 87 D12
Bjärsjölagård S 87 D13
Bjärtrå S 107 F13
Bjästa S 107 E15
Bjela BIH 157 C10
Bjelajci BIH 157 D6
Bjelopolje HR 156 C4
Bjelovar HR 149 E7
Bjerge DK 87 E8
Bjerka N 108 D6
Bjerkvik N 111 C14
Bjerreby DK 86 F7
Bjerregrav DK 86 B5
Bjerringbro DK 86 C5
Bjøllånes N 108 C8
Bjoneroa N 95 A12
Bjønnes N 108 D7
Bjørbo S 97 B12
Bjørboholm S 91 D11
Bjordal N 94 E4
Bjørgen N 105 F9
Bjørgo N 101 E11
Björkå S 107 E13
Bjørkåsen N 111 C17
Bjørkåsen N 111 C12
Björkberg S 103 C9
Björkberg S 107 B13
Björkberg S 118 C5
Björkboda FIN 126 E8
Bjørke N 100 B4
Björke S 107 E13
Bjørke S 103 E13
Björkeflåta N 95 B9
Bjørkelangen N 95 C15
Bjørkeset N 100 C3
Bjørkestrand N 114 C4
Bjørketorp S 91 E12
Björkfors S 119 C10
Björkheden S 109 E10
Björkhöjden S 107 E13
Björkholmen S 109 C17
Björkland S 109 F16
Bjørklia N 105 E9
Björkliden S 111 D16
Björkliden S 99 B9
Bjørkneset N 114 C4
Björkmyren S 103 B9
Bjørknes N 96 B6
Bjørkøy N 114 D6
Bjørkö FIN 126 E8
Björköby FIN 122 D6
Björköby S 92 D5
Björkön S 103 B14
Björksele S 107 B15
Björksele S 107 D12
Björksjön S 107 E12
Björkstugan S 111 D15
Björkvik S 93 B9
Björli N 100 B8
Bjørn N 108 D4
Björna S 107 D15
Bjørnånge S 105 E14
Bjørndalen S 91 C11
Bjørneborg S 97 D11
Bjørnengen N 113 D11

Bjørnera N 111 C12
Bjørnes N 113 B18
Bjørnevatn N 114 D7
Bjørnfjell N 111 D15
Björnhult S 89 A10
Björnliden S 102 B3
Björnlunda S 93 A10
Björnön S 103 A9
Bjørnrå N 111 C10
Björnrike S 102 B6
Björnsjö S 107 D14
Bjørnskinn N 111 B10
Bjørnstad N 105 B14
Bjørnstad N 114 D9
Björsarv S 103 B11
Björsäter S 92 C8
Björsbo S 103 C12
Björsjö S 97 B13
Bjugn N 104 D7
Bjurå S 118 B8
Bjuråker S 103 C12
Bjurberget S 97 A8
Bjurfors S 107 C17
Bjurfors S 118 E5
Bjurholm S 107 D16
Bjursås S 103 E9
Bjurselet S 118 E6
Bjurträsk S 107 B17
Bjuv S 87 C11
Blace MK 164 E3
Blace SRB 164 C3
Blachownia PL 143 E6
Black Bourton GB 13 B11
Black Bull IRL 7 F10
Blackburn GB 3 L12
Blackburn GB 5 D9
Blackburn GB 10 D7
Blackmoor Gate GB 13 C7
Blackpool GB 10 D5
Blackrock IRL 7 E10
Blackstad S 93 D8
Blacktown GB 7 C7
Blackwater IRL 9 D10
Blackwaterfoot GB 4 D6
Blackwood GB 13 B8
Bladel NL 16 F4
Blaenau Ffestiniog GB 10 F4
Blaenavon GB 13 B8
Blagaj BIH 157 F8
Blagaj Japra BIH 156 B5
Blagdon GB 13 C9
Blăgești RO 153 D9
Blăgești RO 153 E12
Blagnac F 33 C8
Blagoevgrad BG 165 E7
Blagoevo BG 166 C6
Blåhøj DK 86 D4
Blaibach D 75 D12
Blain F 23 F8
Blainville-sur-l'Eau F 186 D1
Blainville-sur-Mer F 23 B8
Blair Atholl GB 5 B9
Blairgowrie GB 5 B10
Blaj RO 152 E3
Blajan F 33 D7
Blăjani RO 161 C9
Blăjel RO 152 E4
Blăjeni RO 151 E10
Blakeney GB 13 B10
Blakeney GB 15 B11
Blakstad N 90 C4
Blâmont F 27 C6
Blan F 33 C10
Blanca E 55 C10
Blancafort F 25 E8
Blancas E 47 C10
Blandford Forum GB 13 D10
Blandiana RO 151 F11
Blanes E 43 D9
Blaney GB 7 D7
Blangy-sur-Bresle F 18 E4
Blankaholm S 93 D9
Blankenberg D 83 C11
Blankenberge B 19 B7
Blankenburg (Harz) D 79 C8
Blankenfelde D 80 B4
Blankenhain D 79 E9
Blankenhain D 79 E11
Blankenheim D 21 D7
Blankenrath D 21 D8
Blankensee D 84 D4
Blankenstein D 75 B10
Blanquefort F 28 F4
Blans DK 86 F5
Blansko CZ 77 D11
Blanzac-Porcheresse F 28 E6
Blanzay F 29 C6
Blanzy F 30 B5
Blaricum NL 183 A6
Blarney IRL 8 E5
Blasimon F 28 F5
Blåsjöfallet S 105 B16
Blåsmark S 118 D6
Błaszki PL 142 C5
Blatec MK 164 F6
Blatets BG 167 D7
Blatna BIH 156 C5
Blatná CZ 76 D5
Blatné SK 146 E4
Blatnica BIH 157 D8
Blato HR 162 D2
Blaton B 182 D3
Blattniksele S 109 F14
Blaubeuren D 74 F6
Blaufelden D 74 D6
Blausasc F 37 D6
Blaustein D 187 E8
Blåvik S 92 C6
Blåviksjön S 107 B14
Blavozy F 30 E4
Blaye F 28 E4
Blaževo SRB 163 C10
Błaziny Górne PL 141 H4
Blāzma LV 134 B4
Blažovice CZ 77 D11
Błażowa PL 144 D5
Blázquez E 51 C9
Blažuj BIH 157 E9
Bleckåsen S 105 E15
Bleckede D 83 D9
Blecua E 42 C3
Bled SLO 73 D9
Błędowo PL 138 D6
Bledzew PL 81 A8
Blegny B 19 C12
Bléharies B 19 C7
Bleialf D 20 D6
Bleiburg A 73 C10
Bleicherode D 79 D8
Bleidenstadt D 185 D9
Bleik N 111 B10
Bleikvassli N 108 E6
Bleiswijk NL 182 A5
Blejești RO 161 E6
Blejoi RO 161 D8
Blekendorf D 83 B9
Bleket S 91 D10
Blender D 17 C12
Bléneau F 25 E8
Blénod-lès-Toul F 26 C4
Blenstrup DK 86 B6
Blentarp S 87 D13
Blera I 62 C2
Blérancourt F 19 E7
Bléré F 24 F4
Blerick NL 16 F6
Blesa E 42 E2
Bleskensgraaf NL 182 B5
Blesle F 30 E3
Blessington IRL 7 F9
Blet F 29 B11
Bletchley GB 15 D7
Blīdene LV 134 C5
Blidsberg S 91 D14
Blieskastel D 21 F8
Bligny F 25 D12
Bligny-sur-Ouche F 25 F12
Blikstorp S 91 C15
Bliksund N 90 C3
Blimea E 39 B8
Blindow D 84 D5
Blinja HR 149 F6
Blistrup DK 87 C10
Blixterboda S 97 D13
Blizanów PL 142 C5
Blížejov CZ 76 D3
Blížkovice CZ 77 E9
Bliznatsi BG 167 C9
Bliżyn PL 141 H3
Bllacë RKS 163 E10
Blois F 24 E5
Blokhus DK 86 A5
Blokzijl NL 16 C5
Blombacka S 97 C10
Blomberg D 17 E12
Blome LV 135 B11
Blome LV 135 B13
Blomsøy N 108 E3
Blomstermåla S 89 B10
Błonie PL 141 F3
Błonie PL 143 B7
Blönsdorf D 79 C12
Blötberget S 97 B13
Blousson-Sérian F 33 D6
Blovice CZ 76 C5
Blowatz D 83 C11
Bloxham GB 13 A12
Bludenz A 71 C9
Bludov CZ 77 C11
Blue Ball IRL 7 F7
Blumberg D 27 E10
Blumberg D 80 A5
Blumenhagen D 84 C5
Blumenholz D 84 D4
Blŭskovo BG 167 C8
Blyberg S 102 D7
Blyth GB 5 E13
Blyth GB 11 E9
Blyth Bridge GB 5 D10
Blyton GB 11 E10
Bø N 95 D10
Bø N 110 C8
Bo N 111 B10
Bø N 111 D12
Boada E 45 C8
Boadilla del Monte E 46 D5
Boadilla de Rioseco E 39 D10
Boal E 39 B6
Boalhosa P 38 E3
Boan MNE 163 D7
Boara Pisani I 66 B4
Boat of Garten GB 3 L9
Boa Vista P 44 E3
Boavista P 44 F2
Bobadilla E 53 B7
Bobâlna RO 152 C3
Bobbio I 37 B10
Bobbio Pellice I 31 F11
Bobenheim-Roxheim D 187 B5
Boberg S 107 E9
Boberka UA 145 E6
Bobicești RO 160 E4
Böbing D 71 B12
Bobingen D 71 A11
Bobitz D 83 C10
Bobivtsi UA 153 A7
Böblingen D 27 C11
Bobolice PL 85 C11
Boborás E 38 D3
Boboshevo BG 165 E7
Bobota HR 149 F11
Bobota RO 151 C10
Bobovdol BG 165 E7
Bobove UA 145 G6
Bobowa PL 144 D2
Bobowo PL 138 C6
Bobrov SK 147 C9
Bobrovec SK 147 C9
Bobrowice PL 81 C8
Bobrówko PL 85 E8
Bobrowniki PL 138 E6
Bobrowniki PL 140 D9
Bobryk-Druhyy UA 154 B6
Bocacara E 45 C8
Bocairent E 56 D3
Bočar SRB 150 F5
Bocchigliero I 61 E7
Boceguillas E 40 F4
Bocfölde H 149 C7
Bochnia PL 144 D1
Bocholt B 19 B12
Bocholt D 17 E7
Bochov CZ 76 B4
Bochum D 17 F8
Bockara S 89 A10
Bockenem D 79 B7
Bockenheim an der Weinstraße D 187 B5
Bockhammar S 97 C14
Bockhorn D 17 B10
Bockhorn D 75 F10
Bockhorst D 17 B9
Boćki PL 141 E8
Bocksjö S 92 B5
Bockträsk S 109 F15
Bocognano F 37 G10
Boconád H 150 B5
Bőcs H 145 G2
Bócsa H 150 D3
Bocșa RO 151 C10
Bocșa RO 159 C8
Bocsig RO 151 E8
Boczów PL 81 B7
Bod RO 153 F7
Böda S 89 A12
Boda S 103 A12
Boda S 103 D9
Boda bruk S 103 C12
Bodaczów PL 144 B7
Bodafors S 92 D5
Boda glasbruk S 89 B9
Bodajk H 149 B10
Bodåsgruvan S 98 B6
Bodbacka FIN 122 E6
Bodbyn S 122 B4
Boddam GB 3 F14
Boddam GB 3 L13
Boddin D 83 C10
Bodegraven NL 182 A5
Bodelshausen D 187 E6
Boden S 118 C7
Bodenfelde D 78 C6
Bodenham GB 13 A9
Bodenheim D 21 E10
Bodenkirchen D 75 F11
Bodenmais D 76 D4
Bodenteich D 83 E9
Bodenwerder D 78 C6
Bodenwöhr D 75 D11
Bodești RO 153 C8
Bodman D 27 E11
Bodmin GB 12 E5
Bodnegg D 71 B9
Bodø N 108 B7
Bodom N 105 D11
Bodonal de la Sierra E 51 C6
Bodoney GB 7 C8
Bodony H 147 F10
Bodroghalom H 145 G4
Bodrogkisfalud H 145 G3
Bodrum TR 177 E9
Bodsjö S 102 A8
Bodsjöbyn S 102 A8
Bodträskfors S 118 B5
Bódvaszilas H 145 F2
Bodyke IRL 8 C5
Bodzanów PL 139 E9
Bodzanów PL 142 F3
Bodzentyn PL 143 E10
Boé F 33 B7
Boechout B 19 B9
Boecillo E 39 E10
Boekel NL 16 E5
Boekhoute B 182 C3
Boën-sur-Lignon F 30 D5
Boeslunde DK 87 E8
Boeza E 39 C7
Boffres F 30 F6
Boffzen D 21 A12
Boftsa N 113 C21
Bogács H 145 H2
Bogajo E 45 C7
Bogarra E 55 B8
Bogați RO 160 D6
Bogatić SRB 158 D4
Bogatići BIH 157 E9
Bogatynia PL 81 E7
Boğaziçi TR 177 C10
Bogda RO 151 F8
Bogdan BG 165 D10
Bogdana RO 153 D11
Bogdana RO 160 F6
Bogdanci MK 169 B8
Bogdand RO 151 C10
Bogdănești RO 153 E9
Bogdănești RO 154 E2
Bogdaniec PL 85 E8
Bogdănița RO 153 E11
Bogdan Vodă RO 152 B4
Boge S 93 D13
Bogen D 75 E12
Bogen N 105 A11
Bogen N 111 C12
Bogense DK 86 D6
Boggsjö S 106 E8
Boghești RO 153 E10
Bogilice BIH 158 F3
Bogliasco I 37 C10
Bognanco I 68 A5
Bognelv N 112 C9
Bognes N 111 D11
Bogniebrae GB 3 L11
Bognor Regis GB 15 F7
Bogny-sur-Meuse F 184 E2
Bogø DK 87 F10
Bogodol BIH 157 F8
Bogojevo SRB 157 A11
Bogomilovo BG 166 E5
Bogoria PL 143 E11
Bogorojca MK 169 B8
Bogovina SRB 159 F8
Bogovinje MK 163 F10
Bogoy N 110 E9
Bograngen S 102 E4
Boguchwała PL 144 D4
Bogumiłowice PL 143 D7
Boguszów-Gorce PL 81 E10
Boguty-Pianki PL 141 E6
Bogyiszló H 149 D11
Bohain-en-Vermandois F 19 E7
Bohars F 22 D3
Bohdalov CZ 77 D9
Bohdan UA 152 A4
Bohdíkov CZ 77 B11
Boherboy IRL 8 D4
Boherbue IRL 8 D4
Bohinjska Bistrica SLO 73 D8
Böhl D 187 C5
Böhlen D 79 D11
Böhme D 82 E6
Bohmte D 17 D10
Böhne D 79 A11
Bohola IRL 6 E4
Bohonal de Ibor E 45 E10
Böhönye H 149 D8
Bohoyo E 45 D10
Bohumín CZ 146 B6
Bohuňovice CZ 146 B4
Bohuslavice CZ 146 B6
Bohutín CZ 76 C5
Boianu Mare RO 151 C10
Boiro de Arriba E 38 C2
Boiscommun F 25 D7
Bois-d'Amont F 31 B9
Boisgervilly F 23 D7
Bois-Guillaume F 18 F3
Boișoara RO 160 C4
Boisset-et-Gaujac F 35 B7
Boissezon F 33 C10
Boitzenburg D 84 D5
Boiu Mare RO 152 C3
Boizenburg D 83 D9
Bojadła PL 81 C9
Bojano I 63 E6
Bojanów PL 144 C4
Bojanowo PL 81 C11
Bøjden DK 86 E6
Bojkovice CZ 146 C5
Bojná SK 146 D6
Bojnice SK 147 D7
Bojničky SK 146 E5
Bojnik SRB 164 C4
Bojszów PL 142 F5
Bojszowy PL 143 F7
Boka SRB 159 C6
Bokel D 17 B11
Böklund D 82 A7
Bokod H 149 A10
Bököny H 151 B8
Bokšić HR 149 E10
Boksjön S 109 E10
Bol HR 156 F6
Bölan S 103 D12
Bolanden D 186 B5
Bolandoz F 31 A9
Bolaños de Calatrava E 54 B5
Bolătău RO 153 D8
Bolayir TR 173 C6
Bolbaite E 56 C3
Bolbec F 18 E1
Bolboși RO 159 D11
Bölcske H 150 D2
Boldekow D 84 C5
Bolderslev DK 86 F4
Boldești-Grădiștea RO 161 D9
Boldești-Scăeni RO 161 C8
Boldog H 150 B4
Boldogkőváralja H 145 G3
Boldre GB 13 D11
Boldu RO 161 C10
Boldur RO 159 B8
Boldva H 145 G2
Böle S 99 B9
Böle S 102 B7
Böle S 105 D14
Böle S 105 E15
Böle S 118 C8
Böle S 118 D6
Bolea E 41 D10
Bolekhiv UA 145 E8
Boleráz SK 146 E5
Bolesław PL 143 F7
Bolesław PL 143 F10
Bolesławiec PL 81 D9
Bolesławiec PL 142 D5
Boleszkowice PL 84 E7
Bolga N 108 C5
Bolgatovo RUS 133 C5
Bolhan UA 154 A3
Bolhrad UA 155 B3
Boliden S 118 E4
Bolimów PL 141 F2
Bolintin-Deal RO 161 E7
Bolintin-Vale RO 161 E7
Boliqueime P 50 E3
Boljanić BIH 157 C9
Boljanići MNE 163 C7
Boljevac SRB 159 F8
Boljevci SRB 158 D5
Bölkow D 83 B11
Bolków PL 81 E10
Bollebygd S 91 D12
Bollène F 35 B8
Bollengo I 68 C4
Bollermoen N 108 D6
Bolligen CH 31 B11
Bolling DK 86 D3
Bollingstedt D 82 A6
Bollnäs S 103 D11
Bollsbyn S 91 A12
Bollstabruk S 107 E13
Bollullos Par del Condado E 51 E6
Bolnes NL 182 B5
Bolnhurst GB 15 C8
Bologna I 66 D3
Bologne F 26 D3
Bolognetta I 58 D3
Bolognola I 62 B4
Bolotana I 64 C2
Bolotești RO 153 F10
Bolsena I 62 B1
Bol'shakovo RUS 136 D4
Bolsover GB 11 E9
Bolsward NL 16 B5
Bolszewo PL 138 A5
Boltaña E 33 F6
Boltåsen N 111 C12
Boltenhagen D 83 C10
Boltigen CH 31 B11
Bolton GB 5 D11
Bolton GB 11 D7
Bolüntü TR 181 A7
Bolvașnița RO 159 C9
Bolventor GB 12 D5
Bóly H 149 E11
Bolyarovo BG 167 E7
Bolzano I 72 D3
Bomal B 19 D12
Bomba I 63 C6
Bombarral P 44 F2
Bomlitz D 82 E7
Bompas F 34 E4
Bompensiere I 58 E4
Bompietro I 58 D5
Bomporto I 66 C3
Bomsund S 107 E9
Bona F 30 A3
Bonaduz CH 71 D8
Bonakas N 113 C21
Bönan S 103 E13
Bonanza E 52 C4
Boñar E 39 C9
Bonar Bridge GB 3 K8
Bonarcado I 64 C2
Bonares E 51 E6
Bonäs S 102 D7
Bonäset S 106 D8
Bönäset S 107 E15
Bonassola I 37 C11
Bonawe GB 4 C6
Bonboillon F 26 F4
Bonchamp-lès-Laval F 23 D10
Bonchester Bridge GB 5 E11
Boncourt CH 27 F7
Bondeno I 66 C3
Bondersbyn S 119 C9
Bonderup DK 86 A4
Bondorf D 187 D6
Bondsjö S 103 A14
Bondues F 182 D2
Bönebüttel D 83 B8
Bonefro I 63 D7
Bönen D 17 E9
Bo'ness GB 5 C9
Bonete E 55 B10
Bönhamn S 103 A15
Bonheiden B 19 B10
Boniches E 47 E9
Boniewo PL 138 F6
Bonifacio F 37 J10
Bonifati I 60 D5
Bönigen CH 70 D5
Bonin PL 85 B10
Bonn D 21 C8
Bonnåsjøen N 109 A10
Bonnat F 29 C9
Bonndorf im Schwarzwald D 27 E9
Bønnerup Strand DK 87 B7
Bonnes N 111 C15
Bonnet DK 86 B2
Bonnétable F 24 D3
Bonneuil-Matours F 29 B7
Bonneval F 24 D5
Bonneval F 31 D10
Bonneval-sur-Arc F 31 E11
Bonnevaux F 31 B9
Bonneville F 31 C9
Bonnieux F 35 C9
Bönnigheim D 27 B11
Bonnyrigg GB 5 D10
Bonny-sur-Loire F 25 E8
Bono F 22 E6
Bono I 64 C3
Bonorva I 64 C2
Bons-en-Chablais F 31 C9
Bonson F 30 D5
Bonțida RO 152 D3
Bőny H 149 A9
Bonyhád H 149 D11
Boo S 99 D10
Boock D 84 D6
Boom B 19 B9
Boortmeerbeek B 19 C10
Boos F 18 F3
Boostedt D 83 B8
Bootle GB 10 E6
Bopfingen D 75 E7
Boppard D 21 D9
Bor CZ 75 C12
Bor S 88 A6
Bor SRB 159 E9
Borač SRB 158 F6
Borås S 91 D12
Borăscu RO 160 D2
Borba P 50 B5
Borbjerg DK 86 C3
Borca RO 153 C7
Borča SRB 158 D5
Borcea RO 155 E1
Borchen D 17 E11
Borci BIH 157 C7
Borci BIH 157 E9
Börcs H 149 A9
Borculo NL 17 D7
Bordalba E 41 F7
Bordány H 150 E4
Bordeaux F 28 F4
Bordeira P 50 E2
Bordei Verde RO 161 C11
Bordelum D 82 A5
Bordères-Louron F 33 E6
Bordères-sur-l'Échez F 33 D6
Bordes F 32 D5
Bordes F 33 D6
Bordesholm D 83 B8
Bordești RO 161 B10
Bordighera I 37 D7
Bordils E 43 C9
Bording DK 86 C4
Bordón E 42 F3
Bordușani RO 155 E1
Bore I 69 D8
Boreham GB 15 D10
Borehamwood GB 15 D8
Borek PL 143 F10
Borek Strzeliński PL 81 E12
Borek Wielkopolski PL 81 C12
Boreland GB 5 E10
Børelva N 108 B8
Borensberg S 92 B6
Borg D 20 E6
Borgå FIN 127 E14
Borgafjäll S 106 B8
Borgentreich D 17 E12
Börger D 17 C9
Borger NL 17 C7
Borggård S 92 B7
Borghamn S 92 C5
Borgheim N 90 A7
Borghetto d'Arroscia I 37 C7
Borghetto di Borbera I 37 B9
Borghetto di Vara I 69 E8
Borghetto Santo Spirito I 37 C8
Borgholm S 89 B11
Borgholzhausen D 17 D10
Borgia I 59 B10
Borgloon B 19 C11
Børglum DK 90 E6
Borgo F 37 F10
Borgo a Mozzano I 66 E2
Borgo d'Ale I 68 C5
Borgoforte I 66 B2
Borgofranco d'Ivrea I 68 B4
Borgo Grappa I 61 C10
Borgo-lavezzaro I 68 C6
Borgomanero I 68 B5
Borgomaro I 37 D7
Borgone Susa I 31 E11
Borgonovo Val Tidone I 69 C7
Borgo Pace I 66 E5
Borgorose I 62 C4
Borgo San Dalmazzo I 37 C6
Borgo San Lorenzo I 66 E3
Borgo San Martino I 68 C6
Borgosesia I 68 B5
Borgo Tossignano I 66 D4
Borgo Val di Taro I 69 E8
Borgo Valsugana I 72 D3
Borgo Velino I 62 C4
Borgo Vercelli I 68 C5
Borgsjö S 103 A10
Borgsjö S 107 C13
Borgstedt D 82 B7
Borgstena S 91 D13
Borgue GB 5 F8
Borgvattnet S 107 E9
Borhaug N 94 F5
Boriaeva BG 171 B7
Borike BIH 157 E11
Borino BG 165 F9
Bořitov CZ 77 D11
Borja E 41 E8
Borjabad E 41 E7
Borjana SLO 73 D7
Borjelslandet S 118 C8
Borkan S 106 A8
Borkavichy BY 133 E4
Borken D 17 E7
Borken (Hessen) D 21 B12
Borkenes N 111 C11
Borki PL 141 G7
Borki PL 143 D9
Børkop DK 86 D5
Borkowice PL 141 H3
Borkowo PL 139 D12
Borkum D 17 A7
Borlänge S 97 B13
Borlești RO 153 D9
Bormani LV 135 C10
Børmarka N 104 C8
Bormio I 71 E10
Born D 79 B9
Born NL 183 C7
Borna D 79 D12
Borna D 80 D4
Born am Darß D 83 B13
Borne NL 17 D7
Bornem B 19 B9
Bornerbroek NL 17 D7
Bornes P 39 F6
Bornes de Aguiar P 38 E4
Borne Sulinowo PL 85 C11
Bornheim D 21 C7
Bornhofen D 21 D9
Bornhöved D 83 B8
Bornich D 185 D8
Bornos E 51 F8
Bornova TR 177 C9
Börnsen D 83 D8
Boroaia RO 153 C8
Borobia E 41 E8
Borod RO 151 D10
Borodino UA 154 E4
Borodinskoye RUS 129 C11
Borohrádek CZ 77 B10
Borojevići BIH 157 F8
Boronów PL 143 E6
Borore I 64 C2
Boroșneu Mare RO 153 F8
Boroszów PL 142 E5
Borota H 150 E3
Boroughbridge GB 11 C9
Borovan BG 165 C8
Borovany CZ 77 E7
Borov Dol BG 166 D6
Borovets BG 165 E8
Borovik HR 149 F10
Borovitsa BG 165 B6
Borovka LV 133 E1
Borovnica BIH 157 D9
Borovnica SLO 73 E9
Borovo BG 166 C5
Borovo Selo HR 157 B10
Borovtsi BG 165 C7
Borów PL 81 E11
Borów PL 144 B4
Borowa PL 143 F11
Borowie PL 141 G5
Borox E 46 D5
Borrby S 88 E6
Borre DK 87 F10
Borre N 95 D12
Borrentin D 84 C3
Borrèze F 29 F8
Borriol E 48 D4
Borris DK 86 D3
Borris IRL 9 C9
Borris-in-Ossory IRL 9 C7
Borrisokane IRL 6 G6
Borrisoleigh IRL 9 C7
Borrowdale GB 10 B5
Børrud N 96 C7
Börrum S 93 C9
Borș RO 151 C8
Børsa N 104 E8
Borșa RO 152 B5
Borșa RO 152 D3
Borša SK 145 G4
Borsbeek B 19 B10
Borsec RO 153 D7
Børselv N 113 C16
Borsh AL 168 D2
Borshchi UA 154 B5
Borshchovychi UA 144 D9
Boršice u Buchlovic CZ 146 C4
Borsio GR 174 D3
Borský Svätý Jur SK 77 E12
Borsodbóta H 145 G1
Borsodnádasd H 145 G1
Borsodszentgyörgy H 145 G1
Borsodszirák H 145 G2
Borsosberény H 147 F8
Borssele NL 182 C3
Borstel D 17 C11
Borth GB 10 G3
Bortigali I 64 C2
Bortigiadas I 64 B3
Bort-les-Orgues F 29 E10
Börtnan S 102 A6
Bortnen N 100 C2
Borum DK 86 C6
Borup DK 87 E9
Borve GB 2 L4
Borynya UA 145 E6
Boryslav UA 145 D7
Borzęciczki PL 81 C12
Borzonasca I 37 C10
Borzytuchom PL 85 B12
Bosa I 64 C2
Bošáca SK 146 D5
Bosa Marina I 64 C1
Bosanci RO 153 B8
Bosanka Rača BIH 158 D3
Bosanska Dubica BIH 157 B6
Bosanska Gradiška BIH 157 B7
Bosanska Kostajnica BIH 156 B6
Bosanska Krupa BIH 156 C5
Bosanski Brod BIH 157 B9
Bosanski Kobas BIH 157 B8
Bosanski Novi BIH 156 B5
Bosanski Petrovac BIH 156 C5
Bosanski Šamac BIH 157 B9
Bosansko Grahovo BIH 156 D5
Bošany SK 146 D6
Bősárkány H 149 A8
Bosau D 83 B8
Boscastle GB 12 D5
Bosco I 66 F5
Bosco Chiesanuova I 69 B11
Bosco Marengo I 37 B9
Boscotrecase I 60 B2
Bösdorf D 83 B8
Bösebo S 89 A9
Bösel D 17 B9
Boshulya BG 165 E9
Bosia RO 153 C11
Bosilegrad SRB 164 E5
Bosiljevo HR 148 F4
Boskoop NL 16 D3
Boskovice CZ 77 D11
Bošnjace SRB 164 D4
Bošnjaci HR 157 B10
Bošnjane SRB 159 F7
Bošnjane SRB 159 F7
Boșorod RO 159 B11
Bössbod S 102 D7
Bosset F 29 F6
Bossolasco I 37 B8
Bòssost E 33 E7
Bostad N 110 D6
Bostan BIH 157 F7
Bøstølen N 100 B6
Boston GB 11 F11
Boston Spa GB 11 D9
Bostrak N 90 A4
Bosundet S 107 C10
Botão P 44 D4
Boteå S 107 E13
Boteni RO 160 C6
Botesdale GB 15 C11
Botești RO 153 C9
Botești RO 160 C6
Botevgrad BG 165 D8
Botevo BG 167 C9
Bothel GB 5 F10
Boticas P 38 E4
Botiz RO 151 B10
Botiza RO 152 B4
Botn N 110 E9
Botn N 111 A18
Botn N 112 D4
Botngård N 104 D7
Botnhamn N 111 A14
Botoroaga RO 161 E7
Botorrita E 41 E9
Botoš SRB 158 C6
Botoșana RO 153 B7
Botoșani RO 153 B9
Botoșești-Paia RO 159 E11
Botricello I 61 F7
Bötsle S 103 A14
Botsmark S 118 F4
Bottendorf (Burgwald) D 21 B11
Bottesford GB 11 D10
Bottidda I 64 C3
Bottnaryd S 91 D14
Bottrop D 17 E7
Botun MK 168 B4
Bötzingen D 27 D8
Bouafles F 24 B5
Boucau F 32 C3
Bouc-Bel-Air F 35 D9
Boucé F 23 C11
Bouchain F 19 D7
Bouchemaine F 23 F10
Bouchoir F 18 E6
Boudry CH 31 B10
Boué F 19 D8
Bouglon F 33 B6
Bouguenais F 23 F8
Bouillargues F 35 C7
Bouillon B 19 E11
Bouilly F 25 D10
Bouin F 28 B1
Boujailles F 31 B9
Boujan-sur-Libron F 34 D5
Boulay-Moselle F 26 B5
Boulazac F 29 E7
Boulbon F 35 C8
Bouligny F 19 F12
Bouloc F 33 C8
Boulogne-Billancourt F 25 C7
Boulogne-sur-Gesse F 33 D7
Boulogne-sur-Mer F 15 F12
Bouloire F 24 E4
Boulouris F 36 E5
Boult-aux-Bois F 19 F10
Boulzicourt F 19 E10
Bouniagues F 29 F7
Bøur FO 2 A2
Bourbon-Lancy F 30 B4
Bourbon-l'Archambault F 30 B3
Bourbonne-les-Bains F 26 E4
Bourbourg F 18 C5
Bourbriac F 22 D5
Bourcefranc-le-Chapus F 28 D3
Bourdeaux F 35 A9
Bourdeilles F 29 E7
Bourdonnay F 27 C6
Bouresse F 29 C7
Bourg F 28 E4
Bourg-Achard F 18 F2
Bourganeuf F 29 D9
Bourg-Argental F 30 E6
Bourg-de-Péage F 31 E7
Bourg-de-Thizy F 30 C5
Bourg-de-Visa F 33 B7
Bourg-Dun F 18 E2
Bourg-en-Bresse F 31 C7
Bourges F 29 A10
Bourg-et-Comin F 19 F8
Bourg-Lastic F 29 D11
Bourg-lès-Valence F 30 F6
Bourgneuf-en-Mauges F 23 F10
Bourgneuf-en-Retz F 28 A2
Bourgogne F 19 F9
Bourgoin-Jallieu F 31 D7
Bourg-St-Andéol F 35 B8
Bourg-St-Bernard F 33 C9
Bourg-St-Maurice F 31 D10
Bourgtheroulde-Infreville F 18 F2
Bourguébus F 23 B11
Bourgueil F 23 F12
Bourmont F 26 D4
Bourne GB 11 F11
Bournemouth GB 13 D11
Bournezeau F 28 B3
Bourran F 33 B6
Bourriot-Bergonce F 32 B5
Bourron-Marlotte F 25 D8
Bourscheid L 184 E5
Bourtange NL 17 B8
Bourton GB 13 C10
Boussac F 29 C10
Bousse F 186 C1
Boussens F 33 D7
Boussières F 26 F4
Boussois F 19 D9
Boussu B 19 D8
Boutersem B 19 C10
Bouveret CH 31 C10
Bouvières F 35 A9
Bouvron F 23 F8
Bouxières-aux-Dames F 26 C5
Bouxwiller F 27 C7
Bouy F 25 B11
Bouzonville F 21 F7
Bouzov CZ 77 C11
Bova I 59 C8
Bøvær N 111 B13
Bovalino I 59 C9
Bovallstrand S 91 C9
Bova Marina I 59 D8
Bovan SRB 159 F8
Bovec SLO 73 D8
Bóveda E 38 C5

Boveda E 40 C5
Bovegno I 69 B9
Bovenden D 78 C6
Bøverfjord N 104 E5
Boves I 18 E5
Boves I 37 C7
Bovigny B 20 D5
Boviken S 118 E6
Boville Ernica I 62 D4
Bovino I 60 A4
Bøvlingbjerg DK 86 C2
Bovolone I 66 B3
Bovrup DK 86 F5
Bow GB 3 H10
Bowes GB 11 B7
Bowmore GB 4 D4
Box FIN 127 E13
Boxberg D 81 D7
Boxberg D 187 C8
Boxdorf D 80 D5
Boxholm S 92 C6
Boxmeer NL 16 E5
Boxtel NL 16 E4
Boyadzhik BG 166 E6
Boyanovo BG 167 E7
Boychinovtsi BG 165 C7
Boykovo BG 165 E10
Boyle IRL 6 E6
Bøylefoss N 90 B4
Boynes F 25 D7
Boynitsa BG 159 F10
Bøyum N 100 D5
Božava HR 67 D10
Bozburun TR 181 C8
Bozeat GB 15 C7
Bozel F 31 E10
Boževac SRB 159 D7
Boževo PL 139 E8
Bozhentsi BG 166 D4
Bozhurishte BG 165 D7
Božica SRB 164 D5
Božice CZ 77 E10
Bozieni MD 154 D3
Bozieni RO 153 D10
Bozioru RO 161 C8
Božjakovina HR 148 E6
Bozlar TR 173 D7
Bozouls F 34 B4
Bozovici RO 159 D9
Bozveliysko BG 167 C8
Bozzolo I 66 B1
Bra I 37 B7
Braås S 89 A8
Bråbo S 89 A10
Brabova RO 160 E2
Bracadale GB 2 L4
Bracciano I 62 C2
Brach F 28 E4
Brachbach D 185 C8
Bracieux F 24 E6
Bräcke S 103 A9
Brackenheim D 27 B11
Brackley GB 13 A12
Bracknagh IRL 7 F8
Bracknell GB 15 E7
Braco GB 5 C9
Brad RO 151 E10
Bradashesh AL 168 B3
Brădeanu RO 161 D9
Brădeni RO 152 E5
Brădești RO 152 E6
Brădești RO 160 E3
Bradford GB 11 D8
Bradford-on-Avon GB 13 C10
Bradpole GB 13 D9
Bradu RO 160 D5
Brăduleț RO 160 C5
Brăduț RO 153 E7
Bradwell GB 15 B12
Bradwell Waterside GB 15 D10
Brae GB 3 E14
Brædstrup DK 86 D5
Braehead of Lunan GB 5 B11
Braemar GB 5 A10
Brăești RO 153 B8
Brăești RO 153 C10
Brăești RO 161 C9
Bràfim E 43 E6
Braga P 38 E3
Bragadiru RO 161 E7
Bragadiru RO 161 F7
Bragança P 39 E6
Bragar GB 2 J3
Brăhășești RO 153 E10
Brahlstorf D 83 D9
Brăila RO 155 C1
Brailsford GB 11 E8
Braine F 19 F8
Braine-l'Alleud B 19 C9
Braine-le-Comte B 19 C9
Braintree GB 15 D10
Braives B 19 C11
Brajkovići BIH 157 D8
Brake (Unterweser) D 17 B10
Brakel B 19 C8
Brakel D 17 E12
Bräkne-Hoby S 89 C8
Brålanda S 91 B11
Bralin PL 142 D4
Brallo di Pregola I 37 B10
Bralos GR 174 B5
Braloştiţa RO 160 D3
Bram F 33 D10
Bramberg am Wildkogel
  A 72 B5
Bramdrupdam DK 86 D4
Bramming DK 86 E3
Brampton GB 5 F11
Brampton GB 15 C12
Bramsche D 17 D8
Bramsche D 17 D10
Bramstedt D 17 B11
Bran RO 160 B6
Brånaberg S 109 E11
Branäs S 102 A3
Brancaleone S 59 D9
Brancaster GB 15 B10
Brânceni RO 160 F6
Brâncoveneşti RO 152 D5
Brâncoveni RO 160 E4
Brand A 71 C9
Brand D 75 C10
Brandal N 100 B4
Brändåsen S 102 B4
Brändbo S 103 B11
Brandbu N 95 B13
Brande DK 86 D4
Brande-Hörnerkirchen D 82 C7
Brandenberg A 72 B4
Brandenburg D 79 B12
Brand-Erbisdorf D 80 E4
Branderup DK 86 E4

Brandesburton GB 11 D11
Brandis D 80 C4
Brand-Nagelberg A 77 E8
Brando F 37 F10
Brändö FIN 126 E5
Brandon GB 15 C10
Brändön S 118 C8
Brandshagen D 84 B4
Brandstorp S 92 C4
Brandsvoll N 90 C2
Brandval N 96 B7
Brandvoll N 111 C15
Brandýs nad Labem-Stará
  Boleslav CZ 77 B7
Brandýs nad Orlicí CZ 77 B10
Branes N 96 A6
Brăneşti MD 154 C3
Brăneşti RO 160 C6
Brăneşti RO 160 D2
Brăneşti RO 161 E8
Branice PL 142 F4
Braniewo PL 139 B8
Braník SLO 73 E8
Brănişca RO 151 F10
Branişte RO 152 C4
Branişte RO 155 C1
Brankas LV 134 C7
Branna S 91 B11
Brännåker S 107 B9
Brännäs S 103 B11
Brännberg S 118 C6
Branne F 28 F5
Brännland S 107 D16
Brännland S 122 C4
Brañosera E 40 C3
Brańsk PL 141 E7
Branston GB 11 E11
Brańszczyk PL 139 E12
Brantevik S 88 D6
Brantice CZ 142 F4
Brantôme F 29 E7
Branzi I 69 A8
Braone I 69 B9
Braskereidfoss N 101 E15
Braslaw BY 133 E2
Braşov RO 161 B7
Brassac F 33 C10
Brasschaat B 16 F2
Brassy F 25 F10
Brasta S 105 E16
Brastad S 91 C10
Brastavăţu RO 160 F4
Břasy CZ 76 C5
Brataj AL 168 D2
Bratca RO 151 D10
Bråte N 95 C14
Brateiu RO 152 E4
Brateljevici BIH 157 D10
Brateş RO 153 E8
Bratislava SK 77 F12
Bratkowice PL 144 C4
Bratovoeşti RO 160 E3
Bratsigovo BG 165 E9
Brattåker S 107 A11
Brattbäcken S 107 B14
Bratten S 107 B14
Brattfors S 103 E12
Brattfors S 107 D17
Brattli N 114 D7
Brattmon S 102 E4
Bratton GB 13 C10
Brattsbacka S 107 D16
Brattsele S 107 C12
Brattset N 104 E5
Brattvåg N 100 A4
Bratunac BIH 158 E3
Brătuşeni MD 153 A10
Bratya Daskalovi BG 166 E4
Braubach D 21 D9
Braud-et-St-Louis F 28 E4
Braunau am Inn A 76 F4
Brauneberg D 185 E6
Braunfels D 21 C10
Braunlage D 79 C8
Bräunlingen D 27 E9
Braunsbach D 187 C8
Braunsbedra D 79 D10
Braunschweig D 79 B8
Braunton GB 12 C6
Bravicea MD 154 C2
Bravnica BIH 157 D7
Bray IRL 7 F10
Bray-sur-Seine F 25 D9
Bray-sur-Somme F 18 E6
Brazatortas E 54 B4
Brazey-en-Plaine F 26 F3
Brazii RO 161 D8
Brazii RO 151 E9
Brazii RO 161 D8
Brbinj HR 67 D11
Brčigovo BIH 157 E11
Brčko BIH 157 C10
Brdów PL 138 F6
Bré IRL 7 F10
Brea E 41 E8
Brea de Tajo E 47 D6
Breaghva IRL 8 C3
Breascleit GB 2 J3
Breasta RO 160 E3
Breaza RO 152 C5
Breaza RO 152 D5
Breaza RO 161 C7
Breaza RO 161 C8
Breb RO 152 B3
Brebeni RO 160 E4
Brebu RO 159 C8
Brebu RO 161 C7
Brebu Nou RO 159 C9
Brécey F 23 C9
Brech F 22 E6
Brechfa GB 12 B6
Brechin GB 5 B11
Brecht B 16 F3
Breckerfeld D 185 B7
Břeclav CZ 77 E11
Brecon GB 13 B8
Breda E 43 D9
Breda NL 16 E3
Bredared S 91 D12
Bredaryd S 87 A13
Bredbyn S 107 D15
Breddenberg D 17 C9
Breddin D 83 E12
Bredebo DK 86 E3
Bredene B 18 B6
Bredereiche D 84 D4
Bredevoort NL 17 E7
Bredkälen S 106 D8
Bredsätra S 89 B11
Bredsel S 118 C4
Bredsjö S 97 C12

Bredsjön S 103 A13
Bredstedt D 82 A5
Bredsten DK 86 D4
Bredträsk S 107 D15
Bredvik S 107 D17
Bredviken S 108 C8
Bredviken S 119 C10
Bree B 19 B12
Breese D 83 D11
Bregana HR 148 E5
Breganze I 72 E4
Bregare BG 165 B9
Bregeni MD 153 B9
Bregenz A 71 B9
Breg-Lum AL 163 E9
Breg-Lum AL 168 B2
Bregninge DK 86 F6
Bregovo BG 159 E10
Breguzzo I 69 B10
Bréhal F 23 C8
Bréhan F 22 D6
Brehna D 79 C11
Breidenbach D 21 C10
Breidenbach D 27 B7
Breidstrand N 111 C12
Breidvik N 108 B9
Breidvik N 110 C8
Breidvik N 110 C9
Breidvik N 111 D11
Breiholz D 82 B7
Breil CH 71 D8
Breil-sur-Roya F 37 D7
Breisach am Rhein D 27 D8
Breistein N 94 B2
Breitenbach CH 27 F8
Breitenbach D 21 F8
Breitenbach (Schauenburg)
  D 17 F12
Breitenbach am Herzberg
  D 78 E6
Breitenbach am Inn A 72 B4
Breitenberg D 76 E5
Breitenbrunn D 75 D10
Breitenburg D 82 C7
Breitenfelde D 83 C9
Breitengüßbach D 75 C8
Breitenhagen D 79 C10
Breitnau D 27 E9
Breitscheid D 183 C9
Breitscheid D 185 C7
Breitscheid D 185 C9
Breitungen D 79 F7
Brélès F 22 D2
Brelingen (Wedemark) D 78 A6
Bremdal DK 86 B3
Bremen D 17 B11
Bremerhaven D 17 A11
Bremervörde D 17 B12
Bremgarten CH 27 F9
Bremm D 21 D8
Bremnes N 94 C2
Bremnes N 110 C9
Brem-sur-Mer F 28 B2
Brenderup DK 86 E5
Brenes E 51 D8
Brenguli LV 131 F11
Brenitsa BG 165 C9
Brenna N 108 C5
Brenna N 110 D7
Brenna PL 147 B7
Brennero I 72 C4
Brennes N 112 D5
Brennfjell N 112 E5
Brenngam N 113 B19
Brennhaug N 101 C10
Brennmo N 105 E11
Brennsvik N 113 B13
Breno I 69 B9
Brénod F 31 C8
Brens F 33 C9
Brensbach D 187 B6
Brent Knoll GB 13 C9
Brentwood GB 15 D9
Brenzone I 69 B10
Bresalc RKS 164 E3
Brescello I 66 C2
Brescia I 66 A1
Breskens NL 16 F1
Bresnica SRB 158 F6
Bressana Bottarone I 69 C7
Bressanone I 72 C4
Bressols F 33 C8
Bressuire F 28 B5
Brest GB 160 F5
Brest BY 141 F9
Brest F 22 D3
Brestak BG 167 C9
Brestanica SLO 148 E5
Brestova HR 67 B9
Brestovac SRB 159 E9
Brestovac SRB 164 C4
Brestovac Požeški HR 149 F9
Brestovăţ RO 151 F8
Brestovene BG 161 F9
Brestovets BG 165 C10
Brestovitsa BG 165 E10

Breuilpont F 24 C5
Breukelen NL 16 D4
Breum DK 86 B4
Breuna D 17 F12
Breuvannes-en-Bassigny
  F 26 D4
Brevens bruk S 92 A7
Brevik N 90 A6
Brevik S 92 C4
Brevik S 93 A12
Brevik S 99 C10
Breviken S 96 D7
Brevörde D 78 C5
Breza BIH 157 D9
Breza SLO 148 D4
Brežđe SRB 158 E5
Breze SLO 148 D4
Brezhani BG 165 F7
Březí CZ 77 E11
Brezičani BIH 157 B6
Brežice SLO 148 E5
Brezna SRB 163 B10
Breznica HR 148 D6
Breznica SK 145 E4
Březnice CZ 76 C5
Breznik BG 165 D7
Breznița-Motru RO 159 D11
Breznița-Ocol RO 159 D10
Breznitsa BG 165 F8
Březno CZ 76 B4
Brezno SK 147 D9
Brezoaele RO 161 D7
Brézolles F 24 C5
Březová CZ 146 D5
Březová nad Svitavou CZ 77 C11
Brezová pod Bradlom SK 146 D5
Brezovica SK 145 E2
Brezovica SK 147 C5
Brezovica SLO 73 D9
Brezovo BG 166 E4
Brezovo Polje BIH 157 C10
Brezovo Polje HR 156 B5
Briançon F 31 F10
Briare F 25 E8
Briatexte F 33 C9
Briceni MD 153 A10
Bricherasio I 31 F11
Bricon F 26 D2
Bricquebec F 23 B8
Brides-les-Bains F 31 E10
Brideswell IRL 6 F6
Bridgeland IRL 9 C9
Bridgend GB 4 C6
Bridgend GB 4 D4
Bridgend GB 4 D7
Bridge of Cally GB 5 B10
Bridge of Don GB 3 L12
Bridge of Dye GB 5 B11
Bridge of Earn GB 5 C10
Bridge of Orchy GB 4 B7
Bridge of Weir GB 4 D7
Bridgetown IRL 9 D9
Bridgnorth GB 11 F7
Bridgwater GB 13 C8
Břidličná CZ 146 B4
Bridlington GB 11 C11
Bridport GB 13 D9
Brie F 29 D6
Briec F 22 D4
Brie-Comte-Robert F 25 C8
Briedel D 185 D7
Brielle NL 16 E2
Brienne-le-Château F 25 D12
Briennon F 30 C5
Brienon-sur-Armançon F 25 D10
Brienz CH 70 D6
Brienza I 60 C5
Briesen D 80 A6
Brieske D 80 D5
Brieskow-Finkenheerd D 81 B7
Briesnig D 81 C7
Brietlingen D 83 D8
Briey F 20 F5
Brig CH 68 A4
Brigg GB 11 D11
Brighstone GB 13 D12
Brightlingsea GB 15 D11
Brighton GB 15 F8
Brigi LV 133 C3
Brignais F 30 D6
Brignogan-Plage F 22 C3
Brignoles F 36 E4
Brigstock GB 15 C7
Brihuega E 47 C7
Brijesta HR 162 D4
Brillon-en-Barrois F 26 C3
Brilon D 17 F11
Brimington GB 11 E9
Brimnes N 94 B5
Brinches P 50 C5
Brincones E 45 B8
Brindisi I 61 B9
Brindisi Montagna I 60 B5
Bringsinghaug N 100 B2
Bringsli N 108 B9
Brinian GB 3 G11
Brinje HR 67 B11
Brinkum D 17 B9
Brinkum D 17 B11
Brinlack IRL 6 B6
Brinon-sur-Beuvron F 25 F9
Brinon-sur-Sauldre F 25 E7
Brin-sur-Seille F 26 C5
Brînza MD 155 B2
Brînzeni MD 153 A10
Brion F 30 F3
Briones E 40 C6
Brionne F 24 B4
Brioude F 30 E3
Brioux-sur-Boutonne F 28 C5
Briouze F 23 C11
Briscous F 32 D3
Brisighella I 66 D4
Brissac-Quincé F 23 F11
Bristol GB 13 C9
Britelo P 38 E3
Britof SLO 73 D9
Briton Ferry GB 13 B7
Brittas IRL 7 F10
Brittas Bay IRL 9 C11
Britvica BIH 157 F8
Britz D 84 E5
Brive-la-Gaillarde F 29 E9
Briviesca E 40 C5
Brixen im Thale A 72 B5
Brixham GB 13 E7
Brixworth GB 15 C7
Brka BIH 157 C10
Brløžnik BIH 157 D10
Brna HR 162 D2

Brnaze HR 157 E6
Brněnec CZ 77 C11
Brniště CZ 81 E7
Brnjica SRB 159 D8
Brnjica SRB 163 C9
Brno CZ 77 D11
Bro S 93 D12
Bro S 99 C9
Broadford GB 2 L5
Broadford IRL 8 C5
Broadford IRL 8 D5
Broad Haven GB 9 E12
Broadheath GB 13 A10
Broadstairs GB 15 E11
Broadway GB 13 A11
Broadwey GB 13 D10
Broadwindsor GB 13 D9
Broager DK 86 F5
Broaryd S 87 A12
Broby S 88 C6
Broby S 99 C11
Brobyværk DK 86 E6
Broc CH 31 B11
Bročanac BIH 157 F7
Brocas F 32 B4
Brock CH 31 B11
Brockum D 17 D10
Brockworth GB 13 B10
Broczyno PL 85 C10
Brod BIH 157 C10
Brod MK 168 A5
Brod MK 169 C6
Brodalen S 91 C10
Brodarevo SRB 163 C9
Broddbo S 98 C6
Brodek u Prostějova CZ 77 D12
Broderstorf D 83 B12
Brodica SRB 159 E8
Brodick GB 4 D6
Brodilovo BG 167 E9
Brodina RO 152 B6
Brodnica PL 81 C9
Brodnica PL 139 D8
Brodosané RKS 163 E10
Brodské SK 77 E12
Brody PL 81 B8
Brody PL 81 C7
Broekhuizenvorst NL 183 C8
Broglie F 24 B4
Brohl D 185 D7
Brohm D 84 C5
Broin F 26 F3
Brójce PL 81 B9
Brojce PL 85 C8
Brójce PL 143 C8
Brok PL 139 E12
Brokdorf D 17 A12
Brokind S 92 C7
Brokka N 90 C2
Brokstedt D 83 C7
Brolo I 59 C6
Bromary FIN 127 F9
Brome D 79 A8
Bromes N 112 C2
Bromley GB 15 E9
Bromölla S 88 C6
Brömsebro S 89 C10
Bromsgrove GB 13 A10
Bromyard GB 13 A9
Bron F 30 D6
Bronchales E 47 C9
Brønderslev DK 86 A5
Broni I 69 A11
Bronice PL 81 C7
Brønnøysund N 108 F3
Bronnytsya UA 154 A1
Brøns DK 86 E3
Bronte I 59 D6
Bronzani Majdan BIH 157 C6
Brooke GB 15 B11
Brookeborough GB 7 D8
Broons F 23 D7
Broquiès F 34 B4
Brora GB 3 J9
Brørup DK 86 D4
Brösarp S 88 D6
Broscăuţi RO 153 B8
Broseley GB 10 F7
Broshniv Osada UA 145 F9
Brossac F 28 E5
Brøstadbotn N 111 B14
Broşteni RO 153 C7
Broşteni RO 159 D8
Broşteni RO 159 D10
Brotas P 50 B3
Brötjemark S 92 D4
Broto E 32 E5
Brottby S 99 C10
Brottes F 26 D3
Brotton GB 11 B10
Brøttum N 101 D13
Brou F 24 D5
Brough GB 3 H10
Brough GB 11 B7
Broughshane GB 4 F4
Broughton GB 5 D10
Broughton GB 10 F6
Broughton in Furness GB 10 C5
Broughton GB 3 G11
Broughty Ferry GB 5 C11
Broumov CZ 81 E11
Broussval F 26 D2
Broutzaiika GR 175 D6
Brouvelieures F 26 D6
Brouwershaven NL 16 E1
Brovst DK 86 A5
Brownhills GB 11 F8
Broxburn GB 5 D10
Brozany CZ 76 B6
Brozas E 45 E7
Brožići LT 134 E3
Brozzo I 69 B9
Brštanovo HR 156 E5
Brtnice CZ 77 D9
Bruay-la-Bussière F 18 D6
Bruchhausen-Vilsen D 17 C12
Bruchköbel D 187 A6
Bruchmühlbach D 21 F8
Bruchsal D 27 B10
Bruchweiler-Bärenbach
  D 186 C4
Brück D 79 B12
Bück SK 149 A10
Buca TR 177 C9
Bučany SK 146 E5
Buccheri I 59 E6
Bucchianico I 63 C6
Buccinasco I 69 C7
Buccino I 60 B4

Brückl A 73 C10
Bruckmühl D 72 A4
Brudzeń Duży PL 139 E8
Brudzowice PL 143 E7
Brue-Auriac F 35 C10
Brüel D 83 C11
Bruère-Allichamps F 29 B10
Bruff IRL 8 D5
Brugelette B 182 D3
Bruges B 19 B7
Bruges B 182 C1
Bruggen (Odenwald) D 27 A11
Brugg CH 27 F9
Brugge B 19 B7
Brüggen D 16 F6
Brüggen D 79 B6
Brugnera I 72 E6
Bruguières F 33 C8
Bruguera I 72 E6
Brühl D 21 C7
Brühl D 187 C6
Bruinisse NL 16 E2
Bruiu RO 152 F5
Bruksvallarna S 102 A3
Brûlon F 23 E11
Brûly B 19 E10
Brumath F 27 C8
Brummen NL 183 A8
Brumov-Bylnice CZ 146 C6
Brumunddal N 101 E13
Brumundsag N 101 E13
Brunau D 83 E10
Brunava LV 135 D8
Brundby DK 86 D7
Brundish GB 15 C11
Brunehamel F 19 E9
Brunete E 46 D5
Brunico I 72 C4
Bruniquel F 33 B9
Brunkeberg N 95 D8
Brunn D 84 C4
Brunna S 99 C8
Brunna S 99 C9
Brunn am Gebirge A 77 F10
Brunnberg S 97 B10
Brunnen CH 71 C7
Brunnsberg S 102 D6
Brunnsberg S 97 C8
Brunsbüttel D 17 A12
Brunssum NL 20 C5
Bruntál CZ 142 G3
Bruravik N 94 B5
Bruree IRL 8 D5
Brus SRB 163 C11
Brusago I 69 A11
Brusand N 94 E3
Brušane HR 156 C3
Brusarisi BG 159 F11
Brusartsi BG 159 F11
Brüsewitz D 83 C10
Brusio CH 69 A9
Brüshlen BG 161 F8
Brüshlyanitsa BG 165 B10
Brusnik SRB 159 E9
Brusnika Velika BIH 157 B9
Brusno SK 147 D8
Brusque F 34 C4
Brussel B 19 C9
Brusson I 68 B4
Brüssow D 84 D6
Brusturi RO 151 C9
Brusturiv UA 152 A5
Brusturoasa RO 153 D8
Brusy PL 138 C4
Bruton GB 13 C10
Bruttig-Fankel D 21 D8
Bruvno HR 156 D4
Bruxelles B 19 C9
Bruyères F 26 D6
Bruz F 23 D8
Bruzaholm S 92 D6
Brvnište SK 146 C6
Brwinów PL 141 F3
Bryagovo BG 166 F4
Bryastovo BG 165 F10
Bryggerhaug N 111 B14
Brymbo GB 10 E5
Brynamman GB 13 B7
Bryne N 94 E3
Brynford GB 10 E5
Brynge S 107 E14
Bryngelhögen S 102 B7
Brynje S 102 A8
Brynmawr GB 13 B8
Bryrup DK 86 C5
Bryukhovychi UA 144 D8
Brzan SRB 159 E7
Brza Palanka SRB 159 E9
Brzece SRB 163 C10
Brzeg PL 142 E3
Brzeg Dolny PL 81 D11
Brześć Kujawski PL 138 E6
Brzesko PL 143 G10
Brzeszcze PL 143 G7
Brzezie PL 85 C11
Brzezie PL 138 E6
Brzezinki PL 141 H5
Brzeziny PL 141 G1
Brzeziny PL 142 C5
Brzeziny PL 143 C8
Brzeziny PL 144 D4
Brzeźnica PL 81 C8
Brzeźnica PL 143 F11
Brzeźnica PL 147 B9
Brzeźno PL 85 C9
Brzeźno PL 141 H9
Brzeźno PL 142 B5
Brzostek PL 144 D3
Brzotín SK 145 F1
Brzóza PL 141 G4
Brzozów PL 141 F2
Brzozów PL 144 D6
Brzozowiec PL 81 A8
Brzozowo PL 139 E11

Bucecea RO 153 B8
Bucelas P 50 B1
Buceş RO 151 E10
Bucey-lès-Gy F 26 F4
Buch D 71 A10
Buch am Erlbach D 75 F11
Buchbach D 75 F11
Buchboden A 71 C9
Büchel D 21 D8
Buchen (Odenwald) D 27 A11
Büchenbeuren D 185 E7
Buchholz D 83 D9
Buchholz (Aller) D 82 E7
Buchholz (Westerwald) D 21 C8
Buchin RO 159 C9
Buchin Prohod BG 165 D9
Buch in Tirol A 72 B4
Buchkirchen A 76 F6
Büchlberg D 76 E5
Buchloe D 71 A11
Buchlovice CZ 146 C4
Bucholz in der Nordheide
  D 83 D7
Buchs CH 71 C8
Buchy F 18 E3
Bučim MK 164 F5
Buçimas AL 168 C4
Bucin MK 168 B5
Bucine I 66 F4
Bucinişu RO 160 F4
Bučište MK 164 F5
Bucium RO 151 E11
Buciumeni RO 153 F10
Buciumeni RO 161 C6
Buciumi RO 151 C11
Bučje SRB 159 F9
Bučje SRB 163 C7
Buckden GB 11 C7
Bückeburg D 17 D12
Bücken D 17 C12
Buckfastleigh GB 13 E7
Buckhaven GB 5 C10
Buckie GB 3 K11
Buckingham GB 14 D7
Buckley GB 10 E5
Buckode IRL 6 D6
Buckow Märkische Schweiz
  D 80 A6
Bückwitz D 83 E12
Bucoşniţa RO 159 C9
Bucov RO 161 D8
Bucovăţ MD 154 C2
Bucovăţ RO 160 E3
Bucovica BIH 157 E7
Bučovice CZ 77 D12
Bucsa H 151 C7
Bucşani RO 161 D7
Bucşani RO 161 E7
Bucu RO 161 D11
Bucureşti RO 151 E10
Bucureşti RO 161 E8
Bucy-lès-Pierrepont F 19 E8
Buczek PL 143 D7
Bud N 100 A5
Buda RO 161 B9
Budacu de Jos RO 152 C5
Budakalász H 150 B3
Budakeszi H 149 A11
Budakovo MK 168 B5
Budaörs H 149 B11
Budapest H 150 C3
Bučča SK 147 D8
Buddusò I 64 B3
Bude GB 12 D5
Budeasa RO 160 D5
Budel NL 16 F5
Büdelsdorf D 82 B7
Budenheim D 21 D10
Budens P 50 E2
Büdesheim D 21 D11
Budeşti MD 154 C3
Budeşti RO 152 B3
Budeşti RO 152 D4
Budeşti RO 160 C4
Budeşti RO 161 E8
Budeyi UA 154 A4
Budia E 47 C7
Budila RO 161 B7
Budimci HR 149 F10
Budimlić Japra BIH 156 C5
Budiná SK 147 E8
Büdingen D 21 D12
Budinšćina HR 148 D6
Budišov CZ 77 D9
Budišov nad Budišovkou
  CZ 146 B5
Budkovce SK 145 F5
Budleigh Salterton GB 13 D8
Budmerice SK 146 E4
Budoia I 72 D6
Budoni I 64 B4
Budrio I 66 C4
Budry PL 136 E4
Budureasa RO 151 D10
Budušlău RO 151 C9
Budva MNE 163 E6
Büdvičelait LT 136 D6
Budynĕ nad Ohří CZ 76 B6
Budziszewice PL 141 G1
Budzów PL 147 B9
Budzyń PL 85 E11
Bue S F 47 C10
Bueña E 47 C10
Buenache de Alarcón E 47 E8
Buenache de la Sierra E 47 D8
Buenaventura E 46 D3
Buenavista de Valdavia E 39 C10
Buendía E 47 D7
Buer D 183 B10
Buer N 96 D6
Bueu E 38 D2
Bufleben D 79 D8
Buftea RO 161 D7
Bugac H 150 D4
Bugarra E 48 E3
Buğdaylı TR 173 D8
Bugeat F 29 D9
Buggenhout B 182 C4
Buggerru I 64 E1
Buggingen D 27 E8
Bugiac MD 154 E3
Bugnara I 62 C5
Bugojno BIH 157 D7
Bugøyfjord N 114 D6
Bugøynes N 114 D7
Bugyi H 150 C3
Bühl D 27 C9
Bühl D 27 C9
Bühlertal D 27 C9
Bühlertann D 74 D6
Bühlerzell D 74 D6

Buhoci RO 153 D10
Buhølen N 90 C1
Buhuşi RO 153 D9
Buia I 73 D7
Builth Wells GB 13 A8
Buis-les-Baronnies F 35 B9
Buitenpost NL 16 B6
Buitrago del Lozoya E 46 C5
Buivydiškės LT 137 D11
Buivydžiai LT 137 D12
Buják H 147 F9
Bujalance E 53 A8
Bujan AL 163 E9
Bujaraloz E 42 E3
Buje HR 67 B8
Bujor MD 154 D2
Bujoreni RO 160 C4
Bujoreni RO 161 E7
Bujoru RO 161 F7
Bük H 149 B7
Buk PL 81 B11
Bukaiši LV 134 D6
Bukhava BY 133 E6
Bukhovo BG 165 D8
Bukhovtsi BG 167 C7
Bükkábrány H 145 H2
Bükkösd H 149 D9
Bükkszék H 145 H1
Bükkszentkereszt H 145 G2
Bükkzsérc H 145 H2
Buko D 79 C11
Bukonys LT 135 F8
Bukova Gora BIH 157 E7
Bukovče SRB 159 E10
Bukovets BG 165 D8
Bukovo MK 168 C5
Buków PL 81 B9
Bukowe PL 142 B4
Bukowice PL 81 D12
Bukowiec PL 81 B9
Bukowiec PL 81 B10
Bukowiec PL 138 C5
Bukowina PL 138 B4
Bukowina Tatrzańska PL 145 E1
Bukownica PL 142 D5
Bukowsko PL 145 E5
Bülach CH 27 E10
Bulboaca MD 154 D4
Bulbucata RO 161 E7
Bulçar AL 168 C3
Buldoo GB 3 H9
Bulford GB 13 C11
Bülgarene BG 165 C11
Bülgarevo BG 167 C10
Bülgari BG 167 E9
Bülgarovo BG 166 F5
Bülgarovo BG 167 D8
Bülgarska Polyana BG 166 E6
Bulgnéville F 26 D4
Bülkau D 17 A11
Bulkington GB 13 A12
Bulkowo PL 139 E9
Bullas E 55 C9
Bullaun IRL 6 F5
Bullay D 21 D8
Bulle CH 31 B11
Bullerup DK 86 E6
Büllingen B 20 D6
Bullmark S 122 B4
Bully-les-Mines F 18 D6
Bulqizë AL 168 A3
Bultei I 64 C3
Bulz RO 151 D10
Bulzeşti RO 160 D3
Bulzeştii de Sus RO 151 E10
Bulzi I 64 B2
Bumbeşti-Jiu RO 160 C2
Bumbeşti-Piţic RO 160 C3
Buna BIH 157 F8
Bunacurry IRL 6 E3
Bunalty IRL 6 D3
Bun an Churraigh IRL 6 E3
Bun an Phobail IRL 4 E2
Bun an Tábhairne IRL 8 E6
Bunbeg IRL 6 B6
Bunclody IRL 9 C9
Bun Clóidí IRL 9 C9
Buncrana IRL 4 E2
Bun Cranncha IRL 4 E2
Bunde D 17 B8
Bünde D 17 D11
Bundenbach D 21 E8
Bunderhee D 17 B8
Bun Dobhrain IRL 6 D6
Bundoran IRL 6 D6
Bunessan GB 4 C4
Buneşti RO 152 E6
Buneşti RO 153 B8
Buneşti-Avereşti RO 153 D11
Bungay GB 15 C11
Bunge S 93 D14
Bunić HR 156 C4
Buniel E 40 D4
Bunila RO 159 B10
Bunka LV 134 C3
Bunkeflostrand S 87 D11
Bunkris S 102 C5
Bunmahon IRL 9 D8
Bunnaglass IRL 6 F5
Bun na hAbhna IRL 6 D3
Bunnahowen IRL 6 D3
Bun na Leaca IRL 6 B6
Bunnanaddan IRL 6 D5
Bunnanadden IRL 6 D5
Buñol E 48 F3
Bunschoten-Spakenburg
   NL 16 D4
Bunteşti RO 151 D10
Buntingford GB 15 D8
Bunyola E 49 E10
Buoač BIH 157 C7
Buochs CH 71 D6
Buollannjárga N 113 E15
Buonabitacolo I 60 C5
Buonalbergo I 60 A4
Buonconvento I 66 F3
Buonvicino I 60 D5
Bur DK 86 C2
Buran N 105 D11
Burbach D 21 C10
Burbage GB 13 C11
Burbáguena E 47 B10
Burcei I 64 E3
Bürdarski Geran BG 165 B8
Burdinne B 19 C11
Bureå S 118 E6
Bureåborg S 107 E13
Büren D 17 E11

Büren NL 183 B6
Büren an der Aare CH 27 F7
Bures GB 15 D10
Buresjön S 109 E14
Burfjord N 112 D9
Burford GB 13 B11
Burg D 80 C6
Burg (Dithmarschen) D 82 C6
Burganes de Valverde E 39 E8
Burgas BG 167 E9
Burgau A 148 B6
Burgau D 75 F7
Burgau P 50 E2
Burg auf Fehmarn D 83 B10
Burg bei Magdeburg D 79 B10
Burgbernheim D 75 D7
Burgbrohl D 185 D7
Burgdorf CH 70 C5
Burgdorf D 79 B7
Burgdorf D 79 B7
Burgebrach D 75 C8
Bürgel D 79 E10
Burgess Hill GB 15 F8
Burghausen D 76 F3
Burghclere GB 13 C12
Burghead GB 3 K10
Burgh-Haamstede NL 16 E1
Burgh le Marsh GB 11 E12
Burgio I 58 D3
Burgkirchen an der Alz D 75 F12
Burgkunstadt D 75 B9
Bürglen CH 27 E11
Bürglen CH 71 D7
Burglengenfeld D 75 D11
Burgohondo E 46 D3
Burgos E 40 D4
Burgos I 64 C2
Burgsalach D 75 D9
Burgsinn D 74 B6
Bürgstadt D 21 E12
Burgstädt D 79 E12
Burg Stargand D 84 D4
Burgsvik S 93 E12
Burgthann D 75 D9
Burgtonna D 79 D8
Burgui E 32 E3
Burguillos E 51 D8
Burguillos del Cerro E 51 C6
Burguillos de Toledo E 46 E5
Burgum NL 16 B5
Burgwindheim D 75 C8
Burhaniye TR 173 F6
Burhave (Butjadingen) D 17 A10
Buriasco I 31 F11
Burie F 28 D5
Burila Mare RO 159 E10
Burizanë AL 168 A2
Burjassot E 48 E4
Burjuc RO 151 F10
Burkardroth D 74 B6
Burkhardtsdorf D 80 E3
Burlada E 32 E2
Burladingen D 27 D11
Burlats F 33 C10
Bürmoos A 76 G3
Burnchurch IRL 9 C8
Burness GB 3 G11
Burnfoot GB 4 F3
Burnfoot IRL 4 E2
Burnham GB 15 D7
Burnham Market GB 15 B10
Burnham-on-Crouch GB 15 D10
Burnham-on-Sea GB 13 C9
Burniston GB 11 C11
Burnley GB 11 D7
Burntisland GB 5 C10
Burntwood Green GB 11 F8
Burón E 39 B9
Buronzo I 68 C5
Buros F 32 D5
Burovac SRB 159 E7
Burow D 84 C4
Burøysund N 112 C4
Burravoe GB 3 E14
Burrel AL 168 A3
Burren GB 7 D10
Burren IRL 6 F4
Burriana E 48 E4
Burry Port GB 12 B6
Bürs A 71 C9
Burs S 93 D13
Bursa TR 173 D11
Burscough Bridge GB 10 D6
Burseryd S 87 A12
Bursfelde D 78 C6
Burstow GB 15 E8
Bursuc MD 154 C2
Burtnieki LV 131 F10
Burton-in-Kendal GB 10 C6
Burton Latimer GB 15 C7
Burtonport IRL 6 C6
Burton upon Trent GB 11 F8
Burträsk S 118 E5
Buru RO 152 D3
Burujón E 46 E4
Burwarton GB 13 A9
Burwash GB 15 F9
Burwell GB 15 C9
Burwick GB 3 H11
Bury GB 11 D7
Bury St Edmunds GB 15 C10
Burzenin PL 142 D6
Busachi I 64 C2
Busalla I 37 B9
Busana I 66 D1
Byhleguhre D 80 C6
Bylchau GB 10 E4
Bylderup-Bov DK 86 F4
Byn S 97 B10
Byneset N 104 E8
Byń'ki BY 133 F2
Byenyakoni BY 137 E11
Byershty BY 137 F9
Byfield GB 13 A12
Bygdeå S 122 B5
Bygdeträsk S 118 F5
Bygdsiljum S 118 F5
Bygland N 90 B2
Byglandsfjord N 90 B2
Bygstad N 100 D3
Byhlegruhr D N 94 C7
Byrum DK 87 A7
Byšice I 77 B7
Byske S 118 E6
Bysträsk S 107 C15
Bystřany CZ 80 E5
Bystré CZ 77 C10
Bystré SK 145 E4
Byšta SK 145 F3
Byšička CZ 77 B9
Bystŕec CZ 77 B11
Bystretsovo RUS 132 F5
Bystřičany SK 147 D7
Bystřice CZ 77 C7
Bystřice CZ 147 B7
Bystřice nad Pernštejnem
   CZ 77 C10
Bystřice pod Hostýnem
   CZ 146 C5

Bussi sul Tirino I 62 C5
Büßleben D 79 E9
Bussolengo I 66 B2
Bussoleno I 31 E11
Bussum NL 16 D4
Bussy-en-Othe F 25 D10
Bussy-le-Grand F 25 E12
Buşteni RO 161 C7
Bustillo del Páramo E 39 D8
Busto Arsizio I 69 B6
Bustuchin RO 160 D3
Busturi-Axpe E 41 B6
Büsum D 82 B5
Büta BG 165 E9
Butan BG 160 F3
Buteni MD 154 D3
Buteni RO 151 E9
Butera I 58 E5
Buteşti MD 153 B10
Bütgenbach D 20 D6
Butimanu RO 161 D7
Bütingë LT 134 D2
Butlers Bridge IRL 7 D8
Butoieşti RO 160 D2
Butovo BG 166 C4
Butrimonys LT 137 D9
Butrimonys LT 137 E11
Butryny PL 139 C10
Bütschwil CH 27 F11
Buttapietra I 66 B3
Büttelborn D 187 B6
Buttelstedt D 79 D9
Buttermere GB 10 B5
Buttevant IRL 8 D5
Bütthard D 187 B8
Buttiqliera d'Asti I 37 A7
Buttle S 93 E13
Büttstädt D 79 D9
Büttstedt D 79 D7
Butuceni MD 154 C3
Butuceni MD 154 C3
Buturugeni RO 161 E7
Butzbach D 21 D11
Bützow D 83 C11
Buurse NL 17 D7
Buvåg N 110 D9
Buvik N 111 A15
Buvika N 104 E8
Buxerolles F 29 B6
Buxheim D 71 B10
Buxières-les-Mines F 30 C2
Buxted GB 15 F9
Buxtehude D 82 D7
Buxton GB 11 E8
Buxy F 30 B6
Buynovtsi BG 166 D5
Büyükada TR 173 C11
Büyükaltiağaç TR 171 B10
Büyükanafarta TR 171 D10
Büyükbelen TR 177 B10
Büyükçavuşlu TR 173 B9
Büyükçekmece TR 173 B10
Büyükçiğli TR 177 C9
Büyük Evren TR 171 C10
Büyükgerdelli TR 167 F7
Büyük Kariştiran TR 173 B7
Büyükkarakarlı TR 173 B7
Büyükkariştiran TR 173 B6
Büyükkılıçlı TR 173 B9
Büyükorhan TR 173 E10
Büyükyenice TR 173 F7
Büyükyoncalı TR 173 B8
Buza RO 152 D4
Buzançais F 29 B8
Buzancy F 19 F10
Buzău RO 161 C9
Buzescu RO 160 F5
Buzet HR 67 B8
Buzet-sur-Baïse F 33 B6
Buzet-sur-Tarn F 33 C9
Buziaş RO 159 B8
Buzica SK 145 F3
Bužim BIH 156 B5
Buzoeşti RO 160 D5
Buzsák H 149 C9
By N 104 D8
Byala BG 166 C5
Byala BG 166 D6
Byala BG 167 D9
Byala Cherkva BG 165 F10
Byala Cherkva BG 166 C4
Byala Reka BG 166 E4
Byala Reka BG 167 D7
Byala Slatina BG 165 C8
Byal Izvor BG 171 A8
Byalo Pole BG 166 E5
Byanç CZ 77 B9
Byala Cherkva BG 165 F10

Bystrička SK 147 C7
Bystrzyca PL 142 E3
Bystrzyca Kłodzka PL 77 B11
Bytča SK 147 C7
Bytnica PL 81 B8
Bytom PL 143 F6
Bytom Odrzański PL 81 C9
Bytów PL 85 B12
Byvallen S 102 B7
Byviken S 107 D16
Byxelkrok S 89 A12
Bzenec CZ 146 D4
Bzince pod Javorinou SK 146 D5

C

Cabacés E 42 E5
Cabaj-Čápor SK 146 E6
Cabanac-et-Villagrains F 32 A4
Cabañaquinta E 39 B8
Cabañas del Castillo E 45 E10
Cabanas de Viriato P 44 D5
Cabañas Raras E 39 C6
Cabanes E 48 D5
Cabanillas E 41 D8
Cabannes F 35 C8
Çabar HR 73 E10
Cabação P 50 B3
Cabeça Gorda P 50 D4
Cabeção P 50 B3
Cabeceiras de Basto P 38 E4
Cabeço de Vide P 44 F5
Cabella Ligure I 37 B10
Cabeza de Framontanos E 45 B8
Cabeza del Buey E 51 B9
Cabeza del Caballo E 45 B7
Cabeza la Vaca E 51 C7
Cabezamesada E 47 E6
Cabezarados E 54 B4
Cabezarrubias del Puerto
   E 54 B4
Cabezas del Villar E 45 C10
Cabezas Rubias E 51 D5
Cabezón de Cameros E 41 D6
Cabezón de la Sal E 40 B3
Cabezón de Liébana E 39 B10
Cabezuela del Valle E 45 D9
Çabiny SK 145 E4
Cabo de Palos E 56 F3
Cabolafuente E 47 B8
Cabra E 53 B8
Cabração P 38 E2
Cabra del Camp E 42 E6
Cabra del Santo Cristo E 55 D6
Cabra de Mora E 48 D3
Cabras I 64 D2
Cabrejas del Pinar E 40 E6
Cabrela P 50 B3
Cabrerets F 33 A9
Cabrières-d'Aigues F 35 C10
Cabril P 44 D5
Cabrillanes E 39 C7
Cabrillas E 45 C8
Cabuna HR 149 E9
Cacabelos E 39 C6
Čačak SRB 158 F5
Caçarelhos P 39 E7
Caccamo I 58 D4
Caccuri I 61 E7
Cacém P 50 B1
Cáceres E 45 F8
Cachtice SK 146 D5
Cacica RO 153 B7
Cacín E 53 B9
Cadalso de los Vidrios E 46 D4
Cadamstown IRL 7 F7
Cadaqués E 43 C10
Cadaval P 44 F2
Čadavica BIH 157 C6
Čadavica HR 149 E9
Čadavica Gornja BIH 157 C11
Čadca SK 147 C7
Cadelbosco di Sopra I 66 C2
Cadenazzo CH 69 A6
Cadenberge D 17 A12
Cadenet F 35 C9
Cadeo I 69 D8
Cádiar E 55 F6
Cadillac F 32 A5
Cádiz E 52 C4
Cadolzburg D 75 D8
Cadoneghe I 66 B4
Cadours F 33 C8
Cadreita E 41 D8
Cadrete E 41 E10
Caen F 23 B11
Caerau GB 13 C8
Caerdydd GB 13 C8
Caerfyrddin GB 12 B6
Caergybi GB 10 E2
Caerhun GB 10 E4
Caerleon GB 13 B9
Caernarfon GB 10 E3
Caerphilly GB 13 B8
Cafasse I 31 E11
Caggiano I 60 B5
Çağiş TR 173 E8
Cagli I 42 G4
Cagliari I 64 E3
Čaglin HR 149 F9
Cagnac-les-Mines F 33 C10
Cagnes-sur-Mer F 36 D6
Caherconlish IRL 8 C6
Cahermore IRL 8 E2
Cahir IRL 9 D7
Cahirsiveen IRL 8 E2
Cahul MD 154 F2
Cahuzac-sur-Vère F 33 C9
Căiani RO 152 D3
Căianu Mic RO 152 C4
Caiazzo I 60 A2
Căinari MD 154 D4
Căinarii Vechi MD 153 A12
Căineni RO 160 C4
Căineni-Băi RO 161 C10
Caión E 38 B2
Ciaracla MD 154 F3
Cairanne F 35 B8
Cairnbaan GB 4 C6
Cairnryan GB 4 F6
Cairo Montenotte I 37 C8
Ciaseal IRL 9 C7
Caisleán an Bharraigh IRL 6 E4
Caisleán an Chomair IRL 9 C8
Caisleán Uí Chonaill IRL 8 C5
Caissargues F 35 C7
Caister-on-Sea GB 15 B12

Caistor GB 11 E11
Caivano I 60 B2
Cajarc F 33 B9
Çajetina SRB 158 F4
Čajić BIH 157 E6
Čajkov SK 147 E7
Čajniče BIH 157 E11
Çakır TR 173 D7
Çakıralan TR 172 B6
Cakovec HR 149 D6
Cala E 51 D7
Calabardina E 55 E9
Calabritto I 60 B4
Calaceite E 42 E4
Calacuccia F 37 G10
Cala d'Oliva I 64 A1
Cala d'Or E 57 C11
Calafat RO 159 F10
Calafell E 43 E7
Cala Figuera E 57 C11
Cala Galdana E 57 B12
Calahonda E 53 C10
Calahorra E 32 F1
Calais F 15 F12
Cala Millor E 57 B11
Calamocha E 47 C10
Calamonaci I 58 D3
Calamonte E 51 B7
Cǎlan RO 151 F11
Calañas E 51 D6
Calanda E 42 F3
Calangianus I 64 B3
Calanna I 59 C8
Cala'n Porter E 57 B13
Călăraşi MD 154 C2
Călăraşi RO 152 E3
Călăraşi RO 153 B8
Călăraşi RO 160 F4
Călăraşi RO 161 E10
Cala Ratjada E 57 B11
Calascibetta I 58 D5
Calasetta I 64 E1
Calasparra E 55 C9
Calatafimi I 58 D2
Calatayud E 41 F8
Cǎlǎtele RO 151 D11
Calatorao E 41 F9
Calau D 80 C5
Calbe (Saale) D 79 C10
Calcatoggio F 37 G9
Calcinato I 66 B1
Calcio I 69 B8
Cǎldǎraru RO 160 E5
Caldarola I 67 F7
Caldas da Rainha P 44 F2
Caldas de Reis E 38 C2
Caldas de Vizela P 38 F3
Caldbeck GB 5 F10
Caldearenas E 32 F4
Caldecott GB 11 F10
Caldelas P 38 E3
Caldelas Taipas P 38 F3
Calden D 21 B12
Caldercruix GB 5 D9
Caldes de Malavella E 43 D9
Caldes de Montbui E 43 D8
Caldes d'Estrac E 43 D9
Caldicot GB 13 B9
Caldogno I 72 E3
Caldonazzo I 69 A11
Calella E 43 D9
Calendário P 38 F2
Calenzana F 37 F9
Calenzano I 66 E3
Calera de León E 51 C7
Calera y Chozas E 45 E10
Calerueqa E 40 E5
Calfsound GB 3 G11
Calgary GB 4 B4
Cali TR 173 D10
Calig E 42 G4
Cǎlimǎneşti RO 160 C4
Calimera I 61 C10
Cǎlinǎneşti MD 153 B9
Cǎlinǎneşti RO 152 B3
Cǎlinǎneşti RO 160 D6
Cǎlinǎneşti-Oaş RO 145 H7
Calitri I 60 B4
Calizzano I 37 C8
Çalköy TR 173 E7
Callac F 22 D5
Callan IRL 9 C8
Callander GB 5 C8
Callanish E 2 J3
Callas F 36 D4
Callen F 32 B5
Callian F 36 D5
Callington GB 12 D6
Callosa d'En Sarrià E 56 D4
Callosa de Segura E 56 E3
Calma SRB 158 C4
Cǎlmǎţuiu RO 160 F5
Cǎlmǎţuiu de Sus RO 160 E5
Calmont F 33 B11
Calmont F 33 D9
Calne GB 13 C10
Cǎlnic RO 152 F3
Cǎlnic RO 159 D10
Calolziocorte I 69 B7
Calomarde E 47 D9
Calonge E 43 D10
Calonne I 58 B3
Çalovec HR 146 F5
Calpe E 56 D5
Caltabellotta I 58 D3
Caltagirone I 59 E6
Caltanissetta I 58 E5
Caltavuturo I 58 D4
Caltignaga I 68 B6
Caltilibük TR 173 E10
Caltojar E 40 F6
Caltra IRL 6 F6
Cǎlugǎreni RO 161 E7
Caluso I 68 C4

Calvão P 44 D3
Camporosso I 37 D7
Camporrells E 42 D5
Camporrobles E 47 E10
Campos E 57 C11
Campos P 38 E4
Camposampiero I 66 A4
Composanto I 66 C3
Campotéjar E 53 B9
Campotosto I 62 B4
Campo Tures I 72 C4
Camptown GB 5 E11
Câmpulung RO 160 C6
Câmpulung la Tisa RO 145 H8
Câmpulung Moldovenesc
   RO 153 B7
Câmpuri RO 153 E9
Camrose GB 12 B4
Camuñas E 46 F6
Çamyayla TR 181 B8
Çan TR 173 D7
Caña SK 145 F3
Cañada E 56 D3
Cañada de Benatanduz E 42 F2
Cañada del Hoyo E 47 E9
Cañada Vellida E 42 F2
Čanak HR 156 C3
Çanakçi TR 173 F10
Çanakkale TR 171 D10
Canale I 37 B7
Canale-di-Verde F 37 G10
Canalejas del Arroyo E 47 D8
Canalejas de Peñafiel E 40 E3
Canals E 56 D3
Canals F 33 C8
Canàl San Bovo I 72 D4
Cañamares E 47 D8
Cañamero E 45 F10
Canaples F 18 D5
Canari F 37 F10
Canaro I 66 C4
Cañaveral E 45 E8
Cañaveral de León E 51 C6
Cañaveras E 47 D8
Cañaveruelas E 47 D7
Canazei I 72 D4
Cancale F 23 C8
Cancarix E 55 C9
Cancellara I 60 B5
Cancello ed Arnone I 60 A2
Cancon F 33 A7
Candanchú E 32 E4
Çandarli TR 177 B8
Candás E 39 A8
Candasnos E 42 D4
Candé F 23 E9
Candela I 60 A5
Candelario E 45 D9
Candeleda E 45 D10
Candelo E 68 B5
Candemil P 38 E2
Cândeşti RO 153 B9
Cândeşti RO 153 D9
Candia Lomellina I 68 C6
Candilichera E 41 E7
Candín E 39 C6
Canelli I 37 B8
Canelli I 37 B8
Canena E 55 C6
Canepina I 62 C2
Canero E 39 A7
Cǎneşti RO 161 C9
Canet F 34 C5
Canet F 34 D4
Canet de Mar E 43 D9
Cañete E 47 D9
Cañete de las Torres E 53 A8
Canet-en-Roussillon F 34 E5
Canet lo Roig E 42 F4
Canet-Plage F 34 E5
Cangas E 38 D2
Cangas del Narcea E 39 B6
Cangas de Onís E 39 B9
Cangonj AL 168 C4
Canha P 50 B2
Canhestros P 50 C3
Cania MD 154 E2
Canicattì I 58 E4
Canicattini Bagni I 59 E7
Canicosa de la Sierra E 40 E5
Caniles E 55 E7
Canillas de Aceituno E 53 C8
Canino I 62 C1
Cañizal E 45 B10
Cañizares E 47 C8
Cañizo E 39 E9
Canjáyar E 55 E7
Canlia RO 161 E11
Canna I 61 C7
Cannara I 62 B3
Cannero Riviera I 68 A6
Cannes F 36 D6
Canneto I 59 C6
Canneto I 66 F2
Canneto sull'Oglio I 66 B1
Cannich GB 2 L7
Canninqstown IRL 7 E8
Cannington GB 13 C8
Cannobio I 68 A6
Cannock GB 11 F7
Cano P 50 B4
Canolo I 59 C9
Canonbie GB 5 E11
Canosa di Puglia I 60 A6
Cánovas E 56 F2
Can Pastilla E 49 E10
Can Picafort E 57 B11
Canredondo E 47 C8
Cansano I 62 D6
Cantagallo I 66 D3
Cantalapiedra E 45 B10
Cantalejo E 46 B5
Cantalice I 62 C3
Cantalpino E 45 B10
Cantanhede P 44 D3
Cantavieja E 42 F3
Čantavir SRB 150 F4
Cantemir MD 154 E2
Cantenac F 28 E5
Canteras E 56 F2
Canterbury GB 15 E11
Cantiano I 66 F6
Cantillana E 51 D8
Cantimpalos E 46 B4
Cantoira I 31 E11
Cantoria E 55 E8
Cantù I 69 B7
Canvey Island GB 15 D10
Cany-Barville F 18 E2
Canyelles E 43 E7
Caolas GB 4 B3

Caorle I 73 E6
Capaccio I 60 C4
Capaci I 58 C3
Capafonts E 42 E6
Capalbio I 65 C4
Câpâlna RO 151 D9
Capannoli I 66 E2
Capannori I 66 E2
Caparde BIH 157 D10
Capari MK 168 B5
Caparica E 50 B1
Caparrosa P 44 C4
Caparroso E 32 F2
Cap-Blanc E 48 F4
Capbreton F 32 C3
Cap d'Agde F 34 D6
Capdenac F 33 A10
Capdenac-Gare F 33 A10
Capdepera E 57 B11
Capel Curig GB 10 E4
Capelins P 51 B5
Capelle aan de IJssel NL 16 E3
Capellen L 20 E6
Capel St Mary GB 15 C11
Capendu F 34 D4
Capestang F 34 D5
Capestrano I 62 C5
Cap Ferret F 32 A3
Capileira E 55 F6
Capilla E 54 B2
Capinha P 44 D6
Capistrello I 62 D4
Capizzi I 58 D5
Câpleni RO 151 B10
Câplje BIH 157 C6
Čapljina BIH 157 F8
Capodimonte I 62 B1
Capo di Ponte I 69 A9
Capo d'Orlando I 59 C6
Capoliveri I 65 B2
Capolona I 66 E4
Caposele I 60 B4
Capoterra I 64 E2
Cappadocia I 62 C4
Cappagh White IRL 8 C6
Cappamore IRL 8 C6
Cappawhite IRL 8 C6
Cappeen IRL 8 E5
Cappelle sul Tavo I 62 C6
Cappeln (Oldenburg) D 17 C10
Cappercleuch GB 5 E10
Cappoquin IRL 9 D7
Capracotta I 63 D6
Capraia Isola I 65 A1
Capranica I 62 C2
Caprarola I 62 C2
Câpreni RO 160 D3
Capri I 60 B2
Câpriana MD 154 C2
Capriati a Volturno I 63 E6
Capri Leone I 59 C6
Caprino Bergamasco I 69 B7
Caprino Veronese I 69 B10
Captieux F 32 B5
Capua I 60 A2
Capurso I A7
Câpuşu Mare RO 151 D11
Capvern-les-Bains F 33 D6
Carabaña E 47 D6
Caracal RO 160 E4
Caracuel de Calatrava E 54 B4
Caragas MD 154 D5
Carageie RO 161 D10
Caraglio I 37 C6
Caraman F 33 C9
Caramanico Terme I 62 C6
Caramulo P 44 C4
Cârand RO 151 E9
Caranga E 39 B7
Caranguejeira P 44 E3
Caransebeş RO 159 C9
Carantec F 22 C4
Carapelle I 60 A5
Carapinheira P 44 D3
Carasco I 37 C10
Caraşova RO 159 C8
Caraula RO 159 E11
Caravaca de la Cruz E 55 C9
Caravaggio I 69 C8
Carbajales de Alba E 39 E8
Carballeda de Avia E 38 D3
Carballo E 38 B2
Carballo E 38 D4
Carbellino E 39 F8
Carbonera de Frentes E 41 E6
Carboneras E 55 F9
Carboneras de Guadazaón E 47 E9
Carbonero El Mayor E 46 B4
Carboneros E 54 C5
Carbonia I 64 E2
Carbonin I 72 C5
Carbonne F 33 D8
Carbost GB 2 L4
Carbost GB 2 L4
Cârbunari RO 159 D8
Cârbuneşti RO 161 C8
Carbury IRL 7 F9
Carcaboso E 45 D8
Carcabuey E 53 B8
Carcaixent E 48 F4
Carcaliu RO 155 C2
Carcans F 28 E3
Carcans-Plage F 28 E3
Cárção P 39 E6
Cárcar E 32 F2
Carcare I 37 C8
Carcassonne F 33 D10
Carcastillo E 32 F3
Carcelén E 47 F10
Carcès F 36 E4
Carchelejo E 53 A9
Carcoforo I 68 B5
Cardaillac F 29 F9
Çardak TR 172 D6
Cardedeu E 43 D8
Cardedu I 64 D4
Cardeña E 54 C4
Cardeñadijo E 40 D4
Cardenden GB 5 C10
Cardenete E 47 E9
Cardeñosa E 46 C3
Cardeto I 59 C8
Cardiff GB 13 C8
Cardigan GB 12 A5
Cardigos P 44 E4
Cardinale I 59 B9
Cardito I 62 D5
Cardon RO 155 C5
Cardona E 43 D7
Cardosas P 50 E2
Carei RO 151 B9

Carenas E 41 F8
Carentan F 23 B9
Carentoir F 23 E7
Carevdar HR 149 D7
Carev Dvor MK 168 B5
Cargenbridge GB 5 E9
Cargèse F 37 G9
Carhaix-Plouguer F 22 D4
Caria P 44 D6
Cariati I 61 E7
Caridade P 50 C4
Carife I 60 A4
Carignan F 19 E11
Carignano I 37 B7
Cariñena E 41 F9
Carini I 58 C3
Carinish GB 2 K2
Cariño E 38 A4
Carinola I 60 A1
Carisio I 68 C5
Carisolo I 69 A10
Cârjiţi RO 151 F10
Carland GB 7 C9
Carlanstown IRL 7 E9
Carlantino I 63 D7
Carlat F 29 F11
Carlentini I 59 E7
Carlet E 48 F3
Cârlibaba RO 152 B6
Cârligele RO 153 F10
Carling F 186 C1
Carlingford IRL 7 D10
Carlisle GB 5 F11
Carloforte I 64 E1
Cârlogani RO 160 D4
Cârlomăneşti RO 161 C9
Carlopoli I 59 A9
Carlops GB 5 D10
Carlow D 83 C9
Carlow IRL 9 C9
Carloway GB 2 J3
Carlsberg D 186 C5
Carlton GB 11 F9
Carlton Colville GB 15 C12
Carluke GB 5 D9
Carlux F 29 F8
Carmagnola I 37 B7
Carmanova MD 154 C5
Carmarthen GB 12 B6
Carmaux F 33 B10
Carmena E 46 E4
Cármenes E 39 C8
Carmiano I 61 C10
Carmona E 51 E8
Carmonita E 45 F8
Carmyllie GB 5 B11
Carnac F 22 E5
Carnagh GB 7 D9
Carndonagh IRL 4 E2
Carnew IRL 9 C10
Carnforth GB 10 C6
Carnières F 19 D7
Carnikava LV 135 B8
Carnlough GB 4 F5
Carno GB 10 F4
Carnota I 38 C1
Carnoules F 36 E4
Carnoustie GB 5 B11
Carnoux-en-Provence F 35 D10
Carnteel GB 7 D9
Carnwath GB 5 D9
Carolei I 60 E6
Carolles F 23 C8
Carona I 69 A8
Caronia I 58 C5
C. A. Rosetti RO 155 C5
C. A. Rosetti RO 161 C10
Carosino I 61 C8
Carovigno I 61 B9
Carovilli I 63 D6
Carpaneto Piacentino I 69 D8
Carpegna I 66 E5
Carpen RO 159 E11
Carpenedolo I 66 B1
Carpentras I 35 B9
Carpi I 66 C2
Carpignano Salentino I 61 C10
Carpignano Sesia I 68 B5
Cârpineni MD 154 D2
Cârpinet RO 151 E10
Carpinet I D1
Carpineto Romano I 62 D4
Cârpiniş RO 159 B7
Carpino I 63 D9
Carpinone I 63 D6
Carpio E 40 F1
Carpiquet F 23 B9
Carquefou F 23 F9
Carqueiranne F 36 E4
Carracastle IRL 6 E5
Carracedelo E 39 C6
Carradale East GB 4 D6
Carragh IRL 7 F9
Carraig Airt IRL 7 B7
Carraig na Siuire IRL 9 D8
Carraig Thuathail IRL 8 E6
Carral E 38 B3
Carralevë RKS 163 E10
Carranque E 46 D5
Carrapateira P 50 E2
Carrapichana P 44 C6
Carrara I 69 E9
Carraroe IRL 6 F3
Carrascal del Obispo E 45 C9
Carrascosa E 47 D8
Carrascosa del Campo E 47 D7
Carratraca E 53 C7
Carrazeda de Ansiães P 45 B6
Carrazedo de Montenegro P 38 E5
Carrbridge GB 3 L9
Carreço P 38 E2
Carregado P 50 A2
Carregal do Sal P 44 D5
Carregueiros P 44 E4
Carreira P 44 E3
Carreña E 39 B10
Carreteira P 38 C4
Carriazo E 40 B4
Carrick IRL 6 C5
Carrick IRL 9 D9
Carrickart IRL 7 B7
Carrickfergus GB 4 F5
Carrickmacross IRL 7 E9
Carrickmore GB 4 F3
Carrick-on-Shannon IRL 6 E6
Carrick-on-Suir IRL 9 D8
Carrico P 44 E3
Carrigaholt IRL 8 C3
Carrigallen IRL 7 E7
Carriganimmy IRL 8 E4
Carrigart IRL 7 B7

Carrigkerry IRL 8 D4
Carrig Mhachaire IRL 7 E9
Carrigtohill IRL 8 E6
Carrigtwohill IRL 8 E6
Carrio E 38 B3
Carrión de Calatrava E 54 A5
Carrión de los Céspedes E 51 E7
Carrión de los Condes E 39 D10
Carrizo de la Ribera E 39 C8
Carrizosa E 55 B7
Carronbridge GB 5 E9
Carros F 37 D6
Carrouges F 23 C11
Carrowkeel IRL 4 E2
Carrowkeel IRL 7 B7
Carrowkennedy IRL 6 E3
Carrù I 37 C7
Carryduff GB 7 C11
Carry-le-Rouet F 35 D9
Cars F 28 E4
Carsac-Aillac F 29 F8
Carsluith GB 5 F8
Carsoli I 62 C4
Carspach F 27 E7
Carsphairn GB 5 E8
Carstairs GB 5 D9
Cartagena E 56 F3
Cártama E 53 C7
Cartaxo P 44 F3
Cartaya E 51 E5
Carteleghe F 28 E4
Carteret F 23 B8
Carterton GB 13 B11
Cartes E 40 B3
Cârţişoara RO 152 F5
Cartoceto I 67 E6
Carucedo E 39 D6
Carunchio I 63 D7
Carvalhal P 44 E4
Carvalhal P 50 C2
Carvalho de Egas P 38 F5
Carvalhosa P 38 F3
Carviçais P 45 B7
Carvin F 18 D6
Carvoeira P 44 F2
Carvoeiro P 50 E3
Cáry SK 77 E12
Casabermeja E 53 C8
Casabona I 61 E7
Casa Branca P 50 B3
Casa Branca P 50 B4
Casacalenda I 63 D7
Casagiove I 60 A2
Casaglione F 37 G9
Casa l'Abate I 61 C10
Casalanguida I 63 C6
Casalarreina E 40 C6
Casalbordino I 63 C7
Casalbore I 60 A4
Casalborgone I 68 C4
Casalbuono I 60 C5
Casalbuttano ed Uniti I 69 C8
Casàl Cermelli I 37 B9
Casàl di Principe I 60 A2
Casalecchio di Reno I 66 D3
Casale Monferrato I 68 C5
Casaletto Spartano I 60 C5
Casalfiumanese I 66 D4
Casalgrande I 66 C2
Casalgrasso I 37 B7
Casalmaggiore I 66 C1
Casalnuovo Monterotaro I 63 D8
Casalpusterlengo I 69 C8
Casalvecchio di Puglia I 63 D8
Casàl Velino I 60 C4
Casamassima I 61 B7
Casamozza F 37 F10
Casarabonela E 53 C7
Casarano I 61 C10
Casar de Cáceres E 45 E8
Casar de Palomero E 45 D8
Casarejos E 40 E5
Casares E 39 B7
Casares E 53 D6
Casares de las Hurdes E 45 D8
Casariche E 53 B7
Casarrubios del Monte E 46 D4
Casarsa della Delizia I 73 E6
Casarza Ligure I 37 C10
Casas Altas E 47 D10
Casas Bajas E 47 D10
Casas de Benitez E 47 F8
Casas de Juan Gil E 47 F10
Casas de Juan Núñez E 47 F9
Casas de Lázaro E 55 B8
Casas del Monte E 45 D9
Casas de los Pinos E 47 F8
Casas del Puerto E 56 E2
Casas de Millán E 45 E8
Casas de Reina E 51 C8
Casas de Ves E 47 F10
Casas-Ibáñez E 47 F10
Casasimarro E 47 F8
Casas Novas de Mares P 50 B5
Casasola de Arión E 39 E9
Casatejada E 45 E9
Casatenovo I 69 B7
Casavieja E 46 D3
Cascais P 50 B1
Cascante E 41 D8
Cascante del Río E 47 D10
Cascia I 62 B4
Casciana Terme I 66 E2
Cascina I 66 E2
Cascolevel RO 161 E8
Casebres P 50 B2
Cáseda E 32 E3
Case della Marina I 64 E4
Casei Gerola I 37 A9
Cãşeiu RO 152 C3
Casekow D 84 D6
Casella I 37 B9
Caselle in Pittari I 60 C5
Caselle Torinese I 68 C4
Case Perrone I 61 B7
Caseras E 42 E4
Caserta I 60 A2
Casével P 50 D3
Casével IRL 6 E5
Cashel IRL 6 F3
Cashel IRL 7 B7
Cashel IRL 9 D7
Cashel IRL 9 G7
Cashla IRL 6 F5
Casillas E 46 D3
Casillas de Flores E 45 D7
Casimcea RO 155 D2

Caşin RO 153 E9
Casina I 66 C1
Casinos E 48 E3
Casla IRL 6 F3
Čáslav CZ 77 C8
Casnewydd GB 13 B9
Casola in Lunigiana I 66 D1
Casola Valsenio I 66 D4
Casole d'Elsa I 66 F3
Casoli I 63 C6
Casoria I 60 B2
Caspe E 42 E3
Casperia I 62 C3
Cassà de la Selva E 43 D9
Cassagnes-Bégonhès F 33 B11
Cassaniouze F 29 F11
Cassano allo Ionio I 61 D6
Cassano delle Murge I 61 B7
Cassano Magnano I 69 B6
Cassano Spinola I 37 B9
Cassaro I 59 E6
Cassel F 18 C5
Casseneuil F 33 B7
Casserres E 43 C7
Cassibile I 59 F7
Cassine I 37 B9
Cassino I 62 E5
Cassis F 35 D10
Cassola I 72 E4
Cassuéjouls F 30 F2
Částá SK 146 E4
Castagliona Olona I 69 B6
Castagnaro I 66 B3
Castagneto Carducci I 65 A4
Castagnole delle Lanze I 37 B8
Castagnole Monferrato I 37 B8
Castalla I 56 D3
Castañar de Ibor E 45 E10
Castañares de Rioja E 40 C6
Castanet-Tolosan F 33 C9
Castanheira P 44 C6
Castanheira de Pêra P 44 D4
Castano Primo I 68 B6
Castasegna CH 69 A8
Castejón E 32 F2
Castejón del Puente E 42 D4
Castejón de Monegros E 42 D3
Castejón de Sos E 33 E6
Castejón de Valdejasa E 41 E10
Castelbellino I 67 F7
Castèl Bolognese I 66 D4
Castelbuono I 58 D5
Castelcivita I 60 C4
Castèl d'Ario I 66 B2
Castel de Cabra E 42 F2
Casteldelfino I 36 B6
Castèl del Monte I 62 B5
Castèl del Piano I 65 B5
Castèl del Rio I 66 D4
Castèl di Iudica I 59 D6
Castèl di Lama I 62 B5
Castèl di Lucio I 58 D5
Castèl di Sangro I 62 D6
Casteleiro P 45 D6
Castelfidardo I 67 E8
Castelfiorentino I 66 E3
Castèl Focognano I 66 E4
Castelforte I 62 E5
Castelfranci I 60 B4
Castelfranco di Sopra I 66 E4
Castelfranco di Sotto I 66 E3
Castelfranco Emilia I 66 C3
Castelfranco in Miscano I 60 A4
Castelfranco Veneto I 72 E4
Castèl Frentano I 63 C6
Castèl Gandolfo I 62 D3
Castelginest F 33 C8
Castèl Giorgio I 62 B1
Castèl Goffredo I 66 B1
Castelgrande I 60 B4
Casteljaloux F 33 B6
Castèl Madama I 62 D3
Castèl Maggiore I 66 C3
Castelmassa I 66 B3
Castelmauro I 63 D7
Castelmoron-sur-Lot F 33 B7
Castelnau-Barbarens F 33 C7
Castelnaudary F 33 D9
Castelnau-d'Auzan F 33 C6

Castelnau-de-Médoc F 28 E4
Castelnau-de-Montmiral F 33 C9
Castelnau d'Estréfonds F 33 C8
Castelnau-le-Lez F 35 C6
Castelnau-Magnoac F 33 D7
Castelnau-Montratier F 33 B8
Castelnau-Rivière-Basse F 32 C5
Castelnovo di Sotto I 66 C2
Castelnovo ne'Monti I 66 D1
Castelnuovo Berardenga I 66 F4
Castelnuovo della Daunia I 63 D8
Castelnuovo di Garfagnana I 66 D1
Castelnuovo di Porto I 62 C3
Castelnuovo di Val di Cecina I 66 F2
Castelnuovo Don Bosco I 68 C4
Castelnuovo Rangone I 66 C2
Castelnuovo Scrivia I 37 B9
Castelo Bom P 45 C7
Castelo Branco P 39 F6
Castelo Branco P 44 E6
Castelo de Paiva P 44 B4
Castelo de Vide P 44 F6
Castelo do Neiva P 38 E2
Castelões P 44 B4
Castelplanio I 67 F7
Castelraimondo I 67 F7
Castèl Ritaldi I 62 B3
Castelrotto I 72 C4
Castelsagrat F 33 B7
Castèl San Giovanni I 69 C7
Castèl San Lorenzo I 60 C4
Castèl San Niccolò I 66 E4
Castèl San Pietro Terme I 66 D4
Castèl Sant'Angelo I 62 C3
Castelsantangelo sul Nera I 62 B4
Castelsaraceno I 60 C5
Castelsardo I 64 B2
Castelsarrasin F 33 B8
Castelseras E 42 F3
Casteltermini I 58 D4
Castelu RO 155 E2
Castelverde I 69 C8
Castelvetere in Val Fortore I 60 A3
Castelvetrano I 58 D2
Castèl Viscardo I 62 B2
Castèl Volturno I 60 A1
Castenaso I 66 C3
Castéra-Verduzan F 33 C6
Castetnau-Camblong F 32 D4
Castets F 32 C3
Castiadas I 64 E4
Castiello de Jaca E 32 E4
Castiglioncello I 66 F1
Castiglione dei Pepoli I 66 D3
Castiglione del Lago I 66 F5
Castiglione della Pescaia I 65 B3
Castiglione della Stiviere I 66 B1
Castiglione di Sicilia I 59 D7
Castiglione d'Orcia I 65 A5
Castiglione in Teverina I 62 B2
Castiglione Messer Marino I 63 D6
Castiglion Fiorentino I 66 F4
Castignano I 62 B5
Castilblanco E 45 F10
Castilblanco de los Arroyos E 51 D8
Castiliscar E 32 F3
Castilleja de la Cuesta E 51 E7
Castillejar E 55 D7
Castillejo de Martin Viejo E 45 C7
Castillejo de Mesleón E 40 F4
Castillejo de Robledo E 40 E5
Castillo de Bayuela E 46 D3
Castillo de Garcimuñoz E 47 E8
Castillo de Locubín E 53 A9
Castillon-en-Couserans F 33 E8
Castillon-la-Bataille F 28 F5
Castillonnès F 33 A7
Castilruiz E 41 E7
Cástiони della Presolana I 69 B9
Castións di Strada I 73 E7
Castlebar IRL 6 E4
Castlebay GB 2 L1
Castlebellingham IRL 7 E10
Castleblakeney IRL 6 F6
Castleblayney IRL 7 D9
Castlebridge IRL 9 D10
Castle Carrock GB 5 F11
Castle Cary GB 13 C9
Castlecomer IRL 9 C8
Castleconnell IRL 8 C5
Castlecor IRL 8 D5
Castledawson GB 4 F3
Castlederg GB 4 F1
Castledermot IRL 9 C9
Castle Douglas GB 5 F9
Castleellis IRL 9 D10
Castlefinn IRL 4 F1
Castleford GB 11 D9
Castlegal IRL 6 D6
Castlegregory IRL 8 D2
Castlehill IRL 6 D4
Castleisland IRL 8 D4
Castle Kennedy GB 4 F7
Castlellis IRL 9 D10
Castlemaine IRL 8 D3
Castlemartyr IRL 8 E6
Castleplunket IRL 6 E6
Castlerea IRL 6 E6
Castlereagh GB 7 C11
Castlerock GB 4 E3
Castletown GB 3 H10
Castletown GB 5 F9
Castletown GBM 10 C2
Castletown IRL 8 C6
Castletown Bere IRL 8 E3
Castletownshend IRL 8 E4
Castlewellan GB 7 D11
Castranova RO 160 E4
Castrejón de la Peña E 39 C10
Castres F 33 C10
Castrignano del Capo I 61 D10
Castril E 55 D7
Castrillo de Don Juan E 40 E3
Castrillo de Duero E 40 E3
Castrillo de la Reina E 40 E5
Castrillo de la Vega E 40 E4
Castrillo Tejeriego E 40 E3

Castro E 61 C10
Castrobarto E 40 B5
Castrocalbón E 39 D8
Castro Caldelas E 38 D5
Castrocaro Terme I 66 D4
Castrocontrigo E 39 D7
Castro Daire P 44 C5
Castro dei Volsci I 62 D5
Castro del Río E 53 A8
Castro de Ouro E 38 A5
Castro de Rei E 38 B5
Castrofilippo I 58 E4
Castrogonzalo E 39 E8
Castrojeriz E 40 D3
Castro Laboreiro P 38 D3
Castro Marim P 50 E5
Castromocho E 39 D10
Castromonte E 39 E9
Castronuevo E 39 E8
Castronuño E 39 F9
Castronuovo di Sant'Andrea I 60 C6
Castronuovo di Sicilia I 58 D4
Castropignano I 63 D7
Castropodame E 39 C7
Castropol E 39 A5
Castro-Rauxel D 17 D10
Castroreale I 59 C7
Castro-Urdiales E 40 B5
Castroverde E 38 B5
Castro Verde P 50 D3
Castroverde de Campos E 39 E9
Castrovillari I 60 D6
Castuera E 51 B9
Caţa RO 152 E6
Catadau E 48 F4
Çatalca TR 173 B9
Catalina RO 153 F8
Cataloi RO 155 C3
Catania I 59 E7
Catanzaro I 59 B10
Catanzaro Marina I 59 B10
Catarroja E 48 F4
Cãţcãu RO 152 C3
Cãteasca RO 160 D6
Catenanuova I 59 D6
Caterham GB 15 E8
Cateri F 37 F9
Cathair Dónall IRL 8 E2
Cathair na Mart IRL 6 E3
Cathair Saidhbhín IRL 8 E2
Catherdaniel IRL 8 E2
Catí E 42 G4
Čatići BIH 157 D9
Catignano I 62 C5
Câtina RO 152 D4
Câtina RO 161 C8
Cativelos P 44 C5
Catoira E 38 C2
Caton GB 10 C6
Catral E 56 E3
Cattenom F 20 F6
Catterfeld D 79 E8
Catterick GB 11 C8
Catterline GB 5 B12
Cattolica I 67 E6
Cattolica Eraclea I 58 E3
Cãtunele RO 159 D10
Catus F 33 A8
Cãuaş RO 151 B10
Caudan F 22 E5
Caudebec-lès-Elbeuf F 18 F3
Caudecoste F 33 B7
Caudete E 56 D3
Caudete de las Fuentes E 47 E10
Caudiel E 48 E3
Caudiès-de-Fenouillèdes F 33 E10
Caudry F 19 D7
Caujac F 33 D7
Caulnes F 23 D7
Caulonia I 59 C9
Caumont F 33 D8
Caumont-l'Éventé F 23 B10
Caumont-sur-Durance F 35 C8
Caunes-Minervois F 34 D4
Cauro F 37 H9
Cãuşeni MD 154 D4
Causeway IRL 8 D3
Causeway Head GB 4 E3
Caussade F 33 B9
Cautano I 60 A3
Cauterets F 32 E5
Cava de'Tirreni I 60 B3
Cavadineşti RO 153 E12
Cavaglià I 68 C5
Cavaillon F 35 C9
Cavalaire-sur-Mer F 36 E5
Cavaleiro P 50 D2
Cavalese I 72 D3
Cavallermaggiore I 37 B7
Cavallino I 66 B5
Cava Manara I 69 C7
Cavan IRL 7 E8
Cavanagarven IRL 7 D9
Cavargna I 69 A7
Cavarzere I 66 B5
Cavazzo Carnico I 73 D7
Cave I 62 D3
Cave del Predil I 73 D8
Caveirac F 35 C7
Cavezzo I 66 C3
Cavignac F 28 E5
Cavnic RO 152 B3
Čavle HR 67 B10
Cavour I 68 D3
Cavriago I 66 C2
Cavriglia I 66 E3
Cavtat HR 162 D5
Çavuşköy TR 171 C10
Cawdor GB 3 K9
Cawood GB 11 D9
Cawston GB 15 B11
Caxarias P 44 E3
Çaybaşı TR 177 C9
Çayboyu TR 181 B8
Çayeux-sur-Mer F 18 D4
Çayirdere TR 173 B9
Caylus F 33 B9
Cazalegas E 46 D3
Cazalla de la Sierra E 51 D8
Cazals F 33 A8
Cazals F 33 B10
Cazanuli RO 155 C1
Cazaubon F 32 C5
Cazères E 33 D8
Cazères-Mondenard F 33 B8
Cazilhac F 33 D10
Cazin BIH 156 C4

Cazis CH 71 D8
Cažma HR 149 E7
Cazorla E 55 D7
Cazouls F 29 F8
Cea E 38 D5
Cea E 39 D10
Ceahlãu RO 153 C7
Ceamurlia de Jos RO 155 D3
Ceanannus Mór IRL 7 E9
Ceann Toirc IRL 8 D5
Ceann Trá IRL 8 D2
Ceanu Mare RO 152 D3
Cearsiadar GB 2 J3
Ceathlarlach IRL 9 C9
Ceaucé F 23 D10
Ceauşu de Câmpie RO 152 D5
Céaux-d'Allègre F 30 E4
Cébazat F 30 D3
Cébin CZ 77 D10
Cebolla E 46 E3
Cebreros E 46 D4
Ceccano I 62 D4
Cece I 149 C11
Čečejovce SK 145 F3
Čechtice CZ 77 C7
Čechynce SK 146 E6
Cecina I 66 F2
Ceclavín E 45 E7
Cecuni MNE 163 D8
Cedães P 38 F5
Čedasai LT 135 D10
Cedegolo I 69 A9
Cedeira E 38 A3
Cedillo E 44 E6
Cedillo del Condado E 46 D5
Cedrillas E 48 D3
Cedry Wielkie PL 138 B6
Cedynia PL 84 E6
Cee E 38 C1
Cefa RO 151 D8
Cefalù I 58 C5
Cefn-mawr GB 10 F5
Ceggia I 73 E6
Cegléd H 150 C4
Céglédbercel H 150 C4
Ceglie Messapica I 61 B9
Cegłów PL 141 F5
Ĉegrane MK 163 F10
Cehal RO 151 C10
Cehegín E 55 C9
Cehu Silvaniei RO 151 C11
Ceica RO 151 D9
Ceikiniai LT 135 F12
Ceilhes-et-Rocozels F 34 C5
Ceinos de Campos E 39 D9
Ceintrey F 26 C5
Ceira P 44 D4
Cejč CZ 77 E11
Cejkov SK 145 G4
Cekcyn PL 138 C5
Çekirdekli TR 173 F9
Çekişke LT 134 F7
Ceków-Kolonia PL 142 C5
Celadas E 47 D10
Čeladná CZ 146 B6
Čelákovice CZ 77 B7
Celano I 62 C5
Celanova E 38 D4
Ĉelarevo SRB 158 C4
Celaru RO 160 E4
Celbridge IRL 7 F9
Celeiros P 38 E3
Celenza Valfortore I 63 D7
Celestynów PL 141 F5
Ĉelić BIH 157 C10
Celico I 61 E6
Ĉelinac Donji BIH 157 C7
Celje SLO 148 D4
Cella E 47 D10
Celldömölk H 149 B8
Celle D 79 A7
Celle Ligure I 37 C9
Cellere I 62 C1
Celles B 19 C7
Celles-sur-Belle F 28 C5
Celles-sur-Ource F 25 D11
Cellettes F 24 E5
Cellino Attanasio I 62 B5
Cellole I 62 E5
Ĉelopeci MK 168 B5
Ĉelopek MK 164 F3
Celorico da Beira P 44 C6
Celorico de Basto P 38 F4
Celrà E 43 C9
Ĉeltikçi TR 173 D9
Cembra I 69 A11
Ĉemerno BIH 157 F10
Cempi LV 135 A11
Cénac-et-St-Julien F 29 F8
Cenad RO 150 E6
Cenade RO 152 E4
Cenas LV 134 C7
Cencenighe Agordino I 72 D4
Cendras P 35 B7
Cendrieux F 29 F7
Cenei RO 159 B6
Ceneselli I 66 B3
Cengio I 37 C8
Cenicero E 41 D6
Cenicientos E 46 D4
Ĉenta SRB 158 C5
Centallo I 37 C7
Centelles E 43 D8
Cento I 66 C3
Centola I 60 C4
Centuri F 37 F10
Centuripe I 59 D6
Cepagatti I 62 C6
Cepari RO 160 C5
Ĉepin HR 149 E11
Cepleniţa RO 153 C9
Ĉepovan SLO 73 D8
Ceppaloni I 60 A3
Ceppo Morelli I 68 B5
Ceprano I 62 D5
Ceptura RO 161 C8
Cerami I 58 D5
Ĉeralije HR 149 E9
Cerani BIH 157 C8
Cerano I 68 C6
Ceranów PL 141 E6
Cérans-Foulletourte F 23 E12
Cerasi I 59 C8
Ceraso I 60 C4
Ceraşu RO 161 C8
Cerãt RO 160 E3
Cerauktse LV 135 D8
Ĉeravë AL 168 C4
Cerbãl RO 151 F10

Cerbère F 34 F5
Cercal P 44 F3
Cercal P 50 D2
Čerčany CZ 77 C7
Cercedilla E 46 C4
Cercemaggiore I 63 E7
Cerchezu RO 155 F2
Cerchio I 62 C5
Cercy-la-Tour F 30 B4
Cerda I 58 D4
Cerdanyola del Vallès E 43 E8
Cerdedo E 38 C3
Cerdeira P 44 D5
Cerdon F 25 E7
Cēre LV 134 B5
Cerea I 66 B3
Cered H 147 E9
Ceregnano I 66 B4
Cerekwica PL 85 E13
Cérences F 23 C9
Ceres GB 5 C11
Ceres I 31 E11
Ceresole Reale I 31 E11
Céreste F 35 C10
Céret F 34 F4
Čerević SRB 158 C4
Cerezo de Abajo E 46 B5
Cerezo de Arriba E 40 F4
Cerezo de Riotirón E 40 C5
Cerfontaine B 184 D1
Cergău RO 152 E3
Cergy F 24 B7
Cerhenice CZ 77 B8
Ceriale I 37 C8
Ceriana I 37 D7
Cerignola I 60 A5
Cérilly F 30 B2
Čerín BIH 157 F8
Cerisano I 60 E6
Cerisiers F 25 D9
Cerisy-la-Forêt F 23 B10
Cerisy-la-Salle F 23 B9
Cerizay F 28 B4
Çerkezköy TR 173 B9
Çerkezmüsellim TR 173 B7
Cerklje SLO 73 D9
Cerklje SLO 148 E5
Cerknica SLO 73 E9
Cerkno SLO 73 D8
Cerkwica PL 85 B8
Cermei RO 151 D8
Çermë-Proshkë AL 168 B2
Cermignano I 62 B5
Čërmjan RKS 163 E9
Cerna H 157 B10
Cerna RO 155 C2
Cernache do Bonjardim P 44 E4
Černá Hora CZ 77 D11
Cernat RO 153 F8
Cernătești RO 160 E2
Cernătești RO 161 C9
Cernavodă RO 155 E2
Cernay F 27 E7
Cernay-en-Dormois F 19 F10
Černčice CZ 76 B5
Cernégula E 40 C4
Cernele RO 160 E3
Cernești RO 152 C3
Cernica RO 161 E8
Cernier CH 31 A10
Cernik HR 157 B7
Černilov CZ 77 B9
Cernișoara RO 160 C4
Cernobbio I 69 B7
Cernoleuca MD 153 A11
Černošice CZ 76 C6
Černošín CZ 76 C3
Černilov LV 133 D2
Černovice CZ 77 D7
Černožice CZ 77 B9
Cerová HR 148 E4
Cerovac SRB 159 E6
Cerovak Tušilovički HR 148 F5
Ceroviljani BIH 157 B7
Cerovlje HR 67 B9
Cerovo SK 147 E8
Cerralbo E 45 C7
Cerreto d'Esi I 67 F6
Cerreto di Spoleto I 62 B3
Cerreto Sannita I 60 A3
Cerrigydrudion GB 10 E4
Cërrik AL 168 B2
Cerro al Volturno I 62 D6
Cersay F 28 A5
Cersosimo I 61 C6
Certaldo I 66 E3
Certeju de Sus RO 151 F10
Certești RO 153 E11
Certeze RO 145 H7
Certosa di Pavia I 69 C7
Certosa di Pesio I 37 C7
Ceru-Băcăinți RO 151 F11
Cërujë AL 168 C2
Cerva P 38 F4
Cervaro I 62 E5
Cervatos de la Cueza E 39 D10
Červená Voda CZ 77 B11
Cervenia RO 161 F6
Červená Voda CZ 77 C12
Červený Kostelec CZ 77 B10
Cervera E 42 D6
Cervera de la Cañada E 41 F8
Cervera del Llano E 47 E8
Cervera del Maestre E 48 D5
Cervera de los Montes E 46 D3
Cervera del Río Alhama E 41 D8
Cervera de Pisuerga E 40 C3
Cerveteri I 62 D2
Cervia I 66 D5
Cervignano del Friuli I 73 E7
Cervinara I 60 A3
Červiná Řečice CZ 77 C8
Cervione F 37 G10
Cervo E 38 A5
Cervo I 37 D8
Cervon F 25 F10
Cerzeto I 60 E6
Cesano Boscone I 69 C7
Cesano Maderno I 69 B7
Cesarò I 59 D6
Cesena I 66 D5
Cesenatico I 66 D5
Cesio I 37 C7
Cēsis LV 135 B10
Česká Kamenice CZ 80 E6
Česká Lípa CZ 81 E7
Česká Skalice CZ 77 B10
Česká Ves CZ 77 B12
České Brezovo SK 147 E9
České Budějovice CZ 77 E6
České Meziříčí CZ 77 B10

Český Brod CZ 77 B7
Český Dub CZ 81 E7
Český Krumlov CZ 76 E6
Český Těšín CZ 147 B7
Česljeva Bara SRB 159 D7
Çeşme TR 177 C7
Cespedosa E 45 C9
Cessalto I 73 E6
Cessenon-sur-Orb F 34 D5
Cessole I 37 B8
Cesson F 25 C8
Cesson-Sévigné F 23 D8
Cestas F 28 F4
Čestobrodica SRB 158 F5
Cesuras E 38 B3
Cesvaine LV 135 C12
Cetariu RO 151 C9
Cetate RO 152 C5
Cetate RO 159 E11
Cetatea de Baltă RO 152 E4
Cetățeni RO 160 C6
Cetina E 41 F8
Cetingrad HR 156 B4
Cetinje MNE 163 E6
Ceto I 69 A9
Ceton F 24 D4
Cetona I 62 B1
Cetraro I 60 D5
Ceuta WHAT 53 E6
Ceutí E 56 E2
Ceva I 37 C8
Cevico de la Torre E 40 E3
Cevico Navero E 40 E3
Cevins F 31 D9
Cevio CH 68 A6
Cevizköy TR 173 A8
Čevo MNE 163 D6
Cewice PL 85 B13
Ceyrestre F 35 D10
Ceyzériat F 31 C7
Cezieni RO 160 E4
Chã P 38 E4
Chaam NL 16 F3
Chabanais F 29 D7
Chabeuil F 31 F7
Chabielice PL 143 D7
Chablis F 25 E10
Chabówka PL 147 B9
Chabreloche F 30 D4
Chabris F 24 F6
Chacim P 39 F6
Chagford GB 13 D7
Chagny F 30 B6
Chaïkali GR 174 C4
Chaillac F 29 C8
Chailland F 23 D10
Chaillé-les-Marais F 28 C3
Chailley F 25 D10
Chaintrix-Bierges F 25 C11
Chaironeia GR 175 C6
Chalabre F 33 E10
Chalais CH 31 C12
Chalais F 28 E6
Chalamera E 42 D4
Chalamont F 31 C7
Chalampé F 27 E8
Chalandri GR 175 C8
Chalandritsa GR 174 C4
Chalastra GR 169 C8
Chale GB 13 D12
Chaleix F 29 D7
Châlette-sur-Loing F 25 D8
Chalford GB 13 B10
Chalgrove GB 13 B12
Chaligny F 26 C5
Chalin PL 139 E7
Chalindrey F 26 E3
Chalivoy-Milon F 29 B11
Chalki GR 169 E8
Chalki GR 181 D7
Chalkiades GR 169 F7
Chalkiades GR 174 A2
Chalkida GR 175 C8
Chalkidona GR 169 C8
Chalkio GR 175 D6
Challans F 28 B2
Challerange F 19 F9
Challes-les-Eaux F 31 D8
Chalmoux F 30 B4
Chalonnes-sur-Loire F 23 F10
Châlons-en-Champagne F 25 C11
Chalon-sur-Saône F 30 B6
Châlus F 29 D7
Cham CH 27 F9
Cham D 75 D12
Chamalières F 30 D3
Chamaloc F 31 F7
Chamberet F 29 D9
Chambéria F 31 C8
Chambéry F 31 D8
Chambley-Bussières F 26 B4
Chambois F 23 C12
Chambon-sur-Voueize F 29 C10
Chambord F 24 E6
Chamboulive F 29 E9
Chambray-lès-Tours F 24 F4
Chambry F 19 E8
Chamesson F 25 E12
Chamonix-Mont-Blanc F 31 D10
Chamoux-sur-Gelon F 31 D9
Champagnac F 29 E10
Champagnac-de-Belair F 29 E7
Champagnac-le-Vieux F 30 E4
Champagne-Mouton F 29 C6
Champagne-sur-Seine F 25 D8
Champagney F 26 E6
Champagnole F 31 B8
Champaubert F 25 C10
Champdeniers-St-Denis F 28 C5
Champeix F 30 D3
Champéry CH 31 C11
Champex CH 31 C11
Champforgeuil F 30 B6
Champgenéteux F 23 D11
Champier F 31 E7
Champigné F 23 E10
Champignelles F 25 E9
Champigny F 25 D9
Champlemy F 25 F9
Champlitte F 26 E4
Champniers F 29 D6
Champoléon F 31 F9
Champoluc I 68 B4
Champsecret F 23 C10
Champs-sur-Tarentaine-Marchal F 29 E10
Champs-sur-Yonne F 25 E10
Champ-sur-Drac F 31 E8
Champtoceaux F 23 F9
Chamrousse F 31 E8

Chamusca P 44 F4
Chanac F 34 B5
Chanas F 30 E6
Chança P 44 F5
Chanceaux F 25 E12
Chanceaux-sur-Choisille F 24 F4
Chancelade P 44 F3
Chancelaria P 44 E3
Chandras GR 179 E11
Chañe E 40 F3
Changé F 23 D10
Changé F 23 E12
Changy F 30 C5
Chania GR 178 E6
Chaniotis GR 169 D10
Chantada E 38 C4
Chantelle F 30 C3
Chantilly F 25 B7
Chantonnay F 28 B3
Chanu F 23 C10
Chaource F 25 D11
Chapayevo BG 166 C5
Chapayevka UA 154 A5
Chapel-en-le-Frith GB 11 E8
Chapel-lez-Herlaimont B 182 E1
Chapeltown GB 11 E9
Chapinería E 46 D4
Charakas GR 178 E9
Charavgi GR 169 D6
Charbonnat F 30 B5
Charcenne F 26 F4
Charchilla F 31 C9
Chard GB 13 D9
Chardstock GB 13 D9
Charenton-du-Cher F 29 B11
Charfield GB 13 B10
Chargey-lès-Gray F 26 F4
Charlbury GB 13 B12
Charlemont GB 7 D9
Charleroi B 19 D9
Charlestown IRL 6 E5
Charleville IRL 8 D5
Charleville-Mézières F 19 E10
Charlieu F 30 C5
Charlottenberg S 96 C7
Charlton GB 13 C12
Charlton Kings GB 13 B10
Charly F 25 C9
Charmé F 29 D6
Charmes F 26 D5
Charmes-sur-Rhône F 30 F6
Charmey CH 31 B11
Charmouth GB 13 D9
Charmoy F 25 D9
Charnay-lès-Mâcon F 30 C6
Charny F 25 E9
Charokopeio GR 178 B2
Charolles F 30 C5
Charomkhava BY 133 F3
Charopo GR 169 B9
Chârost F 29 B10
Charquemont F 27 F6
Charrat CH 31 C11
Charrey-sur-Seine F 25 E12
Charrin F 30 B4
Charroux F 29 C6
Charsznica PL 143 F9
Chartres F 24 D5
Charvensod I 31 D11
Charvieu-Chavagneux F 31 D7
Charzyno PL 85 B9
Chassagne-Montrachet F 30 B6
Chasseneuil-sur-Bonnieure F 29 D6
Chasseradès F 35 A6
Chasse-sur-Rhône F 30 D6
Chassigny-Aisey F 26 E3
Chassillé F 23 D11
Chastre B 19 C10
Chastleton GB 13 B11
Cheny F 25 E10
Chepelare BG 165 F10
Chepintsi BG 165 D7
Chepstow GB 13 B9
Chepy F 25 C11
Chera E 48 E3
Chérac F 28 D5
Chéraute F 32 D4
Cherbourg-Octeville F 23 A8
Cheremule I 64 B2
Cherepkivtsi UA 153 A7
Chereshovo BG 161 F8
Cherlenivka UA 133 A8
Cherna BG 155 F1
Cherna Gora BG 166 E4
Chernevo BG 167 C9
Cherni Osŭm BG 165 D10
Cherni Vrŭkh BG 167 E8
Chernivtsi UA 153 A7
Chernogorovo BG 165 E9
Cherno More BG 167 D8
Chernoochene BG 166 F4
Chernyakhovsk RUS 136 D4
Chernyshevskoye RUS 136 D4
Chéroy F 25 D9
Cherskaya RUS 132 F3
Cherso GR 169 B8
Chert E 42 F4
Cherveix-Cubas F 29 E8
Cherven BG 161 F8
Chervena voda BG 161 F8
Cherven Bryag BG 165 C9
Cherventsi BG 167 B8
Cherves-Richemont F 28 D5
Chervona Hreblya UA 154 A4
Chervonoarmiys'ke UA 154 F3
Chervonohrad UA 144 C9
Chesham GB 15 D7
Cheshunt GB 15 D8
Chesley F 25 E11
Chessy-les-Prés F 25 D10
Cheste E 48 F3
Chesterfield GB 11 E9
Chester-le-Street GB 5 F13
Chetani RO 152 E4
Chetrosu MD 153 A11
Chevagnes F 30 B4
Chevanceaux F 28 E5
Chevereșu Mare RO 159 B7
Chevillon F 26 C3
Chevilly F 24 D6
Chevreuse F 24 C7
Chew Magna GB 13 C9
Cheylade F 30 E2
Chezal-Benoît F 29 B10
Chèze F 32 E5
Chiajna RO 161 E8
Chiampo I 66 A3
Chianciano Terme I 62 A1

Chianni I 66 E2
Châtenoy-le-Royal F 30 B6
Chatham GB 15 E10
Châtillon B 19 E12
Châtillon-Coligny F 25 E8
Châtillon-en-Bazois F 30 A4
Châtillon-en-Diois F 35 A9
Châtillon-en-Michaille F 31 C7
Châtillon-la-Palud F 31 D7
Châtillon-sur-Chalaronne F 31 C6
Châtillon-sur-Colmont F 23 D10
Châtillon-sur-Indre F 29 B8
Châtillon-sur-Loire F 25 E8
Châtillon-sur-Marne F 25 B10
Châtillon-sur-Seine F 25 E12
Châtillon-sur-Thouet F 28 B5
Chatte F 31 E7
Chatteris GB 15 C9
Chatton GB 5 D13
Chatuzange-le-Goubet F 31 F7
Chatzis GR 174 E4
Chauchina E 53 B9
Chaudenay F 26 E4
Chaudes-Aigues F 30 F3
Chaudeyrac F 35 A6
Chaudfontaine B 19 C12
Chauffailles F 30 C5
Chauffayer F 31 F9
Chaulnes F 18 E6
Chaumergy F 31 B7
Chaumont F 26 D3
Chaumont-en-Vexin F 18 F4
Chaumont-Porcien F 19 E9
Chaumont-sur-Aire F 26 C3
Chaumont-sur-Loire F 24 F5
Chaunay F 29 C6
Chauny F 19 E7
Chaussin F 31 B7
Chauvigny F 29 B7
Chavanay F 30 E6
Chavanges F 25 C12
Chavanoz F 31 D7
Chavari GR 174 D3
Chavelot F 26 D5
Chaves P 38 E5
Chazelles-sur-Lyon F 30 D5
Cheadle GB 11 F8
Cheb CZ 75 B11
Checa E 47 C9
Chechel'nyk UA 154 A4
Chcjiny PL 143 E9
Chécy F 24 E7
Chedburgh GB 15 C10
Cheddar GB 13 C9
Chef-Boutonne F 28 C5
Chekhpare BG 166 E4
Cheles E 51 B5
Chella E 56 C3
Chełm PL 141 H8
Chełmek PL 143 F7
Chełmiec PL 145 D2
Chełmno PL 138 D5
Chełmno PL 142 B6
Chełmsford GB 15 D9
Chełmża PL 138 D6
Cheltenham GB 13 B10
Chelva E 47 E11
Chemazé F 23 E10
Chémery F 24 F5
Chémery-sur-Bar F 19 E10
Chemillé F 23 F10
Chemin F 31 B7
Cheminon F 25 C12
Chemiré-le-Gaudin F 23 E11
Chemnitz D 80 E3
Chenecey-Buillon F 26 F4
Chénérailles F 29 C10
Cheniménil F 26 D6
Chenôve F 26 F2
Chiari I 69 B8
Chiaromonte I 60 C6
Chiasso CH 69 B7
Chiavari I 37 C10
Chiavenna I 69 A7
Chiché F 28 B5
Chichester GB 15 F7
Chichiș RO 153 F7
Chiclana de la Frontera E 52 D4
Chiclana de Segura E 55 C6
Chieming D 72 A6
Chieri I 72 C4
Chieri I 37 A7
Chiesa in Valmalenco I 69 A8
Chieșd RO 151 C10
Chiesina Uzzanese I 66 E2
Chieti I 63 C6
Chieuti I 63 D8
Chieveley GB 13 C12
Chièvres B 19 C8
Chigwell GB 15 D9
Chiheru de Jos RO 152 D5
Chikhachevo RUS 133 B7
Chilches E 48 E4
Chilcompton GB 13 C9
Chilham GB 15 E10
Chiliile RO 161 C9
Chiliomodi GR 175 D6
Chilleurs-aux-Bois F 24 D7
Chillón E 54 B3
Chilluévar E 55 C6
Chiloeches E 47 C6
Chimay B 19 D9
Chimeneas E 53 B9
Chinanale I 36 B6
Chinchilla de Monte Aragón E 55 B9
Chinchón E 46 D6
Chindrieux F 31 D8
Chinon F 23 F12
Chinteni RO 152 D3
Chiochiș RO 152 D4
Chioggia I 66 B5
Chiojdeni RO 161 B9
Chiojdu RO 161 C8
Chiomonte I 31 E10
Chiona GR 174 C4
Chionata GR 174 C2
Chios GR 177 C7
Chipceren MD 154 E3
Chipiona E 52 C4
Chippenham GB 13 C10
Chipping Campden GB 13 A11
Chipping Norton GB 13 B11
Chipping Ongar GB 15 D9
Chipping Sodbury GB 13 B10
Chippis CH 31 C12
Chiprana E 42 E3
Chiprovtsi BG 165 C6
Chirbury GB 10 F5
Chiren BG 165 B6
Chiriet-Lunga MD 154 E3
Chirivel E 55 D8
Chirk GB 10 F5
Chirnogeni RO 155 F2
Chirnogi RO 161 E9
Chirnside GB 5 D12
Chiroubles F 30 C6
Chirpan BG 166 E4
Chirpăr RO 152 F5
Chirsova MD 154 E3
Chiscani RO 155 C1
Chișcăreni MD 153 B12
Chișcăreni MD 154 C3
Chiselet RO 161 E9
Chișinău MD 154 C3
Chisindia RO 151 E9
Chișineu-Criș RO 151 D8
Chistye-Prudy RUS 136 D3
Chițcani MD 154 D5
Chitcani RO 161 C9
Chitignano I 66 E4
Chitila RO 161 E7
Chiuiești RO 152 C3
Chiuro I 69 A8
Chiusa I 72 C4
Chiusa di Pesio I 37 C7
Chiusaforte I 73 D7
Chiusa Sclafani I 58 D3
Chiusavecchia I 37 D7
Chiusdino I 66 F3
Chiusi I 62 A1
Chiusi della Verna I 66 E4
Chiuza RO 152 C4
Chiva E 48 F3
Chivasso I 68 C4
Chizé F 28 C5
Chlebičov CZ 146 B5
Chlebnice SK 147 C8
Chlebowo PL 81 B7
Chlewiska PL 141 H3
Chłopice PL 144 D6
Chludowo PL 81 A11
Chlumčany CZ 76 C4
Chlumec CZ 80 E5
Chlumec nad Cidlinou CZ 77 B8
Chlum u Třeboně CZ 77 E7
Chmielnik PL 143 E10
Chmielno PL 138 B5
Chmiel Pierwszy PL 144 A6
Chminianske Jakubovany SK 145 F3
Chobienia PL 81 C10
Chobienice PL 81 B9
Choceń CZ 77 B10
Choceń PL 138 F7
Chocholná-Velčice SK 146 D5
Chocianów PL 81 D9
Chocicza PL 81 B12
Chociwel PL 85 D8
Chocz PL 142 C4
Choczewo PL 138 A4
Chodecz PL 138 F7
Chodel PL 141 H6
Chodov CZ 75 B12
Chodów PL 141 F6
Chodów PL 143 B7
Chodzież PL 85 E11
Chojna PL 84 E6
Chojnice PL 85 C13
Chojno PL 81 C12
Chojnów PL 81 D9
Cholet F 28 A4
Chomakovtsi BG 165 C9
Chomelix F 30 E4
Chomérac F 35 A8
Chomutov CZ 76 B4
Chonikas GR 175 D6

Chooz F 19 D10
Chop UA 145 G5
Chora GR 174 E4
Chora GR 175 A8
Chora GR 177 D8
Chora GR 179 B8
Chora GR 179 D9
Chora GR 177 D8
Chorafakia GR 178 D6
Chora Sfakion GR 178 E7
Chorefto GR 169 F9
Chorges F 36 B4
Chorio GR 177 E8
Choristi GR 171 B6
Chorkówka PL 145 D4
Chorley GB 11 D8
Chorna UA 154 B4
Chorna Tysa UA 152 A4
Chornoholova UA 145 F6
Chornomyn UA 154 A4
Chorzele PL 139 D10
Chorzów PL 143 F6
Chorzyna PL 142 D5
Choszczno PL 85 D8
Chotča SK 145 E4
Chotěbořř CZ 77 C9
Chotěšov CZ 76 C4
Chotín SK 149 A10
Chouilly F 25 B11
Chouni GR 174 B4
Chouto P 44 F4
Chouzy-sur-Cisse F 24 E5
Chova P 44 F4
Chove F 26 F4
Choye F 26 F4
Chozas de Abajo E 39 C8
Chrást CZ 76 C4
Chrast CZ 77 C9
Chrastava CZ 81 E7
Chřibská CZ 81 E6
Christchurch GB 13 D11
Christiansfeld DK 86 E4
Christon Bank GB 5 E13
Chropyně CZ 146 C4
Chróścina PL 142 E3
Chrostkowo PL 139 E7
Chroustovice CZ 77 C9
Chrudim CZ 77 C9
Chruślin PL 143 B8
Chruszczobród PL 143 F7
Chrysa GR 171 B7
Chrysafa GR 175 E6
Chryso GR 169 B10
Chrysochorafa GR 169 B9
Chrysochori GR 171 C7
Chrysokellaria GR 178 B2
Chrysoupoli GR 171 C7
Chrzanów PL 143 F7
Chrząstowa Wielka PL 81 D12
Chrząstowice PL 142 E5
Chrzypsko Wielkie PL 81 A10
Chtelnica SK 146 D5
Chuchelná CZ 142 G5
Chudleigh GB 13 D7
Chudoba PL 142 E5
Chulilla E 48 E3
Chulmleigh GB 13 D7
Chuprene BG 165 B6
Chur CH 71 D9
Churchdown GB 13 B10
Church Hill IRL 7 C7
Church Stretton GB 10 F6
Churek BG 165 D8
Churwalden CH 71 D9
Chuzelles F 30 D6
Chvalčov CZ 146 C5
Chvaletice CZ 77 B8
Chvalšiny CZ 76 E6
Chwaszczyno PL 138 B5
Chynadiyeve UA 145 G6
Chyňava CZ 76 B6
Chýnov CZ 77 D7
Chynów PL 141 G4
Chyšky CZ 77 C6

Cill Chomhghaill IRL 7 F10
Cill Chormaic IRL 7 F7
Cill Chuillin IRL 7 F9
Cill Dalua IRL 8 C6
Cill Dara IRL 7 F9
Cill Dhéagláin IRL 7 E10
Cill Droichid IRL 7 F9
Cille Bhrighde GB 2 L2
Cilleros E 45 D7
Cill Mhantáin IRL 7 G10
Cill Mocheallóg IRL 8 D5
Cill na Mallach IRL 8 D5
Cill Orglan IRL 8 D3
Cill Rois IRL 8 C4
Cill Rónáin IRL 6 F3
Cilybebyll GB 13 B7
Cimanes del Tejar E 39 C8
Cimballa E 47 B9
Cimdenieki LV 134 C2
Cimișlia MD 154 D3
Cimolais I 72 D5
Çinarcik TR 173 C11
Cinco Casas E 47 F6
Cinctorres E 42 F3
Cincu RO 152 F5
Cinderford GB 13 B10
Çine TR 181 A8
Ciñera E 39 C8
Cinfães P 44 B4
Cinge TR 177 A9
Cingoli I 67 F7
Cinigiano I 65 B4
Ciniselo Balsamo I 69 B7
Cinn Mhara IRL 6 F3
Cinobaña SK 147 E9
Cinq-Mars-la-Pile F 24 F3
Cinquefrondi I 59 C9
Cintegabelle F 33 D9
Cintrey F 26 E4
Cintruénigo E 41 D8
Ciobăniţa RO 155 E2
Ciobanu RO 155 D1
Ciobiškis LT 137 D10
Ciocănești RO 161 D7
Ciocănești RO 161 E8
Ciocârlia RO 155 E2
Ciocârlia RO 161 D10
Ciochina RO 161 D10
Cìocile RO 161 D8
Cioc-Maidan MD 154 E3
Ciofrângeni RO 160 C5
Cióirtheach IRL 7 F7
Ciolănești RO 160 E6
Ciolpani RO 161 D8
Cionn tSáile IRL 8 E5
Ciorani RO 161 D8
Ciorăşti RO 161 C10
Ciorani RO 161 E7
Cioroiaşi RO 160 E2
Ciorogârla RO 161 E7
Cioroiaşi RO 160 E2
Cioropcani MD 153 C11
Ciortești RO 153 D11
Ciprian Porumbescu RO 153 B8
Cirat E 48 D4
Cirauqui E 32 E2
Cirava LV 134 C2
Circello I 60 A3
Cireşu RO 159 D10
Cireşu RO 161 D10
Cirey-sur-Blaise F 26 D2
Cirey-sur-Vezouze F 27 C3
Ciria E 41 E8
Cirié I 68 C4
Cirigliano I 60 C6
Ciripcău MD 154 A2
Cirkale LV 134 B4
Cirma LV 133 C3
Cirò I 61 E8
Cirò Marina I 61 E8
Çirpi TR 177 C10
Ciacova RO 159 B7
Ciadîr MD 154 D2
Ciadîr-Lunga MD 154 E3
Ciadoux F 33 D7
Ciampino I 62 D3
Cianciana I 58 D3
Ciasna PL 142 E6
Ciążeń PL 142 B4
Cibakháza H 150 D5
Ciborro P 50 B3
Ciboure F 32 D2
Cicagna I 37 C10
Cicârlău RO 151 B11
Cicciano I 60 B3
Cicerale I 60 C4
Čičevac SRB 159 F7
Cicibór Duży PL 141 F8
Ciclova Română RO 159 C8
Čičov SK 149 A9
Cidones E 41 E6
Cidnie RO 160 B4
Ciechanów PL 139 E10
Ciechanowiec PL 141 E7
Ciechocinek PL 138 E6
Cielądz PL 141 G2
Ciempozuelos E 46 D5
Ciepielów PL 141 H4
Ciepłowody PL 81 E11
Cierna nad Tisou SK 145 G5
Čierne SK 147 C7
Cierny Balog SK 147 D9
Cierp-Gaud F 33 E7
Cierznie PL 85 C12
Cieszanów PL 144 C7
Cieszków PL 142 D4
Cieszyn PL 147 B7
Cieutat F 33 D7
Cieux F 29 D8
Cieza E 55 C10
Cifer SK 146 E5
Cıfliq AL 168 E3
Cifuentes E 47 C7
Cigales E 39 E10
Cigliano I 68 C5
Cikó H 149 D11
Cilibia RO 161 C9
Cilieni RO 160 F5
Çilipi HR 162 D5
Çiliżská Radvaň SK 146 F5
Cill Airne IRL 8 D4
Cillas E 47 C9
Cill Chainnigh IRL 9 C5
Cill Charthaigh IRL 6 C5
Cill Chiaráin IRL 6 F3
Cill Choca IRL 7 F9

Cività I 60 D6
Cività Castellana I 62 C2
Civita d'Antino I 62 D5
Civitanova del Sannio I 63 D6
Civitanova Marche I 67 F8
Civitaquana I 62 C5
Civitavecchia I 62 C1
Civitella Casanova I 62 C5
Civitella del Tronto I 62 B5
Civitella di Romagna I 66 D4
Civitella in Val di Chiana I 66 F4

Civitella Roveto I 62 D4
Civray F 29 B10
Civray F 29 C6
Cizer RO 151 C10
Čížkovice CZ 76 B6
Čkyně CZ 76 D5
Clabhach GB 4 B3
Clachan GB 2 L4
Clachan GB 4 C7
Clachan of Glendaruel GB 4 C6
Clachtoll GB 2 J6
Clackmannan GB 5 C9
Clacton-on-Sea GB 15 D11
Cladich GB 4 C6
Clady GB 4 F1
Clady GB 4 F3
Claggan GB 4 B5
Clairac F 33 B6
Clairoix F 18 F6
Clairvaux-les-Lacs F 31 B8
Claix F 31 E8
Clamecy F 25 F10
Clane IRL 7 F9
Clans F 36 C6
Claonadh IRL 7 F9
Claonaig GB 4 D6
Clapham GB 11 C7
Clapham GB 15 C8
Clara IRL 7 F7
Clár Chlainne Mhuiris IRL 6 E5
Clarecastle IRL 8 E5
Claremorris IRL 6 E5
Claret F 35 B10
Claro CH 69 A7
Clary F 19 D7
Clashmore IRL 9 D7
Clashnessie GB 2 J6
Claudy GB 4 F2
Clausnitz D 80 E4
Claußnitz D 80 E3
Clausthal-Zellerfeld D 79 C7
Claut I 72 D6
Clauzetto I 73 D6
Clavering GB 15 D9
Clavier B 19 D11
Clay Cross GB 11 E9
Claydon GB 15 C11
Clayton GB 5 F8
Cleady IRL 8 E3
Cleat GB 3 H11
Cleator Moor GB 10 B4
Clécy F 23 C11
Cléder F 22 C3
Cleethorpes GB 11 D11
Clefmont F 26 D4
Cléguérec F 22 D5
Cleja RO 153 E9
Clelles F 31 F8
Clémency L 20 E5
Clenze D 83 E9
Cleobury Mortimer GB 13 A10
Cléon F 18 F3
Cléon-d'Andran F 35 A8
Cléré-les-Pins F 24 F3
Clères F 18 E3
Clérey F 25 D11
Clermain F 30 C6
Clermont F 18 F5
Clermont F 33 C8
Clermont-en-Argonne F 26 B3
Clermont-Ferrand F 30 D3
Clermont-l'Hérault F 34 C5
Clerval F 26 F6
Clervaux L 20 D6
Cléry-St-André F 24 E6
Cles I 72 D3
Clevedon GB 13 C9
Cleveleys GB 10 D5
Clifden IRL 6 F2
Cliffe GB 15 E9
Cliffoney IRL 6 D6
Clig, RO 153 A11
Clinge NL 16 F2
Clingen D 79 D8
Clion F 29 B8
Clisson F 28 A3
Clitheroe GB 11 D7
Cloch na Rón IRL 6 F3
Clogh GB 4 F3
Clogh IRL 9 C7
Clogh IRL 9 C8
Clogh IRL 9 C10
Cloghan IRL 7 F7
Cloghan IRL 7 F7
Clogheen IRL 8 D7
Clogher GB 7 D8
Clogherhead IRL 7 E10
Cloghy GB 7 D12
Clohars-Carnoët F 22 E4
Clohernagh IRL 9 D8
Cloich na Coillte IRL 8 E5
Clonakilty IRL 8 E5
Clonaslee IRL 7 F7
Clonbern IRL 6 E5
Clonbulloge IRL 7 F8
Clonbur IRL 6 E4
Clondrohid IRL 8 E4
Clondulane IRL 8 D6
Clonea IRL 9 D8
Clonee IRL 7 F10
Cloneen IRL 9 D7
Clones IRL 7 E8
Clonmel IRL 9 D7
Clonmellon IRL 7 E8
Clonoulty IRL 9 C7
Clonroche IRL 9 D9
Clontibret IRL 7 E9
Clonygowan IRL 7 F8
Cloonbannin IRL 8 D4
Cloonboo IRL 6 F4
Cloonfad IRL 6 E5
Cloonfad IRL 6 F6
Cloonkeen IRL 6 E4
Cloppenburg D 17 C10
Closeburn GB 5 E9
Clough GB 7 D11
Cloughjordan IRL 8 C6
Cloughmills GB 4 E4
Cloughton GB 11 C11
Clova GB 5 B10
Clovelly GB 12 D6
Clovullin GB 4 B6
Cloyes-sur-le-Loir F 24 E5
Cloyne GB 8 E6
Cluain Bú IRL 6 D6
Cluain Eois IRL 7 D8
Cluainín IRL 6 D6
Cluain Meala IRL 9 D7
Cluis F 29 B9
Cluj-Napoca RO 152 D3
Clumanc F 36 C4
Clun GB 13 A8
Cluny F 30 C6

Cluses F 31 C10
Clusone I 69 B8
Clydach GB 13 B7
Clydebank GB 5 D8
Clynderwen GB 12 B5
Clyro GB 13 A8
Ćmielów PL 143 E12
Cmolas PL 143 F12
Coachford IRL 8 E5
Coagh GB 4 F3
Coalburn GB 5 D9
Coalisland GB 7 C9
Coalville GB 11 F9
Coaña E 39 A6
Coarnele Caprei RO 153 C10
Coarraze F 32 D5
Coast GB 2 K5
Coatbridge GB 5 D8
Cobadin RO 155 E2
Cobani MD 153 B10
Cobeja E 46 D5
Cobeta E 47 C8
Cobh IRL 8 E6
Cobia RO 160 D6
Coburg D 75 B8
Coca E 46 B3
Cocentaina E 56 D4
Cochem D 21 D8
Cochirleanca RO 161 C10
Cociuba Mare RO 151 D9
Cockburnspath GB 5 D12
Cockenzie and Port Seton GB 5 D11
Cockerham GB 10 D6
Cockermouth GB 5 F10
Cockett GB 12 B7
Cocora RO 161 D10
Cocu RO 160 D5
Cocumont F 32 B6
Codăești RO 153 D11
Code LV 135 D8
Codevigo I 66 B5
Codigoro I 66 C5
Codlea RO 161 B6
Codogno I 69 C8
Codos E 41 F9
Codreanca MD 154 C3
Codroipo I 73 E6
Codrongianos I 64 B2
Codru MD 154 D3
Coesfeld D 17 E8
Coevorden NL 17 C7
Coëx B 28 B2
Cofrentes E 47 F10
Cogealac RO 155 D3
Cogeces del Monte E 40 E3
Coggeshall GB 15 D10
Coggia F 37 G9
Cogîlniceni MD 154 B3
Çöğmen TR 181 C10
Cognac F 28 D5
Cognac-la-Forêt F 29 D8
Cogne I 31 D11
Cognin F 31 D8
Cogolin F 36 E5
Cogollos E 40 D4
Cogollos Vega E 53 B9
Cogolludo E 47 C6
Cogula P 45 C6
Coillan Chollaigh IRL 7 E9
Coimbra P 44 D4
Coimbrão P 44 E3
Coín E 53 C7
Coincy F 25 B9
Coja P 44 D5
Cojasca RO 161 D7
Cojocna RO 152 D3
Čoka SRB 150 F5
Colares P 50 B1
Colayrac-St-Cirq F 33 B7
Colbasna MD 154 B4
Cölbe D 21 C11
Colbitz D 79 B10
Colbordolo I 67 E6
Colceag RO 161 D8
Colchester GB 15 D10
Coldingham GB 5 D12
Colditz D 79 D12
Coldstream GB 5 D12
Coleford GB 13 B9
Coleraine GB 4 E3
Colibași MD 155 B2
Colibași RO 160 D5
Colibași RO 161 E8
Colibița RO 152 C5
Colico I 69 A7
Coligny F 31 C7
Colindres E 40 B5
Colintraive GB 4 D6
Collagna I 66 D1
Collanzo E 39 B8
Collarmele I 62 C5
Collazzone I 62 B4
Collecchio I 66 C1
Collecorvino I 62 B6
Colledara I 62 B5
Collegno I 31 E11
Collesalvetti I 66 E1
Colle Sannita I 60 A3
Collesano I 58 D4
Colletorto I 63 D7
Colliano I 60 B4
Colli a Volturno I 62 D6
Collieston GB 3 L13
Collinas I 64 E2
Collinée F 22 D6
Collinghorst (Rhauderfehn) D 17 B9
Collio I 69 B9
Collioure F 34 C5
Collobrières F 36 E4
Collombey CH 31 C10
Collon IRL 7 E10
Colloney IRL 6 D6
Colmar F 27 D7
Colmars F 36 C5
Colmberg D 75 D7
Colmeal P 44 D5
Colmenar E 53 C8

Colmenar del Arroyo E 46 D4
Colmenar de Montemayor E 45 D9
Colmenar de Oreja E 46 D6
Colmenar Viejo E 46 C5
Colméry F 25 F9
Colmonell GB 4 E7
Colne GB 11 D7
Colobraro I 61 C6
Cologna Veneta I 66 B3
Cologne F 33 C7
Cologno al Serio I 69 B8
Colombelles F 23 B11
Colombey-les-Belles F 26 C4
Colombey-les-Deux-Églises F 25 D12
Colombier CH 31 B10
Colombiès F 33 B10
Colombres E 39 B10
Colomers E 43 C9
Colomiers F 33 C8
Colonești RO 153 D10
Colonești RO 160 D5
Colònia de Sant Jordi E 57 C11
Colònia de Sant Pere E 57 B11
Colonnella I 62 B5
Colorno I 66 C1
Colos P 50 D3
Cólpin D 84 C4
Colquhar GB 5 D10
Colroy-la-Grande F 27 D7
Colsterworth GB 11 F10
Colți RO 161 C8
Coltishall GB 15 B11
Colunga E 39 B9
Colwyn Bay GB 10 E4
Coly F 29 E8
Colyford GB 13 D8
Comacchio I 66 C5
Comana RO 152 F6
Comana RO 155 F2
Comana RO 161 E8
Comana de Sus RO 152 F6
Comandău RO 153 F8
Comănești RO 153 E8
Comares E 53 C8
Comarna RO 153 C11
Comarnic RO 161 C7
Combeaufontaine F 26 E4
Combe Martin GB 12 C6
Comber GB 7 C11
Comberton GB 15 C9
Comblain-au-Pont B 19 D12
Comblanchien F 26 F2
Combles F 18 D6
Combloux F 31 D10
Combourg F 23 D8
Combronde F 30 D3
Comeglians I 73 C6
Comélico Superiore I 72 C6
Comillas E 40 B4
Comines B 182 D2
Comines F 18 C6
Comișani RO 161 D7
Comiso I 59 F6
Comitini I 58 E4
Comloşu Mare RO 150 F6
Commeen IRL 7 C7
Commenailles F 31 B7
Commentry F 30 C2
Commequiers F 28 B2
Commer F 23 D10
Commercy F 26 C4
Como I 69 B7
Cómpeta E 53 C9
Compiano I 37 B11
Compiègne F 18 F6
Compolibat F 33 B10
Comporta P 50 C2
Compreignac F 29 D8
Comps-sur-Artuby F 36 D5
Comrat MD 154 E3
Comrie GB 5 C9
Comunanza I 62 B4
Cona I 66 B5
Conca F 37 H10
Concarneau F 22 E4
Concas I 64 B4
Conceição P 50 E4
Concesio I 69 B9
Concha E 40 B5
Conches-en-Ouche F 24 C4
Concordia Sagittaria I 73 E6
Concorès F 33 A9
Concots F 33 B9
Condat F 30 E2
Condé-en-Brie F 25 B10
Condé-sur-Huisne F 24 D4
Condé-sur-l'Escaut F 182 E3
Condé-sur-Noireau F 23 C10
Condé-sur-Vire F 23 B9
Condino I 69 B10
Condofuri I 59 C8
Condom F 33 C6
Condove I 31 E11
Condrieu F 30 E6
Condrița MD 154 C3
Conegliano I 72 E5
Conflans-en-Jarnisy F 26 B4
Conflans-sur-Lanterne F 26 E5
Conflenti I 59 A9
Confolens F 29 C7
Cong IRL 6 E4
Congaz MD 154 E3
Congdon's Shop GB 12 D6
Congleton GB 11 E7
Congosto E 39 C7
Congosto de Valdavia E 39 C10
Congrier F 23 E9
Conil de la Frontera E 52 D4
Coningsby GB 11 E11
Coniston GB 10 C5
Conlie F 23 D11
Conliège F 31 B8
Conlig GB 4 F5
Connah's Quay GB 10 E5
Connantre F 25 C10
Connaux F 35 B8
Connel GB 4 C6
Connerré F 24 D3
Connolly IRL 8 C4
Connor GB 4 F4
Conon Bridge GB 2 K8
Conop RO 151 E8
Conques F 33 A10
Conques-sur-Orbiel F 33 D10
Conquista E 54 C3
Consandolo I 66 C4
Conselice I 66 C4

Consell E 49 E10
Conselve I 66 B4
Consett GB 5 F13
Constância P 44 F4
Constanța RO 155 E3
Constantí E 42 E6
Constantim P 38 F4
Constantim P 39 E7
Constantina E 51 C6
Constantin Daicoviciu RO 159 B9
Constanzana E 46 C3
Consuegra E 46 F5
Contarina I 66 B5
Contes F 37 D6
Contessa Entellina I 58 D3
Contești RO 161 D7
Contești RO 161 F6
Conthey CH 31 C11
Contigliano I 62 C3
Contis-Plage F 32 B3
Contres F 24 F5
Contrexéville F 26 D4
Controne I 60 B4
Contursi Terme I 60 B4
Contwig D 21 E9
Conty F 18 E5
Conversano I 61 B8
Convoy IRL 7 C7
Conwy GB 10 E4
Conza della Campania I 60 B4
Cookstown GB 4 F3
Coola IRL 6 D6
Coolbaun IRL 6 G6
Coole F 25 C11
Coole IRL 7 E8
Coolmore IRL 6 C6
Coombe Bissett GB 13 C11
Cootehill IRL 7 D8
Copăcel RO 151 D9
Copăcele RO 159 C9
Copăceni MD 153 B10
Copăceni RO 160 D3
Copăcenii de Sus RO 161 E8
Copalnic-Mănăştur RO 152 B3
Copanca MD 154 D5
Copanello I 59 B10
Copceac MD 154 F3
Copertino I 61 C10
Çöpköy TR 173 B6
Copley GB 5 F13
Copons E 43 D7
Copparo I 66 C4
Coppeen IRL 8 E5
Copplestone GB 13 D7
Coppull GB 10 D6
Copşa Mică RO 152 E4
Copythorne GB 13 D12
Corabia RO 160 F4
Cora Chaitlín IRL 8 C5
Cora Droma Rúisc IRL 6 E6
Čoralići BIH 156 C5
Corato I 61 A6
Coray F 22 D4
Corbalán E 47 D11
Corbally IRL 6 D4
Corbasca RO 153 E10
Corbeanca RO 161 D7
Corbeil-Essonnes F 25 C7
Corbeilles F 25 D8
Corbeni RO 160 C5
Corbeny F 19 F8
Corbera E 48 F4
Corbera d'Ebre E 42 E4
Corbi RO 160 C5
Corbie F 18 E6
Corbières CH 31 B11
Corbières F 35 C10
Corbigny F 25 F10
Corbii Mari RO 161 D6
Corbița RO 153 E10
Corbridge GB 5 F12
Corbu RO 153 C8
Corbu RO 155 E3
Corbu RO 160 D5
Corby GB 11 G10
Corcaigh IRL 8 E6
Corcieux F 27 D6
Corcova RO 159 D11
Corcubión E 38 C1
Cordăreni RO 153 B9
Cordemais F 23 F8
Cordenòns I 73 E6
Cordes-sur-Ciel F 33 B9
Córdoba E 53 A7
Cordobilla de Lácara E 45 F8
Corduente E 47 C9
Cordun RO 153 D9
Coreglia Antelminelli I 66 D2
Corella E 41 E8
Coreses E 39 E8
Corești MD 153 B10
Corfe Castle GB 13 D10
Cori I 62 D3
Coria E 45 E7
Coria del Río E 51 E7
Coriano I 66 E6
Corigliano Calabro I 61 D7
Corinaldo I 67 E7
Coripe E 51 F9
Corjeuţi MD 153 A10
Cork IRL 8 E6
Corlăţel RO 159 E10
Corlăţeni RO 153 B9
Corlay F 22 D5
Corlea IRL 7 E7
Corleone I 58 D3
Corleto Perticara I 60 C6
Çorlu TR 173 B8
Cormainville F 24 D6
Cormatin F 30 B6
Cormeilles F 18 F1
Corme Porto E 38 B2
Cormicy F 19 F8
Cormons I 73 E7
Cormontreuil F 20 F7
Cornafulla IRL 6 F6
Cornago E 41 D7
Cornamona IRL 6 E4
Cornaredo I 69 B7
Cornas F 30 F6
Cornăţelu RO 161 D7
Cornau D 17 C10
Cornea RO 159 C9
Corned all'Isarco I 72 D3
Cornedo Vicentino I 69 B11
Cornella-del-Vercol F 34 C5
Cornellà de Llobregat E 43 E8
Cornellà de Terri E 43 C9

Cornellana E 39 B7
Cornereva RO 159 C9
Cornești MD 153 C12
Cornești RO 152 C3
Cornești RO 161 C7
Cornetu RO 161 E7
Corni RO 153 B9
Corni RO 153 F11
Corniglio I 69 E9
Cornimont F 27 E6
Cornu RO 161 C7
Cornuda I 72 E5
Cornudella de Montsant E 42 E5
Cornudilla E 40 C5
Cornu Luncii RO 153 C8
Cornus F 34 C5
Corod RO 153 F11
Corofin IRL 8 C4
Coroieni RO 152 C3
Coroisânmărtin RO 152 E5
Coron F 23 F10
Çorovodë AL 168 C3
Corps F 31 F8
Corps-Nuds F 23 E8
Corral de Almaguer E 47 E6
Corral de Calatrava E 54 B4
Corrales E 39 E8
Corral-Rubio E 55 B10
Corre F 26 E5
Correggio I 66 C2
Corrèze F 29 E9
Corridonia I 67 F8
Corrie GB 4 D6
Corris GB 10 F4
Corr na Móna IRL 6 E4
Corrobert F 25 C10
Corry IRL 6 D6
Corsano I 61 D10
Corseul F 23 D7
Corsham GB 13 C10
Corsico I 69 C7
Corsock GB 5 E9
Cortale I 59 B9
Corte F 37 G10
Cortectoncepción E 51 D7
Corte de Peleas E 51 B6
Cortegada E 38 D3
Cortegana E 51 D6
Cortemaggiore I 69 C8
Cortemilia I 37 B8
Corten RO 155 F2
Corteno Golgi I 69 A9
Corteolona I 69 C8
Cortes E 41 E9
Cortes de Aragón E 42 F2
Cortes de Arenoso E 48 D3
Cortes de Baza E 55 D7
Cortes de la Frontera E 53 C6
Cortes de Pallás E 48 F3
Cortiçadas do Lavre P 50 B3
Cortijo de Arriba E 46 F4
Cortijos Nuevos E 55 C7
Cortina d'Ampezzo I 72 C5
Corton GB 15 B12
Cortona I 66 F4
Coruche I 50 B3
Corullón E 39 C6
Corum RO 152 E6
Corvara in Badia I 72 C4
Corvera E 56 F2
Corwen GB 10 F5
Coryton GB 15 D9
Cosa I 47 C10
Cosâmbești RO 161 D10
Coşăuţi MD 154 A2
Coşbuc RO 152 C4
Cosby GB 11 F9
Coscurita E 41 F7
Coşeiu RO 151 C11
Cosenza I 60 E6
Coşereni RO 161 D9
Coşeşti RO 160 C5
Coshieville GB 5 B9
Cosio di Arroscia I 37 C7
Coslada E 46 D5
Cosmești RO 153 F10
Cosmești RO 161 C7
Cosminele RO 161 C7
Cosne-Cours-sur-Loire F 25 F8
Cosne-d'Allier F 30 C2
Coşniţa MD 154 C5
Cosoleto I 59 C8
Coşoveni RO 160 E3
Cossato I 68 B5
Cossé-le-Vivien F 23 E10
Cossoine I 64 C2
Cossonay CH 31 B10
Costacciaro I 67 F6
Costache Negri RO 153 F11
Cozzano F 37 H10
Craanford IRL 9 C10
Crăciunelu de Jos RO 152 E3
Crăciunești RO 152 E5
Cracow I 61 C6
Craco I 61 C6
Craidorolţ RO 151 B10
Craig GB 2 L6
Craigavad GB 4 F5
Craigavon GB 7 D10
Craigellachie GB 3 L10
Craignure GB 4 C6
Crail GB 5 C11
Crailsheim D 75 D7
Craiova RO 160 E3
Craiva RO 151 D8
Cramlington GB 5 E13
Cranagh GB 4 F2
Cranford IRL 7 B7
Cran-Gevrier F 31 D9
Crângu RO 160 F6
Crângurile RO 160 D6
Cranleigh GB 15 E8
Crans-sur-Sierre CH 31 C11
Craon F 23 E10
Craonne F 19 F8
Craponne-sur-Arzon F 30 E4
Crask Inn GB 2 J7
Crasna RO 151 C11
Crasna RO 160 C3
Crasnoe MD 154 D5
Crathie GB 5 A10
Crato P 44 F5
Cravagliana I 68 B5
Cravant F 25 E10
Craven Arms GB 13 A9
Crawfordjohn GB 5 E9
Crawfordsburn GB 4 F5
Crawley GB 15 E8
Creaca RO 151 C11
Creagh IRL 8 E4

Couëron F 23 F8
Couflens F 33 E8
Coufouleux F 33 C9
Couiza F 33 E10
Coulaines F 23 D12
Coulanges-la-Vineuse F 25 E10
Coulanges-sur-Yonne F 25 E10
Coulaures F 29 E7
Couleuvre F 30 B2
Coullons F 25 E7
Coulmier-le-Sec F 25 E11
Coulmiers F 24 E6
Coulogne F 15 F12
Coulombiers F 29 C6
Coulombs F 24 C6
Coulommiers F 25 C9
Coulonges-sur-l'Autize F 28 C4
Coulounieix-Chamiers F 29 E7
Coulport GB 4 C7
Coupar Angus GB 5 B10
Couptrain F 23 D11
Coura P 38 E2
Courcelles B 182 E4
Courcelles-Chaussy F 26 B5
Courcelles-sur-Nied F 186 C1
Courchaton F 26 E6
Courchevel F 31 E10
Cour-Cheverny F 24 E5
Courcité F 23 D11
Corçon F 28 C4
Courcy F 19 F9
Courgains F 23 D12
Courgenay CH 27 F7
Courgenay F 25 D10
Courlay F 28 B4
Courmayeur I 31 D10
Courmelles F 19 F7
Cournon-d'Auvergne F 30 D3
Courpière F 30 D4
Courrendlin CH 27 F7
Courrensan F 33 C6
Courrières F 182 E1
Coursac F 29 E7
Coursan F 34 D5
Coursegoules F 36 D6
Courseulles-sur-Mer F 23 B11
Cours-la-Ville F 30 C5
Courson-les-Carrières F 25 E10
Court CH 27 F7
Courtalain F 24 D5
Courtelary CH 27 F7
Courtenay F 25 D9
Courthézon F 35 B8
Courtmacsherry IRL 8 E5
Courtomer F 24 C3
Courtown IRL 9 C10
Courtrai B 19 C7
Courtrai F 182 D2
Cousances-les-Forges F 26 C3
Coussac-Bonneval F 29 D8
Coussay-les-Bois F 29 B7
Coussegrey F 25 E11
Coussey F 26 D4
Coustouges F 34 C5
Coutances F 23 B9
Couterne F 23 C11
Couvet CH 31 B10
Couvin B 19 D10
Couze-et-St-Front F 29 F7
Couzeix F 29 D8
Covaleda E 41 F7
Covarrubias E 40 D5
Covasna RO 153 F8
Cove GB 2 K5
Cove Bay GB 3 L12
Coventry GB 13 A11
Covilhã P 44 D6
Cowbit GB 11 F11
Cowbridge GB 5 C10
Cowdenbeath GB 5 C10
Cowes GB 13 D12
Cox F 56 E3
Cox F 33 C8
Coxheath GB 15 E9
Coxhoe GB 5 F13
Coylumbridge GB 3 L9
Cózar E 55 B6
Cozes F 28 D4
Cozești RO 160 C4
Cozieni RO 161 C9
Cozmești RO 153 D11
Cozzano F 37 H10

Creagorry GB 2 L2
Creamhghort IRL 7 B7
Créances F 23 B8
Crécente E 38 D3
Crêches-sur-Saône F 30 C6
Crécy-en-Ponthieu F 18 D4
Crécy-la-Chapelle F 25 C8
Crécy-sur-Serre F 19 E8
Credenhill GB 13 A9
Crediton GB 13 D8
Creeslough IRL 7 B7
Creevagh IRL 6 D4
Creggan GB 4 F2
Creggan GB 7 D9
Cregganbaun IRL 6 E3
Creggs IRL 6 E6
Creglingen D 75 D7
Cregneash GBM 10 C2
Créhange F 186 C2
Creil F 18 F5
Creil NL 16 C5
Creissels F 34 B5
Crema I 69 C8
Cremeaux F 30 D4
Crémenes E 39 C9
Crémieu F 31 D7
Cremlingen D 79 B8
Cremona I 69 C9
Črenšovci SLO 148 C6
Créon F 28 F5
Crepaja SRB 158 C6
Crépey F 26 D4
Crépy F 19 E8
Crépy-en-Valois F 18 F6
Cres HR 67 C9
Crescentino I 68 C5
Crespina I 66 E2
Crespino I 66 C4
Crespos E 46 C3
Cressensac F 29 E9
Crest F 31 F7
Creswell GB 11 E9
Cretas E 42 F4
Créteil F 25 C7
Crețești RO 153 D11
Crețeni RO 160 D4
Creußen D 75 C10
Creutzwald F 21 F7
Creuzburg D 79 D7
Crevalcore I 66 C3
Crevant F 29 C9
Crévéchamps F 26 C5
Crèvecœur-le-Grand F 18 E5
Crevedia RO 161 D7
Crevedia Mare RO 161 E7
Crevenicu RO 161 E7
Crevillente E 56 E3
Crevoladossola I 68 A5
Crewe GB 10 E7
Crewkerne GB 13 D9
Crianlarich GB 4 C7
Cricău RO 152 E3
Criccieth GB 10 F3
Criciova RO 159 B9
Crickhowell GB 13 B8
Cricklade GB 13 B11
Cricova MD 154 C3
Crieff GB 5 C9
Criel-sur-Mer F 18 D3
Crikvenica HR 67 B10
Crimmitschau D 79 E11
Crimond GB 3 K13
Crinan GB 4 C5
Cringleford GB 15 B11
Crinitz D 80 C5
Cripán E 41 D7
Cripp's Corner GB 15 F10
Criquetot-l'Esneval F 18 E1
Crișcior RO 151 E10
Crișeni RO 151 C11
Crispiano I 61 B8
Crissolo I 31 F11
Cristești RO 152 D4
Cristești RO 153 B9
Cristești RO 153 C9
Cristian RO 152 F4
Cristian RO 161 B6
Cristinești RO 153 A8
Criștioru de Jos RO 151 E10
Cristóbal E 45 D9
Cristolț RO 151 C11
Cristuru Secuiesc RO 152 E6
Criuleni MD 154 C4
Criva MD 153 A9
Crivitz D 83 C11
Crkvice HR 67 D8
Crkvice BIH 157 F11
Crkvice HR 163 D6
Crkvina BIH 157 B9
Crkvine SRB 163 C9
Crljivica BIH 156 D5
Črmošnice SLO 73 E11
Črna SLO 73 D10
Crna Bara SRB 150 F5
Crna Bara SRB 158 D3
Crnac HR 149 E9
Crnaja SRB 159 C9
Crna Trava SRB 164 D5
Crnča SRB 158 E3
Crni Lug BIH 156 D6
Crni Lug HR 67 B10
Crnjelovo BIH 157 C11
Crnkovci HR 149 E10
Crnoklište SRB 164 C5
Črnomelj SLO 148 E4
Crock D 75 B8
Crocketford GB 5 E9
Crockets Town IRL 6 D4
Crockmore IRL 7 D7
Crocmaz MD 154 E5
Crocq F 29 D10
Crodo I 68 A5
Crofty GB 12 B6
Croghan IRL 6 E6
Crognaleto I 62 B4
Croisilles F 18 D6
Croithlí IRL 6 B6
Crolles F 31 E8
Crolly IRL 6 B6
Cromadh IRL 8 C5
Cromarty GB 3 K8
Cromer GB 15 B11
Cromhall GB 13 B10
Cronat F 30 B4
Crook GB 5 F13
Crookham GB 5 D12
Crookhaven IRL 8 F3
Crookstown IRL 8 E5
Croom IRL 8 C5
Cropalati I 61 D7
Cropani I 59 B10
Crosbost GB 2 J4

Crosby GB 10 E5
Crosia I 61 D7
Cross IRL 6 E4
Crossaig GB 4 D6
Crossakeel IRL 7 E8
Cross Barry IRL 8 E5
Crosscanonby GB 5 F10
Crossdoney IRL 7 E8
Crossgar GB 7 D11
Crossgare GB 4 E3
Crossgates GB 13 A8
Crosshands GB 5 D8
Crosshaven IRL 8 E6
Crosshill GB 4 E7
Cross Inn GB 12 A6
Cross Keys IRL 7 E9
Crossmaglen GB 7 D9
Crotone I 61 E8
Crots F 36 B4
Crottendorf D 76 B3
Croughton GB 13 B12
Croutelle F 29 B6
Crouy F 19 F7
Crouy-sur-Ourcq F 25 B9
Crowborough GB 15 E9
Crowland GB 11 F11
Crowle GB 11 D10
Crowthorne GB 15 E7
Croy GB 3 K8
Croyde GB 12 C6
Crozant F 29 C9
Crozes-Hermitage F 30 E6
Crozon F 22 D3
Cruas F 35 A8
Crucea RO 153 C7
Crucea RO 155 D2
Crucișor RO 151 B11
Crucoli I 61 E7
Cruden Bay GB 3 L13
Cruglic MD 154 C4
Crumlin GB 4 F4
Cruseilles F 31 C9
Crușeț RO 160 D3
Crusheen IRL 8 C5
Crusnes F 20 F5
Cruzy F 34 D4
Cruzy-le-Châtel F 25 E11
Crvenka SRB 158 B3
Crymych GB 12 B5
Csabacsőd H 150 D6
Csabrendek H 149 B8
Csákánydoroszló H 149 C7
Csákberény H 149 B10
Csákvár H 149 B10
Csanádapáca H 151 D6
Csanádpalota H 150 E6
Csány H 150 B4
Csanytelek H 150 D5
Császár H 149 A10
Császártöltés H 150 E3
Csátalja H 150 E2
Csávoly H 150 E3
Csécse H 147 F9
Csemő H 150 C4
Csengele H 150 D4
Csenger H 151 B10
Csengőd H 150 D3
Csépa H 150 D5
Csepreg H 149 B7
Cserépfalu H 145 H2
Cserhátsurány H 147 F8
Cserkeszőlő H 150 D5
Csernely H 145 G1
Csesztreg H 149 C7
Csetény H 149 B9
Csévharaszt H 150 C3
Csikéria H 150 E3
Csókakő H 149 B10
Csökmő H 151 C7
Csököly H 149 D9
Csokonyavisonta H 149 D8
Csokvaomány H 145 G1
Csolnok H 149 A11
Csólyospálos H 150 E4
Csongrád H 150 D5
Csopak H 149 C9
Csór H 149 B10
Csorna H 149 A8
Csörnyeföld H 149 D7
Csorvás H 150 D6
Csősz H 149 B10
Csót H 149 B9
Csurgó H 149 D8
Cuacos de Yuste E 45 D9
Cuadros E 39 C8
Cualedro E 38 E4
Cuarte de Huerva E 41 E10
Cuba P 50 C4
Cubalhão P 38 D3
Cubells E 42 D5
Cubjac F 29 E7
Cubla E 47 D10
Cubo de Bureba E 40 C5
Cubo de la Solana E 41 E7
Cubolta MD 153 B12
Cubzac-les-Ponts F 28 F5
Cuca RO 153 F11
Cuca RO 160 D5
Cucalón E 47 B10
Cucerdea RO 152 E4
Cuci RO 152 E4
Cuckfield GB 15 E8
Cucuron F 35 C9
Cucuteni RO 153 C9
Cudalbi RO 153 F11
Cudillero E 39 A7
Čudnići BIH 157 D8
Cudos F 32 B5
Cuéllar E 40 F3
Cuenca E 47 D8
Cuenca de Campos E 39 D9
Cuers F 36 E4
Cuerva E 46 E4
Cueva de Agreda E 41 E8
Cuevas Bajas E 53 B8
Cuevas de Almanzora E 55 E9
Cuevas del Becerro E 53 C6
Cuevas del Campo E 55 D7
Cuevas de San Clemente E 40 D4
Cuevas de San Marcos E 53 B8
Cuevas Labradas E 42 G1
Cuffley GB 15 D8
Cugand F 28 A3
Cuges-les-Pins F 35 D10
Cugir RO 151 F11
Cuglieri I 64 C2
Cugnaux F 33 C8
Cuguen F 23 D8
Cuhureștii de Sus MD 154 B3
Cuijk NL 16 E5
Cúil an tSúdaire IRL 7 F8
Cuiseaux F 31 C7
Cuise-la-Motte F 18 F7
Cuisery F 31 B6
Cujmir RO 159 E10
Çukë AL 168 E3
Çukuryurt TR 173 B8
Culan F 29 B10
Culciu RO 151 B11
Culdaff IRL 4 E2
Culdrain GB 3 L11
Culemborg NL 16 E4
Culjković SRB 158 D4
Culla E 48 D4
Cullahill IRL 9 C8
Cúllar-Baza E 55 D7
Cullen GB 3 K11
Cullera E 48 F4
Cullivoe GB 3 D14
Cullompton GB 13 D8
Cully CH 31 C10
Cullybackey GB 4 F4
Cullyhanna GB 7 D9
Culmstock GB 13 D8
Culnaknock GB 2 K4
Culoz F 31 D8
Culswick GB 3 E13
Cumbernauld GB 5 D9
Cumbres de San Bartolomé E 51 C6
Cumbres Mayores E 51 C6
Cumeada P 50 E3
Cumiana I 31 F11
Cumieira P 38 F4
Cuminestown GB 3 K12
Cumlosen D 83 D11
Cumnock GB 5 E8
Cumpăna RO 155 E3
Cunault F 23 F11
Cunegès F 29 F6
Cuneo I 37 C7
Cunewalde D 81 D7
Cunfin F 25 D12
Cungrea RO 160 D4
Cunha P 44 C6
Cunicea MD 154 B3
Čuništa BIH 157 D10
Cunit E 43 E7
Cunningsburgh GB 3 E14
Cuntis E 38 C2
Cuorgnè I 68 C4
Cupar GB 5 C10
Cupcina MD 153 A10
Cupello I 63 C7
Cupra Marittima I 62 A5
Cupramontana I 67 F7
Ćuprija SRB 159 F7
Cupșeni RO 152 B3
Cuq-Toulza F 33 C9
Curățele RO 151 D9
Curcani RO 161 E9
Curcuris I 64 D2
Cureggio I 68 B5
Cureșnița MD 153 A12
Curgy F 30 B5
Curinga I 59 B9
Curon Venosta I 71 D11
Curracloe IRL 9 D10
Curraghroe IRL 6 E6
Curragh West IRL 6 E5
Currás E 38 C2
Curry IRL 6 E5
Curry Rivel GB 13 C9
Cursi I 61 C10
Curtea RO 151 F9
Curtea de Argeș RO 160 C5
Curtici RO 151 E7
Curtișoara RO 160 E4
Curtuișeni RO 151 B9
Čurug SRB 158 C5
Cusano Mutri I 60 A3
Cushendall GB 4 E4
Cushendun GB 4 E4
Cushina IRL 7 F8
Cussac F 29 D7
Cusset F 30 C3
Cussy-les-Forges F 25 F11
Custines F 26 C5
Custonaci I 58 C2
Cutigliano I 66 D2
Cutro I 61 E7
Cutrofiano I 61 C10
Cuxac-Cabardès F 33 D10
Cuxac-d'Aude F 34 D4
Cuxhaven D 17 A11
Cuzăplac RO 151 D11
Cuza Vodă RO 161 E10
Cuzmin MD 154 A3
Cuzorn F 33 A7
Cvikov CZ 81 E7
Cwmafan GB 13 B7
Cwmbrân GB 13 B8
Cybinka PL 81 B7
Cybowo PL 85 D9
Cychry PL 85 E7
Cyców PL 141 H8
Cydweli GB 12 B6
Cynghordy GB 13 A7
Cynwyl Elfed GB 12 B6
Cyprianka PL 138 E7
Cysoing F 182 D2
Czacz PL 81 B11
Czajków PL 142 D5
Czaplinek PL 85 C10
Czarna PL 143 F11
Czarna PL 144 C5
Czarna Białostocka PL 140 D8
Czarna Dąbrówka PL 85 B13
Czarna Górna PL 145 E6
Czarna Woda PL 138 C5
Czarnca PL 143 E8
Czarne PL 85 C11
Czarnia PL 139 D11
Czarnków PL 85 E11
Czarnocin PL 143 F10
Czarnów PL 81 A7
Czarnowąsy PL 142 E4
Czarnożyły PL 142 D6
Czarny Bór PL 81 E10
Czarny Dunajec PL 147 C9
Czastary PL 142 D5
Czaszyn PL 145 E5
Czchów PL 144 D2
Czechowice-Dziedzice PL 147 B8
Czechy PL 85 C11
Czechy PL 143 C6
Czekarzewice PL 143 D12
Czeladź PL 143 F7
Czemierniki PL 141 G7
Czempiń PL 81 B11
Czeremcha PL 141 E8
Czermin PL 142 C4
Czermno PL 141 H2
Czernica PL 81 D12
Czernice Borowe PL 139 D10
Czernichów PL 143 G8
Czernichów PL 147 B8
Czerniejewo PL 85 F12
Czerniewice PL 141 G2
Czernikowo PL 138 E6
Czernina PL 81 C11
Czersk PL 138 C4
Czerwieńsk PL 81 B8
Czerwin PL 139 E12
Czerwińsk nad Wisłą PL 139 F9
Czerwionka-Leszczyny PL 142 F6
Czerwonak PL 81 B11
Czerwone PL 139 D12
Czestków PL 143 C7
Częstochowa PL 143 E7
Czeszów PL 81 D12
Człopa PL 85 D10
Człuchów PL 85 C12
Czmoń PL 81 B12
Czorsztyn PL 145 E1
Czosnów PL 139 F10
Czudec PL 144 D4
Czyże PL 141 E8
Czyżew-Osada PL 141 E6

D

Daaden D 185 C8
Dăbâca RO 152 D3
Dabar HR 156 C3
Dabar HR 156 E6
Dabas H 150 C3
Dabel D 83 C11
Dąbie PL 81 B8
Dąbie PL 141 G6
Dąbie PL 142 B6
Dąbki PL 85 B10
Dabo F 27 C7
Daborgrad BIH 157 C9
Dabrac BIH 157 D7
Dabravolya BY 140 E10
Dabrica BIH 157 F9
Dąbroszyn PL 81 A7
Dąbroszyn PL 142 B5
Dąbrowa PL 138 E4
Dąbrowa PL 142 E4
Dąbrowa PL 142 E4
Dąbrowa Białostocka PL 140 C8
Dąbrowa Biskupia PL 138 E6
Dąbrowa Chełmińska PL 138 D5
Dąbrowa Górnicza PL 143 F7
Dąbrowa Tarnowska PL 143 F10
Dąbrowa Zielona PL 143 E8
Dąbrowice PL 141 G2
Dąbrowice PL 143 B7
Dąbrówka Wielka PL 143 C7
Dąbrówka Wielkopolska PL 81 B9
Dąbrówno PL 139 D9
Dăbuleni RO 160 F4
Dabyeya BY 133 F7
Dachau D 75 F9
Dachnów PL 144 C7
Dachrieden D 79 D7
Dachwig D 79 D8
Dačice CZ 77 D8
Dacre GB 5 F11
Dad H 149 A10
Dadia GR 171 B10
Dådran S 103 E10
Dăeni RO 155 D2
Dăești RO 160 C4
Dåfjord N 112 D3
Dafnes GR 174 C4
Dafni GR 171 D6
Dafni GR 174 D5
Dafni GR 175 C8
Dafni GR 175 F6
Dág H 149 A11
Daganzo de Arriba E 46 C6
Dağardi TR 173 F11
Dagâța RO 153 D10
Dagda LV 133 D3
Dagebüll D 82 A5
Dağkizilca TR 177 C9
Daglan F 29 F8
Daglösen S 97 C11
Dagmersellen CH 27 F8
Dağpinar TR 181 B8
Dagsmark FIN 122 F7
Dahlem D 21 D7
Dahlen D 80 D4
Dahlenburg D 83 D9
Dahlhausen D 183 C10
Dahme D 80 C4
Dahme D 83 B10
Dahn D 27 B8
Dähre D 83 E9
Daia RO 161 F7
Daia Română RO 152 E3
Daikanberg S 107 A10
Daikanvik S 107 A10
Dailly GB 4 E7
Daimiel E 46 F5
Daimonia GR 178 B4
Daingean IRL 7 F8
Daingean Uí Chúis IRL 8 D2
Dainville F 18 D6
Dainville-Bertheléville F 26 D4
Dairsie GB 5 C11
Daknam B 182 C3
Đakovo HR 149 F10
Dal N 95 B14
Dal S 107 E13
Đala SRB 150 E5
Dalaas A 71 C10
Dalabrog GB 2 L2
Dalaman TR 181 C9
Dalarö S 93 A12
Dala Rostock S 91 B11
Dalåsen S 102 A7
Dalasjö S 107 B11
Dalbe LV 135 C7
Dalbeattie GB 5 F9
Dalberg-Wendelstorf D 83 C10
Dalboșet RO 159 D8
Dalby DK 86 D7
Dalby DK 87 E10
Dalby GBM 10 C2
Dalby S 87 D12
Dalbyn S 103 D9
Dalbyover DK 86 B6
Däldenäs S 92 A4
Dale GB 9 E12
Dale N 90 B3
Dale N 100 D2
Dale N 100 E3
Dale N 111 C11
Daleiden D 20 D6
Dalen N 90 A5
Dalen N 94 D7
Dalen NL 17 C7
Daleszyce PL 143 E10
Dalfors S 103 D9
Dalfsen NL 16 C6
Dalgety Bay GB 5 C10
Dalham GB 15 C10
Dalhem B 19 C12
Dalhem S 93 D13
Dalholen N 101 B11
Dalías E 55 F7
Dalików PL 143 C7
Dalj HR 157 B10
Dalkarlsberg S 97 D12
Dalkeith GB 5 D10
Dalkey IRL 7 F10
Dallas GB 3 K10
Dallgow D 80 A4
Dall Villaby DK 86 B5
Dalmally GB 4 C7
Dalmand H 149 D10
Dalmellington GB 5 E8
Dalmine I 69 B8
Dalmose DK 87 E8
Dalovice CZ 76 B3
Dalry GB 4 D7
Dalrymple GB 4 E7
Dalsbruk FIN 126 E8
Dalsbygda N 101 A14
Dalselv N 108 D6
Dalsjöfors S 91 D13
Dals Långed S 91 B11
Dalstein F 20 F6
Dalston GB 5 F11
Dalstorp S 91 D14
Dalstuga S 103 D10
Dalton-in-Furness GB 10 C5
Daluis F 36 C5
Dalum S 91 D13
Dalur FO 2 B3
Dàlvadas FIN 113 D17
Dalwhinnie GB 5 B8
Dalyan TR 181 C9
Dalyokiya BY 135 F13
Dalystown IRL 6 F6
Damachava BY 141 G9
Damas-aux-Bois F 26 D5
Damasi GR 169 E7
Damaskinia GR 168 D5
Damasławek PL 85 E13
Damazan F 33 B6
Dambach-la-Ville F 186 E3
Dambaslar TR 173 B7
Dambeck D 83 D11
Dâmbovicioara RO 160 C6
Damelevières F 26 C5
Damerstown IRL 9 C8
Damery F 25 B10
Damës AL 168 C2
Damgan F 22 E6
Damhead GB 4 E3
Damhliag IRL 7 E10
Dămienești RO 153 D9
Damigny F 23 D12
Damjan RKS 163 E10
Dammarie F 24 D6
Dammartin-en-Goële F 25 B8
Damme B 19 B7
Damme D 17 C10
Damnica PL 85 B12
Damno PL 85 A12
Damp D 83 A7
Dampierre F 26 F4
Dampierre-sur-Linotte F 26 E5
Dampierre-sur-Salon F 26 E4
Damprichard F 27 F6
Damshagen D 83 C10
Damsholte DK 87 F10
Dämsta S 107 E13
Dămuc RO 153 D7
Damüls A 71 C9
Damvant CH 27 F6
Damville F 24 C5
Damvillers F 19 F11
Damwoude NL 16 B6
Damyanovo BG 165 D10
Danaçali TR 173 E10
Danakos GR 177 E6
Danamandira TR 173 B9
Danasjö S 109 E12
Dănciulești RO 160 D3
Dăneasa RO 160 E5
Daneș RO 152 E5
Danesfort IRL 7 E7
Dănești RO 153 D7
Dănești RO 153 D11
Dănești RO 160 D2
Danețí RO 160 F4
Dångebo S 89 B8
Dângeni RO 153 B9
Dangé-St-Romain F 29 B7
Danholn S 103 E10
Dănicei RO 160 D4
Daniec PL 142 E5
Danilovgrad MNE 163 D7
Dänischenhagen D 83 B8
Danişment TR 173 E8
Danjoutin F 27 E6
Dankerode D 79 C9
Danndorf D 79 B8
Dannemare DK 83 A10
Dannemarie F 27 E7
Dannemora S 99 B9
Dannenberg (Elbe) D 83 D10
Dannenwalde D 84 D4
Dány H 150 B4
Daon F 23 E10
Daoulas F 22 D3
Darabani RO 153 A9
Dărăști Ilfov RO 161 E8
Darbėnai LT 134 D2
Dar Ben Karricha el Behri MA 53 E6
Darby's Bridge IRL 8 D2
Dar Chaoui MA 52 E5
Darda HR 149 E11
Dardesheim D 79 C8
Dardhas AL 168 C4
Darè I 69 A10
Darfo Boario Terme I 69 B9
Dargun D 83 C13
Darica TR 173 D8
Darici TR 173 F10
Dârjiu RO 152 E6
Darkley GB 7 D9
Darlington GB 11 B8
Dârlos RO 152 E4
Darłówko PL 85 B10
Darłowo PL 85 B10
Dărmănești RO 153 B8
Dărmănești RO 153 E8
Dârmănești RO 160 C5
Dărmănești RO 161 D7
Darmstadt D 21 E11
Darney F 26 D5
Darnieulles F 26 D5
Darnózseli H 146 F4
Daroca E 47 B10
Darova RO 159 B8
Darque P 38 E2
Darra GB 3 K12
Darragh IRL 8 C4
Darro E 55 E6
Dartford GB 15 E9
Dartmeet GB 13 D7
Dartmouth GB 13 E7
Darton GB 11 D8
Dartsel S 118 C4
Daruvar HR 149 E8
Dârvari RO 159 E11
Darwen GB 10 D7
Dascălu RO 161 D8
Dashava UA 145 E9
Dašice CZ 77 B9
Dasing D 75 F9
Dasochori GR 169 B9
Dasochori GR 171 C7
Dassel D 78 C6
Dassendorf D 83 D8
Dassow D 83 C9
Daszyna PL 143 B7
Datça TR 181 C7
Datteln D 17 E8
Datterode (Ringgau) D 79 D7
Daudzese LV 135 D10
Daudzeva LV 135 C10
Daugai LT 137 E9
Daugailiai LT 135 E11
Daugård DK 86 D5
Daugavpils LV 135 E13
Daugėlaičiai LT 134 E7
Dauguļi LV 135 A10
Daujėnai LT 135 E9
Daumazan-sur-Arize F 33 D8
Daumeray F 23 E11
Daun D 21 D7
Dauphin F 35 C10
Dava GB 3 L9
Daventry GB 13 A12
Davézieux F 30 E6
Davidești RO 160 C6
Davidkovo BG 165 F10
Daviot GB 3 L8
Davle CZ 76 C6
Davleia GR 175 B6
Dávod H 150 E2
Davoli I 59 B9
Davor HR 157 B8
Davos CH 71 D9
Davutlar TR 177 D9
Davydiv UA 144 D9
Dawhinava BY 133 E3
Dawlish GB 13 D8
Dax F 32 C3
Deal GB 15 E11
Dealu RO 152 E6
Dealu Morii RO 153 E10
Dearham GB 5 F10
Deauville F 23 B12
Deba E 32 D1
Debar MK 168 A4
Debeli Lug SRB 159 E8
Debeljača SRB 158 C6
Debenham GB 15 C11
Dębe Wielkie PL 141 F4
Dębica PL 143 F11
De Bilt NL 16 D4
Dęblin PL 141 G5
Debnevo BG 165 D10
Dębnica Kaszubska PL 85 B12
Dębno PL 85 E7
Dębno PL 143 G10
Dęborzeczka PL 141 H2
Debovo BG 165 B10
Dębowa Kłoda PL 141 G8
Dębowa Łąka PL 138 D7
Dębowiec PL 147 B7
Debrc SRB 158 D4
Debrecen H 151 B8
Debrešte MK 168 B5
Debrzno PL 85 C12
Dębsko PL 85 D9
Debŭr BG 166 E4
Deçan RKS 163 D9
Decazeville F 33 A10
Dechtice SK 146 D5
Decimomannu I 64 E2
Decimoputzu I 64 E2
Děčín CZ 80 E6
Decize F 30 B3
De Cocksdorp NL 16 B3
Decollatura I 59 A9
Decs H 149 D11
Deda RO 152 D5
Deddington GB 13 B12
Dedeleben D 79 B8
Dedeler TR 173 F9
Dedelow D 84 D5
Dedelstorf D 83 E9
Dedemsvaart NL 17 C6
Dédestapolcsány H 145 G2
Dedham GB 15 D10
Dedovichi RUS 132 F6
Deensen D 78 C6
Deerlijk B 19 C7
Dég H 149 C10
Degaña E 39 C6
Degeberga S 88 D6
Degerbäcken S 118 C6
Degerby FIN 99 B14
Degerby FIN 127 E11
Degerfors S 92 A4
Degerhamn S 89 C10
Degersjö S 107 D12
Degerträsk S 118 D4
Deggendorf D 76 E3
Deggingen D 74 E6
Değirmen TR 173 B9
Değirmendere TR 177 C9
Değirmendüzü TR 171 D10
Değirmenyeni TR 167 F7
Dego I 37 C8
Degučiai LT 135 E12
Degumnieki LV 135 C13
De Haan B 19 B7
Dehesa de Campoamor E 56 F3
Dehesas de Guadix E 55 D6
Deià E 49 E10
Deidesheim D 21 F10
Deifontes E 53 B9
Deilão P 39 E6
Deining D 75 D10
Deiningen D 75 E8
Deinste D 17 A12
Deinze B 19 C8
Deiva Marina I 37 C11
Dej RO 152 C3
Deje S 97 C9
Dejtár H 147 E8
Dekani SLO 67 A8
Dekeleia GR 175 C8
De Koog NL 16 B3
De Kooy NL 16 C3
Dekov BG 165 B11
Delabole GB 12 D5
Delary S 87 B13
Delbrück D 17 E11
Delčevo MK 165 F6
Delden NL 17 D7
Délegyháza H 150 C3
Deleitosa E 45 E9
Đelekovec HR 149 D7
Delémont CH 27 F7
Delen' UA 154 F4
Deleni RO 153 C9
Deleni RO 155 E2
Deleria GR 169 E7
Delești RO 153 D11
Delfoi GR 175 C6
Delft NL 16 D2
Delfzijl NL 17 B7
Delia I 58 E4
Delianuova I 59 C8
Deliblato SRB 159 D7
Deliceto I 60 A4
Deligrad SRB 159 F8
Deliktaş TR 177 B8
Delingsdorf D 83 C8
Delitzsch D 79 C11
Delle F 27 E7
Delligsen D 78 C6
Dello I 66 B1
Delme F 26 C5
Delmenhorst D 17 B11
Delnice HR 67 B10
Delsbo S 103 C12
Deltebre E 42 F5
Delvin IRL 7 E8
Delvinaki GR 168 E3
Delvinë AL 168 E3
Demandice SK 147 E7
Demange-aux-Eaux F 26 C3
Dembava LT 135 E8
Demecser H 145 G4
De Meern NL 183 A6
Demen D 83 C11
Demene LV 135 E13
Demigny F 30 B6
Demiraj AL 163 E7
Demircihalil TR 167 F8
Demirdere TR 173 D9
Demirhanli TR 167 F7
Demir Hisar MK 168 B5
Demir Kapija MK 169 B7
Demirköy TR 167 F9
Demirli TR 181 C9
Demirtaş TR 173 D11
Demmin D 84 C4
Demonte I 37 C6
Dému F 33 C6
Denain F 19 D7
Denbigh GB 10 E5
Den Bommel NL 182 B4
Den Burg NL 16 B3
Denderleeuw B 182 D4
Dendermonde B 19 B9
Den Dungen NL 16 E4
Denekamp NL 17 D8
Denguin F 32 D5
Den Haag NL 16 D2
Den Haag NL 182 A4
Denham GB 15 D8
Den Ham NL 17 D7
Den Helder NL 16 C3
Denholm GB 5 E11
Denia E 56 D5
Denkendorf D 27 C11
Denkendorf D 75 E9
Denkingen D 27 D10
Denkingen D 27 E11
Denklingen D 71 B11
Dennewitz D 80 C4
Dennhausen (Fuldabrück) D 78 D5
Denny GB 5 C9
Den Oever NL 16 C4
Densow D 84 D4
Densuș RO 159 B10
Denta RO 159 C7
Dentergem B 19 C7
Dentlein am Forst D 75 D7
Denver GB 11 F12
Denzlingen D 27 D8
Déols F 29 B9
De Panne B 18 B6
Deppis S 109 E18
Deråsbrenna N 105 C10
Derby GB 11 F9
Derecske H 151 C8
Dereham GB 15 B10
Derekegyház H 150 D5
Dereköy TR 167 F8
Dereköy TR 173 F7
Derenburg D 79 C8
Derenti TR 173 E7
De Rijp NL 16 C3
Dermantsi BG 165 C9
Dermbach D 79 E7
Dermenas AL 168 C2
Derna RO 151 C9
Dernau D 21 C8
Derreen IRL 6 D4
Derreendaragh IRL 8 E3
Derreeny Bridge IRL 8 E4
Derry GB 4 F2
Derrygonnelly GB 7 D7
Derrylin GB 7 D7
Derrymore IRL 8 D3
Derrynawilt GB 7 D8
Derryrush IRL 6 F3
Derrywode IRL 6 E5
Dersca RO 153 B8
Dersingham GB 11 F13
Dersum D 17 C8
Deruta I 62 B2
Dervaig GB 4 B4
Derval F 23 E8
Dervenakia GR 175 D6
Derveni GR 174 C5
Derventa BIH 157 C8
Derviçan AL 168 D3
Dervio I 69 A7
Derviziana GR 168 F4
Dervock GB 4 E4
Desa RO 159 F11
Desana I 68 C5
Desantne UA 155 B5
Descargamaría E 45 D8
Descartes F 29 B7
Desenzano del Garda I 66 B2
Désertines F 29 C11
Desești RO 152 B3
Desfina GR 175 C6
Deskati GR 169 E6
Deskle SLO 73 D8
Despotovac SRB 159 E7
Despotovo SRB 158 C4
Dessau D 79 C11
Dessel B 16 F4
De Steeg NL 16 D6
Destelbergen B 19 B8
Deštná CZ 77 D7
Destriana E 39 D7
Desulo I 64 C3
Desvres F 15 F12
Deszczno PL 85 E8
Deszk H 150 E5
Deta RO 159 C7
Detern D 17 B9
Detk H 150 B5
Detkovac HR 149 E9
Dětmarovice CZ 146 B6
Detmold D 17 E11
Dettelbach D 75 C7
Dettenhausen D 187 D7
Dettingen an der Erms D 187 D7
Dettmannsdorf D 83 B13
Dettum D 79 B8
Dettwiller F 186 D3
Detva SK 147 D8
Deurne NL 16 F5
Deutsch Evern D 83 D8
Deutschfeistritz A 148 B4
Deutschhof D 84 E3
Deutschkreutz A 149 A7
Deutschlandsberg A 73 C11
Deutschneudorf D 80 E4
Deutsch-Wagram A 77 F11
Deutzen D 79 D11
Deva RO 151 F10
Dévaványa H 151 C6
Devecikonaği TR 173 E10
Devecser H 149 B8
Devene BG 165 C8
Deventer NL 16 D6
Devesel RO 159 E10
Deveselu RO 160 E4
Devetaki BG 165 C10
Deville F 184 E2
Devil's Bridge GB 13 A7
Devin BG 165 F9
Devizes GB 13 C11
Devletliağaç TR 167 F8
Devnya BG 167 C9
Đevrske HR 156 E4
De Wijk NL 16 C6
Dewsbury GB 11 D8
Deza E 41 F7
Dežanovac HR 149 E8
Dezghingea MD 154 E3
Dezna RO 151 E9
Dhërmi AL 168 D2
Dhron D 185 E6
Diafani GR 181 E6
Diakofto GR 174 C5
Dialampi GR 171 B8
Diamante I 60 D5
Dianalund DK 87 D8
Diano d'Alba I 37 B8
Diano Marina I 37 D8
Diavata GR 169 C8
Diavolitsi GR 174 E4
Dichiseni RO 161 E11
Dicomano I 66 E4
Didam NL 16 E6
Didcot GB 13 B12
Didderse D 79 B7
Didești RO 160 E5
Didyma GR 175 E7
Didymoteicho GR 171 B10
Didžiasalis LT 135 F13
Die F 31 F7
Dieblich D 21 D8
Dieburg D 21 E11
Dieci RO 151 E9
Diedorf D 75 F8
Diego Álvaro E 45 C10
Diekhof D 83 C12
Diekholzen D 78 B6
Diekirch L 20 E6
Dielheim D 21 F11
Dielmissen D 78 C6
Dielsdorf CH 27 F9
Diemen NL 16 D3
Diémoz F 31 D7
Dienheim D 185 E9
Dienne F 30 E2
Dienville F 25 D12
Diepenau D 17 D11
Diepenbeek B 19 C11
Diepenheim NL 183 A9
Diepenveen NL 183 A8
Diepholz D 17 C10
Dieppe F 18 E3
Dierdorf D 21 C9
Dieren NL 16 D6
Dierhagen D 83 B12
Diesdorf D 83 E9
Dieskau D 79 D11
Diespeck D 75 C8
Diessen NL 183 C6
Dießen am Ammersee D 72 A3
Diessenhofen CH 27 E10
Diest B 19 C11
Dietachdorf A 77 F6
Dietenheim D 71 A10
Dietersburg D 76 E3
Dietfurt an der Altmühl D 75 D10
Dietikon CH 27 F9
Dietingen D 27 D10
Dietmanns A 77 E7
Dietmanns A 77 E8
Dietmannsried D 71 B10
Dietzenbach D 21 D11
Dietzhölztal-Ewersbach D 185 C9
Dieue-sur-Meuse F 26 B3
Dieulefit F 35 A9
Dieulouard F 26 C5
Dieuze F 26 C6
Dieveniškės LT 137 E12
Diever NL 16 C6
Diex A 73 C10
Diezma E 55 E6
Differdange L 20 E5
Digerberget S 97 B9
Digerberget S 102 A8
Digermulen N 110 D8
Digernes N 100 B5
Dignac F 29 D6
Dignāja LV 135 D12
Dignano I 73 D6
Digne-les-Bains F 36 C4

Digny F 24 C5
Digoin F 30 C4
Dihtiv UA 144 B9
Dijon F 26 F3
Dikaia GR 166 F6
Dikanäs S 107 A10
Dikancë RKS 163 E10
Dikili TR 177 A8
Dikkebus B 18 C6
Dikļi LV 131 F10
Diksmuide B 18 B6
Dilar E 53 B9
Dilbeek B 182 D4
Dilesi GR 175 C8
Dilinata GR 174 C2
Dillenburg D 21 C10
Dilling N 95 D13
Dillingen (Saar) D 21 F7
Dillingen an der Donau D 75 E7
Dilove UA 145 H9
Dilsen B 19 B12
Dimaro I 71 E11
Diminio GR 169 F8
Dimitrie Cantemir RO 153 D12
Dimitritsi GR 169 C9
Dimitrovgrad BG 166 E5
Dimitrovgrad SRB 165 C6
Dimitsana GR 174 D5
Dimovo BG 159 F10
Dimzukalns LV 135 C8
Dinami I 59 B9
Dinan F 23 D7
Dinant B 19 D10
Dinard F 23 C7
Dingé F 23 D8
Dingelstädt D 79 D7
Dingelstedt am Huy D 79 C8
Dingle IRL 8 D2
Dingle S 91 B10
Dingolfing D 75 E12
Dingtuna S 98 C6
Dingwall GB 2 K8
Dinjiška HR 67 D11
Dinkelsbühl D 75 D7
Dinkelscherben D 75 F8
Dinklage D 17 C9
Dinnet GB 5 A11
Dinslaken D 17 E7
Dinteloord NL 16 E2
Dinther NL 183 B6
Dinxperlo NL 17 E6
Diö S 88 B6
Dion GR 169 D7
Diósd H 149 B11
Diosig RO 151 C9
Diósjenő H 147 F8
Dioşti RO 160 E4
Diou F 30 B4
Dipignano I 60 E6
Dipotama GR 171 B7
Dipotamia GR 168 D4
Dippach L 20 E6
Dippoldiswalde D 80 E5
Dirdal N 94 E4
Dirhami EST 130 C7
Dirivaara S 116 E8
Dirkshorn NL 16 C3
Dirksland NL 16 E2
Dirlewang D 71 A11
Dirmstein D 187 B5
Dirvonėnai LT 134 E5
Dischingen D 75 E7
Diseröd S 91 D11
Dison B 19 C12
Diss GB 15 C11
Dissay F 29 B7
Dissay-sous-Courcillon F 24 E3
Dissen am Teutoburger Wald D 17 D10
Distington GB 10 B4
Distomo GR 175 C6
Distrato GR 168 D5
Ditfurt D 79 C9
Diträu RO 153 D7
Ditton GB 15 E9
Ditzingen D 27 C11
Divača SLO 73 E8
Divarata GR 174 C2
Diva Slatina BG 165 C6
Divci SRB 158 E5
Divčibare SRB 158 E5
Dives-sur-Mer F 23 B11
Dividalen N 111 C18
Divieto I 59 C7
Divín SK 147 E9
Divina SK 147 C7
Divion F 18 D6
Divišov CZ 77 C7
Divjakë AL 168 C2
Divonne-les-Bains F 31 C9
Divuša HR 156 C5
Dixmont F 25 D9
Dizy F 25 B10
Dizy-le-Gros F 19 E9
Djäkneboda S 122 B5
Djäkneböle S 122 C4
Djupen N 111 B18
Djupfjord N 110 C9
Djupfors S 109 E11
Djupsjö S 107 E14
Djuptjärn S 107 D15
Djupvik N 109 B10
Djupvik N 112 D5
Djupvik S 89 A11
Djura S 103 E8
Djurås S 97 A13
Djurmo S 97 A13
Djurö S 99 D11
Dlhá nad Oravou SK 147 C8
Dlouhá Loučka CZ 77 C10
Dlouhá Třebová CZ 77 C10
Długołęka PL 81 D12
Długołęka PL 140 D7
Długosiodło PL 139 E11
Dłutów PL 143 C7
Dlŭzhka Polyana BG 166 C6
Dmytrivka UA 154 F3
Dmytrivka UA 154 A3
Dmytrivka UA 155 B4
Dnestrovsc MD 154 D5
Dno RUS 132 F6
Doagh GB 4 F4
Doba RO 151 B10
Dobanovci SRB 158 D5
Dobârceni RO 153 B10
Dobârlău RO 153 F7
Dobbertin D 83 C12
Dobbiaco I 72 C5
Dobczyce PL 144 D1
Dobele LV 134 C6
Döbeln D 80 D4
Dobërçan RKS 164 E4

Doberlug-Kirchhain D 80 C5
Döbern D 81 C7
Dobersberg A 77 E8
Doberschütz D 79 D12
Dobiegniew PL 85 E9
Dobieszewo PL 85 B12
Dobieszyn PL 141 G4
Doboj BIH 157 C7
Dobova SLO 148 E5
Doboz H 151 D7
Dobrá CZ 146 B6
Dobra PL 85 C8
Dobra PL 142 C6
Dobra PL 144 D1
Dobra RO 151 F10
Dobra RO 161 D7
Dobra SRB 159 D8
Dobra Niva SK 147 E8
Dobřany CZ 76 C4
Dobre PL 138 E6
Dobre PL 139 F12
Dobre Miasto PL 136 F1
Dobreni RO 153 D8
Dobrešinci MK 169 A8
Dobrești RO 151 D9
Dobrești RO 160 D6
Dobrești RO 160 F3
Dobrevo MK 164 E5
Dobrica SRB 159 D7
Dobričevo SRB 159 D7
Dobrich BG 155 F1
Dobrich BG 166 E5
Dobri Do SRB 164 D3
Dobri Dol BG 159 F11
Dobrin RO 151 C11
Dobrinishte BG 165 F8
Dobřiš CZ 76 C6
Dobritz D 79 B11
Dobřív CZ 76 C5
Dobrljin BIH 156 B5
Dobrna SLO 73 D11
Dobrnič SLO 73 E10
Dobrna BIH 157 C7
Dobrnja BIH 157 C7
Dobrnje SRB 159 E7
Dobro E 40 C4
Dobrodzień PL 142 E5
Döbrököz H 149 C10
Dobromierz PL 81 E10
Dobromir RO 155 E1
Dobromirka BG 166 C4
Dobromirtsi BG 166 C4
Dobroń PL 143 C7
Dobroń UA 145 G5
Dobronín CZ 77 D9
Dobro Polje BIH 157 E10
Dobro Polje SRB 159 F9
Dobrošane MK 164 E4
Dobrosloveni RO 160 E4
Dobrosyn UA 144 C8
Dobroszyce PL 81 D12
Dobrotesa RO 160 D4
Dobroteşti RO 160 F5
Dobrotić SRB 164 C4
Dobrotich BG 167 C8
Dobrotino BG 165 F8
Dobrotitsa BG 161 F9
Dobrovăţ RO 153 D11
Dobrovce CZ 78 B7
Dobrovnik SLO 149 C7
Dobrovol'sk RUS 136 D5
Dobrowoda PL 143 F10
Dobruchi RUS 132 D2
Dobruška CZ 77 B10
Dobruşa MD 154 B3
Dobruševo MK 169 B5
Dobrzankowo PL 139 E10
Dobrzany PL 85 D8
Dobrzeń Wielki PL 142 E4
Dobrzyca PL 142 C4
Dobrzyków PL 139 F8
Dobrzyń nad Wisłą PL 139 E7
Dobšiná SK 145 F1
Dóc H 150 E5
Docking GB 15 B10
Dockmyr S 103 A10
Docksta S 107 E14
Dockweiler D 21 D7
Doclin RO 159 C8
Doddington GB 5 D12
Dodewaard NL 183 B6
Dodonoupoli GR 168 E4
Dödre S 102 A3
Doesburg NL 16 D6
Doetinchem NL 16 D6
Dofteana RO 153 E9
Doğanbey TR 177 C8
Doğanbey TR 177 D9
Doğancı TR 173 D10
Doğanköy TR 173 D10
Döge H 145 G5
Dogliani I 37 B7
Dognecea RO 159 C8
Döğüşbelen TR 181 C9
Dohna D 80 E5
Dohňany SK 146 C6
Dohren D 17 C9
Doiceşti RO 160 D6
Doïrani GR 169 B8
Doire Iorrais IRL 6 F3
Doische B 19 D10
Dojč SK 146 D4
Dojkinci SRB 165 C6
Dokka N 101 E12
Dokkas S 116 D6
Dokkedal DK 86 B6
Dokkum NL 16 B5
Doksy CZ 76 B6
Doksy CZ 81 E7
Doktor Yosifovo BG 165 C7
Dokupe LV 134 C5
Dolanog GB 10 F5
Dolbenmaen GB 10 F3
Dolceacqua I 37 D7
Dol-de-Bretagne F 23 C8
Dole F 26 F3
Dølemo N 90 B3
Dolenci BIH 157 D10
Dolenja Vas SLO 73 E11
Dolenjske Toplice SLO 73 E11
Dolgarrog GB 10 E4
Dolgellau GB 10 F4
Dolgen D 84 D3
Dolgorukovo RUS 136 E2
Dolhan TR 167 F8
Dolhasca RO 153 C9
Dolheşti RO 153 B9
Dolheşti RO 153 D11

Dołhobyczów PL 144 B9
Dolianova I 64 E3
Dolice PL 85 D8
Dolichi GR 169 D7
Doljani BIH 157 E8
Doljani HR 156 D5
Doljevac SRB 164 C4
Dolla IRL 8 C6
Dolle D 79 B10
Dollern D 82 C7
Döllnitz D 79 D11
Dollnstein D 75 E9
Dollon F 24 D4
Dolna MD 154 C3
Dolna Banya BG 165 E8
Dolna Bela Reka SRB 159 E9
Dolna Dikanya BG 165 E7
Dolna Gradeshnitsa BG 165 F7
Dolná Krupá SK 146 E5
Dolna Lipnitsa BG 166 C4
Dolna Makhala BG 165 E10
Dolna Melna BG 165 D6
Dolna Mitropoliya BG 165 C10
Dolna Oryakhovitsa BG 166 C5
Dolná Strehová SK 147 E8
Dolná Súča SK 146 D6
Dolná Tižina SK 147 C7
Dolné Orešany SK 146 E4
Dolné Vestenice SK 146 D6
Dolneni MK 169 B6
Dolní Bousov CZ 77 B8
Dolní Bukovsko CZ 77 D7
Dolní Čermná CZ 77 C11
Dolni Chiflik BG 167 C9
Dolní Dobrouč CZ 77 C11
Dolni Dŭbnik BG 165 C9
Dolní Dvořiště CZ 77 E6
Dolni Glavanak BG 166 F5
Dolní Kounice CZ 77 D10
Dolní Loučky CZ 77 D10
Dolní Němčí CZ 146 D5
Dolní Podluží CZ 81 E7
Dolní Újezd CZ 77 C10
Dolní Újezd CZ 146 B5
Dolni Voden BG 166 E10
Dolní Žandov CZ 75 B12
Dolno Dupeni MK 168 C5
Dolno Ezerovo BG 167 D8
Dolno Kamartsi BG 165 E7
Dolno Konjare MK 164 F4
Dolno Levski BG 165 E9
Dolno Osenovo BG 165 F7
Dolno Selo BG 164 E5
Dolno Tserovene BG 159 F11
Dolno Uyno BG 164 E6
Dolný Hričov SK 147 C7
Dolný Kubín SK 147 C8
Dolný Pial SK 146 E6
Dolný Štál SK 146 F5
Dolo I 66 B5
Dolomieu F 31 D8
Dolores E 56 F3
Dolovo SRB 159 D6
Dölsach A 73 C6
Dolsk PL 81 C12
Dołubowo PL 141 E7
Dolus-d'Oléron F 28 D3
Dolyna UA 145 F8
Dolynivka UA 154 A5
Dolyns'ke UA 154 B5
Dolzhitsy RUS 132 D5
Domaháza H 147 E10
Domaniewice PL 141 G10
Domaniewice PL 143 B8
Domanín CZ 146 C4
Domaradz PL 144 D4
Domart-en-Ponthieu F 18 D5
Domaševo BIH 162 D5
Domašinec HR 149 D7
Domaşnea RO 159 C9
Domaszek H 150 E5
Domaszków PL 77 B11
Domaszowice PL 142 D4
Domat Ems CH 71 D8
Domats F 25 D9
Domažlice CZ 76 D3
Dombås N 101 B10
Dombegyház H 151 E7
Dombóvár H 149 D10
Dombrád H 145 G4
Dombresson CH 31 A10
Domburg NL 16 E1
Domegge di Cadore I 72 D5
Doméň E 31 E8
Domeikava LT 137 D8
Domène F 31 E8
Domeniko GR 169 E7
Domérat F 29 C11
Domèvre-en-Haye F 26 C4
Domèvre-sur-Vezouze F 27 C6
Domfront F 23 C10
Domgermain F 26 C4
Domínce H 162 D3
Domingo Pérez E 46 E4
Dominowo PL 81 B11
Dömitz D 83 D10
Domlyan BG 165 D10
Dommartin-le-Franc F 26 D2
Dommartin-Varimont F 25 C12
Domme F 29 F8
Dommershausen D 21 D8
Dommitzsch D 80 C3
Domneşti RO 160 C5
Domneşti RO 161 E7
Domnitsa GR 174 B4
Domnovo RUS 136 D3
Domodossola I 68 A5
Domokos GR 174 A5
Domont F 25 B7
Domoroc RKS 164 D4
Domoš H 149 A11
Domoszló H 147 F10
Dompcevrin F 26 C3
Dompierre-les-Ormes F 30 C5
Dompierre-sur-Besbre F 30 B4
Dompierre-sur-Mer F 28 C3
Dompierre-sur-Yon F 28 B3
Domrémy-la-Pucelle F 26 D4
Domsühl D 83 D11
Domus de Maria I 64 F2
Domusnovas I 64 E2
Domžale SLO 73 D9
Donagh GB 7 D8
Donaghadee GB 4 F5
Donaghmore GB 7 D9
Donaghmore IRL 7 F10
Don Álvaro E 51 B7
Doña Mencía E 53 A8
Donard IRL 7 F9

Donaueschingen D 27 E9
Donauwörth D 75 E8
Don Benito E 51 B8
Doncaster GB 11 D9
Donchery F 19 E10
Donegal IRL 6 C6
Doneraile IRL 8 D5
Donerbe E 32 D2
Denfoss N 100 C8
Dongen NL 16 E3
Donges F 23 F7
Dongo I 69 A7
Donici MD 154 C3
Doñinos de Salamanca E 45 C9
Donja Brela HR 157 F6
Donja Bukovica MNE 163 C7
Donja Dubrava HR 149 D7
Donja Kupčina HR 148 E5
Donja Lepenica BIH 157 B8
Donja Mahala BIH 157 B10
Donja Motičina HR 149 F10
Donja Šatornja SRB 159 E6
Donja Stubica HR 148 E5
Donja Višnjica HR 148 D5
Donja Zelina HR 148 E6
Donje Pazarište HR 67 C11
Donjeux F 26 D3
Donji Andrijevci HR 157 B9
Donji Čaglić HR 149 F8
Donji Dubovnik BIH 156 C5
Donji Dušnik SRB 164 C5
Donji Kosinj HR 156 C3
Donji Krčin SRB 159 F7
Donji Krivodol SRB 165 C5
Donji Lapac HR 156 C5
Donji Miholjac HR 149 E10
Donji Milanovac SRB 159 E9
Donji Proložac HR 157 F7
Donji Rujani BIH 157 E7
Donji Seget HR 156 E5
Donji Srb HR 156 D5
Donji Striževac SRB 164 C5
Donji Svilaj BIH 157 C9
Donji Vakuf BIH 157 D7
Donji Vijačani BIH 157 C7
Donji Zemunik HR 156 D3
Donk NL 183 B7
Donkerbroek NL 16 B6
Donnalucata I 59 F6
Donnas I 68 B4
Donnemarie-Dontilly F 25 D9
Donnersbach A 73 B9
Donnersdorf D 75 C7
Donohill IRL 8 C6
Donori I 64 E3
Donostia E 32 D2
Donskoye RUS 139 A8
Donville-les-Bains F 23 C8
Donzdorf D 74 E6
Donzenac F 29 E8
Donzère F 35 B8
Donzy F 25 F9
Dooagh IRL 6 E2
Doochary IRL 6 C6
Dooish GB 4 F2
Doonbeg IRL 8 C3
Doorn NL 16 E3
Doornspijk NL 183 A7
Dorchester GB 13 D10
Dørdal N 90 B5
Dordives F 25 D8
Dordrecht NL 16 E3
Dore-l'Église F 30 E4
Dörentrup D 17 D12
Dores GB 3 L8
Dorfen D 75 F11
Dorfgastein A 73 B7
Dorfmark D 82 E7
Dorf Mecklenburg D 83 C10
Dorf Zechlin D 83 D13
Dorgali I 64 C4
Dorio GR 174 E4
Dorking GB 15 E8
Dorkovo BG 165 E9
Dorlisheim F 186 D3
Dormagen D 21 B7
Dormánd H 150 B5
Dormans F 25 B10
Dor Mărunt RO 161 E9
Dorna-Arini RO 152 C6
Dorna Candrenilor RO 152 C6
Dornava SLO 148 D5
Dornbirn A 71 C9
Dornburg (Saale) D 79 D10
Dornburg-Frickhofen D 185 C9
Dornbusch D 17 A12
Dorndorf D 79 E7
Dorndorf-Steudnitz D 79 D10
Dornelas P 38 E4
Dornes F 30 B3
Dorneşti RO 153 B8
Dornhan D 27 D9
Dornie GB 2 L5
Dornişoara RO 152 C6
Dörnitz D 79 B11
Dorno I 69 C6
Dornoch GB 3 K8
Dornstadt D 74 F6
Dornstetten D 27 D9
Dornum D 17 A8
Dornumersiel D 17 A8
Dorobanţu RO 155 D2
Dorobanţu RO 161 E9
Dorog H 149 A11
Doroghaza H 147 F9
Dorohoi RO 153 B8
Dorohusk PL 141 H9
Dorolţ RO 151 B10
Doroţcaia MD 154 C4
Dorotea S 107 C11
Dörpen D 17 C8
Dörpstedt D 82 A7
Dorras N 112 D4
Dorrington GB 10 F6
Dorsten D 17 E8
Dorstfeld D 185 A7
Dortan F 31 C8
Dortmund D 17 E8
Dörttepe TR 181 C9
Doruchów PL 142 D5
Dorum D 17 A11
Dorupe LV 134 C7

Dörverden D 17 C12
Dörzbach D 74 D6
Dos Aguas E 48 F3
Dosbarrios E 46 E6
Dos Hermanas E 51 E8
Dospat BG 165 F9
Dossenheim D 21 F11
Doştat RO 152 F3
Dostnuva LT 134 F7
Dottenhausen D 27 D10
Döttingen CH 27 E9
Douai F 19 D7
Douarnenez F 22 D3
Doubravice nad Svitavou CZ 77 D11
Doubs F 31 B9
Douchy F 25 E9
Douchy-les-Mines F 19 D7
Doucier F 31 B8
Doudeville F 18 E2
Doudleby nad Orlicí CZ 77 B10
Doué-la-Fontaine F 23 F11
Douglas S 5 D9
Douglas GBM 10 C3
Douglas Bridge GB 4 F2
Doulaincourt-Saucourt F 26 D3
Doulevant-le-Château F 25 D12
Doullens F 18 D5
Dounaiika GR 174 D3
Doune GB 5 C9
Dounreay GB 3 H9
Dour B 19 D8
Dourdan F 24 C7
Dourgne F 33 D10
Douriez F 18 D4
Doussard F 31 D9
Douvaine F 31 C9
Douvres-la-Délivrande F 23 B11
Douzy F 19 E11
Dovadola I 66 D4
Dover GB 15 E11
Dovhe UA 145 G7
Döviken S 103 A9
Dovilai LT 134 E2
Dovre N 101 C10
Dowally GB 5 B9
Downham Market GB 11 F12
Downpatrick GB 7 D11
Downton GB 13 D11
Dowra IRL 6 D6
Dowsby GB 11 F11
Doxato GR 171 B6
Doyet F 30 C2
Doyrentsi BG 165 C10
Dozulé F 23 B11
Drabeši LV 135 B10
Dráby DK 86 C7
Drač RO 161 D8
Drachhausen D 80 C6
Drachselsried D 76 D4
Drachten NL 16 B6
Draga N 105 B10
Dragacz PL 138 C6
Drăgăeşti RO 161 E10
Drăgălina RO 161 E10
Dragalevci SRB 165 C11
Drăganeşti RO 151 D9
Drăgăneşti RO 153 F10
Drăgăneşti RO 153 C10
Drăgăneşti RO 160 D6
Drăgăneşti de Vede RO 160 E6
Drăgăneşti-Olt RO 160 E5
Drăgăneşti-Vlaşca RO 161 E7
Draganići HR 148 E5
Draganovo BG 166 C5
Drăgănu RO 160 D5
Drăgăşani RO 160 D4
Dragash RKS 163 E10
Dragatuš SLO 67 A11
Drage HR 156 E4
Drage D 83 D8
Dragičevo BG 165 D7
Dragijna BIH 157 C7
Draginje SRB 158 D4
Draginovo BG 165 E9
Dragland N 111 C11
Dragnes N 111 C10
Dragnić BIH 157 D7
Dragobi AL 163 E8
Dragočaj BIH 157 C7
Dragocvet SRB 159 F7
Dragodana RO 160 D6
Drăgoeşti RO 160 C6
Drăgoeşti RO 161 D9
Dragoevo MK 164 F5
Dragoevo BG 167 C7
Dragoman BG 165 D6
Dragomer SLO 73 E9
Dragomir BG 165 E9
Dragomireşti RO 152 B4
Dragomireşti RO 153 C9
Dragomireşti RO 160 D6
Dragomirovo BG 166 B4
Dragoni I 60 A2
Dragør DK 87 D11
Dragoş MK 168 B5
Dragoslavele RO 160 C6
Dragoş Vodă RO 161 E10
Drăgoteşti RO 160 E4
Drăgoteşti RO 160 D3
Dragotina HR 156 B5
Dragović HR 149 F8
Dragovishtitsa BG 165 E6
Dragoychintsi BG 164 D5
Dragoynovo BG 166 F4
Dragsfjärd FIN 126 F7
Draguignan F 36 D4
Drăguşeni RO 153 A9
Drăguşeni RO 153 C9
Drăguşeni RO 153 F11
Drăguţeşti RO 159 D11
Drahansdorf D 80 B5
Drahnsdorf D 80 B5
Drahovce SK 146 D5
Drahovo UA 145 G8
Drajna RO 161 C8
Draka BG 167 E8
Drakenburg D 17 C12
Drakšenić BIH 157 B6
Dralfa BG 167 C6
Drama GR 170 B6
Drammen N 95 C12
Drânceni RO 153 D12
Drange N 94 F5
Drangedal N 90 A5

Drangstedt D 17 A11
Drănic RO 160 E3
Dranse D 83 F13
Dransfeld D 78 D6
Dranske D 84 A4
Draperstown GB 4 F3
Drasenhofen A 77 E11
Draßmarkt A 149 A6
Drávafok H 149 E9
Dravagrad SLO 73 C11
Drawno PL 85 D9
Drawsko PL 85 E10
Drawsko Pomorskie PL 85 C9
Drayton GB 5 B11
Drążdżewo PL 139 D11
Dražen Vrh SLO 148 C5
Draževac SRB 158 D5
Dražgoše SLO 73 D9
Drebber D 17 C10
Drebkau D 80 C6
Drégelypalánk H 147 E8
Dreieich D 21 D11
Dreileben D 79 B9
Dreis D 21 E7
Drelów PL 141 G7
Drelsdorf D 82 A6
Drem GB 5 C11
Drenchia I 73 D8
Drenovac SRB 159 F7
Drenovci HR 157 C10
Drenovë AL 168 C4
Drenovets BG 159 F10
Drenovicë AL 168 C2
Drenovo MK 169 B6
Drensteinfurt D 17 E9
Drenta BG 166 D4
Drentwede D 17 C11
Drepano GR 169 D6
Drepano GR 175 D6
Dresden D 80 D5
Dretun' BY 133 E6
Dretyń PL 85 B11
Dreumel NL 183 B6
Dreux F 24 C5
Dreverna LT 134 E2
Drevja N 108 E5
Drevjesætra N 102 D4
Drevsjø N 102 C3
Drewitz D 79 B11
Drezdenko PL 85 E9
Drežnica HR 156 C3
Drežnik SRB 158 F4
Dricēni LV 133 C2
Dridu RO 161 D8
Driebergen NL 16 D4
Driebes E 47 D7
Driedorf D 185 C9
Drienov SK 145 F3
Drietoma SK 146 D5
Driffield GB 11 C11
Drimmo IRL 7 F7
Drimnin GB 4 B5
Drimoleague IRL 8 E4
Drinić BIH 157 D6
Drinjača BIH 157 D11
Drinovci BIH 157 F7
Dripsey IRL 8 E5
Drisht AL 163 E8
Drithas AL 168 E4
Driva N 101 A11
Drivstua N 101 B10
Drmno SRB 159 D7
Drnholec CZ 77 E11
Drniš HR 156 E5
Drnje HR 149 D7
Drnovice CZ 77 D11
Drnovice CZ 77 D11
Dro I 69 B10
Drøbak N 95 C13
Drobeta-Turnu Severin RO 159 D10
Drobin PL 139 E8
Drochia MD 153 A11
Drochtersen D 17 A12
Drogheda IRL 7 E10
Drohiczyn PL 141 F7
Drohobych UA 145 E8
Droichead Abhann IRL 8 C5
Droichead Átha IRL 7 E10
Droichead na Bandan IRL 8 E5
Droichead Nua IRL 7 F9
Droitwich Spa GB 13 A10
Drolshagen D 185 B8
Drolsum N 95 B12
Drömme S 107 E14
Dromod IRL 7 E7
Dromore GB 7 C8
Dromore GB 7 D8
Dromore West IRL 6 D5
Dronero I 37 C6
Dronfield GB 11 E9
Drongan GB 4 E7
Drongen B 182 C3
Dronninglund DK 86 A6
Dronrijp NL 16 B5
Dronten NL 16 C5
Dropla BG 155 F2
Drosato GR 169 B8
Drosbacken S 102 C3
Drösing A 77 E11
Drosia GR 175 C8
Drosopigi GR 168 C5
Droué F 24 D5
Droyßig D 79 D11
Drŭzhba BG 165 E7
Druid GB 10 F5
Druimdrishaig GB 4 D5
Drulingen F 27 C7
Drumandoora IRL 8 C5
Drumaness GB 7 D11
Drumatober IRL 6 F6
Drumbeg GB 2 J6
Drumbilla IRL 7 D10
Drumcard GB 7 D7
Drumcollogher IRL 8 D4
Drumconrath IRL 7 E9
Drumcree IRL 7 E8
Drumettaz-Clarafond F 31 D8
Drumevo BG 167 C8

Drumfree IRL 4 E2
Drumkeeran IRL 6 D6
Drumlea IRL 7 D7
Drumlish IRL 7 E7
Drumlithie GB 5 B12
Drummin IRL 9 D9
Drummore GB 4 F7
Drumnadrochit GB 2 L8
Drumquin GB 4 F1
Drumshanbo IRL 6 D6
Drung IRL 7 D8
Drusenheim F 27 C8
Druskininkai LT 137 F9
Druten NL 183 B7
Druveniena LV 135 B12
Druya BY 133 E2
Druyes-les-Belles-Fontaines F 25 E9
Druysk BY 133 E2
Družbice PL 143 D5
Druzhba RUS 136 D2
Druzhnaya Gorka RUS 132 C7
Druztvená pri Hornáde SK 145 F3
Drvenik HR 157 F7
Drwalew PL 141 G4
Drwinia PL 143 F10
Dryanovets BG 161 F8
Dryanovo BG 166 D4
Dryazhno RUS 132 E6
Drygały PL 139 C13
Drymaia GR 175 B6
Drymen GB 5 C8
Drymos GR 169 C8
Dryna N 100 A5
Dryopida GR 175 E9
Dryos GR 176 E2
Drysvyaty BY 135 E13
Drzewce PL 142 B6
Drzewiany PL 85 C11
Drzewica PL 141 H2
Drzonowo PL 85 C10
Drzycim PL 138 C5
Duagh IRL 8 D4
Dualchi I 64 C2
Dually IRL 9 C7
Duas Igrejas P 39 F7
Dub SRB 158 F4
Dubá CZ 77 A7
Dubăsari MD 154 C4
Dubăsarii Vechi MD 154 C4
Duba Stonska HR 162 D4
Dubău MD 154 C4
Dubeczno PL 141 H8
Düben D 79 C11
Duben D 80 C5
Dübendorf CH 27 F10
Dubeninki PL 136 E6
Dubiecko PL 144 D5
Dubí CZ 80 E5
Dubičiai LT 137 E9
Dubicze Cerkiewne PL 141 E8
Dubienka PL 144 A8
Dubingiai LT 137 C11
Dubino I 69 A7
Dubivka UA 153 A8
Dublin IRL 7 F10
Dublje SRB 158 D4
Dublovice CZ 76 C6
Dublyany UA 144 D7
Dublyany UA 145 D7
Dubna LV 135 D13
Dub nad Moravou CZ 146 C4
Dubňany CZ 77 E12
Dubnica nad Váhom SK 146 D6
Dubník SK 146 F6
Duboštica BIH 157 D9
Dubova RO 159 D9
Dubove UA 145 G8
Dŭbovets BG 166 F5
Dŭbovo BG 166 D5
Dubovac SRB 159 D7
Dubovo SRB 164 D4
Dubovsko BIH 156 C5
Dubrava HR 149 E7
Dubrave BIH 157 C8
Dubrave BIH 157 D6
Dubrave BIH 157 D8
Dubravica BIH 157 D8
Dubravica SRB 159 D7
Dúbravy SK 147 D8
Dubrovka BY 133 F6
Dubrovka RUS 132 F14
Dubrovka RUS 133 D3
Dubrovnik HR 162 D5
Dubrovytsya UA 144 D8
Dubuļi LV 133 D3
Dubynove UA 154 A6
Ducey F 23 C9
Ducherow D 84 C5
Duchcov CZ 80 E5
Duck End GB 15 D9
Duclair F 18 F2
Duda-Epureni RO 153 D12
Dudar H 149 B9
Duddo GB 5 D12
Dudelange L 20 F6
Dudeldorf D 21 E7
Duderstadt D 79 D7
Dudeşti RO 161 D10
Dudeştii Vechi RO 150 E5
Düdingen CH 31 B11
Dudley GB 11 F7
Dudovica SRB 158 E5
Dueñas E 40 E2
Duesund N 100 E2
Dueville I 72 E4
Duffel B 19 B10
Dufftown GB 3 L10
Duga Poljana SRB 163 C9
Dugi Rat HR 156 F6
Dugny-sur-Meuse F 26 B3
Dugopolje HR 156 E6
Dugo Selo HR 148 E6
Düğüncüler TR 173 B7
Duhort-Bachen F 32 C5
Duino I 73 E8
Duirinish GB 2 L5
Duisburg D 17 F7
Dukas AL 168 C2
Dukat AL 168 D1
Dukat i ri AL 168 D1

Dukla PL 145 D4
Dūkštas LT 135 E12
Dúlbok Dol BG 165 D10
Dŭlboki BG 166 E5
Dŭlbok Izvor BG 166 E4
Dulcești RO 153 D9
Duleek IRL 7 E10
Dŭlgodeltsi BG 160 F2
Dŭlgopol BG 167 C8
Dulina BY 133 F2
Duljci BIH 157 D7
Dullingham GB 15 C9
Dülmen D 17 E8
Dulnain Bridge GB 3 L9
Dulovce SK 146 F6
Dulovka RUS 133 A4
Dulovo BG 161 F10
Dulverton GB 13 C7
Dumbarton GB 4 D7
Dumbrava RO 151 F9
Dumbrava RO 159 D11
Dumbrava RO 161 D8
Dumbrava Roșie RO 153 D8
Dumbrăveni RO 152 E5
Dumbrăveni RO 153 B8
Dumbrăveni RO 155 F1
Dumbrăveni RO 161 B10
Dumbrăvești RO 161 C7
Dumbrăvița RO 151 F7
Dumbrăvița RO 152 B3
Dumbrăvița RO 153 F6
Dumbria E 38 B1
Dumești RO 153 C10
Dumești RO 153 D10
Dumfries GB 5 E9
Dumitra RO 152 C4
Dumitrești RO 161 B9
Dummerstorf D 83 C12
Dümpelfeld D 21 D7
Dun F 33 D9
Duna N 105 B11
Dunaegyháza H 149 C11
Dunaföldvár H 149 C11
Dunaharaszti H 150 C3
Dunajská Lužná SK 146 E4
Dunajská Streda SK 146 F5
Dunakeszi H 150 B2
Dunalka LV 134 C2
Dún an Rí IRL 7 E9
Dunapataj H 150 D3
Dunărea RO 155 E2
Dunaszeg H 149 A9
Dunaszekcső H 149 D11
Dunaszentbenedek H 149 C11
Dunaszentgyörgy H 149 C11
Dunasziget H 146 F4
Dunatetétlen H 150 D3
Dunaújváros H 149 C11
Dunava LV 135 D12
Dunavecse H 150 C3
Dunavtsi BG 159 F10
Dunbar GB 5 C11
Dunbeath GB 3 J10
Dunblane GB 5 C9
Dunboyne IRL 7 E10
Dún Búinne IRL 7 F10
Duncannon IRL 9 D9
Dún Chaoin IRL 8 D2
Dunchurch GB 13 A12
Duncormick IRL 9 D9
Dundaga LV 134 A4
Dundalk IRL 7 D10
Dún Dealgan IRL 7 D10
Dun Dealgan IRL 7 D10
Dundee GB 5 C11
Dunderland N 108 D8
Dundonald GB 7 C11
Dundreggan GB 2 L7
Dundrennan GB 5 F9
Dundrum GB 9 D11
Dundrum IRL 8 C6
Dunecht GB 3 L12
Dunes F 33 B7
Dunfanaghy IRL 7 B7
Dunfermline GB 5 C10
Dungannon GB 7 C11
Dún Garbhán IRL 9 D7
Dungarvan IRL 9 D7
Düngenheim D 185 D7
Dungiven GB 4 F3
Dunglow IRL 6 C6
Dungourney IRL 8 E6
Dunholme GB 11 E11
Dunící AL 168 C4
Dunières F 30 E5
Duninowo PL 85 A11
Dunje MK 169 B6
Dunkeld GB 5 B9
Dunkerque F 18 B5
Dunkerrin IRL 9 C7
Dunkitt IRL 9 D7
Dún Laoghaire IRL 7 F10
Dunlavin IRL 7 F9
Dunleer IRL 7 E10
Dún Léire IRL 7 E10
Dun-le-Palestel F 29 C9
Dun-les-Places F 25 F11
Dunlop GB 4 D7
Dunloy GB 4 E4
Dún Mánmhaí IRL 8 E4
Dún Mór IRL 9 D9
Dunmore IRL 6 E5
Dunmore East IRL 9 D9
Dunmurry GB 7 C11
Dunnamanagh GB 4 F2
Dún na nGall IRL 6 C6
Dunoon GB 4 D7
Dunquin IRL 8 D2
Duns GB 5 D12
Dunscore GB 5 E9
Dünsen D 17 C11
Dunshaughlin IRL 7 E9
Dunstable GB 15 D7
Dunster GB 13 C8
Dun-sur-Auron F 29 B11
Dun-sur-Meuse F 19 F11
Dunure GB 4 E7
Dunvant GB 12 B6
Dunvegan GB 2 L3
Duplica SLO 73 D10
Dupnitsa BG 165 E7
Durach D 71 B10
Durak TR 173 E9
Durana E 41 C6
Durance F 33 B6
Durango E 41 B6
Durankulak BG 155 F3
Duras F 33 A6

Durbach D 27 C9
Durban-Corbières F 34 E4
Durbe LV 134 C2
Durbuy B 184 D3
Dúrcal E 53 C9
Durdat-Larequille F 29 C11
Đurđenovac HR 149 F9
Đurđevac HR 149 D8
Đurđevića Tara MNE 163 C7
Đurđevik BIH 157 D10
Đurđevo SRB 158 C5
Đurđevo SRB 159 E6
Düren D 20 C6
Durfort F 35 C6
Durham GB 5 F13
Ďurková SK 145 F3
Durlas IRL 9 C7
Durlești MD 154 C3
Durmanec HR 148 D5
Dürmentingen D 71 A9
Durmersheim D 27 C9
Durness GB 2 H7
Dürnești RO 153 B10
Dürnkrut A 77 F11
Durrës AL 168 B1
Durrington GB 13 C11
Dürrlauingen D 75 F7
Durrow IRL 9 C8
Durrus IRL 8 E3
Dürrwangen D 75 D7
Dursley GB 13 B10
Dursunbey TR 173 E9
Durtal F 23 E11
Duruelo de la Sierra E 40 E6
Duruitoarea MD 153 B11
Durup DK 86 B3
Durusu TR 173 B10
Dusetos LT 135 E11
Dusina BIH 157 E8
Dŭskotna BG 167 D8
Duškovci SRB 158 F5
Dusmenys LT 137 E9
Dusnok H 149 C11
Dusocin PL 138 C6
Düsseldorf D 21 B7
Dussen NL 16 E3
Dußlingen D 187 E7
Duszniki PL 81 B10
Dutluca TR 173 E11
Dutovlje SLO 73 E8
Duvberg S 102 B7
Duved S 105 E13
Düvertepe TR 173 E10
Duži BIH 162 D5
Dvärsätt S 106 E6
Dvaryshcha BY 133 E6
Dve Mogili BG 161 F7
Dverberg N 111 B10
Dviete LV 135 D12
Dvirtsi UA 144 C9
Dvor HR 156 B5
Dvorce CZ 146 B5
Dvornaye Syalo BY 133 E3
Dvorníky SK 146 E5
Dvory nad Žitavou SK 146 F6
Dvůr Králové CZ 77 B9
Dwikozy PL 144 B4
Dwingeloo NL 16 C6
Dyan GB 7 D9
Dyankovo BG 161 F9
Dybvad DK 90 E7
Dyce GB 3 L12
Dychów PL 81 C8
Dydnia PL 144 D5
Dyfjord N 113 B19
Dygowo PL 85 B9
Dyke GB 3 K9
Dykehead GB 5 B11
Dykhtynets' UA 152 A6
Dylągówka PL 144 D5
Dylaki PL 142 E5
Dylewo PL 139 D11
Dymchurch GB 15 E10
Dymock GB 13 B10
Dynäs S 107 F13
Dynów PL 144 D5
Dyo F 30 C5
Dyping N 110 E9
Dyrnes N 104 E3
Dyrøyhamn N 111 B13
Dyrrachi GR 174 E5
Dyulevo BG 167 E8
Dyulino BG 167 D9
Dyviziya UA 154 F5
Dzaczka PL 142 F5
Dzęgiel PL 142 F5
Dzęgiel PL 139 D11
Dzbeniny LV 134 D6
Dzelzava LV 135 C12
Dzeņi LV 135 B12
Dzērbene LV 135 B11
Dzhebel BG 171 A8
Dzherman BG 165 E7
Dzhulynka UA 154 A5
Dzhulyunitsa BG 166 C5
Dzhurivi UA 152 E12
Dzhurovo BG 165 D9
Działdowo PL 142 E5
Działdowo PL 139 D9
Działoszyce PL 143 F9
Działoszyn PL 142 D6
Dziemiany PL 138 B4
Dziergowice PL 142 F5
Dzierzążnia PL 139 E9
Dzierżążno Wielkie PL 85 E10
Dzierzgoń PL 139 C7
Dzierzgowo PL 139 D10
Dzierzkowice-Rynek PL 144 B5
Dzierżoniów PL 81 E11
Dzietrzniki PL 142 D6
Dzietrzychowo PL 136 E3
Dziewierzewo PL 85 E13
Dźęgoli SRB 164 C4
Dzirnavas LV 134 B4
Dzisna BY 133 E4
Dziwnów PL 85 B7
Dzmitravichy BY 141 F9
Dźūkste LV 134 C6
Džumajlija MK 164 F4
Dźwierzuty PL 139 C10
Dźwirzyno PL 85 B8
Dzwola PL 144 B6
Dzwonowice PL 143 F8
Dzyarzhynsk BY 133 E2
Dzyornavichy BY 133 E4

E

Éadan Doire IRL 7 F8
Eaglesfield GB 5 E10
Eardisley GB 13 A8

Earith GB 15 C9
Earl Shilton GB 11 F9
Earlston GB 5 D11
Earl Stonham GB 15 C11
Earsairidh GB 2 L3
Easdale GB 4 C5
Easington GB 5 F14
Easington GB 11 D12
Easingwold GB 11 C9
Easky IRL 6 D5
Eastbourne GB 15 F9
Eastburn GB 11 D11
Eastfield GB 11 C11
East Grinstead GB 15 E8
East Harling GB 15 C10
East Kilbride GB 5 D8
Eastleigh GB 13 D12
East Linton GB 5 D11
East Looe GB 12 E6
Eastoft GB 11 D10
Easton GB 13 D10
East Retford GB 11 E10
Eastriggs GB 5 F10
Eastry GB 15 E11
East Wemyss GB 5 C10
East Wittering GB 15 F7
Eastwood GB 11 E9
Eaton Socon GB 15 C8
Eaunes F 33 D8
Eauze F 33 C6
Ebberup DK 86 E5
Ebbs A 72 A5
Ebbw Vale GB 13 B8
Ebecik TR 181 A9
Ebeleben D 79 D8
Ebelsbach D 75 C8
Ebenal A 73 C9
Ebene Reichenau A 73 C8
Ebenfurth A 77 G10
Eben im Pongau A 73 B7
Ebensee A 73 A8
Ebensfeld D 75 B8
Ebenthal A 73 C9
Ebenweiler D 71 B9
Eberau A 149 B6
Eberbach D 21 F11
Ebergötzen D 79 C7
Ebermannsdorf D 75 D10
Ebermannstadt D 75 C9
Ebern D 75 B8
Eberndorf A 73 C10
Ebersbach D 80 D5
Ebersbach D 81 D7
Ebersbach an der Fils D 74 E6
Ebersberg D 75 F10
Eberschwang A 76 F5
Ebersdorf D 17 A12
Ebersdorf D 79 C10
Ebersdorf bei Graz A 148 B5
Ebersdorf D 83 D8
Eberstein A 73 C9
Eberswalde-Finow D 84 E5
Ebhausen D 27 C10
Ebikon CH 27 F10
Ebnat-Kappel CH 27 F11
Eboli I 60 B4
Ebrach D 75 C8
Ebreichsdorf A 77 G10
Ébreuil F 30 C3
Ébsdorfergrund-Dreihausen D 21 C11
Ebstorf D 83 D8
Écaussinnes-d'Enghien B 182 D4
Ecclefechan GB 5 E10
Eccles GB 5 D12
Eccleshall GB 11 F7
Eceabat TR 171 D10
Echallens CH 31 B10
Echarri E 32 E2
Échauffour F 24 C3
Échenoz-la-Méline F 26 E5
Eching D 75 E11
Eching D 75 F10
Echinos GR 171 B7
Échiré F 28 C5
Échirolles F 31 E8
Échourgnac F 29 E6
Echsenbach A 77 E8
Echt GB 3 L12
Echt NL 19 B12
Echte D 79 C7
Echternach L 20 E6
Éčka SRB 158 C5
Eckartsberga D 79 D10
Eckbolsheim F 186 D4
Eckental D 75 C9
Eckernförde D 83 B7
Eckerö FIN 99 B13
Eckington GB 11 E9
Eckington GB 13 A10
Éclaron-Braucourt-Ste-Livière F 25 C12
Écommoy F 23 E12
Écos F 24 B6
Écouché F 23 C11
Écouflant F 23 E10
Écouis F 18 F3
Écrouves F 26 C4
Écs H 149 A9
Ecséd H 150 B4
Ecseg H 147 F8
Ecsegfalva H 151 C6
Écseri F 150 C3
Écueillé F 29 A8
Écuisses F 30 B6
Écury-sur-Coole F 25 C11
Ed S 91 B10
Ed S 107 E12
Eda glasbruk S 96 C7
Edam NL 16 C4
Edane S 97 C8
Ēdas LV 134 C6
Eddelak D 82 C6
Edderton GB 3 K8
Eddleston GB 5 D10
Ede NL 16 D5
Ede S 103 B12
Edebäck S 97 B10
Edefors S 118 B5
Edegem B 19 B9
Edelény H 145 G2
Edelschrott A 73 B11
Edemissen D 79 B7
Eden S 107 D12
Edenderry IRL 7 F8
Edenkoben D 21 F10
Edermünde D 78 D5
Ederny GB 7 C7

Edesheim D 21 F10
Edewecht D 17 B9
Edewechterdamm D 17 B9
Edgmond GB 11 F7
Ediger-Eller D 21 D8
Edinburgh GB 5 D10
Edincik TR 173 D8
Edineț MD 153 A10
Edirne TR 171 A11
Edland N 94 C7
Edling D 75 F11
Edlingham GB 5 E13
Eik N 94 D3
Éдole LV 134 B3
Edolo I 69 A9
Edremit TR 173 E7
Edrosa P 39 E6
Edroso P 39 E6
Edsbro S 99 C10
Edsbruk S 93 C8
Edsbyn S 103 D10
Edsele S 107 E11
Edsvalla S 97 D9
Edzell GB 5 B11
Eefde NL 183 A8
Eeklo B 19 B8
Eelde-Paterswolde NL 17 B7
Eerbeek NL 16 D6
Eernegem B 182 C2
Eersel NL 16 F4
Eferding A 76 F6
Effelder D 75 B11
Effretikon CH 27 F10
Efkarpia GR 169 B8
Efkarpia GR 169 C10
Eforie RO 155 E3
Efpalio GR 174 C4
Efteni GR 165 B11
Egby S 89 B11
Egebæk DK 86 E3
Egebjerg DK 86 D5
Egebjerg DK 87 D9
Egeln D 79 C9
Egense DK 86 B6
Eger H 145 H1
Egerbakta H 145 H1
Egernsund DK 86 F5
Egersund N 94 F4
Egerszalók H 145 H1
Egervár H 149 C7
Egeskov DK 86 D5
Egestorf D 83 D8
Egga N 111 B19
Eggby S 91 C14
Egge N 105 B11
Eggebek D 82 A6
Eggenburg A 77 E9
Eggenfelden D 75 F12
Eggesin D 84 C6
Eggingen D 27 E9
Eggiwil CH 70 D5
Egglham D 76 E4
Eggolsheim D 75 C9
Eggstätt D 72 A5
Eggum N 110 D6
Eghezée B 19 C10
Eging am See D 76 E4
Eglaine LV 135 E12
Égletons F 29 E10
Egling D 72 A4
Eglingham GB 5 E13
Eglisau CH 27 E10
Eglinton GB 4 E2
Eglisau CH 27 E10
Eglish GB 7 D9
Eglwys Fach GB 10 F4
Eglwyswrw GB 12 A5
Egmond aan Zee NL 16 C3
Egna I 69 A11
Egorovca MD 153 B11
Egremont GB 10 C4
Egsmark DK 86 C7
Egtved DK 86 D4
Éguilles F 35 C9
Eguisheim F 27 D7
Éguzon-Chantôme F 29 C9
Egyek H 151 B6
Egyházaskozár H 149 D10
Ehekirchen D 75 E9
Ehingen D 75 D8
Ehingen (Donau) D 71 A9
Ehlen (Habichtswald) D 17 F12
Ehningen D 187 D6
Ehra-Lessien D 79 A8
Ehrenberg-Wüstensachsen D 74 B7
Ehrenburg D 17 C11
Ehrenfriedersdorf D 80 E3
Ehrenhausen A 148 C5
Ehringshausen D 21 C10
Eibar E 41 B7
Eibelstadt D 74 C7
Eibenstock D 75 B12
Eibergen NL 17 D7
Eibiswald A 148 C4
Eich D 21 E10
Eichenbarleben D 79 B9
Eichenbühl D 27 A11
Eichendorf D 75 E3
Eichenzell D 74 B6
Eichgraben A 77 F9
Eichigt D 75 B11
Eichstätt D 75 E9
Eichwalde D 80 B5
Eickendorf D 79 A7
Eicklingen D 79 A7
Eidapere EST 131 D9
Eide N 100 A6
Eide N 104 E3
Eide N 111 C11
Eidem N 108 E2
Eidet N 105 C15
Eidet N 105 C16
Eidet N 108 A9
Eidet N 110 D8
Eidfjord N 94 B6
Eiði FO 2 A2
Eidkjosen N 111 A16
Eidsbugarden N 101 D8
Eidsdal N 100 B6
Eidsfjord N 110 C8

Eidsfoss N 95 C12
Eidshaug N 105 B10
Eidsnes N 112 C10
Eidsøra N 100 A8
Eidstranda N 111 A19
Eidsvåg N 100 A8
Eidsvåg N 100 A8
Eidsvoll N 95 B14
Eidsvoll Verk N 95 B14
Eidvågeid N 113 B12
Eigeltingen D 27 E10
Eigenrieden D 79 D7
Eijsden NL 183 D7
Eik N 94 C7
Eikelandsosen N 94 B3
Eiken N 94 F6
Eikesdal N 100 B8
Eikjaberg N 100 E3
Eikjeskog N 94 E4
Eikjil N 90 B1
Eiksund N 100 B3
Eilenburg D 79 D12
Eilsleben D 79 B9
Eime D 78 B6
Eimen D 78 C6
Eimke D 83 E8
Eina N 101 E13
Einbeck D 78 C6
Eindhoven NL 16 F4
Einsiedeln CH 27 F10
Einville-au-Jard F 26 C5
Eisden B 183 D7
Eiselfing D 75 F11
Eisenach D 79 E7
Eisenberg D 79 E10
Eisenberg (Pfalz) D 21 E10
Eisenerz A 73 A10
Eisenhüttenstadt D 81 B7
Eisenkappel A 73 C9
Eisenstadt A 77 G11
Eisfeld D 75 B8
Eišiškės LT 137 E10
Eislandet N 100 E3
Eisleben, Lutherstadt D 79 C10
Eislingen (Fils) D 74 E6
Eiterborn D 21 D9
Eiterfeld D 78 E6
Eiternes N 105 B11
Eiterstraum N 108 E5
Eivindvik N 100 E2
Eivissa E 57 D7
Eja P 44 B4
Ejby DK 86 E5
Ejby DK 87 D9
Ejby DK 87 D9
Ejea de los Caballeros E 41 D9
Ejsing DK 86 B3
Ejstrupholm DK 86 D4
Ejulve E 42 C4
Eke B 182 D2
Ekeby S 87 C11
Ekeby S 87 D9
Ekeby S 89 B11
Ekeby S 92 E6
Ekeby S 99 D9
Ekeby-Almby S 97 D13
Ekedalen S 91 C14
Ekenäs FIN 127 F9
Ekenäs S 93 B9
Ekenässjön S 92 E6
Ekerö S 99 D9
Eket S 87 C13
Ekkerøy N 114 C8
Ekmekçi TR 173 D9
Ekola FIN 122 D9
Ekorrträsk S 107 B16
Eksaarde B 182 C3
Eksel B 183 C6
Ekshärad S 97 B9
Eksjö S 92 D5
Eksta S 93 E12
Ekträsk S 118 F3
Ekzarkh-Antimovo BG 167 D8
Ekzarkh Yosif BG 161 F7
Elafos GR 169 D7
Elafotopos GR 168 E4
Elaiochori GR 171 C6
Elaionas GR 169 B9
Elaionas GR 174 A5
Elaionas GR 175 C7
El Álamo E 46 D5
El Algar E 56 F3
El Almendro E 51 D5
El Alquián E 55 F8
Elämäjärvi FIN 123 D15
El Arahal E 51 E8
El Arenal E 45 D10
Elassona GR 169 E7
El Astillero E 40 B4
Elateia GR 175 B6
Elati GR 169 E6
Elati GR 169 E5
Elatou GR 174 C4
El Ballestero E 55 B8
El Barco de Ávila E 45 D9
El Barraco E 46 D3
Elbasan AL 168 B3
Elbergen D 17 D8
Elbeuf F 18 F3
Elbigenalp A 71 C10
Elbingerode (Harz) D 79 C8
Elblag PL 139 B7
El Bodón E 45 D7
El Bonillo E 55 B7
El Bosque E 53 C6
El Bullaque E 46 F4
El Burgo E 53 C7
El Burgo de Ebro E 41 E10
El Burgo de Osma E 40 E5
El Burgo Ranero E 39 D9
El Buste E 41 E8
El Cabaco E 45 C8
El Cabildo y la Campana E 55 E9
El Cabo de Gata E 55 F8
El Campillo E 51 D6
El Campillo de la Jara E 45 E10
El Campo de Peñaranda E 45 C10
El Cañavate E 47 E8
El Carpio E 53 A8
El Carpio de Tajo E 46 E4
El Casar E 46 C6
El Casar de Escalona E 46 D3
El Castellar E 48 D3
El Castillo de las Guardas E 51 D7
El Catllar de Gaià E 43 E6

Eidesheim D 21 F10
El Centenillo E 54 C5
El Cerro de Andévalo E 51 D6
Elche E 56 E3
Elche de la Sierra E 55 C8
Elchingen D 187 E9
Elciego E 41 C6
Elçili TR 172 B6
El Coronil E 51 E8
El Cubo de Don Sancho E 45 C8
El Cubo de Tierra del Vino E 39 F8
El Cuervo E 47 D10
El Cuervo E 51 F7
Elda E 56 E3
Eldalsosen N 100 D4
Eldena D 83 D10
Elderslie E 97 B11
Eldingen D 83 E8
Eldsberga S 87 B12
Eleja LV 134 D7
El Ejido E 55 F7
Elek H 151 D7
Elektrėnai LT 137 D10
Elemir SRB 158 C5
Elena BG 166 D5
Elend D 79 C8
Eleousa GR 168 E4
El Escorial E 46 C4
Eleshnitsa BG 165 F8
El Espinar E 46 C4
El Estrecho E 56 F3
Elexalde E 40 B6
El Fendek MA 53 E5
Elfershausen D 187 A8
El Fresno E 46 C3
Elgå N 101 B15
El Garrobo E 51 D7
Elgershausen (Schauenburg) D 21 B12
Elgeta E 41 B7
Elgin GB 3 K10
Elgoibar E 32 D1
Elgol GB 2 L4
El Grado E 42 C4
El Granado E 50 D5
El Grau de Borriana E 48 E4
Elgsnes N 111 C11
El Herrumblar E 47 F9
El Hito E 47 E7
El Hoyo de Pinares E 46 C4
Elia GR 178 A3
Elice I 62 B5
Elie GB 5 C11
Elika GR 178 B4
Elimäki FIN 127 D15
Eling GB 13 D12
Elini I 64 D4
El Molar E 46 C5
El Molinillo E 46 F4
El Moral E 55 D8
El Morell E 42 E6
Elmshorn D 82 C7
Elne F 34 E4
Elnesvågen N 100 A6
Elorrio E 41 B6
Elorz E 32 E2
Elos GR 178 E6
El Oso E 46 C3
El Palmar E 56 F3
El Palo E 53 C8
El Payo E 45 D7
El Pedernoso E 47 F7
El Pedroso E 51 D8
El Pedroso de la Armuña E 45 B10
El Peral E 47 E9
El Perdigón E 39 F8
El Perelló E 42 F5
El Perelló E 48 F4
El Picazo E 47 E8
El Pinell de Bray E 42 E5
El Piñero E 39 F9
El Pla de Santa María E 43 E6
El Pobo E 42 F3
El Pobo de Dueñas E 47 C9
El Pont d'Armentera E 43 E6
El Port de la Selva E 34 F5
El Prat de Llobregat E 43 E8
El Provencio E 47 F7
El Puente E 40 B5
El Puente de Arzobispo E 45 E10
El Puerto de Santa María E 52 C4
El Real de la Jara E 51 D7
El Real de San Vicente E 46 D3
El Recuenco E 47 C8
El Robledo E 46 F4
El Rocío E 51 E7
El Romeral E 46 E6
El Rompido E 51 E5
El Ronquillo E 51 D7
El Royo E 41 E6
El Rubio E 53 B7
El Sabinar E 41 D9
El Sabinar E 55 C8
El Saler E 48 F4
El Salobral E 55 B9
Els Arcs E 42 E5
El Saucejo E 53 B6
El Saugo E 45 D7
Elsdon GB 5 E12
Elsdorf D 21 C7
Elsenborn B 20 D6
Elsendorf D 75 E11
Elsenfeld D 21 E12
El Serrat AND 33 E9
Elsfjord N 108 D6
Elsfleth D 17 B10
Elshitsa BG 165 E9
Elsloo NL 183 D7
Elsnes N 111 B19
Elsnig D 80 C3
Elsnigk D 79 C11
Elsø N 111 B18
Els Prats de Rei E 43 D7
Elst NL 16 E5
Elst NL 183 B6
Elster D 79 C12
Elsterberg D 79 E11
Elsterwerda D 80 D5
Elstra D 80 D6
El Tiemblo E 46 D4
Eltmann D 75 C8
El Toboso E 47 E7
Elton GB 11 F11
Elton IRL 8 D6
El Torno E 45 D8
El Trincheto E 46 F4
El Tumbalejo E 51 E6
Eltville am Rhein D 21 D10
Elva EST 131 E12
Elvål N 101 C14
Elvanfoot GB 5 E9
Elvas P 51 B5
Elvebakken N 113 D11
Elvegård N 111 D13
Elvekrok N 113 B17
Elvelund N 112 E6
Elvemund N 113 E16
Elven F 22 E6
El Vendrell E 43 E7
El Verger E 56 D5
Elverum N 101 E15
Elvestad N 95 D13
Elve's N 108 B6
Elvevollen N 111 B18
El Villar de Arnedo E 32 F1
Elvington GB 11 D10
El Viso E 54 C3
El Viso del Alcor E 51 E8
Elvnes N 114 D8
Elx E 56 E3
Elxleben D 79 D8
Ely GB 13 C8
Ely GB 15 C9
Elz D 185 D9
Elzach D 27 D9
Elze D 78 B6
Elze (Wedemark) D 78 A6
Embid E 47 C9
Embid de Ariza E 41 F8
Embleton GB 5 E13
Embrun F 36 B4
Emburga LV 135 C7
Embüte LV 134 C3
Emden D 17 B8
Emecik TR 181 C7
Emiralem TR 177 B9
Emirali TR 173 B8
Emlichheim D 17 C7
Emly IRL 8 D6
Emmaboda S 89 B9
Emmaljunga S 87 C13
Emmanouil Pappas GR 169 B10
Emmaste EST 130 D5
Emmeloord NL 16 C5
Emmelshausen D 21 D9
Emmen CH 27 F9
Emmen NL 17 C7
Emmendingen D 27 D8
Emmer-Compascuum NL 17 C8
Emmerich D 16 E6
Emmoo IRL 6 E6
Emőd H 145 H2
Emolahti FIN 123 C15
Empel NL 16 E4
Emponas GR 181 D7
Emporeio GR 179 C9
Emporeios GR 177 C7
Emptinne B 19 D11
Emsbüren D 17 D8
Emsdetten D 17 D9
Emsfors S 89 A10
Emskirchen D 75 C8
Emst NL 16 D5
Emstek D 17 C10
Emsworth GB 15 F7
Emtinghausen D 17 C11
Emtunga S 91 C12
Emyvale IRL 7 D9
Enafors S 105 E12
Enájärvi FIN 128 D7
Enånger S 103 C13
Enånger S 105 D16
Encamp AND 33 E9
Encinas de Abajo E 45 C10
Encinasola E 51 C6
Encinas Reales E 53 B8
Encinedo E 39 D6
Enciso E 41 D7
Encs H 145 G3
Ecsencis H 151 B9
Endingen D 187 D8
Endre S 93 D12
Endrefalva H 147 E9
Endriejavas LT 134 E3
Endrinal E 45 C9

Endzele LV 131 F10
Enebakk N 95 C14
Enego I 72 E4
Eneryda S 88 B6
Enese H 149 A8
Enez TR 171 C10
Enfesta E 38 C2
Enfield IRL 7 F9
Engan N 101 B11
Engan N 104 E4
Engan N 108 D3
Engares GR 176 E5
Engavågen N 108 C6
Engden D 183 A10
Engelberg CH 71 D6
Engelhartstetten A 77 F11
Engelhartszell A 76 E5
Engeln D 17 C11
Engelsberg D 75 F12
Engelskirchen D 21 C8
Engen D 27 E10
Enger D 17 D11
Engerdal N 101 C15
Engerdalssetra N 101 C15
Engerneset N 102 C3
Engesen D 79 A9
Engesland N 90 B3
Engesvang DK 86 C4
Enghien B 19 C9
Engis B 19 C11
Englefontaine F 19 D8
Engomer F 33 E8
Engstingen D 27 D11
Enguera E 56 D3
Enguidanos E 47 E9
Engure LV 134 B6
Engvik N 112 C2
Enhagen-Ekbacken S 98 C7
Enichioi MD 154 E2
Enina BG 166 D4
Eningen unter Achalm D 187 E7
Enitsa BG 165 C9
Enix E 55 F7
Enkenbach D 186 C4
Enkhuizen NL 16 C4
Enkirch D 21 E8
Enklinge FIN 99 B15
Enköping S 98 C8
Enmo N 101 A12
Enna I 58 D5
Ennepetal D 185 B7
Ennery I 186 C1
Ennezat F 30 D3
Ennigerloh D 17 E10
Ennis IRL 8 C5
Enniscorthy IRL 9 C9
Enniscrone IRL 6 D4
Enniskean IRL 8 E5
Enniskerry IRL 7 F10
Enniskillen GB 7 D7
Ennistymon IRL 8 C4
Enns A 77 F6
Eno FIN 125 E14
Enonkoski FIN 125 F11
Enonkylä FIN 119 F17
Enontekiö FIN 117 B11
Ens NL 16 C5
Enschede NL 17 D7
Ensdorf D 75 D10
Ensdorf D 186 C2
Ense D 17 F10
Ensheim D 21 F8
Ensisheim F 27 E7
Enskogen S 103 C9
Ensués-la-Redonne F 35 D9
Enter NL 183 A9
Enterkinfoot GB 5 E9
Entlebuch CH 70 C5
Entracque I 37 C6
Entradas P 50 D3
Entraigues-sur-la-Sorgue F 35 B8
Entrains-sur-Nohain F 25 F9
Entrammes F 23 E10
Entraunes F 36 C5
Entraygues-sur-Truyère F 33 A11
Entrena E 41 D6
Entrevaux F 36 D5
Entroncamento P 44 F4
Envendos P 44 E5
Envermeu F 18 E3
Enviken S 103 E10
Enying H 149 C10
Enzklösterle D 27 C9
Eochaill IRL 9 E7
Eoropaidh GB 2 H4
Épaignes F 18 F1
Épalinges CH 31 C10
Epano Fellos GR 176 D4
Epanomi GR 169 D8
Epe NL 16 D5
Eperjes H 150 D6
Eperjeske H 145 G5
Épernay F 25 B10
Épernon F 24 C6
Epfendorf D 27 D10
Épieds-en-Beauce F 24 E6
Épierre F 31 E9
Épila E 41 E9
Épinac F 30 B6
Épinal F 26 D5
Epiry F 25 F10
Episcopia I 60 C6
Episkopi GR 169 C7
Episkopi GR 178 E7
Episkopi GR 178 E9
Epitalio GR 174 D3
Époisses F 25 E11
Epoo FIN 127 E14
Eppelborn D 21 F7
Eppelheim D 21 F11
Eppenbrunn D 186 C4
Eppertshausen D 21 E11
Eppeville F 19 E7
Epping GB 15 D9
Eppingen D 27 B10
Eppishausen D 71 A11
Eppstein D 21 D10
Epsom GB 15 E8
Eptachori GR 168 D5
Épuisay F 24 E4
Epureni RO 153 E11
Epworth GB 11 D10
Équeurdreville-Hainneville F 23 A8
Eraclea I 73 E6
Eraclea Mare I 47 A6
Eräjärvi FIN 127 B12
Eräjärvi FIN 129 C10
Erastvere EST 131 F13
Erateini GR 174 C5
Eratyra GR 169 D6

Erba I 69 B7
Erbach D 75 C11
Erbach D 74 F6
Erbendorf D 75 C11
Erberge LV 135 D10
Erbiceni RO 153 C10
Erbray F 23 E9
Erchie I 61 C9
Ercsi H 149 B11
Érd H 149 B11
Erdeborn D 79 D10
Erdek TR 173 D8
Erdelli TR 177 B10
Erdeven F 22 E5
Erdőkertes H 150 B3
Erdut HR 157 A11
Erdweg D 75 F9
Erdžilija MK 164 F5
Eréac F 23 D7
Eremitu RO 152 D5
Eremiya BG 165 E6
Erenler TR 173 D10
Eresos GR 177 A6
Eretria GR 169 F8
Eretria GR 175 C8
Erfde D 82 B6
Erftstadt D 21 C7
Erfurt D 79 E9
Ergeme LV 131 F11
Ergersheim D 75 C7
Ergili TR 173 D9
Ergli LV 135 C11
Ergoldsbach D 75 E11
Ergué-Gabéric F 22 D3
Erharting D 75 F11
Eriboll GB 2 J7
Erice E 32 E2
Erice I 58 C2
Ericeira P 50 B1
Eriklice TR 173 C7
Eriksberg S 107 A9
Erikslund S 103 A10
Eriksmåla S 89 B8
Erikssund S 99 C9
Ering D 76 F4
Eringsboda S 89 C8
Eriswil CH 70 C5
Erjova MD 154 B4
Erkelenz D 20 B6
Erkheim D 71 A10
Erkner D 80 B5
Erla E 41 D10
Erlach CH 31 A11
Erlangen D 75 C9
Erlauf A 77 F8
Erlbach D 75 B11
Erlenbach am Main D 187 B7
Erli I 37 C8
Ermelo NL 16 D5
Ermelo P 38 F4
Ermenonville F 25 B8
Ermesinde P 44 B3
Ermidas do Sado P 50 C3
Ermioni GR 175 E7
Ermocila MD 154 B4
Ermoupoli GR 176 E4
Ermsleben D 79 C9
Ermua E 41 B6
Erndtebrück D 21 C10
Ernée F 23 D10
Ernei RO 152 D5
Ernestinovo HR 149 F11
Ernstbrunn A 77 E10
Erp NL 16 E5
Érpatak H 145 H4
Erpel D 21 C8
Erquelinnes B 184 D1
Erquy F 22 C7
Erra P 50 A3
Errenteria E 32 D2
Errezil E 32 D1
Erribera E 41 B7
Errill IRL 9 C7
Errindlev DK 83 A11
Erritsø DK 86 D5
Errogie GB 3 L8
Érsekcsanád H 150 E2
Érsekhalma AL 168 C1
Érsekvadkert H 147 E8
Ersfjord N 111 B13
Ersfjordbotn N 111 A16
Ersmark S 107 A11
Ersmark S 118 C5
Ersmark S 122 C4
Ersnäs S 119 C7
Erstein F 27 D8
Erstfeld CH 71 D7
Ersvik N 108 B7
Ertenvåg N 108 B7
Ertingen D 71 A8
Erto I 72 D5
Ertsjärv S 116 E8
Ertuğrul TR 173 D9
Ertvelde B 182 C3
Erula I 64 B2
Ervalla S 97 D13
Ervasti FIN 121 D9
Ervedosa do Douro P 44 B6
Ervenik HR 156 D4
Ervidel P 50 D3
Ervik N 104 E5
Ervillers F 18 D6
Ervy-le-Châtel F 25 D10
Erwitte D 17 E10
Erxleben D 79 B9
Erxleben D 83 E11
Erythres GR 175 C7
Erzhausen D 21 E11
Eržvilkas LT 134 F5
Esanatoglia I 67 F6
Esbjerg DK 86 E2
Esbo FIN 127 E12
Esbønderup DK 87 C10
Escairón E 38 C4
Escalante E 40 B4
Escalaplano I 64 D3
Escalhão P 45 C7
Escaló E 33 E8
Es Caló E 57 D8
Escalona E 46 D4
Escalona del Prado E 46 B4
Escalonilla E 46 E4
Escalos de Baixo P 44 E6
Escalos de Cima P 44 E6
Escamilla E 47 C7
Es Canar E 57 C8
Escañuela E 53 A8
Escariche E 47 D7
Escarigo P 45 D6
Escároz E 32 E3
Es Castell E 57 B13

Escatrón E 42 E3
Esch NL 183 B6
Eschau D 187 B7
Eschau F 186 E4
Eschborn D 187 A6
Esche D 17 C7
Escheburg D 83 D8
Eschede D 83 E8
Eschenbach CH 27 F9
Eschenburg-Eibelshausen D 21 C10
Eschenstruth (Helsa) D 78 D6
Eschershausen D 78 C6
Eschlkam D 76 D3
Escholzmatt CH 70 D5
Esch-sur-Alzette L 20 E5
Esch-sur-Sûre L 20 E5
Eschwege D 79 D7
Eschweiler D 20 C6
Escombreras E 56 F3
Escorca E 49 E10
Escorihuela E 42 F2
Escos F 32 D3
Escouloubre F 33 E10
Escource F 32 B3
Escout F 32 D4
Escragnolles F 36 D5
Escucha E 42 F2
Escúzar E 53 B9
Esechioi RO 161 E10
Esence TR 173 D10
Esenköy TR 173 C10
Esenler TR 173 B8
Esens D 17 A9
Esenyurt TR 173 B10
Esgos E 38 D4
Esgueira P 44 C3
Esguevillas de Esgueva E 40 E3
Eskdalemuir GB 5 E10
Eskelhem S 93 E12
Eskişehir TR 181 A8
Eskilstrup DK 84 A1
Eskilstuna S 98 D7
Eskioba S 177 C10
Eskişigirçi TR 173 D9
Eskogen S 99 C10
Eskola FIN 123 C12
Eskoriatza E 41 B6
Esku EST 131 C11
Eslarn D 75 C12
Eslava E 32 E3
Eslohe (Sauerland) D 17 F10
Eslöv S 87 D12
Es Mercadal E 57 B13
Es Migjorn Gran E 57 B13
Esnes F 19 D7
Esneux B 19 C12
Espa N 101 E14
Espadañedo E 39 D7
Espalion F 34 A4
Espaly-St-Marcel F 30 E4
Esparragalejo E 51 B7
Esparragosa E 51 B9
Esparragosa de la Serena E 51 B8
Esparreguera E 43 D7
Esparron F 35 C10
Esparza de Salazar E 32 E3
Espe DK 86 E6
Espedal N 94 E4
Espeja E 45 C7
Espeja de San Marcelino E 40 E5
Espejo E 53 A7
Espejón E 40 E5
Espel NL 16 C5
Espeland N 94 B2
Espelette F 32 D3
Espelkamp D 17 D11
Espenau D 78 D5
Espenes N 111 B14
Espera E 51 F8
Esperança P 45 F6
Espéraza F 33 E10
Espergærde DK 87 D11
Esperia I 62 E5
Espevik N 94 C3
Espezel F 33 E10
Espiel E 54 C3
Espinama E 39 B10
Espinasses F 36 C4
Espinhal F 44 E4
Espinho P 44 B3
Espinilla E 40 B3
Espinosa de Cerrato E 40 E4
Espinosa de Henares E 47 C6
Espinosa de los Monteros E 40 B4
Espinoso del Rey E 46 E3
Espira-de-l'Agly F 34 E4
Espírito Santo P 50 D4
Espite P 44 E3
Esplegares E 47 C8
Esplús E 42 D4
Espolla E 34 F5
Espondeilham F 34 D5
Esponellà E 43 C9
Espoo FIN 127 E12
Espoonlahti FIN 127 E12
Esporles E 49 E10
Esposende P 38 E2
Espot E 33 E8
Esprels F 26 E5
Esquivias E 46 D5
Esrange S 116 C6
Essay F 23 C11
Esse FIN 123 C10
Essel D 82 E7
Essen B 16 F2
Essen D 17 F8
Essen (Oldenburg) D 17 C9
Esslingen D 74 E7
Esslingen am Neckar D 27 C11
Essoyes F 25 D12
Essu EST 131 C12
Essvik S 103 B13
Estación de Baeza E 54 C5
Estadilla E 42 C4
Estagel F 34 E4
Estaimpuis B 19 C7
Estaing F 34 A4
Estaires F 18 C6
Estang F 32 C5
Estarreja P 44 C3
Estavayer-le-Lac CH 31 B10
Este I 66 B4
Este P 38 E3
Estela P 38 F2

Estella E 32 E1
Estellencs E 49 E10
Estenfeld D 187 B9
Estepa E 53 B7
Estepar E 40 D4
Estepona E 53 D6
Esteras de Medinaceli E 47 B8
Estercuel E 42 F2
Esternay F 25 C10
Esterri d'Àneu E 33 E8
Esterzili I 64 D3
Estiavreilles F 30 E5
Estissac F 25 D10
Estivareilles F 29 C11
Estói P 50 E4
Estômbar P 50 E3
Estorf D 17 A10
Estorf D 17 C12
Estoril P 51 C5
Estoublon F 36 D4
Estrablin F 31 D6
Estrées-St-Denis F 18 F6
Estreito P 44 E5
Estrela P 51 C5
Estremera E 47 D6
Estremoz P 50 B4
Estriégala E 47 B7
Esvres F 24 F4
Esztár H 151 C8
Esztergom H 149 A11
Étables-sur-Mer F 22 C6
Étagnac F 29 D7
Étain F 19 F12
Étais-la-Sauvin F 25 E9
Étalante F 25 E12
Étalle B 19 E12
Étampes F 24 D7
Étang-sur-Arroux F 30 B5
Étaples F 15 F12
Étaules F 28 D3
Étauliers F 28 E4
Eteläinen FIN 127 C12
Etelä-Vartsala FIN 126 D5
Etelhem S 93 E13
Éternoz F 31 A9
Etes H 147 E9
Ethe B 19 E12
Etholmen N 91 A9
Etili TR 173 E6
Étival F 31 B8
Étival-Clairefontaine F 27 D6
Étivey F 25 E11
Etna N 101 E11
Etne N 94 C3
Étréchy F 24 D7
Étrépagny F 18 F4
Étretat F 23 A12
Étreux F 19 E8
Etrín Bajo E 51 B6
Etropole BG 165 D9
Étroubles I 31 D11
Ettelbruck L 20 E6
Etten-Leur NL 16 E3
Ettington GB 13 A11
Ettlingen D 27 C9
Ettrick GB 5 E10
Ettringen D 21 D8
Etulia MD 155 B2
Étupes F 27 E6
Étuz F 26 F4
Etwall GB 11 F8
Etxalar E 32 D2
Etxarri-Aranatz E 32 E1
Etyek H 149 B11
Eu F 18 D3
Eubigheim D 74 C7
Euerdorf D 74 B7
Eugénie-les-Bains F 32 C5
Eugmo FIN 122 C9
Eulate E 32 E1
Eupen B 20 C6
Euper D 79 C12
Eura FIN 126 C7
Eurajoki FIN 126 C6
Eurasburg D 72 A3
Eurville-Bienville F 26 C3
Euskirchen D 21 C7
Eußenheim D 74 B6
Eutin D 83 B9
Eutingen im Gäu D 187 E6
Eutzsch D 79 C12
Euville F 26 C4
Eva GR 174 E4
Evanger N 100 E4
Evanton GB 3 K8
Évaux-les-Bains F 29 C10
Evciler TR 173 E6
Evciler TR 173 E7
Evdilos GR 177 D7
Évele LV 131 F11
Evenes N 109 C10
Evenesdal N 109 C10
Evenset N 108 B8
Evenskjær N 111 C12
Evenstad N 101 D14
Everdingen NL 183 B6
Everdrup DK 87 E9
Evergem B 19 B8
Everöd S 88 D6
Eversberg S 102 A6
Evertsberg S 102 D6
Evesham GB 13 A11
Évian-les-Bains F 31 C10
Evijärvi FIN 123 D10
Evisa F 37 G9
Evitskog FIN 127 E11
Evje N 90 B2
Evlalo GR 171 C7
Evolène CH 31 C12
Évora P 50 B4
Évora-Monte P 50 B4
Evosmos GR 169 C8
Évran F 23 D8
Évrecy F 23 B10
Evrencik TR 173 A8
Evrenli TR 173 B7
Évreux F 24 B5
Évron F 23 D11
Évropos GR 169 C8
Evrostina GR 174 C5
Évry F 25 C7
Evzonoi GR 169 C8
Ewhurst GB 15 E8
Examilia GR 175 D6
Exaplatanos GR 169 C7
Exarchos GR 175 B6
Excideuil F 29 E8
Exebridge GB 13 C7
Exeter GB 13 D7
Exilles I 31 E10
Exloo NL 17 C7

Exmes F 23 C12
Exminster GB 13 D8
Exmouth GB 13 D8
Exochi GR 169 B10
Exochi GR 169 D7
Exo Chora GR 174 D2
Exo Vathy GR 180 C4
Extremo P 38 E3
Eydehavn N 90 B4
Eydelstedt D 17 C11
Eye GB 11 F11
Eye GB 15 C11
Eyemouth GB 5 D12
Eyeries IRL 8 E3
Eyguians F 35 B10
Eyguières F 35 C9
Eygurande-et-Gardedeuil F 29 E6
Eymet F 33 A6
Eymoutiers F 29 D9
Eynsham GB 13 B12
Eyragues F 35 C8
Eyrans F 28 E4
Eyrarbakki IS 201 G8
Eyrecourt IRL 6 F6
Eyrein F 29 E9
Eyzin-Pinet F 31 E6
Ezcaray E 40 D6
Ezcárate RO 158 D3
Eze F 37 D6
Ezère LV 134 D3
Ežerėlis LT 137 D8
Ezerets BG 155 F3
Ezeriş RO 159 C8
Ezerkalne LV 134 B5
Ezerkalnis LV 134 B5
Ezerkalni LV 133 D3
Ezine TR 171 E10
Ezkurra E 32 D2
Ézy-sur-Eure F 24 C5

F

Faaborg DK 86 E6
Fabara E 42 E4
Fabas F 33 D8
Fåberg N 100 C6
Fåberg N 101 D12
Fabero E 39 C6
Fábiánháza H 145 H5
Fabianki PL 138 E7
Fábiánsebestyén H 150 D5
Fåbodliden S 107 B13
Fåborg DK 86 D3
Fabrègues F 35 C6
Fabrezan F 34 D4
Fabriano I 67 F6
Fabrica di Roma I 62 C2
Fábricas de San Juan de Alcaraz E 55 B8
Fabrizia I 59 C9
Fabro I 62 B2
Făcăeni RO 155 D1
Faches-Thumesnil F 182 D2
Facinas E 52 D5
Fadd H 149 D11
Faedis I 73 D7
Faenza I 66 D4
Fafe P 38 F3
Fagagna I 73 D7
Făgăraş RO 152 F5
Fågelfors S 89 A10
Fågelmara S 89 C9
Fågelsjö S 102 C8
Fågelsta S 92 C6
Fågelsundet S 103 E14
Fagerås S 97 C9
Fagerdal S 106 D8
Fagerhaug N 101 A11
Fagerhult S 91 C11
Fagerhult S 92 C4
Fagerli N 109 B11
Fagernes N 101 E10
Fagernes N 111 A17
Fagersanna S 92 C4
Fagersta S 97 C14
Fagervik FIN 127 E11
Fagervika N 108 D4
Fagervkan S 99 A9
Fäget RO 151 F9
Fågetelu RO 160 D5
Fäggeby S 97 B14
Fagnano Castello I 60 D6
Fagnières F 25 C11
Fahan IRL 4 E2
Fahrdorf D 82 A7
Fahrenkrug D 83 B8
Fahrenzhausen D 75 F10
Fahrland D 80 B4
Faicchio I 60 A2
Faid D 21 D8
Faido CH 71 E7
Failde P 39 E6
Faimes B 19 C11
Fain-lès-Montbard F 25 E11
Fains-Véel F 26 C3
Fairlie GB 4 D7
Fair Oak GB 13 D12
Faissault F 19 E10
Fajão P 44 D5
Fajarda P 50 B2
Fajslawice PL 144 A6
Fajsz H 149 D11
Fakenham GB 15 B10
Fåker S 106 E7
Fakija BG 167 E8
Fakovići BIH 158 E4
Faksdal N 105 B10
Fakse DK 87 E10
Fakse Ladeplads DK 87 E10
Falaise F 23 C11
Falani GR 169 E7
Fålasjö S 107 E13
Falcade I 72 D4
Falcarragh IRL 6 B6
Falces E 32 F2
Fălciu RO 154 E2
Falck F 186 C2
Fålcoiu RO 160 E4
Falconara I 58 E4
Falconara Albanese I 60 E6
Falconara Marittima I 67 E7
Falcone I 59 C7
Faldsled DK 86 E6
Fale N 101 A9
Faleria E 62 C2
Falerna I 59 A9
Falerone I 62 A4
Falerum S 93 C8
Fălești MD 153 B11

Falkekeila N 114 C8
Falkenberg D 75 C11
Falkenberg D 75 F12
Falkenberg D 80 D2
Falkenberg S 87 B11
Falkenhagen D 79 D12
Falkenhain D 79 D12
Falkensee D 80 A4
Falkenstein D 75 A11
Falkenstein D 75 D11
Falkirk GB 5 D9
Falkland GB 5 C10
Falköping S 91 C14
Falla N 97 A8
Falla S 92 B7
Falleron F 28 B2
Fällfors S 118 C5
Fälloheden S 109 E15
Fällsvikhamnen S 103 A15
Falltorp S 97 A8
Falmenta I 68 A5
Falmouth GB 12 E4
Falset E 42 E5
Falstad N 105 D10
Fălticeni RO 153 C8
Falträsk S 107 B15
Falun S 103 E10
Famalicão P 44 D6
Fambach D 79 E7
Fameck F 20 F6
Fanari GR 171 C8
Fanari GR 174 A4
Fanano I 66 D2
Fanari GR 171 C8
Fanbyn S 107 E16
Fångsjöbacken S 107 E11
Fångsjön S 107 D12
Fanjeaux F 33 D10
Fanlo E 32 E5
Fannrem N 104 E7
Fano I 67 E7
Fanore IRL 6 F4
Fanos GR 169 B7
Fântânele RO 151 E5
Fântânele RO 152 E5
Fanthyttan S 97 C13
Fão P 38 E2
Fara Filiorum Petri I 63 C6
Fărăgău RO 152 D5
Fara in Sabina I 62 C3
Faraoani RO 153 D9
Fara San Martino I 63 C6
Farasdues E 41 D9
Fårberget S 107 C15
Fårbo S 93 E8
Farchant D 72 A3
Farciennes B 19 D10
Fardal N 90 A3
Fardella I 60 C6
Fardhem S 93 E12
Fardrum IRL 7 F7
Farébersviller F 186 C2
Fareham GB 13 D12
Faremoutiers F 25 C8
Farfa I 62 B3
Farfara GB 3 L8
Farga d'Alpago I 72 D5
Faringdon GB 13 B11
Farini I 37 B11
Fariza de Sayago E 39 F7
Färjestaden S 89 B10
Farkadona GR 169 E7
Farlete E 41 E10
Färlöv S 88 C6
Fårö S 93 D14
Fårösund S 93 D14
Farr GB 3 L8
Farra d'Alpago I 72 D5
Farranfore IRL 8 D3
Farre DK 86 C4
Farre DK 86 D4
Farsala GR 169 E7
Fårsan S 107 E10
Farsø DK 86 B4
Farstrup DK 86 B4
Farsund N 94 F5
Fârtăţeşti RO 153 F11
Fârtăţeşti RO 160 D3
Farum DK 87 D10
Farvang DK 86 C5
Farynava BY 133 F5
Fasano I 61 B8
Fasgar E 39 C7
Fasnakyle GB 2 L7
Fässbergs RKS 164 E3
Fasty PL 140 D8
Fatela P 44 D6
Fatela GR 171 C10
Fátima P 44 E3
Fatjas S 116 E4
Fatmomakke S 106 A8
Fatnica BIH 157 F9
Fättjaur S 106 A8
Faucogney-et-la-Mer F 26 E6
Faugères F 34 C5
Fauglia I 66 E2
Fauguerolles F 33 B6
Faulbach D 187 B7
Fauldhouse GB 5 D9
Faulenrost D 83 C13
Faulquemont F 26 B6
Fauquembergues F 18 C5
Faura E 48 E4
Făurei RO 153 D9
Făurei RO 155 C1
Fauske N 109 B10
Fauskevåg N 111 C12
Fauville-en-Caux F 18 E2
Faux F 29 F7

Faux-la-Montagne F 29 D9
Favaios P 38 F5
Favale di Malvaro I 37 C10
Fåvang N 101 D12
Favara E 48 F4
Favara I 58 E4
Faverges F 31 D9
Faverney F 26 E5
Faverolles F 30 F3
Faversham GB 15 E10
Favignana I 58 D1
Fawley GB 13 D12
Fay-de-Bretagne F 23 F8
Fayence F 36 D5
Fayl-Billot F 26 E4
Fayón E 42 E4
Fay-sur-Lignon F 30 F5
Fažana HR 67 C8
Fazeley GB 11 F8
Feakle IRL 8 C5
Fécamp F 18 E1
Feda N 94 F5
Fedamore IRL 8 C5
Fedje N 100 E1
Fedosiyivka UA 154 B4
Feeard IRL 8 C3
Feeny GB 4 F2
Fegen S 87 A12
Fégréac F 23 E7
Fegyvernek H 150 C6
Fehérgyarmat H 145 H6
Fehrbellin D 83 E13
Fehring A 148 C6
Feijó P 50 B1
Feilbingert D 21 E9
Feilitzsch D 75 B10
Feillens F 30 C6
Feissons-sur-Isère F 31 D9
Feistritz im Rosental A 73 C9
Feistritz ob Bleiburg A 73 C10
Feiteira P 50 E4
Feketić SRB 158 B4
Felanitx E 57 C11
Feldbach D 34 D6
Felcsút H 149 B11
Feld am See A 73 C8
Feldbach A 148 C5
Feldberg D 84 D4
Feldberg D 84 D4
Felde D 83 B7
Feldebrő H 147 F10
Feldioara RO 153 F7
Feldkirch A 71 C9
Feldkirchen in Kärnten A 73 C9
Feldkirchen-Westerham D 72 A4
Feldru RO 152 C5
Feleacu RO 152 D3
Felgar P 45 B7
Felgueiras P 38 F3
Felgyő H 150 D5
Feliceni RO 152 E6
Felindre GB 13 A8
Félines F 30 E6
Felino I 66 C1
Felitto I 60 C4
Félix E 55 F7
Felixdorf A 77 G10
Felixstowe GB 15 D11
Felizzano I 37 B8
Fell D 21 E7
Fellbach D 27 C11
Felletin F 29 D10
Fellingsbro S 97 D14
Felnac RO 151 E7
Felsberg D 21 B12
Felsberg D 78 D6
Felsődobsza H 145 G3
Felsőlajos H 150 C4
Felsőnyék H 149 C10
Felsőpakeny H 150 C3
Felsőszentiván H 150 E3
Felsőszentmárton H 149 E9
Felsőtárkány H 145 H1
Felsőzsolca H 145 G2
Felsted DK 86 F4
Felton GB 5 E13
Feltwell GB 11 G13
Femundsenden N 101 C15
Femundsundet N 101 C15
Fénay F 26 F3
Fendeille F 33 D9
Fene E 38 B3
Fenerköy TR 173 B9
Fenes N 111 C12
Fenestrelle I 31 E11
Fénétrange F 27 C7
Feneu F 23 E10
Fengersfors S 91 B11
Fenioux F 28 B5
Fenis I 31 D11
Fenit IRL 8 D3
Feniton GB 13 D8
Fensmark DK 87 E9
Fenstanton GB 15 C8
Fenwick GB 5 D13
Fényeslitke H 145 G5
Feofilova Pustyn' RUS 132 E5
Feolin Ferry GB 4 D4
Feonanagh IRL 8 D5
Fépin F 19 D10
Ferbane IRL 7 F7
Ferdinandea I 59 B9
Ferdinandovac HR 149 D8
Ferdinandshof D 84 C5
Fère-Champenoise F 25 C10
Fère-en-Tardenois F 25 B10
Férel F 23 F7
Ferentino I 62 D4
Feres GR 171 C10
Férez E 55 C9
Feričanci HR 149 E9
Ferizaj RKS 164 E3
Ferlach A 73 C9
Fermignano I 66 E6
Fermo I 67 F8
Fermoselle E 39 F7
Fermoy IRL 8 D6
Fernáncaballero E 46 F5
Fernán Núñez E 53 A7
Ferndown GB 13 D11
Ferness GB 3 L9
Ferney-Voltaire F 31 C9
Fernitz A 148 C5
Ferns IRL 9 C9
Feroleto Antico I 59 B9
Ferrals-les-Corbières F 34 D4
Ferrandina I 61 C7
Ferrara I 66 C4
Ferrazzano I 63 D7
Ferreira do Alentejo P 50 C3

Ferreira do Zêzere P 44 E4
Ferrel P 44 F2
Ferreras de Abajo E 39 E7
Ferreras de Arriba E 39 E7
Ferrere I 37 B7
Ferreries E 57 B13
Ferreruela de Huerva E 47 B10
Ferreruela de Tábara E 39 E7
Ferriere I 37 B11
Ferrières B 19 D12
Ferrières F 25 D8
Ferritslet DK 86 E7
Ferrol E 38 B3
Ferrybank IRL 9 C10
Ferryhill GB 5 F13
Ferschweiler D 185 E5
Fertilia I 64 B1
Fertőd H 149 A7
Fertőrákos H 149 A7
Fertőszentmiklós H 149 A7
Ferwert NL 16 B5
Feshiebridge GB 3 L9
Fessenheim F 27 E8
Festieux F 19 E8
Festvåg N 108 B6
Feteşti MD 153 A10
Feteşti RO 155 E1
Feteşti-Gară RO 155 E1
Fethard IRL 9 D7
Fethard IRL 9 D9
Fetsund N 95 C14
Fettercairn GB 5 B11
Feucht D 75 D9
Feuchtwangen D 75 D7
Feugarolles F 33 B6
Feuquières F 18 E4
Feuquières-en-Vimeu F 18 D4
Feurs F 30 D5
Fevåg N 104 D7
Fevik N 90 C4
Feytiat F 29 D8
Ffestiniog GB 10 F4
Ffostrasol GB 12 A6
Fiac F 33 C9
Fiamignano I 62 C4
Fiano I 31 E12
Fiano Romano I 62 C3
Fiavè I 69 B10
Ficarazzi I 58 C3
Ficarolo I 66 C3
Fichtelberg D 75 C10
Fichtenberg D 74 E6
Fichti GR 175 D6
Ficulle I 62 B2
Fiddown IRL 9 D8
Fide S 93 E12
Fidenza I 69 D9
Fidjeland N 94 E5
Fiè allo Sciliar I 72 C4
Fieberbrunn A 72 B6
Fieni RO 160 C6
Fier AL 168 C2
Fiera di Primiero I 72 D4
Fierbinți-Târg RO 161 D8
Fierzë AL 163 E9
Fiesch CH 70 E6
Fiesole I 66 E3
Fiesso Umbertiano I 66 C4
Figaniéres F 36 D4
Figari F 37 J10
Figeac F 33 A10
Figeholm S 93 E9
Figgio N 94 E3
Figline Valdarno I 66 E3
Figueira da Foz P 44 D3
Figueira de Castelo Rodrigo P 45 C7
Figueira e Barros P 44 F5
Figueiredo de Alva P 44 C5
Figueiró da Granja P 44 C6
Figueiró dos Vinhos P 44 E4
Figueres E 43 C9
Figueroles E 48 D4
Figueruela de Arriba E 39 E7
Fijnaart NL 182 B4
Filadelfia I 59 B9
Filakio GR 171 A10
Fiľakovo SK 147 E9
Filatova-Gora RUS 132 F3
Filattiera I 69 E8
Fildu de Jos RO 151 D11
Filettino I 62 D4
Filey GB 11 C11
Filiaşi RO 160 D3
Filiates GR 168 E3
Filiatra GR 174 E4
Filicudi Porto I 59 B6
Filipeni RO 153 D10
Filipeşti RO 153 D9
Filipeştii de Pădure RO 161 D7
Filipeştii de Târg RO 161 D7
Filipjakov HR 156 E3
Filipovtsi BG 165 D6
Filipów PL 136 E6
Filippiada GR 174 A2
Filipstad S 97 C11
Filisur CH 71 D9
Fillan N 104 D5
Fillinges F 31 C9
Fillyra GR 171 B9
Filotio GR 177 E6
Filottrano I 67 F7
Filsbäck S 91 C13
Filskov DK 86 D4
Filsum D 17 B9
Filton GB 13 B9
Filzmoos A 73 B8
Fimber GB 11 C10
Finale I 58 C5
Finale Emilia I 66 C3
Finale Ligure I 37 C8
Fiñana E 55 E7
Finavon GB 5 B11
Finby FIN 99 B14
Finby FIN 127 E8
Findern GB 11 F8
Findhorn GB 3 K9
Findikli TR 172 D6
Findikli TR 173 E8
Findochty GB 3 K11
Findon GB 15 F8
Finestrat E 56 D4
Finhan F 33 C8
Finiq AL 168 E3
Finiş RO 151 D9
Finja S 87 C13
Finkenstein A 73 C8
Finnbacka S 103 D10
Finnbodarna S 102 E7

Finnbyen N 110 D5
Finnea IRL 7 E8
Finneby S 103 B9
Finnentrop D 21 B9
Finnerödja S 92 B4
Finnfors S 118 E4
Finngruvan S 102 E7
Finnholt N 96 B6
Finningham GB 15 C11
Finnkroken N 111 A17
Finnøy N 111 D9
Finnsådal N 90 C2
Finnsäter S 105 D15
Finnset N 101 B8
Finnset N 108 B7
Finnset N 110 D9
Finnseter N 111 C10
Finnshögst S 103 D9
Finnskog N 102 E3
Finntorp S 96 D7
Finnvik N 111 A14
Finnvik N 108 D4
Finnygaud GB 3 K11
Fino Mornasco I 69 B7
Finowfurt D 84 E5
Finse N 100 E7
Finsjö S 89 A10
Finspång S 92 B7
Finsterwalde D 80 C5
Finsterwolde NL 17 B8
Finström FIN 99 B13
Finta RO 161 D7
Fintel D 82 D7
Fintice SK 145 E3
Fintona GB 7 D8
Fintown IRL 6 C6
Finvoy GB 4 E4
Fiodh Ard IRL 9 D7
Fionnphort GB 4 C4
Fiorano Modense I 66 C2
Fiorenzuola d'Arda I 69 D8
Fiplingkroken N 108 F6
Fira GR 179 C9
Firenze I 66 E3
Firenzuola I 66 D3
Firlej PL 141 G7
Firmi F 33 A10
Firminy F 30 E5
Firmo I 60 D6
Fiscal E 32 E5
Fischach D 75 F8
Fischbach D 21 E8
Fischbach D 186 C3
Fischbachau D 72 A4
Fischbach bei Dahn D 27 B8
Fischbeck D 79 A11
Fischen im Allgäu D 71 C10
Fishguard GB 12 B5
Fiskå N 100 B3
Fiskardo GR 174 C2
Fiskarheden S 102 D5
Fiskari FIN 127 E10
Fiskebäckskil S 91 C9
Fiskebøl N 110 D8
Fiskefjord N 110 D8
Fiskö FIN 126 E4
Fiskøy N 111 C11
Fisksätra S 99 D10
Fismes F 19 F8
Fisterra E 38 C1
Fistikli TR 173 D10
Fitionești RO 153 F10
Fitjar N 94 C2
Fitou F 34 E4
Fitz-James F 18 F5
Fiuggi I 62 D4
Fiumalbo I 66 D2
Fiumefreddo Bruzio I 60 E6
Fiumefreddo di Sicilia I 59 D7
Fiumicino I 62 D2
Fiunary GB 4 B5
Fivemiletown GB 7 D8
Fivizzano I 66 D1
Fix-St-Geneys F 30 E4
Fizeșu Gherlii RO 152 C3
Fjær N 108 B8
Fjäl S 106 E7
Fjäll S 96 C7
Fjällåkern S 107 E14
Fjällåsen S 116 C6
Fjällbacka S 91 B9
Fjällnäs S 102 A3
Fjällsjö S 107 D10
Fjällsjönäs S 109 E12
Fjärås Kyrkby S 91 E11
Fjärdhundra S 98 C7
Fjärtervålen S 102 C5
Fjell N 94 B2
Fjellbu N 111 D14
Fjelldal N 111 C12
Fjelle N 105 C10
Fjellerup DK 86 B7
Fjellnes N 108 B9
Fjellstad N 111 C15
Fjelsø N 86 B4
Fjelsted DK 86 E6
Fjelstervang DK 86 C3
Fjelstrup DK 86 E5
Fjennesley DK 87 E9
Fjerritslev DK 86 A4
Fjone N 90 A3
Fjordgard N 111 A14
Fjørvikan N 104 E4
Fjugesta S 92 A5
Flå N 95 B10
Flachau A 73 B7
Flachsmeer D 17 B8
Fladungen D 75 A7
Flagnac F 33 A10
Flaine F 31 C10
Flaka FIN 99 B14
Flakaberg S 116 E7
Flakaträsk S 107 C15
Flakaträsk S 109 F12
Flakk N 104 E8
Flakkebjerg DK 87 E8
Flakstad N 111 B13
Flåm N 100 E6
Flamanville F 23 A8
Flămânzi RO 153 B9
Flamborough GB 11 C11
Flamouria GR 169 C7
Flampouro GR 169 C10
Flärke S 107 D16
Flarken S 118 F5

Flästa S 103 D11
Flatabø N 94 B4
Flåten N 112 D6
Flatøydegard N 101 E11
Flått N 105 B12
Flattach A 73 C7
Flattnitz A 73 C9
Flatval N 104 D5
Flauenskjold DK 86 A6
Flavigny-sur-Moselle F 26 C5
Flavigny-sur-Ozerain F 25 E12
Flavin F 34 B4
Flayosc F 36 D4
Flechtingen D 79 B9
Flecken Zechlin D 83 D13
Fleet GB 15 E7
Fleetmark D 83 E11
Fleetwood GB 10 D5
Flein D 27 B11
Flekkefjord N 94 F5
Flémalle B 19 C11
Flen S 93 A9
Flensburg D 82 A6
Flenstad N 104 D8
Fleringe S 93 D13
Flermoen N 102 D4
Flerohopp S 89 B9
Fléron B 19 C12
Flers F 23 C10
Flers-en-Escrebieux F 182 E2
Flesberg N 95 C10
Flesnes N 111 C10
Flessau D 83 E11
Flesvik N 104 E6
Fleurance F 33 C7
Fleuré F 29 C7
Fleurie F 30 C6
Fleurier CH 31 B10
Fleurus B 19 D10
Fleury F 34 D5
Fleury-les-Aubrais F 24 E6
Fleury-sur-Andelle F 18 F3
Fléville-Lixières F 19 F12
Flieden D 74 B6
Fließ A 71 C11
Flimby GB 5 F9
Flims CH 71 D8
Flines-lez-Raches F 182 E2
Flint GB 10 E5
Flintbek D 83 B8
Flirey F 26 C4
Flisa N 102 E3
Flisby S 92 D5
Fliseryd S 89 A10
Flix E 42 E5
Flixecourt F 18 D5
Flize F 19 E10
Floby S 91 C13
Floda S 91 D11
Floda S 97 D13
Flodden GB 5 D12
Flogned S 96 C7
Flogny-la-Chapelle F 25 E10
Floh D 79 E7
Flöha D 80 E4
Floing F 19 E10
Floirac F 28 F4
Flokenes N 100 D2
Floq AL 168 C4
Flor S 103 B9
Florac F 35 B6
Florange F 20 F6
Forano I 62 C3
Forbach D 27 C9
Forbach F 27 B6
Flores de Ávila E 45 C10
Floresta I 59 D6
Florennes B 19 D10
Florenville B 19 E11
Flores de Ávila E 45 C10
Floresta I 59 D6
Florești MD 154 B2
Florești RO 152 D3
Florești RO 161 C7
Florești-Stoenești RO 161 E7
Floriada GR 174 A3
Florida de Liébana E 45 B9
Floridia I 59 E7
Florina GR 168 C5
Florinas I 64 B2
Florø N 100 C2
Flörsbach D 74 B6
Flörsheim am Main D 187 A5
Flörsheim-Dalsheim D 187 B5
Flosjöhyttan S 97 C12
Flossenbürg D 75 C11
Flöthe D 79 B7
Flötningen S 102 C3
Flötuträsk S 118 D5
Floure F 33 D10
Flovika N 110 D9
Fluberg N 101 E12
Flüelen CH 71 D7
Flühli CH 70 D6
Flumeri I 60 A4
Flumet F 31 D10
Fluminimaggiore I 64 E2
Flums CH 27 F11
Fluren S 103 C11
Flurkmark S 122 C4
Flussio I 64 C2
Fly DK 86 B3
Flyggsjö S 107 D15
Flyinge S 87 D12
Flykälen S 106 D8
Flyn S 107 D12
Fobello I 68 B5
Foča BIH 157 F10
Focant B 19 D11
Fochabers GB 3 K10
Focșani RO 153 F10
Focuri RO 153 C10
Foëcy F 24 F7
Foeni RO 159 B6
Foggia I 63 E9
Foglianise I 60 A3
Föglö FIN 99 B14
Fohnsdorf A 73 B10
Fohrde D 79 B12
Föhren D 21 E7
Foiano della Chiana I 66 F4
Foieni RO 151 B9
Foinikounta GR 178 B2
Foix F 33 E9
Fojnica BIH 157 E8
Foktő H 149 C11
Földeák H 150 E6
Foldereid N 105 B12
Földes H 151 C7
Fole DK 86 E3
Fole S 93 D13
Forøy N 108 C6
Folegandros GR 179 B8
Folgaria I 69 B11
Folgoso de Courel E 38 C5

Folgoso de la Ribera E 39 C7
Folia GR 170 C6
Folignano I 62 B5
Foligno I 62 B3
Folkestad N 100 B4
Folkestone GB 15 E11
Folkingham GB 11 F11
Follafoss N 105 D10
Folldal N 101 B12
Follebu N 101 D12
Føllenslev DK 87 D8
Follina I 72 E5
Follingbo S 93 D12
Föllinge S 106 D7
Follonica I 65 B3
Folly Gate GB 12 D6
Fölsbyn S 96 D7
Folschviller F 26 B6
Folteşti RO 155 B2
Fonâltika GR 174 D3
Fondi I 62 E4
Fondón E 55 F7
Fône S 103 C10
Fônebo S 103 C12
Fonelas E 55 E6
Fonfría E 39 E7
Fonfría E 42 E1
Fønhus N 101 E11
Fonni I 64 C3
Fonroque F 29 F6
Fonsorbes F 33 C8
Fontaine F 31 E8
Fontainebleau F 25 D8
Fontaine-Française F 26 E3
Fontaine-le-Bourg F 18 E3
Fontaine-le-Dun F 18 E2
Fontaine-lès-Dijon F 26 F3
Fontaine-lès-Luxeuil F 26 E5
Fontaine-l'Évêque B 19 D9
Fontainemore I 68 B4
Fontaines E 25 E9
Fontaines F 30 B6
Fontan F 37 C7
Fontanar E 47 C6
Fontanarejo E 46 F3
Fontane I 37 C7
Fontanelice I 66 D4
Fontanellato I 66 C1
Fontanès F 35 C7
Fontanigorda I 37 B10
Fontecchio I 62 C5
Fonte Díaz E 38 C3
Fontellas E 41 D8
Fontenay-le-Comte F 28 C4
Fontenilles F 33 C8
Fontenoy F 25 E9
Fontenoy-le-Château F 26 E5
Fontes P 44 E4
Fontevraud-l'Abbaye F 23 F12
Fontiveros E 46 C3
Font-Romeu-Odeillo-Via F 33 E10
Fontstown IRL 7 F9
Fontvieille F 35 C8
Fonyód H 149 C9
Fonz E 42 C4
Fonzaso I 72 D4
Foppolo I 69 A8
Forano I 62 C3
Forâști RO 153 C8
Forbach D 27 C9
Forbach F 27 B6
Forcall E 42 F3
Forcalquier F 35 C10
Forcarei E 38 C3
Force I 62 B4
Forchheim D 75 C9
Forchtenberg D 187 C8
Forchtenstein A 149 A6
Ford GB 4 C6
Ford GB 5 D12
Ford IRL 9 C10
Førde N 94 C2
Førde N 100 D3
Forderstedt D 79 C10
Fordham GB 15 C9
Fordingbridge GB 13 D11
Fordongianus I 64 D2
Fordoun GB 5 B12
Fore N 110 C7
Foreness N 94 D2
Forenza I 60 B5
Føresvik N 94 D2
Forfar GB 5 B11
Forges-les-Eaux F 18 E4
Forgie GB 3 K10
Forino I 60 B3
Forio I 62 F5
Föritz D 75 B9
Forjães P 38 E2
Forkhill GB 7 D10
Førland N 94 F6
Forlev DK 87 E8
Forlì I 66 D5
Forlimpopoli I 66 D5
Formazza I 71 E6
Formby GB 10 D5
Formello I 62 C2
Formerie F 18 E4
Formia I 62 E5
Formiche Alto E 48 D3
Formigine I 66 C2
Formigliana I 68 C5
Formignana I 66 C4
Formiguères F 33 E10
Formofoss N 105 C12
Fornåsa S 92 C6
Fornelli I 64 A1
Fornells E 57 A13
Fornells de la Selva E 43 D9
Fornes N 111 C10
Fornes N 111 C13
Forni Avoltri I 73 C6
Forni di Sopra I 73 C6
Forni di Sotto I 73 D6
Forno Alpi Graie I 31 E11
Forno di Zoldo I 72 D5
Fornos I 45 B7
Fornos de Algodres P 44 C5
Fornovo del Taro I 66 C1
Foros de Vale Figueira P 50 B3
Foros do Arrão P 44 F4
Forotic RO 159 C8
Forøy N 108 C6
Forra N 111 D13
Forráskút H 150 E4
Forres GB 3 K9

Forró H 145 G3
Fors S 98 B6
Fors S 107 E11
Fors S 107 E15
Forså N 111 C15
Forså N 111 D12
Forsand N 94 E4
Forsåsen S 106 D7
Forsbacka S 103 E12
Forsbacka S 109 F11
Forsbakken N 111 C14
Forsby FIN 122 C9
Forsby FIN 127 E14
Forserum S 92 D4
Forset N 111 C15
Forshaga S 97 C9
Forsheda S 87 A13
Forsinard GB 3 J9
Forsland N 108 D4
Førslev DK 87 E9
Förslöv S 87 C11
Forsmark S 99 B10
Forsmark S 109 F10
Forsmo S 107 E10
Forsnäs S 109 D16
Forsnäs S 109 E13
Forsnäs S 118 B5
Forsøl N 113 B12
Frătăuții Noi RO 153 B7
Frătăuții Vechi RO 153 B7
Forsse S 107 E10
Forssjö S 93 B8
Fort I 32 B10
Forst D 81 C7
Forstinning D 75 F10
Forstråsked S 118 B8
Forsvik S 92 B4
Fortanete E 42 F2
Forte GB 5 B10
Forth GB 5 D9
Fortios P 44 F6
Fort-Mahon-Plage F 18 D4
Fortrose GB 3 K8
Fortuna E 56 E2
Fortuneswell GB 13 D10
Forvik N 108 E3
Fos F 33 E7
Fosdinovo I 69 E9
Foskros S 102 B4
Foskvallen S 102 C4
Fosnavåg N 100 B3
Fosnes N 105 B10
Fossacesia I 63 C6
Fossalta di Portogruaro I 73 E6
Fossano I 37 B7
Fossato di Vico I 67 F6
Fossby N 91 A10
Fosse N 94 B4
Fosser N 95 C14
Fosses-la-Ville B 19 D10
Fossheim N 112 D5
Fossiat F 31 C7
Fossing N 90 B5
Fossmork N 94 E4
Fos-sur-Mer F 35 D8
Fót H 150 B3
Foteina GR 169 D7
Fotherby GB 11 E11
Fotinovo BG 165 F9
Fotolivos GR 170 B6
Foucarmont F 18 E4
Fouesnant F 22 E3
Foug F 26 C4
Fougères F 23 D9
Fougerolles F 26 E5
Fougerolles-du-Plessis F 23 D10
Fouilloy F 33 B7
Foulain F 26 D3
Foulayronnes F 33 B7
Fountain Cross IRL 8 C4
Fouras F 28 D3
Fourchambault F 30 A3
Four Elms GB 15 E9
Fourfouras GR 178 E8
Fourmies F 19 D9
Fourna GR 174 A4
Fournels F 30 F3
Fournes GB 178 E6
Fournoi GR 177 D7
Fourques F 34 E4
Fourques F 35 C8
Fours F 30 B4
Foustani GR 169 B7
Fownhope GB 13 A9
Foxdale GBM 10 C2
Foxford IRL 6 E4
Foyers GB 2 L8
Foygh IRL 7 E7
Foynes IRL 8 C4
Foz E 38 A5
Foz P 44 F4
Foz do Arelho P 44 F2
Foz Giraldo P 44 E5
Frabosa Soprana I 37 C7
Frącki PL 136 F7
Frades de la Sierra E 45 C9
Fraga E 42 E4
Fragagnano I 61 C8
Fraham A 76 F6
Frailes E 53 B9
Fraire B 19 D10
Fraize F 27 D7
Frameries B 19 D8
Framfjord N 100 D7
Framlev DK 86 C6
Framlingham GB 15 C11
Främlingshem S 98 A7
Frammersbach D 187 A7
Främmestad S 91 C12
Frampol PL 144 B6
Frampton GB 11 F11
Francavilla al Mare I 63 B6
Francavilla di Sicilia I 59 D7
Francavilla Fontana I 61 B9
Francavilla in Sinni I 60 C6
Francescas F 33 B6
Frâncești RO 160 C4
Franco P 38 F5
Francofonte I 59 E6
Francorchamps B 20 D5
Francoulès F 33 A8
Francova Lhota CZ 146 C6
Frändefors S 91 B11
Franeker NL 16 B5
Frangy F 31 C8

Frankenau D 21 B11
Frankenberg D 80 E4
Frankenberg (Eder) D 21 B11
Frankenburg am Hausruck A 76 F4
Frankenfels A 77 G3
Frankenheim D 75 A7
Frankenmarkt A 76 G4
Frankenthal (Pfalz) D 21 E10
Frankfurt am Main D 21 D11
Frankfurt an der Oder D 81 B7
Frankowo PL 136 E2
Frankrike S 105 D15
Frânô S 93 A14
Franois F 26 F4
Fränsta S 103 A11
Františkovy Lázně CZ 75 B11
Franzburg D 83 B13
Frascati I 62 D3
Frascineto I 60 D6
Fraserburgh GB 3 K12
Frasin RO 153 B7
Frasin RO 153 B7
Frasne F 31 B9
Frasnes-lez-Buissenal B 19 C8
Frasnes-lez-Gosselies B 19 C9
Frassinoro I 66 D2
Frasso Telesino I 60 A3
Frastanz A 71 C9
Frata RO 152 D4
Frătăuții Noi RO 153 B7
Frătăuții Vechi RO 153 B7
Fratel P 44 E5
Frătești RO 161 F7
Fratta Polesine I 66 B4
Fratta Todina I 62 B2
Fraubrunnen CH 31 A12
Frauenau D 76 E4
Frauenberg CH 27 E10
Frauenfeld CH 27 E10
Frauenkirchen A 77 G11
Frauental an der Laßnitz A 148 C4
Frauenwald D 79 E8
Fraunberg D 75 F10
Frayssinet-le-Gélat F 33 A8
Frecăței RO 155 C3
Frecăței RO 155 D2
Frechas P 38 F5
Frechen D 21 C7
Frechilla E 39 D10
Freckleton GB 10 D6
Fredensborg DK 87 D10
Fredericia DK 86 D5
Frederiks DK 86 C4
Frederiksberg DK 87 D11
Frederiksberg DK 89 E8
Frederikshavn DK 90 E8
Frederikssund DK 87 D10
Frederiksværk DK 87 D10
Fredersdorf D 80 A5
Fredrika S 107 C14
Fredriksberg S 97 B11
Fredriksdal S 92 D5
Fredrikstad N 91 A8
Freemount IRL 8 D5
Fregenal de la Sierra E 51 C6
Fregene I 62 D2
Freginals E 42 F5
Fréhel F 23 C7
Freiberg D 80 E4
Freiburg (Elbe) D 17 A12
Freiburg im Breisgau D 27 D8
Freiensteinau D 74 B5
Freienwill D 82 A6
Freihung D 75 C10
Freila E 55 D7
Freilassing D 73 A6
Freinsheim D 187 B5
Freisen D 21 E8
Freising D 75 F10
Freissinières F 31 F10
Freistadt A 77 E7
Freistatt D 17 C11
Freistroff F 20 F6
Freital D 80 E5
Freixedas P 45 C6
Freixianda P 44 E4
Freixiosa P 44 C5
Freixo P 38 E2
Freixo de Espada à Cinta P 45 B7
Freixo de Espada à Cinta P 45 B7
Freiling S 88 C7
Frejlev DK 86 A5
Fréjus F 36 E5
Frekhaug N 94 A2
Frellstedt D 79 B8
Freluga S 103 D11
Fremdingen D 75 E7
Fremington GB 12 C6
Frenchpark IRL 6 E6
Frencq F 15 F12
Frensdorf D 75 C8
Frenštát pod Radhoštěm CZ 146 B6
Freren D 17 D9
Fresach A 73 C8
Fresagrandinaria I 63 D7
Freshford IRL 9 C8
Freshwater GB 13 D11
Fresnay-sur-Sarthe F 23 D12
Fresneda de la Sierra E 47 D8
Fresnedoso de Ibor E 45 E10
Fresnes-en-Woëvre F 26 B4
Fresnes-sur-Apance F 26 E4
Fresnes-sur-Escaut F 182 E3
Fresne-St-Mamès F 26 E4
Fresno Alhándiga E 45 C9
Fresno de la Ribera E 39 E8
Fresno de Sayago E 39 F8
Fresno el Viejo E 45 B10
Fresnoy-Folny F 18 E3
Fresnoy-le-Grand F 19 E7
Fresse-sur-Moselle F 27 E6
Fressingfield GB 15 C11
Fresvik N 100 D5
Freswick GB 3 H10
Fretigney-et-Velloreille F 26 F4
Freudenberg D 21 C9
Freudenberg D 186 B2
Freudenstadt D 27 D9
Frévent F 18 D5
Freyburg (Unstrut) D 79 D10
Freyenstein D 83 D12
Freyming-Merlebach F 27 B6
Freystadt D 75 D9
Freyung D 76 E5
Friarfjorden N 113 C18
Frías E 40 C5
Fribourg CH 31 B11
Frick CH 27 E9
Fričovce SK 145 E2
Fridafors S 88 C7

Fridalen N 109 B9
Fridaythorpe GB 11 C10
Fridingen an der Donau D 27 D10
Fridlevstad S 89 C9
Fridolfing D 76 G3
Frieda (Meinhard) D 79 D7
Friedberg A 148 B6
Friedberg D 75 F8
Friedberg (Hessen) D 21 D11
Friedeburg D 17 B9
Friedeburg (Saale) D 79 C10
Friedenfels D 75 C11
Friedersdorf D 79 C11
Friedersdorf D 80 B5
Friedewald D 78 E6
Friedewald D 185 C8
Friedland D 79 B6
Friedland D 80 B6
Friedland D 84 C5
Friedrichroda D 79 E8
Friedrichsbrunn D 79 C9
Friedrichsdorf D 187 A6
Friedrichshafen D 71 B9
Friedrichsruhe D 83 C11
Friedrichstadt D 82 B6
Friedrichswalde D 84 D5
Frielendorf D 21 C12
Friemar D 79 E8
Friesach A 73 C9
Friesack D 83 E13
Friesenhagen D 185 C8
Friesenheim D 27 D8
Friesenried D 71 B11
Friesoythe D 17 B9
Frifelt DK 86 E3
Frigento I 60 A4
Friggesund S 103 C12
Frigiliana E 53 C9
Frihetsli N 111 C18
Fritala FIN 126 C6
Frikes GR 174 C2
Frikstad N 90 B2
Frillesås S 91 E11
Frinnaryd S 92 D5
Frinton-on-Sea GB 15 D11
Friockheim GB 5 B11
Friol E 38 B4
Frisange L 20 E6
Fristad S 91 D13
Fritsla S 91 D12
Fritzens A 72 B4
Fritzlar D 21 B12
Friville-Escarbotin F 18 D4
Frizington GB 10 B5
Frošba FO 2 B3
Fröding S 92 D8
Frodsham GB 10 E6
Frœschwiller F 186 D4
Froges F 31 E8
Frogmore GB 15 E7
Frohburg D 79 D12
Frohnleiten A 148 B4
Froidconche F 26 E5
Froissy F 18 E5
Fröjel S 93 E12
Froland N 90 B4
Frolosh BG 165 E6
Frome GB 13 C10
Fromelennes F 184 D2
Fromentine F 28 B1
Frómista E 40 D3
Fröndenberg D 17 F10
Fronhausen D 21 C11
Fronsac F 28 F5
Fronsac F 33 E7
Fronteira P 44 F5
Frontenard F 31 B7
Frontenay-Rohan-Rohan F 28 C4
Frontenhausen D 75 E12
Frontignan F 35 D6
Fronton F 33 C8
Frösakull S 87 B11
Frose D 79 C9
Fröseke S 89 B9
Frosinone I 62 D4
Frøskeland N 110 C9
Frøslev DK 86 B3
Frösö S 106 E7
Frosolone I 63 D6
Frosta N 105 D9
Frostadheia N 104 E4
Frøstrup DK 86 A3
Frouard F 26 C5
Frövi S 97 D13
Frufällan S 91 D12
Fruges F 18 C5
Frumoasa RO 153 E7
Frumoasa RO 161 F6
Frumosu RO 153 B7
Frumușani RO 161 E8
Frumușica RO 153 B9
Frumușița RO 155 B2
Frunzivka UA 154 B5
Frutigen CH 70 D5
Fry GR 181 F5
Frýdek-Místek CZ 146 B6
Frýdlant CZ 81 E8
Frýdlant nad Ostravicí CZ 146 B6
Frygnowo PL 139 C9
Fryksås S 102 D8
Frymburk CZ 76 F6
Fryšták CZ 146 C5
Frysztak PL 144 D4
Fubine I 37 B8
Fucecchio I 66 E2
Fuchstal D 71 B11
Fuencaliente E 54 C4
Fuendejalón E 41 E9
Fuengirola E 53 C7
Fuenlabrada E 46 D5
Fuenmayor E 41 D6
Fuensalida E 46 D4
Fuensanta E 55 D9
Fuensanta de Martos E 53 A9
Fuente-Álamo E 55 B10
Fuente-Álamo E 56 F2
Fuentealbilla E 47 F9
Fuentecambrón E 40 E5
Fuentecén E 40 E4
Fuente de Cantos E 51 C7
Fuente del Arco E 51 C8
Fuente del Maestre E 51 B7
Fuente de Pedro Naharro E 47 E6
Fuente de Piedra E 53 B7
Fuente el Fresno E 46 F5
Fuente el Saz de Jarama E 46 C6

Fuente el Sol E 46 B3
Fuenteguinaldo E 45 D7
Fuentelapeña E 39 F9
Fuentelcésped E 40 E4
Fuentelespino de Haro E 47 E7
Fuentelespino de Moya E 47 E10
Fuentelmonge E 41 F7
Fuentenovilla E 47 D6
Fuente Obejuna E 51 C9
Fuente Palmera E 53 A6
Fuentepelayo E 40 B4
Fuentepinilla E 40 E6
Fuenterodos E 41 F10
Fuenterrebollo E 40 F4
Fuenterroble de Salvatierra
 E 45 C9
Fuentesaúco E 45 B10
Fuentesaúco de Fuentidueña
 E 40 F3
Fuentes-Claras E 47 C10
Fuentes de Andalucía E 51 E9
Fuentes de Ebro E 41 E10
Fuentes de Jiloca E 41 F8
Fuentes de León E 51 C6
Fuentes de Nava E 39 D10
Fuentes de Oñoro E 45 C7
Fuentes de Ropel E 39 E8
Fuentespalda E 42 F4
Fuente-Tójar E 53 A8
Fuente Vaqueros E 53 B9
Fuentidueña E 40 F4
Fuerte del Rey E 53 A9
Fuertescusa E 47 D8
Fügen A 72 B4
Fuglafjørður FO 2 A3
Fugleberg N 111 C12
Fuglebjerg DK 87 E9
Fuglstad N 105 A13
Fuhrberg (Burgwedel) D 78 A6
Fulda D 74 A6
Fulford GB 11 D9
Fulga RO 161 D8
Fulham GB 15 E8
Fullbro S 93 A11
Fulnek CZ 146 B5
Fülöp H 151 B9
Fülöpháza H 150 D3
Fülöpszállás H 150 D3
Fulunäs S 102 D5
Fumay F 19 E10
Fumel F 33 B7
Fumone I 62 D4
Funäsdalen S 102 A4
Fundada E 44 E4
Fundão P 44 D6
Fundata RO 160 C6
Fundeni RO 161 B11
Fundeni RO 161 E8
Funder Kirkeby DK 86 C4
Fundulea RO 161 E9
Fundu Moldovei RO 152 B6
Funes E 32 F2
Funes I 72 C4
Funzie GB 3 D15
Furadouro P 44 C3
Furceni MD 154 C3
Furci I 63 C7
Furci Siculo I 59 D7
Furculeşti RO 160 F6
Furiani F 37 F10
Furnace GB 4 C6
Furnari I 59 C7
Furraleigh IRL 9 D8
Fürstenau D 17 C9
Fürstenberg D 21 A12
Fürstenberg D 84 D4
Fürstenberg (Lichtenfels)
 D 21 B11
Fürstenfeld A 148 B6
Fürstenfeldbruck D 75 F9
Fürstenwalde D 80 B6
Fürstenwerder D 84 D5
Fürstenzell D 76 E4
Furta H 151 C7
Furtan S 97 C8
Furtei I 64 D2
Fürth D 21 E11
Fürth D 75 D8
Fürth D 75 E11
Furth bei Göttweig A 77 F9
Furth im Wald D 76 D3
Furtwangen im Schwarzwald
 D 27 D9
Furuberg S 103 B12
Furuby S 89 B8
Furudal S 103 D9
Furudals bruk S 103 D9
Furuflaten N 111 B19
Furuögrund S 118 E6
Furusjö S 91 D14
Furusund S 99 C11
Furutangvikja N 105 B14
Furuvik S 103 E13
Fusa N 94 B3
Fuscaldo I 60 E6
Fushë-Arrëz AL 163 E9
Fushë-Bardhe AL 168 D3
Fushë Kosovë RKS 164 D3
Fushë-Krujë AL 168 B2
Fushë-Kuqe AL 168 A2
Fusignano I 66 D4
Fußach A 71 C9
Füssen D 71 B11
Fussy F 25 F7
Fustiñana E 41 D9
Futeau F 26 B3
Futog SRB 158 C4
Futrikelva N 111 A17
Füzesabony H 150 B5
Füzesgyarmat H 151 C7
Fužine HR 67 B10
Fyfield GB 15 D9
Fylaki GR 169 F8
Fyli GR 175 C8
Fyllinge S 87 B11
Fyllo GR 169 F7
Fynshav DK 86 F5
Fyrås S 106 E8
Fyrde N 100 B4
Fyresdal N 90 A3
Fyteies GR 174 B3
Fyvie GB 3 L12

G

Gaal A 73 B10
Gaanderen NL 183 B8
Gabaldón E 47 E9
Gabare BG 165 C8
Gabarret F 32 C6
Gabčíkovo SK 146 F5
Gabela BIH 157 F8

Gaber BG 165 D6
Gabia la Grande E 53 B9
Gabicce Mare I 67 E6
Gąbin PL 139 F8
Gablingen D 75 F8
Gáborján H 151 C8
Gabriac F 34 B4
Gabrnik SLO 148 D5
Gabrovnitsa BG 165 B7
Gabrovo BG 166 D4
Gaby I 68 B4
Gać PL 144 C5
Gacé F 23 C12
Gacko BIH 157 F10
Gåda S 103 B10
Gadbjerg DK 86 D4
Gäddede S 105 B16
Gäddträsk S 107 C15
Gadebusch D 83 C10
Gadmen CH 70 D6
Gádor E 55 F8
Gádoros H 150 D6
Gadstrup DK 87 D10
Gadžin Han SRB 164 C5
Gaeiras P 44 F2
Gærum DK 90 E7
Găeşti RO 160 D6
Gaeta I 62 E5
Gafanha da Boa Hora P 44 C3
Gafanha da Nazaré P 44 C3
Gafanha do Carmo P 44 C3
Gafanhoeira P 50 B3
Gáfete P 44 F5
Gaflenz A 73 A10
Gafsele S 107 C12
Gaganitsa BG 165 C7
Găgeşti RO 153 E11
Gaggenau D 27 C10
Gaggi I 59 D7
Gaggio Montano I 66 D2
Gaglianico I 68 B5
Gagliano Castelferrato I 59 D6
Gagliano del Capo I 61 D10
Gagnef S 103 E10
Gagnières F 35 B7
Gagsmark S 118 D6
Găiceana RO 153 E10
Gaigalava LV 133 C2
Gaildorf D 74 E6
Gaillac F 33 C9
Gaillac-d'Aveyron F 34 B4
Gaillard F 31 C9
Gaillimh IRL 6 F4
Gaillon F 24 B5
Gailļmui LV 135 D13
Gaimersheim D 75 E9
Gainsborough GB 11 E10
Gaiole in Chianti I 66 F3
Gaios GR 174 A1
Gairloch GB 2 K5
Gairo I 64 D4
Gais CH 71 C9
Gais I 72 C4
Găiseni RO 161 D7
Gaishorn A 73 A10
Gaismas LV 135 C8
Gaj SRB 159 D7
Gajanejos E 47 C7
Gajary SK 77 F11
Gakovo SRB 150 F3
Galábodarna S 102 A6
Galambok H 149 C8
Galan F 33 D6
Gălăneşti RO 153 B7
Gálaniitu N 112 F10
Galanta SK 146 E5
Galapagar E 46 C5
Galaroza E 51 D6
Galåsen N 102 D4
Galashiels GB 5 D11
Galasjö S 107 E14
Galata BG 167 C9
Galatades GR 169 C7
Galatás GR 175 E7
Gălăţeni RO 160 E6
Galati I 59 B7
Galaţi RO 155 C2
Galaţii Bistriţei RO 152 D4
Galaţi Mamertino I 59 C6
Galatin I 61 C10
Galatina I 61 C10
Galatini GR 169 D6
Galatista SRB 169 D9
Galatone I 61 C10
Gălăuţaş RO 152 D5
Galaxidi GR 174 C5
Galbally IRL 8 D5
Galbarra E 32 E1
Galbenu RO 161 D10
Galbiati I 69 B8
Galda de Jos RO 152 E3
Gáldău RO 161 C9
Gál'din N 113 E12
Galeata I 66 E4
Galende E 39 D6
Galēni LV 135 D13
Galèra E 55 D7
Galéria F 37 G9
Gălești RO 152 E5
Galewice PL 142 D5
Galgagyörk H 150 B3
Galgahévíz H 150 B4
Galgón F 28 E1
Gal'gunjar'ga N 113 F16
Galicea RO 160 D4
Galicea Mare RO 160 E2
Galiche BG 165 B8
Galiny PL 136 E2
Galissas GR 176 E4
Galisteo E 45 E8
Gallardon F 24 C5
Gallargues-le-Montueux
 F 35 C7
Galleberg N 95 C12
Gallegos de Argañan E 45 C7
Gallegos de Solmirón E 45 C10
Galleno I 66 E2
Gälleråsen S 97 D11
Gallese I 62 C2
Gallian-en-Médoc F 28 E4
Galliate I 68 C6
Gallicano I 66 D1
Gallicano nel Lazio I 62 D3
Gallin D 83 C9
Gallin D 83 D12
Gallio I 72 E4
Gallipoli I 61 C10

Garešnica HR 149 E7
Garessio I 37 C8
Garforth GB 11 D9
Gargaliáni GR 174 E4
Gargáligas E 45 F9
Gargallo E 42 F2
Garganta la Olla E 45 D9
Gargazzone I 72 C3
Gargilesse-Dampierre F 29 B9
Gargnano I 69 B10
Gargnäs S 107 A13
Gargogečte N 113 C20
Gargždai LT 134 E2
Garijp NL 16 B5
Garkalne LV 135 B8
Gârla Mare RO 159 E10
Garlasco I 69 C6
Gârleni RO 153 D9
Garliava LT 137 D8
Gârliciu RO 155 D2
Garlieston GB 5 F8
Garlin F 32 C5
Garlitos E 54 B3
Garlstorf D 83 D8
Gama E 40 B5
Gamaches F 18 E4
Gamarde-les-Bains F 32 C4
Gamás H 149 C9
Gambara I 66 B1
Gambarie I 59 C8
Gambassi Terme I 66 E2
Gambateca I 63 D7
Gambettola I 66 D5
Gambolò I 69 C6
Gambsheim F 27 C8
Gaming A 77 G8
Gamleby S 93 D8
Gamlingay GB 15 C8
Gamlitz A 148 C5
Gammalkroppa S 97 C11
Gammelboning S 103 E11
Gammelgården S 119 C10
Gammelgarn S 93 E13
Gammel Ry DK 86 C5
Gammelsdorf D 75 F11
Gammelstaden S 118 C8
Gammelstilla S 98 B7
Gammertingen D 27 D11
Gams CH 71 C8
Gamvik N 112 C9
Gamvik N 113 A21
Gamvik N 113 B11
Gan F 32 D5
Ganagobie F 35 B10
Gand B 19 B8
Gand B 182 C3
Gandarela P 38 F3
Gandellino I 69 B8
Ganderkesee D 17 B11
Gandesa E 42 E4
Gandía E 56 D4
Gandino I 69 B8
Gandra P 38 D2
Gandrup DK 86 A6
Gandvik N 114 C6
Găneasa RO 160 E4
Găneasa RO 161 D8
Găneşti RO 152 E4
Ganfei P 38 D2
Ganges F 35 C6
Gånghester S 91 D13
Gangi I 58 D5
Găngiova RO 160 F3
Gangkofen D 75 F12
Ganløse DK 87 D10
Gannat F 30 C3
Gänserndorf A 77 F11
Ganshoren B 19 C9
Gånsvik S 103 A15
Ganzlin D 83 D12
Gaoth Dobhair IRL 6 B6
Gap F 36 B4
Gąperhult S 91 B13
Gara H 150 E3
Garaballa E 47 E10
Garagarza E 32 D1
Garaguso I 60 B6
Gara Khitrino BG 167 C7
Gara Oreshets BG 159 F10
Gârbău RO 151 C11
Garberg N 105 E10
Gârbou RO 151 C11
Gârbova RO 152 F3
Gârbovi RO 161 D9
Gârbów PL 141 H6
Garbsen D 78 B6
Garching an der Alz D 75 F12
Garching bei München D 75 F10
Garchizy F 30 A3
Garcia E 42 E5
Garciaz E 45 E9
Garciems LV 135 B8
Garcihernández E 45 C10
Garcillán E 46 C4
Garčin HR 157 B9
Gârcina RO 153 D8
Garcinarro E 47 D7
Gârcov RO 160 F5
Garda I 69 B10
Gârda de Sus RO 151 E10
Gardanne F 35 D9
Gârdäs S 102 E6
Gårdby S 89 B11
Garde I 17 C10
Gardejegen D 79 A9
Gardelegen D 79 A9
Gardenstown GB 3 K12
Garderen NL 183 A7
Gardermoen N 95 B14
Gardiki GR 174 B4
Garding D 82 B5
Gärdnäs S 106 C8
Gardone Riviera I 69 B10
Gardone Val Trompia I 69 B9
Gárdony H 149 B11
Gárdos F 26 F4
Gavieze LV 134 C2
Gavik S 103 A15
Gavirate I 68 B6
Gävle S 103 E13
Gavoi I 64 C3
Gavojdia RO 159 B9
Gavorrano I 65 B3
Gâvre F 102 A1
Gavrio GR 176 D5
Gavrolimni GR 174 C4
Gâvsta S 99 B9
Gaweinstal A 77 F11
Gawliki Wielkie PL 136 E5

Gennep NL 16 E5
Genner DK 86 E4
Gennes F 23 F11
Gennes-sur-Seiche F 23 E9
Genola I 37 B7
Génolhac F 35 B6
Genoni I 64 D3
Genouillac F 29 C6
Genouillé F 28 C4
Genouilly F 30 B6
Genova I 37 C9
Genovés E 56 D4
Gensac F 28 F6
Gensingen D 185 E8
Gent B 19 B8
Genthin D 79 B11
Gentioux-Pigerolles F 29 D9
Genzano di Lucania I 60 B6
Genzano di Roma I 62 D3
Geoagiu RO 151 F11
George Enescu RO 153 A9
Georgensgmünd D 75 D9
Georgianoi GR 169 D7
Georgianoi GR 170 C6
Georgi Damyanovo BG 165 C7
Georgioupoli GR 178 E7
Georgitsi GR 174 E5
Georgsheil D 17 B8
Georgsmarienhütte D 17 D10
Ger E 33 F9
Ger F 23 C10
Ger F 32 D5
Gera D 79 E11
Geraardsbergen B 19 C8
Gerabronn D 74 D6
Gerace I 59 C9
Geraci Siculo I 58 D5
Gerakarou GR 169 C9
Geraki GR 175 F6
Gerakini GR 169 D9
Gérardmer F 27 D6
Geras A 77 E9
Gerasdorf bei Wien A 77 F10
Géraudot F 25 D11
Gerbéviller F 186 E2
Gerbrunn D 187 B8
Gerbstedt D 79 C10
Gérce I 149 B8
Gerchsheim D 74 C6
Gerdau D 83 E8
Gerena E 51 D7
Gerendás H 151 D6
Geresdlak H 149 D11
Geretsberg A 76 F3
Geretsried D 72 A3
Gérgal E 55 E7
Gergei I 64 D3
Gergeri GR 178 E8
Gerhardshofen D 75 C8
Gerindote E 46 E4
Geringswalde D 80 D3
Gerjen H 149 D11
Gerlev DK 87 D10
Gerlingen D 27 C11
Gerlos A 72 B5
Germas GR 168 C5
Germay F 26 D3
Germencik TR 177 D10
Germering D 75 F9
Germersheim D 21 F10
Gernika-Lumo E 41 B6
Gernrode D 79 C9
Gernsbach D 27 C9
Gernsheim D 187 B6
Gerola Alta I 69 A8
Gerolimenas GR 178 C3
Gerolsbach D 75 F9
Gerolstein D 21 D7
Gerolzhofen D 75 C7
Gerovo HR 67 A10
Gerpinnes B 19 D10
Gersau CH 71 D7
Gersfeld (Rhön) D 74 B6
Gersheim D 27 B7
Gersten D 17 C9
Gerstetten D 74 E7
Gersthofen D 75 F8
Gerstungen D 79 E7
Gerswalde D 84 D5
Gerswisch D 79 B10
Gerzat F 30 D3
Gerzen D 75 E11
Gesäter S 91 B10
Gescher D 17 E8
Gesico I 64 D3
Gespunsart F 19 E10
Gessertshausen D 75 F8
Gestalgar E 48 E3
Gesté F 23 F9
Gesten DK 86 D4
Gesturi I 64 D3
Gesualdo I 60 A4
Gesunda S 102 E8
Gesves B 19 D11
Geszt H 151 D8
Gesztely H 145 G2
Gesztréd H 151 B8
Geta FIN 99 B13
Getafe E 46 D5
Getaria E 32 D1
Getinge S 87 B11
Getryggen S 103 D10
Getterum S 93 C8
Gettjärn S 97 C8
Gettorf D 83 B7
Gevelsberg D 17 F8
Gévezé F 23 D8
Gevgelija MK 169 B7
Gevrey-Chambertin F 26 F2
Gex F 31 C9
Geyer D 80 E3
Geyikli TR 171 E10
Gezavesh AL 168 B3
Göhl A 77 E8
Ghedi I 66 B1
Ghelari RO 159 B10
Ghelinţa RO 153 F8
Ghemme I 68 B5
Gheorghe Doja RO 161 D10
Gheorghe Lazăr RO 161 D10
Gheorgheni RO 153 D7
Gheorghieni RO 161 D9
Gheorghiţa RO 161 D8
Gherăeşti RO 153 C9
Gherăseni RO 161 C9
Ghercești RO 160 E3
Ghergheasa RO 161 D10
Gherghiţa RO 161 D8
Gherla RO 152 C3
Gherţa Mică RO 145 H7
Ghidfalău RO 153 F7

Ghidigeni RO 153 E10
Ghidighiei MD 154 C3
Ghiffa I 68 B6
Ghilarza I 64 C2
Ghimbav RO 161 B7
Ghimeş-Făget RO 153 D8
Ghimpaţi RO 161 E7
Ghindari RO 152 E5
Ghioroc RO 151 E8
Ghioroiu RO 160 D3
Ghiroda RO 151 F7
Ghislenghien B 19 C8
Ghisonaccia F 37 G10
Ghisoni F 37 G10
Ghizela RO 151 F8
Ghyvelde F 18 B5
Giannades GR 168 E2
Giannitsa GR 169 C7
Giannouli GR 169 C7
Giano dell'Umbria I 62 B3
Giardinetto Vecchio I 60 A5
Giardini-Naxos I 59 D7
Giarmata RO 151 F7
Giarre I 59 D7
Giat F 29 D10
Giaveno I 31 E11
Giave I 64 C2
Gibellina Nuova I 58 D2
Gibostad N 111 B15
Gibraléon E 51 E6
Gibraltar GBZ 53 D6
Giby PL 136 F7
Gibzde LV 134 B4
Gideå S 107 E15
Gideå bruk S 107 E16
Gideåkroken S 107 C12
Gidle PL 143 E7
Giebelstadt D 74 C6
Gieboldehausen D 79 C7
Gieczno PL 143 C7
Giedraičiai LT 137 C11
Gielniów PL 141 H2
Gielow D 83 C13
Gien F 25 E8
Giengen an der Brenz D 75 E7
Giera RO 159 C6
Gierle B 182 C5
Giersleben D 79 C10
Gierstädt D 79 D8
Gierzwałd PL 139 C9
Gièvres F 24 F6
Giffnock GB 5 D8
Gifford GB 5 D11
Gifhorn D 79 B8
Gigean F 35 C6
Gigen BG 160 F4
Gighera RO 160 F3
Giglio Castello I 65 C3
Gignac F 35 C6
Gignac I 35 C10
Gignod I 31 D11
Gijón E 39 A8
Gîkši LV 135 B10
Gilău RO 151 D11
Gilching D 75 F9
Gilena E 53 B7
Gilette F 37 D6
Gilfield GB 7 D10
Gilleleje DK 87 C10
Gillenfeld D 21 D7
Gillhov S 102 A8
Gillingham GB 13 C10
Gillingham GB 15 E8
Gilling West GB 11 C8
Gilly-sur-Isère F 31 D9
Gilly-sur-Loire F 30 B4
Gilmerton GB 5 C9
Gilså N 105 E11
Gilserberg D 21 C12
Gilsland GB 5 F11
Gilten D 82 E7
Gilwern GB 13 B8
Gilze NL 16 E3
Gimåt S 107 E15
Gimdalen S 103 A10
Gimigliano I 59 B10
Gimo S 99 B10
Gimont F 33 C7
Gimouille F 30 B3
Gimsøy N 110 D7
Ginasservis F 35 C10
Ginestas F 34 D4
Gingelom B 19 C11
Gingen an den Fils D 187 D6
Gingst D 84 B4
Ginkūnai LT 134 E6
Ginoles F 33 E10
Ginosa I 61 B7
Ginostra I 59 B7
Ginsheim D 185 E9
Gintsi BG 165 C7
Gioeș P 50 E4
Gioi I 60 C4
Gioia dei Marsi I 62 D5
Gioia del Colle I 61 B7
Gioia Sannitica I 60 A2
Gioia Tauro I 59 C8
Gioiosa Ionica I 59 C9
Gioiosa Marea I 59 C6
Giornico CH 71 E7
Giovinazzo I 61 A7
Gipka LV 130 F5
Giraltovce SK 145 E4
Girancourt F 26 D5
Girasole I 64 D4
Girifalco I 59 B9
Girişu de Criş RO 151 C8
Girkalnis LT 134 F6
Giroc RO 159 C7
Giromagny F 27 E6
Girona E 43 C7
Giroussens F 33 C9
Girov RO 153 D9
Girvan GB 4 E7
Gislaved S 88 A5
Gislingen DK 87 D9
Gisloy N 110 C9
Gisors F 18 F4
Gissi I 63 C7
Gisslarbo S 97 C14
Gistad S 92 C7
Gistel B 18 B6
Gistrup DK 86 B5
Giswil CH 70 D6

Gittelde D 79 C7
Gittun S 109 D16
Giubega RO 160 E2
Giubiasco CH 69 A7
Giugliano in Campania I 60 B2
Giuliano di Roma I 62 D4
Giulianova I 62 B5
Giulvăz RO 153 B1
Giuncugnano I 66 D1
Giurgeni RO 155 D1
Giurgița RO 160 E3
Giurgiu RO 161 F7
Giurgiulești MD 155 C2
Giuvărăști RO 160 F5
Give DK 86 D4
Givet F 19 D10
Givors F 30 D6
Givry B 19 D9
Givry F 30 B6
Givry-en-Argonne F 25 C12
Givskud DK 86 D4
Gižai LT 136 D7
Gizalki PL 142 B4
Gizeux F 23 F12
Giżycko PL 136 E4
Gizzeria I 59 B9
Gjakovë RKS 163 E9
Gjærnes N 90 B5
Gjegjan AL 163 E9
Gjegjan AL 163 F9
Gjengstø N 104 E6
Gjerde N 100 C6
Gjerdebakken N 113 C11
Gjerdrum N 95 B14
Gjerlev DK 86 B6
Gjermundshamn N 94 B3
Gjern DK 86 C5
Gjerrild DK 87 C7
Gjerstad N 90 B5
Gjersvik N 105 B14
Gjesing DK 86 D4
Gjesvær N 113 A15
Gjevaldshaugen N 101 D15
Gjilan RKS 164 E3
Gjirokastër AL 168 D3
Gjógv FO 2 A3
Gjøl DK 86 A5
Gjøljelia N 104 D7
Gjølme N 104 E7
Gjonaj RKS 163 E10
Gjonëm AL 168 A2
Gjøra N 101 A10
Gjorm AL 168 D2
Gjøvåg N 94 B2
Gjøvik N 101 E13
Gjurakoc RKS 163 D9
Gjuvberget N 102 E3
Gkoritsa GR 175 E6
Gladbeck D 17 E7
Gladenbach D 21 C11
Gladsaxe DK 87 D10
Gladstad N 108 E2
Glainans F 26 F6
Glamis GB 5 B11
Glamoč BIH 157 D6
Glâmos N 101 A14
Glamsbjerg DK 86 E6
Glandage F 35 A9
Glandon F 29 E8
Glandore IRL 8 E4
Glandorf D 17 D10
Glanegg A 73 C9
Glanerbrug NL 17 D7
Glanshammar S 97 D13
Glanworth IRL 8 D6
Glarryford GB 4 F4
Glarus CH 71 C8
Glasbury GB 13 A8
Glasgow GB 5 D8
Gläshütten D 21 D10
Glashütten D 75 C9
Glaslough IRL 7 D9
Glassan IRL 7 F7
Glastonbury GB 13 C9
Glaubitz D 80 D4
Glauchau D 79 E12
Glava BG 165 C9
Glava S 97 C8
Glava glasbruk S 96 C7
Glavan BG 166 E6
Glavanovtsi BG 164 D6
Glavatičevo BIH 157 F9
Glavice HR 157 E6
Glavičice BIH 157 C11
Glăvile RO 160 D4
Glavinitsa BG 161 F9
Glavki GR 171 B7
Gleann Cholm Cille IRL 6 C5
Gleann Doirmhin IRL 7 C7
Gleann na Muaidhe IRL 6 D3
Gleđica SRB 163 C9
Glein N 108 D4
Gleina D 79 D10
Gleisdorf A 148 B5
Gleizé F 30 C6
Glejbjerg DK 86 D3
Glemsford GB 15 C10
Glen S 102 A6
Glenade IRL 6 D6
Glenamaddy IRL 6 E5
Glenamoy IRL 6 D3
Glenariff GB 4 E4
Glenarm GB 4 F5
Glenavy GB 7 C10
Glenbarr GB 4 D5
Glenbeg GB 4 B5
Glenbeigh IRL 8 D3
Glencar GB 5 E9
Glencar IRL 6 D6
Glencoe GB 4 B6
Glencolumbkille IRL 6 C5
Glendowan IRL 7 C7
Gleneagles GB 5 C9
Glenealy IRL 7 G10
Gleneely IRL 4 E2
Glenegedale GB 4 D4
Glenelg GB 2 L5
Glenfield GB 11 F9
Glenfinnan GB 4 B6
Glengarriff IRL 8 E3
Glengavlen IRL 7 D7
Glenhead GB 4 E2
Glenluce GB 4 F7
Glenmore IRL 9 D8
Glenoe GB 4 F5
Glenrothes GB 5 C10
Glenties IRL 6 C6
Glère F 27 F6
Glesborg DK 87 C7
Gletsch CH 71 D6
Glewitz D 84 B3

Glibaći MNE 163 C7
Glimåkra S 88 C6
Glimboca RO 159 C9
Glin IRL 8 C4
Glina HR 148 F6
Glina RO 161 E8
Glinde D 83 C8
Glindow D 79 B12
Glinjeni MD 153 B11
Glinojeck PL 139 E9
Glinsce IRL 6 F3
Glinsk IRL 6 F3
Glinton GB 11 F11
Glissjöberg S 102 B7
Gliwice PL 142 F6
Gllamnik RKS 164 D3
Glloboçicë RKS 164 E3
Glodeanu-Sărat RO 161 D9
Glodeanu-Siliștea RO 161 D9
Glodeni MD 153 B11
Glodeni RO 152 D5
Glodeni RO 161 C6
Glödnitz A 73 C9
Głodowa PL 85 C11
Glodzhevo BG 161 F8
Gloggnitz A 148 A5
Głogowa RO 159 D10
Głogów PL 81 C10
Głogówek PL 142 F4
Głogów Małopolski PL 144 C4
Głogowo PL 138 D6
Glomfjord N 108 C6
Glommen S 87 B10
Glommersträsk S 107 A17
Glonn D 75 G10
Glória P 50 B4
Glória do Ribatejo P 44 F3
Glos-la-Ferrière F 24 C4
Glossa GR 175 A8
Glössbo S 103 D12
Glossop GB 11 E8
Glöte S 102 B5
Glöthe D 79 C10
Glottra S 92 B6
Gloucester GB 13 B10
Glounthaune IRL 8 E6
Głowaczów PL 141 G4
Głowczyce PL 85 A12
Glowe D 84 A4
Glöwen D 83 E12
Głowno PL 143 C8
Głožan SRB 158 C4
Glozhene BG 160 F3
Glozhene BG 165 C10
Głubczyce PL 142 F4
Głuchołazy PL 142 F3
Głuchów PL 141 G2
Glücksburg (Ostsee) D 82 A7
Glückstadt D 17 A12
Glud DK 86 D5
Gludsted DK 86 C4
Gluggavasshaugen N 108 E5
Glumslöv S 87 D11
Glumsø DK 87 E9
Glušci SRB 158 D4
Głuszyca PL 81 E10
Glyfa GR 175 B6
Glyfada GR 175 D8
Glyki GR 168 F4
Glyn Ceiriog GB 10 F5
Glyngøre DK 86 B3
Glynn GB 4 F5
Glynn IRL 9 D9
Glynneath GB 13 B7
Gmünd A 73 C8
Gmünd A 77 E11
Gmund am Tegernsee D 72 A4
Gmunden A 73 A8
Gnarp S 103 B13
Gnarrenburg D 17 B12
Gneisenaustadt Schildau D 80 D3
Gnesta S 93 A10
Gniebing A 148 C5
Gniew PL 138 C6
Gniewkowo PL 138 E5
Gniewoszów PL 141 H5
Gnieżdżiska PL 143 E9
Gniezno PL 85 E13
Gnisvärd S 93 D12
Gnocchetta I 66 C5
Gnoien D 83 C12
Gnojna PL 81 E12
Gnojnice BIH 157 F8
Gnojno PL 143 E10
Gnosall GB 11 F7
Gnosjö S 91 E14
Gnotzheim D 75 D8
Gnutz D 83 B7
Göbel TR 173 D9
Gobowen GB 10 F5
Göçbeyli TR 177 A9
Göcek TR 181 C9
Göçerler TR 173 B8
Goch D 16 E6
Gochsheim D 75 B7
Goczałkowice-Zdrój PL 147 B7
Göd H 150 B3
Godačica SRB 159 F6
Godal N 95 D11
Godalming GB 15 E7
Godby FIN 99 B13
Goddelau D 187 B6
Goddelsheim (Lichtenfels) D 21 B11
Godeanu RO 159 D10
Godech BG 165 C7
Godega di Sant'Urbano I 72 E5
Godegård S 92 B6
Godelleta E 48 F3
Godeni RO 160 C5
Goderville F 18 E1
Godiasco I 37 B10
Godimilje BIH 157 E11
Godinești RO 159 C10
Godinje MNE 163 E7
Godkowo PL 139 B8
Godmanchester GB 15 C8
Gödöllő H 150 B3
Godovič SLO 73 E9
Gödre H 149 D9
Godstone GB 15 E8
Goduš BIH 157 C10
Godziesze Wielkie PL 142 C5
Godziszów PL 144 B6
Goes NL 16 E1
Göfritz an der Wild A 77 E8
Göggingen D 187 D8

Gogolin PL 142 F5
Gogołów PL 144 D4
Gogoşari RO 161 F7
Gogoşu RO 159 E10
Gogoşu RO 160 E2
Göhl D 83 B9
Gohor RO 153 E10
Gohrau D 79 C11
Göhrde D 83 D9
Göhren D 84 B5
Göhren-Lebbin D 83 D13
Goian MD 154 C4
Goicea RO 160 F3
Goiești RO 160 E3
Goirle NL 16 E4
Góis P 44 D4
Goito I 66 B2
Goizueta E 32 D2
Gojść PL 143 D7
Gökçealan TR 177 D9
Gökçebayir TR 171 E10
Gökçedağ TR 173 E10
Gökçeören TR 181 B9
Gökçeyazı TR 173 E8
Gokels D 82 B6
Gökova TR 181 B8
Göktepe TR 181 B9
Göktürk TR 173 B10
Gol N 101 E9
Gola HR 149 D8
Gołąb PL 141 H5
Golac HR 67 A9
Golăiești RO 153 C11
Golaj AL 163 E9
Gołańcz PL 85 E12
Gołaszyn PL 141 G6
Golbey F 26 D5
Gölby FIN 99 B13
Gölcük TR 173 F8
Golczewo PL 85 C7
Goldach CH 71 C8
Goldap PL 136 E5
Goldbeck D 83 E11
Goldberg D 83 C12
Goldegg A 73 B7
Goldelund D 82 A6
Golden IRL 9 D7
Golden Pot GB 14 E7
Goldenstedt D 17 C10
Goleen IRL 8 F3
Golegã P 44 F4
Golemanovo BG 159 F9
Golema Rakovitsa BG 165 D8
Golema Rečica MK 163 F10
Golenice PL 85 E7
Goleniów PL 85 C7
Golesh BG 161 F11
Golești RO 153 F10
Golești RO 160 C4
Golfo Aranci I 64 B4
Golina PL 142 B5
Golinhac F 33 A11
Gološeva LV 133 C3
Gölköy TR 177 E9
Gölle H 149 D9
Göllersdorf A 77 F10
Göllheim D 186 B5
Göllin D 83 C11
Gollin D 84 D5
Golling an der Salzach A 73 A7
Göllingen D 79 D9
Gollmitz D 84 D5
Golmes E 42 D5
Golnik SLO 73 D9
Gøløse DK 87 D10
Golovkino RUS 136 D3
Golpejas E 45 B9
Gols A 77 G11
Golspie GB 3 K9
Golßen D 80 C5
Golubac SRB 159 D8
Golub-Dobrzyń PL 138 D7
Golubić HR 156 D5
Golubinje SRB 159 D9
Golyama Zhelyazna BG 165 D9
Golyam Izvor BG 166 F5
Golyam Manastir BG 166 E6
Golyamo Belovo BG 165 E8
Gölyazı TR 173 D10
Gołymin-Ośrodek PL 139 E10
Golzow D 79 B12
Gomadingen D 27 D11
Gómara E 41 E7
Gomaringen D 187 E7
Gomati GR 169 D10
Gomba H 150 C4
Gömeç TR 173 F6
Gomecello E 45 B9
Gomes Aires P 50 D3
Gomirje HR 67 B11
Gommern D 79 B10
Gomotartsi BG 159 D8
Gomunice PL 143 D7
Gönc H 145 G3
Gonçalo P 44 D6
Goncelin F 31 E8
Gondelsheim D 187 C6
Gondershausen D 185 D7
Gondomar E 38 D2
Gondomar P 44 B3
Gondorf D 21 D8
Gondrecourt-le-Château F 26 C4
Gondreville F 26 C4
Gondrin F 33 C6
Goni I 64 D3
Goniądz PL 140 D7
Gonnesa I 64 E1
Gonnoi GR 169 E7
Gonnosfanadiga I 64 E2
Gonnosnò I 64 D2
Gonsans F 26 F5
Gönyő H 149 A9
Gonzaga I 66 C2
Goodwick GB 12 A5
Goole GB 11 D10
Goonhavern GB 12 E4
Goor NL 17 D7
Gopegi E 40 C6
Göppingen D 74 E6
Gor E 55 E7
Góra PL 81 C11
Góra PL 139 E9
Goráfe E 55 E6
Goraj PL 144 B6
Góra Kalwaria PL 141 G4
Góra Puławska PL 141 H5
Gorawino PL 85 C8

Goražde BIH 157 E10
Gorban RO 153 D12
Görbeháza H 151 B7
Görcsöny H 149 E10
Gördalen S 102 C3
Gordaliza del Pino E 39 D9
Gordes F 35 C9
Gordinești MD 153 A10
Gordola CH 69 A6
Gordon GB 5 D11
Gordona I 69 A7
Gorebridge GB 5 D10
Görece TR 177 C9
Gorenja Straža SLO 73 E11
Gorenja vas SLO 73 D9
Gorey IRL 9 C10
Görgeteg H 149 D8
Gorgoglione I 60 C6
Gorgonzola I 69 B7
Gorgota RO 161 D8
Gorgova RO 155 C4
Gorica BIH 157 D7
Gorica BIH 157 F7
Gorica BIH 162 D5
Gorica MNE 163 E7
Goričan HR 149 D7
Gorinchem NL 16 E3
Gorino I 66 C5
Gorishovë AL 168 C2
Goritsa BG 167 D9
Goritsa BG 167 D9
Göritz D 84 D5
Gorleben D 83 D10
Gørlev DK 87 D8
Gorlice PL 144 D3
Görlitz D 81 D7
Gorlosen D 83 D10
Gormanston IRL 7 E10
Gormanston IRL 7 E10
Gormaz E 40 E5
Görmin D 84 C4
Gorna Belica MK 164 F4
Gorna Beshovitsa BG 165 C8
Gorna Breznitsa BG 165 E6
Gorna Koznitsa BG 165 E6
Gorna Kremena BG 165 C8
Gorna Mitropoliya BG 165 C9
Gorna Oryahovitsa BG 166 C5
Gorna Studena BG 166 C4
Gorna Vasilitsa BG 165 E8
Gorna Verenitsa BG 165 C9
Gornești RO 152 D5
Gornet RO 161 C8
Gornet-Cricov RO 161 C8
Gorni Dŭbnik BG 165 C9
Gorni Lom BG 165 C6
Gornja Golubinja BIH 157 D8
Gornja Grabovica BIH 157 F8
Gornja Gračenica HR 149 E7
Gornja Ljubata SRB 164 D5
Gornja Ljuta BIH 157 F9
Gornjane SRB 159 E9
Gornja Ploča HR 156 D4
Gornja Radgona SLO 148 C5
Gornja Sanica BIH 157 C6
Gornja Slatina BIH 157 C9
Gornja Toponica SRB 164 C4
Gornja Trnava SRB 159 E6
Gornje Jelenje HR 67 B10
Gornje Peulje BIH 156 D6
Gornje Ratkovo BIH 157 C6
Gornje Vratno HR 148 D6
Gornji Agići BIH 157 C6
Gornji Dolac HR 157 E6
Gornji Grad SLO 73 D10
Gornji Humac HR 157 F6
Gornji Kosinj HR 156 C3
Gornji Lapac HR 156 C4
Gornji Lukavac BIH 157 F9
Gornji Majkovi HR 162 D4
Gornji Malovan BIH 157 E7
Gornji Matejevac SRB 164 C4
Gornji Milanovac SRB 158 E5
Gornji Podgradci BIH 157 C6
Gornji Rajić HR 157 B6
Gornji Ribnik BIH 157 D6
Gornji Tkalec HR 149 E6
Gornji Vakuf BIH 157 E7
Gorno RO 161 C8
Gorno Ablanovo BG 161 F7
Gorno Aleksandrovo BG 167 D7
Gorno Orizari MK 164 F5
Gorno Ozirovo BG 165 C8
Gorno Pavlikene BG 165 C10
Goro I 66 C5
Gorobinci MK 164 F4
Gorredijk NL 16 B6
Gorron F 23 D10
Görsbach D 79 D8
Gorseinon GB 12 B6
Gorska Polyana BG 167 E7
Gorski Izvor BG 166 F4
Gorsko Novo Selo BG 166 C5
Gorssel NL 16 D6
Gort IRL 6 F5
Gortahork IRL 6 B6
Gort an Choirce IRL 6 B6
Gortavoy Bridge GB 7 C9
Gorteen IRL 6 E5
Gorteen IRL 6 E6
Gorteeny IRL 6 F6
Gortin GB 4 F2
Goruia RO 159 C8
Görükle TR 173 D10
Gorun BG 167 B10
Görvik S 106 D9
Gorzanów PL 77 B11
Gorze F 26 B5
Görzig D 79 C10
Görzke D 79 B11
Gorzkowice PL 143 D8
Gorzków-Osada PL 144 B7
Górzna PL 85 D11
Górzno PL 139 D9
Górzno PL 141 G5
Górzyca PL 81 A7
Górzyca PL 85 C8
Gorzyce PL 144 B4

Gorzyce PL 144 C6
Gorzyce PL 146 B6
Gorzyń PL 81 A9
Górzyn PL 81 C7
Gosaldo I 72 D4
Gosau A 73 A8
Gosberton GB 11 F11
Gościeradów Ukazowy PL 144 B4
Gościm PL 85 E9
Gościno PL 85 B9
Gościszów PL 81 D8
Gosdorf A 148 C5
Gosë AL 168 B2
Goslar D 79 C7
Goślice PL 139 E8
Gosné F 23 D9
Gospić HR 156 C3
Gospodinci BG 165 F9
Gosport GB 13 D12
Gössäter S 91 B13
Gössendorf A 148 C5
Gossau CH 27 F11
Gössitz D 79 E10
Gostavățu RO 160 E5
Gostilj AL 163 E9
Gostilitsa BG 166 C4
Gostinari RO 161 E8
Gostinu RO 161 E8
Gostivar MK 163 F10
Gostovići BIH 157 D9
Gostycyn PL 138 D4
Gostyń PL 81 C12
Gostyń PL 85 B7
Gostynin PL 139 F7
Goszcz PL 142 D3
Goszczanów PL 142 C6
Goszczyn PL 141 G3
Göta S 91 C11
Göteborg S 91 D10
Götene S 91 B13
Gotești MD 154 E2
Gotha D 79 E8
Gothem S 93 D13
Götlunda S 97 D14
Gotse Delchev BG 169 A10
Gottböle FIN 122 F6
Gotteszell D 76 E3
Gottfrieding D 75 E11
Göttingen D 78 C6
Gottmadingen D 27 E10
Gottne S 107 E14
Götzis A 71 C9
Gouarec F 22 D5
Gouda NL 16 D3
Goudswaard NL 182 B4
Gouesnou F 22 D3
Gouhenans F 26 E5
Goult F 35 C9
Goumenissa GR 169 C7
Goumois F 27 F6
Gourdan-Polignan F 33 D7
Gourdon F 29 F8
Gourdon GB 5 B12
Gourette F 32 E5
Gourgançon F 25 C11
Gouria GR 174 C3
Gourin F 22 D4
Gournay-en-Bray F 18 F4
Goussainville F 25 B7
Gout-Rossignol F 29 E6
Gouveia P 44 D5
Gouvia GR 168 E2
Gouvy B 19 D12
Gouzon F 29 C10
Gove P 44 B4
Goveđari HR 162 D3
Govedartsi BG 165 E8
Goven F 23 D8
Gowarczów PL 141 H2
Gowidlino PL 138 B4
Goworowo PL 139 E12
Gowran IRL 9 C8
Goxhill GB 11 D11
Göynükbelen TR 173 E11
Gozd PL 141 H4
Gozdnica PL 81 D8
Gozdowice BIH 162 D5
Gözsüz TR 173 C6
Gozzano I 68 B5
Graal-Müritz D 83 B12
Grab BIH 157 F10
Grab BIH 162 D5
Graben-Neudorf D 187 C5
Grabica PL 143 D8
Grabjan AL 168 C2
Gråbo S 91 D11
Grabovac HR 157 F7
Grabovci SRB 158 D4
Grabovica SRB 159 E10
Grabow D 83 D11
Grabowiec PL 143 D11
Grabowiec PL 144 B8
Grabówka PL 140 D8
Grabów nad Pilicą PL 141 G4
Grabów nad Prosną PL 142 C5
Grabowno PL 85 D12
Grabowno Wielkie PL 142 D3
Grabowo PL 136 D5
Grabowo PL 139 D13
Grabs CH 71 C8
Gračac HR 156 D4
Gračanica BIH 157 C7
Gračanica BIH 157 C9
Gračanica BIH 157 D10
Gračanica BIH 157 E8
Graçay F 24 F6
Gračišće HR 67 B8
Gracze PL 142 E4
Grad SLO 148 C6
Gradac BIH 162 D5
Gradac HR 157 F7
Gradac SLO 148 E4
Gradara I 67 E6
Gradec HR 149 E6
Gradec MK 169 B7
Gradefes E 39 C9
Gradets BG 167 D7
Gradevo BG 165 F7
Gradina BG 166 C5
Gradina BG 166 E4

Gradina BIH 157 F9
Gradina SRB 163 C9
Grădinari RO 159 C8
Grădinari RO 160 D4
Grădinița MD 154 D5
Gradishte BG 166 C4
Gradište HR 157 B10
Gradište SRB 164 B5
Gradište SRB 164 C5
Grădiștea RO 160 D3
Grădiștea RO 161 D8
Grădiștea RO 161 D8
Grădiștea RO 161 E10
Gradište Bekteško HR 149 E9
Gradnitsa BG 165 D10
Grado E 39 B7
Grado I 73 E7
Gradø S 97 B15
Gradojević SRB 158 D3
Gradoli I 62 B1
Gradsko BG 169 A6
Gradskovo SRB 159 E9
Graena E 55 E6
Græsted DK 87 C10
Grafelfing D 75 F9
Grafenau D 76 E4
Gräfenberg D 75 C9
Gräfenhainichen D 79 C11
Grafenhausen D 27 E9
Grafenrheinfeld D 187 B9
Gräfenroda D 79 E8
Grafenstein A 73 C9
Grafenwöhr D 75 C10
Grafenworth A 77 F9
Graffignana I 62 B2
Grafhorst D 79 B8
Graf Ignatievo BG 165 E10
Gräfinau-Angstedt D 79 E9
Grafing bei München D 75 F10
Grafrath D 75 F9
Gräfsnäs S 91 C11
Gräftåvallen S 105 E15
Gragnano I 60 B3
Grahovac MNE 163 D6
Grahovo MNE 163 D6
Grahovo SLO 73 D8
Gráig na Manach IRL 9 C9
Graiguenamanagh IRL 9 C9
Grain GB 15 E10
Grainau D 71 C12
Grainet D 76 E5
Graissac F 30 F2
Graissessac F 34 C5
Graja de Iniesta E 47 E9
Grajal de Campos E 39 D9
Grajduri RO 153 D11
Grajewo PL 140 C6
Grålum N 95 D14
Gram DK 86 E4
Gramada BG 159 F10
Gramastetten A 76 F6
Gramat F 29 F9
Gramatikovo BG 167 E9
Grambow D 84 D6
Grămești RO 153 B8
Grammatiko GR 169 F7
Grammendorf D 83 B13
Grammentsa GR 174 A2
Grammeno GR 168 E4
Grammichele I 59 E6
Gramsbergen NL 17 C7
Gramsh AL 168 C3
Gramzda LV 134 D3
Gramzow D 84 D6
Gran N 95 B13
Granabeg IRL 7 F10
Granada E 53 B9
Granån S 119 C10
Granard IRL 7 E8
Granarolo dell'Emilia I 66 C3
Granátula de Calatrava E 54 B5
Granberg S 118 D3
Granberget N 102 D3
Granbergsdal S 97 D12
Granbergsträsk S 107 A17
Grancey-le-Château-Nouvelle F 26 E3
Grandas E 39 B6
Grandcamp-Maisy F 23 B9
Grand-Champ F 22 E6
Grand-Couronne F 18 F3
Grande-Synthe F 18 B5
Grande-Vabre F 33 A10
Grand-Fort-Philippe F 18 B5
Grand-Fougeray F 23 E8
Grândola P 50 C2
Grandpré F 19 F10
Grandpuits-Bailly-Carrois F 25 C8
Grandrieu F 30 F4
Grandris F 30 C5
Grandson CH 31 B10
Grandtully GB 5 B9
Grandvelle-et-le-Perrenot F 26 E5
Grandvillars F 27 E6
Grandvilliers F 18 E4
Grañén E 41 E11
Grangärde S 97 B12
Grange IRL 7 G8
Grange IRL 9 E7
Grangemouth GB 5 C9
Grange-over-Sands GB 10 C6
Grängesberg S 97 B13
Granges-sur-Vologne F 27 D6
Grâce-Hollogne B 19 C11
Grängshyttan S 97 C12
Grängsjö S 103 B13
Granhult S 116 C7
Granica BIH 162 D5
Grăniceri RO 151 D7
Grănicești RO 153 B8
Graninge S 107 E11
Granitola-Torretta I 58 D2
Granitsa GR 174 A4
Granja P 51 B5
Granja de Moreruela E 39 E8
Granja de Torrehermosa E 51 C8
Granja do Ulmeiro P 44 D3
Gränna S 92 C5
Grannäs S 107 A10
Grannäs S 109 F13
Granneset N 108 E6
Granö S 107 C16

Granollers E 43 D8
Granön S 103 D13
Granowiec PL 142 D4
Granowo PL 81 B11
Granschütz D 79 D11
Gransee D 84 D4
Granselet S 109 E14
Gränsgård S 109 F15
Gransjö S 107 A15
Gransjön S 103 B11
Gränssjö S 108 F8
Grantham GB 11 F10
Grantown-on-Spey GB 3 L9
Granträsk S 107 C14
Granträskmark S 118 D6
Grantshouse GB 5 D12
Gränum S 88 C7
Granvik S 92 B5
Granville F 23 C8
Granvin N 94 A5
Grapska BIH 157 C9
Gräs S 97 C10
Grasbakken N 114 C5
Gräsgård S 89 C11
Grasleben D 79 B9
Gräsmarken S 97 B8
Grasmere GB 10 C5
Gräsmyr S 107 D17
Grassåmoen N 105 C14
Grassano I 60 B6
Grassau D 72 A6
Grasse F 36 D5
Grassington GB 11 C8
Gråsjö S 103 A10
Gråsten DK 86 F5
Gråstorp S 91 C12
Gratallops E 42 E5
Gratangsbotn N 111 C14
Gratens F 33 D8
Gratia RO 161 E6
Gratini GR 171 B8
Gratkorn A 148 B4
Grätnäs S 107 E14
Gråträsk S 118 C4
Gratteri I 58 D4
Gratwein A 148 B4
Grauballe DK 86 C5
Graulhet F 33 C9
Graupa D 80 D5
Graus F 42 F4
Grávalos E 41 D8
Gravberget N 102 E3
Gravbränna S 106 D7
Gravdal N 110 D6
Grave NL 16 E5
Gravedona I 69 A7
Gravelines F 18 C5
Gravellona Toce I 68 B5
Gravelotte F 26 B5
Gravens DK 86 D4
Grävenwiesbach D 21 D10
Gravesend GB 15 E9
Gravia GR 174 B5
Gravigny F 24 C5
Gråvika N 100 C5
Gravina di Catania I 59 D7
Gravina in Puglia I 61 B6
Gravmark S 118 F4
Gray F 26 F4
Grayan-et-l'Hôpital F 28 E3
Grays GB 15 E9
Graz A 148 B4
Grazalema E 53 C6
Grazzanise I 60 A2
Grčak SRB 163 C10
Grdelica SRB 164 D5
Greaca RO 161 E8
Greåker N 95 D14
Gréalou F 33 D7
Great Baddow GB 15 D10
Great Bircham GB 15 B10
Great Clifton GB 5 F10
Great Cornard GB 15 C10
Great Dunmow GB 15 D9
Great Glen GB 11 F10
Great Gonerby GB 11 F10
Greatham GB 11 B9
Great Harwood GB 11 D7
Great Haywood GB 11 E8
Great Linford GB 15 C7
Great Malvern GB 13 A10
Great Ponton GB 11 F10
Great Salkeld GB 5 F11
Great Shelford GB 15 C9
Great Torrington GB 12 D6
Great Wakering GB 15 D10
Great Yarmouth GB 15 B12
Grebănu RO 161 C9
Grebaštica HR 156 E4
Grebbestad S 91 B9
Grebci BIH 162 D5
Grebenac SRB 159 D7
Grebendorf (Meinhard) D 79 D7
Grebenhain D 21 D12
Grebenişu de Câmpie RO 152 D4
Grebenstein D 21 B12
Grebin D 83 B8
Grębków PL 141 F5
Grebo S 92 C7
Grębocin PL 138 D6
Grębów PL 143 F10
Gręboszów PL 143 F10
Greccio I 62 C3
Grecești RO 160 E2
Greci I 60 A4
Greci RO 155 D2
Gredelj BIH 157 F10
Greding D 75 D9
Gredstebro DK 86 E3
Greencastle GB 4 E2
Greencastle GB 7 D10
Greencastle GB 7 D10
Greene D 78 C6
Greengairs GB 5 D9
Greenhead GB 5 F11
Greenigo GB 3 H10
Greenisland GB 4 F5
Greenlaw GB 5 D12
Greenloaning GB 5 C9
Greenock GB 4 D7
Greenodd GB 10 C5
Greenore IRL 7 D10
Greenway GB 12 B5
Greggio I 68 C5
Greifenburg A 73 C7
Greifendorf D 80 D3
Greifenstein D 21 C10
Greiffenberg D 84 D5
Greifswald D 84 B4
Grein A 77 F7

Greiveri LV 135 B11
Greiz D 79 E11
Grejs DK 86 D5
Gremersdorf D 83 B9
Grenaa DK 87 C7
Grenade F 33 C8
Grenade-sur-l'Adour F 32 C5
Grenant F 26 E4
Grenås S 106 D8
Grenchen CH 27 F7
Grenči LV 134 C5
Grenoble F 31 E8
Grense-Jakobselv N 114 D9
Gréoux-les-Bains F 35 C10
Gresenhorst D 83 B12
Gress GB 2 J4
Gressan I 31 D11
Gresse D 83 D9
Gressoney-la-Trinite I 68 B4
Gressvik N 91 A8
Gresten A 77 G8
Grésy-sur-Aix F 31 D8
Grésy-sur-Isère F 31 D9
Gretna GB 5 F10
Greußen D 79 D8
Greux F 26 E4
Grevbäck S 92 C4
Greve in Chianti I 66 E3
Greven D 17 D9
Greven D 83 D9
Grevena GR 168 D5
Grevenbicht NL 183 C7
Grevenbroich D 21 B7
Greveniti GR 168 E5
Grevenmacher L 20 E6
Grevesmühlen D 83 C10
Greve Strand DK 87 D10
Grevie S 87 C11
Grevinge DK 87 D9
Greyabbey GB 7 C11
Greystoke GB 5 F11
Greystones IRL 7 F10
Grez-Doiceau B 19 C10
Grez-en-Bouère F 23 E10
Grgar SLO 73 D8
Grgurevci SRB 158 C4
Griegos E 47 D9
Gries F 27 C8
Gries am Brenner A 72 B3
Griesbach D 27 D9
Griesheim D 21 E11
Grieskirchen A 76 F5
Grießen D 81 C7
Griesstätt D 75 G11
Griffen A 73 C10
Grigiškes LT 137 D11
Grignan F 35 B8
Grigno I 72 D4
Grignols F 32 B5
Grigny F 30 D6
Grigoriopol MD 154 C4
Grijota E 40 D2
Grijpskerk NL 16 B6
Grillby S 98 C8
Grillon F 35 B8
Grimaldi I 60 E6
Grimaud F 36 E5
Grimbergen B 19 C9
Grimma D 79 D12
Grimmen D 84 B4
Grimoldby GB 11 E12
Grimsås S 91 E14
Grimsbu N 101 B12
Grimsby GB 11 D11
Grimslöv S 88 B7
Grimstad N 90 C4
Grimston GB 11 F13
Grimstorp S 92 D5
Grimstrup DK 86 D3
Grindaheim N 101 D9
Grindal N 101 A11
Grindelwald CH 70 D6
Grinder N 96 B7
Grindjord N 111 C12
Grindsted DK 86 A6
Grindsted DK 86 D3
Grindu RO 161 D9
Grinkiškis LT 134 E7
Griñón E 46 D5
Grins A 71 C11
Grinsbol S 97 D8
Grințies RO 153 C7
Gripenberg S 92 D5
Grisén E 41 E9
Griškabūdis LT 136 D7
Grisolia I 60 D5
Grisolles F 33 C8
Grisslehamn S 99 B11
Gritley GB 3 H11
Grivița RO 153 E11
Grivița RO 153 F11
Grivița RO 161 D9
Grivitsa BG 165 C10
Grkinja SRB 164 C4
Grljan SRB 159 F9
Grnčari MK 168 B5
Grobbendonk B 19 B10
Gröbenzell D 75 F9
Grobiņa LV 134 C2
Gröbming A 73 B8
Gröbzig D 79 C10
Grocka SRB 158 D6
Gródby S 93 A11
Gródek PL 140 D9
Gródek nad Dunajcem PL 144 D2
Gröden D 80 D5
Grödig A 73 A7
Gröditz D 80 D4
Gródki PL 139 D9
Grodków PL 142 E3
Grodziczno PL 139 D8
Grodziec PL 142 B5
Grodzisk PL 141 E7
Grodzisk Mazowiecki PL 141 F3
Grodzisk Wielkopolski PL 81 B10
Groenlo NL 17 D7
Groesbeek NL 183 B7
Grohnde (Emmerthal) D 78 B5
Groitzsch D 79 D11
Groix F 22 E5
Grojdibodu RO 160 F4
Grójec PL 141 G3
Grom PL 139 C10
Gromadka PL 81 D9
Grömitz D 83 B9
Gromnik PL 144 D2
Gromo I 69 A8
Gronau (Westfalen) D 17 D8
Grønbjerg DK 86 C3
Grønbo S 118 D5
Gröndal S 108 E8

Grong N 105 C12
Grönhögen S 89 C10
Grønhøj DK 86 C4
Gröningen D 79 C9
Groningen NL 17 B7
Grova N 90 A4
Grove GB 13 B12
Grønnemose DK 86 E6
Grønnes N 100 A6
Grønning N 110 E9
Grønningen N 104 D7
Gronowo PL 138 B5
Grönsinka S 98 B7
Grönskåra S 89 A9
Grönsta S 103 A11
Grønvik N 94 D4
Grönviken S 103 A9
Grönviken S 103 D12
Groomsport GB 4 F5
Grootegast NL 16 B6
Gropello Cairoli I 69 C6
Gropeni RO 155 C1
Gropnița RO 153 C10
Grorud N 95 D13
Groscavallo I 31 E11
Groși RO 152 B3
Grosio I 69 A9
Grošnica SRB 159 F6
Grosotto I 69 A9
Großaitingen D 71 A11
Groß Ammensleben D 79 B10
Großarl A 73 B7
Groß-Bieberau D 21 E11
Groß Börnecke D 79 C9
Großbothen D 79 D12
Großbottwar D 27 C11
Großbreitenbach D 79 E9
Großburgwedel (Burgwedel) D 78 B6
Groß Dölln D 84 E5
Grosselfingen D 27 D10
Großenaspe D 83 C7
Großenbrode D 83 B10
Großenehrich D 79 D8
Groß Engersdorf D 77 F11
Großengottern D 79 D7
Großenhain D 80 D5
Großenkneten D 17 C10
Großenlüder D 78 E6
Großensee D 83 C8
Großenstein D 79 E11
Großenwiehe D 82 A6
Groß-Enzersdorf D 77 F11
Grosseto I 65 B4
Grosseto-Prugna F 37 H9
Groß Fredenwalde D 84 D5
Großfurra D 79 D8
Groß-Gerau D 21 E10
Groß-Gerungs A 77 E7
Groß Glienicke D 80 B4
Großgmain D 73 A6
Groß Grönau D 83 C9
Großhabersdorf D 75 D8
Großhansdorf D 83 C8
Großharras A 77 E10
Großhartmannsdorf D 80 E4
Groß Heere (Heere) D 79 B7
Großhennersdorf D 81 E7
Groß-Hesepe D 17 C7
Großheubach D 187 B7
Grössjö S 107 F14
Großkarolinenfeld D 72 A5
Großklein A 148 C4
Groß Kiesow D 84 C4
Groß Köris D 80 B5
Groß Kreutz D 79 B12
Großkrut A 77 E11
Groß Lafferde (Lahstedt) D 79 B7
Großlangheim D 187 B9
Groß Leine D 80 B6
Groß Leuthen D 80 B6
Großlittgen D 21 D7
Großlohra D 79 D8
Großmaischeid D 185 C8
Großmehlen D 80 D5
Groß Miltzow D 84 C4
Groß Mohrdorf D 84 B3
Großmonra D 79 D9
Groß Naundorf D 80 C3
Großnaundorf D 80 D6
Groß Nemerow D 84 D4
Groß Oesingen D 79 A7
Großolbersdorf D 80 E4
Groß Oßnig D 80 C6
Großostheim D 21 E12
Großpetersdorf A 149 B6
Groß Plasten D 83 C13
Großraming A 73 A10
Großräschen D 80 C6
Großrinderfeld D 74 C6
Groß Roge D 83 C13
Groß-Rohrheim D 21 E10
Großröhrsdorf D 80 D6
Großrosseln D 186 C2
Großrudestedt D 79 D9
Großrußbach A 77 F10
Groß Sankt Florian A 148 C4
Groß Särchen D 80 D6
Großschirma D 80 E4
Großschönau A 77 E7
Groß Schwechten D 83 E11
Groß Schwülper (Schwülper) D 79 B7
Groß-Siegharts A 77 E8
Groß Stieten D 83 C10
Großthiemig D 80 D5
Großtreben D 80 C4
Groß Twülpstedt D 79 B8
Groß-Umstadt D 187 B6
Großwallstadt D 187 B7
Groß Warnow D 83 D11
Groß Welle D 83 D12
Groß Wittensee D 82 B7
Großwudicke D 79 A11
Groß Ziethen D 84 E5
Groß-Zimmern D 187 B6
Grostenquin F 27 C6
Grosuplje SLO 73 E10
Grøtavær N 111 C11
Grong N 111 A16
Grötholen S 102 C4
Grötingen S 103 A9
Grotli N 100 B7
Gröttlingbo S 93 E12
Grøtnesdalen N 111 A18
Grottaferrata I 62 D3
Grottaglie I 61 C9
Grottaminarda I 60 A4
Grottammare I 62 B5
Grottazzolina I 62 A5

Grotte I 58 E4
Grotte di Castro I 62 B1
Grotteria I 59 C9
Grottole I 61 C7
Grou NL 16 B5
Grova N 90 A4
Grove GB 13 B12
Grönnemose DK 86 E6
Grönnes N 100 A6
Grude BIH 157 F7
Gudusk PL 139 C9
Grudziądz PL 138 D6
Gruey-lès-Surance F 26 D5
Grugliasco I 68 C4
Gruia RO 159 E10
Gruissan F 34 D5
Gruiu RO 161 D8
Grullos E 39 B7
Grumăzești RO 153 C8
Grumbach D 80 D5
Grumo Appula I 61 A7
Grums S 97 D9
Grünau S 73 A8
Grünau A 77 F9
Grünberg D 21 C11
Grünburg A 76 G6
Grundagssätern S 102 B4
Grundfors S 106 A8
Grundfors S 107 B13
Grundforsen S 102 A4
Grundsel S 118 C4
Grundsjö S 107 C11
Grundsuna S 107 E16
Grundsund S 91 C9
Grundtjärn S 107 D12
Grundträsk S 107 A16
Grundträsk S 109 F17
Grundträsk S 118 B7
Grundvattnet S 118 C4
Grünendeich D 82 C7
Grünenwald D 80 C5
Grünewalde D 80 C5
Grüngebru N 94 C7
Grünheide D 80 B5
Grünkraut D 71 B9
Grunow D 80 B6
Grünsfeld D 74 C6
Grünstadt D 21 E10
Grünwald D 75 F10
Grupčin MK 164 F3
Grury F 30 B4
Grüšlaukė LT 134 D2
Grußendorf (Sassenburg) D 79 A8
Gruta PL 138 D6
Gruvberget S 103 D11
Gruyères CH 31 B11
Gruža SRB 159 F6
Grüžai LT 135 D8
Gruzdžiai LT 134 D6
Grybów PL 145 D2
Grycksbo S 103 E9
Gryfice PL 85 C9
Gryfino D 84 D6
Gryfów Śląski PL 81 D8
Grygov CZ 146 B4
Grylewo PL 85 E12
Gryllefjord N 111 B13
Grynberget S 107 C11
Gryt S 93 C9
Grytan S 106 E7
Grytgöl S 92 B7
Gryts bruk S 92 B6
Grytsjö S 106 A9
Gryttjom S 99 B8
Gryžliny PL 139 C9
Grzebienisko PL 81 B11
Grzmiąca PL 85 C10
Grzybno PL 84 D7
Grzybno PL 138 D5
Grzymiszew PL 142 B5
Grzywna PL 138 D6
Gschnitz A 72 B3
Gschwandt A 73 A8
Gschwend D 74 C6
Gstaad CH 31 C11
Gsteig CH 31 C11
Guadahortuna E 53 A10
Guadajoz E 51 E8
Guadalajara E 47 C6
Guadalaviar E 47 D9
Guadalcanal E 51 C8
Guadalcázar E 53 A7
Guadalest E 56 D4
Guadalmez E 54 B3
Guadarrama E 46 C4
Guadassuar E 48 F4
Guadix E 55 E6
Guaire (NL) 9 C10
Guájar-Faragüit E 53 C9
Gualav S 88 C6
Gualdo Cattaneo I 62 B3
Gualdo Tadino I 67 F6
Gualtieri I 62 D4
Guarcino I 62 D4
Guarda P 45 C6
Guardamar del Segura E 56 E3
Guardavalle I 59 B9
Guardea I 62 B2
Guardiagrele I 63 D7
Guardia Lombardi I 60 B4
Guardia Perticara I 60 C6
Guardia Piemontese I 60 E6
Guardia Sanframondi I 60 A3
Guardias Viejas E 55 F7
Guardiola de Berguedà E 43 C7
Guardo E 39 C10
Guardramiro E 45 B8
Guareña E 51 B7
Guaro E 53 C7
Guarromán E 54 C5
Guasila I 64 D3
Guastalla I 66 C2
Gubbio I 66 F6
Gubbträsk S 107 A13
Guben D 81 C7
Gübene BG 166 D4

Gubin PL 81 C7
Guča SRB 158 F5
Guča Gora BIH 157 D8
Gudar E 48 D3
Gudavac BIH 156 C5
Gudbjerg DK 86 E7
Gudenieki LV 134 C3
Guderup DK 86 F5
Gudhem S 91 C14
Gudhjem DK 89 E7
Gudiena LT 137 D9
Gudinge S 99 A9
Gudme DK 87 E7
Gudom DK 86 B2
Gudumholm DK 86 B6
Gudvangen N 100 E5
Gudžiūnai LT 134 E7
Guebwiller F 27 E7
Guégon F 22 E6
Güéjar-Sierra E 53 B10
Guémar F 27 D7
Guémené-Penfao F 23 E8
Guémené-sur-Scorff F 22 D5
Guénange F 20 F6
Güeñes E 40 B5
Guenrouet F 23 E8
Guer F 23 E7
Guérande F 22 F7
Guéret F 29 C9
Guérigny F 25 F9
Guerri de la Sal E 33 F8
Güesa E 32 E3
Gueugnon F 30 B5
Gueures I 63 D7
Guglingen D 27 B10
Guglionesi I 63 D7
Gugutka BG 171 B9
Gühlen-Glienicke D 83 D13
Guia P 44 E3
Guia P 50 E3
Guichen F 23 E8
Guidel F 22 E5
Guide Post GB 5 E13
Guidizzolo I 66 B2
Guidonia-Montecelio I 62 D3
Guiglia I 66 D2
Guignen F 23 E8
Guignes F 25 C8
Guignicourt F 19 F8
Guijo de Coria E 45 D8
Guijo de Galisteo E 45 D8
Guijo de Granadilla E 45 D8
Guijuelo E 45 C9
Guildford GB 15 E7
Guilers F 22 D2
Guilherand F 30 F6
Guilhofrei P 38 E3
Guilhovai P 44 C3
Guillaumes F 36 C5
Guillena E 51 D7
Guillestre F 36 B5
Guilliers F 22 D7
Guillon F 25 E11
Guillos F 32 A4
Guilvinec F 22 E3
Guimarães P 38 F3
Guînes F 15 F12
Guingamp F 22 C5
Guipavas F 22 D3
Guipry F 23 E8
Guisando E 45 D10
Guisborough GB 11 B9
Guiscard F 19 E7
Guise F 19 E8
Guissény F 22 C3
Guissona E 42 D6
Guist GB 15 B10
Guitiriz E 38 B4
Guîtres F 28 E5
Gujan-Mestras F 32 A3
Gulács H 145 G5
Gülbahçe TR 177 C8
Gulbene LV 135 B13
Guldager DK 86 D2
Guldborg DK 84 A1
Gulgamme N 113 B16
Gulianca RO 161 C11
Gülitz D 83 D11
Gullabo S 89 C9
Gullane GB 5 C11
Gullberg S 103 D10
Gullbrå N 100 E4
Gullbrandstorp S 87 B11
Gullbranna S 87 B11
Gulleråsen S 103 D9
Gullholmen N 111 C10
Gullön S 109 E15
Gullringen S 92 D7
Gullspång S 91 B15
Gullträsk S 118 B6
Güllübahçe TR 177 D8
Güllüce TR 173 D9
Güllük TR 177 E10
Gullverket N 95 B14
Gulpen NL 183 D7
Gülpinar TR 171 E10
Gulsele S 107 D12
Gulsvik N 95 B10
Gültz D 84 C4
Gülübintsi BG 166 E6
Gülübovo BG 165 E10
Gülübovo BG 166 F5
Gülzow D 83 C12
Gumhöjden S 97 B10
Gumiel de Hizán E 40 E4
Gumiel de Mercado E 40 E4
Gummark S 118 E5
Gummersbach D 21 B9
Gumpelstadt D 79 E7
Gumtow D 83 E12
Günaydın TR 173 D7
Gümüşçay TR 173 D7
Gümüşsuyu TR 177 C9
Gümüşyaka TR 173 B9
Gümzovo BG 159 E10
Gunaroš SRB 150 F4
Gundelfingen D 27 D8
Gundelsheim D 21 F11
Gundershoffen F 27 C8
Gundinci HR 157 B9
Gündoğan TR 173 D8
Gündoğdu TR 173 D7
Güneyli TR 172 B6
Güngörmez TR 173 B8
Gunja HR 157 C10
Gunnarnäs N 113 A13
Gunnarsbo S 103 C11

Gunnarsbyn S 118 B7
Gunnarskog S 97 C8
Gunnarvattnet S 105 C16
Gunnebo S 93 D9
Günstedt D 79 D9
Güntersberge D 79 C8
Guntersdorf A 77 E10
Güntersleben D 187 B8
Guntramsdorf A 77 F10
Günzburg D 75 F7
Gunzenhausen D 75 D8
Gura-Biculuj MD 154 D4
Gura Calițej RO 161 B9
Gura Camencii MD 154 B2
Gura Galbenei MD 154 D3
Gurahonț RO 151 E9
Gura Ocniței RO 161 D7
Gura Râului RO 152 F3
Gurasada RO 151 F10
Gura Teghii RO 161 C8
Gura Vadului RO 161 C8
Gura Văii RO 153 E9
Gura Vitioarei RO 161 C8
Gurbănești RO 161 E9
Gurghiu RO 152 D5
Guri i Bardhë AL 168 B3
Guri i Zi AL 163 E8
Gurk A 73 C9
Gurkovo BG 166 D5
Gurkovo BG 167 C9
Gürlyano BG 166 E6
Gurrea de Gállego E 41 D10
Gurrë e Madhe AL 168 A3
Gurteen IRL 6 E6
Gur'yevsk RUS 136 D2
Gusborn D 83 D10
Güssefeld D 83 E10
Gusev RUS 136 D5
Gusinje MNE 163 D8
Gușoeni RO 160 D4
Gusow D 80 A6
Guspini I 64 D2
Gussago I 69 B9
Gusselby S 97 C13
Güssing A 149 B6
Gussola I 66 B1
Gussvattnet S 105 C16
Gußwerk A 148 A4
Gustavsberg S 99 D10
Gustavsfors S 97 B10
Güsten D 79 C10
Gusterath D 21 E7
Güstrow D 83 C12
Gusum S 93 C8
Gutach (Schwarzwaldbahn) D 187 E5
Gutau A 77 F7
Gutcher GB 3 D14
Güterfelde D 80 B4
Güterglück D 79 C10
Gütersloh D 17 E10
Guthrie GB 5 B11
Gutorfölde H 149 C7
Gutow D 83 C12
Guttannen CH 70 D6
Guttaring A 73 C10
Gützkow D 84 C4
Guvåg N 110 C8
Güvemalanı TR 173 D7
Güvercinlik TR 177 E10
Guxhagen D 78 D5
Güzelbahçe TR 177 C8
Güzelçamlı TR 177 D9
Gvardeysk RUS 136 D3
Gvarv N 95 D10
Gvozd HR 148 F5
Gvozd MNE 163 D7
Gvozdansko HR 156 B5
Gwda Wielka PL 85 C11
Gweedore IRL 6 B6
Gwithian GB 12 E4
Gy F 26 F4
Gyál H 150 C3
Gyarmat H 149 B8
Gyékényes H 149 D8
Gyenesdiás H 149 C8
Gyermely H 149 A11
Gyé-sur-Seine F 25 D11
Gyhum D 17 B12
Gyljen S 118 B9
Gylling DK 86 D6
Gymno GR 175 C8
Gyomaendrőd H 150 D6
Gyömöre H 149 A9
Gyömrő H 150 C3
Gyöngyös H 150 B4
Gyöngyöspata H 150 B4
Gyönk H 149 C10
Győr H 149 A9
Győrság H 149 A9
Györköny H 149 C11
Györsövár H 149 A9
Győrszemere H 149 A9
Györtelek H 145 H5
Győrújbarát H 149 A9
Győrújfalu H 149 A9
Győrzámoly H 149 A9
Gyrstinge S 87 D12
Gysinge S 98 B7
Gytheio GR 178 B4
Gyttorp S 97 C12
Gyueshevo BG 164 E5
Gyula H 151 D7
Gyulaháza H 145 G5
Gyulaj H 149 C10
Gyúró H 149 B10
Gzy PL 139 E10

H

Haabneeme EST 131 B9
Haacht B 19 C10
Häädemeeste EST 131 E8
Haaften NL 183 B6
Haag A 77 F7
Haag am Hausruck A 76 F5
Haag in Oberbayern D 75 F11
Haajainen FIN 124 C7
Haaksbergen NL 17 D7
Haapajärvi FIN 123 D17
Haapa-Kimola FIN 127 D15
Haapakoski FIN 123 E10
Haapakoski FIN 124 F8
Haapakumpu FIN 115 D3
Haapalahti FIN 113 E19
Haapaluoma FIN 123 E10
Haapamäki FIN 123 C16

Haapamäki FIN 123 E17
Haapamäki FIN 123 F12
Haapamäki FIN 125 E10
Haaparanta FIN 115 E3
Haapasalu EST 130 D7
Haar D 75 F10
Haarajoki FIN 123 F17
Haarajoki FIN 127 E13
Haaraoja FIN 119 F16
Haarasaajo FIN 119 B12
Haarby DK 86 E6
Haaren NL 183 B6
Haarlem NL 16 D3
Haastrecht NL 16 E3
Haavisto FIN 127 D11
Habaja EST 131 C10
Habartov CZ 75 B12
Habas F 32 C4
Habay-la-Neuve B 19 E12
Häbbersliden S 118 E4
Habiller TR 167 F7
Hablingbo S 93 E12
Habo S 91 B11
Håbol S 91 B11
Habovka SK 147 C9
Habry CZ 77 C8
Habsheim F 27 E7
Hachenburg D 21 C9
Haciahmetli TR 177 B10
Hacibartov TR 167 F7
Hacigelen TR 172 D6
Hacıköy TR 172 C6
Hacınas F 40 E5
Haciırahmanli TR 177 B10
Haciumur TR 167 F7
Hacivelioba TR 173 D8
Hackås S 102 A8
Hackenheim D 21 E9
Hacketstown IRL 9 C9
Hackleton GB 13 C7
Hacksjö S 107 B12
Hadamar D 21 D10
Hadanberg S 107 D14
Haddeboda S 92 B6
Haddington GB 5 D11
Haddiscoe GB 15 B12
Haderslev DK 86 E4
Haderup DK 86 C3
Hadimköy TR 173 B10
Hadleigh GB 15 C10
Hadley GB 10 F7
Hadol F 26 D5
Hadres A 77 E10
Hadsel N 110 C8
Hadsten DK 86 C6
Hadsund DK 86 B6
Haelen NL 183 C7
Hafnerbach A 77 F8
Haftersbol S 97 C10
Haga S 98 B9
Haganj HR 149 E7
Hagastrøm S 103 E13
Hagby S 89 B10
Hagebyhöga S 92 C5
Hagen D 17 F8
Hagenbach D 187 C5
Hagenow D 83 D10
Hagenwerder D 81 D7
Hageri EST 131 C9
Hägerstad S 92 C7
Hagetaubin F 32 C4
Hagetmau F 32 C4
Hagfors S 97 B10
Hagondange F 20 F6
Hagsta S 103 E13
Haguenau F 27 C8
Hahausen D 79 C7
Hahnbach D 75 C10
Hahnstätten D 185 D9
Hahót H 149 C7
Haibach D 21 E12
Haibach D 75 D12
Haidmühle D 76 E6
Haiger D 21 C10
Haigerloch D 27 D10
Haiming D 76 F3
Haiming A 71 C11
Hailsham GB 15 F9
Hailuoto FIN 119 E13
Haiming D 76 F3
Haina D 75 B8
Haina (Kloster) D 21 B11
Hainburg an der Donau A 77 F11
Hainfeld A 77 F9
Hainichen D 80 E4
Haiterbach D 187 D6
Haitzendorf A 77 E9
Hajala FIN 127 E8
Hajdúböszörmény H 151 B8
Hajdúdorog H 151 B8
Hajdúhadház H 151 B8
Hajdúnánás H 145 H3
Hajdúsámson H 151 B8
Hajdúszoboszló H 151 C7
Hajdúszovát H 151 C7
Hajmáskér H 149 B10
Hajnáčka SK 147 E9
Hajnowka PL 141 E9
Hajnos RKS 164 D4
Hajós H 150 E3
Hakadal N 95 B13
Håkafot S 105 C16
Håkansvallen S 102 B7
Håkvik N 111 C14
Hakkas S 116 E7
Hakenpää FIN 126 D6
Häkkilä FIN 123 E14
Hakokylä FIN 121 E11
Håkøybotn N 111 A16
Håksberg S 97 B13
Hakstabben N 112 C11
Håkvik N 111 D13
Halahora de Sus MD 153 A10
Håland N 94 C4
Halapić BIH 157 D7
Halászi H 146 F5
Halásztelek H 150 C2

Häläucești RO 153 C9
Halbe D 80 C5
Halbenrain A 148 C5
Hålberg S 109 F18
Halberstadt D 79 C9
Halbjerg DK 90 D7
Halblech D 71 B11
Halbturn A 77 F11
Hălchiu RO 153 F7
Hald DK 86 B4
Hald DK 86 B6
Haldarsvik FO 2 A2
Hald Ege DK 86 C4
Halden N 91 A9
Haldensleben D 79 B9
Hale GB 11 E7
Halen B 183 D6
Halenkov CZ 146 C6
Halenkovice CZ 146 C4
Halesowen GB 13 A10
Halesworth GB 15 C12
Halfing D 72 A5
Halfway IRL 8 E5
Halfweg NL 16 D3
Halhjem N 94 B2
Halič SK 147 E9
Halifax GB 11 D8
Halkida FIN 127 E9
Halikarna FIN 119 B9
Halikko FIN 127 E9
Halikirk GB 3 H10
Halkivaha FIN 127 C8
Halkokumpu FIN 124 F7
Hall S 93 D13
Hälla S 107 C12
Halla-aho FIN 124 C9
Hallabro S 89 C8
Hallabrottet S 92 A6
Halla Heberg S 91 E10
Halland GB 15 F9
Hälland S 105 E14
Hallapuro FIN 123 D12
Hällaryd S 89 C7
Hällbacken S 105 E16
Hällbacken S 109 D12
Hällberga S 98 D7
Hällbo S 103 D11
Hällbybrunn S 98 D6
Halle D 78 C6
Halle NL 183 B8
Halle (Saale) D 79 D10
Halle (Westfalen) D 17 D10
Hällefors S 97 C12
Hälleforsnäs S 93 A9
Hallein A 73 A7
Hälleliks S 91 B13
Hällen S 103 E14
Hällen S 105 D16
Hallenberg D 21 B11
Hallencourt F 18 E4
Halle-Neustadt D 79 D10
Hallerndorf D 75 C8
Hällesjö S 103 A11
Hällestad S 92 B7
Hällevadsholm S 91 B10
Hällevik S 88 C7
Hälleviksstrand S 91 C9
Hall-Häxåsen S 106 D8
Hallingby N 95 B12
Hallingeberg S 93 D8
Hällinmäki FIN 124 F9
Hall in Tirol A 72 B4
Hällnäs S 107 C17
Hällnäs S 109 D15
Hällnäs S 109 D13
Hallom S 102 A7
Hallow GB 13 A10
Hällsbäck S 97 D8
Hallsberg S 92 A6
Hällsjö S 107 E13
Hällsta S 98 D6
Hallstahammar S 98 C6
Hallstatt A 73 A8
Hallstavik S 99 B11
Halltorp S 89 C10
Halluin B 19 C7
Hallund DK 86 A6
Hällvik S 109 D14
Hallviken S 106 D8
Hallworthy GB 12 D5
Hälmägel RO 151 E10
Hălmagiu RO 151 E10
Halmeu RO 145 H7
Halmstad S 87 B11
Halna S 92 B4
Halosenniemi FIN 119 D14
Halosenranta FIN 115 E2
Halovo SRB 159 F9
Hals DK 86 B6
Halsa N 104 E4
Halsenbach D 21 D9
Hal'shany BY 137 E13
Hälsingby FIN 122 D7
Hälsjo S 103 C12
Halsøy N 108 D5
Halsskov DK 87 E8
Halstead GB 15 D10
Halstenbek D 83 C7
Halsteren NL 16 E2
Halstroff F 20 F6
Halsua FIN 123 D12
Haltern D 17 E8
Halttula FIN 119 C14
Haltwhistle GB 5 F12
Haluna FIN 125 D10
Hälvä FIN 129 B11
Halvarsgårdarna S 97 B13
Halver D 21 B8
Halvrimmen DK 86 A5
Halwell GB 13 E7
Halže CZ 75 C12
Ham F 19 E7
Ham GB 3 E12
Hamar N 101 E14
Hamari FIN 119 C14
Hamarøy N 108 D5
Hamarøy N 111 D10
Hambach F 27 B7
Hambergen D 17 B11
Hamble-le-Rice GB 13 D12
Hambrücken D 21 F11
Hambühren D 79 A6
Hamburg D 83 C7
Hamburgsund S 91 B9
Hambye F 23 C9
Hamcearca RO 155 C3
Hamdibey TR 173 E7
Hämeenkoski FIN 127 C13

Hämeenkyrö FIN 127 B9
Hämeenlinna FIN 127 D11
Hämelhausen D 17 C12
Hameln D 17 D12
Hämerten D 79 A10
Hamica HR 148 E5
Hamidiye TR 167 F9
Hamidiye TR 172 B6
Hamilton GB 5 D8
Hamilton's Bawn GB 7 D9
Hamina FIN 128 D7
Haminalahti FIN 124 E9
Hamit TR 181 C9
Hamitabat TR 173 A7
Hamlagrø N 94 A4
Hamlot N 111 D10
Hamm D 17 E9
Hamm (Sieg) D 185 C8
Hammar S 92 B5
Hammarland FIN 99 B13
Hammarn S 97 C12
Hammarnäs S 105 E16
Hammarsbyn S 102 E5
Hammarstrand S 107 E10
Hammarvika N 104 D5
Hamme B 19 B9
Hammel DK 86 C5
Hammelburg D 74 B6
Hammelev DK 86 E4
Hammelspring D 84 D4
Hamme-Mille B 19 C10
Hammenhög S 88 D6
Hammer N 105 C12
Hammerbrücke D 75 B11
Hammerdal S 106 D8
Hammerfest N 113 B12
Hammershøj DK 86 C5
Hammerum DK 86 C4
Hamminkeln D 17 E7
Hamn N 108 E3
Hamn N 111 B13
Hamna N 114 B8
Hamnavoe GB 3 D14
Hamnavoe GB 3 E14
Hamnbukt N 112 C8
Hamnbukta N 111 B18
Hamneidet N 112 D6
Hamnes N 105 B10
Hamnes N 108 E4
Hamnes N 112 D6
Hamningberg N 114 B9
Hamnøy N 110 E5
Hamnvågnes N 111 B16
Hamoir B 19 D12
Hamois B 19 D11
Hamont B 16 F5
Hampen DK 86 C4
Hampetorp S 92 A7
Håmpjåkk S 116 D4
Hampont F 26 C6
Hampreston GB 13 D11
Hamra S 93 F12
Hamra S 103 C9
Hamrångefjärden S 103 E13
Hamre N 112 C4
Hamry nad Sázavou CZ 77 C9
Ham-sous-Varsberg F 186 C2
Hamstreet GB 15 E10
Hamsund N 111 D10
Ham-sur-Heure B 19 D9
Hamula FIN 123 D16
Hamula FIN 124 D9
Hamzabeyli TR 167 F7
Hanaskog S 88 C6
Hanau D 187 A6
Handbjerg DK 86 C3
Handeloh D 83 D7
Handen S 93 A12
Handest DK 86 B5
Handewitt D 82 A6
Handlová SK 147 D7
Handog S 106 E7
Handöl S 105 E12
Handrabury UA 154 B5
Handrup D 17 C9
Handsjö S 102 B8
Handstein N 108 D4
Handzame B 182 C2
Hanebo S 103 D12
Hanerau-Hademarschen D 82 B6
Hanestad N 101 C13
Hănești RO 153 B9
Hangastenmaa FIN 128 B7
Hangelsberg D 80 B5
Hånger S 87 A13
Hangö FIN 127 F8
Hangony H 145 G1
Hangu RO 153 C8
Hangvar S 93 D13
Hanhikoski FIN 115 E2
Hanhimaa FIN 117 C14
Han i Elezit RKS 164 E3
Hanikase EST 132 F1
Haniska SK 145 F3
Hankamäki FIN 125 D10
Hankasalem asema FIN 123 F16
Hankasalmi FIN 123 F16
Hankensbüttel D 83 E9
Han Knežica BIH 157 B6
Hanko FIN 127 F8
Hanna PL 141 G9
Hannäs S 93 C8
Hannover D 78 B6
Hannoversch Münden D 78 D6
Hannukainen FIN 117 C11
Hannusperä FIN 119 D15
Hannusranta FIN 121 F10
Hannut B 19 C11
Hanøy N 110 D9
Han-Pijesak BIH 157 D10
Hanshagen D 83 C10
Hańsk Pierwszy PL 141 H8
Hansnes N 112 D4
Hanstedt D 83 D8
Hanstholm DK 86 A3
Han-sur-Nied F 26 C5
Hanušovce nad Topľou SK 145 E4
Hanušovice CZ 77 B11
Hanvec F 22 D3
Haparanda S 119 C12
Hapert NL 183 C6
Häppälä FIN 123 F16
Happburg D 75 D9
Happisburgh GB 15 B12
Haps NL 183 B7
Hapträsk S 118 B4
Hara S 106 E6
Härad S 98 D7
Haradok BY 133 F7
Harads S 118 B5
Häradsbäck S 88 B6
Häradsbygden S 103 E9
Haradshammar S 93 B9
Haradzilavichy Pyershaya BY 133 D4
Haraldseng N 112 B9
Haram N 100 A4
Harang N 104 E6
Harany BY 133 F6
Harasiuki PL 144 C5
Hărău RO 151 F10
Haraudden S 116 E3
Harbacheva BY 133 E6
Harbak N 104 C8
Harbke D 79 B9
Harbo S 98 B8
Harboør DK 86 B2
Harbost GB 2 J4
Harburg (Schwaben) D 75 E8
Harbury GB 13 A12
Hard A 71 C9
Hardbakke N 100 D1
Hardegg A 77 E9
Hardegsen D 78 C6
Hardelot-Plage F 15 F12
Hardenberg NL 17 C7
Harderwijk NL 16 D5
Hardheim D 27 A11
Hardinxveld-Giessendam NL 182 B5
Hardt D 27 D9
Hareid N 100 B4
Harelbeke B 19 C7
Haren NL 17 B7
Haren (Ems) D 17 C8
Hare Street GB 15 D9
Harestua N 95 B13
Harfleur F 23 A12
Harg S 99 B10
Hargesheim D 21 E9
Hargimont B 19 D11
Hargla EST 131 F12
Hargnies F 19 D10
Hargshamn S 99 B10
Harichovce SK 145 F2
Harinkaa FIN 123 E16
Harjakangas FIN 126 B6
Härjåro S 99 D8
Härjåsjön S 102 C7
Harjavalta FIN 126 C7
Harjula FIN 119 C15
Harjumaa FIN 128 B7
Harjunkylä FIN 122 E7
Harjunpää FIN 126 C6
Harju-Risti EST 131 C7
Harka H 149 A7
Härkäjoki FIN 115 D2
Harkakötöny H 150 E4
Harkány H 149 E10
Härkmeri FIN 122 F6
Härkönen FIN 119 C13
Harku EST 131 C9
Hârlău RO 153 C9
Harlech GB 10 F3
Harleston GB 15 C11
Hårlev DK 87 E10
Harlingen NL 16 B4
Harlow GB 15 D9
Harly F 19 E7
Hărman RO 153 F7
Harmånger S 103 C13
Härmänkylä FIN 121 F13
Harmanli TR 173 D9
Härmänmäki FIN 121 F11
Harmannsdorf A 77 F10
Harmelen NL 182 A5
Harmoinen FIN 127 C13
Harmsdorf D 83 C9
Harmston GB 11 E10
Harnes F 18 D6
Härnösand S 103 A14
Haro E 40 C6
Harodz'ki BY 137 E13
Haroldswick GB 3 D15
Harouē F 26 D5
Härpe FIN 127 E14
Harpefoss N 101 C11
Harpenden GB 15 D8
Harplinge S 87 B11
Harpstedt D 17 C11
Harra D 75 B10
Harrachov CZ 81 E8
Harran N 105 B13
Harre DK 86 B3
Harridslev DK 86 C6
Harrietfield GB 5 C9
Harrioja S 119 C11
Harrislee D 82 A6
Harrogate GB 11 D8
Harrsjö S 106 B9
Harrström FIN 122 E6
Harrvik S 107 A10
Harsa S 103 C10
Hårsbäck S 98 C7
Harsefeld D 82 D7
Harșeni RO 152 F6
Hârșești RO 160 D5
Harsleben D 79 C9
Hårslev DK 86 D6
Hârșova RO 155 D1
Harsprånget S 116 E3
Harstad N 111 C12
Harsum D 78 B6
Harsvik N 104 C8
Harta H 150 D3
Hartberg A 148 B5
Hårte S 103 C13
Hartenholm D 83 C8
Hartha D 80 D3
Harthausen D 21 F10
Hartheim D 27 E8
Hârtiești RO 160 C6
Hart im Zillertal A 72 B4
Hartkirchen A 76 F5
Hartland GB 12 D6
Hartlepool GB 11 B9
Hartmanice CZ 76 D4
Hartola FIN 127 B15
Harwich GB 15 D11
Harzgerode D 79 C9
Hasanağa TR 173 D10
Hasbuğa TR 173 A8
Haselünne D 17 C8
Hasirciarnavutköy TR 171 B10
Håsjö S 107 E10
Hasköy TR 173 A6
Hasköy TR 177 C9
Haslach an der Mühl A 76 E6
Haslach im Kinzigtal D 27 D9
Hasle CH 70 C5
Hasle DK 88 E7
Haslemere GB 15 E7
Haslev DK 87 E9
Hasloh D 83 C7
Hasløya N 104 E2
Haslund DK 86 C6
Hășmaș RO 151 D9
Hasparren F 32 D3
Haßbergen D 17 C12
Hassel (Weser) D 17 C12
Hassela S 103 B12
Hassela kyrkby S 103 B12
Hasselfelde D 79 C8
Hasselfors S 92 A5
Hasselt B 19 C11
Hasselt NL 16 C6
Haßfurt D 75 B8
Hassi FIN 127 B13
Hässjö S 103 A14
Haßleben D 79 D9
Haßleben D 84 D5
Hässleholm S 87 C13
Hasslö S 89 C8
Haßloch D 21 F10
Hasslöv S 87 C12
Haßmersheim D 187 C7
Hästbo S 103 E13
Hästholmen S 92 C5
Hastière-Lavaux B 19 D10
Hastings GB 15 F10
Hästnäs S 97 D14
Håstrup DK 86 E6
Hästveda S 87 C13
Hasvåg N 105 C9
Hasvik N 112 C9
Hať CZ 146 B6
Hat' UA 145 G6
Hațeg RO 159 B10
Hatfield GB 11 D10
Hatherleigh GB 12 D6
Hätilä FIN 127 C11
Hatipkişlasi TR 181 B7
Hatsola FIN 128 B8
Hattarvík FO 2 A4
Hattem NL 16 D6
Hattersheim am Main D 21 D10
Hattert D 21 C9
Hattfjelldal N 108 E6
Hatting DK 86 D5
Hattingen D 17 F8
Hatton GB 3 L13
Hattstedt D 82 A6
Hattula FIN 127 C11
Hattuvaara FIN 125 E16
Hatulanmäki FIN 124 C8
Hatunkylä FIN 125 D15
Hatvan H 150 B4
Hatzenbühl D 27 B9
Hatzendorf A 148 C6
Hatzfeld (Eder) D 21 C11
Haubourdin F 18 C6
Hauenstein D 186 C4
Haugan N 105 D9
Haugastøl N 94 A7
Hauge N 94 F4
Hauge N 114 E6
Haugen N 110 D7
Haugesund N 94 D2
Haugh of Urr GB 5 F9
Haugland N 108 D5
Haugli N 111 C15
Haugnes N 111 B11
Haugnes N 112 C6
Haugset N 112 D7
Hauho FIN 127 C12
Haukå N 100 C2
Haukela FIN 125 B14
Haukeligrend N 94 C7
Haukijärvi FIN 127 B9
Haukilahti FIN 121 F13
Haukiniemi FIN 121 C13
Haukipudas FIN 119 D14
Haukivaara FIN 125 E15
Haukivuori FIN 124 F8
Haukøy N 111 D11
Haulerwijk NL 16 B6
Haurukylä FIN 119 E15
Haus A 73 B8
Haus N 94 B2
Hausach D 187 E5
Hausen D 75 E11
Hausen bei Würzburg D 187 B9
Häusern D 27 E9
Hausham D 72 A4
Hausjärvi FIN 127 D12
Hauske N 94 D3
Hausleiten A 77 F10
Hausmannstätten A 148 C5
Hautajärvi FIN 115 E6
Hautakylä FIN 121 D10
Hautakylä FIN 123 E12
Haute-Amance F 26 E4
Hautefort F 29 E8
Hauterives F 31 E7
Hauteville-Lompnes F 31 D8
Haut-Fays B 184 D3
Hautmont F 19 D8
Hautomäki FIN 123 E17
Haux F 32 D4
Hauzenberg D 76 E5
Havant GB 14 F7
Havârna RO 153 A9
Havbro DK 86 B4
Havdhem S 93 E12
Hávdna N 113 C15
Havelange B 19 D11
Havelberg D 83 E12
Havelte NL 16 C6
Håven S 103 C9
Haverdal S 87 B11
Haverfordwest GB 12 B5
Haverhill GB 15 C9
Haverlah D 79 B7
Haverö S 103 B9
Haversin B 19 D11
Haverslev DK 86 B5
Håverud S 91 B11
Havířov CZ 146 B6
Havixbeck D 17 E8
Hävla S 92 B7
Havlíčkův Brod CZ 77 C9
Havndal DK 86 B6
Havneby DK 86 E3
Havnebyen DK 87 D8
Havnsø DK 87 D8
Havøysund N 113 A14
Håvra S 103 C10
Havran TR 173 E7
Havrebjerg DK 87 E8
Havsa TR 173 A6
Havsskogen S 99 B11
Havtun N 94 B2
Hawarden GB 10 E5
Hawes GB 11 C7
Hawick GB 5 E11
Hawkhurst GB 15 E10
Hawkinge GB 15 E11
Haxby GB 11 C9
Hayange F 20 F6
Haybes F 184 D2
Haydarli TR 177 D10
Haydere TR 181 A8
Haydon Bridge GB 5 F12
Haydon Wick GB 13 B11
Hayingen D 71 A8
Hayle GB 12 E4
Hay-on-Wye GB 13 A8
Hayrabolu TR 173 B7
Hayton GB 11 D10
Hayvoron UA 154 A5
Haywards Heath GB 15 F8
Hazebrouck F 18 C6
Hazerswoude-Rijndijk NL 182 A5
Haźlach PL 147 B7
Hažlín SK 145 E3
Hazlov CZ 75 B11
Heacham GB 11 F12
Headcorn GB 15 E10
Headford IRL 6 F4
Healeyfield GB 5 F13
Heanor GB 11 E9
Heathfield GB 15 F9
Hebdów PL 143 F9
Hebenhausen (Neu-Eichenberg) D 78 D6
Heberg S 87 B11
Hebertsfelden D 76 F3
Hebnes N 94 D3
Heby S 98 C7
Hèches F 33 D6
Hechingen D 27 D10
Hecho E 32 E4
Hechtel B 19 B11
Hechthausen D 17 A12
Heckelberg D 84 E5
Heckington GB 11 F11
Hedared S 91 D12
Hedberg S 109 F16
Heddesheim D 21 F11
Hédé F 23 D8
Hede S 98 B6
Hede S 102 B6
Hedekas S 91 B10
Hedel NL 16 E4
Hedemora S 97 B14
Heden DK 86 E6
Heden S 102 C4
Heden S 118 C7
Hedenäset S 119 B11
Hedensbyn S 118 B9
Hedensted DK 86 D5
Hedersleben D 79 C9
Hédervár H 146 F4
Hedesunda S 98 B8
Hedeviken S 102 B6
Hedge End GB 13 D12
Hedlunda S 107 B15
Hedmark S 107 B13
Hedsjön S 103 E12
Hee DK 86 C2
Heeg NL 16 C5
Heek D 17 D8
Heel NL 183 C7
Heemsen D 17 C12
Heemskerk NL 16 C3
Heemstede NL 16 D3
Heenvliet NL 182 B4
Heer B 19 D10
Heerde NL 16 D6
Heerenveen NL 16 C5
Heerewaarden NL 183 B6
Heerhugowaard NL 16 C3
Heerlen NL 20 C5
Heers B 19 C11
Heesch NL 16 E5
Heeslingen D 17 B12
Heeßen D 17 D12
Heeswijk NL 16 E4
Heeten NL 183 A8
Heeze NL 16 F5
Heggeli N 111 B13
Heggem N 104 E4
Heggenes N 101 D10
Heggjabygda N 100 C4
Heggland N 90 A5
Heggmoen N 108 B8
Hegra N 105 E10
Hegyeshalom H 146 F4
Hehlen D 78 C5
Heia N 105 C12
Heia N 111 B17
Heide D 82 B6
Heideck D 75 D9
Heidelberg D 21 F11
Heiden D 17 E7
Heidenau D 80 E5
Heidenheim D 75 D8
Heidenheim an der Brenz D 75 E7
Heidenreichstein A 77 E8
Heigenbrücken D 187 A7
Heikendorf D 83 B8
Heikkilä FIN 121 C14
Heikkilä FIN 122 F7
Heiland N 90 B4
Heilbronn D 27 B11
Heilbrunn A 148 B5
Heiligenberg D 27 E11
Heiligenfelde D 83 E10
Heiligenhafen D 83 B9
Heiligenhaus D 17 F7
Heiligenkreuz am Waasen A 148 C5
Heiligenkreuz im Lafnitztal A 148 C6
Heiligenstadt Heilbad D 79 D7
Heiligenstedten D 82 C6
Heiloo NL 16 C3
Heilsbronn D 75 D8
Heiltz-le-Maurupt F 25 C12
Heim N 104 E6
Heimbach D 21 E8
Heimbuchenthal D 187 B7
Heimdal N 100 E3
Heimdal N 104 E8
Heimertingen D 71 A10
Heimseta N 100 C3
Heimsheim D 187 D6
Heinade D 78 C6
Heinämaa FIN 127 D14
Heinämäki FIN 121 F12
Heinämäki FIN 123 D17
Heinävaara FIN 125 E14
Heinävesi FIN 125 F11
Heinebach (Alheim) D 78 D6
Heinersbrück D 81 C7
Heinersdorf D 80 B6
Heinersreuth D 75 C10
Heinijärvi FIN 119 E14
Heinijoki FIN 126 D7
Heiningen D 79 B8
Heinisuo FIN 119 C16
Heinkenszand NL 16 F1
Heinlahti FIN 128 E6
Heino NL 183 A8
Heinola FIN 127 C15
Heinolan kirkonkylä FIN 127 C15
Heinolanperä FIN 119 E14
Heinoniemi FIN 125 F13
Heinsberg D 20 B6
Heinsen D 78 C5
Heinsnes N 105 B12
Heisingen D 183 C10
Heistadmoen N 95 C11
Heist-op-den-Berg B 19 B10
Heitersheim D 27 E8
Heituinlahti FIN 128 C8
Hejls DK 86 E5
Hejnice CZ 81 E8
Hejnsvig DK 86 D4
Hejőpapi H 145 H2
Hejsager DK 86 E5
Hekelgem B 19 C9
Hel PL 138 A6
Helbra D 79 C9
Helchteren B 183 C6
Heldburg D 75 B8
Heldenbergen D 21 D11
Heldrungen D 79 D9
Helechal E 51 B9
Helegiu RO 153 E9
Helensburgh GB 4 C7
Helfenberg A 76 E6
Helgenes N 110 C9
Helgeroa N 90 B6
Helgum S 107 E11
Hell N 105 E9
Hella N 100 D5
Helland N 104 E5
Helland N 111 D11
Hellanmaa FIN 122 D9
Hellarmo N 109 B10
Helle N 90 B5
Hellebæk DK 87 C11
Hellefjord N 113 B11
Hellendoorn NL 183 A8
Hellenthal D 20 D6
Hellenurme EST 131 E12
Hellesøy N 100 E1
Hellested DK 87 E10
Hellesvik N 104 D5
Hellesylt N 100 B5
Hellevad DK 86 E4
Hellevoetsluis NL 16 E2
Helligskogen N 112 E6
Hellín E 55 B9
Hellingly GB 15 F9
Hellnes N 112 C6
Hellsö FIN 126 F4
Hellvi S 93 D13
Hellvik N 94 F3
Helmbrechts D 75 B10
Helme EST 131 E11
Helmond NL 16 F5
Helmsdale GB 3 J9
Helmsley GB 11 C9
Helmstadt D 74 C6
Helmstedt D 79 B9
Heľpa SK 147 D9
Helppi FIN 117 D13
Helpringham GB 11 F11
Helse D 82 C6
Helsingborg S 87 C11
Helsinge DK 87 C10
Helsingfors FIN 127 E12
Helsingør DK 87 C11
Helsinki FIN 127 E12
Helstad N 105 A12
Helston GB 12 E4
Heltermaa EST 130 D6
Heltersberg D 21 F9
Helvaci TR 177 B9
Helvécia H 150 D4
Helvoirt NL 183 B6
Hem DK 86 B3
Hem F 182 D2
Hemau D 75 D10
Hemavan S 108 E9
Hemeiuș RO 153 D9
Hemel Hempstead GB 15 D8
Hemer D 185 B8
Hemfjäll S 109 E12
Hemfjällstangen S 102 D5
Hemhofen D 75 C8
Hemling S 107 D15
Hemme D 82 B6
Hemmet DK 86 D2
Hemmingen D 78 B6
Hemmingen S 107 B17
Hemmingsmark S 118 D6
Hemmoor D 17 A12
Hemnesberget N 108 D6
Hemnestad N 111 C11
Hempnall GB 15 C11
Hempstead GB 15 C9
Hemsbach D 21 E11
Hemsbünde D 82 D6
Hemsby GB 15 B12
Hemse S 93 E12
Hemsedal N 101 E9
Hemsjö S 107 D14
Hemslingen D 82 D7
Hemsloh D 17 C11
Hemsö S 103 A15
Hemyock GB 13 D8
Henån S 91 C10
Hénanbihen F 23 C7
Henarejos E 47 E10
Hencida H 151 C8
Hendaye F 32 D2
Hendon GB 15 D8
Hengelo NL 16 D6
Hengelo NL 17 D7
Hengersberg D 76 E4
Hengevelde NL 183 A9
Henggart CH 27 E10
Hengoed GB 13 B8
Hénin-Beaumont F 18 D6
Henley-on-Thames GB 15 D7
Hennan S 103 B10
Henndorf am Wallersee A 73 A7
Hennebont F 22 E5
Hennef (Sieg) D 21 C8
Hennes N 110 C9
Henne Stationsby DK 86 D2
Hennezel F 26 D5
Hennickendorf D 80 B4
Hennigsdorf Berlin D 80 A4
Henningskälen S 106 D8
Henningsvær N 110 D7
Henseid N 90 A5
Hennset N 104 E4
Hennstedt D 82 B6
Hennweiler D 21 E8
Henrichemont F 25 F8
Henryków PL 81 E12
Henrykowo PL 139 B9
Henstridge GB 13 D10
Hepola FIN 119 C13
Heppen B 183 C6
Heppenheim (Bergstraße) D 21 E11
Herálec CZ 77 C8
Herálec CZ 77 C9
Herbault F 24 E5
Herbertingen D 27 D11
Herbertstown IRL 8 C6
Herbés E 42 F3
Herbeumont B 184 E3
Herbignac F 23 F7
Herbolzheim D 27 D8
Herborn D 21 C10
Herbrechtingen D 75 E7
Herbstein D 21 C12
Herby PL 142 E6
Herceghalom H 149 A11
Herceg-Novi MNE 162 E6
Hercegovac HR 149 E8
Hercegszántó H 150 F2
Herdecke D 17 F8
Herdorf D 21 C9
Hereclean RO 151 C11
Heréd H 150 B4
Hereford GB 13 A9
Héreg H 149 A11
Herencia E 46 F6
Herend H 149 B9
Herent B 19 C10
Herentals B 19 B10
Herenthout B 182 C5
Hérépian F 34 C5
Herford D 17 D11
Hergatz D 71 B9
Hergiswil CH 70 D6
Herguijuela E 45 F9
Héric F 23 F8
Héricourt F 27 E6
Hérimoncourt F 27 F6
Heringen (Helme) D 79 D8
Heringen (Werra) D 79 E7
Heringsdorf D 83 B10
Heringsdorf D 84 C6
Heriot GB 5 D11
Herisau CH 27 F11
Hérisson F 29 B11
Herk-de-Stad B 19 C11
Herkenbosch NL 183 C8
Herkingen NL 182 B4
Herleshausen D 79 D7
Herlev DK 87 D10
Herlufmagle DK 87 E9
Herm F 32 C3
Hermagor A 73 C7
Hermannsburg D 83 E8
Hermanovce SK 145 E3
Hermanowice PL 144 D6
Hermansverk N 100 D5
Heřmanův Městec CZ 77 C9
Herment F 29 D11
Hermersberg D 186 C4
Hermeskeil D 21 E7
Hermisende E 39 E6
Hermsdorf D 79 E10
Hernád H 150 C3
Hernádnémeti H 145 G2
Hernani E 32 D2
Hernansancho E 46 C3
Herne B 19 C9
Herne D 17 E8
Herne Bay GB 15 E11
Herning DK 86 C3
Heroldsbach D 75 C8
Héron B 19 C11
Hérouville-St-Clair F 23 B11
Herøy N 100 B3
Herpf D 79 E7
Herrala FIN 127 D13
Herramélluri E 40 C5
Herräng S 99 B11
Herré F 32 C5
Herre N 90 A6
Herrenberg D 27 C10
Herrera E 53 B7
Herrera del Duque E 45 F10
Herrera de los Navarros E 42 E1
Herrera de Pisuerga E 40 C3
Herrería E 47 C9
Herreruela E 45 F7
Herrestad S 91 C10
Herrieden D 75 D8
Herringbotn N 108 E6
Herrlisheim F 186 D4
Herrljunga S 91 C13
Herrnhut D 81 D7
Herrö S 102 B7
Herrsching am Ammersee D 75 G9
Herrskog S 103 A15
Hervik S 93 E13
Herry F 25 F8
Hersbruck D 75 C9
Herschbach D 21 C9
Herscheid D 21 B9
Herschweiler-Pettersheim D 186 C3
Herselt B 19 B10
Herslev DK 86 D5
Herstal B 19 C12
Herstmonceux GB 15 F9
Herston GB 3 H11
Herten D 17 E8
Hertford GB 15 D8
Hertník SK 145 E3
Hertsa UA 153 A8
Hertsånger S 118 F6
Hertsjö S 103 D11
Herve B 19 C12
Hervik N 94 D3
Herwijnen NL 183 B6
Herzberg D 80 C4
Herzberg D 83 C11
Herzberg D 84 E3
Herzberg am Harz D 79 C7
Herzebrock-Clarholz D 17 E10
Herzele B 19 C8
Herzfelde D 80 B5
Herzhorn D 17 A12
Herzlake D 17 C9
Herzogenaurach D 75 C8
Herzogenbuchsee CH 27 F8
Herzogenburg A 77 F9
Herzogenrath D 183 D8
Herzsprung D 83 D12
Hesdin F 18 D5
Hesel D 17 B9
Hesjeberg N 111 C13
Hesjestranda N 100 A6
Heskestad N 94 F4
Hespérange L 20 E6
Heßdorf D 75 C8
Hesselager DK 87 E7
Hessen D 79 B8
Hessfjorden N 112 D3
Heßheim D 21 E10
Hessisch Lichtenau D 78 D6
Hessisch Oldendorf D 17 D12
Hest N 100 D3
Hestenesøyri N 100 C4
Hestnes N 104 D5
Hestøy N 108 E3
Hestra S 91 E14
Hestra S 92 D6
Hestvik N 105 B10
Hestvika N 104 D6
Heswall GB 10 E5
Hetekylä FIN 119 D17
Hetés H 149 D9
Hethersett GB 15 B11
Hetlingen D 82 C7
Hettange-Grande F 186 C1
Hettenleidelheim D 186 B5
Hettenshausen D 75 E10
Hettingen D 27 D11
Hetton GB 11 C7
Hettstedt D 79 C10
Hetzerath D 21 E7
Heubach D 187 D8
Heuchelheim D 21 C11
Heuchin F 18 D5
Heudicourt-sous-les-Côtes F 26 C4
Heukelum NL 16 E4
Heusden B 19 B11
Heusden NL 183 B6
Heusenstamm D 21 D11
Heustreu D 75 B7
Heusweiler D 186 C2
Heves H 150 B5
Hévíz H 149 C8
Hevlín CZ 77 E10
Hexham GB 5 F12
Heyrieux F 31 D7
Heysham GB 10 C6
Heythuysen NL 19 B12
Heywood GB 11 D7
Hida RO 151 C11
Hidas H 149 D10
Hidasnémeti H 145 G3
Hiddenhausen D 17 D11
Hiddensee D 84 A4
Hidirköylü TR 177 D10
Hidișelu de Sus RO 151 D9
Hieflau A 73 A10
Hiendelaencina E 47 B7
Hiersac F 28 D5
Hietakangas FIN 115 D3
Hietama FIN 123 E15
Hietanen FIN 117 D11
Hietanen FIN 128 B7
Hietaniemi FIN 115 D6
Hietaniemi FIN 121 B11
Hietaperä FIN 121 F13
Higham Ferrers GB 15 C7
Highampton GB 12 D6
High Bentham GB 10 C6
Highbridge GB 13 C9
Highclere GB 13 C12
High Halden GB 15 E10
High Hawsker GB 11 C10
High Hesket GB 5 F11
High Lorton GB 5 F10
Highnam GB 13 B10
Highworth GB 13 B11
High Wycombe GB 15 D7
Higuera de Arjona E 53 A9
Higuera de la Serena E 51 B8
Higuera de la Sierra E 51 D7
Higuera de Llerena E 51 C8
Higuera de Vargas E 51 C6
Higuera la Real E 51 C6
Higueruela E 55 B10
Higueruelas E 48 E3
Hihnavaara FIN 115 D4
Hiidenkylä FIN 123 C15
Hiidenlahti FIN 125 E10
Hiilikumpu FIN 119 C15
Hiirikylä FIN 125 C10
Hiirola FIN 128 B7
Hiisijärvi FIN 121 F12
Híjar E 42 E3
Hikiä FIN 127 D12
Hilbersdorf D 80 E4
Hilchenbach D 21 C10
Hildburghausen D 75 B8
Hilden D 21 B7
Hilders D 79 E7
Hilderthorpe GB 11 C11
Hildesheim D 78 B6
Hilgertshausen D 75 F9
Hilișeu-Horia RO 153 A8
Hiliuți MD 153 B10
Hillared S 91 D13
Hille D 17 D11
Hille S 103 E13
Hillebola S 99 B9
Hillegom NL 16 D3
Hillerød DK 87 D10
Hillerse D 79 B7
Hillerslev DK 86 A3
Hillerslev DK 86 E6
Hillerstorp S 88 A5
Hilleshamn N 111 C13
Hillesheim D 21 D7
Hillesøy N 111 A15
Hillevik S 103 E13
Hilli FIN 123 C11
Hillilä FIN 123 B11
Hill of Fearn GB 3 K9
Hillosensalmi FIN 128 C6
Hillsand S 106 C8
Hillsborough GB 7 D10
Hillside GB 5 B12
Hillswick GB 3 E14
Hilltown GB 7 D10
Hilpoltstein D 75 D9
Hilsenheim F 186 E4
Hilton GB 11 F8
Hiltpoltstein D 75 C9
Hiltula FIN 129 B9
Hilvarenbeek NL 183 C6
Hilversum NL 16 D4
Himalansaari FIN 128 C8
Himanka FIN 123 B11
Himarë AL 168 D2
Himberg A 77 F10
Himbergen D 83 D9
Himesháza H 149 D11
Himma EST 131 F14

Himmaste EST 131 E14
Himmelberg A 73 C9
Himmelpforten D 17 A12
Hînceşti MD 154 D3
Hinckley GB 11 F9
Hindås S 91 D11
Hindenburg D 83 E11
Hinderwell GB 11 B10
Hindhead GB 15 E7
Hindon GB 13 C10
Hindrem N 104 D8
Hinganmaa FIN 117 D15
Hingham GB 15 B10
Hinnerjöki FIN 126 C6
Hinnerup DK 86 C6
Hinneryd S 87 B13
Hinojal E 45 E8
Hinojales E 51 C6
Hinojares E 55 D7
Hinojosas de Calatrava E 54 B4
Hinojos E 51 E7
Hinojosa E 47 B9
Hinojosa de Duero E 45 C7
Hinojosa de Jarque E 42 F2
Hinojosa del Duque E 51 B9
Hinojosa del Valle E 51 C7
Hinojosa de San Vicente
  E 46 D3
Hinova RO 159 D10
Hinte D 17 B8
Hinterhermsdorf D 80 E6
Hinternah D 75 A8
Hinterrhein CH 71 D8
Hintersee A 73 A7
Hintersee D 84 C6
Hinterweidenthal D 186 C4
Hinterzarten D 27 E9
Hinthaara FIN 127 E13
Hinwil CH 27 F10
Hinx F 32 C4
Hippolytushoef NL 16 C3
Hîrbovăţ MD 154 C2
Hîrjauca MD 154 C2
Hîrka TR 181 B9
Hirnyk UA 144 C9
Hirrlingen D 27 D10
Hirschaid D 75 C9
Hirschau D 75 C10
Hirschberg D 75 B10
Hirschfeld D 80 D5
Hirschhorn (Neckar) D 187 C6
Hirsilä FIN 127 B11
Hirsingue F 27 E7
Hirson F 19 E9
Hîrtop MD 154 D3
Hîrtopul Mare MD 154 C3
Hirtshals DK 90 D6
Hirvas FIN 119 B14
Hirvaskoski FIN 120 D9
Hirvasperä FIN 119 E13
Hirvasvaara FIN 115 E5
Hirvelä FIN 119 D16
Hirvelä FIN 121 F14
Hirvensalmi FIN 128 B6
Hirviäkuru FIN 115 D1
Hirvihaara FIN 127 D13
Hirvijoki FIN 123 E10
Hirvikylä FIN 123 F9
Hirvilahti FIN 124 D8
Hirvineva FIN 119 E14
Hirvivaara FIN 121 E13
Hirvlax FIN 122 D8
Hirwaun GB 13 B7
Hirzenhain D 21 D12
Hisarönü TR 181 C8
Hishult S 87 C12
Hissjön S 122 C4
Histon GB 15 C9
Hita E 47 C6
Hitchin GB 15 D8
Hitis FIN 126 F8
Hittarp S 87 C11
Hittisau A 71 C9
Hitzacker D 83 D10
Hitzendorf A 148 B4
Hitzhusen D 83 C7
Hiukkajoki FIN 129 B12
Hiyche UA 144 C3
Hjåggsjö S 122 C3
Hjallerup DK 86 A6
Hjältevad S 92 D6
Hjärnarp S 87 C11
Hjärsås S 88 C6
Hjärtum S 91 C11
Hjarup DK 86 E4
Hjelle N 100 C6
Hjellestad N 94 B2
Hjellsand N 110 C8
Hjelmeland N 94 D4
Hjelset N 100 A7
Hjerkinn N 101 B11
Hjerm DK 86 C3
Hjo S 92 C4
Hjordkær DK 86 E4
Hjørring DK 90 E7
Hjorted S 93 D10
Hjortkvarn S 92 B6
Hjortsberga S 88 B6
Hjørungavåg N 100 B4
Hjuvik S 91 D10
Hlavani UA 154 F4
Hlebine HR 149 D7
Hligeni MD 154 B3
Hlinaia MD 153 A10
Hlinaia MD 154 C4
Hlinaia MD 154 D5
Hliník nad Hronom SK 147 D7
Hlinné SK 145 E4
Hlinsko CZ 77 C9
Hlohovec SK 146 E5
Hlubočky CZ 146 B4
Hluboká nad Vltavou CZ 77 D6
Hlučín CZ 146 B6
Hlyboka UA 153 A7
Hlybokaye BY 133 F3
Hlyboke UA 155 B5
Hnatkiv UA 154 A2
Hněvotín CZ 77 C12
Hniezdné SK 145 E2
Hnizdychiv UA 145 E9
Hnojník CZ 147 B7
Hnúšťa SK 147 D9
Hobol H 149 D9
Hoboł N 95 C13
Hobro DK 86 B5
Hoburg S 93 F12
Höçe e Qytetit RKS 163 E10
Hoceni RO 153 D12
Hochdonn D 82 B6
Hochdorf CH 27 F9
Hochdorf D 71 A9
Hochfelden F 27 C8

Höchheim D 75 B7
Hochspeyer D 186 C4
Höchstadt (Pfalz) D 187 C5
Höchstadt an der Aisch D 75 C8
Höchstädt an der Donau
  D 75 E8
Hochstetten-Dhaun D 21 E8
Hochs5sovice CZ 142 G4
Höchst im Odenwald D 187 B6
Hoçişti AL 168 C4
Hockenheim D 187 C6
Hockzew PL 145 E5
Hodac RO 152 D5
Hodalen N 101 B14
Hoddesdon GB 15 D8
Hodejov SK 147 E10
Hodenhagen D 82 E7
Hodkovice nad Mohelkou
  CZ 81 E8
Hódmezővásárhely H 150 E5
Hodnet GB 10 F6
Hodod RO 151 C11
Hodonice CZ 77 E10
Hodonín CZ 77 E12
Hodoşa RO 152 D5
Hodruša-Hámre SK 147 E7
Hodsager DK 86 C3
Hodyszewo PL 141 E7
Hoek NL 16 F1
Hoenderloo NL 183 A7
Hœnheim F 186 D4
Hoensbroek NL 19 C12
Hœrdt F 186 D4
Hoeselt B 19 C11
Hoevelaken NL 16 D4
Hoeven NL 16 E3
Hof D 21 C10
Hof D 75 B10
Hof N 95 C12
Hofbieber D 78 E6
Hoffstad N 104 C8
Hofgeismar D 21 B12
Hofheim am Taunus D 21 D10
Hofheim in Unterfranken
  D 75 B8
Höfles N 105 B11
Hofors S 98 A6
Hofsøy N 111 B13
Hofterup S 87 D11
Höganäs S 87 C11
Högås S 108 E9
Högbacka S 103 D12
Högbo S 103 E12
Högboda S 97 C9
Högbränna S 109 F15
Högen S 103 C13
Högfors S 97 B15
Högfors S 97 C13
Hoghilag RO 152 E5
Hoghiz RO 152 F6
Høgild DK 86 C3
Högland S 107 B9
Höglekardalen S 105 E15
Höglunda S 107 E10
Högrun S 105 D16
Högsåra FIN 126 F7
Högsäter S 91 B11
Högsäter S 96 C6
Högsäter S 97 B10
Högsby S 89 A10
Høgset N 104 F3
Högsjö S 92 A7
Högsjö S 103 A14
Hogstad S 92 C6
Hogstorp S 91 C10
Högträsk S 116 D6
Högvålen S 102 B4
Högyész H 149 C10
Hohberg D 186 E4
Hohen-Altheim D 75 E8
Hohenaspe D 82 C7
Hohenau D 76 E5
Hohenau an der March A 77 E11
Hohenberg A 77 G9
Hohenbocka D 80 D6
Hohenbucko D 80 C4
Hohenburg D 75 D10
Hohendorf D 84 B5
Hohenems A 71 C9
Hohenfels D 75 D10
Hohenfurch D 71 B11
Hohengöhren D 79 A11
Hohenhameln D 79 B7
Hohen Wangelin D 83 C13
Hohenwart D 75 E9
Hohenwarth D 76 D3
Hohenwestedt D 82 B7
Höhn D 21 C9
Hohn D 82 B7
Hohne D 79 A7
Hohnhorst D 17 D12
Hohnstorf (Elbe) D 83 D9
Höhr-Grenzhausen D 21 D9
Hohwacht (Ostsee) D 83 B9
Hoikankylä FIN 124 E7
Hoikka FIN 121 D12
Hoisdorf D 83 C8
Hoisko FIN 123 D11
Højby DK 87 E9
Højby DK 86 C2
Højer DK 86 F3
Højmark DK 86 C2
Højslev Stationsby DK 86 B4
Hok S 92 D4
Hökåsen S 98 C7
Hökerum S 91 D13
Hökhuvud S 99 B10
Hokka FIN 128 B6
Hokkaskylä FIN 123 E12
Høksund N 95 C11
Hokland N 111 C11

Hökmark S 118 F6
Hökön S 88 C6
Hol N 101 C11
Hol N 111 C11
Holand N 110 D9
Holandsvika N 108 E5
Holasovice CZ 142 G4
Holbæk DK 86 B6
Holbæk DK 142 B5
Holbeach GB 11 F12
Holboca RO 153 C10
Holbøl DK 86 F4
Holbrook GB 15 D11
Holdorf D 17 C10
Holeby DK 83 A10
Hølen N 95 C13
Holešov CZ 146 C5
Holevik N 100 D1
Holguera E 45 E8
Holič SK 77 E12
Holice CZ 77 B9
Höljes S 102 E4
Holkestad N 110 E8
Holkonkylä FIN 123 E11
Hollabrunn A 77 E10
Hollandscheveld NL 17 C7
Hollange B 19 E12
Hollås N 105 C11
Holle D 79 B7
Hølen N 90 C2
Hollenbach D 75 F9
Hollenbek D 83 C9
Hollenegg A 73 C11
Hollenstedt D 82 D7
Hollenstein an der Ybbs
  A 73 A10
Hollern-Twielenfleth D 82 C7
Hollfeld D 75 C9
Hollingstedt D 82 B6
Hollington GB 15 F10
Hollingworth GB 11 E8
Hollóháza H 145 F3
Hollola FIN 127 D14
Hollum NL 16 B5
Hollybush GB 4 E7
Hollyford IRL 8 C6
Hollywood IRL 7 F9
Holm D 82 C7
Holm DK 86 E5
Holm N 105 A12
Holm N 110 C9
Holm S 103 A13
Holm S 107 E13
Hol'ma UA 154 B5
Holmajärvi S 111 E18
Holme-Olstrup DK 87 A8
Holme-on-Spalding-Moor
  GB 11 D10
Holmestrand N 95 D12
Holmfirth GB 11 D8
Holmfors S 118 D4
Holmisperä FIN 123 D14
Holmsjö S 89 C9
Holmsjö S 103 D12
Holmsund S 122 C4
Holmsvattensel S 118 B6
Holmsveden S 103 D12
Holmträsk S 107 B16
Hölö S 93 A11
Holod RO 151 D9
Hofodowska PL 144 C7
Holoşniţa MD 153 A12
Holoubkov CZ 76 C5
Holovets'ko UA 145 E6
Holovne UA 141 H10
Holsbybrunn S 92 E6
Holslinge S 91 E12
Holsta EST 131 F14
Holstebro DK 86 C3
Holsted DK 86 D3
Hölstein CH 27 F8
Holsworthy GB 12 D6
Holt GB 10 E6
Holt GB 15 B11
Holt N 111 B16
Holt N 101 B17
Holte DK 87 D10
Holten NL 17 D6
Holtet N 102 E3
Holtgast D 17 A9
Holthusen D 83 C10
Holtsee D 83 B7
Holungen D 79 D7
Holwerd NL 16 B5
Holycross IRL 9 C7
Holyhead GB 10 E2
Holywell GB 7 D7
Holywell GB 10 E5
Holywood GB 4 F5
Holzappel D 185 D8
Holzen D 78 C6
Holzgerlingen D 187 D7
Holzhausen an der Haide
  D 21 D9
Holzheim D 21 D11
Holzheim D 75 E8
Holzheim D 75 E8
Holzkirchen D 72 A4
Holzminden D 21 A12
Holzthaleben D 79 D8
Holzweißig D 79 C11
Holzwickede D 17 E9
Høm D 82 B7
Homberg (Efze) D 21 B12
Homberg (Ohm) D 21 C12
Hombourg-Budange F 186 C1
Hombourg-Haut F 186 C2
Homburg D 21 F8
Homécourt F 20 F5
Homersfield GB 15 C11
Homesh AL 168 A3
Hommelstø N 108 F4
Hommelvik N 105 E9
Hommersåk N 94 E3
Homna S 103 D10
Homokmégy H 150 D3
Homokszentgyörgy H 149 D9
Homorode RO 152 E6
Homorod RO 152 E6
Homyel' BY 133 F5
Hønning DK 86 E3
Hondarribia E 32 D2
Hondón de las Nieves E 56 E3
Hondón de los Frailes E 56 E3
Hondschoote F 18 C6
Hône I 68 B4
Hønefoss N 95 B12
Hønefoss N 95 B12
Høng DK 87 D8
Honiton GB 13 D8

Honkajoki FIN 122 G8
Honkakoski FIN 126 B7
Honkakylä FIN 127 E8
Honkilahti FIN 126 D7
Honley GB 11 D8
Honningsvåg N 100 B2
Honningsvåg N 113 B16
Honö S 91 D10
Honoratka PL 142 B5
Honrubia E 47 E8
Honrubia de la Cuesta E 40 F4
Hønseby N 113 B11
Hontacillas E 47 E8
Hontalbilla E 40 F3
Hontanaya E 47 E7
Hontianske Nemce SK 147 E7
Hontoria de la Cantera E 40 D4
Hontoria del Pinar E 40 E5
Hontoria de Valdearados
  E 40 E4
Hoofddorp NL 16 D3
Hoogerheide NL 16 F2
Hoogersmilde NL 16 C6
Hoogeveen NL 17 C6
Hoogezand-Sappemeer
  NL 17 B7
Hoogkarspel NL 16 C4
Hoog-Keppel NL 183 B8
Hoogkerk NL 17 B6
Hoogland NL 183 A6
Hoogstede D 17 C7
Hoogstraten B 16 F3
Hoogvliet NL 16 E2
Hook GB 14 E7
Hooksiel D 17 A10
Höör S 87 D13
Hoorn NL 16 C4
Hoornaar NL 182 B5
Hopârta RO 152 E3
Hope GB 10 E5
Hope N 100 E3
Hopeman GB 3 K10
Hopen N 111 E10
Hopfgarten im Brixental
  A 72 B5
Hopfgarten in Defereggen
  A 72 C6
Hopland N 100 C4
Hoppstädten D 21 E9
Hoppula FIN 115 F2
Hopseidet N 113 B20
Hopsten D 17 D9
Hopton GB 15 C11
Hoptonheath GB 13 A9
Hoptrup DK 86 E4
Horam GB 15 F9
Horažďovice CZ 76 D5
Horb am Neckar D 27 D10
Horbova UA 153 A8
Hörbranz A 71 B9
Hørby DK 90 E7
Hörby S 87 D13
Horcajo de las Torres E 45 B10
Horcajo de los Montes E 46 F3
Horcajo de Santiago E 47 E7
Horcajo Medianero E 45 C10
Horda N 94 C5
Horda S 88 A6
Hörde D 185 B7
Horden GB 11 B9
Hordum DK 86 B3
Horea RO 151 E10
Horeb GB 12 A6
Horeftyci D 27 E11
Horezu RO 160 C3
Horgen CH 27 F10
Horgenzell D 71 B9
Horgeşti RO 153 E10
Horgoš SRB 150 E4
Horia RO 153 C9
Horia RO 155 C2
Horia RO 155 D2
Hořice CZ 77 B9
Horinchove UA 145 G7
Horitschon A 149 A7
Horjul SLO 73 D9
Horka D 81 D7
Hôrka SK 145 E1
Hörken S 97 B12
Horley GB 15 E8
Hörlitz D 80 C5
Hormakumpu FIN 117 C14
Hormilla E 40 D6
Horn N 95 A12
Horn N 108 E3
Horn S 92 D7
Hornachos E 51 B7
Hornachuelos E 51 D9
Horná Kráľová SK 146 E5
Horná Potôň SK 146 E4
Horná Streda SK 146 D5
Horná Štubňa SK 147 D7
Horná Súča SK 146 D5
Horná Ves SK 146 D6
Horndal N 105 C11
Horndal S 98 B6
Horndean GB 14 F6
Horne DK 86 D3
Horne DK 86 E6
Horne DK 90 D6
Horneburg D 82 D7
Hörnefors S 122 C4
Horní Bečva CZ 146 C6
Horní Benešov CZ 146 B5
Horní Bříkovice CZ 77 D8
Horní Cerekev CZ 77 D8
Horní Jiřetín CZ 80 E5
Horní Lideč CZ 146 C6
Horní Maršov CZ 81 E9
Horní Moštěnice CZ 146 C4
Horní Planá CZ 76 E6
Horní Slavkov CZ 75 B12
Horní Štěpánov CZ 77 C11
Horní Stropnice CZ 77 E7
Horní Suchá CZ 146 B6
Hornindal N 100 C5
Hornmyr S 107 C14
Hornnes N 90 B2

Hornön S 103 A14
Hornos E 55 C7
Hornow D 81 C7
Hornsea GB 11 D11
Hørnslet DK 86 C6
Hornstorf D 83 C11
Hornsyld DK 86 D5
Hörnum D 82 A4
Hornum DK 86 B4
Horný Bar SK 146 F4
Horný Tisovník SK 147 E8
Horný Vadičov SK 147 C7
Hoyos E 45 D7
Hoyos de Manzanares E 46 C5
Hoyos del Espino E 45 D10
Höytiä FIN 123 F14
Hoyvík FO 2 A3
Hozha BY 137 F8
Hrabove UA 154 A4
Hrabyně CZ 146 B6
Hradec Králové CZ 77 B9
Hradec nad Moravicí CZ 146 B5
Hradec nad Svitavou CZ 77 C10
Hrádek CZ 147 B7
Hrádek nad Nisou CZ 81 E7
Hradenytsi UA 154 C7
Hradešice CZ 76 D5
Hrádiště SK 146 D6
Hradiště pod Vrátnom SK
  146 D5
Hradištko CZ 76 C6
Hraň SK 145 F4
Hranice CZ 75 B11
Hranice CZ 146 B5
Hranovnica SK 145 F1
Hrastnik SLO 73 D11
Hrastovac N 111 B18
Hrawzhyshki BY 137 E12
Hrebenky UA 154 C10
Hřebíky BY 137 F8
Hreljin HR 67 B10
Hrhov SK 145 F2
Hriňová SK 147 D9
Hristovaia MD 154 A3
Hrnjadi BIH 156 C5
Hrob CZ 80 E5
Hrochův Týnec CZ 77 C9
Hrodna BY 140 C9
Hromnice CZ 76 C4
Hronec SK 147 D9
Hronov CZ 77 B10
Hronovce SK 147 E7
Hronský Beň Beňx SK 147 E7
Hrotovice CZ 77 D10
Hroznová Lhota CZ 146 D4
Hrtkovci SRB 158 D4
Hrubieszów PL 144 B8
Hrusca MD 154 A3
Hrušky CZ 77 E11
Hrušova MD 154 C3
Hrušovany SK 146 E6
Hrušovany nad Jevišovkou
  CZ 77 E10
Hruštín SK 147 C8
Hurezani RO 160 D3
Huriel F 29 B11
Hurissalo FIN 128 C3
Hurler's Cross IRL 8 C5
Hursley GB 13 C12
Hurst Green GB 15 E9
Hurstpierpoint GB 15 F8
Hurteles E 41 D7
Huruieşti RO 153 E10
Hurukselan FIN 128 D6
Hurup DK 86 B2
Hurva S 87 D12
Husà S 105 E14
Husås S 106 E7
Husasău de Tinca RO 151 D8
Husbands Bosworth GB 13 A12
Husberget S 102 A8
Husbondliden S 107 B15
Husby D 82 A7
Husby S 97 B15
Husby S 99 A9
Huschca UA 141 H9
Huşi RO 153 D12
Husinec CZ 76 D5
Husjorda N 111 C9
Huskvarna S 92 D4
Husnes N 94 C3
Husnicioara RO 159 D10
Husøy N 108 D3
Hussjö S 103 A14
Hustopeče CZ 77 E11
Hustopeče nad Bečvou CZ
  146 B5
Husum D 17 C12
Husum D 82 B6
Husum S 107 D16
Husvik N 108 E4
Huta PL 141 H3
Huta Komorowska PL 143 F12
Hutisko-Solanec CZ 146 C6
Hutovo BIH 162 D4
Hütschenhausen D 186 C3
Hüttau A 73 B7
Hüttenberg A 73 C10
Hüttisheim D 74 F6
Hüttlingen D 75 F7
Huttoft GB 11 E12
Hüttschlag A 73 B7
Huttukylä FIN 119 D15
Huttwil CH 27 F8
Huhdasjärvi FIN 127 C16
Huhmarkoski FIN 123 D10
Huhtamo FIN 126 D8
Huhti FIN 127 C10
Huhtilampi FIN 125 F14
Huhus FIN 125 E15
Huijbergen NL 182 C4
Huikola FIN 119 E16
Huisheim D 75 E8
Huisinis GB 2 K2
Huissen NL 16 E6
Huissinkylä FIN 122 E8
Huittinen FIN 126 C8
Huizen NL 16 D4
Hujakkala FIN 128 D8
Hukkajärvi FIN 121 D10
Hukkajärvi FIN 125 B14
Hulín CZ 146 C4
Hulja EST 131 C12
Huljen S 103 B13
Hulkkola FIN 124 E8
Hull GB 11 D11
Hulland GB 11 E8
Hollerich D 17 D8
Hüls D 183 C9
Hulsberg NL 183 D7
Hulst NL 16 F2
Hult S 92 D6
Hult S 91 A15

Hult S 92 D6
Hulterstad S 89 C11
Hultsfred S 92 D7
Hulu S 91 D13
Hulubeşti RO 160 D6
Hulyanka UA 154 C4
Hum BIH 157 F10
Hum BIH 162 D5
Humalajoki FIN 123 D13
Humanes de Madrid E 46 D5
Humanes de Mohernando
  E 47 C6
Humberston GB 11 D11
Humbie GB 5 D11
Humble DK 83 A9
Humenné SK 145 F4
Humilladero E 53 B7
Humlebæk DK 87 D11
Humlegårdsstrand S 103 D13
Humlum DK 86 B3
Hummelholm S 107 D16
Hummelo NL 183 A8
Hummelsta S 98 C7
Hummuli EST 131 F12
Hum na Sutli HR 148 D5
Humpolec CZ 77 C8
Humppila FIN 127 D9
Humshaugh GB 5 E12
Huncovce SK 145 E1
Hundåla N 108 E4
Hundberg N 111 B18
Hundberg S 109 F16
Hundborg DK 86 B3
Hundeluft D 79 C11
Hunderdorf D 75 E12
Hundested DK 87 D9
Hundholmen N 111 D11
Hundorp N 101 C11
Hundsangen D 21 D9
Hundshübel D 79 E12
Hundsjön S 118 C7
Hundslund DK 86 D6
Hundvin N 100 E2
Hune DK 86 A5
Hunedoara RO 151 F10
Hünfeld D 78 E6
Hünfelden-Kirberg D 21 D10
Hunge S 103 A9
Hungen D 21 D11
Hungerford GB 13 C11
Hunnebostrand S 91 C9
Hunsel NL 19 B12
Hunspach F 27 C8
Hunstanton GB 11 F12
Huntingdon GB 15 C8
Huntlosen D 17 C10
Huntly GB 3 L11
Hünxe D 183 B9
Hunya P 151 D6
Huopanankoski FIN 123 D15
Hüpstedt D 79 D7
Hurbanovo SK 146 F6
Hurdal N 95 B14
Hurdalsverk N 95 B14

Hyervyaty BY 137 D13
Hylen N 94 C5
Hylleråsen N 102 C3
Hyllestad N 100 D2
Hyllinge DK 87 E9
Hyllinge S 87 C11
Hyltebruk S 87 A12
Hymont F 26 D5
Hyönölä FIN 127 E10
Hyrkäs FIN 119 E16
Hyry FIN 119 C14
Hyrynsalmi FIN 121 E11
Hysgjokaj AL 168 C2
Hyssna S 91 D12
Hythe GB 13 D12
Hythe GB 15 E11
Hytti FIN 129 D9
Hyttön S 99 B8
Hyväneula FIN 127 D13
Hyväniemi FIN 121 B11
Hyvärilä FIN 119 F15
Hyvikkälä FIN 127 D12
Hyvinkää FIN 127 D12
Hyvölänranta FIN 119 F16
Hyvönmäki FIN 129 B12
Hyypiö FIN 115 E1
Hyyppä FIN 122 F8
Hyžne PL 144 D5

I

Iablaniţa RO 159 D9
Iabloana MD 153 B11
Iacobeni RO 152 C6
Iacobeni RO 152 E5
Ialoveni MD 154 D3
Iam RO 159 C7
Ianca RO 160 F4
Ianca RO 161 C10
Iancu Jianu RO 160 E4
Iara RO 152 D3
Iargara MD 154 E2
Iarova MD 153 A12
Iaşi RO 153 C11
Iasmos GR 171 B8
Ibahernando E 45 F9
Iballë AL 163 E9
Ibăneşti RO 152 D5
Ibăneşti RO 153 A8
Ibarra E 32 D1
Ibbenbüren D 17 D9
Ibdes E 47 B9
Ibë AL 168 B2
Ibeas de Juarros E 40 D4
Ibestad N 111 C13
Ibi E 56 D3
Ibos F 32 D5
Ibrány H 145 G4
Ibriktepe TR 171 B10
Ibros E 53 A10
Ibstock GB 11 F9
Ichenhausen D 75 F7
Ichenheim D 186 E4
Ichtegem B 18 B7
Icking D 72 A3
Icklesham GB 15 F10
Icklingham GB 15 C10
Iclănzel RO 152 D4
Iclod RO 152 D3
Icoana RO 160 E5
Icuşeşti RO 153 D9
Idanha-a-Nova P 45 E6
Idanha-a-Velha P 45 E6
Idar-Oberstein D 21 E8
Ideciu de Jos RO 152 D5
Iden D 83 E11
Idena LV 133 C1
Idenor S 103 C13
Idestrup DK 83 A11
Idiazabal E 32 D1
Idivuoma S 116 B8
Idkerberget S 97 B13
Idmiston GB 13 C11
Idocin E 32 E3
Idom DK 86 C2
Idoš SRB 150 F5
Idre S 102 C4
Idrigill GB 2 K4
Idrija SLO 73 D9
Iditsa RUS 133 D5
Idro I 69 B9
Idstedt D 82 A7
Idstein D 21 D10
Idvattnet S 107 C12
Iecava LV 135 C8
Iedera RO 161 C7
Ieper B 18 C6
Iepureşti RO 161 E7
Ierapetra GR 179 E10
Ieriki LV 135 B10
Ierissos GR 170 D5
Iernut RO 152 E4
Ieromnini GR 168 E4
Ieropigi GR 168 C5
Ieşelniţa RO 159 D9
Ifaistos GR 171 B8
Iffendic F 23 D7
Iffezheim D 187 D5
Ifjord N 113 C19
Ifs F 23 B11
Ifta D 79 D7
Ig SLO 73 E10
Igal H 149 C9
Igalo MNE 162 E6
Igar H 149 C11
Igé F 24 D4
Igea E 41 D7
Igea Marina I 67 E6
Igel D 186 B2
Igelfors S 92 B7
Igelstorp S 91 C14
Igensdorf D 75 C9
Igerøy N 108 E3
Iggersheim D 74 D6
Iggelheim D 187 C5
Iggensbach D 76 E4
Iggesund S 103 C13
Ighiu RO 152 E3
Igis CH 71 D9
Iglesias E 40 E2
Igliauka LT 137 D8
Igling D 71 A11
Igliškėliai LT 137 D8
Ignalina LT 135 F12
Igneada TR 167 F9
Igney F 26 D5
Igornay F 30 A5
Igoumenitsa GR 168 E3
Igralishte BG 169 A9
Igrejinha P 50 B4
Igrici H 145 H2
Igrīve LV 133 B2

Igualada E 43 D7
Igualeja E 53 C6
Igueña E 39 C7
Iguerande F 30 C5
Iharosberény H 149 D8
Ihlienworth D 17 A11
Ihode FIN 126 D6
Iholdy F 32 D3
Ihrhove D 17 B8
Ihrlerstein D 75 E10
Ihsaniye TR 173 B10
Ii FIN 119 D14
Iijärvi FIN 113 E20
Iinattijärvi FIN 121 D9
Iironranta FIN 123 E12
Iisalmi FIN 124 C8
Iisvesi FIN 124 E8
Iitti FIN 127 D15
Iitto FIN 116 A6
Iivantiira FIN 121 F13
IJlst NL 16 B5
IJmuiden NL 16 D3
IJsselmuiden NL 16 C5
IJsselstein NL 16 D4
IJzendijke NL 16 F1
Ikaalinen FIN 127 B9
Ikast DK 86 C4
Ikazn' BY 133 E2
Ikervár H 149 B7
Ikhtiman BG 165 E8
Ikizdere TR 177 D10
Ikkala FIN 119 E13
Ikkala FIN 127 E11
Ikkeläjärvi FIN 122 F9
Ikla EST 131 F8
Ikornes N 100 B5
Ikosenniemi FIN 119 C17
Ikrény H 149 A9
Ikšķile LV 135 C8
Ilandža SRB 159 C6
Ilanz CH 71 D8
Ilava SK 146 D6
Iława PL 139 C8
Ilbono I 64 D4
Ilchester GB 13 C9
Ildir TR 177 C7
Île LV 134 C6
Ileana RO 161 D9
Ileanda RO 152 C3
Ilfeld D 79 C8
Ilford GB 15 D9
Ilfracombe GB 12 C6
Ilgižiai LT 134 F6
Ílhavo P 44 C3
Ilia RO 151 F10
Ilica TR 173 E8
Ilidza BIH 157 E9
Ilieni RO 153 F7
Ilijaš BIH 157 E9
Ilindentsi BG 165 F7
Iliokastro GR 175 E7
Ilirska Bistrica SLO 73 E9
Ilk H 145 G5
Ilkeston GB 11 F9
Ilkley GB 11 D8
Illana E 47 D7
Illar E 55 F7
Illats F 32 A5
Illerrieden D 71 A10
Illertissen D 71 A10
Illescas E 46 D5
Ille-sur-Têt F 34 E4
Illiers-Combray F 24 D5
Illingen D 21 F8
Illingen D 187 D6
Illkirch-Graffenstaden F 27 C8
Illmensee D 27 E11
Illmitz A 149 A7
Íllora E 53 B9
Illschwang D 75 D10
Illueca E 41 E8
Illzach F 27 E7
Ilmajoki FIN 122 E9
Ilmatsalu EST 131 E13
Ilmenau D 79 E8
Ilminster GB 13 D9
Ilmmünster D 75 F10
Ilmola FIN 119 C13
Il'nytsya UA 145 G7
Ilok HR 158 C3
Ilola FIN 127 E14
Ilomantsi FIN 125 E15
Ilosjoki FIN 123 D15
Ins CH 31 A11
Insch GB 3 L11
Insjön S 103 E9
Iński PL 85 D9
Insming F 27 C6
Insteford N 100 E2
Instinción E 55 F7
Însurăţei RO 161 D11
Întepe TR 171 D10
Interlaken CH 70 D5
Întorsura Buzăului RO 161 B8
Întregalde RO 151 E11
Introbio I 69 B7
Inturkė LT 135 F11
Inver GB 16 C6
Inverallochy GB 3 K13
Inveran IRL 6 F4
Inveraray GB 4 C6
Inverarity GB 5 B11
Inverarnan GB 4 C7
Inverbervie GB 5 B12
Invercassley GB 2 K7
Invercharnan GB 4 B6
Invergordon GB 3 K8
Inverkeilor GB 5 B11
Inverkeithing GB 5 C10
Invermoriston GB 2 L7
Inverness GB 3 L8
Inverurie GB 3 L12
Inviken S 106 B8
Inzell D 73 A6
Inzigkofen D 27 D10
Inzing A 72 B3
Inzinzac-Lochrist F 22 E5
Ioannina GR 168 E4
Ion Corvin RO 155 E1
Ion Creangă RO 153 D9
Ioneşti RO 160 D4
Ion Luca Caragiale RO 161 D7
Ion Roată RO 161 D9
Iordăcheanu RO 161 C8
Ioulis GR 175 D9
Ip RO 151 C10
Ipatele RO 153 D10
Iphofen D 187 B9
Ipiki LV 131 E10
Ipoteşti RO 153 B8

Imroz TR 171 D9
Imst A 71 C11
Ina RO 152 D1
Inagh IRL 8 C4
Inancs H 145 G3
Inárcs H 150 C3
Inari FIN 113 F19
Inari FIN 125 D15
Inca E 57 B10
Inch IRL 8 D3
Inch IRL 9 C10
Inchbare GB 5 B11
Incheville F 18 D3
Inchigeelagh IRL 8 E4
Inchnadamph GB 2 J7
Inciems LV 135 B9
Incinillas E 40 C4
İncirliova TR 177 D10
Incisa in Val d'Arno I 66 E3
Incourt B 19 C10
Inčukalns LV 135 B9
Indal S 103 A13
Indalstø N 100 E2
Independenţa RO 155 C1
Independenţa RO 155 F2
Indija SRB 158 C5
Indra LV 133 E3
Indreabhán IRL 6 F4
Indre Arna N 94 B2
Indre Billefjord N 113 C15
Indre Brenna N 113 B16
Indre Kårvik N 111 A16
Indre Kiberg N 114 C19
Indre Kjæss N 113 B16
Indre Sortvik N 113 B15
Indura BY 140 D9
Indzhe Voyvoda BG 167 E8
Inece TR 167 F8
Inecik TR 173 C7
Ineši LV 135 B11
Ineu RO 151 C9
Ineu RO 151 E8
Infiesto E 39 B9
Ingå FIN 127 E11
Ingared S 91 D11
Ingatestone GB 15 D9
Ingatorp S 92 D6
Ingelfingen D 187 C8
Ingelheim am Rhein D 21 E10
Ingelmunster B 19 C7
Ingelstad S 89 B7
Ingenes N 94 B3
Ingersheim F 27 D7
Ingleton GB 5 F13
Ingleton GB 10 C7
Ingoldmells GB 11 E12
Ingolsbenning S 97 B14
Ingolstadt D 75 E9
Ingrandes F 23 F10
Ingrandes F 29 B7
Ingstrup DK 90 E6
Inguiniel F 22 E5
Ingulsvatn N 105 B14
Ingwiller F 27 C7
Inha FIN 123 E12
Ini GR 178 E9
Iniesta E 47 F9
Inis IRL 8 C5
Inis Córthaidh IRL 9 C9
Inis Diomáin IRL 8 C4
Inistioge IRL 9 D8
Injevo MK 169 A7
Inkberrow GB 13 A11
Inke H 149 D8
Inkere FIN 127 E9
Inkoo FIN 127 E11
Inndyr N 108 B7
Innerbraz A 71 C9
Innerleithen GB 5 D10
Innernzell D 76 E4
Innertällmo S 107 D13
Innertavle S 122 C4
Innertkirchen CH 70 D6
Innervik S 109 F14
Innervillgraten A 72 C5
Innhavet N 111 E10
Inniscrone IRL 6 D4
Innishannon IRL 8 E5
Innsbruck A 72 B3
Innset N 111 C16
Inntorget N 108 F3
Inowłódz PL 141 G2
Inowrocław PL 138 E5
Iosona E 42 C6
Iopalo VIN 115 E3
Iorella I 66 B1
Iso-Vimma FIN 126 C7
Ispagnac F 35 B6
Isperikh BG 161 F9
Ispica I 59 F6
Ispoure F 32 D3
Ispra I 68 B6
Ispringen D 27 C10
Issakka FIN 125 C10
Isselburg D 17 E7
Issigeac F 29 F7
Issime I 68 B4
Isso E 55 C9
Issogne I 68 B4
Issoire F 30 D3
Issoudun F 29 B10
Issum D 17 E6
Is-sur-Tille F 26 E3
Issy-l'Évêque F 30 B4
Istalsna LV 133 D3
Istán E 53 C7
İstanbul TR 173 B9
Istead Rise GB 15 E9
Istebna PL 147 B9
Istebné SK 147 C8
Istenmezeje H 147 E10

Ipoteşti RO 153 B9
Ippesheim D 75 C7
Ipplepen GB 13 E7
Ipsala TR 171 C10
Ipsheim D 75 C7
Ipstones GB 11 E8
Ipswich GB 15 C11
Irakleia GR 169 B9
Irakleia GR 176 A5
Irakleia GR 176 F5
Irakleio GR 178 E9
Irancy F 25 E10
Iratoşu RO 151 E7
Irdning A 73 A9
Irechekovo BG 167 E7
Iregszemcse H 149 C10
Irgoli I 64 C4
Iria GR 175 E7
Irig SRB 158 C4
Irishtown IRL 6 E5
Irissarry F 32 D3
Irjanne FIN 126 C6
Irlava LV 134 C5
Irlbach D 75 E12
Irninniemi FIN 121 C13
Irodouër F 23 D8
Ironbridge GB 10 F7
Irrel D 20 E6
Irsch D 21 E7
Irsee D 71 B11
Irshava UA 145 G7
Irši LV 135 C11
Irsina I 60 B6
Irsta S 98 C7
Irueste E 47 C7
Irun E 32 D2
Iruña E 32 E2
Irurita E 32 E3
Irurtzun E 32 E2
Irvine GB 4 D7
Irvinestown GB 7 D7
Irxleben D 79 B9
Isaba E 32 E4
Isaccea RO 155 C2
Isačić BIH 156 C4
İşalniţa RO 160 E3
İsane N 100 C3
Isaris GR 174 E5
Isaszeg H 150 B3
Isàtra S 98 C7
Isbergues F 18 C5
Isbister GB 3 D14
Íscar E 40 F2
Isches F 26 D4
Ischgl A 71 C10
Ischia I 60 B1
Ischia di Castro I 62 B1
Ischitella I 63 D9
Isdes F 25 E7
Iselvmoen N 111 C16
Isen D 75 F11
Is-en-Bassigny F 26 D3
Isenbüttel D 79 B8
Isenvad DK 86 C4
Iseo I 69 B9
Iserlohn D 17 F9
Isernhagen D 78 B6
Isernia I 63 D6
Isfjorden N 100 A7
İshakçelebi TR 177 B10
Ishull-Lezhë AL 163 F8
Isigny-sur-Mer F 23 B9
Isili I 64 D3
Iskele TR 173 F9
Iskender TR 172 A6
İškoras N 113 E16
Iskra BG 166 F4
Iskrets BG 165 D7
Isla Cristina E 51 E5
Islambeyli TR 167 F9
Isla Plana E 56 F2
İšlaužas LT 137 D8
Islaz RO 160 F5
Isle F 29 D8
Isle of Whithorn GB 5 F8
Isl: d RO 160 E2
Isles-sur-Suippe F 19 F9
Tsliče LV 135 D8
İsmailli TR 177 D9
Ismaning D 75 F10
Ismundsundet S 106 E8
Isna P 44 E5
Isnäs FIN 127 E15
Isnello I 58 D5
Isnovăţ MD 154 C3
İsny im Allgäu D 71 B10
Iso-Äiniö FIN 127 C13
Iso-Evo FIN 127 C13
Isohalme FIN 115 E3
Isojoki FIN 122 F7
Isokumpu FIN 121 C11
Isokylä FIN 115 E3
Isokylä FIN 119 F14
Isokyrö FIN 122 D7
Isola F 36 C6
Isola 2000 F 37 C6
Isola della Scala I 66 B3
Isola delle Femmine I 58 C3
Isola del Liri I 62 E5
Isola di Capo Rizzuto I 61 F8
Isole del Cantone I 37 B9
Isona E 42 C6
Isopalo FIN 115 E3
Istibanja MK 164 F5
İstiaia GR 175 B7
Istibanja MK 164 F5
İstog RKS 163 D9
Istres F 35 C8
Istria RO 155 D3
Istrio GR 181 D7
Istunmäki FIN 123 E16
Isuerre E 32 F3
Iszkaszentgyörgy H 149 B10
Itä-Ähtäri FIN 123 E12
Itä-Aure FIN 123 F10
Itä-Karttula FIN 124 E8
Itäkoski FIN 119 C13
Itäkoski FIN 125 C9
Itäkylä FIN 123 D11
Itäranta FIN 115 F2
Itäranta FIN 120 F9
Itea GR 169 C6
Itea GR 169 D6
Itea GR 169 F7
Itea GR 174 C5
Itero de la Vega E 40 D3
Iteuil F 29 C6
Ithaki GR 174 C2
Itrabo E 53 C9
Itri I 62 E5
Itterbeck D 17 C7
Ittireddu I 64 B2
Ittiri I 64 B2
Ittre B 19 C9
Ituero de Azaba E 45 D7
Itzehoe D 82 C7
Itzstedt D 83 C8
Iurceni MD 154 C2
Ivalo FIN 115 A3
Ivalon Matti FIN 117 B15
Iván H 149 B7
Ivana Franka UA 145 E7
Ivancea MD 154 C3
İvančice CZ 77 D10
Ivančići BIH 157 D9
Iváncsa H 149 B11
Ivanec HR 148 D6
Ivănești RO 153 D10
Ivangorod RUS 132 C3
Ivanić-Grad HR 149 E6
Ivanjica SRB 163 B9
Ivanjska BIH 157 C7
Ivankovo HR 149 F11
Ivano-Frankove UA 144 D8
Ivanovice na Hané CZ 77 D12
Ivanovo BG 161 F7
Ivanovo BG 166 F5
Ivanovo BG 167 C7
Ivanovo SRB 159 D6
Ivanska HR 149 E7
Ivanski BG 167 C8
Ivarrud N 108 F6
Ivarsbjörke S 97 C9
Ivars d'Urgell E 42 D5
Ivaylovgrad BG 171 A10
Iveland N 90 C2
Iven D 84 C4
Iver GB 15 D7
Iveşti RO 153 E11
Iveşti RO 153 F11
Ivrea I 68 C4
İvrindi TR 173 E7
Ivry-la-Bataille F 24 C5
Ivry-sur-Seine F 25 C7
Ivybridge GB 13 E7
Iwaniska PL 143 E11
Iwanowice Włościańskie PL 143 F8
Iwkowa PL 144 D2
Iwye BY 137 F12
Ixelles B 19 C9
Ixworth GB 15 C10
Iyaslar TR 177 A10
Iža SK 149 A10
Iza UA 145 G7
Izarra E 40 C6
Izbica PL 144 B7
Izbica Kujawska PL 138 F6
Izbiceni RO 160 F5
Izbicko PL 142 E5
Izbište MD 154 C4
Izbište SRB 159 C7
Izbižno BIH 157 E10
Izeaux F 31 E7
Izeda P 39 E6
Izegem B 19 C7
Izernore F 31 C7
Izeron F 31 E7
Izgrev BG 161 F9
Izgrev BG 167 D9
İž Mali HR 67 D11
Izmayil UA 155 C3
İzmir TR 177 C9
Iznájar E 53 B8
Iznalloz E 53 B9
Izola SLO 67 A8
Izsák H 150 D3
Izsófalva H 145 G2
Izvoarele RO 155 C3
Izvoarele RO 160 E4
Izvoarele RO 160 F6
Izvoarele RO 160 F6
Izvoarele RO 161 E7
Izvoarele Sucevei RO 152 B6
Izvor BG 159 F10
Izvor BG 165 E6
Izvor MK 168 B4
Izvor MK 169 A6
Izvor SRB 159 F8
Izvoru BG 155 F1
Izvoru RO 160 E6
Izvoru Bârzii RO 159 D10
Izvoru Berheciului RO 153 D10
Izvoru Crișului RO 151 D11

Isternia GR 176 D5
Isthmia GR 175 D7
Jäälä FIN 119 D15
Jaakonvaara FIN 125 D14
Jaala FIN 127 C15
Jaalanka FIN 120 D9
Jääli FIN 119 D15
Jaama EST 132 C2
Jääskänjoki FIN 122 E9
Jäätila FIN 119 B14
Jabaga E 47 D7
Jabalanac HR 67 C10
Jabaloyas E 47 D9
Jabalquinto E 53 A9
Jabbeke B 19 B7
Jabel D 83 C13
Jablan Do BIH 162 D5
Jablanica BIH 157 E8
Jablonec nad Jizerou CZ 81 E8
Jablonec nad Nisou CZ 81 E8
Jablonica SK 146 D4
Jabłonka PL 147 C9
Jabłonna Kościelna PL 140 E6
Jabłonna PL 139 F10
Jabłonna PL 141 F6
Jabłonna Lacka PL 141 F6
Jabłonna Pierwsza PL 141 H7
Jablonné nad Orlicí CZ 77 B11
Jablonné v Podještědí CZ 81 E7
Jablonové CZ 77 F12
Jabłonowo Pomorskie PL 139 D7
Jabłonka CZ 146 C5
Jabłonka PL 147 C9
Jabłonkov CZ 147 B7
Jabugo E 51 D6
Jabuka BIH 157 E10
Jabuka SRB 158 D4
Jabuka SRB 163 D7
Jabukovac HR 149 F6
Jabukovac SRB 159 E9
Jabukovik SRB 164 D5
Jaca E 32 E4
Jachenau D 72 A3
Jáchymov CZ 76 B3
Jacovce SK 146 D6
Jäderfors S 103 E12
Jadów PL 139 F12
Jadraås S 103 E11
Jadranska Lešnica SRB 158 D3
Jadraque E 47 C7
Jægerspris DK 87 D9
Jægervatnet N 111 A18
Jaén E 53 A9
Jägala EST 131 C10
Jagare BIH 157 C7
Jagarberg A 148 C5
Jagodina SRB 159 F7
Jagodnjak HR 149 E11
Jagodzin PL 81 D8
Jagstheusen D 27 B11
Jagstzell D 75 D7
Jähdyspohja FIN 123 F11
Jahnsfelde D 80 A6
Jahodná SK 146 E5
Ja-Salih AL 163 E9
Jajce BIH 157 D7
Ják H 149 B7
Jakabszállás H 150 D4
Jäkälävaara FIN 121 C10
Jakkukylä FIN 119 D15
Jakkula FIN 122 E8
Jäkkvik S 109 D12
Jaklovce SK 145 F3
Jakobsbakken N 109 B10
Jakobsnes N 114 D9
Jakobstad FIN 122 C9
Jakokoski FIN 125 E13
Jakovlje HR 148 E5
Jakšić HR 149 F9
Jakštaičiai LT 134 D7
Jaktorów PL 141 F3
Jakubany SK 145 E2
Jakubov SK 77 F11
Jakubów PL 141 F5
Jalance E 47 F10
Jalasjärvi FIN 122 F9
Jalhay B 20 C5
Jaligny-sur-Besbre F 30 C4
Jallais F 23 F10
Jalovik SRB 158 D4
Jalubí CZ 146 C4
Jâmaja EST 130 E4
Jämäs FIN 125 B12
Jämejala EST 131 E11
Jameln D 83 D10
Jamena SRB 157 C11
Jamestown IRL 7 E7
Jamielnik PL 139 C7
Jämijärvi FIN 126 B8
Jamilena E 53 A9
Jäminkipohja FIN 127 B11
Jämjö S 89 C9
Jammerdal N 96 B7
Jamnik SK 145 F2
Jämsä FIN 123 C12
Jämsä FIN 127 B13
Jämsänkoski FIN 127 B13
Jämshög S 88 C7
Jämton S 118 C5
Jamu Mare RO 159 C7
Janakkala FIN 127 D12
Janapole LT 134 E4
Jánd H 145 G5
Jandelsbrunn D 76 E5
Janderup DK 86 D2
Jãneda EST 131 C11
Jänickendorf D 80 B4
Janja BIH 158 D3
Janjevë RKS 164 D3
Janjići BIH 158 F3
Janjina HR 162 D3
Jänkä FIN 123 D13
Jänkälä FIN 115 D3
Jänkisjärvi S 116 E9
Jánkmajtis H 145 H6
Janków PL 143 B7
Jankowo Dolne PL 138 E4
Jänmuiža LV 135 B10
Jännevirta FIN 125 E9
Jánoshalma H 150 E3
Jánosháza H 149 B8
Jánoshida H 150 C5
Jánossomorja H 149 A8
Janów PL 140 D8
Janów PL 143 E7
Janowice Wielkie PL 81 E9
Janowiec PL 141 H5
Janowiec Wielkopolski PL 85 E12
Janów Lubelski PL 144 B5
Janowo PL 139 D10
Janów Podlaski PL 141 F8
Jansjö S 107 D10
Jäniciems LV 135 B13
Jañuciems LV 135 D13
Janville F 24 D6
Janzé F 23 E9
Japca MD 154 B3
Jaraba E 47 B9
Jaraczewo PL 81 C12
Jarafuel E 47 F10
Jaraicejo E 45 E9
Jaraíz de la Vera E 45 D9
Jarãmã S 116 B6
Jarandilla de la Vera E 45 D9
Järbo S 103 E12
Járdánháza H 145 G1
Jard-sur-Mer F 28 C2
Jaren N 95 B13
Jårfjordbotn N 114 D8
Jårgastat N 113 E16
Jargeau F 24 E7
Jarhoinen FIN 117 E11
Jarhois S 117 E11
Jaristea RO 153 F10
Järkvissle S 103 A12
Järlåsa S 98 C8
Järlepa EST 131 C9
Jarmen D 84 C4
Jarménil F 26 D6
Jarmina HR 149 F11
Järna S 93 A11
Järna S 97 A11
Jarnac F 28 D5
Jarnages F 29 C10
Järnäs S 107 E17
Järnforsen S 92 E7
Jarny F 26 B4
Jarocin PL 142 C4
Jarocin PL 144 B5
Jarok SK 146 E5
Jaroměř CZ 77 B9
Jaroměřice CZ 77 C11
Jaroměřice nad Rokytnou CZ 77 D9
Jaroslavice CZ 77 E10
Jarosław PL 144 C6
Jarosławiec PL 85 A11
Jarošov nad Nežárkou CZ 77 D8
Jarovnice SK 145 E3
Järpås S 91 C12
Järpbyn S 105 E14
Järpen S 105 E14
Järpliden S 102 E3
Jarplund-Weding D 82 A6
Jarque E 41 E8
Jarrow S 5 F14
Järva-Jaani EST 131 C11
Järvakandi EST 131 D9
Järvberget S 107 D12
Järvennpää FIN 117 C12
Järvenpää FIN 122 E7
Järvenpää FIN 123 C13
Järvenpää FIN 123 D10
Järvenpää FIN 127 E13
Järvikylä FIN 119 F17
Järvikylä FIN 123 C13
Järvikylä FIN 123 D13
Jarville-la-Malgrange F 26 C5
Järvirova FIN 117 D12
Järvsand S 107 C9
Järvsjö S 107 C9
Järvsö S 103 C11
Järvsta S 103 E13
Järvträsk S 107 A16
Jarzé F 23 E11
Jaša Tomić SRB 159 C6
Jasen BIH 162 D5
Jasenica BIH 156 C5
Jasenovac HR 157 B6
Jasenovo SRB 159 D7
Jasenovo SRB 163 B8
Jasień PL 81 C8
Jasień PL 85 B13
Jasienica PL 139 F11
Jasienica PL 147 B7
Jasienica Rosielna PL 144 D4
Jasieniec PL 141 G3
Jasika SRB 159 F7
Jasionka PL 144 C5
Jasionna PL 143 E9
Jasionówka PL 140 D8
Jasliska PL 145 E4
Jasło PL 144 D3
Jašļūnai LT 137 E11
Jasmuiža LV 135 D13
Jasov SK 145 F3
Jásová SK 146 F6
Jassans-Riottier F 30 D6
Jasseron F 31 C7
Jastarnia PL 138 A6
Jastrebarsko HR 148 E5
Jastrowie PL 85 D11
Jastrząb PL 141 H3
Jastrzębia PL 141 H4
Jastrzębia Góra PL 138 A5
Jastrzębie-Zdrój PL 147 B7
Jászapáti H 150 B5
Jászárokszállás H 150 B4
Jászberény H 150 C4
Jászboldogháza H 150 C4
Jászfényszaru H 150 B4
Jászjákóhalma H 150 B5
Jászkarajenő H 150 C5
Jászkisér H 150 C5
Jászladány H 150 C5
Jászszentandrás H 150 B5
Jászszentlászló H 150 D4
Jásztelek H 150 C5
Jatar E 53 C9
Jättendal S 103 C13
Jättensjö S 103 B12
Jatuni FIN 116 B9
Jatzke D 84 C3
Jatznick D 84 C5
Jaulín E 41 E10
Jaun CH 31 B11
Jaunalūksne LV 133 B2
Jaunanna LV 133 B2
Jaunauce LV 134 D5
Jaunay-Clan F 29 B6
Jaunbērze LV 134 C6
Jaunciems LV 134 B5
Jaundundaga LV 130 F4
Jaungulbene LV 135 B13
Jaunjelgava LV 135 C11
Jaunkalsnava LV 135 C11
Jaunklidzis LV 135 B11
Jaunlaicene LV 131 F13
Jaunlutriņi LV 134 C4
Jaunmārupe LV 135 C8
Jaunpiebalga LV 135 B12
Jaunpils LV 134 C6
Jaunsāti LV 134 C6
Jaunsilava LV 135 D12
Jauntsarats E 32 E2
Jaurakan FIN 119 D10
Jaurakkajärvi FIN 121 D10
Jaurrieta E 32 E4
Jausiers F 36 C5
Javali Viejo E 56 F2
Jávarus FIN 115 E1
Jávea-Xábia E 56 D5

Jävenitz D 79 A10
Javerlhac-et-la-Chapelle-St-Robert F 29 D7
Javgur MD 154 D3
Javier E 32 E3
Javorník CZ 77 B12
Javron-les-Chapelles F 23 D11
Jawor PL 81 D10
Jawornik Polski PL 144 D5
Jaworzno PL 142 D6
Jaworzno PL 143 F7
Jaworzyna Śląska PL 81 E10
Jayena E 53 C9
Jazeneuil F 28 C6
Jebel RO 159 B7
Jebjerg DK 86 B4
Jedlanka PL 141 G6
Jedlicze PL 144 D4
Jedlina-Zdrój PL 81 E10
Jedlińsk PL 141 G4
Jedlnia-Letnisko PL 141 H4
Jedlová CZ 77 C10
Jedľové Kostolany SK 146 E6
Jednorożec PL 139 D11
Jedovnice CZ 77 D11
Jjdrzejewo PL 85 E10
Jjdrzejów PL 143 E9
Jédula E 52 C5
Jedwabne PL 140 D6
Jedwabno PL 139 C10
Jeesiö FIN 117 D16
Jeesijärvi FIN 117 C14
Jegália RO 161 E11
Jegun F 33 C6
Jegunovce MK 164 E3
Jejsing DK 86 F3
Jēkabpils LV 135 C11
Jektvik N 108 C5
Jelah BIH 157 C8
Jelašca BIH 157 F9
Jelcz-Laskowice PL 81 D12
Jelenia Góra PL 81 E9
Jeleniewo PL 136 E6
Jelenin PL 81 C8
Jelenje HR 67 B9
Jeleśnia PL 147 B8
Jelgava LV 134 C7
Jelka SK 146 E5
Jelling DK 86 D4
Jeloboc MD 154 C3
Jelovica SRB 165 C6
Jełowa PL 142 E5
Jels DK 86 E4
Jelsa HR 157 F6
Jelšane SLO 67 A9
Jelšava SK 145 F1
Jelsi I 63 D7
Jemeppe B 19 D10
Jemgum D 17 B8
Jemielnica PL 142 E5
Jemielno PL C11
Jemnice CZ 77 D9
Jena D 79 E10
Jenbach A 72 B4
Jeneč CZ 76 B6
Jengen D 71 B11
Jenikowo PL 85 C8
Jennersdorf A 148 C6
Jenny S 93 D9
Jenő H 149 B10
Jensvoll N 101 A15
Jeppo FIN 122 D9
Jērciens LV 131 F11
Jerchel D 79 B9
Jerez de la Frontera E 52 C4
Jerez del Marquesado E 55 E6
Jerez de los Caballeros E 51 C6
Jerfojaur S 109 E16
Jergol N 113 E14
Jergucat AL 168 E3
Jeri LV 131 F10
Jérica E 48 E3
Jerichow D 79 A11
Jerka PL 81 C11
Jernved DK 86 E3
Jerslev DK 87 D8
Jerslev DK 90 E7
Jerstad N 110 C9
Jerte E 45 D9
Jerup DK 90 D7
Jerzens A 71 C11
Jerzmanowa PL 81 C10
Jerzmanowice PL 143 F8
Jerzu I 64 D4
Jesenice CZ 76 B4
Jesenice CZ 77 C7
Jesenice HR 156 F6
Jesenice SLO 73 D9
Jeseník CZ 77 B12
Jeseník nad Odrou CZ 146 B5
Jesenské SK 147 E10
Jeserig D 79 B11
Jeserig D 79 B12
Jesi I 67 E7
Jesionowo PL 85 D8
Jesolo I 66 A6
Jessen D 80 C3
Jessheim N 95 B14
Jeßnitz D 79 C11
Jesteburg D 83 D7
Jettingen-Scheppach D 75 F7
Jeumont F 19 D9
Jevenstedt D 82 B7
Jever D 17 A9
Jevíčko CZ 77 C11
Jevišovice CZ 77 E10
Jevnaker N 95 B12
Jezera BIH 157 D8
Jezerane HR 67 B11
Jezerc RKS 164 E3
Jezero BIH 157 D7
Jezero HR 156 B3
Jeżewo PL 138 C5
Jeżewo PL 140 D7
Jeziorany PL 136 F2
Jeziorzany PL 141 G6
Jeżów PL 141 G1
Jeżowe PL 144 C5
Jeżów Sudecki PL 81 E9
Jiana RO 159 E11
Jibert RO 152 E6
Jibou RO 151 C11
Jichişu de Jos RO 152 C3
Jičín CZ 77 B8
Jidvei RO 152 E4
Jieznas LT 137 D9
Jihlava CZ 77 D9
Jijila RO 155 C2

Jijona-Xixona E 56 D4
Jilava RO 161 E8
Jilavele RO 161 D9
Jilemnice CZ 81 E9
Jílové CZ 80 E6
Jílové u Prahy CZ 77 C7
Jiltjaur S 109 E12
Jimbolia RO 150 F6
Jimena E 53 A10
Jimena de la Frontera E 53 D6
Jimramov CZ 77 C10
Jina RO 152 F3
Jince CZ 76 C5
Jindřichov CZ 77 B12
Jindřichov CZ 142 F4
Jindřichův Hradec CZ 77 D8
Jiříkov CZ 81 E7
Jirlău RO 161 C10
Jirnsum NL 16 B5
Jirny CZ 77 B7
Jistebnice CZ 77 D7
Jistebník CZ 146 B6
Jitia RO 161 B9
Jlajkovci SRB 163 C10
Joachimsthal D 84 E5
Joane P 38 F3
Job F 30 D4
Jobbágyi H 147 F9
Jobsbo S 97 B13
Jochberg A 72 B5
Jocketa D 79 E11
Jockfall S 116 E9
Jockgrim D 27 B9
Jódar E 55 D6
Jodłowa PL 144 D3
Jodłownik PL 144 D1
Jodoigne B 19 C10
Joensuu FIN 125 E13
Jõepere EST 131 C12
Joesjö S 108 E8
Joeström S 108 E8
Jõesuu EST 131 E9
Jœuf F 20 F6
Jõgeva EST 131 D12
Jõgua EST 131 C11
Johanngeorgenstadt D 75 B12
Johannisfors S 99 B12
Johannishus S 89 C8
Johanniskirchen D 76 E3
Johansfors S 89 B9
John o'Groats GB 3 H10
Johnston GB 12 B5
Johnstone GB 4 D7
Johnstown IRL 9 C7
Johnstown IRL 9 C8
Johovac BIH 158 D3
Jöhstadt D 76 A4
Jõhvi EST 131 C14
Joigny F 25 E9
Joinville F 26 D3
Joița RO 161 E7
Jokela FIN 119 B16
Jokela FIN 119 B18
Jokela FIN 127 D12
Jokelankylä FIN 123 C14
Jøkelfjordeidet N 112 C9
Jokijärvi FIN 121 C12
Jokijärvi FIN 123 D17
Joki-Kokko FIN 119 D16
Jokikunta FIN 127 E11
Jokikylä FIN 121 E11
Jokikylä FIN 122 E8
Jokikylä FIN 123 C15
Jokikylä FIN 123 D15
Jokilampi FIN 121 C12
Jokimaa FIN 127 D12
Jokioinen FIN 127 E9
Jokiperä FIN 122 E8
Jokipii FIN 122 E9
Jokivarsi FIN 123 E11
Jokivarsi FIN 123 C12
Jokkmokk S 116 E3
Jokūbavas S 134 E2
Jolanda di Savoia I 66 C4
Jolanki FIN 117 E13
Jolda P 38 E3
Joloskylä FIN 119 D16
Joltai MD 154 E3
Jomala FIN 99 B13
Jømna N 101 E15
Jona CH 27 F10
Jonava LT 137 C9
Joncy F 30 B6
Jondal N 94 B3
Jonesborough GB 7 D10
Joniec PL 139 E10
Joniškėlis LT 135 D8
Joniškis LT 134 D7
Joniškis LT 137 C12
Jonkeri FIN 125 C13
Jönköping S 92 D4
Jonkowo PL 139 C9
Jonku FIN 120 D8
Jonquières F 35 B8
Jonsberg S 93 B9
Jonsered S 91 D11
Jonslund S 91 C12
Jonstorp S 87 C11
Jonzac F 28 E5
Jõõdre EST 130 D7
Joppolo I 59 B8
Jorăşti RO 153 F11
Jorba E 43 E7
Jorcas E 42 F2
Jordanów PL 147 B9
Jordanów Śląski PL 81 E11
Jordbro S 99 D10
Jordbru N 108 D8
Jordbrua N 108 D8
Jördenstorf D 83 C13
Jordet N 102 D3
Jork D 82 C7
Jörlanda S 91 D10
Jormvattnet S 105 B16
Jörn S 118 D4
Joroinen FIN 125 F9
Jørpeland N 94 D4
Jorquera E 47 F9
Jørstadmoen N 101 D12
Jošanica BIH 157 E9
Jošanička Banja SRB 163 C10
Jošavka BIH 157 C7
Joseni RO 152 E6
Joseni Bârgăului RO 152 C5
Josifovo MK 169 B7
Josipdol HR 156 B3
Josipovac HR 149 E11
Josnes F 24 E6
Jössefors S 96 C7
Josselin F 22 E6
Jossund N 105 C9

Josvainiai LT 134 F7
Jota N 101 D15
Jou P 38 F5
Jouarre F 25 C9
Joué-lès-Tours F 24 F4
Joué-sur-Erdre F 23 E9
Jougne F 31 B9
Joukokylä FIN 121 D10
Jouques F 35 C10
Joure NL 16 C5
Journiac F 29 E7
Joutenniva FIN 123 B15
Joutsa FIN 125 F8
Joutseno FIN 129 C10
Joux-la-Ville F 25 E10
Jouy F 24 C6
Jouy-aux-Arches F 26 B5
Jouy-le-Potier F 24 E6
Jøvik N 111 A13
Jøvik N 111 B13
Joyeuse F 35 B7
Joze F 30 D3
Józefów PL 141 F4
Józefów PL 144 A4
Józefów PL 144 C7
Juankoski FIN 125 D10
Juan-les-Pins F 36 D6
Juban AL 163 E8
Jubė AL 168 B1
Jübek D 82 A6
Jublains F 23 D11
Jubrique E 53 C6
Jüchen D 20 B6
Juchowo PL 85 C10
Jüchsen D 75 B8
Jucu RO 152 D3
Judaberg N 94 D3
Judenbach D 75 B9
Judenburg A 73 B10
Judinsalo FIN 127 B14
Juelsminde DK 86 D6
Jugon-les-Lacs F 23 D7
Jugorje SLO 148 E4
Jugureni RO 161 C8
Juhonpieti S 116 D10
Juhtimäki FIN 127 B9
Juillac F 29 E8
Juillan F 32 D6
Jujurieux F 31 C7
Jukkasjärvi S 116 C5
Juknaičiai LT 134 F3
Juksjaur S 109 E10
Jukua FIN 121 C9
Julåsen S 103 B10
Julbach D 76 E5
Jule N 105 C15
Jülich D 20 C6
Juliénas F 30 C6
Jullouville F 23 C8
Jumaliskylä FIN 121 E13
Jumeaux F 30 E3
Jumilhac-le-Grand F 29 E8
Jumilla E 55 C10
Juminen FIN 125 D9
Jumisko FIN 121 B11
Jumprava LV 135 C9
Jumurda LV 135 C11
Juncal P 44 E3
Juncosa E 42 E5
Juneda E 42 E5
Jung S 91 C13
Jungingen D 27 D11
Junglinster L 20 E6
Jungsund FIN 122 D7
Junik RKS 163 E9
Juniskär S 103 B13
Juniville F 19 F9
Jünkerath D 21 D7
Junkerdal N 109 C10
Junnonoja FIN 119 F15
Junosuando S 116 C9
Junqueira P 50 E5
Junsele S 107 D11
Juntinvaara FIN 121 F15
Juntusranta FIN 121 D12
Juodkrantė LT 134 E2
Juodšiliai LT 137 D11
Juodupė LT 135 D11
Juoksengi S 117 E11
Juokslahti FIN 127 B13
Juokuanvaara FIN 119 C13
Juonto FIN 121 F13
Juorkuna FIN 120 E8
Juornaankylä FIN 127 D14
Juostininkai LT 135 E12
Juotasniemi FIN 117 D17
Jupânești RO 160 D3
Jupilles F 24 E3
Juprelle B 19 C12
Jurançon F 32 D5
Jurbarkas LT 134 F5
Jurbise B 19 C8
Jürgenshagen D 83 C11
Jürgenstorf D 84 C3
Jurgi LV 134 C5
Jūri EST 131 C9
Jurignac F 28 D5
Jurilovca RO 155 D3
Jurjevo HR 67 C10
Jürkalne LV 134 B2
Jurklošter SLO 148 D4
Jurkowice PL 143 E11
Jūrmala LV 134 C7
Jürmalciems LV 134 D2
Jurmo FIN 126 D5
Jurmo FIN 126 F6
Jurmu FIN 121 D10
Jurovski Brod HR 148 E4
Jursla S 93 B8
Jurva FIN 122 E7
Jussac F 29 F11
Jussey F 26 E4
Juta H 149 D9
Jüterbog D 80 C4
Jutis S 109 D13
Jutrosin PL 81 C12
Jutsajaure S 116 D3
Juujärvi FIN 121 B13
Juuka FIN 125 D12
Juuma FIN 121 C12
Juupajoki FIN 127 B11
Juupakylä FIN 123 E9
Juurikka FIN 125 G14
Juurikkalahti FIN 125 B10
Juurikkamäki FIN 125 E10
Juurikorpi FIN 128 D6
Juuru EST 131 C9
Juustovaara FIN 117 D13
Juutinen FIN 123 B17
Juva FIN 128 B8

Juvanådammet S 107 D12
Juvigné F 23 D9
Juvigny-le-Tertre F 23 C9
Juvigny-sous-Andaine F 23 C10
Juvola FIN 125 F11
Juzennecourt F 26 D2
Juzet-d'Izaut F 33 E7
Jūžintai LT 135 E11
Jyderup DK 87 D8
Jylhä FIN 123 D17
Jylhämä FIN 119 E17
Jyllinge DK 87 D10
Jyllinkoski FIN 122 F8
Jyrinki FIN 123 C12
Jyrkänkoski FIN 121 B14
Jyrkänkylä FIN 125 B13
Jyrkkä FIN 125 C9
Jystrup DK 87 D9
Jyväskylä FIN 123 F15

K

Kaagjärve EST 131 F12
Kaakamo FIN 119 C13
Kaalepi EST 131 C11
Kaamanen FIN 113 E19
Kaamasjoki FIN 113 E19
Kaamasmukka FIN 113 E18
Kaanaa FIN 127 B11
Kääntöjärvi S 116 C7
Kääpa EST 131 F14
Kääpälä FIN 128 C6
Kaarakkala FIN 124 C8
Kaaraneskoski FIN 117 E12
Käärdi EST 131 E12
Kaarepere EST 131 D13
Kaaresuvanto FIN 116 B9
Kaarina FIN 126 E7
Kaarlela FIN 123 C10
Käärmelehto FIN 117 D15
Kaarnevaara S 117 C10
Kaarnijärvi FIN 115 F1
Kaarßen D 83 D10
Kaarst D 21 B7
Kaasmarkku FIN 126 C7
Kaatsheuvel NL 16 E4
Kaava FIN 113 D18
Kaavi FIN 125 E10
Kaba H 151 C7
Kabakça TR 173 B9
Kabaklar TR 173 E11
Kabakum TR 177 A8
Kabala EST 131 D11
Käbdalis S 118 B4
Kabelvåg N 110 D7
Kaberneeme EST 131 B10
Kabile LV 134 C4
Kableshkovo BG 167 D9
Kabli EST 131 E8
Kać SRB 158 C4
Kaçanik RKS 164 E3
Kačarevo SRB 158 D6
Kachkivka UA 154 A2
Kachurivka UA 154 B5
Kačice CZ 76 B5
Käckelbäcksmon S 103 A13
Kaczory PL 85 D11
Kadaň CZ 76 B4
Kadarkút H 149 D9
Kadıköy TR 173 B9
Kadıköy TR 173 C6
Kadıköy TR 173 C11
Kadıköy TR 177 B9
Kadila EST 131 C12
Kadrifakovo MK 164 F5
Kadrina EST 131 C12
Kadzidło PL 139 D12
Käenkoski FIN 125 E15
Kaerepere EST 131 D9
Kåfjord N 112 D11
Kåfjord N 113 B16
Kåfjorddalen N 112 C9
Kåge S 118 E5
Kågerod S 87 D12
Kaggebo S 93 D9
Kağıthane TR 173 B10
Kagkadi GR 174 C3
Kahla D 79 E10
Kahl am Main D 187 A7
Kähög S 91 D11
Kahraman TR 181 A8
Kähtävä FIN 119 F12
Kaïafa GR 174 E4
Käina EST 130 D5
Kainach N 105 D7
Kainasto FIN 122 F8
Kainourgio GR 174 B3
Kainulasjärvi S 116 C9
Kainuunkylä FIN 119 C11
Kainuunmäki FIN 124 C9
Kaipiainen FIN 128 D7
Kaipola FIN 127 B13
Kairala FIN 115 D2
Kairiai LT 134 D6
Kairišiai LT 134 C4
Kaisepakte S 111 D17
Kaisersesch D 21 D8
Kaiserslautern D 21 F9
Kaisheim D 75 E8
Kaišiadorys LT 137 D9
Kaisma EST 131 D9
Kaitainen FIN 124 F9
Kaitainsalmi FIN 121 F11
Kaitajärvi FIN 119 B13
Kaitum S 116 C4
Kaivanto FIN 120 F9
Kaive LV 134 B6
Kaive LV 135 B11
Kajaani FIN 121 F10
Kajal SK 146 E5
Kajanki FIN 117 B11
Kajdacs H 149 C11
Kajew PL 143 B7
Kajoo FIN 125 D12
Kájov CZ 76 E6
Kakanj H 149 D11
Kakasd H 149 D11
Kakavi AL 168 E3
Kakenieki LV 134 C6
Kakenstorf D 83 D7
Kakerbeck D 83 E10
Kakhanavichy BY 133 E4
Käkilahti FIN 120 F8
Käkisalmi LV 135 E9
Kaklıç TR 177 C8
Kąkolewnica Wschodnia PL 141 G7
Kąkolewo PL 81 C11
Kakovatos GR 174 E4
Kakrukë AL 168 C3
Kakskerta FIN 126 E7
Kakslauttanen FIN 115 B2

Kakucs H 150 C3
Kál H 150 B5
Kål S 107 D12
Kälä FIN 127 B15
Kalabakbaşı TR 173 E7
Kålaboda S 118 F5
Kalace MNE 163 D9
Kala Dendra GR 169 B9
Kalaja FIN 123 C12
Kalajärvi FIN 123 C14
Kalajoki FIN 119 F11
Kalak N 113 B19
Kalakangas FIN 123 C14
Kalamaki GR 169 E8
Kalamaki GR 174 D2
Kalamaki GR 175 D8
Kalamaria GR 169 C8
Kalamata GR 174 E5
Kalamos GR 175 C8
Kalamoti GR 177 C7
Kalamoto GR 169 C9
Kalampaka GR 169 E6
Kalampaki GR 171 B6
Kalana EST 130 D4
Kalandra GR 169 E9
Kala Nera GR 169 F8
Kalanistra GR 174 C4
Kalanti FIN 126 D6
Kalathos GR 181 D8
Kalavarda GR 181 D7
Kalavryta GR 174 C5
Kalawa PL 81 B9
Kalbe (Milde) D 83 E10
Kalce SLO 73 E9
Kalchevo BG 167 E7
Kaldabruna LV 135 D12
Kaldbak FO 2 A3
Kaldfarnes N 111 B12
Kaldfjord N 111 A16
Kaldslett N 111 A16
Kaldvåg N 111 D10
Kaldvik N 111 A16
Kale TR 181 B9
Kalefeld D 79 C7
Kaleköy TR 171 D9
Kälen S 103 A8
Kälen S 103 B11
Kälen S 108 B6
Kalentzi GR 168 F4
Kalesija BIH 157 D10
Kalesmeno GR 174 B4
Kalety PL 143 E6
Kalevala RUS 121 D17
Kali GR 169 C7
Kali HR 156 D3
Kalianoi GR 175 D5
Kalimanci MK 165 F6
Kalimash AL 163 E9
Kaliningrad RUS 136 D2
Kalinino RUS 136 E6
Kalinovik BIH 157 F9
Kalinovka RUS 136 D4
Kalinowa PL 142 C5
Kalinowo PL 136 F6
Kaliska PL 138 C5
Kalisz PL 142 C5
Kalisz Pomorski PL 85 D9
Kalita EST 131 E9
Kali Vrysi GR 170 B5
Kalix S 119 C10
Kalixforsen S 116 C4
Kalkar D 16 E6
Kalkhorst D 83 C9
Kalki LV 130 F4
Kalkiainen FIN 115 E3
Kalkim TR 173 E7
Kalkkimaa FIN 119 C12
Kalkkinen FIN 127 C14
Kalków PL 79 B12
Kalküni LV 135 E12
Kallaste EST 131 D14
Kallberget S 102 A6
Källby S 91 C13
Kållby S 123 C9
Kalle N 110 D7
Kålleboda S 96 D7
Källekärr S 91 C10
Kållered S 91 D11
Kallerud S 91 A12
Kallham A 76 F5
Kallifoni GR 169 E6
Kallifytos GR 171 B6
Kallimasia GR 177 C7
Kallinge S 89 C8
Kalliojoki FIN 121 F15
Kalliosalmi FIN 117 E17
Kallirachi GR 171 C7
Kallislahti FIN 129 B10
Kallithea GR 169 D8
Kallithea GR 169 E7
Kallithea GR 169 E7
Kallithea GR 174 F4
Kallithea GR 175 D7
Kallithea GR 175 D8
Kallithiro GR 169 F6
Kalljord N 110 C9
Kallmet i Madh AL 163 F8
Kallmünz D 75 D10
Kallo FIN 117 D12
Kálló H 150 B3
Kallön S 109 E15
Kalloni GR 171 F10
Kalloni GR 175 D7
Kalloni GR 176 C5
Kállósemjén H 145 H4
Kallsedet S 105 D13
Källsjön S 103 C11
Kallträsk FIN 122 F7
Kallunki FIN 121 B13
Kálmánháza H 145 H4
Kalmar S 89 B10
Kalmari FIN 123 E14
Kalmthout B 16 F2
Kalna SRB 164 C5
Kalná nad Hronom SK 147 F7
Kalnciems LV 134 C7
Kalni LV 134 B6
Kalnieši LV 133 E2
Kalnujai LT 134 F6

Kalocsa H 150 D2
Kalofer BG 165 D10
Kaloi Limenes GR 178 F8
Kaloneri GR 169 D5
Kalo Nero GR 174 E4
Kalos Agros GR 170 B6
Kalotina BG 165 C6
Kalotintsi BG 165 D6
Kaloyanovets BG 166 E5
Kaloyanovo BG 165 D10
Kalóz H 149 C10
Kalpaki GR 168 E4
Kalpio FIN 121 E10
Kals am Großglockner A 73 B6
Kaltanėnai LT 135 F11
Kaltene LV 134 B5
Kaltenkirchen D 83 C7
Kaltennordheim D 79 E7
Kaltensundheim D 79 E7
Kaltinėnai LT 134 E4
Kaluđerica SRB 158 D5
Kalugerovo BG 165 D8
Kalundborg DK 87 D8
Kalupe LV 135 D13
Kalvarija LT 136 E7
Kalvatn N 100 C1
Kalveliai LT 137 D12
Kalvene LV 134 C3
Kalvi EST 131 C13
Kälviä FIN 123 C10
Kalvik N 109 A10
Kalvitsa FIN 128 B7
Kalvola FIN 127 C11
Kalvsjø N 95 B13
Kälvsträsk S 107 B17
Kalwang A 73 B10
Kalwaria Zebrzydowska PL 147 B9
Kalymnos GR 177 F8
Kalyny UA 145 G7
Kalythies GR 181 D8
Kalyves GR 171 C7
Kalyvia GR 174 B3
Kalyvia GR 174 C4
Kalyvia GR 174 B3
Kalyvia GR 174 B3
Kalyvia Thorikou GR 175 D8
Kamajai LT 135 E11
Kämäränkylä FIN 121 F14
Kamarde LV 135 D8
Kamares GR 174 C4
Kamares GR 175 F10
Kamariotissa GR 171 D8
Kambja EST 131 E13
Kamburovo BG 166 C6
Kamen D 17 E9
Kamenari BG 166 C6
Kamena Vourla GR 175 B6
Kamen Bryag BG 167 C11
Kamencia SRB 158 F6
Kamenec pod Vtáčnikom SK 147 D7
Kamengrad BIH 156 C6
Kamenica BIH 156 D5
Kamenica BIH 157 D9
Kamenica BIH 157 F9
Kamenica BIH 158 F3
Kamenica MK 164 F6
Kamenica SK 145 E2
Kamenica SRB 164 C5
Kamenica nad Cirochou SK 145 F4
Kamenica nad Hronom SK 147 F7
Kameničė AL 168 C4
Kamenice CZ 77 C7
Kamenice CZ 77 D9
Kamenice nad Lipou CZ 77 D8
Kameničná SK 146 F6
Kamenín SK 147 F7
Kamenka RUS 129 E11
Kamennogorsk RUS 129 D11
Kamenný Most SK 147 F7
Kamenný Přívoz CZ 77 C7
Kamenný Újezd CZ 77 E6
Kameno BG 167 D9
Kameno Pole BG 165 C8
Kamenovo BG 161 F10
Kamensko BIH 157 D9
Kamensko HR 157 E6
Kamenskoye RUS 136 D4
Kamenz D 80 D6
Kamëz AL 168 B2
Kamičak BIH 157 C6
Kamień PL 144 C5
Kamieńczyk PL 139 E12
Kamienica PL 145 D1
Kamienica Polska PL 143 E7
Kamieniec PL 81 B10
Kamieniec Ząbkowicki PL 77 A11
Kamienka SK 145 E2
Kamień Krajeńskie PL 85 C13
Kamienna Gora PL 81 E10
Kamiennik PL 81 E12
Kamień Pomorski PL 85 C7
Kamieńsk PL 143 D8
Kamień Wielkie PL 85 E8
Kamilski Dol BG 171 A10
Kamion PL 139 F9
Kamion PL 141 G2
Kamionka PL 141 H6
Kamiros GR 181 D7
Kamlunge S 119 C10
Kammela FIN 126 D5
Kammen N 111 B14
Kamnik SLO 73 D10
Kamøyvær N 113 A16
Kamp D 21 D8
Kampanis GR 169 C8
Kampen D 82 A5
Kampen NL 16 C5
Kampenhout B 182 D5
Kämpfelbach D 187 D6
Kampi GR 174 A3
Kampia GR 177 B6
Kampinkylä FIN 122 E8
Kampinos PL 141 F2
Kampor HR 67 C10
Kampos GR 174 C5
Kampos GR 174 E5
Kampvoll N 111 B14
Kamsjö S 118 F3

Kamula FIN 123 B16
Kamut H 151 D6
Kam''yane UA 154 A5
Kam''yans'ke UA 154 F4
Kamyanyets BY 141 F9
Kamyanyuki BY 141 E9
Kanaküla EST 131 E10
Kanal SLO 73 D8
Kanala FIN 123 D12
Kanala GR 175 E9
Kanali GR 168 F2
Kanali GR 174 A2
Kanalia GR 169 F8
Kanallaki GR 168 F3
Kanan S 109 F17
Kanatlarci MK 169 B6
Kańczuga PL 144 D5
Kandava LV 134 B5
Kandel D 27 B9
Kandelin D 84 B4
Kandern D 27 E8
Kandersteg CH 70 E5
Kandila GR 174 D3
Kandila GR 174 D5
Kandle EST 131 B12
Kanepi EST 131 F13
Kanestraum N 104 E4
Kanfanar HR 67 B8
Kangas FIN 119 F13
Kangas FIN 122 D9
Kangasaho FIN 123 E13
Kangasala FIN 127 C11
Kangaskylä FIN 119 F16
Kangaskylä FIN 123 E11
Kangaskylä FIN 123 C13
Kangaslahti FIN 125 D10
Kangaslampi FIN 125 F11
Kangasniemi FIN 123 G17
Kangasvieri FIN 123 C13
Kangos S 116 C8
Kangosjärvi FIN 117 C11
Kaniánka SK 147 D7
Kaninė N 168 D2
Kanjiža SRB 150 E5
Kånna S 87 B13
Kannas FIN 121 C12
Kannonjärvi FIN 123 E14
Kannonkoski FIN 123 E14
Kannus FIN 123 C11
Kannusjärvi FIN 128 C7
Kannuskoski FIN 128 C7
Kanpantxua E 41 B6
Kanstad N 111 C10
Kanstadbotn N 111 C10
Kantala FIN 124 F8
Kantanos GR 178 E6
Kantele FIN 127 D14
Kantens NL 17 B7
Kantia GR 175 D6
Kantojärvi FIN 119 C12
Kantojoki FIN 121 B13
Kantokylä FIN 123 B13
Kantola FIN 123 D10
Kantomaanpää FIN 119 B12
Kantorneset N 111 B17
Kantserava BY 133 F4
Kantti FIN 122 F9
Kanturk IRL 8 D5
Kaolinovo BG 161 F10
Kaona SRB 158 F5
Kaonik BIH 157 D8
Kaonik SRB 164 B3
Kapakli TR 173 B8
Kapakli TR 173 D10
Kapanbeleni TR 173 D7
Kapanle RKS 164 D4
Kaparelli GR 175 C8
Kapčiamiestis LT 137 F8
Kapela GR 175 C7
Kapelle B 16 F1
Kapelle-op-den-Bos B 182 C4
Kapellskär S 99 C12
Kapfenberg A 148 B4
Kapikargin TR 181 C6
Kapitan-Andreevo BG 166 F6
Kapiz TR 181 B9
Kaplava LV 133 E2
Kaplice CZ 77 E7
Kapljuh BIH 156 C5
Kápolna H 150 B5
Kápolnásnyék H 149 B11
Kaposfő H 149 D9
Kaposmérő H 149 D9
Kaposszekcsö H 149 D10
Kaposvár H 149 D9
Kapp N 101 E13
Kappel D 21 E8
Kappel-Grafenhausen D 186 E4
Kappeln D 83 A7
Kappelrodeck D 186 D5
Kappl A 71 C10
Kápponis S 118 B4
Kaprun A 73 B6
Kapshticë AL 168 C5
Kapsia GR 174 D5
Kaptol HR 149 F9
Kaptsyowka BY 140 C9
Kapušany SK 145 E3
Kapusta FIN 119 B12
Kapuvár H 149 A8
Käpylä FIN 119 F14
Karaağaç TR 173 A6
Karaağaç TR 173 E9
Karaağaçli TR 177 B9
Karabanovo UA 154 C5
Karabiga TR 173 D7
Karaböğürtlen TR 181 B9
Karabunar BG 165 E9
Karaburun TR 173 A9
Karaburun TR 177 B7
Karaca TR 181 C3
Karacabey TR 173 D9
Karacadağ TR 167 F9
Karacakılavuz TR 173 B7
Karacaköy TR 173 B10
Kárád H 149 C9
Karadzhalovo BG 166 C6
Karahalil TR 173 A7
Karaincirli TR 173 C10
Karainebeyli TR 171 D10
Karaisen BG 166 C4
Karakaja BIH 157 D11
Karakasım TR 172 A6
Karakaya TR 173 F9
Karakoca TR 173 D10
Karaköy TR 173 E6
Karaköy TR 177 B9

Karaköy TR 181 B9
Karakurt TR 177 A10
Karala EST 130 E3
Karaman TR 173 E9
Karamanovo BG 166 B5
Karamehmet TR 173 B8
Karamyshevo RUS 132 F4
Karamyshevo RUS 136 E5
Karancsberény H 147 E9
Karancskeszi H 147 E9
Karancslapujtő H 147 E9
Karancsság H 147 E9
Karankamäki FIN 124 C8
Karaoğlanli TR 177 B10
Karaorman TR 173 E9
Karaova TR 177 E10
Karapchiv UA 152 A6
Karapelit BG 161 F11
Karasjok N 113 E15
Karatoulas GR 174 D4
Karats S 109 C16
Karavas GR 178 C4
Karavelovo BG 165 D10
Karavelovo BG 167 E7
Käravete EST 131 C11
Karavomylos GR 175 B6
Karavukovo SRB 157 B11
Karben D 21 D11
Kårberg S 92 B5
Karbinci MK 164 F5
Kårböle S 103 C9
Kårböleskog S 103 C9
Karbow-Vietlübbe D 83 D12
Karbunarë e Vogël AL 168 C2
Karby D 83 A7
Karby DK 86 B3
Karby S 99 C10
Karcag H 151 C6
Karcsa H 145 G4
Karczew PL 141 F4
Karczmiska Pierwsze PL 141 H6
Kärda S 87 A13
Kardakata GR 174 C1
Kardam BG 155 F2
Kardam BG 166 C6
Kardamaina GR 177 F9
Kardamyli GR 174 F5
Kardašova Řečice CZ 77 D7
Karden D 21 D8
Kardiani GR 176 D5
Kardis S 117 E11
Karditsa GR 169 F6
Karditsomagoula GR 169 F6
Kärdla EST 130 D5
Kardon BY 133 F6
Kardos H 150 D6
Kardoskút H 150 E6
Karegasnjarga FIN 113 E16
Kareļi LV 134 D4
Karesuando S 116 B8
Kargowa PL 81 B9
Karhi FIN 123 C10
Karhila FIN 123 F13
Karhujärvi FIN 115 F4
Karhukangas FIN 119 F14
Karhula FIN 128 D6
Kariani GR 170 C5
Karigasniemi FIN 113 E16
Karihaugen N 111 D12
Karijoki FIN 122 F7
Karinainen FIN 126 D8
Käringberg S 107 A12
Käringen N 111 D10
Käringsjön S 102 B3
Käringsjövallen S 102 B4
Karinkanta FIN 119 E13
Karis FIN 127 E10
Karise DK 87 E10
Karisjärvi FIN 127 D11
Karitaina GR 174 E5
Karitsa GR 169 D7
Karjalaisenniemi FIN 121 B11
Karjalan kirkonkylä FIN 126 D7
Karjalankylä FIN 119 D15
Karjalankylä FIN 126 D7
Karjalanvaara FIN 120 B9
Karjalanvaara FIN 121 F10
Karjalohja FIN 127 E10
Kärjenkoski FIN 122 F7
Karjulanmäki FIN 123 C13
Karkalou GR 174 D5
Kärki LV 131 F11
Kärkinen FIN 119 F12
Kärkkäala FIN 123 E16
Kärkkäälä FIN 124 E8
Karkkila FIN 127 D11
Karkku FIN 127 C9
Kärklinieki LV 133 B2
Kärkölä FIN 127 D10
Kärkölä FIN 127 D13
Karksi EST 131 E11
Karksi-Nuia EST 131 E11
Kårkul S 118 B5
Kärla EST 130 E4
Karlå FIN 122 F7
Karlby FIN 126 F4
Karlebotn N 114 C5
Karleby FIN 123 C10
Karlholmsbruk S 99 A9
Karlino PL 85 B9
Kārlmuiža LV 134 B4
Karlobag HR 67 C11
Karlovac HR 148 F5
Karlovasi GR 177 D8
Karlovice CZ 142 F3
Karlovo BG 165 D10
Karlovy Vary CZ 76 B3
Karlowice PL 142 E4
Karlsbäck S 107 D15
Karlsbad D 27 C10
Karlsberg S 103 C9
Karlsborg S 92 B5
Karlsburg D 84 C5
Karlsdal S 97 D12
Karlsdorf-Neuthard D 27 B10
Karlsfeld D 75 F9
Karlsfors S 103 C9
Karlshagen D 84 B5
Karlshamn S 89 C7
Karlshöfen D 17 B12
Karlskoga S 97 D12
Karlskrona S 89 C9
Karlsøy N 112 C4
Karlsruhe D 27 B9
Karlstad S 97 D10
Karlstadt D 74 C6
Karlstein an der Thaya A 77 E8
Karlstetten A 77 F9
Karlukovo BG 165 C9
Karmansbo S 97 C14
Karmas S 109 B17
Karmēlava LT 137 D9
Kärnä FIN 123 D11
Kärnä FIN 123 D15
Kärna S 91 D10
Karnaliyivka UA 154 E6
Karnice PL 85 B8
Karniewo PL 139 E10
Karnjarga FIN 113 D19
Karnobat BG 167 D7
Karojba HR 67 B8
Karolinka CZ 146 C6
Karonsbo S 107 B15
Karoti GR 171 B10
Karousades GR 168 E2
Karow D 79 B11
Karow D 83 C12
Karpacz PL 81 E9
Kärpänkylä FIN 121 C14
Karpathos GR 181 E6
Karpenisi GR 174 B4
Karperi GR 169 B9
Karpero GR 169 E6
Kärppälä FIN 127 C9
Karpuzlu TR 171 C10
Karpuzlu TR 181 A7
Kärrbackstrand S 102 E4
Karrebæksminde DK 87 E9
Karrenzin D 83 D11
Kärrsjö S 107 D15
Karsakiškis LT 135 E9
Kärsämä FIN 119 E15
Kärsämäki FIN 123 C15
Kārsava LV 133 C3
Karsikas FIN 123 C14
Karsikkoniemi FIN 117 C11
Karsikkovaara FIN 124 B9
Karsimus FIN 115 E2
Karsin PL 138 C4
Karşiyaka TR 173 D9
Karşiyaka TR 177 C9
Karsko PL 85 E8
Kårsta S 99 C10
Karstädt D 83 D10
Karstädt D 83 D11
Kärstna EST 131 E11
Karstula FIN 123 E13
Karszew PL 142 B6
Kartal H 150 B4
Kartavoll N 94 E3
Kartena LT 134 E2
Kartitsch A 72 C6
Kartuzy PL 138 B5
Käru EST 131 D10
Käru EST 131 D12
Karuna FIN 126 E8
Karungi S 119 B11
Karunki FIN 119 B12
Karup DK 86 C4
Kårvåg N 104 E3
Karvala FIN 123 D11
Kärväskylä FIN 123 D15
Karvia FIN 122 F9
Kårvikhamn N 111 B15
Karviná CZ 147 B7
Karvoskylä FIN 123 C14
Karvounari GR 168 F3
Karwica PL 139 C11
Karya GR 169 E7
Karya GR 174 B2
Karya GR 175 D6
Karyes GR 171 D6
Karyes GR 175 E5
Karyotissa GR 169 C7
Karyoupoli GR 178 B3
Karystos GR 175 C9
Kås DK 86 A5
Kašalj SRB 163 C10
Kasejovice CZ 76 D5
Kasendorf D 75 B9
Kasepää EST 131 D14
Kasfjord N 111 C11
Kashirskoye RUS 136 D2
Kaşikçi TR 173 B7
Kašina HR 148 E6
Kaskantyú H 150 D3
Kåskats S 116 F4
Kaskii FIN 129 B9
Kaskinen FIN 122 F6
Kaskö FIN 122 F6
Käsmä FIN 121 C12
Kåsmo N 108 B9
Kåsmolia N 108 B9
Käsmu EST 131 B11
Kaspakas GR 171 E8
Kašperské Hory CZ 76 D5
Kaspichan BG 167 C8
Kassa S 117 D11
Kassandreia GR 169 D9
Kasseedorf D 83 B9
Kassel D 78 D6
Kassiopi GR 168 E2
Kastania GR 168 D4
Kastania GR 168 E5
Kastania GR 169 D7
Kastania GR 169 F6
Kastanies GR 171 A10
Kastanochori GR 169 C10
Kastari FIN 127 C13
Kastellaun D 21 D8
Kastelli GR 178 E9
Kastellia GR 174 B5
Kaštel Stari HR 156 E5
Kaštel Sućurac HR 156 E5
Kaštel Šegarski HR 156 D4
Kasterlee B 16 F3
Kastīre LV 135 D13
Kastl D 75 D10
Kastlösa S 89 C10
Kastneshamn N 111 C13
Kastorf D 83 C9
Kastoria GR 168 C5
Kastorio GR 174 E5
Kastraki GR 174 B3
Kastraki GR 176 E5
Kastrāne LV 135 C10
Kastre EST 131 E14
Kastri GR 169 E8
Kastri GR 175 E6
Kastro GR 175 C7
Kastrosykia GR 174 A2
Kastrova BY 133 D4
Kaszaper H 150 E6
Kaszczor PL 81 C10
Katafyto GR 169 B10
Katajamäki FIN 125 D10
Katakolo GR 174 D3
Kåtaliden S 109 F15
Kataloinen FIN 127 C12
Katapola GR 177 F6
Katarraktis GR 177 C7
Kåtaselet S 118 D3
Katastari GR 174 D2
Katerini GR 169 D8
Katerma FIN 125 B12
Kathenoi GR 175 B8
Kathlow D 81 C6
Kätkänjoki FIN 123 E11
Kätkäsuvanto FIN 117 B10
Kätkävaara FIN 119 B13
Kätkesuando S 117 B10
Katlenburg-Lindau D 79 C7
Kátlovce SK 146 D5
Kato Achaïa GR 174 C4
Kato Alepochori GR 175 C7
Kato Asites GR 178 E9
Katochi GR 174 C3
Kato Chorio GR 179 E10
Kato Doliana GR 175 E6
Kato Glykovrysi GR 178 B4
Kato Kamila GR 169 B9
Kato Makrinou GR 174 C4
Kato Nevrokopi GR 169 B10
Kato Sounio GR 175 D9
Kato Tithorea GR 175 B6
Katouna GR 174 B3
Kato Vermio GR 169 C7
Katovice CZ 76 D5
Kato Vlasia GR 174 C4
Kato Vrontou GR 169 B10
Katowice PL 143 F7
Katranca TR 173 B7
Katrineberg S 103 D11
Katrineholm S 93 B8
Katrineholm S 103 E13
Katsdorf A 77 F6
Katsikas GR 168 E4
Kattavia GR 181 E7
Kattbo S 102 E7
Kattelus FIN 123 F11
Kattilasaari S 119 C11
Kättilstad S 92 C7
Kättilstorp S 91 C14
Kattisavan S 107 B14
Kattisträsk S 118 E3
Katundishtë AL 168 D3
Katunets BG 165 C10
Katunitsa BG 165 E10
Katuntsi BG 169 B9
Katwijk aan Zee NL 16 D2
Katyčiai LT 134 F3
Katymár H 150 E3
Kąty Wrocławskie PL 81 D11
Katzenelnbogen D 21 D9
Katzweiler D 21 E9
Kaub D 21 D9
Kaufbeuren D 71 B11
Kaufungen D 78 D6
Kaugurieši LV 135 B11
Kauhajärvi FIN 122 F8
Kauhajärvi FIN 123 D10
Kauhajoki FIN 122 F8
Kauhava FIN 123 D10
Kaukalampi FIN 127 D13
Kaukolikai LT 134 D3
Kaukonen FIN 117 D13
Kauksi EST 131 C14
Kaulille B 183 C7
Kaulinranta FIN 119 B11
Kaulsdorf D 79 E9
Kaunas LT 137 D8
Kaunata LV 133 D3
Kauniainen FIN 127 E12
Kaunisjoensuu S 117 D11
Kaunisvaara S 117 D10
Kaupanger N 100 D6
Kaupiškiai LT 136 D6
Kauppila FIN 123 F17
Kauppilanmäki FIN 124 C8
Kaurajärvi FIN 122 D9
Kaurissalo FIN 126 D5
Kaustinen FIN 123 C11
Kautenbach L 184 E5
Kautokeino N 112 E11
Kautzen A 77 E8
Kauvatsa FIN 126 C8
Kauvosaarenpää FIN 119 B11
Kavacik TR 172 B6
Kavacik TR 173 E9
Kavadarci MK 169 B7
Kavajë AL 168 B2
Kavak TR 173 C6
Kavakdere TR 173 A7
Kavakli TR 173 A7
Kavaklidere TR 181 B8
Kavala GR 171 C6
Kavarna BG 167 C10
Kavarskas LT 135 F9
Kavasilas GR 174 D3
Kavastu EST 131 E14
Kavelstorf D 83 C12
Kävlinge S 87 D12
Kavos GR 168 F3
Kavousi GR 179 E10
Kavs'ke UA 145 E8
Kavyli GR 171 A11
Kaxås S 105 D15
Kåxed S 107 E14
Kaxholmen S 92 D4
Kayabaşi TR 181 B9
Kayalar TR 173 E8
Kayali TR 167 F8
Kayalioğlu TR 177 B10
Kayapa TR 173 F7
Kayatepe TR 173 E7
Käylä FIN 121 B13
Käymäjärvi S 116 D9
Kayna D 79 E11
Kaynaklar TR 177 C9
Kaynarca TR 173 A7
Kaynardzha BG 161 F10
Käyrämö FIN 117 E16
Kaysersberg F 27 D7
Kazanka BG 166 E4
Kazanlŭk BG 166 D4
Kazanów PL 141 H4
Kazár H 147 E9
Kazdanga LV 134 C3
Kazichane BG 165 D7
Kazikli TR 177 E9
Kazimierza Wielka PL 143 F9
Kazimierz Biskupi PL 142 B5
Kazimierz Dolne PL 141 H5
Kazincbarcika H 145 G2
Kazlowshchyna BY 133 E4
Kazlų Rūda LT 137 D7
Kaźmierz PL 81 A11
Kaznějov CZ 76 C4
Kazyany BY 133 E7
Kaz'yany BY 135 F13
Kçirë AL 163 E8
Kcynia PL 85 E12
Kdyně CZ 76 D4
Keadue IRL 6 D6
Keady GB 7 D9
Kealkill IRL 8 E4
Kebal S 91 B9
Kecel H 150 D3
Kecerovce SK 145 F3
Kechrokampos GR 171 B7
Kechros GR 171 B9
Kecskéd H 149 A10
Kecskemét H 150 D4
Kėdainiai LT 135 F7
Kedrös GR 174 A5
Kjdzierzyn-Koźle PL 142 F5
Keele GB 11 E7
Keenagh IRL 7 E7
Keeni EST 131 F12
Kefalos GR 181 C5
Kefalovryso GR 169 E7
Kefenrod D 21 D12
Kefermarkt A 77 F7
Ķegums LV 135 C9
Kegworth GB 11 F9
Kehidakustány H 149 C8
Kehl D 27 C8
Kehlen L 20 E6
Kehra EST 131 C10
Kehrig D 21 D8
Kehtna EST 131 D9
Kehvo FIN 124 D9
Keighley GB 11 D8
Keihärinkoski FIN 123 D15
Keikyä FIN 126 C8
Keila EST 131 C8
Keila-Joa EST 131 C8
Keillmore GB 4 D5
Keinäsperä FIN 119 D17
Ķeipene LV 135 C10
Ķeiprod N 111 C14
Keiss GB 3 H10
Keitele FIN 123 D16
Keitelepohja FIN 123 D15
Keith GB 3 K11
Kék H 145 G4
Ķekava LV 135 C8
Kékcse H 145 G5
Kelankylä FIN 119 C18
Kelberg D 21 D7
Kelbra (Kyffhäuser) D 79 D9
Kelč CZ 146 C5
Këlcyrë AL 168 D3
Kelebia H 150 E4
Kelechyn UA 145 F7
Kelheim D 75 E10
Kelkheim (Taunus) D 187 A5
Kell D 21 E7
Kellas GB 3 K10
Kellas GB 5 B11
Kellenhusen D 83 B10
Kelli GR 169 C6
Kellinghusen D 82 C7
Kellmünz an der Iller D 71 A10
Kello FIN 119 D14
Kellokoski FIN 127 D13
Kelloniemi FIN 115 E3
Kelloniemi FIN 117 D11
Kelloselkä FIN 115 E5
Kells GB 4 F4
Kells IRL 7 E9
Kells IRL 8 E2
Kells IRL 9 C8
Kelmė LT 134 E5
Kelmis B 20 C6
Kelontekemä FIN 117 C15
Kelottijärvi FIN 116 A8
Kelso GB 5 D12
Kelujärvi FIN 115 D2
Kelvä FIN 125 E14
Kelvedon GB 15 D10
Kemalpaşa TR 177 C9
Kemberg D 79 C12
Kemecse H 145 G4
Kemence H 147 E7
Kemenesmagasi H 149 B8
Kemenessömjén H 149 B8
Kemerburgaz TR 173 B10
Kémes H 149 E10
Kemeten A 148 B6
Kemi FIN 119 C13
Kemihaara FIN 115 C5
Kemijärvi FIN 115 E2
Kemilä FIN 121 C14
Keminmaa FIN 119 C13
Keminperä FIN 121 D12
Këmishtaj AL 168 C2
Kemmel B 18 C6
Kemnath D 75 C10
Kemnay GB 3 L12
Kemnitz D 81 D7
Kemnitz D 84 B5
Kempele FIN 119 E15
Kempen D 16 F6
Kempenich D 21 D8
Kempsey GB 13 A10
Kempston GB 15 C8
Kempten (Allgäu) D 71 B10
Kendal GB 10 C6
Kenderes H 150 C6
Kendice SK 145 F3
Kenézlő H 145 G4
Kenfig GB 13 B7
Kengis S 117 D10
Kengyet H 150 C5
Kenilworth GB 13 A11
Kenmare IRL 8 E3
Kenmore GB 5 B9
Kenn D 21 E7
Kennacraig GB 4 D6
Kensaleyre GB 2 L4
Kensworth GB 15 D7
Kentavros GR 171 B7
Kentriko GR 169 B8
Kentro GR 174 D3
Kenyeri H 149 B8
Kenzingen D 27 D8
Kepez TR 171 D10
Kjpice PL 85 B11
Kjpno PL 142 D4
Kepsut TR 173 E9
Keqekollë RKS 164 D3
Keramitsa GR 168 E3
Keramoti GR 171 C7
Keräntöjärvi S 116 C9
Kerasia GR 169 D6
Kerasona GR 168 F4
Keräs-Sieppi FIN 117 B11
Keratea GR 175 D8
Kerava FIN 127 E13
Kerecsend H 147 F10
Kerekegyháza H 150 D3
Kerepestarcsa H 150 B3
Kerets'ky UA 145 G7
Kergu EST 131 D9
Keri GR 174 D2
Kerimäki FIN 129 B11
Kerisalo FIN 125 F9
Kerkdriel NL 16 E4
Kerkejaure S 118 B3
Kerken D 16 F6
Kerkini GR 169 B9
Kerkkoo FIN 127 E14
Kerkonkoski FIN 123 E17
Kerkrade NL 20 C6
Kerkwijk NL 183 B6
Kerkyra GR 168 E2
Kerlouan F 22 C3
Kerma FIN 125 F11
Kermen BG 166 D6
Kernascléden F 22 D5
Kernavė LT 137 D10
Kernhof A 148 A5
Kerns CH 70 D6
Kerpen D 21 C7
Kerrykeel IRL 7 B7
Kershopefoot GB 5 E11
Kersilö FIN 117 C17
Kerspleben D 79 D9
Kerstinbo S 98 B7
Kerteminde DK 86 E7
Kertészsziget H 151 C7
Kertezi GR 174 D4
Kerttuankylä FIN 123 D10
Kerzers CH 31 B11
Kesälahti FIN 129 B12
Keşan TR 172 C6
Kesäniemenkylä FIN 121 B12
Kesarevo BG 166 C5
Kesasjärv S 118 B8
Kesh GB 7 C7
Kesh IRL 6 D6
Kesik TR 177 B8
Keskijärvi FIN 125 E14
Keskikylä FIN 119 E13
Keskikylä FIN 119 E15
Keskikylä FIN 119 F13
Keskikylä FIN 122 F9
Keskikylä FIN 123 E11
Keskinen FIN 121 E13
Keskipiiri FIN 119 E14
Keski-Posio FIN 121 B11
Keskusvankila FIN 124 C8
Kjsowo PL 138 C4
Kessel B 182 C5
Kessel NL 183 C8
Kesselinkylä FIN 125 C14
Kessingland GB 15 C12
Ķesterciems LV 134 B6
Ķesteren NL 183 B7
Kestilä FIN 119 D14
Kestilä FIN 119 F16
Kestrini GR 168 E3
Keswick GB 10 B5
Keszthely H 149 C8
Kesztölc H 149 A11
Kétegyháza H 151 D7
Kéthely H 149 C8
Ketola FIN 115 E2
Ketomella FIN 117 B12
Keträvaara FIN 121 D13
Kjtrzyn PL 136 E3
Ketsch D 21 F11
Kétsoprony H 151 D6
Kettering GB 15 C7
Kettershausen D 71 A10
Kettinge DK 83 A11
Kettletoft GB 3 G11
Kettlewell GB 11 C7
Kettwig D 183 C9
Kjty PL 147 B8
Ketzin D 79 B12
Keula D 79 D8
Keuruu FIN 123 F13
Keutschach am See A 73 C9
Keväjärvi FIN 114 F3
Kevelaer D 16 E6
Ķevele LV 134 D5
Ķevermes H 151 E7
Kevo FIN 113 D19
Keynsham GB 13 C9
Keyritty FIN 125 D10
Kežmarok SK 145 E1
Khadzhidimovo BG 169 A10
Khalamyer"ye BY 133 E7
Kharlu RUS 129 B14
Kharmanli BG 166 F5
Khaskovo BG 166 F5
Khayredin BG 160 F3
Khelyulya RUS 129 B14
Khisarya BG 165 D10
Khiytola RUS 129 C12
Khlivchany UA 144 C8
Kholmets' UA 145 E5
Kholms'ke UA 155 B4
Khorio GR 179 B8
Khrabrovo RUS 136 D2
Khrishteni BG 166 E5
Khust UA 145 G7
Khvoyna BG 165 F10
Khyriv UA 145 D6
Kiannanniemi FIN 121 D13
Kiato GR 175 C6
Kiaunoriai LT 134 E6
Kibæk DK 86 C3
Kibworth Harcourt GB 11 F10
Kiby N 114 C7
Kičevo MK 168 A4
Kichenitsa BG 161 F8
Kichevo BG 167 C9
Kidderminster GB 13 A10
Kidlington GB 13 B12
Kidričevo SLO 148 D5
Kidsgrove GB 11 E7
Kidwelly GB 12 B6
Kiefersfelden D 72 A5
Ķieģeļceplis LV 135 C10
Kiekinkoski FIN 125 B14
Kiekrz PL 81 B11
Kiel D 83 B8
Kielajoki FIN 113 E18
Kielce PL 143 E10
Kiełczygłów PL 143 D6
Kielder GB 5 E11
Kieldrecht B 182 C4
Kiełpino PL 138 B5
Kiemėnai LT 135 D8
Kiemozia PL 141 F1
Kienberg D 75 F11
Kierinki FIN 117 D15
Kierspe D 21 B9
Kieselbach D 79 E7
Kiesilä FIN 128 C7
Kiesimä FIN 123 E17
Kietrz PL 142 F5
Kietz D 81 A7
Kifisia GR 175 C8
Kifjord N 113 B19
Kihelkonna EST 130 E4
Kihlanki FIN 117 C11
Kihlanki S 117 C10
Kihlepa EST 131 E8
Kihlevere EST 131 C12
Kihniö FIN 123 F10
Kiihtelysvaara FIN 125 F14
Kiikala FIN 127 E10
Kiikka FIN 126 C8
Kiikla EST 131 C14
Kiikoinen FIN 126 C8
Kiili EST 131 C9
Kiiminki FIN 119 D15
Kiisa EST 131 C9
Kiiskilä FIN 123 C13
Kiistala FIN 117 C14
Kiiu EST 131 C10
Kiiu-Aabla EST 131 B11
Kije PL 143 E10
Kijevë RKS 163 D10
Kijevo HR 156 E5
Kijewo Królewskie PL 138 D5
Kikerino RUS 132 C6
Kikinda SRB 150 F5
Kików PL 138 E7
Kikorze PL 85 C8
Ķikuri LV 134 C3
Kil N 90 B5
Kil S 97 C9
Kilafors S 103 D12
Kilargue IRL 6 D6
Kilb A 77 F8
Kilbaha IRL 8 C3
Kilbeggan IRL 7 F8
Kilbeheny IRL 8 D6
Kilberry GB 4 D5
Kilberry IRL 7 F8
Kilbirnie GB 4 D7
Kilboghamn N 108 D5
Kilbotn N 111 C12
Kilbrittain IRL 8 E5
Kilby S 99 B10
Kilcar IRL 6 C5
Kilchoan GB 4 B4
Kilchrenan GB 4 C6
Kilcock IRL 7 F9
Kilcolgan IRL 6 F5
Kilcommon IRL 9 D7
Kilconnell IRL 6 F6
Kilconney IRL 7 D8
Kilcoole IRL 7 F10
Kilcormac IRL 7 F7
Kilcreggan GB 4 D7
Kilcullen IRL 7 F9
Kildare IRL 7 F9
Kildavin IRL 9 C9
Kilden DK 90 E7
Kildimo New IRL 8 C5
Kildonan Lodge GB 3 J9
Kile N 90 A2
Kilen N 95 D9
Kilfenora IRL 6 G4
Kilfinan GB 4 D6
Kilfinnane IRL 8 D6
Kilforsen S 107 D11
Kilgarvan IRL 8 E4
Kilgetty GB 12 B5
Kilglass IRL 6 E6
Kilglass IRL 6 F6
Kilham GB 5 D12
Kilidülbahir TR 171 D10
Kilifarevo BG 166 C5
Kilingi-Nõmme EST 131 E9
Kiliya UA 155 C4
Kilkea IRL 9 C9
Kilkee IRL 8 C3
Kilkeel GB 7 D11
Kilkelly IRL 6 E5
Kilkenny IRL 9 C8
Kilkerrin IRL 6 E5
Kilkhampton GB 12 D6
Kilkieran IRL 6 F3
Kilkinlea IRL 8 D4
Kilkis GR 169 C8
Kilkishen IRL 8 C5
Kill IRL 7 F9
Kill IRL 9 D8
Killabunane IRL 8 E3
Killadysert IRL 8 C4
Killagan Bridge GB 4 E4
Killala IRL 6 D4
Killaloe IRL 8 C6
Killamerry IRL 9 D8
Killann IRL 9 C9
Killarga IRL 6 D6
Killarney IRL 8 D4
Killavullen IRL 8 D5
Killeagh IRL 8 E7
Killean GB 4 D5
Killearn GB 5 C8
Killeberg S 88 C6
Killeenleagh IRL 8 E4
Killeigh IRL 7 F8
Killen GB 7 C7
Killenaule IRL 9 C7
Killerrig IRL 9 C9
Killeshandra IRL 7 D7
Killichonan GB 5 B8
Killiecrankie GB 5 B9
Killimor IRL 6 F6
Killin GB 5 C8
Killinaboy IRL 6 G4
Killinchy GB 7 D11
Killinge S 116 C4
Killingworth GB 5 E13
Killinick IRL 9 D10
Killinkoski FIN 123 F11
Killorglin IRL 8 D3
Killough GB 7 D11
Killough IRL 7 F10
Killucan IRL 7 E8
Killukin IRL 6 E6
Killundine GB 4 B5
Killurin IRL 9 D9
Killybegs IRL 6 C6
Killyclogher GB 4 F2
Killylea GB 7 D9
Kilmacanogue IRL 7 F10
Kilmacrenan IRL 7 B7
Kilmacthomas IRL 9 D8
Kilmaganny IRL 9 D8
Kilmaine IRL 6 E4
Kilmaley IRL 8 C4
Kilmallock IRL 8 D5
Kilmaluag GB 2 K4
Kilmarnock GB 4 D8
Kilmartin GB 4 C6
Kilmeague IRL 7 F9
Kilmeedy IRL 8 D5
Kilmelford GB 4 C6
Kilmichael IRL 8 E4
Kilmihill IRL 8 C4
Kilmona IRL 8 E5
Kilmoon IRL 7 E10
Kilmore IRL 8 C5
Kilmore IRL 9 D9
Kilmore Quay IRL 9 D9
Kilmuckridge IRL 9 C10
Kilmurry IRL 8 C5
Kilmurry McMahon IRL 8 C4
Kilnaboy IRL 6 G4
Kilnaleck IRL 7 E8
Kilnamanagh IRL 9 C10
Kilninian GB 4 B4
Kilninver GB 4 C5
Kilnock IRL 6 E5
Kiloran GB 4 C4
Kilpelä FIN 115 D4
Kilpilahti FIN 127 E14
Kilpisjärvi FIN 112 E6
Kilpua FIN 119 F13
Kilquiggin IRL 9 C9
Kilrane IRL 9 D10
Kilrea GB 4 F3
Kilrean IRL 6 C6
Kilreekill IRL 6 F6
Kilrenny GB 5 C11
Kilronan IRL 6 F3
Kilrush IRL 8 C4
Kilsallagh IRL 6 E5
Kilsaran IRL 7 E10
Kilshanchoe IRL 7 F9
Kilshanny IRL 6 G4
Kilskeer IRL 7 E9
Kilsmo S 92 A7
Kilsund N 90 B4
Kilsyth GB 5 D8
Kiltartan IRL 6 F5
Kiltealy IRL 9 C9
Kiltegan IRL 9 C9
Kiltimagh IRL 6 E5
Kiltogan IRL 9 C9
Kiltoom IRL 6 F6
Kiltsi EST 131 C12
Kiltullagh IRL 6 F5
Kilvakkala FIN 127 B9
Kilvenaapa FIN 119 B16
Kilvo S 116 E6
Kilwaughter GB 4 F5
Kilwinning GB 4 D7
Kilworth IRL 8 D6
Kimasozero RUS 121 F17
Kimberley GB 15 B11
Kimbolton GB 15 C8
Kiminki FIN 123 E13
Kimito FIN 126 E8
Kimle H 146 F4
Kimmeria GR 171 B7
Kimo FIN 122 D8
Kimola FIN 127 C15
Kimonkylä FIN 127 D15
Kimovaara RUS 125 C16
Kimpton GB 15 D8
Kimstad S 92 B7
Kinahmo FIN 125 E13
Kinbrace GB 3 J9
Kincardine GB 5 C9
Kincraig GB 3 L9
Kincses H 149 B10
Kindberg A 148 A4
Kindelbrück D 79 D9
Kinderbeuern D 21 D8
Kinding D 75 E9
Kindsbach D 186 C4
Kindsjön S 102 E4
Kineta GR 175 D7
Kingarrow IRL 6 C6
Kingarth GB 4 D6
Kingisepp RUS 132 C4
Kingsbridge GB 13 E7
Kingsclere GB 13 C12
Kingscourt IRL 7 E9
Kingskerswell GB 13 E7
Kingsland IRL 6 E6
King's Lynn GB 11 F12
Kingsnorth GB 15 E10
Kingsteignton GB 13 D7
Kingsthorne GB 13 B9
Kingston GB 3 K10
Kingston Bagpuize GB 13 B12
Kingston Seymour GB 13 C9
Kingston upon Hull GB 11 D11
Kingswear GB 13 E7
Kingswood GB 13 C9
Kings Worthy GB 13 C12
Kington GB 13 A8
Kingussie GB 5 A8
Kingwilliamstown IRL 8 D4
Kinik TR 173 E10
Kinik TR 177 A9
Kinisjärvi FIN 117 D14
Kinloch GB 4 A4
Kinlochard GB 4 C8
Kinlochewe GB 2 K6
Kinlochleven GB 4 B7
Kinloch Rannoch GB 5 B8
Kinloss GB 3 K9
Kinlough IRL 6 D6
Kinn N 111 C10
Kinna S 91 D12
Kinnared S 87 A12
Kinnarp S 91 C14
Kinnarumma S 91 D12
Kinnegad IRL 7 F8
Kinnitty IRL 7 F7
Kinnula FIN 123 D13
Kinnulanlahti FIN 124 D8
Kinrooi B 19 B12
Kinross GB 5 C10
Kinsale IRL 8 E5
Kinsalebeg IRL 9 E7
Kinsarvik N 94 B5
Kintai LT 134 F2
Kintaus FIN 123 F14
Kintbury GB 13 C12
Kintore GB 3 L12
Kinvara IRL 6 F5
Kinvarra IRL 6 F3
Kioni GR 174 C2
Kipen' RUS 132 B6
Kipfenberg D 75 E9
Kipilovo BG 166 D6
Kipinä FIN 119 D17
Kipoi GR 168 E4
Kipoureio GR 168 E5
Kippel CH 70 E5
Kippen GB 5 C8
Kippenheim D 27 D8
Kir AL 163 E8
Kirakkajärvi FIN 114 D5
Kirakkakõngäs FIN 113 F19
Királd H 145 G1
Királyegyháza H 149 D9
Királyhegyes H 150 E6
Kiran N 104 C8
Kiran TR 181 B8
Kirazli TR 172 D6
Kirbla EST 131 D7
Kirby Muxloe GB 11 F9
Kircasalih TR 173 B6
Kirchanschöring D 73 A6
Kirchardt D 21 F11

Kirchbach A 73 C7
Kirchbach in Steiermark
 A 148 C5
Kirchberg CH 27 F11
Kirchberg CH 31 A12
Kirchberg D 76 E4
Kirchberg D 79 E12
Kirchberg (Hunsrück) D 185 E7
Kirchberg am Wagram A 77 F9
Kirchberg am Walde A 77 E8
Kirchberg am Wechsel A 148 A5
Kirchberg an der Jagst D 74 D6
Kirchberg an der Pielach A 77 F8
Kirchberg an der Raab A 148 C5
Kirchbichl A 72 A5
Kirchdorf D 17 C11
Kirchdorf D 83 C10
Kirchdorf an der Iller D 71 A10
Kirchdorf an der Krems A 73 A9
Kirchdorf im Wald D 76 E4
Kirchdorf in Tirol A 72 A5
Kirchehrenbach D 75 C9
Kirchellen D 183 B9
Kirchen (Sieg) D 21 C9
Kirchenlamitz D 75 B10
Kirchenthumbach D 75 C10
Kirchgellersen D 83 D8
Kirchhain D 21 C11
Kirchheim D 74 C6
Kirchheim D 78 E6
Kirchheim am Neckar D 187 C7
Kirchheim bei München
 D 75 F10
Kirchheim-Bolanden D 21 E10
Kirchheim unter Teck D 27 C11
Kirchhundem D 21 B10
Kirchlauter D 75 B8
Kirchlinteln D 17 C12
Kirch Mulsow D 83 C11
Kirchohsen (Emmerthal)
 D 78 B5
Kirchroth D 75 E12
Kirchschlag in der Buckligen
 Welt A 148 A6
Kirchseelte D 17 C11
Kirchtimke D 17 B12
Kirchwalsede D 17 B12
Kirchweidach D 75 F12
Kirchwistedt D 17 B11
Kirchzarten D 27 E8
Kirchzell D 21 E12
Kircubbin GB 7 D11
Kireç TR 173 E9
Kiremitçisalih TR 172 B6
Kirillovskoye RUS 129 E11
Kirjais FIN 126 E6
Kirjavala FIN 129 B12
Kırkağaç TR 177 A10
Kirkbean GB 5 F9
Kirkbride GB 5 F10
Kirkby GB 10 E6
Kirkby in Ashfield GB 11 E9
Kirkby Lonsdale GB 10 C6
Kirkbymoorside GB 11 C10
Kirkby Stephen GB 5 F11
Kirkby Thore GB 5 F11
Kirkcaldy GB 5 C10
Kirkcolm GB 4 F6
Kirkconnel GB 5 E8
Kirkcudbright GB 5 F8
Kirkeby DK 86 E7
Kirkehamn N 94 F5
Kirke Helsinge DK 87 D8
Kirke Hyllinge DK 87 D9
Kirkel-Neuhäusel D 186 C3
Kirkenær N 96 B7
Kirkenes N 114 D8
Kirke Såby DK 87 D9
Kirke Stillinge DK 87 E8
Kirkham GB 10 D6
Kirkinner GB 5 F8
Kirkintilloch GB 5 D8
Kirkjubøur FO 2 B3
Kirkkavak TR 173 B6
Kirkkepenekli TR 173 B8
Kirkkonummi FIN 127 E11
Kirklareli TR 167 F8
Kirkmichael GB 4 E7
Kirkmichael GB 5 B9
Kirk Michael GBM 10 C2
Kirknewton GB 5 D12
Kirkoswald GB 5 F11
Kirkpatrick-Fleming GB 5 E10
Kirkton GB 4 C5
Kirkton of Durris GB 5 A12
Kirkton of Glenisla GB 5 B10
Kirkton of Skene GB 3 L12
Kirktown of Auchterless
 GB 3 L12
Kirktown of Deskford GB 3 K11
Kirkwall GB 3 H11
Kirn D 21 E8
Kirnujärvi S 116 D10
Kirovsk RUS 129 F14
Kirriemuir GB 5 B10
Kirschweiler D 21 E8
Kirtik S 118 B5
Kirtlington GB 13 B12
Kirton GB 11 C11
Kirton in Lindsey GB 11 E10
Kirtorf D 21 C12
Kiruna S 116 C4
Kisa S 92 D7
Kisač SRB 158 C4
Kisar H 145 G6
Kisbér H 149 A10
Kiseljak BIH 157 C10
Kiseljak BIH 157 C11
Kiseljak BIH 157 E8
Kisgyőr H 145 G2
Kishkeam IRL 8 D4
Kisielice PL 139 C7
Kisielnica PL 139 D13
Kisko FIN 127 E9
Kiskőre H 150 B5
Kiskőrős H 150 D3
Kiskunfélegyháza H 150 D4
Kiskunhalas H 150 E2
Kiskunlacháza H 150 C3
Kiskunmajsa H 150 E4
Kişlacık TR 167 E9
Kisláng H 149 C10
Kislőd H 149 B9
Kismarja H 151 C8
Kisnána H 147 F10
Kisovec SLO 73 D10
Kissakoski FIN 128 B6
Kissamos GR 178 E6
Kissenbrück D 79 B8
Kißlegg D 71 B9
Kisszállás H 150 E3
Kist D 187 B8

Kistanje HR 156 E4
Kistelek H 150 E4
Kistokaj H 145 G2
Kistrand N 113 C15
Kisújszállás H 150 C6
Kisvárda H 145 G5
Kisvarsány H 145 G5
Kiszkowo PL 81 A12
Kiszombor H 150 E5
Kitee FIN 125 F14
Kiten BG 167 E9
Kitinoja FIN 122 E9
Kitka FIN 121 B12
Kitkiöjärvi S 116 C10
Kitros GR 169 D8
Kitsi FIN 125 D15
Kittajaur S 118 B3
Kittelfjäll S 106 A8
Kittilä FIN 117 C13
Kittsee A 77 F12
Kitula FIN 127 E10
Kitzbühel A 72 B5
Kitzen D 79 D11
Kitzingen D 75 C7
Kitzscher D 79 D12
Kiuce PL 143 F8
Kiukainen FIN 126 C7
Kiurujärvi FIN 115 D2
Kiuruvesi FIN 123 C17
Kivarinjärvi FIN 115 D2
Kivelä FIN 115 F4
Kiveri GR 175 D6
Kivesjärvi FIN 121 F9
Kiveskylä FIN 121 F9
Kiveslahti FIN 120 F9
Kiviapaja FIN 129 B12
Kivijärvi FIN 123 D14
Kivijärvi S 116 E10
Kivik S 88 D6
Kivikangas FIN 123 D12
Kivilahti FIN 125 E14
Kivilompolo FIN 117 A10
Kivilompolo FIN 119 B12
Kivilompolo N 117 A10
Kivioja FIN 119 B14
Kiviöli EST 131 C13
Kiviperä FIN 121 B14
Kivivaara FIN 121 D11
Kivivaara FIN 125 C14
Kivi-Vigala EST 131 D8
Kivotos GR 168 D5
Kiwity PL 136 E2
Kiyiköy TR 173 A9
Kizilcaova TR 177 C10
Kizilcikdere TR 167 F8
Kizilpinar TR 173 B8
Kizilyaka TR 181 B8
Kjækan N 112 D9
Kjåmes N 111 D11
Kjeldebotn N 111 D12
Kjelkenes N 100 C2
Kjelkvik N 111 D11
Kjelling N 108 B7
Kjemmoen N 102 D3
Kjengsnes N 111 C11
Kjerknesvågen N 105 D10
Kjerret N 96 B7
Kjerringdal N 112 D9
Kjerringøy N 108 A8
Kjerringvåg N 104 D5
Kjerringvik N 111 D9
Kjerringvik N 111 C12
Kjerstad N 101 D9
Kjølebrønn N 90 B5
Kjølen N 91 A9
Kjøllefjord N 113 B19
Kjølstad N 101 D10
Kjøpsvik N 111 D11
Kjøra N 104 E7
Kjøsvika N 105 A12
Kjulaås S 98 D7
Klaaswaal NL 16 E2
Kłačno SK 147 D7
Kladanj BIH 157 D10
Kläden D 79 A10
Kladnica SRB 163 C9
Kladnice HR 156 E5
Kladno CZ 76 B6
Kladovo SRB 159 D10
Kladruby CZ 76 C3
Klæbu N 104 E8
Klagenfurt A 73 C9
Klågerup S 87 D12
Klaipėda LT 134 E2
Kłaj PL 143 F9
Klaksjorda N 110 C8
Klaksvík FO 2 A3
Klamila FIN 128 D7
Klana HR 67 B9
Klanac HR 156 C4
Klanino PL 85 B10
Klanjec HR 148 D5
Klanxbüll D 86 F3
Klapkalnciems LV 134 B6
Kläppsjö S 107 D12
Klärke S 103 A12
Klarup DK 86 A6
Klašnice BIH 157 C7
Klasov SK 146 E6
Kläsbol S 97 C8
Kláštereç nad Ohří CZ 76 B4
Kláštor pod Znievom SK 147 D7
Klátova Nová Ves SK 146 D6
Klatovy CZ 76 D4
Klaukkala FIN 127 E11
Klaus an der Pyhrnbahn A 73 A9
Klausdorf D 80 B4
Klausdorf D 84 B4
Klausen D 21 E7
Klausen Leopoldsdorf A 77 F10
Klausučiai LT 136 C7
Klazienaveen NL 17 C7
Kłębowiec PL 85 D10
Kłecko PL 81 A12
Kleczew PL 138 F5
Kleemola FIN 123 C12
Kleidi GR 169 C8
Kleinarl A 73 B7
Klein Berßen D 17 C8
Kleinblittersdorf D 27 B7
Klein Bünzow D 84 C5
Kleinfurra D 79 D10
Kleinheubach D 21 E12
Kleinjena D 79 D10
Kleinlobming A D 73 D10
Kleinmachnow D 80 B4
Kleinpaschleben D 79 C10
Kleinreifling A 73 A10

Kleinrinderfeld D 187 B8
Klein Rönnau D 83 C8
Klein Sankt Paul A 73 C10
Kleinwallstadt D 21 E12
Kleinwelka D 80 D6
Kleinzell A 77 G9
Kleio GR 171 F10
Kleisoura GR 168 C5
Kleitoria GR 174 D5
Kleiva N 110 C9
Kleive N 100 A7
Klejniki PL 141 E8
Klejtrup DK 86 B5
Klek SRB 158 C5
Klembivka UA 154 A2
Klemenske DK 89 E7
Klenčí pod Čerchovem CZ
 75 D12
Klenica PL 81 C9
Klenike SRB 164 E4
Klenovec SK 147 D10
Klenovice na Hané CZ 77 D12
Kleosin PL 140 D8
Klepacze PL 140 D8
Kleppe N 94 E3
Kleppstad N 110 D7
Kljpsk PL 81 B9
Kleszczele PL 141 E8
Kleszczewo PL 81 B12
Kleszczewo PL 136 F6
Kleszczów PL 143 D7
Klettwitz D 80 C5
Kleve D 16 E6
Klevshult S 92 E4
Kličevac SRB 159 D7
Kličevo MNE 163 D6
Klieken D 79 C11
Klietz D 83 E12
Klikuszowa PL 147 B9
Klim DK 86 A4
Kliment BG 161 F10
Kliment BG 165 D10
Klimentovo BG 167 C9
Klimkovice CZ 146 B6
Klimontów PL 143 E11
Klimontów PL 143 F9
Klimpfjäll S 106 A7
Klin SK 147 C8
Klinča Sela HR 148 E5
Kline RKS 163 D10
Kline e Epërme RKS 163 D10
Klingenberg D 80 E5
Klingenberg am Main D 21 E12
Klingenthal D 75 B11
Klingersel S 118 B7
Klingre S 107 E15
Klink D 83 D13
Klinkby DK 86 B2
Klinte S 93 E12
Klintebjerg D 86 E6
Klintehamn S 93 E12
Kliplev DK 86 F4
Klippan S 87 C12
Klippen S 107 C13
Klippen S 108 E9
Klippinge DK 87 E10
Klis HR 156 E6
Klisura BG 165 D9
Klisura BG 165 E7
Klisura SRB 164 D5
Klitmøller DK 86 A3
Klitten D 81 D7
Klitten S 102 D7
Klixbüll D 82 A5
Kljajićevo SRB 150 F3
Ključ BIH 157 C6
Klłokot RKS 164 E3
Kłobuck PL 143 E6
Klobuk BIH 157 F7
Klöch A 148 C6
Klockestrand S 103 A14
Klockrike S 92 C6
Kłoczew PL 141 G5
Kłodawa PL 85 E8
Kłodawa PL 143 B6
Kłodzko PL 77 B11
Kloetinge NL 16 F1
Kløfta N 95 B14
Klokkarholm DK 86 A6
Klokočevac SRB 159 E9
Klokočevci HR 149 E10
Klokočov SK 147 C7
Klomnice PL 143 E7
Klonowa PL 142 D5
Klooga EST 131 C8
Kloosterhaar NL 17 D7
Kloosterzande NL 16 F2
Klos AL 163 F9
Klos AL 168 B3
Klöse S 107 D16
Kloštar Ivanić HR 149 E6
Kloštar Podravski HR 149 E8
Kloster DK 86 C2
Klosterfelde D 84 E4
Klosterhäseler D 79 D10
Klösterle A 71 C10
Klosterlechfeld D 71 A11
Klostermansfeld D 79 C9
Klosterneuburg A 77 F10
Kloster Zinna D 80 B4
Kloten CH 27 F10
Kloten S 97 C13
Klötze (Altmark) D 79 A9
Kłótno PL 85 B12
Klövsjö S 102 A7

Klynivka UA 153 A7
Knaben N 94 E6
Knåda S 103 D10
Knaften S 107 C15
Knäred S 87 B12
Knarekoski FIN 124 C9
Knaresborough GB 11 C9
Knarrevik N 94 B2
Knarrlagsund N 104 D6
Knätten S 102 B7
Knebel DK 86 C6
Knesebeck D 83 E9
Knesselare B 19 B7
Knetzgau D 75 C8
Knežak SLO 73 E9
Kneževi Vinogradi HR 149 E11
Kneževo HR 149 E11
Knezha BG 165 C9
Knežica BG 165 C9
Knežina BIH 157 D10
Knić SRB 158 F6
Knidi GR 169 D6
Knighton GB 13 A8
Knin HR 156 D5
Knislinge S 88 C6
Knittelfeld A 73 B10
Knittlingen D 27 B10
Kniveri LV 134 D3
Knivsta S 99 C9
Knizhovnik BG 166 F5
Knjaževac SRB 164 B5
Knock GB 4 C5
Knock IRL 6 E5
Knock IRL 8 C4
Knockalough IRL 8 C4
Knockanevin IRL 8 D6
Knockban GB 2 K7
Knockbrack IRL 7 C7
Knockbridge IRL 7 E10
Knockcroghery IRL 6 E6
Knocklong IRL 8 D6
Knockmoyle IRL 6 D4
Knocknacarry GB 4 E4
Knocknacree IRL 9 C9
Knocknagree IRL 8 D4
Knocks IRL 8 E5
Knocktopher IRL 9 D8
Knokke-Heist B 19 B7
Knoppe S 103 B12
Knorrendorf D 84 C4
Knottingley GB 11 D9
Knowle GB 13 A11
Knucklas GB 13 A8
Knud DK 86 B4
Knurów PL 142 F6
Knutbränna S 106 D7
Knutby S 99 C10
Knutsbol S 97 D12
Knutsford GB 11 E7
Knyazevo RUS 133 D5
Knyazhe UA 152 A6
Knyazhevo BG 167 D8
Knyazhitsy RUS 132 E4
Knyszyn PL 140 D7
Kobaky UA 152 A6
Kobarid SLO 73 D7
Kobatovci BIH 157 C7
Kobbelveid N 109 A10
Kobbevågnes N 111 B16
Kobbfoss N 114 E7
Kobela EST 131 F12
København DK 87 D11
Kobenz A 73 B10
Kobeřice CZ 142 F5
Kobern D 185 D7
Kobersdorf A 149 A6
Kobiele Wielkie PL 143 D8
Kobierzyce PL 81 E11
Kobilyane BG 171 A8
Kobiór PL 143 F6
Koblenz D 21 D9
Kobrow D 83 C10
Kobyla Góra PL 142 D4
Kobylanka PL 85 D7
Kobylany PL 145 D4
Kobylin PL 81 C12
Kobyłka PL 139 F11
Kobylnica PL 81 B12
Kobylnica PL 85 B10
Kobylniki PL 139 F9
Kocaavşar TR 173 E8
Kocahidir TR 171 C10
Kočani MK 164 F5
Kocapinar TR 173 E8
Koçarlı TR 177 D10
Kocayazi TR 167 E8
Kocayazı TR 167 F8
Koceljevo SRB 158 E4
Kočeni LV 135 A10
Kočerin BIH 157 F8
Kočevje SLO 73 E10
Kočevska Reka SLO 73 E10
Kochanowice PL 142 E6
Kochel am See D 72 A3
Kocherinovo BG 165 E7
Kochmar BG 161 F10
Kochovo BG 167 C7
Kock PL 141 G6
Kočovce SK 146 D5

Koikkala FIN 128 B8
Koiliomeno GR 174 D2
Koilovtsi BG 165 C10
Koimisi GR 169 B9
Koirakoski FIN 124 C9
Koita GR 178 B3
Koitila FIN 121 C11
Koivu FIN 119 B14
Koivujärvi FIN 123 C16
Koivujärvi FIN 123 D16
Koivumäki FIN 123 C12
Koivumäki FIN 124 D9
Koivumäki FIN 125 F11
Koivuniemi FIN 119 C15
Kõja S 107 F13
Kojanlanti FIN 125 E11
Kojetín CZ 146 C4
Kõka H 150 C4
Kõkeze CZ 77 D9
Kokelv N 113 B14
Kokemäki FIN 126 C7
Kokkala GR 178 B3
Kokkari GR 177 D8
Kokkinochoma GR 171 C6
Kokkino Nero GR 169 E8
Kokkokylä FIN 119 C17
Kokkola FIN 123 C10
Kokkolahti FIN 125 F12
Kokkosniva FIN 115 D2
Kokkotoi GR 175 A6
Kokkovaara FIN 117 D13
Kokni GR 169 C6
Koköt GR 169 C6
Köklot FIN 122 D7
Kokora EST 131 D14
Kokory CZ 146 C4
Kokrica SLO 73 D9
Kola BIH 157 C7
Kolacin PL 141 G1
Kołacz PL 85 C10
Kołacze PL 141 H8
Kołaczkowo PL 142 B4
Kołaczyce PL 144 D3
Kolare SK 147 E8
Kolari FIN 117 C11
Kolari S 117 D11
Kolari SRB 159 D6
Kolárovice SK 147 C7
Kolarovo BG 169 B9
Kolárovo SK 146 F5
Kolåsen S 105 D13
Kolašin MNE 163 D8
Kolbäck S 98 C6
Kolbacz PL 85 D7
Kolbaskowo PL 84 D6
Kolbermoor D 72 A5
Kolbiel PL 141 F4
Kolbotn N 95 C13
Kolbu N 101 E13
Kolbudy Górne PL 138 B5
Kolbuszowa PL 144 C4
Kølby DK 86 B4
Kol'chyne UA 145 G6
Kölcse H 145 G6
Kołczygłowy PL 85 B12
Kolczyn PL 81 A8
Koldby DK 86 B3
Koldere TR 177 B10
Kolding DK 86 E4
Koler S 118 D5
Kõlesd H 149 C11
Kolesjan AL 163 F9
Koleska BIH 157 F9
Kolforsen S 103 E12
Kolga EST 131 C11
Kolga-Aabla EST 131 B11
Kolga-Jaani EST 131 D11
Kolho FIN 123 F13
Koli FIN 125 D13
Kolín CZ 77 B8
Koliňany SK 146 E6
Kolindros GR 169 D7
Kolinec CZ 76 D4
Kolinkivtsi UA 153 A8
Koliri GR 174 D3
Kolisne UA 154 E5
Kolitzheim D 75 C7
Kõljala EST 130 E5
Koljane HR 156 E5
Kolka LV 130 F5
Kolkanlahti FIN 123 E14
Kõlked H 149 E11
Kolkja EST 131 D14
Kolkku FIN 123 D16
Kolkonjärvi FIN 121 B10
Kolkwitz D 80 C6
Kollaja FIN 119 D17
Kölleda D 79 D9
Kollines GR 174 E5
Kölln-Reisiek D 82 C7
Kolno PL 139 D9
Kolo BIH 157 E7
Koło PL 142 B6
Kołobrzeg PL 85 B9
Kolochau D 80 C4
Kolochava UA 145 G8
Kolonje AL 168 C2
Kolonowskie PL 142 E5
Kolosen S 102 A6
Kolpino RUS 129 F14
Kolsätter S 102 B8
Kolsh AL 163 E9
Kölsillre S 103 B11
Kolsko PL 81 C9
Kölsta S 97 C15
Kolsva S 97 C14
Kolszary TR 167 E9
Kõflach A 73 B11
Kog SLO 148 D6
Køge DK 87 E10
Koglhof A 148 B5
Kohila EST 131 C9
Kohlberg D 75 C11
Kohren-Sahlis D 79 D12
Kohtla-Järve EST 131 C14
Koidula EST 132 F2
Koigi EST 131 D11
Koijärvi FIN 127 D10

Kølvrå DK 86 C4
Kolympari GR 178 D6
Kolympia GR 181 D8
Komádi H 151 C7
Komagfjord N 113 C15
Komagvær N 114 C9
Komanos GR 169 D6
Komar BIH 157 D7
Komar GR 171 A10
Komarani SRB 163 C8
Komarevo BG 165 B10
Komarica BIH 157 C8
Kómárno S 149 A10
Komárom H 149 A10
Komárov CZ 76 C5
Komarovo RUS 129 E12
Komarówka Podlaska PL 141 G7
Komarów Osada PL 144 B7
Kombuļi LV 133 E2
Komen SLO 73 E8
Komesi AL 168 A2
Komi GR 176 D5
Komi GR 177 C7
Komin H 148 D6
Komin HR 157 F8
Komiža HR 63 A10
Komjatice SK 146 E5
Komletinci HR 157 B10
Komló H 149 D10
Kömlő H 150 B5
Kömlőd H 149 A10
Kommeno GR 174 A3
Komnina GR 169 C6
Komoran RKS 163 D10
Komorniki PL 81 B11
Komorowo PL 139 E12
Komorzno PL 142 D5
Komoshtitsa BG 160 F2
Komossa FIN 122 D9
Komotini GR 171 B8
Kompakka FIN 125 F13
Kompelusvaara S 116 D8
Kömpöc H 150 E4
Kompoti GR 174 A3
Komprachcice PL 142 E4
Kõmsi EST 130 D7
Komsomol'sk RUS 136 D2
Komsomol'sk RUS 139 E9
Komsomol's'k UA 145 G8
Komu FIN 123 C16
Komula FIN 125 C10
Komunari BG 167 C8
Komuniga BG 166 F4
Komylio GR 174 B2
Konak TR 177 C9
Konakpinar TR 173 F8
Konare BG 155 F2
Konarzewo PL 81 B11
Konarzyce PL 139 D13
Konarzyny PL 85 C12
Koncanica HR 149 F8
Konče MK 169 A7
Kondolovo BG 167 E9
Kondoros H 150 D6
Kondrat'yevo RUS 129 D9
Kondrić HR 157 B8
Koneck PL 138 E6
Kong DK 87 E9
Konga S 89 B8
Köngäs FIN 115 E1
Köngäs FIN 117 C13
Kongasmäki FIN 121 E9
Kongens Lyngby DK 87 D11
Kongerslev DK 86 B6
Konginkangas FIN 123 E15
Kongsberg N 95 C11
Kongselva N 110 D9
Kongsfjord N 114 B6
Kongslia N 101 D9
Kongsmoen N 105 B12
Kongsvik N 111 C11
Kongsvinger N 96 B7
Kongsvoll N 104 D6
Konice CZ 77 C8
Koniecpol PL 143 E8
Königheim D 187 B8
Königsberg in Bayern D 75 B8
Königsborn D 79 B10
Königsbronn D 75 E7
Königsbrück D 80 D5
Königsbrunn D 75 B8
Königsdorf D 72 A3
Königsee D 79 E8
Königsfeld im Schwarzwald
 D 27 D9
Königshofen D 79 C8
Königshütte D 79 C8
Königslutter am Elm D 79 B8
Königsmoos D 75 E9
Königstein D 75 C10
Königstein D 80 E6
Königstein im Taunus D 187 A5
Königswartha D 80 D6
Königswiesen A 77 F7
Königswinter D 21 C8
Königs Wusterhausen D 80 B5
Konin PL 142 B6
Konispol AL 168 E3
Konitsa GR 168 D4
Könitz D 79 E10
Köniz CH 31 B11
Konjevrate HR 156 E5
Konjic BIH 157 E8
Konjsko BIH 157 F7
Konjsko BIH 162 D5
Konnern D 79 C10
Konnevesi FIN 123 E16
Könni FIN 122 E9
Konnunsuo FIN 129 C10
Konnuslahti FIN 125 E11
Könölä FIN 119 C13
Konolfingen CH 70 D5
Konopište MK 169 B7
Konopki PL 139 D9
Konopnica PL 141 H6
Konopnica PL 142 D6
Konotop PL 81 C9
Kon'ovo BG 166 D6
Kon'skie PL 141 H2
Konsko MK 169 B7
Końskowola PL 141 H6
Konsmo N 90 C1
Konstancin-Jeziorna PL 141 F4
Konstantin LV 133 D2
Konstantinovy Lázně CZ 76 C3
Konstantynów PL 141 F8

Konstantynów Łódzki PL 143 C7
Konstanz D 27 E11
Kontariotissa GR 169 D7
Kontiainen FIN 123 E10
Kontias GR 171 E8
Kontinjoki FIN 121 F10
Kontiokoski FIN 119 D15
Kontiolahti FIN 125 E13
Kontiomäki FIN 121 F11
Kontkala FIN 125 E12
Kontopouli GR 171 E8
Kontovazaina GR 174 D4
Konttajärvi FIN 117 E12
Konttila FIN 119 C17
Konttimäki FIN 125 D9
Konush BG 166 F4
Kóny H 149 A9
Konyár H 151 C8
Konyavo BG 165 E6
Konz D 21 E7
Konzell D 75 D12
Koog aan de Zaan NL 16 D3
Koonga EST 131 D8
Köörtilä FIN 126 B6
Koosa EST 131 D14
Kootstertille NL 16 B6
Kootwijkerbroek NL 183 A7
Kopani GR 168 F4
Kopanica PL 81 B9
Kopanos GR 169 C7
Kopardal N 108 D4
Koparnes N 100 B3
Kopčany SK 77 E12
Koper SLO 67 A8
Kopervik N 94 D2
Kópháza H 149 A7
Kopice PL 142 E3
Kopidlno CZ 77 B8
Kopilovtsi BG 165 C6
Köping S 97 C15
Köpingebro S 88 E5
Köpingsvik S 89 B11
Kopisto FIN 119 F12
Kopki PL 144 C5
Koplik AL 163 E7
Koplik i Sipërm AL 163 E7
Köpmanholm S 99 C11
Köpmanholmen S 107 E15
Koporiće RKS 163 C10
Koporiçë RKS 163 C10
Koposperä FIN 123 C14
Koppang N 101 C14
Koppangen N 111 A19
Kopparberg S 97 C13
Kopparmora S 99 C13
Kopparnäs S 118 C6
Koppelo FIN 114 F3
Koppl A 73 A7
Koppom S 96 C7
Koprivets BG 166 C5
Koprivlen BG 169 A10
Koprivnica HR 149 D7
Köprivnice CZ 146 B6
Koprivshtitsa BG 165 D9
Koprzywnica PL 143 E12
Kopsa FIN 119 E13
Kopstal L 186 B1
Kõpu EST 130 D4
Kõpu EST 131 E10
Koraj BIH 157 C10
Koramoniemi FIN 121 B12
Korbach D 17 F11
Korbevac SRB 164 D5
Korbovo SRB 159 D10
Korčanica BIH 156 C5
Korçë AL 168 C4
Korčiv UA 144 C3
Körchow D 83 D10
Korčula HR 162 D3
Korczew PL 141 F7
Korczyna PL 144 D4
Kordel D 185 E6
Korenita SRB 158 E3
Koreňov CZ 81 E8
Korentokylä FIN 120 D9
Korentovaara FIN 125 E16
Koretin RKS 164 E4
Korfantów PL 142 F4
Korfos GR 175 D7
Korgen N 108 D6
Korgene LV 131 F9
Korholanmäki FIN 121 F10
Korhosenniemi FIN 121 C12
Koria FIN 128 D6
Korinos GR 169 D7
Korinth DK 86 E6
Korinthos GR 175 D6
Korisia GR 175 D9
Korisos GR 168 D5
Korita BIH 157 D5
Korita BIH 157 F9
Korita HR 162 D4
Korita MNE 163 E8
Korithi GR 174 D2
Korkana FIN 121 F15
Korkatti FIN 119 F15
Korkeakangas FIN 125 F14
Korkeakoski FIN 127 B11
Korkee FIN 122 D5
Körkvere EST 130 E6
Körle D 78 D6
Körmend H 149 B7
Kormista GR 170 C6
Kormu FIN 127 D12
Korna SK 147 C7
Korneichvyi UA 145 D7
Körner D 79 D8
Korneuburg A 77 F10
Kornevo RUS 136 E1
Kórnik PL 81 B12
Kornitsa BG 165 F9
Kornofolia GR 171 B10
Kornos GR 171 E8
Kornsjø N 91 B10
Kornwestheim D 27 C11
Koroleve UA 145 G7
Koromačno HR 67 C9
Koroncó H 149 A9
Koroni GR 178 B2
Koronia GR 174 A2
Koronos GR 177 E6
Koronouda GR 169 C9
Koronowo PL 138 D4
Koropi GR 175 D8
Körösladány H 151 C7
Körössszakál H 151 C8
Körösszegapáti H 151 C8
Köröstarcsa H 151 D7
Koroviya UA 153 A7

Korpela FIN 117 B14
Körperich D 20 E6
Korpi FIN 123 C12
Korpijärvi FIN 119 B13
Korpijoki FIN 123 C16
Korpikå S 119 C10
Korpikylä FIN 119 B11
Korpikylä FIN 121 E12
Korpikylä S 119 B11
Korpilahti FIN 123 F15
Korpilombolo S 116 E10
Korpilompolo FIN 117 E13
Korpinen FIN 121 D10
Korpinen FIN 125 D10
Korpisel'kya RUS 125 F16
Korpivaara FIN 125 E12
Korpo FIN 126 E6
Korpoström FIN 126 E6
Korsåmon S 103 A12
Korsbäck FIN 122 E6
Korsberga S 89 A8
Korsberga S 91 C15
Korsgården S 103 E10
Korsholm FIN 122 D7
Korskrogen S 103 C10
Korsmyrbränna S 106 E8
Korsnäs FIN 122 E6
Korsnes N 111 D11
Korso FIN 127 E13
Korsør DK 87 E8
Korssjön S 118 F5
Korssund N 100 D1
Korsträsk S 118 C5
Korsveggen N 104 E8
Korsvoll N 104 E4
Korsze PL 136 E3
Kortemark B 19 B7
Korten BG 166 D5
Kortenhoef NL 16 D4
Kortesalmi FIN 121 C14
Kortesjärvi FIN 123 D10
Kortessem B 19 C11
Kortevaara FIN 125 B13
Kortgene NL 16 E1
Korthi GR 176 D4
Kortrijk B 19 C7
Kortteenperä FIN 119 B17
Kortteinen FIN 125 D11
Korubaşi TR 171 E10
Korucu TR 173 F7
Koruköy TR 173 C6
Koruköy TR 177 E10
Korva S 119 B11
Korvakumpu FIN 115 D2
Korvala FIN 117 E16
Korvaluoma FIN 126 B8
Kõrveküla EST 131 E13
Korvenkylä FIN 119 D15
Korvenkylä FIN 119 F14
Korvenkylä FIN 123 B12
Korvua FIN 121 D12
Koryčany CZ 77 D12
Korycin PL 140 D8
Koryfasi GR 174 E4
Koryfi GR 169 C8
Korytnica PL 139 F12
Korzenna PL 144 D2
Korzeńsko PL 81 C11
Korzunovo RUS 114 E9
Korzybie PL 85 B11
Kos GR 177 F9
Kosakowo PL 138 A6
Kosanica MNE 163 C7
Košarovce SK 145 E4
Kösching D 75 E10
Kościan PL 81 B11
Kościelec PL 142 B6
Kościelna Wieś PL 142 C5
Kościernica PL 85 B10
Kościerzyna PL 138 B4
Kosd H 150 B3
Kose EST 131 C10
Kose EST 131 F14
Košeca SK 146 C6
Košecké Podhradie SK 146 D6
Kösedere TR 171 E10
Kösedere TR 177 B8
Köseilyas TR 173 B8
Kosel D 82 A7
Koselji BIH 157 E9
Koserow D 84 B6
Košetice CZ 77 C8
Kosharevo BG 165 D6
Koshava BG 159 E11
Košice SK 145 F3
Kosiv UA 152 A6
Kosivs'ka Polyana UA 145 G9
Kosjerić SRB 158 F4
Koška HR 149 E10
Koskama FIN 117 C14
Koskeby FIN 122 D8
Koskela FIN 119 E15
Koskela FIN 123 D11
Koskenkorva FIN 122 E8
Koskenkylä FIN 117 C16
Koskenkylä FIN 121 C14
Koskenkylä FIN 121 F11
Koskenkylä FIN 124 E8
Koskenkylä FIN 126 D7
Koskenmäki FIN 121 F13
Koskenniska FIN 113 F17
Koskenpää FIN 123 F14
Koskenperä FIN 123 C14
Koski FIN 127 D9
Koski FIN 127 E9
Koskimäki FIN 122 E7
Koskinou GR 181 D8
Koskioinen FIN 127 C9
Koškovce SK 145 E4
Koskue FIN 122 F9
Koskullskulle S 116 D5
Koslovets BG 166 C4
Kosmach UA 152 A5
Kosman BIH 157 F10
Kosmas GR 175 E6
Kosmio GR 171 B8
Kosmonosy CZ 77 B7
Kosola FIN 122 D9
Kosova Hora CZ 77 C6
Kosovo HR 156 E5
Kosovska Kamenicë RKS 164 D4
Kosów Lacki PL 141 E6
Koßdorf D 80 D4
Kössen A 72 A5
Kosta GR 175 E7
Kosta S 89 B8
Kostakioi GR 174 A2
Košťálov CZ 81 E8
Kostamo FIN 115 E2
Kostandenets BG 166 B6
Kostandovo BG 165 E9
Kostanjevac HR 148 E4
Kostanjevica SLO 148 E4
Kostel SLO 67 A10
Kostelec nad Černými Lesy CZ 77 C7
Kostelec nad Orlicí CZ 77 B10
Kostelec na Hané CZ 77 C12
Kostenets BG 165 E8
Kostenets BG 165 E8
Kostice CZ 77 E11
Kostinbrod BG 165 D7
Kostolac SRB 159 D7
Kostolné Kračany SK 146 F5
Kostomłoty PL 81 D11
Kostomuksha RUS 121 E16
Kostrzyn PL 81 A7
Kostrzyn PL 81 B12
Kostyzhitsy RUS 132 F6
Kosula FIN 125 E11
Košute HR 157 E6
Kosy UA 154 B5
Kosyny UA 145 G5
Koszalin PL 85 B10
Koszęcin PL 142 E6
Kőszeg H 149 B7
Koszyce PL 143 F10
Kotajärvi FIN 119 D15
Kotala FIN 115 D5
Kotala FIN 123 F12
Kotalanperä FIN 119 D15
Kotas GR 168 C5
Kotë AL 168 D2
Kötegyán H 151 D7
Kotel BG 167 D6
Kőtelek H 150 C5
Kotelow D 84 C5
Kotešová SK 147 C7
Köthen (Anhalt) D 79 C10
Kotikylä FIN 124 D8
Kotila FIN 121 E10
Kotiranta FIN 121 E13
Kotka FIN 128 E6
Kotlin PL 142 C4
Kotly RUS 132 B4
Kotor MNE 163 E6
Kotoriba HR 149 D7
Kotorsko BIH 157 C9
Kotor Varoš BIH 157 C7
Kotraža SRB 158 F5
Kotronas GR 178 B3
Kötschach A 73 C7
Kotsøy N 105 F9
Kottenheim D 185 D7
Kottes A 77 F8
Köttmannsdorf A 73 C9
Köttsjön S 107 E10
Kotuń PL 141 F6
Koudekerke NL 16 F1
Koudum NL 16 C4
Koufalia GR 169 C8
Koufovouno GR 171 B10
Kougsta S 105 E15
Kouklioi GR 168 E4
Koumanis GR 174 D4
Koura FIN 123 E10
Kouřim CZ 77 C7
Kourkouloi GR 175 B7
Kournas GR 178 E7
Koutaniemi FIN 121 F10
Koutojärvi S 119 B10
Koutsochero GR 169 E7
Koutsopodi GR 175 D6
Koutsouras GR 179 E10
Koutus FIN 117 E12
Kouva FIN 121 C10
Kouvola FIN 128 D6
Kovachevets BG 166 C6
Kovachevitsa BG 165 F8
Kovachevo BG 166 E6
Kovachevtsi BG 165 D6
Kovachitsa BG 160 F2
Kovači BIH 157 E7
Kovačica SRB 158 C6
Kővágószőlős H 149 D10
Kovallberget S 107 B13
Kovanj BIH 157 E10
Kovarce SK 146 E6
Kovářov CZ 76 C6
Kovdor RUS 115 C8
Kovelahti FIN 126 B8
Kovero FIN 125 E15
Kovilj SRB 158 C5
Kovin SRB 159 D6
Kovjoki FIN 122 C9
Kovland S 103 B13
Kövra S 102 A7
Kovren MNE 163 C8
Kowal PL 139 E7
Kowala-Stępocina PL 141 H4
Kowale PL 142 D5
Kowale Oleckie PL 136 E5
Kowale-Pańskie PL 142 C6
Kowalewo Pomorskie PL 138 D6
Kowalów PL 81 B7
Kowary PL 81 E9
Kowiesy PL 141 G2
Köyceğiz TR 181 C9
Köyhäjoki FIN 123 C11
Köyliö FIN 126 C7
Koynare BG 165 C9
Koyundere TR 177 B9
Koyunyeri TR 171 C10
Kozani GR 169 D6
Kozarac BIH 157 C6
Kozarac HR 149 E11
Kozar Belene BG 166 C4
Kozármisleny H 149 D10
Kozárovce SK 147 E7
Kozçeşme TR 173 D6
Kozica HR 157 F7
Koziegłowy PL 143 E7
Kozielice PL 85 D7
Kozienice PL 141 G5
Kozina SLO 73 E8
Kožlany CZ 76 C5
Kozloduy BG 160 F3
Kozłów Biskupi PL 141 F2
Kozłowo PL 139 D9
Kozluk BIH 157 C11
Kozły PL 139 F11
Koźminek PL 142 C5
Koźmin Wielkopolski PL 142 C3
Koz'ove UA 145 F7
Kozubszczyzna PL 141 H6
Kożuchów PL 81 C9
Kožuhe BIH 157 C9
Kozy PL 147 B8
Kozyörük TR 173 B6
Krabbendijke NL 16 F2
Krabi EST 131 F13
Kräckelbäcken S 102 C7
Krackow D 84 D6
Kraddsele S 109 E12
Kraftsdorf D 79 E10
Krag PL 85 B11
Kragelund DK 86 C4
Kragerø N 90 B5
Kragi PL 85 C11
Kragujevac SRB 159 E6
Kraj HR 156 E6
Kraj HR 157 F7
Krajenka PL 85 D12
Krajišnik SRB 159 C6
Krajnik Dolny PL 84 D6
Krakača BIH 156 B4
Kråkberget N 110 C8
Kråken S 122 C3
Kråkenes N 100 B2
Kråkerøy N 91 A8
Krakės LT 134 F7
Krakhella N 100 D2
Kråklingbo S 93 E13
Kråklivollen N 105 E9
Kråkmoen N 111 E10
Krakovets' UA 144 D7
Kraków PL 143 F8
Krakow am See D 83 C12
Kråksmåla S 89 A9
Kråkstad N 95 C13
Kralevo BG 167 C7
Králíky CZ 77 B11
Kraljeva BIH 157 D9
Kraljevica HR 67 B10
Kraljevo SRB 158 F6
Kralovice CZ 76 C4
Kráľovský Chlmec SK 145 G4
Kralupy nad Vltavou CZ 76 B6
Králův Dvůr CZ 76 C6
Kramarzyny PL 85 B12
Kramfors S 103 A14
Kramolin BG 166 C4
Krampenes N 114 C8
Kramsach A 72 B4
Kramsk PL 142 B5
Kramvik N 114 C9
Kranenburg D 16 E6
Kranevo BG 167 C10
Krångfors S 118 E4
Krania GR 168 E5
Krania Elassonas GR 169 E6
Kranichfeld D 79 E9
Kranidi GR 175 E7
Kranj SLO 73 D9
Kranjska Gora SLO 73 D8
Krapanj HR 156 E4
Krapets BG 155 F3
Krąpiel PL 85 D8
Krapina HR 148 D5
Krapinske Toplice HR 148 D5
Krapkowice PL 142 F4
Krašić HR 148 E5
Krasiczyn PL 144 D6
Krasiv UA 145 D8
Krāslava LV 133 E2
Kraslice CZ 75 B12
Krasnagorka BY 133 E2
Krásná Hora nad Vltavou CZ 76 C6
Krasnapollye BY 133 E6
Krasne PL 139 E10
Krasne PL 144 C5
Krasne UA 154 E4
Kraśniczyn PL 144 B7
Kraśnik PL 144 B5
Krasni Okny UA 154 B4
Krasnobród PL 144 B7
Krasnogorodskoye RUS 133 C4
Krásnohorské Podhradie SK 145 F2
Krasnoles'ye RUS 136 E5
Krásno nad Kysucou SK 147 C7
Krasnopol PL 136 E7
Krasno Polje HR 67 C11
Krasnosel'skoye RUS 129 D11
Krasnosielc PL 139 D11
Krasnovo BG 165 E9
Krasnoyil's'k UA 153 A7
Krasnoznamensk RUS 136 D5
Krasnystaw PL 144 B7
Krasocin PL 143 E9
Krastë AL 168 B3
Kraszewice PL 142 C5
Kraszewo PL 136 E2
Kratigos GR 177 A8
Kratiškiai LT 135 D9
Kratovo MK 164 E5
Kratte masugn S 98 B6
Krauchenwies D 27 D11
Krauja LV 135 E13
Kraujas LV 135 D11
Kraukļi LV 135 B12
Krauschwitz D 81 C7
Krautheim D 74 D6
Kravaře CZ 142 G4
Kravarsko HR 148 E6
Kravoder BG 165 C7
Kraymorie BG 167 E8
Kražiai LT 134 E5
Krčina BIH 157 C11
Krefeld D 17 F7
Kreiensen D 78 C6
Krekenava LT 135 E8
Krekhovychi UA 145 E9
Krekilä FIN 123 C11
Kremasti GR 181 D8
Kremen BG 165 F8
Kremena BG 155 F2
Kremintsi UA 152 A5
Kremmydia GR 174 F4
Kremna SRB 158 F4
Kremnica SK 147 D7
Krempe D 82 C7
Kremperheide D 17 A12
Krempna PL 145 D4
Krems an der Donau A 77 F9
Kremsbrücke A 73 C8
Kremsmünster A 76 F6
Křepice CZ 77 E11
Krepoljin SRB 159 E8
Kreševo BIH 157 E9
Kreshpan AL 168 C2
Křešice CZ 76 A6
Kresna BG 165 F7
Kresnice SLO 73 D10
Kressbronn am Bodensee D 71 B9
Krestena GR 174 D4
Kretinga LT 134 E2
Kretingalė LT 134 E2
Kreuth D 72 A4
Kreuzau D 20 C6
Kreuzlingen CH 27 E11
Kreuztal D 21 C9
Kreuzwertheim D 74 C6
Kreva BY 137 E13
Krezluk BIH 157 D7
Krichim BG 165 E9
Krieglach A 148 A5
Kriegstetten CH 27 F8
Krien D 84 C4
Kriens CH 70 C6
Krievciems LV 134 B3
Krieza GR 175 C9
Krikello GR 174 B4
Krikellos GR 174 B3
Krimpen aan de IJssel NL 16 E3
Krimūnas LV 134 C6
Křinec CZ 77 B8
Krinida GR 170 C5
Krinides GR 171 B6
Kriškalni LV 135 C11
Kriškovci BIH 157 C7
Kristberg S 92 B6
Kristdala S 93 E8
Kristiansand N 90 C2
Kristianstad S 88 C6
Kristiansund N 104 E3
Kristiinankaupunki FIN 122 F6
Kristineberg S 107 A15
Kristinefors S 97 B8
Kristinehamn S 97 D11
Kristinestad FIN 122 F6
Kristoni GR 169 C8
Kristvallabrunn S 89 B10
Kritinia GR 181 D7
Kritsa GR 179 E10
Kritzmow D 83 B12
Kriukai LT 134 D7
Kriūkai LT 137 C7
Kriva Bara BG 159 F11
Krivača BIH 157 G9
Kriva Feja SRB 164 D5
Krivaja BIH 157 D9
Kriváň SK 147 D8
Krivany SK 145 E2
Kriva Palanka MK 164 E5
Krivelj SRB 159 E9
Krivi Put HR 67 B10
Krivi Vir SRB 159 F8
Krivodol BG 165 C7
Krivogaštani MK 168 B5
Krivolak MK 169 A7
Križ HR 149 E7
Křižanov CZ 77 D10
Križevci HR 149 D7
Křížová CZ 77 C9
Križpolje HR 67 B11
Krk HR 67 B10
Krka SLO 73 E10
Krmčina HR 156 D3
Krnča SK 146 D6
Krnica HR 67 C9
Krnjača SRB 158 D6
Krnja Jela MNE 163 D7
Krnjak HR 148 F5
Krnjeuša BIH 156 C5
Krnjevo SRB 159 E7
Krnov CZ 142 F4
Krobia PL 81 C11
Kroczyce PL 143 E8
Krøderen N 95 B11
Krofdorf Gleiberg D 21 C11
Krog S 103 B9
Krögis D 80 D4
Krok S 105 E14
Krokees GR 175 F6
Krokeide N 94 B2
Krokek S 93 B8
Kroken N 100 D6
Kroken N 108 F7
Krokfors S 108 E9
Krokfors S 118 B5
Krokio GR 175 A6
Kroknäs S 102 A8
Kroknes N 114 C9
Krokom S 106 E6
Krokos GR 169 D6
Krokowa PL 138 A5
Kroksjö S 107 B13
Kroksjö S 107 D15
Kroksjö S 118 F4
Krokstadelva N 95 C12
Krokstadøra N 104 E7
Krokstranda N 108 D9
Krokströmmen S 102 B8
Kroktjärn S 118 B4
Krokträsk S 118 C6
Królowy Most PL 140 D8
Krölpa D 79 E10
Kroměříž CZ 146 C4
Krommenie NL 16 C3
Krompachy SK 145 F2
Kromsdorf D 79 E9
Kronach D 75 B9
Kronau D 187 C6
Kronauce LV 134 C6
Kronberg im Taunus D 187 A5
Kronlund S 109 E14
Kronoby FIN 123 C10
Kronprinzenkoog D 82 C5
Kronshagen D 83 B8
Kronshtadt RUS 129 F12
Kronstorf A 77 F6
Kropa SLO 73 D9
Kröpelin D 83 B11
Kropp D 82 B7
Kroppenstedt D 79 C9
Kropstädt D 79 C12
Krościenko nad Dunajcem PL 145 E1
Kröslin D 84 B5
Krosna LT 137 E8
Krośnice PL 81 D12
Krośniewice PL 143 B7
Krosno PL 144 D4
Krosno Odrzańskie PL 81 B8
Krossen D 79 E10
Krossen N 90 C2
Krossen N 95 C8
Krossmoen N 94 E4
Krostitz D 79 D11
Krote LV 134 C3
Krotoszyce PL 81 D10
Krotoszyn PL 142 C3
Krottendorf A 148 B5
Krouna CZ 77 C10
Krousonas GR 178 E8
Kröv D 21 E8
Krovik S 111 E19
Krovyli GR 171 C9
Krrabë AL 168 B2
Krš HR 156 C3
Kršan HR 67 B9
Krško SLO 148 E4
Krstac MNE 157 F10
Krstinja HR 156 B4
Krtova BIH 157 C9
Kruchowo PL 138 E4
Krüden D 83 E11
Kruft D 185 D7
Kruibeke B 19 B9
Kruiningen NL 16 F2
Kruishoutem B 19 C8
Krujë AL 168 A2
Krukenychi UA 144 D7
Kruklanki PL 136 E4
Krukowo PL 139 D11
Krumbach A 71 C9
Krumbach A 148 A6
Krumbach (Schwaben) D 71 A10
Krumë AL 163 E9
Krummesse D 83 C9
Krumovgrad BG 171 B9
Krumovo BG 165 E10
Krumovo BG 166 E6
Krumpa (Geiseltal) D 79 D10
Krumvíř CZ 77 E11
Krün D 72 A3
Krunderup DK 86 C3
Kruonis LT 137 D9
Kruopiai LT 134 D6
Krupac BIH 157 E9
Krupac SRB 165 C6
Krupa na Vrbasu BIH 157 C7
Krupanj SRB 158 E3
Krupava BY 137 F11
Krupe PL 144 A7
Krupina SK 147 E8
Krupište MK 164 F5
Krupka CZ 80 E5
Krupnik BG 165 F7
Kruså DK 82 A6
Kruševac SRB 164 B3
Kruševica SRB 158 E5
Kruševo MK 168 B5
Kruševo Grdo BIH 157 D8
Krushari BG 155 F1
Krushë e Madhe RKS 164 E2
Krushel'nytsya UA 145 E8
Krushevets BG 167 E8
Krushevo BG 166 C4
Krushovene BG 160 F4
Krushovitsa BG 160 F3
Krušovce SK 146 D6
Kruszewo PL 85 E11
Kruszwica PL 138 E5
Kruszyna PL 85 B12
Kruszyna PL 143 E7
Krutådal N 108 E7
Krute MNE 163 F7
Kruunupyy FIN 123 C10
Kružlov SK 145 E3
Krya Vrysi GR 169 C7
Kryekuq AL 168 C2
Kryezi AL 163 E9
Kryłów PL 144 B9
Krynica PL 145 E2
Krynica Morska PL 139 B7
Krynice PL 144 B7
Krynki PL 140 D9
Krynychne UA 155 B3
Kryoneri GR 175 D6
Kryoneritis GR 175 B7
Kryopigi GR 169 D9
Krypno Kościelne PL 140 D7
Kryry CZ 76 B4
Krystad N 110 D5
Krystallopigi GR 168 C5
Kryva Balka UA 154 E5
Kryve Ozero UA 154 B6
Kryvorivnya UA 152 A5
Kryzhopil' UA 154 A3
Kržanja MNE 163 D7
Krzanowice PL 142 F5
Krzątka PL 144 C4
Krzczonów-Wójtostwo PL 144 A6
Krzcin PL 85 D9
Krzelów PL 81 D11
Krzemieniewo PL 81 C11
Krzepice PL 142 E6
Krzepielów PL 81 C10
Krzesk-Królowa Niwa PL 141 F7
Krzeszów PL 81 E10
Krzeszów PL 144 C5
Krzeszowice PL 143 F8
Krzeszyce PL 81 A8
Krzętów PL 143 E8
Krzykosy PL 81 B12
Krzynowłoga Mała PL 139 D10
Krzystkowice PL 81 C8
Krzywcza PL 144 D6
Krzywda PL 141 G6
Krzywiń PL 81 C11
Krzywin PL 84 D6
Krzywowierzba PL 141 G8
Krzyżanów PL 143 B7
Krzyżanowice PL 141 H4
Krzyżanowice PL 146 B6
KrzyżKrzyż PL 85 E10
Ksar Sghir MA 53 E5
Książ Wielki PL 143 F9
Książ Wielkopolski PL 81 B12
Księżpol PL 144 C6
Kubanovka RUS 136 D5
Kubbe S 107 D14
Kübekháza H 150 E5
Kublichy BY 133 F4
Küblis CH 71 D9
Kubrat BG 161 F8
Kubuli LV 133 B2
Kuç AL 168 D2
Kučevo SRB 159 E8
Kuchen D 74 E6
Kuchl A 73 A7
Kuchurhan UA 154 D5
Kuchyňa SK 77 F12
Kucice PL 139 E9
Kuciny PL 143 C7
Kučište HR 162 D3
Kuçovë AL 168 C2
Küçükanafarta TR 171 D10
Küçükbahçe TR 177 B7
Küçükçekmece TR 173 B10
Küçükkarıştıran TR 173 B7
Küçükkemerdere TR 177 C10
Küçükköy TR 172 F6
Küçükkumla TR 173 D11
Küçükkuyu TR 172 E6
Küçükyoncali TR 173 B8
Kucura SRB 158 B4
Kuczbork-Osada PL 139 D9
Kudever' RUS 133 C6
Kudirkos Naumiestis LT 136 D6
Kudowa-Zdrój PL 77 B10
Kūdums LV 135 B10
Kufstein A 72 A5
Kuggerud N 96 B6
Kuggören S 103 C14
Kuha FIN 119 C17
Kuhakoski FIN 129 B9
Kühbach D 75 F9
Kuhbier D 83 D12
Kuhfelde D 83 E10
Kühlungsborn D 83 B11
Kuhmalahti FIN 127 B12
Kuhmo FIN 121 F14
Kuhmoinen FIN 127 B13
Kühndorf D 79 E7
Kühren D 79 D12
Kuhs D 83 C12
Kuhstedt D 17 B11
Kuijõe EST 131 C7
Kuimetsa EST 131 C10
Kuinre NL 16 C5
Kuivajärvi FIN 121 E15
Kuivajõe EST 131 C10
Kuivakangas S 119 B11
Kuivalahti FIN 126 C6
Kuivaniemi FIN 119 C14
Kuivanto FIN 127 D15
Kuivasjärvi FIN 123 F9
Kuivastu EST 130 D6
Kujakowice Dolne PL 142 D5
Kūkas LV 135 C12
Kukasjärvi FIN 117 D15
Kukasjärvi S 119 B10
Kukës AL 163 E9
Kukko FIN 123 E12
Kukkola FIN 119 C12
Kukkola S 119 C12
Kuklen BG 165 E10
Kuklin PL 139 D9
Kuklinów PL 81 C12
Kukliš MK 169 B8
Kukljić HR 156 D4
Kukljica HR 156 D3
Kukljin SRB 164 B3
Kukmirn A 148 B6
Kukruse EST 131 C14
Kuktiškės LT 135 F11
Kukulje BIH 157 C7
Kukur AL 168 C3
Kukurečani MK 168 B5
Kula BG 159 F9
Kula HR 149 F9
Kula SRB 158 B4
Kulaši BIH 157 C8
Kulata BG 169 B9
Kulautuva LT 137 D8
Kūlciems LV 134 B6
Kuldīga LV 134 C3
Külefli TR 173 D8
Kuleli TR 173 B6
Kulennoinen FIN 129 B11
Kulen Vakuf BIH 156 C5
Kulesze PL 140 D7
Kulho FIN 125 E13
Kulia N 105 D9
Kuliai LT 134 E3
Kulju FIN 127 C10
Kullaa FIN 126 C7
Kullamaa EST 131 D8
Kulleseid N 94 C2
Kulltorp S 88 A5
Kulmain D 75 C10
Kulmbach D 75 B9
Kuloharju FIN 121 C11
Külsheim D 27 A12
Kultima FIN 116 B9
Kuluntalahti FIN 121 F10
Kulūpėnai LT 134 E2
Kulva LT 137 C9
Kulvemäki FIN 124 C9
Kulykiv UA 144 D9
Kumachevo RUS 139 A9
Kumane SRB 158 B5
Kumanica SRB 163 C9
Kumanovo MK 164 E4
Kumbağ TR 173 C7
Kumberg A 148 B5
Kumbri LV 134 C4
Kumbuļi LV 135 E13
Kumburun TR 171 E10
Kumhausen D 75 E11
Kumkadi TR 173 D9
Kumkale TR 171 E10
Kumköy TR 173 B11
Kumla S 92 A6
Kumla kyrkby S 98 C7
Kumlinge FIN 99 B15
Kummer D 83 D10
Kummerow D 83 C13
Kummersdorf-Alexanderdorf D 80 B4
Kummersdorf Gut D 80 B4
Kummunkylä FIN 123 D16
Kumpuranta FIN 125 G12
Kumpuselkä FIN 123 D16
Kumpuvaara FIN 119 C18
Kumrovec HR 148 D5
Kunadacs H 150 D3
Kunágota H 151 E7
Kunbaja H 150 E3
Kunbaracs H 150 D3
Kunčina CZ 77 C11
Kunda EST 131 B13
Kunes N 113 C18
Kunfehértó H 150 E3
Kungälv S 91 D10
Kungas FIN 123 C11
Kungsängen S 99 D9
Kungsäter S 88 A3
Kungsbacka S 91 E11
Kungsberg S 103 E11
Kungsfors S 103 E13
Kungsgården S 103 D12
Kungsgården S 103 E12
Kungshamn S 91 C9
Kungshult S 87 D12
Kungsör S 98 D6
Kunhegyes H 150 C6
Kunice PL 81 D10
Kunín CZ 146 B5
Kuningaküla EST 132 C2
Kuniów PL 142 E5
Kunmadaras H 150 C6
Kunovice CZ 146 C4
Kunowice PL 81 B7
Kunowo PL 81 C12
Kunpeszér H 150 C3
Kunrade NL 183 D7
Kunrau D 79 A9
Kunštát CZ 77 C11
Kunszállás H 150 D4
Kunszentmárton H 150 D5
Kunszentmiklós H 150 C3
Kunsziget H 149 A9
Kunvald CZ 77 B11
Kunžak CZ 77 D8
Künzell D 74 A6
Künzelsau D 74 D6
Künzing D 76 E4
Kuohatti FIN 125 C12
Kuohu FIN 123 F14
Kuoksajärvi FIN 117 E15
Kuoksu S 116 C7
Kuolayarvi RUS 115 E6
Kuolio FIN 121 C12
Kuomiokoski FIN 128 C7
Kuona FIN 123 C15
Kuopio FIN 124 E9
Kuoppala FIN 122 D9
Kuorevesi FIN 127 B12
Kuortane FIN 123 E11
Kuortti FIN 127 C15
Kuosku FIN 115 D4
Kuossakåbba S 116 D4
Kuouka S 116 E5
Kup PL 142 E4
Kupari HR 162 D5
Küpeler TR 173 E8
Kupferberg D 75 B10
Kupferzell D 74 D6
Kupientyn PL 141 F6
Kupinec HR 148 E5
Kupinovo SRB 158 D5
Kupiškis LT 135 E9
Kupjak HR 67 B10
Küplü TR 171 B10
Kuppenheim D 27 C9
Kuprava LV 133 B3
Kupres BIH 157 D7
Kuprešani BIH 157 D7
Kups D 75 B9
Kurapollye BY 135 F13
Kuratën AL 168 B2
Kurbnesh AL 163 F9
Kurd H 149 D10
Kŭrdzhali BG 171 A8
Kurejoki FIN 123 D11
Kuremaa EST 131 D13
Kuremäe EST 132 C2
Kuressaare EST 130 E4
Kurevere EST 130 E3
Kurienkylä FIN 123 F10
Kurikka FIN 122 E8
Kuřim CZ 77 D11
Kurima SK 145 E3
Kurjala FIN 125 E10
Kurjan AL 168 C2
Kurki FIN 121 D10
Kurkiharju FIN 125 E9
Kurkikylä FIN 121 D11
Kurkimäki FIN 124 E9
Kurmene LV 135 D9
Kürnach D 187 B9
Kŭrnare BG 165 D10
Kürnbach D 27 B10
Kurolanlahti FIN 124 D8
Kuropta RUS 115 D9
Kurort Bad Gottleuba D 80 E5
Kurort Kipsdorf D 80 E5
Kurort Oberwiesenthal D 76 B3
Kurort Schmalkalden D 79 E7
Kurort Steinbach-Hallenberg D 79 E8
Kurów PL 141 H6
Kurowice PL 143 C8
Kurravaara S 116 C4
Kurrokvejk S 109 E14
Kuršėnai LT 134 D5
Kursīši LV 134 D4
Kursu FIN 115 E4
Kuršumlija SRB 164 C3
Kuršumlijska Banja SRB 164 C3
Kurtakko FIN 117 D12
Kurtbey TR 172 B6
Kurtna EST 132 C2
Kurtovo Konare BG 165 E9
Kurtti FIN 121 D11
Kurtto FIN 121 E11
Kurtzea E 40 B6
Kuru FIN 127 B10
Kurvinen FIN 121 C14
Kuryłówka PL 144 C5
Kurzelów PL 143 E8
Kurzeszyn PL 141 G2
Kurzętnik PL 139 D8
Kusa LV 135 C12
Kusadak SRB 159 E6
Kuşadasi TR 177 D9
Kuşçayir TR 172 E6
Kusel D 21 E8
Kusey D 79 A9
Kusfors S 118 E4
Kushnytsya UA 145 G7
Kušići SRB 163 C9
Kuside MNE 163 D6
Kuślin PL 81 B10
Kusmark S 118 E5
Küsnacht CH 27 F10
Küssnacht CH 27 F9
Kustavi FIN 126 D5
Küsten D 83 E10
Kusterdingen D 27 C11
Kuštilj SRB 159 C7
Kuta BIH 157 E10
Kutalli AL 168 C2
Kutas H 149 D8
Kutemajärvi FIN 124 F7
Kutenholz D 17 B12
Kuti MNE 163 D8
Kutina HR 149 F7
Kutjevo HR 149 F9
Kutlovo SRB 159 E6
Kutná Hora CZ 77 C8
Kutno PL 143 B7
Kutrikko FIN 115 E3
Kuttainen S 116 B9
Kuttanen FIN 116 B9
Kuttura FIN 117 B16
Kúty SK 77 E12
Kuty UA 153 A7
Kuukasjärvi FIN 119 C17
Kuumu FIN 121 E14
Kuurne B 19 C7
Kuurtola FIN 121 D12
Kuusaa FIN 123 C15
Kuusaa FIN 123 F15
Kuusajärvi FIN 117 C14
Kuusajoki FIN 117 C14
Kuusalu EST 131 C10
Kuusamo FIN 121 C13
Kuusamonkylä FIN 121 F13
Kuusankoski FIN 128 D6
Kuusijärvi FIN 121 D11
Kuusijoki FIN 126 B8
Kuusiku EST 131 D9
Kuusiranta FIN 120 F9
Kuusirati FIN 119 F14
Kuusivaara FIN 115 E2
Kuusjärvi FIN 125 E11
Kuusjoki FIN 127 D9
Kuuslahti FIN 124 D9
Kuvansi FIN 125 F9
Kuvaskangas FIN 126 B6
Kuyka UA 153 A7
Kuyvozi RUS 129 E13
Kužiai LT 134 E6
Kuzmice SK 145 F4

Kuzmin *SRB* 158 C3
Kuźmina *PL* 145 D5
Kuz'molovskiy *RUS* 129 E13
Kuznechnoye *RUS* 129 C12
Kuźnia Raciborska *PL* 142 F5
Kuźnica *PL* 140 C7
Kuźnica Czarnkowska *PL* 85 E11
Kväcklingen *S* 103 A12
Kværkeby *DK* 87 E9
Kværndrup *DK* 86 E7
Kvalfors *N* 108 E5
Kvalnes *N* 110 D6
Kvalnes *N* 110 E8
Kvalnes *N* 111 B11
Kvalnes *N* 114 C8
Kvaløyhamn *N* 108 E3
Kvaløysletta *N* 111 A16
Kvaløyvågen *N* 111 A16
Kvalsaukan *N* 111 C10
Kvalsund *N* 113 B12
Kvalsvik *N* 100 B3
Kvalvåg *N* 104 E3
Kvam *N* 101 C11
Kvannås *N* 111 B14
Kvanndal *N* 94 F5
Kvanne *N* 101 A9
Kvannli *N* 105 A14
Kvarnberg *N* 102 D8
Kvarnbyn *S* 118 F4
Kvarnriset *S* 118 F5
Kvarnsand *S* 99 B11
Kvarnsjö *S* 102 A7
Kvarntäkt *S* 103 E10
Kvarntorp *S* 92 A6
Kvarv *N* 108 B8
Kvarv *N* 109 B10
Kvasice *CZ* 146 C4
Kvasy *UA* 152 A4
Kveaune *N* 105 C15
Kvédarna *LT* 134 E3
Kveinsjøen *N* 105 A12
Kvelde *N* 90 A6
Kveli *N* 105 B15
Kvenvær *N* 104 D4
Kvevlax *FIN* 122 D7
Kvibille *S* 87 B11
Kvicksund *S* 98 D6
Kvidinge *S* 87 C12
Kvikkjokk *S* 109 C14
Kvillsfors *S* 92 E7
Kvinesdal *N* 94 F5
Kvinlog *N* 94 E5
Kvissleby *S* 103 B13
Kvisvik *N* 104 E3
Kvitblik *N* 109 B10
Kviteberg *N* 112 D8
Kviteseid *N* 95 D8
Kvitnes *N* 110 E8
Kvitnes *N* 112 C5
Kvitsøy *N* 94 F3
Kvívík *FO* 2 A2
Kvorning *DK* 86 C5
Kwaadmechelen *B* 19 B11
Kwidzyn *PL* 138 C6
Kwieciszewo *PL* 138 E5
Kwilcz *PL* 81 A10
Kyan *S* 103 D10
Kybartai *LT* 136 D6
Kycklingvattnet *S* 105 B16
Kydrasivka *UA* 154 A5
Kyjov *CZ* 77 D12
Kylänpää *FIN* 122 E8
Kylänlahti *FIN* 125 D13
Kyläsaari *FIN* 126 B6
Kyleakin *GB* 2 L5
Kyle of Lochalsh *GB* 2 L5
Kylerhea *GB* 2 L5
Kylestrome *GB* 2 J6
Kylland *N* 90 B1
Kyllburg *D* 21 D7
Kyllini *GR* 174 D3
Kylmäkoski *FIN* 127 C10
Kylmälä *FIN* 119 E16
Kymi *GR* 175 B9
Kymina *GR* 169 C8
Kyminlinna *FIN* 128 D6
Kymönkoski *FIN* 123 D15
Kyndby Huse *DK* 87 D9
Kyngäs *FIN* 119 D17
Kynsiperä *FIN* 121 C11
Kynsivaara *FIN* 121 C11
Kynšperk nad Ohří *CZ* 75 B12
Kypäräivaara *FIN* 121 E12
Kyparissia *GR* 174 E4
Kypasjärv *S* 119 B10
Kyprinos *GR* 171 A10
Kypseli *GR* 175 D7
Kyrgia *GR* 171 B6
Kyriaki *GR* 175 C6
Kyritz *D* 83 E12
Kyrkås *S* 106 E7
Kyrkhult *S* 88 C7
Kyrksæterøra *N* 104 E6
Kyrkslätt *FIN* 127 E11
Kyrksten *S* 97 D11
Kyrnychky *UA* 155 C4
Kyröskoski *FIN* 127 B9
Kyrsyä *FIN* 129 B9
Kyslytsya *UA* 155 C4
Kysucké Nové Mesto *SK* 147 C7
Kysucký Lieskovec *SK* 147 C7
Kytäjä *FIN* 127 D12
Kythira *GR* 178 B3
Kythnos *GR* 175 E9
Kytökylä *FIN* 119 F15
Kytömäki *FIN* 121 E11
Kyustendil *BG* 165 E6
Kyyjärvi *FIN* 123 D13
Kyynämöinen *FIN* 123 F14
Kyynärö *FIN* 127 C12

L

Laa an der Thaya *A* 77 E10
Laaber *D* 75 D10
La Adrada *E* 46 D3
Laage *D* 83 C12
Laagri *EST* 131 C9
Laaja *FIN* 121 E12
Laajoki *FIN* 126 D7
Laakajärvi *FIN* 125 C10
La Alberca *E* 45 C8
La Alberca *E* 56 F2
La Alberca de Záncara *E* 47 E8
La Alberguería de Argañán
    E 45 D7
La Albuera *E* 51 B6
La Aldehuela *E* 45 D10
La Algaba *E* 51 D7
La Aliseda de Tormes *E* 45 D10
La Aljorra *E* 56 F2

La Almarcha *E* 47 E8
La Almolda *E* 42 D3
La Almunia de Doña Godina
    E 41 F9
Laanila *FIN* 115 B2
Lääniste *EST* 131 E14
La Antilla *E* 51 E5
Laapas *FIN* 128 D8
Laarkirchen *A* 76 G5
Laarne *B* 19 B8
Laasala *FIN* 123 E12
Laaslich *D* 83 D11
Laatre *EST* 131 E10
Laatre *EST* 131 F12
Laatzen *D* 78 B6
Laax *CH* 71 D8
La Azohía *E* 56 F2
La Baconnière *F* 23 D10
Labajos *E* 46 C3
La Balme-de-Sillingy *F* 31 D9
La Bañeza *E* 39 D8
Labanoras *LT* 135 F11
La Barre-de-Monts *F* 28 B1
La Barre-en-Ouche *F* 24 D4
La Barthe-de-Neste *F* 33 D6
Labarthe-Rivière *F* 33 D7
La Bassée *F* 18 C6
La Bastide-Clairence *F* 32 D3
Labastide-d'Anjou *F* 33 D9
Labastide-d'Armagnac *F* 32 C5
La Bastide-de Bousignac
    F 33 D9
La Bastide-de-Sérou *F* 33 D8
La Bastide-l'Évêque *F* 33 B10
Labastide-Murat *F* 33 A9
La Bastide-Puylaurent *F* 35 A6
Labastide-Rouairoux *F* 34 D4
Labastide-St-Pierre *F* 33 C8
La Bastide-sur-l'Hers *F* 33 E9
La Bâthie *F* 31 D9
La Bâtie-Neuve *F* 36 B4
Lábatlan *H* 149 A10
Labatut-Rivière *F* 32 C6
La Baule-Escoublac *F* 23 F7
La Bazoche-Gouet *F* 24 D4
La Bazoge *F* 23 D12
L'Abbaye *CH* 31 B9
Labégude *F* 35 A7
La Bégude-de-Mazenc *F* 35 A8
Labenne *F* 32 C3
La Bérarde *F* 31 F9
Labergement-lès-Seurre *F* 31 A7
Laberget *N* 111 C13
La Bernerie-en-Retz *F* 28 A1
Laberweinting *D* 75 E11
Labin *HR* 67 B9
La Bisbal de Falset *E* 42 E5
La Bisbal del Penedès *E* 43 E6
La Bisbal d'Empordà *E* 43 D10
Łabiszyn *PL* 138 E4
Lablachère *F* 35 A7
Laboe *D* 83 B8
La Bonneville-sur-Iton *F* 24 C5
La Bouëxière *F* 23 D9
Labouheyre *F* 32 B4
La Bouilladisse *F* 35 D10
La Bourboule *F* 30 D2
Laboutarie *F* 33 C10
La Bóveda de Toro *E* 39 F9
Ladi *GR* 171 B10
Ladignac-le-Long *F* 29 D8
La Brède *F* 32 A4
Le Brôle *F* 36 C4
La Bresse *F* 27 D6
La Brillanne *F* 35 C10
Labrit *F* 32 B4
La Broque *F* 27 D7
La Bruffière *F* 28 A3
Labruguière *F* 33 C10
L'Absie *F* 28 B4
La Buisse *F* 31 E8
Łabunie *PL* 144 B7
La Bussière *F* 25 E8
Läby *S* 99 B9
Laç *AL* 163 F8
Laç *AL* 168 A2
La Cabrera *E* 46 C5
La Caillère-St-Hilaire *F* 28 B4
Lacalahorra *E* 55 E6
La Caletta *I* 64 B4
Lacalm *F* 30 F2
La Calmette *F* 35 C7
La Calzada de Oropesa *E* 45 E10
La Campana *E* 51 D9
La Cañada de San Urbano
    E 55 F8
La Cañada de Verich *E* 42 F3
Lacanau *F* 28 F3
Lacanau-Océan *F* 28 E3
Lacanche *F* 25 F12
La Canourgue *F* 34 B5
La Capelle *F* 19 E8
Lacapelle-Barrès *F* 30 F2
Lacapelle-Marival *F* 29 F9
Laćarak *SRB* 158 C4
La Caridad *E* 39 A6
La Carlota *E* 53 A7
La Carolina *E* 54 C5
Lacaune *F* 34 C3
La Cavada *E* 40 B4
La Cavalerie *F* 34 B5
Lacave *F* 29 F9
Lacco Ameno *I* 62 F5
Laceby *GB* 11 D11
Lacedonia *I* 60 A5
La Cellera de Ter *E* 43 D9
La Celle-St-Avant *F* 29 A7
La Cerca *E* 40 C5
La Cerollera *E* 42 F3
Laces *I* 71 D11
La Chaise-Dieu *F* 30 E4
La Chaize-le-Vicomte *F* 28 B3
La Chambre *F* 31 E9
Lachania *GR* 181 E7
Lachapelle *F* 19 E11
La Chapelle-aux-Bois *F* 26 D5
La Chapelle-aux-Saints *F* 29 F9
La Chapelle-d'Abondance
    F 31 C10
La Chapelle-d'Aligné *F* 23 E11
La Chapelle-d'Angillon *F* 25 F7
La Chapelle-de-Guinchay
    F 30 C6
La Chapelle-des-Fougeretz
    F 23 D8
La Chapelle-en-Valgaudémar
    F 31 F9
La Chapelle-en-Vercors *F* 31 F7
La Chapelle-la-Reine *F* 25 D8
La Chapelle-Laurent *F* 30 E3
Lachapelle-sous-Aubenas
    F 35 A7

La Chapelle-St-André *F* 25 F9
La Chapelle-St-Laurent *F* 28 B5
La Chapelle-St-Luc *F* 25 D11
La Chapelle-St-Quillain *F* 26 F4
La Chapelle-St-Ursin *F* 29 A10
La Chapelle-sur-Erdre *F* 23 F8
Lachar *E* 53 B9
La Charité-sur-Loire *F* 25 F9
La Chartre-sur-le-Loir *F* 24 E4
La Châtaigneraie *F* 28 B5
La Châtre *F* 29 B9
La Châtre-Langlin *F* 29 C8
La Chaume *F* 26 E4
La Chaussée-St-Victor *F* 24 E5
La Chaussée-sur-Marne
    F 25 C12
La Chaux-de-Fonds *CH* 27 F6
La Chaux-du-Dombief *F* 31 B8
Lachendorf *D* 79 A7
La Cheppe *F* 25 B12
La Chèze *F* 22 D6
Lachowo *PL* 139 D13
Laciči *HR* 149 D10
La Cierva *E* 47 D9
La Ciotat *F* 35 D10
La Cisterniga *E* 39 E10
Lack *PL* 139 F8
Lackamore *IRL* 8 C6
Lackeby *S* 89 B10
Łącko *PL* 145 D1
La Clayette *F* 30 C5
La Clusaz *F* 31 D9
La Cluse *F* 35 A10
La Cluse-et-Mijoux *F* 31 B9
La Codosera *E* 45 F6
La Concha *E* 40 B4
La Condamine-Châtelard
    F 36 C5
Laconi *I* 64 D3
La Coquille *F* 29 D7
La Coronada *E* 51 B9
La Coronada *E* 51 C10
La Côte-St-André *F* 31 E7
La-Couarde-sur-Mer *F* 28 C3
La Couronne *F* 28 D6
Lacourt *F* 33 E8
La Courtine *F* 29 D10
La Couture-Boussey *F* 24 C5
La Crau *F* 36 E4
La Crèche *F* 28 C5
Lacroix-Barrez *F* 29 F11
La Croixille *F* 23 D9
La Croix-Valmer *F* 36 E5
Lacrouzette *F* 33 C10
La Cumbre *E* 45 F9
Łączna *PL* 143 E10
Łącznik *PL* 142 F4
Ladánybene *H* 150 C3
Ladce *SK* 146 C6
Lądek *PL* 142 B4
Lądek-Zdrój *PL* 77 B11
Ladelund *D* 82 A6
Ladenburg *D* 21 F11
Lădeşti *RO* 160 D4
Ladignac-le-Long *F* 29 D8
Ladispoli *I* 62 D2
Ladoeiro *P* 45 E6
Ladomirová *SK* 145 E4
Ladon *F* 25 E8
Ladozhskoye Ozero *RUS* 129 E15
Ladushkin *RUS* 139 A9
Ladybank *GB* 5 C10
Ladykirk *GB* 5 D12
Ladysford *GB* 3 K12
Lädzere *LV* 134 B5
Ładzice *PL* 143 D7
Ładzin *PL* 84 C7
Laekvere *EST* 131 C13
La Encina *E* 56 D3
Laer *D* 17 D8
La Ercina *E* 39 C9
Lærdalsøyri *N* 100 D6
Laerma *GR* 181 D7
Laerru *I* 64 B2
La Espina *E* 39 B7
La Estación *E* 43 D8
La Estrella *E* 45 E10
Laeva *EST* 131 D12
La Fare-les-Oliviers *F* 35 C9
La Farlède *F* 36 E4
La Fatarella *E* 42 E4
La Faurie *F* 35 A10
La Faute-sur-Mer *F* 28 C3
La Felipa *E* 47 F9
La Fère *F* 19 E7
La Ferrière *F* 28 B3
La Ferrière-aux-Etangs *F* 23 C10
La Ferté-Alais *F* 25 D7
La Ferté-Bernard *F* 24 D4
La Ferté-Frênel *F* 24 C4
La Ferté-Gaucher *F* 25 C9
La Ferté-Imbault *F* 24 F6
La Ferté-Loupière *F* 25 E9
La Ferté-Macé *F* 23 C11
La Ferté-Milon *F* 25 B9
La Ferté-sous-Jouarre *F* 25 C9
La Ferté-St-Aubin *F* 24 E6
La Ferté-St-Cyr *F* 24 E6
Laferté-sur-Amance *F* 26 E4
La Férte-Vidame *F* 24 C4
La Ferté-Villeneuil *F* 24 E5
Lafitole *F* 33 D6
Lafkos *GR* 175 A7
La Flèche *F* 23 E11
Lafnitz *A* 148 B6
La Fontaine-St-Martin *F* 23 E12
La Font de la Figuera *E* 56 D3
La Force *F* 29 F6
La Forêt-sur-Sèvre *F* 28 B5
La Forge *F* 27 D6
Laforsen *S* 103 C10
La Fortunada *E* 33 E6
La Fouillade *F* 33 B10
La Foux-d'Allos *F* 36 C5
Lafrançaise *F* 33 B8
La Fregeneda *E* 45 C7
La Fresneda *E* 42 F4
La Frontera *E* 47 D8
La Fuente de San Esteban
    E 45 C8
La Fuliola *E* 42 D6
La Gacilly *F* 23 E7
La Galera *E* 42 F4
Lagan *S* 87 B13

La Garde *F* 36 E4
La Garde-Adhémar *F* 35 B8
La Garde-Freinet *F* 36 E4
Lagardelle-sur-Lèze *F* 33 D8
Lagarelhos *P* 38 E5
La Garnache *F* 28 B2
La Garriga *E* 43 D8
Lagarrigue *F* 33 C10
La Garrovilla *E* 51 B7
La Gaubretière *F* 28 B3
Lagavara *GB* 4 E4
Lage *D* 17 D7
Lage *D* 17 E11
Lagedi *EST* 131 C9
Lage Mierde *NL* 16 F4
Lagerfors *S* 91 B15
Lagfors *S* 103 A13
Lagg *GB* 4 E6
Laggan *GB* 5 A8
Lagganulva *GB* 4 B4
Laghey *IRL* 6 F6
Laghtgeorge *IRL* 6 F5
Łagiewniki *PL* 81 E11
Lagkada *GR* 177 C7
Lagkadas *GR* 169 C9
Lagkadia *GR* 174 D5
La Glacerie *F* 23 A8
Lagnieu *F* 31 D7
Lagny-sur-Marne *F* 25 C8
Lago *P* 39 F6
Lagoa *P* 50 E2
Lagoa *P* 50 E2
Lagoaça *P* 45 B7
Lago Menor *E* 57 B11
Lagonegro *I* 60 C5
Lagor *F* 32 D4
Lagorce *F* 28 E5
Lagord *F* 28 C3
La Gornal *E* 43 E7
Lagos *GR* 171 B8
Lagos *P* 50 E2
Lagosanto *I* 66 C5
Lagow *PL* 81 B8
Łagów *PL* 143 E11
Lagrán *E* 41 C6
La Granada de Riotinto *E* 51 D7
La Granadella *E* 42 E5
La Grand-Croix *F* 30 D6
La Grande-Combe *F* 35 B7
La Grande-Motte *F* 35 D7
La Granja d'Escarp *E* 42 E4
La Granjuela *E* 51 C9
Lagrasse *F* 34 D4
La Grave *F* 31 E9
Lägsta *S* 107 D14
La Guarda *E* 51 B8
La Guardia *E* 46 E6
La Guardia de Jaén *E* 53 A9
Laguarta *E* 32 F5
Laguenne *F* 29 E9
Laguépie *F* 33 B9
La Guerche-de-Bretagne
    F 23 E9
La Guerche-sur-l'Aubois *F* 30 B2
Laguiole *F* 30 F2
Laguna Dalga *E* 39 D8
Laguna de Duero *E* 39 E10
Laguna de Negrillos *E* 39 D8
Lagundo *I* 72 C3
Lagunilla *E* 45 D9
Lagyna *GR* 169 C9
Lagyna *GR* 171 B10
La Haba *E* 51 B8
Lahana *TR* 173 B7
La Haye-du-Puits *F* 23 B8
La Haye-Pesnel *F* 23 C9
Lähdejänkkä *FIN* 119 B12
Lähden *D* 17 C9
Lahenpää *S* 116 E10
Laheycourt *F* 26 C3
La Higuera *E* 55 B10
Lahinch *IRL* 8 C4
La Hiniesta *E* 39 E8
La Hinojosa *E* 47 E8
Lahnajärvi *S* 116 E8
Lahnalahti *FIN* 124 F9
Lahnanen *FIN* 123 C16
Lahnasjärvi *FIN* 125 C9
Lahnasuando *S* 116 E9
Lahnstein *D* 21 D9
Laholm *S* 87 C12
Lahonci *SLO* 148 D6
La Horcajada *E* 45 D10
La Horra *E* 40 E4
Lahr (Schwarzwald) *D* 27 D8
Lähte *EST* 131 E13
L'Ametlla de Mar *E* 42 F5
Lahti *FIN* 127 D14
Lahtiranta *FIN* 119 E13
Laichingen *D* 74 F6
Laide *GB* 2 K5
Laidi *LV* 134 C3
Laidze *LV* 134 B5
Laifour *F* 184 E2
L'Aigle *F* 24 C4
La Iglesuela *E* 46 D3
La Iglesuela del Cid *E* 42 G3
Laignes *F* 25 E11
L'Aiguillon-sur-Mer *F* 28 C3
Laihia *FIN* 122 E8
Laikko *FIN* 129 C11
Laiksjö *S* 107 C11
Lailly-en-Val *F* 24 E6
Laimont *F* 26 C3
Lainate *I* 69 B7
La Mongie *F* 33 E6
La Monnerie-le-Montel *F* 30 D4
La Morera *E* 51 B6
Lamothe *F* 30 E3
La Mothe-Achard *F* 28 B2
Lamothe-Cassel *F* 33 A8
La Mothe-St-Héray *F* 28 C5
La Motte-Beuvron *F* 24 E7
La Motte-Chalancon *F* 35 B9
La Motte-du-Caire *F* 35 B11
Lamovita *BIH* 157 C6
Lampaanjärvi *FIN* 124 D7
Lampaul *F* 22 D2
Lampaul-Guimiliau *F* 22 D3
Lampaul-Plouarzel *F* 22 D2
Lampeland *N* 95 C11
Lamperila *FIN* 124 E8
Lampertheim *D* 21 E10
Lampertswalde *D* 80 D5
Lampeter *GB* 12 A6
Lamphun *GR* 169 F9
Lampinsaari *FIN* 119 F14
Lampiselkä *FIN* 115 D1
Lampsijärvi *FIN* 117 E13

Lajkovac *SRB* 158 E5
La Jonchère-St-Maurice *F* 29 C8
La Jonquera *E* 34 F4
Lajoskomárom *H* 149 C10
Lajosmizse *H* 150 C4
La Jumellière *F* 23 F10
Lakaluoma *FIN* 123 E10
Lakatnik *BG* 165 C7
Lakaträsk *S* 118 B6
Lakavica *MK* 163 F10
Lakavica *MK* 164 F5
Lakenheath *GB* 15 C10
Lakhdenpokh'ya *RUS* 129 B13
Laki *MK* 165 F6
Łąkie *PL* 85 D12
Lakki *GR* 177 E8
Lakkoí *GR* 178 E6
Lakkoma *GR* 169 D9
Lakkoma *GR* 171 D9
Lakkopetra *GR* 174 C3
Lakomäki *FIN* 123 E15
Lakselv *N* 113 C14
Lakselvsletta *N* 111 B18
Laksfors *N* 108 E5
Laktaši *BIH* 157 C7
Lakuntza *E* 32 E1
La Lantejuela *E* 51 E9
La Lapa *E* 51 C6
Lalapaşa *TR* 167 F7
Lalas *GR* 174 D4
L'Albagés *E* 42 E5
L'Alcora *E* 48 D4
L'Alcudia *E* 48 F3
L'Alcúdia de Crespins *E* 56 D3
Lalevade-d'Ardèche *F* 35 A7
Lalël *SI* 45 D10
L'Alfàs del Pi *E* 56 D4
Lalín *E* 38 C3
Lalinac *SRB* 164 C5
Lalinde *F* 29 F7
La Línea de la Concepción
    E 53 D6
Lalioti *GR* 175 C6
Lalláing *F* 19 D7
Lalley *F* 31 F8
Lalm *N* 101 C10
La Londe-les-Maures *F* 36 E4
Laloşu *RO* 160 D4
Laloubère *F* 33 D6
La Loupe *F* 24 D5
La Louvière *B* 19 D9
Lalove *UA* 145 G6
La Loye *F* 31 A8
L'Alpe-d'Huez *F* 31 E9
Lalueza *E* 42 D3
La Luisiana *E* 51 D9
Laluque *F* 32 C4
Lam *D* 76 D4
La Machine *F* 30 B3
La Maddalena *I* 64 A3
Lama dei Peligni *I* 63 C6
La Magdalena *E* 39 C8
Lamagistère *F* 33 B7
La Malène *F* 34 B5
Lamalou-les-Bains *F* 34 C5
Lama Mocogno *I* 66 D2
Lamanon *F* 35 C9
La Marche *F* 25 F9
Lamarche *F* 26 D4
Lamarche-sur-Saône *F* 26 F3
Lamargelle *F* 25 E12
Lamarque *F* 28 E4
Lamas *P* 44 C3
La Massana *AND* 33 E9
Lamastre *F* 30 F6
La Mata *E* 46 E4
La Mata de los Olmos *E* 42 F3
La Matilla *E* 46 B5
Lambach *A* 76 F5
Lamballe *F* 22 D6
Lambersart *F* 18 C7
Lambesc *F* 35 C9
Lambia *GR* 174 D4
Łambinowice *PL* 142 E4
Lamborn *S* 103 E10
Lambourn *GB* 13 B11
Lambrecht (Pfalz) *D* 186 C5
Lambsheim *D* 21 E10
Lamego *P* 44 B5
La Meilleraye-de-Bretagne
    F 23 E9
Lameiras *P* 45 C6
Lamerdingen *D* 71 A11
Lamerdingen *D* 71 A11
Lamezia *I* 59 B9
Lamia *GR* 174 B5
Lamiako *E* 40 B6
La Milesse *F* 23 D12
Lamlash *GB* 4 D6
Lammhult *S* 88 A7
Lammi *FIN* 127 C12
Lamminaho *FIN* 123 C16
Lamminmaa *FIN* 122 F8
Lamminperä *FIN* 119 C16
Lamminvaara *FIN* 116 D10
La Mojonera *E* 55 F7
Le Môle *F* 36 E4
Lamon *I* 72 D4

Langnau *CH* 70 D5
Langnes *N* 111 B15
Langnes *N* 114 C4
Langnes *N* 114 D7
Langø *DK* 83 A10
Langogne *F* 30 F4
Langoiran *F* 28 F5
Langon *F* 32 A5
Langport *GB* 13 C9
Langreo *E* 39 B8
Langres *F* 26 E3
Langschlag *A* 77 E7
Längsel *S* 118 B8
Längset *N* 95 B14
Langset *N* 109 B9
Längshyttan *S* 97 B15
Långsjöby *S* 107 A11
Langslett *N* 112 D6
Langstrand *N* 112 B11
Långsund *S* 118 D7
Langsur *D* 186 B2
Langtoft *GB* 11 C11
Långträsk *S* 107 A16
Långträsk *S* 118 C4
Långträsk *S* 118 D4
Langueux *F* 22 D6
Languidic *F* 22 E5
Languilla *E* 40 F5
Langula *D* 79 D7
Långvattnet *S* 107 D11
Långvattnet *S* 107 D13
Långvattnet *S* 118 E4
Långviken *S* 109 E15
Långviksmon *S* 107 D15
Långvinds bruk *S* 103 D13
Langwarden (Butjadingen)
    D 17 A10
Langwathby *GB* 5 F11
Langwedel *D* 17 C12
Langwedel *D* 83 B7
Langweid am Lech *D* 75 F8
Łanięta *PL* 139 F7
Lanivet *GB* 12 E5
Lanjarón *E* 53 C9
Lankojärvi *FIN* 117 E12
Lanloup *F* 22 C6
Lanmeur *F* 22 C4
Lanna *S* 87 A13
Lanna *S* 92 A5
Länna *S* 99 C9
Lannach *A* 148 C4
Lannavaara *S* 116 B7
Lannemezan *F* 33 D6
Lannepax *F* 33 C6
Lannevesi *FIN* 123 E14
Lannilis *F* 22 C2
Lannion *F* 22 C5
Lannoy *F* 19 C7
Lanobre *F* 29 E11
La Neuve-Lyre *F* 24 C4
La Neuveville *CH* 31 A11
La Neuville-au-Pont *F* 25 B12
Laneuville-sur-Meuse *F* 19 F11
Lång *S* 97 D9
Långå *DK* 86 C5
Långå *S* 102 A5
Långå *S* 101 B5
Långa de Duero *E* 40 E5
Langa *S* 99 B10
Långåminne *FIN* 122 E7
Långan *S* 105 D16
Langangen *N* 90 A6
Långås *S* 87 B12
Långsjö *S* 89 B8
Langau *A* 77 E7
Långbäck *S* 107 A11
Långbäcken *S* 107 C14
Langballig *D* 82 A7
Långban *S* 97 C11
Långbo *S* 103 C10
Langbo *S* 103 D12
Langbunes *N* 114 C9
Langdorf *D* 76 D4
Langburkersdorf *D* 80 D6
Langdorf *D* 76 D4
Langeac *F* 30 E4
Langeais *F* 24 F3
Langebæk *DK* 87 F10
Långed *S* 107 D17
Langegeld *NL* 16 C3
Langeid *N* 90 B2
Längelmäki *FIN* 127 B12
Langeln *D* 79 C8
Langelsheim *D* 79 C7
Langemark *B* 18 C6
Langemyr *N* 90 B3
Langen *D* 17 A11
Langen *D* 21 C11
Langenaltheim *D* 75 E8
Langenau *D* 75 F7
Langenaubach *D* 185 C9
Langenberg *D* 17 E10
Langenberg *D* 183 C10
Langenburg *D* 74 D6
Langenenslingen *D* 27 D11
Langenes *N* 110 C8
Längenfeld *A* 71 C11
Langenfeld (Rheinland) *D* 21 B7
Langenhagen *D* 78 B6
Langenhahn *D* 185 C8
Langenhorn *D* 82 A5
Langenleuba-Oberhain *D* 79 E12
Langenlois *A* 77 F9
Langenlonsheim *D* 185 E8
Langennaundorf *D* 80 C4
Langenneufnach *D* 71 A11
Langenorla *D* 79 E10
Langenpreising *D* 75 F10
Langenselbold *D* 21 D12
Langenthal *CH* 27 F8
Langenwang *A* 148 A5
Langenweddingen *D* 79 B10
Langenwetzendorf *D* 79 E11
Langenzenn *D* 75 C8
Langenzersdorf *A* 77 F10
Langeoog *D* 17 A8
Langeskov *DK* 86 E6
Langesund *N* 90 A6
Langevåg *N* 94 C2
Langevåg *N* 100 B4
Langewiesen *D* 79 E8
Langfjordbotn *N* 112 C9
Långgöns *D* 21 D11
Langhagen *D* 83 C12
Langham *GB* 11 F10
Langhamn *N* 111 B14
Länghem *S* 91 D13
Langhirano *I* 66 C1
Langholm *GB* 5 E10
Langhus *N* 95 C13
Långlöt *S* 89 B11
Långnäs *S* 98 A6

La Nucia *E* 56 D4
Luejuols *F* 33 B10
Lanurile *RO* 155 C1
Lanusei *I* 64 D4
Lanuvio *I* 62 D3
Lanvollon *F* 22 C6
Łany *PL* 142 F5
Lánycsók *H* 149 D11
Lanz *D* 83 D11
Lanzahita *E* 46 D3
Lanžhot *CZ* 77 E11
Lanzo Torinese *I* 31 E11
Laon *F* 19 E8
Laons *F* 24 C5
La Paca *E* 55 D9
La Pacaudière *F* 30 C4
Lapajärvi *FIN* 115 E4
Lapalisse *F* 30 C4
La Pallice *F* 28 C3
La Palma *E* 56 F3
La Palma del Condado *E* 51 E6
La Palme *F* 34 E4
Lapalud *F* 35 B8
La Paludsur-Verdon *F* 36 D4
Lapanj *AL* 168 D2
Łapanów *PL* 144 D1
Lapardha *AL* 168 C2
La Parra *E* 51 B6
La Parra de Las Vegas *E* 47 E8
Lapas *GR* 174 C3
La Pellerine *F* 23 D9
La Penne *F* 36 D5
La Peraleja *E* 47 D7
La Pesga *E* 45 D8
La Petite-Pierre *F* 27 C7
La Peza *E* 55 E6
Lapford *GB* 13 D7
Lapinjärvi *FIN* 127 D15
Lapinkylä *FIN* 127 E11
Lapinlahti *FIN* 124 D8
Lapinneva *FIN* 123 C9
Lapinsalo *FIN* 123 C17
La Plagne *F* 31 D10
La Plaza *E* 39 B7
Laplume *F* 33 B7
Lapmezciems *LV* 134 B7
La Pobla de Claramunt *E* 43 D7
La Pobla del Duc *E* 56 D3
La Pobla de Lillet *E* 43 C7
La Pobla de Montornès *E* 43 E6
La Pobla de Segur *E* 42 C5
La Pobla de Vallbona *E* 48 E3
La Pola de Gordón *E* 39 C8
La Pommeraye *F* 23 F10
La Portellada *E* 42 F4
La Portera *E* 47 F10

Lapoş RO 161 C8
La Pouëze F 23 E10
Lapoutroie F 27 D7
Lapovo SRB 159 E7
Lappajärvi FIN 123 D11
Lappe S 92 A7
Lappea FIN 117 D11
Lappeenranta FIN 129 C9
Lappersdorf D 75 D11
Lappetelä FIN 124 D8
Lappfjärd FIN 122 F7
Lappfors FIN 123 C10
Lappi FIN 119 E14
Lappi FIN 121 D13
Lappi FIN 126 C6
Lappila FIN 127 D13
Lappo FIN 126 E5
Lappohja FIN 127 F9
Lappträsk S 119 B11
Lappuluobbal N 113 E13
La Preste F 33 F10
La Proveda de Soria E 41 D7
Lâpseki TR 172 D6
Laptevo RUS 133 C5
Lapua FIN 123 E10
La Puebla de Almoradiel E 47 E6
La Puebla de Arganzón E 40 C6
La Puebla de Cazalla E 51 E9
La Puebla de los Infantes E 51 D9
La Puebla del Río E 51 E7
La Puebla de Montalbán E 46 E4
La Puebla de Valdavia E 39 C10
La Puebla de Valverde E 48 D3
La Puerta de Segura E 55 C7
Lăpugiu de Jos RO 151 F10
La Punt CH 71 D9
Lăpuş RO 152 C4
Lăpuşata RO 160 D4
Lapuşna MD 154 D2
Lăpuşnicel RO 159 D9
Lăpuşnicu Mare RO 159 D8
Łapy PL 140 E7
L'Aquila I 62 C4
Laracha E 38 B2
Laracor IRL 7 E9
Laragh IRL 7 F10
Laragne-Montéglin F 35 B10
La Rambla E 53 A7
Laranueva E 47 C7
La Rasa E 40 E5
La Ravoire F 31 D8
Larbert GB 5 C9
L'Arboç E 43 E7
L'Arbresle F 30 D6
Lärbro S 93 D13
Larceveau-Arros-Cibits F 32 D3
Larchamp F 23 D9
Larchant F 25 D8
Larche F 29 E8
Larche F 36 C5
Lardaro I 69 B10
Larderello I 66 F2
Lardero E 41 D7
Lardos GR 181 D8
Laredo E 40 B5
La Redorte F 34 D4
Laren NL 16 D4
Laren NL 183 A8
La Réole F 32 A5
Larga MD 153 A9
Largan IRL 6 D5
L'Argentière-la-Bessée F 31 F10
Largoward GB 5 C11
Largs GB 4 D7
Largu RO 161 D10
Lari I 66 E2
Lariano I 62 D3
La Riba E 42 E6
La Riba de Escalote E 40 F6
La Ricamarie F 30 E5
La Riche F 24 F4
La Rinconada E 51 E8
Larino I 63 D7
Larionovo RUS 129 D13
Larisa GR 169 E7
Larkhall GB 5 D9
Larkollen N 95 D13
Larling GB 15 C10
L'Armentera E 43 C10
Larmor-Plage F 22 E5
Larne GB 4 F5
La Robla E 39 C8
La Roca de la Sierra E 45 F7
La Roche CH 31 B11
La Roche-Bernard F 23 E7
La Roche-Canillac F 29 E9
La Roche-Chalais F 28 E6
La Roche-de-Rame F 31 F10
La Roche-Derrien F 22 C5
La Roche-des-Arnauds F 35 A10
La Roche-en-Ardenne B 19 D12
La Rochefoucauld F 29 D6
La Rochelle F 28 C3
Larochemillay F 30 B5
La Roche-Posay F 29 B7
La Rochepot F 30 B6
La Roche-sur-Foron F 31 C9
La Roche-sur-Yon F 28 B3
La Rochette F 31 E9
Larochette L 20 E6
La Roda E 47 F8
La Roda de Andalucía E 53 B7
La Roë F 23 E9
Laroles E 55 E7
La Romana E 56 E3
La Romieu F 33 C6
Laroquebrou F 29 F10
Laroque-d'Olmes F 33 E9
La Roque-Ste-Marguerite F 34 B5
Laroque-Timbaut F 33 B7
La Rouquette F 33 B9
Larraga E 32 E2
Larrasoaina E 32 E2
Larrau F 32 D4
Larrazet F 33 C8
Larressore F 32 D3
Larrión E 32 E1
Larsbo S 97 B14
Larseng N 111 A16
Larsmo FIN 122 C9
Larsnes N 100 B3
Laruns F 32 E5
Laruscade F 28 E5
Larv S 91 C13
Larva E 55 D6
Larvik N 90 A7
Larymna GR 175 B7
Lasa I 71 D11
Lasalle F 35 B6
La Salle I 31 D11
La Salle les Alpes F 31 F10
La Salvetat-Peyralès F 33 B10
La Salvetat-sur-Agout F 34 C4
La Salzadella E 48 D5
Läsänkoski FIN 128 B6
Las Arenas E 39 B10
La Sauvetat-du-Dropt F 33 A6
La Savina E 57 D7
Lasberg A 77 F7
Las Berlanas E 46 C3
Låsby DK 86 C5
Las Cabezas de San Juan E 51 F8
Lascari I 58 D4
Las Casas E 48 E4
Lascuarre E 42 C5
La Seca E 39 F10
La Secuita E 43 E6
La Séguinière F 28 A4
La Selva del Camp E 42 E6
La Selve F 33 B11
La Sènia E 42 F4
La Seyne-sur-Mer F 35 D10
Las Herencias E 46 E3
Łasin PL 138 C7
Lasinja HR 148 E5
Łask PL 143 C7
Łaskarzew PL 141 G5
Laško SLO 148 D4
Laskowa PL 144 D1
Laskowice PL 138 D5
Laskowiec PL 139 D12
Las Labores E 46 F5
Laslea RO 152 E5
Las Majadas E 47 D8
Las Menas E 55 E8
Las Mesas E 47 F7
Las Navas de la Concepción E 51 D9
Las Navas del Marqués E 46 C4
Lasne B 182 D4
Las Negras E 55 F9
La Solana E 55 B6
La Souterraine F 29 C8
Lasovo SRB 159 F9
Lasowice Małe PL 142 E5
Las Palas E 56 F2
Las Pedroñeras E 47 F7
Las Pedrosas E 41 D10
La Spezia I 69 E8
Las Plassas I 64 D2
Las Rotas E 56 D5
Las Rozas de Madrid E 46 C5
Lassahn D 83 C9
Lassan D 84 C5
Lassay-les-Châteaux F 23 D11
Lassemoen N 105 B13
Lässerud S 96 C7
Lasseube F 32 D5
Lassigny F 18 E6
Lassila FIN 126 B7
Lassing A 73 A9
Lassing A 73 A10
Laßnitzhöhe A 148 B5
Lastebasse I 69 B11
Las Terreras E 55 D9
Las Torres de Cotillas E 56 E2
Lastours F 33 D10
Lastovo HR 162 D2
Lastra a Signa I 66 E3
Lastras de Cuéllar E 40 F3
Lastrup D 17 C9
Lastukoski FIN 125 D10
Lastva BIH 162 D5
La Suze-sur-Sarthe F 23 E12
Lašva BIH 157 D8
Lasva EST 131 F14
Las Veguillas E 45 C9
Las Ventas con Peña Aguilera E 46 E4
Las Ventas de San Julián E 45 D10
Łaszczów PL 144 B8
Laszki PL 144 C6
Laterza I 61 B7
La Teste-de-Buch F 32 A3
Lathen D 17 C8
Latheron GB 3 J10
Latheronwheel GB 3 J10
La Thuile I 31 D10
Lathus F 29 C7
Latiano I 61 B9
Latikberg S 107 B12
Latillé F 28 B6
Latina I 62 E3
Latisana I 73 E7
Latorpsbruk S 97 D12
La Torre de Cabdella E 33 F7
La Torre de Esteban Hambrán E 46 D4
La Torre de l'Espanyol E 42 E5
La Tour-Blanche F 29 E6
La Tour-d'Auvergne F 29 D11
Latour-de-France F 34 E4
La Tour-du-Crieu F 33 D9
La Tour-du-Pin F 31 D7
La Tour-sur-Orb F 34 C5
Latowicz PL 141 F5
La Tranche-sur-Mer F 28 C3
La Tremblade F 28 D3
La Trimouille F 29 C8
La Trinité F 37 D6
La Trinité-Porhoët F 22 D6
La Trinité-sur-Mer F 22 E5
Latronico I 60 C6
Latronquière F 29 F10
Lattarico I 60 E6
Lattes F 35 C6
Lattomeri FIN 126 C6
Lattrop NL 183 A9
La Turballe F 22 F7
Latva FIN 119 F15
Latva FIN 120 C9
Latvajärvenperä FIN 121 D11
Laubach D 21 C11
Laubach D 21 D8
Lauben D 71 A10
Laubere LV 135 C10
Laubusch D 80 D6
Lauchhammer D 80 D5
Lauchringen D 27 E9
Lauciene LV 134 B5
Lauda-Königshofen D 74 C6
Lauder GB 5 D11
Lauderi LV 133 D4
Laudio E 40 B6
Laudona LV 135 C12
Laudun F 35 B8
Lauenau D 17 D12
Lauenbrück D 82 D7
Lauenburg (Elbe) D 83 D9
Lauenförde D 21 A12
Lauf D 186 D5
Laufach D 187 A7
Lauf an der Pegnitz D 75 C9
Laufen CH 27 F8
Laufenburg CH 27 E9
Lauffen am Neckar D 187 C7
Laugnac F 33 B7
Lauingen (Donau) D 75 E7
Laujar de Andarax E 55 F7
Laukaa FIN 123 F15
Laukeng N 112 D9
Lauker S 118 C3
Laukka FIN 119 E15
Laukkala FIN 123 D17
Laukkoski FIN 127 E13
Laukkuluspa S 111 E18
Laukna EST 131 D8
Lauksargiai LT 134 F4
Lauksletta N 111 A17
Lauksletta N 112 C6
Lauksodis LT 135 D8
Laukuva LT 134 E4
Laukvik N 105 C9
Laukvik N 110 D7
Laukvik N 110 E8
Laukvik N 111 A14
Laukvik N 113 C11
Laukvik N 114 B6
Laukžemė LT 134 D2
Laulasmaa EST 131 C8
Launac F 33 C8
Launceston GB 12 D6
La Unión E 56 F3
Launkalne LV 135 B11
Launonen FIN 127 D12
Laupen CH 31 B11
Laupheim D 71 A9
Laupstad N 110 D8
Lauragh IRL 8 E3
Lauraguel F 33 D10
Laurbjerg DK 86 C5
Laureana di Borrello I 59 C9
Laurencekirk GB 5 B12
Laurencetown IRL 6 F6
Laurens F 34 C5
Laurenzana I 60 C5
Lauria I 60 C5
Laurière F 29 C8
Laurieston GB 5 F8
Laurila FIN 119 C13
Laurino I 60 C4
Lauris F 35 C9
Laurito I 60 C4
Lausanne CH 31 B10
Lauscha D 75 B9
Laußig D 79 C12
Laußnitz D 80 D5
Laussonne F 30 F5
Laussou F 33 A7
Lauta D 80 D6
Lautamaa FIN 119 C12
Lautenbach D 27 C9
Lauter D 79 E12
Lauterbourg F 27 C9
Lauterbrunnen CH 70 D5
Lautere LV 135 C12
Lauterecken D 186 B4
Lauterhofen D 75 D10
Lautersbach (Hessen) D 78 E5
Lauterstein D 187 D8
Lautertal D 75 B8
Lautiosaari FIN 119 C13
Lautrec F 33 C10
Lauttavaara FIN 121 E9
Lauttijärvi FIN 126 B6
Lauve N 90 A7
Lauvsnes N 105 C9
Lauvstad N 100 B3
Lauvuskylä FIN 125 C13
Lauvvik N 94 E4
Lauzerte F 33 B8
Lauzès F 33 A9
Lauzun F 33 A6
Lavagna I 37 C10
Laval F 23 D10
Lavala FIN 121 D14
Lavalette F 33 D10
La Valette-du-Var F 35 D10
La Vall d'Uixó E 48 E4
La Valle I 72 C4
Lavamünd A 73 C10
Lavangen N 111 C14
Lavangsnes N 111 C13
Lavara GR 171 B10
Lavardac F 33 B6
Lavassaare EST 131 D8
Lavaur F 33 C9
Lavaveix-les-Mines F 29 C10
Lavda GR 168 D5
Lavdar i Korçës AL 168 C4
La Vecilla E 39 C9
La Vega E 39 B8
La Vega E 39 B8
La Vega E 39 B10
Lavelanet F 33 E9
La Vellés E 45 B9
Lavello I 60 A5
Laven DK 86 C5
Lavena Ponte Tresa I 69 B6
Lavenham GB 15 C10
Laveno I 68 B6
La Ventosa E 47 D8
La Verdière F 35 C10
La Vernarède F 35 B6
La Verpillière F 31 D7
La Verrie F 28 B4
La Veuve F 25 B11
Lavia FIN 126 B8
Laviano I 60 B4
La Victoria E 53 A7
La Vid E 40 E5
Lavik N 111 B14
La Vila Joiosa E 56 D4
La Villa de Don Fadrique E 47 E6
La Ville-aux-Clercs F 24 E5
La Villedieu F 30 F4
La Villedieu-du-Clain F 29 C6
La Villedieu-en-Fontenette F 26 E5
Lavinio-Lido di Enea I 62 E3
Laviron F 26 F6
Lavis I 69 A11
Lavit F 33 C7
Lavoriškės LT 137 D12
La Voulte-sur-Rhône F 30 F6
Lavoûte-Chilhac F 30 E3
Lavoûte-sur-Loire F 30 E4
Lavradio P 50 B1
Lavre P 50 B3
Lavrio GR 175 D9
Lavsjö S 107 C11
La Wantzenau F 186 D4
Lawers GB 5 B8
Lawford GB 15 D11
Lawrencetown GB 7 D10
Ławsk PL 140 D6
Ławszowa PL 81 D8
Ławy PL 85 E7
Laxå S 92 B5
Laxbäcken S 107 B10
Laxe E 38 B2
Laxey GBM 10 C3
Laxford Bridge GB 2 J6
Laxnäs S 108 E9
Laxne S 93 A10
Laxo GB 3 E14
Laxou F 26 C5
Laxsjö S 106 D7
Laxvik S 87 B11
Laxviken S 106 D7
Layana E 32 F3
La Yesa E 48 E3
Läyliäinen FIN 127 D11
Layos E 46 E4
Layrac F 33 B7
Laz HR 148 E6
Laza E 38 D5
Laza RO 153 D11
Lazagurría E 32 F1
Lazarata GR 174 B2
Lăzarea RO 153 D7
Lăzăreni RO 151 D9
Lazarevac SRB 158 E5
Lazarev Krst MNE 163 D7
Lazarevo SRB 158 C6
Lazdijai LT 137 E8
Lazdininkai LT 134 E2
Lazdona LV 135 C12
Lazdukalns LV 133 C2
Lazeshchyna UA 152 A4
Lazise I 66 B2
Łaziska PL 141 H5
Łaziska Górne PL 142 F6
Lazkao E 32 D1
Lázně Bělohrad CZ 77 B9
Lázně Bohdaneč CZ 77 B9
Lázně Kynžvart CZ 75 B12
Laznica SRB 159 E8
Lazonby GB 5 F11
Lazuri RO 151 B10
Lazuri de Beiuş RO 151 D9
Leabgarrow IRL 6 C5
Leacht Seoirse IRL 6 F5
Leadburn GB 5 D10
Leadenham GB 11 E10
Leadhills GB 5 E9
Leamhcán IRL 7 F10
Leamington Spa, Royal GB 13 A11
Leányfalu H 150 B3
Leap IRL 8 E4
Leasingham GB 11 E11
Leatherhead GB 15 E8
Leavvajohka N 113 D17
Łeba PL 85 A13
Lebach D 21 F7
Lebane SRB 164 D4
Le Ban-St-Martin F 186 C1
Le Barp F 32 A4
Le Bar-sur-Loup F 36 D5
Lebbeke B 19 B9
Le Béage F 30 F5
Le Beausset F 35 D10
Lebedivka UA 154 F6
Lébényimiklós H 149 A8
Lebesby N 113 B18
Le Bez F 33 C10
Lebiez F 18 D4
Le Biot F 31 C10
Le Blanc F 29 B8
Le Bleymard F 35 B6
Łebno PL 138 B5
Le Bois-d'Oingt F 30 D6
Le Bois-Plage-en-Ré F 28 C3
Le Boréon F 37 C6
Lębork PL 85 A13
Le Boulou F 34 E4
Le Boupère F 28 B4
Le Bourg F 29 F9
Le Bourg-d'Oisans F 31 E9
Le Bourget-du-Lac F 31 D8
Le Bousquet-d'Orb F 34 C5
Le Breuil F 25 C10
Le Breuil F 30 B5
Lebrija E 51 F7
Lebring-Sankt Margarethen A 148 C5
Le Brouilh-Monbert F 33 C6
Le Brusquet F 36 C4
Lebução P 38 E5
Le Bugue F 29 F7
Le Buisson F 34 A5
Le Buisson-de-Cadouin F 29 F7
Łebunia PL 138 B4
Lebus D 81 B7
Lebusa D 80 C4
Lebyazh'ye RUS 129 F11
Leça da Palmeira P 44 B3
Leça do Bailio P 44 B3
Le Cannet F 36 D6
Le Cannet-des-Maures F 36 E4
Le Castellet F 35 D10
Le Cateau-Cambrésis F 19 D8
Le Catelet F 19 D7
Le Caylar F 34 C5
Le Cayrol F 34 A4
Lecce I 61 C10
Lecco I 69 B7
Lece SRB 164 D4
Lécera E 42 E2
Lech A 71 C10
Lechaina GR 174 D3
Lechaio GR 175 D6
Le Chambon-Feugerolles F 30 E5
Le Chambon-sur-Lignon F 30 E5
Lechaschau A 71 C11
Le Château-d'Oléron F 28 D3
Le Châtelard F 31 D9
Le Châtelet F 29 B10
Lechbruck D 71 B11
Le Chêne F 25 C11
Le Chesne F 19 E10
Le Cheylard F 30 F5
Le Cheylas F 31 E8
Lechința RO 152 C4
Lechlade GB 13 B11
Lechovo GR 169 C5
Lechtingen (Wallenhorst) D 17 D10
Leciñena E 41 E10
Leck D 82 A5
Leckaun IRL 6 D6
Leckmelm GB 2 K6
Le Clapier F 34 C5
Le Collet-de-Dèze F 35 B6
Le Conquet F 22 D2
Le Coteau F 30 C5
Le Coudray-St-Germer F 18 F4
Lécousse F 23 D9
Le Crès F 35 C6
Le Creusot F 30 B5
Lecrín E 53 C9
Le Croisic F 22 F6
Le Crotoy F 18 D4
Lectoure F 33 C7
Łęczna PL 141 H7
Łęczyca PL 143 B7
Łęczyce PL 138 A4
Ledaig GB 4 C6
Ledaña E 47 F9
Ledanca E 47 C7
Lēdas LV 134 B5
Ledbury GB 13 A10
Lede B 19 C8
Ledeč nad Sázavou CZ 77 C8
Ledegem B 182 D2
Ledenice BIH 157 C9
Ledenice CZ 77 E7
Lédergues F 33 B10
Ledesma E 45 B9
Lédignan F 35 C7
Ledigos E 39 D10
Ledmore GB 2 J7
Lednica SK 146 C6
Lednice CZ 77 E11
Lednické Rovne SK 146 C6
Le Donjon F 30 C4
Le Dorat F 29 C8
Ledrada E 45 D9
Lēdurga LV 135 B9
Ledusjö S 107 D16
Ledvattsfors S 109 F16
Lędyczek PL 85 C11
Lędzin PL 85 B8
Lędziny PL 143 F7
Leeds GB 11 D8
Leedstown GB 12 E4
Leek GB 11 E7
Leek NL 16 B6
Leeming GB 11 C8
Lee Moor GB 12 E6
Leende NL 16 F5
Leer (Ostfriesland) D 17 B8
Leerdam NL 16 E4
Leersum NL 183 A6
Leese D 17 C12
Leeuwarden NL 16 B5
Leevaku EST 131 E14
Leevi EST 131 F14
Leezen D 83 C8
Leezen D 83 C10
Le Faou F 22 D3
Le Faouët F 22 D5
Le Fenouiller F 28 B2
Leffinge B 182 C1
Lefkada GR 174 B2
Lefkes GR 176 E5
Lefkimmi GR 168 F3
Lefkimmi GR 171 B10
Lefkonas GR 169 B10
Lefkopigi GR 169 D6
Lefkothea GR 168 D5
Lefktra GR 175 C7
Le Fleix F 29 F6
Le Folgoët F 22 C3
Leforest F 182 E2
Le Fossat F 33 D8
Le Fousseret F 33 D8
Le Fugeret F 36 C5
Le Fuilet F 23 F9
Leganés E 46 D5
Leganiel E 47 D7
Legau D 71 B10
Le Gault-Soigny F 25 C10
Le Gault-St-Denis F 24 D5
Legazpi E 32 D1
Legde D 83 E11
Legden D 17 D8
Legé F 28 B2
Lège-Cap-Ferret F 28 F3
Le Genest-St-Isle F 23 D10
Leggs GB 7 C7
Legionowo PL 139 F10
Léglise B 19 E12
Legnago I 66 B3
Legnano I 69 B6
Legnica PL 81 D10
Legnickie Pole PL 81 D10
Le Gond-Pontouvre F 29 D6
Łęgowo PL 138 B6
Legrad HR 149 D7
Le Grand-Bornand F 31 D9
Le Grand-Bourg F 29 C9
Le Grand-Lemps F 31 E7
Le Grand-Lucé F 24 E3
Le Grand-Pressigny F 29 B7
Le Grand-Quevilly F 18 F3
Le Grand-Serre F 31 E7
Le Grau-du-Roi F 35 C7
Le Gros Theil F 18 F2
Le Gua F 31 E8
Legutiano E 41 B7
Legyesbénye H 145 G3
Le Havre F 23 A12
Lehe D 82 B6
Lehliu RO 161 E9
Lehliu-Gară RO 161 E9
Lehmäjoki FIN 122 D8
Lehmen D 21 D8
Lehmikumpu FIN 119 B14
Lehmivaara FIN 117 E11
Lehmo FIN 125 E13
Lehndorf D 79 E11
Lehnice SK 146 E4
Lehnin D 79 B12
Le Hohwald F 27 D7
Léhon F 23 D7
Le Horps F 23 D11
Lehota SK 146 E5
Le Houga F 32 C5
Lehrberg D 75 D8
Lehre D 79 B8
Lehrte D 79 B6
Lehsen D 83 D10
Lehtimäki FIN 123 E11
Lehtiniemi FIN 121 B10
Lehto FIN 121 B14
Lehtopää FIN 119 F13
Lehtovaara FIN 117 D17
Lehtovaara FIN 121 C10
Lehtovaara FIN 121 D14
Lehtovaara FIN 121 F14
Lehtovaara FIN 124 B9
Lehtovaara FIN 125 D11
Lehtse EST 131 C11
Leianokladi GR 174 B5
Leibertingen D 27 D11
Leiblfing D 75 E11
Leibnitz A 148 C5
Leicester GB 11 F9
Leichlingen (Rheinland) D 183 C10
Leiden NL 16 D3
Leiderdorp NL 16 D3
Leidschendam NL 16 D2
Leie EST 131 E12
Leifear IRL 4 F2
Leiferde D 79 B7
Leigh GB 10 E6
Leighlinbridge IRL 9 C9
Leighton Buzzard GB 15 D7
Leikanger N 100 B2
Leikanger N 100 D5
Léim an Bhradáin IRL 7 F10
Leimaņi LV 135 D11
Leimen D 21 F11
Leimuiden NL 182 A5
Leinburg D 75 D9
Leine N 101 D9
Leinefelde D 79 D7
Leinfelden-Echterdingen D 187 D7
Leinì I 68 C4
Leino FIN 121 D12
Leinzell D 74 E6
Leioa E 40 B6
Leipalingis LT 137 E8
Leipheim D 75 F7
Leipivaara FIN 121 E10
Leipojärvi S 116 D6
Leipzig D 79 D11
Leira N 101 E10
Leira N 104 E4
Leira N 108 D5
Leirado E 38 D3
Leirämoen N 108 C8
Leiranger N 110 E8
Leirbotn N 113 C11
Leiria P 44 E3
Leirlia N 105 B15
Leiro E 38 D3
Leirvåg N 100 E2
Leirvík FO 2 A3
Leirvik N 94 C2
Leirvik N 100 D2
Leirvik N 105 B11
Leirvika N 108 D6
Leisach A 73 C6
Leisi EST 130 D5
Leisnig D 80 D3
Leißling D 79 D10
Leiston GB 15 C12
Leitir Ceanainn IRL 7 C7
Leitir Mhic an Bhaird IRL 6 C6
Leitrim IRL 6 D6
Leitza E 32 D2
Leitzkau D 79 B10
Leive FIN 119 B14
Leivonmäki FIN 127 B15
Leivset N 108 B9
Leiwen D 21 E7
Leixlip IRL 7 F10
Lejasciems LV 135 B13
Lejasstrazdi LV 134 C6
Leka GR 177 D8
Lekaj AL 168 B2
Lekangen N 111 B13
Lekani GR 171 B7
Łęka Opatowska PL 142 D5
Lekárovce SK 145 F5
Łękawica PL 147 B8
Lekbibaj AL 163 E8
Lekėčiai LT 137 D7
Lekenik HR 148 E6
Lekeryd S 92 D4
Lekhchevo BG 165 B8
Łęki Szlacheckie PL 143 D8
Leknes N 100 B5
Łęknica PL 81 C7
Lekoes N 110 D6
Lekowo PL 85 C9
Leksand S 103 E9
Leksvik N 105 D9
Lekunberri E 32 D2
Leland N 108 D4
Le Langon F 28 C4
Le Lardin-St-Lazare F 29 E8
Le Lauzet-Ubaye F 36 C4
Le Lavandou F 36 E4
Leleasca RO 160 D4
Leles SK 145 G5
Lelești RO 159 C11
Le Leuy F 32 C5
Lelice PL 139 E8
Le Lion-d'Angers F 23 E10
Leliūnai LT 135 F10
Lelkowo PL 139 B9
Lelle EST 131 D9
Le Locle CH 31 A10
Le Louroux-Béconnais F 23 E10
Lelów PL 143 E8
Le Luc F 36 E4
Le Lude F 23 E12
Lelystad NL 16 C4
Lem DK 86 C2
Le Malzieu-Ville F 30 F3
Le Mans F 23 D13
Le Markstein F 27 E7
Le Martinet F 35 B7
Le Mas-d'Agenais F 33 B6
Le Mas-d'Azil F 33 D8
Le Masnau-Massuguiès F 34 C4
Le Massegros F 34 B5
Le Mayet-de-Montagne F 30 C4
Le May-sur-Èvre F 23 F10
Lembach im Mühlkreis A 76 E5
Lembeke B 182 C3
Lemberg D 27 B8
Lemberg F 27 B7
Lembeye F 32 D5
Lembras F 29 F7
Lembruch D 17 C10
Lemele NL 16 D6
Lemelerveld NL 16 D6
Le Mêle-sur-Sarthe F 24 C3
Le Merlerault F 23 C12
Le Mesnil-sur-Oger F 25 C11
Lemetinvaara FIN 121 F12
Lemgo D 17 D11
Lemi FIN 128 C8
Lemierzyce PL 81 A7
Lemland FIN 99 B14
Lemmenjoki FIN 117 A16
Lemmer NL 16 C5
Lemnia RO 153 E8
Le Molay-Littry F 23 B10
Le Monastier F 34 A5
Le Monastier-sur-Gazeille F 30 F4
Le Monêtier-les-Bains F 31 F10
Le Montet F 30 C3
Lempäälä FIN 127 C10
Lempdes F 30 D3
Lempdes F 30 E3
Lempyy FIN 124 E8
Lemu FIN 126 D6
Le Muy F 36 E5
Lemvig DK 86 B2
Lemwerder D 17 B11
Lemybrien IRL 9 D7
Lena N 101 E13
Lenart SLO 148 C5
Lēnas LV 134 C3
Lenauheim RO 150 F6
Lencloître F 29 B6
Lencouacq F 32 B5
Lend A 73 B7
Lendak SK 145 E1
Lendava SLO 149 C6
Lendelede B 182 D2
Lendery RUS 125 D16
Lendinara I 66 B4
Lendum DK 90 E7
Lenë AL 168 B3
Lenešice CZ 76 B5
Le Neubourg F 24 B4
Lengau A 72 B6
Lengau A 76 F4
Lengdorf D 75 F11
Lengefeld D 80 E4
Lengenes N 111 D13
Lengenfeld D 79 E11
Lengenwang D 71 B11
Lengerich D 17 C9
Lengerich D 17 D9
Lenggries D 72 A4
Lengnau CH 27 F7
Lengyeltóti H 149 C9
Lenham GB 15 E10
Lenhovda S 89 B8
Lenine UA 154 C5
Léning F 27 C6
Le Nizan F 32 B5
Lenk CH 31 C11
Lenkimai LT 134 D2
Lenna I 69 B8
Lennartsfors S 96 D6
Lennartsnäs S 99 D9
Lenne D 78 C6
Lennestadt D 21 B10
Lenningen D 27 C11
Lennsjö S 103 B12
Leno I 66 B1
Le Noirmont CH 27 F6
Lenola I 62 E4
Le Nouvion-en-Thiérache F 19 D8
Lens B 19 C8
Lens F 18 D6
Lensahn D 83 B9
Lensvik N 104 D7
Lent F 31 C7
Lent NL 183 B7
Lentas GR 178 F8
Lenti H 149 C7
Lentiai I 72 D5
Lentiira FIN 121 F14
Lenting D 75 E9
Lentini I 59 E7
Lentvaris LT 137 D11
Lenvik N 111 C13
Lenzburg CH 27 F9
Lenzen D 83 D10
Lenzing A 76 G5
Lenzkirch D 27 E9
Leoben A 73 B11
Leoben A 73 C8
Leobendorf A 77 F10
Leobersdorf A 77 G10
Leogang A 73 B6
Léognan F 28 F4
Leominster GB 13 A9
León E 39 C8
Léon F 32 C3
Leonberg D 27 C11
Léoncel F 31 F7
Leonding A 76 F6
Leonessa I 62 B3
Leonforte I 58 D5
Leonidio GR 175 E6
Leontari GR 174 A5
Leontari GR 174 E5
Leopoldov SK 146 E5
Leopoldsburg B 19 B11
Leopoldsdorf im Marchfelde A 77 F11
Leopoldshagen D 84 C5
Leopoldshöhe D 17 D11
Leorda RO 153 B8
Leordeni RO 160 D6
Leordina RO 152 B4
Leova MD 154 E2
Leovo Brdo MNE 157 F11
Lepaa FIN 127 C11
Le Palais F 22 F5
Le Palais-sur-Vienne F 29 D8
Le Pallet F 23 F9
Le Parcq F 18 D5
Lepassaare EST 132 F1
Le Passage F 33 B7
Le Pavillon-Ste-Julie F 25 D10
Lepe E 51 E5
Le Péage-de-Roussillon F 30 E6
Le Pellerin F 23 F8
Le Périer F 31 F8
Le Perthus F 34 F4
Le Pertre F 23 D9
Le Petit-Quevilly F 18 F3
Le Pian-Médoc F 28 F4
Le Pin-au-Haras F 23 C12
L'Épine F 35 B10
Le Pin-la-Garenne F 24 D4
Lepistönmäki FIN 123 D10
Lepitsa BG 165 C9
Le Pizou F 28 E6
Le Plan F 33 D8
Le Plessis-Belleville F 25 B8
Le Poët F 35 B10
Lepoglava HR 148 D6
Le Poinçonnet F 29 B9
Le Poiré-sur-Vie F 28 B2
Le Pont-de-Beauvoisin F 31 D8
Le Pont-de-Claix F 31 E8
Le Pont-de-Montvert F 35 B6
Le Pontet F 35 C8
Leporano I 61 C8
Le Porge F 28 E3
Le Porge-Océan F 28 F3
Le Portel F 15 F12
Leposavić RKS 163 C10
Leposaviq RKS 163 C10
Le Pouldu F 22 E4
Le Pouliguen F 22 F7
Lepoura GR 175 C9

Le Pouzin F 30 F6
Leppäjärvi FIN 117 B10
Leppäkoski FIN 127 D12
Leppälä FIN 113 D19
Leppälä FIN 121 D11
Leppälänkylä FIN 123 E11
Leppälahti FIN 125 F12
Leppälahti FIN 124 D8
Leppälahti FIN 125 F12
Leppäselkä FIN 123 D16
Leppävesi FIN 123 F15
Leppävirta FIN 124 F9
Leppiaho FIN 119 C15
Leppikoski FIN 119 D17
Leppiniemi FIN 119 E16
Leppneeme EST 131 B9
Lepsala FIN 123 F10
Lepsäma FIN 127 E12
Lepsény H 149 B10
Leptokarya GR 169 D8
Le Puy-en-Velay F 30 E4
Le Puy-Notre-Dame F 23 F11
Le Quesnoy F 19 D8
Lequile I 61 C10
Ler N 104 E8
Le Raincy F 25 C8
Léran F 33 E9
Lerberget S 87 C11
Lercara Friddi I 58 D4
Lerdala S 91 C14
Léré F 25 F8
Le Relecq-Kerhuon F 22 D3
Lereşti RO 160 C6
Lerici I 69 E8
Lérida F 42 D5
Lerín E 32 F2
Lerkaka S 89 B11
Lerma E 40 D4
Lerm-et Musset F 32 B5
Lermoos A 71 C11
Lerot S 96 C7
Le Rouget F 29 F10
Lérouville F 26 C4
Le Rozier F 34 B5
Lerum S 91 D11
Le Russey F 26 F6
Lervik N 95 D13
Lerwick GB 3 E14
Lesa I 68 B6
Les Abrets F 31 D8
Les Aix-d'Angillon F 25 F8
Lešak RKS 163 C10
Lesaka E 32 D2
Les Andelys F 18 F3
Les Angles F 33 E10
Les Angles F 35 C8
Lešani MK 168 B4
Les Arcs F 31 D10
Les Arcs F 36 E4
Les Aubiers F 28 B4
Les Avellanes E 42 D5
Les Avenières F 31 D8
Les Bondons F 35 B6
Les Bordes F 25 E7
Les Borges Blanques E 42 D5
Les Borges del Camp E 42 E6
Le Bouchoux F 31 C8
Les Brenets CH 31 A10
Lesbury GB 5 E13
Les Cabannes F 33 E9
L'Escala E 43 C10
L'Escale F 35 B11
Les Cammazes F 33 D10
Lescar F 32 D5
L'Escarène F 37 D6
Les Cases d'Alcanar E 42 F5
Lesce SLO 73 D9
Lesconil F 22 E3
Les Contamines-Montjoie
  F 31 D10
Les Coves de Vinromà E 48 D5
Lescun F 32 E4
Lescure-d'Albigeois F 33 C10
Les Deux-Alpes F 31 E9
Les Diablerets CH 31 C11
Les Échelles F 31 E8
Les Églisottes-et-Chalaures
  F 28 E5
Le Sel-de-Bretagne F 23 E8
Le Sen F 32 B4
Le Sentier CH 31 B9
Les Éparges F 26 B4
Les Epesses F 28 B4
Les Escaldes AND 33 E9
Les Essards-Taignevaux F 31 B7
Les Essarts F 28 B3
Le Seu d'Urgell E 33 F8
Les Eyzies-de-Tayac-Sireuil
  F 29 F8
Les Fins F 31 A10
Les Forges F 26 D5
Les Fourgs F 31 B9
Les Gets F 31 C10
Leshak RKS 163 C10
Leshan RKS 163 C10
Les Hautes-Rivières F 184 E2
Les Herbiers F 28 B3
Les Houches F 31 D10
Lesichevo BG 165 E9
Lesično SLO 148 D5
Lesidren BG 165 D9
Lesina I 63 D8
Les Issambres F 36 E5
Lesja N 101 B9
Lesjöfors S 97 C11
Leskava LT 137 D8
Leskelä FIN 119 F15
Lesko PL 145 E5
Leskoec MK 168 B4
Leskova SRB 163 C9
Leskovac SRB 164 D4
Leskovik AL 168 D4
Leskovo BG 161 F11
Les Landes-Genusson F 28 B3
Leslie GB 5 C10
Les Lucs-sur-Boulogne F 28 B3
Lesmahagow GB 5 D9
Les Maillys F 26 F3
Les Marches F 31 E8
Les Martres-de-Veyre F 30 D3
Les Matelles F 35 C6
Les Mazures F 184 E2
Les Mées F 35 B10
Les Menuires F 31 E10
Lesmont F 25 D11
Les Mureaux F 24 C6
Lešná SK 146 B5
Leśna PL 81 D8
Lesneven F 22 C3
Leśnica PL 142 F5
Leśnica SRB 158 D3
Leśniów Wielki PL 81 C8
Lesogorskiy RUS 129 C11

Lesovaara FIN 121 D13
Lesovo BG 167 F7
Lesparre-Médoc F 28 E4
Les Peintures F 28 E5
Les Pennes-Mirabeau F 35 D9
Lesperon F 32 C3
Lespezi RO 153 C9
Lespignan F 34 D5
Lespinassière F 34 D4
Les Planches-en-Montagne
  F 31 B9
Les Planes d'Hostoles E 43 C9
L'Espluga Calba E 42 E6
L'Espluga de Francolí E 42 E6
Les Ponts-de-Cé F 23 F10
Les Ponts-de-Martel CH 31 A10
Les Preses E 43 C8
Lespugue F 33 D7
Les Rosiers-sur-Loire F 23 F11
Les Rousses F 31 C9
Les Sables-d'Olonne F 28 C2
Les Salles-du-Gardon F 35 B7
Lessay F 23 B8
Lessebo S 89 B8
Les Sièges F 25 D10
Lessines B 19 C8
Les Sorinières F 23 F8
Lestene LV 134 C6
Les Ternes F 30 E3
Les Thuiles F 36 C5
Lestijärvi FIN 123 C13
Lešťina CZ 77 C11
Lestrade F 34 B4
Les Trois-Moutiers F 24 F3
Leşu RO 152 C5
Lesura BG 165 C8
Les Vans F 35 B7
Les Vignes F 34 B5
Leszczyn PL 85 C9
Leszno PL 141 F3
Leszno Górne PL 81 D9
Létavértes H 150 C6
Letca RO 151 C11
Leţcani RO 153 C10
Letca Nouă RO 161 E7
Letchworth Garden City
  GB 15 D8
Letea Veche RO 153 D9
Le Teich F 32 A3
Le Teil F 35 A8
Le Teilleul F 23 C10
Le Temple F 28 E4
Le Theil F 24 D4
Le-Theil-de-Bretagne F 23 E9
Le Thillot F 27 E6
Le Tholy F 27 D6
Le Thor F 35 C8
Letino I 63 E6
Letkés H 147 F7
Letnitsa BG 165 C11
Letoianni I 59 D7
Letonice CZ 77 D11
Le Touquet-Paris-Plage F 15 F12
Le Touvet F 31 E8
Letovice CZ 77 C11
L'Étrat F 30 E5
Le Trayas F 36 E5
Le Tréport F 18 D3
Letsbo S 103 C10
Letschin D 80 A6
Letterfinish IRL 8 E3
Letterkenny IRL 7 C7
Lettermacaward IRL 6 C6
Letterston GB 12 B5
Letur E 55 C8
Le Tuzan F 32 B4
Letzlingen D 79 B9
Leu RO 160 E4
Leuc F 33 D10
Leucate F 34 E5
Leuchars GB 5 C11
Leuchtenberg D 75 C11
Leud RO 152 B4
Leuenberg D 84 E5
Leuglay F 25 E12
Leuk CH 68 A4
Leukerbad CH 70 E5
Leumrabhagh GB 2 J4
Leun D 185 D9
Leuna D 79 D11
Leusden NL 16 D4
Leuşeni MD 154 D3
Leutasch A 72 B3
Leutenberg D 79 E9
Leutershausen D 75 D7
Leutesdorf D 185 D7
Leutkirch im Allgäu D 71 B10
Leuvanjoki FIN 119 D15
Leuven B 19 C10
Leuze-en-Hainaut B 19 C8
Le Val F 36 E4
Levan AL 168 C1
Levänen FIN 128 C8
Levang N 108 D5
Levanger N 105 D10
Levanjska Varoš HR 149 F10
Levanto FIN 127 D13
Levanto I 37 C11
Leva Reka BG 165 D6
Leväsjoki FIN 126 B6
Levél H 146 F4
Levelek H 145 H4
Leven GB 5 C11
Leven GB 11 D11
Levens F 37 D6
Levenwick GB 3 F14
Leverano I 61 C10
Leverburgh GB 2 K2
Le-Verdon-sur-Mer F 28 D3
Leverkusen D 21 B7
Le Vernet F 33 D9
Lèves F 24 D5
Levet F 29 B10
Levice SK 147 E7
Levico Terme I 69 A11
Levidi GR 174 D5
Levie F 37 H10
Levier F 31 B9
Le Vigan F 35 C6
Lévignac F 33 C8
Lévignacq F 32 B3
Levijoki FIN 123 E11
Le Ville I 66 F4
Le-Vivier-sur-Mer F 23 C8
Levka BG 166 F6
Levkogeia GR 170 B6
Levoča SK 145 E2

Levonperä FIN 123 C14
Levo-oja FIN 119 D16
Levroux F 29 B9
Levski BG 165 C10
Lewes GB 15 F9
Lewin Brzeski PL 142 E4
Lewin Kłodzki PL 77 B10
Leyburn GB 11 C8
Leyland GB 10 D6
Leyme F 29 F9
Leysin CH 31 C11
Leytron CH 31 C11
Lézan F 35 B7
Leżajsk PL 144 C5
Lézat-sur-Lèze F 33 D8
Lezay F 28 C5
Lezhë AL 163 F8
Lézignan-Corbières F 34 D4
Lezoux F 30 D3
Lezuza E 55 B8
Lgota Górna PL 143 E7
Lgota Wielka PL 143 D7
Lhenice CZ 76 D6
Lherm F 33 D8
L'Hermenault F 28 B4
L'Honor-de-Cos F 33 B8
L'Hôpital F 186 C4
L'Horme F 30 E6
Lhospitalet F 33 B8
L'Hospitalet de l'Infant E 42 F5
L'Hospitalet de Llobregat
  E 43 E8
L'Hospitalet-du-Larzac F 34 C5
L'Hospitalet-près-l'Andorre
  F 33 E9
L'Hostal del Alls E 42 F5
L'Huissserie F 23 D10
Lhuître F 25 C11
Lia N 111 C14
Liabøen N 104 E4
Liancourt F 18 F5
Liapades GR 168 E2
Liart F 19 E9
Liarvåg N 94 D3
Liatorp S 88 B6
Liatroim IRL 6 D6
Libáň CZ 77 B8
Libatse EST 131 D8
Libberton GB 5 D9
Libčany CZ 77 B9
Libčeves CZ 76 B5
Liberadz PL 139 D9
Liberec CZ 81 E8
Liběšice CZ 80 E6
Libiąż PL 143 F7
Libice nad Cidlinou CZ 77 B8
Libin B 19 E11
Libina CZ 77 C12
Libochovice CZ 76 B6
Libofshë AL 168 C1
Libohovë AL 168 D3
Libouchec CZ 80 E6
Libourne F 28 F5
Libramont B 19 E11
Librazhd AL 168 B3
Librilla E 55 D10
Libros E 47 D10
Licata I 58 E4
Licciana Nardi I 69 E9
Licenza I 62 C3
Liceras E 40 F5
Lich D 21 C11
Lichfield GB 11 F8
Lichnov CZ 142 F4
Lichnowy PL 138 B6
Lichtaart B 182 C5
Lichte D 75 A9
Lichtenau D 17 E11
Lichtenau D 27 C9
Lichtenau im Waldviertel
  A 77 E8
Lichtenstein D 79 E12
Lichtenstein D 74 F6
Lichtentanne D 79 E11
Lichtenvoorde NL 17 E7
Lichtenwörth A 77 G10
Lichterfelde D 84 E5
Lichtervelde B 19 B7
Ličí LV 135 D13
Lički LV 135 D13
Ličko Jesenica HR 156 C3
Lički Osik HR 156 C3
Licodia Eubea I 59 E6
Licques F 15 F12
Ličupe LV 135 C10
Licurici RO 160 D3
Lida BY 137 F11
Lidečko CZ 146 C6
Liden S 103 A12
Lidhult S 87 B12
Lidingö S 99 D10
Lidköping S 91 B13
Lido I 66 B5
Lido Adriano I 66 D5
Lido di Classe I 66 D5
Lido di Foce Verde I 62 E3
Lido di Jesolo I 66 A6
Lido di Metaponto I 61 C7
Lido di Ostia I 62 D2
Lido di Siponto I 63 D9
Lido di Spina I 66 C5
Lidoriki GR 174 B5
Lidsälen S 102 E5
Lidsjöberg S 106 C8
Lidzbark PL 139 D8
Lidzbark Warmiński PL 136 C2
Liebenau D 17 C12
Liebenau D 17 F12
Liebenburg D 79 B7
Liebenfels A 73 C9
Liebenwalde D 84 E4
Lieberose D 80 C6
Liebling RO 159 B7
Liebach A 148 C4
Liebstadt D 80 E5
Liedakkala FIN 119 C13
Liédena E 32 E3
Liedenpohja FIN 123 F11
Liège B 19 C12
Liehittäjä S 119 B10
Liekokylä FIN 119 C16
Lieksa FIN 125 D14
Lielauce LV 134 C5
Lielbērze LV 134 C6
Lielirbe LV 130 F4
Lielklapari LV 135 D13
Lielmēmele LV 135 D10
Lielvārde LV 135 C9

Lielvircava LV 134 C7
Liempde NL 183 B7
Lien S 105 D15
Lien S 107 E10
Lienden NL 183 B7
Lienen D 17 D9
Lienz A 73 C6
Liepa LV 135 B10
Liepāre LV 134 C7
Liepas LV 135 D12
Liepe D 84 E5
Liepene LV 134 B3
Liepgarten D 84 C6
Liepiņas FIN 120 F8 (?) — Liepimäjärvi FIN 117 B11
Liepna LV 133 B2
Lieponys LT 137 E12
Liepupe LV 135 B8
Lier B 19 B10
Lier N 96 B7
Lierbyen N 95 C12
Liernais F 25 F11
Lierneux B 19 D12
Liesek SK 147 C9
Lieser D 21 E8
Lieshout NL 183 B7
Lieso FIN 127 C12
Liessel NL 16 F5
Liestal CH 27 F8
Lieštany SK 146 D6
Liešti RO 161 B11
Lietavská Lúčka SK 147 C7
Lietekylä FIN 121 E11
Lieto FIN 126 D7
Liétor E 55 B9
Lievestuore FIN 123 F16
Lievoperä FIN 119 F16
Liezen A 73 A9
Liezēre LV 135 B12
Liffol-le-Grand F 26 D4
Lifford IRL 4 F2
Liffré F 23 D8
Lifton GB 12 D6
Ligardes F 33 B6
Līgatne LV 135 B10
Ligist A 73 C11
Lignano Pineta I 73 E7
Lignano Sabbiadoro I 73 E7
Lignan-sur-Orb F 34 D5
Ligné F 23 F9
Ligneuville B 20 D6
Lignières F 29 B10
Ligny-en-Barrois F 26 C3
Ligny-le-Châtel F 25 E10
Ligonchio I 66 D1
Ligota PL 142 C4
Ligowo PL 139 E8
Ligueil F 29 A7
Ligugé F 29 B6
Lihme DK 86 B3
Lihula EST 130 D7
Liigvalla EST 131 C12
Liikasenvaara FIN 121 B14
Liikavaara S 116 D6
Liimattala FIN 123 E15
Liimattala FIN 123 E15
Liipantönkkä FIN 122 E9
Liittoperä FIN 123 C16
Liiva EST 130 D6
Lijar E 55 E8
Lijęšće BIH 157 B9
Lijeska BIH 158 F3
Lijeva Rijeka MNE 163 D7
Lijevi Dubravčak HR 149 E6
Likavka SK 147 C9
Likenäs S 102 E5
Liksna LV 135 E12
Lilaia GR 175 B5
Liland N 110 D6
Lilaste LV 135 B8
L'Île-Bouchard F 24 F3
L'Île-Rousse F 37 F9
Lilienfeld A 77 F9
Liljendal FIN 127 D15
Liljendal S 97 B11
Lilkovo BG 165 F10
Lillå S 118 B5
Lilla Edet S 91 C11
Lillåfors S 118 B6
Lilla Tjärby S 87 B12
Lillby FIN 123 D10
Lille B 16 F3
Lille F 19 C7
Lillebo N 102 C3
Lillebonne F 18 E2
Lillehammer N 101 D12
Lillers F 18 C5
Lillesand N 90 C3
Lilleshall GB 11 F7
Lille Skensved DK 87 D10
Lillestrøm N 95 C14
Lille Værløse DK 87 D10
Lillfjäten S 102 C4
Lillhärdal S 102 C7
Lillholmsjö S 105 D16
Lillholmträsk S 107 B18
Lilliesleaf GB 5 D11
Lillkågeträsk S 118 E5
Lillkyrka S 98 C8
Lillmörttsjö S 103 B11
Lillo E 47 E6
Lillögda S 107 C13
Lillpite S 118 D4
Lillsaivis S 118 B7
Lillsele S 107 C16
Lillselet S 116 E9
Lillsjöhögen S 106 E8
Lillskog S 103 C9
Lillström S 102 A7
Lillviken S 109 C11
Lilyache BG 165 C8
Lilyak BG 167 C6
Lilyanovo BG 169 A9
Lima I 72 D5
Limana I 72 D5
Limanköy TR 167 F10
Limanowa PL 144 D1
Limanu RO 155 F3
Limatola I 60 A2
Limavady GB 4 E3
Limay F 24 B6
Limbach D 21 F12
Limbach D 186 C4
Limbach-Oberfrohna D 79 E12
Limbadi I 59 B8

Limbaži LV 135 A9
Limbourg B 20 C5
Limburg an der Lahn D 21 D10
Limburgerhof D 187 C5
Lime DK 86 C6
Limedsforsen S 102 E5
Limenaria GR 171 C7
Limenas GR 177 C6
Limenas Chersonisou GR 178 E9
Limerick IRL 8 C5
Limingen N 105 B15
Liminka FIN 119 E14
Liminpuro FIN 120 F8
Limmared S 91 D13
Limmen NL 16 C3
Limnes GR 175 D6
Limni GR 175 B7
Limnochori GR 169 C6
Limoges F 29 D8
Limogne-en-Quercy F 33 B9
Limone Piemonte I 37 C7
Limone sul Garda I 69 B10
Limons I 63 D7
Limonest F 30 D6
Limosano I 63 D7
Limoux F 33 D10
Limpias E 40 B5
Lin AL 168 B4
Linå DK 86 C5
Lina älv S 116 D4
Linakhamari RUS 114 D10
Linards F 29 D9
Linares E 54 C5
Linares de Mora F 48 D3
Linares de Riofrío E 45 C9
Linaria GR 175 B10
Lincent B 19 C11
Lincoln GB 11 E10
Lind DK 86 C3
Lindas N 100 E2
Lindau D 79 B11
Lindau D 82 A7
Lindau (Bodensee) D 71 B9
Lindberg D 76 D4
Linde DK 86 C2
Lindelse DK 87 F7
Linden D 21 C11
Linden D 82 B6
Lindenberg D 80 B6
Lindenberg D 83 D12
Lindenberg im Allgäu D 71 B9
Lindenfels D 21 E11
Lindern (Oldenburg) D 17 C9
Lindesberg S 97 C13
Lindesnäs S 97 B12
Lindewitt D 82 A6
Lindfield GB 15 E8
Lindhem EST 131 C11
Lindholmen S 99 C10
Lindi EST 131 E8
Lindknud DK 86 D4
Lindkoski FIN 127 D15
Lindlar D 21 B8
Lindome S 91 D11
Lindores GB 5 C10
Lindós GR 181 D8
Lindoso P 38 E3
Lindow D 84 E3
Lindsdal S 89 B10
Lindsjö S 103 B12
Lindstedt D 79 A10
Lindved DK 86 D5
Linge N 100 B6
Lingen (Ems) D 17 C8
Lingenfeld D 21 F10
Lingfield GB 15 E8
Linghed S 103 E10
Linghem S 92 C7
Lingolsheim F 27 C8
Lingrasmo N 111 B18
Linguaglossa I 59 D7
Linguizzetta F 37 G10
Linhares P 44 C6
Liniewo PL 138 B5
Linkmenys LT 135 F11
Linköping S 92 C7
Linksness GB 3 H10
Linkuva LT 135 D7
Linlithgow GB 5 D9
Linna EST 131 E11
Linnamäe EST 130 D7
Linnamäe EST 131 F13
Linnankylä FIN 123 F10
Linneryd S 89 B8
Linnich D 20 C6
Linow D 83 D13
Linsell S 102 B6
Linsidemore GB 2 K8
Linthal CH 71 D8
Linthe D 79 B12
Lintig D 17 A11
Lintrup DK 86 E3
Lintula FIN 117 C14
Linum D 84 E12
Linxe F 32 C3
Linyola E 42 D5
Linz A 76 F6
Linz am Rhein D 21 C8
Lioboml' UA 141 H10
Lioliai LT 134 E5
Lioni I 60 B4
Lion-sur-Mer F 23 B11
Liorac-sur-Louyre F 29 F7
Lios Mór IRL 9 D7
Lios Tuathail IRL 8 D4
Lipa BIH 157 D9
Lipa PL 139 D10
Lipănești RO 161 C8
Lipany SK 145 E2
Lipar SRB 158 B4
Lipari I 59 C6
Lipawki BY 133 E3
Lipce Reymontowskie PL 141 G1
Liperi FIN 125 E12
Liphook GB 15 E7
Lipiany PL 85 D8
Lipik HR 149 F8
Lipka PL 85 D12
Lipki Wielkie PL 85 E9
Lipkovo MK 164 E4
Lipljan RKS 164 D3
Lipnic BIH 157 D9
Lipnica PL 85 C12
Lipnica PL 138 D7
Lipnica PL 143 E9
Lipnik PL 143 E11

Lipník nad Bečvou CZ 146 B5
Lipno CZ 76 E6
Lipno PL 139 E7
Lipolist SRB 158 D4
Liposthey F 32 B4
Lipova RO 151 E8
Lipová SK 146 E6
Lipovac HR 157 B11
Lipovac SRB 164 B4
Lipová-Lázně CZ 77 B12
Lipovăţ RO 153 D11
Lipovec CZ 77 D11
Lipoveni MD 154 D3
Lipovljani HR 149 F7
Lipovo RUS 136 D5
Lipovu RO 160 E3
Lippo FIN 119 D11
Lipsk PL 140 C8
Lipsko PL 141 H5
Liptál CZ 146 C6
Liptovská Kokava SK 147 C9
Liptovská Lúžna SK 147 D8
Liptovská Osada SK 147 D8
Liptovská Teplička SK 147 D10
Liptovské Revúce SK 147 D8
Liptovský Hrádok SK 147 C9
Liptovský Mikuláš SK 147 C9
Lipusz PL 138 B4
Lipůvka CZ 77 D11
Liqenas AL 168 C4
Liré F 23 F9
Lis AL 168 A3
Lisa RO 152 F5
Lisa RO 160 F6
Lisac HR 157 D8
Lisac HR 162 D4
lisaku EST 131 C14
Lisacul IRL 6 E5
Lisbane GB 7 C11
Lisbellaw GB 7 D7
Lisboa P 50 B1
Lisburn GB 7 C10
Liscannor IRL 8 C4
Liscarney IRL 6 E3
Liscarroll IRL 8 D5
Lisciano Niccone I 66 F5
Lişcoteanca RO 161 C11
Lisdoonvarna IRL 6 F4
Liseleje DK 87 C9
Lisets BG 165 C8
Lisewo PL 138 D6
Lisgarode IRL 8 C6
Lisgoold IRL 8 E6
Lisia Góra PL 143 F11
Lisijcice PL 142 F4
Lisieux F 23 B12
Lisiy Nos RUS 129 D13
Lisjö S 97 C15
Liskeard GB 12 E6
Lisková SK 147 C8
Lisków PL 142 C5
Lisky UA 155 C4
Lisle F 29 E7
Lislea GB 4 F3
L'Isle-Adam F 25 B7
L'Isle-de-Noé F 33 C6
L'Isle-d'Espagnac F 29 D6
L'Isle-en-Dodon F 33 D7
L'Isle-Jourdain F 29 C7
L'Isle-Jourdain F 33 C8
L'Isle-sur-la-Sorgue F 35 C9
L'Isle-sur-le-Doubs F 26 F6
L'Isle-sur-Serein F 25 E11
Lisle-sur-Tarn F 33 C9
Lisma FIN 117 B14
Lismakin IRL 9 C7
Lismanaapa FIN 117 D17
Lismarka N 101 D13
Lismore IRL 9 D7
Lisna BY 133 E4
Lisnagry IRL 8 C5
Lisnakill IRL 9 D8
Lisnarrick GB 7 D7
Lisnaskea GB 7 D8
Lisne UA 154 C4
Lišov CZ 77 D7
Lisów PL 142 F5
Lispole IRL 8 D2
Lisronagh IRL 9 D7
Lisryan IRL 7 E8
Liss GB 15 E7
Lissan GB 4 F3
Lisse NL 16 D3
Lissendorf D 185 D6
Lisskogsbränna S 97 A10
Lissone I 69 B7
Lissycasey IRL 8 C4
List D 86 E2
Listed DK 89 E8
Listerby S 89 C8
Listerlin IRL 9 D8
Listowel IRL 8 D4
Listrac-Médoc F 28 E4
Listry IRL 8 D3
Liszki PL 143 F8
Liszkowo PL 85 D12
Lit S 106 E7
Lița RO 160 F5
Litakovo BG 165 D8
Litava SK 147 E8
Litene LV 133 B2
Liteni RO 153 B8
Litér H 149 B9
Lit-et-Mixe F 32 B3
Lith NL 183 B6
Lithakia GR 174 D2
Lithines GR 179 E11
Litija SLO 73 D10
Litke H 147 E9
Litlfjord N 113 B14
Litmalahti FIN 125 E10
Litmaniemi FIN 125 E10
Litochoro GR 169 D8
Litoměřice CZ 76 A6
Litomyšl CZ 77 C10
Litovel CZ 77 C12
Littau CH 70 C6
Littleborough GB 11 D7
Littlehampton GB 15 F7
Littlemill GB 3 K9
Little Oakley GB 15 D11
Littleport GB 15 C9

Littlestone-on-Sea GB 15 F10
Littleton IRL 9 C7
Littoinen FIN 126 E7
Litva BIH 157 D7
Litvínov CZ 80 E5
Litzendorf D 75 C9
Liudinavas LT 136 E7
Liukkunen FIN 125 D14
Liuža LV 133 C2
Livada RO 145 H7
Livada RO 151 B11
Livadaki GR 174 D4
Livadeia GR 175 C6
Livădeni MD 153 A11
Livadero GR 169 D6
Livadero GR 171 B6
Livadi GR 171 B6
Livadi GR 175 D10
Livadia GR 169 B9
Livanates GR 175 B7
Līvāni LV 135 D12
Livari MNE 163 E7
Livarot F 23 B12
Līvbērze LV 134 C7
Livernon F 33 A9
Liverpool GB 10 E6
Livezeni RO 152 D5
Livezi RO 153 E9
Livezi RO 160 D3
Livezile RO 152 C5
Livezile RO 152 E3
Livezile RO 159 D10
Līvi LV 135 B10
Livigno I 71 D10
Livingston GB 5 D9
Livno BIH 157 E7
Livo FIN 119 C17
Livold SLO 73 E10
Livonniska FIN 121 C10
Livorno I 66 E1
Livorno Ferraris I 68 C5
Livron-sur-Drôme F 30 F6
Liw PL 139 F12
Lixing-lès-St-Avold F 186 C2
Lixnaw IRL 8 D3
Lixouri GR 174 C1
Lizard GB 12 F4
Lizarraga E 32 E1
Lizděni LV 131 F10
Lizums LV 135 B12
Lizy-sur-Ourcq F 25 B9
Lizzanello I 61 C10
Lizzano I 61 C8
Ljaljenča BIH 157 C11
Ljeskove Vode BIH 157 C8
Ljig SRB 158 E5
Ljønes N 108 B8
Ljørdal N 102 D4
Ljosland N 90 B1
Ljøsne N 100 D7
Ljubača SRB 164 C5
Ljuberada SRB 164 C5
Ljubija BIH 156 C5
Ljubinje BIH 162 D5
Ljubiš SRB 158 F4
Ljubljana SLO 73 D10
Ljubogošta BIH 157 E10
Ljubovija SRB 158 E3
Ljubuški BIH 157 F8
Ljugarn S 93 E13
Ljung S 91 D13
Ljungå S 103 A11
Ljungaverk S 103 B11
Ljungby S 87 B13
Ljungbyhed S 87 C12
Ljungbyholm S 89 B10
Ljungdalen S 102 A4
Ljungsarp S 91 D14
Ljungsbro S 92 B7
Ljungskile S 91 C10
Ljupina HR 157 B7
Ljuša BIH 157 D7
Ljusci Palanka BIH 156 C5
Ljusdal S 103 C11
Ljusfallshammar S 92 B7
Ljusne S 103 D13
Ljusnedal S 102 A4
Ljustorp S 103 A13
Ljusträsk S 118 D3
Ljusvattnet S 118 E6
Ljuti Dolac BIH 157 F8
Ljutomer SLO 148 C6
Llabjan RKS 164 D3
Llagostera E 43 D9
Llamas de la Ribera E 39 C8
Llanaelhaearn GB 10 F3
Llanarth GB 12 A6
Llanarthney GB 12 B6
Llanbadarn Fawr GB 12 A6
Llanbadrig GB 10 D3
Llanbedr GB 10 F3
Llanbedrog GB 10 F3
Llanberis GB 10 E3
Llanbister GB 13 A8
Llanblethian GB 13 C8
Llançà S 34 F5
Llandanwg GB 10 F3
Llandderfel GB 10 F4
Llandeilo GB 12 B7
Llandissilio GB 12 B5
Llandovery GB 13 B7
Llandrillo GB 10 F5
Llandrindod Wells GB 13 A8
Llandudno GB 10 E4
Llandwrog GB 10 E3
Llandysul GB 12 A6
Llanegwad GB 12 B6
Llaneilian GB 10 D3
Llanelli GB 12 B6
Llanelltyd GB 10 F4
Llanelwy GB 10 E5
Llanes E 39 B10
Llanfaelog GB 10 E3
Llanfair Caereinion GB 10 F5
Llanfairfechan GB 10 E4
Llanfairpwllgwyngyll GB 10 E3
Llanfair Talhaiarn GB 10 E5
Llanfihangel-ar-arth GB
  12 A6
Llanfyllin GB 10 F5
Llangadfan GB 10 F5
Llangefni GB 10 E3
Llangeler GB 12 A6
Llangelynin GB 10 F3
Llangoed GB 10 E3
Llangollen GB 10 F5
Llangurig GB 13 A7
Llanidloes GB 13 A7
Llanilar GB 12 A6
Llanishen GB 13 B8

Llanllwchaiarn GB 10 F5
Llanllyfni GB 10 E3
Llannerch-y-medd GB 10 E3
Llan-non GB 12 B6
Llannon GB 12 B6
Llanrhaeadr-ym-Mochnant GB 10 F5
Llanrhidian GB 12 B6
Llanrhystud GB 12 A6
Llanrug GB 10 E3
Llanrumney GB 13 B8
Llanrwst GB 10 E4
Llansanffraid Glan Conwy GB 10 E4
Llansannan GB 10 E4
Llansawel GB 12 A6
Llantilio Pertholey GB 13 B8
Llantrisant GB 13 B8
Llantwit Major GB 13 C8
Llanuwchllyn GB 10 F4
Llanwddyn GB 10 F5
Llanwenog GB 12 A6
Llanwnda GB 10 E3
Llanwnog GB 10 F5
Llanwrtyd Wells GB 13 A7
Llanybydder GB 12 A6
Llapushnik RKS 163 D10
Llardecans E 42 E5
Llaurí E 48 F4
Llavorsí E 33 E8
Llay GB 10 E5
Lledrod GB 12 A7
Lleida E 42 D5
Llera E 51 C7
Llerena E 51 C7
Lliria E 48 E3
Llívia E 33 F9
Llodio E 40 B6
Llombai E 48 F3
Lloret de Mar E 43 D9
Lloseta E 49 E10
Llubí E 57 B11
Llucmajor E 57 C10
Lniano PL 138 C5
Lo B 18 C6
Loamneş RO 152 F4
Loano I 37 C8
Loarre E 32 F4
Löbau D 81 D7
Lobbæk DK 89 E7
Lobe LV 135 C10
Löbejün D 79 C10
Lobera de Onsella E 32 F3
Löbërgji LV 131 F12
Łobez PL 85 C9
Lobith NL 183 B8
Löbnitz D 83 B13
Łobodno PL 143 E6
Lobón E 51 B6
Lobonäs S 103 C9
Loburg D 79 B11
Łobżenica PL 85 D12
Locana I 31 E11
Locarno CH 68 A6
Locate di Triulzi I 69 C7
Loccum (Rehburg-Loccum) D 17 D12
Loceri I 64 D4
Lochaline GB 4 B5
Lochau A 71 B9
Lochawe GB 4 C6
Lochboisdale GB 2 L2
Lochcarron GB 2 L5
Lochdon GB 4 C5
Lochearnhead GB 5 C8
Lochem NL 16 D6
Lochen A 76 F4
Lochend GB 3 L8
Loches F 24 F4
Lochgelly GB 5 C10
Lochgilphead GB 4 C6
Lochgoilhead GB 4 C7
Lochinver GB 2 J6
Lochmaben GB 5 E10
Lochmaddy GB 2 K2
Lochovice CZ 76 C5
Łochów PL 139 E12
Lochranza GB 4 D6
Lochristi B 19 B8
Loch Sgioport GB 2 L2
Lociki LV 135 E13
Lockenhaus A 149 B6
Lockerbie GB 5 E10
Lockne S 106 E7
Löcknitz D 84 D6
Locks Heath GB 13 D12
Lockton GB 11 C10
Locmaria-Plouzané F 22 D2
Locmariaquer F 22 E6
Locminé F 22 E6
Locorotondo I 61 B8
Locquirec F 22 C4
Locri I 59 C9
Locronan F 22 D3
Loctudy F 22 E3
Loculi I 64 C4
Löddeköpinge S 87 D12
Lödderitz D 79 C10
Loddin D 84 B6
Lødding N 105 B10
Loddiswell GB 13 E7
Loddon GB 15 B11
Lode I 64 B4
Lode LV 135 B10
Loděnice CZ 76 B6
Löderup S 88 E6
Lodève F 34 C5
Lodi I 69 C8
Løding N 108 B8
Lødingen N 111 D10
Lodi Vecchio I 69 C7
Lodosa E 32 F1
Lödöse S 91 C11
Łodygowice PL 147 B8
Łódź PL 143 C7
Loeches E 46 D6
Loenen NL 183 A8
Löf D 21 D8
Løfallstrand N 94 B4
Lofer A 73 A6
Löffingen D 27 E9
Lofos GR 169 D7
Lofsdalen S 102 B5
Loftahammar S 93 D9
Lofthus N 94 B5
Lofthus N 111 E10
Loftus GB 11 B10
Log SLO 73 D8
Loga N 94 F5
Logan GB 5 E8
Logatec SLO 73 E9
Lögda S 107 C14

Lögdeå S 107 D16
Loggerheads GB 11 F7
Loghill IRL 8 C4
Logkanikos GR 174 E5
Logofteni MD 153 B11
Logreşti RO 160 D3
Logron F 24 D5
Logroño E 41 D7
Logrosán E 45 E10
Løgstør DK 86 B4
Løgten DK 86 C6
Løgstrup DK 86 B4
Løgumkloster DK 86 E3
Lohals DK 87 E7
Lohberg D 76 D4
Lohéac F 23 E8
Lohe-Rickelshof D 82 B6
Lohfelden D 78 D6
Lohijärvi FIN 119 B12
Lohilahti FIN 129 B10
Lohiluoma FIN 122 E8
Lohiniva FIN 117 D14
Lohja FIN 127 E11
Lohjan kunta FIN 127 E11
Lohmar D 21 C8
Lohme D 84 A5
Lohmen D 80 E6
Lohmen D 83 C12
Löhnberg D 21 C10
Löhne D 17 D11
Lohne (Oldenburg) D 17 C10
Lohra D 21 C11
Lohr am Main D 74 C6
Lohsa D 80 D6
Lohtaja FIN 123 B11
Loiano I 66 D3
Loigny-la-Bataille F 24 D6
Loimaa FIN 126 D8
Loimaan kunta FIN 127 D8
Loiré F 23 E10
Loiri-Porto San Paolo I 64 B3
Loiron F 23 D10
Loisy-sur-Marne F 25 C12
Loitz D 84 C4
Loivos P 38 E5
Loivos do Monte P 44 B5
Loja E 53 B8
Loja LV 135 B9
Løjt Kirkeby DK 86 E4
Loka brunn S 97 C11
Lokakylä FIN 123 E15
Lokalahti FIN 126 D5
Lokavec SLO 73 E8
Lokca SK 147 C8
Loke S 106 F7
Løken N 95 C14
Lokeren B 19 B9
Loket CZ 75 B12
Lokka FIN 115 C3
Løkken DK 90 E6
Løkken N 104 E7
Lokkiperä FIN 123 C13
Lőkösháza H 151 E7
Lokrume S 93 D13
Loksa EST 131 B11
Løksa N 111 C14
Lokuta EST 131 D10
Lokuti EST 131 C9
Lokve HR 67 B10
Lokve SLO 73 D8
Lokve SRB 159 C7
Lolishniy Shepit UA 152 A6
Lollar D 21 C11
L'Ollería E 56 D3
Lom BG 159 F11
Lom N 101 C9
Łomazy PL 141 G8
Lombez F 33 D7
Lombheden S 119 B9
Lomborg DK 86 B2
Lomello I 68 C6
Lomen N 101 D9
Łomianki PL 139 F10
Lomma S 87 D12
Lommatzsch D 80 D4
Lomme F 18 C6
Lommel B 19 B11
Łomnica PL 81 B9
Lomnice CZ 77 D10
Lomnice nad Lužnicí CZ 77 D7
Lomnice nad Popelkou CZ 77 A8
Lomonosov RUS 129 F12
Lompolo FIN 117 B13
Lomsdalen N 101 E12
Lomsjö S 107 C11
Lörstrand S 103 C14
Lörudden S 103 B14
Lorup D 17 C9
Lorupe LV 135 B9
Los S 103 C9
Losacino E 39 E7
Losa del Obispo E 48 E3
Los Alcázares E 56 F3
Los Algezares E 56 F2
Los Arcos E 32 E1
Losar de la Vera E 45 D9
Los Arenales del Sol E 56 E4
Los Barrios E 53 D6
Los Barrios de Luna E 39 C8
Los Belones E 56 F3
Los Cantareros E 55 D10
Los Corrales E 53 B7
Los Corrales de Buelna E 40 B3
Loscos E 42 E2
Los Dolores E 56 F2
Los Gallardos E 55 E9
Loshchynivka UA 155 C3
Losheim D 21 E7
Los Hinojosos E 47 E7
Łosice PL 141 F7
Łosinka PL 141 E9
Łosiów PL 142 E4
Los Maldonados E 56 F2
Los Molinos E 46 C4
Losna N 101 D12
Los Navalmorales E 46 E3
Los Navalucillos E 46 E3
Losomäki FIN 125 D11
Losone CH 68 A6
Łososina Dolna PL 144 D2
Losova MD 154 C2
Losovaara FIN 121 E11
Los Palacios y Villafranca E 51 E8
Los Pandos E 40 B4

Long Melford GB 15 C10
Longmorn GB 3 K10
Longny-au-Perche F 24 C4
Longobardi I 60 E6
Longobucco I 61 E7
Longomel P 44 F5
Longos GR 168 F3
Longos Vales P 38 D3
Long Preston GB 11 C7
Longré F 28 C5
Longridge GB 10 D6
Long Stratton GB 15 C11
Long Sutton GB 11 F12
Longton GB 10 D6
Longtown GB 5 F10
Longueau F 18 E5
Longué-Jumelles F 23 F11
Longuenesse F 18 C5
Longueville F 25 D9
Longueville-sur-Scie F 18 E3
Longuyon F 19 F11
Longwood IRL 7 F9
Longwy F 19 E12
Lonigo I 66 B3
Lonin N 95 C10
Löningen D 17 C9
Łoniów PL 143 E12
Lonja HR 149 F7
Lonjica HR 149 E6
Lonkan N 110 D3
Lonkka FIN 121 D13
Lonlay-l'Abbaye F 23 C10
Lönneberga S 92 D7
Lonneker NL 183 A9
Lonny F 184 E2
Lons F 32 D5
Lønsdal S 88 C6
Lonsee F 74 E6
Lons-le-Saunier F 31 B8
Lønstrup DK 90 E6
Lontzen B 183 D8
Lónya H 145 G5
Loo EST 131 C9
Loon op Zand NL 16 E4
Loos F 182 D2
Loosdorf A 77 F8
Loose GB 15 E10
Lopadea Nouă RO 152 E3
Lopar HR 67 C10
Lopątari RO 161 C9
Lopate MK 164 E4
Lopatica MK 168 B5
Łopatki PL 143 C7
Lopatnic MD 153 A10
Lopatovo RUS 132 F4
Lopcombe Corner GB 13 C11
Löpe EST 131 D7
Lopera E 53 A8
Łopiennik Górny PL 144 A7
Lopigna F 37 G9
Łopik NL 182 B5
Loppa N 112 C7
Loppersum NL 17 B7
Loppi FIN 127 D11
Lopra FO 2 C3
Lopushna UA 152 A6
Łopuszno PL 143 E9
Lopyan BG 165 D9
Lora N 101 B9
Lora del Río E 51 D8
Loranca de Tajuña E 47 D6
Lorås S 106 D8
Lörby S 88 C7
Lorca E 55 D9
Lorch D 21 D8
Lorch D 74 E6
Lorcha E 56 D4
Lordelo P 38 F4
Lordosa P 44 C5
Lørenskog N 95 C13
Loreo I 66 B5
Loreto I 67 F8
Loreto Aprutino I 62 C5
Lorgues F 36 D4
Lorient F 22 E5
Lorignac F 28 E4
Loriguilla E 48 E3
Lőrinci H 150 B4
Loriol-sur-Drôme F 30 F6
Lormes F 25 F10
Loro Ciuffenna I 66 E4
Loro Piceno I 67 F7
Lorquin F 186 D2
Lörrach D 27 E8
Lorrez-le-Bocage-Préaux F 25 D8
Lorris F 25 E8
Lorsch D 21 E11
Lørslev DK 90 E7

Los Pedrones E 47 F10
Los Pozuelos de Calatrava E 54 B5
Los Rábanos E 41 E7
Los Royos E 55 D8
Los Santos E 45 C9
Los Santos de Maimona E 51 C7
Los Santos de Maimona E 51 C7
Loßburg D 27 D9
Losse F 32 B5
Losser NL 17 D7
Lossiemouth GB 3 K10
Lostallo CH 69 A7
Loštice CZ 77 C11
Los Tojos E 40 B3
Lostwithiel GB 12 E5
Los Villares E 53 A9
Los Yébenes E 46 E5
Lote N 100 C4
Loten N 94 B3
Løten N 101 E14
Lotenhulle B 182 C2
Loth GB 3 G11
Lothmore GB 3 J9
Lotorp S 92 B7
Lotte D 17 D9
Lottefors S 103 D11
Löttorp S 89 A11
Lottstetten D 27 E10
Lottum NL 183 C8
Lotyń PL 85 C11
Lotzorai I 64 D4
Louannec F 22 C5
Louans F 24 F4
Loučeň CZ 77 B8
Loučná nad Desnou CZ 77 B12
Loučovice CZ 76 E6
Loudéac F 22 D6
Loudes F 30 E4
Loudun F 28 A6
Loué F 23 D11
Louejärvi FIN 119 B13
Louejoki FIN 119 B14
Loughanure GB 11 F9
Loughborough GB 11 F9
Loughbrickland GB 7 D10
Lougher IRL 8 D3
Loughgall GB 7 D9
Loughglinn IRL 6 E5
Loughrea IRL 6 F5
Loughton GB 15 D9
Lougratte F 33 A7
Louhans F 31 B7
Louka CZ 146 D4
Loukas GR 174 D5
Loukisia GR 175 C7
Loukkojärvi FIN 119 D15
Loukusa FIN 121 C10
Loulans F 26 F5
Loulé P 50 E3
Loundatte F 33 A8
Louny CZ 76 B5
Loupiac F 32 A5
Lourdes F 32 D5
Lourdoueix-St-Pierre F 29 C9
Louriçal P 44 D3
Lourinhã P 44 F2
Lourmarin F 35 C9
Louros GR 174 A2
Loury F 24 E7
Lousã P 44 D4
Lousa P 50 B1
Lousada P 38 F3
Loué F 24 C6
Loutra GR 175 E9
Loutra GR 177 A8
Loutra Aidipsou GR 175 B7
Loutra Eleftheron GR 170 C6
Loutraki GR 169 C6
Loutraki GR 174 C4
Loutraki GR 175 D6
Loutra Kyllinis GR 174 D3
Loutra Smokovou GR 174 A5
Loutra Ypatis GR 174 B5
Loutro GR 169 C7
Loutro GR 169 E6
Loutro GR 174 B3
Loutros GR 171 C10
Louvain B 19 C10
Louvain B 19 C10
Lubomirno PL 139 B9
Louveigné B 183 D7
Louvern F 23 D10
Louvie-Juzon F 32 D5
Louviers F 18 F3
Louvigné-du-Désert F 23 D9
Louvroil F 19 D8
Louze F 25 D12

Lövtjärn S 103 D11
Lovund N 108 D3
Lövvik S 103 A15
Lövvik S 107 D9
Luciu RO 161 D10
Lőwenberg D 84 E4
Lówenstein D 27 B11
Lower Ballinderry GB 7 C10
Lower Cam GB 13 B10
Lower Kilchattan GB 4 C4
Lowestoft GB 15 C12
Lowick GB 5 D13
Łowicz PL 141 F1
Low Street GB 15 B11
Luçon F 28 C3
Löwenberg D 84 E4
Lozarevo BG 167 D8
Łozar PL 141 G8
Łozen BG 165 D7
Lozen BG 166 C5
Lozenets BG 167 E9
Lozna RO 151 C11
Lozna SRB 159 F6
Loznica SRB 158 D3
Loznitsa BG 161 F9
Loznitsa BG 167 C7
Lozorno SK 77 F12
Lozovac HR 156 E4
Lozovik SRB 159 E7
Lozoya E 46 C5
Lozoyuela E 46 C5
Lozuvata UA 154 A6
Lozzo di Cadore I 72 D5
Lú IRL 7 E9
Luanco E 39 A8
Luarca E 39 A6
Lubaczów PL 144 C7
Lubań PL 81 D8
Lubāna LV 135 C13
Lubanowo PL 84 D7
Lubars D 79 B11
Lubartów PL 141 H7
Lubasz PL 85 E11
Lubawa PL 139 D8
Lubawka PL 81 E10
Lübbecke D 17 D11
Lübben D 80 C5
Lübbenau D 80 C5
Lübbow D 83 E11
Lubczyna PL 85 C7
Lube LV 134 B5
Lübeck D 83 C9
Lubenec CZ 76 B4
Lubeník SK 145 F1
Lubersac F 29 E8
Lübesse D 83 D11
Lubezere LV 134 B5
Lubiąż E 39 D6
Łubianka PL 138 D6
Lubichowo PL 138 C5
Lubicz Dolny PL 138 D6
Lubień PL 147 B9
Lubień PL 147 B9
Lubień Kujawski PL 139 F7
Lubieszewo PL 85 D9
Lubiń PL 81 C11
Lubin PL 81 D10
Lubiszyn PL 85 E7
Lublin PL 141 H7
Lubliniec PL 142 E6
Lubmin D 84 B5
Lubniany PL 142 E5
Lubnica MK 164 E5
Lubnice PL 143 F11
Lubno PL 85 D10
Lubno PL 143 B7
Lubochnia PL 141 G2
Lubomierz PL 81 D9
Lubomino PL 139 B9
Luboń PL 81 B11
Luborzyca PL 143 F9
Lubotice SK 145 E3
Lubotin SK 145 E2
Lubowidz PL 139 D8
Łubowo PL 85 E9
Łubowo PL 85 E12
Lubraniec PL 138 E6
Lubrín E 55 E8
Lubrza PL 81 B8
Lubrza PL 142 F4
Lubsko PL 81 C7
Lübstorf D 83 C10
Lubstów PL 138 F5
Lubsza PL 142 E4
Lübtheen D 83 D10
Luby CZ 75 B11
Lubycza Królewska PL 144 C8
Lübz D 83 D12
Luc F 33 B11
Luc F 35 A6
Lucainena de las Torres E 55 E8
Lucan IRL 7 F10
Lucena del Puerto E 51 E6
Lucena E 53 B8
Lucena de Jalón E 41 E9
Lucena del Cid E 48 D4
Lučenec SK 147 E9
Luceni E 41 E9
Lucéram F 37 D6
Lucey F 26 C4
Lucfalva H 147 E9
Luchapka BY 133 F3
Luché-Pringé F 23 E12
Lucheux F 18 D5
Luchy F 18 E5
Luciana E 54 B4
Lucena Sicula I 58 D3
Lucé F 24 D5
Luče SLO 73 D10
Lučište HR 157 F7
Lucien PL 139 F7
Lucieni RO 161 D6

Lumphanan GB 3 L11
Lumpiaque E 41 E9
Lumpzig D 79 E11
Lumsheden S 103 E11
Luna E 41 E10
Luna RO 152 D3
Lunano I 66 E5
Lunca MD 154 C4
Lunca RO 151 C9
Lunca RO 152 D5
Lunca RO 153 B9
Lunca RO 160 F5
Lunca Banului RO 154 D2
Lunca Bradului RO 152 D6
Lunca Cernii de Jos RO 159 B10
Lunca Corbului RO 160 D5
Lunca de Jos RO 153 D9
Lunca de Sus RO 153 D7
Lunca Ilvei RO 152 C5
Lunca Mureşului RO 152 E3
Luncaviţa RO 155 C2
Luncaviţa RO 159 D9
Luncoiu de Jos RO 151 E10
Lund DK 86 D5
Lund N 105 B11
Lund N 110 E8
Lund N 111 C15
Lund S 87 D12
Lundamo N 104 E3
Lundbjörken S 102 E8
Lundby DK 86 F7
Lundby DK 87 E9
Lunde DK 86 D3
Lunde N 95 D10
Lunde N 111 C16
Lunde S 103 A14
Lundeborg DK 87 E7
Lundegård N 94 F6
Lunden D 82 B6
Lundin Links GB 5 C11
Lundsbrunn S 91 C13
Lundsjön S 106 D7
Lünebach D 20 D6
Lüneburg D 83 D8
Lunel F 35 C7
Lünen D 17 E9
Lunery F 29 B10
Lunéville F 26 C5
Lungani RO 153 C9
Lunger S 97 D14
Lungern CH 70 D6
Lungro I 60 D6
Lungsjön S 107 E10
Lunguleţu RO 161 D7
Lunino RUS 136 D5
L'Union F 33 C8
Lunkkaus FIN 115 D3
Lunna BY 140 D10
Lunnäset S 102 A5
Lünne D 17 D8
Lunneborg N 111 B16
Lunow D 84 E6
Lunteren NL 183 A7
Luogosanto I 64 A3
Luohua FIN 119 E14
Luokë LT 134 E5
Luokkala FIN 121 D11
Luola-aapa FIN 119 C15
Luoma-aho FIN 123 D13
Luopa FIN 122 E9
Luopajärvi FIN 122 E9
Luopioinen FIN 127 C12
Luostari RUS 114 E10
Luosto FIN 115 D1
Luosu FIN 117 C12
Luotolahti FIN 128 D6
Luovankylä FIN 122 F7
Luovttejohka N 113 C21
Lupac RO 159 C8
Lupandi LV 133 E3
Łupawa PL 85 B12
Lupeni RO 152 E6
Lupeni RO 159 C11
Lupiac F 33 C6
Lupiñén E 41 D10
Lupión E 53 A9
Łupków PL 145 E5
Lupoglav HR 67 B9
Łupowo PL 85 E8
Luppa D 80 D3
Luppoperä FIN 121 D9
Luppy F 26 C5
Lupşa RO 151 E11
Lupşanu RO 161 E9
Luque E 53 A8
Lurbe-St-Christau F 32 D4
Lurcy-Lévis F 30 B2
Lure F 26 E5
Lurgan GB 7 D10
Lurgan IRL 6 E6
Luri F 37 F10
Lurøy N 108 D4
Lurs F 35 C10
Lurudal N 105 C13
Lury-sur-Arnon F 24 F7
Lusca IRL 7 E10
Lusciano I 60 B2
Luserna San Giovanni I 31 F11
Lushnjë AL 168 C2
Lusi FIN 127 C15
Lusignan F 29 C6
Lusigny-sur-Barse F 25 D11
Lusk IRL 7 E10
Lus-la-Croix-Haute F 35 A10
Lusminki FIN 121 C14
Lusnić BIH 157 E6
Luso P 44 D4
Luspa FIN 116 B8
Luspebryggan S 109 B18
Lussac F 28 F5
Lussac-les-Châteaux F 29 C7
Lussac-les-Églises F 29 C8
Lussan F 35 B7
Lüssow D 83 C12
Lusta GB 2 K3
Lustad N 105 C12
Lustenau A 71 C9
Lüstrivere EST 131 D12
Lustivere EST 131 D12
Luszkowo PL 81 B11
Luszyn PL 143 B8
Lutago I 72 C4
Lütau D 83 D9
Lütersburg D 17 A8
Lutherstadt Wittenberg D 79 C12

Lütjenburg D 83 B9
Lutnes N 102 D4
Lutocin PL 139 E8
Lutomiersk PL 143 C7
Luton GB 15 D8
Lutowiska PL 145 E6
Lutriņi LV 134 C4
Lutry PL 136 E2
Luttenberg NL 183 A8
Lutter am Barenberge D 79 C7
Lutterbach F 27 E7
Lutterworth GB 13 A12
Lututów PL 142 D5
Lützelbach D 21 E12
Lützen D 79 D11
Lutzerath D 21 D8
Lutzingen D 75 E8
Lutzmannsburg A 149 B7
Lützow D 83 C10
Luua EST 131 D13
Luujoki FIN 119 C14
Luukkola FIN 129 C9
Luukkonen FIN 129 B9
Luumäen kk FIN 128 D8
Luumäki FIN 128 D8
Luunja EST 131 E13
Luupujoki FIN 123 C17
Luupuvesi FIN 123 C17
Luusniemi FIN 124 G7
Luusua FIN 115 F2
Luvia FIN 126 C6
Luvos S 109 C16
Lux F 26 F3
Luxembourg L 20 E6
Luxe-Sumberraute F 32 D3
Luxeuil-les-Bains F 26 E5
Luxey F 32 B4
Luyego de Somoza E 39 D7
Luyksgestel NL 183 C6
Luz P 50 E2
Luz P 50 E4
Luz P 51 C5
Luzaga E 47 C8
Lužani HR 157 B8
Luzarches F 25 B7
Luz-Ardiden F 32 E5
Luže CZ 77 C10
Luzech F 33 B8
Lužec nad Vltavou CZ 76 B6
Luzenac F 33 E9
Luzern CH 70 C6
Luzhany UA 153 A7
Luzhki BY 133 F3
Luzianes P 50 D3
Luz i Madh AL 168 B2
Luzino PL 138 A5
Luzmela E 40 B3
Łużna PL 144 D3
Lūžņa LV 130 F3
Lūznava LV 133 D2
Luzón E 47 B8
Luz-St-Sauveur F 32 E6
Luzy F 30 B4
Luzzara I 66 C2
Luzzi I 60 E6
L'viv UA 144 D9
Lwówek PL 81 B10
Lwówek Śląski PL 81 D9
Lyady RUS 132 D4
Lyaskelya RUS 129 B15
Lyaskovets BG 166 C5
Lyavoshki BY 133 E2
Lybokhora UA 145 F6
Lybster GB 3 J10
Lychen D 84 D4
Lycksaberg S 107 A14
Lycksele S 107 B15
Lydd GB 15 F10
Lyderslev DK 87 E10
Lydford GB 12 D6
Lydney GB 13 B9
Lyeninski BY 141 F10
Lyfjord N 111 A16
Lygna N 95 B13
Lygumai LT 134 D7
Lykofi GR 171 B10
Lykoporia GR 175 C6
Lyly FIN 127 B11
Lylykylä FIN 121 E11
Lyman UA 155 B5
Lyman's'ke UA 154 D5
Lyman's'ka UA 155 C2
Lyme Regis GB 13 D9
Lymington GB 13 D11
Lymm GB 10 E7
Lynäs S 103 D12
Lyndhurst GB 13 D11
Lyne DK 86 D3
Lyneham GB 13 B11
Lynemore GB 3 L9
Lyness GB 3 H10
Lyngby DK 87 C7
Lyngdal N 94 F6
Lyngmoen N 112 D5
Lyngså DK 86 A7
Lyngseidet N 111 A19
Lyngsnes N 105 B10
Lynmouth GB 13 C7
Lynton GB 13 C7
Lyntupy BY 137 C13
Lyökki FIN 126 D5
Lyon F 30 D6
Lyons-la-Forêt F 18 F3
Lyrestad S 91 B15
Lyrkeia GR 175 D6
Lysabild DK 86 F6
Lysá pod Makytou SK 146 C6
Łyse PL 139 D12
Lysebotn N 94 D5
Lysekil S 91 C9
Lyshchytsy BY 141 F9
Lysice CZ 77 D11
Lysnes N 111 B14
Łysomice PL 138 D6
Lysøysund N 104 D7
Lysroll N 111 D11
Lyss CH 31 A11
Lysvik S 97 B9
Łyszkowice PL 141 G1
Lytchett Minster GB 13 D10
Lytham St Anne's GB 10 D5
Lytovezh UA 144 B9
Lyubashivka UA 154 B6
Lyuben BG 165 E10
Lyubimets BG 166 F6
Lyublino RUS 136 D1
Lyubomyrka UA 154 B4
Lyubyntsi UA 145 E8
Lyulyakovo BG 167 D8

M

Maakeski FIN 127 C13
Maalahti FIN 122 E7
Maalismaa FIN 119 D15
Maam IRL 6 E3
Maaninka FIN 124 D8
Maaninkavaara FIN 115 F4
Maanselkä FIN 125 C10
Maaralanpera FIN 123 C16
Maardu EST 131 B10
Maarheeze NL 183 C7
Maaria FIN 126 D7
Maarianvaara FIN 125 E11
Maarn NL 183 A6
Maarssen NL 16 D4
Maarssenbroek NL 183 A6
Maas IRL 6 C6
Maasbracht NL 19 B12
Maasbree NL 16 F6
Maasdam NL 182 B5
Maaseik B 19 B12
Maaselkä FIN 121 F14
Maasen D 17 C11
Maasland NL 16 E2
Maasmechelen B 19 C12
Maassluis NL 16 E2
Maastricht NL 19 C12
Määttälä FIN 123 C12
Määttälänvaara FIN 121 B14
Maavesi FIN 124 F9
Mablethorpe GB 11 E12
Macael E 55 E8
Maçanet de Cabrenys E 34 F4
Maçanet de la Selva E 43 D9
Mação P 44 E5
Măcărești MD 153 C11
Macastre E 48 F3
Maccagno I 68 A6
Macchiagodena I 63 D6
Macclesfield GB 11 E7
Macduff GB 3 K12
Macea RO 151 E7
Maceda E 38 D4
Maceda P 44 C3
Macedo de Cavaleiros P 39 E6
Maceira P 44 C6
Maceira P 44 E3
Macelj HR 148 D5
Macerata I 67 F7
Macerata Feltria I 66 E5
Măceșu de Jos RO 160 F3
Măceșu de Sus RO 160 F3
Machados P 50 C5
Machairas GR 174 B3
Machault F 19 F10
Machecoul F 28 B2
Machelen B 182 D4
Machen GB 13 B8
Machern D 79 D12
Machliny PL 85 D10
Machov CZ 77 A10
Machowa PL 143 F11
Machrihanish GB 4 E5
Machynlleth GB 10 F4
Maciejowice PL 141 G5
Măcin RO 155 C2
Macinaggio F 37 F10
Măciuca RO 160 D4
Mačkatica SRB 164 D5
Mackenbach D 21 F9
Mackenrode D 79 C8
Mačkovci SLO 148 C6
Macomer I 64 C2
Mâcon F 30 C6
Macosquin GB 4 E3
Macotera E 45 C10
Macroom IRL 8 E5
Macugnaga I 68 B4
Mačvanska Mitrovica SRB 158 D4
Mačvanski Pričinović SRB 158 D4
Mád H 145 G3
Madan BG 165 B7
Madan BG 171 A7
Mådan S 103 A15
Madängsholm S 91 C14
Madara BG 167 C8
Madaras H 150 E3
Mădăraș RO 151 D8
Mădărjac RO 153 C10
Maddalena Spiaggia I 64 E3
Maddaloni I 60 A2
Made NL 16 E3
Madekoski FIN 119 E15
Madeley GB 10 F7
Mäder A 71 C9
Madetkoski FIN 115 C1
Madiran F 32 C5
Madley GB 13 A9
Madliena LV 135 C10
Madocsa H 150 D2
Madona LV 135 C12
Madonna di Campiglio I 69 A10
Madrid E 46 D5
Madridejos E 46 F5
Madrigal de las Altas Torres E 45 B11
Madrigal de la Vera E 45 D10
Madrigal del Monte E 40 D4
Madrigalejo E 45 F9
Madrigueras E 47 F9
Madroñera E 45 F9
Mădulari RO 160 D4
Madzharovo BG 171 A9
Mæl N 95 C9
Maël-Carhaix F 22 D5
Maella E 42 E4
Maello E 46 C3
Maenclochog GB 12 B5
Maenza I 62 D4
Mære N 105 D10
Măeriște RO 151 C10
Mäetaguse EST 131 C14
Maeztu E 41 C7
Mafra P 50 B1
Magacela E 51 B8
Magallón E 41 E9
Magaluf E 49 E10
Magaña E 41 E7
Magašići BIH 158 E3
Magaz E 40 E3
Magdala D 79 E9
Magdeburg D 79 B10
Magdeburgerforth D 79 B11
Magenta I 69 C6
Magescq F 32 C3
Măgești RO 151 C9
Maggia CH 68 A6
Maghera GB 4 F3
Magherafelt GB 4 F3
Magheralin GB 7 D10
Măgherani RO 152 D5
Maghery GB 7 C9
Maghull GB 10 D6
Magione I 66 F5
Măgiotsa EST 132 E1
Măgirești RO 153 D9
Magisano I 59 A10
Maglaj BIH 157 C9
Magland F 31 C10
Măglavit RO 159 E11
Magliano de'Marsi I 62 C4
Magliano in Toscana I 65 B4
Magliano Sabina I 62 C2
Magliĉ SRB 158 F6
Maglie I 61 C10
Maglód H 150 C3
Magnac-Laval F 29 C8
Magné F 28 C4
Magnières F 26 D6
Magnor N 96 C7
Magnuszew PL 141 G4
Magny-Cours F 30 B3
Magny-en-Vexin F 24 B6
Mágocs H 149 D10
Magoula GR 174 E5
Magstrup DK 86 E4
Magueija P 44 B5
Maguilla E 51 C8
Maguiresbridge GB 7 D8
Măgura RO 153 D9
Măgura RO 160 E6
Măgura Ilvei RO 152 C5
Magurë RKS 164 D3
Măgurele RO 161 C8
Măgurele RO 161 E8
Măgureni RO 161 C7
Măguri-Răcătău RO 151 D11
Magy H 145 H4
Magyaralmás H 149 B10
Magyaratád H 149 D9
Magyarbánhegyes H 151 E6
Magyarbóly H 149 E10
Magyaregregy H 149 D10
Magyarhomorog H 151 C8
Magyarkeszi H 149 C10
Magyarnándor H 147 F8
Magyarpolány H 149 B9
Magyarszék H 149 D10
Mahala UA 153 A8
Maheriv UA 144 C8
Mahíde E 39 E7
Mahlberg D 186 E4
Mahlsdorf D 83 E10
Mahlu FIN 123 E14
Mahlwinkel D 79 B10
Mahmudia RO 155 C4
Mahmudiye TR 171 E10
Mahmutköy TR 173 C6
Mahón E 57 B13
Mahora E 47 F9
Mahovo HR 149 E6
Mähring D 75 C12
Mahtra EST 131 C10
Maia P 44 B3
Maials E 42 E5
Măicănești RO 161 C10
Maîche F 27 F6
Maida I 59 B9
Maiden Bradley GB 13 C10
Maidenhead GB 15 D7
Maiden Newton GB 13 D9
Maidens GB 4 E7
Maidstone GB 15 E10
Maienfeld CH 71 C9
Maierato I 59 B9
Maierhöfen D 71 B10
Maieru RO 152 C5
Măieruș RO 153 F7
Maigh Chromtha IRL 8 E5
Maigh Cuilinn IRL 6 F4
Maighean Rátha IRL 7 F8
Maignelay-Montigny F 18 E6
Maijanen FIN 117 D14
Maikammer D 186 C5
Maillas F 32 B5
Maillebois F 24 C5
Maillezais F 28 C4
Mailly-le-Camp F 25 C11
Mailly-le-Château F 25 E10
Mailly-Maillet F 18 D6
Mailovac SRB 159 D7
Mainaschaff D 187 B7
Mainbernheim D 75 C7
Mainburg D 75 E10
Mainham IRL 7 F9
Mainhardt D 74 D6
Mainiemi FIN 127 B16
Mainistir Eimhín IRL 7 F8
Mainistir Fhear Maí IRL 8 D6
Mainistir Laoise IRL 9 C8
Mainistir na Búille IRL 6 E6
Mainistir na Corann IRL 8 E6
Mainistir na Feile IRL 8 D4
Männikkö S 116 D8
Mainsat F 29 C10
Maintenon F 24 C6
Mainua FIN 121 F9
Mainvilliers F 24 D5
Mainz D 21 D10
Maiolati Spontini I 67 F7
Maiorca P 44 D3
Maiorga P 44 E3
Mairena del Alcor E 51 E8
Maisach D 75 F9
Maishofen A 73 B6
Maišiagala LT 137 D11
Maissau A 77 E9
Maisse F 25 D7
Maissin B 184 E3
Maivala FIN 121 B14
Maizières-lès-Metz F 186 C1
Majadahonda E 46 D5
Majadas de Tiétar E 45 E9
Majava FIN 121 C12
Majavatn N 105 A14
Majdan BIH 157 D7
Majdan Królewski PL 144 C4
Majdan Niepryski PL 144 C7
Majdanpek SRB 159 E8
Majovakylä FIN 119 C17
Majs H 149 E11
Majšperk SLO 148 D5
Majtum S 109 D18
Makád H 149 B11
Makarove UA 145 G6
Makarove UA 154 C6
Makarska HR 157 F7
Mäkelänranta FIN 121 E13
Makhnovka RUS 133 B6
Mäkikylä FIN 123 E12
Makkola FIN 125 G11
Makkoshotyka H 145 G4
Makkum NL 16 B4
Maklár H 147 F10
Maklјenovac BIH 157 C9
Makó H 150 E5
Makoc RKS 164 D3
Mākoņkalns LV 133 D2
Mąkoszyce PL 142 E4
Makov SK 147 C7
Maków PL 141 G2
Maków PL 141 H4
Mąkowarsko PL 138 D4
Maków Mazowiecki PL 139 E11
Maków Podhalański PL 147 B9
Makrakomi GR 174 B5
Makresh BG 159 F10
Makri GR 171 C9
Makrisia GR 174 D4
Makrochori GR 169 C7
Makrychori GR 169 E7
Makrygialos GR 169 D8
Makrygialos GR 179 E10
Makrynitsa GR 169 F8
Makryrrachi GR 174 A5
Maksamaa FIN 122 D8
Maksniemi FIN 119 C13
Maksymilianowo PL 138 D5
Malá E 53 B9
Mala IRL 8 D5
Mala S 87 C13
Malå S 107 A15
Mala Bosna SRB 150 E4
Mala Čista HR 156 E4
Malacky SK 77 F12
Málaga E 53 C8
Malagón E 46 F5
Malahide IRL 7 F10
Malahvianvaara FIN 121 E14
Malaia RO 160 C4
Mălăiești MD 154 D5
Málainn Bhig IRL 6 C5
Málainn Mhóir IRL 6 C5
Mala Kladuša BIH 156 B4
Malalbergo I 66 C4
Malá Lehota SK 147 D7
Malamocco I 66 B5
Malancourt F 19 F11
Malandrino GR 174 C5
Malangen N 111 B16
Malangseidet N 111 B16
Malanów PL 142 C5
Malansac F 23 E7
Malaryta BY 141 G10
Mäläskä FIN 119 F16
Mala Subotica HR 149 D7
Malaucène F 35 B9
Malaunay F 18 E3
Malaussanne F 32 C5
Malävaara FIN 115 E4
Malåvännäs S 107 A14
Mała Wieś PL 139 F9
Malax FIN 122 E7
Malaya Byerastavitsa BY 140 D9
Malbekkvatn N 114 E7
Malbork PL 138 B7
Malborn D 21 E7
Malbouzon F 30 F3
Malbuisson F 31 B9
Malcesine I 69 B10
Malchin D 83 C13
Malchow D 83 D12
Malcocinado E 51 C8
Malcov SK 145 E3
Malczyce PL 81 D10
Măldăeni RO 160 E5
Măldărești RO 160 C4
Maldegem B 19 B7
Malden NL 16 E5
Maldon GB 15 D10
Małdyty PL 139 C8
Male I 71 E11
Malechowo PL 85 B11
Maleján E 41 E8
Maleme GR 178 D6
Malemort-du-Comtat F 35 B9
Malemort-sur-Corrèze F 29 E9
Malente D 83 B9
Målerås S 89 B9
Males GR 179 E10
Malesco I 68 A6
Malesherbes F 25 D7
Malesina GR 175 B7
Malestroit F 23 E7
Maletto I 59 D6
Malevo BG 166 F5
Malexander S 92 C6
Malfa I 59 B6
Malgersdorf D 75 E12
Malgovik S 107 B10
Malgrat de Mar E 43 D9
Malhadas P 39 E7
Malia GR 178 E9
Malicorne-sur-Sarthe F 23 E11
Malіena LV 133 B2
Mali Iđoš SRB 158 B4
Malijai F 36 C4
Målilla S 92 E7
Mali Lošinj HR 67 C9
Mali Mokryany UA 144 D7
Malin IRL 4 E2
Malin Beg IRL 6 C5
Málinec SK 147 D9
Malines B 19 B9
Malines B 182 C4
Mălini RO 153 C8
Malin More IRL 6 C5
Malinovka LV 135 E13
Malinska HR 67 B10
Maliq AL 168 C4
Malishevë RKS 163 E10
Maliskylä FIN 123 C14
Malissard F 30 F6
Maliuc RO 155 C4
Mali Zvornik SRB 157 D11
Maljasalmi FIN 125 E11
Malkara TR 173 C6
Małkinia Górna PL 139 E13
Malko Gradishte BG 166 F5
Malko Tŭrnovo BG 167 F9
Mallaig GB 4 A5
Mållångsbo S 103 D10
Mallén E 41 E9
Mallentin D 83 C10
Mallersdorf D 75 E11
Malles Venosta I 71 D11
Mallica TR 173 F7
Malling DK 86 C6
Mallißz D 83 D10
Mallnitz A 73 C7
Mallow IRL 8 D5
Mallusjoki FIN 127 D14
Mallwyd GB 10 F4
Malm N 105 C10
Malmån S 107 E12
Malmbäck S 92 D4
Malmberget S 116 D5
Malmby S 98 D8
Malmédy B 20 D6
Malmein N 94 E4
Malmesbury GB 13 B10
Malmköping S 93 A9
Malmö S 87 D12
Malmslätt S 92 C7
Malnaș RO 153 E7
Malnate I 69 B6
Malnava LV 133 C3
Malnes N 110 C8
Malo I 69 B11
Malo Crniće SRB 159 D7
Małogoszcz PL 143 E9
Malo Konare BG 165 E9
Małomice PL 81 C8
Malomir BG 167 E7
Malomozhayskoye RUS 136 D5
Malón E 41 E8
Malona GR 181 D8
Malonno I 69 A9
Malonty CZ 77 E7
Malorad BG 165 C8
Malošište SRB 164 C4
Malo Titavo BIH 156 D5
Malovăț RO 159 D10
Måløy N 100 C2
Maloye-Lugovoye RUS 136 D2
Maloye Sitna BY 133 E6
Malpartida P 45 C7
Malpartida de Cáceres E 45 F8
Malpartida de la Serena E 51 B8
Malpartida de Plasencia E 45 E8
Malpas GB 10 E6
Malpica E 38 B2
Malpica de Tajo E 46 E3
Malpica do Tejo P 44 E6
Mālpils LV 135 B9
Malsch D 27 C9
Målselv N 111 B16
Malsfeld D 78 D6
Malšice CZ 77 D7
Målsnes N 111 B16
Målsryd S 91 D13
Målsta S 106 E7
Malta A 73 C8
Malta LV 133 D2
Malta P 45 C6
Maltas Trūpi LV 135 D13
Maltby GB 11 E9
Maltby le Marsh GB 11 E12
Maltepe TR 173 D7
Malterdingen D 27 D8
Malters CH 70 C6
Malton GB 11 C10
Malu cu Flori RO 160 C6
Maluenda E 41 F8
Malŭk Izvor BG 166 F5
Malu Mare RO 160 E3
Malung S 102 E6
Malungsfors S 102 E6
Mălupe LV 133 B2
Mălureni RO 160 C5
Măluşteni RO 153 E11
Małuszów PL 81 B8
Maluszyn PL 143 E8
Malva E 39 E9
Malvaglia CH 71 E7
Malveira P 50 B1
Malvik N 105 E9
Malý Horeš SK 145 G4
Mályi H 145 G2
Mały Płock PL 139 D13
Malý Šariš SK 145 E3
Malyy Bereznyy UA 145 F5
Mamaia RO 155 E3
Mamarchevo BG 167 E7
Mamarrosa P 44 D3
Mambrilla de Castejón E 40 E4
Mamer L 20 E6
Mamers F 24 D3
Mamići BIH 157 F8
Mamirolle F 26 F5
Mammaste EST 131 E14
Mammendorf D 75 F9
Mammola I 59 C9
Mamoiada I 64 C3
Mamone I 64 B3
Mamonovo RUS 139 B8
Mamuras AL 168 A2
Mamushë RKS 163 E10
Mana MD 154 C3
Maňa SK 146 E6
Manacor E 57 B11
Manage B 19 D9
Manamansalo FIN 120 F9
Mañaria E 41 B6
Månås S 97 A9
Manasia RO 161 D9
Manasterz PL 144 D5
Manastir BG 165 F10
Mănăstirea RO 161 E9
Mănăstirea Cașin RO 153 E9
Mănăstirea Humorului RO 153 B7
Manastirica SRB 159 D7
Manastirsko BG 167 C7
Mănăștiur RO 151 F9
Mancera de Abajo E 45 C10
Mancha Real E 53 A9
Manchester GB 11 E7
Manching D 75 E9
Manchita E 51 B7
Manciano I 65 B5
Manciet F 33 C6
Mandal N 90 C1
Måndalen N 100 A6
Mandalo GR 169 C7
Mandas I 64 D3
Mandatoriccio I 61 E7
Mandayona E 47 C7
Mandelbachtal-Ormesheim D 186 C3
Mandelieu-la-Napoule F 36 D5
Mandello del Lario I 69 B7
Manderscheid D 21 D7
Mandeure F 27 F6
Mandino Selo BIH 157 E7
Mándok H 145 G5
Mandra GR 175 C7
Măndra RO 152 F5
Mandraki GR 181 C6
Mandres-en-Barrois F 26 D3
Mandriko GR 181 D7
Mandritsa BG 171 B10
Manduria I 61 C9
Mane F 33 D7
Mane F 35 C10
Manea GB 11 G12
Măneciu RO 161 C7
Manerbio I 66 B1
Mañeru E 32 E2
Mănești RO 160 D6
Mănești RO 161 D7
Manětín CZ 76 C4
Manfredonia I 63 D9
Mangalia RO 155 F3
Manganeses de la Lampreana E 39 E8
Manganeses de la Polvorosa E 39 D8
Mångberg S 102 E8
Mångbyn S 118 F6
Manger N 100 E2
Mangiennes F 19 F12
Mangotsfield GB 13 C9
Mångsbodarna S 102 D6
Mangualde P 44 C5
Manhay B 19 D12
Manhuelles F 26 B4
Mani GR 171 B10
Maniace I 59 D6
Maniago I 73 D6
Maniakoi GR 168 D5
Manieczki PL 81 B11
Manilva E 53 D6
Manisa TR 177 B9
Manises E 48 E4
Manjärvträsk S 118 C4
Manjaur S 107 B16
Mank A 77 F8
Månkarbo S 99 B8
Mankila FIN 119 E15
Manlay F 25 F11
Manlleu E 43 D8
Manna GR 175 D6
Männamaa EST 130 D5
Mannersdorf an der Rabnitz A 149 B7
Mannheim D 21 F10
Männikuste EST 131 E8
Manningtree GB 15 D11
Manolada GR 174 C3
Manole BG 165 E10
Manoleasa RO 153 B10
Manoppello I 62 C6
Manorbier GB 12 B5
Manorhamilton IRL 6 D6
Manosque F 35 C10
Manowo PL 85 B10
Manresa E 43 D7
Månsåsen S 105 E16
Manschnow D 81 A7
Mansfeld D 79 C9
Mansfield GB 11 E9
Mansfield Woodhouse GB 11 E9
Mansilla E 40 D6
Mansilla de las Mulas E 39 D9
Mansle F 29 D6
Manso F 37 G9
Mansonville F 33 B7
Mansores P 44 C4
Manston GB 13 D10
Månsträsk S 109 E16
Mantamados GR 171 F10
Mantasia GR 174 A5
Manteigas P 44 D5
Mantel D 75 C11
Manternach L 186 B1
Mantes-la-Jolie F 24 C6
Mantes-la-Ville F 24 C6
Manthelan F 24 F4
Mantila FIN 122 F9
Mantoche F 26 F4
Mantorp S 92 C6
Mantoudi GR 175 B7
Mantova I 66 B2
Mäntsälä FIN 127 D13
Mänttä FIN 123 F13
Mäntyharju FIN 128 C6
Mäntyjärvi FIN 117 E14
Mäntyjärvi FIN 121 B10
Mäntylahti FIN 124 D8
Mäntyluoto FIN 126 B5
Mäntyvaara S 116 E7
Manuel E 56 C4
Manulla IRL 6 E4
Mány H 149 A11
Manyas TR 173 D8
Manzac-sur-Vern F 29 E7
Mânzălești RO 161 C9
Manzanal de Arriba E 39 E7
Manzanal del Puerto E 39 C7
Manzanares E 55 A6
Manzanares el Real E 46 C5
Manzaneda E 38 D5
Manzanedo E 40 C4
Manzaneque E 46 E5
Manzanera E 48 D3
Manzanilla E 51 E7
Manzano I 73 E7
Manzat F 30 D2
Manziana I 62 C2
Manziat F 30 C6
Maó E 57 B13
Mão EST 131 D11
Maoča BIH 157 C10
Maqellarë AL 168 A3
Maqueda E 46 D4
Mar P 38 E2
Mara I 64 C2
Marac F 26 E3
Maracalagonis I 64 E3
Marachkova BY 133 E4
Mărăcineni RO 160 D5
Mărăcineni RO 161 C9
Maradik SRB 158 C5
Maråker S 103 D13
Maranchón E 47 B8
Maranello I 66 C2
Marange-Silvange F 186 C1
Maranhão P 50 A4
Marano I 66 D3
Marano di Napoli I 60 B2
Marano sul Panaro I 66 D2
Marans F 28 C4
Maranville F 25 D12
Mărășești RO 153 F10
Mărașu RO 155 D1
Maratea I 60 D5
Marateca P 50 B2
Marathea GR 169 E6
Marathias GR 174 C5
Marathokampos GR 177 D8
Marathonas GR 175 C8
Marathopoli GR 174 E4
Maraussan F 34 D5
Maraye-en-Othe F 25 D10
Marazion GB 12 E4
Marazliyivka UA 154 E6
Marbach CH 70 D5
Marbach am Neckar D 27 C11
Marbäck S 91 D13
Marbella E 53 C7
Marboz F 31 C7
Marburg an der Lahn D 21 C11
Marby S 105 E16
Marça E 42 E5
Marcali H 149 C8
Marcaltő H 149 B8
Marčana HR 67 C8
Marcaria I 66 B2
Mărcăuți MD 153 A10
Marcellina I 62 C3
Marcelová SK 149 A10
Marcenais F 28 E5
Marcenat F 30 E2
March GB 11 F12
Marchamalo E 47 C6
Marchaux F 26 F5
Marche-en-Famenne B 19 D11
Marchegg A 77 F11
Marchena E 51 E9
Marchenoir F 24 E5
Marcheprime F 28 F4
Marchiennes F 19 D7
Marchin B 19 D11
Marchtrenk A 76 F6
Marciac F 33 C6
Marciana I 65 B2
Marciana Marina I 65 B2
Marcianise I 60 A2
Marciano della Chiana I 66 F4
Mārciena LV 135 C12
Marcigny F 30 C5
Marcilhac-sur-Célé F 33 A9
Marcilla E 32 F2
Marcillac F 28 E4
Marcillac-la-Croisille F 29 E10
Marcillac-Vallon F 33 B10
Marcillat-en-Combraille F 29 C11
Marcilly-en-Gault F 24 F6
Marcilly-en-Villette F 24 E7
Marcilly-le-Hayer F 25 D10
Marcilly-sur-Eure F 24 C5
Marcinkonys LT 137 E9
Marcinkowice PL 81 B9
Marcinkowice PL 144 D2
Marcinowice PL 81 E11
Marciszów PL 81 E10
Marck F 18 C4
Marckolsheim F 27 D8
Marco de Canaveses P 44 B4
Marcoing F 19 D7
Marcòn I 66 A5
Marcoux F 36 C4
Marcq-en-Barœul F 19 C7
Mărculești MD 153 B12
Mårdaklev S 87 A11
Mardarivka UA 154 B5
Mardeuil F 25 B10
Mårdsele S 107 B16
Mårdsjö S 106 E9
Mårdsjö S 107 C11
Mårdudden S 118 B6
Marebbe I 72 C4
Marennes F 28 D3
Maresfield GB 15 F9
Mareuil F 29 E6
Mareuil-sur-Arnon F 29 B10
Mareuil-sur-Ay F 25 B11
Mareuil-sur-Lay-Dissais F 28 B3
Marey-sur-Tille F 26 E3
Marga RO 159 B9
Margarites GR 178 E8
Mărgăritești RO 161 C9
Margariti GR 168 F3
Margate GB 15 E11
Mărgău RO 151 D10
Margecany SK 145 F3
Margerie-Hancourt F 25 C12
Margherita di Savoia I 60 A6
Marghita RO 151 C9
Margina RO 151 F9
Marginea RO 153 B7
Mărgineni RO 153 D9
Mărgineni RO 153 D9
Margionys LT 137 F9
Margone I 31 E11
Margonin PL 85 E12
Margraten NL 19 C12
Marguerittes F 35 C7
Margut F 19 E11
Marhaň SK 145 E3
María E 55 D8
Mariac F 30 F5
Mariager DK 86 B5
Maria Lankowitz A 73 B11
Maria Luggau A 73 C6
Marialva P 45 C6
Mariampole LV 133 D2
Mariana E 47 D8
Mariannelund S 92 D7
Mariano Comense I 69 B7
Marianopoli I 58 D4
Marianowo PL 85 D8
Mariánské Lázně CZ 75 C12
Mariapfarr A 73 B8
Maria Saal A 73 C9
Mariazell A 148 A4
Maribo DK 83 A10
Maribor SLO 148 C5
Marieberg S 92 A6
Marieby S 106 E7
Mariefred S 98 D8
Mariehamn FIN 99 B13
Marieholm S 87 D12
Marieholm S 91 E14
Mariembourg B 19 D10
Marienberg D 80 E4
Marienhafe D 17 A8
Marienhagen D 78 B6
Marienheide D 21 B9
Mariental D 79 B8
Mariestad S 91 B14
Marifjøra N 100 D6
Marigliano I 60 B2
Marignana F 37 G9
Marignane F 35 D9
Marigné-Laillé F 24 E3
Marigny F 23 B9
Marigny-le-Châtel F 25 D10
Marijampolė LT 136 D7
Marikaj AL 168 B2
Marikostinovo BG 169 B9
Marín E 38 D2
Marina di Alberese I 65 B4
Marina di Amendolara I 61 D7
Marina di Arbus I 64 D1
Marina di Camerota I 60 C4
Marina di Campo I 65 B2
Marina di Carrara I 69 E9
Marina di Castagneto Donoratico I 66 F2
Marina di Cecina I 66 F1
Marina di Chieuti I 63 D8
Marina di Gioiosa Ionica I 59 C9
Marina di Grosseto I 65 B3
Marina di Leuca I 61 D10
Marina di Massa I 69 E9
Marina di Novaglie I 61 D10

Marina di Palma I 58 E4
Marina di Pulsano I 61 C8
Marina di Ragusa I 59 F6
Marina di Ravenna I 66 C5
Marinaleda E 53 B7
Marina Palmense I 67 F8
Marina Romea I 66 C5
Marina Schiavonea I 61 D7
Marinella I 58 D2
Marineo I 58 D3
Marines E 48 E3
Marines F 24 B6
Maringues F 30 D3
Marinha das Ondas P 44 D3
Marinha Grande P 44 E3
Marinhas P 38 E2
Marinići HR 67 B9
Marinka BG 167 E8
Marinkainen FIN 123 C10
Mārinkalns LV 133 B1
Marino I 62 D3
Mar'insko RUS 132 D4
Mariotto I 61 A7
Mărișelu RO 152 C5
Maritsa GR 181 D8
Marizy F 30 B5
Märja EST 131 E13
Marjaliza E 46 E5
Märjamaa EST 131 D8
Marjaniemi FIN 119 D13
Marjokylä FIN 121 E14
Marjonieemi FIN 127 C14
Marjovaara FIN 125 E15
Marjusaari FIN 123 D12
Mark GB 13 C9
Mark S 107 B10
Markaryd S 87 C13
Markaz H 147 F10
Markby FIN 122 D9
Markdorf D 27 E11
Markebäck S 92 B5
Markelo NL 17 D7
Market Deeping GB 11 F11
Market Drayton GB 10 F7
Market Harborough GB 15 C7
Markethill GB 7 D9
Market Rasen GB 11 E11
Market Warsop GB 11 E9
Market Weighton GB 11 D10
Markgröningen D 27 C11
Markhus N 94 C4
Marki PL 139 F11
Markina-Xemein E 41 B7
Markinch GB 5 C10
Märkisch Buchholz D 80 B5
Markitta S 116 D7
Markivka UA 154 D5
Markkina FIN 116 B8
Markkleeberg D 79 D11
Markkula FIN 123 C12
Marklohe D 17 C12
Marknesse NL 16 C5
Markneukirchen D 75 B11
Markopoulo GR 175 D8
Markovac SRB 159 C7
Markovac SRB 159 E7
Markovac Našički HR 149 E10
Markovac Trojstveni HR 149 E7
Markowa PL 144 C5
Markranstädt D 79 D11
Marksuhl D 79 E7
Markt Allhau A 148 B6
Marktbergel D 75 D7
Markt Berolzheim D 75 D8
Markt Bibart D 75 C7
Marktbreit D 187 B9
Markt Erlbach D 75 D8
Markt Hartmannsdorf A 148 B5
Marktheidenfeld D 74 C6
Markt Indersdorf D 75 F9
Marktjärn S 103 A11
Marktl D 76 F3
Marktleugast D 75 B10
Marktoberdorf D 71 B11
Marktoffingen D 75 E7
Marktredwitz D 75 B11
Markt Rettenbach D 71 B10
Markt Sankt Martin A 149 A6
Markt Schwaben D 75 F10
Marktseft D 75 C7
Markt Wald D 71 A11
Markusevec HR 148 E6
Markušica HR 149 F11
Markušovce SK 145 F2
Markuszów PL 141 H6
Marl D 17 D10
Marl D 17 E8
Marlborough GB 13 C11
Marldon GB 13 E7
Marle F 19 E8
Marlengo I 72 C3
Marlenheim F 27 C8
Marlhes F 30 E5
Marlishausen D 79 E9
Marlow D 83 B13
Marlow GB 15 D7
Marly CH 31 B11
Marly F 19 D8
Marly F 26 B5
Marma S 99 B8
Marmagne F 25 F7
Marmagne F 30 B5
Marmande F 33 A6
Marmara GR 174 B5
Marmara TR 173 C8
Marmaracik TR 173 B8
Marmaraereğlisi TR 173 C8
Marmari GR 175 C9
Marmaris TR 181 C8
Marmaro GR 177 B7
Marmelar P 50 C4
Marmeleira P 44 F3
Marmelete P 50 E2
Marmirolo I 66 B2
Marmolejo E 53 A8
Marmoutier F 27 C7
Marnardal N 90 C2
Marnäs S 103 E10
Marnay F 26 F4
Marne D 82 C6
Marne-la-Vallée F 25 C8
Marnes N 108 B7
Marnheim D 21 E10
Marnitz D 83 D11
Maroldsweisach D 75 B8
Marolles-les-Braults F 23 D12
Maromme F 18 F3
Maroneia GR 171 C9
Maroslele H 150 E5
Marostica I 72 E4
Maroué F 22 D6
Marousi GR 175 C8
Marpingen D 21 F8
Marpissa GR 176 E5
Marple GB 11 E7
Marpod RO 152 F5
Marquartstein D 72 A5
Marquion F 19 D7
Marquise F 15 F12
Marquixanes F 33 E10
Marradi I 66 D4
Marrasjärvi FIN 117 E14
Marraskoski FIN 117 E14
Marrubiu I 64 D2
Marrum NL 16 B5
Mârșa RO 161 E7
Marsac-en-Livradois F 30 E4
Marsac-sur-Don F 23 E8
Marsaglia I 37 B10
Marsal F 26 C6
Marsala I 58 D1
Mârșani RO 160 E4
Marsannay-la-Côte F 26 F2
Marsanne F 35 A8
Marsberg D 17 F11
Marsciano I 62 B2
Marseillan F 35 D6
Marseille F 35 D9
Marseille-en-Beauvaisis F 18 E4
Marsico Nuovo I 60 C5
Marsico Vetere I 60 C5
Marsillargues F 35 C7
Marsjärv S 118 B8
Mårslet DK 86 C6
Mārsnēni LV 135 B11
Marssac-sur-Tarn F 33 C10
Märsta S 99 C9
Marstal DK 83 A9
Märstetten CH 27 E11
Marston GB 13 B12
Marstrand S 91 D10
Marstrup DK 86 E4
Märsylä FIN 123 C11
Marta I 62 B1
Mårtanberg S 103 E9
Martano I 61 C10
Martel F 29 F9
Martelange B 19 E12
Martellago I 66 A5
Martello I 71 D11
Mártély H 150 E5
Marten BG 161 F8
Martfeld D 17 C12
Martfű H 150 C5
Marthon F 29 D6
Martiago E 45 D8
Martignacco I 73 D7
Martigné-Briand F 23 F11
Martigné-Ferchaud F 23 E9
Martigné-sur-Mayenne F 23 D10
Martigny CH 31 C11
Martigny-le-Comte F 30 B5
Martigny-les-Bains F 26 D4
Martigny-les-Gerbonvaux F 26 D4
Martigues F 35 D9
Martiherrero E 46 C3
Martil MA 53 E6
Martim Longo P 50 E4
Martin SK 147 C7
Martina Franca I 61 B8
Martin Brod BIH 156 C5
Martinchel P 44 E4
Martinci SRB 158 C3
Martinci Čepinski HR 149 E10
Martín de la Jara E 53 B7
Martín del Río E 42 F2
Martín de Yeltes E 45 C8
Martinengo I 69 B8
Mărtinești RO 161 F11
Martinet E 33 F9
Martinfeld D 79 D7
Martinganča P 44 E3
Mărtiniș RO 152 E6
Martín Muñoz de las Posadas E 46 B3
Martinniemi FIN 119 D14
Martino GR 175 B7
Martinporra E 39 B8
Martinsberg A 77 F8
Martinšćica HR 67 C9
Martinsicuro I 62 B5
Martis I 64 B2
Martizay F 29 B8
Martley GB 13 A10
Martna EST 130 D7
Martock GB 13 D9
Martonvaara FIN 125 D12
Martorell E 43 E7
Martos E 53 A9
Martres-Tolosane F 33 D8
Mårtsbo S 103 E13
Martti FIN 115 D4
Marttila FIN 127 D8
Marttila FIN 127 D13
Marttisenjärvi FIN 124 C7
Marugán E 46 C4
Maruggio I 61 C9
Marum NL 16 B6
Marum S 99 C12
Mărunței RO 160 E4
Mārupe LV 135 C8
Maruszów PL 143 D12
Maruszów PL 144 B4
Marvão P 44 F6
Marvejols F 34 A5
Marville F 19 F11
Marxheim D 75 E8
Marxzell D 27 C9
Märy FIN 127 E9
Mar"yanivka UA 154 C6
Marykirk GB 5 B11
Marynychi UA 152 A6
Marypark GB 3 L10
Maryport GB 5 F10
Marywell GB 5 A11
Marzabotto I 66 D3
Marzahna D 79 B12
Marzahne D 79 A12
Marzamemi I 59 F7
Marzan F 23 E7
Mărzănești RO 161 F6
Marzling D 75 F10
Masa E 40 C4
Masainas I 64 E2
Masalavés E 48 F3
Masari GR 181 D8
Mas-Cabardès F 33 D10
Mascali I 59 D7
Mascalucia I 59 D7
Mascaraque E 46 E5
Mascarenhas P 38 E5
Maschito I 60 B5
Masclat F 29 F8
Mas de Barberans E 42 F4
Mas de las Matas E 42 F3
Masegosa E 47 C8
Masegoso E 55 B8
Masegoso de Tajuña E 47 C7
Maselheim D 71 A9
Masera I 68 A5
Maserada sul Piave I 72 E5
Masevaux F 27 E6
Masfjorden N 100 E2
Masham GB 11 C8
Masi N 113 E12
Maside E 38 D3
Masi Torello I 66 C4
Maskalyanyaty BY 133 E7
Maskaur S 109 E14
Masku FIN 126 D7
Maslenika HR 156 D4
Maslinica HR 156 F5
Mașloc RO 159 B7
Maslovare BIH 157 C8
Masłowice PL 143 D8
Masone I 37 B9
Masquefa E 43 E7
Massa I 69 E9
Massa Fiscaglia I 66 C5
Massafra I 61 B8
Massa Lombarda I 66 D4
Massa Lubrense I 60 B2
Massamagrell E 48 E4
Massa Marittimo I 65 A3
Massa Martana I 62 B3
Massarosa I 66 E1
Massat F 33 E8
Massay F 24 F6
Maßbach D 75 B7
Masseret F 29 D9
Masseube F 33 D7
Massford GB 7 D10
Massiac F 30 E3
Massiaru EST 131 F9
Massimino I 37 C8
Massing D 75 F12
Mas-St-Chély F 34 B5
Măstăcani RO 155 B2
Mastershausen D 185 D7
Masterud N 96 B7
Mastichari GR 177 F9
Mastrevik N 100 E1
Masua I 64 E1
Masugnsbyn S 116 D8
Masullas I 64 D2
Måsvik N 112 D2
Masyevichy BY 141 G9
Maszewo PL 81 B7
Maszewo PL 85 B13
Maszewo PL 85 D8
Maszewo Duże PL 139 E8
Matabuena E 46 B5
Matadepera E 43 D8
Mataguži MNE 163 E7
Matala FIN 119 C14
Matala GR 178 F8
Matalalahti FIN 124 C8
Matalascañas E 51 E6
Matalebreras E 41 E7
Matallana de Valmadrigal E 39 D9
Matamala de Almazán E 41 E6
Matamorosa E 40 C3
Mataporquera E 40 C3
Matapozuelos E 39 F10
Matara FIN 125 D12
Mataragka GR 169 F7
Mataragka GR 174 B3
Mataraselkä FIN 117 C17
Mataró E 43 D8
Mataruge MNE 163 C7
Mataruška Banja SRB 158 F6
Mătăsari RO 159 D11
Mătăsaru RO 161 D6
Mätäsvaara FIN 125 D13
Matca RO 153 F11
Mateești RO 160 C3
Matei RO 152 D4
Matelica I 67 F7
Matera I 61 B7
Materija SLO 73 E9
Mateševo MNE 163 D8
Mátészalka H 145 H5
Mateuți MD 154 B3
Matfors S 103 B13
Matha F 28 D5
Mathay F 27 F6
Mathi I 68 C4
Matignon F 23 C7
Matigny F 18 E7
Matilda FIN 127 E8
Matinlompolo FIN 117 E12
Matino I 61 C10
Matīši LV 131 F10
Matkaniva FIN 119 F14
Matkavaara FIN 121 E12
Matku FIN 127 D10
Matkule LV 134 C5
Matlock GB 11 E8
Matosinhos P 44 B3
Matour F 30 C5
Mátraballa H 147 F10
Mátraderecske H 147 F10
Mátramindszent H 147 F9
Matrand N 96 B7
Mátraszele H 147 E9
Mátraszőlős H 147 F9
Mátraterenye H 147 E9
Mátraverebély H 147 F9
Matre N 94 C3
Matre N 100 E3
Matrei am Brenner A 72 B3
Matrei in Osttirol A 72 B6
Matsdal S 109 F10
Matsouki GR 174 B3
Matt CH 71 D8
Mattaincourt F 26 D5
Mattersburg A 149 A6
Mattighofen A 76 F4
Mattila S 119 C12
Mattilanmäki FIN 115 E4
Mattinata I 63 D10
Mattinen FIN 119 B13
Mattisudden S 116 E3
Mattmar S 105 E15
Mattsmyra S 103 D9
Måttsund S 118 C7
Matuizos LT 137 E10
Matulji HR 67 B9
Matúškovo SK 146 E5
Matyryna BY 133 F5
Maubert-Fontaine F 19 E9
Maubeuge F 19 D8
Maubourguet F 32 D6
Maubuisson F 28 E3
Mauchline GB 5 D8
Maud GB 3 K12
Mauerbach A 77 F10
Mauerkirchen A 76 F4
Mauerstetten D 71 B11
Maughold GBM 10 C3
Mauguio F 35 C7
Maukkula FIN 125 E15
Maula FIN 119 C13
Maulbronn D 27 C10
Mauléon F 28 B4
Mauléon-Barousse F 33 E7
Mauléon-d'Armagnac F 32 C5
Mauléon-Licharre F 32 D4
Maulévrier F 28 A4
Maum IRL 6 E3
Mauna FIN 116 B8
Maunu S 116 B8
Maunujärvi FIN 117 D14
Maunula FIN 119 D15
Maura N 95 B13
Maure-de-Bretagne F 23 E8
Maureillas-las-Illas F 34 F4
Măureni RO 159 C8
Maurens F 29 F6
Mauriac F 28 F5
Mauriac F 29 E10
Mauricemills IRL 8 C4
Maurik NL 183 B6
Maurnes N 110 C9
Mauron F 23 D7
Mauroux F 33 B8
Maurs F 29 F10
Maurset N 94 B6
Maurstad N 100 C2
Mauru FIN 119 B15
Maury F 34 E4
Mautern an der Donau A 77 F9
Mauterndorf A 73 B8
Mautern in Steiermark A 73 B10
Mauth D 76 E5
Mauthausen A 77 F7
Mauthen A 73 C7
Mauves F 30 E6
Mauvezin F 33 C7
Mauvoisin CH 31 C11
Mauzé-sur-le-Mignon F 28 C4
Mavranaioi GR 168 D5
Mavrochori GR 168 C5
Mavrodendri GR 169 D6
Mavrodin RO 160 E6
Mavrokklisi GR 171 B10
Mavromati GR 174 E4
Mavrommati GR 169 F6
Mavrommati GR 175 C7
Mavrothalassa GR 169 C10
Mavrovë AL 168 D2
Mavrovo MK 163 F10
Mavrovouni GR 169 C7
Mavrovouni GR 169 E7
Maxent F 23 E7
Maxéville F 186 D1
Maxial P 44 F2
Maxieira P 44 E5
Măxineni RO 161 C11
Maxmo FIN 122 D8
Maxsain D 185 C8
Mayakovskoye RUS 136 D5
Maybole GB 4 E7
Maydan UA 145 F7
Mayen D 21 D8
Mayenne F 23 D10
Mayet F 23 E12
Mayfield GB 15 E9
Mayobridge GB 7 D10
Mayorga E 39 D9
Mäyränperä FIN 119 F14
Mayres F 35 A7
Mayrhofen A 72 B4
Mäyry FIN 123 E10
Mayschoss D 21 C8
May's Corner GB 7 D10
Máza H 149 D10
Mazagón E 51 E6
Mazagran F 19 F10
Mažaičiai LT 134 F3
Mazaleón E 42 E4
Mazamet F 33 D10
Mazan F 35 B9
Mazara del Vallo I 58 D2
Mazarakia GR 168 F3
Mazarambroz E 46 E4
Mazarete E 47 C8
Mazarrón E 56 F2
Mazé F 23 F11
Mažeikiai LT 134 D4
Maženiai LT 135 E8
Mazères F 33 D9
Mazerolles F 32 D5
Mazeyrolles F 33 A8
Mazi TR 181 B7
Mazières-en-Gâtine F 28 B5
Mazirbe LV 130 F4
Mažonai LT 134 F4
Mazsalaca LV 131 F10
Mažučište MK 169 B5
Mazzano I 66 A1
Mazzano Romano I 62 C2
Mazzarino I 58 E5
Mazzarrone I 59 E6
Mazzo di Valtellina I 69 A9
Mborje AL 168 C4
Mbrostar AL 168 C2
Mdiq MA 53 E6
Meadela P 38 E2
Mealhada P 44 D4
Mealsgate GB 5 F10
Meana Sardo I 64 D3
Meare GB 13 C9
Measham GB 11 F8
Meåstrand S 107 E11
Meaulne F 29 B11
Méaulte F 18 E6
Meaux F 25 C8
Meauzac F 33 B8
Mechelen B 19 B9
Mechelen NL 183 D7
Mechernich D 21 C7
Mechowo PL 85 C8
Mechterstädt D 79 E8
Mecidiye TR 172 C6
Mecidiye TR 173 C10
Mecidiye TR 177 B10
Měčín CZ 76 D4
Mecina-Bombarón E 55 F6
Męcinka PL 81 D10
Meckenbeuren D 71 B9
Meckenheim D 21 C8
Meckesheim D 187 C6
Meco E 46 C6
Mecseknádasd H 149 D10
Meda P 45 C6
Meda SRB 159 B6
Medåker S 97 D14
Međas BIH 157 D10
Meddersheim D 21 E9
Meddo NL 183 A9
Mede I 68 C6
Medebach D 21 B11
Međeđa BIH 158 F3
Medeikiai LT 135 D9
Medelås S 107 B14
Medelim P 45 D6
Medellín E 51 B8
Medemblik NL 16 C4
Medena-Selišta BIH 157 D6
Medeno Polje BIH 156 C5
Medenychi UA 145 E8
Međeš BIH 158 D3
Medesano I 66 C1
Medgidia RO 155 E2
Medgyesbodzás H 151 D6
Medgyesegyháza H 151 E7
Medhamn S 91 A14
Mediana E 41 F10
Mediaș RO 152 E4
Medicina I 66 D4
Medieșu Aurit RO 151 B11
Medinaceli E 47 B8
Medina de las Torres E 51 C7
Medina del Campo E 39 F10
Medina de Pomar E 40 C5
Medina de Rioseco E 39 E9
Medina-Sidonia E 52 D5
Medingėnai LT 134 E4
Medinilla E 45 D9
Medininkai LT 137 D12
Mediona E 43 E7
Médis F 28 D4
Medkovets BG 159 F11
Medle S 118 E5
Medlov CZ 77 C12
Medneva LV 133 B3
Medolla I 66 C3
Medousa GR 171 B8
Medovoye RUS 136 D1
Mędrzechów PL 143 F10
Medsėdžiai LT 134 D3
Medskog S 103 E12
Medskogsbygget S 102 B5
Medstugan S 105 D12
Međugorje BIH 157 F8
Međuhana SRB 164 C3
Medulin HR 67 C8
Međumajdan HR 156 B5
Medumi LV 135 E12
Meduno I 73 D6
Međurečje SRB 163 B9
Međuvođe BIH 157 B6
Medveđa SRB 159 E7
Medveđa SRB 159 F7
Medveđa SRB 164 D4
Medviđa HR 156 D4
Medvode SLO 73 D9
Medyka PL 144 D6
Medze LV 134 C2
Medzev SK 145 F2
Medzibrod SK 147 D8
Medzilaborce SK 145 E4
Meenaclady IRL 6 B6
Meenavean IRL 6 C5
Meer B 182 C5
Meerane D 79 E11
Meerapalu EST 132 E1
Meerbeck D 17 D12
Meerbusch D 17 F7
Meerhout B 183 C6
Meerkerk NL 182 B5
Meerle B 182 C5
Meerlo NL 183 B8
Meersburg D 27 E11
Meerssen NL 19 C12
Meetkerke B 182 C2
Meeuwen B 19 B12
Mefjordvær N 111 A13
Mega Dereio GR 171 B10
Megala Kalyvia GR 169 F6
Megali Panagia GR 169 D10
Megali Volvi GR 169 C9
Megalochori GR 169 E6
Megalo Chorio GR 174 B4
Megalo Chorio GR 181 D6
Megalo Livadi GR 175 E9
Megalopoli GR 174 E5
Megara GR 175 C7
Megardssætra N 105 C13
Megen NL 183 B7
Megève F 31 D10
Megyaszó H 145 G3
Mehadia RO 159 D9
Mehadica RO 159 C9
Mehamn N 113 A20
Mehedeby S 99 B8
Mehikoorma EST 132 E1
Méhkerék H 151 D7
Mehren D 21 D7
Mehring D 21 E7
Mehrstetten D 74 F6
Mehtäkylä FIN 119 F12
Mehun-sur-Yèvre F 25 F7
Meidrim GB 12 B6
Meigh GB 7 D10
Meigle GB 5 B10
Meijel NL 16 F5
Meikleour GB 5 B10
Meilen CH 27 F10
Meilhan F 32 C4
Meillac F 23 D8
Meillant F 29 B10
Meillerie F 31 C10
Meimoa P 45 D6
Meina I 68 B6
Meine D 79 B8
Meinersen D 79 B7
Meinerzhagen D 185 B8
Meiningen D 79 E7
Meira E 38 B5
Meiringen CH 70 D6
Meisdorf D 79 C9
Meise B 182 D4
Meisenheim D 21 E9
Meißen D 80 D4
Meißenheim D 186 E4
Meitingen D 75 E8
Meix-devant-Virton B 19 E11
Mejlby DK 86 C6
Mejorada E 46 D3
Mejorada del Campo E 46 D6
Mejrup DK 86 C3
Meka Gruda BIH 157 F9
Mekinje SLO 73 D10
Mel I 72 D5
Melalahti FIN 121 F10
Melampes GR 178 E8
Melanthi GR 168 D5
Melay F 23 F10
Melay F 26 E4
Melazzo I 37 B8
Melbå N 111 C11
Melbourn GB 15 C9
Melbu N 110 C8
Melby GB 3 E13
Melchow D 84 E5
Meldal N 104 E7
Meldola I 66 D5
Meldorf D 82 B6
Mele I 37 C9
Melegnano I 69 C7
Melenci SRB 158 B5
Melendugno I 61 C10
Melfi I 60 B5
Melfjordbotn N 108 C6
Melgaço P 38 D3
Melgar de Arriba E 39 D9
Melgar de Fernamental E 40 D3
Melgar de Tera E 39 E7
Melgven F 22 E4
Melhus N 104 E8
Melia GR 169 E8
Meliana E 48 E4
Melick NL 20 B6
Melicucco I 59 C9
Mélida E 32 F2
Melide E 38 C4
Melides P 50 C2
Meligalas GR 174 E4
Meliki GR 169 C7
Melilli I 59 E7
Melinești RO 160 D3
Mélisey F 26 E6
Meliskerke NL 182 B3
Melissa GR 171 B7
Melissa I 61 E8
Melissano I 61 D10
Melissochori GR 175 C7
Melissopetra GR 168 D4
Melitaia GR 174 A5
Meliti GR 169 C6
Melito di Porto Salvo I 59 D8
Melivoia GR 169 E8
Melivoia GR 171 B7
Melk A 77 F8
Melkadalen N 111 D12
Melkefoss N 114 E7
Melksham GB 13 C10
Mellac F 22 E4
Mellajärvi FIN 119 B13
Mellakoski FIN 119 B12
Mellanfjärden S 103 C13
Mellansel S 107 E14
Mellansjö S 103 B10
Mellanström S 109 E15
Mellau A 71 C9
Mellbystrand S 87 B11
Melle B 19 B8
Melle D 17 D10
Melle F 28 C5
Mellen D 83 D11
Mellenbach-Glasbach D 79 E9
Mellendorf (Wedemark) D 78 A6
Mellensee D 80 B4
Mellerud S 91 B11
Mellerup DK 86 B6
Mellgård S 103 A9
Mellilä FIN 127 D8
Mellin D 79 A8
Mellingen D 79 E9
Mellösa S 93 A9
Mellrichstadt D 75 B7
Melmerby GB 5 F11
Melnbārži LV 135 B11
Melnica SRB 159 E7
Melnik BG 169 A9
Mělník CZ 77 B6
Mel'nikovo RUS 129 D12
Melnitsa BG 167 E7
Melnsils LV 130 F5
Melón E 38 D3
Meloy N 110 C9
Meløysund N 108 C6
Melrand F 22 E5
Melres P 44 B4
Melrose GB 5 D11
Mels CH 71 C8
Melsdorf D 83 B8
Melsungen D 78 D6
Melsvik N 112 C11
Meltaus FIN 117 E14
Meltham GB 11 D8
Melton GB 15 C11
Melton Mowbray GB 11 F10
Meltosjärvi FIN 117 E13
Melun F 25 C8
Melvaig GB 2 K5
Melvich GB 3 H9
Mélykút H 150 E3
Melzo I 69 C7
Memaliaj AL 168 D2
Membrey F 26 E4
Membrilla E 55 B6
Membrío E 45 E6
Mēmele LV 135 D8
Memleben D 79 D9
Memmelsdorf D 75 C8
Memmingen D 71 B10
Memmingerberg D 71 B10
Memsie GB 3 K12
Menaggio I 69 A7
Menai Bridge GB 10 E3
Menaldum NL 16 B5
Menars F 24 E5
Menasalbas E 46 E4
Menat F 30 C2
Menata I 66 C5
Mendavia E 32 F1
Mende F 34 A6
Menden (Sauerland) D 17 F9
Mendenitsa GR 175 B6
Menderes TR 177 C9
Mendig D 21 D8
Mendiga P 44 E3
Mendigorría E 32 E2
Menditte F 32 D4
Mendrisio CH 69 B6
Ménéac F 22 D7
Menemen TR 177 B9
Menen B 19 C7
Menesjärvi FIN 117 A16
Ménesplet F 29 E6
Ménessaire F 25 F11
Menet F 29 E11
Menetes GR 181 F6
Menetou-Salon F 25 F7
Menfi I 58 D2
Mengabril E 51 B8
Meņģele LV 135 C10
Mengen D 27 D11
Mengerskirchen D 21 C10
Mengeš SLO 73 D10
Mengíbar E 53 A9
Menidi GR 174 A3
Ménigoute F 28 C5
Ménil-la-Tour F 26 C4
Ménil-sur-Belvitte F 26 D6
Menin B 19 C7
Menin B 182 D2
Menkijärvi FIN 123 E11
Menkulas AL 168 C4
Mennecy F 25 C7
Mennetou-sur-Cher F 24 F6
Menou F 25 F9
Mens F 31 F8
Mensignac F 29 E7
Menslage D 17 C9
Mentana I 62 C3
Menteroda D 79 D8
Menteșe TR 181 B8
Menton F 37 D7
Méntrida E 46 D4
Menznau CH 70 C6
Méobecq F 29 B8
Meolo I 72 E5
Méounes-les-Montrieux F 35 D10
Meppel NL 16 C6
Meppen D 17 C8
Mequinenza E 42 E4
Mer F 24 E6
Mera RO 153 F9
Merag HR 67 C9
Meråker N 105 E11
Meråkervollen N 105 E11
Merano I 72 C3
Méracq F 32 C5
Merasjärvi S 116 C7
Merasjärvi S 117 C10
Merate I 69 B7
Merbes-le-Château B 19 D9
Mercadillo E 40 B5
Mercatale I 66 F5
Mercatello sul Metauro I 66 E5
Mercatino Conca I 66 E6
Mercato San Severino I 60 B3
Mercato Saraceno I 66 E5
Merćez SRB 163 C11
Merching D 71 A11
Merchtem B 19 C9
Mercœur F 29 E9
Mercogliano I 60 B3
Mercuès F 33 B8
Merdrignac F 22 D7
Mērdzene LV 133 C3
Mere B 19 C8
Mere GB 13 C10
Méreau F 24 F7
Merei RO 161 C9
Merelbeke B 19 C8
Meremäe EST 132 F2
Merenberg D 185 C9
Mereni MD 154 D4
Mereni RO 155 E2
Mereni RO 161 E7
Mérens-les-Vals F 33 E9
Merești RO 153 E6
Méréville F 24 D7
Merghindeal RO 152 F5
Mergozzo I 68 B5
Meria F 37 F10
Méribel-les-Allues F 31 E10
Meriç TR 171 B10
Merichas GR 175 E9
Merichleri BG 166 E4
Mérida E 51 B7
Meriden GB 13 A11
Merijärvi FIN 119 F12
Merikarvia FIN 126 B6
Meriläinen FIN 123 D12
Merimasku FIN 126 E6
Měřín CZ 77 D9
Mering D 71 A11
Merișani RO 160 D5
Mérk H 151 B9
Merkendorf A 148 C5
Merkendorf D 75 D8
Merkenes S 109 C11
Merkinė LT 137 E9
Merklín CZ 76 C4
Merklingen D 74 E6
Merksplas B 182 C5
Merlara I 66 B3
Merlevenez F 22 E5
Merlines F 29 D10
Mern DK 87 E10
Mērnieki LV 131 F8
Mernye H 149 C9
Merošina SRB 164 C4
Merrey F 26 D4
Mersch L 20 E6
Merseburg (Saale) D 79 D10
Mersinbeleni TR 177 D10
Mers-les-Bains F 18 D3
Mērsrags LV 134 B6
Mertajärvi S 116 B8
Mertert L 20 E6
Mertesdorf D 186 B2
Merthyr Tydfil GB 13 B8
Mertingen D 75 E8
Mertloch D 185 D7
Mértola P 50 D4
Mertzwiller F 186 D4
Méru F 18 F5
Mervans F 31 B7
Mervent F 28 B4
Merville F 18 C6
Merville F 33 C8
Méry-sur-Seine F 25 C10
Merzen D 17 D9
Merzig D 21 F7
Mesagne I 61 B9
Mesagros GR 175 D8
Mésanger F 23 F9
Mesão Frio P 44 B5
Mesaria GR 177 F6
Meschede D 17 F10
Meschers-sur-Gironde F 28 D4
Mešeišta MK 168 B4
Meselefors S 107 C11
Mesenikolas GR 169 F6
Meseșenii de Jos RO 151 C10
Mesgrigny F 25 D10
Mesi GR 171 C8
Mesići BIH 157 E11
Mesihovina BIH 157 E7
Mesimeri GR 169 D9
Mesinge DK 86 E7
Meskla GR 178 E6
Meškuičiai LT 134 D6
Meslay-du-Maine F 23 E10
Mesocco CH 71 E8
Mesochora GR 168 F5
Mesochori GR 169 E7
Mesochori GR 181 E6
Mesola I 66 C5
Mesolongi GR 174 C3

Mesongi GR 168 F2
Mesopotamia GR 168 C5
Mesopotamos GR 168 E4
Mesoraca I 59 A10
Mesotopos GR 177 A7
Mespelbrunn D 187 B7
Mesquer F 22 F7
Messac F 23 E8
Messanges F 32 C3
Meßdorf D 83 E11
Messei F 23 C10
Messejana P 50 D3
Messina I 59 C8
Messincourt F 19 E11
Messingen D 17 D8
Messini GR 174 E5
Meßkirch D 27 E11
Messlingen S 102 A4
Meßstetten D 27 D10
Mesta GR 165 F8
Mesta GR 177 C6
Mestanza E 54 B4
Městec Králové CZ 77 B8
Mestervik N 111 B16
Mesti GR 171 C9
Mestlin D 83 C11
Město Albrechtice CZ 142 F4
Město Touškov CZ 76 C4
Mestre I 66 B5
Mesves-sur-Loire F 25 F8
Mesztegnyő H 149 C8
Meta I 60 B2
Métabief F 31 B9
Metagkitsi GR 169 D10
Metajna HR 67 C11
Metalliko SK 147 D9
Metallostroy RUS 129 F14
Metaxades GR 171 B10
Metelen D 17 D8
Meteş RO 151 E11
Metfield GB 15 C11
Methana GR 175 D7
Metheringham GB 11 E11
Methlick GB 3 L12
Methoni GR 178 B2
Methven GB 5 C9
Methwold GB 11 F13
Metković HR 157 F8
Metlika SLO 148 E4
Metnitz A 73 C9
Metochi GR 174 C3
Metochi GR 175 B8
Metovnica SRB 159 F9
Mētriena LV 135 C12
Metsäkansa FIN 127 C10
Metsäkylä FIN 121 D11
Metsäkylä FIN 128 D7
Metsälä FIN 120 C9
Metsämaa FIN 127 D9
Metschow D 84 C3
Metsküla EST 130 D5
Metslawier NL 16 B6
Metsovo GR 168 E5
Mettäjärvi S 117 E11
Mettendorf D 20 E6
Mettenheim D 75 F11
Mettet B 19 D10
Mettevoll N 112 D7
Mettingen D 17 D9
Mettlach D 21 F7
Mettmann D 17 F7
Mettray F 24 F4
Metz F 26 B5
Metzervisse F 20 F6
Metzingen D 27 C11
Meudt D 185 D8
Meulan F 24 B6
Meulebeke B 19 C7
Meung-sur-Loire F 24 E6
Meursault F 30 B6
Meuselwitz D 79 D11
Meuzac F 29 D8
Mevagissey GB 12 E5
Mexborough GB 11 E9
Meximieux F 31 D7
Mey GB 3 H10
Meyenburg D 83 D12
Meylan F 31 E8
Meymac F 29 D10
Meyrargues F 35 C10
Meyreuil F 35 D10
Meyronnes F 36 C5
Meyrueis F 34 B5
Meyssac F 29 E9
Meysse F 35 A8
Meythet F 31 D9
Mezapos GR 178 B3
Mežāre LV 135 C12
Mežciems LV 134 C7
Mezdra BG 165 C8
Mèze F 35 D6
Mézel F 36 D4
Mežgale LV 135 D11
Mezhdurech'ye RUS 136 D4
Meziboří CZ 80 E5
Mežica SLO 73 C10
Mézidon-Canon F 23 B11
Mézières-en-Brenne F 29 B8
Mézières-sur-Issoire F 29 C7
Mézilhac F 30 F5
Mézilles F 25 E9
Mézin F 33 B6
Mezio P 44 C5
Mezőberény H 151 D7
Mezőcsát H 147 F11
Mezőcsokonya H 149 D9
Mezőfalva H 149 C11
Mezőgyán H 151 D8
Mezőhegyes H 150 E6
Mezőkeresztes H 145 H2
Mezőkovácsháza H 151 E6
Mezőkövesd H 147 F11
Mezőlak H 149 B8
Mezőnyárád H 145 H2
Mezőörs H 149 A9
Mézos F 32 B3
Mezőszemere H 150 B6
Mezőszentgyörgy H 149 B10
Mezőszilas H 149 C10
Mezőtárkány H 150 B5
Mezőtone LV 135 D8
Mezőtúr H 150 D6
Mezőzombor H 145 G3
Mežvidi LV 133 C3
Mežvidi LV 134 C4
Mezzana I 69 A10
Mezzanego I 37 C10
Mezzano I 72 D4
Mezzocorona I 69 A11

Mezzojuso I 58 D3
Mezzoldo I 69 A8
Mezzolombardo I 69 A11
Mga RUS 129 F15
Miączyn PL 144 B8
Miajadas E 45 F9
Miałet F 29 D7
Miały PL 85 E10
Miasteczko Krajeńskie PL 85 D12
Miastko PL 85 B11
Miastków Kościelny PL 141 G5
Miastkowo PL 139 D12
Miavaig GB 2 J3
Mica RO 152 C3
Mica RO 152 E4
Micăsasa RO 152 E4
Micești RO 160 D5
Miceștii de Câmpie RO 152 D4
Michałany SK 145 F4
Michalová SK 147 D9
Michalovce SK 145 F4
Michałów PL 143 F9
Michałów Górny PL 141 G4
Michałowice PL 142 E3
Michałowice PL 143 F8
Michałowo PL 140 D9
Michelau in Oberfranken
   D 75 B9
Michelbach an der Bilz D 74 D6
Micheldorf A 73 C9
Micheldorf in Oberösterreich
   A 73 A9
Michelfeld D 74 D6
Michelstadt D 21 E12
Michendorf D 80 B4
Michorzewo PL 81 B10
Michów PL 141 G6
Mickelspiltom FIN 127 D15
Mickelsträsk S 118 F4
Mickleton GB 13 A11
Miclești RO 153 D11
Midbea GB 3 G11
Middagsbukt N 111 B17
Middelbeers NL 183 C6
Middelburg NL 16 E1
Middelfart DK 86 D5
Middelharnis NL 16 E2
Middelkerke B 18 B6
Middelstum NL 17 B7
Middenbeemster NL 16 C3
Middenmeer NL 16 C4
Middleham GB 11 C8
Middlemarsh GB 13 D10
Middlesbrough GB 11 B9
Middleton GB 11 D7
Middleton Cheney GB 13 A12
Middleton in Teesdale GB 5 F12
Middletown GB 7 D9
Middlewich GB 10 E7
Midhurst GB 15 F7
Midleton IRL 8 E6
Midlum D 17 A11
Midsund N 100 A5
Midtgård N 114 D8
Midtskogberget N 102 D3
Midwolda NL 17 B8
Mid Yell GB 3 D14
Miechów PL 143 F9
Miechów Charsznica PL 143 F8
Miedes E 41 F9
Miedziana Góra PL 143 E10
Miedzichowo PL 81 B9
Miedzna PL 139 E13
Miedzna PL 143 G7
Miedźno PL 143 E6
Międzybórz PL 142 D4
Międzychód PL 81 A9
Międzylesie PL 77 B11
Międzyrzec Podlaski PL 141 G7
Międzyrzecz PL 81 B9
Międzyzdroje PL 84 C6
Miehikkälä FIN 128 D8
Miehlen D 185 D8
Miejsce Piastowe PL 145 D4
Miejska Górka PL 81 C11
Mijkinia PL 81 D11
Miekojärvi S 119 B10
Miélan F 33 D6
Mielec PL 143 F11
Mielęcin PL 85 E12
Mielęszyn PL 85 E12
Mielno PL 85 B9
Mieluskylä FIN 119 F14
Mielżyn PL 138 F4
Mieming A 71 C12
Mierasjärvi FIN 113 D19
Mieraslompolo FIN 113 D19
Miercurea-Ciuc RO 153 E7
Miercurea Nirajului RO 152 D5
Miercurea Sibiului RO 152 F3
Mieres E 39 B8
Mieres E 43 C9
Mierlo NL 16 F5
Mierojávri N 113 E11
Mieroszów PL 81 E10
Miers F 29 F9
Mierzęcice PL 143 F7
Mierzyn PL 84 D6
Miesau D 186 C3
Miesbach D 72 A4
Mieścisko PL 85 E12
Miesenbach D 186 C4
Mieslahti FIN 121 F10
Miessaure S 116 E6
Mieste D 79 B9
Mieszków PL 142 B3
Mieszkowice PL 84 E6
Mietingen D 71 A9
Mietków PL 81 E11
Mietoinen FIN 126 D6
Miettilä FIN 129 C11
Mieussy F 31 C10
Mieza E 45 B7
Migennes F 25 E10
Migliarino I 66 C4
Migliarino I 66 C4
Miglianico I 61 B6
Mignaloux-Beauvoir F 29 B6
Mignano Monte Lungo I 60 A1
Migné-Auxances F 29 B6
Mignovillard F 31 B9
Miguel Esteban E 47 E6
Miguelturra E 54 B5
Migushino RUS 133 E7
Mihăești RO 160 C4
Mihăești RO 160 D3
Mihăești RO 160 E5
Mihai Bravu RO 155 D5
Mihai Bravu RO 161 E8
Mihăileni RO 152 F4

Mihăileni RO 153 B8
Mihăileni RO 153 E7
Mihăilești RO 161 D9
Mihăilești RO 161 E7
Mihail Kogălniceanu RO 155 C5
Mihail Kogălniceanu RO 155 D3
Mihail Kogălniceanu RO 155 E2
Mihailovca MD 154 D3
Mihai Viteazu RO 152 D3
Mihai Viteazu RO 155 D3
Mihajlovac SRB 159 D6
Mihajlovac SRB 159 E9
Mihajlovo SRB 158 C5
Mihălăşeni RO 153 B10
Miháld H 149 D8
Mihalţ RO 152 E3
Mihályi H 149 A8
Miheșu de Câmpie RO 152 D4
Mihla D 79 D7
Miilüranta FIN 123 C16
Mijares E 46 D3
Mijas E 53 C7
Mijdrecht NL 16 D3
Mijoska MNE 163 D7
Mikalayeva BY 133 F6
Mikepércs H 151 C8
Mikhalishki BY 137 D13
Mikhalkovo BG 165 F9
Mikhaltsi BG 166 C4
Mikhaylovo BG 165 B8
Mikhaylovo BG 166 C5
Mikitamäe EST 132 E2
Mikitsikha BY 133 F6
Mikkeli FIN 128 B7
Mikkelin mlk FIN 128 B7
Mikkelvik N 112 C3
Mikkola FIN 117 D16
Mikladalur FO 2 A3
Miklavž SLO 148 C5
Miklebostad N 111 C13
Mikleuš HR 149 E9
Mikołajki PL 136 F4
Mikołajki Pomorskie PL 139 C7
Mikołów PL 143 F6
Mikoszewo PL 138 B6
Mikre BG 165 C10
Mikri Volvi GR 169 C10
Mikro Dereio GR 171 B10
Mikrokambos GR 169 C8
Mikromilia GR 170 B6
Mikropoli GR 169 B10
Mikrothives GR 169 F8
Mikrovalto GR 169 D6
Mikstat PL 142 C4
Mikulášš CZ 77 C8
Mikulasovice CZ 80 E6
Mikulčice CZ 77 E12
Mikulov CZ 77 E11
Mikulovice CZ 142 F3
Mikuševc S 103 B9
Miladinovci MK 164 F4
Milagro E 41 D8
Milagros E 40 E4
Miłakowo PL 139 B9
Milano I 69 C7
Milano Marittima I 66 D5
Milanówek PL 141 F3
Milaş BG 157 B7
Milas TR 181 B7
Milatkovće SRB 163 C10
Milatos GR 179 E10
Milazzo I 59 C7
Milborne Port GB 13 D10
Milcoiu RO 160 C4
Milcov RO 160 E4
Milcovul RO 161 B10
Mildenhall GB 15 C10
Mildstedt D 82 B6
Mileanca RO 153 A9
Milejczyce PL 141 E8
Milejewo PL 139 B8
Milejów PL 141 H7
Milena I 58 E4
Milești MD 153 C12
Milestone IRL 8 C6
Mileto I 59 B9
Milevsko CZ 76 D6
Milfield GB 5 D12
Milford IRL 7 B7
Milford B 8 D5
Milford Haven GB 12 B4
Milhão P 39 E6
Milhaud F 35 C7
Milići BIH 157 D11
Milicz PL 81 C12
Milies GR 169 F9
Milíkov CZ 147 B8
Milín CZ 76 C6
Milina GR 175 A7
Milis I 64 C2
Militello in Val di Catania
   I 59 E6
Miliyeve UA 152 A6
Milizac F 22 D2
Miljana HR 148 D5
Miljeno BIH 157 E11
Miljevina BIH 157 E10
Milkel D 81 D6
Milki PL 136 E4
Milkovitsa BG 160 F5
Milk'ovtsi BG 165 D6
Millares E 48 F3
Millas F 34 E4
Millau F 34 B5
Millay F 30 B5
Millbrook GB 12 E6
Millbrook IRL 7 E8
Millesimo I 37 C8
Millevaches F 29 D10
Millford GB 7 D9
Millhouse GB 4 D6
Millières F 26 C3
Millingen aan de Rijn NL 183 B8
Millisle GB 7 C11
Millom GB 10 C5
Milloshevë RKS 164 D3
Millport GB 4 D7
Millstatt A 73 C8
Millstreet IRL 8 D4
Milltown GB 5 F10
Milltown IRL 7 F9
Milltown IRL 8 D3
Milltown IRL 8 D3
Milltown Malbay IRL 8 C4
Milly-la-Forêt F 25 D7
Milmarcos E 47 B9
Milmersdorf D 84 D5
Milmort B 183 D7
Milna HR 156 F5
Milnathort GB 5 C10

Milngavie GB 5 D8
Milnthorpe GB 10 C6
Milo I 59 D7
Miłocice PL 85 C11
Milohnić HR 67 B9
Miłomłyn PL 139 C8
Miłoradz PL 138 B6
Miloš I 59 D7
Miloșeşti RO 161 D10
Milovaig GB 2 L3
Milovice CZ 77 B7
Milow D 79 A11
Milow D 83 D11
Miłówka PL 147 B8
Miltach D 75 D12
Miltenberg D 21 E12
Milţini LV 134 C6
Milton GB 2 L8
Milton GB 5 B9
Milton Keynes GB 15 C7
Miltzow D 84 B4
Milutinovac SRB 159 F7
Milverton GB 13 C8
Milz D 75 B8
Mimetiz E 40 B5
Mimizan F 32 B3
Mimizan-Plage F 32 B3
Mimoň CZ 81 E7
Mina de São Domingos P 50 D5
Mín an Chladaigh IRL 6 B6
Minas de Riotinto E 51 D6
Minateda E 55 C9
Minaya E 47 F8
Minde P 44 E3
Mindelheim D 71 A10
Mindelstetten D 75 E10
Minden D 17 D11
Minderhout B 182 C5
Mindnes N 108 E3
Mindresunde N 100 C3
Mîndreşti MD 154 B2
Mindszent H 150 D5
Mindszentgodisa H 149 D10
Mindtangen N 108 E3
Mindya BG 166 C5
Minehead GB 13 C8
Mineo I 59 E6
Mineralni Bani BG 166 F4
Minerbio I 66 C3
Minervino Murge I 60 A6
Minfeld D 27 B9
Minfordd GB 10 F3
Minger MD 154 D2
Minglanilla E 47 E9
Mingorría E 46 C3
Miniac-Morvan F 23 C8
Miničevo SRB 159 F9
Mín na bhFiann IRL 6 C5
Minne S 103 B9
Minnertsga NL 16 B5
Minnesund N 95 B14
Minnigaff GB 4 F8
Minot F 25 E12
Mińsk Mazowiecki PL 141 F5
Minsterley GB 10 F6
Mintiloglio GR 174 C4
Mintiu Gherlii RO 152 C3
Mintlaw GB 3 K13
Mintraching D 75 E11
Minturno I 62 E5
Minucciano I 66 D1
Minusio CH 68 A6
Mioarele RO 160 C6
Mionica SRB 158 E5
Mionnay F 30 D6
Mios F 32 A4
Mira I 66 B5
Mira I 66 B5
Mira P 44 D3
Mirabeau F 35 C10
Mirabel E 45 E8
Mirabel F 33 B8
Mirabel-aux-Baronnies F 35 B9
Mirabella Eclano I 60 A4
Mirabella Imbaccari I 58 E5
Miraflores de la Sierra E 46 C5
Miralcamp E 42 D5
Miramare I 66 D6
Miramas F 35 C9
Mirambeau F 28 E4
Mirambel E 42 F3
Miramont-de-Guyenne F 33 A6
Miranda de Arga E 32 F2
Miranda de Ebro E 40 C6
Miranda do Corvo P 44 D4
Miranda do Douro P 39 E7
Mirande F 33 C6
Mirandela P 38 F5
Mirandilla E 51 A7
Mirandola I 66 C3
Mirandol-Bourgnounac
   F 33 B10
Miranje HR 156 E4
Mirano I 66 B5
Miras AL 168 C4
Mirash RKS 164 E3
Mirăslău RO 152 E3
Miratovac SRB 164 D4
Miravci MK 169 B7
Miravet E 42 E5
Miravete de la Sierra E 42 F2
Mircea Vodă RO 155 D2
Mircea Vodă RO 161 C10
Mirceşti RO 153 C9
Mircze PL 144 B8
Mirebeau F 26 F3
Mirebeau F 29 B6
Mirecourt F 26 D5
Miren SLO 73 E8
Mirepoix F 33 D9
Mireşu Mare RO 151 C11
Mireval F 35 C6
Miričina BIH 157 C9
Mirkovci HR 157 B10
Mirkovo BG 165 D9
Mirlović Zagora HR 156 E5
Mirna SLO 73 E11
Mirna Peč SLO 73 E11
Mirocin PL 144 C5
Mirocin Górny PL 81 C9
Mironeasa RO 153 D10
Mirosăuce SRB 164 D4
Miroşi RO 160 E5
Mirosława RO 153 C9
Mirosławiec PL 85 D10
Mirosloveşti RO 153 C9
Mirošov CZ 76 C5
Mirotice CZ 76 D6
Mirovice CZ 76 C6

Mirovtsi BG 167 C8
Mirow D 83 D13
Mirşid RO 151 C11
Mirsk PL 81 E8
Mirto Crosia I 61 D7
Mirueña de los Infanzones
   E 45 C10
Mirzec PL 141 H4
Misano Adriatico I 67 E6
Mişca RO 151 D8
Mischii RO 160 E3
Miserey-Salines F 26 F4
Mishnyevichy BY 133 F7
Misi FIN 117 E17
Misilmeri I 58 C3
Miske H 150 E3
Miskolc H 145 G2
Mislina HR 162 D4
Mislinja SLO 73 D11
Mišnjak HR 67 C10
Mison F 35 B10
Missanello I 60 C6
Missenträsk S 107 A17
Missillac F 23 F7
Misso EST 131 F14
Mistelbach A 77 E11
Mistelgau D 75 C9
Mistelbach BIH 157 C8
Misten N 108 B8
Misterbianco I 59 D7
Misterhult S 93 E9
Misterton GB 11 E10
Mistretta I 58 D5
Mistros GR 175 B8
Misurina I 72 C5
Misvær N 108 B9
Mitandersfors S 96 B7
Mitchelstown IRL 8 D6
Mithymna GR 171 F10
Mitoc RO 153 A10
Mitreni RO 161 E9
Mitropoli GR 169 F6
Mitrousi GR 169 B9
Mitrova Reka SRB 163 C9
Mitrovicë RKS 163 D10
Mitry-Mory F 25 C8
Mittädalen S 102 A4
Mittelberg A 71 C10
Mittelberg A 71 D11
Mittelbiberach D 71 A9
Mittelkalbach D 74 B6
Mittelsinn D 187 A8
Mittenwald D 72 B3
Mittenwalde D 80 B5
Mittenwalde D 84 D5
Mitterbach am Erlaufsee
   I 148 A4
Mitterding A 76 F4
Mitterdorf im Mürztal A 148 A5
Mittersheim F 27 C6
Mittersill A 72 B5
Mitterskirchen D 75 F12
Mitterteich D 75 C11
Mittet N 100 A7
Mittiliden S 105 B16
Mittweida D 80 E3
Mitwitz D 75 B9
Mizhhir"ya UA 145 F7
Mizil RO 161 C8
Miziya BG 160 F3
Mjäldrunga S 91 C14
Mjäll S 107 A17
Mjällby S 88 C7
Mjällom S 107 F14
Mjehë AL 163 F8
Mjohira H 147 F8
Mjohorn D 80 E4
Mjølfjell N 100 D7
Mjöljby S 92 C6
Mjölkbäck S 88 A3
Mjolby S 92 C6
Mjönäs S 97 C10
Mjøndalen N 95 C12
Mjønes N 108 B8
Mjösjöby S 107 D15
Mjösund FIN 126 E7
Mjöträsk S 119 B9
Mjøvattnet S 103 A14
Mjøvattnet S 118 E5
Mladá Boleslav CZ 77 B7
Mladá Vožice CZ 77 C7
Mladé Buky CZ 81 E9
Mladenovac SRB 158 E6
Mladenovo SRB 158 C3
Mladikovine BIH 157 D8
Mladinovo BG 166 F6
Mlado Nagoričane MK 164 E4
Mława PL 139 D9
Mlekarevo BG 166 E6
Mlinište BIH 157 D7
Mliniste BIH 157 D7
Mlodzieszyn PL 141 F2
Młynary PL 139 B8
Mlynarze PL 139 E11
Mlynky'ka UA 145 E9
Mnichovice CZ 77 C7
Mnichovo Hradiště CZ 77 A7
Mnichów PL 143 E9
Mniów PL 143 D9
Mníšek nad Hnilcom SK 145 F2
Mníšek pod Brdy CZ 76 C6
Mniszew PL 141 G4
Mniszków PL 141 H2
Mo N 100 E3
Mo S 103 D12
Mo S 103 D12
Mo S 107 D11
Mo S 107 D11
Moaça RO 153 F7
Moaña E 38 D2
Moara RO 153 B8
Moara Domnească MD 153 B10
Moara Vlăsiei RO 161 D8
Moate IRL 7 F7
Mobberley GB 11 E7
Moča SK 149 A10
Moçarria P 44 F3
Mocejón E 46 E5
Močenok SK 146 E5
Mochales E 47 B9
Mochos GR 178 E9
Mochy PL 81 B10
Möckern D 79 B10
Mockfjärd S 97 A12
Möckmühl D 27 B11
Mockrehna D 79 C12
Mockträsk S 118 C7
Moclín E 53 A9
Moclinejo E 53 C8
Mocra MD 154 B4
Mócsa H 149 A10
Modane F 31 E10

Modave B 19 D11
Modbury GB 13 E7
Modelu RO 161 E10
Modena I 66 C2
Modi GR 175 B6
Modica I 59 F6
Modigliana I 66 D4
Modliborzyce PL 144 B5
Modliszewice PL 141 H2
Modra SK 146 E4
Modran BIH 157 C8
Modrany SK 146 F6
Modreeny IRL 8 C6
Modriach A 73 C11
Modrica BIH 157 C9
Modrište MK 168 A5
Modruš HR 156 B3
Modrý Kameň SK 147 E8
Modugno I 61 A7
Moëlan-sur-Mer F 22 E4
Moelfre GB 10 E3
Moen N 101 E13
Moen N 111 B16
Moena I 72 D4
Moerbeke B 182 C3
Moergestel NL 16 E4
Moerkerke B 182 C2
Moers D 17 F7
Moffat GB 5 E10
Mofreita P 39 E6
Mogadouro P 39 F6
Mogata S 93 C8
Mögelin D 79 A11
Møgeltønder DK 86 F3
Mogenstrup DK 87 E9
Moggio Udinese I 73 D7
Mögglingen D 187 D8
Mogielnica PL 141 G3
Mogila MK 168 B5
Mogilany PL 147 B9
Mogilishte BG 167 C10
Mogilno PL 138 E4
Moglia I 66 C2
Mogliano I 67 F7
Mogliano Veneto I 66 A5
Möglingen D 187 D7
Mogón E 55 C6
Mogorella I 64 D2
Mogoro I 64 D2
Mogoşani RO 160 D6
Mogoşeşti RO 153 C10
Mogoşeşti-Siret RO 153 C9
Mogoşoaia RO 161 D7
Moguer E 51 E6
Mohács H 149 E11
Moharque E 55 C9
Mohed S 103 D12
Mohedas de Granadilla E 45 D8
Mohedas de la Jara E 45 E10
Mohelnice CZ 77 C11
Mohelno CZ 77 D10
Mohernando E 47 C6
Mohill IRL 9 C8
Mohill IRL 7 E7
Möhnö FIN 125 E16
Möhlau D 79 C11
Möhlin CH 27 E8
Moholm S 91 B15
Mohora H 147 F8
Mohorn D 80 E4
Mohyliv Podil's'kyy UA 154 A1
Moi N 94 F5
Moi N 94 F6
Moià E 43 D8
Moiano I 60 A3
Moieciu RO 160 C6
Moimenta da Beira P 44 C5
Moineşti RO 153 E8
Móinteach Milic IRL 7 F8
Moira GB 7 D10
Moi i Rana N 108 D7
Moirax F 33 B7
Moires GR 178 E8
Mõisaküla EST 131 E10
Moisburg D 82 D7
Moisdon-la-Rivière F 23 E9
Moisei RO 152 B5
Moisiovaara FIN 121 E13
Moislains F 18 E6
Moissac F 33 B8
Moissac-Bellevue F 36 D4
Moissey F 26 F4
Moïta F 37 G10
Moita P 44 D4
Moita P 44 F3
Moita P 50 B2
Moixent-Mogente E 56 D3
Mojácar E 55 E9
Mojados E 39 F10
Mojkovac MNE 163 D8
Mojmírovce SK 146 E6
Mojstrana SLO 73 D8
Mojzesovo SK 146 E6
Møkekvik N 110 D6
Möklinta S 98 B7
Mokobody PL 141 F6
Mokra Hora CZ 77 D11
Mokrance SK 145 F3
Mokre PL 143 F10
Mokren BG 167 D7
Mokresh BG 160 F3
Mokrievo MK 169 B8
Mokrin SRB 150 F5
Mokro BIH 157 E10
Mokronog BIH 156 D5
Mokronoge BIH 157 E9
Møksy FIN 123 D12
Mol B 19 B11
Mol SRB 150 F5
Mola di Bari I 61 A8
Molaoi GR 178 B4
Molare I 37 B9
Molares P 38 F4
Molares E 51 E7
Molat HR 67 D10
Molbergen D 17 C9
Mølby DK 86 E4
Mold GB 10 E5
Moldava nad Bodvou SK 145 F2
Molde N 100 A6
Moldjord N 108 B8
Moldova Nouă RO 159 D8
Moldova-Sulița RO 152 B6
Moldoveni RO 153 D9
Moldoviţa RO 153 B7

Møldrup DK 86 B5
Moldvik N 111 C11
Moledo P 38 E2
Moledo P 44 C5
Molelos P 44 C4
Molenbeek-St-Jean B 182 D4
Molenstede B 183 C6
Molescroft GB 11 D11
Molesmes F 25 E11
Molești MD 154 D3
Moletai LT 135 F10
Molfetta I 61 A7
Molfsee D 83 B8
Moliden S 107 E14
Molières F 29 F9
Molières F 33 B8
Molières-sur-Cèze F 35 B7
Moliets-et-Maa F 32 C3
Molina Aterno I 62 C5
Molina de Aragón E 47 C9
Molina de Segura E 56 E2
Molina di Ledro I 69 B10
Molinara I 60 A3
Molinaseca E 39 C7
Molinella I 66 C4
Molines-en-Queyras F 31 F10
Molinet F 30 C4
Molinges F 31 C8
Molinicos E 55 C8
Molini di Tures I 72 C4
Molino de Villobas E 32 F5
Molinos E 42 F3
Molins de Rei E 43 E8
Moliterno I 60 C5
Molitg-les-Bains F 33 E10
Molkojärvi FIN 117 D14
Molkom S 97 C10
Mollas AL 168 C3
Mölle S 87 C11
Molledo E 40 B3
Möllenbeck D 84 D4
Möllenhagen D 84 C3
Mollerussa E 42 D5
Mollet del Vallès E 43 D8
Molliens-Dreuil F 18 E5
Mollis CH 27 F11
Mölln A 73 A9
Mölln D 83 C9
Mölln D 84 C4
Molló E 33 F10
Mollösund S 91 C9
Mölltorp S 92 C4
Mölnbo S 93 A10
Mölnlycke S 91 D11
Molnytsya UA 153 A8
Moloha UA 154 E6
Molompize F 30 E3
Molos GR 175 B6
Moloy F 26 E2
Molpe FIN 122 D6
Mölschleben D 79 D8
Molsheim F 186 D3
Molunat HR 162 E5
Molve HR 149 D8
Molveno I 69 A10
Molvízar E 53 C9
Mombaldone I 37 B8
Mombaroccio I 67 E6
Mombeltrán E 45 D10
Mombercelli I 37 B8
Mombris D 21 D12
Mombuey E 39 D7
Momchilgrad BG 171 A8
Momignies B 19 D9
Momo I 68 B6
Mona FIN 122 D8
Monachil E 53 B9
Monaghan IRL 7 D9
Monamolin IRL 9 C10
Monäs FIN 122 D8
Monashi UA 154 E6
Monasterace I 59 C10
Monasterevin IRL 7 F8
Monastir I 64 E3
Monastiraki GR 174 B2
Monbahus F 33 A7
Monbazillac F 29 F6
Moncada E 48 E4
Moncalieri I 37 A7
Moncalvo I 68 C5
Monção P 38 D3
Moncarapacho P 50 E4
Moncaut F 33 B6
Moncel-sur-Seille F 26 C5
Mönchengladbach D 20 B6
Mönchhof A 77 G11
Monchio delle Corti I 66 D1
Monchique P 50 E2
Mönchsdeggingen D 75 E8
Monclar F 33 B7
Moncofa E 48 E4
Moncontour F 22 D6
Moncontour F 28 B4
Moncrabeau F 33 B6
Monda E 53 C7
Mondariz E 38 D3
Mondariz-Balneario E 38 D3
Mondavezan F 33 D8
Mondavio I 67 E6
Mondéjar E 47 D6
Mondeville F 23 B11
Mondolfo I 67 E7
Mondoñedo E 38 B5
Mondorf-les-Bains L 20 E6
Mondoubleau F 24 E4
Mondovì I 37 C7
Mondragon F 35 B8
Mondragone I 62 E5
Mondsee A 73 A7
Monea GB 7 D7
Moneasa RO 151 E9
Moneen IRL 6 F5
Moneglia I 37 C10
Monegrillo E 41 E11
Monein F 32 D4
Monesi I 37 C7
Monemvasia GR 178 B5
Monesiglio I 37 C8
Monesterio E 51 C7
Monestier-de-Clermont F 31 F8
Monestiés F 33 B10
Monêtier F 25 E10
Moneygall IRL 9 C7
Moneymore GB 4 F3
Moneyneany IRL 4 F3
Moneyreagh GB 7 C11
Monfalcone I 73 E8
Monfero E 38 B3
Monforte P 44 F6

Monforte da Beira P 45 E6
Monforte d'Alba I 37 B7
Monforte del Cid E 56 E3
Monforte de Lemos E 38 C4
Monforte de Moyuela E 42 E2
Monfortinho P 45 D7
Monghidoro I 66 D3
Mongrando I 68 B5
Mongstad N 100 E2
Monguelfo I 72 C5
Monheim D 75 E8
Moniaive GB 5 E9
Monieux F 35 B9
Monifieth GB 5 C11
Monilea IRL 7 E8
Mõniste EST 131 F13
Monistrol-d'Allier F 30 F4
Monistrol de Calders E 43 D8
Monistrol de Montserrat
  E 43 D7
Monistrol-sur-Loire F 30 E5
Monivea IRL 6 F5
Mönkeberg D 83 B8
Mońki PL 140 D7
Monkokehampton GB 12 D6
Monléon-Magnoac F 33 D7
Monmouth GB 13 B9
Monnaie F 24 E4
Mönni FIN 125 E14
Monninkylä FIN 127 E14
Monok H 145 G3
Monolithos GR 181 D7
Monopoli I 61 B8
Monor H 150 C3
Monor RO 152 C5
Monostorapáti H 149 C9
Monostorpályi H 151 C8
Monóvar E 56 E3
Monpazier F 33 A7
Monreal E 32 E3
Monreal del Campo E 47 C10
Monreale I 58 C2
Monreith GB 4 F7
Monroy E 45 E8
Monroyo E 42 F3
Mons B 19 D8
Mons F 34 C4
Mons F 36 D5
Monsampolo del Tronto I 62 B5
Monsaraz P 51 C5
Monschau D 20 C6
Monsec F 29 E7
Monségur F 33 A6
Monselice I 66 B4
Monsempron-Libos F 33 B7
Monserrat E 48 F3
Monsheim D 187 B5
Mönsheim D 187 D6
Mønsted DK 86 C4
Monster NL 16 D2
Mönsterås S 89 A10
Monsummano Terme I 66 E2
Monta I 37 B7
Montabaur D 21 D9
Montaberner E 56 D4
Montady F 34 D5
Montagnac F 34 D5
Montagnana I 66 B3
Montagne F 28 F5
Montagney F 26 F4
Montagnol F 34 C5
Montagrier F 29 E6
Montaigu F 28 B3
Montaigu-de-Quercy F 33 B8
Montaigut F 30 C2
Montaigut-sur-Save F 33 C8
Montaione I 66 E2
Montalbán E 42 F2
Montalbán de Córdoba E 53 A7
Montalbano Elicona I 59 C7
Montalbano Jonico I 61 C7
Montalbo E 47 E7
Montale I 66 E3
Montalegre P 38 E4
Montalieu-Vercieu F 31 D7
Montalivet-les-Bains F 28 E3
Montallegro I 58 E3
Montalto delle Marche I 62 B5
Montalto di Castro I 65 B5
Montalto Marina I 65 C5
Montalto Uffugo I 60 E6
Montalvão P 44 E5
Montamarta E 39 E8
Montana BG 165 C7
Montana CH 31 C11
Montanejos E 48 D3
Montaner F 32 D5
Montanquila I 62 D6
Montargil P 44 F4
Montargis F 25 E8
Montastruc-la-Conseillère
  F 33 C9
Montataire F 18 F5
Montauban F 33 B8
Montauban-de-Bretagne
  F 23 D7
Montaudin F 23 D10
Montauriol F 33 A7
Montauroux F 36 D5
Montaut F 32 C4
Montaut F 33 D6
Montaut F 33 D9
Montayral F 33 B7
Montazzoli I 63 D6
Montbard F 25 E11
Montbarrey F 31 A8
Montbazens F 33 B10
Montbazin F 35 C6
Montbazon F 24 F4
Montbéliard F 27 E6
Montbenoît F 31 B9
Montbeton F 33 B8
Montblanc E 42 E6
Montboucher-sur-Jabron
  F 35 A8
Montbozon F 26 F5
Montbrió del Camp E 42 E6
Montbrison F 30 D5
Montbron F 29 D7
Montbrun F 33 A9
Montbrun-les-Bains F 35 B9
Montcada i Reixac E 43 E8
Montcavrel F 15 F12
Montceau-les-Mines F 30 B5
Montcenis F 30 B5
Montchanin F 30 B5
Montcornet F 19 E9
Montcresson F 25 E8
Montcuq F 33 B8
Montcy-Notre-Dame F 19 E10

Montdardier F 35 C6
Mont-Dauphin F 36 B5
Mont-de-Marsan F 32 C5
Montdidier F 18 E6
Mont-Dore F D2
Monteagudo E 41 E8
Monteagudo de las Salinas
  E 47 E9
Monteagudo de las Vicarías
  E 41 F7
Montealegre del Castillo
  E 55 B10
Montebello Ionico I 59 D8
Montebello Vicentino I 66 B3
Montebelluna I 72 E5
Montebourg F 23 B9
Montebruno I 37 B10
Montecalvo in Foglia I 66 E6
Montecalvo Irpino I 60 A4
Monte-Carlo MC 37 D6
Montecarotto I 67 E7
Montecassiano I 67 F7
Monte Castello di Vibio I 62 B2
Montecastrilli I 62 B2
Montecatini Terme I 66 E2
Montecatini Val di Cecina
  I 66 F2
Montecchio I 67 E6
Montecchio Emilia I 66 C1
Montecchio Maggiore I 66 A3
Montech I 33 C8
Montechiaro d'Asti I 37 A8
Montechiarugolo I 66 C1
Montecilfone I 63 D7
Montecorice I 60 C3
Montecosaro I 67 F8
Montecreale Valcellina I 73 D6
Montecreto I 66 D2
Monte da Pedra P 44 F5
Montederramo E 38 D5
Monte di Procida I 60 B2
Monte do Trigo P 50 C4
Montefalco I 62 B3
Montefalcone di Val Fortore
  I 60 A4
Montefalcone nel Sannio
  I 63 D7
Montefano I 67 F7
Montefelcino I 67 E6
Montefiascone I 62 B2
Montefiore dell'Aso I 62 A5
Montefiorino I 66 D1
Montefortino I 62 B4
Montefranco I 62 B3
Montefrío E 53 B8
Montegiordano I 61 C7
Montegiorgio I 67 F8
Monte Gordo P 50 E5
Montegranaro I 67 F8
Montegrotto Terme I 66 B4
Montehermoso E 45 D8
Monteiasi I 61 C8
Monteils F 33 B10
Montejaque E 53 C6
Montejícar E 53 A10
Montejo de la Sierra E 46 B5
Montelabbate I 67 E6
Montelanico I 62 D4
Montelavar P 50 B1
Montel-de-Gelat F 29 D11
Monteleone di Puglia I 60 A4
Monteleone d'Orvieto I 62 B2
Monteleone Rocca Doria I 64 C2
Montelepre I 58 C3
Montelibretti I 62 C3
Montélier F 31 F7
Montélimar F 35 A8
Montella I 60 B4
Montellano E 53 B6
Montels F 33 D8
Montelupo Fiorentino I 66 E3
Montelupone I 67 F8
Montemaggiore Belsito I 58 D4
Montemagno I 37 B8
Montemarciano I 67 E7
Montemayor E 53 A7
Montemayor de Pililla E 40 E3
Montemesola I 61 C8
Montemiletto I 60 A3
Montemilone I 60 A5
Montemolín E 51 C7
Montemonaco I 62 B4
Montemor-o-Novo P 50 B3
Montemurlo I 66 E3
Montemurro I 60 C5
Montenay F 23 D10
Montendre F 28 E5
Montenegro de Cameros
  E 40 D6
Montenero di Bisaccia I 63 D7
Montenerodomo I 63 D6
Monte Porzio I 67 E7
Monteprandone I 62 B5
Montepulciano I 62 A1
Monterblanc F 22 E6
Monterchi I 66 F5
Monte Real P 44 E3
Montereale I 62 B4
Montereau-fault-Yonne F 25 D8
Monte Redondo P 44 E3
Monterenzio I 66 D3
Monteriggioni I 66 F3
Monteroduni I 63 D6
Monte Romano I 62 C1
Monteroni d'Arbia I 66 F3
Monteroni di Lecce I 61 C10
Monterosso Almo I 59 E6
Monterosso Calabro I 59 B9
Monterotondo I 62 C3
Monterotondo Marittimo
  I 66 F2
Monterrei E 38 E5
Monterroso E 38 C4
Monterrubio de la Serena
  E 51 B9
Monterubbiano I 62 A5
Montesa I 56 D3
Monte San Biagio I 62 E4
Monte San Giovanni Campano
  I 62 D5
Montesano Salentino I 61 D10
Montesano sulla Marcellana
  I 60 C5
Monte San Savino I 66 F4
Monte Santa Maria Tiberina
  I 66 F5
Monte Sant'Angelo I 63 D9
Monte San Vito I 67 E7
Montesarchio I 60 A3

Montescaglioso I 61 B7
Montesclaros E 46 D3
Montescudaio I 66 F2
Montese I 66 D2
Montesilvano I 63 B6
Montespertoli I 66 E3
Montesquieu F 33 B8
Montesquieu-Volvestre F 33 D8
Montesquiou F 33 C6
Montes Velhos P 50 D3
Monteux F 35 B8
Montevago I 58 D2
Montevarchi I 66 F4
Montevecchia I 64 D2
Monteverde I 60 A5
Montevil P 50 C2
Montfaucon F 23 B9
Montfaucon F 29 F9
Montfaucon-d'Argonne F 19 F11
Montfaucon-en-Velay F 30 E5
Montferran-Savès F 33 C7
Montferrat F 36 D4
Montferrier F 33 E9
Montfoort NL 182 A5
Montfort F 23 B8
Montfort F 32 D4
Montfort NL 183 B7
Montfort-en-Chalosse F 32 C4
Montfort-l'Amaury F 24 C6
Montfort-le-Gesnois F 24 D3
Montfort-sur-Risle F 18 F2
Montgai E 42 D5
Montgaillard F 33 D6
Montgaillard F 33 E9
Montgenèvre F 31 F10
Montgeron F 25 C7
Montgiscard F 33 D8
Montgivray F 29 B9
Montgomery GB 10 F5
Montguyon F 28 E5
Monthermé F 19 E10
Monthey CH 31 C10
Monthois F 19 F9
Monthureux-sur-Saône F 26 D4
Monti I 64 B3
Monticelli d'Ongina I 69 C8
Monticello F 37 F9
Montichiari I 66 B1
Monticiano I 65 A4
Montiel E 55 B7
Montier-en-Der F 25 D12
Montieri I 65 A4
Montiers-sur-Saulx F 26 C3
Montiglio I 68 C5
Montignac F 29 E8
Montignies-le-Tilleul B 19 D9
Montignoso I 66 D1
Montigny F 27 C6
Montigny-la-Resle F 25 E10
Montigny-le-Roi F 26 D3
Montigny-lès-Metz F 26 B5
Montigny-Mornay-Villeneuve-
  sur-Vingeanne F 26 E3
Montigny-sur-Aube F 25 E12
Montijo E 51 B6
Montijo P 50 B2
Montilla E 53 A7
Montillana E 53 A9
Montivilliers F 23 A12
Montizón E 55 C8
Montjaux F 34 B4
Montjean F 23 D10
Montjovet I 68 B4
Montlauar F 34 C4
Montlieu-la-Garde F 28 E5
Mont-Louis F 33 E10
Montluçon F 29 C11
Montluel F 31 D7
Montmarault F 30 C2
Montmartin-sur-Mer F 23 C8
Montmédy F 19 E11
Montmélian F 31 D9
Montmelo E 43 D8
Montmeyran F 31 F6
Montmeyran F 35 A8
Montmirail F 24 D4
Montmirail F 25 C10
Montmirey-le-Château F 26 F4
Montmoreau-St-Cybard F 29 E6
Montmorillon F 29 C7
Montmorin F 35 B10
Montmort F 31 B9
Montoir-de-Bretagne F 23 F7
Montoire-sur-le-Loir F 24 E4
Montoison F 30 F6
Montoito P 50 B4
Montola FIN 124 F8
Montón E 47 D10
Montone I 66 F5
Montopoli di Sabina I 62 C3
Montorio al Vomano I 62 B5
Montoro E 53 A8
Montory F 32 D4
Montournais F 28 B4
Montpelier IRL 8 C6
Montpellier F 35 C6
Montpeyroux F 34 A4
Montpezat F 33 B8
Montpezat F 33 D7
Montpezat-de-Quercy F 33 B8
Montpezat-sous-Bauzon F 30 F5
Montpon-Ménesterol F 29 E6
Montpont-en-Bresse F 31 B7
Mont-ras E 43 D10
Montréal F 25 E11
Montréal F 33 C6
Montréal F 33 D10
Montredon-Labessonnié
  F 33 C10
Montregard F 30 E5
Montréjeau F 33 D7
Montrésor F 24 F5
Montresta I 64 C2
Montret F 31 B7
Montreuil F 15 G12
Montreuil-Bellay F 23 F11
Montreuil-Juigné F 23 E10
Montreux CH 31 C10
Montrevault F 23 F9
Montrevel-en-Bresse F 31 C7
Montrichard F 24 F5
Montricoux F 33 B9
Montriond F 31 C10
Mont-roig del Camp E 42 E5
Montrond F 31 B8
Montrond-les-Bains F 30 D5
Montrose GB 5 B12
Montroy E 48 F3
Monts F 24 F4
Montsalvy F 29 F10
Montsauche-les-Settons
  F 25 F11

Montségur F 33 E9
Montseny E 43 D8
Montsoué F 32 C5
Mont-sous-Vaudrey F 31 B8
Monts-sur-Guesnes F 29 B6
Mont-St-Aignan F 18 F3
Mont-St-Jean F 25 F11
Mont-St-Martin F 19 E12
Mont-St-Vincent F 30 B5
Montsûrs F 23 D10
Montsuzain F 25 D11
Montuïri E 57 B10
Montuïri E 57 B10
Montvalent F 29 F9
Montville F 18 E3
Montzen B 183 D7
Montzéville F 20 F4
Monza I 69 B7
Monzingen D 21 E9
Monzón E 42 D4
Monzón de Campos E 40 D3
Mook NL 183 B7
Moone IRL 7 G9
Moordorf (Südbrookmerland)
  D 17 B8
Moorends GB 11 D10
Moorenweis D 75 F9
Moorfields GB 4 F5
Moorrege D 82 C7
Moorslede B 19 C7
Moorweg D 17 A9
Moos D 76 E3
Moosbach D 75 C11
Moosburg A 73 C9
Moosburg an der Isar D 75 F10
Moosinning D 75 F10
Mooste EST 131 E14
Mór H 149 B10
Mora E 46 E5
Mora P 50 B3
Mora S 97 B14
Mora S 102 D8
Móra d'Ebre E 42 E5
Mora de Rubielos E 48 D3
Morag PL 139 C8
Mórahalom H 150 E4
Moraice MNE 163 C7
Moraira E 56 D5
Morais P 39 E6
Moraïtika GR 168 E2
Morakovo MNE 163 D7
Moral de Calatrava E 54 B5
Moraleda de Zafayona E 53 B9
Moraleja E 45 D7
Moraleja del Vino E 39 F8
Moraleja de Sayago E 39 F7
Morales de Campos E 39 E9
Morales del Vino E 39 F8
Morales de Toro E 39 E9
Morales de Valverde E 39 E8
Moralina E 39 F7
Morano Calabro I 60 D6
Morano sul Po I 68 C5
Morar GB 4 B5
Mörarp S 87 C11
Morasverdes E 45 C8
Morata de Jalón E 41 F9
Morata de Tajuña E 46 D6
Moratalla E 55 C9
Morava BG 166 C4
Morava SLO 73 E10
Moravany CZ 77 B9
Moravany CZ 77 D11
Moravany SK 145 F4
Moravče SLO 73 E10
Moravice HR 67 B11
Moravița RO 159 C7
Moravka BG 166 C6
Morávka CZ 147 B7
Moravská Třebová CZ 77 C11
Moravské Budějovice CZ 77 D9
Moravské Lieskové SK 146 D5
MoravskýMoravskýx CZ 146 B4
Moravský Svätý Ján SK 77 E12
Morawica PL 143 E10
Morbach D 21 E8
Morbegno I 69 A8
Morbier F 31 B9
Mörbisch am See A 149 A7
Mörby S 99 C10
Mörbylånga S 89 B10
Morcenx F 32 B4
Morciano di Leuca I 61 D10
Morciano di Romagna I 66 E6
Morcone I 60 A3
Mordelles F 23 D8
Mordoğan TR 177 B8
Mordy PL 141 F7
More LV 135 B10
Moréac F 22 E6
Moréanes P 50 D4
Morebattle GB 5 D12
Morecambe GB 10 C6
Moreda E 39 B8
Moreda E 55 E6
Morée F 24 E5
Mörel CH 70 E6
Morella E 42 F3
Moreni RO 161 D7
Morenish GB 5 C8
Morentín E 32 E1
Morerruela de Tábara E 39 E8
Mores I 64 B2
Morestel F 31 D7
Moretonhampstead GB 13 D7
Moreton-in-Marsh GB 13 B11
Moret-sur-Loing F 25 D8
Moretta I 37 B7
Moreuil F 18 E5
Morez F 31 B9
Morfa Nefyn GB 10 F2
Morfasso I 69 D8
Morfi GR 168 D5
Morfou CY 134 F5
Morfovouni GR 169 F6
Morgat F 22 D2
Morgedal N 95 D8
Morges CH 31 B10
Morgex I 31 D11
Morgongåva S 98 C7
Morhange F 26 C6
Mori I 69 B10
Moria GR 177 A8
Moricone I 62 C3
Morienval F 18 F6
Moriles S 53 B7
Morină AL 163 E10
Morină RKS 163 E9

Moringen D 78 C6
Morino I 62 D4
Moritzburg D 80 D5
Morjärv S 118 B9
Mørke DK 86 C6
Morkkaperä FIN 115 E1
Mørkøv DK 87 D9
Morkovice CZ 77 D12
Mörkret S 102 C4
Morlaàs F 32 D5
Morlanne F 32 C4
Mörlenbach D 21 E11
Morley F 26 C3
Morley GB 11 D8
Morley's Bridge IRL 8 E4
Mörlunda S 89 A9
Mormanno I 60 D6
Mormant F 25 C8
Mormoiron F 35 B9
Mornant F 30 D6
Mornas F 35 B8
Mornese I 37 B9
Moroeni RO 161 C6
Morolo I 62 D4
Morón de Almazán E 41 F7
Morón de la Frontera E 51 E9
Moros E 41 F8
Morosaglia F 37 G10
Morottaja FIN 115 E4
Morović SRB 158 C3
Morozova RUS 129 F14
Morozovo BG 166 D4
Morozzo I 37 C7
Morpeth GB 5 E13
Mørrevatnet N 104 D8
Morrfjord N 110 D8
Morriston GB 13 B7
Morrovalle I 67 F8
Mörrum S 89 C7
Morsbach D 21 C9
Morschen D 78 D6
Morshyn UA 145 E8
Mörsil S 105 E15
Morskoga S 97 C13
Morskogen N 95 B14
Morsum D 17 C12
Mørsvikbotn N 111 E10
Mortagne-au-Perche F 24 C4
Mortagne-sur-Gironde F 28 E4
Mortagne-sur-Sèvre F 28 A4
Mortágua P 44 D4
Mortain F 23 C10
Mortara I 68 C6
Morteau F 31 A10
Morteau-Coulibœuf F 23 C11
Mórtebo S 103 C12
Mortegliano I 73 E7
Mortelle I 59 C7
Morteni RO 160 D6
Mortensnes N 112 C11
Mortensnes N 114 C4
Mortimer's Cross GB 13 A9
Morton GB 11 F11
Mortrée F 23 C12
Mortsel B 19 B9
Mörtschach A 73 C6
Mortsund N 110 D6
Morud DK 86 E6
Morunglav RO 160 E4
Morville GB 10 F7
Mor'ye RUS 129 E15
Moryń PL 84 E6
Morzeszczyn PL 138 C6
Morzine F 31 C10
Moșana MD 153 A11
Mosar BY 133 F2
Mosàs S 92 A6
Mosàtt S 102 B7
Mosbach D 21 F12
Mosberg DK 90 D7
Mosborough GB 11 E9
Mosby N 90 C2
Moscavide P 50 B1
Moschopotamos GR 169 D7
Mosciano Sant'Angelo I 62 B5
Móscicha PL 140 C8
Moscovei MD 154 E2
Moscow GB 5 D8
Moseby DK 86 A5
Mosédis LT 134 D3
Mosel D 79 E11
Möser D 79 B10
Mosina PL 81 B11
Mosjø S 107 E13
Mosjøen N 108 E5
Moskaret N 101 B12
Mosko BIH 162 D5
Moskorzew PL 143 E8
Moskosel S 109 F17
Moskuvaara FIN 115 C1
Moslavna Podravska HR 149 E9
Moșna MD 154 C4
Moșna RO 153 D11
Moșnița Nouă RO 159 B7
Moșoaia RO 160 D5
Moso in Passiria I 72 C3
Mosonmagyaróvár H 146 F4
Mosonszolnok H 146 F4
Mošovce SK 147 D7
Mosqueruela E 48 D3
Moss N 95 D13
Mossala FIN 126 E5
Mossat GB 3 L11
Mossbo S 103 D11
Mössingen D 27 D11
Mossley D 4 E5
Mossley GB 11 D7
Møslav IRL 6 D4
Moss-side GB 4 E4
Mosstakan S 96 C7
Most BG 166 F5
Most CZ 76 A5
Mostar BIH 157 F8
Mosteiro E 38 B5
Mosteiro P 44 E5
Mosteiro P 50 D4
Mostek CZ 77 B9
Mosterhamn N 94 C2
Mosti FIN 126 E7
Mostkowo PL 85 B12
Mostkowo PL 139 C9
Most na Soči SLO 73 D8
Mosty PL 141 G8
Mosty u Jablunkova CZ 147 B7
Mosty'ka UA 144 D7
Mosvik N 105 D10
Mosyr UA 144 A9

Moszczenica PL 143 C8
Mota del Cuervo E 47 F7
Mota del Marqués E 39 E9
Moțăieni RO 160 C6
Motala S 92 B6
Motarzyno PL 85 B12
Moțățeni RO 159 C11
Moțca RO 153 C9
Motherwell GB 5 D9
Motike BIH 156 D6
Motike BIH 157 C7
Motilla del Palancar E 47 E9
Motilleja E 47 F9
Motjärnshyttan S 97 C10
Motoșeni RO 153 D10
Motovun HR 67 B8
Motril E 53 C9
Motru RO 159 D10
Motta Montecorvino I 63 D8
Motta San Giovanni I 59 C8
Motta Visconti I 69 C6
Motten D 74 B6
Mottola I 61 B8
Möttingen D 75 E8
Möttönen FIN 123 D13
Mötz A 71 C11
Mou DK 86 B6
Moucha GR 174 A4
Mouchamps F 28 B3
Mouchan F 33 C6
Moudon CH 31 B10
Moudros GR 171 E8
Mougins F 36 D6
Mouhijärvi FIN 127 B9
Moularès F 33 B10
Moulay F 23 D10
Mouleydier F 29 F7
Moulherne F 23 F12
Moulin-Neuf F 33 D9
Moulins F 30 B3
Moulins-Engilbert F 30 B4
Moulins-la-Marche F 24 C3
Moulis-en-Médoc F 28 E4
Moulismes F 29 C7
Moult F 23 B11
Moulton GB 15 C9
Moulton GB 15 C9
Mountbellew IRL 6 F6
Mountbenger GB 5 D10
Mountcharles IRL 6 C6
Mountcollins IRL 8 D4
Mount Hamilton GB 4 F2
Mountjoy GB 4 F2
Mountjoy GB 7 D9
Mountmellick IRL 7 F8
Mount Norris GB 7 D10
Mount Nugent IRL 7 E8
Mountrath IRL 7 F8
Mountshannon IRL 8 C6
Mountsorrel GB 11 F9
Moura P 50 C5
Mourão P 51 C5
Moure LV 135 C8
Mourenx F 32 D4
Mouriès F 35 C8
Mouries GR 169 B8
Mouriki GR 175 C7
Mourisca do Vouga P 44 C4
Mouriscas P 44 E4
Mournies GR 178 E7
Mouscron B 19 C7
Moussac F 35 C7
Moussey F 27 D6
Moussoulens F 33 D10
Moussy F 25 F9
Moustéru F 22 C5
Moustey F 32 B4
Mousteni GR 170 C6
Moustiers-Ste-Marie F 36 D4
Mouthe F 31 B9
Mouthier-Haute-Pierre F 31 A9
Mouthiers-sur-Boëme F 29 D6
Mouthoumet F 34 E4
Moutier CH 27 F7
Moutier-d'Ahun F 29 C10
Moûtiers F 31 E10
Moutiers-les-Mauxfaits F 28 C3
Moutnice CZ 77 D11
Moutsouna GR 177 E6
Moux F 34 D4
Moux-en-Morvan F 25 F11
Mouy F 18 F5
Mouzaki GR 169 F6
Mouzaki GR 174 D4
Mouzay F 19 E11
Mouzon F 19 E11
Moviken S 103 C12
Movila RO 155 D1
Movila Miresii RO 155 C1
Movileni RO 153 C10
Movileni RO 153 F10
Movileni RO 161 D8
Movilița RO 153 F10
Moville IRL 4 E2
Movollen N 105 F11
Mowtie GB 5 B12
Moy GB 3 L8
Moy GB 7 D9
Moya E 48 E3
Moyard IRL 6 E2
Moyasta IRL 8 C3
Moycullen IRL 6 F4
Moy-de-l'Aisne F 19 E7
Moyenmoutier F 27 D6
Moyenneville F 18 D4
Moygashel GB 7 D9
Moyivka UA 154 A2
Möykkylänperä FIN 119 E13
Möykkyylänperä FIN 119 F17
Moylaw IRL 6 D4
Moylett IRL 7 E8
Moylough IRL 6 F5
Moymore IRL 8 C5
Moyne IRL 7 E7
Moyvalley IRL 7 F9
Moyvore IRL 7 E7
Mozac F 30 D3
Mozăceni RO 160 D6
Mozárbez E 45 C9
Mozelos P 50 D4
Mozirje SLO 73 D10
Mozoncillo E 46 B4
Mozsgó H 149 D9
Mozyr RUS 136 E3
Mračaj BIH 157 E7
Mragowo PL 136 F3
Mrákov CZ 76 D3
Mrakovica BIH 157 B6

Mramor BIH 157 F8
Mramorak SRB 159 D6
Mratinje MNE 157 F10
Mrčajevci SRB 158 F5
Mrežičko MK 169 B6
Mrkalji BIH 157 D10
Mrkonjić–Grad BIH 157 D7
Mrkopalj HR 67 B10
Mrmoš SRB 164 B3
Mrocza PL 85 D13
Mroczeń PL 142 D4
Mroczków PL 141 H3
Mroczno PL 139 D8
Mrozy PL 141 F5
Mścice PL 85 B10
Mściwojów PL 81 D10
Mšené Lázně CZ 76 B6
Mšeno CZ 77 B7
Mshinskaya RUS 132 C6
Mstów PL 143 E7
Mszana PL 147 B7
Mszana Dolna PL 144 D1
Mszczonów PL 141 G3
Muccia I 62 A4
Much D 21 C8
Muchalls GB 5 A12
Mucharz PL 147 B9
Müchelen (Geiseltal) D 79 D10
Muchów D 81 D11
Muchówka PL 144 D1
Much Wenlock GB 10 F6
Mucientes E 39 E10
Mücka D 81 D7
Muckross IRL 8 D4
Múcsony H 145 G2
Mudanya TR 173 D10
Mudau D 187 B6
Müdelheim D 183 C7
Müden (Aller) D 79 A7
Müden (Örtze) D 83 E8
Mudersbach D 185 C8
Mûdrets BG 166 E6
Muel E 41 F9
Muelas del Pan E 39 E8
Muff IRL 4 E2
Muga de Sayago E 39 F7
Mugardos E 38 B3
Muge P 44 F3
Mügeln D 80 C4
Mügeln D 80 B10
Mugeni RO 152 E6
Muggensturm D 187 D5
Muggia I 73 E8
Muglia TR 181 B8
Müglen BG 167 D8
Müglizh BG 166 D5
Mugron F 32 C4
Mühlacker D 27 C10
Mühlanger D 79 C12
Mühlbachl A 72 B3
Mühlberg D 79 E8
Mühlberg D 80 D4
Mühldorf A 73 C7
Mühldorf am Inn D 75 F12
Mühldorf bei Feldbach A 148 C5
Mühlen A 73 B9
Mühlenbeck D 84 E4
Mühlhausen D 21 F11
Mühlhausen D 75 D9
Mühlhausen (Thüringen)
  D 79 D7
Mühltroff D 75 A10
Muhola FIN 123 D14
Muhos FIN 119 E15
Muhr am See D 75 D8
Muhur AL 163 F9
Muineachán IRL 7 D9
Muine Bheag IRL 9 C9
Muiños E 38 E4
Muirdrum GB 5 B11
Muirhead GB 5 C10
Muirkirk GB 5 D8
Muir of Ord GB 2 K8
Muizon F 19 F8
Mujdić BIH 157 D7
Mujejärvi FIN 125 C12
Mukacheve UA 145 G6
Mukařov CZ 77 C5
Mukhavyets BY 141 F9
Mukhovo BG 165 E8
Mukkala FIN 115 D5
Mukkavaara FIN 115 D4
Mula E 55 C10
Mulbarton GB 15 B11
Muleby DK 88 E7
Mulešiči BIH 157 C9
Mulfingen D 74 D6
Mülheim an der Ruhr D 17 F7
Mülheim-Kärlich D 185 D7
Mulhouse F 27 E7
Muljava SLO 73 E10
Mullach Íde IRL 7 F10
Mullagh IRL 7 F4
Mullagh IRL 7 F9
Mullaghroe IRL 6 E6
Mullany's Cross IRL 6 D5
Mullartown GB 7 D11
Müllheim D 27 E8
Mullhyttan S 92 A5
Mullingar IRL 7 E8
Mullion GB 12 F4
Müllrose D 80 B6
Mullsjö S 91 D14
Mulrany IRL 6 E3
Mulsanne F 23 E12
Mulseryd S 91 D14
Multia FIN 123 F13
Multiperä FIN 121 C15
Mümliswil CH 27 F8
Munakka FIN 122 E9
Muñana E 45 C10
Munapirtti FIN 128 E6
Münchberg D 75 B10
Müncheberg D 80 A6
München D 75 F9
Münchenbernsdorf D 79 E10
Münchenbuchsee CH 31 A11
Münchhausen D 21 C11
Münchsteinach D 75 C8
Münchweiler an der Rodalb
  D 186 C4
Münchwilen CH 27 F11
Mundaka E 41 B6
Munderkingen D 187 E8
Mundesley GB 15 B11
Mundford GB 15 B10
Mundheim N 94 B3
Mundolsheim F 27 C8
Munebrega E 41 F8
Munera E 55 A8

Mungia E 40 B6
Mungret IRL 8 C5
Muñico E 45 C10
Muniesa E 42 E2
Munilla E 41 D7
Munka-Ljungby S 87 C11
Munkbyn S 103 B11
Munkebo DK 86 E7
Munkedal S 91 C10
Munken N 104 D6
Munkflohögen S 106 D7
Munkfors S 97 C10
Munklia N 111 D14
Munksund S 118 D7
Munktorp S 98 C6
Munkzwalm B 19 C8
Munne FIN 128 C7
Münnerstadt D 75 B7
Munningen D 75 E8
Muñogalindo E 46 C3
Munsala FIN 122 D8
Münsingen D 31 B12
Münsingen D 74 F5
Münster A 72 B4
Münster CH 70 E6
Münster D 17 E9
Münster D 21 E11
Münster D 83 E8
Munster F 27 D7
Münsterdorf D 82 C7
Munstergeleen NL 183 D7
Münsterhausen D 75 F7
Münstermaifeld D 185 D7
Muntendam NL 17 B7
Munteni RO 153 F10
Munteni-Buzău RO 161 D9
Muntenii de Jos RO 153 D11
Münzenberg D 21 D11
Münzkirchen A 76 F5
Muodoslompolo S 117 C10
Muonio FIN 117 C11
Muonionalusta S 117 C11
Muotathal CH 71 D7
Muotkajärvi FIN 117 B10
Muotkavaara FIN 117 C12
Mur SRB 163 C9
Muradiye TR 173 D9
Muradiye TR 177 B9
Murakeresztúr H 149 D7
Muráň SK 147 D10
Muras E 38 B4
Murasson F 34 C4
Muraste EST 131 C8
Muraszemenye H 149 D7
Murat F 30 E2
Muratlar TR 181 B9
Muratli TR 173 B7
Murato F 37 F10
Murat-sur-Vèbre F 34 C4
Murau A 73 B9
Muravera I 64 E4
Murazzano I 37 C8
Murça P 38 F5
Murchante E 41 D8
Murcia E 56 F2
Murczyn PL 138 E4
Mur-de-Barrez F 29 F11
Mûr-de-Bretagne F 22 D6
Mur-de-Sologne F 24 F6
Mureck A 148 C5
Mürefte TR 173 C7
Muret F 33 D8
Murgeni RO 153 E12
Murgenthal CH 27 F8
Murgeşti RO 161 C9
Murgia E 40 C6
Muri CH 27 F9
Muri CH 31 B11
Murias de Paredes E 39 C7
Muriedas E 40 B4
Murighiol RO 155 C4
Murillo de Río Leza E 32 F1
Murillo el Fruto E 32 F3
Murino MNE 163 D8
Murisengo I 68 C5
Murjāni LV 135 B9
Murjek S 116 F5
Murley GB 7 D8
Murlo I 66 B2
Murmastiene LV 135 C13
Murnau am Staffelsee D 72 A3
Muro E 57 B11
Muro F 37 F9
Muro P 38 F2
Muro de Alcoy E 56 D4
Murol F 30 D2
Murole FIN 127 B10
Muro Lucano I 60 B4
Muron F 28 C4
Murony H 151 D7
Muros E 38 C1
Muros E 39 A7
Muros I 64 B2
Murovane UA 144 C9
Murów PL 142 E4
Murowana Goślina PL 81 A12
Murrë AL 168 A3
Murrhardt D 74 E6
Murronkylä FIN 119 E16
Murroogh IRL 6 F4
Mursalli TR 177 D10
Mûrs-Erigné F 23 F10
Mursko Sobota SLO 148 C6
Mursko Središče HR 149 C6
Murtas E 55 F6
Murtede P 44 D4
Murten CH 31 B11
Murter HR 156 E4
Murto FIN 119 E15
Murtolahti FIN 125 D9
Murtomäki FIN 124 B9
Murtovaara FIN 121 C13
Murumoen N 105 C16
Murvica HR 156 D3
Murviel-lès-Béziers F 34 D5
Mürzsteg A 148 A5
Murzynowo PL 81 A8
Mürzzuschlag A 148 A5
Mûsa LV 135 D8
Musbury GB 13 D8
Müschenbach D 185 C8
Musei I 64 E2
Muselievo BG 160 F5
Mushtisht RKS 163 E10
Musile di Piave I 72 E6
Muskö S 93 B12
Mussalo FIN 128 D6
Musselburgh GB 5 D10
Musselkanaal NL 17 C8

Mussidan F 29 E6
Mussomeli I 58 D4
Musson B 19 E12
Mussy-sur-Seine F 25 E12
Mustafakemalpaşa TR 173 D9
Müstair CH 71 D10
Mustamaa FIN 119 F17
Mustamaa FIN 123 D10
Mustasaari FIN 122 D7
Mustavaara FIN 121 D12
Mustavaara FIN 121 F12
Mustinlahti FIN 125 E10
Mustjala EST 130 E4
Mustla EST 131 E11
Mustola FIN 114 F4
Mustolanmäki FIN 125 C10
Mustolanmutka FIN 125 B10
Mustvee EST 131 D13
Muszaki PL 139 D10
Muszyna PL 145 E2
Muta SLO 73 C11
Mutala FIN 127 B10
Mutalahti FIN 125 F16
Mütevelli TR 177 B10
Muthill GB 5 C9
Mutilva Baja E 32 E2
Mutné SK 147 C8
Mutriku E 32 D1
Mutterstadt D 21 F10
Mutxamel E 56 E4
Mutzig F 27 C7
Mutzschen D 80 D3
Muuga EST 131 C13
Muukajärvi S 116 E10
Muuksi EST 131 B11
Muurame FIN 123 F15
Muurasjärvi FIN 123 C14
Muurikkala FIN 128 D8
Muurla FIN 127 E9
Muurola FIN 119 B14
Muurola FIN 128 D8
Muuruvesi FIN 125 D10
Muxía E 38 B1
Muzillac F 22 E7
Mužla SK 149 A11
Myahuny BY 137 C14
Myakishevo RUS 133 C5
Myaretskiya BY 137 C14
Myazhany BY 135 E13
Mybster GB 3 J10
Myckelgensjö S 107 D13
Myckle S 118 E5
Myedna BY 141 G9
Myggenäs S 91 C10
Myggsjö S 102 C8
Myhinpää FIN 124 F7
Myjava SK 146 D5
Mykanów PL 143 E7
Mykhal'cha UA 153 A7
Mykhaylivka UA 154 F5
Myki GR 171 B7
Myklebostad N 110 E9
Mykolayiv UA 145 D8
Mykolayivka UA 154 E4
Mykolayivka-Novorosiys'ka UA 154 E5
Mykonos GR 176 E5
Mykulychyn UA 152 A5
Mykytychi UA 144 B9
Myllykoski FIN 128 D6
Myllykylä FIN 122 E8
Myllykylä FIN 127 D10
Myllykylä FIN 128 D7
Myllylahti FIN 121 D13
Myllymäki FIN 123 E12
Myloi GR 175 D6
Mylopotamos GR 178 C4
Mynämäki FIN 126 D6
Mynttilä FIN 128 C6
Myon F 31 A8
Myory BY 133 E3
Myra GR 181 C9
Myräs S 109 E14
Myre N 110 C9
Myre N 111 B10
Myresjö S 92 E5
Myrhaug N 101 A14
Myrheden S 118 D4
Myrhult S 92 B4
Myrina GR 171 E8
Myriokefala GR 178 E7
Myrkky FIN 122 F7
Myrland N 110 D5
Myrland N 110 C9
Myrland N 111 C10
Myrlandshaugen N 111 C13
Myrmoen N 101 A15
Myrne UA 155 B4
Myrnes N 112 C9
Myrnopillya UA 154 E4
Myrsini GR 174 F5
Myrsini GR 178 B3
Myrskylä FIN 127 D14
Myrties GR 177 F8
Myrtos GR 179 E10
Myrviken S 105 E16
Mysen N 95 C14
Myshall IRL 9 C9
Myślachowice PL 143 F7
Myślakowice PL 81 E9
Myślenice PL 147 B9
Myślibórz PL 85 E7
Myślice PL 139 C8
Mysłowice PL 143 F7
Mysovka RUS 134 F2
Myssjö S 102 A7
Mystegna GR 177 A7
Mystras GR 174 E5
Myszków PL 143 E7
Myszyniec PL 139 D11
Mytikas GR 174 B2
Mytilini GR 177 A8
Mytilinioi GR 177 D8
Mýtna SK 147 E9
Mýto CZ 76 C5

N

Nå N 94 B5
Naaldwijk NL 16 E2
Naamankylä FIN 119 E17
Naamijoki FIN 117 E11
Naantali FIN 126 E7
Naarden NL 183 A6
Näärinki FIN 128 B8
Naarn im Machlande A 77 F7
Naartijärvi S 119 C11
Naarva FIN 125 D16
Naas IRL 7 F9
Näätämö FIN 114 D6
Näätänmaa FIN 125 F10
Näätävaara FIN 121 E13

Nabburg D 75 D11
Nábrád H 145 G5
Na Cealla Beaga IRL 6 C6
Načeradec CZ 77 C7
Nacha BY 137 E10
Náchod CZ 77 B10
Nacina Ves SK 145 F4
Nackel D 83 E13
Nackenheim D 185 E9
Näcksjö S 103 C12
Na Clocha Liathe IRL 7 F10
Nacpolsk PL 139 E9
Nad IRL 8 D5
Nadalj SRB 158 C4
Nadarzyce PL 85 D11
Nadarzyn PL 141 F3
Naddvik N 100 D7
Nadeș RO 152 E5
Nădlac RO 150 E6
Nădrag RO 159 B9
Nadrichne UA 154 E4
Nádudvar H 151 C7
Năeni RO 161 C8
Nærbø N 94 E3
Nærøset N 101 E13
Nærsnes N 95 C13
Næsbjerg DK 86 D3
Næstved DK 87 E9
Näfels CH 27 F11
Nafferton GB 11 C11
Nafpaktos GR 174 C4
Nafplio GR 175 D6
Nagele NL 16 C5
Naggen S 103 B11
Naglarby S 97 B14
Na Gleannta IRL 6 C6
Nagli LV 133 C1
Nagłowice PL 143 E9
Nagold D 27 C10
Nagore E 32 E3
Nago-Torbole I 69 B10
Nagu FIN 126 E6
Nagyatád H 149 D8
Nagybajom H 149 D9
Nagybánhegyes H 151 E6
Nagybaracska H 149 D11
Nagybarca H 145 G2
Nagyberény H 149 C10
Nagyberki H 149 D10
Nagycenk H 149 A7
Nagycsécs H 145 H2
Nagycserkesz H 145 H4
Nagydobos H 145 G5
Nagydorog H 149 C11
Nagyecsed H 145 H5
Nagyfüged H 150 B5
Nagyhalász H 145 G4
Nagyharsány H 149 E10
Nagyhegyes H 151 B7
Nagyigmánd H 149 A10
Nagyiván H 151 C6
Nagykálló H 145 H4
Nagykanizsa H 149 D7
Nagykapornak H 149 C7
Nagykáta H 150 C4
Nagykereki H 151 C8
Nagykónyi H 149 C10
Nagykőrös H 150 C4
Nagykőrű H 150 C5
Nagykovácsi H 149 A11
Nagylak H 150 E6
Nagylóc H 147 E9
Nagylók H 149 C11
Nagylózs H 149 A7
Nagymágocs H 150 D5
Nagymaros H 149 A11
Nagynyárád H 149 E11
Nagyoroszi H 147 E8
Nagyréde H 150 B4
Nagyszénás H 150 D6
Nagyszokoly H 149 C10
Nagytarcsa H 150 B3
Nagytőke H 150 D5
Nagyvarjány H 145 G5
Nagyvázsony H 149 C9
Nagyvisnyó H 145 G1
Naha EST 132 E1
Naharros E 47 D8
Nahe D 83 C8
Nahirne UA 155 C2
Nahrendorf D 83 D9
Naidăș RO 159 D8
Naila D 75 B10
Nailloux F 33 D9
Nailsworth GB 13 B10
Naimakka S 116 A7
Naintré F 29 B6
Naipköy TR 173 C7
Nairn GB 3 K9
Naives-Rosières F 26 C3
Naizin F 22 E6
Najac F 33 B9
Nájera E 40 D6
Näkkälä FIN 117 A11
Nakkerud N 95 B12
Nakkila FIN 126 C7
Náklo CZ 77 C12
Nakło PL 143 E8
Naklo SLO 73 D9
Nakło nad Notecią PL 85 D13
Nakomiady PL 136 E3
Näkotne LV 134 C6
Nakovo SRB 150 F6
Nakskov DK 83 A10
Nalbach D 186 C2
Nalband RO 155 C3
Nalda E 41 D7
Nälden S 105 E16
Nałęczów PL 141 H6
Nálepkovo SK 145 F2
Näljänkä FIN 121 D11
Nalkki FIN 121 E10
Nalliers F 28 C3
Nalžovské Hory CZ 76 D5
Namborn D 21 E8
Nambroca E 46 E5
Namdalseid N 105 C10
Náměšť nad Oslavou CZ 77 D10
Náměšť na Hané CZ 77 C12
Námestovo SK 147 C8
Nampnis F 126 E3
Nampnes-Dizy FIN 105 C11
Namsos N 105 C10
Namsskogan N 105 B14
Namsvatn N 105 B15
Namur B 19 D12
Namysłów PL 142 D4
Nana RO 161 E10
Nána SK 147 F7
Nançay F 24 F7
Nanclares de la Oca E 40 C6
Nancy F 26 C5

Nabburg D 75 D11
Nandrin B 183 D6
Nănești RO 161 B10
Nangis F 25 C9
Nannestad N 95 B13
Nanov RO 160 F6
Nans-les-Pins F 35 D10
Nant F 34 B5
Nanterre F 25 C7
Nantes F 23 F8
Nanteuil-le-Haudouin F 25 B8
Nantiat F 29 C8
Nantua F 31 C8
Nantwich GB 10 E6
Naousa GR 169 C7
Naousa GR 176 E5
Napajedla CZ 146 C5
Napiwoda PL 139 D9
Napkor H 145 H4
Napola I 58 D2
Napp N 110 D6
Năpradea RO 151 C11
Năquera E 48 E4
Når S 93 E13
Nåra N 100 D1
Nárai H 149 B7
Narberth GB 12 B5
Narbolia I 64 C2
Narbonne F 34 D5
Narbonne-Plage F 34 D5
Narborough GB 15 B9
Narbuvoll N 101 B14
Narcao I 64 E2
Narcy F 25 F9
Nardò I 61 C10
Narechenski Bani BG 165 F10
Narew PL 140 E9
Narewka PL 141 E9
Närhilä FIN 123 E16
Narin IRL 6 C6
Nāriņciems LV 134 B5
Narkaus FIN 119 B16
Narken S 116 E9
Narlidere TR 177 C9
Narni I 62 B3
Naro I 58 E4
Narol PL 144 C7
Närpes FIN 122 F6
Narrosse F 32 C3
Narta HR 149 E7
Nartë AL 168 D1
Năruja RO 153 F9
Naruska FIN 115 D6
Naruszewo PL 139 E9
Narva EST 132 C3
Narva FIN 127 C10
Narva-Jõesuu EST 132 C3
Närvijoki FIN 122 E7
Narvik N 111 D13
Narzole I 37 B7
Narzym PL 139 D9
Näs FIN 99 B14
Nås N 90 A5
Näs S 93 E12
Näs S 97 B12
Näs S 102 A8
Näsåker S 107 E11
Näsåud RO 152 C5
Nasavrky CZ 77 C9
Näsberg S 103 C10
Nasbinals F 34 A5
Näs bruk S 98 B6
Näsby S 89 C10
Na Sceirí IRL 7 E10
Näset S 103 D9
Nashec RKS 163 E10
Našice HR 149 F10
Nasielsk PL 139 E10
Näske S 107 E15
Näsliden S 107 A16
Naso I 59 C6
Nassau D 21 D9
Nassereith A 71 C11
Nassjö S 92 C5
Nässjö S 92 D5
Nässjö S 107 D10
Nassogne B 19 D11
Nästansjö S 107 B11
Nästätten D 185 D8
Nastola FIN 127 D14
Nasūm S 88 C7
Nasutów PL 141 H6
Näsviken S 103 C12
Näsviken S 106 D9
Naszály H 149 A10
Natalinci SRB 159 E6
Nateby GB 11 C7
Naters CH 68 A4
Nattavaara S 116 E5
Nattavaara by S 116 E5
Nattheim D 75 E7
Nättraby S 89 C9
Naturno I 71 D11
Naucelle F 33 B10
Naucelles F 29 F10
Naudaskalns LV 133 B2
Nauders A 71 D11
Naudīte LV 134 C6
Nauen D 79 A12
Nauendorf D 79 C10
Nauheim D 21 E10
Naujac-sur-Mer F 28 E4
Naujamiestis LT 135 E8
Naujasis Daugėliškis LT 135 F12
Naujoji Akmenė LT 134 D6
Naujoji Vilnia LT 137 D11
Naukšēni LV 131 F10
Naul IRL 7 E10
Naulaperä FIN 121 E10
Naulavaara FIN 125 C10
Naumburg D 17 F12
Naumburg (Hessen) D 17 F12
Naumburg (Saale) D 79 D10
Naundorf D 80 D4
Naundorf D 80 E4
Naunhof D 79 D12
Nauroth D 21 C9
Naustbukta N 105 B11
Naustdal N 100 C3
Nauste N 101 A8
Nautijaur S 109 C17
Nautsi RUS 114 E6
Nautsund N 100 D2
Nava E 39 B9
Navacepeda de Tormes E 45 D10
Navaconcejo E 45 D9
Nava de Arévalo E 46 C3
Nava de la Asunción E 46 B4
Nava del Rey E 39 F9
Nava de Sotrobal E 45 C10

Navadrutsk BY 133 F2
Navafría E 46 B5
Navahermosa E 46 E4
Navajas E 48 E4
Naval E 42 C4
Navalagamella E 46 D4
Navalcaballo E 41 E6
Navalcán E 45 D10
Navalcarnero E 46 D4
Navalero E 40 E6
Navalmanzano E 46 B4
Navalmoral E 46 D3
Navalmoral de la Mata E 45 E9
Navalonguilla E 45 D9
Navalosa E 46 D3
Navalperal de Pinares E 46 C4
Navalpino E 46 F3
Navaluenga E 46 D3
Navalvillar de Ibor E 45 E10
Navalvillar de Pela E 45 F10
Navamorcuende E 46 D3
Navan IRL 7 E9
Navapolatsk BY 133 E5
Navarcles E 43 D7
Navardún E 32 E3
Navarredonda de la Rinconada E 45 C8
Navarrenx F 32 D4
Navarrés E 48 F3
Navarrete E 41 D6
Navarreviaca E 46 D3
Navàs E 43 D7
Navascués E 32 E3
Navas de Estrena E 46 E3
Navas de Jorquera E 47 F9
Navas del Madroño E 45 E7
Navas del Rey E 46 D4
Navas de Oro E 46 B4
Navas de San Juan E 55 C6
Navasfrías E 45 D7
Navata E 43 C9
Navatalgordo E 46 D3
Nave I 69 B9
Nave P 50 E2
Nave de Haver P 45 C7
Năvekvarn S 93 B9
Navelli I 62 C5
Năverdal N 101 A12
Năverede S 106 E8
Nave Redonda P 50 E3
Năverkärret S 97 C14
Năverrys FIN 119 C15
Naverstad S 91 B10
Navès E 43 D7
Naves F 29 E9
Navezuelas E 45 E10
Navia E 39 A6
Navilly F 31 B7
Navit N 112 D8
Năvodari RO 155 E3
Năvrăgol S 89 C9
Nawojowa PL 145 D2
Naxos GR 176 E5
Nay-Bourdettes F 32 D5
Nazaré P 44 E2
Nazelles-Négron F 24 F4
Nazza D 79 D7
Ndroq AL 168 B2
Nea Agathoupoli GR 169 D8
Nea Alikarnassos GR 178 E9
Nea Anchialos GR 169 F8
Nea Apollonia GR 169 C10
Nea Artaki GR 175 B8
Nea Efesos GR 169 D7
Nea Epidavros GR 175 D7
Nea Figaleia GR 174 E4
Nea Fokaia GR 169 D9
Nea Ionia GR 169 F8
Nea Iraklitsa GR 171 C6
Nea Kallikrateia GR 169 D9
Nea Karvali GR 171 C6
Nea Karya GR 177 C7
Nea Kerdylia GR 169 C10
Nea Kios GR 175 D6
Nea Koroni GR 174 F4
Nea Lampsakos GR 175 C8
Neale IRL 6 E4
Nea Liosia GR 175 C8
Nea Madytos GR 169 C10
Nea Makri GR 175 C8
Nea Malgara GR 169 C8
Nea Mesimvria GR 169 C8
Nea Michaniona GR 169 D8
Nea Moudania GR 169 D9
Nea Olynthos GR 169 D9
Nea Pella GR 169 C8
Nea Peramos GR 171 C6
Nea Peramos GR 175 C7
Nea Plagia GR 169 D9
Nea Roda GR 170 D5
Nea Santa GR 169 C8
Nea Santa GR 171 B9
Nea Silata GR 169 D9
Nea Styra GR 175 D9
Neath GB 13 B7
Nea Tiryntha GR 175 D6
Nea Triglia GR 169 D9
Neaua RO 152 E5
Nea Vravrona GR 175 D9
Nea Vyssa GR 171 A11
Nea Zichni GR 169 B10
Nebel D 82 A4
Nébias F 33 E10
Nebljusi HR 156 C4
Nebra (Unstrut) D 79 D10
Nebreda E 40 E4
Nechanice CZ 77 B9
Neckarbischofsheim D 187 C6
Neckargemünd D 21 F11
Neckargerach D 21 F12
Neckarsteinach D 21 F11
Neckarsulm D 21 F12
Neckartenzlingen D 27 C11
Necşeşti RO 160 E6
Necton GB 15 B10
Nečujam HR 156 F5
Neda E 38 B3
Nedansjö S 103 B12
Nedašov CZ 146 C6
Neddemin D 84 C4
Nedde F 29 D9
Nedelišče HR 149 D6
Nederby DK 86 B4
Nederhögen S 102 A7
Nederhorst den Berg NL 183 A6
Neder Hvam DK 86 C4
Nederlangbroek NL 183 A6
Nedervetil FIN 123 C10

Neder Vindinge DK 87 E9
Nederweert NL 16 F5
Nedlitz D 79 B11
Nedožery-Brezany SK 147 D7
Nedrebø N 94 E4
Nedre Saxnäs S 109 F14
Nedre Soppero S 116 B7
Nedstrand N 94 D3
Nedvědice CZ 77 D10
Nedyalsko BG 167 E7
Neede NL 17 D7
Needham Market GB 15 C11
Neer NL 183 C7
Neerijnen NL 183 B6
Neeroeteren B 183 C7
Neerpelt B 19 B11
Neetze D 83 D9
Negenborn D 78 C6
Negomir RO 159 D10
Negorci MK 169 B7
Negoslavci HR 157 B11
Negotin SRB 159 E10
Negotino MK 163 F10
Negotino MK 169 B7
Negrar I 66 A2
Negrași RO 160 D6
Negredo E 47 B7
Negreira E 38 C2
Nègrepelisse F 33 B9
Negrești RO 153 D10
Negrești-Oaș RO 145 H7
Negri RO 153 D9
Negru Vodă RO 155 F2
Nehoiu RO 161 C8
Neiden N 114 D6
Neidín IRL 8 E3
Neinstedt D 79 C9
Neietaskaite S 116 E8
Neitsuanto S 116 D6
Neittävä FIN 119 E17
Neive I 37 B8
Nejdek CZ 75 B12
Nekėzseny H 145 G1
Nekla PL 81 B12
Nekso DK 89 E8
Nelas P 44 C5
Nellim FIN 114 F4
Nellingen D 74 E6
Nelson GB 11 D7
Nemaitonys LT 137 D9
Neman RUS 136 D5
Nemanjica MK 164 F4
Nemanskoye RUS 136 C5
Nembro I 69 B8
Nemea GR 175 D6
Nemenčinė LT 137 D11
Nemesgulács H 149 C8
Nemesnádudvar H 150 E3
Nemesvámos H 149 B9
Nemesvid H 149 C8
Németkér H 149 C11
Neméžis LT 137 D11
Nemours F 25 D8
Nemsdorf-Göhrendorf D 79 D10
Nemšová SK 146 D6
Nemunaitis LT 137 E9
Nemunėlio Radviliškis LT 135 D9
Nenagh IRL 8 C6
Nenince SK 147 E8
Nenita GR 177 C7
Nennhausen D 79 A12
Nennslingen D 75 D9
Nenonpelto FIN 124 F8
Nentershausen D 21 D9
Nentershausen D 78 D6
Nenthead GB 5 F12
Nenzing A 71 C9
Neo Agioneri GR 169 C8
Neochoraki GR 175 C7
Neochori GR 169 F6
Neochori GR 171 C6
Neochori GR 174 A3
Neochori GR 174 C3
Neo Erasmio GR 171 C7
Neoi Epivates GR 169 C8
Neo Monastiri GR 169 F7
Neoneli I 64 C2
Neo Petritsi GR 169 B9
Neorić HR 156 E6
Neos Kafkasos GR 168 C5
Neos Marmaras GR 169 D10
Neos Mylotopos GR 169 C7
Neo Souli GR 169 B10
Neos Pagontas GR 175 B8
Neos Pyrgos GR 175 B7
Neos Skopos GR 169 B10
Néoules F 36 E4
Nepi I 62 C2
Nepomuk CZ 76 D5
Nérac F 33 B6
Neratovice CZ 77 B7
Nerău RO 150 F6
Neravai LT 137 E9
Nerchau D 79 D12
Nercillac F 28 D5
Nerdal N 101 A9
Nerde Gärdsjö S 103 E9
Néré F 28 D5
Nereju RO 153 F9
Neresheim D 75 E7
Neresnica SRB 159 E8
Neresnytsya UA 145 G8
Nereta LV 135 D11
Nereto I 62 B5
Nerezine HR 67 C9
Nerežišče HR 156 F6
Néris-les-Bains F 29 C11
Nerja E 53 C9
Nerkoo FIN 124 D8
Nerlia N 108 E7
Nerokouros GR 178 E7
Néronde F 30 D5
Nérondes F 30 B2
Neroth D 21 D7
Nerpio E 55 C8
Nersac F 28 D6
Nersingen D 75 F7
Nerskogen N 101 A11
Nerushay UA 155 B5
Nerva E 51 D6
Nervesa della Battaglia I 72 E5
Nervieux F 30 D5
Nes FO 2 A3
Nes N 95 D9
Nes N 96 A2
Nes N 110 D9

Nes N 111 D10
Nes NL 16 B5
Nesbyen N 101 E10
Neschwitz D 80 D6
Nesebür BG 167 D9
Neset N 112 C7
Nes Flaten N 94 C5
Nesgrenda N 90 B4
Nesheim N 94 D3
Nesje N 110 D6
Nesjegjerde N 100 A6
Nesland N 110 D5
Neslandsvatn N 90 B5
Nesle F 18 E6
Nesna N 108 D5
Nesovice CZ 77 D12
Nessa F 37 F9
Nesse D 17 A8
Nesseby N 114 C6
Nesselwang D 71 B11
Nesslau CH 27 F11
Nessodtangen N 95 C13
Nestani GR 175 D5
Nestby N 108 B9
Nesterov RUS 136 D6
Neston GB 10 E5
Nestorio GR 168 D5
Nestoyita UA 154 B4
Nesttun N 94 B3
Nesvady SK 146 F6
Nesvatnstemmen N 90 B3
Nesvik N 94 D4
Nethy Bridge GB 3 L9
Netolice CZ 76 D6
Netphen D 21 C10
Netra (Ringgau) D 79 D7
Netretić HR 148 E4
Netstal CH 71 C8
Nettancourt F 25 C12
Nettersheim D 21 D7
Nettetal D 16 F6
Nettuno I 62 E3
Netvořice CZ 77 C7
Neu-Anspach D 21 D11
Neubeckum D 82 A7
Neuberg an der Mürz A 148 A5
Neubeuern D 72 A5
Neubiberg D 75 F10
Neubrandenburg D 84 C4
Neubruchhausen D 17 C11
Neubrunn D 187 B8
Neubukow D 83 B11
Neubulach D 27 C10
Neuburg am Rhein D 187 D5
Neuburg an der Donau D 75 E9
Neuburg-Steinhausen D 83 C11
Neuburxdorf D 80 D4
Neuchâtel CH 31 B10
Neu Darchau D 83 D9
Neudietendorf D 79 E8
Neudorf A 146 C2
Neudrossenfeld D 75 B10
Neuenburg D 27 C10
Neuendettelsau D 75 D8
Neuenhagen Berlin D 80 A5
Neuenhaus D 17 D7
Neuenhof CH 27 F9
Neuenkirch CH 27 F9
Neuenkirchen D 17 A11
Neuenkirchen D 17 C11
Neuenkirchen D 17 D8
Neuenkirchen D 17 D9
Neuenkirchen D 82 B6
Neuenkirchen D 82 D7
Neuenkirchen D 84 A4
Neuenkirchen D 84 B4
Neuenkirchen (Oldenburg) D 17 C10
Neuenkirchen-Seelscheid D 21 C8
Neuenrade D 185 B8
Neuenstadt am Kocher D 27 B11
Neuenstein D 187 C8
Neuenwalde D 17 A11
Neuerburg D 20 D6
Neufahrn bei Freising D 75 F10
Neufahrn in Niederbayern D 75 E11
Neufchâteau B 19 E11
Neufchâteau F 26 D4
Neufchâtel-en-Bray F 18 E3
Neufchâtel-Hardelot F 15 F12
Neufchâtel-sur-Aisne F 19 F9
Neufeld D 17 A12
Neufeld an der Leitha A 77 G10
Neuffen D 27 C11
Neufmanil F 184 E2
Neufra D 27 D11
Neugersdorf D 81 E7
Neuharlingersiel D 17 A9
Neuhaus A 73 A11
Neuhaus A 73 D13
Neuhaus (Oste) D 17 A12
Neuhaus am Inn D 76 F4
Neuhaus am Klausenbach A 148 C6
Neuhaus am Rennweg D 75 A9
Neuhaus an der Pegnitz D 75 C10
Neuhausen CH 27 E10
Neuhausen D 80 E4
Neuhausen D 187 D6
Neuhausen ob Eck D 27 E10
Neuhof D 74 B6
Neuhof an der Zenn D 75 D8
Neuhofen D 187 C5
Neuhofen an der Krems A 76 F6
Neuillé-Pont-Pierre F 24 E4
Neuilly F 25 F10
Neuilly-en-Thelle F 18 F5
Neuilly-l'Évêque F 26 E3
Neuilly-le-Réal F 30 C3
Neuilly-St-Front F 25 B9
Neu-Isenburg D 187 A6
Neukalen D 83 C13
Neu Kaliß D 83 D10
Neukirch D 80 D6
Neukirchen D 21 C12
Neukirchen D 80 E3
Neukirchen D 86 F3
Neukirchen am Großvenediger A 72 B5
Neukirchen an der Enknach A 76 F4
Neukirchen an der Vöckla A 76 F5
Neukirchen-Balbini D 75 D11
Neukirchen beim Heiligen Blut D 76 D3
Neukirchen vorm Wald D 76 E4
Neukloster D 83 C11

Neulengbach A 77 F9
Neuler D 75 E7
Neulewin D 84 E6
Neulikko FIN 121 E10
Neulise F 30 D5
Neu Lübbenau D 80 B5
Neum BIH 162 D4
Neumagen D 185 E6
Neumark D 79 E11
Neumarkt am Wallersee A 73 A7
Neumarkt im Mühlkreis A 77 F6
Neumarkt in der Oberpfalz D 75 D9
Neumarkt in Steiermark A 73 B9
Neumarkt-Sankt Veit D 75 F12
Neu Mukran D 84 B5
Neumünster D 83 B7
Neunburg vorm Wald D 75 D11
Neundorf D 75 A11
Neung-sur-Beuvron F 24 E6
Neunkirch CH 27 E10
Neunkirchen A 148 A6
Neunkirchen D 21 C10
Neunkirchen D 21 F8
Neunkirchen am Brand D 75 C9
Neunkirchen am Sand D 75 C9
Neuötting D 75 F12
Neupetershain D 80 C6
Neupölla A 77 E8
Neureichenau D 76 E5
Neuruppin D 83 E13
Neuschönau D 76 E4
Neusiedl am See A 77 G11
Neusorg D 75 C10
Neuss D 21 B7
Neussargues-Moissac F 30 E2
Neustadt D 27 E9
Neustadt D 79 E10
Neustadt D 83 E12
Neustadt (Harz) D 79 C8
Neustadt (Hessen) D 21 C12
Neustadt (Wied) D 21 C8
Neustadt am Kulm D 75 C10
Neustadt am Rübenberge D 78 A5
Neustadt an der Aisch D 75 C8
Neustadt an der Donau D 75 E10
Neustadt an der Waldnaab D 75 C11
Neustadt an der Weinstraße D 21 F10
Neustadt bei Coburg D 75 B9
Neustadt-Glewe D 83 D11
Neustadt in Holstein D 83 B9
Neustadt in Sachsen D 80 D6
Neustift im Stubaital A 72 B3
Neustrelitz D 84 D4
Neutraubling D 75 E11
Neutrebbin D 80 A6
Neu-Ulm D 74 F7
Neuvéglise F 30 F2
Neuves-Maisons F 186 D1
Neuvic F 29 E6
Neuvic F 29 E10
Neuville-aux-Bois F 24 D7
Neuville-de-Poitou F 29 B6
Neuville-les-Dames F 31 C7
Neuville-lès-Dieppe F 18 E3
Neuville-sur-Saône F 30 D6
Neuvilly-en-Argonne F 26 B3
Neuvy-Grandchamp F 30 B4
Neuvy-le-Roi F 24 E4
Neuvy-Pailloux F 29 B9
Neuvy-St-Sépulchre F 29 B9
Neuvy-sur-Barangeon F 25 F7
Neuweiler D 27 C10
Neuwied D 21 D8
Neuwittenbek D 83 B8
Neu Wulmstorf D 83 D7
Neu Zauche D 80 C6
Neuzelle D 81 B7
Neu Zittau D 80 B5
Névache F 31 E10
Nevarėnai LT 134 D4
Neveja LV 130 F4
Neveklov CZ 77 C7
Nevel' RUS 133 D7
Nevele B 19 B8
Neverfjord N 113 C12
Nevernes N 108 F4
Neverness N 110 C9
Neveronys LT 137 D9
Nevers F 30 A3
Nevesinje BIH 157 F9
Nevestino BG 165 E6
Névez F 22 E4
Neviano I 61 C10
Néville F 18 E2
Nevlunghavn N 90 B6
Nevsha BG 167 C8
New Abbey GB 5 F9
New Aberdour GB 3 K12
New Alresford GB 13 C12
Newark-on-Trent GB 11 E10
Newbawn IRL 9 D9
Newbiggin-by-the-Sea GB 5 E13
Newbliss IRL 7 D8
Newborough GB 11 F11
Newbridge GB 13 B8
Newbridge IRL 7 F9
New Buildings GB 4 F2
Newburgh GB 3 L12
Newburgh GB 5 C10
Newbury GB 13 C12
Newby Bridge GB 10 C6
Newcastle GB 7 D11
Newcastle GB 13 A8
Newcastle IRL 7 F10
Newcastle IRL 7 F10
Newcastle Emlyn GB 12 A6
Newcastleton GB 5 E11
Newcastle-under-Lyme GB 11 E7
Newcastle upon Tyne GB 5 F13
Newcastle West IRL 8 D4
New Cumnock GB 5 E8
New Deer GB 3 K12
Newel D 21 E7
Newent GB 13 B10
New Galloway GB 5 E8
New Inn IRL 6 F6
New Inn IRL 7 E8
Newinn IRL 9 D7
New Kildimo IRL 8 C5
Newmarket GB 2 J4
Newmarket GB 15 C9
Newmarket IRL 8 D4
Newmarket IRL 9 D8
Newmarket-on-Fergus IRL 8 C5
Newmill GB 3 K11
New Milton GB 13 D11
Newnham GB 13 B10
New Pitsligo GB 3 K12
Newport GB 3 J10
Newport GB 11 F7
Newport GB 12 A5
Newport GB 13 B9
Newport GB 13 D12
Newport GB 15 D9
Newport IRL 6 E3
Newport IRL 8 C6
Newport-on-Tay GB 5 C11
Newport Pagnell GB 15 C7
Newport Trench GB 4 F3
New Quay GB 12 A6
Newquay GB 12 E4
New Radnor GB 13 A8
New Romney GB 15 F10
New Ross IRL 9 D9
Newry GB 7 D10
Newton GB 4 C6
Newton GB 10 D7
Newton Abbot GB 13 D7
Newton Aycliffe GB 5 F13
Newton Ferrers GB 12 E6
Newtonhill GB 5 A12
Newton-le-Willows GB 10 E6
Newton Mearns GB 5 D8
Newtonmore GB 5 A8
Newton Stewart GB 4 F8
Newtown GB 10 F5
Newtown GB 13 A9
Newtown IRL 6 F6
Newtown IRL 8 D5
Newtown IRL 8 D6
Newtown IRL 9 C8
Newtownabbey GB 4 F5
Newtownards GB 7 C11
Newtownbarry IRL 9 C9
Newtownbutler GB 7 D8
Newtown Crommelin GB 4 F4
Newtown Forbes IRL 7 E7
Newtown Mount Kennedy IRL 7 F10
Newtown St Boswells GB 5 D11
Newtownstewart GB 4 F2
Nexon F 29 D8
Neyland GB 12 B5
Nezamyslice CZ 77 D12
Nezavertailovca MD 154 D5
Nézsa H 147 F8
Nezvěstice CZ 76 C5
Nianfors S 103 C12
Niata GR 175 F6
Nibbiano I 37 B10
Nibe DK 86 B5
Nīca LV 134 D2
Nicastro I 59 B9
Nice F 37 D6
Nīcgale LV 135 D12
Nichelino I 37 A7
Nickelsdorf A 77 G12
Nicolae Bălcescu RO 153 B9
Nicolae Bălcescu RO 153 E9
Nicolae Bălcescu RO 155 D3
Nicolae Bălcescu RO 155 E2
Nicolae Bălcescu RO 160 D4
Nicolae Bălcescu RO 161 E9
Nicolae Titulescu RO 160 E5
Nicolaevca MD 154 B2
Nicolosi I 59 D7
Nicoreni MD 153 B11
Nicorești RO 153 F10
Nicosia I 58 D5
Nicotera I 59 B8
Nicșeni RO 153 B9
Niculești RO 161 D7
Niculițel RO 155 C2
Nida LT 134 F1
Nidau CH 27 F7
Nidda D 21 D12
Nidzica PL 139 D9
Niebla E 51 E6
Nieborów PL 141 F2
Niebüll D 82 A5
Niebylec PL 144 D4
Niechanowo PL 138 F4
Niechcice PL 143 D8
Niechłonin PL 139 D9
Niechlów PL 81 C10
Niechorze PL 85 B8
Niederaichbach D 75 E11
Niederanven L 20 E6
Niederau D 80 D5
Niederaula D 78 E6
Niederbipp CH 27 F8
Niederbrechen D 21 D10
Niederbreitbach D 185 C7
Niederbronn-les-Bains F 27 C8
Niederfinow D 84 E5
Niederfischbach D 185 C8
Niedergörsdorf D 80 C3
Niederkassel D 21 C8
Niederkirchen D 21 E9
Niederkrüchten D 20 B6
Niederndorf A 72 A5
Niederneisen D 21 D10
Niedernhall D 74 D6
Niedernhausen D 21 D10
Niederoderwitz D 81 E7
Nieder-Olm D 185 E9
Nieder-Rodenbach D 21 D12
Niederroßla D 79 D9
Niedersachswerfen D 79 C8
Niederselters D 21 D10
Niederstetten D 74 D6
Niederurnen CH 27 F11
Niederviehbach D 75 E11
Niederwerrn D 75 B7
Niederwörresbach D 186 B3
Niederzissen D 21 D8
Niedrzwica Duża PL 141 H6
Niedźwiada PL 141 G7
Niedźwiadna PL 139 C13
Niefern-Öschelbronn D 27 C10
Niegosław PL 85 E9
Niegosławice PL 81 C9
Niegowa PL 143 E7
Niegripp D 79 B10
Nieheim D 17 E12
Niekerk NL 16 B6
Niekłań Wielki PL 141 H3
Niekursko PL 85 D10
Niel B 182 C4
Nielisz PL 144 B7
Niemberg D 79 C11
Niemce PL 141 H7
Niemcza PL 81 E11
Niemegk D 79 B12
Niemelä FIN 113 C20
Niemelä FIN 115 E5
Niemelänkylä FIN 119 F12
Niemenkylä FIN 122 E7
Niemenkylä FIN 126 C6
Niemenpää FIN 119 B11
Niemis S 119 B11
Niemisel S 118 B7
Niemisjärvi FIN 123 F16
Niemisjärvi FIN 124 E8
Niemiskylä FIN 123 C17
Niemodlin PL 142 E4
Niemysłów PL 142 C6
Nienadówka PL 144 C5
Nienburg (Saale) D 79 C10
Nienburg (Weser) D 17 C12
Niepars D 84 B3
Niepołomice PL 143 F9
Nieporjt PL 139 F11
Nierstein D 21 E10
Niesa FIN 117 D11
Niesi FIN 117 D15
Niesky D 81 D7
Nieświń PL 141 H2
Nieszawa PL 138 E6
Nietsak S 116 D4
Nietulisko Duże PL 143 E11
Nieul F 29 D8
Nieuw-Amsterdam NL 17 C7
Nieuw-Bergen NL 16 E6
Nieuwegein NL 16 D4
Nieuwe-Niedorp NL 16 C3
Nieuwe Pekela NL 17 B7
Nieuwerkerk NL 16 E2
Nieuwerkerk aan de IJssel NL 16 E3
Nieuwerkerken B 19 C11
Nieuwe-Tonge NL 16 E2
Nieuw-Heeten NL 16 D6
Nieuwkoop NL 16 D3
Nieuw-Loosdrecht NL 183 A6
Nieuw-Milligen NL 183 A7
Nieuw-Namen NL 182 C4
Nieuwolda NL 17 B7
Nieuwpoort B 18 B6
Nieuwveen NL 182 A5
Nieuw-Vennep NL 16 D3
Nieuw-Vossemeer NL 182 B4
Nieuw-Weerdinge NL 17 C7
Nievern D 185 D8
Niewjgłosz PL 141 G7
Niezabyszewo PL 85 B12
Nigrán E 38 D2
Nīgrande LV 134 D4
Nigrita GR 169 C10
Nigüelas E 53 C9
Niherne F 29 B9
Niinilahti FIN 123 E15
Niinimaa FIN 123 E10
Niinimäki FIN 125 F10
Niinisalo FIN 126 B8
Niinivaara FIN 125 D11
Niinivesi FIN 123 E16
Niirokumpu FIN 121 B11
Níjar E 55 F8
Nijemci HR 157 B11
Nijkerk NL 16 D4
Nijlen B 19 B10
Nijmegen NL 16 E5
Nijverdal NL 17 D6
Nikaia GR 169 E7
Nikaranperä FIN 123 E14
Nikel' RUS 114 E8
Niki GR 168 C5
Nikisiani GR 170 C6
Nikiti GR 169 D10
Nikkala S 119 C11
Nikkaluokta S 111 E17
Nikkaroinen FIN 127 C14
Nikkeby N 112 C6
Nikodin MK 169 B6
Nikokleia GR 169 C9
Nikolaevo BG 165 C10
Nikolaevo BG 166 D5
Nikola-Kozlevo BG 161 F10
Nikolovo BG 161 F8
Nikolsdorf A 73 C6
Nikopol BG 160 F5
Nikopoli GR 174 A2
Nīkrāce LV 134 C3
Nikšić MNE 163 D6
Nikyup BG 166 C5
Nilivaara FIN 117 C14
Nilivaara S 116 D7
Nilsiä FIN 125 D10
Nilvange F 20 F6
Nim DK 86 D5
Nîmes F 35 C7
Nimigea RO 152 C4
Nimis I 73 D7
Nimisenkangas FIN 125 C11
Nimisjärvi FIN 119 E17
Nimtofte DK 86 C7
Nin HR 67 D11
Nina EST 131 D14
Nindorf D 82 B6
Ninemile Bar GB 5 E9
Ninemilehouse IRL 9 D8
Ninove B 19 C9
Niort F 28 C5
Nirza LV 133 D3
Niš SRB 164 C4
Nisa P 44 E5
Nisbet GB 5 D11
Niscemi I 58 E5
Niška Banja SRB 164 C5
Niskankorpi FIN 123 C13
Niskanpera FIN 119 B15
Nisko PL 144 B5
Niskos FIN 123 F10
Nismes B 19 D10
Nispen NL 16 F2
Nisporeni MD 154 C2
Nissafors S 91 E14
Nissan-lez-Enserune F 34 D5
Nissilä FIN 123 C17
Nissinvaara FIN 121 B13
Nissoria I 58 D5
Nissumby DK 86 B2
Nissum Seminarieby DK 86 B2
Nistelrode NL 16 E5
Nistorești RO 153 F9
Nītaure LV 135 B10
Nitra SK 146 E6
Nitrianske Hrnčiarovce SK 146 E6
Nitrianske Pravno SK 147 D7
Nitrianske Rudno SK 146 D6
Nitrianske Sučany SK 146 D6
Nitry F 25 E10
Nitta S 91 D13
Nittedal N 95 B13
Nittel D 20 E6
Nittenau D 75 D11
Nittendorf D 75 D10
Nittorp S 91 D14
Niukkala FIN 129 B12
Nivå DK 87 D11
Niva FIN 121 F14
Nivala FIN 123 C13
Nivankylä FIN 117 E15
Nivanpää FIN 117 E11
Nivelles B 19 C9
Nivenskoye RUS 136 D2
Nivillac F 23 E7
Nivillers F 18 F5
Nivnice CZ 146 D5
Nivolas-Vermelle F 31 D7
Nivyanin BG 165 C8
Niwiska PL 143 F12
Nižbor CZ 76 C6
Nižná SK 147 C9
Nižná Slaná SK 145 F1
Nižný Hrabovec SK 145 F4
Nižný Hrušov SK 145 F4
Nižný Šipov SK 145 F4
Nizza di Sicilia I 59 D7
Nizza Monferrato I 37 B8
Njavve S 109 C15
Njegovuđa MNE 163 C7
Një Maj AL 168 C3
Njetjavare S 116 E4
Njivice HR 67 B10
Njurundabommen S 103 B13
Njutånger S 103 C13
No DK 86 C2
Noaillan F 32 B5
Noailles F 18 F5
Noain E 32 E2
Noale I 66 A5
Noalejo E 53 A9
Noasca I 31 E11
Nöbbele S 89 B8
Nobber IRL 7 E9
Nobitz D 79 E11
Noblejas E 46 E6
Noćaj SRB 158 D4
Nocé F 24 D4
Nocera Inferiore I 60 B3
Nocera Terinese I 59 A9
Nocera Umbra I 62 A3
Noceto I 66 C1
Noci I 61 B8
Nociglia I 61 C10
Nociūnai LT 135 F8
Nocrich RO 152 F4
Nødebo DK 87 D10
Nodeland N 90 C2
Nödinge S 91 D11
Nodland N 94 F4
Nods F 26 F5
Noé F 33 D8
Noepoli I 61 C6
Noer D 83 B8
Nœux-les-Mines F 18 D6
Noez E 46 E4
Nofuentes E 40 C5
Nogales E 51 B6
Nogara I 66 B3
Nogaro F 32 C5
Nogent F 26 D3
Nogent-le-Bernard F 24 D3
Nogent-le-Roi F 24 C6
Nogent-le-Rotrou F 24 D4
Nogent-sur-Aube F 25 D11
Nogent-sur-Oise F 18 F5
Nogent-sur-Seine F 25 D10
Nogent-sur-Vernisson F 25 E8
Nogersund S 89 C7
Nógrád H 147 F8
Nógrádmegyer H 147 E9
Nógrádsáp H 147 F8
Nograles E 40 F6
Noguera de Albarracín E 47 D9
Noguères F 32 D4
Nogueruelas E 48 D3
Nohant-Vic F 29 B9
Nohfelden D 21 E8
Nohic F 33 C8
Noia E 38 C2
Noicattaro I 61 A7
Noidans-lès-Vesoul F 26 E5
Noilhan F 33 C7
Noirétable F 30 D4
Noirmoutier-en-l'Île F 28 A1
Noisseville F 26 B5
Noja E 40 B4
Nojorid RO 151 C8
Nokia FIN 127 C10
Nol S 91 D11
Nolay F 30 B6
Noli I 37 C8
Nolimo FIN 121 B11
Nolmyra S 99 B8
Nólsoy FO 2 A3
Nombela E 46 D4
Nomeland N 90 A2
Nomenj SLO 73 D9
Nomeny F 26 C5
Nomexy F 26 D5
Nomia GR 178 B5
Nonancourt F 24 C5
Nonantola I 66 C3
Nonaspe E 42 E4
None I 37 B7
Nonnenweier D 186 E4
Nonnweiler D 21 E7
Nontron F 29 D7
Nonza F 37 F10
Nõo EST 131 E13
Noordwijk aan Zee NL 182 A4
Noordwijk-Binnen NL 16 D2
Noordwijkerhout NL 16 D3
Noordwolde NL 16 C6
Noormarkku FIN 126 B6
Nootdorp NL 182 A4
Nopankylä FIN 122 E8
Noppikoski S 102 D8
Nor S 103 C11
Nora S 97 C13
Nora S 103 A12
Nørager DK 86 B5
Noragugume I 64 C2
Norberg S 97 B14
Norcia I 62 B4
Nordagutu N 95 D10
Nordanå S 103 A13
Nordanås S 107 C14
Nordanås S 109 E16
Nordanås S 109 F11
Nordanede S 103 A11
Nordankäl S 107 D10
Nordannälden S 105 E16
Nordano S 98 B6
Nordborg DK 86 E5
Nordbotn N 112 D9
Nordby DK 86 D7
Nordby DK 86 E2
Norddeich D 17 A8
NorŠdepil FO 2 A3
Norddorf D 82 A4
Norddyrøy N 104 D5
Nordeide N 100 D3
Nordeidet N 112 D4
Norden D 17 A8
Nordendorf D 75 E8
Nordenham D 17 B10
Nordenskov DK 86 D3
Norderåsen S 106 E7
Norderney D 17 A8
Norderö S 105 E16
Norderstedt D 83 C8
Nordfjord N 114 B8
Nordfjordbotn N 111 B17
Nordfjordeid N 100 C3
Nordfold N 110 E9
Nordhalben D 75 B10
Nordhallen S 105 E13
Nordhastedt D 82 B6
Nordhausen D 79 D8
Nordheim D 27 B11
Nordholz D 17 A11
Nordhorn D 17 D8
Nordhuglo N 94 C3
Nordingrå S 103 A15
Nordkil N 111 D10
Nordkirchen D 17 E9
Nordkisa N 95 B14
Nordkjosbotn N 111 B18
Nordland N 110 E4
Nord-Leirvåg N 114 D7
Nordlenangen N 111 A19
Nordli N 105 C15
Nördlingen D 75 E7
Nordmaling S 107 D17
Nordmannvik N 112 D5
Nordmela N 111 B10
Nordnesøy N 108 C4
Nordøyvågen N 108 D4
NorŠragøta FO 2 A3
Nordråk N 101 E12
Nordsand N 111 C12
Nordsinni N 101 E11
Nordsjö S 103 C12
Nordsjö S 107 D10
Nordsjona N 108 D5
NorŠskáli FO 2 A2
Nordskjør N 104 C8
Nordskot N 110 E8
Nordstemmen D 78 B6
Nord-Værnes N 108 C5
Nordvågen N 113 B17
Nordvik N 108 B9
Nordvik S 103 A14
Nordvika N 104 E4
Nordwalde D 17 D8
Nore S 103 C11
Noreikiškės LT 137 D8
Norem N 105 D10
Noreña E 39 B8
Noresund N 95 B11
Norg NL 17 B6
Norheimsund N 94 B4
Norinkylä FIN 122 E8
Norje S 88 C7
Norma I 62 D3
Norn S 97 B14
Nornäs S 102 D5
Noroy-le-Bourg F 26 E5
Norppa FIN 123 C11
Norra Åsum S 88 D6
Norra Blommaberg S 103 C9
Norra Bredåker S 118 C6
Norra bro S 92 A6
Norra Fjällnäs S 109 E10
Norra Holmnäs S 118 C3
Norråker S 106 C9
Norra Klagshamn S 87 D11
Norra Malånäs S 107 A15
Norra Prästholm S 118 C8
Norra Rödupp S 118 B9
Norra Skärvången S 105 D16
Norra Vallgrund FIN 122 D6
Norra Vi S 92 D6
Norrbäck S 103 B12
Norrbäck S 107 B13
Norrbo S 103 C12
Norrboda S 99 B10
Norrboda S 103 D9
Norrby FIN 122 C9
Norrby S 99 B11
Norrbyberg S 107 B14
Norrbyn S 122 C3
Norrbyskär S 122 C3
Nørre Aaby DK 86 E5
Nørre Alslev DK 84 A1
Nørreballe DK 83 A10
Nørre Bork DK 86 D2
Nørre Broby DK 86 E6
Nørre Felding DK 86 C3
Nørre Halne DK 86 A5
Nørre Kongerslev DK 86 B6
Nørre Nebel DK 86 D2
Norrent-Fontes F 18 C5
Nørre Snede DK 86 D4
Nørresundby DK 86 A5
Nørre Vejrup DK 86 D3
Nørre Vorupør DK 86 B2
Norrfällsviken S 107 F15
Norrfjärden S 103 B13
Norrfjärden S 118 D7
Norrfjärden S 122 C5
Norrflärke S 107 D14
Norrfors S 107 C14
Norrfors S 107 D15
Norrgårdssälen S 102 E6
Norr-Greningen S 106 E8
Norrhult-Klavreström S 89 A8
Norrköping S 93 B8
Norrlångträsk S 118 D5
Norr-Moflo S 107 E11
Norrnäs FIN 122 E6
Norrsjön S 106 B8
Norrskedika S 99 B10
Norrstig S 103 A14
Norrstrand S 109 E16
Norrsundet S 103 E13
Norrtälje S 99 C11
Norrtjärn S 103 E12
Norrvåge S 107 E15
Norrvik S 107 B13
Nors DK 86 A3
Norsholm S 92 B7
Norsjö S 107 B17
Nörten-Hardenberg D 78 C6
Northallerton GB 11 C9
Northam GB 12 C6
Northampton GB 15 C7
North Berwick GB 5 C11
Northborough GB 11 F11
North Cave GB 11 D10
North Dell GB 2 J4
North Duffield GB 11 D10
Northeim D 79 C6
North Ferriby GB 11 D10
North Grimston GB 11 C10
North Hykeham GB 11 E10
North Leigh GB 13 B12
North Shields GB 5 E14
North Somercotes GB 11 E12
North Sunderland GB 5 D13
North Tidworth GB 13 C11
Northton GB 2 K2
North Walsham GB 15 B11
Northwich GB 10 E6
Nortmoor D 17 B9
Norton GB 11 C10
Norton GB 15 C10
Norton Fitzwarren GB 13 C8
Nortorf D 83 B7
Nortrup D 17 C9
Nort-sur-Erdre F 23 F8
Norup DK 86 B6
Norvasalmi FIN 117 E15
Norwich GB 15 B11
Norwick GB 3 D15
Noșlac RO 152 E3
Nøss N 111 B10
Nossa Senhora da Boa Fé P 50 B3
Nossa Senhora da Graça de Póvoa e Meadas P 44 E5
Nossa Senhora da Graça do Divor P 50 B4
Nossa Senhora da Graça dos Degolados P 45 F6
Nossa Senhora das Neves P 50 C4
Nossa Senhora de Machede P 50 B4
Nossebro S 91 C12
Nossen D 80 D4
Nossendorf D 84 C3
Nossentiner Hütte D 83 C12
Noszlop H 149 B8
Noszvaj H 145 H1
Notaresco I 62 B5
Notia GR 169 B7
Nőtincs H 147 F8
Nötö FIN 126 F6
Noto I 59 F7
Notodden N 95 C10
Notre-Dame-de-Bellecombe F 31 D10
Notre-Dame-de-Gravenchon F 18 F2
Notre-Dame-de-Monts F 28 B1
Notre-Dame-d'Oé F 24 F4
Nötsch im Gailtal A 73 C8
Nottensdorf D 82 D7
Nottingham GB 11 F9
Nottuln D 17 E8
Notviken S 118 C8
Nouan-le-Fuzelier F 24 E7
Nouans-les-Fontaines F 24 F5
Nouart F 19 F11
Nõuni EST 131 E13
Nousiainen FIN 126 D7
Nousionmäki FIN 125 D10
Nousu FIN 115 D5
Nouvion F 18 D4
Nouzilly F 24 E4
Nouzonville F 19 E10
Nõva EST 130 C7
Nova H 149 C7
Nová Baňa SK 147 E7
Nova Breznica MK 164 F3
Nova Bukovica HR 149 E9
Nová Bystřice CZ 77 D8
Nová Cerekev CZ 77 D8
Novachene BG 165 B10
Novachene BG 165 D8
Novaci MK 168 B5
Novaci RO 160 C3
Nova Crnja SRB 158 B6
Nová Dedina SK 147 E7
Novadnieki LV 134 C4
Nová Dubnica SK 146 D6
Novafeltria I 66 E5
Nova Gorica SLO 73 E8
Nova Gradiška HR 157 B7
Nova Ivanivka UA 154 F4
Novaj H 145 H1
Novajidrány H 145 G3
Nova Kamena BG 161 F10
Nova Kasaba BIH 157 D11
Novaki HR 148 E5
Novakovo BG 166 F4
Nováky SK 147 D7
Novales E 40 B3
Novales E 41 D11
Nova Levante I 72 D4
Novalja HR 67 C10
Novallas E 41 E8
Nová Ľubovňa SK 145 E2
Nova Makhala BG 165 F9
Nova Nadezhda BG 166 E5
Nova Nekrasivka UA 155 C3
Nová Paka CZ 77 B9
Nova Pazova SRB 158 D5
Nova Pokrovka UA 155 B4
Novara I 68 C6
Novara di Sicilia I 59 C7
Nová Role CZ 75 B12
Nova Sela HR 157 F8
Nova Siri I 61 C7
Nova Siri Scalo I 61 C7
Novate Mezzola I 69 A7
Nova Topola BIH 157 B7
Nova Varoš SRB 163 C8
Nova Vas SLO 73 E9
Nová Včelnice CZ 77 D8
Nová Ves CZ 77 B8
Nová Ves nad Šitavou SK 146 E6
Nova Zagora BG 166 E6
Nové Hrady CZ 77 E7
Novelda E 56 E3
Novellara I 66 C2
Nové Město nad Metuj CZ 77 B10
Nové Mesto nad Váhom SK 146 D5
Nové Město na Moravé CZ 77 C10
Nové Město pod Smrkem CZ 81 E8
Nove Misto UA 145 D6
Noventa di Piave I 72 E6
Noventa Vicentina I 66 B4
Novés E 46 D4
Noves F 35 C8
Nové Veselí CZ 77 C9
Nové Zámky SK 146 F6
Novgorodka RUS 133 B5
Novgrad BG 161 F7
Novi Banovci SRB 158 D5
Novi Bečej SRB 158 B5
Novi di Modena I 66 C2
Novi Dojran MK 169 B8
Noviergas E 41 E7
Novi Grad BIH 157 B9
Novigrad HR 67 B8
Novigrad HR 156 D4
Novigrad Podravski HR 149 D7
Novi Iskŭr BG 165 D7
Novi Karlovci SRB 158 C5
Novi Khan BG 165 D8
Novi Kneževac SRB 150 E5
Novi Kozarci SRB 150 F6
Novi Ligure I 37 B9
Novillars F 26 F5
Noville B 182 D5
Novi Marof HR 149 D6
Novion-Porcien F 19 E9
Novi Pazar BG 167 C8
Novi Pazar SRB 163 C10
Novi Sad SRB 158 C4
Novi Šeher BIH 157 C9
Novi Slankamen SRB 158 C5
Novi Travnik BIH 157 D8
Novi Vinodolski HR 67 B10
Novo Beograd SRB 158 D5
Novoborysivka UA 154 C5
Novočići BIH 157 F9
Novo Delchevo BG 169 B9
Novokhovansk RUS 133 E7
Novo Korito SRB 159 F9
Novo Mesto SLO 73 E11
Novo Miloševo SRB 158 B5
Novomoskovskiy RUS 139 A9
Novomykolayivka UA 155 B5
Novo Orahovo SRB 150 F4
Novo Oryakhovo BG 167 D9
Novopetrivka UA 154 C5
Novorzhev RUS 133 B6
Novosamarka UA 154 B5
Novosedly CZ 77 E11
Novoselë AL 163 F10
Novoselë AL 168 C1
Novoselec HR 149 E7
Novoselets BG 166 E6
Novoselija BIH 157 C7
Novoselivka UA 154 B5
Novoselivka UA 154 D5
Novo Selo BG 159 E10
Novo Selo BG 161 F8
Novo Selo BG 165 E6
Novo Selo BG 166 F6
Novo Selo BIH 157 B8
Novo Selo BIH 157 B9
Novo Selo MK 169 B8
Novo Selo SRB 159 F6
Novoselovo RUS 139 B9
Novoseltsi BG 167 E8
Novosel'ye RUS 132 E4
Novoselytsya UA 153 A8
Novoselytsya UA 154 A6
Novosil's'ke UA 155 C3
Novostroyevo RUS 136 E4
Novot SK 147 C8
Novo Virje HR 149 D8
Novovolyns'k UA 144 B9
Novoyavorivs'ke UA 144 D8
Novska HR 149 F7
Nový Bor CZ 81 E7
Nový Bydžov CZ 77 B8
Novy-Chevrières F 19 E9
Novy Dvor BY 137 F10
Nový Hrozenkov CZ 146 C6
Nový Jičín CZ 146 B5
Nový Knín CZ 76 C6
Nový Malín CZ 77 C12
Novy Pahost BY 133 F2
Nový Rychnov CZ 77 D8
Novyya Kruki BY 133 E3
Novyy Izborsk RUS 132 F2
Novyy Rozdil UA 145 E9
Nový Šivot SK 146 E4
Nowa Brzeźnica PL 143 D7
Nowa Cerekwia PL 142 F4
Nowa Chodorówka PL 140 C8
Nowa Djba PL 143 F12
Nowa Karczma PL 138 B5
Nowa Ruda PL 81 E11
Nowa Sarzyna PL 144 C5
Nowa Słupia PL 143 E11
Nowa Sól PL 81 C9
Nowa Sucha PL 141 F2
Nowa Wieś Ełcka PL 140 C6
Nowa Wieś Ljborskie PL 85 A13
Nowa Wieś Wielka PL 138 E5
Nowa Wola PL 140 D9
Nowa Wola Gołjbiowska PL 141 H4
Nowe PL 138 C6
Nowe Brusno PL 144 C7
Nowe Brzesko PL 143 F9
Nowe Czarnowo PL 84 D6
Nowe Miasteczko PL 81 C9
Nowe Miasto PL 139 E10
Nowe Miasto Lubawskie PL 139 D8
Nowe Miasto nad Pilicą PL 141 G3
Nowe Miasto nad Wartą PL 81 B12
Nowe Ostrowy PL 143 B7
Nowe Piekuty PL 141 E7
Nowe Skalmierzyce PL 142 C4
Nowe Warpno PL 84 C6
Nowinka PL 136 F6
Nowogard PL 85 C8
Nowogród PL 139 D12
Nowogród Bobrzański PL 81 C8
Nowogródek Pomorski PL 85 E8
Nowogrodziec PL 81 D8
Nowosady PL 141 E9
Nowosielce PL 145 D5
Nowosolna PL 143 C8
Nowotaniec PL 145 D5
Nowowola PL 140 D8
Nowy Bartków PL 141 F7
Nowy Duninów PL 139 E7
Nowy Dwór PL 138 D4
Nowy Dwór PL 140 C9
Nowy Dwór Gdański PL 138 B7
Nowy Dwór Mazowiecki PL 139 F10
Nowy Kawjczyn PL 141 G2
Nowy Korczyn PL 143 F10
Nowy Lubliniec PL 144 C7
Nowy Sącz PL 145 D2
Nowy Staw PL 138 B7
Nowy Targ PL 147 C10
Nowy Tomyśl PL 81 B10
Nowy Wiśnicz PL 144 D1
Nowy Żmigród PL 145 D4
Noyal-Muzillac F 22 E7
Noyalo F 22 E6
Noyal-Pontivy F 22 D6
Noyant F 23 E12

Noyarey F 31 E8
Noyen-sur-Sarthe F 23 E11
Noyers F 25 E10
Noyers-sur-Cher F 24 F5
Noyers-sur-Jabron F 35 B10
Noyon F 18 E6
Nozay F 23 E8
Nozdrzec PL 144 D5
Nozeroy F 31 B9
Nuaillé-d'Aunis F 28 C4
Nuasjärvi FIN 117 E13
Nubledo E 39 A8
Nucet RO 151 E10
Nuci RO 161 D8
Nucşoara RO 160 C5
Nudersdorf D 79 C12
Nüdlingen D 75 B7
Nudyzhe UA 141 H10
Nueil-les-Aubiers F 28 B4
Nuenen NL 16 F5
Nueno E 41 D11
Nueva E 39 B10
Nueva-Carteya E 53 A8
Nueva Jarilla E 52 C4
Nuez de Ebro E 41 E10
Nufăru RO 155 C3
Nughedu di San Nicolò I 64 B3
Nuijamaa FIN 129 D10
Nuillé-sur-Vicoin F 23 E10
Nuits F 25 E11
Nuits-St-Georges F 26 F2
Nukari FIN 127 D12
Ņukši LV 133 D3
Nuland NL 16 E4
Nule I 64 C3
Nules E 48 E4
Nulvi I 64 B2
Numana I 67 E8
Numansdorp NL 16 E2
Nummela FIN 127 E11
Nummi FIN 127 E10
Nummijärvi FIN 122 F8
Nummikoski FIN 122 F9
Nünchritz D 80 D4
Nuneaton GB 11 F9
Nunkirchen D 186 C2
Nunnanen FIN 117 B12
Nunnanlahti FIN 125 D12
Nuñomoral E 45 D8
Nunsdorf D 80 B4
Nunspeet NL 16 D5
Nuojua FIN 119 E17
Nuoksujärvi S 116 E9
Nuolijärvi FIN 125 C11
Nuoramoinen FIN 127 C14
Nuorgam FIN 113 C20
Nuoritta FIN 119 D16
Nuoro I 64 C3
Nuorunka FIN 120 C9
Nuottavaara FIN 117 D12
Nuottikylä FIN 121 E12
Nur PL 141 E6
Nuragus I 64 D3
Nurallao I 64 D3
Nuraminis I 64 E3
Nureci I 64 D2
Nuriye TR 177 B10
Nurmaa FIN 128 C6
Nurmes FIN 125 C12
Nurmesperä FIN 123 C15
Nurmijärvi FIN 125 C13
Nurmijärvi FIN 127 E12
Nurmo FIN 123 E9
Nürnberg D 75 D9
Nurney IRL 7 F9
Nurri I 64 D3
Nurste EST 130 D4
Nürtingen D 27 C11
Nurzec-Stacja PL 141 F8
Nus I 31 D11
Nusco I 60 B4
Nuşeni RO 152 C4
Nuşfalău RO 151 C10
Nusfjord N 110 D5
Nusnäs S 102 E8
Nusplingen D 27 D10
Nußbach A 76 G6
Nußdorf D 73 A6
Nußdorf am Inn D 72 A5
Nuštar HR 149 F11
Nustrup DK 86 E4
Nuth NL 19 C12
Nutheim N 95 C9
Nuttuperä FIN 123 C15
Nuuksujärvi S 116 C8
Nuupas FIN 119 B16
Nuutajärvi FIN 127 C9
Nuutila FIN 119 F16
Nuutilanmaki FIN 128 B8
Nuvsvåg N 112 C9
Nuvvus FIN 113 D17
Nuxis I 64 E2
Nüziders A 71 C9
Nya Bastuselet S 109 F16
Nyåker S 107 D13
Nyåker S 107 D16
Nyárád H 149 B8
Nyáregyháza H 150 C4
Nyárlőrinc H 150 D4
Nyársapát H 150 C4
Nybble S 91 A15
Nybergsund N 102 D3
Nyborg DK 87 E7
Nyborg N 114 C5
Nyborg S 119 C10
Nybro S 89 B9
Nybrostrand S 88 E5
Nyby FIN 122 E6
Nyby N 113 C15
Nyby S 106 E8
Nybyn S 103 C9
Nybyn S 107 E14
Nybyn S 118 D6
Nýdek CZ 147 B7
Nydri GR 174 B2
Nye S 89 A8
Nyékládháza H 145 H2
Nyelv N 114 C5
Nyergesújfalu H 149 A11
Nyhammar S 97 B12
Nyhem S 103 A10
Nyhem S 109 E14
Ny Højen DK 86 D5
Nyhus N 111 B15
Nyhyttan S 97 C12
Nyírábrány H 151 B9
Nyíracsád H 151 B8
Nyírád H 149 B8
Nyíradony H 151 B8
Nyírbátor H 151 B9
Nyírbéltek H 151 B9
Nyírbogát H 151 B9
Nyírbogdány H 145 G4
Nyíregyháza H 145 H4
Nyírgelse H 151 B8
Nyírgyulaj H 145 H5
Nyíribrony H 145 G4
Nyírkáta H 145 H5
Nyírmada H 145 G5
Nyírmeggyes H 145 H5
Nyírmihálydi H 151 B8
Nyírpazony H 145 H4
Nyírtass H 145 G5
Nyírtelek H 145 G4
Nyírtét H 145 G4
Nyírtura H 145 G4
Nyírvasvári H 151 B9
Nykarleby FIN 122 C9
Nyker DK 89 E7
Nykil S 92 C6
Nykøbing DK 83 A11
Nykøbing Mors DK 86 B3
Nykøbing Sjælland DK 87 D9
Nyköping S 93 B10
Nykrogen S 98 B6
Nykroppa S 97 C11
Nyksund N 110 C9
Nykvåg N 110 C7
Nykvarn S 93 A10
Nykyrke S 92 B5
Nyland S 107 D16
Nyland S 107 E13
Nyland S 122 C3
Nylars DK 89 E7
Nyliden S 107 D15
Nymburk CZ 77 B8
Nymfes GR 168 E2
Nymindegab DK 86 D2
Nymoen N 112 C6
Nynäshamn S 93 B11
Nyneset N 105 C13
Ny Nørup DK 86 D4
Nyoiseau F 23 E10
Nyon CH 31 C9
Nyons F 35 B9
Nyråd DK 87 E9
Nýřany CZ 76 C4
Nýrsko CZ 76 D4
Nyrud N 114 E6
Nysa PL 142 F3
Nysäter S 97 D8
Nysätern S 102 A5
Nysättra S 99 C11
Nysted DK 83 A11
Nysted N 111 C15
Nystrand S 118 C5
Nyträsk S 118 E4
Nytrøa N 111 B16
Nyúl H 149 A9
Nyvoll N 113 C11
Nyzhankovychi UA 144 D6
Nyzhni Petrivtsi UA 153 A7
Nyzhni Vorota UA 145 F7
Nyzhniy Bystryy UA 145 G8
Nyzhnya Vysots'ke UA 145 E7
Nyzhnya Yablun'ka
UA 145 E6

O

Oadby GB 11 F9
Oakengates GB 10 F7
Oakham GB 11 F10
Oakley GB 13 B12
Oakley GB 13 C12
Oakley GB 15 C7
Oancea RO 154 F2
Oandu EST 131 C13
Oarja RO 160 D5
O Arrabal E 38 D2
Oarța de Jos RO 151 C11
Obal' BY 133 E7
Obal' BY 133 F6
Obalj BIH 157 F9
Oban GB 4 C6
O Barco E 39 D6
Obârșia RO 160 F4
Obârșia-Cloșani RO 159 C10
Obârșia de Câmp RO 159 E11
Obbola S 122 C4
Obdach A 73 B10
Obecnice CZ 76 C5
Obedinenie BG 166 C5
Obejo E 54 C3
Obeliai LT 135 E11
Oberaich A 73 B11
Oberalm A 73 A7
Oberammergau D 71 B12
Oberasbach D 75 D8
Oberau D 72 A3
Oberaudorf D 72 A5
Obercunnersdorf D 81 D7
Oberderdingen D 27 B10
Oberding D 75 F10
Oberdorla D 79 D7
Oberdrauburg A 73 C6
Oberegg CH 71 C9
Oberelsbach D 75 B7
Oberfell D 185 D7
Obergebra D 79 D8
Obergösgen CH 27 F8
Ober-Grafendorf A 77 F9
Obergriesbach D 75 F9
Obergünzburg D 71 B10
Obergurgl A 72 C3
Obergurig D 80 D6
Oberhaag A 148 C4
Oberhaid D 75 C8
Oberharmersbach D 27 D9
Oberhausen D 17 F7
Oberhausen D 75 E9
Oberhausen-Rheinhausen
D 187 C5
Oberheldrungen D 79 D9
Oberhof D 79 E8
Oberhofen CH 70 D5
Oberhoffen-sur-Moder F 186 D4
Oberkirch D 27 C9
Oberkochen D 75 E7
Oberkotzau D 75 B10
Oberlangen D 17 C8
Oberlungwitz D 79 E12
Obermarchtal D 71 A9
Obermaßfeld-Grimmenthal
D 75 A7
Obermoschel D 21 E9
Obernai F 27 D7
Obernberg am Inn A 76 F4
Obernburg am Main D 187 B7
Oberndorf D 17 A12
Oberndorf am Lech D 75 E8
Oberndorf am Neckar D 27 D10
Oberndorf bei Salzburg A 73 A6
Oberneukirchen A 76 F6
Obernfeld D 79 C7
Obernheim D 27 D10
Obernheim-Kirchenarnbach
D 186 C4
Obernkirchen D 17 D12
Obernzell D 76 E5
Ober-Olm D 185 E9
Oberpullendorf A 149 A7
Oberried D 27 E8
Oberrieden D 71 A10
Oberriet CH 71 C9
Ober-Roden D 21 E11
Oberrot D 187 C8
Oberrotweil D 27 D8
Oberschneiding D 75 E12
Oberschützen A 148 B6
Obersiebenbrunn A 77 F11
Obersinn D 74 B6
Obersontheim D 187 C8
Oberspier D 79 D8
Oberstadion D 71 A9
Oberstaufen D 71 B10
Oberstdorf D 71 C10
Oberstenfeld D 27 B11
Oberthal D 21 E8
Oberthulba D 187 A8
Obertilliach A 73 C6
Obertraubling D 75 E11
Obertrubach D 75 C9
Obertshausen D 21 D11
Oberursel (Taunus) D 21 D11
Obervellach A 73 C7
Oberviechtach D 75 D11
Oberwald CH 70 D6
Oberwart A 148 B6
Oberwesel D 21 D9
Oberwolfach D 187 E5
Oberwölz A 73 B9
Óbidos P 44 F2
Obiliq RKS 164 D3
Obing D 75 F11
Obinitsa EST 132 F1
Obitel BG 167 C7
Objat F 29 E8
Objazda PL 85 A12
Öblarn A 73 B8
Oblešеvo MK 164 F5
Oblikë e Madhe AL 163 E7
Obnova BG 165 C10
Obodivka UA 154 A4
Oboga RO 160 E4
O Bolo E 38 D5
Obón E 42 F2
Oborci BIH 157 D7
Oborín SK 145 F4
Oborishte BG 165 D9
Oborniki PL 81 A11
Oborniki Śląskie PL 81 D11
Obrazów PL 143 E12
Obreja RO 159 C9
Obrenovac SRB 158 D5
Obretenik BG 166 B5
Obrež SRB 158 D4
Obrež SRB 159 F7
Obrigheim D 21 F12
Obrigheim (Pfalz) D 187 B5
Obrnice CZ 76 A5
Obrochishte BG 167 C10
Obrov SLO 67 A9
Obrovac HR 156 D4
Obrovac SRB 158 C3
Obrowo PL 138 E6
Obrtići BIH 157 E10
Obruchishte BG 166 E5
Obryte PL 139 E11
Obrzycko PL 85 E11
Obsza PL 144 C6
Obudovac BIH 157 C10
Obyce SK 146 E6
Obzor BG 167 D9
O Cádavo E 38 B5
Ocaklar TR 173 D8
O Campo da Feira E 38 B3
Ocaña E 46 E6
Ocana F 37 H9
O Carballiño E 38 D3
O Castelo E 38 D3
O Castro E 38 C3
O Castro de Ferreira E 38 C4
Occhiobello I 66 C4
Occimiano I 68 C6
Očevlja BIH 157 D9
Ochagavía E 32 E3
O Chao E 38 B4
Ochiltree GB 5 E8
Ochla PL 81 C8
Ochodnica SK 147 C7
Ocholt D 17 B9
Ochsenfurt D 75 C7
Ochsenhausen D 71 A9
Ochtrup D 17 D8
Ocke S 105 E15
Ockelbo S 103 E12
Öckerö S 91 D10
Ockholm D 82 A5
Ocksjön S 102 A8
Ocland RO 152 E6
Ocna de Fier RO 159 C8
Ocna Mureș RO 152 E3
Ocna Sibiului RO 152 F4
Ocna dugatag RO 152 B3
Ocnele Mari RO 160 C4
Ocnița RO 161 D7
Ocolina MD 154 A2
Ocoliș RO 151 E11
O Convento E 38 D2
O Corgo E 38 C5
Ocrkavlje BIH 157 E10
Öcsa H 150 C3
Öcsény H 149 D11
Öcsöd H 150 D5
Octeville-sur-Mer F 23 A12
Ocypel PL 138 C5
Odăile RO 161 C9
Ödåkra S 87 C11
Odda N 94 B5
Odden N 112 D5
Oddense DK 86 B3
Odder DK 86 D6
Oddsta GB 3 D15
Ödeborg S 91 B10
Odeceixe P 50 E2
Odeleite P 50 E5
Odelouca P 50 E3
Odelzhausen D 75 F9
Odemira P 50 D2
Ödena E 43 D7
Ödensbacken S 92 A7
Ödensberg S 91 C13
Odense DK 86 E6
Ödensjö S 92 D4
Ödensvi S 93 D8
Oderberg D 84 E6
Oderin D 80 B5
Odernheim am Glan D 21 E9
Oderzo I 72 E5
Ödeshog S 92 C5
Odiáxere P 50 E2
Odiham GB 15 E7
Ødis DK 86 E4
Odivelas P 50 B1
Odivelas P 50 C3
Ödkarby FIN 99 B13
Odobești RO 153 F10
Odobești RO 161 D7
Odolanów PL 142 C4
Odolena Voda CZ 76 B6
Odón E 47 C9
Odoorn NL 17 C7
Odorheiu Secuiesc RO 152 E6
Odry CZ 146 B5
Odrzywół PL 141 G3
Ödsmål S 91 C10
Ødsted DK 86 D4
Odűrne BG 165 C10
Odžaci BIH 157 E9
Odžaci SRB 158 B3
Odžak BIH 157 B9
Odžak BIH 157 E6
Odžak BIH 157 F9
Odžak MNE 163 C7
Odziena LV 135 C11
Oebisfelde D 79 B8
Oedelem B 182 C2
Oedelsheim (Oberweser) D 78 C6
Oederan D 80 E4
Oeffelt NL 16 E5
Oegstgeest NL 16 D3
Oeiras P 50 B1
Oelde D 17 E10
Oelixdorf D 82 C7
Oelsnitz D 75 B11
Oelsnitz D 79 E12
Oene NL 183 A8
Oenkerk NL 16 B5
Oensingen CH 27 F8
Oerel D 17 B12
Oering D 83 C8
Oerlenbach D 75 B7
Oerlinghausen D 17 E11
Oestrich-Winkel D 21 D9
Oettersdorf D 79 E10
Oettingen in Bayern D 75 E8
Oetz A 71 C11
Oetzen D 83 D9
Oeversee D 82 A6
Œyreluy F 32 C3
Ofatinți MD 154 B4
Öfehértó H 145 H5
Ofena I 62 C5
Offanengo I 69 C8
Offemont F 27 E6
Offenbach am Main D 21 D11
Offenbach an der Queich
D 187 C5
Offenberg D 76 E3
Offenburg D 27 D8
Offerdal S 105 E16
Offersøy N 111 D10
Offida I 62 B5
Offingen D 75 F7
Offranville F 18 E3
O Forte E 38 C3
Ofte N 95 D8
Ofterdingen D 27 D11
Oftersheim D 21 F11
Ogenbargen D 17 A9
Oger F 25 C11
Ogeu-les-Bains F 32 D4
Ogéviller F 26 C6
Oggevatn N 90 C3
Ogliastro F 37 F10
Ogliastro Cilento I 60 C4
Ogmore GB 13 C7
Ognyanovo BG 169 A10
Ogonelloe IRL 8 C6
Ogoya BG 165 D8
Ogra RO 152 E4
Ogre LV 135 C9
Ogren AL 168 D3
Ogresgals LV 135 C9
Ogrezeni RO 161 E7
Ogrodniki PL 139 E12
Ogrodzieniec PL 143 F8
Ogrosen D 80 C6
O Grove E 38 D2
Ogulin HR 67 B11
Oğulpaşa TR 172 A6
Ohaba RO 152 E3
Ohaba Lungă RO 151 F8
Ohanes E 55 E7
Ohey B 19 D11
Ohkola FIN 127 D13
Ohlsbach D 27 D8
Ohlstadt D 72 A3
Ohne D 17 D8
Ohorn D 80 D6
Ohrady SK 146 E5
Ohrdruf D 79 E8
Ohrid MK 168 B4
Öhringen D 27 B11
Ohtaanniemi FIN 125 E11
Ohtanajärvi S 116 E10
Ohukotsu EST 131 C9
Oia GR 179 C9
Oiã P 44 C3
Oiartzun E 32 D2
Oichalia GR 169 E6
Øie N 105 B12
Oignies F 18 D6
O Igrexario E 38 D3
Oijärvi FIN 119 C15
Oijen NL 183 B6
Oijusluoma FIN 121 C13
Oikarainen FIN 119 B16
Oileán Ciarrái IRL 8 D4
Oilgate IRL 9 D9
Oímbra E 38 E5
Oinacu RO 161 F8
Oinas FIN 115 E2
Oinasjärvi FIN 124 C9
Oinofyta GR 175 C8
Oinoi GR 175 C7
Oion E 41 C7
O Irixo E 38 C3
Oiron F 28 B5
Oirschot NL 183 B6
Oiselay-et-Grachaux F 26 F4
Oisemont F 18 E4
Oisseau F 23 D10
Oissel F 18 F3
Oisterwijk NL 183 B6
Oisu EST 131 D11
Õisu EST 131 E11
Oitti FIN 127 D13
Oituz RO 153 E9
Oitylo GR 178 B3
Oivanki FIN 121 B13
Oizon F 25 F8
Öja FIN 123 C9
Öja S 93 E12
Ojakkala FIN 127 E11
Ojakylä FIN 119 D13
Ojakylä FIN 119 D14
Ojakylä FIN 119 F15
Ojanperä FIN 120 F8
Öjarn S 106 D8
Ojdula RO 153 F8
Öje S 102 E6
Öjebyn S 118 D6
Öjeforsen S 103 B9
Ojén E 53 C7
Öjingsvallen S 103 C8
Ojos Negros E 47 C10
Ojrzeń PL 139 E10
Öjung S 103 C10
Okalewo PL 139 D8
Okány H 151 D7
Okçular TR 181 C9
Økdal N 101 A12
Okehampton GB 12 D6
Okhotnoye RUS 136 D4
Oklaj HR 156 E5
Öknö S 89 A11
Okoč SK 146 F5
Okonek PL 85 C11
Okopy PL 141 H9
Ököritófülpös H 145 H6
Okorsh BG 161 F10
Okříšky CZ 77 D9
Okrouhlice CZ 77 C8
Okrúhle SK 145 E4
Oksa PL 143 E9
Öksajärvi S 116 C8
Oksakoski FIN 123 D12
Oksava FIN 123 C14
Oksbøl DK 86 D2
Oksbøl DK 86 E5
Øksfjord N 112 C9
Øksnes N 110 C8
Øksneshamn N 110 D9
Oksvoll N 104 D7
Oktonia GR 175 B9
Okučani HR 157 B7
Ola E 38 D2
Olague E 32 E2
Olaine LV 135 C7
Olalhas P 44 E4
Oland N 90 B3
Olănești MD 154 E5
Olanu RO 160 D4
Olargues F 34 C4
Olari RO 151 E8
Olaszliszka H 145 G3
Olave E 32 E2
Oława PL 81 E12
Olazti E 32 E1
Olba E 48 D3
Olbendorf A 148 B6
Olbernhau D 80 E4
Olbersdorf D 81 E7
Olbersleben D 79 D9
Olbia I 64 B3
Olbijcin PL 144 B5
Olbramovice CZ 77 C7
Olcea RO 151 D8
Oldcastle IRL 7 E8
Old Dailly GB 4 E7
Oldebroek NL 16 D5
Oldedalen N 100 C5
Oldehove NL 16 B6
Oldeide N 100 C2
Oldemarkt NL 16 C5
Olden N 100 C5
Olden S 105 D15
Oldenbrok D 17 B10
Oldenburg D 17 B10
Oldenburg in Holstein D 83 B9
Oldendorf D 17 A12
Oldenswort D 82 B5
Oldenzaal NL 17 D7
Olderdalen N 112 D6
Oldereid N 108 B8
Olderfjord N 113 C15
Oldernes N 113 C13
Oldervik N 108 C5
Oldervik N 111 A18
Oldervik N 113 B13
Oldham GB 11 D7
Old Head IRL 8 E5
Oldisleben D 79 D9
Old Leake GB 11 E12
Oldmeldrum GB 3 L12
Oldsum D 82 A4
Oldtown IRL 7 E10
Oleby S 97 B9
Olecko PL 136 E6
Oleggio I 68 B6
Oleiros P 44 E5
Oleksandrivka UA 154 C6
Olekseyivka UA 154 B3
Olemps F 33 B11
Olen B 19 B10
Ølen N 94 C3
Olesa de Montserrat E 43 D7
Oleśnica PL 142 D3
Oleśnica PL 143 F11
Olešnice CZ 77 C10
Olesno PL 142 E5
Olesno PL 143 F10
Oleszyce PL 144 C7
Olette F 33 E10
Olevano Romano I 62 D4
Olfen D 17 E8
Olgina EST 132 C3
Olginate I 69 B7
Ølgod DK 86 D3
Olgrinmore GB 3 J9
Olhalvo P 44 F2
Olhão P 50 E4
Olhava FIN 119 D14
Ølholm DK 86 D5
Olho Marinho P 44 F2
Ol'hopil' UA 154 A5
Oliana E 43 C6
Olías del Rey E 46 E5
Oliena I 64 C3
Oliete E 42 E2
Oligastro Marina I 60 C3
Olingdal S 102 C7
Olingsjövallen S 102 C7
Oliola E 42 D6
Olite E 32 F2
Oliva E 56 D4
Oliva de la Frontera E 51 C6
Oliva de Mérida E 51 B7
Olival P 44 E3
Olivares E 51 E7
Olivares de Júcar E 47 E8
Oliveira de Azeméis P 44 C4
Oliveira de Frades P 44 C4
Oliveira do Arda P 44 B4
Oliveira do Bairro P 44 C4
Oliveira do Conde P 44 D5
Oliveira do Douro P 44 B3
Oliveira do Hospital P 44 D5
Olivenza E 51 B5
Oliveri I 59 C7
Olivet F 24 E6
Oliveto Citra I 60 B4
Oliveto Lucano I 60 B6
Olivone CH 71 D7
Oľka SK 145 E4
Olkijoki FIN 119 E13
Olkiluoto FIN 126 C5
Olkkajärvi FIN 117 E16
Olkusz PL 143 F8
Ollaberry GB 3 D14
Ollerton GB 11 E9
Ollerup DK 86 E7
Olliergues F 30 D4
Ollila FIN 121 B13
Ollila FIN 127 D8
Ollilanniemi FIN 121 E12
Ollioules F 35 D10
Ollo E 32 E2
Öllölä FIN 125 F15
Ollolai I 64 C3
Ollon CH 31 C10
Ollsta S 106 E8
Ölmbrotorp S 97 D13
Ölme S 97 D11
Olmedilla de Roa E 40 E4
Olmedo E 46 B3
Olmedo I 64 B1
Olmeta-di-Tuda F 37 F10
Olmeto F 37 H9
Olmos de Ojeda E 40 C3
Olney GB 15 C7
Olocau E 48 E3
Olocau del Rey E 42 F3
Olofsfors S 107 D16
Olofstorp S 91 D11
Olofström S 88 C7
Olombrada E 40 F3
Olomouc CZ 146 B4
Olonne-sur-Mer F 28 B2
Olonzac F 34 D4
Oloron-Ste-Marie F 32 D4
Olost E 43 D8
Olot E 43 C8
Olovi CZ 75 B12
Olovo BIH 157 D10
Olpe D 21 B9
Olřišov CZ 142 G4
Olšany CZ 77 C11
Olšany u Prostějova CZ 77 C12
Olsätter S 97 C10
Olsbenning S 97 B15
Olsberg D 17 F10
Olsberg N 111 B16
Ölsboda S 92 A4
Olsfors S 91 D12
Olshammar S 92 B5
Olsøy N 104 D8
Olst NL 16 D6
Ølsted DK 86 D5
Ølsted DK 87 D10
Ølstykke DK 87 D10
Olszanica PL 145 E5
Olszanka PL 142 E3
Olszany PL 144 D6
Olszewo-Borki PL 139 D12
Olsztyn PL 136 F1
Olsztyn PL 143 E7
Olsztynek PL 139 C9
Olszyn PL 141 F8
Olszyna PL 81 D8
Olszyny PL 144 D2
Oltedal N 94 E4
Olten CH 27 F8
Oltenești RO 153 D11
Olteni RO 160 E6
Oltenița RO 161 E9
Oltina RO 155 E1
Olula del Río E 55 E8
Olustvere EST 131 D11
Olvan E 43 C7
Olvasjärvi FIN 120 D9
Ólvega E 41 E8
Olvena E 42 C4
Olvera E 51 F9
Olympiada GR 169 C10
Olympiada GR 169 E7
Olympos GR 181 E6
Olzai I 64 C3
Oma N 94 B3
Omagh GB 4 F2
Omalos GR 178 E6
Omarchevo BG 166 E6
Omarska BIH 157 C6
Ombersley GB 13 A10
Omedu EST 131 D14
Omegna I 68 B5
Ömerköy TR 173 E9
Ömerli TR 173 D9
O Mesón do Vento E 38 B3
Omessa F 37 G10
Omiš HR 157 F6
Omišalj HR 67 B10
Ommen NL 16 C6
Omne S 107 F14
Omolio GR 169 E8
Omoljica SRB 159 D6
Omont F 19 E10
Ömossa FIN 122 F7
O Mosteiro E 38 C2
Omurtag BG 167 C6
Omvriaki GR 174 A5
Oña E 40 C5
Ona N 100 A5
Onani I 64 C3
Onano I 62 B1
Oñati E 32 D1
Oncala E 41 E7
Oncești RO 153 E10
Onchan GBM 10 C3
Onda E 48 E4
Ondara E 56 D5
Ondarroa E 32 D1
Ondřejov CZ 77 C7
Ondres F 32 C3
Oneglia I 37 D8
Onesse-et-Laharie F 32 B3
Onești RO 153 E9
Onet-le-Château F 33 B11
Ongles F 35 B10
Oniceni RO 153 D10
Onich GB 4 B6
Onifai I 64 C4
Oniferi I 64 C3
Onițcani MD 154 C4
Onkamaa FIN 128 D7
Onkamo FIN 115 E6
Onkamo FIN 119 D15
Onkamo FIN 125 F14
Onkiniemi FIN 127 C15
Önnestad S 88 C6
Önningby FIN 99 B14
Ónod H 145 G2
Onøya N 108 D4
Onsala S 91 E11
Onsbjerg DK 86 D7
Ønslev DK 83 A11
Onslunda S 88 D6
Onstmettingen D 27 D10
Onstwedde NL 17 B8
Ontiñena E 42 D4
Ontinyent E 56 D3
Ontojoki FIN 125 B11
Ontronvara RUS 125 E16
Onttola FIN 125 E13
Ontur E 55 B10
Onuškis LT 135 D11
Onuškis LT 137 E10
Onzain F 24 E5
Onzonilla E 39 C8
Oola IRL 8 C6
Ooltgensplaat NL 16 E2
Oonurme EST 131 C13
Oostakker B 19 B8
Oostburg NL 19 B7
Oostende B 18 B6
Oostendorp NL 16 D5
Oosterbeek NL 183 B7
Oosterend NL 16 B3
Oosterhesselen NL 17 C7
Oosterhout NL 16 E3
Oosterland NL 16 E2
Oosterwolde NL 16 C6
Oosterzele B 19 C8
Oostham B 183 C6
Oosthuizen NL 16 C3
Oostkamp B 19 B7
Oostkapelle NL 16 E1
Oostmalle B 182 C5
Oost-Souburg NL 16 F1
Oostvleteren B 18 C6
Oost-Vlieland NL 16 B4
Oostvoorne NL 182 B4
Ootmarsum NL 17 D7
Opaka BG 166 C6
Opalenica PL 81 B10
Opalenie PL 138 C6
Ópályi H 145 H5
Opan BG 166 E5
Opařany CZ 77 D6
Opatija HR 67 B9
Opatov CZ 77 C10
Opatovice nad Labem CZ 77 B9
Opatów PL 142 D5
Opatów PL 142 E6
Opatów PL 143 E11
Opatówek PL 142 C5
Opatowiec PL 143 F10
Opava CZ 146 B5
O Pazo E 38 D3
O Pazo de Irixoa E 38 B3
Ope S 106 E7
O Pedrouzo E 38 C3
Opeinde NL 16 B6
Opfenbach D 71 B9
Opglabbeek B 183 C7
Opheusden NL 183 B7
Opi I 62 D5
Opitter B 183 C7
Oploo NL 183 B7
Oplotnica SLO 148 D4
Opmeer NL 16 C3
Opochka RUS 133 C5
Opočno CZ 77 B10
Opoczno PL 141 H3
Opoeteren B 183 C7
Opole PL 142 E4
Opole Lubelskie PL 141 H5
Oporelu RO 160 D4
Oporets' UA 145 F7
O Porriño E 38 D2
Opoul-Périllos F 34 E4
Opovo SRB 158 C5
Oppach D 81 D7
Oppala S 103 E13
Oppdal N 101 A11
Oppeano I 66 B3
Oppeby S 92 C7
Oppedal N 100 D3
Oppegard N 95 C13
Oppenau D 27 D9
Oppenheim D 21 E10
Oppenweiler D 187 C7
Opphaug N 104 D7
Opphus N 101 D14
Oppido Lucano I 60 B5
Oppido Mamertina I 59 C8
Oppin D 79 C11
Oppinitz A 73 A10
Oppurg D 79 E10
Oprisavci HR 157 B9
Oprișor RO 159 E11
Oprtalj HR 67 B8
Opsa BY 135 E13
Opsaheden S 97 B10
Optași-Măgura RO 160 D5
Ópusztaszer H 150 E5
Opuzen HR 157 F8
Opwijk B 19 C9
Ör H 145 H5
Ora I 72 D3
Øra N 112 C8
Orada P 50 B5
Oradea RO 151 C8
Oradour-sur-Glane F 29 D8
Oradour-sur-Vayres F 29 D7
Orah BIH 157 F7
Orah BIH 162 D5
Orahavičko Polje BIH 157 D8
Orahova BIH 157 B7
Orahov Do BIH 162 D4
Orahovica HR 149 E9
Oraio GR 171 B7
Oraiokastro GR 169 C8
Oraison F 35 C10
Orajärvi FIN 117 E12
Orakylä FIN 115 D1
Orange F 35 B8
Orani I 64 C3
Oranienburg D 84 E4
Órán Mór IRL 6 F5
Oranmore IRL 6 F5
Orašac BIH 156 C5
Orašac HR 162 D5
Orašac SRB 164 C5
Orašje BIH 157 B10
Orăștie RO 151 F11
Orăștioara de Sus RO 151 F11
Orașu Nou RO 145 H7
Öratjärn S 103 C10

Orava EST 132 F1
Orava FIN 123 D10
Oravainen FIN 122 D8
Oravais FIN 122 D8
Oravala FIN 128 D6
Oravan S 107 B14
Oravankylä FIN 123 C15
Oravattnet S 106 E9
Oravi FIN 125 F11
Oravikoski FIN 124 E9
Oravisalo FIN 125 F13
Oravița RO 159 C8
Oravivaara FIN 121 E11
Oravská Polhora SK 147 B8
Oravské Veselé SK 147 C8
Oravský Podzámok SK 147 C8
Orba E 56 D4
Orbacém P 38 E2
Orbäck S 97 C15
Orbaden S 103 C11
Ørbæk DK 86 E7
Orbais-l'Abbaye F 25 C10
Orbara E 32 D1
Orbe CH 31 B10
Orbeasca RO 160 E6
Orbec F 24 B3
Orbeni RO 153 E10
Orbetello I 65 C4
Örbyhus S 99 B9
Orca P 44 D6
Orce E 55 D8
Orcera E 55 C7
Orchamps-Vennes F 26 F6
Orchies F 19 D7
Orchomenos GR 175 C6
Orchów PL 143 C7
Orchowo PL 138 E5
Orciano di Pesaro I 67 E6
Orcières F 36 B4
Orcival F 30 D2
Ordan-Larroque F 33 C6
Ordes E 38 B3
Ordizia E 32 D1
Ordona I 60 A3
Ordzhonikidze UA 154 C6
Orea E 47 C9
O Real E 38 B3
Örebäcken S 102 C4
Orebić HR 157 G7
Örebro S 97 D13
Ořechov CZ 77 D11
Öregcsertő H 150 D3
Öreglak H 149 C9
Øregrund S 99 B10
Orehoved DK 87 F9
Oreini GR 169 B10
Orekhovitsa BG 165 B9
Orellana de la Sierra E 51 A9
Orellana la Vieja E 51 A8
Ören TR 177 C10
Ören TR 181 B7
Orenhofen D 185 E6
Oreoi GR 175 B7
Orés E 32 F3
Oresh BG 166 B4
Oreshak BG 165 D10
Orestiada GR 171 B11
Öreström S 107 C16
Öretjändalen S 103 A10
Oreye B 19 C11
Orezu RO 161 D9
Orford GB 15 C12
Organi GR 171 B9
Organyà E 43 C9
Orgaz E 46 E5
Orgelet F 31 B8
Ørgenvika N 95 B11
Orgères-en-Beauce F 24 D6
Orgita EST 131 D8
Orgiva E 53 C10
Orgon F 35 C9
Orgosolo I 64 C3
Orhaneli TR 173 E10
Orhaniye TR 171 C10
Orhaniye TR 181 C8
Orhanlar TR 173 E8
Orhei MD 154 C3
Oria E 55 E8
Oria I 61 C9
O Rial E 38 D2
Origny-Ste-Benoîte F 19 E7
Orihuela E 56 E3
Orihuela del Tremedal E 47 C9
Orikhivka UA 154 F3
Orikum AL 168 D1
Orimattila FIN 127 D14
Oriniemi FIN 127 C9
Orio E 32 D1
Oriola P 50 C4
Oriolo I 61 C6
Oriolo Romano I 62 C2
Oripää FIN 126 D8
Orismala FIN 122 E8
Orissaare EST 130 D6
Oristà E 43 D8
Oristano I 64 D2
Oristown IRL 7 E9
Őriszentpéter H 149 C6
Oriv UA 145 E8
Oriveden asema FIN 127 B11
Orivesi FIN 127 B11
Orizare BG 167 D9
Orizari MK 164 F5
Orjavik N 104 F2
Ørje N 96 D6
Orkanger N 104 E7
Ørkelljunga S 87 C12
Ørkény H 150 C3
Orla PL 141 E8
Orlamünde D 79 E10
Orlat RO 152 F3
Orlea RO 160 F4
Orléans F 24 E6
Orleşti RO 160 D4
Orlivka UA 155 D2
Orllan RKS 164 D3
Orlová CZ 146 B6
Orlov Dol BG 166 E6
Orlovets BG 166 C5
Orły PL 144 D6
Orlyak BG 161 F10
Orlyane BG 165 C9
Orma GR 169 C6
Ormanli TR 173 B9
Ormaryd S 92 D5
Ormea I 37 C8
Örményes H 150 C6
Örménykút H 150 D6
Ormos GR 176 D4
Ormos Panormou GR 176 D3
Ormos Prinou GR 171 C7
Ormož SLO 148 D6

Ormskirk GB 10 D6
Ormylia GR 169 D10
Ornaisons F 34 D4
Ornans F 26 F5
Ornäs S 97 A14
Örnäsudden S 109 E13
Ornavasso I 68 B5
Ornbau D 75 D8
Ornes N 105 B15
Ørnes N 108 C6
Orneta PL 139 B9
Ørnhøj DK 86 C3
Ornö S 93 A12
Orontowice PL 142 F6
Ornsköldsvik S 107 E15
Orødel RO 159 E11
Orolik HR 157 B11
Orom SRB 150 F4
Oron-la-Ville CH 31 B10
Oronoz E 32 D2
Orońsko PL 141 H3
Oropa I 68 B4
Oropesa E 45 E10
Oropesa del Mar E 48 D5
Ororbia E 32 E2
Orosei I 64 C4
Orosháza H 150 D6
Oroslavje HR 148 E5
Oroszlány H 149 B10
Orpierre F 35 B10
Orreaga E 32 D3
Orrefors S 89 B9
Orrios E 42 F2
Orrmo S 102 C7
Orroli I 64 D3
Orrviken S 106 E9
Orsa S 102 D7
Orsara di Puglia I 60 A4
Orsay F 24 C7
Örsbäck S 107 D17
Orsennes F 29 C9
Örserum S 92 C5
Orsières CH 31 C11
Örsjö S 89 B11
Ørslev DK 87 E9
Ørsnes N 100 A5
Orsogna I 63 C6
Orsomarso I 60 D5
Ørsta N 100 B4
Ørsted DK 86 C6
Örsundsbro S 99 C8
Ortaca TR 181 C9
Ortacesus I 64 D3
Ortakent TR 177 E9
Ortaklar TR 177 D9
Ortaköy TR 173 B9
Ortala S 99 C11
Orta Nova I 60 A5
Orte I 62 C2
Orten N 100 A6
Ortenberg D 21 D12
Ortenburg D 76 E4
Orth an der Donau A 77 F11
Orthez F 32 D4
Ortholmen S 102 B6
Orthouvani GR 168 E5
Ortigosa E 41 D6
Ortigueira E 38 A4
Ørting DK 86 D6
Ortisei I 72 C4
Orțişoara RO 151 F7
Ortnevik N 100 D4
Orton GB 10 C6
Ortona I 63 C6
Ortovera I 37 C8
Ortrand D 80 D5
Örträsk S 107 C15
Ørtueri I 64 C3
Örtülüce TR 173 D7
Ørum DK 86 C5
Ørum DK 86 C7
Orune I 64 C3
Orusco E 47 D6
Orval F 29 B10
Orvalho P 44 D5
Orvault F 23 F8
Orvieto I 62 B2
Orviken S 118 E6
Orvinio I 62 C3
Oryakhovo BG 160 F3
Orzesze PL 142 F6
Orzinuovi I 69 C8
Orzyny PL 139 C11
Orzysz PL 136 F4
Os N 101 B14
Osa N 100 E6
Osa de Vega E 47 E7
Ošani LV 135 D11
Osaonica SRB 163 C9
Osbaldwick GB 11 D9
Os Blancos E 38 D4
Osburg D 186 B3
Øsby DK 86 E5
Osby S 88 C5
Osbyholm S 87 D13
Oščadnica SK 147 C7
Oschatz D 80 D4
Oschersleben (Bode) D 79 B9
Oschiri I 64 B3
Ościsłowo PL 139 E9
Os Dices E 38 C2
Osdorf D 83 B8
Osečina SRB 158 E4
Oseja de Sajambre E 39 B9
Osek CZ 76 B5
Osek CZ 82 B6
Osen N 105 C9
Osen N 108 D6
Osenets BG 166 B6
Ošenieki LV 134 C4
Osera E 41 E10
Oşeşti RO 153 D9
Osetno PL 81 C10
Ósi H 149 B10
Osica de Sus RO 160 E4
Osidda I 64 B3
Osie PL 138 C5
Osięciny PL 138 E6
Osieck PL 141 G4
Osieczna PL 81 C11
Osiecznica PL 81 D8
Osiek PL 138 C5
Osiek PL 139 D7
Osiek PL 143 E12
Osiek PL 147 B8
Osiek Jasielski PL 145 D3
Osiek Mały PL 142 B6
Osiek nad Notecią PL 85 D12

Osielsko PL 138 D5
Osiglia I 37 C8
Osijek HR 149 E11
Osikovitsa BG 165 D9
Osilo I 64 B2
Osimo I 67 F7
Osina PL 85 C8
Osini I 64 D3
Osiny PL 141 H6
Osio Sotto I 69 B8
Osipaonica SRB 159 D7
Osjaków PL 142 D6
Oskar-S 89 B9
Oskar-Fredriksborg S 99 D10
Oskarshamn S 93 E8
Öskarström S 87 B11
Oskava CZ 77 C12
Oskořínek CZ 77 B8
Ošľany SK 146 D6
Oslättfors S 103 E12
Osli H 149 A8
Oslo N 95 C13
Osloß D 79 B8
Osma E 40 C5
Osma FIN 117 D15
Osmancali TR 173 A7
Osmancık TR 173 E11
Osmangazi TR 173 D11
Osmaniye TR 173 E10
Osmaniye TR 173 F10
Osmanlı TR 173 A6
Osmanli TR 173 B7
Os'mino RUS 132 C5
Ösmo S 93 B11
Osmolin PL 141 G1
Osmoloda UA 145 F9
Osnabrück D 17 D10
Osno Lubuskie PL 81 B7
Osny F 24 B7
Osoblaha CZ 142 F4
Osogna CH 69 A6
Osojnik HR 162 D5
Osoppo I 73 D7
Osor E 43 D9
Osor HR 67 C10
Osorhei RO 151 C9
Osorno E 40 D3
Osowa PL 136 E6
Osowa Sień PL 81 C10
Osøyri N 94 B2
Ospitaletto I 69 B9
Oss NL 16 E5
Ossa GR 169 C2
Ossa de Montiel E 55 B7
Ossana I 69 A10
Osséja F 33 F9
Ossendrecht NL 182 C4
Ossès F 32 D3
Ossiach A 73 C8
Oßmannstedt D 79 D9
Ossun F 32 D5
Østa S 98 B7
Ostanå S 88 C6
Ostanfjärden S 119 C10
Östansjö S 92 A5
Östansjö S 109 E16
Östanskär S 103 A13
Östanvik S 103 D9
Oštarije HR 156 B3
Ostaszewo PL 138 B6
Ostavall S 103 A9
Østbevern D 17 D9
Østbirk DK 86 D5
Östbjörka S 103 E9
Østby N 91 A9
Østby N 102 B8
Östby S 107 D13
Osted DK 87 E9
Ostellato I 66 C4
Osten D 17 A12
Ostend B 18 B6
Ostend B 182 C1
Ostenfeld (Husum) D 82 B6
Österås S 107 E12
Øster Assels DK 86 B3
Øster Bjerregrav D 86 C5
Øster Brønderslev DK 86 A5
Osterburg (Altmark) D 83 E11
Osterburken D 27 B11
Østerby D 82 B7
Østerby DK 86 A5
Østerbybruk S 99 B9
Østerbymo S 92 D6
Østerede S 107 E12
Österfärnebo S 98 B7
Osterfeld D 79 D10
Osterforse S 107 E14
Östergarn S 93 E13
Östergraninge S 107 F12
Osterheverr D 82 B5
Osterhofen D 76 E4
Øster Højst DK 86 F4
Øster Hornum DK 86 B5
Osterholz-Scharmbeck D 17 B11
Øster Hurup DK 86 B6
Østerild DK 86 A3
Østerø DK 86 B3
Österjörn S 118 D4
Østerlars DK 89 E7
Øster Lindet DK 86 E4
Österlisa S 99 C11
Ostermarie DK 89 E8
Østermark FIN 126 E8
Ostermiething A 76 F3
Ostermundigen CH 31 B11
Östernoret S 107 C12
Östero FIN 122 D8
Osterode am Harz D 79 C7
Osterrönfeld D 82 B7
Österskucku S 102 A8
Östersund S 106 E8
Östersundom FIN 127 E13
Øster Tørslev DK 86 B6
Øster Ulslev DK 83 A11
Östervåla S 98 B8
Øster Vedsted DK 86 E3
Østervrå DK 90 E7
Osterwieck D 79 C8
Østese N 94 B4
Ostfildern D 187 D7
Östhammar S 99 B10
Ostheim vor der Rhön D 75 B7
Osthofen D 21 E10
Ostia I 62 D2
Ostiano I 66 B1
Ostiglia I 66 B3
Ostiz E 32 E2
Östloning S 103 A13
Östmark S 97 B8
Östmarkum S 107 E14

Ostnor S 102 D7
Ostojićevo SRB 150 F5
Ostoros H 145 H1
Ostra I 67 E7
Ostra RO 153 C7
Östra Åliden S 118 D4
Ostrach D 27 E11
Östra Ed S 93 C9
Östra Frölunda S 91 E13
Östra Granberg S 118 C4
Östra Grevie S 87 E12
Östra Husby S 93 B9
Östra Ljungby S 87 C12
Östra Lovsjön S 97 C13
Östra Ormsjö S 107 C10
Östra Ryd S 93 C8
Östra Skrämträsk S 118 A5
Östra Sönnarslöv S 88 D6
Östra Stugusjö S 103 A9
Ostrau D 80 D4
Östrau D 80 D4
Ostrava CZ 146 B6
Östra Vemmerlöv S 88 D6
Ostravice CZ 146 B6
Östra Yttermark FIN 122 E6
Oštrelj BIH 157 D7
Ostren AL 168 B3
Ostříltín CZ 77 B10
Ostritsa BG 166 B5
Ostróda PL 139 C8
Ostrołęka PL 140 D5
Ostromecko PL 138 D5
Ostroměř CZ 77 B9
Ostroróg PL 81 A10
Ostrov BG 160 F4
Ostrov CZ 76 B3
Ostrov RO 155 D2
Ostrov RO 161 D8
Ostrov RUS 133 B4
Ostroveni RO 160 F3
Ostrovo BG 161 F9
Ostrów PL 143 F12
Ostrówek PL 141 G7
Ostrówek PL 142 D6
Ostrowice PL 85 C9
Ostrowiec PL 85 B11
Ostrowiec Świętokrzyski PL 143 E11
Ostrowite PL 138 F5
Ostrowite PL 139 D7
Ostrów Lubelski PL 141 H7
Ostrów Mazowiecka PL 139 E12
Ostrowo PL 138 E5
Ostrów Wielkopolski PL 142 C4
Ostrowy nad Okszą PL 143 E7
Ostrożac BIH 156 C4
Ostrožac BIH 157 E8
Ostrożeń PL 141 G5
Østrup DK 86 B4
Ostrzeszów PL 142 D4
Ostuni I 61 B9
Ostvik S 118 E6
Ostwald F 186 D4
Osula EST 131 F13
Osuna E 53 B6
Oşupe LV 135 C13
Osvallen S 102 A4
Osvica BIH 157 C8
Ovada I 37 B9
Ovanåker S 103 D10
Ovanmo S 107 D10
Ovar P 44 C3
Ovaro I 73 D6
Ovča SRB 158 D6
Ovcha Mogila BG 166 C4
Ovcharovo BG 166 E6
Ovchepoltsi BG 165 E9
Ove DK 86 B5
Ovelgönne D 17 B10
Överammer S 107 E9
Overäng S 105 D14
Øverås N 100 A8
Overath D 21 C8
Overberg N 111 B18
Overbister GB 3 G11
Overbyn S 103 C12
Överdinkel NL 183 A10
Over Feldborg DK 86 C3
Overflakkee NL 182 B4
Övergård N 111 B18
Øvergård N 111 A18
Överhalla N 105 B11
Ötigheim D 27 C9
Ötisheim D 27 C10
Otišić HR 156 E5
Otívar E 53 C9
Otley GB 11 D8
Otlis S 95 C11
Otmuchów PL 77 B12
Otnes N 101 C14
Otočac HR 156 C3
Otok HR 157 B10
Otok HR 157 E6
Otoka BIH 156 C5
Otopeni RO 161 D8
Otorowo PL 81 A10
O Toural E 38 D2
Otovica MK 164 F4
Otradnoye RUS 129 F14
Otranto I 61 C10
Otricoli I 62 B2
Otrokovice CZ 146 C5
Otta N 101 C11
Ottana I 64 C3
Ottaviano I 60 B2
Ottenby S 89 C10
Ottendorf-Okrilla D 80 D5
Ottenheim D 186 E4
Ottenhöfen im Schwarzwald D 27 C9
Ottenschlag A 77 F8
Ottensheim A 76 F6
Ottenstein D 78 C5
Otterbach D 186 C4
Otterbäcken S 91 B15
Otterberg D 21 E9
Otterburn GB 5 E12
Otter Ferry GB 4 C6
Otterfing D 75 G9
Otterlo NL 16 D5
Otterndorf D 17 A11
Ottersberg D 17 B12
Ottersøy N 105 B10
Otterstad S 91 B13
Ottersweier D 27 C9
Otterswick GB 3 D11
Otterup DK 86 D6

Otterwisch D 79 D12
Öttevény H 149 A9
Öttignies B 19 C10
Ottmarsheim F 27 E8
Ottobeuren D 71 B10
Ottobrunn D 75 F10
Öttömös H 150 E4
Ottone I 37 B10
Ottrau D 21 C12
Ottsjö S 105 E14
Ottsjön S 106 D7
Ottweiler D 21 F8
Otwock PL 141 F4
Otxandio E 41 B6
Otyń PL 81 C9
Otzing D 76 E3
Ouanne F 25 E9
Ouarville F 24 D6
Ouca P 44 C3
Oucques F 24 E5
Oud-Beijerland NL 16 E2
Ouddorp NL 182 B3
Oudehaske NL 16 C5
Oudemirdum NL 16 C5
Oudenaarde B 19 C8
Oudenbosch NL 16 E3
Oudenburg B 18 B7
Oudeschild NL 16 B3
Oude-Tonge NL 16 E2
Oudewater NL 182 A5
Oud-Gastel NL 16 E2
Oudon F 23 F9
Oud-Turnhout B 16 F3
Oud-Vossemeer NL 16 E2
Oudzele B 182 C2
Oued Laou MA 53 F6
Ouffet B 19 D11
Oughterard IRL 6 F4
Ougney F 26 F4
Ouguela P 45 F6
Ouistreham F 23 B11
Oulainen FIN 119 F13
Oulanka FIN 115 F5
Oulchy-le-Château F 25 B9
Oulder B 20 D6
Oullins F 30 D6
Oulton GB 15 C12
Oulu FIN 119 D14
Oulunsalo FIN 119 E14
Oulx I 31 E10
Oundle GB 15 C8
Oupeye B 19 C11
Ouranoupoli GR 170 D5
Oure DK 87 E7
Ourém P 44 E3
Ourense E 38 D4
Ourique P 50 D3
Ourol E 38 A4
Ouroux-en-Morvan F 25 F10
Ouroux-sur-Saône F 31 B6
Ourville-en-Caux F 18 E2
Oust F 33 E8
Outakoski FIN 113 D16
Outarville F 24 D7
Outeiro P 38 E2
Outeiro P 39 E6
Outeiro de Rei E 38 B4
Outeiro Seco P 38 E5
Outokumpu FIN 125 E12
Outomuro E 38 D4
Outreau F 15 F12
Outwell GB 11 F12
Ouveillan F 34 D4
Ouzouer-le-Marché F 24 E6
Ouzouer-sur-Loire F 25 E7
Ovesp S 107 C15
Pää-aho FIN 121 D10
Pääjärvi FIN 123 E13
Paakinmäki FIN 121 F11
Paakkila FIN 125 E11
Paakkola FIN 119 C13
Paal B 183 C6
Paalasmaa FIN 125 D12
Paaso FIN 127 C15
Paasvere EST 131 C13
Paatela FIN 129 B9
Paattinen FIN 126 D7
Paatus FIN 113 D17
Paavola FIN 119 E14
Pabaiskas LT 135 F9
Paberžė LT 137 D11
Pabianice PL 143 C8
Pabillonis I 64 D2
Pabiržė LT 135 D9
Pabneukirchen A 77 F7
Pabradė LT 137 D12
Pabu F 22 C5
Pacanów PL 143 F11
Paceco I 58 D2
Pacheia Ammos GR 179 E10
Pachino I 59 F7
Pachni GR 171 B7
Paciano I 62 A2
Pácin H 145 G4
Pačir SRB 150 F3
Pack A 73 C10
Paços de Ferreira P 38 F3
Pacov CZ 77 D8
Pacsa H 149 C8
Păcureți RO 161 C8
Pacy-sur-Eure F 24 B5
Paczków PL 77 B12
Padasjoki FIN 127 C13
Padborg DK 82 A6
Padbury GB 14 D7
Padej SRB 150 F5
Padene HR 156 D5
Paderborn D 17 E11
Padern F 34 E4
Paderne P 50 E3
Paderne de Allariz E 38 D4
Padeş RO 159 C10
Padew Narodowa PL 143 F11
Padežine BIH 157 F8
Padiham GB 11 D7
Pădina RO 159 E11
Padina RO 161 D10
Padina SRB 159 C6
Padinska Skela SRB 158 D5
Padiraç F 29 F9
Padise EST 131 C8
Padoby BY 133 F2
Padoux F 26 D6
Padova I 66 B3
Padria I 64 C2
Padrón E 38 C2
Padru I 64 B4
Padstow GB 12 D5
Padsvillye BY 133 F3
Paduł E 53 B9
Padula I 60 C5
Padure LV 134 C3
Pădureni RO 153 D12
Paesana I 37 B6
Paese I 72 E5
Pag HR 67 D11
Pagani I 60 B3

Paganica I 62 C4
Paganico I 65 B4
Pagégiai LT 134 F3
Pagiriai LT 135 E9
Pagiriai LT 137 D11
Paglieta I 63 C6
Pagny-sur-Moselle F 26 C5
Pagondas GR 177 D8
Pagouria GR 171 B8
Pagramantis LT 134 F4
Paharova S 116 E8
Páhi H 150 D3
Pahkakoski FIN 119 D16
Pahkakumpu FIN 115 E3
Pahkakumpu FIN 121 C12
Pahkala FIN 119 F11
Pahkamäki FIN 123 D16
Pähl D 72 A3
Pahlen D 82 B6
Pahranichny BY 140 D9
Pahtaoja FIN 119 C14
Paião P 44 D3
Paide EST 131 D11
Paignton GB 13 E7
Paihola FIN 125 E13
Päijälä FIN 127 B12
Paikuse EST 131 E9
Pailhès F 33 D8
Paillet F 32 A4
Paimbœuf F 23 F7
Paimela FIN 127 C14
Paimio FIN 126 E8
Paimpol F 22 C5
Paimpont F 23 D7
Painswick GB 13 B10
Painten D 75 E10
Paipis FIN 127 E13
Paisley GB 5 D8
Paistu EST 131 E11
Paisua FIN 124 C9
Päivajoki FIN 115 F3
Päiväjoki FIN 119 E13
Pajala S 117 D10
Pajares de la Lampreana E 39 E8
Pajarón E 47 E9
Pajęczno PL 143 D6
Pajukoski FIN 125 C11
Pajukoste FIN 113 C20
Pajūris LT 134 F4
Pajuskylä FIN 124 D7
Pajuvaara FIN 121 D14
Påka H 149 C7
Pakaa FIN 127 D14
Pakalné LT 134 F2
Pakalniai LT 135 F10
Pakapė LT 134 E6
Pakarila FIN 123 E17
Pakila FIN 127 E13
Pakisjärvi FIN 117 C12
Pakkala FIN 127 C11
Pakod H 149 C8
Pakość PL 138 E5
Pakosław PL 81 C12
Pakoštane HR 156 E4
Pákozd H 149 B11
Pakrac HR 149 F8
Pakruojis LT 134 E7
Paks H 149 C11
Paksuniemi S 116 C5
Pala S 107 D15
Pala EST 131 D12
Palacios del Sil E 39 C7
Palacios de Sanabria E 39 D6
Palaciosrubios E 45 B10
Palade EST 130 D5
Palafrugell E 43 D10
Palagianello I 61 B7
Palagiano I 61 B7
Palagonía I 59 E6
Palaia I 66 E2
Palaia Fokaia GR 175 D8
Palaikastro GR 179 E11
Palaiochora GR 169 C9
Palaiochora GR 178 E6
Palaiochori GR 169 D10
Palaiochori GR 175 C7
Palaiokastritsa GR 168 E2
Palaiokastro GR 177 D9
Palaiokipos GR 177 A7
Palaiokomi GR 170 C6
Palaiomonastiro GR 169 F6
Palaiopoli GR 176 D4
Palaiopyrgos GR 169 E6
Palaiopyrgos GR 169 E8
Palaiopyrgos GR 174 C4
Palaiovracha GR 174 B5
Palairos GR 174 B2
Palaiseau F 25 C7
Palamas GR 169 F7
Palamós E 43 D10
Palamuse EST 131 D13
Palanca RO 153 D8
Palanga LT 134 E2
Pålänge S 119 C9
Palanzano I 66 D1
Palárikovo SK 146 E6
Palas de Rei E 38 C4
Palata RO 152 D4
Palata I 63 D7
Palau I 64 A3
Palavas-les-Flots F 35 C6
Palazzo Adriano I 58 D3
Palazzolo Acreide I 59 E6
Palazzolo sull'Oglio I 69 B8
Palazzo San Gervasio I 60 B6
Pale BIH 157 E10
Pâle LV 131 F9
Paleičiai LT 134 F4
Palena I 63 D6
Palencia E 40 D3
Palenciana E 53 B7
Palenzuela E 40 D3
Palermo AL 168 D2
Palermo I 58 C3
Palešnica PL 144 D2
Palestrina I 62 D3
Palēvenēlė LT 135 E10
Palež BIH 158 E3
Palhaça P 44 C3
Pálháza H 145 G4
Palia Kavala GR 171 C6
Paliano I 62 D4
Palić SRB 150 E4
Palinges F 30 B5
Palinuro I 60 C4
Paliouri GR 169 E10
Paliouria GR 169 E6
Palis F 25 D10
Paliseul B 19 E11
Palivere EST 131 D7
Palizzi I 59 D9
Paljakka FIN 121 B14
Paljakka FIN 121 E11

Pälkäne FIN 127 C11
Pälkem S 118 B7
Palkino RUS 132 F3
Palkisoja FIN 115 A2
Palkovice CZ 146 B6
Palladio GR 171 B8
Pallagorio I 61 E7
Pallarés E 51 C7
Pallas Green New IRL 8 C6
Pallas Green IRL 8 C6
Pälli FIN 119 E16
Palling D 75 F12
Palluau F 28 B2
Palluau-sur-Indre F 29 B8
Palma P 50 C2
Palma Campania I 60 B3
Palma del Río E 51 D9
Palma de Mallorca E 49 E10
Palma di Montechiaro I 58 E4
Palmadula I 64 B1
Palmanova E 49 E10
Palmanova I 73 E7
Palmaz F 44 C4
Palmeira P 38 E3
Palmela P 50 B2
Palmi I 59 C8
Pálmonostora H 150 D4
Palmse EST 131 B11
Palnackie GB 5 F9
Palneca F 37 H10
Palo del Colle I 61 A7
Palohuornas S 116 E6
Palojärvi FIN 115 E2
Palojärvi FIN 117 A10
Palojärvi FIN 117 D13
Palojoensuu FIN 116 B10
Palokki FIN 125 E11
Palomaa FIN 113 E19
Palomäki FIN 125 D11
Palomar de Arroyos E 42 F2
Palomares del Río E 51 E7
Palomas E 51 B7
Palombara Sabina I 62 C3
Palombaro I 63 C6
Palomene LT 137 D9
Palomera E 47 D8
Palomeras del Campo E 47 E7
Palomonte I 60 B4
Palonoja FIN 115 F4
Palonselkä FIN 117 D13
Palonurmi FIN 125 D10
Paloperä FIN 115 F4
Palos de la Frontera E 51 E6
Palosenjärvi FIN 124 C8
Palotabozsok H 149 D11
Palotáshalom H 150 B4
Palovaara FIN 119 B12
Palovaara FIN 119 B16
Palovaara FIN 121 E13
Palovaara FIN 125 E14
Pals E 43 D10
Pålsboda S 92 A6
Palsmane LV 135 B12
Palsselkä FIN 117 D16
Pålsträsk S 118 C6
Paltamo FIN 121 F10
Paltanen FIN 124 F7
Paltaniemi FIN 121 F10
Paltin RO 153 F9
Păltiniş RO 153 A9
Păltiniş RO 159 C9
Păltinoasa RO 153 B7
Paludi I 61 D7
Paluel F 18 E2
Paluknys LT 137 E10
Paluzza I 73 C7
Palyatskishki BY 137 E11
Palyessye BY 135 F12
Palzem D 20 E6
Pambukovica SRB 158 E4
Pameče SLO 73 C11
Pamfylla GR 177 A8
Pamhagen A 149 A7
Pamiers F 33 D9
Pampāļi LV 134 C4
Pamparato I 37 C7
Pampelonne F 33 B10
Pampilhosa P 44 D4
Pampilhosa da Serra P 44 D5
Pampliega E 40 D4
Pamplona E 32 E2
Pampow D 83 C10
Pamproux F 28 C5
Pamukçu TR 173 E8
Panaci RO 152 C6
Panagia GR 171 C7
Panagia GR 171 E8
Panagia GR 178 E8
Panagyurishte BG 165 D9
Panagyurski Kolonii BG 165 D9
Panahor AL 168 C1
Panaitolio GR 174 B3
Panaja AL 168 C1
Pănăşeşti MD 154 C3
Panassac F 33 D7
Pănătău RO 161 C8
Panazol F 29 D8
Pancalieri I 37 B7
Pancar TR 177 C9
Pancarköy TR 173 B7
Păncești RO 153 E10
Pančevo SRB 158 D6
Pancharevo BG 165 D7
Panciu RO 153 F10
Pancorbo E 40 C5
Pâncota RO 151 E8
Pancrudo E 42 F1
Pánd H 150 C4
Pandélys LT 135 D10
Pandino I 69 C8
Pandrup DK 86 A5
Pandy GB 13 B9
Panelia FIN 126 C6
Panemunė LT 136 C4
Panemunėlis LT 135 D12
Panes E 39 B10
Pănet RO 152 D4
Panevėžys LT 135 E8
Panga EST 130 D4
Pange F 186 C1
Panicale I 62 A2
Panichkovo BG 166 F4
Panissières F 30 D5
Paniza E 41 F9
Panjas F 32 C5
Panjevac SRB 159 E8
Panjik BIH 157 C9
Pankakoski FIN 125 D14
Pankajärvi FIN 125 D13
Panker D 83 B9

Panki PL 142 E6
Pannarano I 60 A3
Pannes F 25 D8
Panni I 60 A4
Panningen NL 16 F5
Pannonhalma H 149 A9
Panóias P 50 D3
Panorama GR 169 C9
Panormos GR 178 E3
Pansarau D 75 D10
Panschwitz-Kuckau D 80 D6
Pantanassa GR 178 B4
Pántáne FIN 122 F8
Panteinsee D 84 C6
Pantelimon I 55 D2
Pantelimon RO 161 E10
Panticeu RO 152 C3
Pántoa E 46 D5
Pantoja E 46 D5
Panttikylä FIN 122 F8
Panttila FIN 122 E8
Pant-y-dwr GB 13 A8
Paola I 60 E6
Pap H 145 G5
Pápa H 149 B8
Papadianika GR 178 B4
Papasidero I 60 D5
Pápateszér H 149 B9
Papenburg D 17 B8
Papendorf D 83 B12
Papendrecht NL 16 E3
Papile LT 134 D5
Papilys LT 135 D10
Papín SK 145 E5
Papkeszi H 149 B10
Paplaka LV 134 D2
Papowo Biskupie PL 138 D6
Pappades GR 175 B8
Pappados GR 177 A8
Pappenheim D 75 E8
Paprado SK 146 C6
Paprotnia PL 141 F6
Par GB 12 E5
Parabita I 61 C10
Parača SRB 159 F7
Paracuellos E 47 E9
Paracuellos de Jarama E 46 C5
Parád H 147 F10
Parada P 45 C6
Parada de Ester P 44 C4
Parada de Pinhão P 38 F4
Parada de Rubiales E 45 B10
Parada de Sil E 38 D4
Paradas E 51 E9
Paradeisi GR 181 D8
Paradeisia GR 174 E5
Paradeisos GR 171 B7
Paradela E 38 C5
Paradela P 38 E4
Paradela P 44 B5
Paradyż PL 141 H2
Parainen FIN 126 E7
Parakalamos GR 168 E4
Parakka S 116 D7
Parakoila GR 177 A7
Paralepa EST 130 D7
Paralia GR 174 C4
Paralia GR 175 F6
Paralia Avdiron GR 171 C7
Paralia Saranti GR 175 C6
Paralia Tyrou GR 175 E6
Paralio Astros GR 175 E6
Paramé F 23 C8
Parâmio P 39 E6
Páramo del Sil E 39 C7
Paramythia GR 168 F4
Paranesti GR 171 B6
Paranhos P 44 B5
Parantala FIN 123 E15
Parapotamos GR 168 E3
Paras N 111 B19
Părău RO 152 F6
Parava RO 153 E9
Paravola RO 153 E9
Paray-le-Monial F 30 C5
Parcani MD 154 B3
Parcent E 56 D4
Parcé-sur-Sarthe F 23 E11
Parchen D 79 B11
Parchim D 83 D11
Parchovany SK 145 F4
Parchów PL 81 D9
Parchowo PL 85 B13
Parciaki PL 139 D11
Parczew PL 141 G7
Pardais P 50 B5
Pardies F 32 D4
Pardilhó P 44 C3
Pardoşi RO 161 C8
Pardubice CZ 77 B9
Parechcha BY 137 F9
Paredes de Coura P 38 E2
Paredes de Nava E 39 D10
Pareja E 47 C7
Parempuyre F 28 E4
Parenti I 61 E6
Parentis-en-Born F 32 B3
Parets del Vallès E 43 D8
Parey D 79 B10
Parga GR 168 F3
Pargas FIN 126 E7
Parghelia I 59 B8
Pargny-sur-Saulx F 25 C12
Pargolovo RUS 129 E13
Parhalahti FIN 119 F12
Päri EST 131 E11
Parigné-l'Évêque F 24 E3
Parikkala FIN 129 B12
Parincea RO 153 E10
Paris F 25 C7
Parisot F 33 B9
Parisot F 33 C9
Parissavaara FIN 125 E16
Pärjänsuo FIN 120 C9
Pärjol RO 153 D9
Park GB 4 F2
Parkajoki S 117 C10
Parkalompolo S 116 C9
Parkano FIN 123 F10
Parkkila FIN 121 C14
Parkkila FIN 123 C14
Parkkila FIN 123 C15
Parkkima FIN 123 C15
Parkkuu FIN 127 B10
Parksepa EST 131 F13
Parla E 46 D5
Parława F 46 D5
Parma I 66 C1
Parndorf A 77 G11
Pärnu EST 131 E8

Pärnu-Jaagupi EST 131 D9
Paroikia GR 176 E5
Parola FIN 127 C11
Paron F 25 D9
Parowa PL 81 D8
Parrillas E 45 D10
Parsau D 79 B8
Parsberg D 75 D10
Pârscov RO 161 C9
Pârscoveni RO 160 E4
Parsçicko PL 85 C11
Partaloa E 55 E8
Parteboda S 103 A10
Partenen A 71 D10
Pârteştii de Jos RO 153 B7
Parthenay F 28 B5
Partheni GR 177 E8
Partinello F 37 G9
Partinico I 58 C3
Partizani BG 167 C8
Partizani SRB 158 D5
Partizánska Ľupča SK 147 C8
Partizánske SK 146 D6
Partney GB 11 E12
Parton GB 10 B4
Partry IRL 6 E4
Partsi EST 131 E14
Parudaminys LT 137 D11
Pårup DK 86 C4
Parva RO 152 C5
Parviainen S 119 C11
Pâryd S 89 B9
Parysów PL 141 G5
Parzjczew PL 143 C7
Pasai Donibane E 32 D2
Pasaköy TR 171 E10
Paşaköy TR 173 E8
Paşaköy TR 177 B10
Pasalankylä FIN 125 D10
Paşayiğit TR 172 C5
Paşcani RO 153 C9
Pasching A 76 F6
Paseka CZ 77 C12
Pas-en-Artois F 18 D5
Pasewalk D 84 C6
Pasi FIN 128 D7
Pasiano di Prato I 73 D7
Pasieki PL 139 C10
Pasiene LV 133 D4
Pasikovci HR 149 F9
Páskallavik S 89 A10
Pasłęk PL 139 B8
Pasmajärvi FIN 117 D12
Pašman HR 156 E3
Passage East IRL 9 D9
Passail A 148 B5
Passais F 23 C10
Passau D 76 E4
Passignano sul Trasimeno I 66 F5
Passow D 84 D6
Passy F 31 D10
Pastavy BY 135 F11
Pastende LV 134 B5
Pasto FIN 123 E10
Pastoriza E 38 B5
Pastrana E 47 D7
Pastriveni RO 153 C9
Pašuliene LV 135 E12
Pasvalys LT 135 D8
Pašvitinys LT 134 D7
Pasym PL 139 C10
Pasytsely UA 154 A5
Paszab H 145 G4
Paszowice PL 81 D10
Pásztó H 147 F9
Pasztowa Wola PL 141 H4
Pata SK 146 E5
Pataias P 44 E3
Patak H 147 E8
Patana FIN 123 D10
Pătârlagele RO 161 C8
Patay F 24 D6
Patchway GB 13 B9
Pateley Bridge GB 11 C8
Patensöre FIN 122 C9
Patergassen A 73 C8
Paterna E 48 E4
Paterna del Campo E 51 E7
Paterna del Madera E 55 B8
Paterna del Río E 55 E7
Paternión A 73 C8
Paternò I 59 D6
Paterno I 60 C5
Paternopoli I 60 B4
Patersdorf D 76 D3
Pătêurud S 96 C7
Patiška Reka MK 164 F3
Pátka H 149 B11
Patmos GR 177 E8
Patna GB 4 E7
Pątnów PL 142 D6
Păuca RO 152 E3
Paudorf A 77 F9
Pauilhac F 33 B7
Pauillac F 28 E4
Paukarlahti FIN 124 E9
Paukkaja FIN 125 E14
Paukkeri FIN 120 F9
Paul F 44 D5
Paularo I 73 C7

Păuleni-Ciuc RO 153 E7
Păuleşti MD 154 C2
Păuleşti RO 151 B10
Paulhac-en-Margeride F 30 F3
Paulhan F 34 C5
Paulilatino I 64 C2
Paulinenaue D 83 E13
Pauliş RO 151 E8
Paulström S 92 E7
Paüls E 42 F4
Paulx F 28 B2
Păuneşti RO 153 E10
Pausa D 79 E11
Păuşeşti RO 160 C4
Păuşeşti-Măglaşi RO 160 C4
Pautrăsk S 107 B13
Pauvres F 19 F10
Pavel BG 166 C5
Pavel Banya BG 166 D4
Pavia I 69 C7
Pavia P 50 B3
Pavia di Udine I 73 E7
Pavías E 48 E4
Pavie F 33 C7
Pavilly F 18 E3
Păvilosta LV 134 C2
Pavlikeni BG 166 C5
Pavliani GR 174 B5
Pavlikeni BG 166 C5
Pavliš SRB 159 C7
Pavlos GR 175 B7
Pavlovac HR 149 E8
Pavlovce nad Uhom SK 145 F5
Pavullo nel Frignano I 66 D2
Payerne CH 31 B10
Paymogo E 51 D5
Payrac F 29 F9
Payrin-Augmontel F 33 C10
Payzac F 29 E8
Pazardzhik BG 165 E9
Pazarič BIH 157 E9
Pazarköy TR 173 E7
Pazin HR 67 B8
Paziols F 34 E4
Pázmánd H 149 B11
Pazos E 38 D2
Pchelarovo BG 166 F4
Pchelin BG 165 E8
Pčinja MK 164 E4
Peacehaven GB 15 F8
Peal de Becerro E 55 D6
Péaule F 23 E7
Pébrac F 30 E4
Peccia CH 71 E7
Peccioli I 66 E2
Pécel H 150 C3
Pecenega RO 155 C2
Pechea RO 155 B1
Pechenga RUS 114 D10
Pechina S 55 F8
Pechory RUS 132 F2
Peci BIH 156 D5
Pecica RO 151 E7
Pečigrad BIH 156 B4
Pečinci SRB 158 D4
Pecineaga RO 155 F2
Peciu Nou RO 159 B7
Pecka CZ 77 B9
Pecka SRB 158 E4
Pečky CZ 77 B8
Pjctaw PL 81 C10
Pecq B 19 C7
Pécs H 149 D10
Pécsvárad H 149 D10
Pjczniew PL 142 C6
Pedaso I 62 A5
Pededze LV 133 B2
Pederobba I 72 E4
Pedersker DK 89 E7
Pedersöre FIN 122 C9
Pedino GR 169 C5
Pedrafita do Cebreiro E 38 C5
Pedrajas de San Esteban E 40 F2
Pedralba E 48 E3
Pedralba de la Pradería E 39 D6
Pedraza de Campos E 39 E10
Pedrera E 53 B7
Pedro Abad E 53 A8
Pedro Bernardo E 46 D3
Pedroche E 54 C3
Pedrógão P 44 E3
Pedrógão P 45 D6
Pedrógão P 50 C4
Pedrógão Grande P 44 E4
Pedrógão Pequeno P 44 E4
Pedro-Martínez E 55 D6
Pedro Muñoz E 47 F7
Pedrosa E 40 B4
Pedrosa del Príncipe E 40 D3
Pedrosillo de los Aires E 45 C9
Pedroso E 41 D6
Pedroso P 44 B3
Pedrouzos E 38 C2
Peebles GB 5 D10
Peel GBM 10 C2
Peenemünde D 84 B5
Peer B 19 B11
Peera FIN 112 F7
Peetri EST 131 D11
Pefki GR 175 A7
Pefkofyto GR 168 D4
Pefkoi GR 179 E10
Pefkos GR 178 E9
Pega P 45 D6
Pegalajar E 53 A9
Pegau D 79 D11
Peggau A 148 B4
Pegli I 37 C9
Pegnitz D 75 C9
Pego E 56 D4
Pego P 44 F4
Pegões P 50 B2
Pigów PL 81 D11
Peguera E 49 E9
Pehčevo MK 165 F6
Pehkolanlahti FIN 120 F9
Pehlivanköy TR 173 B6

Peine D 79 B7
Peio I 71 D11
Peipin F 35 B10
Peipohja FIN 126 C7
Peira-Cava F 37 D6
Peirais GR 175 D8
Peißen D 79 C10
Peißen D 79 C11
Peißenberg D 72 A3
Peiting D 71 B11
Peitz D 80 C6
Pejë RKS 163 D9
Pepeni MD 154 B2
Pepingen B 19 C9
Pepinster B 19 C12
Peplos GR 171 C10
Pjpowo PL 81 C12
Pëqin AL 168 B2
Peque E 39 D7
Pêra P 50 E3
Perabroddzye BY 133 E2
Perachora GR 175 C6
Perafita E 43 C10
Perä-Hyyppä FIN 122 F8
Peraia GR 169 C6
Peraia GR 169 D8
Perais P 44 E5
Perälä FIN 122 F7
Peralada E 43 C10
Peraleda de la Mata E 45 E10
Peraleda del Zaucejo E 51 C8
Peralejos E 42 G1
Peralejos de las Truchas E 47 C9
Perales del Alfambra E 42 F2
Perales del Puerto E 45 D7
Peralta E 32 F2
Peralta de Alcofea E 42 D3
Peralta de la Sal E 42 D4
Peraltilla E 42 C3
Peralva P 50 E4
Peralveche E 47 C8
Perama GR 168 E4
Perama GR 175 D8
Perama GR 178 E8
Perämäki FIN 122 D9
Peramola E 42 D6
Peranka FIN 121 D13
Peränne FIN 123 F11
Perä-Posio FIN 121 B10
Perarolo di Cadore I 72 D5
Peräseinäjoki FIN 123 E10
Perast MNE 163 E6
Perävaara FIN 115 C2
Perbál H 149 A11
Perchtoldsdorf A 77 F10
Percy F 23 C9
Perdasdefogu I 64 D3
Perdaxius I 64 E2
Perdifumo I 60 C4
Perdiguera E 41 D10
Perdika GR 168 F3
Perdika GR 175 D7
Perdika GR 175 D7
Perdikkas GR 169 C6
Perduhovo Selo BIH 157 D6
Perechyn UA 145 F5
Peredo P 39 F6
Peregu Mare RO 151 E6
Perehins'ke UA 145 F9
Pereiras P 50 E3
Pereiro E 38 A4
Pereiro P 50 E4
Pereiro de Aguiar E 38 D4
Perekhrestove UA 154 C5
Pererîta MD 153 A9
Pereruela E 39 F8
Peresecina MD 154 C3
Peressaare EST 131 C13
Peretu RO 160 E6
Pereyma UA 154 A5
Perfugas I 64 B2
Perg A 77 F7
Pergine Valdarno I 66 F4
Pergine Valsugana I 69 A11
Pergola I 67 E6
Perho FIN 123 D12
Periam RO 151 E6
Periana E 53 C8
Pericei RO 151 C10
Périers F 23 C9
Perieţi RO 160 E5
Perieţi RO 161 D10
Périgueux F 29 E7
Perikleia GR 169 B7
Perila EST 131 C10
Perilla de Castro E 39 E8
Perín-Chym SK 145 F3
Periprava RO 155 C5
Periş RO 161 D7
Perişani RO 160 C4
Perişor RO 160 E2
Perişoru RO 161 E11
Perissa GR 179 C9
Peristasi GR 169 D8
Peristera GR 169 C10
Peristeri GR 175 C8
Perithori GR 169 B10
Perivoli GR 168 F3
Perivoli GR 168 F3
Perivoli GR 174 A5
Perivoli GR 174 B5
Perivolia GR 178 E7
Perjasica HR 156 B3
Perkáta H 149 B11
Perkiömäki FIN 123 D9
Perl D 20 F6
Perlat AL 163 F8
Perleberg D 83 D11
Perlejevo PL 141 E7
Perlez SRB 158 C5
Perloja LT 137 E9
Perły PL 136 E5
Permani HR 67 B9
Permatokoski FIN 117 F16
Pärmet AL 168 D3
Pernå FIN 127 E15
Pernarava LT 134 F7
Pernegg an der Mur A 148 B4
Pernersdorf A 77 E10
Pernes F 44 F3
Pernes-les-Fontaines F 35 C9
Perni GR 171 B7
Pernik BG 165 D7
Perniö FIN 127 E9
Perniön asema FIN 127 E9
Pernitz A 77 G9
Perný FIN 121 B10
Pero I 69 B7
Peroguarda P 50 C3
Pérols F 35 C6
Pero Viseu P 44 D6
Péronnas F 31 C7

Péronne F 18 E6
Perosa Argentina I 31 F11
Pero Viseu P 44 D6
Perpignan F 34 E4
Perranporth GB 12 E4
Perrecy-les-Forges F 30 B5
Perreux F 30 C5
Perrigny F 31 B8
Perrogney-les-Fontaines F 26 E3
Perros-Guirec F 22 C5
Perrum-Åbmir FIN 113 E19
Persan F 25 B7
Persåsen S 102 A7
Persberg S 97 C11
Persbo S 97 B13
Persenbeug A 77 F8
Pershagen S 93 A11
Pershamawskaya BY 133 E4
Pershore GB 13 A10
Pershotravneve UA 155 C4
Pershyttan S 97 D13
Persnäs S 89 A11
Persön S 118 C8
Perstorp S 87 C12
Perth GB 5 C10
Perthes F 25 D8
Pertouli GR 168 E5
Perttaus FIN 117 D15
Pertteli FIN 127 E9
Perttula FIN 127 E12
Pertuis F 35 C10
Pertunmaa FIN 127 C15
Pertusa E 42 C3
Peruc CZ 76 B5
Perućac SRB 158 F3
Perugia I 66 F5
Perukka FIN 119 F17
Perunkajärvi FIN 117 E15
Perushtitsa BG 165 E10
Perušić HR 156 C3
Péruwelz B 19 C8
Pervalka LT 134 F2
Pervenchères F 24 D3
Pervomaisc MD 154 D5
Pervomayskoye RUS 129 E12
Perwez B 19 C10
Pesadas de Burgos E 40 C4
Pesaro I 67 E6
Pescaglia I 66 E1
Pescantina I 66 B2
Pescara I 63 C6
Pescasseroli I 62 D5
Pesceana RO 160 D4
Peschadoires F 30 D3
Peschici I 63 D10
Peschiera del Garda I 66 B2
Peschina I 62 C5
Pescocostanzo I 62 D6
Pescolanciano I 63 D6
Pescopennataro I 62 C4
Pescosolido I 62 D6
Pesco Sannita I 60 A3
Peseux CH 31 B10
Peshkopi AL 163 F9
Peshtera BG 165 E9
Pesiökylä FIN 121 E12
Pesiönranta FIN 121 E12
Pesmes F 26 F4
Pesnica SLO 148 C5
Pesochnyy RUS 129 E13
Peso da Régua P 44 B5
Pesquera de Duero E 40 E3
Pessac F 28 F4
Pessalompolo FIN 117 F12
Pessan F 33 C7
Pesse NL 17 C6
Pessin D 80 A1
Peştani MK 168 B4
Peştera RO 155 E2
Peştişani RO 159 C11
Peştişu Mic RO 151 F10
Pesués E 40 B3
Pešurići BIH 157 E11
Petacciato I 63 C7
Petäikkö FIN 119 C17
Petäikylä FIN 125 C12
Petäjajärvi FIN 119 C17
Petäjäkangas FIN 119 D17
Petäjäskoski FIN 119 B14
Petäjäskoski FIN 119 F13
Petäjävesi FIN 123 F14
Petalax FIN 122 E6
Petalidi GR 174 F4
Pétange L 20 F5
Petas GR 174 A3
Petelea RO 152 D5
Peteranec HR 149 D7
Peterborough GB 11 F11
Peterculter GB 3 L12
Peterhead GB 3 K13
Péteri H 150 C3
Peterlee GB 5 F14
Petersberg D 74 A6
Petersdorf D 75 E9
Petersdorf auf Fehmarn D 83 B10
Petersfield GB 15 E7
Petershagen D 17 D11
Petershagen D 80 B6
Peterswell IRL 6 F5
Pétervására H 147 E10
Pethelinos GR 169 C10
Petilia Policastro I 59 A10
Petín E 38 D5
Petisträsk S 107 B17
Petite-Rosselle F 186 C2
Petit-Mars F 23 F9
Petitmont F 186 D2
Petit-Noir F 31 B7
Petko Karavelovo BG 166 C5
Petko Slaveykov BG 165 C10
Petkula FIN 115 C1
Petkus D 80 C4
Petlovača SRB 158 D3
Petneháza H 145 G5
Petöfibánya H 150 B4
Petra GR 171 A8
Petra GR 171 F10
Petrăchioaia RO 161 D8
Petrades GR 172 B6
Petralia-Soprana I 58 D5
Petran AL 168 D3
Petrana GR 169 D6
Petrella Salto I 62 C4
Petrella Tifernina I 63 D7
Petrer E 56 D3
Petreşti RO 151 B9
Petreşti RO 160 D6
Petreştii de Jos RO 152 D3

Petreto-Bicchisano F 37 H9
Petriano I 67 E6
Petricani RO 153 C8
Petrich BG 169 B9
Petrijevci HR 149 E11
Petrila RO 152 B3
Petriş RO 151 E9
Petritoli I 62 A5
Petrivka UA 154 D4
Petrivs'k UA 154 E3
Petrochori GR 174 B4
Petrodvorets RUS 129 F12
Pétrola E 55 B9
Petromäki FIN 125 E9
Petronà I 59 A10
Petroşani RO 160 C2
Petrota GR 166 F6
Petrov CZ 146 B6
Petrova RO 152 B4
Petrovac MNE 163 E6
Petrovac SRB 159 E7
Petrovany SK 145 F3
Petrovaradin SRB 158 C4
Petrovec MK 164 F4
Petrovice CZ 76 C6
Petrovice u Karvine CZ 147 B7
Petrovići BIH 157 D10
Petrovići MNE 162 D6
Petrovo BG 169 B9
Petrovo Selo SRB 159 D9
Petruma FIN 125 F11
Petru Rareş RO 152 C4
Petruşeni MD 153 B10
Petřvald CZ 146 B6
Petřvald CZ 146 B6
Petsakoi GR 174 C5
Petsmo FIN 122 D7
Petten NL 16 C3
Pettigo GB 7 C7
Pettineo I 58 D5
Petting D 73 A6
Pettneu am Arlberg A 71 C10
Pettorano sul Gizio I 62 D5
Petürzh BG 165 D7
Petworth GB 15 F7
Peuerbach A 76 F5
Peujard F 28 E5
Peura FIN 119 B14
Peurajärvi FIN 119 B16
Peurasuvanto FIN 115 C1
Pevensey GB 15 F9
Peveragno I 37 C7
Pewsey GB 13 C11
Pewsum (Krummhörn) D 17 B8
Pexonne F 27 D6
Peymeinade F 36 D5
Peynier F 35 C10
Peypin F 35 D10
Peyrat-le-Château F 29 D9
Peyrehorade F 32 D4
Peyrieu F 31 D8
Peyrins F 31 E7
Peyrolles-en-Provence F 35 C10
Peyruis F 35 B10
Pézenas F 34 D5
Pizino PL 85 D8
Pezinok SK 146 E4
Pezuls F 29 F7
Pfaffenberg D 75 E11
Pfaffendorf D 80 B6
Pfaffenhausen D 71 A10
Pfaffenhofen an der Ilm D 75 E10
Pfaffenhofen an der Roth D 187 B5
Pfaffenhoffen F 27 C8
Pfäffikon CH 27 F10
Pfaffing D 75 F11
Pfalzfeld D 185 D8
Pfalzgrafenweiler D 27 C10
Pfarrkirchen D 76 F3
Pfarrweisach D 75 B8
Pfarrwerfen A 73 B7
Pfedelbach D 27 B11
Pflach A 71 B11
Pfons A 72 B3
Pförring D 75 E10
Pforzen D 71 B11
Pforzheim D 27 C10
Pfreimd D 75 D11
Pfronstetten D 27 D11
Pfronten D 71 B11
Pfullendorf D 27 E11
Pfullingen D 27 D11
Pfunds A 71 D11
Pfungstadt D 21 E11
Pfyn CH 27 E10
Phalsbourg F 27 C7
Philippeville B 19 D10
Philippine NL 182 C3
Philippsburg D 187 C5
Philippsreut D 76 E5
Piacenza I 69 C8
Piadena I 66 B1
Piana F 37 G9
Piana GR 174 D5
Piana Crixia I 37 C8
Piana degli Albanesi I 58 D3
Piancastagnaio I 62 B1
Piandimeleto I 66 E5
Piàn di Scò I 66 E4
Pianella I 62 C6
Pianello Val Tidone I 37 B10
Piano del Voglio I 66 D3
Pianoro I 66 D3
Pianosa I 65 B2
Pianotolli-Caldarello F 37 J10
Pians A 71 C11
Piansano I 62 B1
Pianu RO 152 F2
Pias P 50 C5
Piaseczno PL 85 D7
Piaseczno PL 141 F4
Piasek PL 84 E6
Piaski PL 81 C12
Piaski PL 141 H7
Piastów PL 141 F3
Piątek PL 143 B7
Piątnica Poduchowna PL 139 D13
Piatra RO 160 F6
Piatra Neamţ RO 153 D8
Piatra Olt RO 160 E4
Piatra şoimului RO 153 D8
Piau-Engaly F 33 E6
Piazza al Serchio I 66 D1
Piazza Armerina I 58 E5
Piazza Brembana I 69 B8
Piazzatorre I 69 B8

Piazzola sul Brenta I 66 A4
Pibrac F 33 C8
Pićan HR 67 B9
Picar AL 168 D3
Picassent E 48 F4
Picauville F 23 B9
Picerno I 60 B5
Picher D 83 D10
Pichl bei Wels A 76 F5
Pickering GB 11 C10
Pico I 62 E5
Picón E 54 A4
Picoto P 44 B3
Picquigny F 18 E5
Pidbuzh UA 145 E7
Pidhorodtsi UA 145 E7
Pidlisne UA 153 A7
Piebalgas LV 135 B10
Piechcin PL 138 E5
Piechowice PL 81 E9
Piecki PL 139 C11
Piecnik PL 85 D10
Piedicorte-di-Gaggio F 37 G10
Piedicroce F 37 G10
Piedimonte Etneo I 59 D7
Piedimonte Matese I 60 A2
Piedimulera I 68 A5
Piedrabuena E 54 A4
Piedrafita de Babia I 39 C7
Piedrahíta E 45 D10
Piedralaves E 46 D3
Piedras Albas E 45 E7
Piedras Blancas E 39 A8
Piedruja LV 133 E2
Piegaro I 62 B2
Piégut-Pluviers F 29 D7
Piehinki FIN 119 E12
Piekary Śląskie PL 143 F6
Piekielnik PL 147 C9
Piekoszów PL 143 E9
Pieksämäen mlk FIN 124 F8
Pieksämäki FIN 124 F8
Pielavesi FIN 123 D17
Pieleşti RO 160 E3
Pielgrzymka PL 81 D9
Pienava LV 134 C6
Pienięznica PL 85 C11
Pieniężno PL 139 B9
Pieńkowo PL 85 B11
Piennes F 19 F12
Pieńsk PL 81 D8
Pienza I 62 A1
Piera E 43 D7
Pierowall GB 3 G11
Pierre-Buffière F 29 D8
Pierre-Châtel F 31 F8
Pierre-de-Bresse F 31 B7
Pierrefeu-du-Var F 36 E4
Pierrefitte-Nestalas F 32 E5
Pierrefitte-sur-Aire F 26 C3
Pierrefonds F 18 F6
Pierrefontaine-les-Varans F 26 F6
Pierrefort F 30 F2
Pierrelatte F 35 B8
Pierrepont F 19 F12
Pierres F 24 C6
Pierrevert F 35 C10
Piershil NL 182 B4
Piertinjaure S 109 C17
Pierzchnica PL 143 E10
Piesau D 75 A9
Pieścirogi PL 139 E10
Piesendorf A 73 B6
Pieski PL 81 B8
Piesport D 185 E6
Pieštany SK 146 D5
Pieszkowo PL 136 E2
Pieszyce PL 81 E11
Pietrabbondante I 63 D6
Pietracatella I 63 D7
Pietracorbara F 37 F10
Pietra-di-Verde F 37 G10
Pietragalla I 60 B5
Pietralba F 37 F10
Pietra Ligure I 37 C8
Pietralunga I 66 F5
Pietramelara I 60 A2
Pietramontecorvino I 63 D8
Pietraperzia I 58 E5
Pietraporzio I 36 C6
Pietrari RO 160 C4
Pietrasanta I 66 E1
Pietravairano I 60 A2
Pietroasa RO 151 D10
Pietroasele RO 161 C9
Pietroşani RO 161 F7
Pietrosella F 37 H9
Pietroşiţa RO 161 C6
Pietrowice Wielkie PL 142 F5
Pievene Rocchette I 69 B11
Piperskärr S 93 D9
Pipirig RO 153 C8
Pipriac F 23 E8
Piqeras AL 168 D2
Pir RO 151 C9
Piraino I 59 C6
Piran SLO 67 A8
Pirčiupiai LT 137 E9
Pirdop BG 165 D9
Pirg AL 168 C4
Pirgovo BG 161 F7
Piriac-sur-Mer F 22 F6
Piricse H 151 B9
Pirin BG 169 A10
Pirinççi TR 173 B10
Pîrjolteni MD 153 C11
Pirkkala FIN 127 C10
Pîrlița MD 153 C11
Pîrlița MD 154 A2
Pirmasens D 21 F9
Pirna D 80 E5
Pirnmill GB 4 D6
Pirot SRB 164 C6
Pirovac HR 156 E4
Pirtó H 150 E3
Pirttijoki FIN 121 E9
Pirttikoski FIN 119 B18
Pirttikoski FIN 119 D18
Pirttikoski FIN 123 C10
Pirttikylä FIN 122 E7
Pirttimäki FIN 124 E7
Pirttimäki FIN 125 C10
Pirttinen FIN 119 E16
Pirttivaara FIN 121 D14
Pirttivuopio S 111 E17
Pirsalu EST 131 C8
Piispa FIN 125 D11
Piispajärvi FIN 121 D11
Piittisjärvi FIN 119 B17
Pijnacker NL 16 D2
Pikkara FIN 119 E15
Pikkula FIN 119 D17
Pikutėniai LT 134 F3
Pila I 66 C5

Piła PL 85 D11
Pilar de la Mola I E 57 D8
Pilas E 51 E7
Piława PL 141 G5
Piława Górna PL 81 E11
Pilchowice PL 142 F5
Pilda LV 133 D3
Piles E 56 D4
Pilica I 147 B7
Pili GR 175 B8
Pilica PL 143 F8
Pilis H 150 C4
Piliscsaba H 149 A11
Pilisszántó H 149 A11
Pilisszentiván H 149 A11
Pilisvörösvár H 149 A11
Pill A 72 B4
Pilling GB 10 D6
Pilníkov CZ 77 B9
Pilpala FIN 127 D11
Pilsach D 75 D10
Pilskalns LV 135 B13
Pilsting D 75 E12
Piltene LV 134 B3
Piltränk S 118 C4
Pilu RO 151 D7
Pilviškiai LT 136 D7
Pilzno PL 143 G11
Pimentel I 64 E3
Pimperne GB 13 D11
Pimpiö S 117 E10
Piña de Campos E 40 D3
Piña de Esgueva E 40 E3
Piñar E 53 B10
Pinarbaşı TR 171 E10
Pinarca TR 173 B9
Pinarejo E 47 E8
Pinarhisar TR 173 A8
Pinarköy TR 181 B7
Pinarlibelen TR 177 E10
Pinasca I 31 F11
Pincehely H 149 C10
Pinchbeck GB 11 F11
Pińczów PL 143 E10
Pindstrup DK 86 C6
Pineda de Cigüela E 47 D7
Pineda de la Sierra E 40 D5
Pineda de Mar E 43 D9
Pinela P 39 E6
Piñel de Abajo E 40 E3
Pinerolo I 31 F11
Pineto I 62 C6
Piney F 25 D11
Pinggau A 148 B6
Pinhal Novo P 50 B2
Pinhanços P 44 D5
Pinhão P 44 B5
Pinheiro P 50 C2
Pinheiro Grande P 44 F4
Pinhel P 45 C6
Pinhoe GB 13 D8
Pinilla de Molina E 47 C9
Pinilla de Toro E 39 E9
Pinkafeld A 148 B6
Pinneberg D 82 C7
Pinnow D 81 C7
Pino E 39 B7
Pino F 37 F10
Pino del Río E 39 C10
Pinofranqueado E 45 D8
Pinols F 30 E3
Piñor E 38 C3
Pinoso E 56 E2
Pinos-Puente E 53 B9
Pinsac F 29 F9
Pinsió FIN 127 B9
Pinsoro E 41 D9
Pintamo FIN 121 D10
Pintano E 32 E3
Pinto E 46 D5
Pinwherry GB 4 E7
Pinzano al Tagliamento I 73 D6
Pinzio P 45 C6
Pinzolo I 69 A10
Piobbico I 66 E6
Piolenc F 35 B8
Pioltello I 69 C7
Piombino I 65 B3
Piombino Dese I 72 E4
Pionerskiy RUS 139 A9
Pionki PL 141 H4
Pionsat F 29 C11
Pioraco I 67 F6
Piornal E 45 D9
Piossasco I 31 F11
Piotrkowice PL 81 D7
Piotrków Kujawski PL 138 E5
Piotrków Trybunalski PL 143 D8
Piove di Sacco I 66 B5
Piovene Rocchette I 69 B11
Pischelsdorf in der Steiermark A 148 B5
Pischia RO 151 F7

Pisciotta I 60 C4
Pişcolt RO 151 B9
Piscu RO 155 B1
Piscu Vechi RO 159 F11
Pişece SLO 148 D5
Piešćná CZ 77 B12
Písek CZ 76 D6
Písek CZ 147 B7
Pishcha UA 141 G9
Pishchana UA 154 A5
Pishchanka UA 154 A3
Pisisaare EST 131 D11
Piskokefalo GR 179 E11
Piškorevci HR 157 B9
Pisodri GR 168 C5
Pisogne I 69 B9
Pissos F 32 B4
Pissonas GR 175 B8
Pisticci I 61 C7
Pisto FIN 121 D13
Pistoia I 66 E2
Pisz PL 139 C12
Piszczac PL 141 G8
Pitagowan GB 5 B9
Pitäjänmäki FIN 123 C15
Pitarque E 42 F2
Piteå S 118 D6
Piteşti RO 160 D5
Pithiviers F 25 D7
Pitigliano I 65 B5
Piteşcop F 22 C6
Pleşcuţa RO 151 E9
Pitkäjärvi FIN 127 D9
Pitkälä FIN 129 B11
Pitkälahti FIN 124 E9
Pitkäsenkylä FIN 119 E11
Pitkyaranta RUS 129 B15
Pitlochry GB 5 B9
Pitomača HR 149 E8
Pitrags LV 130 F4
Pitres F 55 F6
Pîtres F 18 F3
Pitscottie GB 5 C11
Pitsinaiika GR 174 C4
Pitstone GB 15 D7
Pitsund S 118 D6
Pitt GB 13 C12
Pittem B 19 C7
Pitten A 148 A6
Pittentrail GB 3 K8
Pittenweem GB 5 C11
Pitvaros H 150 E6
Pivašiūnai LT 137 E9
Pivka SLO 73 E9
Pivnice SRB 158 C3
Piwniczna-Zdrój PL 145 E2
Pizarra E 53 C7
Pizzighettone I 69 C8
Pizzo I 59 B9
Pizzoferrato I 63 D6
Pizzoli I 62 C4
Pjedsted DK 86 D5
Pjelax FIN 122 F6
Pjenovac BIH 157 D10
Pjesker S 118 C3
Plaaz D 83 C12
Plabennec F 22 C3
Placencia de las Armas E 32 D1
Plachkovtsi BG 166 D4
Pläcis LV 135 B9
Plaffeien CH 31 B11
Plagiá GR 169 B8
Plaidt D 21 D8
Plăieşii de Jos RO 153 E8
Plaintel F 22 D6
Plaisance F 33 C6
Plaisance-du-Touch F 33 C8
Plaisir F 24 C6
Plaka GR 168 F5
Plaka GR 171 D8
Plaka GR 175 E6
Plaka GR 179 B7
Plakhtiyivka UA 154 E5
Plakias GR 178 E7
Plakovo BG 166 D5
Plana BIH 157 G9
Planá CZ 75 C12
Plana GR 169 D10
Planá nad Lužnicí CZ 77 D7
Plaňany CZ 77 B8
Plancher-Bas F 27 E6
Plancoët F 23 C7
Plancy-l'Abbaye F 25 C10
Plop MD 153 A11
Plopana RO 153 D10
Plopeni RO 161 C7
Plopi MD 154 B4
Plopii-Slăviteşti RO 160 F5
Plopşoru RO 160 D2
Plopu RO 161 C8
Plosca RO 160 E6
Ploscoş RO 152 D3
Ploska UA 152 B6
Ploskinia PL 139 B8
Płośnica PL 139 D9
Plötzin D 79 B12
Plötzky D 79 B10
Plou F 42 F2
Plouagat F 22 C5
Plouaret F 22 C5
Plouarzel F 22 D2
Plouay F 22 E5
Ploubalay F 23 C7
Ploubazlanec F 22 C5
Plouberzre F 22 C5
Ploudalmézeau F 22 C2
Ploudiry F 22 D3
Plouescat F 22 C3
Plouézec F 22 C6
Ploufragan F 22 D6
Plougasnou F 22 C4
Plougastel-Daoulas F 22 D3
Plougonven F 22 C4
Plougonver F 22 D5
Plougrescant F 22 C5
Plouguenast F 22 D6
Plouguerneau F 22 C2
Plouguernével F 22 D5
Plouguiel F 22 C5
Plouguin F 22 C2
Plouha F 22 C6
Plouhinec F 22 D2
Plouhinec F 22 E5
Plouigneau F 22 C4
Ploumagoar F 22 C5
Ploumilliau F 22 C4
Plounéour-Trez F 22 C3
Plounévez-Moëdec F 22 C4
Plounévez-Quintin F 22 D5
Plouray F 22 D5
Plouvorn F 22 C4
Plouyé F 22 D4
Plouzané F 22 D2

Plau D 83 D12
Plaue D 79 B8
Plauen D 75 A11
Plav MNE 163 D8
Plavě RKS 163 E10
Plaveč SK 145 E2
Plaviņas LV 135 C11
Plavna SRB 159 E9
Plavni UA 155 C3
Plavnica SK 145 E2
Plavno HR 156 D5
Plavy CZ 81 E8
Plawno PL 85 C10
Plaza E 40 B6
Płazów PL 144 C7
Plech D 75 C9
Plecka Dąbrowa PL 143 B8
Pleine-Fougères F 23 C8
Pleikšni LV 133 D3
Plélan-le-Grand F 23 D7
Plélo F 22 C6
Plémet F 22 C12
Plénée-Jugon F 23 D7
Pléneuf-Val-André F 22 C6
Pleniţa RO 159 E11
Plentzia E 40 B6
Plérin F 22 C6
Plescop F 22 E6
Pleşeni MD 154 E2
Plešivec SK 145 F1
Plesná CZ 75 B11
Pleśna PL 144 D2
Plessé F 23 E8
Plestin-les-Grèves F 22 C4
Pleszew PL 142 C4
Pleternica HR 157 B8
Plettenberg D 21 B9
Pleubian F 22 C5
Pleudihen-sur-Rance F 23 C8
Pleumartin F 29 B7
Pleumeur-Bodou F 22 C4
Pleurs F 25 C10
Pleuven F 22 E3
Plevljе MNE 163 C7
Pljevlja MNE 163 C7
Plobannalec F 22 E3
Ploemeur F 22 E5
Ploeren F 22 E6
Ploërmel F 23 E7
Plœuc-sur-Lié F 22 D6
Plogonnec F 22 D3
Plogshagen D 84 A4
Ploieşti RO 161 D8
Plomari RO 177 B7
Plombières-les-Bains F 26 E5
Plomeur F 22 E3
Plomin HR 67 B9
Plomodiern F 22 D3
Plön D 83 B8
Plonéour-Lanvern F 22 E3
Plonévez-du-Faou F 22 D4
Plonevez-Porzay F 22 D3
Płońsk D 139 E9
Plop MD 153 A11
Plopana RO 153 D10
Plopeni RO 161 C7
Plopi MD 154 B4
Plopii-Slăviteşti RO 160 F5
Plopşoru RO 160 D2
Plopu RO 161 C8
Plosca RO 160 E6
Ploscoş RO 152 D3
Ploska UA 152 B6
Ploskinia PL 139 B8
Płośnica PL 139 D9
Plötzin D 79 B12
Plötzky D 79 B10
Plou F 42 F2
Plouagat F 22 C5
Plouaret F 22 C5
Plouarzel F 22 D2
Plouay F 22 E5
Ploubalay F 23 C7
Ploubazlanec F 22 C5
Ploubezre F 22 C5
Ploudalmézeau F 22 C2
Ploudiry F 22 D3
Plouescat F 22 C3
Plouézec F 22 C6
Ploufragan F 22 D6
Plougasnou F 22 C4
Plougastel-Daoulas F 22 D3
Plougonven F 22 C4
Plougonver F 22 D5
Plougrescant F 22 C5
Plouguenast F 22 D6
Plouguerneau F 22 C2
Plouguernével F 22 D5
Plouguiel F 22 C5
Plouguin F 22 C2
Plouha F 22 C6
Plouhinec F 22 D2
Plouhinec F 22 E5
Plouigneau F 22 C4
Ploumagoar F 22 C5
Ploumilliau F 22 C4
Plounéour-Trez F 22 C3
Plounévez-Moëdec F 22 C4
Plounévez-Quintin F 22 D5
Plouray F 22 D5
Plouvorn F 22 C4
Plouyé F 22 D4
Plouzané F 22 D2

Plouzévédé F 22 C3
Plovdiv BG 165 E10
Plozévet F 22 E3
Pluck IRL 7 C7
Plugari RO 153 C10
Plumbridge GB 4 F2
Plumelec F 22 E6
Pluméliau F 22 E6
Plumergat F 22 E6
Plumlov CZ 77 D12
Pluneret F 22 E6
Plungė LT 134 E3
Pluszkiejmy PL 136 E5
Pluvigner F 22 E5
Plužine BIH 157 F9
Plužine MNE 163 C7
Plzeň CZ 76 C4
Pług SK 147 D10
Pługi PL 142 E4
Pniewo PL 85 D11
Pniewo PL 139 E11
Pniewo PL 143 B8
Pniewy PL 81 A10
Pniewy PL 141 G3
Poarta Albă RO 155 E2
Pobedim SK 146 D5
Pobedino RUS 136 D6
Pobeni RUS 136 D6
Poběžovice CZ 75 C12
Pobierowo PL 85 B7
Pobiedno RUS 145 E5
Pobiedziska PL 81 B12
Pobierowo PL 85 B7
Pobikry PL 141 E7
Pobladura del Valle E 39 D8
Poblete E 54 B5
Pobłocie PL 85 A13
Poboleda E 42 E5
Poboru RO 160 D5
Pobožje MK 164 E3
Počátky CZ 77 D8
Poceirão P 50 B2
Pöchlarn A 77 F8
Pociems LV 131 F9
Pociumbeni MD 153 B10
Pöcking D 75 G9
Pocking D 76 F4
Pocklington GB 11 D10
Pocola RO 151 D9
Pocrnje BIH 157 F9
Pocsaj H 151 C8
Pócspetri H 145 H4
Poczesna PL 143 E7
Podareš MK 169 A8
Podari RO 160 E3
Podayva BG 161 F9
Podbiel SK 147 C8
Podbořany CZ 76 B4
Podborov'ye RUS 132 F4
Podbožur MNE 163 D6
Podbrdo BIH 157 F7
Podbrdo SLO 73 D8
Podbrezová SK 147 D9
Podčetrtek SLO 148 D5
Poddębice PL 143 C6
Poděbrady CZ 77 B8
Podedwórze PL 141 G8
Podegrodzie PL 145 D2
Podelzig D 81 B7
Podem BG 165 B10
Podeni RO 159 D9
Podenii Noi RO 161 C8
Podensac F 32 B5
Podenzano I 69 E8
Podersdorf am See A 77 G11
Podgajci Posavski HR 157 C10
Podgaje PL 85 D11
Podgora HR 157 F8
Podgorač HR 149 E10
Podgorac SRB 159 F8
Podgoria RO 161 C10
Podgorica MNE 163 E7
Podgorica SLO 73 D10
Podgorie AL 168 C4
Podgoritsa BG 167 C6
Podgórze PL 139 C11
Podgrab BIH 157 E10
Podgrad SLO 67 A9
Podhorod SK 145 F5
Podhum BIH 157 E7
Podil's'k UA 154 B5
Podkova BG 171 B8
Podkrajowo PL 139 D9
Podkum SLO 73 D11
Podlehnik SLO 148 D5
Podles MK 169 A6
Podlipoglav SLO 73 D10
Podmilečje BIH 157 D7
Podnanos SLO 73 E9
Podnovljie BIH 157 C9
Podochori GR 170 C6
Podoima MD 154 A3
Podoleni RO 153 D9
Podolí CZ 77 D11
Podolie SK 146 D5
Podolínec SK 145 E2
Podorozhnye UA 145 E9
Podosoje BIH 162 D5
Podrašnica BIH 157 D6
Podravske Sesvete HR 149 D8
Podromanija BIH 157 E10
Podsreda SLO 148 D5
Podstrana HR 156 F6
Podturen HR 149 D7
Podu Iloaiei RO 153 C10
Podujevo RKS 164 D3
Podu Turcului RO 153 E10
Poduševi BIH 157 H8
Podveleži BIH 157 F8
Podvrška SRB 159 D9
Podvysoká SK 147 C7
Podwilk PL 147 C9
Poederlee B 182 C5
Poeni RO 160 E6
Poeniţa MD 153 A11
Pofi I 62 D4
Pogăceaua RO 152 D4
Pogana RO 153 E11

Pogar BIH 157 D9
Poggendorf D 84 B4
Poggiardo I 61 C10
Poggibonsi I 66 F3
Poggio Berni I 66 D5
Poggio Bustone I 62 B3
Poggio Catino I 62 C3
Poggiodomo I 62 B3
Poggio Imperiale I 63 D8
Poggio-Mezzana F 37 G10
Poggio Mirteto I 62 C3
Poggio Moiano I 62 C3
Poggio Picenze I 62 C5
Poggio Renatico I 66 C4
Poggiorsini I 60 B6
Poggio Rusco I 66 C3
Pöggstall A 77 E8
Pogny F 25 C11
Pogoanele RO 161 D9
Pogoniani GR 168 E3
Pogorzela PL 81 C12
Pogorzelice PL 85 B13
Pogradec AL 168 C4
Pogrodzie PL 139 B8
Pohja FIN 127 C12
Pohja FIN 127 D10
Pohja-Lankila FIN 129 C11
Pohjasenvaara FIN 117 D11
Pohjaslahti FIN 119 B17
Pohjaslahti FIN 123 F12
Pohjavaara FIN 121 F11
Pohjois-li FIN 119 D14
Pohjoisjärvi FIN 123 F13
Pohorelá SK 147 D10
Pohořelice CZ 77 E11
Pohronská Polhora SK 147 D9
Pohronský Ruskov SK 147 F7
Poian RO 153 E8
Poiana RO 160 D7
Poiana Blenchii RO 152 C3
Poiana Câmpina RO 161 C7
Poiana Cristei RO 161 B9
Poiana Lacului RO 160 D5
Poiana Mare RO 159 F11
Poiana Mărului RO 160 B6
Poiana Sibiului RO 152 F3
Poiana Stampei RO 152 C6
Poiana Teiuliu RO 153 C7
Poiana Vadului RO 151 C9
Poibrene BG 165 E8
Poiana RO 160 D7
Poienari RO 153 D10
Poienarii Burchii RO 161 D8
Poienarii de Argeş RO 160 C5
Poieneşti RO 153 D11
Poieni RO 151 D10
Poienile de Sub Munte RO 152 B4
Poijula FIN 121 D10
Poikajärvi FIN 117 E15
Pöikva EST 131 D10
Poinçon-lès-Larrey F 25 E11
Poing D 75 F10
Pointis-Inard F 33 D7
Poirino I 37 B7
Poiseux F 25 F9
Poissons F 26 D3
Poissy F 24 C7
Poitiers F 29 B6
Poix-de-Picardie F 18 E4
Poix-Terron F 19 E10
Pojan AL 168 C4
Pojanluoma FIN 122 E9
Pojatno H 148 E5
Pojejena RO 159 D8
Pojo FIN 127 E10
Pojorâta RO 152 B6
Pókaszepetk H 149 C7
Poki LV 134 C7
Pokka FIN 117 B15
Poklečani BIH 157 E7
Pokoj BIH 156 C4
Pokój PL 142 E4
Pokrówka PL 141 H8
Pokrzywnica PL 139 E10
Polac RKS 163 D10
Polača HR 156 D5
Pola de Allande E 39 B6
Pola de Laviana E 39 B8
Pola de Lena E 39 B8
Pola de Siero E 39 B8
Pola de Somiedo E 39 B7
Polaincourt-et-Clairefontaine F 26 E5
Połajewo PL 85 E11
Polán E 46 E4
Polanica-Zdrój PL 77 B10
Połaniec PL 143 F11
Polanów PL 85 B11
Polatsk BY 133 F5
Polch D 21 D8
Polcirkeln S 116 E6
Polczyno PL 138 A5
Połczyn Zdrój PL 85 C10
Polegate GB 15 F9
Polena BG 165 F7
Poleñino E 41 E11
Polepy CZ 76 A6
Polesella I 66 C4
Polessk RUS 136 D3
Polgár H 145 H3
Polgárdi H 149 B10
Polgaste EST 131 F13
Polia I 59 B9
Poliçan AL 168 C3
Poliçan AL 168 C4
Police D 84 C7
Police nad Metují CZ 81 E10
Polichni GR 169 C8
Polichnitos GR 177 A7
Polička CZ 77 C10
Policoro I 61 C7
Policzna PL 141 H5
Polientes E 40 C4
Poligny F 31 B8
Polikrayshte BG 166 C5
Polisot F 25 D11
Polistena I 59 C9
Politika GR 175 B8
Politz D 83 C8
Polizzi Generosa I 58 D5
Põlja FIN 124 C8
Poljana RO 153 D9
Poljanak HR 156 C4
Poljana Pakračka HR 149 F7
Poljane SLO 73 D9
Poljčane SLO 148 D5
Poljice BIH 157 C6
Poljica HR 156 D3
Poljice BIH 157 D10
Poljice-Popovo BIH 162 D5

Polkowice PL 81 D10
Polla I 60 B4
Pölläkkä FIN 125 F11
Pöllau A 148 B5
Pöllauberg A 148 B5
Polle D 78 C5
Pollença E 57 B11
Pollenfeld D 75 E9
Pollenza I 67 F7
Pollfoss N 100 C7
Polliat F 31 C7
Pollica I 60 C4
Pollina I 58 D5
Pollitz D 83 E11
Pollos E 39 F9
Polmak N 113 C20
Polminhac F 29 F11
Polmont GB 5 D9
Polo FIN 121 C12
Polomka SK 147 D9
Polop E 56 D4
Pölöske H 149 C7
Połoski PL 141 G8
Polovragi RO 160 C3
Polperro GB 12 E5
Pöls A 73 B10
Polsbroek NL 182 B5
Polsingen D 75 E8
Polska Cerekiew PL 142 F5
Polski Gradets BG 166 E6
Polski Trŭmbesh BG 166 C5
Polsko Kosovo BG 166 C5
Polso FIN 123 D12
Poltár SK 147 E9
Põltsamaa EST 131 D11
Põlula EST 131 C13
Polumir SRB 163 B10
Połupin PL 81 B8
Põlva EST 131 E14
Polvela FIN 125 D12
Polvenkylä FIN 122 E8
Polverigi I 67 E7
Polvijärvi FIN 125 E12
Polyana UA 145 F6
Polyanets'ke UA 154 A6
Polyantho GR 171 B8
Polyany RUS 129 E11
Polyatsite BG 167 D8
Polydendro GR 169 D7
Polydrosos GR 175 B6
Polygyros GR 169 D9
Polykarpi GR 169 C7
Polykastano GR 168 D5
Polykastro GR 169 C8
Polymylos GR 169 D7
Polyneri GR 168 D5
Polypotamo GR 168 C5
Polzela SLO 73 D11
Pölzig D 79 E11
Pomaluengo E 40 B4
Pomarance I 66 F2
Pomarão P 50 D4
Pomarez F 32 C4
Pomarico I 61 B7
Pomarkku FIN 126 B7
Pomârla RO 153 A8
Pomáz H 150 B3
Pombal P 38 F5
Pombal P 44 E3
Pomer E 41 E8
Pomeroy GB 7 C9
Pomezeu RO 151 D9
Pomezí CZ 77 C10
Pomezia I 62 D3
Pomi RO 151 B11
Pomiechówek PL 139 F10
Pömiö FIN 119 C14
Pommard F 30 A6
Pommelsbrunn D 75 C10
Pommersfelden D 75 C8
Pomol BIH 157 D11
Pomorie BG 167 D9
Pomorsko PL 81 B8
Pompaire F 28 B5
Pompei I 60 B3
Pompey F 26 C5
Pompia GR 178 E8
Pompignan F 35 C6
Pomysk Mały PL 85 B13
Poncin F 31 C7
Ponferrada E 39 C6
Poniatowa PL 141 H6
Poniatowo PL 139 D8
Poniec PL 81 C11
Poniklá CZ 81 E8
Poniky SK 147 D8
Ponoarele RO 159 D10
Ponor RO 151 E11
Ponoshec RKS 163 E9
Pons F 28 D4
Ponsa FIN 127 B11
Ponsacco I 66 E2
Pont-à-Celles B 19 C9
Pontacq F 32 D5
Pontailler-sur-Saône F 26 F3
Pontaix F 31 F7
Pont-à-Marcq F 19 C7
Pont-à-Mousson F 26 C5
Pontardawe GB 13 B7
Pontarion F 29 D9
Pontarlier F 31 B9
Pontassieve I 66 E3
Pontaubault F 23 C9
Pont-Audemer F 18 F2
Pontault-Combault F 25 C8
Pontaumur F 29 D11
Pont-Aven F 22 E4
Pont-Canavese I 68 C4
Pontcharra F 31 E9
Pontchâteau F 23 F7
Pont-Croix F 22 D3
Pont-d'Ain F 31 C7
Pont-de-Buis-lès-Quimerch F 22 D3
Pont-de-Chéruy F 31 D7
Pont-de-Larn F 33 C10
Pont-de-l'Isère F 30 E6
Pont-de-Loup B 182 E5
Pont-de-Poitte F 31 B8
Pont-de-Roide F 27 F6
Pont-de-Salars F 34 B4
Pont de Suert E 33 F7
Pont-de-Vaux F 31 C6
Pont-de-Veyle F 30 C6
Pont-d'Hérault F 35 B6
Pont-d'Ouilly F 23 C11
Pont-du-Casse F 33 B7
Pont-du-Château F 30 D3
Pont-du-Navoy F 31 B8
Ponte I 60 A3
Ponte Aranga E 38 B4
Ponteareas E 38 D3
Pontebba I 73 C7
Pontecagnano Faiano I 60 B3
Ponte Caldelas E 38 D3
Ponteceso E 38 B2
Pontechianale I 36 B6
Pontecorvo I 62 E5
Pontecurone I 37 B9
Ponte da Barca P 38 E3
Pontedassio I 37 D8
Pontedecimo I 37 B9
Ponte de Lima P 38 E2
Ponte dell'Olio I 37 B11
Pontedera I 66 E2
Ponte de Sor P 44 F4
Pontedeume E 38 B3
Ponte di Legno I 69 A10
Ponte di Piave I 72 E5
Ponte do Rol P 44 F2
Pontefract GB 11 D9
Ponte Gardena I 72 C4
Pontelagoscuro I 66 C4
Ponteland GB 5 E13
Pontelandolfo I 60 A3
Ponte-Leccia F 37 G10
Pontelongo I 66 B5
Ponte nelle Alpi I 72 D5
Ponte Nizza I 37 B10
Ponte Nossa I 69 B8
Ponte Nova I 72 D3
Pont-en-Royans F 31 E7
Pontenure I 69 C8
Pontenx-les-Forges F 32 B3
Ponte San Nicolò I 66 B4
Ponte San Pietro I 69 B8
Ponte Valga E 38 C2
Pontevedra E 38 D2
Pontével P 44 F3
Pont-Évêque F 30 D6
Pontevico I 66 B1
Pont-Farcy F 23 C9
Pontfaverger-Moronvilliers F 19 F9
Pontgibaud F 30 D2
Pont-Hébert F 23 B9
Pontinha P 50 B1
Pontinia I 62 E4
Pöntiö FIN 120 F2
Pontivy F 22 D6
Pont-l'Abbé F 22 E3
Pont-la-Ville F 25 D12
Pont-les-Moulins F 26 F5
Pont-l'Évêque F 23 B12
Pontlevoy F 24 F5
Pontoise F 24 B7
Pontokomi GR 169 D6
Pontones E 55 C7
Pontonnyy RUS 129 F14
Pontonx-sur-l'Adour F 32 C4
Pontoon IRL 6 E4
Pontorson F 23 C8
Pontpoint F 18 F6
Pontremoli I 69 E8
Pontresina CH 71 E9
Pontrhydfendigaid GB 13 A7
Pontrieux F 22 C5
Pontrilas GB 13 B9
Ponts E 42 D6
Pöntsö FIN 117 C12
Pont-Ste-Marie F 25 D11
Pont-Ste-Maxence F 18 F6
Pont-St-Esprit F 35 B8
Pont-St-Martin I 68 B4
Pont-sur-Yonne F 25 D9
Pontvallain F 23 E12
Pontyberem GB 12 B6
Pontycymer GB 13 B7
Pontypool GB 13 B8
Pontypridd GB 13 B8
Ponyativka UA 154 D6
Ponza I 62 F3
Ponzone I 37 B8
Poola FIN 122 E7
Poole GB 13 D11
Poolewe GB 2 K5
Pooley Bridge GB 5 F11
Pool of Muckhart GB 5 C9
Pootsi EST 131 E8
Pope LV 134 B3
Popeasca MD 154 D5
Poperinge B 18 C6
Popești RO 151 C9
Popești RO 153 C10
Popești RO 160 C4
Popești RO 160 E6
Popești-Leordeni RO 161 E8
Popielów PL 142 E4
Popina BG 161 E9
Popintsi BG 165 E9
Popitsa BG 165 C8
Poplaca RO 152 F4
Popoli I 62 C5
Popovača HR 149 E7
Popovica SRB 159 E9
Popovitsa BG 166 E4
Popovo BG 166 C6
Popów PL 141 F1
Popów PL 143 D6
Poppenhausen D 75 B7
Poppenricht D 75 D10
Poppi I 66 E4
Poprad SK 145 E1
Popricani RO 153 C11
Poproč SK 145 F2
Popsko BG 171 A9
Pópulo P 38 F5
Populonia I 65 B2
Porąbka PL 147 B8
Poraj PL 143 E7
Porcari I 66 E2
Porcia I 73 E6
Porcsalma H 145 H6
Porcuna E 53 A8
Pordenone I 73 E6
Pordim BG 165 C10
Porjba PL 143 F7
Porjba-Kocjby PL 139 E12
Poreč HR 67 B8
Pori FIN 126 C6
Porice BIH 157 D7
Porjus S 116 E3
Porkhov RUS 132 F6
Porkkala FIN 127 F11
Porkuni EST 131 C12
Porlammi FIN 127 D15
Porlezza I 69 A7
Porlock GB 13 C7
Pornainen FIN 127 E13
Pornassio I 37 C7
Pornic F 23 F7
Pornichet F 23 F7
Poroina Mare RO 159 E10
Poros GR 174 C2
Poros GR 175 D7
Poroschia RO 160 F6
Poroshkove UA 145 F6
Poroszló H 150 B6
Porozina HR 67 B9
Porpi GR 171 B8
Porqueres E 43 C9
Porras FIN 127 D10
Porraskoski FIN 127 C12
Porrentruy CH 27 F7
Porreres E 57 B11
Porretta Terme I 66 D2
Porsangmoen N 113 D14
Pörsänmäki FIN 124 D8
Porsåsen N 102 E3
Porsgrunn N 90 A6
Porsi S 118 B5
Porspoder F 22 C2
Port N 113 D17
Porta F 33 E9
Portadown GB 7 D10
Portaferry GB 7 D11
Portaje E 45 E7
Portakallik TR 181 B8
Portalegre P 44 F6
Portals Vells E 49 F10
Portaria GR 169 D9
Portaria GR 169 F8
Portarlington IRL 7 F8
Port Askaig GB 4 D4
Portavogie GB 7 D12
Portbail F 23 B8
Port-Barcarès F 34 E5
Portbou E 34 F5
Port Brillet F 23 D10
Portchester GB 13 D12
Port d'Andratx E 49 E9
Port-de-Bouc F 35 D8
Port-de-Piles F 29 A7
Port de Pollença E 57 B11
Port-des-Barques F 28 D3
Port de Sóller E 49 E10
Portel P 50 C4
Portel-des-Corbières F 34 D4
Portell de Morella E 42 F3
Port Ellen GB 4 D4
Port-en-Bessin-Huppain F 23 B10
Portencross GB 4 D7
Port Erin GBM 10 C2
Portes-lès-Valence F 30 F6
Portets F 28 F5
Portet-sur-Garonne F 33 C8
Port Eynon GB 12 B6
Port Glasgow GB 4 D7
Porth GB 13 B8
Porthcawl GB 13 C7
Port Henderson GB 2 K5
Porthleven GB 12 E4
Porthmadog GB 10 F3
Porticcio F 37 H9
Portici I 60 B2
Portieux F 26 D5
Portilla E 47 D8
Portilla de la Reina E 39 B10
Portillo E 40 F2
Portillo de Toledo E 46 D4
Portimão P 50 E2
Portimo FIN 119 B16
Portimojärvi FIN 119 B11
Portishead GB 13 C9
Portknockie GB 3 K11
Port Láirge IRL 9 D8
Portland IRL 6 F6
Port-la-Nouvelle F 34 D5
Port Laoise IRL 7 F8
Portlaoise IRL 7 F8
Portlethen GB 5 A12
Port-Leucate F 34 E5
Port Logan GB 4 F7
Port-Louis F 22 E5
Portmagee IRL 8 E2
Portmahomack GB 3 K9
Portman E 56 F3
Portmarnock IRL 7 F10
Port Mearnóg IRL 7 F10
Portmuck GB 4 F5
Port-na-Con GB 2 H7
Portnaguran GB 2 J4
Portnahaven GB 4 D3
Portnalong GB 2 L4
Port-Navalo F 22 E6
Porto E 39 D6
Porto F 37 G9
Porto P 44 B3
Porto Alto P 50 B2
Porto Azzurro I 65 B2
Porto Botte I 64 E2
Portobravo E 38 C2
Porto Cervo I 64 A4
Porto Cesareo I 61 C9
Portocheli GR 175 E7
Portocolom E 57 C11
Porto Covo da Bandeira P 50 D2
Porto Cristo E 57 B11
Porto d'Ascoli I 62 B5
Porto de Lagos P 50 E2
Porto de Mós P 44 E3
Porto do Barqueiro E 38 A4
Porto do Son E 38 C1
Porto Empedocle I 58 E4
Porto Ercole I 65 C4
Portoferraio I 65 B2
Portofino I 37 C10
Port of Ness GB 2 J4
Porto Garibaldi I 66 C5
Porto Germeno GR 175 C7
Portogruaro I 73 E6
Porto Koufo GR 170 E5
Porto Levante I 59 C6
Porto Levante I 66 B5
Pörtom FIN 122 E7
Portomaggiore I 66 C4
Portomarín E 38 C4
Port Omna IRL 6 F6
Portopalo di Capo Passero I 59 F7
Porto Petro E 57 C11
Portør N 90 B5
Porto Rafti GR 175 D9
Porto Recanati I 67 F8
Porto Rotondo I 64 A4
Portorož SLO 67 A8
Porto San Giorgio I 67 F8
Porto San Paolo I 64 B4
Porto Sant'Elpidio I 67 F8
Porto Santo Stefano I 65 C4
Portoscuso I 64 E1
Porto Tolle I 66 C5
Porto Torres I 64 B1
Porto-Vecchio F 37 H10
Portovenere I 69 E8
Porto Viro I 66 B5
Portpatrick GB 4 F6
Portrane IRL 7 F10
Port Reachrann IRL 7 F10
Portreath GB 12 E4
Portree GB 2 L4
Portroe IRL 8 C6
Portrush GB 4 E3
Portsalon IRL 4 E1
Portsmouth GB 13 D12
Portsoy GB 3 K11
Port-Ste-Marie F 33 B6
Portstewart GB 4 E3
Port-St-Louis-du-Rhône F 35 D8
Port St Mary GBM 10 C2
Port-St-Père F 23 F8
Port-sur-Saône F 26 E5
Port Talbot GB 13 B7
Portugalete E 40 B5
Portumna IRL 6 F6
Port-Vendres F 34 E5
Port William GB 4 F7
Poruba SK 147 D7
Porubne UA 153 A8
Porumbacu de Jos RO 152 F4
Porvoo FIN 127 E14
Porządzie PL 139 E11
Porzuna E 46 F4
Posada E 39 B8
Posada I 64 B4
Posada de Valdeón E 39 B10
Posadas E 53 A6
Poșaga RO 151 E11
Poschiavo CH 69 A9
Posedarje HR 156 D3
Poseidonia GR 176 E4
Poseritz D 84 B4
Posești RO 161 C8
Pösing D 75 D12
Posio FIN 121 B11
Positano I 60 B2
Possagno I 72 E4
Posseberg S 97 D11
Possendorf D 80 E5
Possesse F 25 C12
Pößneck D 79 E10
Posta I 62 B4
Poșta Câlnău RO 161 C9
Postal I 72 C3
Posta Piana I 60 A5
Postau D 75 E11
Posterholt NL 20 B6
Postiglione I 60 B4
Postojna SLO 73 E9
Postoliska PL 139 F11
Postoloprty CZ 76 B5
Postomino PL 85 B11
Postřelmov CZ 77 C11
Postupice CZ 77 C7
Posušje BIH 157 F7
Poświętne PL 140 E7
Poświętne PL 141 G2
Potamia GR 171 C7
Potamia GR 174 F5
Potamochori GR 171 B8
Potamoi GR 170 B6
Potamos GR 168 E2
Potamos GR 178 C4
Potashnya UA 154 A5
Potcoava RO 160 E5
Potęgowo PL 85 B12
Potenza I 60 B5
Potenza Picena I 67 F8
Potes E 39 B10
Potidania GR 174 C5
Potigny F 23 C11
Potkraj BIH 157 E7
Potku FIN 119 E17
Potlogi RO 161 D7
Potočac SRB 159 F7
Potočani BIH 157 E7
Potoci BIH 156 D6
Potoci BIH 157 F8
Potok Złoty PL 143 E7
Potsdam D 80 B4
Pötsönvaara FIN 125 D16
Potštát CZ 146 B5
Pottendorf A 77 G10
Pottenstein A 77 G10
Pottenstein D 75 C9
Potterne GB 13 C10
Potters Bar GB 15 D8
Pöttmes D 75 E9
Potton GB 15 C8
Pöttsching A 146 F2
Potworów PL 141 G3
Pouancé F 23 E9
Pougny F 25 F9
Pougues-les-Eaux F 30 A3
Pougy F 25 D11
Pouillon F 32 C4
Pouilly-en-Auxois F 25 F12
Pouilly-sous-Charlieu F 30 C5
Pouilly-sur-Loire F 25 F8
Pouilly-sur-Saône F 31 A7
Poulaines F 24 F6
Pouldreuzic F 22 E3
Poulgorm Bridge IRL 8 E4
Pouligny-St-Pierre F 29 B8
Poulithra GR 175 E6
Poullaouen F 22 D4
Poulnamucky IRL 9 D7
Poulstrup DK 90 E7
Poulton-le-Fylde GB 10 D6
Pounta GR 176 E5
Poupas F 33 C7
Pourcieux F 35 D10
Pouri GR 169 F9
Pourrain F 25 E9
Pourrières F 35 C10
Pousada P 45 C6
Pousos P 44 E3
Poussan F 35 D6
Poussay F 26 D5
Poussu FIN 121 C13
Pouxeux F 26 D6
Pouyastruc F 33 D6
Pouydesseaux F 32 C5
Pouzauges F 28 B4
Pouzay F 24 F4
Považská Bystrica SK 146 C6
Povedilla E 55 B7
Poviglio I 66 C2
Povlja HR 157 F6
Póvoa de Lanhoso P 38 E3
Póvoa de São Miguel P 51 C5
Póvoa de Varzim P 38 F2
Póvoa do Concelho P 45 C6
Povoletto I 73 D7
Povrly CZ 80 E6
Powburn GB 5 E13
Power's Cross IRL 6 F6
Powick GB 13 A10
Powidz PL 138 F4
Powmill GB 5 C9
Poyales del Hoyo E 45 D10
Poyatos E 47 D8
Poyntz Pass GB 7 D10
Poyrazcik TR 177 A9
Poysdorf A 77 E11
Pöytyä FIN 126 D8
Poza de la Sal E 40 C5
Pozaldez E 39 F10
Požarevac SRB 159 D7
Požarnica BIH 157 C10
Požega HR 149 F9
Požega SRB 158 F5
Požerė LT 134 E4
Pozezdrze PL 136 E4
Pozharan RKS 164 E3
Pozherevitsy RUS 133 B7
Poznań PL 81 B11
Pozo Alcón E 55 D7
Pozoamargo E 47 F8
Pozoantiguo E 39 E9
Pozoblanco E 54 C3
Pozo Cañada E 55 B9
Pozo de Guadalajara E 47 D6
Pozohondo E 55 B9
Pozo-Lorente E 47 F10
Pozondón E 47 C10
Pozořice CZ 77 D11
Pozorrubio E 47 E7
Poźrzadło Wielkie PL 85 D9
Pozuel del Campo E 47 C10
Pozuelo E 55 B8
Pozuelo de Alarcón E 46 D5
Pozuelo de Aragón E 41 E9
Pozuelo del Páramo E 39 D8
Pozuelo del Rey E 46 D6
Pozuelo de Zarzón E 45 D8
Pozuelos de Calatrava E 54 B4
Pozza di Fassa I 72 D4
Pozzallo I 59 F6
Pozzolo Formigaro I 37 B9
Pozzomaggiore I 64 C2
Pozzuoli I 60 B2
Pozzuolo del Friuli I 73 E7
Prabuty PL 139 C7
Prača BIH 157 E10
Prachatice CZ 76 D6
Pracht D 21 C9
Prackenbach D 76 D3
Prádanos de Ojeda E 40 C3
Pradejón E 32 F1
Pradelles F 30 F4
Prádena E 46 B5
Prades F 33 E9
Prades F 33 E10
Prades-d'Aubrac F 34 A4
Pradillo E 41 D6
Pradines F 33 B8
Prado P 38 E3
Prado de la Guzpeña E 39 C9
Prado del Rey E 53 C5
Pradoluengo E 40 D5
Præstbro DK 86 A6
Præstø DK 87 E10
Pragelato I 31 E10
Pragersko SLO 148 D5
Prägraten A 72 B5
Praha CZ 77 B6
Prahecq F 28 C5
Prahovo SRB 159 E10
Praia a Mare I 60 D5
Praia da Barra P 44 C3
Praia da Rocha P 50 E2
Praia da Tocha P 44 D3
Praia de Esmoriz P 44 C3
Praia de Mira P 44 D3
Praiano I 60 B3
Praid RO 152 D6
Prăjeni RO 153 B10
Prakovce SK 145 F2
Pralognan-la-Vanoise F 31 E10
Pralyetarsk BY 133 E7
Pramanta GR 168 E5
Prambachkirchen A 76 F5
Pranjani SRB 158 E5
Prapatnica HR 156 E5
Prašice SK 146 D6
Praszka PL 142 D5
Prata di Pordenone I 73 E6
Pratau D 79 C12
Prat de Comte E 42 F4
Pratdip E 42 E5
Pratella I 60 A2
Prato I 66 E3
Prato allo Stelvio I 71 D11
Pratola Peligna I 62 C5
Pratovecchio I 66 E4
Prats de Lluçanès E 43 C8
Prats-de-Mollo-la-Preste F 33 F10
Pratteln CH 27 E8
Prauliena LV 135 C12
Prauthoy F 26 E3
Pravda BG 161 F10
Pravdinsk RUS 136 E3
Pravets BG 165 D8
Pravia E 39 B7
Prayssas F 33 B7
Prazaroki BY 133 F4
Praz-sur-Arly F 31 D10
Prebold SLO 73 D11
Préchac F 32 B5
Preci I 62 B4
Précigné F 23 E11
Prečín SK 147 C7
Précy-sous-Thil F 25 F11
Predappio I 66 D4
Predazzo I 72 D4
Predeal RO 161 B7
Predeal-Sărari RO 161 C8
Predejane SRB 164 D5
Predești RO 160 E3
Preding A 148 C4
Predlitz A 73 B8
Predmeja SLO 73 E8
Předměřice nad Labem CZ 77 B9
Predosa I 37 B9
Pré-en-Pail F 23 D11
Prees GB 10 F6
Preetz D 83 B8
Préfailles F 23 F7
Preganziol I 72 E5
Pregarten A 77 F7
Pregrada HR 148 D5
Preignan F 33 C7
Preiļi LV 135 D13
Preitenegg A 73 C10
Preiviiki FIN 126 C6
Preixan F 33 D10
Prejmer RO 153 F7
Prekaja BIH 156 D6
Preko HR 156 D3
Prekopa HR 148 F6
Preljina SRB 158 F5
Prelog HR 149 D7
Prelošćica HR 149 F6
Přelouč CZ 77 B9
Prem SLO 73 E9
Premantura HR 67 C8
Prémery F 25 F9
Premia I 68 A5
Premià de Mar E 43 E8
Premilcuore I 66 E4
Prémilhat F 29 C11
Premnitz D 79 A11
Premosello Chiovenda I 68 A5
Prenzlau D 84 D5
Préporché F 30 B4
Přerov CZ 146 C4
Prerow D 83 B13
Preselentsi BG 155 F2
Preševo SRB 164 E4
Presicce I 61 D10
Prešov SK 145 F3
Pressac F 29 C7
Pressath D 75 C10
Pressbaum A 77 F10
Presseck D 75 B10
Pressel D 79 C12
Pressig D 75 B9
Prestatyn GB 10 E5
Prestbakken N 111 C15
Prestbury GB 13 B10
Pre-St-Didier I 31 D10
Prestebakke N 91 B10
Presteigne GB 13 A8
Prestfoss N 95 B11
Přeštice CZ 76 C4
Preston GB 5 D12
Preston GB 10 D6
Prestwick GB 4 E7
Prettin D 80 C3
Pretushë AL 168 C4
Pretzfeld D 75 C9
Pretzier D 83 E10
Pretzsch D 79 C12
Pretzschendorf D 80 E5
Preuilly-sur-Claise F 29 B7
Preutești RO 153 C8
Prevalje SLO 73 C10
Prévenchères F 35 A6
Préveranges F 29 C10
Prevešt SRB 159 F7
Preveza GR 174 B2
Prevršac HR 156 B5
Prežganje SLO 73 D10
Prezid HR 73 E10
Prez-sous-Lafauche F 26 D3
Priaranza del Bierzo E 39 C6
Pribelja BIH 157 D6
Pribeta SK 146 F6
Pribinić BIH 157 C8
Pribislavec HR 149 D6
Priboieni RO 160 D6
Priboj BIH 157 C10
Priboj SRB 163 B8
Příbor CZ 146 B6
Priborn D 83 D13
Priboy BG 165 D6
Příbram CZ 76 C6
Pribrezhnoye RUS 136 D1
Pribude HR 156 E5
Pribylina SK 147 C9
Přibyslav CZ 77 C9
Prichaly RUS 134 F2
Prichsenstadt D 75 C7
Pridvorci BIH 157 F9
Priedaine LV 134 C3
Priedes LV 131 F9
Priego E 47 D8
Priego de Córdoba E 53 B8
Priekulė LT 134 E2
Priekule LV 134 D3
Priekuļi LV 135 B10
Prienai LT 137 D8
Prienai LT 137 D12
Prien am Chiemsee D 72 A5
Prieros D 80 B5
Prießnitz D 79 D10
Prießnitz D 79 D12
Priestewitz D 80 D5
Prievidza SK 147 D7
Priežmale LV 133 D2
Prignac-et-Marcamps F 28 E5
Prigor RO 159 D9
Prigoria RO 160 C3
Prigradica HR 162 D2
Prigrevica SRB 158 B3
Prijeboj HR 156 C4
Prijedor BIH 157 C6
Prijepolje SRB 163 C8
Prikuļi LV 135 D13
Priladozhskiy RUS 129 F15
Prilep MK 169 B6
Prilike SRB 158 F5
Prillimäe EST 131 C9
Priluka BIH 157 E6
Přimda CZ 75 C12
Primišlje HR 156 B3
Primolano I 72 E4
Primorsk RUS 129 E10
Primorsk RUS 139 A9
Primorsko BG 167 E9
Primor'ye RUS 139 A9
Primošten HR 156 E4
Princes Risborough GB 15 D7
Princetown GB 12 D7
Prinos GR 171 C7
Prinsenbeek NL 16 E3
Prinzhöfte D 17 C11
Priolithos GR 174 D5
Priolo Gargallo I 59 E7
Prioro E 39 C10
Priozersk RUS 129 C13
Priponești RO 153 E10
Prirechnyy RUS 114 E8
Prisăcani RO 153 C11
Priseaca RO 160 D4
Priseltsi BG 167 C9
Prishtinë RKS 164 D3
Prisjan SRB 164 C6
Prisoja MNE 163 D8
Prisoje BIH 157 E7
Příšovice CZ 81 E8
Prissac F 29 B8
Prissé F 30 C6
Priština RKS 164 D3
Pristol RO 159 E10
Prittriching D 71 A11
Pritzerbe D 79 B11
Pritzier D 83 D10
Pritzwalk D 83 D12
Privas F 30 F6
Priverno I 62 E4
Privlaka HR 67 D11
Privlaka HR 157 B10
Prizna HR 67 C10
Prizren RKS 163 E10
Prizzi I 58 D3
Prkosi BIH 156 C5
Prnjavor BIH 157 C8
Prnjavor SRB 158 D3
Proaza E 39 B7
Probištip MK 164 E5
Probota RO 153 C10
Probsteierhagen D 83 B8
Probus GB 12 E5
Proceno I 62 B1
Prochoma GR 169 C8
Prochowice PL 81 D10
Procida I 60 B2
Prodromos GR 175 C6
Produlești RO 161 D7
Proença-a-Nova P 44 E5
Proença-a-Velha P 45 D6
Profen D 79 D11
Profesor-Ishirkovo BG 161 F10
Profilia GR 181 D7
Profitis GR 169 C9
Profitis Ilias GR 178 E9
Profondeville B 19 D10
Progonat AL 168 D2
Prohn D 84 B4
Prokhladnoye RUS 134 F2
Prokopi GR 175 B7
Prokuplje SRB 164 C4
Prolaz BG 167 C6
Prolog BIH 157 E6
Promachoi GR 169 B7
Promachonas GR 169 B9
Promna PL 141 G3
Promyri GR 175 A7
Pronsfeld D 20 D6
Propriano F 37 H9
Proseč CZ 77 C10
Prosek AL 163 F8
Prosenik BG 167 D8
Prosenjakovci SLO 149 C6
Prosetín CZ 77 C9
Proshkava BY 133 F4
Proskynites GR 171 C8
Prosotsani GR 170 B5
Prosperous IRL 7 F9
Prossedi I 62 D4
Prostějov CZ 77 D12
Prostki PL 140 C6
Prostřední Bečva CZ 146 C6
Prószków PL 142 E4
Proszowice PL 143 F9
Proszówki PL 143 F9
Proti GR 170 C5
Protići BIH 157 D6
Protivanov CZ 77 D11
Protivín CZ 76 D6
Protokklisi GR 171 B10
Protoria GR 178 E9
Prötzel D 80 A5
Provadiya BG 167 C8
Provatas GR 169 B9
Provenchères-sur-Fave F 27 D7
Provins F 25 C9
Provo SRB 158 D4
Prozor BIH 157 E8
Prozor HR 156 C3
Prrenjas AL 168 B4
Pruchnik PL 144 D6
Prudhoe GB 5 F13
Prudnik PL 142 F4
Prudzinki BY 133 E4
Prugoc RKS 164 D3
Prügy H 145 G3
Prüm D 20 D6
Pruna E 51 F9
Prundeni RO 160 D4
Prundu RO 161 E8
Prundu Bârgăului RO 152 C5
Prunières F 36 B4
Pruniers-en-Sologne F 24 F6
Prunișor RO 159 D10
Prusac BIH 157 D7
Prušánky CZ 77 E11
Prusice PL 81 D11
Prusinovice CZ 146 C5
Prūšīši LV 135 B13
Pruszcz PL 138 D4
Pruszcz PL 138 D5
Pruszcz Gdański PL 138 B6
Pruszków PL 141 F3
Prutz A 71 C11
Pružina SK 146 C6
Prvačina SLO 73 E8
Pryamobalka UA 154 F4
Prymors'ke UA 155 B5
Prymors'ke UA 155 B5
Pryozerne UA 155 B5
Prypruttya UA 153 A8
Przasnysz PL 139 D10
Przechlewo PL 85 C12
Przeciszów PL 143 F7
Przecław PL 143 F11
Przedbórz PL 143 D8
Przedecz PL 138 F6
Przejazdowo PL 138 B6
Przelewice PL 85 D8
Przemęt PL 81 B10
Przemków PL 81 C9
Przemyśl PL 144 D6
Przerośl PL 136 E6
Przewale PL 144 B8
Przewłoka PL 141 G8
Przeworno PL 81 E12
Przeworsk PL 144 C5
Przewóz PL 81 D7
Przeździatka PL 141 F6
Przezdzijk Wielki PL 139 D10
Przezmark PL 139 C7
Przine-Zdralovac BIH 156 D6
Przodkowo PL 138 B5
Przybiernów PL 85 C7
Przyborów PL 81 C9
Przyborowice PL 139 E9
Przybranowo PL 138 E6
Przygodzice PL 142 C4
Przykona PL 142 C6
Przyłęk PL 141 G1
Przylep PL 81 C8
Przylesie PL 142 E3
Przyrów PL 143 E8
Przysieki PL 144 D3
Przystajń PL 142 E6
Przystałowice Duże PL 141 H3
Przysucha PL 141 H3
Przyszów PL 144 C4
Przytoczna PL 81 A9
Przytoczno PL 141 G6
Przytuły PL 140 D6
Przytyk PL 141 H3

Przywidz PL 138 B5
Psača MK 164 E5
Psachna GR 175 B8
Psara GR 177 B6
Psarades GR 168 C5
Psari GR 174 E4
Psari GR 175 D10
Psathopyrgos GR 181 D8
Psinthos GR 181 E8
Pskov RUS 132 F3
Psychiko GR 169 B10
Psczew PL 81 B9
Pszczółki PL 138 B6
Pszczonów PL 141 G1
Pszczyna PL 147 B7
Pteleos GR 175 A6
Pteri GR 174 C5
Ptolemaida GR 169 C6
Ptuj SLO 148 D5
Publier F 31 C10
Puchberg am Schneeberg
  A 146 F1
Pucheni RO 160 C6
Puchenii Mari RO 161 D8
Puchheim D 75 F9
Púchov SK 146 C6
Pucioasa RO 161 C6
Pučišče HR 157 F6
Puck PL 138 A5
Pucol E 48 E4
Pudasjärven kirkko FIN 119 D17
Pudasjärvi FIN 119 D17
Puddletown GB 13 D10
Puderbach D 185 C8
Pudinava LV 133 C3
Pudsey GB 11 D8
Puebla de Albortón E 41 F10
Puebla de Alcocer E 51 B9
Puebla de Alfindén E 41 E10
Puebla de Almenara E 47 E7
Puebla de Beleña E 47 C6
Puebla de Don Fadrique
  E 55 D8
Puebla de Don Rodrigo E 46 F3
Puebla de Guzmán E 51 D5
Puebla de la Calzada E 51 B6
Puebla de la Reina E 51 B7
Puebla de Lillo E 39 B9
Puebla del Maestre E 51 C7
Puebla del Príncipe E 55 B7
Puebla del Prior E 51 B7
Puebla del Salvador E 47 E9
Puebla de Obando E 45 F7
Puebla de Sanabria E 39 D6
Puebla de Sancho Pérez E 51 C7
Puebla de San Miguel E 47 E10
Puebla de Yeltes E 45 C8
Puente de Domingo Flórez
  E 39 D6
Puente de Génave E 55 C7
Puente del Congosto E 45 D9
Puente de Montañana E 42 C5
Puente de San Miguel E 40 B3
Puente-Genil E 53 B7
Puente la Reina E 32 E2
Puentenansa E 40 B3
Puente Viesgo E 40 B4
Puerto de Béjar E 45 D9
Puerto de Mazarrón E 56 F2
Puerto de San Vicente E 45 E10
Puerto Lápice E 46 F6
Puerto Lumbreras E 55 D9
Puertomingalvo E 48 D4
Puerto Real E 52 C4
Puerto Seguro E 45 C7
Puerto Serrano E 51 F8
Pueyo E 32 E2
Pueyo de Santa Cruz E 42 D4
Pufeşti RO 153 E10
Puget-Théniers F 36 D5
Puget-Ville F 36 E4
Pugnochiuso I 63 D10
Puhja EST 131 E12
Puhoi MD 154 D4
Puhos FIN 121 D10
Puhos FIN 125 F13
Puhovac BIH 157 D9
Pui RO 159 B11
Puieşti EST 131 E10
Puieşti RO 153 E11
Puieşti RO 161 C10
Puig E 48 E4
Puigcerdà E 33 F9
Puigpunyent E 49 E10
Puig-reig E 43 D7
Puikkola FIN 115 E3
Puikule LV 131 F9
Puimoisson F 36 D4
Puiseaux F 25 D7
Puisieux F 18 D6
Puisseguin F 28 F5
Puisserguier F 34 D5
Puivert F 33 E10
Pujaut F 35 B8
Pujols F 28 F5
Pujols F 33 B7
Puka EST 131 E12
Pukanec SK 147 E7
Pukaro FIN 127 D15
Pukavik S 88 C7
Pukë AL 163 E8
Pukiš BIH 157 C10
Pukkila FIN 127 D14
Pula HR 67 C8
Pula I 64 E3
Pułatwy PL 141 H5
Pulborough GB 15 F7
Pulfero I 73 D7
Pulgar E 46 E4
Pulheim D 21 B7
Pulju FIN 117 B13
Pulkau A 77 E9
Pulkkaviita FIN 115 D5
Pulkkila FIN 119 F15
Pulkkinen FIN 123 D10
Pulkonkoski FIN 124 D8
Pulpí E 55 E9
Pulsa FIN 128 D8
Pulsano I 61 C8
Pulsen D 80 D4
Pulsnitz D 80 D6
Pulsujärvi S 116 B6
Pułtusk PL 139 E11
Pulversheim F 27 E7
Pumpėnai LT 135 E8
Pumpuri LV 134 C4
Pumsaint GB 13 A7
Pūņas LV 134 B4
Punat HR 67 B10

Pundsvik N 111 D12
Punduri LV 133 D3
Pungeşti RO 153 D10
Punghina RO 159 E10
Punia LT 137 D9
Punkaharju FIN 129 B11
Punkalaidun FIN 127 C9
Punkka FIN 128 C7
Punta Ala I 65 B3
Punta Križa HR 67 C9
Punta Sabbioni I 66 B5
Punta Umbría E 51 E6
Puokio FIN 120 E9
Puolakka FIN 115 D1
Puolanka FIN 121 E10
Puolivälä FIN 124 C9
Puoltikasvaara S 116 C6
Puottaure S 118 B4
Pūpoli LV 133 D2
Puraći BIH 157 C8
Puračič BIH 157 C10
Purani RO 161 F6
Puras FIN 121 E14
Purba LV 138 B4
Purbach am Neusiedler See
  A 77 G11
Purcari MD 154 D5
Purchena E 55 E8
Pūre LV 134 B5
Purgstall an der Erlauf A 77 F8
Purila EST 131 C9
Purkersdorf A 77 F10
Purkijaur S 109 C18
Pürksi EST 130 C7
Purley GB 15 E8
Purmerend NL 16 C3
Purmo FIN 123 C9
Purmojärvi FIN 123 D10
Purmsäti LV 134 D3
Purnu S 116 E6
Purnumukka FIN 115 B2
Purnuvaara FIN 121 C12
Purnuvaara S 116 D6
Purola FIN 128 E6
Purontaka FIN 123 C12
Purujosa E 41 E8
Purullena E 55 E6
Pürvenets BG 165 E10
Purviniškė LT 137 D7
Pürvomay BG 166 E4
Pürvomay BG 169 B9
Puša LV 133 D2
Pušalotas LT 135 E8
Puschendorf D 75 C8
Pushkinskiye Gory RUS 133 B3
Pušmucova LV 133 C3
Püspökladány H 151 C7
Püssi EST 131 C14
Pusté Úľany SK 146 E5
Pustków PL 143 F11
Pustomyty UA 144 D8
Pustoshka RUS 133 D6
Pūstrovo BG 166 E4
Pusula FIN 127 E10
Puszcza Mariańska PL 141 G2
Puszczykowo PL 81 B11
Pusztaföldvár H 150 D6
Pusztakovácsi H 149 C9
Pusztamérges H 150 E4
Pusztamonostor H 150 B4
Pusztaszabolcs H 149 B11
Pusztaszer H 150 D4
Pusztavacs H 150 C4
Pusztavám H 149 B10
Putaja FIN 126 C8
Putanges-Pont-Écrepin F 23 C11
Putbus D 84 B4
Putifigari I 64 B1
Putignano I 61 B8
Putikko FIN 129 B11
Putinci SRB 158 C4
Putineiu RO 160 F5
Putineiu RO 161 F7
Putkivaara FIN 119 B17
Putlitz D 83 D12
Putna RO 153 B7
Putnok H 145 G1
Putte B 19 B10
Putte NL 16 F2
Puttelange-aux-Lacs F 27 B6
Putten NL 16 D5
Puttgarden D 83 A10
Püttlingen D 21 F7
Putula FIN 127 C13
Putyla UA 152 B6
Putzar D 84 C5
Putzkau D 80 D6
Puukari FIN 125 C11
Puukkokumpu FIN 119 C14
Puumala FIN 129 B9
Puurmani EST 131 D12
Puurs B 19 B9
Puurtila FIN 125 F9
Puutossalmi FIN 124 E9
Puutturinjärvi FIN 119 E17
Puybrun F 29 F9
Puycasquier F 33 C7
Puygouzon F 33 C10
Puylaroque F 33 B9
Puylaurens F 33 C10
Puy-l'Évêque F 33 A8
Puymirol F 33 B7
Puymoyen F 29 D6
Puyôo F 32 C4
Pwllheli GB 10 F3
Pyaozerskiy RUS 121 C17
Pyatidorozhnoye RUS 139 B9
Pyatirech'ye RUS 129 D14
Pyelishcha BY 141 F9
Pyershamayski BY 137 F11
Pyhäjärvi FIN 113 F16
Pyhäjärvi FIN 115 C12
Pyhäjärvi FIN 119 F12
Pyhäjoki FIN 119 F12
Pyhäjoki FIN 126 C7
Pyhäkylä FIN 121 D12
Pyhältö FIN 128 D7
Pyhämaa FIN 126 C5
Pyhänkoski FIN 119 F12
Pyhäntä FIN 119 F16
Pyhäntä FIN 121 F11
Pyhäranta FIN 126 D5
Pyhäsalmi FIN 123 D15
Pyhäselkä FIN 125 F13
Pyhe FIN 126 D5
Pyhra A 77 F9
Pyhtää FIN 128 E7
Pyle GB 13 B7
Pyles GR 181 E6
Pyli GR 169 F6
Pyli GR 175 C8
Pyli GR 177 E9

Pylkönmäki FIN 123 E13
Pylos GR 174 F4
Pylypets' UA 145 F7
Pyntäinen FIN 126 B6
Pyrbaum D 75 D9
Pyrgetos GR 169 E8
Pyrgi GR 177 C6
Pyrgiotika GR 175 D6
Pyrgoi GR 169 C6
Pyrgoi GR 170 B6
Pyrgos GR 174 D3
Pyrgos GR 176 D5
Pyrgos GR 177 D8
Pyrgos GR 178 B3
Pyrgos Dirou GR 178 B3
Pyrrönperä FIN 123 B15
Pyrsogianni GR 168 D4
Pyrzyce PL 85 D7
Pyskowice PL 142 F6
Pyssyperä FIN 121 D10
Pystan' UA 145 A6
Pysznica PL 144 B5
Pytalovo RUS 133 B3
Pythagoreio GR 177 D8
Pythio GR 169 D7
Pythio GR 172 B6
Pyykkölänvaara FIN 121 E12
Pyykköskylä FIN 121 D13
Pyyli FIN 125 F11

Q

Qafzez AL 168 D4
Qelëz AL 163 E8
Qeparo AL 168 D2
Qerret AL 168 B2
Quadrazais P 45 D7
Quadri I 63 D6
Quakenbrück D 17 C9
Qualiano I 60 B2
Quaregnon B 182 E3
Quarona I 68 B5
Quarrata I 66 E2
Quarré-les-Tombes F 25 F10
Quarteira P 50 E3
Quartell E 48 E4
Quarten CH 27 F11
Quartu Sant'Elena I 64 E3
Quatre-Champs F 19 F10
Quatretonda E 56 D4
Quattro Castella I 66 C1
Quedlinburg D 79 C9
Queenborough GB 15 E10
Queensbury GB 11 D8
Queenstown IRL 8 E6
Queidersbach D 21 F9
Queige F 31 D9
Queipo P 44 C5
Quelaines-St-Gault F 23 E10
Quellendorf D 79 C11
Queluz P 50 B1
Quemada E 40 E4
Quend F 18 D4
Quendorf D 17 D8
Queralbs E 33 F10
Quercianella I 66 F1
Querenhorst D 79 B8
Querfurt D 79 D10
Quérigut F 33 E10
Quern D 82 A7
Quernheim D 17 D10
Quero E 47 E6
Quero I 72 E4
Querrieu F 18 E5
Quesada E 48 F3
Quesada E 55 D6
Quesnoy-sur-Deûle F 18 C7
Quessoy F 22 D6
Questembert F 22 E7
Quettehou F 23 A9
Quettreville-sur-Sienne F 23 C9
Quevauvillers F 18 E5
Queyrac F 28 E4
Quézac F 29 F10
Quiaios P 44 D3
Quiberon F 22 F5
Quickborn D 83 C7
Quierschied D 21 F8
Quiévrain B 19 D8
Quiévrechain F 182 E3
Quiliano I 37 C8
Quillan F 33 E10
Quillebeuf-sur-Seine F 18 F2
Quimper F 22 E3
Quimperlé F 22 E4
Quin IRL 8 C5
Quincinetto I 68 B4
Quincy-Voisins F 25 C8
Quingey F 26 F4
Quinson F 36 D4
Quinssaines F 29 C11
Quintana de la Serena E 51 B8
Quintana del Castillo E 39 C7
Quintana del Pino E 40 E2
Quintana del Puente E 40 D3
Quintana de Rueda E 39 C9
Quintana-Martín Galíndez
  E 40 C5
Quintanapalla E 40 D4
Quintanar de la Orden E 47 E6
Quintanar de la Sierra E 40 E5
Quintanar del Rey E 47 E9
Quintana Redonda E 41 E6
Quintanilla de Onésimo E 40 E3
Quintenas F 30 E6
Quintin F 22 D6
Quinto CH 71 D7
Quinto E 41 F11
Quintos P 50 C4
Quinzano d'Oglio I 69 C9
Quiroga E 38 D5
Quiruelas de Vidriales E 39 D8
Quismondo E 46 D4
Quissac F 35 C7
Quittebeuf F 24 B4
Qukës AL 168 B3

R

Raab A 76 F5
Raabs an der Thaya A 77 E8
Raahe FIN 119 E12
Raajärvi FIN 115 E1
Rääkkylä FIN 125 F13
Raalte NL 16 D6
Raamsdonksveer NL 16 E3
Raanujärvi FIN 117 E12
Raappananmäki FIN 121 E10
Raasiku EST 131 C10
Raate FIN 121 E14

Raattama FIN 117 B12
Rab HR 67 C10
Rabac HR 67 B9
Rabaçal P 44 D4
Rabaçal P 45 C6
Rabade E 38 B4
Rábahidvég H 149 B7
Rábakecöl H 149 B8
Rabanales E 39 E7
Rábapaty H 149 B7
Rabastens F 33 C9
Rabastens-de-Bigorre F 33 D6
Rábatamási H 149 A8
Raba Wyżna PL 147 B9
Rabbalshede S 91 B9
Rabča SK 147 B9
Rabčice SK 147 B9
Rabe SRB 150 E5
Rabenstein an der Pielach
  A 77 F8
Raben Steinfeld D 83 C11
Råberg S 107 B13
Rąbino PL 85 C9
Rabisha BG 159 F10
Rabivere EST 131 C9
Rabka PL 147 B9
Råbke D 79 B8
Rabrovo BG 159 E10
Rabrovo SRB 159 D8
Rača SRB 159 E6
Rača SRB 164 D3
Răcăciuni RO 153 E9
Racale I 61 D10
Răcălmás H 149 B11
Racalmuto I 58 E4
Răcari RO 161 D7
Răcăşdia RO 159 D8
Racconigi I 37 B7
Rače SLO 148 D5
Rachanie PL 144 B8
Rachecourt-sur-Marne F 26 C3
Raches GR 175 B6
Raches GR 177 D7
Răchiţi RO 153 B9
Răchitoasa RO 153 E10
Răchitova RO 159 B10
Rachoni GR 171 C7
Raciąż PL 138 C4
Raciąż PL 139 E9
Racibórz PL 142 F5
Raciechowice PL 144 D1
Racimierz PL 85 C7
Račinovci HR 157 C10
Račišče HR 162 D3
Rǎciu RO 152 D4
Rǎciula MD 154 C2
Ráckeve H 149 B11
Racksätter S 97 C14
Racksund S 109 D14
Rǎcǎwice PL 143 F9
Rahden D 17 D11
Rahikka FIN 123 C12
Rahkio FIN 126 C8
Rahkonen FIN 123 C12
Rahman RO 155 D2
Råholt N 95 B14
Rahovec RKS 163 E10
Rahumäe EST 132 E1
Raiano I 62 C5
Raikuu FIN 125 F12
Räimä FIN 124 D9
Rain D 75 E8
Rain D 75 E11
Rainbach im Mühlkreis A 77 E6
Raippo FIN 129 D9
Räisälä FIN 115 E3
Raisdorf D 83 B8
Raisio FIN 126 E7
Raiskio FIN 115 D2
Raismes F 19 D7
Raistakka FIN 121 B11
Raitajärvi S 119 B10
Raitajärvi S 119 D13
Raja EST 131 D13
Raja-Jooseppi FIN 115 B4
Rajala FIN 117 C16
Rajamäki FIN 127 D12
Rajastrand S 106 B8
Rajcza PL 147 B8
Rájec CZ 77 D11
Rajec SK 147 C7
Rajecká Lesná SK 147 C7
Rajgród PL 140 C7
Rajhrad CZ 77 D11
Rajka H 146 E4
Raka SLO 148 E4
Rakamaz H 145 G3
Rakek SLO 73 E9
Rakevo BG 165 C7
Rakhiv UA 152 A4
Rakh'ya RUS 129 E13
Rakita BG 165 C9
Rakita RO 165 D6
Rakitna SLO 73 E9
Rakitovec SLO 67 B8
Rakitovo BG 165 F9
Rakke EST 131 D12
Rakkeby DK 90 E6
Rakkestad N 95 D14
Raklitsa BG 167 D7
Rákóczifalva H 150 C5
Rákócziújfalu H 150 C5
Rakoniewice PL 81 B10
Rakoshyn UA 145 G6
Rakova Bara SRB 159 D8
Rakovica HR 156 C4
Rakovinë RKS 163 E10
Rakovitsa BG 159 F9
Rakovník CZ 76 B5
Rakovo BG 165 D6
Rakovski BG 165 D10
Rakow D 84 B4
Raków PL 143 E11
Rakvere EST 131 C12
Ralingen D 21 E7
Ralja SRB 158 D6
Rålla S 89 B11
Ram SRB 159 D7
Ramacca I 59 E6
Rămâlă FIN 123 E12
Ramales de la Victoria E 40 B5

Radovići MNE 163 E6
Radoviš MK 169 A7
Radovljica SLO 73 D9
Radovnica SRB 164 E5
Radstadt A 73 B7
Radstock GB 13 C10
Răducăneni RO 153 D11
Raducič HR 156 D5
Raduil BG 165 E8
Radujevac SRB 159 E10
Radun' BY 137 E10
Radvanice CZ 81 E10
Radvaň nad Laborcom SK
  145 E4
Radviliškis LT 134 E7
Radwanice PL 81 C9
Radymno PL 144 D6
Radzanów PL 139 E9
Radzanów PL 141 G3
Radzanowo PL 139 E8
Radzice Duże PL 141 H2
Radzicz PL 85 D12
Radzieje PL 136 E4
Radziejów PL 138 E6
Radziejowice PL 141 F3
Radziemice PL 143 F9
Radzików PL 81 B7
Radzymin PL 139 F11
Radzyń DK 86 B3
Radzyń Chełmiński PL 138 D6
Radzyń Podlaski PL 141 G7
Ræhr DK 86 A3
Rækker Mølle DK 86 C3
Raeren B 20 C6
Raesfeld D 17 E7
Rafelbunyol E 48 E4
Raffadali I 58 E4
Rafford GB 3 K9
Rafina GR 175 C9
Råförsen S 97 B10
Råfov RO 161 D8
Rafsbotn N 113 C12
Raften N 110 D9
Raftsjöhöjden S 106 D8
Ragaciems LV 134 B6
Rágama E 45 C10
Ragana LV 135 B9
Rageliai LT 135 E11
Răgelin D 83 D13
Raglan GB 13 B9
Raguhn D 79 C11
Ragunda S 107 E10
Ragunda S 107 E10
Ragusa I 59 F6
Raguva LT 135 E9
Rahden D 17 D11
Rahikka FIN 123 C12
Rahkio FIN 126 C8
Rahkonen FIN 123 C12
Rahman RO 155 D2
Råholt N 95 B14
Rahovec RKS 163 E10
Rahumäe EST 132 E1
Raiano I 62 C5
Raikuu FIN 125 F12
Räimä FIN 124 D9
Rain D 75 E8
Rain D 75 E11
Rainbach im Mühlkreis A 77 E6
Raippo FIN 129 D9
Räisälä FIN 115 E3
Raisdorf D 83 B8
Raisio FIN 126 E7
Raiskio FIN 115 D2
Raismes F 19 D7
Raistakka FIN 121 B11
Raitajärvi S 119 B10
Räitälä FIN 126 E7
Raittijärvi S 112 D6
Raivala FIN 126 B7
Raja EST 131 D13
Raja-Jooseppi FIN 115 B4
Rajakorpi FIN 123 E11
Rajala FIN 117 C16
Rajamäki FIN 127 D12

Ramillies B 182 D5
Ramingstein A 73 B8
Ramirás E 38 D4
Ramløse DK 87 C10
Ramme DK 86 C2
Rammelsbach D 186 B3
Rammingen D 75 E7
Râmna RO 159 C8
Ramnäs S 102 D6
Ramnes N 95 D12
Râmnicelu RO 161 C10
Râmnicelu RO 161 C11
Râmnicu Sărat RO 161 C10
Râmnicu Vâlcea RO 160 C4
Ramonville-St-Agne F 33 C8
Ramosch CH 71 D10
Rämpsänkylä FIN 121 F13
Rampside GB 10 C5
Ramså N 111 B10
Ramsau im Zillertal A 72 B4
Ramsberg S 97 C13
Ramsbottom GB 11 D7
Ramsele S 107 C17
Ramsele S 107 D10
Ramsen CH 27 E10
Ramsey GB 15 C8
Ramsey GBM 10 C3
Ramsey St Mary's GB 15 C8
Ramsgate GB 15 E11
Ramsi EST 131 E11
Ramsjö S 103 B10
Ramsloh (Saterland) D 17 B9
Ramstadlandet N 105 B10
Ramstein D 21 F9
Ramsund N 111 D12
Ramundberget S 102 A3
Ramvik S 103 A14
Ramygala LT 135 E8
Råna N 111 D13
Rånäs S 99 C10
Rånäs S 102 C5
Rånåsfoss N 95 B14
Rance B 19 D9
Randaberg N 94 E3
Randalstown GB 4 F4
Randan F 30 C3
Randaträsk S 118 B6
Randazzo I 59 D6
Rânddalen S 102 B8
Randegg A 77 F7
Randen N 101 C9
Randen N 101 C8
Randers DK 86 C6
Randersacker D 187 B8
Randijaur S 109 C17
Randonnai F 24 C4
Randsjö S 102 B6
Randsverk N 101 C10
Råne N 111 E11
Rånes F 23 C11
Rångedala S 91 D13
Rangendingen D 187 E6
Rangersdorf A 73 C6
Rangsby FIN 122 E6
Rangsdorf D 80 B4
Ranhados P 44 C5
Ranis D 79 E10
Ranizów PL 144 C4
Ranka LV 135 B12
Rankil GB 11 E9
Ranskill GB 11 E9
Ranst B 182 C5
Ranta FIN 113 F19
Rantajärvi S 117 E11
Rantakangas FIN 123 E11
Rantasalmen asema FIN 125 F10
Rantasalmi FIN 125 F10
Ranta-Töysä FIN 123 E11
Ranten A 73 B9
Rantsila FIN 119 E15
Rantila FIN 113 E16
Rantum D 82 A4
Rantzausminde DK 86 E7
Ranua FIN 119 C17
Ranum DK 86 B4
Rånvassbotn N 111 D13
Raon-l'Étape F 27 D6
Raossi I 69 B11
Rapakkojoki FIN 123 C17
Rapallo I 37 C10
Raphoe IRL 4 F1
Rapice PL 81 B7
Räpina EST 132 E1
Rapla EST 131 C9
Rapolano Terme I 66 F4
Rapolla I 60 B5
Rapoltu Mare RO 151 F11
Raposa P 44 F3
Raposeira P 50 E2
Rapotín CZ 77 B12
Rappenswil CH 27 F10
Rappin D 84 B4
Raron CH 68 A4
Râşa HR 67 B9
Râsăle FIN 125 E9
Rasanovci BIH 156 D5
Râşca RO 153 C8
Rascafría E 46 C5
Răscăieţi MD 154 D5
Raschau D 79 E12
Raseiniai LT 134 F6
Râsele S 107 C11
Rasen I 72 C5
Rasharkin GB 4 F4
Rašica SLO 73 E10
Rasina EST 131 E14
Râşinari RO 160 B4

Rasines E 40 B5
Rasinja HR 149 D7
Rasinkylä FIN 121 E10
Rasinvaara FIN 121 D14
Rasivaara FIN 125 F13
Rsjö S 103 C12
Raška SRB 163 C10
Rask Mølle DK 86 D5
Raskovice CZ 146 B6
Raslavice SK 145 E3
Răsmireşti RO 161 F7
Rasno BG 163 C9
Râşnov RO 161 B6
Rasony BY 133 E5
Rasova RO 155 E1
Rasovo BG 159 F7
Raspenava CZ 81 E8
Rasquera E 42 E5
Rast RO 160 F2
Raštani BIH 157 F8
Rastatt D 27 C9
Rastdorf D 17 C9
Rasteby N 111 B19
Rästed DK 86 B5
Rastede D 17 B10
Rastenfeld A 77 E8
Raštević HR 156 D4
Rasti FIN 117 C14
Rasti FIN 125 G13
Rastinkylä FIN 125 C13
Râstoliţa RO 152 D5
Rastošnica BIH 157 C10
Rastovac MNE 163 D6
Rastow D 83 D10
Råstrand S 107 A14
Răsuceni RO 161 E7
Rasueros E 45 B10
Rasvåg N 94 F5
Raszków PL 142 C4
Raszyn PL 141 F3
Rataje SRB 164 C3
Rătan S 102 B8
Ratan S 122 C5
Rătansbyn S 102 B8
Ratasjärvi FIN 117 E11
Rateče SLO 73 C8
Ratekau S 83 C9
Rătești RO 160 D6
Rathangan IRL 7 F9
Ráth Bhoth IRL 4 F1
Ráth Caola IRL 8 C5
Rathconrath IRL 7 F7
Rathcoole IRL 7 F10
Ráth Cúil IRL 7 F10
Ráth Domhnaigh IRL 9 C7
Rathdowney IRL 9 C7
Ráth Droma IRL 9 C10
Rathdrum IRL 9 C10
Rathenow D 79 A11
Rathfriland GB 7 D10
Rathgormuck IRL 9 D7
Ráth Iomgháin IRL 7 F9
Rathkeale IRL 8 C5
Rathkeevin IRL 9 D7
Rathlee IRL 6 D4
Rathluirc IRL 8 D5
Ráth Mealtain IRL 7 B7
Rathmolyon IRL 7 F9
Rathmore IRL 8 D4
Rathmullan IRL 4 E1
Ráth Naoi IRL 7 G10
Rathnew IRL 7 G10
Rathnure IRL 9 D9
Ratho GB 5 D10
Rathowen IRL 7 E7
Rathstock D 81 A7
Rathumney IRL 9 D9
Rathvilly IRL 9 C9
Ratiboř CZ 146 C5
Ratič BIH 158 D3
Ratingen D 17 F7
Ratiškovice CZ 77 E12
Rátka H 145 G3
Ratkoc RKS 163 E10
Ratkovo SRB 158 C3
Ratnieki LV 133 D2
Ratoath IRL 7 E10
Rattelsdorf D 75 B8
Ratten A 148 B5
Rattenberg A 72 B4
Rattosjärvi FIN 117 E13
Rattray GB 5 B10
Rättsel S 118 C3
Rättvik S 103 E9
Ratzeburg D 83 C9
Rätzlingen D 79 B9
Raubach D 185 C8
Rauda LV 135 E12
Raudåna N 90 B4
Raudanjoki FIN 117 D16
Raudaskylä FIN 123 D13
Raudasmäki FIN 123 D13
Raudeberg N 100 C3
Råu de Mori RO 159 C10
Raudénai LT 134 D5
Raudondvaris LT 137 D8
Raudonė LT 136 C7
Rauen D 80 B6
Raufoss N 101 E13
Rauha FIN 129 C10
Rauhala FIN 117 C12
Raulhac F 29 F11
Rauma FIN 126 C6
Rauna LV 135 B11
Raunds GB 15 C7
Rauris A 73 B6
Râu Sadului RO 160 B4
Rauschenberg D 21 C11
Raussila FIN 128 D6
Rautajärvi FIN 127 C12
Rautalampi FIN 124 E7
Rautapera FIN 114 E4
Rautas S 111 D18
Rautavaara FIN 125 C10
Rautenkranz D 75 B11
Rautila FIN 119 F11
Rautila FIN 126 D6
Rautio FIN 120 F7
Rautionmäki FIN 123 E16
Rautjärven kk FIN 129 C11
Rautjärvi FIN 129 C11
Rautuskylä FIN 117 C13
Rauvanniemi FIN 129 B11
Rauzan F 28 F5
Ravadinovo BG 167 E9
Ravanusa I 58 E4
Rava-Rus'ka UA 144 C8
Ravasd H 149 A9
Ravča HR 157 F7
Ravda BG 167 D9
Ravels B 16 F3

Ravelsbach A 77 E9
Rävemåla S 89 B8
Ravenglass GB 10 C5
Ravenna I 66 D5
Ravensburg D 71 B9
Ravenstein NL 16 E5
Ravières F 25 E11
Ravijoki FIN 128 D8
Ravik N 108 B7
Rävlanda S 91 D12
Ravna Dubrava SRB 164 C5
Ravna Gora HR 67 B10
Ravna Reka SRB 159 E8
Ravne SLO 73 D11
Ravne na Koroškem SLO 73 C10
Ravnets BG 167 D8
Ravni BIH 157 F8
Ravnište SRB 164 C3
Ravnje SRB 158 D3
Ravnkilde DK 86 B5
Ravno BIH 157 E7
Ravno BIH 162 D4
Ravnogor BG 165 F9
Ravno Selo SRB 158 C4
Ravnshøj DK 90 E7
Ravnstrup DK 86 C4
Rävsön S 103 A15
Ravsted DK 86 E4
Rawa Mazowiecka PL 141 G2
Rawicz PL 81 C11
Rawmarsh GB 11 E9
Rawtenstall GB 11 D7
Raykovo BG 171 A7
Rayleigh GB 15 D10
Rayol-Canadel-sur-Mer F 36 E4
Räyrinki FIN 123 D11
Ražana SRB 158 E4
Ražanac HR 156 D3
Ražanj SRB 159 F8
Războieni RO 153 C9
Razboj BIH 157 B7
Razbojna SRB 164 C3
Razdelna BG 167 C9
Razdol BG 169 A9
Razdrto SLO 73 E9
Razès F 29 C8
Razgrad BG 160 F2
Razgrad BG 167 B7
Ražljevo BIH 157 C10
Razlog BG 165 F7
Razlovci MK 165 F6
Ražňany SK 145 E3
Ráztočno SK 147 D7
Răzvad RO 161 D6
Reading GB 14 E7
Reaghstown IRL 7 E9
Real P 38 F3
Réalmont F 33 C10
Realmonte I 58 E3
Réalville F 33 B8
Rear Cross IRL 8 C6
Réaup F 33 B6
Reay GB 3 H9
Rebais F 25 C9
Rebbenesbotn N 112 C2
Rebecq B 19 C9
Rébénacq F 32 D5
Rebild DK 86 B5
Rebollosa de Jadraque E 47 B7
Reboly RUS 125 C15
Rebordelo E 38 B3
Rebordelo P 38 E5
Rebra RO 152 C4
Rebricea RO 153 D11
Rebrișoara RO 152 C4
Rebrovo BG 165 D7
Rebŭrkovo BG 165 C8
Reca SK 146 E4
Reçan RKS 163 E10
Recanati I 67 F8
Recaș RO 151 F8
Recco I 37 C10
Recea MD 153 B11
Recea MD 154 C3
Recea RO 151 B12
Recea RO 152 F5
Recea RO 160 D6
Recea-Cristur RO 152 C3
Recess IRL 6 F3
Recey-sur-Ource F 25 E12
Réchicourt-le-Château F 27 C6
Rechlin D 83 D13
Rechnitz A 149 B6
Recht B 20 D6
Rechtenbach D 74 C6
Reci RO 153 F7
Rečica SLO 73 D11
Rečice BIH 157 F8
Recke D 17 D9
Reckingen CH 70 E6
Recklinghausen D 17 E8
Recoaro Terme I 69 B11
Recoubeau-Jansac F 35 A9
Recsk H 147 F10
Recuerda E 40 F6
Recz PL 85 D9
Rjczno PL 141 H1
Reda PL 138 A5
Redalen N 101 E13
Redange L 20 E5
Redcar GB 11 B9
Redcastle IRL 4 E2
Redcross IRL 9 C10
Reddelich D 83 B11
Redditch GB 13 A11
Réde H 149 B9
Redea RO 160 E4
Redefin D 83 D10
Redhill GB 15 E8
Rédics H 149 C6
Réding F 27 C7
Redinha P 44 D3
Rediu RO 153 C11
Rediu RO 153 D9
Rediu RO 153 F11
Rediul Mare MD 153 A11
Rednitzhembach D 75 D9
Redon F 23 E7
Redondela E 38 D2
Redondelo P 38 E4
Redondo P 50 B4
Redován E 56 E3
Red Point GB 2 K5
Redruth GB 12 E4
Redsted DK 86 B3
Reduzum NL 16 B5
Rjdzikowo PL 85 B12
Rjdziny PL 143 E7
Reen IRL 8 E3
Reens IRL 8 C5
Reepham GB 15 B11
Rees D 16 E6
Reeßum D 17 B12
Reetz D 79 B11
Reetz D 83 D11
Reftele S 87 A13
Regalbuto I 59 D6
Regen D 76 E4
Regensburg D 75 D11
Regensdorf CH 27 F9
Regenstauf D 75 D11
Reggello I 66 E4
Reggio di Calabria I 59 C8
Reggiolo I 66 C2
Reggio nell'Emilia I 66 C2
Reghin RO 152 D5
Reghiu RO 153 F9
Regna S 92 B7
Regnitzlosau D 75 B11
Régny F 30 D5
Regöly H 149 C10
Regozero RUS 121 D17
Regstrup DK 87 D9
Reguengo E 38 D2
Reguengos de Monsaraz P 50 C4
Rehau D 75 B11
Rehburg (Rehburg-Loccum) D 17 D12
Rehden D 17 C10
Rehling D 75 F8
Rehlingen-Siersburg D 21 F7
Řehlovice CZ 80 E5
Rehmsdorf D 79 D11
Rehna D 83 C10
Rehula FIN 129 C9
Reibitz D 79 C11
Reichelsheim (Odenwald) D 187 B6
Reichenau an der Rax A 148 A5
Reichenbach CH 70 D5
Reichenbach D 79 E11
Reichenbach D 187 B6
Reichenberg D 74 C6
Reichenfels A 73 B10
Reichenthal A 76 E6
Reichertsheim D 75 F11
Reichia GR 178 B5
Reichling D 71 B11
Reichmannsdorf D 75 A9
Reicholzheim D 74 C6
Reichraming A 73 A9
Reichshoffen F 27 C8
Reichstett F 186 D4
Reiden CH 27 F8
Reigada P 45 C7
Reigate GB 15 E8
Reignac F 28 E4
Reignier F 31 C9
Reil D 21 D8
Reilingen D 187 C6
Reillanne F 35 C10
Reillo E 47 E9
Reims F 19 F9
Reina E 51 C8
Reinach CH 27 F8
Reinach CH 27 F9
Reinbek D 83 C8
Reinberg D 84 B4
Reine N 110 E5
Reinfeld (Holstein) D 83 C8
Reinheim D 21 E11
Reinosa E 40 C3
Reinøysund N 114 D8
Reinsfeld D 21 E7
Reinskard N 112 D4
Reinskloster N 104 D7
Reinstad N 111 C10
Reinsvik N 104 E3
Reinsvoll N 101 E13
Reipa N 108 C6
Reisbach D 75 E12
Reischach D 75 F12
Reisjärvi FIN 123 C13
Reiskirchen D 21 C11
Reiss GB 3 J10
Reitan N 100 B8
Reitan N 101 A14
Reitano I 58 D5
Reith bei Seefeld A 72 B3
Reit im Winkl D 72 A5
Reittiö FIN 125 D9
Reivyčiai LT 134 D4
Rejmyre S 92 B7
Rejowiec PL 141 H8
Rejsby DK 86 E3
Reka HR 149 D7
Rekava LV 133 B3
Rekavice BIH 157 C7
Reken D 17 E8
Rekijoki FIN 127 E9
Rekken NL 17 D7
Reklynets' UA 144 C9
Rekovac SRB 159 F7
Rekowo PL 85 B12
Rekvik N 111 A15
Rėkyva LT 134 E6
Relíquias P 50 D3
Relletti FIN 119 E13
Relleu E 56 D4
Rellingen D 83 C7
Rém H 150 E3
Remagen D 21 C8
Rémalard F 24 D4
Rembercourt-Sommaisne F 26 C3
Remda D 79 E9
Remels (Uplengen) D 17 B9
Remennikovo RUS 133 C5
Remeskylä FIN 123 C16
Remetea RO 151 D9
Remetea RO 152 D6
Remetea Chioarului RO 152 B3
Remetea Mare RO 151 F7
Remeţi RO 145 H8
Remetinec HR 149 D6
Remetské Hámre SK 145 F5
Remich L 20 E6
Remicourt B 183 D6
Remiremont F 26 D6
Remmam S 107 D14
Remmen S 102 B8
Remmet S 102 B7
Remnes N 108 E4
Remolinos E 41 E9
Remouchamps B 183 E7
Remoulins F 35 C8
Remplin D 83 C13
Remptendorf D 75 A10
Remscheid D 21 B8
Remte LV 134 C5
Remungol F 22 E6
Rémuzat F 35 B9
Rena E 45 F9
Rena N 101 D14
Renaison F 30 C4
Renålandet S 106 D8
Renazé F 23 E9
Rencēni LV 131 F10
Renchen D 27 C9
Renda LV 134 B4
Rende I 60 E6
Rendsburg D 82 B7
Renedo E 39 E10
Renedo E 40 B4
Renedo de la Vega E 39 D10
Renens CH 31 B10
Renesse NL 16 E1
Renfrew GB 5 D8
Renginio GR 175 B6
Rengsdorf D 21 C8
Rengsjö S 103 D12
Renholmen S 118 D6
Reni UA 155 C2
Renko FIN 127 D11
Renkomäki FIN 127 D14
Renkum NL 183 B7
Renndal N 104 E5
Rennerod D 21 C10
Rennertshofen D 75 E9
Rennes F 23 D8
Rennes-les-Bains F 33 E10
Renningen D 27 C10
Renneg A 73 B8
Renòn I 72 C3
Rens DK 86 F4
Rensjön S 111 D18
Reńska Wieś PL 142 F5
Renström S 118 E4
Renswoude NL 183 A7
Rentina GR 174 A4
Rentjärn S 107 A15
Rentweinsdorf D 75 B8
Renwez F 19 E10
Renzow D 83 C10
Repbäcken S 97 A13
Répcelak H 149 B8
Repedea RO 152 B4
Repino RUS 129 E12
Repki PL 141 F6
Replot FIN 122 D6
Repojoki FIN 117 B15
Repolka RUS 132 C6
Reposaari FIN 126 B5
Repparfjord N 113 C13
Reppelin D 83 B12
Reppen N 108 C6
Reppenstedt D 83 D8
Reps AL 163 F9
Repton GB 11 F8
Repvåg N 113 B16
Requejo E 39 D6
Requena E 47 F10
Réquista F 33 B11
Rerik D 83 B11
Resana I 72 E4
Resarö S 99 D10
Resavica SRB 159 E8
Resele S 107 E12
Resen BG 166 C5
Resen MK 168 B5
Resenbro DK 86 C5
Resende P 44 B5
Rešetari HR 157 B7
Reșița RO 159 C8
Resko PL 85 C8
Resna MNE 163 E6
Resolven GB 13 B7
Respenda de la Peña E 39 C10
Resse (Wedemark) D 78 A6
Ressons-sur-Matz F 18 E6
Restelicë RKS 163 F10
Restinga MA 53 E6
Reston GB 5 D12
Resuttano I 58 D5
Retamal E 51 B8
Retford GB 11 E10
Rethel F 19 E9
Rethem (Aller) D 17 C12
Rethymno GR 178 E7
Retie B 16 F4
Retiers F 23 E9
Retje SLO 73 E10
Retortillo E 45 C8
Retortillo de Soria E 40 F6
Retournac F 30 E5
Rétság H 147 F8
Retuerta del Bullaque E 46 F4
Retunen FIN 125 E11
Retz A 77 E9
Reuden D 79 B11
Reuilly F 24 F7
Reurieth D 75 B8
Reus E 42 E6
Reusel NL 16 F4
Reut D 76 F3
Reute D 27 D8
Reuţel MD 153 B11
Reuterstadt Stavenhagen D 84 C3
Reutlingen D 27 D11
Reutte A 71 C11
Reutuaapa FIN 119 B15
Reuver NL 16 F6
Revel F 33 D10
Revello I 37 B6
Revest-du-Bion F 35 B10
Révfülöp H 149 C9
Revholmen N 91 A8
Reviga RO 161 D10
Revigny-sur-Ornain F 26 C2
Revilla de Collazos E 40 C3
Revilla del Campo E 40 D4
Revin F 19 E10
Revine-Lago I 72 E5
Řevnice CZ 76 C6
Řevničov CZ 76 B5
Revò I 72 D3
Revonlahti FIN 119 E13
Revsnes N 100 D6
Revsnes N 111 C11
Revsund S 103 A9
Revúca SK 147 D10
Rewal PL 85 B8
Rexbo S 103 E9
Reyrieux F 30 D6
Rezé F 23 F8
Rēzekne LV 133 C2
Rezi H 149 C8
Rezina MD 154 B3
Rēzna LV 133 D2
Rezovo BG 167 F10
Rezzato I 66 A1
Rezzo I 37 C7
Rezzoaglio I 37 B10
Rgotina SRB 159 E9
Rhade D 17 B12
Rhaunen D 21 E8
Rhayader GB 13 A7
Rheda-Wiedenbrück D 17 E10
Rhede D 17 E7
Rhede (Ems) D 17 B8
Rheden NL 183 A8
Rheinau D 27 C8
Rheinbach D 21 C7
Rheinberg D 17 E7
Rheinböllen D 185 E8
Rheinbreitbach D 21 C8
Rheinbrohl D 185 D7
Rheine D 17 D8
Rheinfelden (Baden) D 27 E8
Rheinsberg D 84 D3
Rheinstetten D 27 C9
Rheinzabern D 187 C5
Rhêmes-Notre-Dame I 31 D11
Rhêmes-St-Georges I 31 D11
Rhenen NL 16 E5
Rhens D 185 D8
Rhiconich GB 2 J7
Rhinau F 27 D8
Rhinow D 83 E12
Rhisnes B 182 D5
Rho I 69 B7
Rhode IRL 7 F8
Rhoden (Diemelstadt) D 17 F12
Rhoon NL 182 B4
Rhoose GB 13 C8
Rhosllanerchrugog GB 10 E5
Rhôs-on-Sea GB 10 E4
Rhossili GB 12 B6
Rhuddlan GB 10 E5
Rhydaman GB 12 B7
Rhyl GB 10 E5
Rhymney GB 13 B8
Riace I 59 C9
Riachos P 44 F3
Riaillé F 23 E9
Rialp E 33 F8
Riaño E 39 C10
Riano I 62 C3
Rians F 35 C10
Riantec F 22 E5
Rianxo E 38 C2
Riaz CH 31 B11
Riba E 40 B4
Ribadavia E 38 D3
Ribadelago E 39 D6
Riba de Mouro P 38 D3
Ribadeo E 38 A5
Riba de Saelices E 47 C8
Ribadesella E 39 B9
Ribaforada E 41 D8
Ribafrecha E 32 F1
Ribarci SRB 164 E6
Ribare SRB 164 C4
Ribari SRB 158 D3
Ribaritsa BG 165 D9
Riba-roja d'Ebre E 42 E4
Riba-roja de Turia E 48 E3
Ribbåsen S 102 D7
Ribchester GB 10 D6
Ribe DK 86 E3
Ribeauvillé F 27 D7
Ribécourt-Dreslincourt F 18 E6
Ribeira E 38 C2
Ribeira P 38 E3
Ribeira de Pena P 38 E4
Ribemont F 19 E7
Ribera I 58 E3
Ribérac F 29 E6
Ribera del Fresno E 51 B7
Ribesalbes E 48 D4
Ribes de Freser E 33 F10
Ribița RO 151 E10
Ribnica BIH 157 D9
Ribnica SLO 73 E10
Ribnica SLO 148 C4
Ribnica SRB 158 F4
Ribnik HR 148 E4
Rîbnița MD 154 B4
Ribnitz-Damgarten D 83 B12
Ribnovo BG 165 F8
Ribota E 40 F5
Ricadi I 59 B8
Říčany CZ 77 C7
Říčany CZ 77 D10
Riccia I 63 E7
Riccio I 66 F5
Riccione I 66 D6
Riccò del Golfo di Spezia I 69 E8
Richardménil F 26 C5
Richelieu F 29 A6
Richhill GB 7 D9
Richka UA 152 A5
Richmond GB 11 C8
Richvald SK 145 E3
Rickebo S 103 D11
Rickenbach D 27 E8
Rickinghall GB 15 C10
Rickling D 83 B8
Rickmansworth GB 15 D8
Ricla E 41 E9
Ricse H 145 G4
Ridasjärvi FIN 127 D13
Riddarhyttan S 97 C14
Ridderkerk NL 16 E3
Riddes CH 31 C11
Riđica SRB 150 F3
Rīdzene LV 135 B10
Riebiņi LV 135 D13
Riebnesluspen S 109 D13
Riec-sur-Belon F 22 E4
Ried CH 68 A5
Riede D 17 C11
Riedenburg D 75 E10
Rieder D 79 C9
Ried im Innkreis A 76 F4
Ried im Oberinntal A 71 C11
Ried im Zillertal A 72 B4
Ried in der Riedmark A 77 F7
Riedlingen D 71 A8
Riegelsberg D 21 F7
Riegersburg A 148 B5
Riego de la Vega E 39 D8
Riehe (Suthfeld) D 78 B5
Riehen CH 27 E8
Rielasingen-Worblingen D 27 E10
Riello E 39 C8
Rielves E 46 E4
Riemst B 19 C12
Rieneck D 187 A8
Rieni RO 151 D9
Rieponlahti FIN 124 E7
Riepsdorf D 83 B9
Riesa D 80 D4
Rieseby D 83 A7
Riesi I 58 E5
Riestedt D 79 D9
Rietavas LT 134 E3
Rietberg D 17 E10
Rieth D 84 C6
Riethoven NL 183 C6
Rieti I 62 C3
Rietschen D 81 D7
Rieumes F 33 D8
Rieupeyroux F 33 B10
Rieutort-de-Randon F 34 A5
Rieux F 23 E7
Rieux F 33 D8
Riez F 36 D4
Rifiano I 72 C3
Rīga LV 135 C8
Rigaio GR 169 F8
Rigaud F 36 D5
Riggisberg CH 31 B11
Rignac F 33 B10
Rignano Flaminio I 62 C2
Rignano Garganico I 63 D9
Rignano sull'Arno I 66 E3
Rigny-le-Ferron F 25 D10
Rigny-sur-Arroux F 30 B5
Rigny-Ussé F 24 F3
Rigside GB 5 D9
Rihtniemi FIN 126 C5
Riihimäki FIN 127 D12
Riihivaara FIN 125 C14
Riikonkumpu FIN 117 C14
Riipi FIN 117 D16
Riippi FIN 122 F7
Riisipere EST 131 C8
Riistavesi FIN 125 E10
Riitiala FIN 127 B8
Riječa BIH 157 E10
Rijeka BIH 157 D9
Rijeka BIH 157 F11
Rijeka HR 67 B9
Rijeka Crnojevića MNE 163 E7
Rijen NL 16 E3
Rijkevorsel B 16 F3
Rijnsburg NL 16 D2
Rijsbergen NL 16 E3
Rijsel F 19 C7
Rijssen NL 17 D7
Rijswijk NL 16 D2
Rikava LV 133 C2
Riksgränsen S 111 D15
Rila BG 165 E7
Rilhac-Rancon F 29 D8
Rilland NL 182 C4
Rillé F 23 F12
Rillieux-la-Pape F 30 D6
Rillo E 42 F2
Rillo de Gallo E 47 C9
Rimavská Baňa SK 147 D9
Rimavská Seč SK 145 G1
Rimavská Sobota SK 147 E10
Rimavské Janovce SK 147 E10
Rimbach D 76 D3
Rimbach D 187 B6
Rimbo S 99 C10
Rimetea RO 152 E3
Rimforsa S 92 C7
Rimicāni LV 135 D12
Rimini I 66 D6
Rimjokk S 118 B5
Rimmilä FIN 127 D11
Rimóc H 147 E9
Rimogne F 184 E2
Rimont F 33 E8
Rimpar D 74 C6
Rimsbo S 103 D11
Rimšė LT 135 E12
Rimšėnai LT 135 F12
Rimske Toplice SLO 73 D11
Rimsting D 72 A5
Rinchnach D 76 E4
Rincón de la Victoria E 53 C8
Rincón de Soto E 41 D8
Rinda LV 134 A3
Rindal N 104 E6
Rindsholm DK 86 C4
Rineia GR 176 E5
Rinella I 59 B6
Ringarum S 93 C8
Ringaudai LT 137 D8
Ringe D 17 C7
Ringe DK 86 E6
Ringebu N 101 C12
Ringelia N 101 E12
Ringen N 95 B12
Ringford GB 5 F8
Ringhals S 87 A10
Ringkøbing DK 86 C2
Ringleben D 79 D9
Ringsend GB 4 E3
Ringsta S 106 E7
Ringsted DK 87 E9
Ringvattnet S 106 C8
Ringville IRL 9 D7
Ringwood GB 13 D11
Rinkaby S 88 D6
Rinkabyholm S 89 B10
Rinkenæs DK 86 F5
Rinkilä FIN 129 B10
Rinloan GB 5 A10
Rinn S 97 B9
Rinneen IRL 8 C4
Rinøyvåg N 111 D10
Rintala FIN 123 D10
Rinteln D 17 D12
Rio GR 174 C4
Rio Caldo P 38 E3
Rio de Mel P 44 C6
Rio de Moinhos P 50 B4
Rio de Moinhos P 50 C3
Rio de Moinhos P 50 D3
Rio de Onor P 39 E6
Rio di Pusteria I 72 C4
Riofrío E 46 C3
Riofrío de Aliste E 39 E7
Riogordo E 53 C8
Rioja E 55 F8
Riola Sardo I 64 D2
Riolobos E 45 E8
Riolo Terme I 66 D4
Riols F 34 C4
Riom F 30 D3
Riomaggiore I 69 E8
Rio Maior P 44 F3
Rio Marina I 65 B2
Riom-ès-Montagnes F 29 E11
Rion-des-Landes F 32 C4
Rionegro del Puente E 39 D7
Rio nell'Elba I 65 B2
Rionero in Vulture I 60 B5
Rionero Sannitico I 63 D6
Rions F 32 A5
Riorges F 30 C5
Ríos E 38 E5
Rioseco de Tapia E 39 C8
Rio Tinto P 44 B3
Rio Torto P 38 E5
Rioz F 26 F5
Ripač BIH 156 C4
Ripacandida I 60 B5
Ripalimosano I 63 D7
Ripanj SRB 158 D6
Riparbella I 66 F2
Ripatransone I 62 B5
Ripe I 67 E7
Ripi I 62 D4
Ripiceni RO 153 B10
Ripley GB 11 C8
Ripley GB 11 E9
Ripoll E 43 C8
Ripon GB 11 C8
Riposto I 59 D7
Rips NL 183 B7
Riquewihr F 27 D7
Risan MNE 163 D6
Risarven S 103 C10
Risbäck S 106 B9
Risberg S 102 D6
Risca GB 13 B8
Rișca RO 151 D11
Rîșcani MD 153 B11
Riscle F 32 C5
Risdal N 90 B3
Risede S 106 C8
Rish BG 167 D7
Risinge S 92 B7
Risliden S 107 B16
Risnabben S 118 D3
Risnes N 94 E5
Risør N 90 B5
Risøyhamn N 111 C10
Rissa N 104 D7
Rissna S 106 E8
Rissnaben S 118 D4
Riste FIN 126 C7
Risteli FIN 125 B12
Risti EST 131 D8
Ristiina FIN 128 B7
Ristijärvi FIN 121 F11
Ristilä FIN 121 B11
Ristilampi FIN 117 E17
Ristinen FIN 124 D7
Ristinkylä FIN 125 E12
Ristioja FIN 117 E13
Ristonmännikkö FIN 117 D16
Risträsk S 107 B12
Risudden S 119 B11
Risum-Lindholm D 82 A5
Rītausmas LV 135 D8
Rite LV 135 D10
Rīteri LV 135 C11
Ritini GR 169 D7
Ritola FIN 123 E11
Ritterhude D 17 B11
Rittersdorf D 185 D5
Rittersgrün D 75 B12
Riudarenes E 43 D9
Riudecols E 42 E5
Riudoms E 42 E6
Riutta FIN 123 C12
Riutula FIN 113 F18
Rīva LV 134 C2
Riva del Garda I 69 B10
Riva di Solto I 69 B9
Riva di Tures I 72 C5
Rivanazzano I 37 B10
Rivardo Ligure I 37 C9
Rivarolo Canavese I 68 C4
Rivarolo Mantovano I 66 B1
Rivas-Vaciamadrid E 46 D6
Rive-de-Gier F 30 D6
Rivedoux-Plage F 28 C3
Rivello I 60 C5
Riverchapel IRL 9 C10
Rivergaro I 37 B11
Rivero E 40 B3
Riverstown IRL 7 F7
Riverstown IRL 8 E6
Rivery F 18 E5
Rives F 31 E8
Rivesaltes F 34 E4
Rivière-sur-Tarn F 34 B5
Rivignano I 73 E7
Rivinperä FIN 119 F16
Rivodutri I 62 B3
Rivoli I 68 C4
Rivolta d'Adda I 69 C8
Rixensart B 19 C10
Rixheim F 27 E7
Rixö S 91 C9
Riza GR 175 C6
Rizes GR 174 E5
Rizia GR 171 A10
Rizomata GR 169 D7
Rizomylos GR 169 F8
Rizziconi I 59 C8
Rjånes N 100 B3
Rjukan N 95 C9
Rø DK 89 E7
Ro I 66 C4
Rö S 103 A14
Roa E 40 E4
Roa N 95 B13
Roade GB 15 C7
Roadside GB 3 H10
Roadside of Kinneff GB 5 B12
Roager DK 86 E3
Roaillan F 32 B5
Roald N 100 A4
Roan N 104 C8
Roanne F 30 C5
Roata de Jos RO 161 E7
Roath GB 13 C8
Röbäck S 122 C4
Robănești RO 160 E4
Robbio I 68 C6
Robeasca RO 161 C10
Robecco d'Oglio I 69 C9
Röbel D 83 D13
Robella I 68 C5
Robert-Espagne F 26 C3
Roberton GB 5 D9
Roberton GB 5 E11
Robertsfors S 118 F5
Robežnieki LV 133 E3
Robiac-Rochessadoule F 35 B7
Robilante I 37 C6
Robin Hood's Bay GB 11 C10
Robion F 35 C9
Robledo E 55 B8
Robledo de Chavela E 46 C4
Robledo del Mazo E 46 E3
Robledollano E 45 E9
Robles de la Valcueva E 39 C9
Robliza de Cojos E 45 C9
Robșle N 101 E11
Robregordo E 46 B5
Robres E 41 E11
Robres del Castillo E 32 F1
Roč HR 67 B9
Rocafort de Queralt E 43 E6
Rocamadour F 29 F9
Roca Vecchia I 61 C10
Roccabianca I 66 B1
Roccadaspide I 60 C4
Rocca d'Evandro I 60 A1
Rocca di Cambio I 62 C4
Rocca di Mezzo I 62 C5
Rocca di Neto I 61 E7
Rocca di Papa I 62 D3
Roccafranca I 69 C8
Roccagloriosa I 60 C4
Roccagorga I 62 D4
Rocca Grimalda I 37 B9
Rocca Imperiale I 61 C7
Roccalbegna I 65 B5
Roccalumera I 59 D7
Roccamandolfi I 63 D6
Rocca Massima I 62 D3
Roccamena I 58 D3
Roccamonfina I 60 A1
Roccamontepiano I 62 C6
Roccanova I 60 C6
Roccapalumba I 58 D4
Rocca Pia I 62 D5
Roccaraso I 62 D6
Rocca San Casciano I 66 D4
Rocca San Giovanni I 63 C6
Roccasecca I 62 D5
Roccasecca dei Volsci I 62 E4
Rocca Sinibalda I 62 C3
Roccastrada I 65 A4
Roccavione I 37 C6
Roccella Ionica I 59 C9
Rocchetta Sant'Antonio I 60 A4
Rochdale GB 11 D7
Roche GB 12 E5
Rochechouart F 29 D7
Rochefort B 19 D11
Rochefort F 28 D4
Rochefort-en-Terre F 23 E7
Rochefort-Montagne F 30 D2
Rochefort-sur-Nenon F 26 F4
Rochehaut B 184 E3
Roche-la-Molière F 30 E5
Rochemaure F 35 A8
Roches-Bettaincourt F 26 D3
Rocheservière F 28 B2
Rochester GB 5 E12
Rochester GB 15 E10
Rochetaillée F 26 E3
Rochford GB 15 D10
Rochfortbridge IRL 7 F8
Rochin F 19 C7
Rochlitz D 79 D12
Rociana del Condado E 51 E6
Ročinj SLO 73 D8
Rociu RO 160 D6
Rockanje NL 182 B4
Rockchapel IRL 8 D4
Rockcliffe GB 5 F9
Rockcorry IRL 7 D8
Rockenhausen D 21 E9
Rockesholm S 97 C12
Rockhammar S 97 C13
Rockhill IRL 8 D5
Rockingham GB 11 F10
Rockmills IRL 8 D6
Rockneby S 89 B10
Röcknitz D 79 D12
Rocourt-St-Martin F 25 B9
Rocroi F 19 E10
Roda de Bara E 43 E6
Roda de Ter E 43 D8
Rodalben D 21 F9
Rodaljice HR 156 D4
Rödåsel S 118 F3
Rodberg N 95 B9
Rødbergshamn N 111 B15
Rødby DK 83 A10
Rødbyhavn DK 83 A10
Rødding DK 86 B3
Rødding DK 86 C5
Rødding DK 86 E4
Rödeby S 89 C9
Rodeiro E 38 C4
Rødekro DK 86 E4
Rodel GB 2 K3
Rodellar E 32 F5
Rodelle F 34 A4
Roden NL 17 B6
Ródenas E 47 C10
Rodenkirchen (Stadland) D 17 B10
Rödental D 75 B9
Rodewald D 82 E6
Rodewisch D 75 A11
Rodez F 33 B11
Rodi Garganico I 63 D9
Roding D 75 D12
Rodingträsk S 107 C14
Rödjebro S 98 B8
Rødkærsbro DK 86 C4
Rodleben D 79 C11
Rødlia N 108 E7
Rödmyra S 103 C11
Rodna RO 152 C5
Rododafni GR 174 C5
Rodolivos GR 170 C5
Rödön S 105 E16
Rodopoli GR 169 B9
Rodopos GR 178 D6
Rodos GR 181 D8
Rødovre DK 87 D10
Rødsand N 111 B13
Rødsand N 114 D8
Rødseidet N 105 B11
Rödvattnet S 107 D13
Rødvig DK 87 E10
Roela EST 131 C13
Roermond NL 20 B5
Roeselare B 19 C7
Roești RO 160 D4
Roetgen D 20 C6
Röfors S 92 B5
Rofrano I 60 C4
Rogač HR 156 F5
Rogačica SRB 158 E4
Rogaška Slatina SLO 148 D5
Rogaszyce PL 142 D4
Rogate GB 15 E7
Rogatec SLO 148 D5
Rogatica BIH 157 E11
Rogätz D 79 B10
Roggel NL 16 F5
Roggenburg D 75 F7
Roggendorf D 83 C10
Roggentin D 84 D3
Roggiano Gravina I 60 D6
Roghudi I 59 C8
Rogienice Wielkie PL 139 D13
Rogil P 50 E2
Rogliano F 37 F10
Rogliano I 61 E6
Rognac F 35 D9

Rognan N 108 B9
Rognes F 35 C9
Rognes N 104 E8
Rognonas F 35 C8
Rogova RO 159 E10
Rogovka LV 133 C2
Rogów PL 141 G1
Rogowo PL 138 E4
Rogowo PL 139 E7
Rogozen BG 165 B8
Rogoznica HR 156 E4
Rogoźnica PL 81 D10
Rogoźniczka PL 141 F7
Rogoźno PL 85 E12
Rogslösa S 92 C5
Rogsta S 103 C13
Rohan F 22 D6
Röhlingen D 75 E7
Rohlsdorf D 83 E10
Rohlsdorf D 83 D12
Rohod H 145 G5
Rohovce SK 146 E4
Rohožník S 77 F12
Rohr D 79 E8
Rohrau A 77 F11
Rohrbach D 75 E10
Rohrbach in Oberösterreich A 76 E5
Rohrbach-lès-Bitche F 27 B7
Rohrberg D 83 E10
Rohr in Niederbayern D 75 E10
Röhrmoos D 75 F9
Röhrnbach D 76 E5
Rohrsen D 17 C12
Rohuküla EST 130 D6
Roiffieux F 30 E6
Roisel F 19 E7
Roismala FIN 127 C8
Roivainen FIN 115 B2
Roiz E 40 B3
Roja LV 134 A5
Rojales E 56 E3
Röjan S 102 B7
Röjdåfors S 97 B8
Rojewo PL 138 E5
Rôkå S 107 A15
Rokai LT 137 D8
Rokiciny PL 143 C8
Rokietnica PL 81 A11
Rokietnica PL 144 D6
Rokiškis LT 135 E11
Rokitno PL 141 F8
Rokksøy N 111 C10
Røkland N 101 A8
Røkland N 108 C9
Roklum D 79 B8
Roknäs S 118 D6
Rokycany CZ 76 C5
Rokytnice CZ 146 C4
Rokytnice v Orlických Horách CZ 77 B10
Rolampont F 26 E3
Rold DK 86 B5
Røldal N 94 C5
Rolde NL 17 C7
Rolfs S 119 C10
Rolfstorp S 87 A10
Rollag N 95 B10
Rollán E 45 C9
Rolle CH 31 C9
Rolsted DK 86 E7
Rolvåg N 108 D3
Rolvsnes N 94 C2
Rolvsøy N 95 D14
Rom D 83 D11
Rom F 29 C6
Roma I 62 D3
Roma RO 153 B9
Roma S 93 D12
Romagnano Sesia I 68 B5
Romagné F 23 D9
Romainmôtier CH 31 B9
Romakkajärvi FIN 117 E13
Roman BG 165 C8
Roman RO 153 D9
Romana I 64 C2
Romanàsl RO 151 C11
Românesti RO 153 B10
Români RO 153 D9
Romanija BIH 157 E10
Romano d'Ezzelino I 72 E4
Romano di Lombardia I 69 B8
Romanones E 47 C7
Romanovce MK 164 E4
Romanovo RUS 136 D1
Romanowo PL 85 E11
Romanshorn CH 27 E11
Romans-sur-Isère F 31 E7
Romanu RO 155 C1
Romazy F 23 D9
Rombas F 20 F6
Rombiolo I 59 B9
Romeira P 44 F3
Rometta I 59 C7
Romeu P 38 E5
Romford GB 15 D9
Romhány H 147 F8
Römhild D 75 B8
Romillé F 23 D8
Romilly-sur-Seine F 25 C10
Rommerskirchen D 21 B7
Romont CH 31 B10
Rømonysæter N 102 C3
Romorantin-Lanthenay F 24 F6
Romos RO 151 F11
Romppala FIN 125 E13
Romrod D 21 C12
Romsey GB 13 D12
Rømskog N 96 D6
Romsley GB 13 A10
Romstad N 105 C10
Romuli RO 152 B4
Rona de Jos RO 145 H9
Rona de Sus RO 145 H9
Rönäs S 108 E8
Rønbjerg DK 86 B3
Roncade I 72 E5
Roncadelle I 66 A1
Roncal E 32 E4
Roncegno I 69 A11
Ronce-les-Bains F 28 D3
Ronchamp F 26 E6
Ronchi dei Legionari I 73 E7
Ronciglione I 62 C2
Ronco Canavese I 68 C4
Ronco Scrivia I 37 B9
Ronda E 53 C6
Rønde DK 86 C6
Rondissone I 68 C4

Rone S 93 E12
Ronehamn S 93 E12
Rong N 94 A1
Rôngu EST 131 E12
Rönnäng S 91 D10
Rönnbacken S 103 E11
Rönnberg S 118 D6
Rønne DK 88 E7
Rønnebæk DK 87 E9
Ronneburg D 79 E11
Ronneby S 89 C8
Rønnede DK 87 E10
Ronnenberg D 78 B6
Rönninge S 93 A11
Rönnliden S 109 F17
Rönnöfors S 105 D15
Rönö S 93 C9
Ronov nad Doubravou CZ 77 C9
Ronsberg D 71 B10
Ronse B 19 C8
Ronshausen D 78 E6
Ronvik N 108 B7
Rooaun IRL 6 F6
Roodeschool NL 17 B7
Rookchapel IRL 8 D4
Roosendaal NL 16 E2
Roosinpohja FIN 123 F13
Roosky IRL 7 E7
Roosna-Alliku EST 131 C11
Ropa PL 145 D3
Ropažl LV 135 C9
Ropcha UA 153 A7
Ropczyce PL 143 F12
Ropeid N 94 D4
Roperuelos del Páramo E 39 D8
Ropienka PL 145 D5
Ropinsalmi FIN 116 A7
Ropotovo MK 168 B5
Roquebillière F 37 C6
Roquebrun F 34 C5
Roquebrune-Cap-Martin F 37 D6
Roquebrune-sur-Argens F 36 E5
Roquecor F 33 B7
Roquecourbe F 33 C10
Roquefort F 32 B5
Roquemaure F 35 B8
Roquesteron F 36 D6
Roquetas E 42 F5
Roquetas de Mar E 55 F7
Roquevaire F 35 D10
Rörberg S 103 E12
Rörby DK 87 D8
Rore BIH 157 D6
Røros N 101 A14
Rorschach CH 71 C9
Rörvattnet S 105 D16
Rørvig DK 87 D9
Rørvik N 94 F5
Rørvik N 105 B10
Rørvik N 110 D7
Rörvik S 88 A7
Rosà I 72 E4
Rosala FIN 126 F7
Rosal de la Frontera E 51 D5
Rosans F 35 B9
Rosapenna IRL 7 B7
Rosário P 50 D3
Rosarno I 59 C8
Rosavci BIH 157 C6
Rosbach vor der Höhe D 21 D11
Roscanvel F 22 D2
Ros Cathail IRL 6 F4
Rosche D 83 E9
Roscigno I 60 C4
Rościszewo PL 139 E8
Roscoff F 22 C4
Ros Comáin IRL 6 E6
Roscommon IRL 6 E6
Ros Cré IRL 9 C7
Roscrea IRL 9 C7
Rosdorf D 78 D6
Rose I 60 E6
Rose MNE 162 E6
Rosée B 184 D2
Rosehearty GB 3 K12
Rosemarkie GB 3 K8
Rosen BG 167 E9
Rosenallis IRL 7 F8
Rosendal N 94 C4
Rosenfeld D 27 D10
Rosenfors S 92 E7
Rosengarten D 83 D7
Rosenheim D 72 A5
Rosenlund S 91 D13
Rosenow D 84 C4
Rosenthal D 21 C11
Roserberg S 99 C9
Roses E 43 C10
Roseti RO 161 E10
Roseto Capo Spulico I 61 D7
Roseto degli Abruzzi I 62 B5
Roseto Valfortore I 60 A4
Roshchino RUS 129 E12
Rosheim F 27 C7
Roshven GB 4 B5
Rosia RO 151 D9
Rosia RO 152 F4
Rosia de Amaradia RO 160 C3
Rosia de Secaş RO 152 E3
Rosia Montană RO 151 E11
Rosica LV 133 D3
Rosice CZ 77 C9
Rosice CZ 77 D10
Rosières F 30 F5
Rosières-en-Santerre F 18 E6
Roşieşti RO 153 E11
Rosignano Marittimo I 66 F1
Roşiile RO 160 D3
Roşiori RO 153 D10
Roşiori RO 161 D10
Roşiori de Vede RO 160 E6
Rositsa BG 155 F11
Rositsa BY 133 E3
Rositz D 79 D11
Rosiyanivka UA 154 C5
Roskhill GB 2 L3
Roskilde DK 87 D10
Rosko PL 85 E10
Roskow D 79 B12
Röslau D 75 B10
Roslev DK 86 B3
Rosmalen NL 16 E4
Rosmaninhal P 45 E6
Ros Mhic Thriúin IRL 9 D9
Rosnowo PL 85 B10
Rosolina I 66 B5

Rosolina Mare I 66 B5
Rosolini I 59 F6
Rosoman MK 169 A6
Rosoy F 25 D9
Rosporden F 22 E4
Rösrath D 21 C8
Rossano I 61 D7
Rossano Veneto I 72 E4
Roßbol S 118 B11
Rosscahill IRL 6 F4
Ross Carbery IRL 8 E4
Rosscarbery IRL 8 E4
Rosscor GB 6 D6
Roßdorf D 21 E11
Rossell E 42 F4
Rosselló E 42 D5
Rosses Point IRL 6 D5
Rossett GB 10 E6
Rossfjord N 111 B15
Roßhaupten D 71 B11
Rossiglione I 37 B9
Rossignol B 19 E11
Rössing (Nordstemmen) D 78 B6
Rossington GB 11 E9
Rossio ao Sul do Tejo P 44 F4
Roßla D 79 D9
Rosslare IRL 9 D10
Rosslare Harbour IRL 9 D10
Roßlau D 79 C11
Rosslea GB 7 D8
Roßleithen A 73 A9
Rossnowlagh IRL 6 C6
Rossön S 107 D10
Ross-on-Wye GB 13 B9
Rossosz PL 141 G8
Rossoszyca PL 142 C6
Rossow D 83 D13
Roßtal D 75 D8
Rossum NL 183 B6
Røssvassbukta N 108 E7
Rossvik N 105 A11
Rossvoll N 104 E4
Rossvoll N 111 B15
Roßwein D 80 D4
Røst N 108 A3
Röstabo S 103 D11
Röstånga S 87 C12
Rostarzewo PL 81 B10
Röste S 103 D11
Rostellan IRL 8 E6
Rostock D 83 B12
Rostrenen F 22 D5
Rostrevor GB 7 D10
Röström S 107 C10
Rostrup DK 86 B5
Rostundelva N 112 D6
Rosturk IRL 6 E3
Rostuša MK 168 A4
Røstvollen N 102 B3
Røsvik S 118 D7
Rosvik S 118 D6
Roszki-Wodźki PL 140 D6
Roszków PL 142 C4
Röszke H 150 E5
Rot S 102 D7
Rota E 52 C4
Rota N 111 E10
Rota Greca I 60 E6
Rot am See D 74 D7
Rot an der Rot D 71 A10
Rotava CZ 75 B12
Rotberget N 97 A8
Roteberg S 103 D12
Rotello I 63 D7
Rotenburg (Wümme) D 17 B12
Rotenburg an der Fulda D 78 D6
Rötgesbüttel D 79 B8
Rotgülden A 73 B7
Roth D 75 D9
Röthenbach an der Pegnitz D 75 D9
Rothenberg D 21 E11
Rothenbuch D 74 C5
Rothenburg (Oberlausitz) D 81 D7
Rothenburg ob der Tauber D 75 D7
Rothéneuf F 23 C8
Rothenfels D 74 C6
Rothenschirmbach D 79 D10
Rothenstein D 79 E10
Rotherham GB 11 E9
Rothes GB 3 K10
Rothesay GB 4 D6
Rotheux-Rimière B 19 C11
Rothiesholm GB 3 G11
Rothley GB 11 F9
Rothrist CH 27 F8
Rothwell GB 15 C8
Rothwell GB 11 D7
Rothwesten (Fuldatal) D 78 D6
Rotimlja BIH 157 F8
Rotimjoki FIN 123 C17
Rotnäset S 106 C9
Rotonda I 60 D6
Rotondella I 61 C7
Rotselaar B 19 C10
Rotsjö S 103 A10
Rotsjön S 118 F4
Rotsund N 112 D6
Rott D 71 B11
Rottach-Egern D 72 A4
Rott am Inn D 75 G11
Røttangen N 111 E10
Rottenacker D 71 A9
Röttenbach D 75 D9
Rottenbach D 79 E9
Rottenbuch D 71 B11
Rottenburg am Neckar D 27 D10
Rottenburg an der Laaber D 75 E11
Rottendorf D 74 C7
Rottenmann A 73 A9
Rotterdam NL 16 E3
Rotthalmünster D 76 F4
Röttingen D 74 C6
Rottleberode D 79 C9
Rottne S 89 A7
Rottnemon S 96 B8
Rottofreno I 69 C8
Rottweil D 27 D10
Rötz D 75 D12
Rouans F 23 F8
Roubaix F 19 C7
Roúddaas Sámit FIN ... [Roude EST 131 D13]
Roudnice nad Labem CZ 76 B6

Rouen F 18 F3
Rouffach F 27 E7
Rouffignac F 29 E7
Rôuge EST 131 F13
Rougé F 23 E9
Rougemont F 26 F5
Rougemont-le-Château F 27 E6
Roughton GB 15 B11
Rougnac F 29 D6
Rouillac F 29 D6
Rouillé F 28 C6
Roujan F 34 C5
Roukala FIN 119 F11
Roukalahti FIN 125 F13
Roulans F 26 F5
Roulers B 19 C7
Roulers B 182 D2
Roumazières-Loubert F 29 D7
Roumoules F 36 D4
Roundstone IRL 6 F3
Roundway GB 13 C11
Roundwood IRL 7 F10
Rouravaara FIN 117 C14
Roure I 31 E11
Rousínov CZ 77 D11
Rousky GB 4 F2
Rousset F 35 D10
Roussillon F 30 E6
Roussillon F 35 C9
Rousson F 35 B7
Routot F 18 F2
Rouvroy F 182 E1
Rouvroy-sur-Audry F 19 E10
Rouy F 30 A4
Rovala FIN 115 C5
Rovala FIN 115 C5
Rovaniemi FIN 117 F15
Rovanpää FIN 117 C15
Rovanpää FIN 117 E12
Rovapää FIN 119 B9
Rovastinaho FIN 119 C16
Rovato I 69 B9
Rovegno I 37 B10
Roverbella I 66 B2
Roveredo CH 69 A7
Rovereto I 69 B11
Rö,vershagen D 83 B12
Roverud N 96 B7
Roviano I 62 C3
Rovies GR 175 B7
Rovigo I 66 B4
Rovinari RO 159 D11
Rovine BIH 157 B7
Rovinj HR 67 B8
Rovinka SK 146 E4
Rovišče HR 149 E7
Rovisuvanto FIN 113 E16
Rovšättra S 99 B10
Rów PL 85 E7
Rowde GB 13 C10
Równa PL 142 C6
Rownaye F 28 C6
Roxmo S 93 A8
Roxton GB 15 C8
Royal Wootton Bassett GB 13 B11
Royan F 28 D3
Royat F 30 D3
Roybon F 31 E7
Roybridge GB 4 B7
Roydon GB 15 C11
Roye F 18 E6
Royère-de-Vassivière F 29 D9
Røyken N 95 C12
Røykenes N 111 C10
Røykkä FIN 127 E12
Roylyanka UA 154 E5
Røyrvik N 105 B15
Røyse N 95 B12
Royston GB 15 C8
Royton GB 11 D7
Röyttä FIN 119 C12
Roytvollen N 105 A12
Royuela E 47 D10
Roza BG 166 E6
Rožaje MNE 163 D9
Rozalén del Monte E 47 E7
Rozalimas LT 134 E7
Rózan PL 139 E11
Rózanki PL 85 E8
Rozavlea RO 152 B4
Rozay-en-Brie F 25 C8
Roždalovice CZ 77 B8
Rozdil UA 145 E8
Rozdil'na UA 154 D6
Rozdrażew PL 142 C4
Rozenburg NL 182 B4
Rozendaal NL 183 A7
Roženica HR 148 E5
Rozes LV 135 B11
Rozhniv UA 152 A6
Rozhnyativ UA 145 F9
Rozino BG 165 D10
Rožmitál pod Třemšínem CZ 76 C5
Rožňava SK 145 F2
Rožniatów PL 142 B6
Roznov RO 153 D9
Rožnov pod Radhoštěm CZ 146 C6
Roznowo PL 85 E11
Rozogi PL 139 D11
Rozovets BG 166 E4
Rozoy-sur-Serre F 19 E9
Rozprza PL 143 D8
Rozptoka Wielka PL 145 E2
Roztoky CZ 76 B5
Roztoky UA 152 A6
Rozula LV 135 B9
Rožupe LV 135 D12
Rozzano I 69 C7

Rubielos de la Cérida E 47 C10
Rubielos de Mora E 48 D3
Rubiera I 66 C2
Rubik AL 163 F8
Rubkow D 84 C5
Rucăr RO 160 C6
Rucava LV 134 D2
Rucphen-Nida PL 139 C12
Rückersdorf D 80 C5
Ruda PL 142 B6
Ruda S 89 B11
Rudabánya H 145 G2
Ruda Maleniecka PL 141 H2
Rudamina LT 137 D11
Rudamina LT 137 E7
Rudartsi BG 165 D7
Ruda Śląska PL 142 F6
Rudbārzl LV 134 C3
Rudbjerg DK 87 F7
Rudka PL 141 E7
Rudkøbing DK 87 F7
Rudky UA 145 D7
Rudná CZ 76 B6
Rudna PL 81 C10
Rudna Glava SRB 159 E9
Rudňany SK 145 F2
Rudne UA 144 D8
Rudnica RO 160 C3
Rudnica SRB 163 C10
Rudnik BG 167 D9
Rudnik PL 142 F5
Rudnik SRB 158 E5
Rudniki PL 142 D6
Rudnik nad Sadem PL 144 C5
Rudno PL 81 A10
Rudno PL 138 C5
Rudnya UA 145 E8
Rudnytsya UA 154 A3
Rudo BIH 158 F3
Rudolfov CZ 77 E7
Rudolstadt D 79 E9
Rudozem BG 171 B7
Rudsgrendi N 95 C9
Rudsjön S 107 D10
Rudston GB 11 C11
Ruds Vedby DK 87 D8
Rudzāti LV 135 D13
Rudziczka PL 142 F4
Rudziniec PL 142 F5
Rue F 18 D4
Rueda E 39 F10
Rueda de Jalón E 41 E9
Rueil-Malmaison F 24 C7
Ruelle-sur-Touvre F 29 D6
Ruen BG 167 D8
Ruente E 40 B3
Ruffano I 61 D10
Ruffec F 26 F5
Ruffec F 29 C6
Ruffey-lès-Echirey F 26 F3
Ruffiac F 23 E7
Ruffieu F 31 C8
Ruffieux F 31 D8
Rufford GB 10 D6
Rufina I 66 E3
Rugāji LV 133 B2
Rugby GB 13 A12
Rugeley GB 11 F8
Rugge N 110 C8
Rugince MK 164 E4
Ruginesti RO 153 E10
Ruginoasa RO 153 C9
Rügland D 75 D8
Rugles F 24 C4
Rugvica HR 148 E6
Ruha FIN 123 E9
Ruhala FIN 124 G2
Ruhla D 79 E7
Ruhland D 80 D5
Ruhmannsfelden D 76 E3
Rühn D 83 C11
Ruhpolding D 73 A6
Ruhsdorf an der Rott D 76 F4
Ruidera E 55 B7
Ruikka FIN 119 B14
Ruinas I 64 D2
Ruinen NL 16 C6
Ruinerwold NL 16 C6
Ruiselede B 19 C8
Ruismäki FIN 123 D10
Ruivães P 38 E3
Ruja PL 81 D10
Rüjiena LV 131 F10
Rujišta BIH 157 F8
Ruka FIN 121 B13
Rukajärvi FIN 121 B13
Rukkisperä FIN 119 E14
Rulbo S 102 A7
Rullbo S 102 E7
Rullnäs S 107 D15
Rully F 30 B6
Rülzheim D 27 B9
Rum A 72 B3
Rum BY 133 E6
Rum H 149 B7
Ruma SRB 158 C4
Rumboci BIH 157 E7
Rumburk CZ 81 E7
Rumelange L 20 F6
Rumelifeneri TR 173 B11
Rumenka SRB 158 C4
Rumes B 19 C7
Rumia PL 138 A5
Rumigny F 19 E9
Rumilly F 31 D8
Rummu EST 131 C8
Rummukkala FIN 125 F12
Rumo FIN 125 C11
Rumont F 26 C3
Rumšiškes LT 137 D9
Rumskulla S 92 D7
Rumyantsevo BG 165 C9
Runaberg S 107 E11
Runcorn GB 10 E6
Runcu RO 160 C4
Runcu RO 160 C6
Rundēni LV 133 D3
Rundfloen N 102 D4

Rundhaug N 111 B16
Rundmoen N 108 D8
Rundvik S 107 D16
Rungsted DK 87 D11
Runhällen S 98 B7
Runik RKS 163 D10
Runkel D 185 D9
Runni FIN 123 C17
Runovic HR 157 F7
Runsten S 89 B11
Runtuna S 93 B10
Ruohokangas FIN 115 A3
Ruohola FIN 119 C15
Ruokojärvi FIN 117 D11
Ruokojärvi FIN 129 B11
Ruokojärvi S 117 D11
Ruokolahti FIN 129 C10
Ruokoniemi FIN 125 F11
Ruokotaipale FIN 128 C8
Ruolahti FIN 127 B13
Ruoms F 35 B7
Ruona FIN 119 B17
Ruona FIN 123 E11
Ruonajärvi FIN 117 D13
Ruopsa FIN 115 E2
Ruorasmäki FIN 127 B15
Ruotaanmäki FIN 124 D7
Ruoti I 60 B5
Ruotsalo FIN 123 C10
Ruotsinkylä FIN 127 E12
Ruottisenharju FIN 120 D9
Ruovesi FIN 123 G12
Rupa HR 67 B9
Rupea RO 152 E6
Ruppovaara FIN 125 F14
Rupt-sur-Moselle F 26 E6
Rus E 55 C6
Rus RO 152 C3
Rusãnes N 108 C9
Rusãneşti RO 160 F5
Rusca Montană RO 159 B9
Ruscova RO 152 B4
Ruse BG 161 F7
Ruse SLO 148 C5
Rusele S 107 B14
Ruselė S 107 B14
Ruseni MD 153 A10
Ruşeţu RO 161 D10
Ruševo HR 149 F9
Rush IRL 7 E10
Rushden GB 15 C7
Rusiec PL 143 D6
Rusii-Munţi RO 152 D5
Rusinovo MK 165 F6
Rusinów PL 141 H3
Rusinowo PL 85 D10
Ruskeala RUS 129 B14
Ruskele S 107 B15
Ruski Krstur SRB 158 B3
Rusko FIN 126 D7
Rusko Selo SRB 150 F6
Ruskov SK 145 F3
Rusksträsk S 107 B15
Ruşteşti RO 153 E11
Rusokastro BG 167 E8
Rušona LV 133 D2
Rüsselsheim D 21 D10
Russelluft N 113 C11
Russelv N 112 D5
Russhaugen N 111 D11
Russi I 66 D5
Rust A 77 G11
Rustad N 95 B13
Rustad N 101 D14
Rustrel F 35 C9
Ruswil CH 27 F9
Ruszów PL 81 D8
Rutalahti FIN 123 G15
Rute E 53 B8
Rute S 93 D13
Rutesheim D 187 D6
Rüthen D 17 F10
Ruthin GB 10 E5
Rüti CH 27 F10
Rutigliano I 61 A8
Rutino I 60 C4
Rutka-Tartak PL 136 E6
Rutki-Kossaki PL 140 D6
Rutledal N 100 D2
Rutoš SRB 163 B8
Rutten NL 16 C5
Rütten-Scheid D 183 C9
Rutvik S 118 C8
Ruuhenso FIN 121 C9
Ruuhijärvi FIN 117 D13
Ruuhijärvi FIN 127 D15
Ruukki FIN 119 E14
Ruunaa FIN 125 D14
Ruurlo NL 17 D6
Ruusa EST 131 E14
Ruusmäe EST 131 F14
Ruutana FIN 123 C17
Ruvanaho FIN 115 E5
Ruvaslahti FIN 125 E12
Ruvo del Monte I 60 B5
Ruvo di Puglia I 61 A6
Ruy F 31 D7
Ruynes-en-Margeride F 30 F3
Rüzhevo Konare BG 165 E10
Ruzhintsi BG 159 F10
Ružina LV 133 D2
Ružindol SK 146 E5
Ružomberok SK 147 C8
Ruzsa H 150 E4
Ry DK 86 C5
Ryabovo RUS 129 E10
Ryakhovo BG 161 F8
Ryakhovtsite BG 165 C11
Rybachiy RUS 134 F1
Rybany SK 146 D6
Rybczewice Drugie PL 144 A6
Rybitví CZ 77 B9
Rybnik PL 142 F6
Rybnica LV 135 D12
Rybno PL 139 D8
Rybno PL 139 C11
Rybno PL 141 F2
Ryboly PL 141 E8
Rychliki PL 139 C8
Rychnov nad Kněžnou CZ 77 B10
Rychnowa PL 139 D11
Rychtal PL 142 D4
Rychvald CZ 146 B6
Rychwał PL 142 B5
Ryczywół PL 85 E11
Ryczywół PL 141 G4
Ryd S 88 C7
Rydaholm S 88 B6
Rydal S 91 D12
Rydboholm S 91 D12

Ryde DK 86 C3
Ryde GB 13 D12
Rydet S 91 E11
Rydöbruk S 87 B12
Rydsgård S 87 E13
Rydsnäs S 92 D6
Ryduttowy PL 142 F5
Rydzyna PL 81 C11
Rye GB 15 F10
Ryen N 90 C3
Ryeng N 114 D8
Ryes F 23 B10
Rygge N 95 D13
Ryggesbro S 103 D13
Ryglice PL 144 D3
Rygnestad N 94 D6
Ryhälä FIN 129 B9
Ryhall GB 11 F11
Ryjewo PL 138 C6
Rykene N 90 C4
Ryki PL 141 G5
Rymań PL 85 C9
Rymanów PL 145 D4
Rymarov CZ 81 G12
Rymättylä FIN 126 E6
Rymnio GR 169 D6
Ryn PL 136 F4
Rynarzewo PL 138 D4
Rynkeby DK 86 E7
Rynsk PL 138 D6
Ryomgård DK 86 C7
Rypefjord N 113 B12
Rypin PL 139 D7
Rysjedal N 100 D2
Ryslinge DK 86 E7
Ryssby S 88 B6
Rysum (Krummhörn) D 17 B8
Rytel PL 138 C4
Rytilahti FIN 115 E3
Rytinki FIN 120 C9
Rytky FIN 123 C17
Rytkynkylä FIN 119 F14
Ryttylä FIN 127 D12
Rytwiany PL 143 E11
Rżanovo MK 168 B4
Rząśnik PL 139 E11
Rzeczenica PL 85 C12
Rzeczyca PL 141 G2
Rzeczyca PL 142 C6
Rzjgnowo PL 139 D10
Rzejowice PL 143 D8
Rzekuń PL 139 D12
Rzepiennik Strzyżewski PL 144 D3
Rzepin PL 81 B8
Rzerzjczyce PL 143 E7
Rzesznikowo PL 85 C8
Rzeszów PL 144 C5
Rzgów PL 143 C8
Rzgów Pierwszy PL 142 B5
Rzuców PL 141 H3

S

Sääksjärvi FIN 123 D11
Sääksjärvi FIN 127 C10
Sääksjärvi FIN 127 D13
Sääksmäki FIN 127 C11
Saal D 83 B12
Saal an der Donau D 75 E10
Saalbach-Hinterglemm A 73 B6
Saalburg D 75 B10
Saales F 27 D7
Saalfeld D 79 E9
Saalfelden am Steinernen Meer A 73 B6
Saanen CH 31 C11
Saarbrücken D 21 F7
Saarburg D 21 E7
Säare EST 130 F4
Saarela FIN 125 C13
Saaren kk FIN 129 B12
Saarenkylä FIN 117 E15
Saaresmäki FIN 124 B7
Saari FIN 129 B12
Saariharju FIN 120 C9
Saarijärvi FIN 123 C14
Saari-Kämä FIN 119 B16
Saarikoski FIN 112 F7
Saarikoski FIN 119 C15
Saarikoski FIN 119 E14
Saarikylä FIN 121 D13
Saario FIN 125 F14
Saaripudas FIN 117 D11
Saarivaara FIN 121 C9
Saarivaara FIN 121 E14
Saarivaara FIN 125 F15
Saarlouis D 21 F7
Saarwellingen D 21 F7
Saas CH 71 D6
Sääse EST 131 C12
Saas Fee CH 68 A4
Saas Grund CH 68 A4
Sääskjärvi FIN 127 D15
Säävälä FIN 119 D16
Šabac SRB 158 D4
Sabadell E 43 D8
Sãbãoani RO 153 C9
Sabarat F 33 D7
Sabatynivka UA 154 A6
Sabaudia I 62 E4
Sabbioneta I 66 C1
Sabero E 39 C9
Sabile LV 134 B5
Sabiñánigo E 32 E5
Sabinov SK 145 E3
Sabiote E 55 C6
Sables-d'Or-les-Pins F 23 C7
Sablé-sur-Sarthe F 23 E11
Sablet F 35 B9
Sabnie PL 141 E6
Sabres F 32 B4
Sabro DK 86 C6
Sabrosa P 38 F4
Sabugal P 45 D6
Sabugueiro P 44 D5
Sabugueiro P 50 B3
Sãcãdat RO 151 C9
Sãcãlãşeni RO 152 B3
Sãcãlaz RO 151 F7
Sacañet E 48 E3
Sãcãşeni RO 151 C10
Sacavém P 50 B1
Sacecorbo E 47 C8
Sãcel RO 152 B4
Sãcel RO 152 E5
Sãcele RO 155 E3
Sãcele RO 161 B7
Sãcelu RO 160 C4
Sãceni RO 160 E6
Sacramenia E 40 E4
Sacruela E 54 B3
Sachseln CH 70 D6

Sachsenberg (Lichtenfels) D 21 B11
Sachsenbrunn D 75 B8
Sachsenburg A 73 C7
Sachsenhagen D 17 D12
Sachsenhausen (Waldeck) D 17 F12
Sachsenheim D 27 C11
Sacile I 72 E5
Sacoşu Turcesc RO 159 B7
Sacović BIH 156 E6
Sacquenay F 26 E3
Sacramenia E 40 E4
Sacu RO 159 B9
Săcueni RO 151 C9
Săcuieu RO 151 D10
Sačurov SK 145 F4
Sada E 38 B3
Sádaba E 32 F3
Sadala EST 131 D13
Sadali I 64 D3
Saddell GB 4 D5
Sadina BG 166 C6
Sadki PL 85 D12
Sadkowice PL 141 G3
Sadkowo PL 85 C10
Sadlinki PL 138 C6
Sadova MD 154 C2
Sadova RO 152 B6
Sadova RO 160 F3
Sadove UA 154 E4
Sadovec BG 165 C9
Sadovo BG 165 E10
Sadowie PL 143 E11
Sadowne PL 139 E12
Sadská CZ 77 B7
Sadu RO 160 B4
Sädvaluspen S 109 D12
Sæbo N 94 B6
Sæbø N 100 B4
Sæbøvik N 94 C3
Sæby DK 87 D8
Sæby DK 90 E8
Sæd DK 86 F3
Saelices E 47 E7
Saelices de la Sal E 47 C8
Saelices del Rio E 39 C9
Saelices de Mayorga E 39 D9
Saerbeck D 17 D9
Særslev DK 86 D6
Sæter N 104 C8
Sætra N 104 E6
Sætre N 95 C13
Saeul L 20 E5
Sævareid N 94 B3
Safaalan TR 173 B9
Safara P 51 C5
Säffle S 91 A12
Saffré F 23 E8
Saffron Walden GB 15 C9
Săg RO 151 C10
Săg RO 159 B7
Sagama I 64 C2
Sagard D 84 A5
Sage D 17 C10
Săgeata RO 161 C9
Sågen S 97 B11
Sagiada GR 168 E3
Sağirlar TR 173 F9
Sağlamtaş TR 173 C7
Sågmyra S 103 E9
Sagna RO 153 D10
Sagone F 37 G9
Sagres P 50 E2
Sagstua N 95 B15
Săgu RO 151 E7
Sagunto E 48 E4
Sagvåg N 94 C2
Ságvár H 149 C10
Sagy F 31 B7
Sahagún E 39 D9
Sahaidac MD 154 D3
Sahalahti FIN 127 C11
Sahankylä FIN 122 F8
Saharna Nouă MD 154 B3
Săhăteni RO 161 C8
Şahin TR 173 B6
Şahinli TR 172 D6
Sahl DK 86 C5
Sahrajärvi FIN 123 F14
Sahun E 33 E6
Sahune F 35 B9
Šahy SK 147 E7
Saiakopli EST 131 C12
Saighdinis GB 2 K2
Saija FIN 115 D5
Säijä FIN 127 C10
Saikari FIN 124 E7
Saillagouse F 33 F10
Saillans F 35 A9
Sail-sous-Couzan F 30 D4
Saimaanharju FIN 129 C9
Säimen FIN 125 F12
Sains-Richaumont F 19 E8
St Abbs GB 5 D12
St-Affrique F 34 C4
St-Agnan F 30 B4
St-Agnan-en-Vercors F 31 F7
St-Agnant F 28 D4
St-Agnant-de-Versillat F 29 C9
St Agnes GB 12 E4
St-Agrève F 30 E5
St-Aignan F 24 F5
St-Aignan-sur-Roë F 23 E9
St-Aigulin F 28 E5
St-Albain F 30 C6
St-Alban F 22 C6
St-Alban-Leysse F 31 D8
St Albans GB 15 D8
St-Alban-sur-Limagnole F 30 F3
St-Amand-en-Puisaye F 25 E9
St-Amand-les-Eaux F 19 D7
St-Amand-Longpré F 24 E5
St-Amand-Montrond F 29 B11
St-Amand-sur-Fion F 25 C12
St-Amans F 34 A5
St-Amans-des-Cots F 30 F2
St-Amans-Soult F 33 D10
St-Amant-de-Boixe F 29 D6
St-Amant-Roche-Savine F 30 D4
St-Amant-Tallende F 30 D3
St-Amarin F 27 E7
St-Ambroix F 35 B7
St-Amour F 31 C7
St-Andiol F 35 C8
St-André F 34 E4
St-André-de-Corcy F 31 D6
St-André-de-Cruzières F 35 B7
St-André-de-Cubzac F 28 F5
St-André-de-l'Eure F 24 C5
St-André-de-Sangonis F 34 C6
St-André-de-Valborgne F 35 B6
St-André-le-Gaz F 31 D8
St-André-les-Alpes F 36 D5
St-André-les-Vergers F 25 D11
St Andrews GB 5 C11
St-Angel F 29 D10
St Anne GBG 23 A7
St-Anthème F 30 D4
St-Antonin-Noble-Val F 33 B9
St-Août F 29 B9
St-Apollinaire F 26 F3
St-Arcons-d'Allier F 30 E4
St-Arnoult-en-Yvelines F 24 C6
St Asaph GB 10 E5
St-Astier F 29 E7
St-Astier F 29 F6
St Athan GB 13 C8
St-Auban F 36 D5
St-Auban-sur-l'Ouvèze F 35 B9
St-Aubin F 31 A7
St-Aubin-Château-Neuf F 25 E9
St-Aubin-d'Aubigné F 23 D8
St-Aubin-de-Blaye F 28 E4
St-Aubin-du-Cormier F 23 D9
St-Aubin-lès-Elbeuf F 18 F3
St-Aubin-sur-Mer F 23 B11
St-Aulaye F 29 E6
St Austell GB 12 E5
St-Avé F 22 E6
St-Avertin F 24 F4
St-Avold F 26 B6
St-Ay F 24 E6
St-Aygulf F 36 E5
St-Barthélemy-d'Agenais F 33 A6
St-Barthélemy-de-Vals F 30 E6
St-Bauzille-de-Putois F 35 C6
St-Béat F 33 E7
St-Beauzély F 34 B4
St Bees GB 10 C4
St-Benin-d'Azy F 30 A3
St-Benoît F 29 B6
St-Benoît F 33 D10
St-Benoît-du-Sault F 29 C8
St-Benoît-sur-Loire F 25 E7
St-Béron F 31 D8
St-Berthevin F 23 D10
St-Bertrand-de-Comminges F 33 D7
St-Blaise CH 31 A10
St-Blaise-la-Roche F 27 D7
St-Blin-Semilly F 26 D3
St-Boil F 30 B6
St-Bonnet-de-Bellac F 29 C7
St-Bonnet-de-Joux F 30 C5
St-Bonnet-en-Bresse F 31 B7
St-Bonnet-en-Champsaur F 36 B4
St-Bonnet-le-Château F 30 E5
St-Bonnet-le-Froid F 30 E5
St-Bonnet-sur-Gironde F 28 E4
St-Branchs F 24 F4
St Brelade GBJ 23 B7
St-Brevin-les-Pins F 23 F7
St-Briac-sur-Mer F 23 C7
St-Brice-en-Coglès F 23 D9
St Brides Major GB 13 C7
St-Brieuc F 22 C6
St-Bris-le-Vineux F 25 E10
St-Brisson F 25 F11
St-Broing-les-Moines F 25 E12
St Buryan GB 12 E3
St-Calais F 24 E4
St-Cannat F 35 C9
St-Céré F 29 F9
St-Cergue CH 31 C9
St-Cergues F 31 C9
St-Cernin F 29 E10
St-Chaffrey F 31 F10
St-Chamarand F 33 A8
St-Chamas F 35 C9
St-Chamond F 30 E6
St-Chaptes F 35 C7
St-Chef F 31 D7
St-Chély-d'Apcher F 30 F3
St-Chély-d'Aubrac F 34 A4
St-Chinian F 34 D4
St-Christol F 35 B9
St-Christol-lès-Alès F 35 B7
St-Christoly-Médoc F 28 E4
St-Christophe I 31 D11
St-Christophe-en-Bazelle F 24 F6
St-Christophe-en-Brionnais F 30 C5
St-Ciers-sur-Gironde F 28 E4
St-Cirq-Lapopie F 33 B9
St-Clair-du-Rhône F 30 E6
St-Clar F 33 C7
St-Claud F 29 D6
St-Claude F 31 C8
St Clears GB 12 B6
St-Clément F 25 D9
St-Clément F 26 C6
St-Clément F 29 E9
St Clement GBJ 23 B7
St-Clément-de-Rivière F 35 C6
St Columb Major GB 12 E5
St Combs GB 3 K13
St-Constant F 29 F10
St-Cosme-en-Vairais F 24 D3
St-Cricq-Chalosse F 32 C4
St-Cyprien F 29 F8
St-Cyprien F 33 B8
St-Cyprien F 34 E5
St-Cyr-sur-Loire F 24 F4
St-Cyr-sur-Mer F 35 D10
St Cyrus GB 5 B12
St David's GB 9 E12
St Day GB 12 E4
St-Denis F 25 C7
St-Denis-d'Anjou F 23 E11
St-Denis-de-Gastines F 23 D10
St-Denis-de-Jouhet F 29 B9
St-Denis-de-Pile F 28 F5
St-Denis-d'Oléron F 28 C3
St-Denis-en-Bugey F 31 D7
St-Denis-lès-Bourg F 31 C7
St Dennis GB 12 E5
St-Désert F 30 B6
St-Didier-en-Velay F 30 E5
St-Didier-sur-Chalaronne F 30 C6
St-Dié F 27 D6
St-Dier-d'Auvergne F 30 D3
St-Dizier F 25 C12
St-Dizier-Leyrenne F 29 C9
St-Dolay F 23 E7
St-Donat-sur-l'Herbasse F 31 E6
St-Doulchard F 25 F7
Ste-Adresse F 23 A12
Ste-Alvère F 29 F7
Ste-Bazeille F 33 A6
Ste-Cécile-les-Vignes F 35 B8
Ste-Croix CH 31 B10
Ste-Croix F 31 B7
Ste-Croix F 31 F7
Ste-Croix-Volvestre F 33 D8
Ste-Engrâce F 32 D4
Ste-Énimie F 34 B5
Ste-Eulalie d'Olt F 34 B4
Ste-Eulalie-en-Born F 32 B3
Ste-Feyre F 29 C9
Ste-Foy-de-Peyrolières F 33 D8
Ste-Foy-la-Grande F 29 F6
Ste-Foy-l'Argentière F 30 D5
Ste-Foy-lès-Lyon F 30 D6
Ste-Foy-Tarentaise F 31 D10
Ste-Geneviève F 18 F5
Ste-Geneviève-sur-Argence F 30 F2
St-Ègrève F 31 E8
Ste-Hélène F 28 F4
Ste-Hermine F 28 B3
Ste-Livrade-sur-Lot F 33 B7
St-Élix-le-Château F 33 D8
St-Élix-Theux F 33 D6
Ste-Lizaigne F 29 A10
St-Éloy-les-Mines F 30 C2
Ste-Lucie-de-Tallano F 37 H10
Ste-Marguerite F 186 E2
Ste-Marie F 34 E5
Ste-Marie-aux-Mines F 27 D7
Ste-Maure-de-Peyriac F 33 B6
Ste-Maure-de-Touraine F 24 F4
Ste-Maxime F 36 E5
Ste-Menehould F 25 B12
Ste-Mère-Église F 23 B9
St-Émiland F 30 B5
St Endellion GB 12 D5
St Enoder GB 12 E5
Ste-Orse F 29 E8
Ste-Pazanne F 23 F8
Ste-Radegonde F 28 B5
St-Erme-Outre-et-Ramecourt F 19 E8
St Erth GB 12 E4
Saintes F 28 D4
Ste-Sabine F 25 F12
Ste-Savine F 25 D11
Ste-Sévère-sur-Indre F 29 C10
St-Esteben F 32 D3
St-Estèphe F 28 E4
St-Estève F 34 E4
Ste-Suzanne F 23 D11
St-Étienne F 30 E5
St-Étienne-de-Baïgorry F 32 D3
St-Étienne-de-Fontbellon F 35 A7
St-Étienne-de-Fursac F 29 C9
St-Étienne-de-Montluc F 23 F8
St-Étienne-de-St-Geoirs F 31 E7
St-Étienne-de-Tinée F 36 C5
St-Étienne-du-Bois F 31 C7
St-Étienne-du-Rouvray F 18 F3
St-Étienne-en-Dévoluy F 35 A10
St-Étienne-les-Orgues F 35 B10
St-Étienne-lès-Remiremont F 26 D6
St-Étienne-Vallée-Française F 35 B6
Ste-Tulle F 35 C10
Ste-Vertu F 25 E10
St-Fargeau F 25 E9
St-Félicien F 30 E6
St-Félix-Lauragais F 33 D9
St Fergus GB 3 K13
St-Ferme F 28 F6
Saintfield GB 7 D11
St Fillans GB 5 C8
St-Firmin F 26 D5
St-Firmin F 31 F9
St-Flavy F 25 D10
St-Florent F 37 F10
St-Florent-des-Bois F 28 B3
St-Florentin F 25 D10
St-Florent-le-Vieil F 23 F9
St-Florent-sur-Cher F 29 B10
St-Flour F 30 E3
St-Flovier F 29 B8
St-Fons F 30 D6
St-Fort-sur-Gironde F 28 E4
St-Frajou F 33 D7
St-François-Longchamp F 31 E9
St-Front-de-Pradoux F 29 E6
St-Fulgent F 28 B3
St-Galmier F 30 D5
St-Gaudens F 33 D7
St-Gaultier F 29 B8
St-Gein F 32 C5
St-Gély-du-Fesc F 35 C6
St-Genest-Malifaux F 30 E5
St-Geniez F 36 C4
St-Geniez-d'Olt F 34 B4
St-Genis-de-Saintonge F 28 E4
St-Genis-Laval F 30 D6
St-Genis-Pouilly F 31 C9
St-Genix-sur-Guiers F 31 D8
St-Genou F 29 B8
St-Geoire-en-Valdaine F 31 E8
St-Georges-Buttavent F 23 D10
St-Georges-d'Aurac F 30 E4
St-Georges-de-Commiers F 31 E8
St-Georges-de-Didonne F 28 D4
St-Georges-de-Luzençon F 34 B4
St-Georges-de-Mons F 30 D2
St-Georges-de-Reneins F 30 C6
St-Georges-des-Groseillers F 23 C10
St-Georges-d'Oléron F 28 D3
St-Georges-du-Vièvre F 18 F2
St-Georges-en-Couzan F 30 D4
St-Georges-lès-Baillargeaux F 29 B6
St-Georges-sur-Baulche F 25 E10
St-Georges-sur-Cher F 24 F5
St-Georges-sur-Loire F 23 F10
St-Geours-de-Maremne F 32 C3
St-Gérand-le-Puy F 30 C4
St-Germain-Chassenay F 30 B3
St-Germain-de-Calberte F 35 B6
St-Germain-de-la-Coudre F 24 D4
St-Germain-des-Fossés F 30 C3
St-Germain-d'Esteuil F 28 E4
St-Germain-du-Bel-Air F 33 A8
St-Germain-du-Bois F 31 B7
St-Germain-du-Corbéis F 23 D12
St-Germain-du-Plain F 31 B6
St-Germain-du-Puy F 25 F7
St-Germain-du-Teil F 34 B5
St-Germain-en-Laye F 24 C7
St-Germain-Laval F 30 D5
St-Germain-Lembron F 30 E3
St-Germain-les-Belles F 29 D8
St-Germain-les-Vergnes F 29 E9
St-Germain-l'Herm F 30 E4
St Germans GB 12 E6
St-Germé F 32 C5
St-Gervais F 28 B1
St-Gervais F 31 E7
St-Gervais-d'Auvergne F 30 C2
St-Gervais-la-Forêt F 24 E5
St-Gervais-les-Bains F 31 D10
St-Gervais-les-Trois-Clochers F 29 B6
St-Gervais-sur-Mare F 34 C5
St-Géry F 33 B9
St-Ghislain B 19 D8
St-Gildas-de-Rhuys F 22 E6
St-Gildas-des-Bois F 23 E7
St-Gilles F 35 C7
St-Gilles-Croix-de-Vie F 28 B2
St-Gingolph F 31 C10
St-Girons F 33 E8
St-Girons-Plage F 32 C3
St-Gobain F 19 E7
St-Guénolé F 22 E3
St-Guilhem-le-Désert F 35 C6
St-Haon-le-Châtel F 30 C4
St-Héand F 30 D5
St Helens GB 10 E6
St Helier GBJ 23 B7
St-Herblain F 23 F8
St-Hilaire F 33 D10
St-Hilaire-de-Brethmas F 35 B7
St-Hilaire-de-Riez F 28 B2
St-Hilaire-des-Loges F 28 C4
St-Hilaire-de-Villefranche F 28 D4
St-Hilaire-du-Harcouët F 23 C9
St-Hilaire-du-Rosier F 31 E7
St-Hilaire-Fontaine F 30 B4
St-Hilaire-le-Grand F 25 B11
St-Hilaire-St-Florent F 23 F11
St-Hippolyte F 27 D7
St-Hippolyte F 27 F6
St-Hippolyte-du-Fort F 35 C6
St-Honoré-les-Bains F 30 B4
St-Hostien F 30 E5
St-Hubert B 19 D11
St-Imier CH 27 F6
St-Ismier F 31 E8
St Ive GB 12 E6
St Ives GB 12 E4
St Ives GB 15 C8
St-Izaire F 34 C4
St-Jacques-de-la-Lande F 23 D8
St-James F 23 C9
St-Jean F 33 C8
St-Jean-Bonnefonds F 30 E5
St-Jean-Brévelay F 22 E6
St-Jean-d'Angély F 28 D4
St-Jean-d'Assé F 23 D12
St-Jean-de-Bournay F 31 D7
St-Jean-de-Braye F 24 E6
St-Jean-de-Daye F 23 B9
St-Jean-de-la-Ruelle F 24 E6
St-Jean-de-Losne F 26 F3
St-Jean-de-Luz F 32 D2
St-Jean-de-Marsacq F 32 C3
St-Jean-de-Maurejols-et-Avéjan F 35 B7
St-Jean-de-Maurienne F 31 E9
St-Jean-de-Monts F 28 B1
St-Jean-de-Sixt F 31 D9
St-Jean-de-Védas F 35 C6
St-Jean-d'Illac F 28 F4
St-Jean-du-Bruel F 34 B5
St-Jean-du-Falga F 33 D9
St-Jean-du-Gard F 35 B6
St-Jean-le-Centenier F 35 A8
St-Jean-Pied-de-Port F 32 D3
St-Jean-Poutge F 33 C6
St-Jean-sur-Erve F 23 D11
St-Jeoire F 31 C9
St-Jeure-d'Ay F 30 E6
St-Jeures F 30 E5
St-Joachim F 23 F7
St John GBJ 23 B7
St John's Chapel GB 5 F12
St John's Town of Dalry GB 5 E8
St-Jores F 23 B9
St-Jorioz F 31 D9
St-Jory F 33 C8
St-Jouan-des-Guérets F 23 C8
St-Jouin-Bruneval F 23 A12
St-Jouin-de-Marnes F 28 B5
St-Julien F 31 C7
St-Julien F 33 D8
St-Julien-Beychevelle F 28 E4
St-Julien-Boutières F 30 F5
St-Julien-Chapteuil F 30 E5
St-Julien-de-Concelles F 23 F9
St-Julien-de-Vouvantes F 23 E9
St-Julien-du-Sault F 25 D9
St-Julien-du-Verdon F 36 D5
St-Julien-en-Beauchêne F 35 A10
St-Julien-en-Born F 32 B3
St-Julien-en-Genevois F 31 C9
St-Julien-l'Ars F 29 B7
St-Junien F 29 D7
St-Just F 35 B8
St Just GB 12 E3
St-Just-en-Chaussée F 18 E5
St-Just-en-Chevalet F 30 D4
St-Just-Ibarre F 32 D3
St-Justin F 32 C5
St Just in Roseland GB 12 E4
St-Just-la-Pendue F 30 D5
St-Just-Luzac F 28 D3
St-Just-Sauvage F 25 C10
St-Just-St-Rambert F 30 E5
St Keverne GB 12 E4
St-Lambert-des-Levées F 23 F11
St-Lary-Soulan F 33 E6
St-Laurent F 36 C5
St-Laurent-Bretagne F 32 D5
St-Laurent-d'Aigouze F 35 C7
St-Laurent-de-Carnols F 35 B8
St-Laurent-de-Cerdans F 34 F4
St-Laurent-de-Chamousset F 30 D5
St-Laurent-de-la-Cabrerisse F 34 D4
St-Laurent-de-la-Salanque F 34 E4
St-Laurent-de-Neste F 33 D6
St-Laurent-des-Autels F 23 F9
St-Laurent-du-Pont F 31 E8
St-Laurent-du-Var F 37 D6
St-Laurent-en-Caux F 18 E2
St-Laurent-en-Grandvaux F 31 B8
St-Laurent-les-Bains F 35 A6
St-Laurent-Médoc F 28 E4
St-Laurent-Nouan F 24 E6
St-Laurent-sur-Gorre F 29 D7
St-Laurent-sur-Sèvre F 28 B4
St-Léger B 19 E12
St-Léger-des-Vignes F 30 B3
St-Léger-en-Yvelines F 24 C6
St-Léger-sous-Beuvray F 30 B5
St-Léonard F 27 D6
St-Léonard-de-Noblat F 29 D8
St Leonards GB 13 D11
St-Lizier F 33 D8
St-Lô F 23 B9
St-Lon-les-Mines F 32 C3
St-Loubès F 28 F5
St-Louis-lès-Bitche F 186 D3
St-Loup-Géanges F 30 B6
St-Loup-Lamairé F 28 B5
St-Loup-sur-Semouse F 26 E5
St-Lubin-des-Joncherets F 24 C5
St-Lunaire F 23 C7
St-Lupicin F 31 C8
St-Lyé F 25 D11
St-Lys F 33 C8
St-Macaire F 32 A5
St-Macaire-en-Mauges F 23 F10
St-Magne F 32 A4
St-Magne-de-Castillon F 28 F5
St-Maime F 35 C10
St-Maixent-l'École F 28 C5
St-Malo F 23 C7
St-Malo-de-la-Lande F 23 B8
St-Mamert-du-Gard F 35 C7
St-Marcel F 24 B5
St-Marcel F 29 B9
St-Marcel F 30 B6
St-Marcel-d'Ardèche F 35 B8
St-Marcel-lès-Annonay F 30 E6
St-Marcel-lès-Sauzet F 35 A8
St-Marcel-lès-Valence F 31 F6
St-Marcellin F 31 E7
St-Marc-sur-Seine F 25 E12
St-Mards-en-Othe F 25 D10
St Margaret's Hope GB 3 H11
St-Marsal F 34 E4
St-Mars-d'Outillé F 24 E3
St-Mars-du-Désert F 23 F9
St-Mars-la-Brière F 24 D3
St-Mars-la-Jaille F 23 E9
St-Martial F 35 B6
St-Martial-de-Nabirat F 29 F8
St-Martial-de-Valette F 29 D7
St-Martin F 35 C10
St Martin GBG 22 B6
St Martin GBJ 23 B7
St-Martin-Boulogne F 15 F12
St-Martin-d'Ablois F 25 B10
St-Martin-d'Arrossa F 32 D3
St-Martin-d'Auxigny F 25 F7
St-Martin-de-Belleville F 31 E10
St-Martin-de-Castillon F 35 C10
St-Martin-de-Crau F 35 C8
St-Martin-de-Landelles F 23 C9
St-Martin-de-Londres F 35 C6
St-Martin-d'Entraunes F 36 C5
St-Martin-de-Ré F 28 C3
St-Martin-des-Besaces F 23 B10
St-Martin-des-Champs F 22 C4
St-Martin-de-Seignanx F 32 C3
St-Martin-de-Valamas F 30 F5
St-Martin-de-Valgalgues F 35 B7
St-Martin-d'Hères F 31 E8
St-Martin-d'Oney F 32 C4
St-Martin-du-Mont F 31 C7
St-Martin-du-Var F 37 D6
St-Martin-en-Bresse F 31 B7
St-Martin-le-Beau F 24 F4
St-Martin-sur-Ouanne F 25 E9
St-Martin-Valmeroux F 29 E10
St-Martin-Vésubie F 37 C6
St-Martory F 33 D7
St Mary's GB 3 H11
St-Mathieu F 29 D7
St-Mathurin F 28 B2
St-Maur F 29 B9
St-Maurice CH 31 C10
St-Maurice-de-Lignon F 30 E5
St-Maurice-des-Lions F 29 D7
St-Maurice-la-Souterraine F 29 C8
St-Maurice-l'Exil F 30 E6
St-Maurice-Navacelles F 35 C6
St-Maurin F 33 B7
St Mawes GB 12 E4
St-Max F 26 C5
St-Maximin-la-Ste-Baume F 35 D10
St-Médard-en-Jalles F 28 F4
St-Méen-le-Grand F 23 D7
St-Méloir-des-Ondes F 23 C8
St-Memmie F 25 C11
St-Menoux F 30 B3
St Merryn GB 12 D5
St-Mesmin F 25 D10
St-Mesmin F 29 E8
St-Michel F 19 E9
St-Michel F 28 D6
St-Michel F 33 D6
St-Michel-Chef-Chef F 23 F7
St-Michel-de-Castelnau F 32 B5
St-Michel-de-Maurienne F 31 E9
St-Michel-en-l'Herm F 28 C3
St-Michel-sur-Meurthe F 27 D6
St-Mihiel F 26 C4
St Monans GB 5 C11
St-Montant F 35 B8
St-Nabord F 26 D6
St-Nauphary F 33 C8
St-Nazaire F 23 F7
St-Nazaire-le-Désert F 35 A9
St-Nectaire F 30 D2
St Neots GB 15 C8
St-Nicolas B 183 D7
St-Nicolas F 18 D6
St-Nicolas-d'Aliermont F 18 E3
St-Nicolas-de-la-Grave F 33 B8
St-Nicolas-de-Port F 26 C5
St-Nicolas-de-Redon F 23 E7
St-Nicolas-du-Pélem F 22 D5
St-Oedenrode NL 16 E4
St-Omer F 18 C5
St-Orens-de-Gameville F 33 C9
St-Ost F 33 D6
St Osyth GB 15 D11
St-Ouen F 18 D5
St-Ouen F 24 E5
St Ouen GBJ 23 B7
St-Ouen-des-Toits F 23 D10
St-Pair-sur-Mer F 23 C8
St-Palais F 32 D3
St-Palais-sur-Mer F 28 D3
St-Pal-de-Chalancon F 30 E4
St-Pal-de-Mons F 30 E5
St-Pantaléon F 30 B5
St-Pantaléon F 33 B8
St-Papoul F 33 D10
St-Pardoux-Isaac F 33 A6
St-Pardoux-la-Rivière F 29 E7
St-Parize-le-Châtel F 30 B3
St-Parres-lès-Vaudes F 25 D11
St-Paterne F 23 D12
St-Paterne-Racan F 24 E3
St-Paul F 36 B5
St-Paul-Cap-de-Joux F 33 C9
St-Paul-de-Fenouillet F 33 E11
St-Paul-de-Jarrat F 33 E9
St-Paul-en-Born F 32 B3
St-Paul-en-Forêt F 36 D5
St-Paul-et-Valmalle F 35 C6
St-Paulien F 30 E4
St-Paul-le-Jeune F 35 B7
St-Paul-lès-Dax F 32 C3
St-Paul-lès-Durance F 35 C10
St-Paul-Trois-Châteaux F 35 B8
St-Pé-de-Bigorre F 32 D5
St-Pée-sur-Nivelle F 32 D2
St-Péray F 30 F6
St-Père F 25 F10
St-Père-en-Retz F 23 F7
St Peter in the Wood GBG 22 B6
St Peter Port GBG 22 B6
St-Phal F 25 D10
St-Philbert-de-Bouaine F 28 B2
St-Philbert-de-Grand-Lieu F 28 A2
St-Pierre I 31 D11
St-Pierre-d'Albigny F 31 D9
St-Pierre-de-Chignac F 29 E7
St-Pierre-de-Côle F 29 E7
St-Pierre-de-la-Fage F 34 C5
St-Pierre-de-Maillé F 29 B7
St-Pierre-de-Plesguen F 23 D8
St-Pierre-des-Champs F 34 D4
St-Pierre-des-Corps F 24 F4
St-Pierre-des-Échaubrognes F 28 A4
St-Pierre-des-Landes F 23 D9
St-Pierre-des-Nids F 23 D11
St-Pierre-de-Trivisy F 33 C10
St-Pierre-d'Irube F 32 D3
St-Pierre-d'Oléron F 28 D3
St-Pierre-du-Chemin F 28 B4
St-Pierre-du-Mont F 32 C4
St-Pierre-Église F 23 A9
St-Pierre-en-Faucigny F 31 C9
St-Pierre-en-Port F 18 E1
St-Pierre-le-Moûtier F 30 B3
St-Pierre-lès-Elbeuf F 18 F3
St-Pierre-lès-Nemours F 25 D8
St-Pierre-Montlimart F 23 F9
St-Pierre-Quiberon F 22 E5
St-Pierre-sur-Dives F 23 B11
St-Plancard F 33 D7
St-Pois F 23 C9
St-Poix F 23 E9
St-Pol-de-Léon F 22 C4
St-Pol-sur-Mer F 18 B5
St-Pol-sur-Ternoise F 18 D5
St-Pompont F 29 F8
St-Pons F 36 C5
St-Pons-de-Thomières F 34 D4
St-Porchaire F 28 D4
St-Pourçain-sur-Sioule F 30 C3
St-Prex CH 31 C9
St-Priest F 30 D6
St-Priest-de-Champs F 30 D2
St-Priest-Laprugne F 30 D4
St-Priest-Taurion F 29 D8
St-Privat F 29 E10
St-Privat-d'Allier F 30 F4
St-Prix F 30 C4
St-Projet F 33 B9
St-Puy F 33 C6
St-Quentin F 19 E7
St-Quentin-la-Poterie F 35 B7
St-Quirin F 27 C7
St-Rambert-d'Albon F 30 E6
St-Rambert-en-Bugey F 31 D7
St-Raphaël F 36 E5
St-Remèze F 35 B7
St-Rémy F 30 B6
St-Rémy-de-Provence F 35 C8
St-Remy-en-Bouzemont-St-Genest-et-Isson F 25 C12
St-Rémy-sur-Avre F 24 C5
St-Rémy-sur-Durolle F 30 D4
St-Renan F 22 D2
St-Révérien F 25 F10
St-Rhemy I 31 D11
St-Riquier F 18 D4
St-Romain-en-Gal F 30 D6
St-Romain-sur-Cher F 24 F5
St-Romans F 31 E7
St-Rome-de-Cernon F 34 B4
St-Rome-de-Tarn F 34 B4
St-Saëns F 18 E3
St Sampson GBG 22 B6
St-Saturnin-lès-Apt F 35 C9
St-Saud-Lacoussière F 29 D7
St-Saulge F 25 F10
St-Sauves-d'Auvergne F 29 D11
St-Sauveur F 22 D3
St-Sauveur F 26 E5
St-Sauveur-de-Montagut F 30 F6
St-Sauveur-en-Puisaye F 25 E9
St-Sauveur-Gouvernet F 35 B9
St-Sauveur-Lendelin F 23 B9
St-Sauveur-le-Vicomte F 23 B8
St-Sauveur-sur-Tinée F 36 C6
St-Sauvy F 33 C7
St-Savin F 28 E5
St-Savin F 29 B7
St-Savinien F 28 D4
St Saviour GBJ 23 B7
St-Sébastien-de-Morsent F 24 B5
St-Sébastien-sur-Loire F 23 F8
St-Seine-l'Abbaye F 25 F12
St-Sernin F 35 A7
St-Sernin-sur-Rance F 34 C4
St-Seurin-sur-l'Isle F 28 E5
St-Sever F 32 C4
St-Sever-Calvados F 23 C9
St-Siméon-de-Bressieux F 31 E7
St-Simon F 19 E7
St-Simon F 29 F11
St-Sorlin-d'Arves F 31 E9
St-Soupplets F 25 B8
St-Sulpice F 33 C9
St-Sulpice-Laurière F 29 C8
St-Sulpice-les-Champs F 29 D10
St-Sulpice-les-Feuilles F 29 C8
St-Sulpice-sur-Lèze F 33 D8
St-Sulpice-sur-Risle F 24 C4
St-Sylvain F 23 B11
St-Symphorien F 30 F4
St-Symphorien F 32 B5
St-Symphorien-de-Lay F 30 D5
St-Symphorien-sur-Coise F 30 D5
St Teath GB 12 D5
St-Thégonnec F 22 C4
St-Thibéry F 34 D5
St-Thiébault F 26 D4
St-Thurien F 22 E4
St-Trivier-de-Courtes F 31 C7
St-Trivier-sur-Moignans F 30 C6
St-Trojan-les-Bains F 28 D3
St-Tropez F 36 E5
St-Uze F 30 E6
St-Valérien F 25 D9
St-Valery-en-Caux F 18 E2
St-Valery-sur-Somme F 18 D4
St-Vallier F 30 B5
St-Vallier F 30 E6
St-Vallier-de-Thiey F 36 D5
St-Varent F 28 B5
St-Vaury F 29 C9
St-Victor F 30 E6
St-Victor-de-Cessieu F 31 D7
St-Victoret F 35 D9
St-Victor-la-Coste F 35 B8
St Vigeans GB 5 B11
St-Vigor-le-Grand F 23 B10
St-Vincent I 68 B4
St-Vincent-de-Connezac F 29 E6
St-Vincent-de-Paul F 32 C4
St-Vincent-les-Forts F 36 C4
St-Vit F 26 F4
St-Vite F 33 B7
St-Vith B 20 D6
St-Vivien-de-Médoc F 28 E3
St-Xandre F 28 C3
St-Yan F 30 C5
St-Ybars F 33 D8
St-Yorre F 30 C3
St-Yrieix-la-Perche F 29 D8
St-Yrieix-sur-Charente F 29 D6
St-Yvy F 22 E4
St-Zacharie F 35 D10
Sainville F 24 D6
Saissac F 33 D10
Saittarova S 116 D8
Saivomuotka S 116 B10
Saïx F 33 C10
Sajaniemi FIN 127 D11
Šahyajince SRB 164 E5
Šajkaš SRB 158 C5
Sajóbábony H 145 G2
Sajókaza H 145 G2
Sajókeresztúr H 145 G2
Sajólád H 145 G2
Sajószentpéter H 145 G2
Sajószöged H 145 H3
Sajóvámos H 145 G2
Säjvis S 119 C11
Saka LV 134 C2
Sakajärvi S 116 D5
Sakalishcha BY 133 E5
Sakaravaara FIN 121 E12
Šakiai LT 136 D7
Säkinmäki FIN 123 F16
Sakizköy TR 173 B7
Säkkilä FIN 121 B13
Sakshaug N 105 D10
Saksild DK 86 D6
Saksköbing DK 83 A11
Saksun FO 2 A2
Saku EST 131 C9
Sakule SRB 158 C6
Säkylä FIN 126 C7
Šakyna LT 134 D6
Sala LV 134 C7
Sala LV 135 C11
Sala S 98 C7
Šal'a SK 146 E5
Salaca LV 131 F10
Sălacea RO 151 C9
Salacgrīva LV 131 F8
Sala Consilina I 60 C5
Salagnac F 29 E8
Salahmi FIN 124 C7
Salaise-sur-Sanne F 30 E6
Salakas LT 135 E12
Salakos GR 181 D7
Salakovac BIH 157 F8
Salamajärvi FIN 123 D13
Salamanca E 45 C9
Salamina GR 175 D7
Salandra I 61 B6
Salanki FIN 117 B13
Salantai LT 134 D3
Salar E 53 B8
Sălard RO 151 C9
Salardu E 33 E7
Salarli TR 172 B6
Salas E 39 B7
Salaš SRB 159 E9
Salas de los Infantes E 40 D5
Salash BG 164 B6
Salaspils LV 135 C8
Sălașu de Sus RO 159 C10
Sălătig RO 151 C11
Sălătrucel RO 160 C4
Sălătrucu RO 160 C5
Salaunes F 28 F4
Salberg S 107 D16
Salbertrand I 31 E10
Sälboda S 97 C8
Salbohed S 98 C6
Salbris F 24 F7
Salbu N 100 D2
Salcea RO 153 B8
Salching D 75 E12
Salcia RO 159 E10
Salcia RO 160 F5
Salcia RO 161 C8
Salcia Tudor RO 161 C10
Sălciile RO 161 D8
Šalčininkai LT 137 E11
Šalčininkėliai LT 137 E11
Sălciua RO 151 E11
Salcombe GB 13 E7
Sălcuța MD 154 D4
Sălcuța RO 160 E2
Saldaña E 39 C10
Saldenburg D 76 E4
Saldón E 47 D10
Salduero E 40 E6
Saldus LV 134 C4
Sale GB 11 E7
Sale I 37 B9
Saleby S 91 C13
Salem D 27 E11
Salem D 83 C9
Salemi I 58 D2

Salen GB 4 B5
Salen GB 4 B5
Sälen S 102 D5
Salernes F 36 D4
Salerno I 60 B3
Salers F 29 E10
Salettes F 30 F4
Saleux F 18 E5
Salford GB 11 E7
Şalgamli TR 173 B6
Salgótarján H 147 E9
Salgueiro P 44 E5
Salhus N 94 A2
Sali HR 156 E3
Salice Salentino I 61 C9
Saliceto I 37 C8
Saliena LV 135 C7
Saliena LV 135 E13
Salies-de-Béarn F 32 D4
Salies-du-Salat F 33 D7
Salignac-Eyvignes F 29 F8
Salillas de Jalón E 41 E9
Salinas E 39 A8
Salinas E 56 D3
Salinas del Manzano E 47 D9
Salinas de Pamplona E 32 E2
Salinas de Pisuerga E 40 C3
Salin-de-Giraud F 35 D8
Saline di Volterra I 66 F2
Sälinkää FIN 127 D13
Salins F 29 E10
Salins-les-Bains F 31 B8
Salir P 50 E3
Salisbury GB 13 C11
Săliște RO 152 F3
Săliștea RO 151 F11
Săliștea de Sus RO 152 B4
Salka SK 147 F7
Sal'kove UA 154 A5
Sall DK 86 C5
Salla EST 131 D12
Salla FIN 115 E5
Sallanches F 31 D10
Sallent E 43 D7
Sallent de Gállego E 32 E5
Salles F 32 A4
Salles-Curan F 34 B4
Salles-d'Angles F 28 D5
Salles-la-Source F 33 B11
Salles-sur-l'Hers F 33 D9
Sallgast D 80 C5
Sälliku EST 131 C14
Sallingberg A 77 F8
Sallins IRL 7 F9
Sällsjö S 105 E15
Sallypark IRL 8 C6
Salme EST 130 E4
Salmerón E 47 C8
Salmeroncillos de Abajo E 47 C7
Salmi FIN 123 E10
Salmi S 119 B10
Salmijärvi FIN 121 D10
Salminen FIN 121 B12
Salminen FIN 124 E8
Salmivaara FIN 115 E4
Salmiyarvi RUS 114 E8
Salmoral E 45 C10
Salmtal D 21 E7
Salnava LV 133 C3
Salnö S 99 C11
Salo FIN 127 E9
Salò I 69 B10
Salobre E 55 B7
Salobreña E 53 C9
Saločiai LT 135 D8
Saloinen FIN 119 E12
Salon F 25 C11
Salon-de-Provence F 35 C9
Salonkylä FIN 123 C11
Salonpää FIN 119 E14
Salonta RO 151 D8
Salorino E 45 F6
Salornay-sur-Guye F 30 B6
Salorno I 69 A11
Salou E 42 E6
Salouël F 18 E5
Šalovci SLO 148 C6
Salsåker S 107 F14
Salsbruket N 105 B11
Salsburgh GB 5 D9
Salses-le-Château F 34 E4
Sâlsig RO 151 B11
Salsomaggiore Terme I 69 D8
Salt E 43 D9
Saltara I 67 E6
Saltash GB 12 E6
Saltburn-by-the-Sea GB 11 B10
Saltcoats GB 4 D7
Salteras E 51 E7
Salthill IRL 6 F4
Salto P 38 E4
Saltoniškės LT 137 D11
Saltrød N 90 C4
Saltsjöbaden S 99 D10
Saltum DK 90 E6
Saltvik FIN 99 B14
Saltvik S 103 C13
Saludecio I 67 E6
Saluggia I 68 C5
Salur TR 173 D8
Salussola I 68 C5
Salutaguse EST 131 C9
Saluzzo I 37 B6
Salva RO 152 C4
Salvacañete E 47 D10
Salvagnac F 33 C9
Salvaleón E 51 B6
Salvaterra de Magos P 50 A2
Salvaterra do Extremo P 45 E7
Salvatierra E 32 E1
Salvatierra de los Barros E 51 C6
Salvatierra de Santiago E 45 F8
Salve I 61 D10
Salviac F 33 A8
Sály H 145 H2
Salzburg A 73 A7
Salzgitter D 79 B7
Salzhausen D 83 D8
Salzhemmendorf D 78 B6
Salzkotten D 17 E11
Salzmünde D 79 C10
Salzwedel D 83 E10
Salzweg D 76 E4
Samadet F 32 C5
Samaila SRB 158 F6
Samarate I 68 B6
Samarica HR 149 E7
Samarina GR 168 D5
Samarinești RO 159 D11
Samassi I 64 E2
Samatan F 33 D7
Sambade P 39 F6
Sâmbăta RO 151 D9
Sambiase I 59 B9
Sambir UA 145 D7
Samboal E 40 F3
Samborzec PL 143 E12
Sambuca di Sicilia I 58 D3
Sambuca Pistoiese I 66 D3
Sambuco I 36 C6
Sâmbureşti RO 160 D4
Samedan CH 71 D9
Sameiro P 44 D6
Samer F 15 F12
Sames E 39 B9
Sami GR 174 C2
Samil P 39 E6
Samir de los Caños E 39 E7
Şamli TR 173 E8
Sammakko S 116 E7
Sammakkola FIN 125 C10
Sammaljoki FIN 127 C9
Sammatti FIN 127 E10
Sammichele di Bari I 61 B7
Samnaun CH 71 D10
Samobor HR 148 E5
Samoëns F 31 C10
Samões P 38 F5
Samokov BG 165 E8
Samokov MK 164 F3
Samolaco I 69 A7
Samora Correia P 50 B2
Šamorín SK 146 E4
Samos E 38 C5
Samos GR 177 D8
Samoš SRB 159 C6
Samothraki GR 171 D9
Samovodene BG 166 C5
Samper de Calanda E 42 E3
Sampeyre I 37 B6
Sampierdarena I 37 C9
Sampieri I 59 F6
Sampigny F 26 C4
amșud RO 151 C10
Samswegen D 79 B10
Samtens D 84 B4
Samuelsberg N 112 D6
Samugheo I 64 D2
Samuil BG 167 B7
Samuilovo BG 166 E5
San Adrián E 32 F2
San Agustín de Guadalix E 46 C5
Sanaigmore GB 4 D4
San Amaro E 38 D3
Sânandrei RO 151 F7
San Andrés del Rabanedo E 39 C8
San Antolín E 39 B6
San Antonio E 47 E10
Sanary-sur-Mer F 35 D10
San Asensio E 40 C6
San Bartolomé de las Abiertas E 46 E3
San Bartolomé de la Torre E 51 E5
San Bartolomé de Pinares E 46 C3
San Bartolomeo al Mare I 37 D8
San Bartolomeo in Galdo I 60 A4
San Basilio I 64 D3
San Benedetto dei Marsi I 62 C5
San Benedetto del Tronto I 62 B5
San Benedetto Po I 66 B2
San Benito E 54 B3
San Benito de la Contienda E 51 B5
San Biagio di Callalta I 72 E5
San Biago Platani I 58 D4
San Bonifacio I 66 B3
San Buono I 63 D7
San Candido I 72 C5
San Carlos del Valle E 55 B6
San Casciano dei Bagni I 62 B1
San Casciano in Val di Pesa I 66 E3
San Cataldo I 58 E4
San Cataldo I 61 C10
San Cebrián de Castro E 39 E8
Sâncel RO 152 E3
Sancergues F 25 F8
Sancerre F 25 F8
San Cesario sul Panaro I 66 C3
Sancey-le-Grand F 26 F6
Sancheville F 24 D6
Sanchidrián E 46 C3
San Chirico Nuovo I 60 B6
San Chirico Raparo I 60 C6
San Cibrão das Viñas E 38 D4
San Cipirello I 58 D3
San Cipriano d'Aversa I 60 B2
San Clemente E 47 F8
San Clodio E 38 D5
Sancoins F 30 B2
San Colombano al Lambro I 69 C7
San Cosme E 38 A5
San Costantino Albanese I 61 C6
San Costanzo I 67 E7
Sâncrăieni RO 153 E7
Sâncraiu RO 151 D10
Sâncraiu de Mureș RO 152 D5
San Cristóbal de Entreviñas E 39 D8
San Cristóbal de la Vega E 46 B3
Sancti-Spíritus E 45 C8
Sancti-Spíritus E 51 B9
Sand N 94 D4
Sand N 95 B15
Sand N 110 D5
Sand (Bad Emstal) D 17 F12
Sanda S 93 E12
Sandager DK 86 E5
Sandamendi E 40 B5
San Damiano d'Asti I 37 B8
San Damiano Macra I 37 C6
Sandane N 100 C4
San Daniele del Friuli I 73 D7
San Daniele Po I 66 B1
Sandanski BG 169 A9
Sandared S 91 D12
Sandarne S 103 D13
Sandau D 83 E12
Sandbach GB 11 E7
Sandberg D 74 B7
Sandby DK 87 F8
Sande D 17 B10
Sande N 95 C12
Sande N 100 D3
Sande P 44 B4
Sandefjord N 90 A7
Sandeggen N 111 A17
Sandeid N 94 C3
Sandelva N 112 D7
San Demetrio Corone I 61 D6
San Demetrio ne Vestini I 62 C5
Sander N 96 B6
Sandersdorf D 79 C11
Sandershausen (Niestetal) D 78 D6
Sandersleben D 79 C10
Sandes N 110 C8
Sandes N 110 C9
Sandfjord N 114 B9
Sandfors S 118 E5
Sandgarth GB 3 G11
Sandhausen D 21 F11
Sandhead GB 4 F7
Sandhem S 91 D14
Sandhult S 91 D12
Sandhurst GB 15 E7
Sandiás E 38 D4
Sandillon F 24 E7
Sandkrug D 84 E5
Sandl A 77 E7
Sandland N 112 C8
Sandnäset S 102 A8
Sandnes N 90 A5
Sandnes N 94 E3
Sandnes N 105 C12
Sandneshamn N 111 A15
Sandness N 111 C11
Sandnessjøen N 108 D4
Sando E 45 C8
Sandomierz PL 143 E12
Sândominic RO 153 D7
San Donaci I 61 C9
San Donà di Piave I 72 E6
San Donato di Lecce I 61 C10
San Donato di Ninea I 60 D6
San Donato Milanese I 69 C7
San Donato Val di Comino I 62 D5
Sándorfalva H 150 E5
Sandown GB 13 D12
Sandøy N 100 A5
Sandplace GB 12 E6
Šandrovac HR 149 E8
Sandsele S 107 A13
Sandsend GB 11 B10
Sandsjö S 102 C8
Sandsjöfors S 92 E5
Sandsjönäs S 107 A13
Sandslån S 107 E13
Sandstad N 104 D6
Sandstedt D 17 B11
Sandstrak N 108 D3
Sandstrand N 111 C12
Sandtangen N 114 D7
Sandtorg N 111 C12
Sandträsk S 118 B6
Sânduleni RO 153 E9
Săndulești RO 152 D3
Sandur FO 2 B3
Sandvatn N 94 F5
Sandved DK 87 E9
Sandvik FO 2 B3
Sandvik N 101 D15
Sandvik N 108 B7
Sandvik N 111 A16
Sandvik N 111 B14
Sandvik N 113 B16
Sandvik S 103 C11
Sandvika N 95 C13
Sandvika N 105 D12
Sandviken S 103 E12
Sandviken S 107 E15
Sandviken S 107 F13
Sandviksjön S 106 D7
Sandvikvåg N 94 C2
Sandwich GB 15 E11
Sandwick GB 3 F14
Sandy GB 15 C8
Sanem L 20 E5
San Emiliano E 39 C8
San Esteban de Gormaz E 40 E5
San Esteban de la Sierra E 45 C9
San Esteban de Litera E 42 D4
San Esteban del Molar E 39 E8
San Esteban del Valle E 46 D3
San Fele I 60 B5
San Felice a Cancello I 60 A2
San Felice Circeo I 62 E4
San Felices de los Gallegos E 45 C7
San Felice sul Panaro I 66 C3
San Ferdinando I 59 C8
San Ferdinando di Puglia I 60 A6
San Fernando E 52 D4
San Fernando de Henares E 46 D5
San Fili I 60 E6
San Filippo del Mela I 59 C7
Sanfins do Douro P 38 F5
San Francisco Javier E 57 D7
San Fratello I 59 C6
Sanfront I 37 B6
Sånga S 107 E13
Sangarcía E 46 C4
Sangaste EST 131 F12
Sangatte F 15 F12
San Gavino Monreale I 64 D2
Sangbäcken S 102 B7
San Gemini I 62 B3
Sângeorgiu de Mureș RO 152 D5
Sângeorgiu de Pădure RO 152 E5
Sângeorz-Băi RO 152 C5
Sânger RO 152 D4
Sangerhausen D 79 D9
San Germano Chisone I 31 F11
Sângeru RO 161 C8
Sangijän S 119 C11
San Gimignano I 66 F3
San Ginesio I 62 A4
Sanginjoki FIN 119 E16
Sanginkylä FIN 119 E17
San Giorgio a Liri I 62 E5
San Giorgio della Richinvelda I 73 D6
San Giorgio del Sannio I 60 A3
San Giorgio di Lomellina I 68 C6
San Giorgio di Nogaro I 73 E7
San Giorgio di Piano I 66 C3
San Giorgio Ionico I 61 C8
San Giorgio la Molara I 60 A3
San Giorgio Lucano I 61 C6
San Giovanni a Piro I 60 C4
San Giovanni Bianco I 69 B8
San Giovanni d'Asso I 66 F4
San Giovanni Gemini I 58 D4
San Giovanni Incarico I 62 D4
San Giovanni in Croce I 66 B1
San Giovanni in Fiore I 61 E7
San Giovanni in Persiceto I 66 C3
San Giovanni Lupatoto I 66 B3
San Giovanni Rotondo I 63 D9
San Giovanni Suegiu I 64 E2
San Giovanni Teatino I 63 C6
San Giovanni Valdarno I 66 E4
Sangis S 119 C10
San Giuliano Terme I 66 E1
San Giuseppe Jato I 58 D3
San Giuseppe Vesuviano I 60 B3
San Giustino I 66 E5
San Godenzo I 66 E4
San Gregorio I 59 C8
San Gregorio Magno I 60 B4
San Gregorio Matese I 60 A2
Sangüesa E 32 E3
San Guiliano Milanese I 69 C7
San Guim de Freixenet E 43 D6
Sanguinet F 32 B3
Sanguinetto I 66 B3
Sani GR 169 D9
San Ildefonso E 46 C5
Sanislău RO 151 B9
Sanitz D 83 B12
San Javier E 56 F3
San Jordi E 42 F4
San Jorge de Alor E 51 B5
San José E 55 F8
San José del Valle E 52 C5
San José de Malcocinado E 52 D5
San Juan E 41 B6
San Juan de Alicante E 56 E4
San Juan de Aznalfarache E 51 E7
San Juan de la Nava E 46 D3
San Juan del Puerto E 51 E6
San Justo de la Vega E 39 D7
Sankt Aegyd am Neuwalde A 77 G9
Sankt Andrä A 73 C10
Sankt Andrä am Zicksee A 149 A7
Sankt Andreasberg D 79 C8
Sankt Anna S 93 C9
Sankt Anna am Aigen A 148 C5
Sankt Anton an der Jeßnitz A 77 G8
Sankt Augustin D 21 C8
Sankt Gallen A 73 A10
Sankt Gallen CH 27 F11
Sankt Gallenkirch A 71 C9
Sankt Gangloff D 79 E10
Sankt Georgen am Walde A 77 F7
Sankt Georgen im Schwarzwald D 27 D9
Sankt Gilgen A 73 A7
Sankt Goar D 21 D9
Sankt Goarshausen D 21 D9
Sankt Ingbert D 21 F8
Sankt Jakob im Rosental A 73 C9
Sankt Jakob im Walde A 148 B5
Sankt Jakob in Defereggen A 72 C5
Sankt Johann am Tauern A 73 B9
Sankt Johann im Pongau A 73 B7
Sankt Johann im Walde A 73 C6
Sankt Johann in Tirol A 72 A5
Sankt Julian D 21 E9
Sankt Katharinen D 185 C7
Sankt Lambrecht A 73 B9
Sankt Leonhard am Forst A 77 F8
Sankt Leonhard am Hornerwald A 77 E9
Sankt Leonhard im Pitztal A 71 C11
Sankt Lorenz A 73 A7
Sankt Lorenzen im Gitschtal A 73 C7
Sankt Lorenzen im Lesachtal A 73 C6
Sankt Lorenzen im Mürztal A 148 B4
Sankt Lorenzen ob Murau A 73 B9
Sankt Marein im Mürztal A 148 B4
Sankt Margarethen D 17 A12
Sankt Margarethen an der Raab A 148 B5
Sankt Margarethen bei Knittelfeld A 73 B10
Sankt Margarethen im Burgenland A 77 G11
Sankt Märgen D 27 D9
Sankt Martin A 73 B7
Sankt Martin A 77 E7
Sankt Martin im Mühlkreis A 76 F6
Sankt Michael im Burgenland A 148 B6
Sankt Michael im Lungau A 73 B8
Sankt Michael in Obersteiermark A 73 B11
Sankt Michaelisdonn D 82 C6
Sankt Moritz CH 71 D9
Sankt Nikolai im Saustal A 148 C4
Sankt Nikolai im Sölktal A 73 B9
Sankt Olof S 88 D6
Sankt Oswald bei Freistadt A 77 E7
Sankt Oswald ob Eibiswald A 73 C11
Sankt Pankraz A 73 A9
Sankt Paul im Lavanttal A 73 C10
Sankt Peter am Kammersberg A 73 B9
Sankt Peter am Ottersbach A 148 C5
Sankt-Peterburg RUS 129 F13
Sankt Peter-Freienstein A 73 B11
Sankt Peter in der Au A 77 F7
Sankt Peter-Ording D 82 B5
Sankt Pölten A 77 F9
Sankt Radegund A 76 F3
Sankt Ruprecht an der Raab A 148 B5
Sankt Stefan im Gailtal A 73 C8
Sankt Stefan ob Leoben A 73 B10
Sankt Stefan ob Stainz A 148 C4
Sankt Ulrich bei Steyr A 76 F6
Sankt Valentin A 77 F7
Sankt Veit am Vogau A 148 C5
Sankt Veit an der Glan A 73 C9
Sankt Veit an der Gölsen A 77 F9
Sankt Veit im Pongau A 73 B7
Sankt Veit in Defereggen A 72 C5
Sankt Wendel D 21 F8
Sankt Wolfgang D 75 F11
Sankt Wolfgang im Salzkammergut A 73 A7
San Lazzaro di Savena I 66 D3
San Leo I 66 E5
San Leonardo de Yagüe E 40 E5
San Leonardo in Passiria I 72 C3
San Lorenzo I 59 D8
San Lorenzo al Mare I 37 D7
San Lorenzo Bellizzi I 61 D6
San Lorenzo de Calatrava E 54 C5
San Lorenzo de El Escorial E 46 C4
San Lorenzo de la Parrilla E 47 E8
San Lorenzo di Sebato I 72 C4
San Lorenzo in Campo I 67 E6
San Lorenzo Nuovo I 62 B1
San Luca I 59 C9
Sanlúcar de Barrameda E 52 C4
Sanlúcar de Guadiana E 50 E5
Sanlúcar la Mayor E 51 E7
San Lucido I 60 E6
Sanluri I 64 D2
San Maddalena Vallalta I 72 C5
San Mamés de Campos E 40 D2
San Marcello I 67 E7
San Marcello Pistoiese I 66 D2
San Marco Argentano I 60 D6
San Marco dei Cavoti I 60 A3
San Marco in Lamis I 63 D9
San Marcos E 38 B3
San Marino RSM 66 E5
San Martín E 32 D1
San Martín E 40 B4
Sânmartin RO 151 C8
Sânmartin RO 152 C4
Sânmartin RO 153 E7
San Martín de la Vega E 46 D5
San Martín de la Vega del Alberche E 45 D10
San Martín del Pimpollar E 45 D10
San Martín de Montalbán E 46 E4
San Martín de Pusa E 46 E3
San Martín de Unx E 32 E2
San Martín de Valdeiglesias E 46 D4
San Martino Buon Albergo I 66 B3
San Martino di Castrozza I 72 D4
San Martino di Lupari I 72 E4
San Martino di Venezze I 66 B4
San Martino in Badia I 72 C4
San Martino in Passiria I 72 C3
San Martino in Pensilis I 63 D8
San Mateo de Gállego E 41 E10
San Mauro Castelverde I 58 D5
San Mauro Forte I 60 C6
San Mauro Marchesato I 61 E7
San Mauro Pascoli I 66 D5
San Mauro Torinese I 68 C4
San Menaio I 63 D9
San Michele al Tagliamento I 73 E6
San Michele Mondovì I 37 C7
San Michele Salentino I 61 B9
San Miguel de Arroyo E 40 F3
San Miguel de Bernuy E 40 F4
San Miguel de Salinas E 56 F3
Sânmihaiu Almașului RO 151 C11
Sânmihaiu de Câmpie RO 152 D4
Sânmihaiu Român RO 159 B7
San Millán de la Cogolla E 40 D6
San Miniato I 66 E2
Sänna S 92 B5
Sannahed S 92 A6
Sannazzaro de'Burgondi I 69 C6
Sannicandro di Bari I 61 B7
Sannicandro Garganico I 63 D9
Sannicola I 61 C10
San Nicola dell'Alto I 61 E7
San-Nicolao F 37 G10
San Nicolás del Puerto E 51 C8
Sânnicolau Mare RO 150 E6
San Nicolò I 66 C4
San Nicolò d'Arcidano I 64 D2
San Nicolò Gerrei I 64 E3
Sanniki PL 139 F8
Sanok PL 145 D5
San Pablo de los Montes E 46 E4
San Pancrazio I 72 C3
San Pancrazio Salentino I 61 C9
San Paolo di Civitate I 63 D8
Sânpaul RO 151 D11
Sânpaul RO 152 E4
San Pedro E 55 B8
San Pedro de Alcántara E 53 D7
San Pedro de Ceque E 39 D7
San Pedro del Arroyo E 46 C3
San Pedro de Latarce E 39 E9
San Pedro del Pinatar E 56 F3
San Pedro del Romeral E 40 B4
San Pedro de Rozados E 45 C9
San Pedro Manrique E 41 D7
San Pedro Palmiches E 47 D8
San Pellegrino Terme I 69 B8
Sânpetru RO 153 F7
Sânpetru de Câmpie RO 152 D4
Sânpetru Mare RO 150 E6
San Piero a Sieve I 66 E3
San Piero Patti I 59 C6
San Pietro I 59 B7
San Pietro di Cadore I 73 C6
San Pietro in Cariano I 66 A2
San Pietro in Casale I 66 C3
San Pietro in Guarano I 61 E6
San Pietro Vernotico I 61 C10
San Polo d'Enza I 66 C1
San Prospero I 66 C3
Sanquhar GB 5 E9
San Quirico d'Orcia I 65 A5
San Rafael del Río E 42 F4
San Remo I 37 D7
San Román E 38 C5
San Román de Cameros E 41 D7
San Román de la Cuba E 39 D10
San Román de los Montes E 46 D3
San Roque E 38 B2
San Roque E 38 D3
San Roque E 53 D6
San Rufo I 60 C4
Sansac-de-Marmiesse F 29 F10
San Salvador de Cantamunda E 40 C3
San Salvatore I 64 D1
San Salvatore Monferrato I 37 B9
San Salvatore Telesino I 60 A2
San Salvo I 63 C7
San Sebastián E 32 D2
San Sebastián de los Ballesteros E 53 A7
San Sebastián de los Reyes E 46 C5
San Secondo Parmense I 66 C1
Sansepolcro I 66 E5
San Severa I 62 C1
San Severino Lucano I 60 C6
San Severino Marche I 67 F7
San Severo I 63 D8
San Silvestre de Guzmán E 51 E5
Sânsimion RO 153 E7
Sanski Most BIH 157 C6
Sansol E 32 E1
San Sosti I 60 D6
San Sperate I 64 E3
San Spirito I 61 A7
Sanț RO 152 C5
Santa Amalia E 51 A7
Santa Ana E 55 B9
Santa Ana de Pusa E 46 E3
Santa Ana la Real E 51 D6
Santa Bàrbara E 42 F5
Santa Bárbara de Casa E 51 D5
Santacara E 32 F2
Santa Catalina de Armada E 38 B2
Santa Catarina P 50 C3
Santa Catarina da Fonte do Bispo P 50 E4
Santa Caterina dello Ionio I 59 B10
Santa Caterina di Pittinuri I 64 C2
Santa Caterina Villarmosa I 58 D5
Santa Cesarea Terme I 61 C10
Santa Cilia de Jaca E 32 E4
Santa Clara-a-Nova P 50 E3
Santa Clara-a-Velha P 50 D3
Santa Clara de Louredo P 50 D4
Santa Coloma de Farners E 43 D9
Santa Coloma de Queralt E 43 D6
Santa Colomba de Somoza E 39 D7
Santa Columba de Curueño E 39 C9
Santa Comba Dão P 44 D4
Santa Comba de Rossas P 39 E6
Santa Cristina d'Aro E 43 D9
Santa Cristina de la Polvorosa E 39 D8
Santa Croce Camerina I 59 F6
Santa Croce del Sannio I 60 A3
Santa Croce di Magliano I 63 D8
Santa Croce sull'Arno I 66 E2
Santa Cruz P 50 C2
Santa Cruz da Tapa P 44 C4
Santa Cruz de Bezana E 40 B4
Santa Cruz de Campézo E 32 E1
Santa Cruz de la Serós E 32 E4
Santa Cruz de la Sierra E 45 F9
Santa Cruz de la Zarza E 47 E6
Santa Cruz de los Cáñamos E 55 B7
Santa Cruz del Retamar E 46 D4
Santa Cruz de Moya E 47 E10
Santa Cruz de Mudela E 55 B6
Santadi I 64 E2
Santa Domenica Talao I 60 D5
Santa Domenica Vittoria I 59 D6
Santa Elena E 55 C5
Santa Elena de Jamuz E 39 D8
Santa Elisabetta I 58 E4
Santaella E 53 A7
Santa Engracia E 32 F1
Santa Eufemia E 54 B3
Santa Eugènì E 49 E10
Santa Eulalia E 39 B8
Santa Eulalia E 39 B9
Santa Eulalia E 47 C10
Santa Eulália P 51 A5
Santa Eulalia del Río E 57 D8
Santa Eulalia de Oscos E 38 B5
Santa Eulàlia de Riuprimer E 43 D8
Santa Fé E 53 B9
Santa Fiora I 65 B5
Sant'Agata de'Goti I 60 A3
Sant'Agata del Bianco I 59 C9
Sant'Agata di Esaro I 60 D5
Sant'Agata di Militello I 59 C6
Sant'Agata di Puglia I 60 A4
Sant'Agata Feltria I 66 E5
Santa Giusta I 64 D2
Santa Giustina I 72 D5
Sant'Agostino I 66 C3
Sant Agustí de Lluçanès E 43 C8
Santahamina FIN 127 E13
Santa Iria P 50 D4
Santa Justa P 50 A3
Sant'Alberto I 66 C5
Santalha P 38 E5
Santa Liestra y San Quílez E 33 F6
Santa Luce I 66 F2
Santa Lucia I 64 B4
Santa Lucia del Mela I 59 C7
Santa Lucía de Moraña E 38 C2
Santa Luzia P 50 D3
Santa Magdalena de Pulpís E 48 D5
Santa Mare RO 153 B10
Santa Margalida E 57 B11
Santa Margarida da Serra P 50 C2
Santa Margarida de Montbui E 43 D7
Santa Margarida do Sádão P 50 C3
Santa Margherita di Belice I 58 D3
Santa Margherita Ligure I 37 C10
Santa Maria CH 71 D10
Santa María E 32 F4
Santa Maria Capua Vetere I 60 A2
Santa Maria da Feira P 44 C3
Santa María de Cayón E 40 B4
Santa María de Corcó E 43 C8
Santa María de Huertas E 41 F7
Santa Maria del Berrocal E 45 C10
Santa Maria del Camí E 49 E10
Santa María del Campo E 40 D4
Santa María del Campo Rus E 47 E8
Santa Maria del Cedro I 60 D5
Santa Maria della Versa I 37 B10
Santa María de los Llanos E 47 F7
Santa María del Páramo E 39 D8
Santa María del Val E 47 C8
Santa María de Nieva E 55 E9
Santa María de Palautordera E 43 D8
Santa Maria di Castellabate I 60 C3
Santa Maria di Sala I 66 A5
Santa María la Real de Nieva E 46 B4
Santa Maria Maggiore I 68 A5
Santa Maria Navarrese I 64 D4
Santa Maria Nuova I 67 F7
Sântămăria-Orlea RO 159 B10
Santa Maria Rezzonico I 69 A7
Santa-Maria-Siché F 37 H9
Santa Marina I 60 C5
Santa Marina del Rey E 39 C8
Santa Marina Salina I 59 B6
Santa Marinella I 62 C1
Santa Marta E 47 F8
Santa Marta E 51 B6
Santa Marta de Penaguião P 44 B5
Santa Marta de Tormes E 45 C9
Sant'Ambroggio F 37 F9
Santana P 44 D3
Santana P 50 C1
Sântana RO 151 E8
Santana da Serra P 50 D3
Santana de Cambas P 50 D4
Santana do Mato P 50 B3
Sant'Anastasia I 60 B2
Sant'Anatolia di Narco I 62 B3
Santander E 40 B4
Sant'Andrea Apostolo dello Ionio I 59 B10
Sant'Andrea Frius I 64 E3
Sântandrei RO 151 C8
Sant'Angelo I 59 B9
Sant'Angelo a Fasanella I 60 C4
Sant'Angelo dei Lombardi I 60 B4
Sant'Angelo di Brolo I 59 C6
Sant'Angelo in Lizzola I 67 E6
Sant'Angelo in Vado I 66 E5
Sant'Angelo Lodigiano I 69 C7
Sant'Angelo Muxaro I 58 E4
Santa Ninfa I 58 D2
Sant'Anna Arresi I 64 E2
Sant'Antimo I 60 B2
Sant'Antioco I 64 E1
Sant Antoni de Portmany E 57 D7
Sant'Antonio Abate I 60 B3
Sant'Antonio di Gallura I 64 B3
Sant'Antonio di Santadi I 64 D1
Santanyí E 57 C11
Santa Olalla E 46 D4
Santa Oliva E 43 E7
Santa Olalla del Cala E 51 D7
Santa Pau E 43 C9
Santa Pola E 56 E3
Santar P 44 C5
Sant'Arcangelo I 60 C6
Santarcangelo di Romagna I 66 D5
Santarém P 44 F3
Sant'Arsenio I 60 C4
Santa Severina I 61 E7
Santas Martas E 39 D9
Santa Sofia I 66 E4
Santa Sofia P 50 B3
Santa Sofia d'Epiro I 61 D6
Santa Susana P 50 B4
Santa Susana P 50 C3
Santa Teresa di Gallura I 64 A3
Santa Teresa di Riva I 59 D7
Santău RO 151 C10
Santa Uxía E 38 C2
Santa Venerina I 59 D7
Santa Vitória P 50 D3
Santa Vitória do Ameixial P 50 B4
Sant Boi de Llobregat E 43 E8
Sant Carles de la Ràpita E 42 F5
Sant Celoni E 43 D8
Sant Cugat del Vallès E 43 E8
Sant'Egidio alla Vibrata I 62 B5
Sant'Elia a Pianisi I 63 D7
Sant'Elia Fiumerapido I 62 D5
Sant Elm E 49 E9
San Telmo E 51 D6
Sant'Elpidio a Mare I 67 F8
San Teodoro I 64 B4
Santeramo in Colle I 61 B7
Santervás de la Vega E 39 C10
Santes Creus E 43 E6
Sant Feliu de Guíxols E 43 D10
Sant Feliu de Pallerols E 43 C9
Sant Feliu Sasserra E 43 D8
Santhià I 68 C5
Sant Hilari Sacalm E 43 D9
Sant Hipòlit de Voltregà E 43 C8
Santiago de Alcántara E 45 E6
Santiago de Calatrava E 53 A8
Santiago de Compostela E 38 C2
Santiago de Covelo E 38 D3
Santiago de la Espada E 55 C7
Santiago de la Ribera E 56 F3
Santiago del Campo E 45 E8
Santiago do Cacém P 50 C2
Santiago do Escoural P 50 B3
Santiagomillas E 39 D7
Santibáñez de Béjar E 45 D9
Santibáñez de la Peña E 39 C10
Santibáñez de la Sierra E 45 C9
Santibáñez de Tera E 39 E8
Santibáñez de Vidriales E 39 D7
Santibáñez el Bajo E 45 D8
Santibáñez Zarzaguda E 40 D4
Sant'Ilario d'Enza I 66 C1
Santillana E 40 B3
Sântimbru RO 152 E3

Santiponce E 51 E7
Santisteban del Puerto E 55 C6
Santiuste de San Juan Bautista E 46 B3
Santiz E 45 B9
Sant Jaime Mediterráneo E 57 B13
Sant Jaume d'Enveja E 42 F5
Sant Joan de Labritja E 49 F8
Sant Joan de les Abadesses E 43 C8
Sant Joan de Vilatorrada E 43 D7
Sant Joan les Fonts E 43 C9
Sant Josep de sa Talaia E 57 D7
Santi Julià de Lòria AND 33 F9
Sant Llorenç de Morunys E 43 C7
Sant Llorenç des Cardassar E 57 B11
Sant Lluís E 57 B13
Sant Martí de Tous E 43 D7
Sant Martí Sarroca E 43 E7
Sant Mateu E 42 G4
Sant Miquel de Balansat E 57 C7
Santo Aleixo P 50 B5
Santo Aleixo da Restauração P 51 C5
Santo Amador P 51 C5
Santo André P 50 C2
Santo Antonio E 38 C2
Santo Antonino dos Cavaleiros P 50 B1
Santo António da Calzada E 40 D6
Santo Domingo de la Calzada E 40 D6
Santo Domingo de Silos E 40 E5
Santo Estêvão E 50 B2
Santo Estêvão P 50 C2
Santo Isidro de Pegões P 50 B2
Santok PL 85 E8
Santomera E 56 E2
Sant Omero I 62 B5
Santoña E 40 B5
Santo Pietro I 58 E6
Santo-Pietro-di-Tenda F 37 F10
Santo-Pietro-di-Venaco F 37 G10
Santo Stefano al Mare I 37 D7
Santo Stefano Belbo I 37 B8
Santo Stefano d'Aveto I 37 B10
Santo Stefano di Cadore I 72 C6
Santo Stefano di Camastra I 58 C5
Santo Stefano di Magra I 69 E8
Santo Stefano Quisquina I 58 D3
Santo Stino di Livenza I 73 E6
Santo Tirso P 38 F3
Santo Tomé E 55 C6
Santovenia E 39 E8
Santpedor E 43 D7
Sant Pere de Ribes E 43 E7
Sant Pere de Torelló E 43 C9
Sant Pol de Mar E 43 D9
Santpoort NL 182 A5
Sant Privat d'en Bas E 43 C8
Sant Quintí de Mediona E 43 E7
Sant Quirze de Besora E 43 C8
Sant Sadurní d'Anoia E 43 E7
Santullano E 39 B8
Santu Lussurgiu I 64 C2
Santurtzi E 40 B5
Sant Vicenç dels Horts E 43 E8
Sant Vicenç de Castellet E 43 D7
San Venanzo I 62 B2
San Vendemiano I 72 E5
San Vero Milis I 64 C2
San Vicente de Alcántara E 45 F6
San Vicente de Arana E 32 E1
San Vicente de la Barquera E 40 B3
San Vicente de la Sonsierra E 40 C6
San Vicente del Raspeig E 56 E3
San Vicente de Palacio E 46 B3
San Vicente de Toranzo E 40 B4
San Vicenzo E 38 C2
San Vincenzo I 59 B7
San Vincenzo I 65 A3
San Vincenzo Valle Roveto I 62 D5
San Vitero E 39 E7
San Vito I 64 E4
San Vito al Tagliamento I 73 E6
San Vito Chietino I 63 C6
San Vito dei Normanni I 61 B9
San Vito di Cadore I 72 D6
San Vito lo Capo I 58 B2
San Vito Romano I 62 D3
San Vito sullo Ionio I 59 B9
San Vittoria in Matenano I 62 A4
Sanxenxo E 38 D2
Sanxhax AL 168 A2
Sanza I 60 C5
Sânzieni RO 153 E8
Sanzoles E 39 F8
São Barnabé P 50 E3
São Bartolomeu P 44 F5
São Bartolomeu da Serra P 50 C2
São Bartolomeu de Messines P 50 E3
São Bento do Cortiço P 50 B4
São Brás P 50 D4
São Brás de Alportel P 50 E4
São Brás do Regedouro P 50 C3
São Brissos P 50 C4
São Cosmado P 44 B5
São Domingos P 50 D2
São Facundo P 44 F4
São Francisco da Serra P 50 C2
São Geraldo P 50 B3
São Gregório P 50 B4
São Jacinto P 44 C3
São João da Madeira P 44 C4
São João da Pesqueira P 44 B6
São João da Venda P 50 E4
São João do Campo P 44 D4
São João dos Caldeireiros P 50 D4
São José da Lamarosa P 44 F4
São Lourenço de Mamporção P 50 B4
São Luís P 50 D2
São Manços P 50 C4
São Marcos da Ataboeira P 50 D4
São Marcos da Serra P 50 E3
São Marcos do Campo P 50 C4

São Martinho da Cortiça P 44 D4
São Martinho das Amoreiras P 50 D3
São Martinho de Angueira P 39 E7
São Martinho do Porto P 44 E2
São Matias P 50 C4
São Miguel de Acha P 45 D6
São Miguel de Machede P 50 B4
São Miguel do Rio Torto P 44 F4
São Miguel do Outeiro P 44 C4
São Miguel do Pinheiro P 50 D4
Saône F 26 F5
São Pedro da Cadeira P 44 F2
São Pedro de Muel P 44 E2
São Pedro de Solis P 50 D4
São Pedro do Sul P 44 C4
Saorge F 37 D7
São Romão P 51 B5
São Romão do Sado P 50 C3
São Sebastião dos Carros P 50 D4
São Teotónio P 50 D2
Saou F 35 A9
São Vicente P 38 E5
São Vicente da Beira P 44 D5
Sáp H 151 C7
Sapanca TR 173 B9
Săpânța RO 145 H8
Sapareva Banya BG 165 E7
Saparevo BG 165 E7
Săpata RO 160 D5
Sapes GR 171 B9
Sa Pobla E 57 B11
Săpoca RO 161 C9
Sapotskin BY 137 F8
Sappada I 73 C6
Sap'parjäkka N 113 D17
Sappee FIN 127 C11
Sappen N 112 D7
Sappetavan S 107 A13
Sappetsele S 107 A13
Sappisaasi S 116 C7
Sapri I 60 C5
Sapsalampi FIN 123 F11
Sapsoperä FIN 125 B11
Sara FIN 122 F9
Saraby N 113 C12
Saracena I 60 D6
Saračinec HR 148 D6
Sarafovo BG 167 D9
Saraiķi LV 134 C2
Säräisniemi FIN 119 F17
Saraiu RO 155 D2
Sarajärvi FIN 120 C9
Sarajärvi FIN 129 B11
Sarajevo BIH 157 E9
Saramo FIN 125 C12
Saramon F 33 C7
Saran F 24 E6
Sáránd H 151 C8
Sarandë AL 168 E3
Sarantaporo GR 169 D7
Sarantsi BG 165 D8
Sa Ràpita E 57 C10
Sărăsău RO 145 H8
Sarata UA 154 E5
Sărata Galbenă MD 154 D2
Sărata-Monteoru RO 161 C9
Sărata Nouă MD 154 E2
Sărăteni MD 154 C2
Sărăteni MD 154 D2
Sărătenii Vechi MD 154 B3
Saray TR 173 B8
Sarayakpinar TR 167 F7
Saraylar TR 173 C8
Šarbanovac SRB 159 F9
Sárbogárd H 149 C11
Sarcelles F 25 C7
Sarconi I 60 C5
Sardara I 64 C2
Šardice CZ 77 E11
Sardinia GR 174 B3
Sardoal P 44 E4
Sare F 32 D2
S'Arenal E 49 E10
Sarentino I 72 C3
Sarezzo I 69 B9
Sargans CH 71 C8
Sariai LT 134 C3
Saribeyler TR 173 F8
Saricaali TR 171 C10
Sariçam TR 177 B9
Saridioni TR 173 B8
Saridinişment TR 167 F7
Sariegos E 39 C8
Sarikemer TR 177 D9
Sariköy TR 173 D8
Sariñena E 42 D3
Sariñena E 42 D3
Šariská Michaľany SK 145 E3
Sariyer TR 173 B11
Sarjankylä FIN 123 B14
Sarkad H 151 D7
Sarkadkeresztúr H 151 D7
Särkelä FIN 121 C12
Sárkeresztúr H 149 C11
Särkijärvi FIN 117 C11
Särkijärvi FIN 119 C15
Särkijärvi FIN 120 E9
Särkikorpi FIN 125 D12
Särkikylä FIN 123 D11
Särkilahti FIN 127 B14
Särkilahti FIN 129 B11
Särkiluoma FIN 121 B14
Särkimo FIN 122 D8
Särkisalmi FIN 129 B11
Särkisalo FIN 123 E16
Särkisalo FIN 127 E10
Şarköy TR 173 C7
São Barnabé P 50 E3

Särö S 91 D10
Sarochyna BY 133 F5
Saronno I 69 B7
Sárosd H 149 B11
Sárospatak H 145 G4
Šarovce SK 147 E7
Sarow D 84 C4
Sarpsborg N 95 D14
Sarracín E 40 D4
Sarral E 42 E6
Sarralbe F 27 C7
Sarrance F 32 D4
Sarrancolin F 33 E6
Sarraquinhos P 38 E4
Sarras F 30 E6
Sarre GB 15 E11
Sarre I 31 D11
Sarreaus E 38 D4
Sarrebourg F 27 C7
Sarreguemines F 27 B7
Sárrétudvari H 151 C7
Sarre-Union F 27 C7
Sarria E 38 C5
Sarrià de Ter E 43 C9
Sarrians F 35 B8
Sarrión E 48 D3
Sarroca de Lleida E 42 E5
Sarròch I 64 E3
Sarród H 149 A7
Sarrola-Carcopino F 37 G9
Sarron F 32 C5
Sarry F 25 C11
Sarsina I 66 E5
Sárszentágota H 149 C11
Sárszentlőrinc H 149 C11
Sart B 183 D7
Sartaguda E 32 F1
Sarteano I 62 B1
Sartène F 37 H9
Sarti GR 170 E5
Sartilly F 23 C9
Sartininkai LT 134 F3
Sarud H 150 B6
Saru Dornei RO 152 C6
Šaruhanli TR 177 B10
Sarule I 64 C3
Sărulești RO 161 C9
Sărulești RO 161 E9
Sárvár H 149 B7
Sarvela FIN 122 F9
Sarvijoki FIN 122 E7
Sarvikumpu FIN 125 F12
Sarviluoma FIN 122 F8
Sarvinki FIN 125 E14
Sarvisé E 32 F5
Sarvisvaara S 116 E6
Särvsjön S 102 A5
Sar"ya BY 133 E3
Sarzana I 69 E8
Sarzeau F 22 E6
Sarzedas P 44 E5
Sarzedo P 44 B5
Sasa MK 164 E6
Sasalli TR 177 C3
Sasamón E 40 D3
Sasbach D 27 D9
Sasbachwalden D 186 D5
Sasca Montană RO 159 D8
Saschiz RO 152 E5
Săsciori RO 152 F3
Sascut RO 153 E10
Sásd H 149 D10
Sasina BIH 157 C6
Sasnava LT 137 D7
Sassali FIN 117 D15
Sassano I 60 C5
Sassari I 64 B2
Sassello I 37 C8
Sassen D 84 B4
Sassenage F 31 E8
Sassenberg D 17 E10
Sassenheim NL 16 D3
Sassetta I 65 A3
Sassnitz D 84 A5
Sassocorvaro I 66 E5
Sassoferrato I 67 F6
Sasso Marconi I 66 D3
Sassuolo I 66 D2
Sástago E 41 F11
Šaštín-Stráže SK 77 E12
Sas Van Gent NL 16 F1
Sáta H 145 G1
Satão P 44 C5
Satchinez RO 151 F7
Šateikiai LT 134 E3
Sätenäs villastad S 91 C12
Säter S 97 B14
Säterväilen S 102 A5
Säti LV 134 C5
Satikl LV 134 C5
Sätila S 91 D11
Satillieu F 30 E6
Satkūnai LT 134 D7
Satnica Đakovačka HR 149 F10
Sätofta S 87 D13
Sátoraljaújhely H 145 G4
Satovcha BG 170 A5
Satow D 83 C11
Satriano di Lucania I 60 B5
Satrup D 82 A7
Sattanen FIN 117 D17
Satteins A 71 C9
Sattledorf D 75 D7
Satter S 116 E7
Sattledt A 76 F6
Satulung RO 151 B11
Satu Mare RO 151 B10
Satu Mare RO 151 B10
Saubusse F 32 C3
Saúca E 47 B7
Sauca MD 154 A1
Sâuca RO 151 C9
Săucești RO 153 D10
Sauclières F 34 C5
Sauda N 94 C4
Saue EST 131 C9
Sauerlach D 75 G10
Sauga EST 131 E8
Saugnacq-et-Muret F 32 B4
Saugos LT 134 F2
Saugues F 30 F4
Saujon F 28 E4
Sauk AL 168 B2
Sauka LV 135 D10
Šaukėnai LT 134 E5
Saukko FIN 125 C11
Saukkoaapa FIN 115 D2
Saukkojärvi FIN 119 B16
Saukkola FIN 127 E10

Saukkoriipi FIN 117 E12
Saukonkylä FIN 123 E11
Sauland N 95 C9
Saulce-sur-Rhône F 35 A8
Sauldorf D 27 E11
Saulepi EST 130 E7
Săulești RO 160 D2
Saulgau D 71 A9
Saulgrub D 71 B12
Saulheim D 21 E10
Šaulia E 25 F11
Saulieu F 25 F11
Saulkalne LV 135 C8
Saulkrasti LV 135 B8
Sault F 35 B9
Sault-de-Navailles F 32 C4
Sault-lès-Rethel F 19 F9
Saulx F 26 E5
Saulxures-sur-Moselotte F 27 E6
Saulzais-le-Potier F 29 B11
Saumos F 28 F3
Saumur F 23 F11
Saunajärvi FIN 125 C13
Saunakylä FIN 123 D13
Saunavaara FIN 115 D3
Saundersfoot GB 12 B5
Saura FIN 119 E15
Saurat F 33 E9
Šauriešl LV 135 C8
Sauris I 73 D6
Saursfjord N 110 E9
Sausnėja LV 135 C11
Sausset-les-Pins F 35 D9
Saussy F 26 F2
Sautens A 71 C11
Sautiņi LV 135 B8
Sautron F 23 F8
Sautso Kraftverk N 113 D14
Sauvagnon F 32 D4
Sauvagnon F 32 B3
Sauve F 35 C6
Sauveterre-de-Béarn F 32 D4
Sauveterre-de-Guyenne F 28 F5
Sauveterre-la-Lémance F 33 A8
Sauviat-sur-Vige F 29 D9
Sauvo FIN 126 E8
Sauxillanges F 30 D3
Sauzé-Vaussais F 29 C6
Sauzon F 22 F5
Sava I 61 C9
Sava SLO 73 D10
Săvădisla RO 151 D11
Savalia GR 174 D3
Savaloja FIN 119 E15
Savar S 122 C5
Sävärsjön RO 151 E9
Sävast S 118 C7
Savastepe TR 173 F8
Säve S 91 D10
Savelli I 61 E7
Savenay F 23 F8
Săveni RO 153 B9
Săveni RO 161 D11
Saverdun F 33 D9
Saverne F 27 C7
Sävi FIN 126 B8
Sävjä FIN 123 D17
Saviaho FIN 125 C10
Savières F 25 D10
Savigliano I 37 B7
Savignac-les-Églises F 29 E7
Savignano Irpino I 60 A4
Savignano sul Rubicone I 66 D5
Savigné-l'Évêque F 23 D12
Savigneux F 30 D5
Savigny-en-Sancerre F 25 F8
Savigny-lès-Beaune F 25 F12
Savigny-sur-Braye F 24 E4
Savijärvi FIN 125 C13
Savikylä FIN 125 C11
Savilahti FIN 129 C10
Savimäki FIN 124 C7
Savines-le-Lac F 36 B4
Săvinești RO 153 D8
Savino Selo SRB 158 B4
Savira FIN 121 F10
Savirata FIN 121 F10
Saviselkä FIN 123 B16
Savitaipale FIN 128 C8
Sävja S 99 C9
Šavnik MNE 157 G11
Savognin CH 71 D9
Savoisy F 25 E11
Savona I 37 C8
Savonlinna FIN 129 B10
Savonranta FIN 125 F12
Savran' UA 154 A6
Sävsjö S 92 E6
Sävsjön S 97 C12
Savudrija HR 67 B10
Savukoski FIN 115 D4
Sawin PL 141 H8
Sawston GB 15 C9
Sax E 56 D3
Saxdalen S 97 B12
Saxen A 77 F7
Saxhyttan S 97 C11
Saxilby GB 11 E10
Saxmundham GB 15 C11
Saxnäs S 106 B8
Saxon CH 31 C11
Saxthorpe GB 15 B11
Saxvallen S 105 D12
Sayalonga E 53 C8
Sayatón E 47 D7
Sayda D 80 E4
Säynäjä FIN 121 B13
Säynätsalo FIN 123 F15
Säyneinen FIN 125 D10
Săzava CZ 77 C7
Sazli TR 171 E10
Sazli TR 177 D9
Sazoba TR 173 D7
Sazoba TR 177 B10
Scaër F 22 D4
Scăești RO 160 E3
Scafa I 62 C5
Scalasaig GB 4 C4
Scalby GB 11 C11
Scalea I 60 D5
Scaletta Zanclea I 59 C7
Scalloway GB 3 E14
Scandale I 61 E7
Scandiano I 66 D2
Scandicci I 66 E3
Scandriglia I 62 C3
Scanno I 62 D5
Scano di Montiferro I 64 C2
Scansano I 65 B4
Scanzano Jonico I 61 C7
Scapa GB 3 H11

Scarborough GB 11 C11
Scardovari I 66 C5
Scarinish GB 4 B3
Scario I 60 C5
Scârișoara RO 160 F5
Scarlino I 65 B3
Scarperia I 66 E3
Scartaglen IRL 8 D4
Scartaglin IRL 8 D4
Ščenica-Bobani BIH 162 D5
Scerni I 63 C7
Scey-sur-Saône-et-St-Albin F 26 E4
Schaafheim D 187 B7
Schaan FL 71 C9
Schaarsbergen NL 183 A7
Schaerbeek B 19 C9
Schaesberg NL 20 C5
Schaffhausen CH 27 E10
Schafflund D 82 A6
Schafstädt D 79 D10
Schafstedt D 82 B6
Schagen NL 16 C3
Schaijk NL 183 B7
Schalchen A 76 F4
Schalkau D 75 B9
Schalkhaar NL 183 A8
Schalksmühle D 17 F9
Schänis CH 27 F11
Schapen D 17 D9
Schaprode D 84 A4
Scharbeutz D 83 B9
Schardenberg A 76 E4
Schärding D 76 F4
Scharendijke NL 16 E1
Scharnebeck D 83 D9
Scharnitz A 72 B3
Scharnstein A 73 A8
Schattendorf A 149 A7
Schebheim D 75 C7
Scheemda NL 17 B7
Scheer D 27 D11
Scheeßel D 82 D6
Schefflenz D 21 F12
Scheggia e Pascelupo I 67 F6
Scheggino I 62 B3
Scheia RO 153 B8
Scheia RO 153 D11
Scheibbs A 77 F8
Scheiblingkirchen A 148 A6
Scheidegg D 71 B9
Scheifling A 73 B9
Scheinfeld D 75 C8
Schela RO 155 B1
Schela RO 160 C2
Schelklingen D 74 F6
Schellerten D 79 B7
Schemmerhofen D 71 A9
Schenefeld D 82 B6
Schenefeld D 83 C7
Schenkenfelden A 76 E6
Schenkenzell D 187 D5
Schenklengsfeld D 78 E6
Schermbeck D 17 E7
Schermen D 79 B10
Schermerhorn NL 16 C3
Scherpenheuvel B 19 C10
Scherpenzeel NL 16 D4
Scherwiller F 27 D7
Scherzingen CH 27 E11
Scheßlitz D 75 C9
Schiavi di Abruzzo I 63 D6
Schiedam NL 16 E2
Schieder-Schwalenberg D 17 E12
Schieren L 20 E6
Schierling D 75 E11
Schiermonnikoog NL 16 B5
Schiers CH 71 D9
Schiffdorf D 17 A11
Schifferstadt D 21 F10
Schifflange L 20 E6
Schiffweiler D 186 C3
Schijndel NL 16 E4
Schilde B 16 F3
Schillingen D 186 B2
Schillingsfürst D 75 D7
Schilpario I 69 A9
Schiltach D 27 D9
Schiltigheim F 27 C8
Schimatari GR 175 C8
Schinnen L 20 D5
Schinos GR 174 B3
Schinveld NL 20 C5
Schio I 69 B11
Schipkau D 80 C5
Schipluiden NL 182 B4
Schirmeck F 27 D7
Schirmitz D 75 C11
Schitu RO 160 E5
Schitu RO 161 E7
Schitu Duca RO 153 C11
Schitu Golești RO 160 C6
Schkeuditz D 79 D11
Schkölen D 79 D10
Schkona D 79 C12
Schkopau D 79 D10
Schlabendorf D 80 C5
Schladen D 79 B8
Schlangen D 17 E11
Schlangenbad D 21 D10
Schleching D 72 A5
Schleiden D 20 C6
Schleife D 81 C7
Schleiz D 79 E10
Schlema D 79 E12
Schlepzig D 80 B5
Schleswig D 82 A7
Schleusingen D 75 A8
Schlieben D 80 C4
Schliengen D 27 E8
Schlier D 71 A9
Schlierbach D 73 A9
Schlieren CH 27 F9
Schliersee D 72 A4
Schlitters A 72 B4
Schlitz D 78 E6
Schlossberg A 148 C4
Schloss Holte-Stukenbrock D 17 E11
Schlossvippach D 79 D9
Schlosswil CH 70 D5
Schlotheim D 79 D7
Schluchsee D 27 E8
Schlüchtern D 74 B6
Schlüsselfeld D 75 C8
Schmalkalden D 79 E7

Schmelz D 21 F7
Schmidgaden D 75 D11
Schmidmühlen D 75 D10
Schmiedeberg D 80 E5
Schmiedeberg D 83 D11
Schmölln D 79 E11
Schmölln D 84 D6
Schnabelwaid D 75 C10
Schnackenburg D 83 D11
Schnaittach D 75 C9
Schneeberg D 79 E12
Schneidlingen D 79 B10
Schnelldorf D 187 C9
Schnellmannshausen D 79 D7
Schneverdingen D 82 D7
Schnürpflingen D 187 E8
Schobüll D 82 A6
Schodnia PL 142 E5
Schoenberg B 20 D6
Scholen D 17 C11
Schollene D 83 E12
Schöllkrippen D 187 A7
Schöllnach D 76 E4
Schömberg D 27 D10
Schömberg D 187 D6
Schönaich D 187 D7
Schönau D 76 F3
Schönau im Schwarzwald D 27 E8
Schönbach D 84 D5
Schönberg D 83 C9
Schönberg D 84 E3
Schönberg (Holstein) D 83 B8
Schönberg am Kamp A 77 E9
Schönberg im Stubaital A 72 B3
Schönborn D 80 C5
Schondra D 74 B6
Schönebeck D 83 D12
Schönebeck (Elbe) D 79 B10
Schöneck D 75 B11
Schönecken D 20 D6
Schönenberg-Kübelberg D 186 C3
Schönermark D 84 D5
Schönewalde D 80 C5
Schönewörde D 79 A8
Schongau D 71 B11
Schönhausen D 79 A11
Schöningen D 79 B8
Schönkirchen D 83 B8
Schönow D 84 E5
Schönsee D 75 C12
Schöntal D 74 D6
Schönthal D 75 D12
Schönwalde D 80 D5
Schönwalde am Bungsberg D 83 B9
Schönwies A 71 C11
Schoondijke NL 16 F1
Schoonebeek NL 17 C8
Schoonhoven NL 16 E3
Schoorl NL 16 C3
Schopfheim D 27 E8
Schopfloch D 75 D7
Schöppenstedt D 79 B8
Schoppernau A 71 C10
Schöppingen D 17 D8
Schörfling am Attersee A 73 A8
Schorndorf D 74 E6
Schorndorf D 75 D12
Schortens D 17 A9
Schoten B 16 F2
Schotten D 21 D12
Schramberg D 27 D9
Schreckbach D 21 C12
Schrems A 77 E8
Schrepkow D 83 E12
Schriesheim D 21 F11
Schrobenhausen D 75 E9
Schröder A 73 B9
Schrozberg D 74 D6
Schruns A 71 C9
Schübelbach CH 27 F10
Schuby D 82 A6
Schulenberg im Oberharz D 79 C7
Schull IRL 8 E3
Schulzendorf D 84 E6
Schüpfheim CH 70 D6
Schuttertal D 186 E4
Schutterwald D 186 E4
Schüttorf D 17 D8
Schwaan D 83 C12
Schwabach D 75 D9
Schwäbisch Gmünd D 74 E6
Schwäbisch Hall D 74 D6
Schwabmünchen D 71 A11
Schwabstedt D 82 B6
Schwaförden D 17 C11
Schwaigern D 21 F11
Schwalbach D 21 F7
Schwalmstadt-Treysa D 21 C12
Schwalmstadt-Ziegenhain D 21 C12
Schwanberg A 73 B11
Schwanden CH 71 C8
Schwandorf D 75 D11
Schwanebeck D 79 C9
Schwanenstadt A 76 F5
Schwanewede D 17 B11
Schwangau D 71 B11
Schwanstetten D 75 D9
Schwarme D 17 C12
Schwarmstedt D 82 E7
Schwarz D 83 D13
Schwarza D 79 E8
Schwarzach D 76 E3
Schwarzau im Gebirge A 148 A5
Schwarzenau A 149 A6
Schwarzenbach A 148 A6
Schwarzenbach D 79 E12
Schwarzenborn D 78 E5
Schwarzenburg CH 31 B11
Schwarzenfeld D 75 D11
Schwarzheide D 80 D5
Schwaz D 72 B4
Schwechat A 77 F10
Schwedeneck D 83 B8
Schwedt an der Oder D 84 D6
Schwegenheim D 187 C5
Schwei (Stadland) D 17 B10
Schweiburg D 17 B10
Schweigen-Rechtenbach D 27 B8
Schweighouse-sur-Moder F 186 D4
Schweinfurt D 75 B7
Schweinitz D 80 C4
Schweinrich D 83 D13

Schwelm D 17 F8
Schwendau A 72 B4
Schwendi D 71 A9
Schwenningen D 27 D10
Schwepnitz D 80 D5
Schwerin D 83 C10
Schwerte D 17 F8
Schwichtenberg D 84 C5
Schwieberdingen D 27 C11
Schwiesau D 79 A9
Schwindegg D 75 F11
Schwinkendorf D 83 C13
Schwoich A 72 A5
Schwyz CH 71 C7
Sciacca I 58 D3
Sciara I 58 D4
Scicli I 59 F6
Sciez F 31 C9
Scigliano I 61 E6
Scilla I 59 C7
Ścinawa PL 81 D10
Scionzier F 31 C10
Scoarța RO 160 C2
Scobinți RO 153 C9
Scoglitti I 58 F5
Scolaticci I 59 C6
Scole GB 15 C11
Sconser GB 2 L4
Scopello I 68 B5
Scorbé-Clairvaux F 29 B6
Scordia I 59 E6
Scornicești RO 160 D5
Scorrano I 61 C10
Scorțaru Nou RO 161 C11
Scorțeni MD 154 C3
Scorțeni RO 153 D9
Scorțeni RO 161 C7
Scorțoasa RO 161 C9
Scorton GB 11 C8
Scorzè I 66 A5
Scotch Corner GB 11 C8
Scotch Corner IRL 7 D9
Scotshouse IRL 7 D8
Scourie GB 2 J6
Scousburgh GB 3 F14
Scrabster GB 3 H9
Screeb IRL 6 F3
Screggan IRL 7 F7
Scremerston GB 5 D13
Scribbagh GB 6 D6
Scrioaștea RO 160 E5
Scriob IRL 6 F3
Sculeni MD 153 C11
Scundu RO 160 D4
Scunthorpe GB 11 D10
Scuol CH 71 D11
Scurcola Marsicana I 62 C4
Scurtu Mare RO 160 E6
Scutelnici RO 161 D9
Seaca RO 160 E5
Seaca RO 160 F6
Seaca de Pădure RO 160 E2
Seaford GB 15 F9
Seaham GB 5 F14
Seahouses GB 5 D13
Seamer GB 11 C11
Seapatrick GB 7 D10
Seara P 38 E2
Seascale GB 10 C5
Seaton GB 13 D8
Seaton Delaval GB 5 E13
Seaton Sluice GB 5 E14
Seaview GB 13 D12
Sebal P 44 D3
Sébazac-Concourès F 34 B4
Sebbersund DK 86 B5
Sebechleby SK 147 E7
Sebedražie SK 147 D7
Sebeş RO 152 F3
Şebinkarahisar TR 173 B11 [?]
Sebezh RUS 133 D4
Sebiş RO 151 E9
Sebnitz D 80 E6
Seč CZ 77 C9
Sečanj SRB 159 C6
Seča Reka SRB 158 E4
Secăria RO 161 C7
Secaş RO 151 F8
Sece LV 135 C10
Secemin PL 143 E8
Seckach D 21 F12
Seckau A 73 B10
Seclin F 19 C7
Secondigny F 28 B5
Sečovce SK 145 F4
Sečovská Polianka SK 145 F4
Secu RO 160 E2
Secueni RO 152 E5
Secuieni RO 153 D9
Secusigiu RO 151 E6
Seda E 44 F5 [?]
Seda LV 131 F11
Sedan F 19 E10
Sedano E 40 C4
Sedbergh GB 10 C6
Seddülbahir TR 171 D10
Seden DK 86 E6
Sedere LV 135 E12
Séderon F 35 B10
Sedgefield GB 5 F14
Sedico I 72 D5
Sedini I 64 B2
Sedlarica HR 149 E8
Sedlčany CZ 77 C6
Sedlec Prčice CZ 77 C7
Sedlice CZ 76 D5
Sedlice SK 145 F3
Sedliská SK 145 F4
Sedlnice CZ 146 B6
Sedrina I 69 B8
Šeduva LT 134 E7
Sjdziejowice PL 143 C7
Sjdzin PL 138 E6
Sjdziszów PL 143 E9
Sjdziszów Małopolski PL 143 F12
See A 71 C10
See A 73 B7
Seebach D 79 E7
Seebergen D 79 E8
Seeboden A 73 C8
Seebruck D 72 A5
Seeburg D 79 C7
Seedorf A 73 C9
Seefeld D 75 F9
Seefeld D 83 B7 [?]
Seefeld (Stadland) D 17 B10

Seefeld in Tirol A 72 B3
Seeg S 73 B11
Seehausen D 79 B9
Seehausen D 84 D5
Seehausen (Altmark) D 83 E11
Seeheim-Jugenheim D 21 E11
Seekirchen am Wallersee
   A 73 A7
Seelow D 80 A6
Seelze D 78 B6
Seend GB 13 C10
Seeon D 72 A5
Sées F 23 C12
Seesen D 79 C7
Seeshaupt D 72 A3
Seethal A 73 B8
Seevetal D 83 D8
Seewiesen A 148 A4
Séez F 31 D10
Seferihisar TR 177 C8
Sefkerin SRB 158 C6
Sefrivatn N 105 A14
Seftigen CH 31 B12
Segalstad N 101 D12
Șegarcea RO 160 E3
Șegarcea-Vale RO 160 F5
Segeletz D 83 E13
Segersäng S 93 A11
Segersta S 103 D12
Segerstad S 89 C11
Segesd H 149 D8
Seggiano I 65 B5
Séglien F 22 D5
Seglinge FIN 99 B15
Seglingsberg S 98 C6
Seglodden N 114 C9
Seglvik N 112 C7
Segmon S 97 D9
Segni I 62 D4
Segonzac F 28 D5
Segorbe E 48 E4
Segovia E 46 C4
Segré F 23 E10
Ségur F 34 B4
Ségrie F 23 D12
Segura P 45 E7
Segura de la Sierra E 55 C7
Segura de León E 51 C6
Segura de los Baños E 42 F2
Segurilla E 46 D3
Sehlde D 79 B7
Sehma D 76 A3
Sehnde D 79 B6
Seia P 44 D5
Șeica Mare RO 152 E4
Șeica Mică RO 152 E4
Seiches-sur-le-Loir F 23 E11
Seiersberg A 148 B4
Seierstad N 105 B10
Seifhennersdorf D 81 E7
Seignelay F 25 E10
Seignelégier CH 27 F6
Seilhac F 29 E9
Seillans F 36 D5
Seilles B 183 E6
Seimeni RO 155 E2
Seinäjoki FIN 122 E9
Seini RO 151 B11
Seinsheim D 75 C7
Seipäjärvi FIN 117 D16
Seirijai LT 137 E8
Seissan F 33 D7
Seitajärvi FIN 115 C3
Șeitin RO 150 E6
Șeix F 33 E8
Seixal P 50 B1
Sejerby DK 87 D8
Sejerslev DK 86 B3
Sejet DK 86 D5
Sejny PL 136 E7
Sekkemo N 112 D8
Šekovići BIH 157 D10
Sjkowa PL 145 D3
Sjkowo PL 81 A10
Sel S 107 E10
Sel S 107 E13
Sela HR 149 E6
Selånger S 103 B13
Selanovtsi BG 160 F3
Selänpää FIN 128 C6
Selargius I 64 E3
Șelaru RO 161 D6
Šelattyn GB 10 F5
Selaya E 40 B4
Selb D 75 B11
Selbekken N 104 E7
Selbitz D 75 B10
Selbu N 105 E10
Selbustrand N 105 E9
Selby GB 11 D9
Selce AL 163 D8
Selce HR 67 B10
Selce SK 147 D8
Selci Đakovački HR 149 F10
Selçuk TR 177 D9
Selde DK 86 B4
Selegas I 64 D3
Selenicë AL 168 C2
Selent D 83 B8
Selero GR 171 B7
Sélestat F 27 D7
Selet S 118 C7
Selet S 122 B3
Seleuș RO 151 E8
Seleuš SRB 159 C6
Selevac SRB 159 E6
Selfjord N 110 D5
Selí LV 131 F10
Selice SK 146 E5
Seligenstadt D 187 A6
Șelimbăr RO 152 F4
Șelimiye TR 177 E10
Selimpașa TR 173 B9
Selimşahlar TR 177 B9
Selishtë AL 168 A3
Selishte BG 165 E7
Selište SRB 159 E9
Selitë AL 168 C2
Selja S 102 D7
Selje N 100 B2
Seljeli N 108 D6
Seljelynes N 111 B17
Seljenes N 113 B15
Seljord N 95 D9
Selkäjärvi S 116 E8
Selkälä FIN 115 E6
Selkirk GB 5 D11
Selkopp N 113 B12
Sella E 56 D4
Sellano I 62 B3
Sellasia GR 174 E5

Selles-St-Denis F 24 F6
Selles-sur-Cher F 24 F6
Sellia GR 178 E7
Sellia Marina I 59 B10
Sellières F 31 B8
Sellin D 84 B5
Sellindge GB 15 E10
Selling DK 86 C6
Sellingen NL 17 C8
Sellrain A 72 B3
Sellye H 149 E9
Selm D 17 E8
Selmes P 50 C4
Selmsdorf D 83 C9
Selnes N 104 D7
Selnes N 111 B12
Selnes N 111 C13
Selo BIH 157 D10
Selommes F 24 E5
Selongey F 26 E3
Selonnet F 36 C4
Selow D 83 C11
Selsey GB 15 F7
Selsingen D 17 B12
Selsjön S 107 E12
Selsøyvika N 108 C4
Selters (Westerwald) D 21 C9
Seltjärn S 107 D13
Seltz F 27 C9
Selva E 57 B10
Selva I 61 B8
Selva N 104 D7
Selva dei Molini I 72 C4
Selva di Progno I 69 B11
Selva di Val Gardena I 72 C4
Selvær N 108 C3
Selvåg N 104 D6
Selvazzano Dentro I 66 B4
Selvino I 69 B8
Selyatyn UA 152 B6
Selzthal A 73 A9
Sem N 95 D12
Seman AL 168 C1
Sembadel F 30 E4
Sembrancher CH 31 C11
Šěme LV 134 B6
Séméac F 33 D6
Sémelay F 30 B4
Semeljci HR 149 F11
Semeni MD 153 C11
Semenivka UA 154 E6
Semerovo SK 146 E6
Semič SLO 73 E11
Semide P 44 D4
Semily CZ 81 E8
Semizovac BIH 157 E9
Semlac RO 151 E6
Semlow D 83 B13
Semmenstedt D 79 B8
Semoutiers-Montsaon F 26 D3
Sempach CH 27 F9
Šempeter SLO 73 D9
Semproniano I 65 B5
Semriach A 148 B4
Šemša SK 145 F3
Šemševo MK 164 E3
Semur-en-Auxois F 25 F11
Semur-en-Brionnais F 30 C5
Semussac F 28 E4
Sena E 42 D3
Seňa SK 145 F3
Senales I 71 D11
Senarpont F 18 E4
Sénas F 35 C9
Sencelles E 57 B10
Sencur SLO 73 D9
Send GB 15 E7
Senden D 75 F7
Sendenhorst D 17 E9
Sendets F 32 D5
Sendim P 38 F6
Sendim P 39 F7
Șendreni RO 155 B2
Șendriceni RO 153 B8
Senec SK 146 E4
Seneffe B 19 C9
Seneghe I 64 C2
Senerchia I 60 B4
Senes GB 11 E9
Senez F 36 D4
Senftenberg A 77 F9
Senftenberg D 80 D6
Sengouagnet F 33 E7
Senhora do Rosário P 45 F6
Senica SK 146 D5
Senice na Hané CZ 77 C12
Senigallia I 67 E7
Senis I 64 D2
Senise I 60 C6
Senj HR 67 C10
Senje SRB 159 F7
Senjehesten N 111 B12
Senjehopen N 111 B13
Senjski Rudnik SRB 159 F8
Sen'kava BY 133 D3
Šenkvice SK 146 E4
Senlis F 25 B8
Sennan S 87 B11
Sennariolo I 64 C2
Sennecey-le-Grand F 30 B6
Sennels DK 86 B3
Sennen GB 12 E3
Sennik BG 165 D11
Sennori I 64 B2
Sennwald CH 71 C8
Sennybridge GB 13 B7
Senohrad SK 147 E8
Senokos BG 161 F3
Senonches F 24 C5
Senones F 27 D6
Senorbì I 64 D3
Senouillac F 33 C9
Senovo BG 161 F8
Senožeče SLO 73 E9
Sens F 25 D9
Sens-de-Bretagne F 23 D8
Senta SRB 150 F5
Sentein F 33 E7
Senterada E 33 F7
Šentilj SLO 148 C5
Šentjernej SLO 148 E4
Šentjur pri Celju SLO 148 D4
Senuc F 19 F10
Seon CH 27 F9
Šepak BIH 157 C11
Sepekov CZ 77 D6
Sepino I 60 A3
Sępólno Krajeńskie PL 85 D13
Sępolno Wielkie PL 85 C11
Seppois-le-Bas F 27 E7
Șepreuș RO 151 D8

Septèmes-les-Vallons F 35 D9
Septemvri BG 165 E9
Septemvriytsi BG 160 F2
Septeuil F 24 C6
Septfonds F 33 B9
Septmoncel F 31 C8
Sepúlveda E 40 F4
Sequals I 73 D6
Sequeros E 45 D8
Seraincourt F 19 E9
Seraing B 19 C12
Séranon F 36 D5
Seravezza I 66 E1
Șerbănești RO 160 E5
Șerbettar TR 173 B6
Sërboc RKS 163 D10
Șercaia RO 152 F6
Serdiana I 64 E3
Seredka RUS 132 F3
Seredyne UA 145 F6
Seredžius LT 137 C7
Seregélyes H 149 B11
Seregno I 69 B7
Séreilhac F 29 D8
Šerene LV 135 C10
Sérent F 22 E6
Serényfalva H 145 G1
Serfaus A 71 D11
Sergen TR 167 F9
Sergines F 25 D9
Sergnano I 69 C8
Serhat TR 172 E6
Serhiyivka UA 154 B6
Seriate I 69 B8
Sérifontaine F 18 F4
Serifos GR 175 E10
Sérignan F 34 D5
Sérignan-du-Comtat F 35 B8
Serina I 69 B8
Serino I 60 B3
Serinyà E 43 C9
Sermaises F 25 D7
Sermano I 62 D4
Sermenin MK 169 B7
Sermide I 66 C3
Sermoneta I 62 D4
Sermoyer F 31 B6
Sërmükšl LV 135 B11
Sernancelhe P 44 C6
Serno D 79 C11
Serock PL 138 D5
Serock PL 138 E11
Serokomla PL 141 G6
Serón E 55 E8
Serón de Nájima E 41 F7
Seroskoberre NL 182 B3
Seròs E 42 E4
Serpa P 50 D4
Serpins P 44 D4
Serpneve UA 154 E4
Serqueux F 26 E4
Serquigny F 24 B4
Serra E 48 E4
Serracapriola I 63 D8
Serrada E 39 F10
Serra de'Conti I 67 E7
Serradifalco I 58 E4
Serra-di-Ferro F 37 H9
Serradilla E 45 E8
Serradilla del Arroyo E 45 C8
Serra-di-Scopamène F 37 H10
Serramanna I 64 E2
Serramazzoni I 66 D2
Serranillos E 46 D3
Serra Riccò I 37 C9
Serra San Bruno I 59 B9
Serrastretta I 59 A9
Serravalle RSM 66 E5
Serravalle di Chienti I 62 A3
Serravalle Scrivia I 37 B9
Serre I 60 B4
Serrejón E 45 E9
Serrenti I 64 E2
Serres F 35 B10
Serres GR 169 B10
Serres-Castet F 32 D5
Serri I 64 D3
Serriera F 37 G9
Serrière-de-Briord F 31 D7
Serrières F 30 E6
Serrig D 21 E7
Serritslev DK 90 E6
Serrungarina I 67 E6
Sers F 29 D6
Sersale I 59 A10
Sertã P 44 E4
Sertolovo RUS 129 E13
Servance F 26 E6
Serverette F 30 F3
Servia GR 169 D7
Servian F 34 D5
Serviana GR 168 E4
Servigliano I 62 A4
Servon-sur-Vilaine F 23 D9
Servoz F 31 D10
Sery F 19 E9
Serzedo P 44 B3
Sesa E 42 D3
Sesava LV 134 D7
Seseña E 46 D5
Seskarö S 119 C11
Seskinore GB 7 C8
Sesma E 32 F1
Sessa Aurunca I 60 A1
Sessa Cilento I 60 C4
Ses Salines E 57 C11
Seßlach D 75 B8
Sesta Godano I 69 E8
Šeštanovac HR 157 F6
S'Estanyol de Migjorn E 57 C10
Sestao E 40 B6
Sestino I 66 E5
Sesto I 72 C5
Sesto al Reghena I 73 E6
Sesto Calende I 68 B6
Sesto Campano I 60 A2
Sesto Fiorentino I 66 E3
Šeštokai LT 137 E7
Sestola I 66 D2
Sesto San Giovanni I 69 B7
Sestri Levante I 37 C10
Sestrimo BG 165 E8
Sestri Ponente I 37 C9
Sestu I 64 E3
Šešuoliai LT 135 F9
Sesvete HR 148 E6
Seta GR 175 B8
Šėta LT 135 F8
Sète F 35 D6

Setenil E 51 F9
Setermoen N 111 C15
Seternes N 100 A6
Setiles E 47 C9
Setivoho BIH 158 F3
Šetonje SRB 159 E7
Setter B 3 E14
Settimo San Pietro I 64 E3
Settimo Torinese I 68 C4
Settimo Vittone I 68 B4
Settle GB 11 C7
Setúbal P 50 B2
Seubersdorf in der Oberpfalz
   D 75 D10
Seui I 64 D3
Seuil-d'Argonne F 26 C3
Seulo I 64 D3
Seurre F 31 A7
Seva E 43 D8
Sevar BG 161 F9
Sevaster AL 168 D2
Sevel DK 86 C3
Sevenoaks GB 15 E9
Sevenum NL 16 F6
Sévérac-le-Château F 34 B5
Sever do Vouga P 44 C4
Severin HR 149 E7
Severinovca MD 154 A3
Severnyak BG 155 F1
Seveso I 69 B7
Ševětín CZ 77 D7
Sevid HR 156 E5
Sévignacq F 32 D5
Sevilla E 51 E8
Sevilla la Nueva E 46 D4
Sevilleja de la Jara E 46 E3
Șeketiye TR 173 D8
Sevlievo BG 166 C4
Sevnica SLO 148 D4
Sevojno SRB 158 F4
Sévrier F 31 D9
Sexdrega S 91 D13
Seyches F 33 A6
Seyda D 79 C12
Seymen TR 173 B8
Seymen TR 173 B9
Seyne F 36 C4
Seynes F 35 B7
Seynod F 31 D9
Seyrek TR 177 C9
Seyssel F 31 D8
Seysses F 33 C8
Sežana SLO 73 E8
Sézanne F 25 C10
Sezemice CZ 77 B9
Sezimovo Ústí CZ 77 D7
Sezze I 62 E4
Sfaka GR 179 E11
Sfântu Gheorghe RO 153 F7
Sfântu Gheorghe RO 161 D9
Sfendami GR 169 D8
Sfințești RO 160 E5
Sgiogarstaigh GB 2 J4
's-Gravendeel NL 16 E3
's-Gravenhage NL 16 D2
's-Gravenmoer NL 16 E3
's-Gravenpolder NL 16 F1
's-Gravenvoeren B 183 D7
's-Gravenzande NL 16 E2
Sgurgola I 62 D4
Shabla BG 155 F3
Shaftesbury GB 13 C10
Shalfleet GB 13 D12
Shalwy IRL 6 C5
Shanacrane IRL 8 E4
Shanagolden IRL 8 C4
Shanavogh IRL 8 C4
Shankill IRL 7 F10
Shanklin GB 13 D12
Shanlaragh IRL 8 E4
Shantonagh IRL 7 D9
Shanvus IRL 6 D6
Shap GB 10 B6
Sharashova BY 141 E10
Sharavogue IRL 7 F7
Sharkawshchyna BY 133 F2
Sharkovo BG 167 E7
Shatilava BY 133 F6
Shats'k UA 141 H9
Shawbost GB 2 J3
Shchyrets' UA 145 D8
's-Heerenberg NL 16 E6
's-Heerenhoek NL 182 C3
Sheerness GB 15 E10
Sheffield GB 11 E9
Shefford GB 15 C8
Shelekhove UA 154 B6
Shëmri AL 163 E9
Shëngjergj AL 168 B3
Shëngjin AL 163 F8
Shepit UA 152 B6
Shepshed GB 11 F9
Shepton Mallet GB 13 C9
Sherborne GB 13 D9
Sherborne St John GB 13 C12
Sherburn in Elmet GB 11 D9
Shercock IRL 7 E9
Sheringham GB 15 B11
Sherston GB 13 B10
's-Hertogenbosch NL 16 E4
Shetaj AL 168 A2
Shevchenkove UA 155 B4
Shieldaig GB 2 K5
Shifnal GB 11 F7
Shijak AL 168 B2
Shildon GB 5 F8
Shillelagh IRL 9 C9
Shinfield GB 15 E7
Shinness Lodge GB 2 J8
Shinrone IRL 7 G7
Shipka BG 166 D4
Shipkovo BG 165 D10
Shipley GB 11 D8
Shipston on Stour GB 13 A11
Shipton GB 10 F6
Shiroka Lŭka BG 165 F10
Shirokë AL 163 E7
Shivachevo BG 166 D6
Shkodër AL 163 E8
Shkorpilovtsi BG 167 D9
Shlissel'burg RUS 129 F15
Shmoylovo RUS 132 F4
Sho BY 133 F4
Sigean F 34 D4
Sigerfjord N 110 D8
Siggelkow D 83 D11
Siggerud N 95 C13
Sigglesthorne GB 11 D11
Sighetu Marmației RO 145 H8
Sighișoara RO 152 E5
Sigillo I 67 E6
Sigmaringen D 27 D11

Shtërmen AL 168 C3
Shtërpcë RKS 164 E3
Shtime RKS 164 E3
Shtiqën AL 163 E9
Shtit BG 166 F6
Shumen BG 167 C7
Shumilina BY 133 F7
Shushicë AL 168 B3
Shymkove UA 154 B6
Shyroke UA 145 G7
Shyroke UA 154 C6
Shyryayeve UA 154 C6
Siamanna I 64 D2
Sianów PL 85 B10
Siatista GR 169 D6
Šiauliai LT 134 E6
Šiauliai LT 134 E6
Sibari I 61 D6
Sibbhult S 88 C6
Sibbo FIN 127 E13
Šibenik HR 156 E4
Sibinj HR 157 B8
Sibiu RO 152 F4
Sible Hedingham GB 15 D10
Sibnica SRB 158 E5
Sibo S 103 D12
Șibot RO 151 F11
Šibsey GB 11 E12
Sicevo E 40 E6
Siciny PL 81 C10
Sickte D 79 B8
Sicula RO 151 E8
Siculeni RO 153 E7
Siculiana I 58 E3
Šid S 147 E9
Šid SRB 158 C3
Sidari GR 168 E2
Sidbury GB 13 D8
Sidcup GB 15 E9
Siddeburen NL 17 B7
Siddi I 64 D2
Sideby FIN 122 F6
Sidensjö S 107 E14
Siderno I 59 C9
Sidgunda LV 135 C9
Sidirokastro GR 169 B9
Sidirokastro GR 174 E4
Sidironero GR 171 B7
Sidmouth GB 13 D8
Sidrabiņi LV 135 C11
Sidzina PL 147 B9
Siebe N 112 F11
Siebengewald NL 183 B8
Siebenlehn D 80 D4
Siecieborzyce PL 81 C8
Siechnice PL 81 E12
Sieci PL 143 F12
Siedlanka PL 143 F12
Siedlce PL 141 F6
Siedlec PL 81 B10
Siedlice PL 85 C8
Siedliska PL 144 D3
Siedlisko PL 81 C9
Siedlisko PL 85 E8
Siedliszcze PL 141 H8
Siedliszcze PL 144 A8
Siegburg D 21 C8
Siegen D 21 C10
Siegenburg D 75 E10
Sieggraben A 149 A6
Sieghartskirchen A 77 F10
Siegsdorf D 73 A6
Sieima N 112 E8
Siek D 83 C8
Siekasjärvi S 117 E10
Siekkinen FIN 121 C11
Sielec PL 144 A4
Sielnica SK 147 D8
Siemianowice Śląskie PL 143 F7
Siemianówka PL 141 E9
Siemiatycze PL 141 F7
Siemien PL 141 G7
Siemkowice PL 143 D6
Siemyśl PL 85 B9
Siena I 66 F3
Sieniawa PL 144 C6
Sieniec PL 142 D6
Siennica PL 141 F5
Siennica Różana PL 144 A7
Sienno PL 143 D11
Sieppijärvi FIN 117 D11
Siepraw PL 147 B9
Sieradz PL 142 C6
Sieraków PL 81 A10
Sieraków PL 142 E6
Sierakówek PL 139 F7
Sierakowice PL 138 B4
Sierck-les-Bains F 20 F6
Sierentz F 27 E7
Sierksdorf D 83 B9
Siernczyno PL 85 C10
Sierndorf A 77 F10
Sierning A 76 F6
Sieroszewice PL 142 C4
Sierpc PL 139 E8
Sierra de Fuentes E 45 F8
Sierra de Luna E 41 D10
Sierra de Yeguas E 53 B7
Sierra Engarcerán E 48 D5
Sierre CH 31 C12
Sierro E 55 E8
Siershahn D 185 D8
Siersleben D 79 C10
Siete Iglesias de Trabancos
   E 39 F9
Sietow D 83 D13
Șieu RO 152 C5
Șieu-Măgheruș RO 152 C4
Șieu-Odorhei RO 152 C4
Șieuț RO 152 D5
Sieversdorf D 83 E12
Sieverstedt D 82 A6
Sievi FIN 123 C13
Sievin asema eli Korhoskylä
   FIN 123 C13
Siewierz PL 143 F7
Sifferbo S 97 A13
Sifjord N 111 B13
Sig D 86 D3

Sigmaringendorf D 27 D11
Sigmen BG 167 D7
Sigmundsherberg A 77 E9
Signa I 66 E3
Signau CH 70 D5
Signes F 35 D10
Signy-l'Abbaye F 19 E9
Signy-le-Petit F 19 E9
Sigogne F 28 D5
Sigoulès F 29 F6
Sigri GR 177 A6
Sigtuna S 99 C9
Sigüeiro E 38 C3
Sigüenza E 47 B7
Sigües E 32 E3
Sihlea RO 161 C9
Sihtuuna FIN 119 B13
Sihva EST 131 E12
Siikainen FIN 126 B6
Siikajoki FIN 119 E13
Siika-Kämä FIN 119 B16
Siikakoski FIN 128 B8
Siilinjärvi FIN 124 D9
Siimusti EST 131 D12
Siironen FIN 119 F11
Sijarinska Banja SRB 164 D4
Sijekovac BIH 157 B8
Sijsele B 182 C2
Sikås S 106 D8
Sikeå S 118 F6
Sikfors S 118 C6
Sikirevci HR 157 B9
Siklós H 149 F9
Sineşti RO 161 D3
Sinetäinsalmi FIN 117 E14
Sinetä EST 114 E5
Sineu E 57 B11
Singen (Hohentwiel) D 27 E10
Sîngera MD 154 D3
Sîngerei MD 153 B12
Singhofen D 21 D9
Singsjön S 106 E8
Singureni RO 161 E7
Singusdal N 90 A4
Sinimäe EST 132 C2
Siniscola I 64 B4
Sinj HR 157 E6
Sinlabajos E 46 B3
Sin-le-Noble F 19 D7
Sinn D 21 C10
Sinnai I 64 E3
Sinnes N 94 F5
Sinoie RO 155 D3
Sinole LV 135 B12
Sinopoli I 59 C8
Sins CH 27 F9
Sinsheim D 21 F11
Sint Annaland NL 16 E2
Sint Annaparochie NL 16 B5
Sint Anthonis NL 16 E5
Sintautai LT 136 D7
Šintava SK 146 E5
Sintea Mare RO 151 D8
Şintereag RO 152 C4
Şinteu RO 151 C10
Sint-Genesius-Rode B 182 D4
Sint-Gillis-Waas B 16 F2
Sint-Huibrechts-Lille B 183 C6
Sint Jansteen NL 182 C4
Sint-Katelijne-Waver B 19 B10
Sint-Laureins B 182 C3
Sint-Lenaarts B 182 C5
Sint Maartensdijk NL 16 E2
Sint-Margriete B 182 C3
Sint-Maria-Lierde B 19 C8
Sint-Martens-Latem B 19 C8
Sint Michielsgestel B 183 B6
Sint Nicolaasga NL 16 C5
Sint-Niklaas B 19 B9
Sint Odilienberg NL 183 C8
Sint-Pauwels B 182 C4
Sint Philipsland NL 16 E2
Sint-Pieters-Leeuw B 19 C9
Sintra P 50 B1
Sint-Truiden B 19 C11
Sint Willebrord NL 16 E3
Sinzheim D 27 C9
Sinzig D 21 C8
Sióagárd H 149 D11
Siófok H 149 C10
Sion CH 31 C11
Sion RO 161 C8
Sion Mills GB 4 F2
Šipacă MD 154 C3
Šipinen FIN 121 F12
Šipkovica MK 163 E10
Sipola FIN 119 F15
Șipote RO 153 C10
Șipotina MD 154 C2
Sipovo BIH 157 D7
Sipplingen D 27 E11
Sippola FIN 128 D7
Sira N 94 F5
Sirač HR 149 E8
Siracusa I 59 E7
Siran F 29 F10
Sirbmá N 113 C19
Siret RO 153 B8
Şireţel RO 153 C9
Sirevåg N 94 F3
Sirgala EST 132 C2
Siria RO 151 E8
Širig SRB 158 C4
Sirineasa RO 160 D4
Širitovci HR 156 E5
Siriu RO 161 C8
Sirkka FIN 117 C13
Sirkkakoski FIN 117 E12
Sirkkamäki FIN 123 E16
Sirmione I 66 B2
Şirna RO 161 D7
Sirnach CH 27 F11
Siriniö FIN 121 C11
Sirnitz A 73 C9
Sirod F 31 B8
Sirogojno SRB 158 F4
Sirok H 145 H1
Široki Brijeg BIH 157 F8
Sirolo I 67 E8
Siròr I 72 D4
Sirotsina BY 133 F7
Siruela E 54 B2
Sirutiškis LT 135 F7
Širvintos LT 137 C10
Sisak HR 149 F6
Sisante E 47 F8
Șişcani MD 154 D2
Sisco F 37 F10
Șişeşti RO 152 B3
Șişeşti RO 159 D10
Şişli TR 173 B10
Sissa I 66 C1

Sissach CH 27 F8
Sisses GR 178 E8
Sissonne F 19 E8
Şiştarovăţ RO 151 E8
Sisteron F 35 B10
Sistranda N 104 D5
Sistrans A 72 B3
Sita Buzăului RO 161 B8
Sitaniec PL 144 B7
Siteia GR 179 E11
Sitges E 43 E7
Sitkówka-Nowiny PL 143 E10
Sitnica BIH 157 C7
Sitochori GR 169 C10
Sitovo BG 161 E10
Sitsyenyets BY 133 E6
Sittard NL 19 C12
Sittensen D 82 D7
Sittersdorf A 73 C10
Sittingbourne GB 15 E10
Sitzendorf an der Schmida A 77 E9
Sitzenroda D 80 D3
Siulaisiadar GB 2 J4
Siuntio FIN 127 E11
Siuro FIN 127 C9
Siurua FIN 119 D16
Siurunmaa FIN 115 D1
Sivac SRB 158 B3
Sivakka FIN 125 C13
Sivakkajoki FIN 119 B13
Sivakkavaara FIN 125 E11
Siverić HR 156 E5
Siverskiy RUS 132 C7
Sivertgården N 108 E7
Sivry B 19 D9
Sivry-sur-Meuse F 19 F11
Sixarby S 99 B9
Six-Fours-les-Plages F 35 D10
Sixmilebridge IRL 8 C5
Sixmilecross GB 7 C8
Six Road Ends GB 4 F5
Sixt-Fer-à-Cheval F 31 C10
Sizun F 22 D3
Sjemeć BIH 158 F3
Sjenica SRB 163 C9
Sjetlina BIH 157 E10
Sjoa N 101 C11
Sjøåsen N 105 C10
Sjöbo S 87 D13
Sjöbotten S 118 E6
Sjöbrånet S 107 C17
Sjøholt N 100 B5
Sjølund DK 86 E5
Sjömarken S 91 D12
Sjonbotn N 108 D6
Sjørring DK 86 B3
Sjørslev DK 86 C4
Sjørup DK 86 C4
Sjösa S 93 B10
Sjösäter S 99 B11
Sjötofta S 91 E13
Sjötorp S 91 B14
Sjoutnäset S 106 B7
Sjøvassbotn N 111 B17
Sjøvegan N 111 C14
Sjövik S 91 D11
Sjulsåsen S 106 C7
Sjulsmark S 118 C7
Sjunnen S 92 E6
Sjuntorp S 91 C11
Sjursvik N 111 B12
Skademark S 107 E16
Skælsør DK 87 E8
Skærbæk DK 86 E3
Skævinge DK 87 D10
Skaftung FIN 122 F6
Skagen DK 90 D8
Skagersvik S 91 B15
Skäggebyn S 91 A12
Skagshamn S 107 E16
Skaidi N 113 C13
Skaidiškės LT 137 D11
Skaill GB 3 H11
Skaista LV 133 E2
Skaistgiriai LT 135 E8
Skaistgirys LT 134 D6
Skaistkalne LV 135 D9
Skala GR 174 C2
Skala GR 175 B7
Skala GR 175 F6
Skala GR 177 E8
Skała PL 143 F8
Skala Eresou GR 177 A6
Skala Kallonis GR 177 A7
Skala Marion GR 171 C7
Skålan S 102 A7
Skaland N 111 B13
Skala Oropou GR 175 C8
Skálavík FO 2 B3
Skalbmierz PL 143 F9
Skåle N 105 C15
Skålevik N 90 C3
Skälgården S 103 A12
Skáli FO 2 A3
Skalica SK 146 D4
Skalice CZ 81 E7
Skalité SK 147 C7
Skalitsa BG 166 E6
Skallelv N 114 C8
Skällinge S 87 A10
Skallvik S 93 C9
Skalmodal S 108 F8
Skalmsjö S 107 D13
Skalná CZ 75 B11
Skålö S 97 A11
Skaloti GR 171 B6
Skals DK 86 B4
Skålsjön S 103 D10
Skalstugan S 105 D12
Skålsvik N 108 B7
Skålvallen S 103 C10
Skån S 103 B11
Skanderåsen S 102 A7
Skanderborg DK 86 C5
Skånes-Fagerhult S 87 C12
Skåne-Tranås S 88 D5
Skånevik N 94 C3
Skåningen N 112 C4
Skaņkalne LV 131 F10
Skänninge S 92 C6
Skanör med Falsterbo S 87 E11
Skansbacken S 97 B11
Skansen N 105 D9
Skansholm S 107 B10
Skansnäs S 107 A10
Skansnäs S 109 E13
Skansnäset S 106 C9
Skåpafors S 91 A11
Skąpe PL 81 B8
Skapiškis LT 135 E10
Skår N 94 D4
Skara S 91 C13
Skäran S 118 F6
Skarberget N 111 D11
Skärblacka S 92 B7
Skarda S 107 C15
Skardmodalen N 108 F7
Skardmunken N 111 A18
Skardstein N 111 B11
Skardsvåg N 113 A16
Skare N 94 C5
Skåre S 97 D9
Skärhamn S 91 D10
Skarkdalen S 102 A4
Skärkind S 92 C7
Skarnes N 96 B6
Skärplinge S 99 B9
Skarp Salling DK 86 B4
Skarrild DK 86 D3
Skärså S 103 D13
Skarsfjord N 112 D2
Skärsjövålen S 102 B5
Skarstad N 111 D11
Skärstad S 92 D4
Skarsvåg N 111 B15
Skarszewy PL 138 B5
Skårup DK 86 E7
Skarv N 112 C11
Skärvången S 105 D16
Skarvfjordhamn N 112 B11
Skarvsjöby S 107 B12
Skaryszew PL 141 H4
Skarżysko-Kamienna PL 141 H3
Skasenden N 96 B7
Skästra S 103 C11
Skatamark S 118 C7
Skatan S 103 B13
Skattkärr S 97 D10
Skattungbyn S 102 D8
Skatvik N 111 B14
Skaudvilė LT 134 F5
Skaugvoll N 108 C7
Skaulo S 116 D6
Škaune LV 133 D3
Skavdal N 111 B10
Skave DK 86 C3
Skavnakk N 112 C7
Skawina PL 143 G8
Skebobruk S 99 C11
Skebokvarn S 93 A9
Skeda udde S 92 C7
Skēde LV 134 C4
Skede S 92 E6
Skedevi S 92 B7
Skedsmokorset N 95 B14
Skee S 91 B9
Skegness GB 11 E12
Skegrie S 87 E12
Skei N 100 C4
Skei N 105 A11
Skela SRB 158 D5
Skelby DK 87 E9
Skelde DK 82 A7
Skelhøje DK 86 C4
Skellefteå S 118 E5
Skelleftehamn S 118 E6
Skelmersdale GB 10 D6
Skelton GB 11 B10
Šķeltova LV 133 D2
Skelund DK 86 B6
Skelwick GB 3 G11
Skėmiai LT 134 E7
Skenderaj RKS 163 D10
Skender Vakuf BIH 157 D7
Skenfrith GB 13 B9
Skepasto GR 174 C5
Skjpe PL 139 E7
Skepplanda S 91 D11
Skeppshamn S 103 B14
Skeppshult S 87 A12
Skeppsmalen S 107 E16
Skerries IRL 7 E10
Skhidnytsya UA 145 E7
Ski N 95 C13
Skiathos GR 175 A7
Skibbereen IRL 8 E4
Skibbild DK 86 C3
Skibby DK 87 D9
Šķibe LV 134 C6
Skibinge DK 87 E10
Skibotn N 111 B19
Skidal' BY 140 C10
Skiemonys LT 135 F10
Skien N 90 A6
Šķeneri LV 135 B13
Skierbieszów PL 144 B7
Skierniewice PL 141 G2
Skiippagurra N 114 C4
Šķilbēni LV 133 B3
Skillebotn N 108 F3
Skillefjordnes N 113 C11
Skillingaryd S 92 E4
Skillinge S 88 E6
Skillvassbakk N 111 D10
Skinias GR 178 E9
Skinnarud N 101 E12
Skinnskatteberg S 97 C14
Skipmannvik N 109 B9
Skipness GB 4 D6
Skipsea GB 11 D11
Skipton GB 11 D7
Skiptvet N 95 D14
Skirlaugh GB 11 D11
Skitenelv N 111 A17
Skiti GR 169 E8
Skivarp S 87 E13
Skive DK 86 B4
Skivjan RKS 163 E9
Skivsjön S 107 C16
Skiwy Duże PL 141 F7
Skjærhalden N 91 A9
Skjåholmen N 113 B12
Skjånes N 113 B18
Skjånes N 113 B21
Skjåvika N 108 E6
Skjeberg N 91 A9
Skjeggedal N 90 B3
Skjelelv N 111 C13
Skjellbreid N 105 C14
Skjelman N 111 A17
Skjelnes N 111 A18
Skjelstad N 105 D10
Skjelvik N 108 B7
Skjern DK 86 D3
Skjern N 105 C9
Skjerstad N 108 B9
Skjervøy N 112 C6
Skjød DK 86 C5
Skjold N 111 B17
Skjoldastraumen N 94 D3
Skjolden N 100 D7
Skjombotn N 111 D13
Skjøtningberg N 113 A19
Sklithro GR 169 E8
Skobelevo BG 166 D4
Skoby S 99 B10
Skočivir MK 169 C6
Škocjan SLO 148 E4
Skoczów PL 147 B7
Skodborg DK 86 E4
Skodje N 100 A5
Skøelv N 111 B15
Škofja Loka SLO 73 D9
Škofljica SLO 73 E10
Skog S 103 D12
Skogaholm S 92 A6
Skoganvarri N 113 D15
Skoger N 95 C12
Skogfoss N 114 E7
Skoghall S 97 D9
Skogly N 114 E6
Skogmo N 105 B12
Skogn N 105 D10
Skogså S 118 C7
Skogsby S 89 B11
Skogsfjord N 112 C3
Skogshöjden S 91 C11
Skogstorp S 87 B10
Skogstorp S 98 D6
Skogstue N 112 D11
Skogum N 114 E6
Skoki PL 85 E12
Sköldinge S 93 A8
Skole UA 145 E8
Skollenborg N 95 C11
Sköllersta S 92 A6
Skoltenes N 110 C8
Skoltevatn N 114 E7
Skołyszyn PL 144 D3
Skomlin PL 142 D5
Skonseng N 108 D7
Skönvik S 103 E12
Skopelos GR 175 A8
Skopelos GR 177 A7
Skopi GR 179 E11
Skopje MK 164 F3
Skopos GR 169 C6
Skopos GR 171 B7
Skopun FO 2 B3
Skórcz PL 138 C6
Skorica SRB 159 F8
Skorild N 104 E6
Skorogoszcz PL 142 E4
Skoroszyce PL 142 E3
Skorovatn N 105 B14
Skorped S 107 E13
Skorpetorp S 89 A10
Skørping DK 86 B5
Skorstad N 105 B10
Skórzec PL 141 F6
Skoteini GR 174 D5
Skotfoss N 90 A6
Skotina GR 169 D8
Skotoussa GR 169 B9
Skotselv N 95 C11
Skotterud N 96 C7
Skottsund S 103 B13
Skoura GR 175 E5
Skourta GR 175 C8
Skoutari GR 169 B10
Skoutari GR 178 B4
Skoutaros GR 171 F10
Skovby DK 86 C5
Skövde S 91 C14
Skoved S 107 E14
Skovlund DK 86 D3
Skovsgård DK 86 A4
Skra GR 169 B7
Skräddrabo S 103 D10
Skradin HR 156 E4
Skråmestø N 100 E1
Skranstad N 110 E9
Skravena BG 165 D8
Skrea S 87 B11
Skreia N 101 E13
Skriaudžiai LT 137 D8
Skrinyano BG 165 E6
Skřipov CZ 146 B5
Skrīveri LV 135 C10
Skröven S 116 E7
Skrøytnes N 114 E7
Skrudaliena LV 135 E13
Skrunda LV 134 C4
Skruv S 89 B8
Skrwilno PL 139 D8
Skrzatusz PL 85 D11
Skrzyńsko PL 141 H3
Skrzyszów PL 143 G11
Skucani BIH 157 E6
Skudeneshavn N 94 D2
Skuhrov nad Bělou CZ 77 B10
Skujene LV 135 B10
Skujetnieki LV 133 C2
Skuķi LV 133 E3
Skuldelev DK 87 D10
Skule S 107 E14
Skulerud N 95 C15
Skulgammen N 111 A17
Skulsfjord N 111 A16
Skulsk PL 138 F5
Skulte LV 135 B8
Skulte LV 135 C7
Skultorp S 91 C14
Skultuna S 98 C6
Skuodas LT 134 D3
Skurträsk S 107 C16
Skurup S 87 E13
Skuteč CZ 77 C9
Skutskär S 103 E13
Skutvik N 110 D9
Skutvik N 111 B16
Skwierzyna PL 81 A9
Skýcov SK 146 D6
Skydra GR 169 C7
Skyllberg S 92 B6
Skylnäs S 103 A9
Skyros GR 175 B10
Skyttmon S 106 E9
Skyttorp S 99 B9
Slabodka BY 133 E2
Słaboszów PL 143 F9
Sládkovičovo SK 146 E5
Slagavallen S 102 B5
Slagelse DK 87 E8
Slagnäs S 109 E15
Slaidburn GB 10 D7
Slaka S 92 C7
Slampe LV 134 C6
Slane IRL 7 E9
Slanec SK 145 F3
Slangerup DK 87 D10
Slănic RO 161 C7
Slănic Moldova RO 153 E8
Slano HR 162 D4
Slantsy RUS 132 C3
Slaný CZ 76 B6
Slap BIH 158 F3
Slap MNE 163 D7
Slap SLO 73 D8
Šlapaberžė LT 135 F7
Šlapanice CZ 77 D11
Släppträsk S 107 A15
Slate LV 135 D12
Slatina BIH 157 C7
Slatina BIH 157 C8
Slatina BIH 157 E8
Slatina BIH 157 E10
Slatina HR 149 E9
Slatina RO 153 C8
Slatina RO 160 E4
Slatina SRB 158 E4
Slatiňany CZ 77 C9
Slatina-Timiş RO 159 C9
Slatino MK 168 B4
Slatinski Drenovac HR 149 E9
Slătioara RO 160 C3
Slătioara RO 160 E4
Slato BIH 157 F9
Slättberg S 102 D8
Slåttholmen N 110 D8
Slåttmon S 103 A13
Slattum N 95 C13
Slava Cercheză RO 155 D3
Slava Rusă RO 155 D3
Slaveino BG 165 F10
Slavičín CZ 146 C5
Slavinja SRB 165 C6
Slavkov CZ 146 B5
Slavkovichi RUS 132 F5
Slavkov u Brna CZ 77 D11
Slavonice CZ 77 E8
Slavonski Brod HR 157 B9
Slavošovce SK 145 F1
Slavotin BG 165 B7
Slavovitsa BG 160 F4
Slavovitsa BG 165 E9
Slavsk RUS 136 C4
Slavs'ke UA 145 F7
Slavsko Polje HR 148 F5
Slavyani BG 165 C10
Slavyanovo BG 165 C10
Slavyanovo BG 166 C6
Slavyanovo BG 166 F5
Sława PL 81 C10
Sławatycze PL 141 G9
Sławięcin PL 85 C13
Sławków PL 143 F7
Sławno PL 85 B11
Sławoborze PL 85 C9
Sławsko PL 85 B11
Sleaford GB 11 F11
Sledmere GB 11 C10
Sleen NL 17 C7
Sleidinge B 182 C3
Sleights GB 11 C10
Slemmestad N 95 C12
Ślesin PL 138 D4
Ślesin PL 138 F5
Sletta N 112 C9
Slevik N 91 A8
Sliač SK 147 D8
Slidre N 101 D9
Sliedrecht NL 16 E3
Šlienava LT 137 D9
Sligachan GB 2 L4
Sligeach IRL 6 D6
Sligo IRL 6 D6
Slimminge DK 87 E9
Slimnic RO 152 F4
Slinfold GB 15 E8
Slipra N 105 D9
Slišane SRB 164 D4
Slite S 93 D13
Sliven BG 166 D6
Slivileşti RO 159 D11
Slivnitsa BG 165 D7
Slivo Pole BG 161 F8
Śliwice PL 138 C5
Sllatinë e Madhe RKS 164 D3
Slobidka UA 154 B4
Slobozia MD 154 D5
Slobozia RO 160 D6
Slobozia RO 161 D10
Slobozia RO 161 F7
Slobozia Bradului RO 161 C10
Slobozia Ciorăşti RO 161 B10
Slobozia Conachi RO 155 B1
Slobozia Mândra RO 160 F5
Slobozia Mare MD 155 B2
Slobozia Moară RO 161 D7
Slochteren NL 17 B7
Slöinge S 87 B11
Słomniki PL 143 F9
Slonowice PL 85 C9
Słońsk PL 81 A7
Slootdorp NL 16 C3
Slottsskogen S 99 C9
Slough GB 15 D7
Sloupnice CZ 77 C10
Sløvåg N 100 E2
Slovenj Gradec SLO 73 C11
Slovenska Bistrica SLO 148 D5
Slovenská Ľupča SK 147 D8
Slovenská Ves SK 145 E1
Slovenske Konjice SLO 148 D4
Slovenské Nové Mesto SK 145 G4
Slovenský Grob SK 146 E4
Slovinci HR 157 B6
Slovinky SK 145 F2
Sløvra N 110 D8
Slov''yanoserbka UA 154 D5
Słowik PL 143 C7
Słubice PL 81 B7
Słubice PL 139 F8
Sluderno I 71 D11
Sluis NL 19 B7
Sluiskil NL 16 F1
Šluknov CZ 81 D6
Slunj HR 156 B4
Słupca PL 142 B4
Słupcza PL 144 B4
Słupia PL 141 G1
Słupia PL 143 D9
Słupia PL 143 E8
Słupno PL 139 E8
Słupsk PL 85 B12
Slušovice CZ 146 C5
Slussfors S 109 F11
Słuszków PL 142 C5
Slyuda RUS 115 D8
Smailholm GB 5 D11
Smålandsstenar S 87 A12
Smalåsen N 105 A14
Smalfjord N 113 C21
Smalininkai LT 136 C6
Smalvos LT 135 E12
Smârdan RO 155 C1
Smârdan RO 155 C2
Smārde LV 134 C6
Smârdioasa RO 161 F6
Smardzewice PL 141 H2
Smardzewo PL 81 B9
Smardzko PL 85 C9
Smarhon' BY 137 E13
Šmarje pri Jelšah SLO 148 D5
Šmarjeta SLO 148 E4
Šmartno SLO 73 D10
Šmartno SLO 73 D11
Smarves F 29 B6
Smedby S 89 B10
Smederevo SRB 159 D6
Smederevska Palanka SRB 159 E6
Smedjebacken S 97 B13
Smedsbyn S 118 C8
Smedvik N 110 D6
Smeeni RO 161 C9
Smęgorzów PL 143 F11
Smelror N 114 C10
Smelteri LV 135 D13
Smętowo Graniczne PL 138 C6
Smidary CZ 77 B8
Smidstrup DK 86 D5
Smidstrup DK 87 C10
Śmigiel PL 81 B11
Smilčić HR 156 D4
Smilde NL 17 C6
Smilets BG 165 E9
Smilevo MK 168 B5
Smilgiai LT 135 D9
Smilgiai LT 135 E8
Smilgiai LT 137 D8
Smilgynai LT 134 E2
Smilovci SRB 165 C6
Śmiłowice PL 138 E7
Śmiłowo PL 85 D11
Smiltene LV 135 B11
Smiltynė LT 134 E2
Smilyan BG 171 A7
Smines N 110 C8
Smiřice CZ 77 B9
Smirnenski BG 159 F11
Smirnenski BG 161 F8
Smiugard N 101 D11
Smižany SK 145 F2
Smögen S 91 C9
Smokvica HR 162 D2
Smokvica MK 169 B7
Smołdzino PL 85 A12
Smolenice SK 146 D4
Smolice PL 81 C12
Smolmark S 96 C7
Smolnica PL 84 E7
Smolník SK 145 F2
Smolyan BG 171 A7
Smolyanovtsi BG 165 C6
Smørfjord N 113 B15
Smulţi RO 153 F11
Smyadovo BG 167 C8
Smygehamn S 87 E12
Smyków PL 143 D9
Snagov RO 161 D8
Snainton GB 11 C10
Snaith GB 11 D9
Snålroa N 102 E2
Snappertuna FIN 127 E10
Snaptun DK 86 D6
Snarby N 111 A18
Snåre FIN 123 C10
Snartemo N 94 F6
Snåsa N 105 C12
Snave Bridge IRL 8 E4
Snedsted DK 86 B3
Sneek NL 16 B5
Sneem IRL 8 E3
Snejbjerg DK 86 C3
Snēpele LV 134 C3
Snerta N 101 C15
Snertinge DK 87 D8
Snesslinge S 99 B10
Snesudden S 118 B4
Snettisham GB 11 F13
Śniadowo PL 139 D12
Snikere LV 134 D6
Snina SK 145 F5
Šnjegotina Velika BIH 157 C8
Snøde DK 87 E7
Snøfjord N 113 B14
Snogebæk DK 89 E8
Snoghøj DK 86 D5
Snoldelev DK 87 D10
Soajo P 38 E3
Şoarş RO 152 F5
Soave I 66 B3
Søberg N 110 C7
Soběslav CZ 77 D7
Sobienie-Jeziory PL 141 G4
Sobolew PL 141 G5
Sobota PL 143 B8
Soboth A 73 C11
Sobotín CZ 77 B12
Sobotište SK 146 D4
Sobotka CZ 77 B8
Sobótka PL 81 E11
Sobótka PL 142 C4
Sobótka PL 143 E12
Sobowidz PL 138 B6
Sobra HR 162 D4
Sobradelo E 39 D6
Sobradiel E 41 E9
Sobrado E 38 B3
Sobrado E 38 D3
Sobral da Adiça P 51 C5
Sobral de Monte Agraço P 50 A1
Sobrance SK 145 F5
Sobreira Formosa P 44 E5
Søby DK 86 F6
Soča SLO 73 D8
Sočanica RKS 163 C10
Soçanicë RKS 163 C10
Socchieve I 73 D6
Sočerga SLO 67 B8
Sochaczew PL 141 F2
Sochaux F 27 E6
Sochocin PL 139 E9
Sochos GR 169 C9
Socodor RO 151 D7
Socol RO 159 D7
Socond RO 151 B10
Socovos E 55 C9
Socuéllamos E 47 F7
Sodankylä FIN 117 D17
Söderåkra S 89 C10
Söderala S 103 D12
Söderås S 103 E9
Söderbärke S 97 B14
Söderboda S 99 B10
Söderby-Karl S 99 C11
Söderfors S 98 B8
Söderhamn S 103 D13
Söderköping S 93 C8
Söderkulla FIN 127 E13
Södersvik S 99 C11
Södertälje S 93 A11
Södra Åbyn S 118 E5
Södra Brännträsk S 118 C4
Södra Drängsmark S 118 E5
Södra Harads S 118 B5
Södra Johannisberg S 109 F15
Södra Löten S 102 E4
Södra Sandby S 87 D12
Södra Sandträsk S 107 A16
Södra Sunderbyn S 118 C7
Södra Tresund S 107 B11
Södra Vallgrund FIN 122 D6
Södra Vi S 92 D7
Sodražica SLO 73 E10
Soerendonk NL 16 F5
Soest D 17 E10
Soest NL 16 D4
Soesterberg NL 183 A6
Sofades GR 169 F7
Sofia BG 165 D7
Sofia MD 153 B11
Sofiko GR 171 B11
Sofiko GR 175 D7
Sofporog RUS 121 C17
Şofrâncani MD 153 A10
Şofronea RO 151 E7
Şofronievo BG 160 F3
Søften DK 86 C6
Søftestad N 90 A4
Sofular TR 181 A9
Sögel D 17 C9
Sogndalsfjøra N 100 D6
Søgne N 90 C2
Soğucak TR 173 A8
Soğucak TR 173 F8
Soğucak TR 177 D9
Soğukoluk TR 181 A7
Söğüt TR 181 C8
Söğütalan TR 173 D10
Soham GB 15 C9
Sohatu RO 161 E9
Soheit-Tinlot B 19 D11
Sohland D 80 D6
Sohodol RO 151 E11
Sohren D 21 E8
Soidinkumpu FIN 121 B12
Soidinvaara FIN 121 F12
Soignies B 19 C9
Soikko FIN 119 C14
Şoimari RO 161 C8
Şoimi RO 151 D9
Şoimuş RO 151 F10
Soing F 26 E4
Soings-en-Sologne F 24 F6
Soini FIN 123 E12
Soinilansalmi FIN 125 F10
Soinlahti FIN 124 C8
Soissons F 19 F7
Soivio FIN 121 C13
Soizy-aux-Bois F 25 C10
Sójkowa PL 144 C5
Söjtör H 149 C7
Sokal' UA 144 C9
Söke TR 177 D9
Soklot FIN 122 C9
Sokna N 95 B11
Soknedal N 104 F8
Sokobanja SRB 159 F8
Sokojärvi FIN 125 D14
Sokolac BIH 157 E10
Sokolany PL 140 D8
Sokolce SK 146 F5
Sokolivka UA 154 A3
Sokółka PL 140 D9
Sokółki PL 136 E5
Sokolnice CZ 77 D11
Sokolniki PL 142 D5
Sokolov CZ 75 B12
Sokolovac HR 149 D7
Sokolovce SK 146 D5
Sokolovici BIH 157 E10
Sokolovo BG 166 C5
Sokolovo BG 167 C10
Sokolovo BIH 157 C6
Sokołów Małopolski PL 144 C5
Sokołów Podlaski PL 141 F6
Sokoły PL 140 E7
Sokorópátka H 149 B9
Sokyrnytsya UA 145 G7
Sól PL 144 B6
Soľ SK 145 F4
Sola N 94 E3
Solacolu RO 161 E9
Solana de los Barros E 51 B6
Solana del Pino E 54 C4
Solana de Rioalmar E 45 C11
Søland N 95 B10
Solarino I 59 E7
Solaro F 37 H10
Solberg N 101 E15
Solberg N 111 B14
Solberg S 107 D11
Solberg S 107 D13
Solberga S 92 D5
Solbjerg DK 86 C6
Solca RO 153 B7
Solčava SLO 73 D10
Solda I 71 D11
Şoldăneşti MD 154 B3
Şoldanu RO 161 E9
Soldatnes N 113 D14
Sölden A 71 D12
Soldeu AND 33 E9
Solec Kujawski PL 138 D5
Solec-Zdrój PL 143 F10
Solenzara F 37 H10
Solesino I 66 B4
Solesmes F 19 D7
Solesmes F 23 E11
Soleşti RO 153 D11
Soleto I 61 C10
Solf FIN 122 D7
Solférino F 32 B4
Solferino I 66 B2
Solfjellsjøen N 108 D4
Soliera I 66 C2
Solignano I 69 D8
Solihull GB 13 A11
Solin HR 156 E5
Solina PL 145 E5
Solingen D 21 B8
Solivella E 42 E6
Soljani HR 157 C10
Sölje S 97 D8
Solkei FIN 128 C8
Söll A 72 A5
Sollacaro F 37 H9
Sollas GB 2 K2
Sollebrunn S 91 C12
Sollefteå S 107 E12
Sollenau A 77 G10
Sollenkroka S 99 D11
Sollentuna S 99 D9
Söller E 49 E10
Sollerön S 102 E8
Søllested DK 83 A10
Söllichau D 79 C12
Solliès-Pont F 36 E4
Solliès-Toucas F 36 E4
Sollihøgda N 95 C12
Söllingen D 79 B8
Sollstedt D 79 D8
Solmaz TR 181 B9
Solms D 21 C10
Solnice CZ 77 B10
Solnik BG 167 D9
Solofra I 60 B3
Solojärvi FIN 113 F18
Solomiac F 33 C7
Solomos GR 175 D6
Solopaca I 60 A3
Solórzano E 40 B4
Solosancho E 46 C3
Sološnica SK 146 E4
Solothurn CH 27 F8
Solotvyna UA 145 H8
Soløy N 111 C14
Solre-le-Château F 19 D9
Solrød Strand DK 87 D10
Solsem N 105 A11
Solskjela N 104 E4
Sølsnes N 100 A6
Solsona E 43 D7
Solsvik N 94 B1
Solt H 150 D3
Soltau D 83 E7
Soltendieck D 83 E9
Sol'tsy RUS 132 E7
Soltszentimre H 150 D3
Soltvadkert H 150 E3
Solumshamn S 103 A14
Solva GB 9 E12
Solvalla S 99 C10
Solvarbo S 97 B14
Sölvesborg S 88 C7
Solvorn N 100 D6
Solymár H 149 A11
Soma TR 177 A10
Somain F 19 D7
Somberek H 149 D11
Sombernon F 25 F12
Sombor SRB 150 F3
Sombreffe B 19 C10
Şomcuţa Mare RO 151 B11
Somercotes GB 11 E9
Someren NL 16 F5
Somerniemi FIN 127 D10
Somero FIN 127 D10
Someronkylä FIN 119 F12
Somerovaara FIN 119 D16
Sõmerpalu EST 131 F13
Somerton GB 13 C9
Sõmeru EST 131 C12
Someş-Odorhei RO 151 C11
Somianka PL 139 E11
Sominy PL 85 B13
Somlóvásárhely H 149 B8
Sommacampagna I 66 B2
Somma Lombardo I 68 B6
Sommariva del Bosco I 37 B7
Sommarøy N 110 C9
Sommarøy N 111 A15
Sommarset N 109 A10
Sommatino I 58 E4
Somme-Leuze B 19 D11
Sommen S 92 C5
Sommepy-Tahure F 19 F10
Sömmerda D 79 D9
Sommerfeld D 84 E4
Sommersted DK 86 E4
Sommesous F 25 C11
Somme-Suippe F 25 B12
Sommevoire F 25 D12
Sommières F 35 C7
Sommières-du-Clain F 29 C6
Somogyapáti H 149 D9
Somogyjád H 149 D9
Somogyszob H 149 D8
Somogyudvarhely H 149 D8
Somogyvár H 149 C9
Somonino PL 138 B5
Somontín E 55 E8
Somotor SK 145 G4
Somova RO 155 C3
Sompa EST 131 C14
Sompolno PL 138 F6
Sompujärvi FIN 119 C14
Somzée B 19 D9
Son N 95 C13
Son NL 16 E4
Sona I 66 B2
Sona N 105 E10
Şona RO 152 E4
Sonceboz CH 27 F7
Soncillo E 40 C4
Soncino I 69 C8
Sonda EST 131 C13
Sondalo I 69 A9
Søndeled N 90 B5
Sønder Balling DK 86 B3
Sønder Bjerre DK 86 D5
Sønder Bjert DK 86 E5
Sønderborg DK 86 F5
Sønderby DK 87 D10
Sønder Dråby DK 86 B3
Sønder Felding DK 86 D3
Sønderho DK 86 E2
Sønderholm DK 86 A5
Sønder Hygum DK 86 E3
Sønder Nissum DK 86 C2
Sønder Omme DK 86 D3
Sønder Onsild DK 86 B5
Sønder Rubjerg DK 90 E6
Sondershausen D 79 D8
Sondersø DK 86 E6
Sønder Stenderup DK 86 E5
Sønder Vilstrup DK 86 E5
Sønder Vissing DK 86 C5
Sønder Vium DK 86 D2
Sondori LV 133 C2
Sondrio I 69 A8
Soneja E 48 E4
Songe N 90 B5
Songeons F 18 E4
Sonim P 38 E5
Sonka FIN 117 E14
Sonkajärvi FIN 124 C9
Sonkakoski FIN 124 C9
Sonkamuotka FIN 117 B10
Sonneberg D 75 B9
Sonneborn D 79 E8
Sonnefeld D 75 B9
Sonnewalde D 80 C5
Sonnino I 62 E4
Sonntag A 71 C9

Sonntagberg A 77 G7
Sonseca E 46 E5
Son Servera E 57 B11
Sońsk PL 139 E10
Sonstorp S 92 B7
Sonta SRB 157 A11
Sonthaim an der Brenz D 75 E7
Sonthofen D 71 B10
Sontra D 78 D6
Soodla EST 131 C10
Söörmarkku FIN 126 B6
Soorts-Hossegor F 32 C3
Sopeira E 33 F7
Sopelana E 40 B6
Sopilja BIH 157 F9
Sopište MK 164 F3
Soponya H 149 B10
Šoporňa SK 146 E5
Sopot BG 165 C9
Sopot PL 138 B6
Sopot RO 160 E3
Sopot SRB 158 D6
Sopotnica MK 168 B5
Şopotu Nou RO 159 D8
Šoppela FIN 115 C13
Sopron H 149 A7
Sopronkövesd H 149 A7
Sora I 62 D5
Soraga I 72 D4
Soragna I 66 C1
Sörarp S 103 A14
Söräng S 103 D11
Sorano I 62 B1
Sørarnøy N 108 B6
Sør-Audnedal N 90 C1
Sorbas E 55 E8
Sorbie GB 5 F8
Sorbiers F 30 E5
Sörbo S 103 D11
Sörböle S 103 B13
Sorbolo I 66 C1
Sörby S 97 C9
Sörbygden S 103 A11
Sørbymagle DK 87 E8
Sörbyn S 118 B7
Sörbyn S 118 B14
Sorcy-St-Martin F 26 C4
Sord IRL 7 F10
Sørdal N 109 C10
Sorde-l'Abbaye F 32 C3
Sore F 32 B4
Sørebø N 100 D3
Sören S 118 C8
Søreng N 111 B19
Soresina I 69 C8
Sorèze F 33 D10
Sörfjärden S 103 B13
Sørfjord N 111 C10
Sørfjord N 111 C14
Sørfjorden N 111 C10
Sørfjordmoen N 109 A10
Sörflärke S 107 E13
Sörfors S 103 B13
Sörfors S 122 C4
Sörforsa S 103 C12
Sorge D 79 C8
Sorges F 29 E7
Sorgono I 64 C3
Sorgues F 35 B8
Sørheim N 100 D6
Soria E 41 E7
Soriano Calabro I 59 B9
Soriano nel Cimino I 62 C2
Sorihuela E 45 D9
Sorihuela del Gaudalimar E 55 C6
Sorisdale GB 4 B4
Sørkjosen N 112 D6
Sørkjosen N 112 D6
Sorkwity PL 136 F3
Sørland N 110 E4
Sørlenangen N 111 A19
Sörli N 105 C15
Sørli N 111 B14
Sörmark S 97 B8
Sörmjöle S 122 C4
Sørmo N 111 C16
Sorn GB 5 D8
Sornac F 29 D10
Sörnoret S 107 C12
Sørø DK 87 E9
Soroca MD 154 A2
Sorokino RUS 133 B7
Soroni GR 181 D7
Sorradile I 64 C2
Sørreisa N 111 B15
Sorrento I 60 B2
Sorring DK 86 C5
Sørrollnes N 111 C12
Sorsakoski FIN 124 F9
Sorsele S 109 E14
Sörsjön S 102 D5
Sorso I 64 B2
Sörstafors S 98 C6
Sørstraumen N 112 D8
Sort E 33 F8
Sortavala RUS 129 B14
Sortelha P 45 D6
Sortino I 59 E7
Sörtjärn S 102 B8
Sortland N 110 C9
Sør-Tverrfjord N 112 C8
Sôru EST 130 D5
Sørum N 101 E11
Sorumsand N 95 C14
Sorunda S 93 A11
Sörup D 82 A7
Sørvad DK 86 C3
Sørvær N 112 B8
Sörvåge S 107 E15
Sørvågen N 110 E5
Sørvágur FO 2 A2
Sörvattnet S 102 B4
Sørvik N 111 C13
Sörvik S 97 B13
Sørvika N 101 B15
Sörviken S 107 D9
Sorvilán E 55 F6
Sos F 33 B6
Sosandra GR 169 C7
Sösdala S 87 C13
Sos del Rey Católico E 32 E3
Soses E 42 D4
Soshe-Ostrivs'ke UA 154 C5
Sösjö S 103 A9
Sóskút H 149 B11
Sośnica RS 85 D10
Sośno PL 138 D4
Sosnovka RUS 136 D3
Sosnovo RUS 129 D13

Sosnovyy Bor RUS 129 F11
Sosnowica PL 141 G8
Sosnowiec PL 143 F7
Sosnówka PL 141 G8
Soso FIN 119 E15
Sospel F 37 D6
Šoštanj SLO 73 D11
Sostis GR 171 B8
Sot N 96 C6
Șotânga RO 160 D6
Sotés E 41 D6
Sotiel Coronada E 51 D6
Sotillo de la Adrada E 46 D3
Sotillo del Rincón E 41 E6
Sotin HR 157 B11
Sotkajärvi FIN 119 E16
Sotkamo FIN 121 F11
Soto E 39 A7
Soto de la Vega E 39 D8
Soto del Real E 46 C5
Soto de Ribera E 39 B8
Soto en Cameros E 41 D7
Sotopalacios E 40 D4
Sotos E 47 D8
Sotoserrano E 45 D8
Soto y Amio E 39 C8
Sotres E 39 B10
Sotresgudo E 40 C3
Şotrile RO 161 C7
Sotrondio E 39 B8
Sotta F 37 H10
Sottomarina I 66 B5
Sottrum D 17 B12
Sottunga FIN 99 B15
Sotuélamos E 55 A7
Soual F 33 C10
Soubès F 34 C5
Soucy F 25 D9
Souda GR 178 E7
Soudan F 23 E9
Soueix E 33 E8
Souesmes F 24 F7
Soufflenheim F 27 C8
Soufli GR 171 B10
Sougia GR 178 E6
Souillac F 29 F8
Souilly F 26 B3
Souk el Had el Rharbia MA 52 E5
Souk-Khémis-des-Anjra MA 53 E6
Soukolojärvi S 119 B11
Souk Tleta Taghramet MA 53 E6
Soulac-sur-Mer F 28 D3
Soulaines-Dhuys F 25 D12
Soulatgé F 33 E11
Souli GR 175 D6
Soullans F 28 B2
Soulom F 32 E5
Soumagne B 19 C12
Soumoulou F 32 D5
Souppes-sur-Loing F 25 D8
Souprosse F 32 C4
Soure P 44 D3
Sournia F 33 E10
Souro Pires P 45 C6
Sourpi GR 175 A6
Sours F 24 D5
Sourzac F 29 E6
Sousceyrac F 29 F10
Sousel P 50 B4
Soustons F 32 C3
Southam GB 13 A12
Southampton GB 13 D12
South Anston GB 11 E9
South Bank GB 11 B9
Southborough GB 15 E9
South Cave GB 11 D10
South Chard GB 13 D9
Southend GB 4 E5
Southend-on-Sea GB 15 D10
Southery GB 11 F12
Southgate GB 15 D8
South Harting GB 15 F7
South Kelsey GB 11 E11
South Kirkby GB 11 D9
Southminster GB 15 D10
South Molton GB 13 C7
South Ockendon GB 15 D9
Southport GB 10 D5
South Queensferry GB 5 D10
South Shields GB 5 F14
Southwell GB 11 E10
Southwold GB 15 C12
South Woodham Ferrers GB 15 D10
Souto E 38 C4
Souto P 38 E2
Souto P 44 E4
Souto P 45 D7
Souto da Casa P 44 D5
Soutuperä FIN 123 B14
Souvala GR 175 D9
Souvigny F 30 B3
Șovarna RO 159 D10
Sovata RO 152 D6
Soveja RO 153 E9
Soverato I 59 B10
Soveria F 37 G10
Soveria Mannelli I 59 A9
Sovetsk RUS 136 C4
Sovetskiy RUS 129 D13
Sovič BIH 157 F7
Sovicille I 66 F3
Søvik N 100 A4
Søvind DK 86 D5
Sowno PL 85 B11
Sowno PL 85 D7
Soyaux F 29 D6
Soye F 26 F6
Soylu TR 173 B7
Soymy UA 145 F7
Soyons F 30 F6
Sozopol BG 167 E9
Spa B 19 D12
Spa IRL 8 D3
Spaßbrücken D 21 E9
Spaichingen D 27 D10
Spalding GB 11 F11
Spálené Poříčí CZ 76 C5
Spalt D 75 D8
Spangenberg D 78 D6
Spanish Point IRL 8 C4

Spantekow D 84 C5
Spanțov RO 161 E9
Sparanise I 60 A2
Sparbu N 105 D10
Spåre LV 134 B4
Sparreholm S 93 A9
Spartà I 59 C7
Sparti GR 174 E5
Sparto GR 174 E3
Spartylas GR 168 E2
Spasovo BG 155 F2
Spata GR 175 D8
Spay D 185 D8
Spean Bridge GB 4 B7
Specchia I 61 D10
Speen GB 13 C12
Speia MD 154 D4
Speicher D 21 E7
Speicherdorf D 75 C10
Spello I 62 B3
Spenge D 17 D10
Spennymoor GB 5 F13
Spentrup DK 86 B6
Spercheiada GR 174 B5
Sperlinga I 58 D5
Sperlonga I 62 E4
Spermezeu RO 152 C4
Spetalen N 95 D13
Spetses GR 175 E7
Spey Bay GB 3 K10
Speyer D 21 F10
Spezzano Albanese I 61 D6
Spiczyn PL 141 H7
Spiddal IRL 6 F4
Spielberg bei Knittelfeld A 73 B10
Spiere B 182 D2
Spiesen-Elversberg D 21 F8
Spiez CH 70 D5
Spigno Monferrato I 37 B8
Spigno Saturnia I 62 E4
Spiiniigied'di N 113 E15
Spijk NL 17 B7
Spijkenisse NL 16 E2
Spikberg S 118 B5
Spilamberto I 66 C3
Spili GR 178 E8
Spilimbergo I 73 D6
Spilinga I 59 B8
Spillersboda S 99 C11
Spillum N 105 C11
Spilsby GB 11 E12
Spinazzola I 60 B6
Spincourt F 19 F12
Spineni RO 160 D5
Spinetoli I 62 B5
Spink IRL 9 C8
Spinus RO 151 C9
Špionica BIH 157 C9
Špišić-Bukovica HR 149 E8
Spiss A 71 D10
Spišská Belá SK 145 E1
Spišská Nová Ves SK 145 F2
Spišská Stará Ves SK 145 E1
Spišská Teplica SK 145 F1
Spišské Bystré SK 145 F1
Spišské Podhradie SK 145 F2
Spišské Vlachy SK 145 F2
Spišský Hrušov SK 145 F2
Spital am Pyhrn A 73 A9
Spital am Semmering A 148 A5
Spitsyno RUS 132 D2
Spittal GB 3 J10
Spittal an der Drau A 73 C7
Spittal of Glenshee GB 5 B10
Spitz A 77 F8
Spjald DK 86 C3
Spjelkavik N 100 B4
Spjutsbygd S 89 C9
Spjutsund FIN 127 E14
Split HR 156 F5
Splügen CH 71 D8
Spodnja Idrija SLO 73 D9
Spodnje Hoče SLO 148 C5
Spodsbjerg DK 87 F7
Spofforth GB 11 D9
Spoleto I 62 B3
Spoltore I 63 B6
Spondigna I 71 D11
Spontin B 19 D11
Spornitz D 83 D11
Spotorno I 37 C8
Spraitbach D 74 E6
Sprakensehl D 83 E9
Sprâncenata RO 160 E5
Sprângsviken S 103 A14
Spreenhagen D 80 B5
Spremberg D 80 D6
Sprendlingen D 185 D6
Spresiano I 72 E5
Spriana I 69 A8
Sprimont B 19 D12
Spring RO 152 F3
Springe D 78 B6
Springholm GB 5 E9
Springliden S 107 A16
Sproatley GB 11 D11
Sprockhövel D 17 F8
Sproge S 93 E12
Sprogø! LV 135 D10
Sprova N 105 C10
Sprowston GB 15 B11
Sproxton GB 11 C9
Spunģēni LV 135 C11
Spuž MNE 163 D7
Spychowo PL 139 C11
Spydeberg N 95 C14
Spytihněv CZ 146 C5
Spytkowice PL 143 G7
Spytkowice PL 147 B9
Squillace I 59 B10
Squinzano I 61 C10
Sráid an Mhuilinn IRL 8 D4
Sraith Salach IRL 6 F3
Sranea IRL 6 D6
Srath an Urláir IRL 7 C7
Srbac BIH 157 B7
Srbobran SRB 158 B4
Srbovac RKS 163 C10
Srđevići BIH 8 D3
Srebrenica BIH 157 D11
Srebrenik BIH 157 C10
Srebŭrna BG 161 E10
Sredets BG 166 E5
Sredets BG 167 E8
Središče SLO 148 D6
Srednie BIH 157 D9
Srednjevo SRB 159 D8
Sredno Gradishte BG 166 E4

Śrem PL 81 B12
Sremčica SRB 158 D5
Sremska Kamenica SRB 158 C4
Sremska Mitrovica SRB 158 D4
Sremski Karlovci SRB 158 C4
Srenica BIH 156 D6
Srnice BIH 157 C9
Srockowo PL 136 E4
Środa Śląska PL 81 D11
Środa Wielkopolska PL 81 B12
Srpska Crnja SRB 159 B6
Srpski Itebej SRB 159 B6
Srpski Miletić SRB 157 A11
Sta S 105 E13
Staatz A 77 E10
Stabbfors S 108 E8
Stabbursnes N 113 C14
Stabroek B 16 F2
Stabulnieki LV 133 D2
Staburags LV 135 C11
Staburnäs S 107 B11
Staby DK 86 C2
Stachy CZ 76 D5
Stade D 17 A12
Staden B 18 C7
Stadl-Paura A 76 F5
Stadra S 97 C12
Stadsbygd N 104 E7
Stadskanaal NL 17 C7
Stadtallendorf D 21 C12
Stadtbergen D 75 F8
Stadthagen D 17 D12
Stadtilm D 79 E9
Stadtkyll D 21 D7
Stadtlauringen D 75 B7
Stadtlohn D 17 E7
Stadtoldendorf D 78 C6
Stadtprozelten D 74 C5
Stadtroda D 79 E10
Stadtschlaining A 148 B6
Stadum D 82 A6
Staffanstorp S 87 D12
Staden B 18 C7
Stadra S 97 C12
Stadthagen D 17 D12
Staicele LV 131 F9
Staig D 74 F6
Stainach A 73 A9
Staindrop GB 11 B8
Staines-upon-Thames GB 15 E7
Stainforth GB 11 C7
Stainforth GB 11 D9
Staintondale GB 11 C11
Stainville F 26 C3
Stainz A 148 C5
Staiti I 59 D9
Stakčín SK 145 E5
Stąkļi LV 135 B13
Stakkai LT 134 F6
Stakkvik N 112 D4
Staklevtsi BG 164 B6
Stakliškės LT 137 D9
Stakroge DK 86 D3
Stalać SRB 159 F7
Stalbe LV 135 B10
Stålbo S 98 B7
Stalbridge GB 13 D10
Stalden CH 68 A4
Staldzene LV 134 B3
Stalgėnai LT 134 E3
Stalgene LV 135 C7
Stalham GB 15 B12
Stalheim N 100 E4
Stalidzani LV 135 C13
Staliogargo N 113 B12
Stall A 73 C7
Stallarholmen S 98 D8
Stållberg S 97 C12
Ställdalen S 97 C12
Stallwang D 75 D12
Stalon S 107 B9
Stâlpeni RO 160 C5
Stâlpu RO 161 C9
Stâmboliyski BG 165 E10
Stâmbulčič BIH 157 E10
Stamford GB 11 F11
Stamford Bridge GB 11 D10
Stamford CZ 76 D5
Stammham D 75 E9
Stamnes GR 174 B3
Stamovo BG 166 E5
Stams A 71 C11
Stamstik N 110 D6
Stamsund N 110 D6
Standish GB 10 D6
Ștănești RO 159 C11
Ștănești RO 160 D3
Ștănești RO 161 F7
Stânga S 93 E12
Stângăceaua RO 160 D2
Stangnes N 111 B10
Stångviken S 105 D16
Stanhoe GB 15 B10
Stanhope GB 5 F12
Ștănilești RO 154 D2
Stanin PL 141 G6
Ștănișești RO 153 E10
Stanišić SRB 150 F3
Stanišinci SRB 163 B10
Stanisław CZ 76 C4
Stanišinci SRB 163 B10
Stanisławów PL 141 F5
Ștănița RO 153 C10
Štavalj SRB 163 C9
Stankov CZ 76 C4
Stankovany SK 147 C8
Stanley GB 5 C10
Stanley GB 5 F13
Staveley GB 11 E9
Stannington GB 5 E13
Stanomino PL 85 C9
Stanos GR 169 C10
Stanos GR 174 B3
Stan'ovsti BG 165 D6
Stans CH 71 D6
Stansted Mountfitchet GB 15 D9
Stantăr RKS 163 D10
Stanton GB 15 C10
Stanzach A 71 C11
Stanz im Mürztal A 148 B5
Stapar SRB 158 B3
Stapel D 83 D9
Stapelburg D 79 C8
Stapelfeld D 83 C8
Stąpork NL 16 C6
Stąporków PL 141 H2
Stara Błotnica PL 141 G3
Stará Bystrica SK 147 C8
Stara Gradina HR 149 E9

Stará Huť CZ 76 C6
Stara Kamienica PL 81 E9
Stara Kamionka PL 140 D9
Stara Kiszewa PL 138 C5
Stará Kuřna UA 154 B4
Stara Lubianka PL 85 D11
Stará Ľubovňa SK 145 E2
Stara Moravica SRB 150 F3
Stara Novalja HR 67 C10
Starcross GB 13 D8
Stare Babice PL 141 F3
Stare-Bogaczowice PL 81 E10
Stare Budkowice PL 142 E5
Stareč CZ 77 D9
Stare Czarnowo PL 85 D7
Stare Dąbrowa PL 85 D8
Stare Dolistowo PL 140 C7
Stare Hołowczyce PL 141 F7
Stare Kurowo PL 85 E9
Staré Město CZ 77 B11
Staré Město u Uherského Hradiště CZ 146 C4
Stare Miasto PL 142 B5
Stare Pole PL 139 B7
Stare Puchały PL 141 E7
Stare Selo UA 144 D9
Stare Strącze PL 81 C10
Stargard Szczeciński PL 85 D8
Staroglavice BIH 158 E3
Starokozache UA 154 D5
Staro Oryakhovo BG 167 C9
Staropatitsa BG 159 F9
Staro Petrovo Selo HR 157 B8
Starosel BG 165 E10
Staro Selo BG 161 F9
Staro Selo BG 166 D5
Staro Selo SRB 159 E7
Staroseltsi BG 165 B9
Starosiedle PL 81 C7
Starowa Góra PL 143 C7
Staroye Syalo BY 133 F7
Staro Zhelezare BG 165 E10
Starozřeby PL 139 E8
Startforth GB 11 B8
Starup DK 86 E5
Stary Brus PL 141 H8
Stary Cykarzew PL 143 E7
Stary Dzierzgoń PL 139 C7
Stary Dzikowiec PL 144 C4
Stary Kisielin PL 81 C9
Stary Kobrzyniec PL 139 E7
Starý Kolín CZ 77 B8
Stary Majdan PL 144 C4
Starynovichy BY 133 F6
Stary Pahost BY 133 E3
Starý Plzenec CZ 76 C4
Stary Sącz PL 145 D2
Stary Szelków PL 139 E11
Stary Targ PL 139 C7
Staryy Sambir UA 145 E6
Stary Zamość PL 144 B7
Starzyno PL 138 A5
Staškov SK 147 C7
Staßfurt D 79 C10
Staszów PL 143 E11
Stathelle N 90 A6
Statland N 105 C10
Statsås S 107 B11
Statzendorf A 77 F9
Stăuceni MD 154 C3
Stăuceni RO 153 B9
Stelpe LV 135 C9
Staufenberg D 21 C11
Staupitz D 80 C5
Staveley GB 11 E9
Stavang N 100 C2
Stavanger N 94 E3
Stavatrăsk S 118 D4
Stavby UA 144 A9
Stave N 111 B10
Staveley GB 11 E9
Stavelot B 20 D5
Stavenisse NL 16 E2
Stavern N 90 B7
Stavertsi BG 165 B9
Stavky UA 144 A9
Stavning DK 86 D2
Stavoren NL 16 C4
Stavre S 103 A9
Stavre S 105 E16
Staveviken S 103 A13
Stavrodromi GR 174 D4
Stavros GR 169 C7
Stavros GR 169 C10
Stavros GR 169 F7
Stavros GR 174 B3
Stavroupoli GR 171 B7
Stavsjö S 93 B8
Stavsnäs S 99 D11
Stavtrup DK 86 C6
Stawiguda PL 139 C9
Stawiski PL 139 D13
Stawiszyn PL 142 C5
Steane N 95 D9
Ștębark PL 139 C9
Steblevë AL 168 B3
Stebnyk UA 145 E8
Steccato I 61 F7
Štěchovice CZ 76 C6
Stechow D 79 A11
Steckborn CH 27 E10
Stedesdorf D 17 A9
Stedten D 79 D10
Steeg A 71 C10
Steenbergen NL 16 E2
Steenderen NL 183 A8
Steenvoorde F 18 C6
Steenwijk NL 16 C6
Steeton GB 11 D8
Stefanaconi I 59 B9
Ștefan cel Mare RO 153 C9
Ștefan cel Mare RO 153 D11
Ștefan cel Mare RO 155 D1
Ștefan cel Mare RO 155 E1
Ștefan cel Mare RO 160 F4
Ștefănești MD 154 B3
Ștefănești RO 153 B10
Ștefănești RO 160 D5
Ștefănești RO 161 D9
Ștefănești de Jos RO 161 D8
Ștefani GR 175 C8
Ștefanje HR 149 E7
Stefan Karadzha BG 167 C8
Stefan-Karadzhovo BG 167 E7
Ștefanovikeio GR 169 F8
Stefanovo BG 167 C9
Ștefanovouno GR 169 E7
Stefan Vodă MD 154 D5
Ștefan Vodă RO 161 E10
Ștefești RO 161 C7
Steffisburg CH 70 D5
Stege DK 87 F10
Stegelitz D 79 B10
Stegersbach A 148 B6
Stegna PL 138 B7
Stegny PL 139 D8
Stehag S 87 D12
Ștei RO 151 D9
Steigen N 110 E8
Steimbke D 17 C12
Stein D 75 D9
Stein D 75 D11
Stein D 82 A7
Steinach A 72 B3
Steinach D 21 C11
Steinach D 186 E5
Steinach an Brenner A 72 B3
Stein am Rhein CH 27 E10
Steinau D 17 A11
Steinau an der Straße D 74 B5
Steinbach D 21 C11
Steinbach D 80 E4
Steinbach am Attersee A 73 A8
Steinbach am Wald D 75 B9
Steinbakk N 114 C7
Steinberg D 75 D11
Steinberg D 82 A7
Steine N 105 D11
Steine N 110 C9
Steinfeld A 73 C7
Steinfeld D 186 E5
Steinfeld D 17 C10
Steinfeld (Oldenburg) D 17 C10
Steinfjord N 111 B13
Steinfort L 20 E5
Steinfurt D 17 D8
Steingaden D 71 B11
Steinhagen D 17 C10
Steinhagen D 84 B3
Steinheim D 17 E12
Steinheim D 111 B15
Steinheim am Albuch D 187 D9
Steinheim an der Murr D 187 D7
Steinhöring D 75 F11
Steinhorst D 83 E8
Steinigtwolmsdorf D 80 D6
Steinkirchen D 82 C7
Steinkjer N 105 C11
Steinland N 110 C9
Steinløysa N 100 A7
Steinsdorf D 81 B7
Steinsfeld D 75 D7
Steinshamn N 100 A5
Steinsholt N 95 D11
Steinskjærnes N 114 C7
Steinsland N 94 B2
Steinsvik N 100 C3
Steinwenden D 186 C4
Steinwiesen D 75 B9
Stejari RO 155 D3
Stejaru RO 160 E5
Stekene B 19 B9
Stelle D 83 D8
Stellendam NL 16 E2
Stelnica RO 155 E1
Stelpe LV 135 C9
Stemland N 108 B9
Stemmen D 82 D7
Stemnes N 111 D13
Stemnitsa GR 174 D5
Stemshorn D 17 D10
Stemwede D 17 D10
Stenåsa S 89 B11
Stenay F 19 F11
Stenbacken S 111 D17
Stenbjerg DK 86 B2
Stenbo S 93 D9
Stendal D 79 A10
Stende LV 134 B4
Stenderup DK 86 D3
Steneset N 108 D4
Stengelse N 113 D11
Stenhamarra S 98 D8
Stenhamra S 99 D9
Stenhousemuir GB 5 C9
Stenico I 69 A10
Steninge S 87 B11
Steninge S 99 C10
Stenis S 102 E7
Stenkullen S 91 D11
Stenkumla S 93 D13
Stenkyrka S 93 D13
Stenlille DK 87 D10
Stenløse DK 87 D10
Stennäs S 107 C14
Stenness GB 3 E13
Steno GR 174 D5
Steno GR 175 E5
Stenon S 103 B9
Stensân S 103 B9
Stensele S 107 A12
Stenshede S 91 B10
Stensjön S 92 D5
Stenskär S 99 B10
Stenstorp S 91 C14
Stensträsk S 107 A17
Stenstrup DK 86 E6
Stensund S 109 D15
Stensund S 109 F13
Stenton GB 5 D11
Stenträsk S 118 B3
Stenudden S 109 C14
Stenum DK 90 E6
Stenungsund S 91 C10
Stenvad DK 86 C7
Stenzharychi UA 144 B9
Stepanci MK 169 B6
Stepanivka UA 144 D5
Štěpánov CZ 77 C12
Stepen BIH 157 F10
Stepnica PL 84 C7
Stepojevac SRB 158 D5
Stepping DK 86 E4
Sterdyń-Osada PL 141 E6
Sterławki-Wielkie PL 136 E4
Sterna GR 171 A10
Sterna GR 175 D6
Sterna HR 67 B8
Sternberg D 83 C11
Šternberk CZ 146 B4
Sternes GR 178 D7
Stes-Maries-de-la-Mer F 35 D7
Stișzew PL 81 B11
Štěti CZ 76 B6
Stetten am kalten Markt D 27 D11
Steuerberg A 73 C9
Steutz D 79 C11
Stevenage GB 15 D8
Stevning DK 86 E5
Stevrek BG 166 D6
Stewarton GB 4 E7
Stewartstown GB 7 C9
Steyerberg D 17 C12
Steyning GB 15 F8
Steyr A 76 F6
Steyregg A 76 F6
Steżery CZ 77 B9
Steżerovo BG 166 C4
Stężyca PL 138 B4
Stężyca PL 141 G5
Stia I 66 E4
Stibb Cross GB 12 D6
Stickney GB 11 E12
Stidsvig S 87 C12
Stiege D 79 C9
Stiens NL 16 B5
Stienta I 66 C4
Stigen S 91 B11
Stigliano I 60 C6
Stignano I 59 C9
Stigsjö S 103 A14
Stigtomta S 93 B9
Stijena BIH 156 C5
Stikli LV 134 B4
Stilligarry GB 2 L2
Stilling DK 86 C6
Stillington GB 11 C9
Stillorgan IRL 7 F10
Stilo I 59 C9
Stilton GB 11 G11
Stimpfach D 75 D7
Stintino I 64 B1
Stio I 60 C4
Štip MK 164 F5
Stirfaka GR 174 B5
Stiring-Wendel F 21 F7
Stirling GB 5 C9
Štitar HR 157 B10
Štitar SRB 158 D4
Štitina CZ 146 B6
Štítnik SK 145 F1
Štíty CZ 77 C11
Štiubieni RO 153 B9
Štiuca RO 159 B8
Stjær DK 86 C5
Stjärnhov S 97 C13
Stjärnhov S 93 A9
Stjärnorp S 92 B7
Stjørdalshalsen N 105 E9
Støa N 101 E14
Støa N 102 D4
Stobiecko Miejskie PL 143 D7
Stobreč HR 156 E6
Stoby S 87 C13
Stochov CZ 76 B5
Stocka S 103 C13
Stockach D 27 E11
Stockamöllan S 87 D12
Stockaryd S 88 A7
Stöcke S 122 C4
Stockelsdorf D 83 C8
Stockenboi A 73 C8
Stockerau A 77 F10
Stockheim D 75 B9
Stockholm S 99 D10
Stocking A 148 C5
Stockport GB 11 E7
Stocksfield GB 5 F13
Stockstadt am Rhein D 21 E10
Stockton-on-Tees GB 11 B9
Stockvik S 103 B13
Stoczek PL 139 E12
Stoczek Łukowski PL 141 G5
Stod CZ 76 C4
Stöde S 103 B12
Stoenești RO 160 C4
Stoenești RO 160 C6
Stoenești RO 160 E5
Stoenești RO 161 E7
Stoer GB 2 J6
Stoholm DK 86 C4
Stoianovca MD 154 E2
Stoičinești RO 160 E5
Stoilești RO 160 C4
Stoina RO 160 D3
Stojakovo MK 169 B8
Stojdraga HR 148 D5
Stojnci SLO 148 D5
Stoke Ash GB 15 C11
Stoke-on-Trent GB 11 E7
Stokesay GB 13 A9
Stokite BG 166 D4
Stokka N 108 E3
Stokkasjøen N 108 E4
Stokkdal N 111 D12
Stokke N 90 A7
Stokkemarke DK 83 A10
Stokkvågen N 108 D5
Stokmarknes N 110 C8
Štoky CZ 77 D9

Stolac BIH 157 F8
Stolberg (Harz) Kurort D 79 C8
Stolberg (Rheinland) D 20 C6
Stołczno PL 85 C12
Stolerova LV 133 D3
Stollberg D 79 E12
Stöllet S 97 B9
Stolmen N 94 B2
Stolnicei MD 154 D3
Stolniceni-Prăjescu RO 153 C9
Stolnici RO 160 D5
Stolnik BG 165 D8
Stolno PL 138 D6
Stolpe D 83 B8
Stolpe D 84 E6
Stolpen D 80 D6
Stolzenau D 17 C12
Stomio GR 169 E8
Stömne S 97 D8
Ston HR 162 D4
Stone GB 11 F7
Stone GB 13 B10
Stonehaven GB 5 B12
Stonehouse GB 5 D9
Stong N 94 D3
Stongfjorden N 100 D2
Stonglandseidet N 111 B13
Stonybreck GB 3 F13
Stoob A 149 A7
Stöpen S 91 C14
Stopiče SLO 148 E4
Stopki PL 136 E3
Stopnica PL 143 F10
Storå N 111 D11
Storå S 97 C13
Storå Åby S 92 C5
Storåbränna S 106 D7
Stora Höga S 91 C10
Stora Levene S 91 C12
Stora Melby S 91 C12
Stora Mellösa S 92 A6
Storarmsjö S 107 C16
Storås N 104 E7
Storåsen S 103 A10
Störåsen S 106 D7
Stora Skedvi S 97 B14
Stora Tallberg S 109 E17
Stora Vika S 93 B11
Storbäck S 106 B9
Storbacka FIN 123 D10
Storbäcken S 102 C4
Storberg S 109 E16
Stor-Blåsjön S 105 B16
Storbo S 102 C3
Storbogaren S 107 D14
Storbränna S 106 D7
Storbränna S 118 E4
Storbukt N 113 B12
Storby FIN 99 B13
Stordal N 100 B6
Štore SLO 148 D4
Storebø N 94 B2
Storebro S 92 D7
Storebru N 100 C3
Store Damme DK 84 A2
Store Darum DK 86 E3
Store Heddinge DK 87 E10
Storeidet N 111 E10
Storekorsnes N 112 C11
Storelv N 112 B10
Store Merløse DK 87 D9
Store Molvik N 114 B5
Støren N 104 E8
Storenga N 112 D7
Store Rise DK 83 A8
Store Rørbæk DK 86 B5
Storfjäten S 102 C5
Storfjord N 111 B18
Storfjordbotn N 113 C18
Storfors S 97 D12
Storforshei N 108 D8
Storhågna S 102 A7
Storhallaren N 104 C9
Stor-Hallen S 102 A7
Storhogen S 106 E8
Stor-Hullsjön S 103 A12
Štorje SLO 73 E8
Storjola S 106 B7
Storjord N 109 C9
Storjorda N 108 C6
Storjorda N 111 C11
Storkow D 80 B5
Storli N 101 A10
Storlien S 105 E12
Stormi FIN 127 C9
Stornara I 60 A5
Stornarella I 60 A5
Stornäs S 106 A8
Stornäs S 107 A11
Stornäset S 107 C10
Stornes N 111 C11
Storneshamn N 112 D7
Stornoway GB 2 J4
Storo I 69 B10
Storobăneasa RO 161 F6
Storodden N 104 E6
Storöhamn S 119 C10
Storrington S 15 F8
Storrøsta N 101 B13
Storsand S 103 C13
Storsand S 118 B5
Storsandsjö S 107 C17
Störsätern S 102 B3
Storsävarträsk S 118 F3
Storsele S 107 D14
Storseleby S 107 B11
Storseløy N 108 C4
Storsjö S 102 A5
Storskog S 109 E10
Storslett N 112 D6
Storsletta N 112 D6
Storsteinnes N 111 A18
Storsteinnes N 111 B17
Storsund S 118 C5
Storuman S 107 A12
Storvik N 108 C6
Storvik N 110 C9
Storvik N 112 D7
Storvik S 103 D13
Storvorde DK 86 A6
Storvreta S 99 C9
Štós SK 145 F2
Stößen D 79 D10
Stössing A 77 F9
Stoszowice PL 81 E11
Støtt N 108 C5
Stötten am Auerberg D 71 B11
Stotternheim D 79 D8
Stouby DK 86 D5
Stoumont B 19 D12
Stourbridge GB 13 A10

Stourport-on-Severn GB 13 A10
Støvran N 108 B8
Støvring DK 86 B5
Støvset N 108 B8
Stow GB 5 D11
Stowicjno PL 85 A12
Stowmarket GB 15 C10
Stow-on-the-Wold GB 13 B11
Stoyan Mikhaylovski BG 167 C8
Stoyanovo BG 165 C10
Stoykite BG 165 F10
Stozher BG 167 C9
Stożne PL 136 E5
Stra I 66 B5
Straach D 79 C12
Strabane GB 4 F2
Strabla PL 141 E8
Strachan GB 5 A11
Strachówka PL 139 F11
Strachur GB 4 C6
Stracin MK 164 E5
Stračiūnai LT 137 E9
Stradalovo BG 165 E6
Stradbally IRL 7 F8
Stradbroke GB 15 C11
Stradella I 69 C7
Stradi LV 135 B8
Stradishall GB 15 C10
Stradone IRL 7 E8
Stradsett GB 11 F12
Straelen D 16 F6
Stragari SRB 158 E6
Strai N 90 C2
Straimont B 19 E11
Straja RO 153 B7
Strakhilovo BG 166 C5
Strakonice CZ 76 D5
Straldzha BG 167 D7
Stralki BY 133 E4
Straloch GB 5 B9
Strålsnäs S 92 C6
Stralsund D 84 B4
Strambino I 68 C4
Stramproy NL 19 B12
Strâmtura RO 152 B4
Stráňavy SK 147 C7
Strančice CZ 77 C7
Strand N 101 D15
Strand N 110 C9
Strand S 106 D9
Stranda N 100 B5
Strandå N 108 A8
Strandby DK 86 B4
Strandby DK 90 E8
Strande D 83 B8
Strandnorum S 91 C10
Strandval N 105 B10
Strangford GB 7 D11
Stranghele N 100 E3
Strängnäs S 98 D8
Strangolagalli I 62 D4
Strångsjö S 93 B9
Stráni CZ 146 D5
Stranocum GB 4 E2
Stranorlar IRL 7 C7
Stranraer GB 4 F6
Străoane RO 153 F10
Strasatti I 58 D2
Strasbourg F 27 C8
Strasburg D 84 D5
Strășeni MD 154 C3
Stratice CZ 76 C5
Stråssa S 97 C13
Straßberg D 27 D11
Straßberg D 79 C9
Straßburg A 73 C9
Strassen L 20 E6
Straßengel A 148 B4
Straßenhaus D 21 C7
Strasshof an der Nordbahn A 77 F11
Straßkirchen D 75 E12
Straßwalchen A 76 G4
Stratford IRL 7 G9
Stratford-upon-Avon GB 13 A11
Strathaven GB 5 D8
Strathblane GB 5 D8
Strathpeffer GB 2 K7
Strathy GB 3 H9
Strathyre GB 5 C8
Stratinska BIH 157 C6
Stratiyivka UA 154 A4
Stratoni GR 169 C10
Stratoniki GR 169 C10
Stratos GR 174 B3
Stratton GB 12 D5
Stratton St Margaret GB 13 B11
Straubing D 75 E12
Straum N 104 D5
Straum N 108 E5
Straume N 90 A2
Straume N 110 C7
Straumen N 104 E4
Straumen N 105 D10
Straumen N 108 B8
Straumen N 109 B10
Straumen N 111 A19
Straumen N 111 C11
Straumen N 114 B7
Straumfjord N 110 C9
Straumgjerde N 100 B5
Straumsnes N 110 D7
Straumsnes N 110 C8
Straumsnes N 111 B13
Straumstad N 111 B17
Straunen N 111 B7
Straupe LV 135 B9
Straupitz D 80 C6
Strausberg D 80 A5
Straußfurt D 79 D8
Stravaj AL 168 C3
Strawczyn PL 143 E9
Straža SRB 159 D7
Strazhitsa BG 166 C5
Stráž nad Nežárkou CZ 77 D7
Stráž nad Nisou CZ 81 E8
Strážnice CZ 146 D4
Stráž pod Ralskem CZ 81 E7
Strážske SK 145 F4
Štrba SK 147 C10
Streatley GB 13 B12
Strečno SK 147 C7
Streda nad Bodrogom SK 145 G4
Streek D 17 B10
Street GB 13 C9
Strehaia RO 159 D11
Strehla D 80 D4
Strejeşti RO 160 D4
Strekov SK 146 F6

Strelac SRB 164 D5
Strelcě AL 168 C4
Strelcha BG 165 D9
Strellc i Epërm RKS 163 D9
Strëlnieki LV 135 C8
Strem A 149 B6
Strembo I 69 A10
Stremţ RO 152 E3
Strenči LV 131 F11
Strendur FO 2 A3
Strengberg A 77 F7
Strengelvåg N 110 C9
Strengen N 95 D9
Stresa I 68 B6
Stretford GB 11 E7
Stretham GB 15 C9
Streufdorf D 75 B8
Strezimirovtsi BG 164 D5
Strib DK 86 D5
Striberg S 97 C12
Stříbro CZ 76 C3
Strichen GB 3 K12
Strigno I 72 D4
Štrigova HR 148 C6
Strijen NL 16 E3
Strimasund S 108 D8
Strimoniko GR 169 B9
Strinda N 111 E10
Strittjomvare S 109 E16
Strizivoja HR 157 B9
Strmec HR 148 E5
Strmen HR 149 F7
Strmica BIH 156 D5
Strmica HR 156 D5
Ströbeck D 79 C8
Strobl A 73 A7
Strøby DK 87 E10
Strøby Egede DK 87 E10
Stroești RO 160 C3
Stroevo BG 165 E10
Strofylia GR 175 B8
Ströhen D 17 C11
Stroiești RO 153 B8
Strokestown IRL 6 E6
Ström S 108 E8
Strömbäck S 122 C4
Strömbacka S 103 C12
Stromberg D 185 E8
Stromeferry GB 2 L5
Strömfors S 118 E4
Strömholm S 109 E15
Stromiec PL 141 G4
Strommen N 95 C13
Strömmer S 96 C6
Strömnäs S 107 B10
Strömnäs S 118 D5
Stromness GB 3 H10
Strömsberg S 99 B9
Strömsbro S 103 E13
Strömsbruk S 103 C13
Strömsholden S 98 D8
Strömsnes N 111 C16
Strömsnäs S 107 E9
Strömsnäsbruk S 87 B13
Strömstad S 91 B9
Strömsund S 106 D9
Strömsund S 107 A11
Ströoane RO 153 F10
Stroncone I 62 C3
Strongoli I 61 E8
Stronie Śląskie PL 77 B11
Stronsdorf A 77 E10
Strontian GB 4 B5
Stropi LV 135 E13
Stropkov SK 145 E4
Stroppiana I 68 C5
Stroppo I 36 B6
Stroud GB 13 B10
Strövelstorp S 87 C11
Strovija MK 168 A5
Stróża PL 147 B9
Štrpce RKS 164 E3
Strücklingen (Saterland) D 17 B9
Struer DK 86 B3
Strugi-Krasnyye RUS 132 E5
Strullendorf D 75 C8
Strumë AL 168 C2
Strumica MK 169 B8
Strumień PL 147 B7
Strumkiva UA 145 G5
Strumok UA 155 B4
Strumyani BG 169 A9
Strunkovice nad Blanicí CZ 76 D6
Struplľ LV 133 C1
Struth D 79 D7
Štružani UA 153 C2
Stružec HR 149 F7
Stryama BG 165 E10
Stryków PL 143 C8
Stryksele S 107 C16
Stryn N 100 C5
Stryy UA 145 E8
Strzała PL 141 F6
Strzałkowo PL 142 B4
Strzebień PL 143 E6
Strzegocin PL 139 E10
Strzegom PL 81 E10
Strzegowo PL 139 E9
Strzelce PL 143 B7
Strzelce Krajeńskie PL 85 E9
Strzelce Opolskie PL 142 E5
Strzelce Wielkie PL 143 D7
Strzeleczki PL 142 F4
Strzelin PL 81 E12
Strzelno PL 138 E5
Strzepcz PL 138 B5
Strzyżewice PL 144 A5
Strzyżów PL 144 D4
Sts-Geosmes F 26 E3
Stubbæk DK 86 F4
Stubbekøbing DK 84 A2
Stubben D 17 B11
Stubel BG 165 C7
Stubno PL 144 D6
Stuchowo PL 85 C8
Studena BG 165 D7
Studena BG 166 F6
Studená CZ 77 D8
Studena UA 154 A3
Studençan RKS 163 E10
Studenci HR 157 E7
Studenec CZ 81 E8
Stüdenitz D 83 E12
Stredno I 69 A10
Studénka SK 77 E12
Studina RO 160 F4

Studley GB 13 A11
Studsvik S 93 B10
Studsviken S 107 D14
Studzienice PL 85 B13
Studzieniec PL 81 C9
Stugubacken S 103 D11
Stuguflåten N 100 B8
Stugun S 106 E9
Stühlingen D 27 E9
Stuhr D 17 B11
Stukmaṇl LV 135 C11
Stulpicani RO 153 C7
Stumm A 72 B4
Stumsnäs S 102 E8
Stuorajavrre N 112 E10
Stuorragår'žl N 113 E16
Stupava SK 77 F12
Stupsk PL 139 D9
Stupurai LT 134 D7
Sturefors S 92 C7
Sturkö S 89 C9
Šturlić BIH 156 B4
Šturmai LT 134 F2
Sturminster Newton GB 13 D10
Šturovo MK 164 F5
Šturovo SK 149 A11
Sturry GB 15 E11
Sturzelbronn F 27 B8
Stützerbach D 27 C11
Stützerbach D 79 E8
Styggedalen N 111 B19
Stylida GR 175 B6
Stypsi GR 171 F10
Styra GR 175 C9
Styrkesnes N 109 B9
Styrnäs S 107 E13
Styrrmanstø N 110 A18
Suances E 40 B3
Suaningi S 117 E10
Suatu RO 152 D3
Subačius LT 135 E9
Subaşı TR 171 B10
Subaşı TR 173 B8
Subaşı TR 177 C9
Subate LV 135 D5
Subbiano I 66 E4
Suben A 76 F4
Subiaco I 62 D4
Subkowy PL 138 C6
Subotica SRB 150 E4
Subotište SRB 158 D4
Subotniki BY 137 E12
Sučany SK 147 C7
Suceava RO 153 C8
Suceveni RO 155 E12
Sučević HR 156 D5
Suceviţa RO 153 B7
Sucha Beskidzka PL 147 B9
Suchacz PL 138 B7
Suchá Hora SK 147 C9
Suchá Loz CZ 146 D5
Suchań PL 85 D8
Suchá nad Parnou SK 146 E4
Suchdol CZ 77 E7
Suchdol nad Lužnicí CZ 77 E7
Suchdol nad Odrou CZ 146 B5
Suchedniów PL 141 D10
Suchowola PL 140 C8
Suchożebry PL 141 F6
Suchy Dąb PL 138 B6
Suchy Las PL 81 B11
Sucina E 56 F3
Suciu de Sus RO 152 C4
Suckow D 83 D11
Sucleia MD 154 D5
Sučuraj HR 157 F7
Sudanell E 42 D5
Sudargas LT 136 C5
Sudbury GB 15 C10
Suddendorf D 183 A10
Süden D 82 B5
Süderbrarup D 82 A7
Süderhastedt D 82 B6
Süderlügum D 86 F3
Süderstapel D 82 B6
Suderve LT 137 D11
Sudiţi RO 161 D11
Sudkov CZ 77 C11
Südlohn D 17 E7
Sudok S 118 B4
Sudoměřice CZ 146 D4
Sudova Vyshnya UA 144 D7
Sudovec HR 149 D6
Sudrabkalns LV 135 D12
Suđurađ HR 162 D4
Sudwalde D 17 C11
Sueca E 48 F4
Südinedinie BG 165 E10
Suelli I 64 E3
Suèvres F 24 E5
Sugag RO 152 F3
Suha BIH 157 D9
Suha BIH 157 F10
Suhaia RO 160 F6
Suhărău RO 153 A8
Suharekë RKS 163 E10
Suhl D 79 E8
Suhlendorf D 83 E9
Suhmura FIN 125 F13
Suho Polje BIH 157 C11
Suhopolje HR 149 E8
Šuica BIH 157 E7
Šuici RO 160 C5
Šuijavaara S 116 B9
Suolijärvi FIN 121 D11
Suolijoki FIN 119 B14
Suoluvuobmi N 113 D12
Suomela FIN 119 C15
Suomenniemi FIN 121 E12
Suomijärvi FIN 122 F9
Suomu FIN 115 E4
Suomusjärvi FIN 127 E10
Suomussalmi FIN 121 E12
Suonenjoki FIN 124 E8
Suoniemi FIN 124 F8
Suonnankylä FIN 121 B11
Suontee FIN 124 F8
Suopajärvi FIN 117 E15
Suorajärvi FIN 121 E13
Suorsa FIN 120 B9
Suosjavri N 113 E13
Suostola FIN 115 D2
Suovaara FIN 121 F14
Suovanlahti FIN 123 D16
Superdévoluy F 35 A10
Supersano I 61 C10
Supetar HR 156 F5
Süleymaniye TR 173 B6
Süleymaniye TR 173 C6
Supino I 62 D4

Süleymanlı TR 177 B10
Sulików PL 81 D8
Sulingen D 17 C11
Suliszewo PL 85 D9
Suliţa RO 153 B9
Sulitjelma N 109 B11
Sulkava FIN 123 D17
Sulkava FIN 129 B9
Sulkavanjärvi FIN 123 D16
Sulkavanjärvi FIN 123 E16
Sulkavankylä FIN 123 F11
Sułkowice PL 147 B9
Sullington GB 15 F8
Sully F 30 A5
Sully GB 13 C8
Sully-sur-Loire F 25 E7
Sulmierzyce PL 142 C4
Sulmierzyce PL 143 D7
Sulmona I 62 C5
Sulniac F 22 E6
Süloğlu TR 167 F7
Sułoszowa PL 143 F8
Sułów PL 81 D12
Sułów PL 144 B6
Sulsted DK 86 A5
Sultaniça TR 171 C10
Sultaniye TR 173 D9
Sultanköy TR 171 C10
Sultanköy TR 173 B8
Suluca TR 171 C10
Suluca TR 172 D6
Sulvik S 96 C7
Suluviken S 105 D14
Sulz D 83 D11
Sulz am Neckar D 27 D10
Sulzbach am Main D 21 E12
Sulzbach an der Murr D 27 B11
Sulzbach-Laufen D 74 E6
Sulzbach-Rosenberg D 75 C10
Sulzbach/Saar D 186 C3
Sulzdorf an der Lederhecke D 75 B8
Sulzemoos D 75 F9
Sulzfeld D 75 B7
Sulzfeld D 187 C6
Sulzheim D 75 C7
Sulzthal D 75 B7
Sumartin HR 157 F6
Šumatrac BG 166 C5
Šumče CZ 146 C5
Sümeg H 149 C8
Sümeġ FIN 123 E16
Sumburgh GB 3 F14
Šumećani HR 149 E6
Sümeg H 149 C8
Sumelhaka S 93 A9
Šumende S 103 B13
Sumiainen FIN 123 E16
Šumice CZ 146 C5
Sumiswald CH 70 C5
Šumjaca MK 164 E4
Summer Bridge GB 11 C8
Summerhill IRL 7 F9
Šumperk CZ 77 C11
Šumsa FIN 121 F14
Šumvald CZ 77 C12
Sumvitg CH 71 D7
Sunäkste LV 135 D11
Šuňava SK 147 C10
Sunbilla E 32 D2
Şuncuiuş RO 151 D10
Sund N 108 B7
Sund N 110 D5
Sund N 110 D5
Sund S 92 D6
Sund S 103 B10
Sund S 107 E14
Sundborn S 103 E10
Sundby DK 86 B3
Sundby DK 86 B3
Sundby FIN 122 C9
Sundby N 108 B9
Sunde N 94 C3
Sunde N 104 E6
Sunderland GB 5 F14
Sundern (Sauerland) D 17 F10
Sundet S 105 D13
Sundklakk N 110 D7
Sundnäs S 109 D14
Sundom FIN 122 D7
Sundom S 118 C8
Sundre S 93 F12
Sunds DK 86 C4
Sundsbruk S 103 B13
Sundsjö S 103 A9
Sundsli N 90 A3
Sundsvall S 103 B13
Sundvollen N 95 B12
Sungurlare BG 167 D7
Sunhultsbrunn S 92 D5
Suni I 64 C2
Sunja HR 149 F7
Sünna D 79 E7
Sunnan N 105 C11
Sunnanfors S 97 C13
Sunnansjö S 97 B12
Sunnansjö S 107 E14
Sunnäs S 103 A12
Sunndal N 94 B4
Sunndalsøra N 101 A9
Sunne N 97 C9
Sunne S 103 A14
Sunne S 106 E6
Sunnemo S 97 C10
Sunnersta S 107 D12
Sunningen S 91 C10
Suntaži LV 135 C9
Suodenniemi FIN 126 B8
Suojanperä FIN 114 E4
Suojoki FIN 122 F7

Süleymaniye TR 173 C6
Supino I 62 D4

Suplac RO 152 E5
Suplacu de Barcău RO 151 C10
Suplai RO 152 C4
Supraśl PL 140 D8
Supru FIN 114 E4
Supur RO 151 C10
Súr H 149 B9
Surahammar S 98 C6
Suraia RO 153 F10
Şura Mare RO 152 F4
Şura Mică RO 152 F4
Şurani RO 161 C8
Suraż PL 140 E7
Surbo I 61 C10
Surčin SRB 158 D5
Surdegis LT 135 E9
Surdila-Găiseanca RO 161 C10
Surdila-Greci RO 161 C10
Surduc RO 151 C11
Surdulica SRB 164 D5
Surfleet GB 11 F11
Surgères F 28 C4
Surhuisterveen NL 16 B6
Súria E 43 D7
Surju EST 131 D10
Surmaduk N 104 F5
Sürmevets BG 166 F6
Sürnevo BG 166 E5
Sürnitsa BG 165 F9
Šúrovce SK 146 E5
Sursee CH 27 F9
Surte S 91 D11
Survilišķis LT 135 F8
Surwold D 17 C9
Surzur F 22 E6
Susa I 31 D11
Suşani RO 160 D4
Susa šara SRB 159 E7
Susch CH 71 D10
Susegana I 72 E5
Susek SRB 158 C4
Süsel D 83 B9
Suseni RO 152 D5
Suseni RO 153 D7
Suseni RO 160 D5
Sushitsa BG 166 C5
Sušice CZ 76 D5
Susiec PL 144 C7
Šuškova LV 133 D4
Susleni MD 154 C3
Susort N 94 D2
Susteren NL 19 B12
Sustinente I 66 B3
Sustrum D 17 C8
Susurluk TR 173 E9
Suszezmüsellim TR 173 B7
Susz PL 139 C7
Sutera I 58 D4
Suteşti RO 160 D4
Suteşti RO 161 C10
Sutina BIH 157 E7
Sutivan HR 156 F5
Sutjeska SRB 158 C6
Sütlüce TR 173 A8
Sutri I 62 C2
Sutri LV 135 D12
Sutterton GB 11 F11
Sutton GB 15 C9
Sutton Bridge GB 11 F12
Sutton Coldfield GB 11 F8
Sutton in Ashfield GB 11 E9
Sutton-on-the-Forest GB 11 C9
Suure-Jaani EST 131 D10
Suurejõe EST 131 D10
Suuremõisa EST 130 D5
Suurimäki FIN 124 D9
Suur-Miehikkälä FIN 128 D8
Suurpea EST 131 B11
Suutarinkylä FIN 119 E16
Suutarinkylä FIN 119 F17
Suvainiškis LT 135 D10
Suvanto FIN 115 D2
Suvantokumpu FIN 117 C15
Suvereto I 65 A3
Suviekas LT 135 E10
Sütlüce TR 173 A8
Suvodol MK 168 A5
Suvodol MK 169 B6
Suvorov MD 155 B2
Suvorove UA 155 B4
Suvorovo BG 167 C9
Suwałki PL 136 E6
Suydamevo RUS 133 C10
Suzdol HR 149 D6
Suze-la-Rousse F 35 B8
Suzzara I 66 C2
Svabensverk S 103 D10
Svalboviken S 93 A8
Svalenik BG 166 B6
Svalöv S 87 D12
Svalsta S 93 B9
Svalyava UA 145 F6
Svanå S 98 C6
Svanabyn S 107 C11
Svanberga S 99 C11
Svaneke DK 89 E8
Svanesund S 91 C10
Svängsta S 89 C7
Svannäs S 109 D15
Svannäs S 109 D15
Svansele S 107 B17
Svansele S 107 D15
Svanskog S 91 A12
Svanstein S 117 E11
Svanström S 118 E5
Svanträsk S 107 A12
Svanvik N 114 E8
Svanvik S 91 C10
Svappavaara S 116 C6
Svardal N 101 A12
Svärdsjö S 103 E10
Svarinci LV 133 D5
Svarstad N 95 D11
Svartå FIN 127 E10
Svartå S 92 A5
Svartbo S 103 D11
Svartbyn S 119 C9
Svarte S 87 E13
Svartemyr N 100 D3
Svärtinge S 92 B8
Svartidalshytta N 108 D7
Svartlå S 118 B8
Svartnes N 108 B8
Svartnes N 111 B17
Svartnes N 114 C10
Svartöstaden S 118 C8
Svärtträsk S 107 A12
Svartvik S 103 A14

Svartvik S 103 B13
Svartvik S 103 D13
Svatava CZ 75 B12
Svätuše SK 145 G4
Svätý Jur SK 146 E4
Svätý Peter SK 146 F6
Svebølle DK 87 D8
Svedala S 87 D12
Svédasai LT 135 E10
Svedja S 103 C12
Svedje S 106 C9
Svedje S 107 D15
Svedjebo S 103 C12
Svedjebo S 103 C12
ŠveđlarSK 145 F2
Sveg S 102 B7
Sveggesundet N 104 E3
Šveicarija LT 137 C9
Sveindal N 90 C1
Sveio N 94 D2
Svejbæk DK 86 C5
Svekl LV 135 B13
Švekšna LT 134 E3
Švenčionėliai LT 135 F11
Švenčionys LT 135 F12
Svendborg DK 86 E7
Svene N 95 C11
Svenes N 90 B3
Svenljunga S 91 E13
Svenningdal N 108 F5
Svensbu N 111 A18
Svensbyn S 118 D6
Svenshögen S 91 C10
Svenstavik S 102 A7
Svenstrup DK 86 B5
Svenstrup DK 86 E5
Svenstrup DK 87 E8
Svente LV 135 E12
Šventeżeris LT 137 E8
Šventoji LT 134 D2
Sverepec SK 146 C6
Sveta Marija HR 149 D7
Svētciems LV 131 F8
Svēte LV 134 C7
Sveti Nikola BG 167 C10
Sveti Nikola MNE 163 F7
Sveti Nikole MK 164 F4
Sveti Rok HR 156 D4
Sveti Stefan MNE 163 E6
Světlá Hora CZ 142 F3
Světlá nad Sázavou CZ 77 C8
Svetlen BG 166 C6
Svetlogorsk RUS 139 A9
Svetlyy RUS 139 A9
Svetogorsk RUS 129 C10
Svetozar Miletić SRB 150 F3
Svetvinčenat HR 67 B8
Svezhen BG 165 D11
Švica HR 67 C11
Svídník SK 145 E4
Svihov CZ 76 D4
Sviiebi EST 130 D6
Svilajnac SRB 159 E7
Svilengrad BG 166 F6
Svindinge DK 86 E7
Svinesund S 91 A9
Svingen N 111 A18
Svingstad N 100 E12
Svingvoll N 101 D12
Svinhult S 92 D6
Svinia SK 145 E3
Sviniţa RO 159 D9
Svinnersta S 92 A5
Svinninge DK 87 D8
Svinninge DK 87 D9
Svinninge S 99 D10
Svínoy FO 2 A4
Svinvika N 104 E6
Svir BY 137 D13
Svirkos LT 135 F12
Svishtov BG 160 F6
Svislach BY 140 D10
Svit SK 145 E1
Svitávka CZ 77 C11
Svitavy CZ 77 C10
Svitene LV 135 D7
Svitlodolyns'ke UA 154 E5
Svityaz' UA 141 H9
Svoboda BG 155 F1
Svoboda BG 166 E4
Svoboda RUS 136 D4
Svoboda nad Úpou CZ 81 E9
Svobodinovo BG 166 F4
Svođe SRB 164 D5
Svodín SK 146 F6
Svodna BIH 156 B6
Svoge BG 165 D7
Svogerslev DK 87 D10
Svolvær N 110 D8
Svorkmo N 104 E7
Svratka CZ 77 C10
Svrčinovec SK 147 C7
Svrljig SRB 164 C5
Svullrya N 96 B7
Swadlincote GB 11 F8
Swaffham GB 15 B10
Swalmen NL 20 B6
Swan IRL 9 C8
Swanage GB 13 D11
Swanley GB 15 E9
Swanlinbar IRL 7 D7
Swansea GB 13 B7
Swanton Morley GB 15 B10
Swarożyn PL 138 B6
Swarzędz PL 81 B12
Swatragh GB 4 F3
Sway GB 13 D11
Świątki PL 139 C9
Świbno PL 138 B6
Świderki PL 141 G6
Świdnica PL 81 E10
Świdnica PL 81 E10
Świdnik PL 141 H7
Świdwin PL 85 C9
Świebodzice PL 81 E10
Świebodzin PL 81 B9
Świecie PL 138 C5
Świeciechowa PL 81 C11
Świeciechów-Duży PL 144 B4
Świedziebnia PL 139 D8
Świekatowo PL 138 D5
Świeradów-Zdrój PL 81 E8
Świercze PL 139 E10
Świerczów PL 142 E4
Świerklaniec PL 143 F6
Świerklany Górne PL 142 F6
Świerże PL 141 H9
Świerzenko PL 85 B11
Świerzno PL 85 C7

Świeszyno PL 85 B10
Świjtajno PL 136 E5
Świjtajno TR 139 C11
Świjtochłowice PL 143 F6
Świjtoszów PL 85 B8
Świlcza PL 144 C4
Swindon GB 13 B11
Swineshead GB 11 F11
Swinford IRL 6 E5
Świnna PL 147 B8
Świnoujście PL 84 C6
Swinton GB 5 D12
Swinton GB 11 D7
Swobnica PL 84 D7
Swords IRL 7 F10
Swornegacie PL 85 C13
Syalyawshchyna BY 133 E5
Sycewice PL 85 B11
Syców PL 142 D3
Sydalen N 110 D7
Sydänmaa FIN 123 E10
Sydänmaankylä FIN 123 C16
Sydnes N 94 C3
Syelishcha BY 133 F4
Syfteland N 94 B2
Sykaminia GR 171 F10
Sykäräinen FIN 123 C12
Syke D 17 C11
Sykea GR 178 B4
Syki GR 169 F9
Sykia GR 169 E7
Sykia GR 170 D5
Sykies GR 169 F7
Sykkylven N 100 B5
Sykorrachi GR 171 C9
Sykourio GR 169 E8
Sylling N 95 C12
Sylte N 100 B6
Symbister GB 3 E14
Symi GR 181 C7
Synej AL 168 B2
Synevyr UA 145 G8
Synevyrs'ka Polyana UA 145 F8
Synod Inn GB 12 A6
Synsiö FIN 123 F17
Synyak UA 145 F6
Syötekylä FIN 121 C10
Sypniewo PL 85 D11
Sypniewo PL 139 D11
Syrau D 75 A11
Syre GB 3 J8
Syrgenstein D 75 E7
Syri FIN 123 C13
Syrjä FIN 125 F10
Sysmä FIN 127 B14
Sysslebäck S 102 E4
Syston GB 11 F9
Syväjärvi FIN 117 C15
Syvänniemi FIN 124 E8
Syvärinpää FIN 125 D9
Syvde N 100 B3
Sydsnes N 100 B3
Syvota GR 168 F3
Syvros GR 174 B2
Syvsten DK 90 E7
Syyspohja FIN 129 C10
Szabadegyháza H 149 B11
Szabadhidvég H 149 C10
Szabadkígyós H 151 D7
Szabadszállás H 150 D3
Szabolcsbáka H 145 G5
Szada H 150 B3
Szadek PL 143 C6
Szaflary PL 147 C10
Szajol H 150 C5
Szakály H 149 C10
Szakmár H 150 D3
Szákszend H 149 A10
Szalánta H 149 E10
Szalaszend H 145 G3
Szalkszentmárton H 150 D3
Szalonna H 145 G2
Szamocin PL 85 D12
Szamossegg H 145 G6
Szamotuły PL 81 A11
Szank H 150 D4
Szany H 149 B8
Szár H 149 B10
Szarvas H 150 D6
Szászberek H 150 C5
Szatymarcseke H 145 G6
Szatymaz H 150 E5
Százhalombatta H 149 B11
Szczaniec PL 81 B9
Szczawin Kościelny PL 139 F8
Szczawne PL 145 E5
Szczawnica PL 145 E2
Szczawno-Zdrój PL 81 E10
Szczebrzeszyn PL 144 B6
Szczecin PL 84 D7
Szczecinek PL 85 C11
Szczekociny PL 143 E8
Szczepankowo PL 139 D12
Szczepanowo PL 138 E4
Szczerców PL 143 D7
Szczucin PL 143 F11
Szczuczyn PL 140 C6
Szczurkowo PL 136 E2
Szczurowa PL 143 F10
Szczutowo PL 139 E8
Szczyrk PL 147 B8
Szczytna PL 77 B10
Szczytniki PL 142 C5
Szczytno PL 139 C10
Szécsény H 147 E9
Szederkény H 149 D10
Szedres H 149 D11
Szeged H 150 E5
Szeghalom H 151 C7
Szegi H 145 G3
Szegvár H 150 D5
Székely H 145 G4
Székesfehérvár H 149 B10
Székkutas H 150 D6
Szekszárd H 149 D11
Szemud PL 138 B5
Szendehely H 147 F8
Szendrő H 145 G2
Szendrőlád H 145 G2
Szentendre H 150 B3
Szentes H 150 D5
Szentgál H 149 B9
Szentgotthárd H 148 C6
Szentistván H 150 B6
Szentkirály H 150 D4
Szentlászló H 149 D9
Szentörinc H 149 D9
Szentpéterfa H 149 B6
Szepetnek H 149 D7
Szepietowo PL 141 E7

Szecseny H 149 B9
Szeremle H 149 D11
Szerencs H 145 G3
Szerep H 151 C7
Szerzyny PL 144 D3
Szestno PL 136 F3
Szigetbecse H 149 B11
Szigethalom H 150 C2
Szigetszentmiklós H 150 C3
Szigetvár H 149 C8
Szigliget H 149 C8
Szihalom H 150 B5
Sziksző H 145 G2
Szil H 149 A8
Szilvásvárad H 145 G1
Szirák H 147 F9
Szirmabesenyő H 145 G2
Szkaradowo PL 81 C12
Szklarska Porjba PL 81 E8
Szklary Górne PL 81 D10
Szlichtyngowa PL 81 C10
Szob H 147 F7
Sződ H 150 B3
Szőgliget H 145 F2
Szokolya H 147 F8
Szolnok H 150 C5
Szőlősgyörök H 149 C9
Szombathely H 149 B7
Szomód H 149 A10
Szomolya H 145 H1
Szówsko PL 144 C6
Szpetal Górny PL 138 E7
Szprotawa PL 81 C9
Szreńsk PL 139 D9
Szropy PL 139 C7
Sztabin PL 140 C8
Sztum PL 138 C7
Szubin PL 138 D4
Szczyrzyc PL 140 D9
Szügy H 147 E8
Szuhogy H 145 G2
Szulborze Wielkie PL 141 E6
Szumowo PL 139 E13
Szurdokpüspöki H 147 F9
Szydłów PL 143 E11
Szydłowiec PL 141 H3
Szydłowo PL 85 D11
Szydłowo PL 139 D9
Szymanów PL 141 F7
Szymonka PL 136 F4
Szynkielów PL 142 D6
Szypliszki PL 136 E7

T

Taagepera EST 131 F11
Taalintehdas FIN 126 E8
Taapajärvi FIN 117 D13
Taastrup DK 87 D10
Tab H 149 C10
Tabajd H 149 B11
Tabaky UA 155 B3
Tabanera de Cerrato E 40 D3
Tábara E 39 E8
Tabarz D 79 E8
Tabasalu EST 131 C9
Tabdi H 150 D3
Taberg S 91 D15
Tabernas E 55 E8
Taberno E 55 E8
Tabivere EST 131 D13
Taboada E 38 C4
Taboadela E 38 D4
Tábor CZ 77 D7
Táborfalva H 150 C3
Tábua P 44 D4
Tabuaço P 44 B5
Tabuenca E 41 E8
Täby S 99 D10
Tác H 149 B10
Tacen SLO 73 D9
Tacherting D 75 F12
Tachov CZ 75 C12
Tackåsen S 103 C9
Tăcuta RO 153 D11
Tadasuni I 64 C2
Tadcaster GB 11 D9
Tadley GB 13 C12
Taebla EST 130 D7
Tælavåg N 94 B1
Tafalla E 32 F2
Tafers CH 31 B11
Taff's Well GB 13 B8
Tafjord N 100 B6
Täfteå S 107 E15
Täfteå S 122 C4
Taga RO 152 D4
Tagananna EST 130 D4
Taggia I 37 D7
Taghmon IRL 9 D9
Tagliacozzo I 62 C4
Taglio di Po I 66 B5
Taglio-Isolaccio F 37 G10
Tagnon F 19 F9
Tágszöberg S 107 D11
Tahal E 55 E8
Tähemaa EST 131 E14
Tahilla IRL 8 E3
Tahitótfalu H 150 B3
Tähtelä FIN 117 D17
Taibón Agordino I 72 D5
Taíde P 38 E3
Tain GB 3 K8
Tainiemi FIN 119 C15
Tainijoki FIN 119 C15
Tain-l'Hermitage F 30 E6
Taintrux F 27 D6
Taio I 71 D11
Taipale FIN 119 B15
Taipale FIN 119 C14
Taipale FIN 123 D17
Taipale FIN 123 D13
Taipale FIN 126 B8
Taipaleenharju FIN 119 C17
Taipalsaari FIN 129 C9
Taipalus FIN 123 E10
Taivalkoski FIN 121 C11
Taivassalo FIN 126 D6
Taizé F 30 B6
Tajmište MK 168 A4
Tajno Łanowe PL 140 C7
Takácsi H 149 B8
Takamaa FIN 127 B10
Takeley GB 15 D9
Takene S 97 C9
Takene S 97 D10
Taklax FIN 122 E6
Taktakenéz H 145 G3

Taktaszada H 145 G3
Talais F 28 E3
Talamantes E 41 E8
Talamona I 69 A8
Talamone I 65 B4
Talange F 186 C1
Talant F 26 F3
Talarrubias E 51 A9
Talaván E 45 E8
Talavera de la Reina E 46 E3
Talavera la Real E 51 B6
Talayuela E 45 E9
Talayuelas E 47 E10
Talea RO 161 C7
Talence F 28 F4
Talensac F 23 D8
Tales E 48 E4
Taleža BIH 162 D5
Talgarreg GB 12 A6
Talgarth GB 13 B8
Talhadas P 44 C4
Tali EST 131 E9
Taliard F 36 C4
Taliesin GB 10 F4
Táliga E 51 B5
Tälje S 103 A10
Talla I 66 E4
Tallås S 103 E11
Tallås S 109 E14
Tallåsen S 103 C10
Tällberg S 103 E8
Tallberg S 118 B8
Taller F 32 C3
Tallinn EST 131 C9
Talljärv S 118 B8
Talloires F 31 D9
Tallone F 37 G11
Tallós E 48 E4
Tallow IRL 8 D6
Tallsjö S 107 C14
Talluskylä FIN 124 D7
Tallvik S 119 B9
Tállya H 145 G3
Tålmaciu RO 160 B4
Talmay F 26 F3
Talmaz MD 154 D5
Talmont F 28 C4
Talmont-St-Hilaire F 28 C2
Talpa RO 160 E6
Talsano I 61 C8
Talsi LV 134 B5
Taluskylä FIN 119 F12
Talviainen FIN 127 B12
Talvik N 112 C10
Tama E 39 B10
Tămădău Mare RO 161 E9
Tamajón E 47 B6
Tamames E 45 C8
Tamarë AL 163 E8
Tamarino BG 167 E7
Tamarite de Litera E 42 D4
Tamashowka BY 141 G9
Tamási H 149 C10
Tamaşi RO 153 D10
Tambach-Dietharz D 79 E8
Tâmboeşti RO 161 B10
Tâme S 118 E6
Tamins CH 71 D8
Tamiş TR 171 E10
Tamm D 27 C11
Tammela FIN 121 C15
Tammela FIN 127 D10
Tammensiel D 82 A5
Tammijärvi FIN 127 B14
Tammiku EST 131 C12
Tammisaari FIN 127 F9
Tammispää EST 131 D14
Tâmna RO 159 D11
Tamnay-en-Bazois F 30 A4
Tamnes N 101 A15
Tamnič SRB 159 E9
Tampere FIN 127 C10
Tamsalu EST 131 C12
Tamsweg A 73 B8
Tamurejo E 54 B3
Tamworth GB 11 F8
Tana Bru N 113 C21
Tanacu RO 153 D11
Tanaji LV 135 E13
Tananes N 114 B4
Tananger N 94 E3
Tanaqual GR 153 E10
Tanaunella I 64 B4
Tancarville F 18 F1
Tǎndǎdalen S 102 D4
Tandamo S 106 E7
Tăndărei RO 161 D11
Tando S 102 E5
Tandragee GB 7 D10
Tandsbyn S 106 E7
Tandsjöborg S 102 C8
Tang H 1 T E7
Tångaberg S 87 A10
Tangelo S 102 D4
Tangbüle S 105 E13
Tange DK 86 C5
Tangen N 95 A12
Tangen N 101 E14
Tangen N 111 B14
Tanger MA 52 E5
Tångeråsen S 105 D15
Tangerhütte D 79 B10
Tangermünde D 79 A10
Tängstamon S 107 E11
Tangstedt D 83 C8
Tängvattnet S 108 E8
Tanhua FIN 115 C3
Taninges F 31 C10
Tankapirtti FIN 115 B2
Tankavaara FIN 115 B2
Tanlay F 25 E11
Tann H 76 T3
Tann (Rhön) D 79 E7
Tanna D 75 B10
Tannadice GB 5 B11
Tännäs S 102 B4
Tannay F 25 F10
Tännäsbergsthal D 75 B11
Tanne D 79 C8
Tannenbergsthal D 75 B11
Tännesberg D 75 C11
Tannhausen D 75 E7
Tannheim A 71 C11
Tannila FIN 119 D15
Tånnö S 88 A6
Tannroda D 79 E9
Tannsjön S 106 D9
Tanowo PL 84 C6
Tansa RO 153 D10
Tañtǎreni RO 160 D2
Tantonville F 26 D5
Tanumshede S 91 B9
Tanvald CZ 81 E8

Taormina I 59 D7
Tapa EST 131 C11
Tapanikylä FIN 121 F13
Tapfheim D 75 E8
Tapia de Casariego E 39 A6
Tápióbicske H 150 C4
Tápiógyörgye H 150 C4
Tapionkylä FIN 117 E14
Tapionniemi FIN 115 E2
Tápióság H 150 C4
Tápiószecső H 150 C4
Tápiószele H 150 C4
Tápiószentmárton H 150 C4
Tápiószőlős H 150 C4
Táplánszentkereszt H 149 B7
Tapojärvi FIN 117 C11
Tapolca H 149 C8
Tappeluft N 112 C9
Tappenbeck D 79 B8
Tappernøje DK 87 E9
Taps DK 86 E4
Tapsony H 149 D8
Tar H 147 F9
Taracena E 47 C6
Tarack BIH 157 C6
Tǎrada AL 168 C3
Tǎradell E 43 D8
Tarancón E 47 D6
Tarano I 62 C3
Taranto I 61 C8
Tarany H 149 D8
Tarare F 30 D5
Tarascon F 35 C8
Tarascon-sur-Ariège F 33 E9
Tarashany UA 153 A8
Tarazona E 41 E8
Tarazona de la Mancha E 47 F9
Tárbena E 56 D4
Tarbert GB 2 K3
Tarbert GB 4 D5
Tarbert GB 4 D6
Tarbert IRL 8 C4
Tarbes F 33 D6
Tarbja EST 131 D11
Tarbolton GB 4 D8
Tǎrcaia RO 151 D9
Tarcal H 145 G3
Tǎrcǎu RO 153 D8
Tarcea RO 151 C9
Tarcento I 73 D7
Tarčin BIH 157 E9
Tarczyn PL 141 G3
Tard H 145 H2
Tardajos E 40 D4
Tardelcuende E 41 E6
Tardets-Sorholus F 32 D4
Tardienta E 41 E10
Tardona H 145 G2
Târendö S 116 D9
Tǎreuca MD 154 B3
Tárgale LV 134 B3
Targon F 28 F5
Târgovişte RO 161 D6
Targowa Górka PL 81 F12
Târgu Bujor RO 153 F11
Târgu Cărbuneşti RO 160 D3
Târgu Frumos RO 153 C9
Târgu Jiu RO 159 C11
Târgu Lăpuş RO 152 C3
Târgu Mureş RO 152 D5
Târgu Neamţ RO 153 C8
Târgu Ocna RO 153 E9
Târgu Secuiesc RO 153 E8
Târguşor RO 155 E2
Tǎrgu Trotuş RO 153 E9
Tarhos H 151 D7
Tarifa E 53 D5
Tarigrad MD 153 A11
Tǎrian H 149 A11
Tárkány H 149 A9
Tarleton GB 10 D6
Târlişua RO 152 C4
Tarłów PL 141 H5
Tarm DK 86 D3
Tarmstedt D 17 B12
Târnaby S 108 E9
Tarnala FIN 129 B12
Tarnalelesz H 145 G1
Tarna Mare RO 145 G7
Tarnaméra H 150 B5
Tarnaörs H 150 B5
Tarnaszentmiklós H 150 B5
Târnăveni RO 152 E4
Tarnawa Duża PL 144 B6
Tarnawatka PL 144 B7
Tarnazsadány H 150 B5
Târnelv N 111 B15
Tårnes N 104 D7
Târnet N 114 D8
Tarnobrzeg PL 143 E12
Tainoloan GB 4 C5
Tarnogród PL 144 C6
Târnok H 149 B10
Tarnos F 32 C3
Tarnoszyn PL 144 C8
Tarnow D 83 C12
Tarnów PL 85 E7
Tarnów PL 85 D7
Tarnowiec PL 144 D4
Tarnówka PL 85 D10
Tarnówko PL 85 D11
Tarnowo Podgórne PL 81 B12
Tarnów Opolski PL 142 E5
Tarnowskie Góry PL 142 F6
Tarnów RO 151 E8
Tarnova RO 151 E8
Tarnow F 25 B7
Tarnowska E 41 B8
Tarora I 59 C9
Tarouca P 44 B5
Tarp D 82 A6
Tarp DK 86 D2
Tarpa H 145 G5
Tarprubežiai LT 136 E7
Tarquinia I 62 C1
Tarquinia Lido I 62 C1
Tarragona E 42 E6
Tàrrajaur S 109 D18
Tàrrega E 42 D6
Tarrel GB 3 K9
Tarrenz A 71 C11
Tarrio E 38 B3
Tarroja de Segarra E 42 D6
Tårs DK 87 F8
Tårs DK 90 E7
Tarsele S 107 C13
Tarsia I 60 D6
Târşolţ RO 145 H7

Tårstad N 111 D12
Tartas F 32 C4
Tărtăşeşti RO 161 D7
Tartu EST 131 E13
Tǎrup DK 87 E7
Tarutyne UA 154 E4
Tarvaala FIN 123 E15
Tarvasjoki FIN 126 D8
Tarves GB 3 L12
Tarvisio I 73 C8
Tarvola FIN 123 D11
Taşağıl TR 173 A7
Taşca RO 153 D8
Tǎşjö S 107 C9
Tass H 150 C3
Tassagh GB 7 D9
Tassin-la-Demi-Lune F 30 D6
Taszár H 149 D9
Tåt H 149 A11
Tata H 149 A10
Tatabánya H 149 A10
Tataháza H 150 E3
Tǎtǎrǎni RO 153 D11
Tǎtǎrani RO 160 D6
Tǎtǎranu RO 161 B10
Tǎtǎrǎşti RO 153 E10
Tǎtǎrǎşti de Jos RO 160 E4
Tǎtǎrǎşti de Sus RO 160 E5
Tǎtǎrǎuca MD 153 A12
Tatarbunary UA 154 F5
Tatarevo BG 166 E4
Tatarköy TR 173 B7
Tatarlar TR 167 F7
Tatárszentgyörgy H 150 C3
Tatišli TR 173 D8
Tatranská Javorina SK 145 E1
Tattershall GB 11 E11
Tǎtuleşti RO 160 D5
Tau N 94 D3
Tauberbischofsheim D 74 C6
Taucha D 79 D11
Tauche D 80 B6
Tauer D 81 C6
Taufkirchen D 75 F10
Taufkirchen D 75 F11
Taufkirchen (Vils) D 75 F11
Taujénai LT 135 F9
Taulé F 22 C4
Taulignan F 35 B8
Taulov DK 86 E4
Tauplitz A 73 A9
Taurage LT 134 F4
Tauragnai LT 135 F11
Tauralaukis LT 134 E2
Taurasi I 60 B4
Taurene LV 135 B11
Taurisano I 61 D10
Taurupe LV 135 C10
Tauste E 41 E9
Tǎuţ RO 151 E9
Tǎuteu RO 151 C9
Tǎuţii-Mǎgherǎuş RO 151 B12
Tauves F 29 D11
Tavankut SRB 150 E4
Tavannes CH 27 F7
Tavant F 24 F3
Tavarnelle Val di Pesa I 66 E3
Tavastila FIN 128 D6
Tavastkenkä FIN 119 F16
Tavaux F 31 A7
Taveiro P 44 D4
Tavel F 35 B8
Tavelsjö S 122 B4
Tavera F 37 G9
Taverham GB 15 B11
Taverna I 59 A10
Tavernay F 30 A5
Tavernelle I 62 A2
Tavernes F 36 D4
Tavernes de la Valldigna E 56 C4
Tavernspite GB 12 B5
Taverny F 25 B7
Tavertet E 43 D8
Taviano I 61 D10
Tavira P 50 E4
Tavistock GB 12 D6
Tavullia I 67 E6
Tawern D 186 B2
Tawern D 186 B2
Taxenbach A 73 B6
Taxiarchis GR 169 D10
Taxobeni MD 153 C11
Tayfur TR 171 D10
Tayinloan GB 4 D5
Taylor's Cross IRL 7 F7
Taynuilt GB 4 C6
Tayport GB 5 C11
Tayvallich GB 4 C5
Tázlár H 150 D4
Tazlău RO 153 D9
Tazones E 39 A9
Tczew PL 138 B6
Tczów PL 141 H4
Teaca RO 152 D5
Teano I 60 A2
Tearce MK 164 E3
Teasc RO 160 E3
Teba E 53 C7
Tebar E 47 E8
Tebay GB 10 C6
Tebra E 38 D2
Tebstrup DK 86 D5
Techendorf A 73 C7
Techirghiol RO 155 E3
Tecuci RO 153 F10
Tedavnet IRL 7 D8
Tefeli GR 178 E9
Tegelen NL 16 F6
Tegelträsk S 107 D13
Teggiano I 60 C5
Téglás H 151 B8
Teglio I 69 A9
Tegnäset S 107 C16
Tegover CZ 76 B6
Teichwolframsdorf D 79 E11
Teignmouth GB 13 D7
Teijo FIN 126 E8
Teikosuvanto FIN 117 C11
Teillay F 23 E8
Teillet F 33 C10
Teisendorf D 73 A6

Teisko FIN 127 B10
Teisnach D 76 D4
Teistungen D 79 D7
Teiu RO 160 D6
Teius RO 152 E3
Teixeiro E 38 B3
Teixoso P 44 D6
Tejadillos E 47 D9
Tejado E 41 E7
Tejeda de Tiétar E 45 D9
Tejn DK 89 E7
Tekeler TR 181 A7
Tekeli TR 177 C9
Tekeriš SRB 158 D4
Tekija BIH 157 D11
Tekija SRB 159 D9
Tekirdağ TR 173 C7
Tekovské Lužany SK 147 E7
Teksdal N 104 D7
Telaki TR 144 B8
Telatyn PL 144 B8
Telč CZ 77 D8
Telciu RO 152 C4
Teldau D 83 D9
Teleĉka SRB 150 F3
Telega RO 161 C7
Telekgerendás H 151 D6
Teleneşti MD 154 B2
Telerig BG 161 F11
Telese I 60 A3
Teleşti RO 159 C11
Telford GB 10 F7
Telfs A 72 B3
Telgárt SK 147 D9
Telgte D 17 E9
Telhado P 44 D5
Telish BG 165 C9
Teliu RO 153 F7
Teliucu Inferior RO 159 B10
Teljo FIN 125 C13
Telkkälä FIN 119 C17
Tellancourt F 19 E12
Tellejåk S 118 B3
Tellin B 19 D11
Tellingstedt D 82 B6
Telnice CZ 77 D11
Telões P 38 F4
Telšiai LT 134 E4
Telti I 64 B3
Teltow D 80 B4
Tembleque E 46 E6
Temeleuţi MD 153 C12
Temelin CZ 77 D7
Temenin BG 161 F10
Temerin SRB 158 C4
Temmes FIN 119 E15
Tempi GR 169 E8
Tempio Pausania I 64 B3
Temple Bar GB 12 A6
Templeboy IRL 6 D5
Temple Ewell GB 15 E11
Templemore IRL 9 C7
Templepatrick GB 4 F4
Temple Sowerby GB 5 F11
Templeton GB 12 B5
Templetuohy IRL 9 C7
Templeuve F 182 D2
Templin D 84 D5
Tempo GB 7 D8
Temse B 19 B9
Temska SRB 164 C6
Tenancingen CH 27 F7
Tenay F 31 D8
Ten Boer NL 17 B7
Tenbury Wells GB 13 A9
Tenby GB 12 B5
Tence F 30 E5
Tende F 37 C7
Tendilla E 47 C7
Tendu F 29 B9
Teneniai LT 134 F3
Tenevo BG 167 E7
Tengelic H 149 C11
Tengen D 27 E10
Tengesdal N 94 C4
Tenhult S 92 D4
Teningen D 27 D8
Tenja HR 149 F11
Tenk H 150 B5
Tennänget S 102 D6
Tennevik N 111 C12
Tennevoll N 111 C14
Tennilä FIN 119 B16
Tennilä FIN 127 D13
Tennsjer N 111 B15
Tennstrand N 110 D9
Tenterden GB 15 E10
Tentúgal P 44 D3
Teora I 60 B4
Teovo MK 169 A6
Tepasto FIN 117 C13
Tépe H 151 C7
Tepeboz TR 177 B2
Tepecik TR 173 E10
Tepecik TR 173 E10
Tepelenë AL 168 D3
Teplá CZ 76 C3
Teplice CZ 80 E5
Teplice nad Metují CZ 81 E10
Teplička SK 145 F2
Teplička nad Váhom SK 147 C7
Tepsa FIN 117 C15
Ţepu RO 153 F10
Ter Aar NL 182 A5
Terama I 62 B5
Térande LV 134 B3
Ter Apel NL 17 C8
Teratyn PL 144 B8
Tèrbaç AL 168 D2
Terborg-Silvolde NL 16 E6
Terchová SK 147 C8
Terebeşti RO 151 B10
Tereblya UA 145 G8
Teregova RO 159 C9
Teremia Mare RO 150 E4
Terena P 50 B5
Teresa E 48 E3
Teresa de Cofrentes E 47 F10
Teresin PL 141 F2
Terespol PL 141 F9
Teresva UA 145 G8
Terezín CZ 76 B6
Terezino Polje HR 149 E8
Tergnier F 19 E7
Tergu I 64 B2
Terhijärvi FIN 123 C10
Terheijden NL 182 B5
Terherne NL 16 B5
Teriberka RUS 114 C10
Terikeste EST 131 E14
Terjärv FIN 123 C11
Terka PL 145 E5
Terlan I 72 C3

Těrlicko CZ 146 B6
Terlizzi I 61 A7
Terme Luigiane I 60 E5
Térmens E 42 D5
Termignon F 31 E10
Terminiers F 24 D6
Termini Imerese I 58 D4
Termoli I 63 D7
Termon IRL 7 B7
Termonfeckin IRL 7 E10
Ternaard NL 16 B5
Ternavka UA 153 A8
Ternberg A 76 G6
Terndrup DK 86 B6
Terneuzen NL 16 F1
Terni I 62 B3
Ternitz A 148 A6
Ternove UA 145 G8
Terovo GR 168 F4
Terpezita RO 160 E3
Terpni GR 169 C9
Terpsithea GR 169 E7
Terpyllos GR 169 B8
Terracina I 62 E4
Terrades E 34 F4
Terrak N 105 A12
Terralba I 64 D2
Terranova da Sibari I 61 D6
Terranova di Pollino I 60 D6
Terranuova Bracciolini I 66 E4
Terrasini I 58 C3
Terrassa E 43 D8
Terrasson-Lavilledieu F 29 E8
Terraube F 33 C7
Terravecchia I 61 E7
Terricciola I 66 E2
Terriente E 47 D10
Terrin IRL 7 E8
Terrinches E 55 B7
Terrou F 29 F9
Terrugem P 31 E10
Terrugem P 51 B5
Terryglass IRL 6 F6
Terslev DK 87 E9
Tèrstenik RKS 164 D2
Tertenia I 64 D4
Teruel E 47 D10
Tervajoki FIN 122 D8
Tervakoski FIN 127 D12
Tervavaara FIN 121 D11
Tervel BG 161 F10
Terves F 28 B4
Tērvete LV 134 D6
Tervo FIN 123 E17
Tervola RO 119 B13
Tervolan asema FIN 119 B13
Tervuren B 19 C9
Tés H 149 B9
Tešanj BIH 157 C8
Tešany CZ 77 D11
Tešedíkovo SK 146 E5
Tesero I 72 D4
Tešica SRB 164 C4
Tesimo I 72 C3
Tesjoki FIN 127 E15
Teslič BIH 157 C8
Teslui RO 160 D4
Teslui RO 160 E4
Tespe D 83 D8
Tessenderlo B 19 C11
Tessin D 83 B12
Tesson F 28 D4
Tessy-sur-Vire F 23 C7
Testa del Gargano I 63 D10
Testa dell'Acqua I 59 F6
Testelt B 182 C5
Teşvikiye TR 173 C11
Tét H 149 A9
Tetbury GB 13 B10
Teţcani MD 153 A9
Teţchea RO 151 C9
Teteringen NL 182 B5
Teterow D 83 C13
Tetétlen H 151 C7
Teteven BG 165 D9
Teti I 64 C3
Tetney GB 11 E11
Tetoiu RO 160 D3
Tétouan MA 53 E6
Tetovo BG 161 F8
Tetovo MK 163 E10
Tettens D 17 A9
Tettnang D 71 B9
Tetyri PL 85 D7
Teublitz D 75 D11
Teuchern D 79 D11
Teufen CH 27 F7
Teufenbach A 73 B9
Teulada I 64 F2
Teulada E 56 D6
Teunz D 75 D11
Teupitz D 80 B5
Teurajärvi FIN 117 D11
Teurajärvi S 116 E9
Teuro FIN 127 D10
Teuschnitz D 75 B9
Teutschenthal D 79 D10
Teuva FIN 122 F7
Tevaniemi FIN 127 B10
Tevansjö S 103 B9
Tevel H 149 D10
Tēvenāni LV 133 C1
Tevfikiye TR 171 E10
Teviothead GB 5 E11
Tewkesbury GB 13 B10
Teyssieu F 29 F9
Thal D 79 E7
Thale (Harz) D 79 C9
Thaleischweiler-Fröschen D 186 C4
Thalfang D 21 E7
Thalheim D 79 C11
Thalheim bei Wels A 76 F6
Thaljina BIH 157 F7
Thalmässing D 75 D9
Thalwil CH 27 F10
Thame GB 14 D7
Thann F 27 E7
Thannhausen D 75 F7
Thaon-les-Vosges F 26 D5
't Harde NL 16 D5
Tharsis E 51 D5
Thasos GR 171 C7
Thatcham GB 13 C12
Thaumiers F 29 B11
Thaxted GB 15 D9
Thaya A 77 E8
Thayngen CH 27 E10
Theale GB 13 C12
Thedinghausen D 17 C12
Theillay F 24 F7
Theißen D 79 D11

Theix F 22 E6
Them DK 86 C5
Themar D 75 A8
The Mumbles GB 12 B6
Thenay F 29 B8
Thénezay F 28 B5
Thenon F 29 E8
Theologos GR 171 C7
Théoule-sur-Mer F 36 D5
The Pike IRL 9 D7
Therma GR 171 D9
Thermi GR 169 C9
Thermisia GR 175 E7
Thermo GR 174 B4
Thermopyles GR 175 B6
Thérouanne F 18 C5
The Sheddings GB 4 F4
Thespies GR 175 C7
Thesprotiko GR 168 F4
Thessaloniki GR 169 C8
The Stocks GB 15 E10
Thetford GB 15 C10
Theth AL 163 E8
Theux B 19 C12
Thèze F 32 D5
Thèze F 35 B10
Thiaucourt-Regniéville F 26 C4
Thiberville F 24 B3
Thibie F 25 C11
Thiéblemont-Farémont F 25 C12
Thiendorf D 80 D5
Thiene I 72 E3
Thierhaupten D 75 E8
Thierrens CH 31 B10
Thiers F 30 D4
Thiersee A 72 A5
Thiersheim D 75 B11
Thiesi I 64 B2
Thießow D 84 B5
Thiézac F 29 E11
Thimert-Gâtelles F 24 C5
Thin-le-Moutier F 19 E10
Thionville F 20 F6
Thiron Gardais F 24 D4
Thirsk GB 11 C9
Thisted DK 86 B3
Thisvi GR 175 C6
Thiva GR 175 C7
Thivars F 24 D5
Thiviers F 29 E7
Thizy F 30 C5
Thoirette F 31 C8
Thoiry F 24 C6
Thoissey F 30 C6
Tholen NL 16 E2
Tholey D 21 F8
Thomastown IRL 9 C8
Thommen B 20 D6
Thônes F 31 D9
Thonnance-lès-Joinville F 26 D3
Thonon-les-Bains F 31 C9
Thorame-Haute F 36 C5
Thoras F 30 F4
Thoré-la-Rochette F 24 E4
Thorenc F 36 D5
Thorigny-sur-Oreuse F 25 D9
Thörl A 73 A11
Thorn NL 19 B12
Thornaby-on-Tees GB 11 B9
Thornbury GB 13 B9
Thorne GB 11 D10
Thorney GB 11 F11
Thornhill GB 5 E9
Thorning DK 86 C4
Thornton GB 10 D5
Thorpe-le-Soken GB 15 D11
Thorpe Market GB 15 B11
Thorpeness GB 15 C12
Thorsager DK 86 C6
Thorshøj DK 90 E7
Thorsø DK 86 C5
Thouarcé F 23 F11
Thouaré-sur-Loire F 23 F9
Thouars F 28 B5
Thouria GR 174 E5
Thourotte F 18 F6
Thrapston GB 15 C7
Threshfield GB 11 C7
Thropton GB 5 E13
Thrumster GB 3 J10
Thuès-entre-Valls F 33 E10
Thueyts F 35 A7
Thuin B 19 D9
Thuine D 17 D9
Thuir F 34 E4
Thum D 80 E3
Thun CH 70 D5
Thundersley GB 15 D10
Thüngen D 74 C6
Thüngersheim D 74 C6
Thuré F 29 B6
Thuret F 30 D3
Thurey F 31 B7
Thüringen A 71 C9
Thurins F 30 D6
Thürkow D 83 C13
Thurlby GB 11 F11
Thurles IRL 9 C7
Thurnau D 75 B9
Thursby GB 5 F10
Thurso GB 3 H9
Thury-Harcourt F 23 C11
Thusis CH 71 D8
Thwaite GB 11 C7
Thyborøn DK 86 B2
Thyez F 31 C10
Thymiana GR 177 C7
Thyregod DK 86 D4
Thyrnau D 76 E5
Tia Mare RO 160 F5
Tiana I 64 C3
Ţibana RO 153 D10
Ţibăneşti RO 153 D10
Tibble S 99 D9
Tiberget S 102 D6
Tibi E 56 D3
Tibolddaróc H 145 H2
Tibro S 92 C4
Ţibucani RO 153 C9
Tice BIH 156 D6
Ticehurst GB 15 E9
Ticha BG 167 D6
Tichá CZ 146 B6
Tichileşti RO 155 C1
Tičići BIH 157 D9
Ticknall GB 11 F9
Ţicleni RO 160 D2
Ţicuşu RO 152 F6
Ticvaniu Mare RO 159 C8
Tidaholm S 91 C14
Tidan S 91 B15
Tiddische D 79 A8
Tidenham GB 13 B9
Tidersrum S 92 D7
Tiebas E 32 E2
Tiedra E 39 E9
Tiefenbach D 75 D12
Tiefenbach D 76 E4
Tiefenbronn D 27 C10
Tiefencastel CH 71 D9
Tiefensee D 84 E5
Tiel NL 16 E4
Tielen B 182 C5
Tielt B 19 C7
Tiemassaari FIN 125 F10
Tienen B 19 C10
Tiengen D 27 E9
Tiercé F 23 E11
Tierga E 41 E8
Tierp S 99 B9
Tierzo E 47 C9
Ţifeşti RO 153 F10
Ţigănaşi RO 153 C10
Ţigăneşti RO 160 F6
Tigare BIH 158 E3
Tighina MD 154 D4
Tighira MD 153 C11
Tighnabruaich GB 4 D6
Tignale I 69 B10
Tignes F 31 E10
Tigveni RO 160 C5
Tigy F 25 E7
Tiha Bârgăului RO 152 C5
Tihany H 149 C9
Tihemetsa EST 131 E10
Tihilä FIN 123 C16
Tihusniemi FIN 124 F9
Tiistenjoki FIN 123 E10
Tiitilänkylä FIN 123 E17
Tijesno HR 156 E4
Tijnje NL 16 B5
Tíjola E 55 E8
Tikkakoski FIN 123 F15
Tikkala FIN 123 F14
Tikkala FIN 125 F14
Tikkurila FIN 127 E13
Tikob DK 87 C10
Tilburg NL 16 E4
Tilbury GB 15 E9
Til-Châtel F 26 E3
Tildarg GB 4 F4
Tileagd RO 151 C9
Tilehurst GB 13 C12
Tilh F 32 C4
Tilişca RO 152 F3
Tillac F 33 D6
Tillberga S 98 C7
Tillicoultry GB 5 C9
Tillières-sur-Avre F 24 C5
Tilloy-et-Bellay F 25 B12
Tillyfourie GB 3 L11
Tilly-sur-Seulles F 23 B10
Tilvikai LT 134 E3
Tilža LV 133 C2
Tim DK 86 C2
Timahoe IRL 7 G8
Timár H 145 G3
Timau I 73 C7
Timelkam A 76 F5
Timiryazevo RUS 136 C4
Timişeşti RO 153 C9
Timişoara RO 151 F7
Timmele S 91 D13
Timmendorfer Strand D 83 C9
Timmernabben S 89 B10
Timmersdala S 91 B14
Timola FIN 125 F9
Timoleague IRL 8 E5
Timolin IRL 7 G9
Timoniemi FIN 121 F13
Timovaara FIN 125 D12
Timrå S 103 A13
Timring DK 86 C3
Timsgearraidh GB 2 J2
Tinahely IRL 9 C10
Tinajas E 47 D7
Tinalhas P 44 E5
Tinca RO 151 D8
Tinchebray F 23 C10
Tineo E 39 B7
Tiņģere LV 134 B5
Tinglev DK 86 F4
Tingsryd S 89 B7
Tingstad S 93 B8
Tingstäde S 93 D13
Tingvatn N 94 F6
Tingvoll N 100 A8
Tingwall GB 3 G10
Tinja BIH 157 C10
Tinjan HR 67 B8
Tinn N 95 C9
Tinnoset N 95 C10
Tinos GR 176 D5
Tiñosillos E 46 C3
Tinosu RO 161 D8
Tinqueux F 19 F8
Tintagel GB 12 D5
Tinténiac F 23 D8
Tintern Parva GB 13 B9
Ţinteşti RO 161 C9
Tintigny B 19 E12
Tīnūži LV 135 C9
Tiobraid Árann IRL 8 D6
Tione di Trento I 69 A10
Tipasoja FIN 125 B11
Tipperary IRL 8 D6
Tiptree GB 15 D10
Tipu EST 131 E10
Tira MD 154 B2
Tiranë AL 168 B2
Tiranges F 30 E4
Tirano I 69 A9
Tiraspol MD 154 D5
Tiraspolul Nou MD 154 D5
Tire TR 177 C10
Tiream RO 151 B9
Tireļi LV 134 C7
Tirgo E 40 C6
Tiriez E 55 B8
Tirig E 48 D5
Tiriolo I 59 B10
Tirkšliai LT 134 D4
Tîrnova MD 153 A11
Tirrenia I 66 E1
Tirro FIN 113 F18
Tirschenreuth D 75 C11
Tirstrup DK 86 C7
Tirteafuera E 54 B4
Tirza LV 135 B12
Tisău RO 161 C9
Tišća BIH 157 D10
Tishevitsa BG 165 C8
Tishono RUS 136 E2
Tišice CZ 77 B7
Tismana RO 159 C10
Tišnov CZ 77 D10
Tisovec SK 147 D9
Tistrup Stationsby DK 86 D3
Tisvilde DK 87 C10
Tiszaalpár H 150 D4
Tiszabecs H 145 G6
Tiszabezdéd H 145 G5
Tiszabő H 150 C5
Tiszabura H 150 C5
Tiszacsege H 151 B7
Tiszadada H 145 G3
Tiszaderzs H 150 B6
Tiszadob H 145 G3
Tiszaeszlár H 145 G3
Tiszaföldvár H 150 D5
Tiszafüred H 150 B6
Tiszagyenda H 150 C6
Tiszaigar H 150 B6
Tiszajenő H 150 C5
Tiszakanyár H 145 G4
Tiszakarád H 145 G4
Tiszakécske H 150 D5
Tiszakerecseny H 145 G5
Tiszakeszi H 151 B6
Tiszakürt H 150 D5
Tiszalök H 145 G3
Tiszalúc H 145 G3
Tiszanagyfalu H 145 G3
Tiszanána H 150 B6
Tiszaörs H 150 B6
Tiszapalkonya H 145 H3
Tiszapüspöki H 150 C5
Tiszaroff H 150 C5
Tiszasas H 150 D5
Tiszasüly H 150 C5
Tiszaszalka H 145 G5
Tiszaszentimre H 150 C6
Tiszasziget H 150 E5
Tiszatarján H 147 F12
Tiszatelek H 145 G4
Tiszatenyő H 150 C5
Tiszaug H 150 D5
Tiszaújváros H 145 H3
Tiszavárkony H 150 C5
Tiszavasvári H 145 H3
Titaguas E 47 E10
Titel SRB 158 C5
Ţiţeşti RO 160 C6
Tithorea GR 175 B6
Tito I 60 B5
Titova Korenica HR 156 C4
Titov Drvar BIH 156 D5
Titran N 104 D4
Tittelsnes N 94 C3
Titting D 75 E9
Tittmoning D 76 F3
Titu RO 161 D7
Titulcia E 46 D5
Tiukuvaara FIN 117 C13
Tiurajärvi FIN 117 C12
Tivat MNE 163 E6
Tivenys E 42 F5
Tiverton GB 13 D8
Tivissa E 42 E5
Tivoli I 62 D3
Tizzano F 37 H9
Tjæreborg DK 86 E3
Tjäkkjokk S 109 E15
Tjällmo S 92 B6
Tjåmotis S 109 C16
Tjappsåive S 109 E17
Tjärmyrberget S 106 C9
Tjärn S 107 D13
Tjärnäs S 98 A6
Tjärnberg S 107 A15
Tjärstad S 92 C7
Tjäruträsk S 118 B8
Tjautas S 116 D5
Tjeldnes N 111 D11
Tjeldstø N 100 E1
Tjelle N 100 A7
Tjentište BIH 157 F10
Tjöck FIN 122 F6
Tjøme N 90 A7
Tjønnefoss N 90 B4
Tjorhom N 94 E5
Tjörnarp S 87 D13
Tjøtta N 108 E3
Tjuda FIN 126 E8
Tjuvskjær N 111 C13
Tkon HR 156 E3
Tleń PL 138 C5
Tlmače SK 147 E7
Tłuchowo PL 139 E7
Tlumačov CZ 146 C5
Tłuszcz PL 139 F11
Toab GB 3 F14
Toaca RO 152 D5
Tóalmás H 150 C4
Toano I 66 D2
Tobar an Choire IRL 6 D5
Tobarra E 55 B9
Tobercurry IRL 6 D5
Tobermore GB 4 F3
Tobermory GB 4 B4
Tobo S 99 B9
Tobyn S 97 C8
Tocane-St-Apre F 29 E6
Tocco da Casauria I 62 C5
Tocha P 44 D3
Töcksfors S 96 C6
Tocón E 53 B9
Todal N 104 E5
Toddington GB 13 B11
Todi I 62 B2
Todireni RO 153 B10
Todireşti RO 153 B8
Todireşti RO 153 C9
Todireşti RO 153 D10
Todmorden GB 11 D7
Todolella E 42 F3
Todorići BIH 157 D7
Todor-Ikonomovo BG 161 F10
Todorovo BG 161 F9
Todtmoos D 27 E8
Todtnau D 27 E8
Toén E 38 D4
Toft GB 3 E14
Toft N 108 F3
Tofta S 87 A10
Tofta S 93 D12
Tofte N 95 C13
Töftedal S 91 B10
Tofterup DK 86 D3
Toftir FO 2 A3
Toftlund DK 86 E4
Tofyeli BY 133 E5
Togher IRL 7 E10
Togher IRL 7 F7
Togher IRL 8 E4
Togston GB 5 E13
Tohmajärvi FIN 125 F14
Tohmo FIN 115 E2
Toholampi FIN 123 C12
Toija FIN 127 E9
Toijala FIN 127 C10
Toila EST 132 C2
Toirano I 37 C8
Toivakka FIN 119 B17
Toivakka FIN 123 F16
Toivala FIN 124 E9
Toivola FIN 128 C6
Tojaci MK 169 B6
Töjby FIN 122 E6
Tök H 149 A11
Tokachka BG 171 B9
Tokaj H 145 G3
Tokarnia PL 143 E9
Tokarnia PL 147 B9
Tokod H 149 A11
Tököl H 149 B11
Tokrajärvi FIN 125 E15
Toksovo RUS 129 E14
Tolastadh Úr GB 2 J4
Tolbaños E 46 C3
Tolbert NL 16 B6
Tolcsva H 145 G3
Toledo E 46 E4
Tolentino I 67 F7
Tolfa I 62 C1
Tolga N 101 B14
Toliejai LT 135 F10
Tolja FIN 119 B17
Tolk D 82 A7
Tolkmicko PL 139 B8
Tollarp S 88 D5
Tollered S 91 D11
Tollesbury GB 15 D10
Tollo I 63 C6
Tølløse DK 87 D9
Töllsjö S 91 D12
Tolmachevo RUS 132 D6
Tolmezzo I 73 D7
Tolmin SLO 73 D8
Tolna H 149 D11
Tolnanémedi H 149 C10
Tolne DK 90 E7
Tolo GR 175 D6
Toločănești MD 153 A11
Tolonen FIN 117 E14
Tolosa E 32 D1
Tolosa P 44 F5
Tolosenmäki FIN 125 F14
Tolox E 53 C7
Tolšići BIH 157 D10
Tolva E 42 C5
Tolva FIN 121 B12
Tolvayarvi RUS 125 F16
Tolve I 60 B6
Tomai MD 154 D2
Tomai MD 154 E3
Tomar P 44 E4
Tomares E 51 E7
Tomaševac SRB 158 C6
Tomaševo MNE 163 C8
Tomašica BIH 157 C6
Tomášikovo SK 146 E5
Tomášovce SK 147 E9
Tomaszów Lubelski PL 144 C7
Tomaszów Mazowiecki PL 141 G2
Tomatin GB 3 L9
Tombebœf F 33 A6
Tomelilla S 88 D5
Tomelloso E 47 F6
Tomești RO 151 E10
Tomești RO 151 F9
Tomești RO 153 C11
Tomice PL 147 B8
Tomiño E 38 E2
Tomintoul GB 3 L10
Tomislavgrad BIH 157 E7
Tømmerneset N 111 E10
Tommerup DK 86 E6
Tomnavoulin GB 3 L10
Tömörkény H 150 D5
Tompa H 150 E4
Tomra N 100 A5
Tomșani RO 161 D8
Tona E 43 D8
Tonara I 64 C3
Tonbridge GB 15 E9
Tondela P 44 C4
Tønder DK 86 F3
Tonezza del Cimone I 69 B11
Tongeren B 19 C11
Tongland GB 5 F8
Tongue GB 2 J8
Tönisvorst D 183 C8
Tonkopuro FIN 115 E4
Tonna GB 13 B7
Tonnay-Boutonne F 28 D4
Tonnay-Charente F 28 D4
Tonneins F 33 B6
Tonnerre F 25 E10
Tonnes N 108 C5
Tönning D 82 B5
Tønsberg N 95 D12
Tönsen S 103 D12
Tonstad N 94 E5
Tonsvik N 111 A17
Toombeola IRL 6 F3
Toomebridge GB 4 F4
Tootsi EST 131 D9
Topalu RO 155 D2
Topana RO 160 D5
Topares E 55 D8
Toparlar TR 181 C9
Topchii BG 161 F9
Topchin D 80 B5
Topčić-Polje BIH 157 D8
Topcliffe GB 11 C9
Töpen D 75 B10
Topeno FIN 127 D11
Tophisar TR 173 D9
Toplet RO 159 D9
Topliceni RO 161 C10
Topli Do SRB 165 C6
Toplița RO 152 D6
Toplița RO 159 B10
Töplitz D 79 B12
Topojë AL 168 C1
Topola SRB 158 E6
Topolčani MK 168 B5
Topoľčany SK 146 D6
Topoľčianky SK 146 E6
Topolia GR 178 E6
Topólka PL 138 E6
Topolnica SRB 159 E9
Topoľníky SK 146 F5
Topolog RO 155 D2
Topolovac HR 149 F6
Topolovățu Mare RO 151 F8
Topoloveni RO 160 D6
Topolovgrad BG 166 E6
Topolovnik SRB 159 D7
Topolovo BG 166 F4
Topolšica SLO 73 D11
Toponica SRB 158 F6
Toporec SK 145 E1
Toporivtsi UA 153 A8
Toporów PL 81 B8
Toporu RO 161 E7
Toporzyk PL 85 C10
Toppenstedt D 83 D8
Topraisar RO 155 E2
Topsham GB 13 D8
Topusko HR 156 B4
Torá E 43 D6
Toral de los Guzmanes E 39 D8
Toral de los Vados E 39 C6
Torano Castello I 60 E6
Torasalo FIN 125 F10
Toras-Sieppi FIN 117 C11
Torbali TR 177 C9
Torbjörntorp S 91 C14
Torbygget S 102 A4
Torchiara I 60 C4
Torchiarolo I 61 C10
Torcy F 30 B5
Torda SRB 158 B5
Tordas H 149 B11
Tordehumos E 39 E9
Tordera E 43 D9
Tordesillas E 39 E10
Tordesilos E 47 C9
Töre S 118 C9
Töreboda S 91 B15
Toreby DK 83 A11
Torekov S 87 C11
Torella del Sannio I 63 D7
Torellano E 56 E3
Torelló E 43 C8
Toreno E 39 C6
Torestorp S 91 E12
Torgau D 80 C3
Torgelow D 84 C6
Torgiano I 62 A2
Torhamn S 89 C9
Torhout B 19 B7
Tori EST 131 E9
Torigni-sur-Vire F 23 B10
Torija E 47 C6
Torino I 68 C4
Toritto I 61 B7
Torkanivka UA 154 A4
Torkovichi RUS 132 D7
Torla E 32 E5
Torma EST 131 D13
Tormac RO 159 B7
Törmänen FIN 113 E19
Törmänen FIN 115 A2
Törmänki FIN 117 E13
Törmänmäki FIN 121 E10
Törmäsenvaara FIN 121 C13
Törmäsjärvi FIN 119 B12
Tormestorp S 87 C13
Tormón E 47 D10
Tormore GB 4 D6
Tornadizos de Ávila E 46 C3
Tornaľa SK 145 F1
Tornavacas E 45 D9
Tornby DK 90 D6
Tornemark DK 87 E9
Tornes N 100 A6
Tørnes N 111 D11
Tornesch D 82 C7
Torneträsk S 111 D18
Tornimäe EST 130 D6
Tornio FIN 119 C12
Tornjoš SRB 150 F4
Torno I 69 B7
Tornos E 47 C10
Tornow D 84 D4
Toro E 39 E9
Torö S 93 B11
Törökbálint H 149 B11
Törökszentmiklós H 150 C5
Torony H 149 B7
Toros BG 165 C9
Toroshino RUS 132 F4
Torp FIN 99 B13
Torpa S 92 D6
Torphins GB 3 L11
Torpo N 101 E9
Torpoint GB 12 E6
Torpsbruk S 88 A7
Torpshammar S 103 B11
Torquay GB 13 E7
Torquemada E 40 D3
Torraiba de Calatrava E 54 A5
Torralba E 47 D8
Torralba I 64 B2
Torralba de Aragón E 41 E10
Torralba de El Burgo E 40 E6
Torralba de los Sisones E 47 C10
Torralba de Oropesa E 45 E10
Torrão P 50 C3
Torrböle S 107 D17
Torre-Alháquime E 51 F9
Torre Annunziata I 60 B2
Torrebaja E 47 D10
Torreblanca E 48 D5
Torreblascopedro E 53 A9
Torrebruna I 63 D7
Torrecaballeros E 46 C4
Torrecampo E 54 C3
Torre Canne I 61 B8
Torre-Cardela E 55 D6
Torrecilla de Alcañiz E 42 F3
Torrecilla de la Jara E 46 E3
Torrecilla de la Orden E 45 B10
Torrecilla del Rebollar E 42 F1
Torrecillas de la Tiesa E 45 E9
Torrecuso I 60 A3
Torre da Gadanha P 50 B3
Torre das Vargens P 44 F5
Torre de Coelheiros P 50 C4
Torre de Dona Chama P 38 E5
Torre de Embesora E 48 D4
Torredeita P 44 C4
Torre de Juan Abad E 55 B6
Torre del Bierzo E 39 C7
Torre del Burgo E 47 C6
Torre del Campo E 53 A9
Torre del Greco I 60 B2
Torre del Mar E 53 C8
Torredembarra E 43 E6
Torre de Miguel Sesmero E 51 B6
Torre de Moncorvo P 45 B6
Torre de'Passeri I 62 C5
Torre de Santa María E 45 F8
Torredonjimeno E 53 A9
Torre do Terrenho P 44 C6
Torrefarrera E 42 D5
Torregamones E 39 F7
Torregrossa E 42 D5
Torreiglesias E 46 B4
Torreira P 44 C3
Torrejoncillo E 45 E8
Torrejoncillo del Rey E 47 D7
Torrejón de Ardoz E 46 D6
Torrejón del Rey E 46 C6
Torrejón el Rubio E 45 E9
Torrelacarcel E 47 C10
Torrelaguna E 46 C5
Torrelapaja E 41 E8
Torrelavega E 40 B3
Torrellas E 41 E8
Torrelles de Foix E 43 E7
Torrelobatón E 39 E9
Torrelodones E 46 C5
Torremaggiore I 63 D8
Torremanzanas-La Torre de les Macanes E 56 D4
Torremayor E 51 B6
Torremegía E 51 B7
Torre Mileto I 63 D9
Torremocha E 45 F8
Torremocha de Jiloca E 47 C10
Torremolinos E 53 C7
Torrenostra E 48 D5
Torrent E 48 F4
Torrente del Cinca E 42 E4
Torrenueva E 55 B6
Torreorgaz E 45 F8
Torre Orsaia I 60 C4
Torre-Pacheco E 56 F3
Torre Pellice I 31 F11
Torreperogil E 55 C6
Torres E 53 A9
Torresandino E 40 E4
Torre San Giovanni I 61 D10
Torre Santa Susanna I 61 C9
Torres de Albánchez E 55 C7
Torres de Berrellén E 41 E9
Torres de la Alameda E 46 D6
Torres del Carrizal E 39 E8
Torresmenudas E 45 B9
Torres Novas P 44 F3
Torres Vedras P 44 F2
Torrevelilla E 42 F3
Torrevieja E 56 F3
Torrice I 62 D4
Torricella I 61 C9
Torricella in Sabina I 62 C3
Torricella Peligna I 63 C6
Torricella Sicura I 62 B5
Torricella Taverne CH 69 A6
Torrico E 45 E10
Torri del Benaco I 69 B10
Torridon GB 2 K5
Torriglia I 37 B10
Torrijas E 48 D3
Torrijo E 41 F8
Torrijo del Campo E 47 C10
Torrijos E 46 E4
Torrin GB 2 L4
Tørring DK 86 D4
Tørring N 105 C10
Torrita di Siena I 66 F4
Torroal P 50 C2
Torroella de Montgrí E 43 C10
Torrox E 53 C9
Torrubia del Campo E 47 E7
Torrubia de Soria E 41 E7
Tørrvika N 104 C7
Torsåker S 98 A6
Torsång S 97 B14
Torsås S 89 C10
Tørsbøl DK 86 F4
Törsbole S 107 E15
Torsborg S 102 A5
Torsby S 97 B9
Torsby S 97 C9
Torsebro S 88 C6
Torshälla S 98 D6
Tórshavn FO 2 A3
Torsholma FIN 126 E5
Torsken N 111 B13
Torslanda S 91 D10
Torsminde DK 86 C2
Torsö S 91 B14
Torsvåg N 112 C4
Törtel H 150 C4
Tortellà E 43 C9
Torteval GBG 22 B6
Torthorwald GB 5 E9
Tortinmäki FIN 126 D7
Tórtola de Henares E 47 C6
Tórtoles de Esgueva E 40 E3
Tortolì I 64 D4
Tortomanu RO 155 E2
Tortona I 37 B9
Tortora I 60 D5
Tortoreto I 62 B5
Tortorici I 59 C6
Tortosa E 42 F5
Tortozendo P 44 D5
Tortuera E 47 C9
Tortuna S 98 C7
Toruń PL 138 D6
Torun' UA 145 F8
Torup S 87 B12
Tõrva EST 131 E11
Tor Vaianica I 62 D2
Tõrvandi EST 131 E13
Torvenkylä FIN 119 F11
Torvik N 100 B3
Torvik N 104 F4
Torvikbukt N 104 F3
Tørvikbygd N 94 B4
Torvinen FIN 117 D17
Torvizcón E 55 F6
Torvsjö S 107 C12
Torysa SK 145 E2
Torzym PL 81 B8
Tosbotn N 108 F4
Toscolano-Maderno I 69 B10
Tossa E 43 D9
Tossåsen S 102 A5
Tossåsen S 102 A7
Tossavanlahti FIN 123 D16
Tosse F 32 C3
Tösse S 91 B12
Tossicia I 62 B5
Tosside GB 11 C7
Tõstamaa EST 131 E7
Tostedt D 82 D7
Tószeg H 150 C5
Toszek PL 142 F6
Totana E 55 D10
Totebo S 93 D8
Tôtes F 18 E3
Totești RO 159 B10
Tótkomlós H 150 E6
Totland GB 13 D11
Totnes GB 13 E7
Totra S 103 E13
Tótszerdahely H 149 D7
Tøttdal N 105 C10
Tottijärvi FIN 127 C9
Totton GB 13 D12
Tótvázsony H 149 B9
Touça P 45 B6
Toucy F 25 E9
Touffailles F 33 B8
Touget F 33 C7
Toul F 26 C4
Toulon F 35 D10
Toulon-sur-Allier F 30 B3
Toulon-sur-Arroux F 30 B5
Toulouges F 34 E4
Toulouse F 33 C8
Tounj HR 156 B3
Touques F 23 B12
Tourch F 22 D4
Tourcoing F 19 C7
Tourlaville F 23 A8
Tournai B 19 C7
Tournan-en-Brie F 25 C8
Tournay F 33 D6
Tournecoupe F 33 C7
Tournefeuille F 33 C8
Tournon-d'Agenais F 33 B7
Tournon-St-Martin F 29 B7
Tournon-sur-Rhône F 30 E6
Tournus F 30 B6
Tourny F 24 B6
Tourouvre F 24 C4
Tours F 24 F4
Tourteron F 19 E10
Tourtoirac F 29 E8
Toury F 24 D6
Tous E 48 F3
Tõusi EST 131 D7
Touvois F 28 B2
Toužim CZ 76 B3
Tovačov CZ 146 C4
Tovariševo SRB 158 C3
Tovarné SK 145 F4
Tovarnik HR 157 B11
Toven N 108 D5
Tovrljane SRB 164 C3
Towcester GB 14 C7
Tower IRL 8 E5
Toymskardlia N 106 A5
Töysä FIN 123 E11
Traar D 183 C9
Trabada E 38 B5
Trabanca E 45 B8
Trabazos E 39 E7
Traben D 21 E8
Trąbki PL 144 D1
Trąbki Wielkie PL 138 B6
Traboch A 73 B10
Trabotivište MK 165 F6
Traby BY 137 E12
Trachili GR 175 B9
Tradate I 69 B6
Trädet S 91 D14
Trædal N 111 D14
Trafrask IRL 8 E3
Tragacete E 47 D9
Tragana GR 175 B7
Tragano GR 174 D3
Tragjas AL 168 D2
Tragwein A 77 F7
Traian RO 153 D10
Traian RO 155 C1
Traian RO 155 C2
Traian RO 160 E4
Traian RO 160 F6
Traian Vuia RO 151 F9
Traid E 47 C9
Traiguera E 42 F4
Train D 75 E10
Traînel F 25 D9
Traînou F 24 E7
Traisen A 77 F9
Traiskirchen A 77 F10
Traismauer A 77 F9
Traitsching D 75 D12
Trakai LT 137 D10
Trakovice SK 146 E5
Trakšėdžiai LT 134 F2
Tralee IRL 8 D3
Trá Li IRL 8 D3
Tramacastilla E 47 D9
Tramagal P 44 F4
Tramariglio I 64 B1
Tramatza I 64 C2
Tramayes F 30 C6
Tramelan CH 27 F7
Trá Mhór IRL 9 D8
Tramonti di Sopra I 73 D6
Tramonti di Sotto I 73 D6
Tramore IRL 9 D8
Tramutola I 60 C5
Tranås S 92 C5
Tranbjerg DK 86 C6
Trancoso P 44 C6
Tranebjerg DK 86 D7
Tranemo S 91 E13
Trången S 105 D15
Trånghalla S 92 D4
Trängslet S 102 D6
Trångsviken S 105 E16
Trani I 61 A6
Trannes F 25 D12
Tranovalto GR 169 D6
Tranøy N 111 D10
Trans F 23 D8
Trans-en-Provence F 36 D4
Transtrand S 102 D5
Transtrand S 102 E5
Tranum DK 86 A4
Tranvik S 99 D11
Trapani I 58 C2
Trapene LV 135 B13
Traplice CZ 146 C4
Trappes F 24 C7
Trarbach D 185 E7
Traryd S 87 B13
Trasacco I 62 D5
Träskvik FIN 122 F7
Trasmiras E 38 D4
Trasobares E 41 E8
Tratalias I 64 E2
Traun A 76 F6
Traunreut D 73 A6
Traunstein A 77 F8
Traunstein D 73 A6
Traupis LT 135 E9
Trava SLO 73 E10
Tråvad S 91 C13
Travagliato I 66 A1
Travanca do Mondego P 44 D4
Travassô P 44 C4
Travemünde D 83 C9
Travenbrück D 83 C8
Travers CH 31 B10
Traversetolo I 66 C1
Trávnica SK 146 E6
Travnik BIH 157 D8
Travo I 37 B11

Trawniki *PL* **141** H8
Trawsfynydd *GB* **10** F4
Trbovlje *SLO* **73** D11
Trbuk *BIH* **157** C9
Trebaseleghe *I* **72** E5
Trebatice *SK* **146** D5
Trebatsch *D* **80** B6
Třebechovice pod Orebem *CZ* **77** B9
Trebel *D* **83** E10
Treben *D* **79** D11
Třebenice *CZ* **76** B5
Trebenow *D* **84** D5
Trèbes *F* **33** D10
Trébeurden *F* **22** C4
Třebíč *CZ* **77** D9
Trebinje *BIH* **162** D5
Trebisacce *I* **61** D7
Trebišov *SK* **145** F4
Trebnje *SLO* **73** E11
Trebolle *E* **38** C4
Třeboň *CZ* **77** F6
Trebsen *D* **79** D12
Trebujena *E* **51** F7
Trebur *D* **21** E10
Trecastagni *I* **59** D7
Trecate *I* **68** C6
Trecchina *I* **60** C5
Trecenta *I* **66** B3
Tredegar *GB* **13** B8
Tredington *GB* **13** A11
Tredozio *I* **66** D4
Treehoo *IRL* **7** D8
Trefaldwyn *GB* **10** F5
Trefeglwys *GB* **10** F4
Treffen *A* **73** C8
Treffort-Cuisiat *F* **31** C7
Treffurt *D* **79** D7
Trefriw *GB* **10** E4
Trefynwy *GB* **13** B9
Tregaron *GB* **13** A7
Trégastel *F* **22** C4
Tregde *N* **90** C2
Tregnago *I* **66** A3
Tregony *GB* **12** E5
Trégueux *F* **22** D6
Tréguier *F* **22** C5
Trégunc *F* **22** E4
Tregynon *GB* **10** F5
Trehörna *S* **92** C5
Trehörningsjö *S* **107** D15
Treia *D* **82** A6
Treia *I* **67** F7
Treignac *F* **29** D9
Treigny *F* **25** E9
Treimani *EST* **131** F8
Treis *D* **185** D7
Trekanten *S* **89** B10
Treklyano *BG* **165** D6
Trélazé *F* **23** F11
Trelech *GB* **12** B6
Trélissac *F* **29** E7
Trelleborg *S* **87** E12
Trelleck *GB* **13** B9
Trélon *F* **19** D9
Tremadog *GB* **10** F3
Tremblay-les-Villages *F* **24** C5
Tremedal de Tormes *E* **45** B8
Tremelo *B* **19** C10
Trémentines *F* **23** F10
Tremês *F* **44** F3
Tréméven *F* **22** E4
Tremezzo *I* **69** B7
Trémolat *F* **29** F7
Třemošná *CZ* **76** C4
Trémouilles *F* **34** B4
Tremp *E* **42** C5
Trenance *GB* **12** E4
Trenčianska Turná *SK* **146** D6
Trenčianske Jastrabie *SK* **146** D6
Trenčianske Stankovce *SK* **146** D5
Trenčianske Teplice *SK* **146** D5
Trenčín *SK* **146** D6
Trendelburg *D* **21** A12
Trengereid *N* **94** B3
Trensacq *F* **32** B4
Trent *D* **84** A4
Trenta *SLO* **73** D8
Trentels *F* **33** B7
Trento *I* **69** A11
Tréon *F* **24** C5
Treorchy *GB* **13** B7
Trepča *HR* **148** F5
Treppeln *D* **81** B7
Trept *F* **31** D7
Trepuzzi *I* **61** C10
Trequanda *I* **66** F4
Tres Cantos *E* **46** C5
Trescléoux *F* **35** B10
Trescore Balneario *I* **69** B8
Tresenda *I* **69** A9
Tresfjord *N* **100** A6
Tresigallo *I* **66** C4
Tresjuncos *E* **47** E7
Treski *EST* **132** F2
Treskog *S* **97** C8
Trešnjevica *SRB* **158** F5
Tresnuraghes *I* **64** C2
Trespaderne *E* **40** C5
Tressait *GB* **5** B9
Třešť *CZ* **77** D9
Tretower *GB* **13** B8
Trets *F* **35** D10
Tretten *N* **101** D12
Treuchtlingen *D* **75** E8
Treuenbrietzen *D* **79** B12
Treungen *N* **90** A4
Trévé *F* **22** D6
Trevélez *E* **55** F6
Tréveray *F* **26** C3
Trèves *F* **34** B5
Trevi *I* **62** B3
Treviana *E* **40** C5
Trévières *F* **23** B10
Treviglio *I* **69** B8
Trevignano Romano *I* **62** C2
Trévillers *F* **27** F6
Treviño *E* **40** C6
Treviso *I* **72** E5
Trevllazër *AL* **168** C2
Trevões *P* **44** B6
Trévoux *F* **30** D6
Trézelles *F* **30** C4
Trgovište *SRB* **164** E5
Trhová Hradská *SK* **146** F5
Trhové Sviny *CZ* **77** E7
Trhoviště *SK* **145** F4
Trhový Štěpánov *CZ* **77** C8
Triacastela *E* **38** C4
Triaize *F* **28** C3

Trianta *GR* **181** D8
Triantaros *GR* **176** D5
Tribalj *HR* **67** B10
Tribanj-Krušćica *HR* **156** D3
Tribehou *F* **23** B9
Tribsees *D* **83** B13
Tribunj *HR* **156** E4
Tricarico *I* **60** B6
Tricase *I* **61** D10
Tricesimo *I* **73** D7
Trichiana *I* **72** D5
Tricot *F* **18** E6
Trieben *A* **73** A9
Triebes *D* **79** E11
Trie-Château *F* **18** F4
Trier *D* **21** E7
Trierweiler *D* **186** B2
Trieste *I* **73** E8
Trie-sur-Baïse *F* **33** D6
Trieux *F* **20** F5
Trifeşti *RO* **153** C10
Trifeşti *RO* **153** D9
Triftern *D* **76** F4
Trigaches *P* **50** C4
Trigance *F* **36** D4
Triggiano *I* **61** A7
Triglitz *D* **83** D12
Trignac *F* **23** F7
Trigrad *BG* **165** F9
Triguères *F* **25** E8
Trigueros *E* **51** E6
Trigueros del Valle *E* **39** E10
Triigi *EST* **130** D5
Trikala *GR* **169** E6
Trikáta *LV* **131** F11
Trikeri *GR* **175** A7
Trilj *HR* **157** E6
Trillevallen *S* **105** E14
Trillick *GB* **7** D8
Trillo *E* **47** C7
Trilofo *GR* **174** E5
Trilofos *GR* **169** D8
Trilport *F* **25** C8
Trim *IRL* **7** E9
Trimdon *GB* **5** F14
Trimley St Mary *GB* **15** D11
Trimmis *CH* **71** D9
Trimsaran *GB* **12** B6
Trindade *P* **38** F5
Trindade *P* **50** D4
Třinec *CZ* **147** B7
Tring *GB* **15** D8
Trinità d'Agultu *I* **64** B2
Trinitapoli *I* **60** A6
Trino *I* **68** C5
Trins *A* **72** B3
Trinta *P* **45** C6
Trinwillershagen *D* **83** B13
Triollo *E* **39** C10
Triora *I* **37** D7
Tripkau *D* **83** D10
Tripoli *GR* **174** D5
Tripotama *GR* **174** D4
Tripotamos *GR* **169** C7
Trippstadt *D* **21** F9
Triptis *D* **79** E10
Tritenii de Jos *RO* **152** D4
Trittau *D* **83** C8
Trittenheim *D* **21** E7
Trivalea-Moşteni *RO* **160** E6
Trivento *I* **63** D7
Trivero *I* **68** B5
Trivigno *I* **60** B5
Trizac *F* **29** E11
Trnakovac *HR* **157** B7
Trnava *CZ* **146** D5
Trnava *SK* **146** E5
Trnava *SRB* **158** F5
Trnavá Hora *SK* **147** D7
Trnjani *BIH* **157** C6
Trnovci *MK* **168** B5
Trnovec Bartolovečki *HR* **149** D6
Trnovec nad Váhom *SK* **146** E5
Trnovica *BIH* **157** F9
Trnovo *BIH* **157** E9
Tro *N* **108** E4
Troarn *F* **23** B11
Tröbitz *D* **80** C4
Trochtelfingen *D* **27** D11
Tröbje *S* **103** E13
Troense *DK* **86** E7
Trofa *P* **38** F2
Trofaiach *A* **73** B11
Trofors *N* **108** E5
Trogir *HR* **156** E5
Trøgstad *N* **95** C14
Troia *I* **60** A4
Tróia *P* **50** C2
Troianul *RO* **160** F6
Troina *I* **59** D6
Troisdorf *D* **21** C8
Troisfontaines *F* **186** D3
Trois-Ponts *B* **19** D12
Troissereux *F* **18** F5
Trois-Vèvres *F* **30** A3
Troisvierges *L* **20** D6
Troïtsoe *MD* **154** D4
Trojane *SLO* **73** D10
Trojanów *PL* **141** G6
Troldhede *DK* **86** D3
Trollbukta *N* **113** C19
Trollhättan *S* **91** C11
Trollvik *N* **112** D6
Tromello *I* **69** C6
Tromsdalen *N* **111** A16
Tromsø *N* **111** A16
Tromvik *N* **111** A15
Tronco *P* **38** E5
Trondenes *N* **111** C12
Trondheim *N* **104** E8
Trones *N* **105** B13
Trongisvágur *FO* **2** B3
Tronnes *N* **108** C8
Trönninge *S* **87** B11
Trönningeby *S* **87** A10
Trönö *S* **103** C12
Trontano *I* **68** A5
Tronvik *N* **105** D9
Tronville-en-Barrois *F* **26** C3
Troo *F* **24** E4
Troon *GB* **4** D7
Trooz *B* **183** D7
Tropaia *GR* **174** D4
Tropea *I* **59** B8
Trory *GB* **7** D7
Trosa *S* **93** B11
Troshan *AL* **163** F8
Trösken *S* **98** B7
Troškūnai *LT* **135** E9
Trošmarija *HR* **148** F4
Trossin *D* **79** C12
Tübingen *D* **27** C11
Tubize *B* **19** C9
Tubre *I* **71** D10
Tučepi *HR* **157** F7
Tüchen *D* **83** D12
Tüchorn *D* **79** B11
Tuchola *PL* **138** C4
Tuchomie *PL* **85** B11
Tuchów *PL* **144** D3
Tuchowicz *PL* **141** G6
Tuckur *FIN* **122** D8
Tuczna *PL* **141** G8
Tuczno *PL* **85** D10
Tudela *E* **41** D8

Tröstau *D* **75** B10
Trostberg *D* **75** F12
Trostyanets' *UA* **145** E9
Trostyanets' *UA* **153** A12
Troszyn *PL* **139** D12
Troubky *CZ* **146** C4
Troubsko *CZ* **77** D10
Troutbeck *GB* **10** C6
Trouville-sur-Mer *F* **23** B12
Trouy *F* **29** A10
Troviscal *P* **44** E4
Trowbridge *GB* **13** C10
Troyan *BG* **165** D10
Troyanovo *BG* **167** D8
Troyes *F* **25** D11
Troyits'ke *UA* **154** B6
Troyits'ke *UA* **154** D6
Troyon *F* **26** B3
Trpanj *HR* **157** F7
Trpezi *MNE* **163** D9
Trpinja *HR* **157** B10
Trsa *MNE* **157** F10
Trstená *SK* **147** C9
Trstené pri Hornáde *SK* **145** F3
Trstenik *HR* **162** D3
Trstenik *SRB* **163** B8
Trstice *SK* **146** E5
Trstín *SK* **146** D4
Trubar *BIH* **156** D5
Trubia *E* **39** B7
Truchas *E* **39** D7
Truchtershein *F* **27** C8
Trud *BG* **165** E10
Trudovets *BG* **165** D8
Trudy *BY* **133** F6
Trujillanos *E* **51** B7
Trujillo *E* **45** F9
Trulben *D* **27** B8
Trůn *BG* **165** D6
Trun *CH* **71** D7
Trun *F* **23** C12
Trůnchovitsa *BG* **165** C11
Trusetal *D* **79** E7
Truşeşti *RO* **153** B10
Trush *AL* **163** F7
Truskava *LT* **135** E8
Truskavets' *UA* **145** E8
Trústenik *BG* **161** F7
Trůstenik *BG* **165** C9
Trustrup *DK* **87** C7
Trutnov *CZ* **81** E9
Try *N* **90** C2
Tryavna *BG* **166** D4
Trybusivka *UA* **154** A3
Tryfos *GR* **174** B3
Tryggelev *DK* **83** A9
Trygona *S* **108** E5
Tryńcza *PL* **144** C5
Tryserum *S* **93** C9
Trysil *N* **102** D3
Tryškiai *LT* **134** D5
Trysunda *S* **107** E16
Tržac *BIH* **156** C4
Trzcianka *PL* **85** D10
Trzcianka *PL* **139** E12
Trzcianne *PL* **140** D7
Trzciel *PL* **81** B9
Trzebiatów *PL* **85** B8
Trzebiechów *PL* **81** B9
Trzebiel *PL* **81** C7
Trzebielino *PL* **85** B12
Trzebień *PL* **81** D7
Trzebieszów *PL* **141** G7
Trzebieszowice *PL* **77** B11
Trzebież *PL* **84** C7
Trzebinia *PL* **143** F7
Trzebiszewo *PL* **81** A8
Trzebnica *PL* **81** D12
Trzebownisko *PL* **144** C5
Trzeciewiec *PL* **138** D5
Trzemeszno *PL* **138** E4
Trzemeszno Lubuskie *PL* **81** B8
Trześcianka *PL* **140** E8
Trześniów *PL* **145** D4
Trzeszczany Pierwsze *PL* **144** B8
Tržič *SLO* **73** D9
Trzcińsko-Zdrój *PL* **84** E7
Trzyciąż *PL* **143** F8
Trzydnik Duży *PL* **144** B5
Tsagkarada *GR* **169** F9
Tsakarisianos *GR* **174** C2
Tsalapitsa *BG* **165** E10
Tsamantas *GR* **168** E3
Tsaparevo *BG* **169** A9
Tsareva Livada *BG* **166** D4
Tsarev Brod *BG* **167** C8
Tsarevo *BG* **167** E9
Tsarimir *BG* **165** E10
Tsaritsani *GR* **169** E7
Tsar Kaloyan *BG* **161** F9
Tsar-Petrovo *BG* **159** F10
Tschagguns *A* **71** C9
Tschernitz *D* **81** C7
Tsebrykove *UA* **154** C6
Tselina *BG* **166** E4
Tsenovo *BG* **166** C5
Tserovo *BG* **165** C7
Tsiistre *EST* **131** F14
Tsirguliina *EST* **131** F12
Tsivaras *GR* **178** E7
Sooru *EST* **131** F13
Tsotili *GR* **168** D5
Tsoukalades *GR* **174** B2
Tsvetino *BG* **165** F9
Tsyatserki *BY* **133** E2
Tua *N* **105** B13
Tuaim *IRL* **6** E5
Tuaim Beola *IRL* **6** F3
Tuam *IRL* **6** E5
Tuamgraney *IRL* **8** C5
Tubbercurry *IRL* **6** D5
Tubbergen *NL* **17** D7
Tubilla del Agua *E* **40** C4

Tudela de Duero *E* **40** E2
Tudora *RO* **153** B9
Tudor Vladimirescu *RO* **155** B1
Tudu *EST* **131** C13
Tudulinna *EST* **131** C13
Tudweiliog *GB* **10** F2
Tuejar *E* **47** E10
Tufeni *RO* **160** E5
Tufeşti *RO* **155** D1
Tuffé *F* **24** D4
Tufjord *N* **113** A12
Tuhkakylä *FIN* **125** B10
Tui *E* **38** D2
Tuili *I* **64** D2
Tuin *MK* **168** A5
Tuiskula *FIN* **122** E8
Tūja *LV* **135** B8
Tukhkala *RUS* **121** C16
Tukhol'ka *UA* **145** F7
Tukums *LV* **134** C6
Tula *I* **64** B2
Tulach Mhór *IRL* **7** F8
Tulare *SRB* **164** D3
Tuľawki *PL* **136** F2
Tulbing *A* **77** F10
Tulca *RO* **151** D8
Tulce *PL* **81** B12
Tulcea *RO* **155** C3
Tulčík *SK* **145** E3
Tulette *F* **35** B8
Tulghes *RO* **153** D7
Tuli *BIH* **162** D5
Tuliszków *PL* **142** B5
Tulje *BIH* **162** D5
Tulka *S* **99** B11
Tulla *IRL* **8** C5
Tullaghan *IRL* **6** D6
Tullamore *IRL* **7** F8
Tulle *F* **29** E9
Tulleby *DK* **87** F7
Tulleng *N* **111** A15
Tulleråsen *S* **105** E16
Tullingsås *S* **106** D9
Tullins *F* **31** E7
Tulln *A* **77** F10
Tullow *IRL* **9** C9
Tully *IRL* **7** E10
Tully *GB* **7** D8
Tullyallen *IRL* **7** E10
Tullyvin *IRL* **7** D8
Tulnici *RO* **153** C11
Tulos *RUS* **125** C14
Tulovo *BG* **166** D5
Tułowice *PL* **139** F9
Tułowice *PL* **142** E4
Tulppio *FIN* **115** C6
Tulsk *IRL* **6** E6
Tulstrup *DK* **87** D10
Tuluceşti *RO* **155** B2
Tumba *S* **93** A11
Tumbo *S* **98** D6
Tume *LV* **134** C6
Tummel Bridge *GB* **5** B8
Tumşupe *LV* **135** B9
Tun *S* **91** C12
Tunadal *S* **103** B13
Tuna-Hästberg *S* **97** B13
Tunari *RO* **161** D8
Tungozero *RUS* **121** C17
Tunnerstad *S* **92** C4
Tunnhovd *N* **95** B9
Tunnsjø-Røyrvika *N* **105** B14
Tunsjön *S* **107** E12
Tunstall *GB* **15** C11
Tuntenhausen *D* **72** A5
Tunvågen *S* **102** A8
Tuohikotti *FIN* **128** C7
Tuohikylä *FIN* **115** E5
Tuolluvaara *S* **116** C4
Tuomikylä *FIN* **122** E9
Tuomioja *FIN* **119** E14
Tuorila *FIN* **126** B6
Tuoro sul Trasimeno *I* **66** F5
Tuovilanlahti *FIN* **124** D3
Tupilați *RO* **153** C9
Tuplice *PL* **81** C7
Tuppurinmäki *FIN* **125** E10
Tura *H* **150** B4
Turanlar *TR* **177** D10
Turany *SK* **147** C8
Turawa *PL* **142** E5
Turba *EST* **131** C8
Turbe *BIH* **157** D8
Turbenthal *CH* **27** F10
Turburea *RO* **160** D3
Turceni *RO* **160** D2
Turcia *E* **39** C8
Turčianske Teplice *SK* **147** D7
Turcifal *P* **44** F2
Turcineşti *RO* **160** C2
Turcoaia *RO* **155** C2
Turda *RO* **152** D3
Turdaş *RO* **151** F11
Turégano *E* **46** B4
Turek *PL* **142** B6
Tureni *RO* **152** D3
Turenki *FIN* **127** D12
Turew *PL* **81** B11
Turgeliai *LT* **137** E12
Türgovishte *BG* **167** C7
Turgut *TR* **181** B8
Turgutbey *TR* **173** B7
Turgutlu *TR* **177** C10
Turgutreis *TR* **177** E9
Türi *EST* **131** D10
Turia *RO* **153** E8
Turić *BIH* **157** C10
Turie *SK* **147** C7
Turija *BIH* **157** C9
Turija *SRB* **158** B4
Turija *SRB* **159** D8
Turís *E* **48** F3
Turiya *BG* **166** D4
Türje *H* **149** C8
Turka *UA* **145** E7
Túrkeve *H* **150** C6
Türkgücü *TR* **173** B8
Turki *LV* **135** D12
Türkmenli *TR* **171** E10
Turkova *BY* **133** E4
Turkovići *BIH* **162** D4
Turku *FIN* **126** E7
Turlava *LV* **134** C3
Turleque *E* **46** E5
Turmantas *LT* **135** E12
Turmenti *BIH* **162** D5

Turna *LV* **131** F11
Tŭrnak *BG* **165** C9
Turnau *A* **148** A4
Tŭrnava *BG* **165** B8
Turnberry *GB* **4** E7
Turners Hill *GB* **15** E8
Turnhout *B* **16** F3
Turnišće *SLO* **149** C6
Turnov *CZ* **81** E8
Turnu Măgurele *RO* **160** F5
Turnu Roşu *RO* **152** F5
Turnu Ruieni *RO* **159** C9
Turobin *PL* **144** B6
Turosl *PL* **139** C12
Turośl *PL* **139** D12
Turów *PL* **141** G7
Turowo *PL* **85** C11
Turquel *P* **44** F3
Turrach *A* **73** C8
Turre *E* **55** E9
Turri *I* **64** D2
Turriff *GB* **3** K12
Turt *RO* **145** H7
Turtel *MK* **164** F6
Turtola *FIN* **117** E11
Turup *DK* **86** E5
Turupe *LV* **131** F11
Turzovka *SK* **147** C7
Tusa *I* **58** D5
Tuscania *I* **62** C1
Tuse *DK* **87** D9
Tušet *N* **105** A10
Tushilović *HR* **148** F5
Tuşnad *RO* **153** E7
Tussenhausen *D* **71** A11
Tüßling *D* **75** F12
Tuszów Narodowy *PL* **143** F11
Tuszyma *PL* **143** F12
Tuszyn *PL* **143** C8
Tutbury *GB* **11** F8
Tuţora *RO* **153** C11
Ţuţova *RO* **153** E11
Tutow *D* **84** C4
Tutrakan *BG* **161** E9
Tuttlingen *D* **27** E10
Tütüncü *TR* **173** D8
Tützpatz *D* **84** C4
Tuudi *EST* **130** D7
Tuukkala *FIN* **127** B16
Tuuliharju *FIN* **117** D13
Tuulimäki *FIN* **121** F11
Tuulos *FIN* **127** C12
Tuupovaara *FIN* **125** F15
Tuuri *FIN* **123** E11
Tuusjärvi *FIN* **125** E10
Tuusniemi *FIN* **125** E10
Tuusula *FIN* **127** E12
Tuv *N* **101** E8
Tuv *N* **108** B3
Tuvattnett *S* **106** D7
Tuvnes *N* **104** D5
Tuvnes *N* **108** E4
Tuvträsk *S* **107** B15
Tuxford *GB* **11** E10
Tuzburgazi *TR* **177** D9
Tuzculu *TR* **177** B8
Tŭzha *BG* **166** D4
Tuzi *MNE* **163** E7
Tužina *SK* **147** D7
Tuzla *BIH* **157** C10
Tuzla *RO* **155** E3
Tuzla *TR* **171** E10
Tužno *HR* **148** D6
Tuzora *MD* **154** C2
Tuzsér *H* **145** G5
Tvååker *S* **87** B11
Tváran *S* **118** C4
Tvärån *S* **118** C4
Tvärälund *S* **107** C17
Tvärråbäck *S* **107** A13
Tvärsele *S* **106** B8
Tvärskog *S* **89** B10
Tvede *DK* **86** B6
Tvedestrand *N* **90** B4
Tveit *N* **90** C3
Tveit *N* **94** D4
Tverai *LT* **134** E4
Tverečius *LT* **135** F13
Tverråga *N* **108** D7
Tverråmo *N* **109** B10
Tverrelmo *N* **111** C18
Tversted *DK* **90** D7
Tving *S* **89** C8
Tvis *DK* **86** C3
Tvøroyri *FO* **2** B3
Tvrdošín *SK* **147** C9
Tvrdošovce *SK* **146** E6
Tvŭrditsa *BG* **166** D5
Twardogóra *PL* **142** D3
Twatt *GB* **3** G10
Tweedmouth *GB* **5** D12
Tweedsmuir *GB* **5** D10
Twello *NL* **16** D6
Twist *D* **17** C9
Twistringen *D* **17** C11
Two Mile Borris *IRL* **9** C7
Twomileborris *IRL* **9** C7
Two Mile Bridge *IRL* **7** F8
Tworóg *PL* **142** E6
Twyford *GB* **13** C12
Twyford *GB* **15** E7
Twyning *GB* **13** A10
Tyachiv *UA* **145** G8
Tychero *GR* **171** B10
Tychówko *PL* **85** C10
Tychowo *PL* **85** C10
Tychy *PL* **143** F6
Tydal *N* **105** E11
Tydavnet *IRL* **7** D8
Tyfors *S* **97** B11
Tygelsjö *S* **87** D11
Tyinkrysset *N* **101** D8
Tylawa *PL* **145** E4
Tylissos *GR* **178** E9
Tyllinge *S* **93** B10
Tylmanowa *PL* **145** D1

Tylstrup *DK* **86** A5
Tymbark *PL* **144** D1
Tymień *PL* **85** B9
Tympaki *GR* **178** E6
Tynderö *S* **103** B14
Tyndrum *GB* **4** C7
Týnec nad Labem *CZ* **77** B8
Týnec nad Sázavou *CZ* **77** C7
Tynemouth *GB* **5** E14
Tyngsjö *S* **97** B10
Tyniewicze Małe *PL* **141** E8
Týniště nad Orlicí *CZ* **77** B10
Tynkä *FIN* **119** F12
Týn nad Vltavou *CZ* **77** D6
Tynset *N* **101** B13
Typpö *FIN* **119** F12
Typpyrä *FIN* **117** E14
Tyrämäki *FIN* **121** D12
Tyrawa Wołoska *PL* **145** D5
Tyresö *S* **99** D10
Tyringe *S* **87** C13
Tyristrand *N* **95** B12
Tyrjänsaari *FIN* **125** E15
Tyrnävä *FIN* **119** E15
Tyrnavos *GR* **169** E7
Tyrrellspass *IRL* **7** F8
Tyrväntö *FIN* **127** C11
Tysnes *N* **111** C19
Tysse *N* **94** B3
Tysse *N* **100** D2
Tyssebotnen *N* **100** E3
Tyssedal *N* **94** B5
Tystberga *S* **93** B10
Tyszowce *PL* **144** B8
Tytuvėnai *S* **134** E6
Tyukod *H* **145** H6
Tyulenovo *BG* **167** B10
Tywyn *GB* **10** F3
Tyykiluoto *FIN* **119** D14
Tzermiado *GR* **178** E9
Tzummarum *NL* **16** B5

U

Uachdar *GB* **2** L2
Uachtar Ard *IRL* **6** F4
Ub *SRB* **158** E5
Übach-Palenberg *D* **183** D8
Ubby *DK* **87** D8
Úbeda *E* **53** A10
Überherrn *D* **21** F7
Überlingen *D* **27** E11
Übersee *D* **72** A5
Ubli *HR* **162** D2
Ubli *MNE* **163** D7
Ubrique *E* **53** C6
Ubstadt-Weiher *D* **21** F11
Ucciani *F* **37** G9
Uccle *B* **19** C9
Ucea *RO* **152** F5
Uceda *E* **46** C5
Ucel *F* **35** A7
Ucero *E* **40** E5
Ucha *P* **38** E2
Uchanie *PL* **144** B8
Uchaux *F* **35** B8
Uchizy *F* **30** B6
Uchte *D* **17** D11
Üchtelhausen *D* **75** B7
Uchtspringe *D* **79** A10
Uckange *F* **186** C1
Uckfield *GB* **15** F9
Uckro *D* **80** C5
Uclés *E* **47** E7
Üçpınar *TR* **177** B9
Uda *RO* **160** D5
Udanin *PL* **81** D10
Udavské *SK* **145** F4
Udbina *HR* **156** C4
Udbyhøj *DK* **87** C7
Uddebo *S* **91** E13
Uddeholm *S* **97** B10
Uddel *NL* **183** A7
Uddevalla *S* **91** C10
Uddheden *S* **97** C8
Uddington *GB* **5** D9
Uden *NL* **16** E5
Udenhout *NL* **16** E4
Udenisht *AL* **168** C4
Uderns *A* **72** B4
Üdersdorf *D* **21** D7
Udeşti *RO* **153** B8
Udiča *SK* **146** C6
Udine *I* **73** D7
Udorpie *PL* **85** B13
Üdruma *EST* **131** D8
Udrycze *PL* **144** B7
Uebigau *D* **80** C4
Ueckermünde *D* **84** C6
Uehlfeld *D* **75** C7
Uelsen *D* **17** D7
Uelzen *D* **83** E9
Uetendorf *CH* **31** B12
Uetersen *D* **82** C7
Uettingen *D* **74** C6
Uetze *D* **79** B7
Uffculme *GB* **13** D8
Uffenheim *D* **75** C7
Uffing am Staffelsee *D* **72** A3
Uftrungen *D* **79** C8
Ugāle *LV* **134** B4
Ugao *SRB* **163** C9
Ugarana *E* **40** B6
Uge *DK* **86** F4
Ugelbølle *DK* **86** C6
Ugento *I* **61** D10
Ugerløse *DK* **87** D9
Uggdal *N* **94** B2
Uggelheden *S* **102** E3
Uggelhuse *DK* **86** C6
Uggerby *DK* **90** D7
Uggersløv *DK* **86** D7
Uggiano la Chiesa *I* **61** C10
Ugíjar *E* **55** F6
Ugine *F* **31** D9
Uglev *DK* **86** B3
Ugljan *HR* **67** D11
Ugljane *HR* **157** E6
Ugod *H* **149** B9
Ugŭrchin *BG* **165** D10
Uğurlu *TR* **171** D9
Uharte-Arakil *E* **32** E2
Uhingen *D* **74** E6
Uhldingen *D* **27** E11
Uhlířské Janovica *CZ* **77** C8
Uhlstädt *D* **79** E9

Uhniv *UA* **144** C8
Uhtna *EST* **131** C13
Uhyst *D* **81** D7
Uig *GB* **2** K4
Uimaharju *FIN* **125** E14
Uimila *FIN* **127** C15
Uitgeest *NL* **16** C3
Uithoorn *NL* **16** D3
Uithuizen *NL* **17** B7
Uivar *RO* **159** B6
Ujazd *PL* **141** G1
Ujazd *PL* **142** F5
Ujezd *CZ* **77** C12
Ujezd *CZ* **146** C5
Újfehértó *H* **151** B8
Újhartyán *H* **150** C3
Újkér *H* **149** B7
Újkígyós *H* **151** D7
Újléta *H* **151** C8
Újsoły *PL* **147** C8
Újszalonta *H* **151** D7
Újszász *H* **150** C5
Újszentiván *H* **150** E5
Újszentmargita *H* **151** B7
Újszilvás *H* **150** C5
Újtikos *H* **145** H3
Újudvar *H* **149** C7
Ukhozhany *UA* **154** A5
Ukkola *FIN* **125** E14
Ukmergė *LT* **135** F9
Ukri *LV* **134** D6
Ula *BY* **133** F6
Ula *I* **103** A14
Ulan-Majorat *PL* **141** G6
Ulanów *PL* **144** C5
Ulaş *TR* **173** B8
Ulassai *I* **64** D4
Ula Tirso *I* **64** C2
Ulbjerg *DK* **86** B4
Ulbroka *LV* **135** C8
Ulcinj *MNE* **163** F7
Uldum *DK* **86** D5
Ulefoss *N* **95** D10
Uleila del Campo *E* **55** E8
Ülenurme *EST* **131** E13
Ulëz *AL* **163** F8
Ulfborg *DK* **86** C2
Ulft *NL* **16** E6
Ulhówek *PL* **144** C8
Uličь *SK* **145** F5
Ulicoten *NL* **182** C5
Ulies *RO* **152** E6
Ulieşti *RO* **161** D6
Ulila *EST* **131** E12
Uljanik *HR* **149** E8
Uljma *SRB* **159** C7
Ullånger *S* **107** E14
Ullapool *GB* **2** K6
Ullared *S* **87** A11
Ullatti *S* **116** C7
Ullava *FIN* **123** C11
Ullbergsträsk *S* **107** A17
Ulldecona *E* **42** F4
Ulldemolins *E* **42** E5
Ullersløv *DK* **86** E7
Ullervad *S* **91** B14
Üllés *H* **150** E4
Ulleskelf *GB* **11** D9
Ullisjaur *S* **107** A13
Ullits *DK* **86** B4
Üllő *H* **150** C3
Ullsfjord *N* **111** A18
Ulm *D* **74** F6
Ulma *RO* **152** B6
Ulmbach *D* **74** B5
Ulme *P* **44** F4
Ulmen *D* **21** D7
Ulmeni *RO* **151** C11
Ulmeni *RO* **161** D10
Ulmeni *RO* **161** E9
Ulmi *RO* **161** D6
Ulmu *RO* **161** D10
Ulmu *RO* **161** E9
Ulog *BIH* **157** F9
Uløybukta *N* **112** D6
Ulricehamn *S* **91** D13
Ulrichsberg *A* **76** E5
Ulrichstein *D* **21** C12
Ulrika *S* **92** C5
Ulriksberg *S* **97** B12
Ulriksfors *S* **106** D9
Ulrum *NL* **16** B6
Ulsberg *N* **101** A11
Ulsta *GB* **3** D14
Ulsted *DK* **86** A6
Ulsteinvik *N* **100** B3
Ulstrup *DK* **86** C5
Ulstrup *DK* **87** D7
Ulsvåg *N* **111** D10
Ultrå *S* **107** E16
Uluabat *TR* **173** D9
Ulucak *TR* **177** C9
Ulucak *TR* **181** A7
Ulvåker *S* **91** C14
Ulvenhout *NL* **16** E3
Ulverston *GB* **10** C5
Ulvik *N* **100** E5
Ulvila *FIN* **126** C6
Ulvöhamn *S* **107** E15
Ulvsjön *S* **102** C7
Ulvsjön *S* **103** B11
Ulvvik *S* **103** A14
Ul'yanovka *UA* **154** A4
Ul'yanovo *RUS* **136** D5
Umag *HR* **67** B8
Umberleigh *GB* **12** D7
Umbertide *I* **66** F5
Umbrărești *RO* **153** F10
Umbriatico *I* **61** E7
Umbukta *N* **108** D4
Umčari *SRB* **158** D6
Umeå *S* **122** C4
Umfors *S* **108** D4
Umgransele *S* **107** B14
Umhausen *A* **71** C11
Umin Dol *MK* **164** E4
Umka *SRB* **158** D5
Umkirch *D* **27** D8
Umljanović *HR* **156** E5
Ummeljoki *FIN* **128** D6
Ummern *D* **79** A7
Umnäs *S* **109** F14
Ümraniye *TR* **173** D11
Umurbey *TR* **172** D6
Umurga *LV* **135** A9
Uña *E* **47** D9
Uña de Quintana *E* **39** D7

Unaja FIN 126 C6
Únanov CZ 77 E10
Unapool GB 2 J6
Unari FIN 117 D15
Unbyn S 118 C7
Uncastillo E 32 F3
Undenäs S 92 B4
Undereidet N 112 D9
Underfossen N 113 C18
Undersåker S 105 E14
Undingen D 27 D11
Undløse DK 87 D9
Undva EST 130 D3
Undy GB 13 B9
Unelanperä FIN 120 F9
Ungerhausen D 71 A10
Ungheni MD 153 C11
Ungheni RO 152 E4
Ungheni RO 160 E5
Ungra RO 152 F6
Unguraşl RO 152 C4
Ungureni RO 153 B9
Ungureni RO 153 D10
Ungurpils LV 131 F9
Unhais da Serra P 44 D5
Unhais-o-Velho P 44 D5
Unhošť CZ 76 B6
Uničov CZ 77 C12
Uniejów PL 142 C6
Unieux F 30 E5
Unín SK 146 D4
Unirea RO 152 E3
Unirea RO 155 C1
Unirea RO 155 F3
Unirea RO 159 B10
Unirea RO 159 E11
Unirea RO 161 E11
Unisław PL 138 D5
Unkel D 21 C8
Unken A 73 A6
Unlingen D 71 A9
Unna D 17 E9
Unnaryd S 87 B13
Unnau D 185 C8
Unntorp S 102 D7
Unset N 101 C14
Unsholtet N 101 A14
Unstad N 110 D6
Untamala FIN 122 D9
Untamala FIN 126 D6
Unțeni RO 153 B9
Unterägeri CH 27 F10
Unterammergau D 71 B12
Unterdießen D 71 B11
Untergriesbach D 76 E5
Unterhaching D 75 F10
Unterkulm CH 27 F9
Unterlüß D 83 E8
Untermaßfeld D 75 A7
Untermerzbach D 75 B8
Untermünkheim D 74 D6
Unterneukirchen D 75 F12
Unterpleichfeld D 75 C7
Unterreit D 75 F11
Unterschächen CH 71 D7
Unterschleißheim D 75 F10
Untersiemau D 75 B8
Untersteinach D 75 B10
Unterweißenbach A 77 F7
Unterwössen D 72 A5
Unverre F 24 D5
Upavon GB 13 C11
Upenieki LV 134 C5
Upenieki LV 135 D12
Upesgrīva LV 134 B6
Upgant-Schott D 17 A8
Úpice CZ 77 A10
Upinniemi FIN 127 E11
Uplyme GB 13 D9
Upninkai LT 137 C10
Upper Knockando GB 3 L10
Upperlands GB 4 F3
Upphärad S 91 C11
Uppingham GB 11 F10
Upplanda S 99 B9
Upplands-Väsby S 99 C9
Uppsala S 99 C9
Uppsälje S 97 A11
Uppsete N 100 E5
Uppsjö S 103 C12
Upton upon Severn GB 13 A10
Upyna LT 134 E5
Upyna LT 134 F4
Upytė LT 135 E8
Urafirth GB 3 E14
Urago d'Oglio I 69 B8
Uraiújfalu H 149 B7
Uras I 64 D2
Ura Vajgurore AL 168 C2
Uraz PL 81 D11
Urbach D 21 C9
Urbania I 66 E6
Urbar D 185 D8
Urbe I 37 C9
Urberach D 187 B6
Urbino I 66 E6
Urbisaglia I 67 F7
Urbise F 30 C4
Určice CZ 77 D12
Urda E 46 F5
Urdari RO 160 D2
Urdax-Urdazuli E 32 D2
Urdorf CH 27 F9
Urdos F 32 E4
Urduña E 40 C6
Ure N 110 D6
Urecheni RO 153 C9
Urechești RO 153 E10
Urechești RO 161 B10
Urë e Shtrenjtë AL 163 E8
Urepel F 32 D3
Ureterp NL 16 B6
Urga LV 131 F9
Úrhida H 149 B10
Úri H 150 C4
Uri I 64 B2
Uricani RO 159 C11
Uriménil F 26 D5
Uringe S 93 A11
Uriu RO 152 C4
Urjala FIN 127 C10
Urk NL 16 C5
Ürkmez TR 177 C8
Úrkút H 149 B9
Urla TR 177 C8
Urlațl RO 161 D8
Urlingford IRL 9 C7
Urmeniș RO 152 D4
Urmince SK 146 D6
Urnäsch CH 27 F11
Urnieta E 32 D2
Üröm H 150 B3
Urovica SRB 159 E9
Urrea de Gaén E 42 E3
Urrea de Jalón E 41 E9
Urretxu E 32 D1
Urriés E 32 E3
Urros P 45 B6
Urroz E 32 E3
Urrugne F 32 D2
Ursberg D 71 A10
Ursensollen D 75 D10
Urshult S 89 B7
Ursviken S 118 E6
Urszulin PL 141 H8
Urt F 32 D3
Urtenen CH 31 A11
Urtimjaur S 116 E5
Urueña E 39 E9
Ururi I 63 D8
Urville Nacqueville F 23 A8
Urzjdów PL 144 B5
Urzica RO 160 F4
Urziceni RO 151 B9
Urziceni RO 161 D9
Urzicuța RO 160 E3
Urzulei I 64 C4
Urzy F 30 A3
Usagre E 51 C7
Ušari BIH 157 C7
Ušće SRB 163 C10
Uschlag (Staufenberg) D 78 D6
Uście Gorlickie PL 145 D3
Uście Solne PL 143 F10
Uscio I 37 C10
Usedom D 84 C5
Usellus I 64 D2
Useras E 48 D4
Ushachy BY 133 F5
Ušl LV 130 F5
Usingen D 21 D11
Usini I 64 B2
Usk GB 13 B9
Uskali FIN 125 F14
Uskedal N 94 C3
Üsküdar TR 173 B11
Üsküp TR 167 F8
Uslar D 78 C6
Usma LV 134 B4
Úsov CZ 77 C12
Uspenivka UA 154 E5
Usquert NL 17 B7
Ussana I 64 E3
Ussassai I 64 D3
Usseglio I 31 E11
Ussel F 29 D10
Ussel F 30 E2
Usson-du-Poitou F 29 C7
Usson-en-Forez F 30 E4
Ustaoset N 95 B8
Ustaritz F 32 D3
Ust'-Chorna UA 145 G8
Ust'-Dolyssy RUS 133 D7
Úštěk CZ 80 E6
Uster CH 27 F10
Ustibar BIH 163 B7
Ustica I 58 B3
Ustikotlina BIH 157 E10
Ústí nad Labem CZ 80 E6
Ústí nad Orlicí CZ 77 C10
Ustiprača BIH 157 E11
Ustirama BIH 157 E8
Ustka PL 85 A11
Ust'-Luga RUS 132 B3
Ustou F 33 E8
Ustovo BG 171 A7
Ustrem BG 167 E6
Ustroń PL 147 B7
Ustronie Morskie PL 85 B9
Ustrzyki Dolne PL 145 E6
Ustya UA 154 A5
Ustyluh UA 144 B9
Usurbil E 32 D1
Uszew PL 144 D2
Uszód H 149 C11
Utajärvi FIN 119 E16
Utåker N 94 C3
Utakleiv N 110 D6
Utanede S 103 A12
Utanen FIN 119 E16
Utansjö S 103 A14
Utanskog S 107 E14
Utarp D 17 A8
Utbjoa N 94 C3
Utebo E 41 E10
Utelle F 37 D6
Utena LT 135 F11
Utersum D 82 A4
Uthaug N 104 D7
Uthleben D 79 D8
Uthlede D 17 B11
Utiel E 47 E10
Utne N 94 B5
Utö S 93 B12
Utoropy UA 152 A6
Utrecht NL 16 D4
Utrera E 51 E8
Utrillas E 42 F2
Utrine SRB 150 F4
Utro N 104 C8
Utsjoki FIN 113 D18
Utskor N 110 C8
Uttendorf A 72 B6
Uttendorf A 76 F4
Uttenweiler D 71 A9
Utterbyn S 97 B9
Utterliden S 109 F17
Uttersberg S 97 C14
Uttersjö S 107 D14
Utterslev DK 87 F8
Utti FIN 128 D6
Utting am Ammersee D 71 A12
Uttoxeter GB 11 F8
Utula FIN 129 C9
Utvalnäs S 103 E13
Utvik N 100 C5
Utvorda N 105 B9
Utzedel D 84 C4
Uuemõisa EST 130 D7
Uukuniemi FIN 129 B13
Uulu EST 131 E9
Uura FIN 121 F10
Uurainen FIN 123 E14
Uuro FIN 122 F8
Uusikaarlepyy FIN 122 C9
Uusikartano FIN 126 D7
Uusikaupunki FIN 126 D5
Uusikylä FIN 123 D12
Uusikylä FIN 127 D15
Uusi-Värtsilä FIN 125 F14
Uva FIN 121 E11
Uvac BIH 158 F4
Uvåg N 110 C8
Úvaly CZ 77 B7
Uvanå S 97 B10
Uvdal N 95 B9
Üvecik TR 171 E10
Uvernet-Fours F 36 C5
Uv'jaråtto N 113 D12
Uxbridge GB 15 D8
Uxeau F 30 B5
Üxheim D 21 D7
Uyeasound GB 3 D15
Uza F 32 B3
Užava LV 134 B2
Uzdin SRB 158 C6
Uzel F 22 D6
Uzer F 35 A7
Uzerche F 29 E9
Uzès F 35 B7
Uzhhorod UA 145 F5
Uzhok UA 145 F6
Užice SRB 158 F4
Uzlovoye RUS 136 D5
Uznovë AL 168 C2
Užpaliai LT 135 E11
Uzrechcha BY 133 F3
Uzundzhovo BG 166 F5
Uzunköprü TR 172 B6
Uzunkuyu TR 177 C8
Užventis LT 134 E5

V

Vaadinselkä FIN 115 E5
Vaajakoski FIN 123 F15
Vaajasalmi FIN 124 E7
Vääkiö FIN 121 D12
Vaala FIN 119 E17
Vaalajärvi FIN 117 D16
Vaale D 82 C6
Vaalimaa FIN 128 D8
Vaals NL 20 C6
Vaarakylä FIN 121 C11
Vaarankylä FIN 121 F10
Vaaranniva FIN 121 D11
Vaaraperä FIN 121 C13
Vaaraslahti FIN 123 D17
Väärinmaja FIN 124 G2
Vaas F 24 E3
Vaasa FIN 122 D7
Vaassen NL 16 D5
Väätäiskylä FIN 123 E13
Väätsa EST 131 D10
Vaattojärvi FIN 117 D12
Vabalninkas LT 135 E9
Vabole LV 135 D12
Vabre F 33 C10
Vabres-l'Abbaye F 34 C4
Vác H 150 B3
Văcărești RO 161 D6
Vaccarizzo Albanese I 61 D6
Váchartyán H 150 B3
Vacheresse F 31 C10
Vachlia GR 174 D4
Väckelsång S 89 B7
Vacov CZ 76 D5
Vacqueyras F 35 B8
Vácrátót H 150 B3
Văculești RO 153 B8
Vad RO 152 C3
Vad S 97 B14
Vadakste LV 134 D5
Vadaktai LT 135 E7
Vădastra RO 160 F4
Vădăstrița RO 160 F4
Vaddas gruver N 112 D8
Vădeni RO 155 C1
Väderstad S 92 C5
Vad Foss N 90 B5
Vadheim N 100 D3
Vadla N 94 D4
Vadocondes E 40 E4
Vadokliai LT 135 F8
Vado Ligure I 37 C8
Vadskinn N 111 C11
Vadsø N 114 C7
Vadstena S 92 C5
Vadu Crișului RO 151 D10
Vadu lui Isac MD 155 B2
Vadu Izei RO 145 H8
Vadul lui Vodă MD 154 C4
Vadul Turcului MD 154 B3
Vadum DK 86 A5
Vadu Moldovei RO 153 C8
Vadu Moților RO 151 E10
Vadu Pașii RO 161 C9
Vaduz FL 71 C9
Vadžgirys LT 134 F5
Væggerløse DK 83 A11
Vafaiika GR 171 B7
Vafiochori GR 169 B8
Våg N 94 D2
Vågaholmen N 108 C5
Vågåmo N 101 C10
Vagan BIH 157 D6
Vågan N 111 B14
Vågdalen S 106 D9
Våge N 94 B3
Våge N 94 G6
Vaggatem N 114 E6
Vaggeryd S 92 E4
Vågholmane N 100 A4
Vagia GR 175 C7
Văgiulești RO 159 D11
Vaglia I 66 E3
Vaglio Basilicata I 60 B5
Vagli Sotto I 66 D1
Vagney F 26 D6
Vagnhärad S 93 B11
Vagnsunda S 99 C11
Vagos P 44 C3
Vågseidet N 100 E2
Vägsele S 107 B14
Vågsodden N 108 E3
Vágur FO 2 C3
Vähäjoki FIN 119 B14
Vähäkangas FIN 123 B13
Vähäkyrö FIN 122 D8
Vähäniva FIN 116 B9
Vahanka FIN 123 E13
Vahastu EST 131 D10
Vahenurme EST 131 D8
Vähikkälä FIN 127 D12
Vahojärvi FIN 127 B9
Váhovce SK 146 E5
Vahterpää FIN 127 E15
Vahto FIN 126 D7
Vaiamonte P 44 F6
Vaiano I 66 E3
Vaickūniškės LT 137 D10
Vaida EST 131 C9
Vaidava LV 135 B10
Vaideeni RO 160 C3
Vaidotai LT 137 D11
Vaiges F 23 D11
Vaiguva LT 134 E5
Väike-Maarja EST 131 C12
Väike-Pungerja EST 131 C14
Vaikijaur S 116 E3
Vaikko FIN 125 D11
Vailly-sur-Aisne F 19 F8
Vailly-sur-Sauldre F 25 F8
Vaimastvere EST 131 D12
Väimela EST 131 F14
Vaimõisa EST 131 D8
Vainikkala FIN 129 D9
Vaiņode LV 134 D3
Vainotiškiai LT 134 F7
Vainupea EST 131 B12
Vairano Patenora I 60 A2
Vairano Scalo I 60 A2
Väisälä FIN 121 E11
Vaison-la-Romaine F 35 B9
Vaïssac F 33 B9
Vaišvydava LT 137 D9
Vaivio FIN 125 E12
Vaivre-et-Montoille F 26 E5
Vaja H 145 H5
Vajangu EST 131 C12
Vajdácska H 145 G4
Våje N 90 B4
Våje N 110 D5
Vajkal AL 168 A3
Vajmat S 109 C18
Vajska SRB 157 B11
Vajszló H 149 E9
Vajta H 149 C11
Vakarel BG 165 D8
Vakern S 97 B11
Vakiflar TR 173 B8
Vaklino BG 155 F2
Vaksdal N 94 B3
Vaksevo BG 165 E6
Vaksince MK 164 E4
Vál H 149 B11
Valada P 44 F3
Vålådalen S 105 E13
Valadares P 38 D3
Valajanaapa FIN 119 C15
Valajaskoski FIN 119 B14
Valaliky SK 145 F3
Valand N 90 C2
Valandovo MK 169 B8
Vålånger S 103 A14
Valanida GR 169 E7
Valanjou F 23 F10
Valareña E 41 D9
Vålåsjø N 101 B10
Valaská SK 147 D9
Valaská Belá SK 146 D6
Valašská Bystřice CZ 146 C6
Valašská Polanka CZ 146 C5
Valašské Klobouky CZ 146 C6
Valašské Meziříčí CZ 146 C5
Vålax FIN 127 E14
Valberg F 36 C5
Valberg N 110 D6
Vålberg S 97 D9
Valbiska HR 67 B9
Valbo S 103 E13
Valbom P 44 B3
Valbona E 48 D3
Valbondione I 69 A9
Valbonë AL 163 E8
Valbonnais F 31 F8
Valbonne F 36 D6
Valbuena de Duero E 40 E3
Valča SK 147 C7
Valcabrère F 33 D7
Valcău de Jos RO 151 C10
Vâlcele RO 153 F7
Vâlcele RO 160 E5
Vâlcelele RO 161 C10
Vâlcelele RO 161 E10
Valdagno I 69 B11
Valdahon F 26 F5
Valdaora I 72 C5
Valddak N 113 C14
Valdealgorfa E 42 E3
Valdeblore F 37 C6
Valdecaballeros E 45 F10
Valdecañas de Tajo E 45 E9
Valdecarros E 45 C10
Valdecilla E 40 B4
Valdecuenca E 47 D10
Valdefuentes E 45 F8
Valdeganga E 47 F9
Valdekl LV 134 C5
Valdelacasa E 45 C9
Valdelacasa de Tajo E 45 E10
Valdelamusa E 51 D6
Valdelinares E 48 D3
Valdemanco del Esteras E 54 B3
Valdemārpils LV 134 B5
Valdemarsvik S 93 C9
Valdemeca E 47 D9
Valdemorillo E 46 C4
Valdemoro E 46 D5
Valdemoro-Sierra E 47 D9
Valdenoches E 47 C6
Valdeobispo E 45 D8
Valdeolivas E 47 C8
Valdepeñas E 55 B6
Valdepeñas de Jaén E 53 A9
Valderas E 39 D9
Val-de-Reuil F 18 F3
Valderice I 58 C2
Valderiès F 33 B10
Valderøy N 100 A4
Valderrobres E 42 F4
Val de Santo Domingo E 46 D4
Valdestillas E 39 F10
Valdetormo E 42 F4
Valdetorres E 51 B7
Valdeverdeja E 45 E10
Valdevimbre E 39 D8
Valdgale LV 134 B5
Valdice CZ 77 B8
Valdidentro I 71 E10
Valdilecha E 47 D6
Val-d'Isère F 31 E10
Valdisotto I 71 E10
Valdivienne F 29 B7
Val-d'Izé F 23 D9
Valdobbiadene I 72 E4
Valdoie F 27 E6
Valdunquillo E 39 D9
Vale GBG 22 B6
Våle N 95 D12
Våle S 103 A8
Valea Adîncă MD 154 A3
Valea Argovei RO 161 E9
Valea Călugărească RO 161 D8
Valea Chioarului RO 151 C11
Valea Ciorii RO 161 D11
Valea Crișului RO 153 F7
Valea Danului RO 160 C5
Valea Doftanei RO 161 C7
Valea Dragului RO 161 E8
Valea Ierii RO 151 D11
Valea Largă RO 152 D4
Valea lui Mihai RO 151 B9
Valea Lungă RO 152 E4
Valea Lungă RO 161 C7
Valea Măcrișului RO 161 D9
Valea Mare MD 153 C11
Valea Mare RO 160 D3
Valea Mare RO 160 D6
Valea Mare RO 160 E4
Valea Mare-Pravăț RO 160 C6
Valea Mărului RO 153 F11
Valea Moldovei RO 153 C8
Valea Nucarilor RO 155 C3
Valea Râmnicului RO 161 C10
Valea Salciei RO 161 C9
Valea Sării RO 153 F9
Valea Seacă RO 153 C9
Valea Seacă RO 153 E10
Valea Stanciului RO 160 F3
Valea Teilor RO 155 C3
Valea Ursului RO 153 D10
Valea Viilor RO 152 E4
Valea Vinului RO 151 B11
Vale da Rosa P 50 E4
Vale das Mós P 44 F4
Vale de Açor P 44 F5
Vale de Açor P 50 D4
Vale de Cambra P 44 C4
Vale de Cavalos P 44 F3
Vale de Espinho P 45 D7
Vale de Estrela P 45 C6
Vale de Figueira P 44 F3
Vale de Lobo P 50 E3
Vale de Prazeres P 44 D6
Vale de Reis P 50 C3
Vale de Salgueiro P 38 E5
Vale de Santarém P 44 F3
Vale do Peso P 44 F5
Válega P 44 C3
Valeggio sul Mincio I 66 B2
Valen N 94 C3
Valença P 38 D2
Valença do Douro P 44 B5
Valençay F 24 F6
Valence F 30 F6
Valence F 33 B7
Valence-d'Albigeois F 33 B10
Valence-sur-Baïse F 33 C6
Valencia E 48 F4
Valencia de Alcántara E 45 F6
Valencia de Don Juan E 39 D8
Valencia de las Torres E 51 C7
Valencia del Mombuey E 51 C5
Valencia del Ventoso E 51 C7
Valenciennes F 19 D8
Văleni RO 153 D11
Văleni RO 160 E5
Vălenii de Munte RO 161 C8
Valensole F 35 C10
Valentano I 62 B1
Valentigney F 27 F6
Valenza I 37 A9
Valenzano I 61 A7
Valenzuela E 53 A8
Valenzuela de Calatrava E 54 B5
Våler N 95 D13
Våler N 101 E15
Valera de Arriba E 47 E8
Valernes F 35 B10
Vales Mortos P 50 D5
Valestrand N 94 A2
Valevåg N 94 C2
Valfabbrica I 66 F6
Valfarta E 42 D3
Valfroicourt F 26 D5
Valfurva I 71 E10
Valga EST 131 F12
Valgalciems LV 134 B5
Valgale LV 134 B4
Valgrisenche I 31 D11
Valgu EST 131 D9
Valguarnera Caropepe I 58 E5
Valgunde LV 134 C7
Valhelhas P 44 D6
Valhermoso E 47 C9
Vålhovd N 101 E12
Välijoki FIN 119 B15
Välikangas FIN 119 B16
Väli-Kannus FIN 123 C11
Valikardhë AL 168 A3
Välikylä FIN 123 C11
Valimi GR 174 C5
Välitalo FIN 117 C16
Văliug RO 159 C9
Väli-Viirre FIN 123 C11
Valjala EST 130 E5
Valjevo SRB 158 E4
Valjok N 113 D16
Valjunquera E 42 F4
Valka LV 131 F12
Valkeajärvi FIN 123 F12
Valkeakoski FIN 127 C11
Valkeakoski S 117 E11
Valkeala FIN 128 D6
Valkeiskylä FIN 124 C8
Valkeiskylä FIN 125 D10
Valkenburg NL 19 C12
Valkenswaard NL 16 F4
Valkininkai LT 137 E10
Valkla EST 131 C10
Valko FIN 127 E15
Valkó H 150 B4
Valla S 93 A8
Valla S 107 E10
Valladolid E 39 E10
Valladolises E 56 F2
Vállaj H 151 B9
Vallåkra S 87 D11
Vallargärdet S 97 D10
Vallata I 60 A4
Vallauris F 36 D6
Vallberga S 87 C12
Vallbo S 105 E14
Vallbona d'Anoia E 43 D7
Vallda S 91 E10
Valldal N 100 B6
Vall d'Alba E 48 D4
Valldemossa E 49 E10
Valle E 40 B3
Valle LV 135 C9
Valle N 90 A2
Valle N 90 B6
Valle N 108 B6
Valle Castellana I 62 B5
Vallecorsa I 62 E4
Valle de Abdalajís E 53 C7
Valle de la Serena E 51 B8
Valle de Matamoros E 51 C6
Valle de Santa Ana E 51 C6
Valle di Cadore I 72 D5
Valledolmo I 58 D4
Valledoria I 64 B2
Valleiry F 31 C8
Vallelunga Pratameno I 58 D4
Valle Mosso I 68 B5
Vallen S 107 D11
Vallen S 118 F6
Vallenca E 47 D10
Vallendar D 185 D8
Vallentuna S 99 C10
Vallerås S 102 E6
Valleraugue F 35 B6
Vallermosa I 64 E2
Vallerotonda I 62 D5
Vallersund N 104 D7
Vallervatnet N 105 B15
Vallet F 23 F9
Valley D 72 A4
Valley GB 10 E2
Vallfogona de Riucorb E 42 D6
Vallières F 29 D10
Vallioniemi FIN 121 B12
Vallmoll E 42 E6
Valløby DK 87 E10
Vallo della Lucania I 60 C4
Vallo di Nera I 62 B3
Valloire F 31 E9
Vallombrosa I 66 E4
Vallon-en-Sully F 29 B11
Vallon-Pont-d'Arc F 35 B7
Vallorbe CH 31 B9
Vallorcine F 31 C10
Vallouise F 31 F9
Vallrun S 105 D16
Valls E 42 E6
Vallsbo S 103 E12
Vallsjön S 103 A11
Vallsta S 103 C11
Vallstena S 93 D13
Vallvik S 103 D13
Valmadrera I 69 B7
Valmadrid E 41 F10
Valmen N 101 D15
Valmiera LV 131 F10
Valmiermuiža LV 131 F10
Valmojado E 46 D4
Valmont F 18 E2
Valmontone I 62 D3
Valmorel F 31 E9
Valmy F 25 B12
Valnes N 108 B7
Valognes F 23 A9
Valongo P 44 B4
Valongo P 44 F5
Válor E 55 F6
Valoria la Buena E 40 E2
Valøy N 105 B9
Valøy N 105 C11
Valpaços P 38 E5
Valpalmas E 41 D10
Valpelline I 31 D11
Valperga I 68 C4
Valpovo HR 149 E10
Valpperi FIN 126 D7
Valras-Plage F 34 D5
Valréas F 35 B8
Valros F 34 D5
Vals CH 71 D8
Valsavarenche I 31 D11
Vålse DK 87 F9
Valseca E 46 B4
Valsequillo E 51 C9
Valsgård DK 86 B5
Valsgarth GB 3 D15
Valshed S 103 E9
Valsinni I 61 C6
Valsjöbyn S 105 C16
Valsjön S 103 B11
Valška SRB 158 E6
Valskog S 97 D14
Vals-les-Bains F 35 A7
Valsøybotn N 104 E5
Välsta S 103 C13
Valstagna I 72 E4
Val-Suzon F 26 F2
Valtablado del Río E 47 C8
Valtero GR 169 B9
Valtesiniko GR 174 D5
Valtice CZ 77 E11
Valtiendas E 40 F4
Valtierra E 41 D8
Valtimo FIN 125 C11
Valtola FIN 128 C7
Valtopina I 62 A3
Valtos GR 171 A10
Valtotopi GR 169 C10
Valtournenche I 68 B4
Valtura HR 67 C8
Valu lui Traian RO 155 E2
Valun HR 67 C9
Väluste EST 131 E11
Valverde de Burguillos E 51 C6
Valverde de Júcar E 47 E8
Valverde de la Virgen E 39 C8
Valverde del Camino E 51 D6
Valverde de Leganés E 51 B6
Valverde del Fresno E 45 D7
Valverde de Llerena E 51 C8
Valverde del Majano E 46 C4
Valverde de Mérida E 51 B7
Valvika N 108 B8
Valvträsk S 118 B7
Valyra GR 174 E4
Vama RO 145 H7
Vama RO 153 B7
Vama Buzăului RO 161 B7
Vamberk CZ 77 B10
Vamdrup DK 86 E4
Våmhus S 102 D7
Vamlingbo S 93 F12
Vammala FIN 127 C8
Vammen DK 86 B5
Vamos GR 178 E7
Vámosmikola H 147 F7
Vámospércs H 151 B8
Vámosújfalu H 145 G3
Vampula FIN 126 C8
Vamvakofyto GR 169 B9
Vamvakou GR 169 F7
Vanaja FIN 127 D12
Vana-Koiola EST 131 F14
Vânători RO 152 E5
Vânători RO 153 C9
Vânatori RO 153 F10
Vânători RO 155 B2
Vânători RO 159 E10
Vânătorii Mici RO 161 E7
Vânători-Neamț RO 153 C8
Vanault-les-Dames F 25 C12
Vana-Vigala EST 131 D8
Vana-Võidu EST 131 E11
Váncsod H 151 C8
Vanda FIN 127 E12
Vandel DK 86 D4
Vandellós E 42 E5
Vandenesse F 30 B4
Vandenesse-en-Auxois F 25 F12
Vandœvre-lès-Nancy F 186 D1
Vandoies I 72 C4
Vändra EST 131 D10
Vändträsk S 118 C6
Vandzene LV 134 B5
Vandžiogala LT 135 F7
Vāne LV 134 C5
Väne-Åsaka S 91 C11
Vänersborg S 91 C11
Vañes E 40 C3
Vang N 101 D9
Vånga S 92 B7
Vangažl LV 135 B9
Vänge S 93 E13
Vängel S 107 D10
Vangshamn N 111 B15
Vangshylla N 105 D10
Vangsnes N 100 D5
Vangsvik N 111 B14
Vanha-Kihlanki FIN 117 C10
Vanhakylä FIN 122 F7
Vänjaurbäck S 107 C15
Vänjaurträsk S 107 C15
Vânjuleț RO 159 E10
Vânju Mare RO 159 E10
Vannareid N 112 C4
Vännäs S 122 C3
Vännäsberget S 118 B9
Vännäsby S 122 C3
Vannavalen N 112 C4
Vånne N 90 B2
Vannes F 22 E6
Vannvåg N 112 C4
Vannvikan N 104 D8
Vänö FIN 126 F7
Vansbro S 97 A11
Vanse N 94 F5
Vänsjö S 103 C9
Vantaa FIN 127 E12
Vanttausjärvi FIN 119 B17
Vanttauskoski FIN 119 B17
Vanvey F 25 E12
Vanyarc H 147 F8
Vanzone I 68 B5
Vaour F 33 B9
Vápenná CZ 77 B12
Vaplan S 105 E16
Vaqueiros P 50 E4
Vara EST 131 D13
Vara S 91 C12
Vara del Rey E 47 F8
Varades F 23 F9
Vărădia RO 159 C8
Vărădia de Mureș RO 151 E9
Varages F 35 C10
Varaire F 33 B9
Varajärvi FIN 119 B13
Varajoki FIN 121 F14
Varakļāni LV 135 C13
Varallo I 68 B5
Varangerbotn N 114 C5
Varano de'Melegari I 69 D8
Varapayeva BY 133 F2
Varapodio I 59 C8
Vărăști RO 161 E8
Văratec RO 153 C8
Varaždin HR 149 D6
Varaždinske Toplice HR 149 D6
Varazze I 37 C9
Varberg S 87 A10
Vărbilău RO 161 C7
Varbla EST 130 E7
Varbó H 145 G2
Varbola EST 131 C8
Varces-Allières-et-Risset F 31 E8
Vârciorog RO 151 D9
Varda GR 174 C3
Vardali GR 174 A5
Varde DK 86 D2
Vardim BG 161 F6
Vardište BIH 158 F3
Vårdö FIN 99 B14
Vardø N 114 C10
Várdomb H 149 D11
Varejoki FIN 119 B13
Varekil S 91 C10
Varel D 17 B10
Varėna LT 137 E10
Varengeville-sur-Mer F 18 E2
Varenna I 69 A7
Varennes-en-Argonne F 19 F11
Varennes-St-Sauveur F 31 C7
Varennes-sur-Allier F 30 C3
Varennes-Vauzelles F 30 A3
Vareš BIH 157 D9
Varese I 69 B6
Varese Ligure I 37 C11
Varetz F 29 E8
Vârfu Câmpului RO 153 B8
Vârfuri RO 161 C7
Vârfurile RO 151 E10
Vårgårda S 91 C12
Vărgata RO 152 D5
Vârghiș RO 153 E7
Vargön S 91 C11
Vargträsk S 107 C15
Varhaug N 94 E3
Vari GR 175 D8
Vari GR 176 E4
Variaș RO 151 E6
Varik NL 183 B6
Variku EST 130 C7
Varilhes F 33 D9
Varimbombi GR 175 C8
Varín SK 147 C7
Väring S 91 B14
Varinl LV 135 B12
Variskylä FIN 121 F9
Varislahti FIN 125 E11
Varistaipale FIN 125 E11
Varjakka FIN 119 E14
Varjisträsk S 109 D18
Varkaliai LT 134 E3
Varkaus FIN 125 F9
Vārkava LV 135 D13
Varkhi BY 133 E7
Vârlezi RO 153 F11
Varlosen (Niemetal) D 78 D6
Vārme LV 134 C4
Värmlandsbro S 91 A13
Varna BG 167 C9
Varna I 72 C4
Varna SRB 158 D4
Värnamo S 88 A6
Värnäs S 97 B9
Varnavas GR 175 C8
Varnhem S 91 C14
Varniai LT 134 E4
Varnja EST 131 E14
Varnsdorf CZ 81 E7
Varntresken N 108 E7
Varnyany BY 137 D13
Väröbacka S 87 A10

Varonichy BY 133 F5
Varonka BY 133 F2
Városföld H 150 D4
Varoška Rijeka BIH 156 B5
Városlőd H 149 B9
Varpaisjärvi FIN 124 D9
Várpalota H 149 B10
Varpanen FIN 128 C6
Varparanta FIN 125 G11
Varpasalo FIN 125 F12
Varpsjö S 107 C11
Varpuselkä FIN 115 E5
Varpuvaara FIN 115 E4
Värriö FIN 115 D3
Varrio FIN 115 E2
Vars F 29 D6
Vars F 36 B5
Vărșand RO 151 D7
Varsány H 147 E8
Värsås S 91 C15
Varsi I 69 D8
Värska EST 132 F2
Vârșolț RO 151 C10
Varsseveld NL 17 E6
Värst DK 86 B6
Vårsta S 93 A11
Varstu EST 131 F13
Varteig N 95 D14
Vartemyagi RUS 129 E13
Vârteșcoiu RO 153 F10
Vartholomio GR 174 D3
Vartius FIN 121 E14
Vårtoape RO 160 E6
Vartofta S 91 C14
Vårtop RO 160 E2
Värtsilä FIN 125 F15
Varuträsk S 118 E5
Varvara BG 165 E9
Varvara BG 167 D8
Varvara GR 169 C10
Varvarin SRB 159 F7
Varvasaina GR 174 D4
Värve LV 134 B3
Varvikko FIN 115 E4
Várvölgy H 149 C8
Vârvoru de Jos RO 160 E3
Varyazh UA 144 B9
Vărzărești MD 154 C2
Varzi I 37 B10
Varzo I 68 A5
Varzy F 25 F9
Vasa FIN 122 D7
Vasalemma EST 131 C8
Vasanello I 62 C2
Vasaniemi FIN 115 D2
Vasankari FIN 119 F11
Vasaraperä FIN 121 B12
Vásárosdombó H 149 D10
Vásárosnamény H 145 G5
Vașcău RO 151 E10
Väse S 97 D10
Vashkivtsi UA 153 A7
Vashtëmi AL 168 C4
Vasilați RO 161 E8
Vasilika GR 169 D9
Vasilika GR 177 A7
Vasiliki GR 174 B2
Vasiliko GR 175 C8
Vasilikos GR 174 D2
Vasilis GR 169 F7
Vasilitsi GR 178 B2
Vasil Kolarov BG 165 F10
Vasil Levski BG 166 E5
Vasilopoulo GR 174 B3
Vasilovtsi BG 159 F11
Vasil'yevo RUS 132 F2
Vaški LT 135 D8
Vaski LV 134 C6
Vaškiai LT 134 E2
Väskinde S 93 D12
Vaskio FIN 127 E9
Vaskivesi FIN 123 F11
Vaskút H 150 E2
Vaskuu FIN 123 F11
Vasles F 28 B5
Vaslui RO 153 D11
Vasmegyer H 145 G4
Vassaras GR 175 E6
Vassbo S 102 C4
Vassbotn N 111 C13
Vassbygdi N 100 E6
Vassdalen N 111 C14
Vassdalsvik N 108 C6
Vassenden N 100 D4
Vassieux-en-Vercors F 31 F7
Vassmolösa S 89 B10
Vassnäs S 105 C14
Vassor FIN 122 D8
Vasstrand N 111 A15
Vassy F 23 C10
Vasszécseny H 149 B7
Västansta S 103 A12
Västanå S 103 B13
Västanå S 107 E16
Västanbäck S 107 D12
Västanfjärd FIN 126 E8
Västannäs S 118 B9
Västansjö S 103 A12
Västansjö S 103 C12
Västansjö S 107 A9
Västansjö S 107 C13
Västansjö S 107 E12
Västansjö S 108 E9
Västansjön S 103 B12
Västanvik S 103 C8
Vastemõisa EST 131 E10
Västerås S 98 C7
Västeråsen S 107 F11
Västerberg S 103 E12
Västerby S 97 B14
Västerbyn S 99 B10
Västerfärnebo S 98 C6
Västerhållan S 102 A5
Västerhaninge S 93 A12
Västerhejde S 93 D12
Västerhus S 107 E15
Västerlandsjö S 107 E15
Västerljung S 93 B10
Västermyckeläng S 102 D7
Västerottna S 97 C8
Västerrtråsjö S 103 C11
Västervik S 93 D9
Västilä FIN 127 B12
Vastinki FIN 123 E13
Västinniemi FIN 125 E10
Vasto I 63 C7
Vastorf D 83 D9
Västra Ämtervik S 97 C9
Västra Bodarna S 91 D11
Västra Eneby S 92 C7
Västra Fagelberget S 105 C17
Västra Harg S 92 C6

Västra Hjåggböle S 118 E5
Västra Husby S 93 C8
Västra Karup S 87 C11
Västra Kiilisjärvi S 119 B10
Västra Lainejaure S 107 A15
Västra Ormsjö S 107 C10
Västra Sjulsmark S 118 F5
Västra Stugusjö S 103 A9
Västra Tåsjö S 106 C9
Västra Torup S 87 C13
Västra Yttermark FIN 122 E6
Vastse-Kuuste EST 131 E13
Vastseliina EST 132 F1
Vasvár H 149 B7
Vasylivka UA 155 B3
Vasylivka UA 155 B4
Vaszar H 149 B9
Vatan F 29 A9
Vâtava RO 152 D5
Väte S 93 E12
Vatera GR 177 A7
Vatero GR 169 D6
Vaterstetten D 75 F10
Vatheia GR 178 C5
Vathy GR 177 D8
Vathy GR 177 D8
Vathylakkos GR 169 C8
Vathylakkos GR 169 D6
Vathys GR 177 F9
Vati GR 181 D7
Vatican City E 62 D2
Vatici MD 154 C3
Vatjusjärvi FIN 123 B14
Vatla EST 130 D7
Vatland N 94 F6
Vatnahalsen N 100 E6
Vātnas S 103 C13
Vatne N 94 E3
Vatne N 100 A5
Vatolakkos GR 169 D5
Vatoussa GR 177 A7
Vatra Dornei RO 152 C6
Vatra Moldoviței RO 153 B7
Vats N 101 E8
Vatta H 145 H2
Vattholma S 99 B9
Vattjom S 103 B11
Vattlång S 103 C13
Vattrång S 103 C13
Vattukylä FIN 119 F14
Vatula FIN 127 B8
Vätvoll N 111 C10
Vaubadon F 23 B10
Vaubecourt F 26 C3
Vauchassis F 25 D10
Vauclaix F 25 F10
Vauconcourt-Nervezain F 26 E4
Vaucouleurs F 26 C4
Vaudémont F 26 D5
Vaugneray F 30 D6
Vauldalen N 101 A16
Vaulx-en-Velin F 30 D6
Vaulx-Milieu F 31 D7
Vauvenargues F 35 C10
Vauvert F 35 C7
Vauvillers F 26 E5
Vaux-le-Pénil F 25 C8
Vaux-sur-Mer F 28 D3
Vaux-sur-Sûre B 19 E12
Vavdos GR 169 D9
Växbo S 103 D12
Vaxholm S 99 D10
Växjö S 89 B7
Växtorp S 87 C12
Väylä FIN 113 E20
Väylänpää FIN 117 D11
Vayrac F 29 F9
Vayres F 29 D7
Väyrylä FIN 121 E10
Väystäjä FIN 119 B12
Včelná CZ 77 E6
Veåskoonjarga FIN 113 F20
Veauche F 30 D5
Veavägen N 90 D2
Vebbestrup DK 86 B5
Veberöd S 87 D12
Veblungsnes N 100 A7
Vebomark S 118 E5
Vebron F 35 B6
Vecate LV 131 F10
Vecauce LV 134 D6
Vecbebri LV 135 C10
Vecchiano I 66 E1
Vechelde D 79 B7
Vechta D 17 C10
Vecinos E 45 C9
Veckerhagen (Reinhardshagen)
  D 78 D6
Veckrape LV 135 C9
Veclaicene LV 131 F14
Vecmikeļi LV 134 D6
Vecpiebalga LV 135 B11
Vecpils LV 134 C2
Vecsaikava LV 135 C12
Vecsalaca LV 131 F8
Vecsés H 150 C3
Vecskulte LV 135 B8
Vecslabada LV 133 D3
Vecumnieki LV 135 C9
Veda S 103 A14
Vedde DK 87 D10
Veddelev DK 87 D10
Veddige S 88 A2
Veddum DK 86 B6
Vēde LV 134 B3
Vedea RO 160 D5
Vedea RO 161 F7
Vedelago I 72 E5
Vedevåg S 97 C13
Vedjeön S 106 C8
Vedra E 38 C3
Védrines-St-Loup F 30 E3
Vedro Polje BIH 156 D5
Vedsted DK 86 E4
Vedum S 91 C13
Veendam NL 17 B7
Veenendaal NL 16 D5
Veenhusen D 17 B8
Veensgarth GB 3 E14
Veere NL 182 B3
Veerle B 182 C5
Veflinge DK 86 E6
Vegacervera E 39 C8
Vega de Espinareda E 39 C6
Vegadeo E 38 B5
Vega de Pas E 40 B4
Vega de Tirados E 45 B9
Vega de Valcarce E 39 C6
Vega de Valdetronco E 39 E9
Veganzones E 46 B5

Vegaquemada E 39 C9
Vegarienza E 39 C7
Vegarshei N 90 B4
Vegas del Condado E 39 C9
Vegas de Matute E 46 C4
Vegby S 91 D13
Végegyháza H 151 E6
Veggen N 111 D13
Vegger DK 86 B4
Veghel NL 16 E5
Vegli LV 134 B4
Veglie I 61 C9
Vegset N 105 C12
Vehkajärvi FIN 127 B12
Vehkalahti FIN 121 B15
Vehkalahti FIN 128 D7
Vehkataipale FIN 129 C9
Vehlow D 83 D12
Vehmaa FIN 126 D6
Vehmaa FIN 128 B8
Vehmasjärvi FIN 125 C10
Vehmersalmi FIN 125 E10
Vehniä FIN 123 F15
Vehu FIN 123 E12
Vehvilä FIN 124 E8
Veidholmen N 104 D3
Veidneset N 113 B18
Veigy-Foncenex F 31 C9
Veihtivaara FIN 121 E11
Veikkola FIN 127 E11
Veimo N 105 D11
Veinge S 87 B12
Veiros P 50 B4
Veisiejai LT 137 E8
Veitastrond N 100 E6
Veitsbronn D 75 C8
Veitsch A 148 A5
Veitservasa FIN 117 C13
Veiveriai LT 137 D8
Veivirženai LT 134 E3
Vejano I 62 C2
Vejby DK 87 C10
Vejen DK 86 E4
Vejenò DK 84 E4
Vejer de la Frontera E 52 D5
Vejle DK 86 D5
Vejle DK 86 E6
Vejprnice CZ 76 C4
Vejrum DK 86 C3
Vejstrup DK 87 E7
Vekilski BG 161 F10
Vela RO 160 E2
Velagići BIH 157 C6
Vela Luka HR 162 D2
Velamazán E 41 F6
Velanda S 91 C11
Velanidia GR 178 C5
Veľaty SK 145 F4
Velaux F 35 C9
Velbastaður FO 2 B3
Velbert D 17 F8
Velburg D 75 D10
Velden D 75 F11
Velden am Wörther See A 73 C9
Veldhoven NL 16 F4
Veldrome I 64 C4
Velefique E 55 E8
Velehrad CZ 146 C4
Velen D 17 E7
Velence H 149 B11
Velenje SLO 73 D11
Veles MK 164 F4
Veleševec HR 148 E6
Velešín CZ 77 E6
Velešta MK 168 B4
Velestino GR 169 F8
Vélez-Blanco E 55 D9
Vélez de Benaudalla E 53 C10
Vélez-Málaga E 53 C8
Vélez-Rubio E 55 D8
Velgast D 83 B13
Velika HR 149 F9
Velika Brijesnica BIH 157 C9
Velika Drenova SRB 159 F7
Velika Gorica HR 148 E6
Velika Greda SRB 159 C7
Velika Ilova BIH 157 C8
Velika Ivanča SRB 158 D6
Velika Kladuša BIH 156 B4
Velika Kopanica HR 157 B9
Velika Krsna SRB 159 D6
Velika Mlaka HR 148 E6
Velika Obarska BIH 157 C11
Velika Pisanica HR 149 E8
Velika Plana SRB 159 D7
Velika Plana SRB 164 C3
Velika Račna SLO 73 E10
Velike Lašč SLO 73 E10
Veliki Crljeni SRB 158 E5
Veliki Drvenik HR 156 F5
Veliki Gaj SRB 159 C7
Veliki Preslav BG 166 C7
Veliki Kupci SRB 164 C3
Veliki Prolog HR 157 F7
Veliki Radinci SRB 158 C4
Veliki Troyany UA 154 A6
Velikiy Lyubin' UA 144 D3
Veliki Zdenci HR 149 F8
Veliko Gradište SRB 159 D8
Veliko Laole SRB 159 E7
Veliko Središte SRB 159 C7
Veliko Trojstvo HR 149 E7
Velikönly TR 173 B8
Velilla de Cinca E 42 D4
Velilla del Río Carrión E 39 C10
Veli Lošinj HR 67 D9
Velimeşe TR 173 B8
Velimlje MNE 163 D7
Vélines F 28 F6
Velingrad BG 165 E9
Velipojë AL 163 F7
Velise EST 131 D9
Veliuona LT 136 C7
Velje Duboko MNE 163 D7
Veljun HR 156 B4
Velká Bíteš CZ 77 D10
Velká Bystřice CZ 146 B4
Velká Dobrá CZ 76 B6
Velká Hleďsebe CZ 75 C12
Veľká Ida SK 145 F3
Veľká Lomnica SK 145 E1
Veľká Mača SK 146 E5
Veľká nad Ipľom SK 147 E9
Velká Polom CZ 146 B6
Velké Bílovice CZ 77 E11
Velké Březno CZ 80 E6

Velké Heraltice CZ 146 B5
Veľké Kapušany SK 145 F5
Veľké Kapošany SK 145 F5
Veľké Leváre SK 77 E12
Velké Losiny CZ 77 B11
Veľké Lovce SK 146 E6
Velké Ludince SK 146 E6
Velké Meziříčí CZ 77 D10
Velké Němčice CZ 77 E11
Velké Opatovice CZ 77 C11
Velké Pavlovice CZ 77 E11
Veľké Ripňany SK 146 E5
Velké Svatoňovice CZ 81 E10
Veľké Uherce SK 146 D6
Veľké Úľany SK 146 E5
Veľký Blh SK 147 E10
Veľký Ďur SK 146 E6
Veľký Kýr SK 146 E5
Veľký Meder SK 146 F5
Veľký Šenov CZ 80 D6
Velký Osek CZ 77 B8
Veľký Slavkov SK 145 E1
Veľký Týnec CZ 146 B4
Velký Újezd CZ 146 B4
Vellahn D 83 D9
Vellberg D 74 D6
Velletri I 62 D3
Vellevans F 26 F6
Velling DK 86 C2
Vellinge S 87 E12
Vellisca E 47 D7
Vellmar D 78 D6
Velo GR 175 D6
Velosnes F 19 E11
Velp NL 183 B7
Velpke D 79 B8
Velten D 84 E4
Veltruby CZ 77 B8
Vejbystrand S 87 C11
Velturno I 72 C4
Velušina MK 168 C5
Velvary CZ 76 B6
Velventos GR 169 D7
Velyatyn UA 145 G7
Velyka Horozhanna UA 145 D8
Velyka Kisnytsya UA 154 A2
Velyka Kopanya UA 145 G7
Velyka Mykhaylivka UA 154 C5
Velyka Tur"ya UA 145 E9
Velyki Kom"yaty UA 145 G6
Velyki Luchky UA 145 G6
Velyki Mosty UA 144 C9
Velykokomarivka UA 154 C5
Velykoploske UA 154 C5
Velykozymenove UA 154 C6
Velykyy Bereznyy UA 145 F6
Velykyy Bychkiv UA 145 H9
Velykyy Rakovets' UA 145 G7
Velžys LT 135 E9
Vemb DK 86 C2
Vemdalen S 102 B6
Vemdalsskalet S 102 B6
Véménd H 149 D11
Vemhån S 102 B7
Vemmenaes DK 87 E7
Vemmetofte DK 87 E9
Vemundvik N 105 B11
Vena S 92 D7
Venaco F 37 G10
Venafro I 62 E6
Venansault F 28 B2
Venarey-les-Laumes F 25 E11
Venaria I 68 C4
Venarotta I 62 B4
Venås S 103 C13
Venasca I 37 B6
Venčane SRB 158 E5
Vence F 36 D6
Venčiūnai LT 137 E9
Venda Nova P 38 E4
Vendargues F 35 C6
Vendas Novas P 50 B3
Vendays-Montalivet F 28 E3
Vendenheim F 186 D4
Vendeuvre-du-Poitou F 29 B6
Vendeuvre-sur-Barse F 25 D11
Vendinha P 50 C4
Vendœuvres F 29 B8
Vendôme F 24 E5
Veneheitto FIN 119 F17
Venejärvi FIN 117 D12
Venelles F 35 C9
Vénès F 33 C10
Venesjärvi FIN 126 B7
Veneskoski FIN 123 E10
Venetmäki FIN 124 D7
Venetmäki FIN 124 F7
Venetpalo FIN 123 C15
Venets BG 167 B7
Venets BG 167 D7
Venevere EST 131 C13
Venezia I 66 B5
Vengasaho FIN 119 D16
Vengsoy N 111 A16
Venhuizen NL 16 C4
Venialbo E 39 F8
Vénissieux F 30 D6
Venizel F 19 F7
Venjan S 102 D6
Venlo NL 16 F6
Venna GR 171 B9
Vennesla N 90 C2
Vennesund N 105 A12
Venosa I 60 B5
Venoy F 25 E9
Venray NL 16 E5
Vensac F 28 E3
Venta LV 134 D5
Venta LV 134 C4
Venta de Baños E 40 E3
Venta del Charco E 54 C3
Venta del Moro E 47 F10
Venta de los Santos E 55 C6
Venta las Ranas E 39 B8
Venta Nueva E 39 B6
Ventas de Huelma E 53 B9
Ventas de Zafarraya E 53 C8
Ventavon F 35 B10
Venteuges F 30 F4
Ventimiglia I 37 D7
Ventiseri F 37 H10
Ventnor GB 13 D12
Ventry IRL 8 D2
Ventschow D 83 C11
Ventspils LV 134 B3
Venzone I 73 D7
Vép H 149 B7
Vepriai LT 137 C10
Vepsä FIN 119 E16
Vepsä FIN 125 C12

Vepsä FIN 125 F14
Vera E 55 E9
Vera Cruz P 50 C4
Verbania I 68 B6
Verberie F 18 F6
Verbicaro I 60 D5
Verbier CH 31 C11
Verbița RO 159 E11
Verbka UA 154 A4
Verceia I 69 A7
Vercelli I 68 C5
Vercel-Villedieu-le-Camp
  F 26 F5
Verchen D 84 C3
Verd SLO 73 E9
Verdaches F 36 C4
Verdalen N 94 E3
Verdalsøra N 105 D10
Verden (Aller) D 17 C12
Verdikoussa GR 169 E7
Vërdovë AL 168 C4
Verdun F 26 B3
Verdun-sur-Garonne F 33 C8
Verdun-sur-le-Doubs F 31 B7
Verebiejai LT 137 E8
Vereşti RO 153 B8
Verfeil F 33 B9
Verfeil F 33 C7
Vērgale LV 134 C2
Vergato I 66 D3
Vergaville F 27 C6
Vergèze F 35 C7
Verghereto I 66 E5
Vergi EST 131 B12
Vergi GR 169 C9
Vergigny F 25 E10
Vergina GR 169 D7
Vergongheon F 30 E3
Veria GR 169 D7
Vērī D 84 E4
Verín E 38 E5
Veringenstadt D 27 D11
Veriora EST 132 F1
Verkebro S 98 A8
Verkhivka UA 154 A4
Verkhni Petrivtsi UA 153 A7
Verkhniy Bereziv UA 145 E8
Verkhniy Yaseniv UA 152 A5
Verkhnya Vysots'ke UA 145 F6
Verkhnya Vyznytsya UA 145 F6
Verkhnya Yablun'ka UA 145 E6
Verkhnye Syn'ovydne
  UA 145 E8
Verkhovyna UA 152 A5
Verl D 17 E11
Verla FIN 128 C6
Verlaine B 19 C11
Verma N 100 B8
Vermand F 19 E7
Vermenton F 25 E10
Vermeş RO 159 B8
Vermiglio I 69 A10
Vermiosa P 45 C7
Vermoil P 44 E3
Vermosh AL 163 D8
Vermuntila FIN 126 C6
Vernantes F 23 F12
Vernayaz CH 31 C11
Vern-d'Anjou F 23 E10
Verneřice CZ 80 E6
Vernești RO 161 C9
Vernet F 33 D9
Vernet-les-Bains F 33 E10
Verneuil-sur-Avre F 24 C4
Verneuil-sur-Vienne F 29 D8
Vernier CH 31 C9
Verningen N 90 A7
Verniolle F 33 D9
Vernole I 61 C10
Vernon F 24 B5
Vernouillet F 24 C5
Vernoux-en-Vivarais F 30 F6
Vern-sur-Seiche F 23 D8
Verny F 26 B5
Vero F 37 G9
Veröcemaros H 147 F8
Veroia GR 169 C7
Verolanuova I 69 C9
Veroli I 62 D4
Verona I 66 B3
Verosvres F 30 C5
Verpelét H 145 H1
Verrabotn N 105 D9
Verran N 105 D9
Verres I 68 B4
Verrières F 29 C7
Versailles F 24 C7
Verseg H 150 B4
Vers-en-Montagne F 31 B8
Versmold D 17 D10
Versoix CH 31 C9
Versols-et-Lapeyre F 34 C4
Verson F 23 B11
Vers-Pont-du-Gard F 35 C8
Vert F 32 B4
Verteillac F 29 E6
Vértesacsa H 149 B11
Vértesboglár H 149 B10
Vértessomló H 149 A10
Vértesszőlős H 149 A10
Verteuil-d'Agenais F 33 B6
Vertheuil F 28 E4
Verton F 18 D4
Vertou F 23 F9
Vertus F 25 C11
Verucchio I 66 E5
Verviers B 19 C12
Vicarstown IRL 7 F8
Verwood GB 13 D11
Verzino I 61 E7
Verzy F 25 B11
Vesajärvi FIN 126 B8
Vesala FIN 119 D16
Vesamäki FIN 123 D15
Vesanka FIN 123 F15
Vesanto FIN 123 E16
Vescovato F 37 F10
Vése H 149 D8

Vesijärvi FIN 122 F7
Vesilahti FIN 127 C10
Vesime I 37 B8
Vesivehmaa FIN 127 C14
Vesløs DK 86 A3
Vesnovo RUS 136 D5
Vesoul F 26 E5
Vespolate I 68 C6
Vessa SF 177 C7
Vessem NL 16 F4
Vessigebro S 87 B11
Vestad N 101 C13
Vestbjerg DK 86 A5
Vestby N 95 C13
Vestby N 102 D2
Vestbygd N 111 D10
Vester Åby DK 86 E6
Vesterby DK 87 F8
Vester Hassing DK 86 A6
Vester Herborg DK 86 C3
Vester Hjermitslev DK 90 E6
Vester Hornum DK 86 B4
Vestermarie DK 89 E7
Vester Nebel DK 86 D4
Vesterø Havn DK 87 A7
Vestertana N 113 C20
Vester Torup DK 86 A4
Vester Vedsted DK 86 E3
Vestervig DK 86 B2
Vestfossen N 95 C11
Vestmanna FO 2 A2
Vestnes N 100 A6
Vestone I 69 B9
Vestpollen N 110 D8
Vestre Gausdal N 101 D12
Vestre Jakobselv N 114 C6
Vestvågen N 108 E4
Veszkény H 149 A8
Veszprém H 149 B9
Veszprémvarsány H 149 B9
Vésztő H 151 D7
Vetca RO 152 E5
Vețel RO 151 F10
Veteli FIN 123 D11
Vetersko MK 164 F4
Vétheuil F 24 B6
Vetiş RO 151 B10
Vetlanda S 92 D6
Vetlefjorden N 100 D5
Vetovo BG 161 F8
Vetovo HR 149 F9
Vetralla I 62 C2
Vetren BG 165 E9
Vetren BG 167 D8
Vetrino BG 167 C8
Vetrişoaia RO 154 E2
Větřní CZ 76 E6
Vetschau D 80 C6
Vetskojärvi S 116 D7
Vettasjärvi S 116 D7
Vettelschoss D 185 C7
Vetterslev DK 87 E9
Vetto I 69 D1
Veulettes-sur-Mer F 18 E2
Veurne B 18 B6
Vevang N 104 E3
Vevčani MK 168 B4
Veverská Bítýška CZ 77 D10
Vevey CH 31 C10
Vevi GR 169 C6
Vex CH 31 C11
Vexala FIN 122 D8
Veynes F 35 A10
Veyre-Monton F 30 D3
Vézac F 29 F8
Vézelay F 25 F10
Vézelise F 26 D5
Vézénobres F 35 B7
Vezins F 23 F11
Vézins-de-Lévézou F 34 B4
Vezzani F 37 G10
Vezzano I 69 A11
Vezzano sul Crostolo I 66 C2
Viadana I 66 C2
Viala du Tarn F 34 B4
Vialas F 35 B6
Viana E 32 E1
Viana de Cega E 39 E10
Viana do Alentejo P 50 C4
Viana do Bolo E 38 E2
Viana do Castelo P 38 E2
Vianden L 20 E6
Viane F 34 C4
Vianen NL 16 E4
Viannos GR 178 E9
Viano F 66 C2
Viaño Pequeno E 38 B3
Vianos E 55 B7
Viantie FIN 119 C13
Viareggio I 66 E1
Viarmes F 25 B7
Vias F 34 D5
Viasvesi FIN 126 C6
Viatodos P 38 F2
Viator E 55 F8
Viaur F 33 A10
Vibble S 93 D12
Vibbyn S 118 C7
Vibonati I 60 C5
Viborg DK 86 C4
Vibo Valentia I 59 B9
Vibraye F 24 D4
Viby DK 87 D10
Viby S 88 C6
Vic E 43 D8
Vícar E 55 F7
Vicari I 58 D4
Vicchio I 66 E3
Vicdessos F 33 E8
Vic-en-Bigorre F 33 D6
Vicenza I 66 A4
Vic-Fezensac F 33 C6
Vichy F 30 C3
Vickan S 91 E11
Vic-le-Comte F 30 D3
Vico F 37 G9
Vico del Gargano I 63 D9
Vico Equense I 60 B2
Vicoforte I 37 C7
Vico nel Lazio I 62 D4
Vicovaro I 62 C3
Vicovu de Jos RO 153 B7
Vicovu de Sus RO 153 B7
Vicq-Exemplet F 29 B10
Vic-sur-Cère F 29 F11
Vic-sur-Seille F 26 C5
Victoria RO 153 C11

Victoria RO 160 B5
Victoria RO 161 D11
Victor Vlad Delamarina RO
  159 B7
Vidaga LV 135 B12
Vidago P 38 E4
Vidais P 44 F3
Vidåle LV 130 F4
Vidamlya BY 141 F9
Vidángoz E 32 E3
Vidauban F 36 E4
ViŠareišl FO 2 A3
Vidauchy BY 141 F9
Vidče CZ 146 C6
Viddal N 100 B5
Viddalba I 64 B2
Videbæk DK 86 C3
Videle RO 161 E7
Videm SLO 148 E6
Videmonte P 44 C6
Videniškiai LT 135 F10
Vidhas AL 168 B3
Vidigueira P 50 C4
Vidin BG 159 E10
Vidiškiai LT 135 F10
Vidlin GB 3 E14
Vidnava CZ 77 B12
Vidovec HR 148 D6
Vidovice BIH 157 C10
Vidra RO 151 E10
Vidra RO 153 F9
Vidra RO 161 E8
Vidrare BG 165 C9
Vidreres E 43 D9
Vidrek N 111 D13
Vidrenjak HR 149 E7
Vidrieres E 43 D9
Vidrižī LV 135 B9
Vidsala LV 135 D11
Vidsel S 118 C5
Vidstrup DK 90 D6
Vidzy BY 135 F13
Viechtach D 76 D3
Vieille-Brioude F 30 E3
Vieira de Leiria P 44 E3
Vieira do Minho P 38 E3
Vieki FIN 125 D11
Viekšniai LT 134 D5
Vielank D 83 D10
Vielha E 33 E7
Vielle-Aure F 33 E6
Vielle-St-Girons F 32 C3
Vielmur-sur-Agout F 33 C10
Vielsalm B 20 D5
Vielverge F 26 F3
Vienenburg D 79 C8
Vieníba LV 134 C5
Vienne F 30 D6
Viereck D 84 C6
Vieremä FIN 124 C8
Viereth-Trunstadt D 75 C8
Vierlingsbeek NL 16 E5
Viernau D 79 E8
Viernheim D 21 E11
Vierraden D 84 D6
Viersen D 16 F6
Vierumäki FIN 127 C14
Vierville-sur-Mer F 23 B10
Vierzon F 25 F7
Viesecke D 83 D12
Viesīte LV 135 D11
Vieste I 63 D10
Viešvénai LT 134 E4
Viešvilė LT 134 C6
Vietas S 109 A15
Vietri di Potenza I 60 B5
Vietri sul Mare I 60 B3
Vieux-Boucau-les-Bains F 32 C3
Vieux-Condé F 182 E2
Vievis LT 137 D10
Vif F 31 E8
Vig DK 87 D9
Viganti LV 135 D13
Vigarano Mainarda I 66 C3
Vigasio I 66 B2
Vigaun A 73 A7
Vigdenes N 105 D10
Vigeland N 94 F6
Vigeois F 29 E9
Vigevano I 69 C6
Vigge S 102 A7
Vigge S 103 B12
Viggianello F 37 H9
Viggiano I 60 C6
Viggiano I 62 C5
Viglaš SK 147 D8
Vignacourt F 18 D5
Vignale Monferrato I 37 A8
Vignanello I 62 C2
Vigneulles-les-Hattonchâtel
  F 26 C4
Vignola I 66 D3
Vignola Mare l'Agnata I 64 A3
Vignory F 26 D3
Vigny F 24 B6
Vigo E 38 D2
Vigodarzere I 66 B4
Vigo di Cadore I 72 D5
Vigo di Fassa I 72 D4
Vigone I 37 B6
Vigonza I 66 B4
Vigo Rendena I 69 A10
Vigrestad N 94 E3
Viguzzolo I 37 B9
Vigy F 20 F6
Vihalsen N 104 E5
Vihanti FIN 119 F13
Vihiers F 23 F11
Vihtari FIN 125 F11
Vihtasuo FIN 125 D12
Vihtavuori FIN 123 F15
Vihteljärvi FIN 126 B8
Vihti FIN 127 E11
Vihtijärvi FIN 127 E12
Vihula EST 131 B12
Viiala EST 131 C9
Viiksimo FIN 121 F15
Viile Satu Mare RO 151 B10
Viimsi EST 131 B9
Viinamäki FIN 125 D12
Viinijärvi FIN 125 E12
Viinikka FIN 123 D10
Viinikoski FIN 119 D16
Viiratsi EST 131 E11
Viirinkylä FIN 119 B17
Viirre FIN 119 F12
Viisarimäki FIN 123 F16
Viişoara MD 153 B10
Viişoara RO 151 C9
Viişoara RO 152 D3
Viişoara RO 152 E5

Vojakkala FIN 119 C12
Vojakkala FIN 127 D11
Vojčice SK 145 F4
Vojens DK 86 E4
Vojka SRB 158 D5
Vojkovic BIH 157 E9
Vojnić HR 148 F1
Vojnik SLO 148 D4
Vojtjajaure S 108 E9
Voka EST 132 C2
Vokány H 149 E10
Vokil BG 161 F10
Voknavolok RUS 121 E16
Voksa N 100 B2
Volakas GR 170 B5
Volary CZ 76 E5
Volda N 100 B4
Voldby DK 86 C5
Voldby DK 87 C7
Voldum DK 86 C6
Volendam NL 16 D4
Volgsele S 107 B11
Volimes GR 174 D2
Volintiri MD 154 E5
Volissos GR 177 C6
Voljevac BIH 157 E8
Voljice BIH 157 E8
Volkach D 75 C7
Völkel NL 183 B7
Völkermarkt A 73 C10
Volketswil CH 27 F10
Völklingen D 21 F7
Volkmarsen D 17 F12
Volkovija MK 163 F10
Voll N 101 E13
Völlen D 17 B8
Vollenhove NL 16 C5
Vollersode D 17 B11
Vollsjö S 87 D13
Volmunster F 27 B7
Voloiac RO 159 D11
Voloka UA 153 A7
Volonne F 35 B11
Volos GR 169 F8
Voloshcha UA 145 D8
Volosovo RUS 132 C5
Volosyanka UA 145 F6
Volovăț RO 153 B7
Volovets' UA 145 F7
Volovo BG 166 B5
Volpago del Mòntello I 72 E5
Volpiano I 68 C4
Völs A 72 B3
Völschow D 84 C4
Voltaggio I 37 B9
Volta Mantovana I 66 B2
Volterra I 66 F2
Voltlage D 17 D9
Voltri I 37 C9
Voltti FIN 122 D9
Volturara Appula I 63 E8
Volturara Irpina I 60 B3
Volturino I 63 E8
Voluntari RO 161 E8
Volvic F 30 D3
Volx F 35 C10
Volya Arlamivs'ka UA 144 D9
Volyně CZ 76 D5
Vomp A 72 B4
Voneshta Voda BG 166 D5
Vonge DK 86 D4
Vonges F 26 F3
Voni GR 178 E9
Vonitsa GR 174 B2
Võnnu EST 131 E14
Võõpste EST 131 E14
Võõpsu EST 132 E2
Voorburg NL 16 D2
Voore EST 131 D13
Voorhout NL 182 A4
Voorschoten NL 16 D2
Voorst NL 16 D6
Voorthuizen NL 183 A7
Voose EST 131 C10
Võra FIN 122 D8
Voranava BY 137 E11
Vorau A 148 B5
Vorbasse DK 86 D4
Vorchdorf A 76 F5
Vorden NL 16 D6
Vordernberg A 73 A10
Vordorf D 79 B8
Vorë AL 168 B2
Voreppe F 31 E8
Vorey F 30 E4
Vorgod DK 86 C3
Vormsele S 107 B15
Vormstad N 104 E7
Vormsund N 95 B14
Vormträsk S 107 B15
Vorna FIN 119 F15
Vorniceni RO 153 B9
Voroi GR 178 E8
Vorokhta UA 152 A5
Vorona RO 153 B9
Vorra D 75 C9
Vorst B 19 B11
Vorța RO 151 E10
Võru EST 131 F14
Vorwerk D 17 B12
Voskopojë AL 168 C4
Vosláběni RO 153 D7
Voss N 100 E4
Vosselaar B 16 F3
Voštane HR 157 E6
Võsu EST 131 B11
Votice CZ 77 C7
Votonosi GR 168 E5
Voudia GR 179 B8
Vougeot F 26 F2
Vouillé F 28 C5
Vouillé F 29 B6
Voukolies GR 178 E6
Voula GR 175 D8
Voulaines-les-Templiers
  F 25 E12
Vouliagmeni GR 175 D8
Voulpi GR 174 A4
Voulx F 25 D8
Vouneuil-sous-Biard F 29 B6
Vouneuil-sur-Vienne F 29 B7
Vourgareli GR 168 F5
Vourvourou GR 169 D10
Voutenay-sur-Cure F 25 E10
Voutezac F 29 E8
Voutianoi GR 174 E5
Vouvant F 28 B4
Vouvray F 24 F4
Vouvry CH 31 C10
Vouzela P 44 C4

Vouzi GR 174 A5
Vouziers F 19 F10
Vouzon F 24 E7
Voves F 24 D6
Vowchyn BY 141 F8
Vowkawshchyna BY 133 E2
Voxna S 103 D10
Voynika BG 167 E7
Voynitsa RUS 121 D15
Voynovo BG 161 F10
Vozmediano E 41 E8
Voznesenska-Persha UA 154 E4
Vrå DK 90 E6
Vrabevo BG 165 D10
Vráble SK 146 E6
Vračev Gaj SRB 159 D7
Vračevšnica SRB 158 E6
Vrachasi GR 179 E10
Vrachati GR 175 D6
Vrachesh BG 165 D8
Vrachnaiika GR 174 C4
Vrachos GR 168 E5
Vracov CZ 146 D4
Vrådal N 95 D8
Vrakúň SK 146 F5
Vrané nad Vltavou CZ 76 C6
Vrani RO 159 C8
Vranino BG 167 B10
Vranisht AL 168 D2
Vranisht AL 168 D2
Vranjak BIH 157 C8
Vranje SRB 164 D4
Vranjska Banja SRB 164 D5
Vranov nad Topľou SK 145 F4
Vransko SLO 73 D10
Vrapčište MK 163 F10
Vrapčići BIH 157 F8
Vrasene S 182 C4
Vrasna GR 169 C10
Vratarnica SRB 159 F9
Vratimov CZ 146 B6
Vratnica MK 164 E3
Vratsa BG 165 C8
Vrattsa BG 165 E6
Vražogrnac SRB 159 F9
Vrbanja BY 133 F7
Vrbanja HR 157 C10
Vrbanjci BIH 157 C7
Vrbas SRB 158 B4
Vrbaška BIH 157 B7
Vrbica SRB 150 E5
Vrbice CZ 77 E11
Vrbnik HR 67 B10
Vrbnik HR 156 D5
Vrbno pod Pradědem CZ 142 F3
Vrbovac SRB 159 F9
Vrbovce SK 146 D4
Vrbové SK 146 D5
Vrbovec HR 149 E6
Vrbovsko HR 67 B11
Vrchlabí CZ 81 E9
Vrčin SRB 158 D6
Vrdy CZ 77 C8
Vrebac HR 156 C4
Vrécourt F 26 D4
Vreden D 17 D7
Vreeland NL 183 A6
Vrees D 17 C9
Vrellë RKS 163 D9
Vrelo SRB 164 C4
Vrena S 93 B9
Vrensted DK 90 E6
Vřesina CZ 146 B6
Vresse B 19 E10
Vresthena GR 175 E6
Vretstorp S 92 A5
Vrgorac HR 157 F7
Vrhnika SLO 73 E9
Vrhopolje BIH 157 C6
Vridsted DK 86 C4
Vries NL 17 B7
Viezenveen NL 17 D7
Vrigstad S 92 E4
Vrinners DK 86 C6
Vrisa GR 177 A7
Vrizy F 19 F10
Vrlika HR 156 E5
Vrnjačka Banja SRB 163 B10
Vrnograč BIH 156 B4
Vron F 18 D4
Vrontados GR 177 C7
Vrontero GR 168 C5
Vrontou GR 169 D7
Vroomshoop NL 17 D7
Vrosina GR 168 E4
Vrouchas GR 179 E10
Vrouwenpolder NL 16 E1
Vrpolje HR 156 E5
Vrpolje HR 157 B9
Vrrin AL 168 B1
Vršac SRB 159 C7
Vršani BIH 157 C11
Vrsar HR 67 B8
Vrsi HR 156 D3
Vrtoče BIH 156 C5
Vitojba SLO 73 E8
Vrulja MNE 163 C7
Vrútky SK 147 C7
Vrutok MK 163 F10
Vrův BG 159 E10
Vrysia GR 169 F7
Vrysoula GR 174 B4
Všeruby CZ 76 C4
Všestary CZ 146 C5
Všetín CZ 146 C5
Vsevolozhsk RUS 129 E14
Vŭbel BG 160 F5
Vučitjak BIH 157 C8
Vučja Lokva SRB 163 C10
Vučje SRB 164 D4
Vught NL 16 E4
Vŭglevtsi BG 166 D5
Vuka HR 149 F10
Vukova Gorica HR 148 F4
Vukovar HR 157 B11
Vuku N 105 D11

Vulturu RO 155 D2
Vulturu RO 161 B10
Vuobmaved FIN 113 E16
Vuohijärvi FIN 128 C6
Vuohtomäki FIN 123 C16
Vuojärvi FIN 117 D17
Vuokatti FIN 121 F11
Vuokko FIN 125 D12
Vuokoski FIN 127 C15
Vuolijoki FIN 120 F8
Vuolle FIN 123 C11
Vuollerim S 118 B5
Vuonisjärvi FIN 125 D14
Vuonislahti FIN 125 D13
Vuonos FIN 125 E12
Vuontisjärvi FIN 117 B11
Vuorenmaa FIN 124 G9
Vuorenmaa FIN 126 C8
Vuoreslahti FIN 121 F9
Vuorimäki FIN 123 F12
Vuorimäki FIN 124 C9
Vuoriniemi FIN 129 B11
Vuosaari FIN 127 E13
Vuosanka FIN 121 F13
Vuostimo FIN 115 E2
Vuostimojärvi FIN 115 E2
Vuotner S 118 C3
Vuotso FIN 115 B2
Vuottas S 118 B7
Vŭrbitsa BG 166 E4
Vŭrbitsa BG 167 D7
Vurpær RO 152 F4
Vŭrshets BG 165 C7
Vushtrri RKS 164 D2
Vustsye BY 133 E3
Vutcani RO 153 E11
Vuzlove UA 145 G6
Vvedenka UA 154 E5
Vyalets BY 133 F7
Vyalikaya Byerastavitsa BY
  140 D10
Vyalikaya Stayki BY 133 F7
Vyalikaye Syalo BY 133 F3
Vyarkhovichy BY 141 F8
Vyartsilya RUS 125 F15
Vyaz RUS 133 C7
Vyborg RUS 129 D10
Vyčapy-Opatovce SK 146 E6
Východná SK 147 C9
Vydeniai LT 137 E10
Vydrany SK 146 F5
Vyerkhnyadzvinsk BY 133 E3
Vyetryna BY 133 F4
Vyhne SK 147 D7
Vyhoda UA 145 F8
Vy-lès-Lure F 26 E5
Vylkove UA 155 C5
Vylok UA 145 G6
Vynnyky UA 144 D9
Vynohradiv UA 145 G7
Vynohradivka UA 154 F4
Vyritsa RUS 132 C7
Vyroneia GR 169 B9
Vyronas GR 175 D8
Vyshgorodok RUS 133 B3
Vyshka UA 145 F6
Vyshkiv UA 145 G8
Vyshkove UA 145 G7
Vyshneve UA 154 F5
Vyshniv UA 141 H10
Vyskoď RUS 132 F7
Vyškov CZ 77 D12
Vyšná Ružbachy SK 145 E2
Vyšný Mirošov SK 145 E3
Vyšný Orlík SK 145 E4
Vyšný Šipov SK 145 E4
Vysoká nad Kysucou SK 147 C7
Vysokaye BY 141 F8
Vysoké Mýto CZ 77 C10
Vysokoye RUS 136 D4
Vysotsk RUS 129 D10
Vyšší Brod CZ 76 E6
Vyssinia GR 168 C5
Vytina GR 174 D5
Vyzhnytsya UA 152 A6
Vyžuonos LT 135 E11
Vzmor'ye RUS 139 A9

W

Waabs D 83 A7
Waal D 71 B11
Waalre NL 16 F4
Waalwijk NL 16 E4
Waarschoot B 19 B8
Wabern D 21 B12
Wąbrzeźno PL 138 D6
Wachenheim an der Weinstraße
  D 187 C5
Wąchock PL 143 D11
Wachow D 79 A12
Wachtebeke B 19 B8
Wächtersbach D 21 D12
Wacken D 82 B6
Wackersdorf D 75 D11
Waddeweitz D 83 D9
Waddington GB 11 E11
Waddinxveen NL 16 D3
Wadebridge GB 12 D5
Wädenswil CH 27 F10
Wadern D 21 E7
Wadersloh D 17 E10
Wadgassen D 21 F7
Wadhurst GB 15 E9
Wadlew PL 143 C7
Wadowice PL 147 B9
Wadowice Górne PL 143 F11
Wądroże Wielkie PL 81 D10
Waganiec PL 138 E6
Wagenfeld D 17 C11
Wagenhoff D 79 A8
Wageningen NL 16 E5
Waghäusel D 21 F11
Waging am See D 73 A6
Wagna A 148 C5
Wagrain A 73 B7
Wągrowiec PL 85 E12
Wahlhausen D 79 D6
Wahlsdorf D 80 C4
Wahlstedt D 83 C8
Wahrenholz D 79 A8
Waiblingen D 27 C11
Waibstadt D 187 C6
Waidhofen an der Thaya A 77 E8
Waidhofen an der Ybbs A 77 G7
Waigolshausen D 75 C7
Waimes B 20 D6
Wain D 71 A10
Wainfleet All Saints GB 11 E12
Wainhouse Corner GB 12 D5

Waischenfeld D 75 C9
Waizenkirchen A 76 F5
Wakefield GB 11 D8
Wakendorf II D 83 C8
Walberswick GB 15 C12
Wałbrzych PL 81 E10
Walburg D 78 D6
Walchum D 17 C8
Walcourt B 19 D9
Walcz PL 85 D10
Wald CH 27 F10
Wald D 27 E11
Wald D 75 D11
Waldachtal D 27 D10
Waldböckelheim D 185 E8
Waldbreitbach D 185 C7
Waldbröl D 21 C9
Waldbrunn-Lahr D 21 C10
Waldburg D 71 B9
Waldbüttelbrunn D 74 C6
Walddegg A 77 G10
Walddrehna D 80 C5
Waldeck D 17 F12
Waldenbach D 27 C11
Waldenburg CH 27 F8
Waldenburg D 74 D6
Walderbach D 75 D11
Waldershof D 75 C11
Waldesch D 185 D7
Waldfischbach-Burgalben
  D 21 F9
Waldhausen A 77 E8
Waldhausen im Strudengau
  A 77 F7
Waldheim D 80 D4
Walding A 76 F6
Waldkappel D 78 D6
Waldkirch D 27 D8
Waldkirchen D 76 E5
Waldkraiburg D 75 F11
Wald-Michelbach D 187 B6
Waldmohr D 21 F8
Waldmünchen D 76 D3
Wałdowo-Szlacheckie PL 138 D6
Waldrach D 21 E7
Waldsassen D 75 B11
Waldsee D 187 C5
Waldshut D 27 E9
Waldstatt CH 27 F11
Waldstetten D 75 F7
Waldstetten D 187 D8
Walenstadt CH 27 F11
Walferdange L 20 E6
Walim PL 81 E10
Walkendorf D 83 C13
Walkenried D 79 C7
Wallasey GB 10 E5
Walldorf D 21 D11
Walldorf D 21 F11
Walldorf D 79 E7
Walldürn D 27 A11
Wallenfels D 75 B9
Wallerfing D 76 E3
Wallern im Burgenland
  A 149 A7
Wallersdorf D 75 E12
Wallerstein D 75 E8
Wallgau D 72 A3
Wallhausen D 75 D7
Wallhausen D 185 E8
Wallisellen CH 27 F10
Walls GB 3 E13
Wallsbüll D 82 A6
Wallstawe D 83 E9
Walmer GB 15 E11
Wałowice PL 81 C7
Wals A 73 A6
Walsall GB 11 F8
Walschleben D 79 D8
Walsleben D 83 E13
Walsoken GB 11 F12
Walsrode D 82 E7
Waltenhofen D 71 B10
Waltershausen D 79 E8
Waltham on the Wolds GB
  11 F10
Walton-on-Thames GB 15 E8
Walton on the Naze GB 15 D11
Wamba E 39 E10
Wamel NL 183 B6
Wanderup D 82 A6
Wandlitz D 84 E4
Wandre B 183 D7
Wang A 77 F9
Wangen CH 27 F8
Wangen im Allgäu D 71 B9
Wängi CH 27 E10
Wankendorf D 83 B8
Wanna D 17 A11
Wanne-Eikel D 183 B10
Wanroij NL 183 B7
Wanssum NL 183 B8
Wantage GB 13 B12
Wanze B 19 C11
Wanzleben D 79 B9
Wapenveld NL 16 D6
Wąpiersk PL 139 D8
Waplewo PL 139 C9
Wapnica PL 85 D8
Wapno PL 85 E12
Warberg D 79 B8
Warboys GB 15 C9
Warburg D 17 F12
Warcop GB 11 B7
Warcq F 20 F5
Wardenburg D 17 B10
Wardington GB 13 A12
Ware GB 15 D8
Waregem B 19 C7
Wareham GB 13 D11
Waren D 83 C13
Warendorf D 17 E9
Warffum NL 17 B7
Warin D 83 C11
Waringstown GB 7 D10
Wark GB 5 E12
Warka PL 141 G4
Warkworth GB 5 E13
Warlingham GB 15 E8
Warloy-Baillon F 18 D6
Warlubie PL 138 C6
Warmeriville F 19 F9
Warmington GB 13 A12
Warminster GB 13 C10
Warmond GB 182 A5
Warmsen D 17 D11
Warngau D 72 A4
Warnice PL 85 D7
Warnice PL 85 E7
Warnino PL 85 C10
Warnow D 83 C11
Warnsveld NL 16 D6
Warrenpoint GB 7 D10

Warrington GB 10 E6
Warsingsfehn D 17 B8
Warslow GB 11 E8
Warstein D 17 F10
Warszawa PL 141 F4
Warszkowo PL 85 B11
Warta PL 142 C6
Warta Bolesławiecka PL 81 D9
Wartberg an der Krems A 76 G6
Wartenberg D 75 F10
Wartenberg-Angersbach
  D 78 E5
Warth A 71 C10
Wartin D 84 D6
Wartkowice PL 143 C7
Wartmannsroth D 74 B6
Warwick GB 13 A11
Warwick Bridge GB 5 F11
Warzyce PL 144 D4
Wasbek D 83 B7
Wasbister D 3 G10
Wäschenbeuren D 74 E6
Washington GB 5 F13
Wasigny F 19 E9
Wasilków PL 140 D8
Waśniów PL 143 E11
Wąsosz PL 81 C11
Wąsosz PL 140 C6
Wąsowo PL 81 B10
Waspik NL 16 E3
Wasselonne F 27 C7
Wassen CH 71 D7
Wassenaar NL 16 D2
Wassenberg D 20 B6
Wasseralfingen D 75 E7
Wasserbillig D 186 B2
Wasserburg am Inn D 75 F11
Wasserliesch D 186 B2
Wasserlosen D 74 B7
Wassertrüdingen D 75 D8
Wassigny F 19 D8
Wassy F 26 C2
Wasungen D 79 E7
Watchet GB 13 C8
Watchgate GB 10 C6
Waterbeck GB 5 E10
Waterford IRL 9 D8
Watergrasshill IRL 8 D6
Wateringen NL 182 A4
Waterland-Oudeman B 182 C3
Waterloo B 19 C9
Waterlooville GB 14 F6
Waterville IRL 8 E3
Watford GB 15 D8
Wathlingen D 79 A7
Watlington GB 14 D6
Watten F 18 C5
Wattenbeck D 83 B8
Wattens A 72 B4
Watten-Scheid D 183 C10
Wattenwil CH 31 B12
Wattlebridge GB 7 D8
Watton GB 15 B10
Wattwil CH 27 F11
Wavre B 19 C10
Wavrin F 18 C6
Waweln PL 85 D13
Wąwelno PL 142 C4
Wąwolnica PL 141 H6
Wawrów PL 85 E8
Wawrzeńczyce PL 143 F9
Waxweiler D 20 D6
Waziers F 182 E2
Weaverham GB 10 E6
Wechmar D 79 E8
Wechselburg D 79 D12
Wedde NL 17 B8
Weddingstedt D 82 B6
Wedel (Holstein) D 82 C7
Wedemore GB 13 C9
Wednesbury GB 11 F7
Wednesfield GB 11 F7
Weede D 83 C8
Weedon Bec D 13 A12
Weelde B 182 C5
Weem GB 5 B9
Weener D 17 B8
Weerberg A 72 B4
Weerselo NL 17 D7
Weert NL 16 F5
Weesen CH 27 F11
Weesp NL 16 D4
Weeze D 16 E6
Weferlingen D 79 B9
Wegberg D 20 B6
Wegenstedt D 79 B9
Weggis CH 71 C6
Wegscheid D 76 E5
Wehdel D 17 A11
Wehl NL 16 E6
Wehr D 27 E8
Wehrbleck D 17 C11
Wehringen D 71 A11
Wehrum D 183 D11
Weibersbrunn D 74 C5
Weichering D 75 E9
Weichs D 75 F9
Weida D 79 E11
Weidenberg D 75 C10
Weiden in der Oberpfalz
  D 75 C11
Weidenstetten D 187 D8
Weidenthal D 21 F10
Weiding D 75 D12
Weiersbach D 186 B3
Weigersdorf D 81 D7
Weihmichl D 75 E11
Weikersheim D 74 C6
Weil D 75 F11
Weil am Rhein D 27 E8
Weilbach D 21 E12
Weilburg D 21 D10
Weil der Stadt D 27 C10
Weilerbach D 186 C4
Weilerswist D 21 C7
Weilheim an der Teck D 74 E6
Weilheim in Oberbayern
  D 72 A3
Weilmünster D 21 D10
Weimar D 79 E9
Weinbach D 80 D5
Weinböhla D 80 D5
Weinfelden CH 27 E11
Weingarten D 71 B9
Weingarten (Baden) D 187 C6
Weinheim D 21 E11
Weinsberg D 21 F12
Weinsheim D 20 D6
Weinsheim D 21 E9
Weinstadt D 27 C11

Weischlitz D 75 B11
Weisen D 83 D11
Weiskirchen D 21 E7
Weismain D 75 B9
Weissach D 27 C10
Weißbriach A 73 C7
Weißenbach am Lech A 71 C11
Weißenberg D 81 D7
Weißenbrunn D 75 B9
Weißenfels D 79 D10
Weißenhorn D 75 F7
Weißensee D 79 D9
Weißenstadt D 75 B10
Weißenstein A 73 C8
Weißenthurm D 185 D7
Weißkirchen in Steiermark
  A 73 B10
Weißkollm D 80 D6
Weißwasser D 81 C7
Weistrach A 77 F7
Weiswampach L 20 D6
Weisweil D 27 D8
Weitbruch F 186 D4
Weitefeld D 185 C8
Weiten A 77 F8
Weitensfeld A 73 C9
Weitersfeld A 77 E9
Weiterstadt D 187 B6
Weitra A 77 E7
Weixdorf D 80 D5
Weiz A 148 B5
Wejherowo PL 138 A5
Wekerom NL 16 D5
Welkenraedt B 20 C5
Well NL 16 E6
Wellaune D 79 C12
Welle D 82 D7
Wellen B 183 D6
Wellesbourne GB 13 A11
Wellheim D 75 E9
Wellin B 19 D11
Welling D 21 D8
Wellingborough GB 15 C7
Wellington GB 10 F6
Wellington GB 13 C8
Wellingtonbridge IRL 9 D9
Wellington Bridge IRL 9 D9
Wells GB 13 C9
Wells-next-the-Sea GB 15 B10
Welney GB 11 F12
Wels A 76 F6
Welschbillig D 21 E7
Welshpool GB 10 F5
Welsickendorf D 80 C4
Welsleben D 79 C10
Welver D 17 E9
Welwyn GB 15 D8
Welwyn Garden City GB 15 D8
Welzheim D 74 E6
Welzow D 80 C6
Wem GB 10 F6
Wembdon GB 13 C8
Wemding D 75 E8
Wemeldinge NL 182 B4
Wemyss Bay GB 4 D7
Wendeburg D 79 B7
Wendelsheim D 21 E10
Wendelstein D 75 D9
Wenden D 75 C9
Wendens Ambo GB 15 D9
Wendisch Priborn D 83 D12
Wendisch Rietz D 80 B6
Wendlingen am Neckar
  D 27 C11
Wendover GB 15 D7
Wenduine B 182 C2
Wengen CH 70 D5
Wengsel (Isterberg) D 17 D8
Wennigsen (Deister) D 78 B6
Wenningstedt D 86 F2
Wenns A 71 C11
Wentorf D 83 C8
Wentorf bei Hamburg D 83 D8
Wenzenbach D 75 D11
Wenzlow D 79 B11
Wépion B 182 E5
Werbach D 74 C6
Werben D 80 C6
Werben (Elbe) D 83 E11
Werbig D 80 C4
Werbkowice PL 144 B8
Werbomont B 19 D12
Werdau D 79 E11
Werder D 79 B12
Werder D 84 C4
Werdohl D 17 F9
Werfen A 73 B7
Werlte D 17 C9
Werl D 17 E9
Wermelskirchen D 185 B7
Wermsdorf D 80 D3
Wernau D 27 C11
Wernberg-Köblitz D 75 C11
Werne D 17 E9
Werneck D 75 C7
Werneuchen D 80 A5
Wernigerode D 79 C7
Wernshausen D 79 E7
Werpeloh D 17 C9
Wertach D 71 B10
Wertheim D 74 C6
Werthenstein CH 70 C6
Werther (Westfalen) D 17 D10
Wertingen D 75 E8
Werveshoof NL 16 C4
Wervik B 182 D1
Wesel D 17 E7
Wesenberg D 84 D3
Wesendorf D 79 A8
Wesepe NL 183 A8
Wesoła PL 141 F4
Wessel PL 82 B5
Wesselburen D 82 B5
Wessling D 82 B6
Weßling D 75 F9
Wessobrunn D 71 B11
West Auckland GB 5 F13
West Bridgford GB 11 F9
West Bromwich GB 11 F8
Westbury GB 13 C10
Westendorf A 72 B5
Westenholz D 17 C11
Westerbeck (Sassenburg)
  D 79 A8
Westerbork NL 17 C7

Westerburg D 21 C9
Westerdale GB 3 J10
Westeregeln D 79 C9
Westerende-Kirchloog (Ihlow)
  D 17 B8
Westergate GB 15 F7
Westergellersen D 83 D8
Westerhaar NL 17 D7
Westerheim D 187 D8
Westerholt D 17 A8
Westerhorn D 82 C7
Westerhoven NL 183 C6
Westerland D 86 F2
Westerlo B 19 B10
Westerrönfeld D 82 B7
Westerstede D 17 B9
Westerstetten D 74 E6
Westervoort NL 16 E5
Westgate GB 5 F12
West Grinstead GB 15 E8
West Haddon GB 13 A12
Westhausen D 75 E7
Westhill GB 3 L12
Westhofen D 187 B5
Westhoffen F 186 D3
Westkapelle NL 16 E1
West Kilbride GB 4 D7
West Kirby GB 10 E5
West Knapton GB 11 C10
West Lavington GB 13 C11
Westleton GB 15 C12
West Linton GB 5 D10
West Looe GB 12 E6
West Lulworth GB 13 D10
Westmalle B 16 F3
West Malling GB 15 E9
West Meon Hut GB 15 C12
West Mersea GB 15 D10
West Moors GB 13 D11
Westness GB 3 G10
Westnewton GB 5 F10
Weston GB 11 F7
Weston GB 13 D10
Weston-super-Mare GB 13 C9
Westonzoyland GB 13 C9
Westport IRL 6 E3
Westport Quay IRL 6 E3
West Somerton GB 15 B12
West Tarbert GB 4 D6
West-Terschelling NL 16 B4
Westward Ho! GB 12 C6
West Wellow GB 13 D11
West Winch GB 11 F12
Wethau D 79 D10
Wetheral GB 5 F11
Wetherby GB 11 D9
Wetlina PL 145 E5
Wetter (Hessen) D 21 C11
Wetter (Ruhr) D 185 B7
Wetteren B 19 B8
Wetterzeube D 79 D11
Wettin D 79 C10
Wettingen CH 27 F9
Wettrup D 17 C9
Wetzikon CH 27 F10
Wetzlar D 21 C11
Wevelgem B 19 C7
Wewelsfleth D 17 A12
Wexford IRL 9 D10
Weyarn D 72 A4
Weybridge GB 15 E8
Weyerbusch D 21 C9
Weyer Markt A 73 A10
Weyersheim F 27 C8
Weyhausen D 79 B8
Weyhe D 17 C11
Weymouth GB 13 D10
Whalton GB 5 E13
Whauphill GB 4 F8
Wheddon Cross GB 13 C7
Wherwell GB 13 C12
Whiddon Down GB 13 D7
Whitburn GB 5 D9
Whitby GB 11 C10
Whitchurch GB 10 F6
Whitchurch GB 13 B8
Whitchurch GB 15 D7
Whitecross GB 7 D10
Whitegate GB 8 E6
Whitegate IRL 8 E6
Whitehall GB 3 G11
Whitehall IRL 9 C8
Whitehaven GB 10 B4
Whitehead GB 4 F5
Whitehill GB 15 C7
Whitfield GB 15 E11
Whithorn GB 5 F8
Whiting Bay GB 4 E6
Whitland GB 12 B5
Whitley Bay GB 5 E14
Whitstable GB 15 E11
Whittington GB 10 F5
Whittlesey GB 11 F11
Wiartel PL 139 C12
Wiatrowo PL 85 E12
Wiązów PL 81 E12
Wiązownica PL 144 C6
Wichelen B 19 B8
Wick GB 3 J10
Wick GB 13 C7
Wick GB 15 F7
Wickede (Ruhr) D 185 B8
Wickenrode (Helsa) D 78 D6
Wickford GB 15 D10
Wickham GB 13 D12
Wickham Market GB 15 C11
Wicklow IRL 7 G10
Wicko PL 85 A13
Widawa PL 143 C7
Widecombe in the Moor
  GB 13 D7
Widnau CH 71 C9
Widnes GB 10 E6
Widuchowa PL 84 D6
Więcbork PL 85 D12
Wieck am Darß D 83 B13
Wieczfnia Kościelna PL 139 D9
Wieda D 79 C7
Wiedensahl D 17 D12
Wiederau D 80 E3
Wiednitz D 80 D6
Wiefelstede D 17 B10
Wiehe D 79 D9
Wiehl D 21 C9
Wiek D 84 A4
Wijkszyce PL 142 F5
Wielbark PL 139 D10
Wieleń PL 85 E10
Wielenbach D 72 A3
Wielgie PL 139 E7
Wielgomłyny PL 143 D8

Wielichowo PL 81 B10
Wielczna PL 143 G9
Wieliczki PL 136 F6
Wielka Wieś PL 143 F8
Wielkie Oczy PL 144 C7
Wielki Klincz PL 138 B5
Wielopole Skrzyńskie PL 143 G12
Wielowieś PL 142 E6
Wieluń PL 142 D6
Wiemersdorf D 83 C7
Wien A 77 F10
Wienerbruck A 77 G8
Wiener Neustadt A 77 G10
Wieniawa PL 141 H3
Wieniec PL 138 E6
Wienrode D 79 C8
Wiepke D 79 A9
Wieprz PL 147 B8
Wieprz PL 147 B8
Wiercień Duży PL 141 F7
Wierden NL 17 D7
Wieren D 83 E9
Wieringerwerf NL 16 C4
Wiernsheim D 187 D6
Wieruszów PL 142 D5
Wierzawice PL 144 C5
Wierzbica PL 141 H4
Wierzbica PL 141 H8
Wierzbica Górna PL 142 D4
Wierzbicin PL 85 C8
Wierzbinek PL 138 F6
Wierzbnik PL 142 E3
Wierzbno PL 139 F12
Wierzbowa PL 81 D9
Wierzchlas PL 142 D6
Wierzchosławice PL 138 E5
Wierzchosławice PL 143 F10
Wierzchowo PL 85 C11
Wierzchowo PL 85 D10
Wierzchucino PL 138 A5
Wies A 148 C4
Wiesa D 80 E3
Wiesau D 75 C11
Wiesbaden D 21 D10
Wieselburg A 77 F8
Wiesen A 149 A6
Wiesen D 21 E7
Wiesen D 74 B5
Wiesenau D 81 B7
Wiesenburg D 79 B11
Wiesenfelden D 75 D12
Wiesensteig D 187 D8
Wiesent D 75 C9
Wiesenthau D 75 C9
Wiesentheid D 75 C7
Wiesloch D 21 F11
Wiesmath A 148 A6
Wiesmoor D 17 B9
Wieszowa PL 142 F6
Wietmarschen D 17 C8
Wietze D 78 A6
Wietzen D 17 C12
Wietzendorf D 83 E7
Wiewiórczyn PL 143 C7
Wigan GB 10 D6
Wiggensbach D 71 B11
Wigierska Górka PL 147 B8
Wijgliniec PL 81 D8
Wigmore GB 13 A9
Wigorzewo PL 136 E4
Wigorzyno PL 85 C9
Wigrów PL 139 F13
Wigrzynice PL 81 B8
Wigrzynowo PL 139 F9
Wigston GB 11 F9
Wigton GB 5 F10
Wigtown GB 5 F8
Wijchen NL 16 E5
Wijewo PL 81 C10
Wijhe NL 183 A8
Wijk aan Zee NL 16 D3
Wijk bij Duurstede NL 16 E4
Wijk en Aalburg NL 183 B6
Wil CH 27 F11
Wilamowice PL 147 B8
Wilczjta PL 139 B8
Wilczogóra PL 138 F5
Wilczyn PL 138 F5
Wildalpen A 73 A10
Wildau D 80 B5
Wildberg D 27 C10
Wildberg D 83 E13
Wildberg D 84 C4
Wildeck-Richelsdorf D 79 E7
Wildendürnbach A 77 E10
Wildenfels D 79 E12
Wildeshausen D 17 C10
Wildflecken D 74 B6
Wildon A 148 C5
Wildpoldsried D 71 B10
Wildshut A 76 F3
Wilga PL 141 G4
Wilhelminadorp NL 183 C6
Wilhelmsburg A 77 F9
Wilhelmsburg D 84 C5
Wilhelmsdorf D 27 E11
Wilhelmshaven D 17 A10
Wilkau-Haßlau D 79 E12
Wilkinstown IRL 7 E9
Wilkołaz Pierwszy PL 144 A5
Wilków PL 141 H5
Wilków PL 142 D4
Wilkowice PL 147 B8
Wilkowo PL 81 B8
Willand GB 13 D8
Willebadessen D 17 E12
Willebroek B 19 B9
Willemstad NL 16 E2
Willich D 17 F7
Willingdon GB 15 F9
Willingen (Upland) D 17 F11
Willingshausen D 21 C12
Willisau CH 27 F9
Williton GB 13 C8
Willstätt D 27 C8
Wilmersdorf D 84 D5
Wilmslow GB 11 E7
Wilnis NL 182 A5
Wilnsdorf D 21 C10
Wilp NL 183 A8
Wilsdruff D 80 D5
Wilsickow D 84 D5
Wilster D 82 C6
Wilsum D 17 C7
Wiltersdorf A 77 E11
Wiltingen D 21 E7
Wilton GB 13 C11
Wiltz L 20 E5
Wimblington GB 11 F12
Wimborne Minster GB 13 D11
Wimereux F 15 F12
Wimmelburg D 79 C10

Wimmis CH 70 D5
Wimpassing A 148 A6
Wincanton GB 13 C10
Winchburgh GB 5 D10
Winchelsea GB 15 F10
Wincheringen D 186 B1
Winchester GB 13 C12
Wincrange L 20 D5
Winda PL 136 E3
Windach D 71 A12
Windeby D 83 B7
Windermere GB 10 C6
Windesheim D 21 E9
Windhagen D 21 C8
Windigsteig A 77 E8
Windischeschenbach D 75 C11
Windischgarsten A 73 A9
Windorf D 76 E4
Windsbach D 75 D8
Windsor GB 15 E7
Wingate GB 5 F14
Wingene B 19 B7
Wingen-sur-Moder F 27 C7
Winklarn D 75 D11
Winkleigh GB 13 D7
Winklern A 73 C6
Winklern bei Oberwölz A 73 B9
Winnenden D 27 C11
Winnert D 82 B6
Winnica PL 139 E10
Winningen D 79 C9
Winningen D 185 D8
Winnweiler D 186 B4
Winschoten NL 17 B8
Winsen (Aller) D 83 E7
Winsen (Luhe) D 83 D8
Winsford GB 10 E6
Wińsko PL 81 D11
Winslow GB 15 D7
Winssen NL 183 B7
Winston GB 11 B8
Winsum NL 16 B5
Winterberg D 21 B11
Winterbourne Abbas GB 13 D9
Winterfeld D 83 E10
Winterswijk NL 17 E7
Winterthur CH 27 E10
Winterton GB 11 D10
Winton GB 11 C7
Wintrich D 185 E6
Wintzenheim F 27 D7
Winwick GB 15 C8
Winzenburg D 78 C6
Winzer D 76 E4
Wipperdorf D 79 D8
Wipperfürth D 21 B8
Wippra Kurort D 79 C8
Wirdumer (Wirdum) D 17 B8
Wirges D 185 D8
Wirksworth GB 11 E8
Wirsberg D 75 B10
Wisbech GB 11 F12
Wischhafen D 17 A12
Wishaw GB 5 D9
Wiskitki PL 141 F2
Wisła PL 147 B7
Wiślica PL 143 F10
Wismar D 83 C10
Wiśniew PL 141 F6
Wiśniewo PL 139 D9
Wiśniowa PL 144 D1
Wiśniowa PL 144 D4
Wissant F 15 F12
Wissembourg F 27 B8
Wissen D 21 C9
Wissenkerke NL 16 E1
Wistedt D 82 D7
Wisznia Mała PL 81 D12
Wisznice PL 141 G8
Witaszyce PL 142 C4
Witham GB 15 D10
Witheridge GB 13 D7
Withernsea GB 11 D12
Witkowo PL 85 D8
Witkowo PL 138 F4
Witley GB 15 E7
Witmarsum NL 16 B4
Witney GB 13 B12
Witnica PL 84 E6
Witnica PL 85 E7
Witonia PL 143 B7
Witosław PL 85 D12
Witry-lès-Reims F 19 F9
Wittdün D 82 A4
Witten D 17 F8
Wittenbach CH 27 F11
Wittenberge D 83 E11
Wittenburg D 83 C10
Wittenförden D 83 C10
Wittenhagen D 84 B4
Wittenheim F 27 E7
Wittibreut D 76 F3
Wittichenau D 80 D6
Wittighausen D 74 C6
Wittingen D 83 E9
Wittlich D 21 E7
Wittmund D 17 A9
Wittstock D 83 D12
Witzenhausen D 78 D6
Witzin D 83 C11
Witzwort D 82 B5
Wiveliscombe GB 13 C8
Wivenhoe GB 15 D10
Wiżajny PL 136 E6
Wizna PL 140 D6
Władysławowo PL 142 B5
Władysławowo PL 138 A5
Wleń PL 81 D9
Włocławek PL 138 E7
Włodawa PL 141 G9
Włodzienin PL 142 F4
Włodzimierzów PL 143 D8
Włostów PL 143 E11
Włoszakowice PL 81 C10
Włoszczowa PL 143 E8
Wöbbelin D 83 D11
Woburn GB 15 D7
Wodynie PL 141 F5
Wodzierady PL 143 C7
Wodzisław PL 143 E9
Wodzisław Śląski PL 142 F5
Woensdrecht NL 182 C4
Woerden NL 16 D3
Wœrth F 27 C8
Wohlen CH 27 F9
Wohlen CH 31 B11
Wohlmirstedt D 79 D9
Wohltorf D 83 C8
Wöhrden D 82 B6
Wohyń PL 141 G7
Woippy F 26 B5

Wojaszówka PL 144 D4
Wojcieszków PL 141 G6
Wojcieszów PL 81 E9
Wójcin PL 138 E5
Wojkowice PL 143 F7
Wojnicz PL 143 G10
Wojnowo PL 138 D4
Wojsławice PL 144 B8
Woking GB 15 E7
Wokingham GB 15 E7
Wola PL 138 E7
Wola Mołodycka PL 144 C6
Wola Mysłowska PL 141 G5
Wolanów PL 141 H3
Wola-Rjbkowska PL 141 G5
Wola Uhruska PL 141 H9
Wola Wierzbowska PL 139 E10
Wolbórz PL 141 H1
Wolbrom PL 143 F8
Wołczyn PL 142 D5
Woldegk D 84 D5
Woldendorp NL 17 B8
Wolfach D 27 D9
Wolfegg D 71 B9
Wolfen D 79 C11
Wolfenbüttel D 79 B8
Wolfersheim D 21 D11
Wolfhagen D 17 F12
Wölfis D 79 E8
Wolfpassing A 77 F8
Wolfratshausen D 72 A3
Wolfsberg A 73 C10
Wolfsburg D 79 B8
Wolfstein D 21 E9
Wolfurt A 71 C9
Wolgast D 84 B5
Wolhusen CH 70 C6
Wolin PL 84 C7
Wólka PL 85 D12
Wólka PL 141 H7
Wólka Dobryńska PL 141 F8
Wolkersdorf A 77 F11
Wollbach D 75 B7
Wollerau CH 27 F10
Wolmirstedt D 79 B10
Wolnzach D 75 E10
Wołomin PL 139 F11
Woloskowola PL 141 H8
Wołów PL 81 D11
Wolpertshausen D 74 D6
Wolpertswende D 71 B9
Wolphaartsdijk NL 182 B3
Wolsingham GB 5 F13
Wolsztyn PL 81 B10
Woltersdorf D 80 B4
Woltersdorf D 83 E10
Wolvega NL 16 C6
Wolverhampton GB 11 F7
Wombwell GB 11 D9
Wommelgem B 19 B10
Wommels NL 16 B5
Wonfurt D 75 B7
Wonsees D 75 C9
Woodbridge GB 15 C11
Woodcote GB 13 B12
Woodford IRL 6 F6
Woodhall Spa GB 11 E11
Woodland GB 5 F13
Woodley GB 15 E7
Woodstock GB 13 B12
Woodton GB 15 C11
Woodtown IRL 7 E9
Wool GB 13 D10
Wooler GB 5 D12
Wootton Bassett GB 13 B11
Worb CH 31 B12
Worbis D 79 D7
Worcester GB 13 A10
Wördern A 77 F10
Worfield GB 11 F7
Wörgl A 72 B5
Workington GB 5 F9
Worksop GB 11 E9
Workum NL 16 C4
Wörlitz D 79 C11
Wormeldange L 20 E6
Wormerveer NL 16 D3
Wormhout F 18 C5
Worms D 21 E10
Worpswede D 17 B11
Wörrstadt D 21 E10
Wörschach A 73 A9
Wörtel B 182 C5
Wörth A 73 B6
Worth GB 15 E8
Wörth am Main D 187 B7
Wörth am Rhein D 27 B9
Worthing GB 15 F8
Woudenberg NL 183 A6
Woudrichem NL 16 E3
Woudsend NL 16 C5
Woustviller F 27 B7
Wouw NL 16 E2
Woźniki PL 143 E7
Wragby GB 11 E11
Wrangle GB 11 E12
Wrecsam GB 10 E6
Wręczyca Wielka PL 143 E6
Wredenhagen D 83 D13
Wrelton GB 11 C10
Wremen D 17 A11
Wrestedt D 83 E9
Wrexham GB 10 E6
Wriedel D 83 E8
Wriezen D 84 E6
Wrist D 82 C7
Wróblew PL 142 C6
Wrocław PL 81 D12
Wrohm D 82 B6
Wronki PL 85 E10
Wronki PL 136 E5
Wrotnów PL 139 E13
Wrząkelka PL 142 B6
Wrzelowiec PL 144 A4
Wrzeście PL 85 A12
Września PL 85 F13
Wrzosowo PL 85 B9
Wschowa PL 81 C10
Wulfen D 79 C10
Wulferstorf D 83 D10
Wülfershausen an der Saale D 75 B7
Wulfsen D 83 D8
Wulften D 79 C7
Wulkau D 83 E12
Wüllersdorf A 77 E10
Wundschuh A 148 C4
Wünnenberg D 17 E11
Wünsdorf D 80 B4
Wunsiedel D 75 B11
Wunstorf D 78 B5

Wuppertal D 17 F8
Wurmlingen D 27 D10
Würselen D 20 C6
Wurzbach D 75 B10
Würzburg D 74 C6
Wurzen D 79 D12
Wüstenrot D 27 B11
Wusterhausen D 83 E12
Wusterhusen D 84 B5
Wustermark D 79 A12
Wusterwitz D 79 B11
Wustrau-Altfriesack D 84 E3
Wustrow D 83 E10
Wustrow D 84 D3
Wustrow D 83 B12
Wutha D 79 E7
Wutöschingen D 27 E9
Wuustwezel B 16 F3
Wyczechy PL 85 C12
Wydminy PL 136 F5
Wye GB 15 E10
Wygoda PL 143 E7
Wygon PL 85 D9
Wyhl D 27 D8
Wyk auf Föhr D 82 A5
Wylatowo PL 138 E5
Wylye GB 13 C11
Wymondham GB 15 B11
Wyre Piddle GB 13 A10
Wyrozjby-Konaty PL 141 E7
Wyry PL 143 F6
Wyryki-Połód PL 141 G8
Wyrzysk PL 85 D12
Wyśmierzyce PL 141 G3
Wysoka PL 85 D12
Wysoka PL 85 A8
Wysoka Kamieńska PL 85 C7
Wysokie PL 136 F6
Wysokie PL 144 B6
Wysokie Mazowieckie PL 141 E7
Wysowa PL 145 E3
Wyszanów PL 142 D5
Wyszki PL 141 E7
Wyszków PL 139 E11
Wyszogród PL 139 F9
Wyszyny PL 85 E11
Wythall GB 13 A11
Wytyczno PL 141 H8

X

Xanceda E 38 B3
Xanten D 17 E6
Xanthi GR 171 B7
Xarrê AL 168 E3
Xátiva E 56 D3
Xeraco E 56 C4
Xeresa E 56 C4
Xermade E 38 B4
Xerta E 42 F5
Xertigny F 26 D5
Xifiani GR 169 C7
Xino Nero GR 169 C6
Xinzo de Limia E 38 D4
Xirivella E 48 F4
Xirochori GR 174 D4
Xirokampi GR 174 F5
Xirokampo GR 177 E8
Xiropotamos GR 170 B6
Xixón E 39 A8
Xonrupt-Longemer F 27 D6
Xove E 38 A4
Xunqueira de Ambía E 38 D4
Xylagani GR 171 C8
Xylokastro GR 175 C6
Xyloupoli GR 169 C9

Y

Yablanitsa BG 165 C9
Yablanovo BG 167 D7
Yabluniv UA 152 A5
Yabŭlchevo BG 167 D8
Yabŭlkovo BG 166 E4
Yağci TR 173 C7
Yağcilar TR 173 F9
Yağcili TR 173 F8
Yagoda BG 166 D5
Yakimovo BG 160 F2
Yakoruda BG 165 E8
Yakovo BG 169 A9
Yaliçiftlik TR 173 D10
Yalikavak TR 177 E9
Yaliköy TR 173 B9
Yalova TR 173 C8
Yambol BG 167 E7
Yamkino RUS 132 F5
Yamm RUS 132 E3
Yampil' UA 154 A2
Yangi TR 181 C9
Yanguas E 41 D7
Yanikağil TR 173 B8
Yaniskoski RUS 114 F5
Yankavichy BY 133 E5
Yankovo BG 167 C8
Yantarnyy RUS 139 A8
Yapildak TR 172 D6
Yaraş TR 181 B8
Yareva BY 135 F13
Yarlovo BG 165 E7
Yarm GB 11 B9
Yarmouth GB 13 D12
Yarnton GB 13 B12
Yarove UA 154 E4
Yarrow GB 5 D10
Yasen BG 165 C10
Yasen' UA 145 F9
Yasenkovo BG 167 B7
Yasenovets BG 161 F9
Yasinya UA 145 F8
Yas'ky UA 154 D6
Yasna Polyana BG 167 E9
Yassiören TR 173 B10
Yasski RUS 132 F7
Yatağan TR 181 B8
Yate GB 13 B10
Yatova E 48 F3
Yavora UA 145 E7
Yavoriv UA 144 D7
Yavoriv UA 152 A5
Yaxley GB 11 F11
Yaylagöne TR 172 C6
Yazibaşi TR 177 C9
Yaziköy TR 181 B8
Yazna BY 133 F4
Yazvina BY 133 F7
Ybbs an der Donau A 77 F8
Ybbsitz A 77 G7
Ychoux F 32 B4
Ydby DK 86 B2
Ydes F 29 E10

Ydra GR 175 E7
Ydrefors S 92 D7
Y Drenewydd GB 10 F5
Yeadon GB 11 D8
Yealmpton GB 13 E7
Yebra E 47 D7
Yebra de Basa E 32 F5
Yecla E 56 D2
Yecla de Yeltes E 45 C8
Yedy BY 133 F2
Yémeda E 47 E9
Yemişendere TR 181 B9
Yenice TR 171 C10
Yenice TR 173 D7
Yenice TR 173 D9
Yenice TR 181 B8
Yeniçiftlik TR 173 B8
Yeniçiftlik TR 173 B8
Yeniçiftlik TR 177 C9
Yenifoça TR 177 B8
Yenihisar TR 177 E9
Yeniköy TR 173 B6
Yeniköy TR 173 E8
Yeniköy TR 173 B9
Yeniköy TR 177 B9
Yeniköy TR 177 C9
Yeniköy TR 177 C9
Yeniköy TR 177 E9
Yeniköy TR 181 B8
Yenimuhacirköy TR 172 C6
Yenişakran TR 177 B9
Yenne F 31 D8
Yeovil GB 13 D9
Yepes E 46 E5
Yerkesik TR 181 B8
Yerseke NL 16 F2
Yershovo RUS 132 F3
Yerville F 18 E2
Yesa E 32 E3
Yeşilsırt TR 173 B7
Yeşilyurt TR 181 B8
Yeste E 55 C8
Yevtodiya UA 154 B4
Yezyaryshcha BY 133 E7
Y Fenni GB 13 B8
Ygos-St-Saturnin F 32 C4
ygrande F 30 B2
Ykspihlaja FIN 123 C10
Ylakiai LT 134 D3
Yläköngäs FIN 113 D17
Ylä-Luosta FIN 125 D11
Ylämaa FIN 129 D9
Ylämylly FIN 125 E13
Yläne FIN 126 D7
Ylä-Valtimo FIN 125 C11
Ylihärmä FIN 122 D9
Ylijärvi FIN 128 D8
Yli-Kärppä FIN 119 C15
Ylikiiminki FIN 119 D16
Yli-Körkkö FIN 119 B16
Ylikulma FIN 127 E9
Yli-Kurki FIN 121 D10
Ylikylä FIN 115 E2
Ylikylä FIN 117 E15
Ylikylä FIN 123 D12
Ylikylä FIN 123 D10
Ylikylä FIN 125 C12
Yli-Kyrö FIN 117 B12
Yli-Lesti FIN 123 D13
Yli-Liakka FIN 119 C12
Yli-Livo FIN 120 C9
Yli-Muonio FIN 117 B10
Yli-Nampa FIN 117 E16
Ylinenjärvi S 117 E10
Yli-Olhava FIN 119 C15
Ylipää FIN 119 E12
Ylipää FIN 119 E13
Ylipää FIN 119 E13
Ylipää FIN 119 E16
Ylipää FIN 119 F13
Ylipää FIN 123 C14
Ylipää FIN 123 D11
Yli-Paakkola FIN 119 B13
Yli-Siurua FIN 119 C17
Yli-Tannila FIN 119 D16
Ylitornio FIN 119 B11
Yli-Utos FIN 120 E8
Yli-Valli FIN 123 F9
Ylivieska FIN 123 D13
Yli-Vuotto FIN 119 E17
Ylläsjärvi FIN 117 C12
Ylöjärvi FIN 127 B10
Ylönkylä FIN 127 E9
Ylvingen N 108 E3
Ymonville F 24 D6
Yngsjö S 88 D6
Yöğuntaş TR 167 F8
Yolageldi TR 173 A6
Yonkovo BG 161 F9
York GB 11 D9
Youghal IRL 9 E7
Yovkovo BG 155 F2
Yoxford GB 15 C12
Ypäjä FIN 127 D9
Ypäjänkylä FIN 127 D9
Ypati GR 174 B5
Yport F 18 E1
Yppäri FIN 119 F12
Ypsos GR 168 E2
Ypso TR 123 C13
Yrittäperä FIN 121 D10
Yrttivaara S 116 E7
Ysane S 88 C7
Ysbyty Ystwyth GB 13 A7
Ysselsteyn NL 183 C7
Yssingeaux F 30 E5
Ystad S 87 E13
Ystalyfera GB 13 B7
Ytre Arna N 94 B2
Ytre Billefjord N 113 C15
Ytre Kjæs N 113 B16
Ytre Sandvik N 113 C15
Ytterån S 105 E16
Ytteräng S 105 D14
Ytterberg S 102 B7
Ytter-Busjö S 107 B13
Ytteresse FIN 123 C9
Ytterhogdal S 102 B6
Ytterjeppo FIN 122 D9
Yttermalung S 102 E6
Yttersta S 118 D6
Ytterträsk S 118 F4
Ytterturingen S 103 B9
Yttervik S 109 E10
Yttre Lansjärv S 116 E14
Yukaribey TR 177 A9
Yukarikizilca TR 177 C9

Yukhavichy BY 133 D5
Yuncler E 46 D5
Yuncos E 46 D5
Yundola BG 165 E8
Yunquera E 53 C7
Yunquera de Henares E 47 C6
Yuper BG 161 F8
Yurasishki BY 137 E12
Yuratsishki BY 137 E12
Yürücekler TR 173 E10
Yürük TR 173 C7
Yutz F 20 F6
Yuzhnyy RUS 136 D2
Yverdon CH 31 B10
Yvetot F 18 E2
Yvignac F 23 D7
Yvoir B 19 D10
Yvoire F 31 C9
Yvonand CH 31 B10
Yxnerum S 93 C8
Yxsjö S 107 C13
Yxsjöberg S 97 B12
Yxskaftkälen S 106 D8
Yzeure F 30 B3
Yzeures-sur-Creuse F 29 B7

Z

Zaamslag NL 182 C3
Zaandam NL 16 D3
Zaazyer"ye BY 133 F5
Žabalj SRB 158 C5
Žabari SRB 159 E7
Zabeltitz-Treugeböhla D 80 D5
Žabia Wola PL 141 F3
Žabica BIH 162 D5
Žabiče SLO 67 A9
Zabiele PL 139 D12
Zabierzów PL 143 F8
Ząbki PL 141 F4
Ząbkowice Śląskie PL 81 E11
Žabljak MNE 163 D7
Żabno PL 143 F10
Žabno HR 148 D5
Żabok PL 85 D7
Žabokreky SK 147 C7
Žabokreky nad Nitrou SK 146 D6
Żabolova UA 133 A2
Zábor PL 81 C9
Zabor"ye BY 133 E6
Żabów PL 85 D7
Zabowo PL 85 C8
Zábřani PL 143 F10
Zabrđe BIH 157 C10
Zábřeh CZ 77 C11
Zăbriceni MD 153 A10
Zabrze PL 142 F6
Zabŭrdo BG 165 F10
Zabuzhzhya UA 141 H9
Zacharo GR 174 E4
Zaclau RUS 155 C2
Žacléř CZ 81 E9
Zaczopki PL 141 F8
Zadar HR 156 D3
Zadunayivka UA 154 F4
Zádveřice CZ 146 C5
Zadzim PL 142 C6
Zadzyezhzha BY 133 E4
Zafarraya E 53 C8
Zaffarana Etnea I 59 D7
Zafirovo BG 161 F9
Zafra E 51 C7
Zafra de Záncara E 47 E7
Zafrilla E 47 D9
Žaga SLO 73 D8
Żagań PL 81 C8
Zagår RO 152 E5
Żagare LT 134 D6
Zagkliveri GR 169 C9
Žaglav HR 67 E11
Zagnańsk PL 143 E10
Zagon RO 153 F8
Zagora GR 169 F9
Zagorë AL 163 E8
Zagorje SLO 73 E9
Zagorje ob Savi SLO 73 D10
Zagórów PL 142 B4
Zagortsi BG 167 E8
Zagra PL 145 D5
Zagra RO 152 C4
Zagrazhden BG 160 F5
Zagrazhden BG 166 F3
Zagrodno PL 81 D9
Zagrović HR 156 D5
Žagubica SRB 159 E8
Zagvozd HR 157 F7
Zagyvaréskas H 150 C5
Zahara E 51 F9
Zahara de los Atunes E 52 D5
Zahinos E 51 C6
Zahna D 79 C12
Zahnitkiv UA 154 A3
Záhony H 145 G5
Záhorská Ves SK 77 F11
Zahor"ye BY 133 F5
Žăicani MD 153 B10
Zaiceva LV 133 B2
Zaidín E 42 D4
Žaiginys LT 134 F6
Zaim MD 154 D4
Zajas MK 168 A4
Zaječar SRB 159 F9
Zaječov CZ 76 C5
Zajezierze PL 81 C8
Zákamenné SK 147 C8
Zákány H 149 D7
Zákányszek H 150 E4
Zakharnichy BY 133 E5
Zakliczyn PL 144 D2
Zaklików PL 144 B5
Zaklopača BIH 157 D11
Zakoma BIH 157 D8
Zakopane PL 147 C9
Zakros GR 179 E11
Zakrzew PL 141 H4
Zakrzewo PL 85 D8
Zakrzewo PL 138 E6
Zakrzówek-Wieś PL 144 B5
Zákupy CZ 81 E7
Zalaapáti H 149 C8
Zalaegerszeg H 149 C7
Zalakaros H 149 C8

Zalakomár H 149 C8
Zalalövő H 149 C7
Zalamea de la Serena E 51 B8
Zalamea la Real E 51 D6
Zalaszántó H 149 C7
Zalaszentbalázs H 149 C7
Zalaszentgrót H 149 C8
Zalaszentiván H 149 C7
Zalău RO 151 C11
Zalavár H 149 C8
Zalavas LT 135 F11
Zalazy PL 141 H5
Zaldibar E 41 B6
Žalec SLO 73 D11
Zalenieki LV 134 C7
Zalesie PL 85 E13
Zalesie PL 141 F8
Zalesie Śląskie PL 142 F5
Zalesje LV 133 D4
Zales'ye RUS 136 D4
Zaleszany PL 144 B4
Zalewo PL 139 C8
Zalha RO 152 C3
Žalīte LV 135 C8
Zalivnoye RUS 136 D2
Zall-Dardhë AL 163 F9
Żalno PL 138 C4
Zalogovac SRB 159 F7
Zaltbommel NL 16 E4
Załuski PL 139 E10
Zalužje BIH 158 E3
Zalužnica HR 156 C3
Zalve LV 135 D10
Zalyessye BY 133 E4
Zalyessye BY 137 E13
Zam RO 151 F10
Zamárdi H 149 C9
Zamarte PL 85 C12
Zámbreasca RO 160 E6
Zambrów PL 140 D6
Zambujal de Cima E 50 C1
Zambujeira do Mar E 50 D2
Zamjcin PL 85 D9
Zamfirovo BG 165 C7
Zamogil'ye RUS 132 D2
Zámoly H 149 B10
Zamora E 39 E8
Zamość PL 139 D12
Zamość PL 144 B7
Zamoshsha BY 133 F2
Zamostea RO 153 B8
Zams A 71 C11
Zámutov SK 145 F4
Zandhoven B 19 B10
Žandov CZ 80 E6
Zandvliet B 16 F2
Zandvoort NL 16 D3
Žănești RO 153 D9
Zănești RO 161 C9
Žarnovica SK 147 D7
Żarnów PL 141 H2
Zarnowiec PL 143 F8
Zaronsza B 137 F7
Żarošīce CZ 77 D11
Żarów PL 81 E10
Zarpen D 83 C9
Zarra E 47 F10
Zarren B 182 C1
Zarrentin D 83 C9
Żarszyn PL 145 D5
Żary PL 81 C8
Żarki Wielkie PL 81 C7
Zărnești RO 160 B6
Zărnești RO 161 C9
Zaronowicz BY 133 F8
Zaronowiec PL 143 F8
Zaronasa B 137 F7
Zas E 38 B2
Zasa LV 135 D11
Zaskarki BY 133 F5
Žaškov SK 147 C7
Zasliai LT 137 D10
Zásmuky CZ 77 C8
Zasów PL 143 F11
Zastrażiště HR 157 F6
Žatec CZ 76 B4
Zaton HR 156 D4
Zaton HR 162 D5
Zátor CZ 142 F4
Zator PL 143 G7
Zatory PL 139 E11
Zătreni RO 160 D3
Zatyshshya UA 154 C5
Zaube LV 135 C10
Zau de Câmpie RO 152 D4
Zavadka UA 145 E2
Závadka nad Hronom SK 147 D9
Zavala BIH 162 D4
Zavala HR 157 F6
Zavalje BIH 156 C4
Zavallya UA 153 A7
Zavallya UA 154 A6
Zavattarello I 37 B10

Závažná Poruba SK 147 C9
Zaventem B 19 C9
Zavet BG 161 F9
Zavidovići BIH 157 D9
Zavlaka SRB 158 E3
Závoaia RO 161 D10
Závod SK 77 E12
Zavoj RO 159 B9
Zavoj BIH 157 C6
Zavutstsye BY 133 F4
Zavyachellye BY 133 F5
Zavydovychi UA 144 D8
Zawada PL 81 C9
Zawada PL 141 G1
Zawada PL 142 E4
Zawada PL 143 E7
Zawada PL 144 B7
Zawady PL 140 D7
Zawadzkie PL 142 E5
Zawichost PL 144 B4
Zawidów PL 81 D8
Zawidz Kościelny PL 139 E8
Zawiercie PL 143 F7
Zawoja PL 147 B9
Zawonia PL 81 D12
Zaytsevo RUS 132 F4
Zažina HR 148 E6
Zázrivá SK 147 C8
Zažvlč HR 156 E4
Zbąszyn PL 81 B9
Zbąszynek PL 81 B9
Zbehy SK 146 E6
Zberoaia MD 153 D12
Zbiczno PL 139 D7
Zbiersk PL 142 C5
Zbiroh CZ 76 C5
Zblewo PL 138 C5
Zbludowice PL 143 F10
Zbójna PL 139 D12
Zbójno PL 139 D7
Zborov SK 145 E3
Zborovice CZ 146 C4
Zborov nad Bystricou SK 147 C7
Zbraslav CZ 77 D10
Zbraslavice CZ 77 C8
Zbrzeźnica PL 140 D6
Zbuczyn Poduchowny PL 141 F6
Ždala PL 149 D8
Žďánice CZ 77 D12
Žďár CZ 77 A8
Žďár nad Sázavou CZ 77 C9
Zdenci HR 149 E9
Ždiar SK 145 E1
Zdice CZ 76 C5
Zdihovo HR 67 B11
Zdíkov CZ 76 D5
Ždírec nad Doubravou CZ 77 C9
Zdounky CZ 146 C4
Zdralovac BIH 157 E6
Zdravets BG 167 C9
Zdravinje SRB 164 C3
Ždrelac HR 67 D11
Ždrelo SRB 159 E8
Zdunje MK 164 F3
Zduńska Wola PL 143 C6
Zduny PL 81 C12
Zduny PL 141 F1
Zdynia PL 145 E3
Zdziarzec PL 143 F11
Zdziechowa PL 85 E13
Zdzieszowice PL 142 F5
Zdziłowice PL 144 B6
Zbjowice PL 142 E5
Žebrák CZ 76 C5
Žebreira P 45 E6
Zebrene LV 134 C5
Zebrzydowa PL 81 D8

Zechlinerhütte D 84 D3
Zeddam NL 183 B8
Zeddiani I 64 D2
Zedelgem B 19 B7
Zederhaus A 73 B8
Žednik SRB 150 F4
Zeebrugge B 19 B7
Zeeland NL 16 E5
Zeewolde NL 183 A7
Zegama E 32 E1
Żegiestów PL 145 E4
Żegljane MK 164 E4
Żegocina PL 144 D1
Žehra SK 145 F2
Zehdenick D 84 D4
Zehna D 83 C12
Žehra SK 145 F2
Zehren D 80 D4
Zeilarn D 76 F3
Žeimelis LT 135 D8
Žeimiai LT 135 F8
Zeiselmauer A 77 F10
Zeiskam D 187 C5
Zeist NL 16 D4
Zeithain D 80 D4
Zeitlofs D 74 B6
Zeitz D 79 D11
Zejmen AL 163 F8
Żelazków PL 142 C5
Zele B 19 B9
Żelechlinek PL 141 G2
Żelechów PL 141 G5
Zelena UA 152 A5
Zelena UA 152 B5
Zelena UA 153 A9
Zeleneč SK 146 E5
Zeleni Jadar BIH 158 E3
Zelenikovo BG 166 E4
Zelenikovo MK 164 F4
Zelenogorsk RUS 129 C12
Zelenogradsk RUS 136 D1
Zelenohirs'ke UA 154 B6
Želetava CZ 77 D9
Železná Ruda CZ 76 D4
Železné SK 147 D8
Železnica CZ 77 B8
Železnice CZ 77 B8
Železný Brod CZ 81 E8
Zelhem NL 16 D6
Żeliszowce SK 147 E7
Zelina HR 148 E6
Zelinja BIH 157 C9
Želino MK 164 F3
Żeliv CZ 77 C8
Żeljuša BIH 157 F8
Żelków-Kolonia PL 141 F6
Zell D 75 B10
Zell (Mosel) D 21 D8
Zella-Mehlis D 79 E8
Zell am Harmersbach D 27 D9
Zell am Main D 187 B8
Zell am See A 73 B6
Zell am Ziller A 72 B4
Zell im Wiesental D 27 E8
Zellingen D 74 C6
Zell-Pfarre A 73 D9
Zelmeņi LV 134 D6
Żelowce SK 147 E8
Zelów PL 143 D7
Zeltingen-Rachtig D 21 E8
Zeltiņi LV 135 B13
Zeltweg A 73 B10
Zelva LT 135 F10
Zelzate B 19 B8
Žemaičiu Naumiestis LT 134 F3
Žemberovce SK 147 E7
Zemblak AL 168 C4

Zembrów PL 141 E6
Zembrzyce PL 147 B9
Zemen BG 165 E6
Zemeno GR 175 C6
Zemes RO 153 D8
Zemianska Olča SK 146 F5
Zemītė LV 134 C5
Zemmer D 21 E7
Zemné SK 146 F5
Zemplénagárd H 145 G5
Zemplínske Hámre SK 145 F5
Zemst B 19 C9
Zemun SRB 158 D5
Zenica BIH 157 D8
Zennor GB 12 E3
Zentene LV 134 B5
Žepa BIH 157 E11
Žepče BIH 157 D8
Žeravice CZ 146 C4
Zerbst D 79 C11
Zerf D 21 E7
Zerind RO 151 D8
Žerkov PL 142 B4
Zernez CH 71 D10
Zernien D 83 D9
Zernitz D 83 E12
Zero Branco I 72 E5
Zerpenschleuse D 84 D4
Zerrenthin D 84 D6
Zestoa E 32 D1
Žetale SLO 148 D5
Zetea RO 152 E6
Zetel D 17 B9
Zet'ovo BG 166 E4
Zeulenroda D 79 E10
Zeven D 17 B12
Zevenaar NL 16 E6
Zevenbergen NL 16 E3
Zevgolatio GR 175 D6
Zevio I 66 B3
Zeytinalani TR 181 C9
Zeytinbağı TR 177 B9
Zeytineli TR 177 C8
Zeytinli TR 173 E6
Zeytinliova TR 177 B10
Zgierz PL 143 C8
Zgłobice PL 143 G10
Zgornje Bitnje SLO 73 D7
Zgornje Jezersko SLO 73 D9
Zgornji Duplek SLO 148 C5
Zgorzelec PL 81 D8
Zgropolci MD 169 A6
Zguriţa MD 153 A11
Zhabinka BY 141 F10
Zhabka UA 154 A3
Zhabokrychka UA 154 A3
Zhdenievo UA 145 G7
Zhegěr RKS 164 E3
Zhelezdovno PL 136 E7
Zhelezdovorozhnyy RUS 136 E3
Zhelyazkovo BG 167 E8
Zhelyu Voyvoda BG 167 D6
Zheravna BG 167 D6
Zhilino RUS 136 D4
Zhitkovo RUS 129 C11
Zhitnitsa BG 167 C9
Zhitom AL 168 C3
Zhodzishki BY 137 D13
Zhorany UA 141 H9
Zhovkva UA 144 C8
Zhovtantsi UA 144 D9
Zhovtneve UA 144 B9
Zhovtneve UA 155 B3
Zhovtyy Yar UA 154 F5
Zhuprany BY 137 E13
Zhur RKS 164 E2
Zhvyrka UA 144 C9

Zhydachiv UA 145 E9
Zhyrmuny BY 137 E11
Žiar nad Hronom SK 147 D7
Zibalai LT 137 C10
Zibello I 66 B1
Zibreira P 44 F3
Zicavo F 37 H10
Žichovice CZ 76 D5
Zickhusen D 83 C10
Zidani Most SLO 73 D11
Zidikai LT 134 D4
Ziduri RO 161 C10
Zijbice PL 81 E12
Ziedkalne LV 134 D6
Ziegelroda D 79 D9
Ziegendorf D 83 D11
Ziegenrück D 79 E10
Ziegra D 80 D4
Zieleniewo PL 85 B9
Zieleniewo PL 85 D9
Zielitz D 79 B10
Zielkowice PL 141 F2
Zielona PL 139 D8
Zielona Chocina PL 85 C12
Zielona Góra PL 81 C9
Zielona Góra PL 85 E11
Zielonka PL 139 F11
Zielonki PL 143 F8
Zieluń PL 139 D8
Ziemeri LV 131 F14
Ziemnice Wielkie PL 142 E4
Ziemupe LV 134 C2
Zierenberg D 17 F12
Zierikzee NL 16 E1
Zierow D 83 D11
Ziesar D 79 B11
Ziežmariai LT 137 D9
Žigljen HR 67 C10
Žiguri LV 133 B3
Žihárec SK 146 E5
Žihle CZ 76 B4
Zilaiskalns LV 131 F9
Žilina SK 147 C7
Žilinai LT 137 E10
Zillis CH 71 D8
Ziltendorf D 81 B7
Zilupe LV 133 D4
Zimandu Nou RO 151 E7
Zimbor RO 151 C11
Zimmersrode (Neuental) D 21 B12
Zimnicea RO 160 F6
Zimnitsa BG 167 D7
Žindaičiai LT 134 F5
Zingst D 83 B13
Zinkgruvan S 92 B6
Zinnowitz D 84 B5
Ziras LV 134 B3
Zirc H 149 B9
Zirchow D 84 C6
Zirndorf D 75 D8
Zîrneşti MD 154 E2
Zirņl LV 134 C4
Ziros GR 179 E11
Žirovnice CZ 77 D8
Zistersdorf A 77 E11
Žitište SRB 158 C6
Žitkovac SRB 164 B4
Žitni Potok SRB 164 D4
Žitomislić BIH 157 F8
Žitorsđa SRB 164 C4
Žitoše MK 168 B5
Zitsa GR 168 E4

Zittau D 81 E7
Zitz D 79 B11
Živaja HR 157 B6
Živinice BIH 157 D10
Žiželice CZ 77 C8
Zizers CH 71 D9
Zizurkil E 32 D1
Zlarin HR 156 E4
Zlata SRB 164 C4
Zlatar HR 148 D6
Zlatar-Bistrica HR 148 D6
Zlataritsa BG 166 C5
Zlaté Hory CZ 142 F3
Zlaté Klasy SK 146 E5
Zlaté Moravce SK 146 E6
Zlaten Rog BG 159 E10
Zlatna RO 151 E11
Zlatna Panega BG 165 C9
Zlatograd BG 171 B8
Zlatokop SRB 164 D4
Zława Wielka PL 138 D5
Žlebič SLO 73 E10
Žleby CZ 77 C8
Zlēkas LV 134 B3
Zletovo MK 164 F5
Žlibinai LT 134 E4
Zlín CZ 146 C5
Zliv CZ 76 D6
Žljebovi BIH 157 D10
Złlakuqan RKS 164 D2
Żłocieniec PL 85 C10
Żłoczew PL 142 D6
Złokuchene BG 165 E6
Żłonice CZ 76 B5
Żłota PL 141 G2
Żłota PL 143 F10
Złotniki Kujawskie PL 138 E5
Złotoryja PL 81 D9
Złotów PL 85 D12
Złoty Stak PL 77 B11
Złozela BIH 157 D7
Žlutice CZ 76 B4
Zmajevac HR 149 E11
Zmajevac HR 149 E11
Zmajevo SRB 158 C4
Zmeyovo BG 166 E5
Żmigród PL 81 D11
Zmijavci HR 157 F7
Żminj HR 67 B8
Zmudź PL 144 A8
Znamensk RUS 136 D3
Znin PL 138 E4
Znojmo CZ 77 E10
Zoagli I 37 C10
Zoelen NL 183 B6
Zoersel B 16 F3
Zoetermeer NL 16 D2
Zofingen CH 27 F8
Zogno I 69 B8
Zografou GR 175 D8
Zola Predosa I 66 C3
Zolder B 19 B11
Zoldo Alto I 72 D5
Żółkow D 83 C11
Zollikofen CH 31 A11
Zollikon CH 27 F10
Zolotkovychi UA 144 D6
Zófthica PL 85 D11
Żofynia PL 144 C5
Zomba H 149 D11
Zomergem B 19 B8
Zonhoven B 19 C11

Zoni GR 171 A10
Zoniana GR 178 E8
Zonza F 37 H10
Zórawina PL 81 E12
Zörbig D 79 C11
Zorita E 45 F9
Zorita del Maestrazgo E 42 F3
Zorleni RO 153 E11
Zorlentu Mare RO 159 C8
Zorneding D 75 F10
Zornheim D 21 E10
Zörnigal D 79 C12
Zornitsa BG 167 C9
Zornitsa BG 167 E7
Żory PL 142 F6
Zossen D 80 B4
Zottegem B 19 C8
Zoutkamp NL 16 B6
Zoutleeuw B 183 D6
Zovi Do BIH 157 F9
Zovka RUS 132 E4
Zreče SLO 148 D4
Zrenjanin SRB 158 C5
Zrin HR 156 B5
Zrinski Topolovac HR 149 D7
Zrmanja Vrelo HR 156 D5
Zruč CZ 76 C4
Zruč nad Sázavou CZ 77 C8
Zsadány H 151 D7
Zsáka H 151 C7
Zsámbék H 149 A11
Zsámbok H 150 B4
Zsana H 150 E4
Zschaitz D 80 D4
Zscherben D 79 D10
Zschopau D 80 E4
Zschortau D 79 D11
Zsombó H 150 E4
Zuberec SK 147 C9
Zubia E 53 B9
Zubiaur E 40 B6
Zubići BIH 157 D8
Zubiena I 68 C5
Zubieta E 32 D2
Zubieta E 32 D2
Zubin Potok RKS 164 D2
Zubiri E 32 E2
Zubří CZ 146 C6
Zubrohlava SK 147 C9
Zubrów PL 81 B8
Żuc SRB 164 C3
Zucaina E 48 D4
Zuchwil CH 27 F8
Zudaire E 32 E1
Zudar D 84 B4
Zuera E 41 E10
Zufre E 51 D7
Zug CH 27 F10
Zuhatza-Kuartango E 40 C6
Zuheros E 53 A8
Zuid-Beijerland NL 182 B4
Zuidhorn NL 16 B6
Zuidland NL 182 B4
Zuidlaren NL 17 B7
Zuidwolde NL 17 C6
Zuienkerke B 182 C2
Zújar E 55 D7
Żuków PL 141 F2
Żuków PL 141 G8
Żukowice PL 81 C9
Żukowo PL 138 B5
Żuljana HR 162 D3
Żulová CZ 77 B12
Zülpich D 21 C7

Zumaia E 32 D1
Zumarraga E 32 D1
Zundert NL 16 F3
Zungri I 59 B8
Zunzarren E 32 E3
Zuoz CH 71 D10
Żupanja HR 157 B10
Żúras LV 134 B3
Zúrgena E 55 E8
Zürich CH 27 F10
Zurndorf A 77 G12
Zürnevo BG 161 F10
Zuromin PL 139 D8
Zurow D 83 C11
Zusmarshausen D 75 F8
Züsow D 83 C11
Züssow D 84 C5
Žuta Lokva HR 67 C11
Žutautai LT 134 E2
Zutendaal B 19 C12
Zutphen NL 16 D6
Żużemberk SLO 73 E10
Zveçan RKS 164 D2
Zvejniekciems LV 135 B8
Zverino BG 165 C8
Zvezdé AL 168 C4
Zvezdel BG 171 B8
Zvezdets BG 167 E8
Zvolen SK 147 D8
Zvolenská Slatina SK 147 D8
Zvonce SRB 164 D6
Zvorište RO 153 B8
Zvornik BIH 157 D11
Zwartemeer NL 17 C8
Zwartsluis NL 16 C6
Zweeloo NL 17 C7
Zweibrücken D 21 F8
Zweisimmen CH 31 B11
Zwenkau D 79 D11
Zwethau D 80 C4
Zwettl A 77 E8
Zwevegem B 19 C7
Zwevezele B 182 C2
Zwickau D 79 E12
Zwiefalten D 27 D11
Zwierzyn PL 85 E9
Zwierzyniec PL 144 B6
Zwiesel D 76 D4
Zwijndrecht B 19 B9
Zwijndrecht NL 16 E3
Zwinge D 79 C7
Zwingen CH 27 F8
Zwingenberg D 21 E11
Zwochau D 79 D11
Zwoleń PL 141 H5
Zwolle NL 16 C6
Zwönitz D 79 E12
Zwota D 75 B11
Zyabki BY 133 F4
Zyal'ki BY 133 E4
Zyalyonka BY 133 E5
Zychlin PL 143 B8
Żydowo PL 85 B11
Żydowo PL 85 F13
Żygaičiai LT 134 F4
Zygos GR 171 B6
Żyniai LT 134 F2
Zyrakow PL 143 F11
Żyrardów PL 141 F3
Zyrzyn PL 141 H6
Żytkiejmy PL 136 E6
Żytniów PL 142 D6
Żytno PL 143 E8
Żywiec PL 147 B8
Żywocice PL 142 F4

Æ

Ærøskøbing DK 86 F6

Ø

Ødis DK 86 E4
Ødsted DK 86 D4
Øie N 105 B12
Økdal N 101 A12
Øksfjord N 112 C9
Øksnes N 110 C8
Øksneshamn N 110 D9
Ølen N 94 C3
Ølgod DK 86 D3
Ølholm DK 86 D5
Ølsted DK 86 D5
Ølsted DK 87 D10
Ølstykke DK 87 D10
Ønsnes N 83 A11
Øra N 112 C8
Ørbæk DK 86 E7
Ørgenvika N 95 B11
Ørjavik N 104 F2
Ørje N 96 D6
Ørnes N 108 C6
Ørnhøj DK 86 C3
Ørslev DK 87 E9
Ørsnes N 100 A5
Ørsta N 100 B4
Ørsted DK 86 C6
Ørting DK 86 D6
Ørum DK 86 C5
Ørum DK 86 D7
Øsby DK 86 E5
Østbirk DK 86 D5
Østby N 91 A9
Østby N 102 D4
Østengård DK 86 D4
Øster Assels DK 86 B3
Øster Bjerregrav DK 86 C5
Øster Brønderslev DK 86 A5
Østerby DK 86 A5
Øster Hornum DK 86 B5
Øster Hurup DK 86 B6
Øster Højst DK 86 E4
Østerild DK 86 A3
Øster Jølby DK 86 B3
Østerlars DK 89 E7
Øster Lindet DK 86 E4
Østermarie DK 89 E8
Øster Tørslev DK 86 C6
Øster Ulslev DK 83 A11
Øster Vedsted DK 86 E3
Østervrå N 90 E7
Øster Vrøgum DK 86 D2
Østese N 94 B4
Østrup DK 86 B4
Øverbygd N 111 C17
Øvergard N 111 B18
Øvre Alta N 113 D11

Øvre Kildal N 112 D7
Øvrella N 95 C10
Øvre Rendal N 101 C14
Øvre Årdal N 100 D7
Øvre Åstbru N 101 D13
Øyangen N 104 E7
Øydegarden N 104 E4
Øyenkilen N 91 A8
Øyer N 101 D12
Øyeren N 96 B7
Øyjord N 108 B9
Øynes N 108 B9
Øynes N 111 C11
Øyslebø N 90 C2
Øyvatnet N 111 C12

Å

Å N 104 F7
Å N 110 E4
Å N 111 B12
Å N 111 C13
Åberget S 109 E18
Åbo S 103 C10
Åbodarna S 107 E14
Åbogen N 96 B7
Åbosjö S 107 D12
Åby S 89 A7
Åby S 93 B8
Åbyen DK 90 D7
Åbyggeby S 103 E13
Åbyn S 118 D6
Åbytorp S 92 A6
Ådalsliden S 107 E11
Ådum DK 86 D3
Åfarnes N 100 A7
Åfjord N 104 D8
Åfoss N 90 A6
Ågerup DK 87 D10
Ågotnes N 94 B2
Ågskaret N 108 C2
Åheim N 100 B3
Åhus S 88 D6
Åkarp S 87 D12
Åkerbränna S 107 D11
Åkerby S 99 B9
Åkerholmen S 118 C6
Åkersberga S 99 D10
Åkers styckebruk S 98 D8
Åknes N 110 C9
Åkran N 105 D12
Åkrehamn N 94 D2
Åkullsjön S 118 C3
Åkvisslan S 107 E13
Ål N 101 E9
Ålberga S 93 B9
Ålbo S 98 B7
Ålbæk DK 90 D7
Åle DK 86 D5
Åled S 87 B11

Ålem S 89 B10
Ålen N 101 A14
Ålesund N 100 B4
Ålgnäs S 103 D12
Ålgård N 94 E4
Ålhult S 92 D7
Ålloluokta S 109 B17
Ålmo N 104 E4
Ålsrode DK 87 C7
Ålstad N 108 C9
Ålund S 118 D6
Ålvik N 94 B4
Ålvund N 101 A9
Ålvundeid N 101 A9
Ålåsen S 106 D7
Åminne FIN 122 E7
Åminne S 87 A14
Åmland N 94 F5
Åmli N 90 A3
Åmli N 90 B3
Åmmeberg S 92 B6
Åmot N 94 C7
Åmot N 95 B11
Åmot N 95 C8
Åmot N 95 C11
Åmot S 103 E11
Åmotfors S 96 C7
Åmsele S 107 B16
Åmsosen N 94 D8
Åmynnet S 107 E15
Åmål S 91 A12
Åmål S 91 A12
Åmøyhamn N 108 C5
Åna-Sira N 94 F4
Åndalsnes N 100 A7
Åneby N 95 B13
Ånes N 104 E4
Ånge S 103 A10
Ånge S 109 E14
Ångelsberg S 97 C15
Ångersjö S 102 C8
Ångsö S 105 E13
Ånimskog S 91 A11
Ånn S 105 E13
Ånset N 104 E6
Ånsnes N 104 F5
Ånäset S 118 C6

Årosjåkk S 111 E17
Årre DK 86 D3
Årrenjarka S 109 C15
Årsandøy N 105 A12
Årsdale DK 89 E8
Årset N 105 A11
Årsunda S 98 A7
Årvik N 100 B3
Årviksand N 112 C10
Årvågen N 104 E5
Åryd S 89 B7
Åryd S 89 C8
Årøybukta N 111 A19
Årøysund N 90 A7
Ås N 95 C13
Ås N 105 E11
Ås N 96 C7
Ås S 97 C3
Ås S 106 E7
Ås S 107 E11
Åsa N 95 B12
Åsa S 91 B11
Åsan S 105 B12
Åsarna S 102 A7
Åsby S 87 A10
Åse N 111 B10
Åsebyn S 96 D7
Åseda S 89 A8
Åsegg N 105 C9
Åsele S 107 C12
Åselet S 118 D4
Åsen S 102 C7
Åsen N 105 D10
Åsen S 102 C7
Åsen S 106 E7
Åsen S 107 E11
Åsenbruk S 91 B11
Åsensbruk S 91 B11
Åshammar S 103 E12
Åskilje S 107 B13
Åskogen S 118 C7
Åsli N 101 E11
Åsljunga S 87 C12
Åsmansbo S 97 B14
Åsmarka N 101 D13
Åsmark N 104 E5
Åskard N 104 E5
Åskö S 92 A8
Åssjö S 103 B12
Åtran S 87 A11
Åyskoski FIN 123 D17
Åystö FIN 122 F8
Äänekoski FIN 123 E15

Ä

Äetsä FIN 126 C8
Ähtäri FIN 123 E12
Ähtärinranta FIN 123 E12
Äijäjoki FIN 116 B10
Äijälä FIN 123 E12
Äkäsjokisuu FIN 117 D11
Äkäslompolo FIN 117 C12
Älandsbro S 103 A14
Älgarås S 92 B4
Älgered S 103 B12
Älghult S 89 A9
Älmestad S 91 D13
Älmhult S 88 B6
Älmsta S 99 C11
Älvdalen S 102 D7
Älvho S 102 D8
Älvkarleby S 103 E13
Älvkarleö S 99 A8
Älvros S 102 B8
Älvsbyn S 118 C6
Älvsered S 87 A11
Älvängen S 91 D11
Ämmälänkylä FIN 123 E9
Ämmänsaari FIN 121 E12
Åmådalen S 102 D8
Ång S 92 D5
Änge S 105 E16
Ängebo S 103 C11
Ängelholm S 87 C11
Ängersjö S 122 C3
Ängeslevä FIN 119 E15
Ängesån S 116 E8
Ångom S 103 B13
Äppelbo S 97 B11
Ärla S 98 D7
Ärnäs S 102 D5
Ärnäs S 102 D5
Ärtled S 103 E9
Ärtrik S 107 E11
Äsbacka S 103 D11
Äsköping S 92 A8
Ässjö S 103 B12
Ätran S 87 A11
Äyskoski FIN 123 D17

Ö

Öckerö S 91 D10
Ödeborg S 91 B10
Ödeshog S 92 C5
Ödkarby FIN 99 B13
Ödsmål S 91 C10

Öja FIN 123 C9
Öja S 93 E12
Öjarn S 106 D8
Öje S 97 B12
Öjebyn S 118 D6
Öjeforsen S 103 B9
Öjingsvallen S 103 C8
Öjung S 103 C10
Öksajärvi S 116 C8
Öllölä FIN 125 F15
Ölmbrotorp S 97 D13
Ölme S 97 C12
Olsboda S 92 A4
Ömossa FIN 122 F7
Önnestad S 88 C2
Önningeby FIN 99 B14
Öratjärn S 103 C10
Öravan S 107 B14
Öravattnet S 106 C10
Örbyhus S 99 B9
Örbäck S 97 C15
Örebro S 97 C13
Örebäcken S 102 C4
Öregrund S 99 B10
Öreström S 107 C13
Öretjändalen S 103 A10
Örkelljunga S 87 C12
Örnsköldsvik S 107 E15
Örnsudden S 109 E13
Örsbäck S 107 D17
Örserum S 92 C5
Örsjö S 89 B9
Örsundsbro S 99 C8
Örträsk S 107 C15
Örviken S 118 C6
Östa S 98 B7
Östanfjärden S 119 C10
Östansjö S 92 A5
Östanskär S 103 A13
Östanvik S 103 D9
Östanå S 88 C6
Östbjörka S 103 E9
Östby S 107 D13
Österbybruk S 99 B9
Österbymo S 92 D6
Österede S 107 E11
Österforse S 107 E12
Österfärnebo S 98 B7
Östergar S 93 E13
Östergraninge S 107 F12
Österhankmo FIN 122 D7
Österjörn S 118 C3
Österlisa S 99 C11
Östermark FIN 126 E8
Östernoret S 107 C12
Östero FIN 122 D8
Österskucku S 102 A3

Östersund S 106 E7
Östersundom FIN 127 E13
Östervåla S 98 B8
Österås S 107 E12
Östhammar S 99 B10
Östlöning S 103 A13
Östmark S 97 B8
Östmarkum S 107 E14
Östnor S 102 D7
Östra Ed S 93 C9
Östra Frölunda S 91 E13
Östra Granberg S 118 C4
Östra Grevie S 87 D12
Östra Husby S 93 B9
Östra Ljungby S 87 C11
Östra Lõa S 97 C13
Östra Ormsjö S 107 C10
Östra Ryd S 93 C8
Östra Skrämträsk S 118 E5
Östra Stugusjö S 103 A9
Östra Sönnarslöv S 88 D6
Östra Vemmerlöv S 88 D6
Östra Yttermark FIN 122 E6
Östra Äliden S 118 C4
Överammer S 107 E8
Överberg S 102 B7
Överbyn S 103 C12
Överhogdal S 102 B8
Överhörnäs S 107 E15
Överkalix S 119 B9
Överlida S 91 E12
Överlännäs S 107 E12
Övermalax FIN 122 E7
Övermark FIN 122 E6
Övermorjärv S 118 B9
Övernäs S 109 D14
Överstbyn S 118 B7
Övertorneå S 119 B11
Överturingen S 102 B8
Övertänger S 103 D10
Överum S 93 D8
Överäng S 105 D14
Överö FIN 99 B15
Öv Långträsk S 109 E16
Övra S 107 D11
Övre Bredåker S 118 C4
Övre Flåsjön S 118 B7
Övre-Konäs S 105 D13
Övre Soppero S 116 B7
Övre Tväräsel S 118 C5
Övsjöbyn S 107 E9
Öxabäck S 91 E12

i-SPY

Collins

Look around you and discover the world with i-SPY

i-SPY In the countryside
What can you spot?

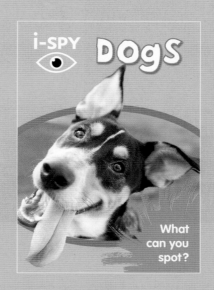

i-SPY DOGS
What can you spot?

i-SPY Creepy crawlies
What can you spot?

Spy it
up to 200 fun things to spot around you

Spot it
tick off what you see as you go

Score it
score points for each spot and receive your super-spotter certificate and badge!

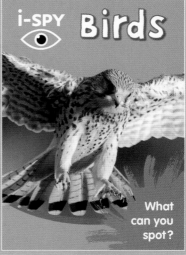

i-SPY Birds
What can you spot?

collins.co.uk/i-SPY

@Collins4Parents   f facebook.com/collins4parents

What can you spot?

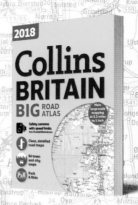
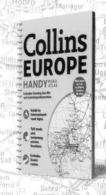

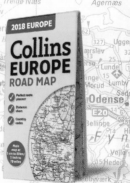
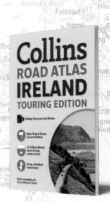 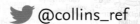

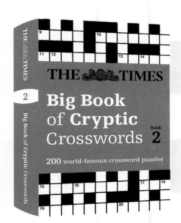

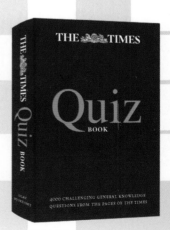